ENCYCLOPEDIA OF
The Korean War

A Political, Social, and Military History

ENCYCLOPEDIA OF
The Korean War

A Political, Social, and Military History

Spencer C. Tucker, *Editor*

Jinwung Kim,
Michael R. Nichols,
Paul G. Pierpaoli, Jr.,
Priscilla Roberts,
and Norman R. Zehr,
Assistant Editors

☑®
Checkmark Books®
An imprint of Facts On File, Inc.

Encyclopedia of the Korean War

Copyright © 2002 by Spencer C. Tucker

Checkmark Books
An imprint of Facts On File, Inc.
132 West 31st Street
New York NY 10001

Library of Congress Cataloging-in-Publication Data

 Encyclopedia of the Korean War : a political, social, and military history / Spencer C. Tucker, editor; Jinwung Kim . . . [et al.], assistant editors

   p. cm.
   Originally published: Santa Barbara, Calif. : ABC-CLIO, c2000. Vols. 1–2 of the 3 volume original are combined into this one volume.
  Includes bibliographical references and index.
   ISBN 0-8160-4682-4 (pbk. : alk. paper)
  1. Korean War, 1950–1953—Encyclopedias. I. Tucker, Spencer, 1937– . II Kim, Jinwung.
 II. Title.
  DS918 E53 2002
  951.904'2'03—dc21

                       2001037155

THE CONTRIBUTORS

Brian A. Arnold II
Virginia Military Institute

Robert J. Arvin
Virginia Military Institute

Jonathan D. Atkins
Virginia Military Institute

Lt. Col. Joseph C. D. (Geoff) Babb
U.S. Army (ret.)

Dr. Mark Beasley
Department of History
Texas Christian University

Dr. John L. Bell, Jr.
Department of History
Western Carolina University

Jason B. Berg
Virginia Military Institute

Col. Daniel Randall Beime
U.S. Army (ret.)

Col. Don Boose, Jr.
U.S. Army (ret.)

Walter Boyne
Ashburn, Virginia

Dean Brumley
Department of History
Texas Christian University

David R. Buck
Department of History
West Virginia University

Dr. Robert J. Bunker
National Security Studies
California State University,
  San Bernardino

Dr. Paul R. Camacho
University of Massachusetts—
  Boston

Phillip A. Cantrell II
West Virginia University

Matthew S. Carman
Virginia Military Institute

Professor Chan Lau Kit-ching
Department of History
University of Hong Kong

Dr. Sunghun Cho
Dankook University, Korea

Col. To-Woong Chung
Department of Military History
Korea Military Academy

Richard E. Coate
Brooklyn, New York

Dr. Don Coerver
Department of History
Texas Christian University

Dr. Finnie D. Coleman
Department of English
Texas A&M University

Jeffrey C. Colvin
United States Naval Academy

Dean Corey
U.S. Air Force Historian
Warner Robins AFB, Georgia

JLTC Conrad C. Crane
Professor of History
United States Military Academy

Dr. David R. Dorondo
Department of History
Western Carolina University

Dr. Timothy G. Dowling
Department of History
Tulane University

Dr. Joe P. Dunn
Department of History and Politics
Converse College

Dr. Blake Dunnavent
Lubbock Christian University

W. D. (Bill) Ehrhart
Philadelphia, Pennsylvania

Brig. Gen. Uzal W. Ent, PNG (ret.)
Philadelphia, Pennsylvania

Mark Esposito
Department of History
West Virginia University

Dr. Matt Esposito
Department of History
Drake University

Ronald A. Fiocca
Virginia Military Institute

LTC Mark Franklin, U.S. Army
Montclair, Virginia

Dr. Don Frazier
Department of History
McMurry University

Dr. John C. Fredricksen
Salem, Massachusetts

Kevin J. Fromm
Virginia Military Institute

Dr. Richard A. Garver
Fairfax, Virginia

Richard Z. Groen
Virginia Military Institute

William B. Harrington
Virginia Military Institute

Dr. William Head
U.S. Air Force Historian

Dr. Richard Weixing Hu
Department of Politics and
  Public Administration
University of Hong Kong

v

Professor Man-Ho Huh
Department of Political Science
& Diplomacy
Kyungpook National University

William Van Husen
Kaiserlauten, Germany

Arnold Isaacs
Pasadena, Maryland

Dr. Eric Jarvis
Department of History
King's College

Major Kelly Jordan
Department of History
United States Military Academy

Mary Kelley
Department of History
Texas Christian University

Dr. Hakjoon Kim
President
The University of Inch'ŏn

Dr. Youngho Kim
Department of Political Science
and Diplomacy, College of
Social Sciences
Sungshin Women's University

Professor Jinwung Kim
Department of History,
Teachers College
Kyungpook National University

Dr. Jeff Kinard
Guilford Technical Community
College

Dr. Clayton D. Laurie
Histories Division
United States Army Center of
Military History

Professor Hochul Lee
Department of Political Science
The University of Inch'ŏn

Dr. Jack McCallum
Department of History
Texas Christian University

Alec McMorris
Virginia Military Institute

Dr. Stanley S. McGowen
Department of History
Sam Houston State University

Lt. Col. Kevin W. T. Madden
U.S. Army Command and General
Staff College

James R. Mahala
Virginia Military Institute

Colin Mahle
Virginia Military Institute

Dr. Edward J. Marolda
Senior Historian
Naval Historical Center

Matthew V. Martin
Virginia Military Institute

Professor Allan R. Millett
Department of History
Ohio State University

Dr. Akitoshi Miyashita
Political Science Department
Drake University

Dr. Malcolm Muir, Jr.
Austin Peay State University

Michael D. Mulé
Virginia Military Institute

Clint Mundinger
Virginia Military Institute

Dr. Michael R. Nichols
Tarrant County College

William Robert O'Neal, Jr.
Virginia Military Institute

Dr. Mark O'Neill
Tallahassee Community College

Eric Osborne
Department of History
Texas Christian University

Dr. Insook Park
Pusan, Republic of Korea

Natalia Petrouchkevitch
London, Ontario, Canada

Dr. Paul G. Pierpaoli, Jr.
Department of History
Virginia Military Institute

LTC Sherman W. Pratt,
U.S. Army (ret.)
Alexandria, Virginia

LTC Susan M. Puska
U.S. Army

Robert B. Richards
United States Military
Academy

Dr Priscilla Roberts
University of Hong Kong

Dr. Rodney J. Ross
Harrisburg, Pennsylvania

Dr. Claude R. Sasso
William Jewell College

Dr. Elizabeth D. Schafer
Loachapoka, Alabama

Dr. Edward Sharp
History Department
University of North Carolina
at Greensboro

Dr. Charles R. Shrader
Carlisle, Pennsylvania

Timothy A. Sikes
United States Military Academy

Frank Skidmore
Department of History
Howard Payne University

Monica Spicer
Andrews AFB, Maryland

Chuck Steele
Falls Church, Virginia

Dr. Suh, Choo Suk
Research Fellow
Korea Institute for Defense
  Analyses

Dr. Suh, Dong-Man
Institute of Foreign Affairs and
  National Security
Republic of Korea

Larry Swindell
Moraga, California

Dr. Richard C. Thornton
George Washington University

Dr. David Trask
Department of History
Guilford Technical Community
  College

Zsolt Varga
Department of History
Texas Christian University

Dr. Patricia Wadley
Colleyville, Texas

Jack Walker
Antioch, Tennessee

Duane Wesolick
Western Carolina University

Dr. James Willbanks
U.S. Army Command and General
  Staff College

Sean Williams
Virginia Military Institute

Bradford A. Wineman
Virginia Military Institute

Carol J. Yee
Department of the Army

Colonel David Zabecki
American Military University

Norman R. Zehr

CONTENTS

LIST OF ENTRIES

FOREWORD

The war that raged over the Korean peninsula during the early 1950s was one of the pivotal events of the twentieth century. Forces of the United Nations, led by those of the United States, were pitted against those of Communist North Korea and China at great and possibly unnecessary cost to both sides. The results were twofold: South Korea, the victim of North Korean aggression, was restored to its previous borders, and the nations of the West were awakened to the fact that the struggle against the Communist bloc would be long, expensive, and hazardous.

Yet this war—officially called a "police action" because it was undeclared—has largely faded from memory, even from the consciousness of those who live through those dramatic years. At first glance that fact seems nearly unbelievable.

Korea is not our only "forgotten" war. Other examples abound. The average American citizen is constantly reminded of the Civil War, the Second World War, and the Vietnam war but knows little of the War of 1812, in which a fledgling nation (the United States) defied the most powerful nation on earth (Britain), and fought her to a standstill. They give little thought to the fact that the entire southwestern portion of the United States was expropriated from Mexico as the result of the Mexican-American War (1846–1848). Also dim in memory is the First World War, in which this country mobilized four million men and sent two million to France to assist in the defeat of the Kaiser's imperial Germany. There is some logic behind this phenomenon: By and large our "forgotten" wars have preceded episodes of even greater impact on our society. People have selective memories.

Nevertheless, the Korean War provides a rewarding area of study. Because of the neglect it has suffered in the public print, there is much for the general reader to learn about it. But far more important is the fact that it constituted a highly significant milestone in the development of America's relations with the rest of the world. It was also a period of intense drama, a time when military defeats drove home to Americans the serious nature of the communist threat. If for only these reasons, the Korean War should provide a fertile ground for general readers who are interested in rounding out their knowledge of American history.

Let us go back a few years. At the end of World War II in 1945, the Western powers—the United States, Britain, and France—nurtured a hope that the former enemies of Nazi Germany, including the Soviet Union, might retain their policies of cooperation for the cre-

ation of a better world. It was to their credit that the nations of the Western world made every effort to promote that mutual cooperation. But the "honeymoon" was short-lived. The Soviet Union and her satellites withdrew into isolation, which grew to the point that Winston Churchill, in 1946, coined the apt phrase "iron curtain" to describe the new cleavage between the Communist bloc and the West.

Still, the Western World reacted passively to belligerent actions on the part of the Communists. We reacted to the Soviet siege of Berlin in 1948 by the dramatic Berlin Airlift which, though successful in defusing that particular crisis, did nothing to discourage further communist ventures. Between late 1945 and 1950 we maintained in Europe a pitiful military force—only one division—to occupy all of Germany and Austria, presumably based on the unrealistic assumption that any military confrontation with the Communists was unthinkable. But then, when President Harry S. Truman sent U.S. forces into Korea to resist the first overt Communist military aggression, the United States had taken a positive stand for the first time. The American people, despite the grim prospects of sacrifice, heaved a collective sigh of relief.

The sacrifice that followed was real indeed. The first U.S. ground troops sent into Korea, the 24th Division, were almost wiped out. Meeting the North Korean aggressors just south of Seoul, they were pursued relentlessly, losing units at every defensive position. American citizens followed the action hourly, many of us remembering the very spot where we learned of the capture of the American commander, Major General William F. Dean. President Truman called on General Douglas MacArthur, then military governor of Japan and commander of U.S. forces in the Far East, to take command of the forces fighting on the Korean peninsula. The United States was into the so-called police action all the way.

Then began a race against time, the North Koreans trying to push the United Nations forces into the sea, while the UN—and particularly the Americans, one division after another—moved to the southern port of Pusan to build up a bridgehead called the Pusan Perimeter. First went the 1st Cavalry and the 25th Division from Japan. The 2d Division and the 1st Marine followed soon after. Later came others such as the 3d, 40th, and 45th. At first it looked as if the Pusan Perimeter would be overrun, with the UN forces driven into the sea. But with North Korean supply lines stretched and the United Nations forces built up, the

Americans, South Korean, British, French, Dutch, Belgian, Turkish, and Greek forces eventually burst out of the perimeter and, with a brilliant amphibious landing at Inch'ŏn, near Seoul, sent the North Koreans in headlong flight.

Then came near disaster. General MacArthur overstretched his lines into North Korea, ignoring the presence of Chinese "volunteers" sent to protect Chinese territory from feared Western invasion, and his exposed spearheads reached as far north as the Yalu River, the border between North Korea and Manchuria. When the Chinese hit in force around Thanksgiving 1950, the American forces were forced to fight their way back to the eastern coast of Korea in sub-zero weather. They were eventually evacuated by sea and delivered back to Pusan, in the south, where they began fighting their way up the peninsula once more.

Once again the UN forces, now pursuing an overstretched enemy, were victorious in the field. But by later 1951 war-weariness had set in on both sides, and the respective governments were now looking for peace. So when the UN Army reached the present-day Demilitarized Zone, which approximates the original border between North and South Korea, the Communists proposed peace talks and the United States agreed. The war of maneuver stopped, and military action settled down to trench warfare in the mode of the First World War or the siege of Petersburg, both sides killing each other across a no-man's land every day.

The stalemate went on for a tragic twenty-one additional months, longer than the mobile phase of the war. It was a situation nearly unique in military history, with two opposing forces fighting in the knowledge that a conference for truce was being conducted over a long stretch of time. When peace finally came, the United States had suffered a loss of 36,000 dead. The Communists, both North Korean and Chinese, lost countless thousands more. Some call the outcome of the conflict a defeat for the United Nations; more regard it as a stalemate. But it should not be forgotten that the United Nations forces accomplished what they set out to do, to free South Korea from the aggressor from the north.

To me, the outcome of the Korean conflict was quite satisfactory. If it appears to be less, that is because the nature of war has changed. Korea was our first "limited war," in in which the survival of neither side was deemed to be at stake, certainly as it pertained to China and the United States. That was a new concept for Americans, fighting without the intention of utterly destroying the enemy. But in the atomic age, that pol-

icy has become the norm. It is the only way for nations to survive in this new world. In Vietnam, the Persian Gulf, and even in the recent actions in the former Yugoslavia, there has been no intention of destroying the government of the enemy; the objectives have been more realistic than that.

The fighting itself, however, constitutes only part of the story of the Korean War. Of perhaps greater importance was the impact the Korean war had on American attitudes. Now awakened to the reality of the global Communist threat, the United States and Canada joined the nations of Western Europe to put teeth into the North Atlantic Treaty Organization (NATO), which had previously been little more than a sheet of paper. The West built up a respectable fighting force with which to resist possible Communist aggression in Europe, raising its defensive strength from a single division to one of six, backed up by overwhelming air power. General Dwight Eisenhower was called out of retirement to organize the new Western armies. In the course of a couple of years, as a direct result of the new East-West confrontation, the rehabilitation of Germany was accelerated, and that previously wayward nation was given the right and obligation to contribute to the Western defense.

The war had its impact on domestic politics. The American people bore the price controls with good humor, but when the prospects for a satisfactory culmination of the blood-letting faded, the war engendered grave dissatisfaction in the public. President Truman was temporarily discredited, even in his own party, when he relieved General MacArthur for patent insubordination. The "firing MacArthur" matter, incidentally, is probably better remembered in the public mind than the policy issues that brought it about—the prudent limiting of the war to Asia, sparing a threat to Western Europe.

The Korean War, in conclusion, is a rewarding subject for study—significant for its impact on American foreign policy, full of military controversies, and overflowing with such colorful characters as South Korean President Syngman Rhee, North Korean President Kim Il Sung, and Generals Matthew Ridgway, Ned Almond, Douglas MacArthur, James Van Fleet, and Maxwell Taylor, not to mention President Harry Truman himself. This encyclopedia will make such studies easier by providing a handy reference for the general reader who was not alive at the time or whose memory has faded. It will be a significant contribution to the benefits of studying the Korean War.

—John S. D. Eisenhower

PREFACE

The Korean War is a key event in world history and is well deserving of further study. The first shooting confrontation of the Cold War and the first limited war in the nuclear age, it was the only time since the Second World War that two of the world's major military powers have fought one another, in this case the United States and China. Diplomatically the war is interesting for the miscalculations and ineptitude on both sides that led up to it. It also saw the United Nations play a leading role and prisoners used as pawns.

The Korean War had a profound impact on the countries involved. For Koreans it brought great suffering, catastrophic civilian and military casualties, and widespread damage. It also resulted in the continued division of their country. In fact, it added greatly to the existing enmity between the two Korean states, lengthening the odds against political reunification.

The war was also important in U.S. history. One of America's least understood wars, it nonetheless marked an important transition to the Cold War national security state. Previously the United States had disarmed after every war. World War II was no exception, and the United States was woefully unprepared militarily to fight the Korean War; but with the Korea War, the United States came to maintain a powerful military for the indefinite future. This was a fundamental change and politically perilous.

The war is worth studying also for its two-phase nature of maneuver and stalemate and for the restrictions placed on its conduct by political leaders, a process that would be repeated in Vietnam. Militarily the war saw many innovations. It marked the first extensive use of the helicopter on the battlefield. The helicopter demonstrated its potential in reconnaissance, evacuation, resupply, and rescue work. The war witnessed history's first battles between jet aircraft. It was a reminder that air power alone can not bring about final decisions in land warfare, and it revealed the importance of command of the sea, especially in resupply from Japan. It also saw considerable improvements in the treatment of wounded.

Certainly the Korean War casts a long shadow. During the later Vietnam War, planners in Washington were haunted by fears of Chinese military intervention partly based on mistaken notions of that nation's military power born in the Korean War.

Strangely, in the United States the Korean War came to be known as the "Forgotten War." World War II veterans were lionized, but Korean veterans never received the measure of praise they too deserved. Indicative of the desire of Americans to forget is that Korean War veterans did not have a memorial in Washington until 1995. It is hoped that this encyclopedia will in some small measure help Americans to remember all those individuals who fought in Korea.

Technically, the Korean War continues today; only an armistice agreement halted the fighting in 1953. The Korean peninsula remains one of the world's most dangerous flash points, and the West knows less about the Democratic People's Republic of Korea (North Korea) than about any nation on earth. The intentions and behavior of its leaders remain shrouded in mystery. To maintain the uneasy armistice, today some 37,000 U.S. troops, centered on the 2d Infantry Division, remain in the Republic of Korea (South Korea).

We believe this *Encyclopedia of the Korean War* is the most comprehensive encyclopedia of the war to appear to date. It includes many topics and individuals not covered in other encyclopedias of the conflict, and we are proud of its extensive 200,000-word documents section, a feature not available in most other encyclopedias of the war.

Regarding the form of the Korean names, we have chosen to follow the McCune-Reischauer system now used in the Republic of Korea, with the exception of such well-known names as Seoul (Sŏul), Syngman Rhee (Yi Sŭng-man), Kim Il Sung (Kim Il-sŏng), and Park Chung Hee (Pak Chŏng-hŭi). Also, family names precede personal names, which usually consist of two syllables and are hyphenated. Also, although many people are aware that President Harry Truman had no middle name and the S should thus properly be without a period, we have decided to use the generally accepted practice of including the period: thus Harry S. Truman.

Statistics are always difficult and this is especially true with casualty totals. We have worked hard to reconcile differences, but there are discrepancies, depending on the source used.

I am especially appreciative of the hard work of my assistant editors, all of whom made valuable contributions. Professor Jinwung Kim, of Kyungpook National University in Taegu, Republic of Korea, contributed entries, did herculean work in correcting accents and spellings, and caught many factual errors. Mike Nichols, my doctoral student in history at Texas Christian University, now professor at Tarrant County College, compiled and scanned in all the documents and wrote the brief introductions to each. Professor

Paul G. Pierpaoli, Jr., a valued colleague at the Virginia Military Institute (VMI) with a vast knowledge of the Truman administration and the impact of the war on the United States, helped in those areas and also assisted in editing. Professor Priscilla Roberts of the University of Hong Kong wrote more entries than any one individual and was immensely helpful in tracking down sources and information; she also secured a number of obscure documents. Norm Zehr, a U.S. Army aviator with the 40th Infantry Division during the war, has one of the finest reference libraries on the war and a near-encyclopedic knowledge of the conflict. He provided valuable assistance in chasing down factual details and in catching errors.

Don Frazier of McMurray University, and his associate, Richard J. Thompson, Jr., produced the excellent maps that are such an important part of this encyclopedia. I am also grateful for assistance provided by Brad Arnold, my former cadet assistant at VMI and now a graduate student in history at James Madison University, and Cadet Colin Mahle, my current assistant at VMI. Both helped run down elusive information in the editing process. Certainly, I am most appreciative of the hard work of the 120 contributors, including a number of scholars from the Republic of Korea.

I am appreciative also of the support provided to me by the Virginia Military Institute, as well as the many wonderful people on the staff of ABC-CLIO for their encouragement and support in a difficult project. I am grateful also to Dr. Henry S. Bausum, retired editor of *The Journal of Military History*, for allowing me to reprint Professor Allan R. Millett's review article on the historiography of the war, which appeared in that journal but is here extensively revised.

Despite all the preceding, I take full responsibility for any errors. Finally, I am also most grateful to my wife Beverly for her forbearance and patience for the long hours that I spend at the computer.

—*Spencer C. Tucker*

LIST OF MAPS

Cartography by Donald Frazier and Richard J. Thompson, Jr.

China

Najin

Ch'ŏngjin

YANGGANG

Hyesanjin

HAMGYŎNG

Kanggye

Pujŏn
Reservoir

CHAGANG

Changjin
Reservoir

Sinŭiju

Hamhŭng

P'YŎNGAN

Hŭngnam

Anju

**East Sea
(Sea of Japan)**

Sinanju

P'yŏngyang

Chinnamp'o

Wŏnsan

KANGWŎN

Sariwŏn

HWANGHAE

Kimhwa

Haeju

Ch'ŏrwŏn

Kaesŏng

Ongjin

Ŭijŏngbu

Ch'unch'ŏn

Kangnŭng

Seoul

Samch'ŏk

Inch'ŏn

KYŎNGGI

Suwŏn

Wŏnju

Yellow Sea

Osan

Ch'ŏnan

Andong

CH'UNGCH'ŎNG

Yŏngdŏk

Kimch'ŏn

P'ohang

Taejŏn

Waegwan

Yŏngch'ŏn

Kunsan

Taegu

Chŏnju

KYŎNGSANG

CHŎLLA

Masan

Pusan

Kwangju

Mokp'o

Korean
Peninsula

Political

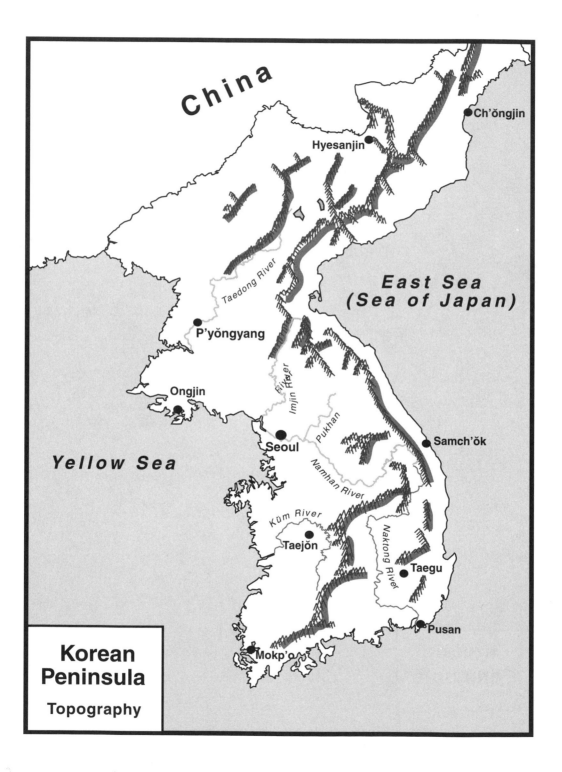

China

Ch'ŏngjin

Hyesanjin

East Sea
(Sea of Japan)

Taedong River

P'yŏngyang

Ongjin

Imjin River

Pukhan River

Seoul

Samch'ŏk

Yellow Sea

Namhan River

Küm River

Naktong River

Taejŏn

Taegu

Pusan

Mokp'o

**Korean
Peninsula**

Topography

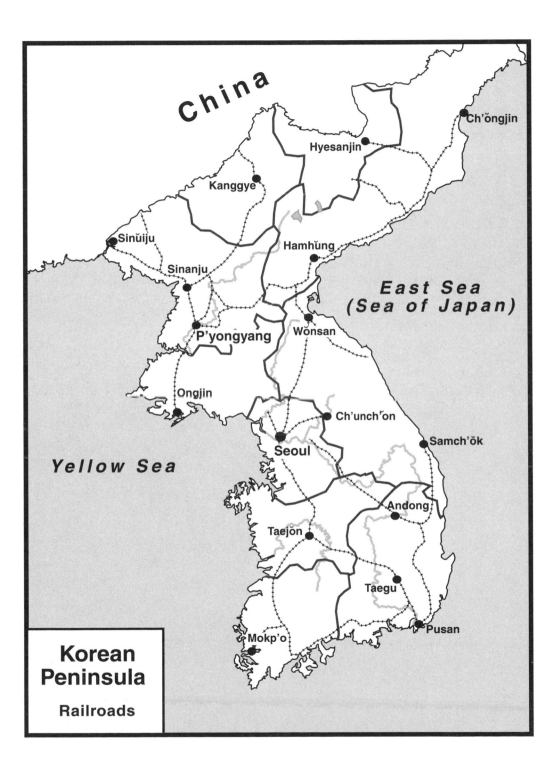

China

Ch'ŏngjin

Hyesanjin

Kanggye

Sinŭiju

Sinanju

Hamhŭng

East Sea
(Sea of Japan)

P'yongyang

Wŏnsan

Ongjin

Ch'unch'on

Samch'ŏk

Seoul

Yellow Sea

Andong

Taejŏn

Taegu

Mokp'o

Pusan

**Korean
Peninsula**

Railroads

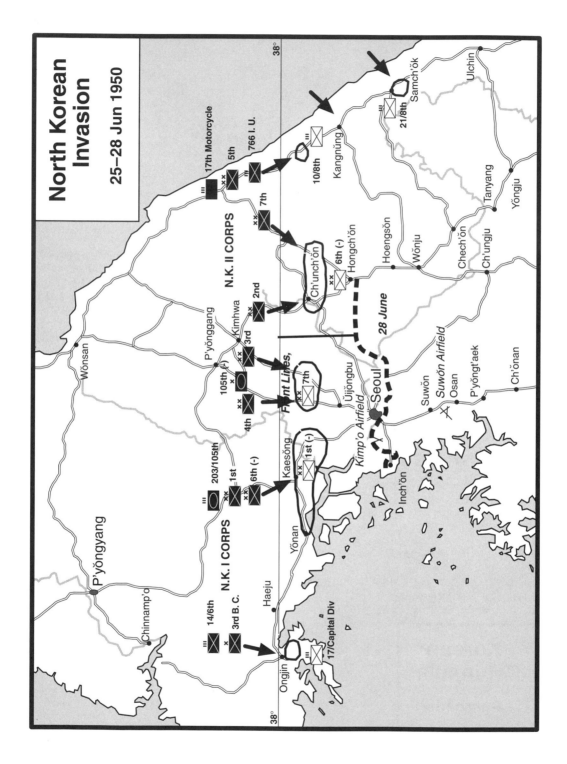

North Korean Invasion 25–28 Jun 1950

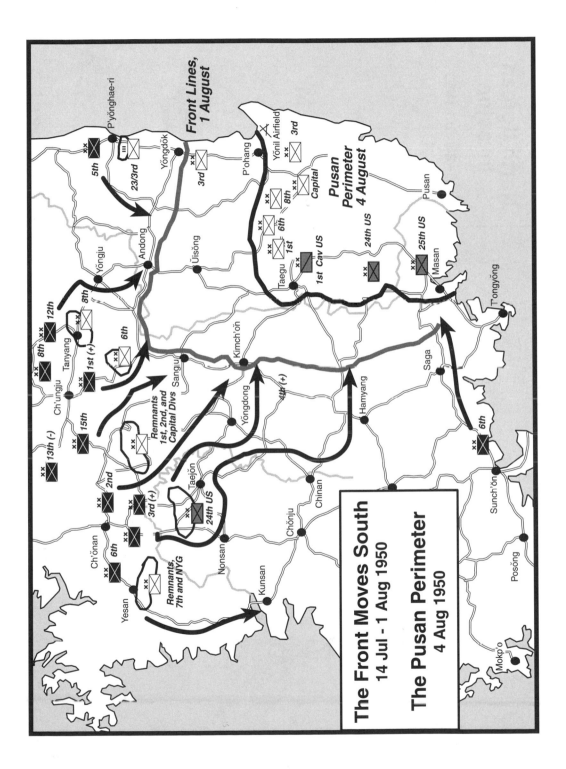

The Front Moves South
14 Jul - 1 Aug 1950

The Pusan Perimeter
4 Aug 1950

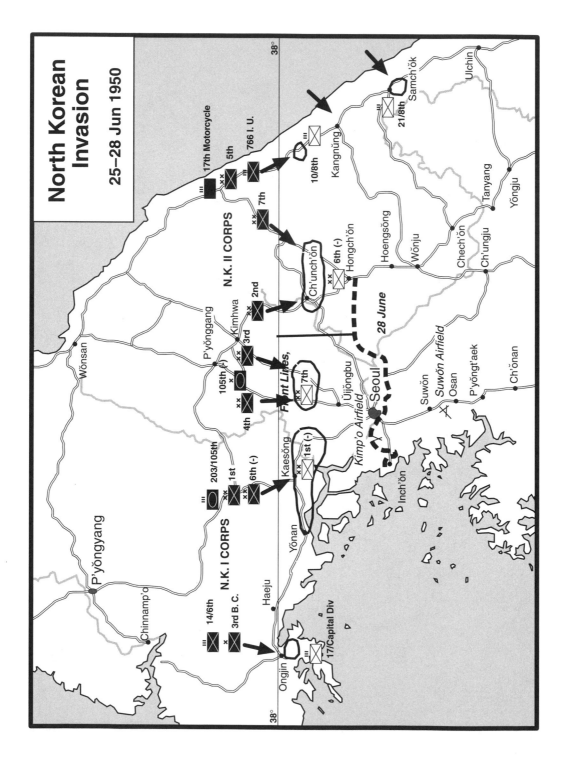

North Korean Invasion
25–28 Jun 1950

N.K. II CORPS

N.K. I CORPS

17th Motorcycle
5th
766 I. U.
7th
10/8th
21st
Samch'ŏk
Ulchin
Kangnŭng
38°
Hoengsŏng
Hongch'ŏn
6th (-)
Ch'unch'ŏn
Wŏnju
Chech'ŏn
Ch'ungju
Yŏngju
Tanyang
2nd
3rd
Kimhwa
P'yŏnggang
105th (-)
4th
7th
Front Lines,
28 June
Ŭijŏngbu
Seoul
Kimp'o Airfield
Suwŏn
Suwŏn Airfield
Osan
P'yŏngt'aek
Ch'ŏnan
Wŏnsan
203/105th
1st
6th (-)
Kaesŏng
1st (-)
Yŏnan
Inch'ŏn
P'yŏngyang
Chinnamp'o
Haeju
14/6th
3rd B. C.
Ongjin
17/Capital Div
38°

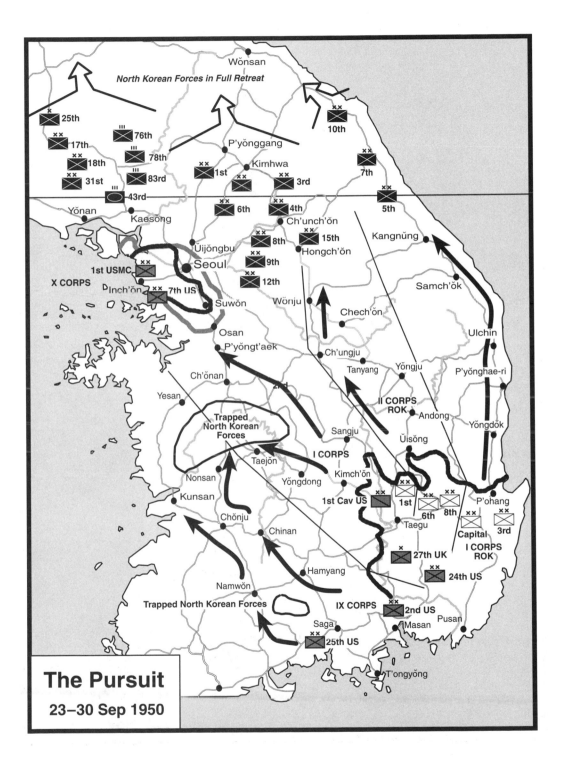

The Pursuit

23–30 Sep 1950

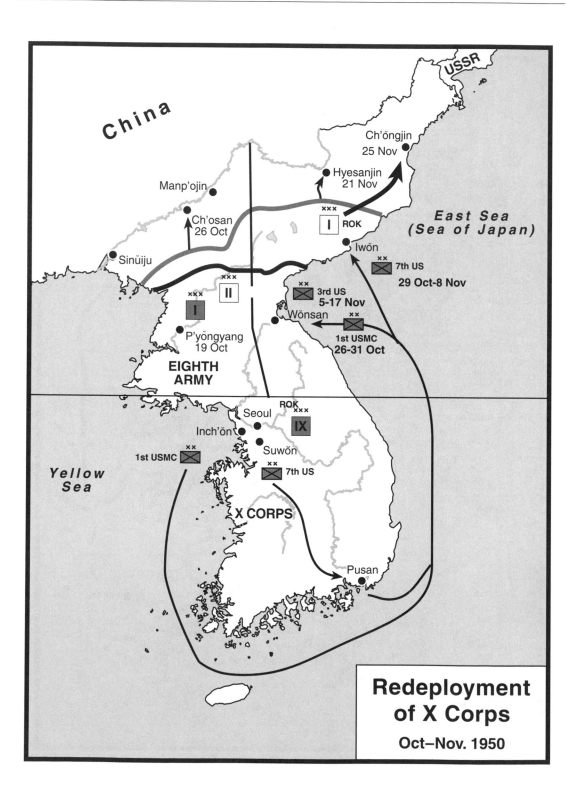

China

USSR

Ch'ŏngjin
25 Nov

Manp'ojin

Hyesanjin
21 Nov

Ch'osan
26 Oct

I ROK

East Sea
(Sea of Japan)

Sinŭiju

Iwŏn

7th US
29 Oct-8 Nov

II

3rd US
5-17 Nov

I

Wŏnsan

1st USMC
26-31 Oct

P'yŏngyang
19 Oct

EIGHTH
ARMY

ROK

Seoul

IX

Inch'ŏn

Yellow
Sea

Suwŏn

1st USMC

7th US

X CORPS

Pusan

**Redeployment
of X Corps**

Oct–Nov. 1950

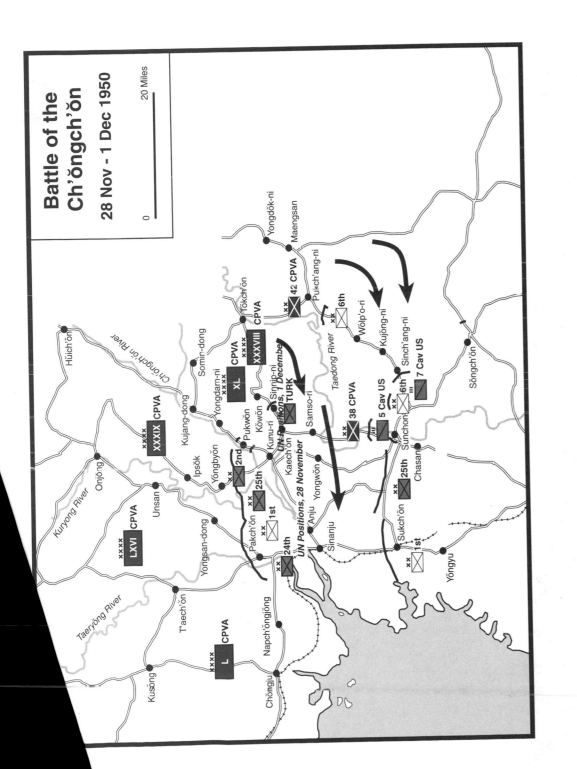

Battle of the Ch'ŏngch'ŏn

28 Nov - 1 Dec 1950

0   20 Miles

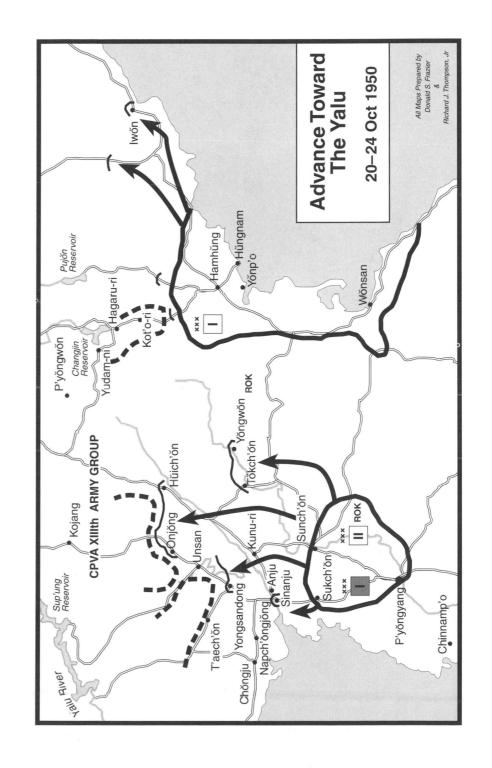

Advance Toward The Yalu

20–24 Oct 1950

All Maps Prepared by
Donald S. Frazier
&
Richard J. Thompson, Jr

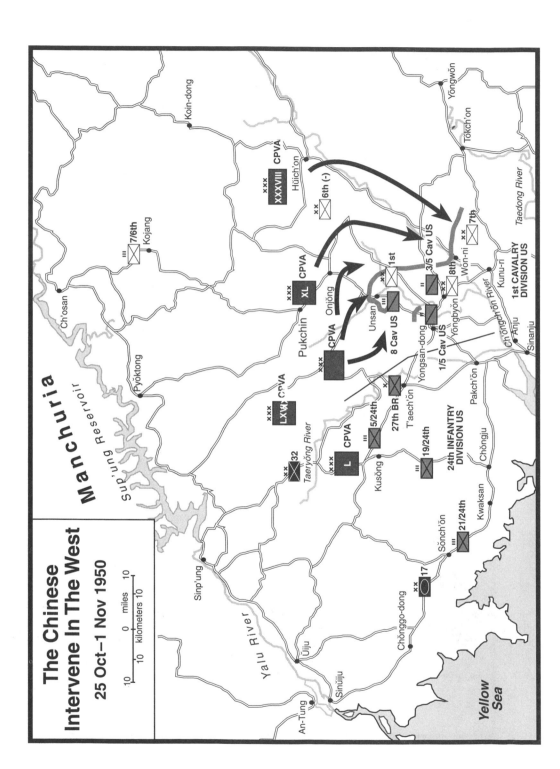

The Chinese Intervene In The West
25 Oct–1 Nov 1950

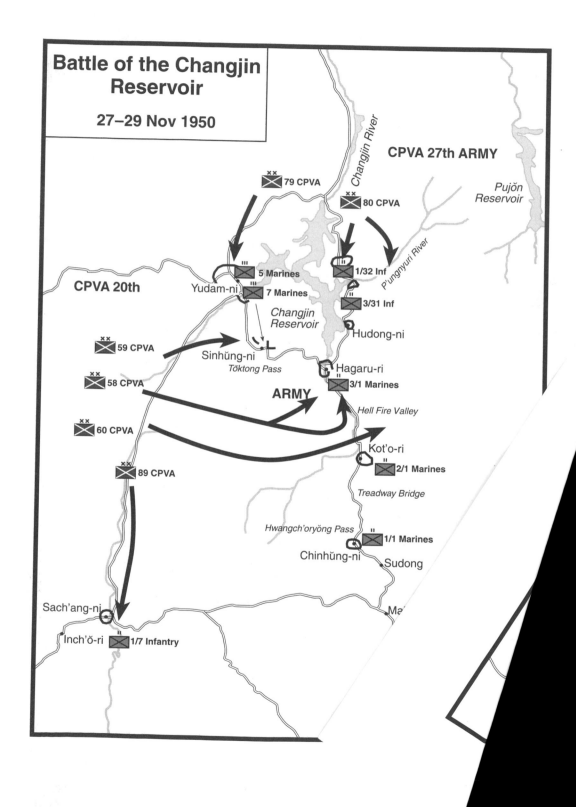

Battle of the Changjin Reservoir
27–29 Nov 1950

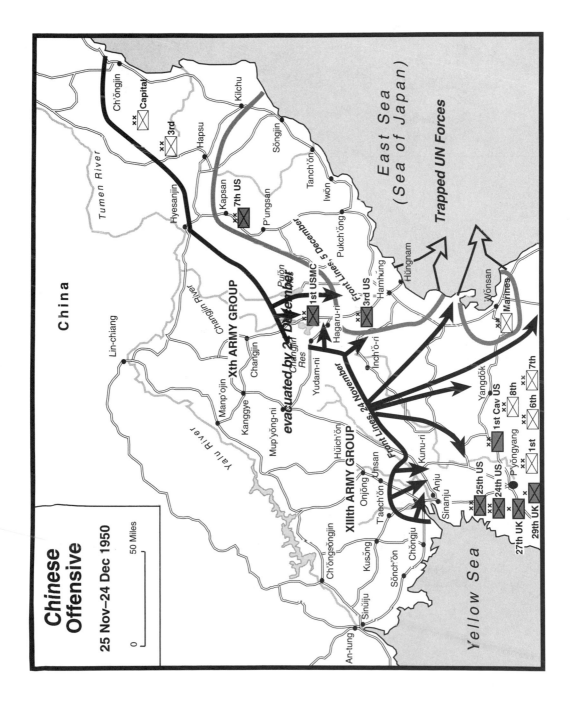

Chinese Offensive

25 Nov–24 Dec 1950

0   50 Miles

China

Tumen River

Ch'ŏngjin

Capital

3rd

Hapsu

Kilchu

Songjin

Tanch'on

*East Sea
(Sea of Japan)*

Kapsan

7th US

P'ungsan

Iwŏn

Pukch'ŏng

Trapped UN Forces

Hyesanjin

Changjin River

Lin-chiang

Xth ARMY GROUP

Pujon

1st USMC

Front Lines, 5 December

3rd US

Hamhung

Hŭngnam

Wŏnsan

Marines

evacuated by 24 December

Changjin
Res

Hagaru-ri

Manp'ojin

Changjin

Yudam-ni

Inch'o-ri

Kanggye

Mup'yong-ni

Hŭich'ŏn

Front Lines, 24 November

Yangdŏk

7th

Yalu River

XIIIth ARMY GROUP

Kunu-ri

1st Cav US

8th

6th

Onjŏng

Unsan

Anju

P'yŏngyang

1st

Ch'ŏngsŏngjin

Kusŏng

T'aech'ŏn

Sinanju

25th US

24th US

Kusang

Sŏnch'ŏn

Chŏngju

27th UK

29th UK

Sinŭiju

An-tung

Yellow Sea

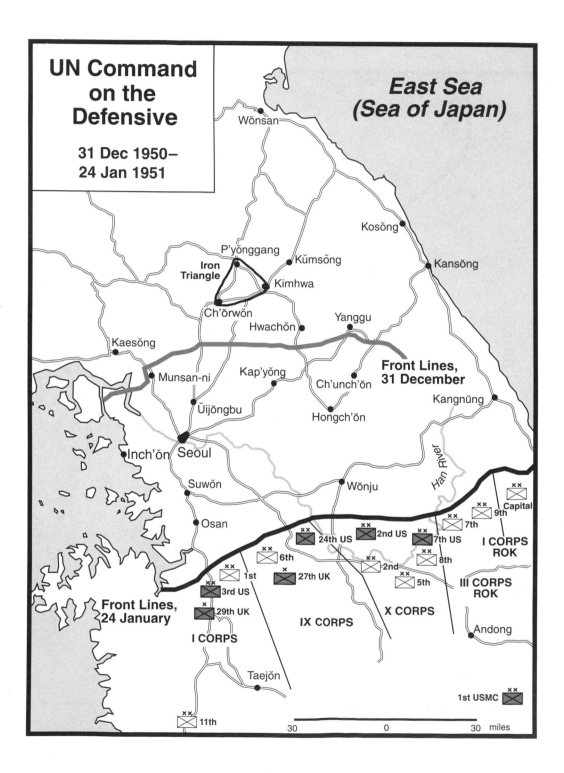

UN Command
on the
Defensive

31 Dec 1950–
24 Jan 1951

*East Sea
(Sea of Japan)*

Wŏnsan

Kosŏng

Kansŏng

P'yŏnggang

Kŭmsŏng

**Iron
Triangle**

Kimhwa

Ch'ŏrwŏn

Hwachŏn

Yanggu

Kaesŏng

Munsan-ni

Kap'yŏng

Ch'unch'ŏn

**Front Lines,
31 December**

Ŭijŏngbu

Kangnŭng

Hongch'ŏn

Han River

Inch'ŏn

Seoul

Suwŏn

Wŏnju

Capital

9th

7th

Osan

24th US

2nd US

7th US

**I CORPS
ROK**

6th

2nd

8th

**Front Lines,
24 January**

1st

27th UK

5th

**III CORPS
ROK**

3rd US

X CORPS

29th UK

IX CORPS

Andong

I CORPS

Taejŏn

1st USMC

11th

30   0   30   miles

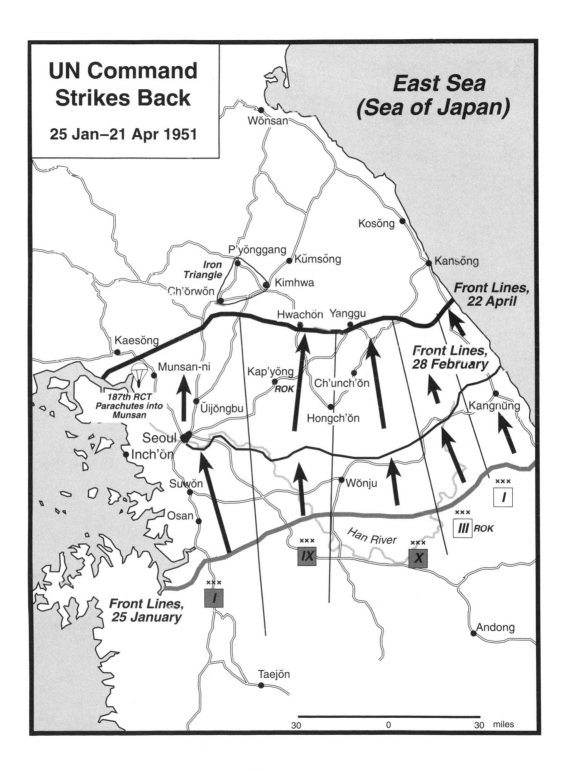

UN Command Strikes Back

25 Jan–21 Apr 1951

East Sea (Sea of Japan)

Wŏnsan

Kosŏng

Kansŏng

P'yŏnggang
Kŭmsŏng

Iron Triangle
Kimhwa

Ch'ŏrwŏn

Front Lines, 22 April

Hwachŏn   Yanggu

Kaesŏng

Front Lines, 28 February

Munsan-ni

Kap'yŏng

Ch'unch'ŏn

187th RCT Parachutes into Munsan

ROK

Kangnŭng

Ŭijŏngbu

Hongch'ŏn

Seoul
Inch'ŏn

Suwŏn

Wŏnju

xxx

I

Osan

Han River

xxx

III ROK

xxx

IX

xxx

X

xxx

I

Front Lines, 25 January

Andong

Taejŏn

30   0   30   miles

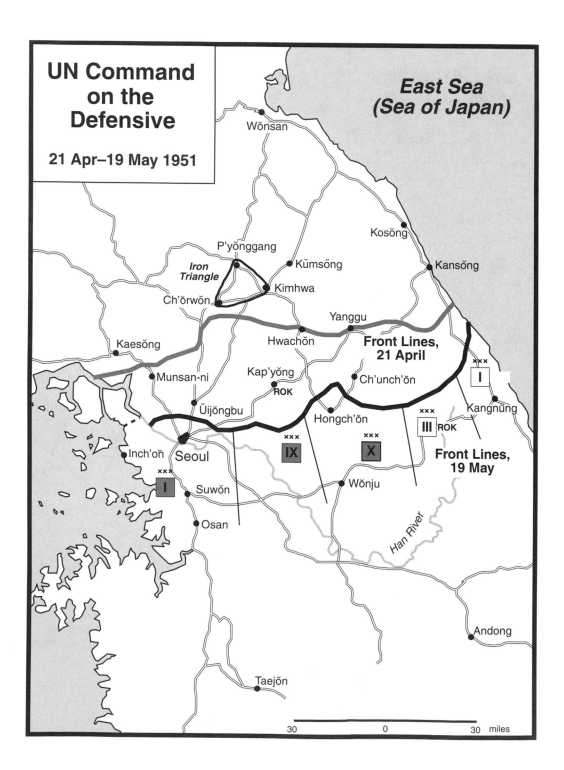

UN Command on the Defensive

21 Apr–19 May 1951

East Sea (Sea of Japan)

Wŏnsan

Kosŏng

Kansŏng

P'yŏnggang

Kŭmsŏng

Iron Triangle

Kimhwa

Ch'ŏrwŏn

Yanggu

Hwachŏn

Front Lines, 21 April

Kaesŏng

Kap'yŏng

Ch'unch'ŏn

×××
I

ROK

Munsan-ni

Ŭijŏngbu

Hongch'ŏn

Kangnŭng

×××
III ROK

×××
IX

×××
X

Front Lines, 19 May

Inch'ŏn

Seoul

×××
I

Suwŏn

Wŏnju

Osan

Han River

Andong

Taejŏn

30   0   30 miles

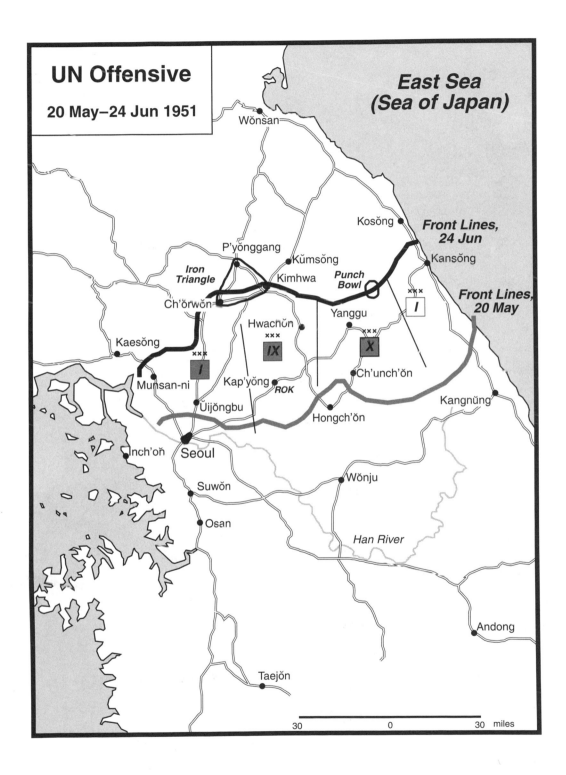

UN Offensive

20 May–24 Jun 1951

East Sea (Sea of Japan)

Wŏnsan

Kosŏng

Front Lines, 24 Jun

Kansŏng

P'yŏnggang

Kŭmsŏng

Iron Triangle

Kimhwa

Punch Bowl

Front Lines, 20 May

Ch'ŏrwŏn

×××
I

Hwachŏn

×××
IX

Yanggu

×××
X

Kaesŏng

×××
I

Kap'yŏng

ROK

Ch'unch'ŏn

Munsan-ni

Ŭijŏngbu

Hongch'ŏn

Kangnŭng

Inch'oŏ

Seoul

Suwŏn

Wŏnju

Osan

Han River

Andong

Taejŏn

30   0   30   miles

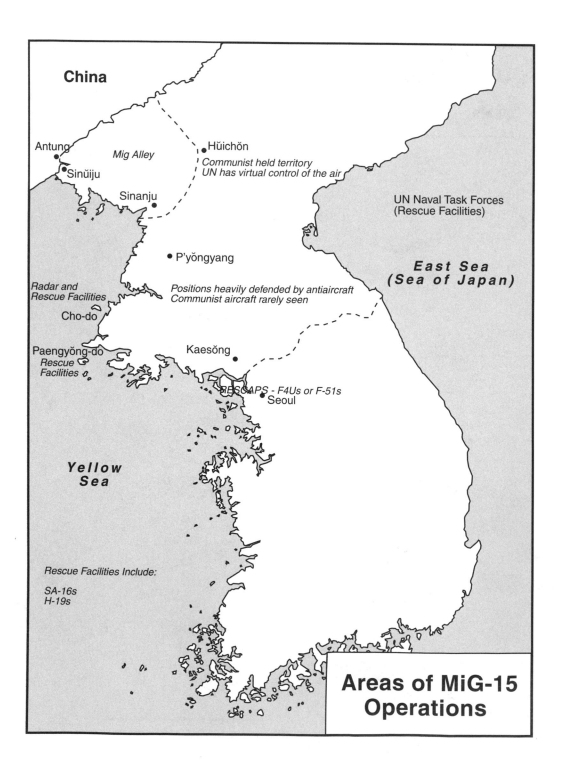

China

Antung

Mig Alley

Sinŭiju

Sinanju

Hŭichŏn

Communist held territory
UN has virtual control of the air

UN Naval Task Forces
(Rescue Facilities)

East Sea
(Sea of Japan)

P'yŏngyang

Positions heavily defended by antiaircraft
Communist aircraft rarely seen

Radar and
Rescue Facilities

Cho-do

Paengyŏng-do
Rescue
Facilities

Kaesŏng

RESCAPS - F4Us or F-51s

Seoul

Yellow
Sea

Rescue Facilities Include:

SA-16s
H-19s

Areas of MiG-15 Operations

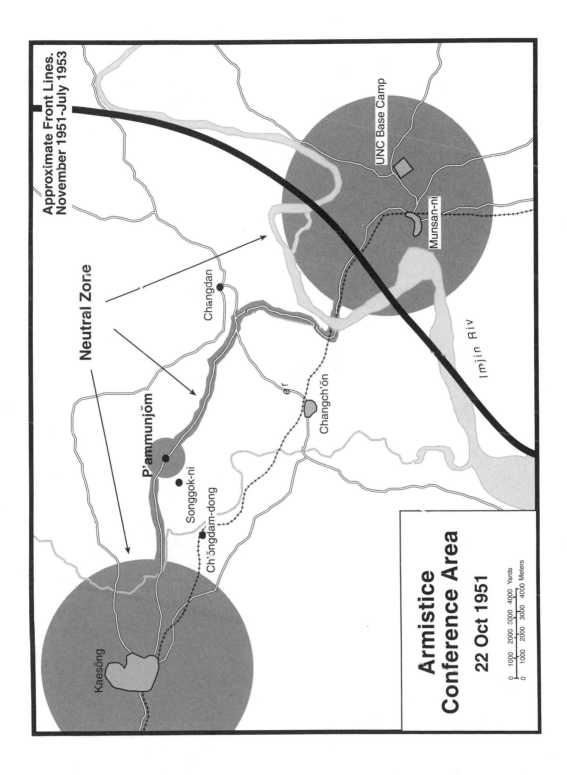

Approximate Front Lines.
November 1951-July 1953

Neutral Zone

UNC Base Camp

Munsan-ni

Changdan

Imjin Riv

P'anmunjŏm

Changch'ŏn

Songgok-ni

Ch'ŏngdam-dong

Kaesŏng

**Armistice
Conference Area**
22 Oct 1951

0   1000   2000   3000   4000 Yards
0   1000   2000   3000   4000 Meters

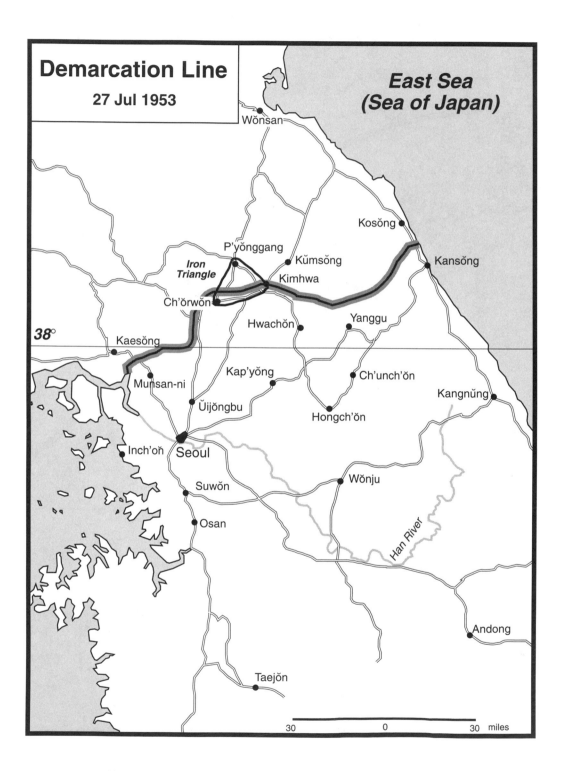

Demarcation Line
27 Jul 1953

Wŏnsan

East Sea
(Sea of Japan)

Kosŏng

P'yŏnggang

Kŭmsŏng

Iron
Triangle

Kimhwa

Kansŏng

Ch'ŏrwŏn

Hwachŏn

Yanggu

38°

Kaesŏng

Munsan-ni

Kap'yŏng

Ch'unch'ŏn

Kangnŭng

Ŭijŏngbu

Hongch'ŏn

Inch'ŏn

Seoul

Suwŏn

Wŏnju

Osan

Han River

Andong

Taejŏn

30   0   30   miles

ENCYCLOPEDIA OF

The Korean War

A Political, Social, and Military History

A

Aces, U.S. Air Force

The term "ace" comes from pre–World War I French slang "as," referring originally to an athletic champion. Early in World War I, French pilots called their top pilots "aces." By 1915 France officially recognized any pilot with ten or more aerial victories as an "ace." British and German air forces soon followed this.

Because the United States entered the conflict so late, it reduced the number of confirmed aerial kills necessary to become an ace to five. This soon became the standard for all aerial aces. It is generally accepted that only fighter pilots can be aces. The first U.S. ace was World War I fighter pilot Captain Edward V. "Eddie" Rickenbacker. He ended the war with twenty-six kills.

The U.S. Air Force (USAF) had thirty-eight jet-versus-jet aces during the Korean War. In addition, one U.S. Marine Corps (USMC) pilot flying in an F-86 with USAF units became an ace. One U.S. Navy pilot flying a propeller aircraft out of a USAF base against propeller aircraft also became an ace. Of these aces, six had been aces in World War II. U.S. aces were credited with 305.5 of the total of 810 air-to-air combat victories credited to U.S. pilots during the war.

In the order in which they became an ace, the first American ace in Korea was Colonel James Jabara (1923–1966). He was also the first jet-versus-jet ace in the world. (There were twenty-two German jet aces in World War II against only propeller aircraft.) In World War II, Jabara flew P-51s over Europe, scoring 1.5 kills during 108 combat sorties. Jabara first went to Korea as a captain in 1950 and flew F-80s and F-86s with the 4th Fighter Interceptor Wing (4FIW) of the Fifth Air Force (5AF). During this first tour, he shot down six MiG-15s, becoming an ace on 20 May 1951.

Early in the war, aces were automatically rotated back to the United States. This policy was changed in 1952 at the request of pilots such as Jabara. Jabara, then a major, returned to down nine more MiG-15s during May–July 1953. He was the second-ranking Korean War ace with fifteen total kills, and he was one of only two triple aces. Overall, he had 16.5 victories during his career.

First Lieutenant (later Captain) Richard S. Becker of the 4FIW became the second ace on 9 September 1951, when he shot down his fifth MiG. Getting his fifth enemy jet on the same day was the third U.S. ace, First Lieutenant (later Captain) Ralph D. Gibson, also of the 4FIW. Nearly two months later, on 27 November 1951, Major Richard D. Creighton of the

4th became the fourth ace. With a total of five kills each, all three pilots were rotated home and never returned.

The fifth ace was Lieutenant Colonel (then Major) George A. Davis (1920–1952). Davis was the first American ace in two wars. He became a pilot in 1942. Flying 266 combat sorties in a P-47 in the Pacific, he scored seven victories. Davis went to Korea in 1951 as the commander of the 334th Fighter Interceptor Squadron (334FIS) flying F-86s. Between 1 November 1951 and 10 February 1952 Davis shot down eleven MiGs and three Tu-2 twin-engine medium bombers. He became an ace on 30 November. On 10 February, Davis downed two enemy jets, thus becoming the leading U.S. ace at the time, but he himself was shot down and killed. For his heroism, he received the Medal of Honor. He was one of only four airmen to earn this honor in Korea.

The sixth ace was Major Winton W. Marshall of the 51st Fighter Wing (51FW). He was credited with 6.5 kills, among them a Tu-2 bomber, a La-9 fighter, and 4.5 MiG-15s. He gained his last two kills on 30 November.

Major (later Colonel) William T. Whisner, Jr. (1923–1989) of the 51st became the U.S.'s second two-war ace on 23 February 1952, with the last of 5.5 victories. He received his wings in 1943, and, flying P-47s and P-51s over Europe, he was credited with 15.5 kills. On 21 November 1944, he downed seven enemy Fw-190s in one engagement. He tied for sixteenth on the all-time list of American aces with his total of 21 kills.

Colonel Francis S. "Gabby" Gabreski (1919–   ) became the Korean War's eighth American jet ace on 1 April 1952. By the time he returned home, he had been credited with 34.5 kills (some sources say 37.5) in two wars, ranking him third on the all-time U.S. aces list. During World War II, he flew 166 combat sorties over Europe, shooting down 28 (some sources say 31) German fighters between 22 May and 20 July 1944. During a strafing run on 20 July he crashed and spent the rest of the war in a German prisoner-of-war (POW) camp. Gabreski went to Korea in 1950 as the deputy commander of the 4FIW, and the next year he became commander of the 51FW. He had 6.5 kills in Korea.

Eight additional F-86 pilots became aces in the spring of 1952. First Lieutenant (later Captain) Robert H. Moore gained the distinction on 3 April; he had five total kills. Three days later, Captain Ivan C. Kincheloe became the tenth ace, also totaling five kills. On the 21st, Captain Robert J. Love became an ace. On the

26th, Major William H. Wescott got his fifth kill. Love totaled six kills. Wescott ended his tour with five kills, as did Captain Robert T. Latshaw, Jr., who became an ace on 3 May. Major Donald E. Adams became an ace the same afternoon as Latshaw and went on to total 6.5 kills. Adams was followed on 15 May by Lieutenant James H. Kasler who ultimately had six victories.

The U.S.'s sixteenth ace was Brigadier General (then Colonel) Harrison R. Thyng (1919–1983), another of the six Americans to become an ace in two wars. He became a pilot in 1940 and flew for the 309th Fighter Squadron, which flew British-made Spitfires. He scored victories over six German, one Italian, and one Vichy French aircraft while flying 162 combat missions in Europe. At age 26, Thyng became a colonel, commanding the 413th Long Range Fighter Group, flying P-47s in the Pacific. There he shot down one Japanese fighter.

In Korea, Colonel Thyng commanded the 4FIW and became an ace on 20 May 1952. He eventually shot down five MiG-15s while flying 114 combat sorties. In April 1966 he flew a handful of sorties in Vietnam just before his retirement.

Lieutenant John F. Low, who eventually totaled nine kills, became an ace on 15 June 1952, after only six months as a pilot. Low was followed on 8 August by Captain Clifford D. Jolley, who ultimately got seven MiG kills.

Ace nineteen was Major General Frederick C. "Boots" Blesse (1921–). As a captain and major he spent two tours in Korea flying F-51s and F-80s during his first tour and F-86s during the second. During his second, he downed nine MiG-15s and one La-9. Blesse was shot down in September but rescued. When he returned home in October 1952, Blesse was the leading U.S. ace. His total of ten kills made him the first jet double ace in U.S. history and made him the U.S.'s sixth-ranked jet ace. Blesse flew 156 more combat sorties over Vietnam (1967–1968) and retired in 1975 with 650 combat sorties and 6,500 flying hours.

As MiG-15 activities increased over MiG Alley, U.S. kills also rose. On 21 September 1952, Captain (later Major) Robinson Risner became the U.S.'s twentieth ace, ultimately totaling eight victories. On 17 November 1952, Colonel Royal N. Baker, commander of the 4th Fighter Group (4FG), shot down his fifth Communist fighter. By the time he rotated home on 17 March 1953, he had been credited with shooting down 12 MiGs and one La-9. With his 3.5 kills in World War II, he ended his career with 16.5 total victories. When he left Korea he was the U.S.'s top jet ace.

The day after Baker became an ace, Captain Leonard W. Lilley, flying with the 334th Squadron, downed his fifth MiG. He totaled seven kills. Four days later, First Lieutenant (later Captain) Cecil G.

Foster of the 51FW became the twenty-third U.S. ace. Foster eventually downed nine Communist fighters.

On 24 January 1953, Captain Dolphin D. Overton, III, and First Lieutenant (later Captain) Harold E. Fischer, Jr., both of the 51FW, became aces. Overton had the record for the shortest time span for becoming an ace, shooting all five of his MiGs during his last four missions. Fischer, on the other hand, went on to get ten kills and become a double ace. Captain Manuel J. Fernandez, 4FIW, not only became the U.S.'s twenty-sixth ace on 18 February but ultimately was credited with 14.5 kills, becoming a double ace.

The U.S.'s ace of aces in Korea was its twenty-seventh ace, First Lieutenant (later Captain) Joseph McConnell, Jr. (1922–1954) of the 51FW. He enlisted as a private in the U.S. Army in 1940. He became an officer and navigator in 1944, flying B-24 combat missions in Europe. In 1948 he became a fighter pilot. In 1952, he arrived in Korea as flight leader for the 16th Squadron of the 51FW. He was an aggressive pilot, getting his fifth kill in less than two months. He had shot down eight MiGs before flak forced him to parachute into the Yellow Sea on 12 April. After his rescue he went on to get eight more kills, six during 13–18 May 1953. His 16 victories in 106 combat sorties made him the U.S.'s top Korean War ace as well as its top jet ace for all wars. He was also one of only two triple aces in Korea. McConnell was killed in 1954 while testing a newly modified F-86H at Edwards Air Force Base, California. Not long after, his life story was made into a movie, *The McConnell Story,* starring Alan Ladd and June Allison.

On 27 March 1953, Major James P. Hagerstram became the twenty-eighth American ace and the 18th Fighter Bomber Wing's only ace. Flying an F-86F, he totaled 5.5 kills.

A day later Colonel James K. Johnson and Lieutenant Colonel George L. Jones, both of the 4FIW, became aces. Johnson became a double ace with ten kills, and Jones was credited with 6.5 victories.

For F-86 Sabre pilots, May and June 1953 recalled the "Mariannas Turkey Shoot" in June 1944 when U.S. Naval aviators shot down so many Japanese planes of World War II. During June more pilots, five, became aces than in any other month of the Korean War. On 18 May, Lieutenant Colonel George L. Ruddell of the Fifty-first shot down his fifth of his total of eight MiGs to become the thirty-first ace.

On 5 June, thirty-seven-year-old Major (later Lieutenant Colonel) Vermont L. Garrison became the U.S.'s thirty-second ace and the oldest ace of the Korea War. Flying Spitfires and Hurricanes with the Royal Air Force at the beginning of World War II, Garrison transferred to the U.S. Army Air Forces in 1943 and was credited with 7.33 kills before being shot down in 1944 and spending the remainder of the war in a German POW camp. Garrison returned to combat in Korea in November 1952 and eventually shot down ten MiGs. He not only became a double ace in Korea but an ace in two wars with 17.33 victories.

Captains Lonnie R. Moore and Ralph S. Parr both became aces on 18 June. Both men became double aces with ten kills each. Four days later Colonel Robert P. Baldwin became the thirty-fifth U.S. ace, and on 30 June Lieutenant Henry Buttelmann, the youngest ace in Korea (not yet twenty-four years old), became the thirty-sixth American ace. Buttelmann also had the shortest flight time to become an ace. He had arrived in Korea on 19 June and eleven days later was an ace. Baldwin totaled five kills; Buttelmann got seven.

Major John F. Bolt was the only USMC pilot to become an ace in the war. Flying with the 51FW, on 11 July he shot down his fifth and sixth MiGs, his final total for the war.

The last two jet aces of the war were Captain Clyde A. Curtin and Major Stephen L. Bettinger both of the 4FIW. On 19–20 July both shot down their fifth and final MiGs to become the thirty-eighth and thirty-ninth U.S. aces of the war.

The last jet engagements of the war came on 22 July when Lieutenant Sam P. Young downed the last two MiGs.

The only propeller and U.S. Navy ace of the Korean War was Lieutenant Gary Bordelon, who flew off the carrier *Princeton* in a F-4U-5N Corsair. Flying from a 5AF field, he downed five Yak-18 and La-11 night raiders, known as "Bed-Check Charlies."

Most aces of the Korean War flew F-86s, and most flew patrols against massed formations of MiG-15s over MiG Alley. The battles there, which captured popular attention in the United States, saw superior veteran U.S. pilots, including eighteen former World War II aces, turn their experience, training, ever-improving technology, and superior tactics into one of the most one-sided air victories in airpower history. Although the United States lost 1,166 airmen and 750 planes in Korea, only a relative few of these were F-86 pilots or aircraft. These pilots received credit for 792 MiG kills and 18 others. They lost 218 F-86s: 76 to MiGs, 19 to ground fire, 15 to unknown enemy action, 13 to unknown operational causes, and the remainder to mechanical failure or accidents. Because there were fewer air-to-air engagements during the Vietnam and the Persian Gulf Wars, the records of the top aces of the Korean War remain intact to this day.

—*William Head*

References:
Bright, Charles D., ed. *Historical Dictionary of the U.S. Air Force.* Westport, CT: Greenwood Press, 1992.

Futrell, Robert F. *The United States Air Force in Korea, 1950–1953.* Rev. ed. Washington, DC: Office of the Chief of Air Force History, 1983.

Haulman, Daniel L., and Col. William C. Stancik. *Air Force Victory Credits: World War I, World War II, Korea, and Vietnam.* Maxwell Air Force Base, AL: U.S. Historical Research Center, 1988.

Thompson, Wayne. "The Air War over Korea." In *Winged Shield, Wing Sword: A History of the United States Air Force,* edited by Bernard C. Nalty. Washington, DC: U.S. Air Force History and Museum Program, 1997, 3-52.

Toliver, Raymond F., and Trevor J. Constable. *Fighter Aces of the United States of America.* Fallbrook, CA: Aero Publishers, 1979.

See also: Aerial Combat; Air Power in the War; Aircraft (Principal Combat); "Bed-Check Charlies"; Medal of Honor Winners; MiG Alley.

Acheson, Dean Goodersham
(1893–1971)

One of the primary architects of U.S. foreign policy during the initial stages of the Cold War and Secretary of State during the Korean War. Dean Goodersham Acheson was born on 11 April 1893 in Middletown, Connecticut. His father was an English immigrant Episcopal minister and later bishop; his mother was the daughter of a Canadian whiskey distiller and bank president. Educated at Groton, Yale

Dean G. Acheson, Truman's top advisor during the Korean War. (Harry S. Truman Library)

President Truman at his desk in the Oval Office with Secretary of State Dean Acheson, discussing Acheson's recent meetings with NATO foreign and defense ministers in Brussels, 21 December 1950. (National Park Service Photograph. Harry S. Truman Library)

University, and Harvard Law School, Acheson clerked under Supreme Court Justice Louis D. Brandeis and by the mid-1920s was a partner in one of Washington's most prestigious law firms. He served briefly as undersecretary of the Treasury in 1933 before resuming private practice. At the beginning of World War II, he returned to government service as assistant secretary of state for economic affairs, where he managed the Lend-Lease program and played a leading role in establishing several postwar international organizations, including the International Monetary Fund, United Nations Relief and Rehabilitation Agency, and World Bank.

In April 1945 President Harry S. Truman promoted Acheson to undersecretary of state. Serving under James F. Byrnes and then George C. Marshall, Acheson was a key player in the development of the Truman Doctrine and the Marshall Plan. Acheson left the State Department in June 1947 but returned when Truman named him secretary of state on 21 January

1949. Among his early achievements were contributing to the formation of the North Atlantic Treaty Organization and negotiations that resulted in the creation of the Federal Republic of Germany in June 1949. He also avidly supported the recommendations of National Security Council Memorandum 68 (NSC-68), "United States Objectives and Programs for National Security."

On 12 January 1950, in the course of a speech before the National Press Club in Washington, Acheson remarked that South Korea was not within the direct defense perimeter of the United States. However, he also made clear that the United States had a strong interest in the country. Republican critics later argued that this statement invited the North Korean invasion, which occurred on 25 June 1950.

Operating from a Cold War perspective, Acheson interpreted the invasion as a direct Soviet challenge to the United States. He quickly emerged as Truman's top advisor on the war. Acheson secured a United

Nations (UN) Security Council emergency-session resolution on 25 June that condemned the action, and he secured the first UN-sanctioned authorization to employ military action to halt infringement on another country's sovereignty. With Acheson's encouragement, the president extended the Truman Doctrine to the Pacific region, thereby providing increased military aid to the Philippines and South Vietnam, and Truman ordered the U.S. Seventh Fleet to the Straits of Formosa.

On 30 June 1950, U.S. forces under UN authority and under the command of General Douglas MacArthur entered combat in Korea. At first, Acheson sought restoration of the antebellum status quo, but under severe pressure from Congress, which blamed the administration for allowing the invasion, he adopted General MacArthur's call for a decisive victory in the war. On 7 October 1950, U.S. forces, endorsed by a UN resolution, crossed the 38th parallel, the dividing line between North and South Korea.

Acheson and Truman, however, viewed the conflict in very different perspective than did General MacArthur. Truman and Acheson were apprehensive about a larger war with China; MacArthur discounted this. The secretary of state endorsed the president's order to MacArthur to employ only South Korean forces near the Chinese border. However, MacArthur insisted on sending U.S. troops to the border and the right to bomb bridges over the Yalu River, which separated China and North Korea.

When the Chinese entered the war in November 1950, sending MacArthur's forces into retreat, Acheson regretted that he had not articulated more emphatically his concerns about MacArthur's actions. He did not intend to be outflanked by the general in the future. In March 1951, when Truman and Acheson were prepared to accept a negotiated settlement along the 38th parallel, MacArthur disobeyed another presidential directive. Acheson completely agreed with Truman and the Joint Chiefs of Staff that MacArthur must be relieved.

Interpreting the Korean War as part of a worldwide challenge, Truman and Acheson initiated a number of actions to shore up the U.S. national security posture. These included reviving the draft, quadrupling the defense budget, nearly doubling air force wings to 100 and army personnel to 3.5 million, establishing new bases worldwide, developing the thermonuclear bomb, and signing a peace treaty with Japan that provided U.S. bases in the country.

Despite his hard-line Cold War foreign policy, Acheson was a central target of Senator Joseph McCarthy and the Republican right wing known as the China lobby. Focusing on a white paper directed by Acheson and that was highly critical of Jiang Jieshi (Chiang Kai-shek), they blamed the State Department for the "fall of China" to the Communists. McCarthy also lambasted Acheson for his support of Alger Hiss. Those critical of the Truman administration's conduct of the Korean War especially blamed Acheson. The secretary of state's patrician demeanor and patronizing manner infuriated many of his detractors.

At the close of the Truman administration in January 1953, Acheson retired from public office. However, he reemerged as one of the former State and Defense Department intellectuals, known as the "Wise Men," who served as informal advisers to Presidents John Kennedy and Lyndon Johnson throughout the 1960s. Acheson wrote several books, including his memoir, *Present at the Creation: My Years at the State Department* (1969), which won the Pulitzer Prize in history in 1970. From this larger volume, Acheson wrote *The Korean War* (1971), his personal account of the conflict. This esteemed elder statesmen died on 12 October 1971 in Sandy Spring, Maryland.

—*Joe P. Dunn*

References:
Acheson, Dean. *The Korean War*. New York: W. W. Norton, 1971.
— —, *Present at the Creation: My Years at the State Department*. New York: W. W. Norton, 1969.
Brinkley, Douglas, ed. *Dean Acheson and the Making of U.S. Foreign Policy*. New York: St. Martin's Press, 1993.
Chace, James. *Acheson: The Secretary of State Who Created the American World*. New York: Simon & Schuster, 1998.
See also: China Lobby; Jiang Jieshi (Chiang Kai-Shek); MacArthur, Douglas; Marshall, George C.; McCarthy, Joseph R.; NATO (North Atlantic Treaty Organization); Truman, Harry S.; Truman's Cease-Fire Initiative; Truman's Recall of MacArthur; Yalu Bridges Controversy.

Active Defense Strategy

According to U.S. Army *Field Service Regulations*, "An effective defense consists of active and passive components combined to deprive the enemy of the initiative." Commander of the U.S. Eighth Army in Korea Lieutenant General Walton H. Walker used the active defense most effectively early in the war along the Pusan perimeter.

Active defense includes:

1. Reconnaissance patrols, the mission of which is to seek information.

2. Combat patrols, the mission of which is usually to capture prisoners, as well as to gather information on the enemy.

3. Raids, made by company or larger forces, designed to attack designated points or identified enemy positions or units. The objective of a raid is to disrupt enemy plans and inflict casualties and the loss of weapons and/or equipment.

4. Reconnaissance in force, usually conducted by a reinforced battalion or larger command. This maneu-

ver is designed to develop the enemy's strength and disposition in a given sector. The force usually consists of mobile infantry, armor, self-propelled artillery, and helicopter or other air support on station or on call.

5. Spoiling attack, made by a relatively large combined-arms force, designed to create the impression of a much larger attack. It is an attempt to inflict casualties, take prisoners, destroy enemy weapons and equipment, and disrupt enemy planned attack. Operations THUNDERBOLT and ROUNDUP, outlined below, were spoiling attacks.

These are a few examples of the results of aggressive patrolling and reconnaissances in force during the Korean War:

During 10–25 January 1951, Major General Edward M. Almond's U.S. X Corps in the west-central portion of the United Nations (UN) line across Korea employed aggressive reconnaissance and combat patrols against the four advancing divisions of the Korean People's Army (KPA, North Korean) II Corps. So well did these numerous patrols disrupt, disorganize, and delay the KPA divisions, inflicting high casualties, that by the 24th the KPA corps commander withdrew them from contact. X Corps estimated that up to half of the North Korean troops in the four divisions were casualties in those two weeks.

Between 7 and 15 January 1951, numerous and far-ranging patrols of the U.S. I and IX Corps (Major Generals Frank W. Milburn and John B. Coulter, respectively) confirmed that no large body of Communist troops were immediately in front of the two corps.

On 15 January 1951, in Operation WOLFHOUND the U.S. I Corps sent a tank-infantry team built around 1st Battalion, 27th Infantry on a deep reconnaissance in force. The force met little resistance but discovered elements of three Chinese armies nearby. A similar reconnaissance by elements of the 8th Cavalry Regiment and the 70th Tank Battalion (Task Force Jackson) in the IX Corps sector revealed that Chinese forces were deployed north of the corps along the main north-south highway.

In Operation THUNDERBOLT, UN and U.S. Eighth Army commander Lieutenant General Matthew B. Ridgway, who wanted to learn more about enemy dispositions before launching an all-out counteroffensive, ordered I and IX Corps to each send a reinforced division-sized force on a phased reconnaissance in force north to the Han River. These forces moved out on 25 January 1951 in a tightly controlled advance amply supported by tactical air. Elements of General Almond's X Corps protected the right flank of the IX Corps during the operation.

Operation THUNDERBOLT soon took on the aspects of a controlled offensive. U.S. forces soon discovered that the Chinese Fiftieth Army had been deployed as a reconnaissance screen. THUNDER-

BOLT forces reached the Han River by 10 February. Meantime, Operation ROUNDUP, staged by elements of the U.S. X Corps and ROK III Corps, and designed to disrupt the KPA V and II Corps, got under way on 4 February. The troops faced ever-increasing resistance in rugged terrain, limiting ROUNDUP's advance to about ten miles.

These aggressive and massive "reconnaissances" threw Communist forces off balance, created heavy casualties, and ultimately led to Operations KILLER, designed to inflict maximum casualties on the enemy, and RIPPER, which included the successful assault crossing of the Han River by elements of the 25th Infantry Division. Without these active defensive efforts, the initiative would have remained with the Chinese and North Koreans, with perhaps very different results for the UN in Korea.

On 12 November 1951, General Ridgway ordered Lieutenant General James A. Van Fleet, commanding UN troops in Korea, to assume an "active defense." This led to six months of patrols, raids, and ambushes by UN troops and counteraction by Communist forces. However, by April 1952 the Communists were stronger and better prepared to continue the war than in November 1951. This active defense may have prevented Communist forces from mounting an offensive, but it did little to inflict heavy casualties and punish them.

—Uzal W. Ent

References:

Ent, Uzal W. *Fighting on the Brink: Defense of the Pusan Perimeter.* Paducah, KY: Turner, 1996.

"Fundamentals of the Defense." In *Field Service Regulations, Operations.* Washington, DC: Department of the Army, 1993.

Hermes, Walter G. *United States Army in the Korean War: Truce Tent and Fighting Front.* Washington, DC: Office of the Chief of Military History, 1966.

Mossman, Billy C. *U.S. Army in the Korean War: Ebb and Flow, November 1950–July 1951.* Washington, DC: U.S. Army Center of Military History, 1990.

See also: Almond, Edward Mallory; Coulter, John Breitling; KILLER, Operation; Milburn, Frank William; Ridgway, Matthew Bunker; RIPPER, Operation; ROUNDUP, Operation; THUNDERBOLT, Operation; Van Fleet, James Alward; Walker, Walton Harris; WOLFHOUND, Operation.

ADCOM (General Headquarters Advance Command, Korea)

U.S. fact-finding mission on the situation in the Republic of Korea (ROK, South Korea) dispatched there after the 25 June 1950 Korean People's Army (KPA, North Korean) invasion of the ROK (South Korea). U.S. President Harry S. Truman and his advisors agreed on the necessity of defending South Korea, but they were unaware of the details of the attack and whether or not the ROK military needed assistance.

Upon arriving in Washington from his home in Missouri on the night of 25 June, the president called a meeting at Blair House with Secretary of State Dean Acheson and most of the senior foreign policy and military advisors. Here Truman approved the suggestion of State Department officials that a survey team be dispatched to report on the situation.

General Douglas MacArthur dispatched the survey mission and named Brigadier General John H. Church as its commander. Upon learning of the decision of the Joint Chiefs of Staff to commit air and naval support to the defense of the ROK, MacArthur changed the designation of the team to the Advance Command and Liaison Group in Korea (ADCOM). MacArthur expanded the duties of Church's command to include direction of U.S. military forces in the defense of South Korea.

Church and his command arrived in South Korea on 27 June 1950 at the city of Suwŏn, south of the capital of Seoul. U.S. Ambassador John Muccio met Church at the airfield and briefed him on the situation. Church immediately established his headquarters in a nearby agricultural college. He then met with ROK Army (ROKA) Chief of Staff General Ch'ae Pyŏng-dŏk and stressed the need for rallying the ROK's badly shaken army to mount an effective defense.

The situation, however, continued to deteriorate rapidly despite Church's efforts, which did, however, result in a better organized defense. On 28 June, KPA forces captured Seoul and continued to drive south. Church reported to MacArthur that the United States must commit ground forces to stop the North Koreans. This report prompted MacArthur to fly from Japan to Korea on 29 June to view the conflict himself. Before MacArthur left, he issued orders to Church's command to continue its efforts to keep the ROK forces from disintegrating in the face of the North Korean advance. MacArthur's appraisal of the condition of the ROKA on 30 June, combined with another report from Church on the same day, painted a somber picture. Upon MacArthur's request, Truman gave him the authority to commit ground troops under his command in South Korea. ADCOM's role largely ended at this point as the U.S. Army readied for combat in Korea.

—*Eric W. Osborne*

References:

Spanier, John W. *The Truman-MacArthur Controversy and the Korean War.* Cambridge, MA: Harvard University Press, 1959.

Toland, John. *In Mortal Combat: Korea, 1950–1953.* New York: William Morrow, 1991.

U.S. Department of State, Bureau of Public Affairs. *Foreign Relations of the United States, 1950.* Vol. 7, *Korea.* Washington, DC: U.S. Government Printing Office, 1976.

See also: Ch'ae Pyŏng-dŏk ; Church, John H.; Joint Chiefs of Staff (JCS); MacArthur, Douglas; Muccio, John J.; Truman, Harry S.

Aerial Combat

Early Days

As with every other element of the Department of Defense, the U.S. Air Force and the U.S. Navy were completely surprised by President Harry S. Truman's decision to oppose militarily the June 1950 North Korean invasion of South Korea. Neither service had yet recovered from the devastating effects of demobilization after World War II, and neither had adequate equipment or personnel on hand in the Far East to engage in a war against the military forces of the Democratic People's Republic of Korea (DPRK, North Korea), which had been well equipped and well trained by the Soviet Union.

In sharp contrast, military forces of the Republic of Korea (ROK, South Korea) lacked both equipment and training. U.S. policy had been to provide South Korea with only a minimum of heavy equipment—armor, artillery, and aircraft—because of concern that a well-equipped ROK would invade North Korea to unify the two halves of Korea. As the Korean People's Army (KPA, North Korea) swept south, threatening to overrun completely the peninsula and capture the few U.S. ground forces there, the only immediate military response available was U.S. air power.

Fortunately for the United Nations Command (UNC), the DPRK possessed fewer than 200 aircraft. These consisted of some 65 Ilyushin Il-2 and 10 Sturmovik ground attack planes; a mixed bag of 70 fighters, Yakolev Yak-9s and Lavochkin La-7s and La-11s; and a handful of Yakolev Yak-18 and Polikarpov PO-2 trainers. Available U.S. airpower in the theater was mostly World War II vintage, consisting of 32 North American F-82s, 26 Douglas B-26s, 22 Boeing B-29s, and 365 postwar Lockheed F-80s. These were joined a month later by Grumman F9F Panthers, Vought F4-U Corsairs, and Douglas AD-2 Skyraiders flying from the carrier *Valley Forge.*

During the Korean War, the U.S. Navy would see the character of carrier warfare change from fast attack groups that functioned so well against Japan into a system of portable airfields that launched attack after attack, day after day. Carriers would relieve each other, but both the number of sorties and the level of munitions expended were a dramatic increase from past navy practice.

Despite the handicaps of operating from Japan, the U.S. Air Force (USAF) quickly established air superiority over Korea. Working with the U.S. Navy and the Marine Corps, the USAF provided both close air support and effective interdiction. Air power first halted the flow of KPA supplies and then permitted the successful invasion at Inch'ŏn and the near-simultaneous breakout from the Pusan perimeter in which the UN forces had been confined.

Fighter Saga

Operating under an umbrella of growing air power, UNC forces drove through North Korea, undeterred by threats of intervention by the Communist Chinese. This complacency was shaken on 1 November 1950, when MiG-15 jet fighters made their first appearance. The MiG-15 was by far the most effective aircraft in the theater, and the USAF hastily responded with the North American F-86 Sabres of the Fourth Fighter Interceptor Wing.

The two fighters were evenly matched, but the training and aggressiveness of their pilots were not. As a result, the USAF reestablished air superiority, and the Sabres eventually compiled a seven-to-one victory ratio over their MiG-15 opponents. If all the non-Sabre engagements are counted, the victory ratio would be in the approximate four-to-one range. The MiG-15s were flown primarily by Russian pilots but also by Chinese and North Koreans. Most of the Communist pilots were Russians and the air war became not so much a contest for air superiority as an advanced training school for Soviet pilots. At their peak, MiGs in the theater outnumbered the F-86s by a factor of five to one or more.

U.S. politics dictated the difficult rules of engagement that hampered U.S. actions. Communist air forces operated from a sanctuary behind the Yalu River. This permitted them to launch their planes without concern of air attack and then climb to an altitude from which they could choose whether or not to engage in combat. U.S. forces, in contrast, had to fly almost to the limit of their range to reach the so-called MiG Alley, and often had to lure the enemy into combat.

The U.S. fighter force nonetheless maintained a complete air superiority that prevented the Communists from operating from North Korean airfields. Air superiority also allowed UNC bomber forces to conduct the interdiction and strategic bombing efforts that eventually forced the Chinese and North Koreans to sign the armistice terms.

Bombers Press On

A relative handful of USAF and U.S. Navy bombers had stemmed the tide of the first KPA onslaught. Suitably reinforced, they performed the same mission during the massive People's Volunteer Army (Chinese Communist) ground intervention that threatened a South Korean "Dunkirk." Under the umbrella of UNC air superiority, U.S. and ROK ground forces fought their way north again, eventually reaching a point just north of the 33d parallel where the Communist side agreed to peace negotiations.

The employment of the forces to achieve this advance began a controversy that extends to this day. The U.S. Marines were provided extensive close air support by Marine Corps and U.S. Navy fighters. The U.S. Army demanded the same from the USAF, but in this it was to be disappointed. The USAF believed that using its fighters and bombers to interdict enemy supplies was far more effective than employing them in close air support. This was particularly true after the two sides had halted and dug in while the peace talks dragged on.

Communist forces were expert at digging bunkers to shelter both personnel and supplies. The bunkers were difficult to attack from the air, and results of air attacks were often inconclusive. In contrast, attacks against ground and rail traffic could be conducted night and day, and results were much more verifiable. The consequence of these attacks was to immobilize the Communist armies and inhibit them from the style of massive ground attack for which they were trained.

B-29 bombers, never more than 106 in number, operated by day until September 1951, when heavy losses to MiG-15s forced them to shift to night operations. Despite being a piston-engine bomber in a jet-age war, the B-29s served nobly, taking out strategic targets all over North Korea and in spring 1953 wiping out many airfields that the Communists had built in North Korea.

Lessons Learned and Not Learned

Sadly, the lessons not learned were the most important. The air force and the navy never succeeded in operating together on an extended basis. Neither service recognized that extensive training was essential against enemy tactics and the kinds of aircraft the enemy might employ. USAF ground support was also lacking.

On a more positive note, the United States learned once again that a second-best air force is terribly expensive; that air superiority is essential to successful ground operations, whether offensive or defensive; and that the day of the citizen air force was over. It was now manifestly evident that both the air force and the navy had to maintain professional air forces, fully equipped and staffed for immediate service.

The United States had begun the war with forces that were once again too little and almost too late; it never built its armed forces to the levels they might have been because the United States was focused on the protracted Cold War. The majority of the nation's military assets were devoted to deterring the Soviet Union, and it fought the war in Korea as it would later fight in Vietnam, with only a portion of its attention and its power.

—*Walter J. Boyne*

References:

Boyne, Walter J. *Beyond the Wild Blue. A History of the USAF, 1947–1997.* New York: St. Martin's Press, 1997.

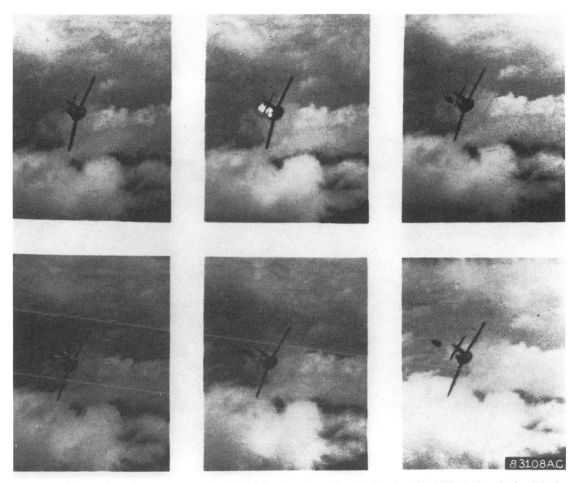

Sequence of photos from the gun camera of an F-86 Sabre showing a pilot ejecting from his MiG-15 aircraft after it had been hit with gunfire from the Sabre. (National Archives)

Futrell, Robert F. *The United States Air Force in Korea, 1950–1953*. Rev. ed. Washington, DC: Office of the Chief of Air Force History, 1983.

Goulden, Joseph C. *Korea: The Untold Story of the War*. New York: Times Books, 1982.

Hallion, Richard P. *The Naval Air War in Korea*. Baltimore: Nautical and Aviation Publishing Co. of America, 1986.

Mark, Edward. *Aerial Interdiction in Three Wars*. Washington, DC: Center for Air Force History, 1994.

Momyer, William. *Air Power in Three Wars: WWII, Korea, Vietnam*. Washington, DC: Department of the Air Force, 1978.

See also: Aircraft (Principal Combat); Aircraft Carriers; United States: Air Force (USAF); United States: Navy.

Aeromedical Evacuation

Attempts to create a military air ambulance date to 1910, and the first U.S. Army aircraft used specifical- ly to transport patients (a remodeled Curtis Jenny) went into service in 1919. The first U.S. Army aircraft specifically designed as an air ambulance was deployed in 1920. By World War II, fixed-wing trans- port of the sick and wounded was standard military procedure. In 1942 the Fifth Air Force evacuated 13,000 patients from New Guinea to Australia, and 383,676 patients were air-evacuated from Europe in the last six months of the war. In 1943 a Sikorsky R-6 helicopter was the first rotorcraft used for air evacua- tion. It carried a pilot, a medic, and the two patients in litters attached to the outside of the aircraft.

When the Military Air Transport Service was char- tered after World War II, patient transport was one of its designated missions. In 1949 U.S. Secretary of Defense Louis A. Johnson declared air transport the

A wounded soldier in a litter capsule receives blood plasma as an H-5 helicopter of the 3d Air Rescue Squadron takes off en route to a hospital. (National Archives)

method of choice in moving those injured in battle. The rough terrain and inadequate land transport facilities in Korea and the need to transport patients to remote specialized medical facilities affirmed this decision and sped its implementation.

Late in July 1950, a helicopter detachment of the 3d Air Rescue Squadron commanded by Captain Oscar N. Tibbetts was sent to Korea to retrieve downed pilots. Because air superiority was established early in the war, the unit was underutilized and Colonel Chauncey Dovell, commanding Eighth Army Medical Services, requisitioned the helicopters for transport of sick and wounded. The first trial flight, with the portly Dovell as a passenger, was from a school yard in Taegu to the 8054th Evacuation Hospital at Pusan on 3 August 1950.

After the Chinese offensive of late November 1950, General Douglas MacArthur decided that helicopters

should be a routine part of his medical units' equipment, and he convinced the Surgeon General to establish and equip two helicopter ambulance companies of twenty-four craft each—a deployment that was well under way by that month. The Marine Corps was routinely using helicopter evacuation by November 1950; the U.S. Army, by January 1951.

From the beginning, Sikorsky H-5 helicopters were the most popular for air evacuation, but they were fragile and, because they were no longer in production, parts were scarce. For these reasons, they were initially reserved to move patients from aid stations to Mobile Army Surgical Hospital units and were used only for those patients believed unlikely to survive without air transport. As the war progressed and their unique suitability to their mission became clear, helicopters were used closer to the front lines and for less urgent cases. Ultimately, helicopter transport from the site of trauma to an appropriate treatment facility became not only a military, but also a civilian, standard of care.

The navy realized that air transport to rear area hospitals was faster and more efficient than transport by sea. Hospital ships, which had initially been earmarked to transport and treat patients, became floating stationary hospitals with helipads to receive the wounded.

Single-engine, fixed-wing aircraft were also used to move patients. The L5-B could carry one litter and one ambulatory patient and the C-64 could carry 3 litters and 2 ambulatory patients. Transport from Pusan to Japan and then to the United States was principally by aircraft of World War II vintage: the C-47 (which could carry 18–24 litters or 25 ambulatory patients), the C-54 (18–36 litters or 31–45 ambulatory patients), the C-46 (24 litters and 9 ambulatory patients or 37 ambulatory patients), and the C-82 (14 litters and 6 ambulatory patients or 19 ambulatory patients). Late in the war, the newer C-119 and C-124 became available. The C-124 could be configured to carry 136 litters, 35 medical personnel, and a portable operating facility. Its lack of soundproofing and insulation and the length of time required to load and unload such a large contingent limited its usefulness in combat situations, but did not seriously detract from its ability to transport stable patients the long distances from Japan to the United States.

—*Jack McCallum*

References:

Cleaver, Frederick. *U.S. Army Battle Casualties in Korea.* Chevy Chase, MD: Operations Research Office, 1956.

Cowdrey, Albert A. *United States Army in the Korean War: The Medic's War.* Washington, DC: U.S. Army Center of Military History, 1987.

Smith, Allen D. "Air Evacuation—Medical Obligation and Military Necessity." *Air University Quarterly* 6 (1953): 98–111.

See also: Hospital Ships; MacArthur, Douglas; Military Medicine; Mobile Army Surgical Hospital (MASH).

African-Americans and the Korean War

For African-American service members and civilians alike, the Korean War represented much more than a campaign to protect U.S. foreign interests by checking the spread of communism abroad. The war served as the first viable challenge to an established system of social apartheid in the United States.

On 23 November 1947, with the support of prominent black civil rights politicians, A. Phillip Randolph and Grant Reynolds founded the Committee Against Jim Crow in Military Service and Training. It devised an aggressive tripartite plan to eliminate segregation in the U.S. armed forces. The first phase of the plan called for black youths to openly refuse to register for the draft. The committee realized that it would be difficult to convince blacks to defy the law in large numbers without some reassurance that the consequences for such action would not result in serious harm. The second phase of the plan called for the retention of lawyers to defend blacks charged with draft evasion should the need arise. Finally, the committee put together a marketing plan that centered around the slogan "Don't Join a Jim Crow Army!"

In private meetings with U.S. President Harry S. Truman and in testimony before the Senate Armed Services Committee on 31 March 1948, Randolph and Reynolds made it clear that African-Americans would no longer be content to "shoulder a gun and fight for democracy abroad unless full democracy was obtained at home." Compounding Truman's plight was that a liberal wing of the Democratic Party, led by Senator Hubert Humphrey, had forced him to accept a liberal platform that contained a strong civil rights plank. Bowing to the threats of Randolph and Reynolds's committee and recognizing the desires of liberals within the Democratic Party, on 26 July 1948, President Truman signed Executive Order 9981.

The order called for "equality of treatment and opportunity for all persons in the Armed Services without regard to race, color, religion, or national origin." To facilitate this change without "impairing the efficiency or morale" of the armed forces, the order also established the President's Committee on Equality of Treatment and Opportunity in the Armed Services. This seven-person committee was organized on 18 September 1948 and held its first official meeting on 12 January 1949. The committee was headed by former Solicitor General Charles Fahy. Members of the "Fahy Committee" were President of General Cable Corporation and member of the Urban League Dwight R. G. Palmer, President of Oberlin College William E. Stevenson, "Negro Head" of the Urban League Lester Granger, publisher of the *Chicago Defender* John H. Sengstacke, Catholic layman Alphonsus Donohue, Lever Brothers executive Charles Luckman, and former newspaperman E. W. Kenworthy. Because Donohue was ailing and Luckman had business obligations, neither participated actively on the committee. Sengstacke and Granger were the committee's only African-American members. The committee functioned as an advisory body to the secretary of defense and reported directly to the president.

In March 1949 the committee found an unexpected ally in newly named Secretary of Defense Louis A. Johnson. Immediately upon succeeding then-ailing Secretary of Defense James Forrestal, Johnson ordered the secretaries of the U.S. Army and U.S. Navy to submit detailed plans for their compliance with the presi-

First Lieutenant Alvin Anderson, one of the many repatriated POWs to return home aboard the *Marine Phoenix*, embracing his mother and sister as other members of his family look on, 14 September 1953. (National Archives)

dent's executive order no later than 1 May 1949. The U.S. Air Force led the way in adhering to Truman's executive order by submitting a plan for racial integration in mid-January 1949. Its subsequent plan, although less than what the Fahy Committee would have liked, was far more progressive than the plans grudgingly submitted by the navy and later the army— plans that Johnson would initially reject.

The navy, under the leadership of Secretary Francis P. Matthews, eventually submitted an acceptable plan on 23 June, but the senior leadership of the army remained recalcitrant. Not until 1 October 1949 did Secretary Johnson accept a proposal from the army. It called for the abolition of quotas for units and schools, the development of a merit-based promotion system that did not take race into account, the desegregation of

Reserve Officers' Training Corps summer camp training, and the establishment of a race policy review board. This plan fell short of Secretary Johnson's and the Fahy Committee's most important caveat, the unconditional and complete desegregation of all military units. Citing past failures of black units and theories of racial inferiority, the senior leadership of the army expressed the view that black soldiers would severely diminish the combat effectiveness of units to which they were assigned. The Fahy Committee was not provided with a copy of the new proposal that Johnson sent immediately to all levels of command for implementation.

The army's plan called for the retention of segregated units, but promised that black soldiers would be given the opportunity to receive training in military occupational specialties (MOS) that would presumably lead them to assignments outside of segregated units. In effect, blacks who did not meet minimum criteria for retraining would by default remain in segregated units. The army did not countenance the fact that such a policy would only heighten the stigma placed on soldiers, especially those who did not "qualify" for additional training and reassignment. This policy reduced morale and esprit de corps in units that could ill afford it.

The 1 October plan, although it did not effectively challenge segregation, still proved too radical for the army's ranking leadership. On 27 October 1949, an anonymous informant provided Secretary of the Army Gordon Gray with a copy of a second order that countermanded the 1 October plan.

Members of the Fahy Committee were outraged that Johnson never submitted the plan for their review and shocked by the insubordination manifest in the issuance of a countermanding second order. The committee demanded that any future plans or orders concerning the desegregation of the army pass before it before dissemination and implementation. For the next eight months, the committee struggled against the army's insistence upon "protective measures" such as quotas and special assignment of black recruits. The army provided strong support for the 10 percent quota that was designed to protect individual units and the military in general from inundation by African-American recruits. In concentrations of 10 percent or less, military leaders believed that the inefficiency of black soldiers could be absorbed by their white counterparts. The quota also protected the military services from being overwhelmed by a tide of blacks who could not find gainful employment in the private sector. The navy and the air force eventually abandoned this method of de facto segregation, but as of 25 June 1950, when the Korean People's Army (KPA) streamed across the 38th parallel, the army still had not come into compliance with President Truman's 1948 executive order.

Many blacks believed that the Korean conflict would provide opportunities for young black men and women to demonstrate their dedication to the country. Americans took acts of patriotism and heroism as signal markers of good citizenship. As during previous military conflicts, blacks and black leaders reasoned that if black Americans could effectively demonstrate their willingness to fight for and perhaps die for the country then white Americans would recognize that blacks deserved the rights and privileges that accrue to good citizenship in a democracy.

The U.S. Army's reluctance to desegregate ground forces punctuated the country's failure to come to this realization after World War II. Moreover, that the senior leadership of the army resorted to using theories of black inferiority and reports of cowardice under fire to undergird their arguments against segregating ground forces proved particularly galling to the black community. Not only were these claims patently racist, but many of their recollections of the combat ineffectiveness of black units were distorted or untrue. Active black World War II veterans, such as Louis Stukes, had continued to chafe under accusations that black soldiers performed poorly under fire. Stukes, a former Buffalo Soldier, recalled that black soldiers fought as bravely as any other soldiers, but their failures were unfairly highlighted by senior officials.

Black soldiers were often poorly trained, poorly equipped, and maliciously provided with faulty intelligence. On the eve of the Korean conflict, recollections by senior officers of black performance in World War II centered on failures rather than successes of black units, such as the legendary 99th Fighter Squadron of the 339th Fighter Group. As the political struggle gave way to the realities of war in the summer of 1950, U.S. ground forces entered the war with black and white soldiers fighting in separate units.

The first major all-black unit in Korea was the 25th Infantry Division's 24th Infantry Regiment. It was followed by the 2d Infantry Division's 3d Battalion, 9th Infantry Regiment, the 3d Infantry Division's 3d Battalion, 15th Infantry Regiment, and the 64th Tank Battalion.

Initially the Republic of Korea Army and U.S. ground forces fared poorly against the overwhelming numbers and firepower of the KPA. The 24th Infantry Regiment of the 25th Infantry Division, the first black unit to see combat duty, also performed poorly in the early days of the conflict. Black units were severely criticized for inefficiency and accused of cowardliness under fire. While advancing near Sangju on 22 July 1950, members of one company from the 2d Battalion broke under fire. On 12 August, the 3d Battalion was cited as being unreliable under fire. On 15 August, the 3d Battalion, while attempting to occupy Obong-san Mountain ridge, broke contact with the KPA and withdrew to Battle Mountain and the ridge west of Haman. In September an unspecified number of black soldiers of the 1st Battalion were reported to have fled to the rear.

While certain of these allegations were unsupported, they were held up as absolute truths. Moreover, unlike white units with similar combat records, the 24th Infantry Regiment was held up as a model of what black soldiers were capable of achieving. That the regiment produced two Medal of Honor winners, Private First Class William Thompson (the first person to win the medal in Korea) and Sergeant

Cornelius H. Charlton, did not carry as much weight as negative accusations.

In an unfortunate moment of overexaggeration, Major General William B. Kean suggested that the 24th Infantry's performance under fire jeopardized the United Nation's mission at large. Kean's striking accusation filtered down to black and white ground troops, where it lowered morale and heightened racial tension between black units and their counterparts. All parties concerned agreed that, for whatever reasons, the combat effectiveness of all-black units was undesirably low.

Segregationists argued that the ineffectiveness of black units was the result of innate inferiority on the part of blacks, whereas desegregationists pointed to inadequate or poor training and the absence of mutual trust between black soldiers and the white officers who led them. As the war progressed, it became clear that segregated units would have to be integrated, but the first significant move toward the integration of the army came in the United States.

The army had long held to the 10 percent quota where blacks were concerned. The Fahy Committee argued that the quota was discriminatory and persuaded the army to abolish it in April 1950. Before the abolishment of the quota, black recruits made up 8.2 percent of all trainees. By July 1950, this percentage had increased to 25 percent. Training stations were literally overwhelmed by the number of black troops. By August 1950, commanders at Fort Jackson, South Carolina, found that it was impossible to effectively train troops in segregated units. Citing U.S. Army policy as of January 1950, the post commander justified the full integration of training units in his command.

As these troops began to filter into combat units, the 10 percent quota that helped to justify and maintain segregation became problematic. The army was left with few options: either create more segregated units or overstaff existing units. Neither option was practical, given that many existing white units were dramatically understrength. Black troops held in garrison had a lower chance of seeing combat than their white peers.

Before long, the logic undergirding the myth of the white soldier's inherent superiority came into question. Many white infantrymen had been trained alongside black troops. Even though they had received the same training, white soldiers were more likely than their equally well-trained black counterparts to be sent into combat. The army's decision to comply with Executive Order 9981 in Korea was based on four principles: training efficiency, combat-line strength, unit uniformity, and equality of opportunity for battlefield casualty.

On 1 October 1951, the army began the hard work of integrating its units. This process would take more than three years to complete. On 31 October 1954, the U.S. Army reported that no segregated units remained within its ranks.

—Finnie D. Coleman

References:

Bogart, Leo, ed. *Project Clear: Social Research and the Desegregation of the United States Army.* New Brunswick, NJ: Transaction Publishers, 1992.

———. *Social Research and the Desegregation of the U.S. Army: Two Original 1951 Field Reports by Leo Bogart, John Morsell, Robert Bower, Ira Cisin, Leila Sussmann and Elmo C. Wilson.* Chicago: Markham, 1969.

Dalfiume, Richard M. *Desegregation of the U.S. Armed Forces: Fighting on Two Fronts, 1939–1953.* Columbia: University of Missouri Press, 1969.

Fletcher, Marvin. *The Black Soldier and Officer in the United States Army, 1891–1917.* Columbia: University of Missouri Press, 1974.

Greene, Robert Ewell. *Black Defenders of America, 1775–1973: A Reference and Pictorial History.* Chicago: Johnson, 1974.

Johnson, Jesse J., ed. *Black Women in the Armed Forces, 1942–1974: A Pictorial History.* Hampton, VA: Hampton Institute Press, 1974.

Nalty, Bernard C. *Strength for the Fight: A History of Black Americans in the Military.* New York: Free Press, 1986.

Stillman, Richard J., III. *Integration of the Negro in the U.S. Armed Forces.* New York: Praeger, 1968.

See also: Johnson, Louis A.; Kean, William Benjamin; Matthews, Francis P.; Truman, Harry S.

Agenda Controversy

When the United Nations Command (UNC) and the Korean People's Army/Chinese People's Volunteer Army (KPA/CPVA, North Korean) truce negotiators began their first plenary session on 10 July 1951, both sides anticipated a quickly arranged cease-fire. But the process of negotiating an agenda revealed serious disagreement on two fundamental issues.

At the first meeting, UNC senior negotiator U.S. Vice Admiral C. Turner Joy stated that he intended to discuss only military matters relating to Korea and indicated that hostilities would continue until a military armistice commission was in place and functioning. In his opening statement, KPA General Nam Il proposed an immediate cease-fire, the establishment of the 38th parallel as the military demarcation line (MDL), a 20-kilometer-wide demilitarized zone (DMZ), and the withdrawal of foreign armed forces from Korea.

The UNC then presented a proposed nine-point agenda: (1) adoption of the agenda; (2) location of, and authority for, International Red Cross representatives to visit prisoner-of-war (POW) camps; (3) limitation of discussions to purely military matters related to Korea only; (4) cessation of hostilities under conditions that would ensure against resumption of hostilities in Korea; (5) agreement on a DMZ across Korea;

(6) composition, authority, and function of a Military Armistice Commission; (7) agreement on the principle of inspection within Korea by military observer teams functioning under a Military Armistice Commission; (8) composition and functioning of these teams; and (9) arrangements pertaining to POWs.

Just as the UNC agenda had identified its key issues, the KPA/CPVA agenda proposal reflected the issues important to them: (1) adoption of an agenda; (2) establishment of the 38th parallel as the MDL and establishment of a DMZ as basic conditions for the cessation of hostilities in Korea; (3) withdrawal of all armed forces of foreign countries from Korea; (4) concrete arrangements for the realization of a cease-fire and armistice; and (5) arrangements pertaining to POWs.

The UNC immediately accepted KPA/CPVA agenda items 1, 4, and 5, but it was not prepared to change any of its own agenda items. There was discussion but no progress on the agenda during the next few days as the two sides argued over access and security in the conference site. On 15 July the UNC dropped its agenda item limiting the talks to Korea-related military matters because the KPA/CPVA side had already agreed on this point. The UNC also acknowledged that Red Cross visits could be discussed as part of the arrangements for POWs. The next day the KPA/CPVA side agreed to delete specific reference to the 38th parallel as the MDL while reserving the right to pursue this issue in the subsequent negotiations.

By 18 July the only remaining issue was the withdrawal of foreign troops, on which both sides remained adamant. On 19 July U.S. Secretary of State Dean G. Acheson released a statement that UN forces had to remain in Korea until a genuine peace was established. On 24 July U.S. Secretary of Defense George C. Marshall said that troop withdrawal was not a subject for the truce talks but would "naturally follow" a satisfactory peace settlement. On 25 July the UNC suggested that, although foreign troops should eventually be withdrawn from Korea, the arrangements for the withdrawal must be considered at the governmental level as part of a permanent political settlement. The KPA/CPVA side then proposed a new agenda item, "recommendations to the governments of the countries concerned on both sides," a formula that cleared the way to a mutually acceptable agenda.

At the tenth plenary session on 26 July 1951, the two sides agreed to a five-item agenda that provided the format for the eventual Armistice Agreement: (1) adoption of the agenda; (2) fixing a MDL between both sides so as to establish a DMZ as a basic condition for a cessation of hostilities in Korea (Armistice Agreement Article I); (3) concrete arrangements for the realization of a cease-fire and armistice in Korea,

including the composition, authority, and functioning of a supervising organization for carrying out the terms of a cease-fire and armistice (Article II); (4) arrangements relating to POWs (Article III); and (5) recommendations to the governments of the countries concerned on both sides (Article IV).

Compared with the grueling two-year-long negotiation process that would follow, the agenda was resolved with remarkable ease and swiftness. But to the negotiators and observers at the time, the resolution of the agenda seemed unduly lengthy and contentious. UNC negotiators complained that the KPA/CPVA inclusion of specific, substantive material in their agenda proposals was inappropriate and inconsistent with the purpose of an agenda, although the UNC agenda also incorporated specifics on Red Cross visits, the nature of the armistice supervisory mechanism, and inspections. KPA/CPVA efforts to portray the UNC as defeated supplicants; the clash over access and security in the conference area; the tone and content of KPA/CPVA statements; and Chinese and North Korean radio reporting on the talks angered the UNC commander and his negotiators and reinforced their perceptions of Communist perfidy and insincerity.

For their part, the KPA/CPVA side appears to have been surprised at the immediate and determined UNC rejection of a 38th parallel truce line and the withdrawal of foreign forces from Korea. Based on public statements by Dean Acheson, UN Security General Trygve Lie, and Soviet Deputy Foreign Minister Jacob A. Malik, the Chinese seem to have believed that both these issues had already been agreed to and only the details remained to be worked out at the truce talks. The Chinese concluded that the Americans had misrepresented their position in prenegotiation discussions with third country interlocutors, and this reinforced Chinese suspicion and distrust of the UNC.

The first two weeks of the truce talks were thus disconcerting to both sides. In many ways the agenda controversy and the accompanying confrontation over access and security were harbingers of the bitter and difficult negotiations to follow.

—*Donald W. Boose, Jr.*

References:

Goodman, Allan E., ed. *Negotiating While Fighting: The Diary of Admiral C. Turner Joy at the Korean Armistice Conference.* Stanford, CA: Hoover Institute Press, 1978.

Hermes, Walter G. *United States Army in the Korean War: Truce Tent and Fighting Front.* Washington, DC: Office of the Chief of Military History, 1966.

U.S. Department of State, Bureau of Public Affairs. *Foreign Relations of the United States, 1951.* Vol. 7, *China and Korea.* Washington, DC: U.S. Government Printing Office, 1983.

Wilhelm, Alfred D., Jr. *The Chinese at the Negotiating Table: Style and Characteristics.* Washington, DC: National Defense University Press, 1991.

See also: Acheson, Dean Goodersham; Cease-Fire Negotiations; Joy, Charles Turner; Kaesŏng Neutral Zone Controversy; Kaesŏng Truce Talks; Kennan-Malik Conversations; Lie, Trygve; Malik, Jacob (Iakov) Alexandrovich; Marshall, George C.; Nam Il; P'anmunjŏm Security Agreement; Truce Talks.

Air Power in the War

The concept of air power has been debated endlessly from the flight of the Wright Brothers' Military Flyer to the B-2; it will go on being debated for the foreseeable future. Two extensions of the concept, true air power and absolute air power, have rarely been mentioned and are a necessary background to this discussion. As defined here, true air power means the ability to use bombers with conventional munitions to hammer an enemy into submission. Absolute air power means the ability to employ nuclear or thermonuclear weapons totally to destroy the enemy.

In a purely abstract sense, there is a terrible irony in the fact that true air power was so transitory. Its coming was prophesied for four decades without fulfillment. It finally arrived in 1945 when air superiority permitted the unfettered bombing of Japan by the Boeing B-29, when it achieved all that had been predicted for it by air power advocates Giulio Douhet, Hugh Trenchard, William Mitchell, and others. True air power was translated into absolute air power in a three-day period in 1945, from 6 August at Hiroshima to 9 August at Nagasaki.

As the Cold War intensified, absolute air power became the vehicle for the concept of mutual deterrence. The two superpowers maintained an uneasy truce as they built massive arsenals of nuclear and thermonuclear weapons. Because *both sides* soon possessed it, absolute air power would be useful only as a means of deterrence, creating a strategic stalemate. This situation remained relatively unchanged until the time of the Gulf War, when space-age technology created a new, nonnuclear true air power.

During the Korean War, the United States possessed absolute air power but elected not to use it, for both moral and practical reasons. Morally, any administration using nuclear weapons without the greatest provocation would have been severely reprimanded by the electorate; practically, the Soviet Union now had nuclear weapons and let it be known that it would have no hesitation in using them. Instead, the United States relied on the creation of the superb Strategic Air Command (SAC) as an instrument of absolute air power and, as such, as a prevention of the Soviet Union's making a first strike. SAC bombers were later supplemented by intercontinental ballistic missiles and then by submarine-launched ballistic missiles. The strategy worked at two levels. On one level, it succeeded in deterring the Soviet Union and effectively prevented a nuclear exchange. At another level, it was an important instrument in the destruction of the shaky Soviet economy.

Also, there were economic side effects for the United States, which had to use the remainder of its military budget to fund the army, navy, and conventional forces of the air force. The level of this funding was inadequate, and it invited Soviet expansion by its traditional methods, which included exportation of communism by client states. U.S. Air Force (USAF) Chief of Staff General Hoyt S. Vandenberg stated that the inadequate funding resulted in a "shoe-string Air Force," one not capable of meeting all the demands placed upon it.

Thus the war in Korea, and the subsequent war in Southeast Asia, found the United States equipped with a superb nuclear force that it dared not use and conventional forces that were inadequate in numbers, technology, and logistical support. These conventional forces were obtained only after vicious infighting over the defense budget that remained after the funding of the strategic forces.

The war could have been won by air power if the decision had been made to use nuclear weapons and to accept all the risks and public condemnation that such use would have brought about. The United States undoubtedly possessed sufficient nuclear power to have neutralized the Democratic People's Republic of Korea (North Korean) and People's Republic of China (PRC, Communist Chinese) forces, and *probably* possessed enough to deter both the PRC and the Soviet Union from attacking. Fortunately, a natural moral repugnance at the use of nuclear weapons and the uncertainty of the Communist side's reaction made the point moot. It is said, however, that the Chinese reacted positively to a warning during the prolonged armistice negotiations that U.S. patience was wearing thin and that nuclear weapons might be used unless an agreement was reached.

Although neither true nor absolute air power was used in the Korean War, the concept of conventional air power was demonstrated in many ways, and it proved absolutely decisive in three instances. (Note that the term used is "decisive," not "war-winning.")

The first instance in which air power was decisive was the interdiction and ground support that prevented the Korean People's Army (KPA, North Koreans) from overrunning the Pusan perimeter in the summer of 1950. Few Americans recall just how close the KPA came to achieving a complete victory in South Korea, one that would have seen the unification of the peninsula under Communist rule. The prosecution of the war would then have been much more difficult and expensive, involving a massive buildup in Japan before an invasion of Korea.

U.S. B-29s strike an oil refinery at Wŏnsan, 10 August 1950. (National Archives)

USAF assets available in Japan and U.S. Navy forces that could be brought to the scene were just enough to stem the North Korean tide. Although aircraft and ordnance were in short supply, the U.S. forces were largely composed of veterans with World War II combat experience. They were able to make the best use of the arms they had on hand and interdict the KPA supply lines.

The second instance of the decisive application of air power came after the intervention of Chinese People's Volunteer Army (Communist Chinese) forces in November 1950, an event that General Douglas MacArthur had predicted would not happen because the PRC lacked an air force. In the ensuing disaster, every element of the United Nations Command (UNC) air forces was called upon. The combination of interdiction, close air support, aerial resupply, and strategic bombing again managed to slow, then stop, the Communist military advance.

The third instance in which air power was decisive was less dramatic but equally effective. When resurgent UNC forces succeeded in stabilizing the front just north of the 38th parallel, armistice negotiations began. Communist forces maintained an overwhelming superiority in number of personnel, but were unable to build up their supplies to the level needed for yet another massive offensive because of an effective UNC air interdiction campaign. This was possible only because the handful of North American F-86 Sabres (never more than about 125 aircraft in the theater) maintained air superiority. Hundreds of MiG-15s, Ilyushin IL-28s, Tupelov Tu-2s and, other first-line aircraft available to the Chinese could not be brought into use.

In both Korea and later in Vietnam, political leaders made the decision to fight a ground war in Asia with conventional weapons. Conventional air power was called upon to supplement the ground operations.

A fond farewell from his family sends Captain Johnnie Gosnell of Borger, Texas, off on another mission over Korea. Gosnell is a pilot flying with the 68th All-Weather Fighter Interception Squadron at a U.S. Far East Air Force base in Southern Japan. He is preparing to take off in his twin-engine F-82 Mustang. (National Archives)

Sadly, in both wars air power was limited to a strength and to methods that could not win a victory and could only stave off defeat. In Korea the joint decisions to fight a ground war in Asia and not to use nuclear weapons resulted in a new fact of life: the United States would not always win wars. Stalemate became an acceptable substitute for victory, primarily because military and political attention were focused on mutual deterrence.

Despite this, military planners learned a number of lessons in Korea. Among the least recognized but most significant of these was the realization that aircraft were not only a unique weapon systems but platforms that could employ a whole series of systems. In Korea a number of World War II aircraft received new equipment and new duties, and they performed these duties well. Such missions included Grumman

F6F Hellcats as pilotless bombs and Grumman TBMs used as antisubmarine warfare aircraft. The U.S. Navy Douglas F3D Skyknight entered the war as a night-fighter, but over the years it was modified to perform many other tasks. The Douglas AD operated in a variety of roles in Korea and, later, in Southeast Asia. The concept of the aircraft as platform would begin a trend toward retaining aircraft for new roles. Two examples of this might be the Boeing B-52s and KC-135s, now slated to remain in service until well into the twenty-first century.

A second set of lessons learned involved the logistics of supporting large military forces at the end of a 10,000-mile pipeline. Much had been learned during World War II, of course, but conditions had changed greatly, and there was a far greater requirement to manage logistics more effectively than in the past.

assigned to relieve the paratroopers was halted by dense Chinese minefields some fifteen miles to the south of the linkup point.

Overcoming several minor complications, the 187th began to rapidly consolidate at the northern DZ. Because of the misdrop, the DZ was overcrowded, but unit commanders swiftly organized their units and secured the regiment's perimeter. As they moved out from the DZ, the paratroopers met only minor and sporadic resistance from scattered, isolated KPA infantry units supported by a few mortars. Local civilians complicated matters by coming into the DZ to carry away the scattered parachutes.

Bowen directed his unit skillfully, and by 1800 the regiment secured all its assigned objectives. The RCT occupied high ground north of Munsan-ni and cleared the town of Communist soldiers. Bowen sent one company to rescue the 1st Battalion's command group and linked up with them by 1600. About two hours later the entire group joined the regiment at the north DZ.

Because of negligible Communist resistance the regiment suffered relatively few casualties in the operation. Combat casualties totaled 19, and of the 84 jump casualties, almost half returned to duty after treatment. Communist casualties totaled 136 dead and 149 prisoners. Interrogations indicated that most Communist military units had withdrawn north of the Imjin River before the landings. The North Korean I Corps had retreated too rapidly to be caught in Ridgway's trap of dropping the 187th behind the lines.

Delayed by mines and artillery fire, the relieving armored task force did not completely close with the 187th until 0700 on 24 March. Complying with his orders, Bowen joined his troops with the tanks of the task force to patrol and reconnoiter ferry sites along the Imjin River. During the reconnaissance patrols, U.S. forces encountered only minor enemy contact. The 1st Cavalry Division advanced much faster than the 1st Republic of Korea (South Korean) Division and relieved the 187th by 1700 on 24 March.

Instead of immediately reverting to Eighth Army reserve, the 187th joined the rush to cut off the CPVA forces retreating north. Milburn alerted the 187th to prepare for an attack east on a Chinese division blocking Route 3 and 33 north from Ŭijŏngbu. He assigned the RCT the objective of holding the high ground ten miles north of Ŭijŏngbu, bordering Route 33. Milburn ordered the regiment to prevent the Chinese from withdrawing in front of the U.S. 3d Division attacking up Route 33. At 1800 on 24 March, Bowen initiated his advance with a forced march. Because of a shortage of fuel, only Company C of the 64th Tank Battalion accompanied the 187th until later.

At 0600 on 25 March, the regiment arrived at its jump off point for the attack. Landslides, rain, and poor roads had stopped the tanks. Without armored support the regiment started up Hill 228 on the left side of Route 33. Meeting heavy small arms, machine gun, and mortar fire and hampered by a driving rain, the 187th was still two miles short of its objective by day's end. Even after several tanks from the 3d Division managed to reinforce the regiment's attack, the 187th was not able to capture Hill 228 until 27 March.

After an all-day battle on 28 March, the 187th finally cut Route 33 by capturing high ground on both sides of the road. Despite U.S. forces' valiant attempts to cut off their retreat, the Chinese held Route 33 open long enough to withdraw their main forces. With the failure to trap the retreating Communist forces, the 187th RCT became part of the general UN advance. By the end of March, UN forces closed on the 38th parallel almost across the entire Korean peninsula, almost where the war began—and ended, with the armistice in 1953.

—*Stanley S. McGowen*

References:
Blair, Clay. *The Forgotten War: America in Korea, 1950–1953.* New York: Times Books, 1987.
Mossman, Billy C. *U.S. Army in the Korean War: Ebb and Flow, November 1950–July 1951.* Washington, DC: U.S. Army Center of Military History, 1990.
See also: Almond, Edward Mallory; COURAGEOUS, Operation; Joint Chiefs of Staff (JCS); KILLER, Operation; MacArthur, Douglas; Milburn, Frank William; Ridgway, Matthew Bunker; RIPPER, Operation; Sukch'ŏn and Sunch'ŏn Airborne Operation.

Aircraft (Principal Combat)

Aircraft of the U.S. Air Force

Fighters and Fighter-Bombers

Lockheed F-80. The Shooting Star was the U.S. Air Force's (USAF's) first operational jet fighter, making its first flight in January 1944. It operated extensively in Korea in a ground attack role and as the RF-80 reconnaissance plane. Although technically obsolete, on 8 November 1950 it bested the MiG-15 in the world's first jet-versus-jet air combat when Lieutenant Russell Brown shot down the swept-wing MiG. Powered by a 4,600-pound, static-thrust Allison J33 engine, the F-80 did remarkable work at a variety of tasks in Korea.

Lockheed F-94. A development of the T-33, in turn a development of the F-80, the F-94 was a two-place night fighter first flown in 1949. (A later version, the F-94C, was called the Starfire.) The power plant was an Allison J33 of 6,000 pounds of thrust in afterburner. Because it carried a highly secret airborne radar system, F-94s were at first not permitted to fly deep into enemy territory. Ironically, the F-94's radar was not

Budgets were limited, weapons cost more, and most important, the number of merchant ships available had declined. Large cargo aircraft such as the C-124 were just coming into the fleet. Shortages resulting from inadequate transport induced planners to examine ways better to manage inventories, improve shipping procedures, and plan procurement more rationally. The ability to improve logistics management would be limited until the arrival of effective computer systems.

It was patently obvious that better, more efficient transport aircraft were required, and the specifications to create them ultimately resulted in the brilliant series of Lockheed transports, including the C-130, C-141, and C-5A. This array of specially designed military transports would prove to be vital not only in the Vietnam conflict but in meeting U.S. military and compassionate mission requirements around the world.

The U.S. government and the American people learned from the Korean War that it would be essential in the future to maintain large professional military forces. It was no longer possible to allow six months to a year to build up armed forces in response to a foreign threat. More important, perhaps, was the concept that National Guard and Reserve personnel had to be more proficient. The National Guard and Reserve forces were a long way from today's concept of "total force" readiness, but a trend had been established. One particular grievance that had been manifested during the Korean War was the unfair situation in which regular members of the air force were retained in state-side positions while called-up reservists were sent to Korea. The new concept of a professional military force in being resolved the grievance over time.

The most obvious lesson *not* learned was effective army/navy/air force cooperation. The term "joint operations" is more current now, but the concept goes back to World War I. It was achieved intermittently during World War II, often more as a consequence of overlapping needs than the desire to cooperate. The general problem of the services operating together in Korea was solved as it would later be in Southeast Asia: by assigning defined geographical areas of responsibility. This eased communication problems and helped avoid duplication, but it prevented the exercise of air power at its fullest.

In summary, air power did all that could have been expected of it during the Korean War, given the strategic situation and decisions on allocating resources. Unfortunately, precisely the same thing could be said about air power during the Vietnam War. Air power advocates would not see their claims vindicated in full until the Gulf War, when leadership, technology, timing, and training all came together and air power was at last employed as it should be used.

—*Walter J. Boyne*

References:
Boyne, Walter J. *Beyond the Wild Blue. A History of the USAF, 1947–1997.* New York: St. Martin's Press, 1997.
Futrell, Robert F. *The United States Air Force in Korea, 1950–1953.* Rev. ed. Washington, DC: Office of the Chief of Air Force History, 1983.
Mark, Edward. *Aerial Interdiction in Three Wars.* Washington, DC: Center for Air Force History, 1994.
Momyer, William. *Air Power in Three Wars: WWII, Korea, Vietnam.* Washington, DC: Department of the Air Force, 1978.
See also: MacArthur, Douglas; United States Air Force (USAF); Vandenberg, Hoyt S.

Airborne Operations

United Nations Command (UNC) forces conducted few large airborne operations during the Korean War. The jagged ridgelines that ran down the spine of the peninsula offered little in the way of suitable drop zones (DZs) large enough to deliver regimental-sized units by parachute drops. The operations that did take place, as with most previous airborne assaults, met with limited success. Generally, airborne units fought as regular infantry or remained in tactical reserve for the Eighth Army.

In July 1950 General Douglas MacArthur, to halt the North Korean drive south, forwarded substantial requests for reinforcements to the Joint Chiefs of Staff (JCS). In his communication he requested a regimental combat team (RCT) from the highly trained 82d Airborne Division. U.S. military planners considered an intact 82d Airborne Division as an indispensable component of the strategic defense plan for Western Europe, and the JCS ordered the 187th RCT (Airborne), from the 11th Airborne Division, to South Korea. The 187th became the only airborne infantry regiment to serve in Korea.

MacArthur had hoped to use airborne forces in conjunction with his amphibious landing at Inch'ŏn, but none was then available in the theater of operations. The 4,000-man 187th, commanded by Colonel Frank S. Bowen, Jr., did not arrive in Japan until 20 September. Its operational readiness date was 21 October; pending this, MacArthur held the 187th under his control in general headquarters reserve at Kimpŏ Airfield near Seoul. During 20–23 October 1950, the 187th RCT was employed in the first airborne drop of the war at Sukch'ŏn and Sunch'ŏn, twenty-five miles north of the Democratic People's Republic capital of P'yŏngyang. MacArthur hoped that the RCT would be able to block Korean People's Army (KPA, North Korean) escape routes north and rescue UNC prisoners held by the KPA, but the operation came too late and was only moderately successful.

Men and equipment parachuting to earth, probably Operation TOMAHAWK, March 1951. (National Archives)

Paratroopers of the 187th Airborne Regimental Combat Team, seated in the cargo compartment of a 314th Troop Carrier Group C-199 (Flying Boxcar), during the flight to the dropzone at Munsan-ni, Korea, March 1951. (National Archives)

On 13 February 1951, as part of Operation KILLER, Eighth Army commander Lieutenant General Matthew B. Ridgway released the 187th RCT from Eighth Army to X Corps. X Corps commander Lieutenant General Edward M. Almond deployed the 187th in the center of his line across Route 29, two miles north of Wǒnju, to prevent Chinese People's Volunteer Army (CPVA, Communist Chinese) forces from advancing southward. Almond instructed the commander of the 187th, Brigadier General Frank S. Bowen, to be prepared to move his regiment from Wǒnju, southeast of Ch'unch'ǒn, in support of the U.S. 7th Division's attack to the north.

Ridgway, however, did not allow Almond complete operational control of the parachute regiment. He ordered Almond not to commit the regiment to any attack without his specific approval. If KILLER proved successful, Ridgway intended to relocate the 187th near Taegu Airfield for refresher jump training. As a contingency of Operation RIPPER, the code name for the overall plan to envelope Seoul, Ridgway intended to employ the regiment in an airborne operation north of the city. After refresher training, the 187th RCT refitted and rearmed for a drop at Munsan-ni, twenty miles from Seoul.

On 18 March 1951, Ridgway ordered U.S. IX Corps to continue its advance against Chinese withdrawals in the vicinity of Ch'unch'ǒn. As UN forces drove northward, the paratroopers readied for a drop near Ch'unch'ǒn. Landing Plan HAWK called for the regiment, reinforced by the 2d and 4th Ranger Companies, to drop north of the town on March 22 to block Chinese movements out of Ch'unch'ǒn Basin. Ridgway ordered IX Corps to link up with the airborne forces within twenty-four hours. A rapid advance north by the 1st Cavalry Division, along with continued Chinese retreats, however, negated the necessity for the jump.

The 187th remained at a high state of alert and was immediately available for Operation COURAGEOUS, the UN attack across the Han River. Ridgway planned to drop the 187th RCT with its two attached Ranger companies at Munsan-ni to block Route 1 and hold until relieved by advancing U.S. forces. According to the operational time table, linkup would take twenty-four hours, after which the 187th RCT would come under Lieutenant General Frank W. Milburn's I Corps command. When the armored task force Milburn had assembled passed through the lines, the 187th was to revert to Eighth Army reserve.

On 23 March favorable weather permitted commencement of Operation TOMAHAWK, code name for the vertical envelopment of retreating CPVA units. At 0700, C-46s and C-119s took off from Taegu with the paratroopers. Engine trouble forced the lead aircraft carrying the 1st Battalion commander and his staff to return to the airfield, causing some confusion in the initial stages of the operation. General Bowen had designated two DZs, one a mile northeast of Munsan-ni and the other three miles southeast of the town. The 1st Battalion was scheduled to be dropped in the southern DZ, while the remainder of the RCT would jump into the northern DZ. Because of inadequate pilot briefings, the aircraft transporting the bulk of the 1st Battalion, without a formation leader, joined the formations heading for the northern DZ. As a result, the Air Force mistakenly dropped almost the entire airborne force into the north DZ. The first paratroopers leapt into the cold slipstream at 0900, and the 674th Airborne Field Artillery Battalion followed in a heavy drop at 1000 hours.

Poor coordination and Communist reaction continued to interrupt the operation's schedule. A replacement aircraft ferried the 1st Battalion commander and his staff back to the proper DZ. Shortly after 1000 hours, this single stick of troops jumped into the southern DZ, the only U.S. troops there. Luckily only a few KPA troops remained in the vicinity of the DZ. The 187th completed its drop, but the armored task force

F-51 fighter taking off in adverse conditions. (National Archives)

very effective on night missions against MiGs, although a victory was scored late in the war. The major task of the F-94 was to protect Korean air bases against enemy intruders.

North American F-51. The single-seat Mustang was first flown in 1940; many consider it to have been the premier piston-engine fighter of World War II. It was especially valuable in Korea because it could be employed from rough South Korean airfields. Powered by a 1,695-horsepower, liquid-cooled, Packard-built Rolls-Royce Merlin power plant, the F-51 proved a capable ground attack and reconnaissance aircraft, the latter as the F-6/RF-51D.

North American F-82. Called the Twin Mustang, the F-82 appeared to be essentially two halves of an F-51 joined together with a wing center section and horizontal stabilizer. Its design was actually more specialized than it appeared. The aircraft first flew in 1945, intended for use as an ultra–long-range escort fighter and as a night fighter. F-82s gained the first victories

for the USAF in Korea, when they shot down two Yak-9s on 27 June 1950. The F-82s were powered by two 1,600-horsepower Allison V-1710 engines. Used initially for air and ground counterattack work, their importance as night fighters caused them to be withdrawn for defense purposes until a shortage of spare parts forced their retirement.

North American F-86. The North American F-86 Sabre incorporated much German research into its design, employing a 35-degree swept wing and automatic leading edge slots. Flown for the first time in October 1947, the Sabre survived many initial problems to become the premier USAF fighter of the Korean War. The first model to see combat, the F-86A, was powered by a 5,270-pound, static-thrust General Electric J47 engine. Later F-86s were more powerful and were used both for air-to-air and ground support. The F-86F, with a 5,970-pound, static-thrust J47 engine and the "6-3" wing had superior high-altitude performance. In combat, F-86s destroyed 792

Fifth Air Force F-86 Sabre flying over North Korea. (National Archives)

MiGs while suffering 110 losses. The RF-86 was used for reconnaissance.

Republic F-84. The Thunderjet was first flown in February 1946 and arrived in Korea in December 1950. Initially assigned as escorts for the B-29s, the F-84s soon gained fame in ground attack operations. Powered by a single 5,000-pound, static-thrust Allison J35 engine, the F-84's heavily laden takeoffs from Korean airfields were sometimes augmented by the use of jet-assisted takeoff, or JATO. In a jet-assisted

Fighter aircraft specifications

	Span	Length	Height	Gross Weight (pounds)	Top Speed (mph)	Range (miles)	Ceiling (feet)
Lockheed F-80	39'11"	34'6"	11'4"	16,856	580	1,380	42,750
Lockheed F-94	38'11"	40'1"	12'8"	16,844	606	905	48,000
N.A. F-51	37'1¼"	32'3"	8'8"	11,600	437	950	41,900
N.A. F-82	51'3"	42'5"	13'10"	25,891	461	2,250	38,900
N.A. F-86A	37'1"	37'6"	14'8"	16,357	672	785	48,300
N.A. F-86F	37'1"	37'6"	14'8"	17,921	690	1,270	50,000
Republic F-84	36'5"	38'5"	12'7"	23,525	613	1,500	43,230

takeoff, a pack of rockets attached to the fuselage centerline was ignited to add speed for liftoff and then jettisoned as soon as the rocket thrust was exhausted. F-84s were used to attack enemy airfields and even large targets such as irrigation dams. Although unable to cope with the MiG-15 at high altitude, the F-84s were more effective at medium or low altitudes, and scored several kills. RF-84s were used for reconnaissance.

Bombers

Boeing B-29. The Superfortress first flew in September 1942. It contributed substantially to the victory over Japan. The B-29 was recalled to service for the Korean War, when many aircraft were plucked from storage and refurbished. Powered by four Wright Cyclone R-3350 engines, B-29s were effective as day bombers until the appearance of the MiG-15. Thereafter, it was confined to night bombing against strategic and tactical targets, flying all but twenty-one days during the entire three years and one month of the war. In 21,000 sorties, B-29s dropped 167,100 tons of bombs and claimed 16 MiGs and 17 other fighters shot down. At least 16 B-29s were shot down over North Korea, and as many as 48 were lost in crash landings or written off because of heavy damage after returning to base. Superfortresses were also used as reconnaissance, weather, and rescue aircraft. The KB-29 was used to refuel RF-80 fighters and F-84 Thunderjets.

Douglas B-26. Originally designated the A-26, the Invader first flew in July 1942, but a protracted development period kept it out of combat until 1944. Its performance during the war was exceptional, but after the war the type was gradually retired. The 26 Invaders in Japan proved to be invaluable in a night interdiction role, and it fell to the B-26 to fly the first and the last bombing missions of the Korean War. Powered by Wright R-2800 engines, Invaders flew some 55,000 sorties and were credited with the destruction of 38,500 vehicles, 3,700 railway cars, and 406 locomotives. The Invader would again see service in Vietnam.

North American RB-45. The Tornado was the first USAF four-jet bomber, making its first flight in March 1947. The RB-45 reconnaissance version used in Korea first flew in April 1950. It was powered by four 5,200-pound, static-thrust General Electric J47 jet engines

The Tornado carried out risky night reconnaissance missions over North Korea. Only a small number of RB-45s were available and, although they were not adequately supported logistically, they did yeoman work.

Transports

Curtiss C-46. A derivative of a commercial passenger transport, the first Commando prototype flew in March 1940. The Commando was a radical departure from previous Curtiss transport designs and performed exceptionally well in the "Hump" supply operation during World War II. The C-46 was powered by two 2,000-horsepower Pratt & Whitney R-2800 engines and was operated both by the USAF and by civil operators. It served again in Southeast Asia during the Vietnam War.

Douglas C-47. Officially known as the Skytrain, but more affectionately referred to as the "Gooneybird," the C-47 served as well in Korea as it had done during World War II and would do again during the Vietnam War. First flown as the Douglas Sleeper Transport (DST) in December 1935, and produced by the thousands during World War II, the C-47 was powered by two 1,200-horsepower Pratt & Whitney R-1830 engines. It was and is a classic aircraft. The U.S. Navy operated it as the R4D.

Douglas C-54. Originally designed as the DC-4A passenger transport, the C-54 was quickly adopted for military use and served brilliantly in World War II and during the Berlin airlift. A C-54 was the first USAF aircraft destroyed in the Korean War, when strafed at Kimpŏ Airfield on 25 June 1950. The C-54 was powered by four 1,290-horsepower Pratt & Whitney R-2000 engines and was a Military Air Transport Service workhorse throughout the war. The U.S. Navy operated basically similar aircraft as the R5D.

Douglas C-124. The Globemaster II first flew on 27 November 1949. Production models were fitted with "corn-cob" Pratt & Whitney R-4360 engines, and "Old Shakey," as it was affectionately called, soon became the premier U.S. heavy transport. While only 447 C-124s were produced, they were ubiquitous and also served well in the Vietnam War.

Fairchild C-119. The Fairchild C-119 Flying Boxcar was a development of the earlier C-82.

	Span	Length	Height	Gross Weight (pounds)	Top Speed (mph)	Range (miles)	Ceiling (feet)
Boeing B-29	141'3"	99'0"	29'7"	137,500	364	4,200	32,000
Douglas B-26	70'0"	50'0"	18'6"	35,000	355	1,400	22,100
N.A. RB-45	96'0"	75'11"	25'2"	110,721	570	2,530	40,250

Bomber Specifications

Transport Specifications

	Span	Length	Height	Gross Weight (pounds)	Top Speed (mph)	Range (miles)	Ceiling (feet)
Curtiss C-46	108'1"	76'4"	21'9"	56,000	269	1,200	27,600
Douglas C-47	95'6"	63'9"	17'0"	26,000	230	1,600	24,000
Douglas C-54	117'6"	93'10"	27'6"	62,000	265	2,000	22,000
Douglas C-124	173'3"	127'2"	48'3"	175,000	298	6,280	22,050
Fairchild C-119	109'3"	86'6"	26'6"	72,700	281	1,630	21,580

Distinguished by its twin-boom, podded fuselage layout, the C-119 first flew in November 1947. It was powered by the new and trouble-prone Pratt & Whitney R-4360 in some versions and by the Wright R-3350 in others. Despite logistics problems that kept monthly flying time averages low, the C-119 worked well in Korea, dropping supplies, paratroops, and outsize equipment that included artillery, vehicles, and two-ton bridge spans. No one envisioned that it would one day be modified as a "gunship."

Reconnaissance/Observation Planes/Rescue

(Note: There were reconnaissance versions of the B-26, B-29, B-45, F-51, F-80, F-84, and F-86, all of which are described earlier. In a similar way, there were rescue versions of many aircraft including the SC-47, SB-17G, and SB-29A.)

Boeing RB-17. The Boeing B-17 Flying Fortress was adapted for photographic mapping, reconnaissance, and, as the SB-17, for rescue work. First flown in July 1935, the B-17 went on to become a workhorse of the Second World War. Powered by four 1,200-horsepower Wright Cyclone R-1820 engines, the RB-17 operated for three months in 1950 before being replaced.

Boeing RB-50A. An updated version of the B-29, the RB-50A was used for strategic reconnaissance. First flown in June 1947, it was powered by four Pratt & Whitney R-4360 engines.

Convair RB-36. The huge six-engine Peacemaker was also used for strategic reconnaissance. As with the RB-50A, the RB-36 operated out of Yakota by the Ninety-first Strategic Reconnaissance Squadron. The XB-36 prototype was first flown in August 1946 and was powered by six Pratt & Whitney R-4360 engines.

Grumman SA-16. The Albatross first flew in October 1947. It saw service with the USAF, U.S. Navy, and the Coast Guard. A traditional "Iron-works" product, the Albatross had two 1,425-horsepower Wright R-1820 engines to pull it off the rough seas, in which it could land.

North American AT-6G. The famed Texan trainer found a new life in Korea as a forward air controller (FAC). Operating under the Mosquito call-sign, T-6s performed invaluable work. Its Pratt & Whitney R-1340 engine was rated at 600 horsepower. The airplane was also operated as the LT-6G in Korea. The Navy SNJ version was also operated as a FAC.

Aircraft of the U.S. Navy and Marine Corps

Chance Vought F4U-4/AU-1. The Corsair was in production longer than any other U.S. fighter of World War II, and it proved to be a rugged, reliable ground attack aircraft in Korea. The prototype of the F4U first flew in May 1940, and the last Corsair left the Vought plant in December 1952, destined for the French naval air arm. Powered by a 2,100-horsepower Pratt & Whitney R-2800, the F4U could carry a huge and

Reconnaissance/Observation Planes/Rescue Specifications

	Span	Length	Height	Gross Weight (pounds)	Top Speed (mph)	Range (miles)	Ceiling (feet)
Boeing RB-17	103'9"	74'4"	19'1"	65,500	287	2,000	35,600
Boeing RB-50	141'3"	99'0"	32'8"	168,400	385	4,650	37,000
Convair RB-36	230'0"	162'1"	46'8"	328,000	381	8,000	42,500
Grumman SA-16	96'8"	61'3"	25'10"	35,700	236	2,850	21,500
N.A. AT-6G	42'0"	27'9"	14'0"	5,200	207	665	24,100

widely varied armament load. The Vought AU-1 was designed specifically for ground support work.

Consolidated PB4Y (PB4Y-2). One regular squadron and two reserve squadrons operated Privateers in Korea, where they were used for electronic intelligence gathering and flare-dropping missions. Powered by four 1,350-horsepower Pratt & Whitney R-1830 engines, the Privateers were a development of the famous Liberator of World War II.

Douglas AD. The famous Skyraider was the product of Ed Heinemann's genius and would serve well in Korea and subsequently during the Vietnam War. Powered by a Wright R-3350 piston engine, it appeared in a number of models specialized for specific roles. Its ability to carry a wide variety of ordnance, ranging from rockets to napalm to depth charges ensured that it saw almost continuous combat. Many consider it to be the best close-support aircraft of the Korean War, and it served in several variants.

Douglas F3D. The Skyknight was one of the least pugnacious looking warplanes of all times, but it would have a distinguished career that extended beyond Korea into Vietnam. The first flight of the prototype took place in March 1948. Production models, powered by Westinghouse J34 engines, had a surprisingly good performance that belied their looks. On 2 November 1952, one downed an enemy jet (identified as a Yak-15), the first time one jet fighter had destroyed another on a night interception. Ultimately, the Skyknight (or "Blue Whale," as it was known to its crews) was credited with the destruction of more enemy aircraft than any other U.S. Navy or Marine Corps type.

Grumman AF-2. The little-remembered "Guardian" was a development of the hunter/killer antisubmarine warfare teams initiated with the Grumman TBM Avenger. A mid-wing monoplane (similar to its ancestor the F4F), the Guardian was powered by a 2,400-horsepower Pratt & Whitney R-2800 engine. Several squadrons flew the AF-2 between March 1951 and May 1953 during the Korean War.

Grumman F6F-K. Designed as an antidote to the Japanese Zero in World War II, the Grumman F6F-K Hellcat soldiered on as a pilotless guided bomb (today an "uninhabited aerial vehicle") in Korea. Equipped with a television camera and carrying a 2,000-pound bomb, it was guided to its target by a Douglas AD aircraft. All six Hellcats committed to the theater were expended on high-value targets. In effect, they were early smart bombs.

Grumman F7F. The handsome Tigercat arrived too late to see combat in World War II, despite having made its first flight in November 1943. It was the first navy fighter to have tricycle landing gear and was powered by two Pratt & Whitney R-2800 engines. The

last of 364 Tigercats was delivered in November 1946. Two Marine squadron used F3F-3N variants as ground support and night fighters in Korea from September 1951 through November 1952.

Grumman F9F-2. The Panther was first flown in November 1947 and would prove to be as rugged and capable an aircraft as the previous piston-engine fighters from Grumman. Powered by a Pratt & Whitney J42 engine (essentially a Rolls-Royce Nene built under license) of 5,750 pounds static thrust, the Panther was the first U.S. Navy jet ever in combat, flying off the USS *Valley Forge* on 3 July 1950. An F9F became the first navy aircraft to shoot down a MiG-15, on 9 November 1950. (Ironically, the MiG was also powered by a license-built version of the Nene.) Several variants of the Panther were used in Korea.

Grumman TBM. The classic Avenger torpedo plane of World War II was pressed into service in a variety of roles, including airborne early warning, antisubmarine warfare, and general utility. Powered by a 1,750-horsepower Wright R-2600 engine, the Avenger (all manufactured by General Motors) did excellent, if unsung, service in Korea.

Lockheed P2V. The Lockheed Neptune served as a search and reconnaissance patrol plane, its presence heralding the ultimate demise of the traditional flying boat in that role. Powered by two Wright R-3350 engines, the Neptune had a remarkable range and carried a wide variety of ordnance.

Martin PBM-5. The beautiful gull-wing Martin Mariner flying boat had a distinguished career during World War II and soldiered on in Korea. Powered by two 2,100-horsepower Pratt & Whitney R-2800 engines, the Mariner was effective in a wide range of activities that included rescue, routine maritime patrol, detecting and destroying minefields, and, when the situation demanded, engaging in shootouts with enemy antiaircraft batteries.

Martin P4M. The Mercator was unusual in that it had two 3,000-horsepower Pratt & Whitney R-4360 piston engines and two Allison J33 4,600-pound, static-thrust jet engines. The piston and jet engines were paired in a clean cowling installation that gave the airplane the appearance of having only two engines. Mercators were used for highly classified intelligence-gathering missions.

McDonnell F2H. The Banshee was a development of the successful Phantom, McDonnell's first jet fighter, and it first flew in January 1947. The Banshee first saw service in Korea aboard the carrier *Essex*, entering combat on 23 August 1951. During the next two years, Banshees operated both from carriers and from P'ohang Airfield in Korea. Powered by two 3,250-pound, static-thrust Westinghouse J34 turbojets, the Banshee had an excellent high-altitude per-

U.S. Navy and Marine Corps Aircraft Specifications

	Span	Length	Height	Gross Weight (pounds)	Top Speed (mph)	Range (miles)	Ceiling (feet)
C. Vought F4U-4	41'0"	33'8"	14'9"	14,670	446	1,005	41,500
Consol PB4Y-2	110'0"	74'7"	29'1½"	60,000	249	2,630	18,300
Douglas AD-2	50'¼"	38'2"	15'7½"	18,263	321	915	32,700
Douglas F3D	50'0"	45'5"	16'1"	27,681	565	1,540	38,200
Grumman AF-2	60'8"	43'4"	16'2"	25,500	317	1,500	32,500
Grumman F6F-K	42'10"	33'10"	14'5"	12,000	375	1,500	39,900
Grumman F7F-3N	51'6"	45'6½"	13'9"	21,857	447	1,750	40,600
Grumman F9F-2	38'0"	37'3"	11'4"	19,494	575	1,353	44,600
Grumman TBM	54'2"	40'0"	16'5"	18,250	267	1,130	23,400
Lockheed P2V	100'0"	77'10"	28'1"	63,078	320	3,985	26,000
Martin PBM-5	118'0"	79'10"	27'6"	56,000	215	2,700	20,200
Martin P4M	114'0"	84'0"	26'1"	83,378	415	3,800	34,600
McDonnell F2H-2	44'10"	40'2"	14'6"	22,312	575	1,475	44,800
N.A. AJ-2	71'5"	63'1"	21'5"	50,963	449	1,723	40,800

formance. It was also used as the F2H-2P photo reconnaissance aircraft.

North American AJ-1. The Savage was initially designed as the U.S. Navy's atomic bomber. Powered by two Pratt & Whitney R-2800 piston engines, with an Allison J33 jet engine in the tail to boost speeds over short distances, the XAJ-1 was first flown in July 1948. About 140 AJ-1 and AJ-2 aircraft were procured, of which some 30 were AJ-2P reconnaissance aircraft that were operated by squadron VJ-61.

Aircraft of the U.S. Army

Cessna L-19. The Cessna L-19 Bird Dog was used in both the Korean and Vietnam Wars as a liaison aircraft and forward air controller (FAC). Powered by a 213-horsepower, air-cooled Continental engine, the

Bird Dog was easy to fly and reliable. More than 3,000 were procured for the U.S. Army.

de Havilland L-20. The Beaver entered the Korean War late but proved to be a superb liaison aircraft and also served later in Vietnam. The rugged bush-born Beaver's wide landing gear made it useful in off-field applications. (In 1962 the L-20 was designated the U-6.)

North American/Ryan L-17. The classic Navion was used extensively in the Far East during the Korean War for troop and VIP transport, aeromedical evacuation, and reportedly, on some occasions, even for ground attack. It was later redesignated U-18.

Piper L-4A. A derivative of the famous Piper Cub, the L-4A served with distinction in both World War II and Korea. About 5,375 were built for the army in various models from 1941 on; they were powered by a

U.S. Army Aircraft Specifications

	Span	Length	Height	Gross Weight (pounds)	Top Speed (mph)	Range (miles)	Ceiling (feet)
Cessna L-19	36'0"	25'10"	7'4"	2,100	135	600	18,500
de Havilland U-6	48'0"	30'4"	9'0"	5,100	163	690	20,000
N.A./Ryan L-17	33'5"	27'6"	8'8"	2,905	155	650	15,600
Piper L-4	35'3"	22'4"	6'8"	1,220	110	230	13,500
Stinson L-5E	34'0"	24'1"	7'11"	2,020	130	425	15,800

variety of engines ranging from 65-horsepower Franklins to 100-horsepower Lycomings.

Stinson L-5E. The Sentinel was a development of the civil Stinson 105 Voyager. Sentinels were used from the start of the Korean War, and one ferried South Korean President Syngman Rhee from Seoul when the North Koreans attacked. Substantially larger and more powerful than the L-4s, the L-5 had a 185-horsepower Lycoming engine and could be equipped to carry a stretcher for wounded.

Aircraft of Great Britain

Auster A.O.P.6. Descended from the U.S.-designed Taylorcraft, the Auster A.O.P.6 was first produced in 1945. Powered by a 145-horsepower de Havilland Gipsy Major engine, it was used in small numbers during the Korean War as a liaison plane.

Fairey Firefly. The Firefly flew its first combat sortie in Korea from the decks of the light-fleet carrier HMS *Theseus*, continuing a distinguished combat record that had begun in World War II. Mark 5 Fireflies of the Fleet Air Arm (FAA) were powered by a 2,245-horsepower Rolls-Royce Griffon engine. Six FAA squadrons used the Firefly, which was noted for its reliability and high sortie rate.

Handley Page Hastings. First flown on 7 May 1946, the Hastings was powered by four 1,675-horsepower Bristol Hercules radial engines. The Royal Air Force procured a total of 147 Hastings, and they were used for transport and medical evacuation duties in Korea.

Hawker Sea Fury. The Fleet Air Arm's last piston-engine fighter, the Sea Fury, may still be seen each year at the Reno Air Races, contending for the top position with Mustangs and Bearcats. Derived from the World War II Hawker Tempest, it was powered by a 2,550-horsepower Bristol Centaurus engine. The Sea Fury went into action from the HMS *Theseus* and fought with distinction throughout the entire Korean War, being used in conjunction with the Fairey Firefly in close air support duties. The Sea Furies mixed up in air-to-air combat with MiG-15s and, although several Sea Furies were shot down, they destroyed a number of Communist aircraft.

Short Sunderland GR.5. The famous Flying Porcupine of World War II served in two Royal Air Force squadrons, 88 and 209, in Korea. The Sunderland performed many roles, but starred in rescue work. Powered by four Pratt & Whitney R-1830 Twin Wasp 1,230-horsepower engines, the Sunderland was a welcome sight to a downed aviator.

Supermarine Seafire. A derivative of the immortal Battle of Britain Spitfire, the Seafire operated off the HMS *Triumph* during the early months of the war, when Seafires flew 360 sorties. The Seafire Mk 47 was powered by the Rolls-Royce Griffon engine of 2,375 horsepower and equipped with four 20-mm guns and eight 60-pound air-to-ground rockets.

Aircraft of Other United Nations Command Nations and the Republic of Korea Air Force

A variety of aircraft were operated by the various UN allies; the specifications for most of them are covered in other sections. The Republic of Korea Air Force flew L-19A and T-6 FAC aircraft and F-51D fighters. It also had a few Tachikawa 55 trainers left behind by the Japanese. The Turkish Army used the Piper L-18B for artillery spotting. The Royal Australian Air Force flew Gloster F.8 Meteor fighters. The South African Air Force flew F-51Ds and F-86Fs.

Gloster F.8. The Meteor was Great Britain's first operational jet fighter and was used in World War II against the V-1 buzz bomb. The Mk.8 Meteor first flew in October 1948 and had a longer fuselage. Powered by two Rolls-Royce Derwent engines of 3,600-pound static thrust, the Meteor engaged in some air-to-air combat, but was primarily dedicated to ground support.

Piper L-18. An upgraded version of the classic Piper L-4, the L-18 was furnished to the Turkish Air Force under the Mutual Security Program.

Great Britain Aircraft Specifications

	Span	Length	Height	Gross Weight (pounds)	Top Speed (mph)	Range (miles)	Ceiling (feet)
Auster A.O.P.6	36'0"	23'9"	8'4½"	2,160	124	315	14,000
Fairey Firefly	41'2"	37'11"	14'4"	16,096	386	1,300	28,400
H.P. Hastings	113'0"	82'8"	22'6"	80,000	348	1,690	26,540
Hawker Sea Fury	38'4¾"	34'8"	15'10½"	12,500	460	700	41,000
Short Sunderland	112'9½"	85'4"	32'10½"	60,000	213	2,880	17,900
Supermarine Seafire	36'0"	33'7"	12'9"	11,615	452	400	43,100

Other UNC and Republic of Korea Aircraft Specifications

	Span	Length	Height	Gross Weight (pounds)	Top Speed (mph)	Range (miles)	Ceiling (feet)
Gloster F.8	37'2"	44'7"	13'0"	15,700	598	600	43,000
Piper L-18	35'3"	22'4½"	6'7"	1,500	110	450	13,500
Tachikawa Ki 55	38'8¾"	26'3"	11'11¾"	3,660	216	750	26,740

Helicopter Specifications

	Main Rotor (diameter)	Length	Height	Gross Weight (pounds)	Top Speed (mph)	Range (miles)	Ceiling (feet)
Bell H-13	35'1"	27'4"	9'6"	2,600	85	200	13,000
Hiller H-23A	35'5"	27'9"	9'9½"	2,700	82	224	13,200
Piasecki HRP	41'0"	54'9"	14'11"	6,907	99	265	8,530
Piasecki HUP-1	35'	31'10"	12'6"	6,005	120	273	12,467
Sikorsky H-5	49'0"	40'10"	13'0"	4,989	103	298	11,000
Sikorsky H-19	53'0"	62'7"	13'4"	7,200	100	400	11,000

Tachikawa Ki 55. Many Japanese aircraft, left behind after World War II, were used in Indo-China, Thailand, and Korea. The Tachikawa was a pleasant-looking, pleasant-flying trainer, powered by a 510-horsepower Hitachi radial engine.

Helicopters of United Nations Forces

Bell H-13. The Bell H-13 was the first army model of the classic Bell Model 47 helicopter. It was later called the Sioux. The H-13 went through a long development process as it was adapted to task after task. It is most remembered for its medical evacuation work. It was powered by a 265-horsepower Avco Lycoming flat six engine.

Hiller H-23. The Raven was developed for training and observation work and was powered by a variety of engines, with the early models using a 178-horsepower Franklin engine. The Raven was distinguished by its bubble canopy and sharply canted tail boom.

Piasecki HRP-1/-2. Immediately nicknamed the "flying banana" because of the unusual shape of the twin-rotor fuselage, the Piasecki helicopters were at the time of their debut the world's largest. The twin-rotor layout permitted loads to be distributed within a wide center of gravity. A 525-horsepower Continental engine powered the aircraft.

Piasecki HUP-1/-2. Smaller, cleaner, and more compact than the HRP-1, the HUP-1 retained the twin-rotor configuration but offered much improved per-formance. It performed well in Korea for transport and rescue, and it operated from aircraft carriers to pick up downed pilots.

Sikorsky H-5/HO3S-1. The Sikorsky Model 51 was a development of the pioneering R-4 and R-5 models. It served the air force as the H-5 and the navy as the HO3S-1. Although most were powered by 450-horsepower Pratt & Whitney R-985 engines, some received larger Pratt & Whitney R-1340 engines of 600 horsepower and were fitted with a larger diameter main rotor. Other variants included HO4S-1 and HRS.

Sikorsky H-19. The Model S-55 helicopter was built in large numbers by Sikorsky and served with the USAF and the U.S. Army as the H-19, with the U.S. Navy as the HO4S-1, and with the Marine Corp as the HRS-2. Powered by the 600-horsepower Pratt & Whitney R-1340, these helicopters were used as troop transports, for carrying cargo, for recovering damaged vehicles, and even for clandestine "exfiltration" of secret agents from behind Communist lines.

Aircraft of the Democratic People's Republic of Korea (DPRK, North Korea) and People's Republic of China (PRC, Communist China)

Ilyushin Il-2 and Il-10. The famed Sturmovik was said by Stalin to be as important as "air or bread" to the Red Army as a ground-support aircraft in World War II, and so it was. The Il-2 was powered by a variety of engines, with later versions receiving the liquid-cooled

Mikulin AM-38F of 1,770 horsepower. It was succeeded by the Il-10, which looked much like the Il-2, but was a very different aircraft. With its 2,000-horsepower AM-42 engine, it proved to be even more effective, and was well liked by air and ground crews. Nearly as many Sturmoviks (estimated at about 40,000) were produced as the PO-2, and many were sent to Soviet client states. Heavily armored, it was difficult to shoot down, but it found no place during the Korean War, in which U.S. air superiority prevented its effective use.

Ilyushin Il-28. Although never used in combat, the Beagle was in place on Manchurian airfields and, as such, represented a considerable threat, particularly to U.S. carriers. The Il-28 was powered by two Klimov RD-45 turbojets of 5,000-pound static thrust. The aircraft was efficient and reliable and widely used through out the Soviet bloc.

Lavochkin La-7 and La-11. Developments of the wartime series of Lavochkin fighters, the La-7 and L-11 were used extensively in the Soviet Union and by client states. The La-11 was the last of the piston-engine Lavochkin fighters, being powered by a 1,775-horsepower Shvetsov M-82FN radial engine. A tandem version of the La-11 was the La-11-UTI. The La-7, La-11, and La-11-UTI had similar dimensions and performance.

MiG-15. The MiG-15 stunned the Western world when it was introduced into combat in Korea in November 1950. It was a precursor of the future for air and space technology in the Soviet Union, which would go from triumph to triumph in aeronautical design. The MiG-15 first flew in December 1947 and was powered by the RD-45, a 5,000-pound, static-thrust, Soviet-built version of the Rolls-Royce Nene.

While the MiG-15 was on the short end of a seven-to-one victory ratio in combat with the F-86, it wreaked havoc with lesser aircraft, including the B-29 and F-84.

Polikarpov PO-2. While no exact statistics exist, the Polikarpov PO-2 is generally conceded with the Il-2 Sturmovik to have been one of the two aircraft manufactured in greater quantity than any other in history, as many as 41,000 having been built. It was affectionately called Kukuruznik ("corn cutter") by the Soviets. First flown in 1927, it served in World War II and in Korea in a variety of roles, powered by an M-11 engine of 115 horsepower. It became notorious as "Bed-Check Charlie" on night bombing missions. Intended more to harass and force defenders to lose sleep than to do damage, the PO-2 was very effective.

Tupelov Tu-2. This handsome twin-engine bomber first flew in 1943, and some 3,000 were built in a wide variety of marks. It was powered by two 1,850-horsepower A SH-82 radial engines. As with the MiG-15, it was supplied to many of the Soviet Union's client states. Despite having the MiG-15 to back it up, the Tu-2 never was a significant threat to UNC forces during the Korean War.

Yakolev-9. The Yak-9 was the most important Soviet fighter of World War II, and it served after the war in many of the Soviet Union's client states. Powered by a liquid-cooled 1,620-horsepower Klimov VK-107A engine, the more advanced Yak-9U was a highly maneuverable fighter, and, despite being sparsely equipped, it was otherwise fully up to Western standards of performance. More than 33,000 Yak fighters of all series were produced, including almost 17,000 Yak-9s.

Yakolev-15. A simple single-engine jet fighter based essentially on the Yak-3 piston engine forerunner, the

DPRK and PRC Aircraft Specifications

	Span	Length	Height	Gross Weight (pounds)	Top Speed (mph)	Range (miles)	Ceiling (feet)
Ilyushin Il-2	47'10¾"	38'3½"	13'8"	14,021	255	496	15,000
Ilyushin Il-10	43'11½"	36'3½"	13'8½"	14,407	329	497	23,790
Ilyushin Il-28	70'4½"	57'10¾"	21'0"	46,297	559	1,350	40,300
Lavochkin La-11	32'7¾"	28'2½"	9'2"	8,810	429	466	33,640
MiG-15	33'1"	33'2"	12'1¾"	7,456	652	882	49,869
Polikarpov PO-2	37'4¾"	26'9¾"	10'2"	1,962	93	250	13,125
Tupelov Tu-2	61'10½"	45'3½"	14'11"	18,257	342	870	29,500
Yakolev-9	32'¾"	28'½"	9'8½"	6,830	435	550	34,450
Yakolev-15	30'2¼"	28'9¾"	8'0"	5,809	505	220	43,800
Yakolev-18	33'9½"	26'5¼"	8'0"	2,425	154	652	13,123

Yak-15 was powered by an RD-10 engine of 1,980-pound static thrust. It had a modest performance and only a few hundred were built. It was followed by the essentially similar Yak-17, which was slightly heavier and had a tricycle landing gear.

Yakolev-18. From the flight of the prototype in 1945, the Yak-18 has been used in a variety of roles, from basic training to aerobatic competition. The Yak-18 was essentially a PO-2 replacement and was used by both civil and military air components in the Soviet Union and its client states. It was also offered for sale outside the Communist bloc. The Yak-18 used in Korea had a 160-horsepower M-11FR radial engine with a pressed aluminum helmeted cowling.

—*Walter J. Boyne*

References:

Boyne, Walter J. *Beyond the Wild Blue. A History of the USAF, 1947–1997.* New York: St. Martin's Press, 1997.

Dorr, Robert F., and Warren E. Thompson. *The Korean Air War.* Osceola, WI: Motorbooks International, 1994.

Flintham, Victor. *Air Wars and Aircraft.* New York: Facts on File, 1990.

Swanborough, Gordon, and Peter Bowers. *United States Military Aircraft Since 1909.* Washington, DC: Smithsonian Press, 1986.

———. *United States Navy Aircraft Since 1911.* New York: Funk & Wagnalls, 1968.

Thetford, Owen. *Aircraft of the Royal Air Force Since 1918.* New York: Funk & Wagnalls, 1968.

See also: China, People's Republic of: Air Force; Korea, Democratic People's Republic of: Air Force (Korean People's Air Force [KPAF]); Korea, Republic of: Air Force (ROKAF); United States: Air Force (USAF).

Aircraft Carriers

In June 1950 the aircraft carrier was a weapons system in trouble. Despite its assumption of the sea control mission during World War II, the aircraft carrier after 1945 was widely derided in press and government circles as vulnerable to nuclear attack and as dispensable in a confrontation against a land-based Communist foe. During the defense drawdown after the war, Harry Truman's administration cut the U.S. Navy's air arm drastically by mothballing many World War II–era ships and in 1949 cancelling on the stocks the supercarrier *United States*.

The outbreak of the Korean War immediately proved the naysayers wrong. Far from being superfluous, the four active Essex-class carriers rapidly deployed to the theater and gave close air support to hard-pressed soldiers ashore. Other carriers were quickly recommissioned. Ultimately eleven carriers of the Essex class made at least one combat tour: the *Antietam*, *Bon Homme Richard*, *Boxer*, *Essex*,

Navy Grumman F9F Panther, the first U.S. Navy jet ever in combat, preparing to land on the USS *Valley Forge*. (U.S. Naval Institute)

Kearsarge, Lake Champlain, Leyte, Oriskany, Philippine Sea, Princeton, and *Valley Forge.* Also making at least one combat tour during the Korean War were one Independence-class light carrier, the *Bataan,* and two escort carriers, the *Badoeng Strait* and *Sicily.* The last were employed principally in antisubmarine duty and in close air support. Many of these warships made more than one deployment, the record being held by *Boxer* and *Valley Forge* with four tours each. Five Royal Navy light carriers—the *Glory, Ocean, Theseus, Triumph,* and *Warrior,* which usually operated in the Yellow Sea—also assisted the United Nations' effort. The Australians provided the light carrier *Sydney.*

Essentially mobile airfields, carriers remained in the war zone for weeks on end. The ships carried a heavy share of the air war with their aviation groups of mixed propeller and jet aircraft. The newer planes brought certain problems along with their greatly increased performance. They were physically bigger, which reduced the size of air groups. Because of the relatively slow response time of the early jet engines, the aircraft needed catapult assistance on launching, but the existing hydraulic catapults provided only marginal thrust. Recovery of the jets aboard the axial-deck carriers was particularly hazardous, with flight deck accidents distressingly frequent. Despite these handicaps, by 1953 the U.S. Navy was flying more jet than propeller sorties.

The aircraft carriers undertook a wide variety of missions. These included striking at strategic targets in North Korea, conducting antisubmarine screens against possible Soviet intervention, and ferrying air force fighters from the United States to the operational theater.

U.S. carriers suffered no damage from enemy action. The most serious operational casualty occurred in August 1952 aboard the *Boxer,* when a fuel tank exploded on the hangar deck, starting a fire that killed nine sailors and burned out eighteen planes.

As the carrier showed its worth early in the conflict, Congress reversed course and in January 1951 authorized construction of another supercarrier, soon named the *Forrestal.* It was followed quickly by three more ships. These vessels incorporated the advanced design elements (initiated by the Royal Navy) that the Korean War showed were needed to make jet operations easier and safer: the steam catapult, the angled flight deck, and mirror landing lights. All three would remain standard features of carrier design over the next half-century.

—Malcolm Muir, Jr.

References:
Cagle, Malcolm W., and Frank A. Manson. *The Sea War in Korea.* Annapolis, MD: Naval Institute Press, 1957.
Field, James A., Jr. *History of United States Naval Operations: Korea.* Washington, DC: U.S. Government Printing Office, 1962.
Hallion, Richard P. *The Naval Air War in Korea.* Baltimore: Nautical and Aviation Publishing Co. of America, 1986.
Polmar, Norman. *Aircraft Carriers.* New York: Doubleday, 1969.
See also: Naval Forces Far East (NAVFE); United States Navy; U.S. Naval Air Operations.

Airfields

Airfields were used by all United Nations Command (UNC) air assets in varying degrees during the Korean War. This included the U.S. Air Force (USAF), Army, Navy, and Marine Corps. In the early months of the conflict, most air activity was conducted out of airfields in Japan, Okinawa, and the Philippines.

Early on, the U.S. Army established airfields in South Korea for use by its liaison light aircraft, especially for artillery spotting. These fields were often just a wide place in a road, but it was important to have these aircraft close to the scene of action. Some airfields, such as the one at P'ohang, were used by the USAF and the Marine Corps until Korean People's Army (North Korean) forces advanced too close for safe operation.

After the Inch'ŏn invasion and the Pusan perimeter breakout, airfields were established close behind advancing UNC infantry units. These were simply dirt strips, adequate for U.S. Army light aircraft, but generally not suitable for high-performance fighter aircraft, especially jets.

As the front moved forward into North Korea the USAF, Navy, and Marines positioned high-performance aircraft at better developed airfields in Korea. Most of these airfields required considerable work to bring them up to adequate standards after they had been severely damaged by bombing raids by UNC aircraft.

All airfields required a proper designation other than just the name of a nearby town or village. The USAF established a system designating their fields with a K- (for Korea) and then a number. The U.S. Army chose to designate their fields as A- (army) with a number and also designated some less–well-developed fields as AE- (army emergency) with a number.

Although the AE- designation remained throughout the war, many of these fields were used by the army for daily operations and by navy and marine aircraft when they were short on fuel or developed mechanical problems. On the east-central front in 1951, the Marines designated their airfields for helicopter and fixed wing liaison aircraft as X- fields. When the Marines moved to the western front, they used the army and air force designations.

As time passed and the airfields were improved, many of them were used for regular operations. The Pusan West Airfield became K-1, and Taegu 1 became K-2. In some cases an airfield had both army (A-) and air force (K-) designations. Taegu 2 was both

K-37 and A-3. K-38 at Wŏnju was also A-34. Usually the air force designation superseded the army designation as the field was improved to accept air force operations, but the dual designation created little confusion for pilots of either service. At times navy and Marine aircraft operated out of K- airfields, usually on a temporary basis when they were not operating from aircraft carriers.

Many airfields were built by army engineer combat and construction battalions. The air force employed special category army with air force engineer units for airfield construction and maintenance. These units were actually U.S. Army Corps of Engineers units, designated engineer aviation battalions and groups and assigned to the air force.

As military operations moved into North Korea, some existing airfields were captured by UNC forces and used by all services, usually after extensive repairs. Several airfields in the P'yŏngyang area were examples of this. However, with the rapid withdrawal of UNC forces from most of North Korea in late 1950, these airfields were abandoned.

In addition to fixed-wing aircraft, rotary wing (helicopter) aircraft operated out of many Korean airfields, especially the army airfields. These army airfields varied from 900 to several thousand feet in length. A few were paved, but most were dirt strips. Air force airfields were much longer and were usually paved, especially later in the war. Some used pierced steel plank surfaces in the early months.

By July 1953 with the battle line generally just north of the 38th parallel, there were approximately forty A- (able) airstrips in Korea. In addition there were some seventy AE (able easy) airfields in operation. At that time there were about forty K- (king) airfields, although perhaps seven of these also carried an army (able) designation. By custom the USAF called their airfields just K- (rather than king), whereas the army continued to use able and able easy designations orally.

These airfields had a mixture of facilities. Most had control towers of varying sophistication; others did not. Most had refueling and some maintenance facilities. Many air force airfields also had the capability of radar controlled approach and air traffic control.

One of the most interesting army fields was A-2 in Seoul. It was called the "Racetrack" because it was a horse-racing track that had been converted to airfield use. One flat side of the racetrack was used as the runway; the rest, as a taxiway and parking area. This was the location of the Eighth Army Flight Detachment in the latter part of the war. It was a challenge for pilots flying in there, as was most aviation activity during the war.

—*Norman R. Zehr*

References:

Army Engineers, EUSAK. "United Nations Airfields in Korea" [Map], 1953.

Field, James A., Jr. *History of United States Naval Operations: Korea.* Washington, DC: U.S. Government Printing Office, 1962.

Futrell, Robert F. *The United States Air Force in Korea, 1950–1953.* Rev. ed. Washington, DC: Office of the Chief of Air Force History, 1983.

Montross, Lynn, Hubard D. Kuokka, and Norman W. Hicks. *U.S. Marine Operations in Korea, 1950–1953: The East-Central Front.* Vol. 4. Washington, DC: U.S. Marine Corps Historical Branch, 1962.

Politella, Dario. *Operation Grasshopper.* Wichita, KS: Robert R. Longo, 1958.

See also: Air Power in the War; Aircraft (Principal Combat); United States Air Force (USAF).

Alexander-Lloyd Mission
(June 1952)

In June 1952, British Prime Minister Winston Churchill sent Minister of Defense William Alexander Sterling, Lord Alexander, and Minister of State for Foreign Affairs John Selwyn Lloyd to Tokyo and Korea. This mission was intended to reassure the British public that the Conservative government would be able to restrain the U.S.-led United Nations Command (UNC) and avoid widening the Korean War.

The prelude to the mission was the UNC suppression of the Kŏje-do prisoner-of-war (POW) uprising, in which Commonwealth units had been deployed without British approval. Another incentive of the mission was a rumor concerning Chiang Kai-shek's growing influence in U.S. policy toward China while the Korean truce talks in P'anmunjŏm remained deadlocked.

While in South Korea, Lloyd was critical of South Korean President Syngman Rhee's declaration of martial law and the situation in POW camps. Still, he did not oppose strong U.S. measures to restore political freedom among Communist prisoners. Before they left Korea, the two emissaries endorsed the U.S. POW policy and thus avoided confrontation over this sensitive issue.

In Tokyo the major issue during meetings with Commander in Chief United Nations Command General Mark W. Clark was British representation on Clark's staff and on the UNC delegation at P'anmunjŏm. Alexander and Lloyd wanted to gain more control over UNC policy formation and also wanted London kept better informed of developments.

The Tokyo negotiations occurred in a friendly atmosphere as Clark and Alexander had been comrades-in-arms on the Italian front during World War II. Nevertheless, Clark refused to alter the composition of the armistice negotiating team. He emphasized that "a change such as that during the critical stage of negotiations would only be an indication of weakness and indecision to the Communists." Moreover, if the United States yielded to British demands, then all other countries with troops in Korea would have the right to press identical demands. Publicly Alexander expressed his disappointment with the U.S. opposition but privately wrote Clark saying that he agreed with the general's reasoning about the composition of the negotiating team.

As a compromise, General Clark suggested that a British general officer be assigned to his UN staff in Tokyo. The Americans agreed and Alexander soon selected Major General Stephen N. Shoosmith as a deputy chief to Clark's staff. Prime Minister Churchill in his speech on 1 July 1952, however, emphasized that Shoosmith was to serve in a normal staff capacity rather than as a liaison.

The Alexander-Lloyd Mission achieved its objective of relieving domestic political pressure on the British Conservatives and restoring public faith in the Anglo-American alliance. Shoosmith and Clark worked harmoniously until the end of the war and their cooperation served as an example for other members of the UNC.

—Zsolt Varga

References:

Clark, Mark W. *From the Danube to the Yalu.* New York: Harper & Row, 1954.

U.S. Department of State, Bureau of Public Affairs. *Foreign Relations of the United States, 1952–1954.* Vol. 15, *Korea.* Washington, DC: U.S. Government Printing Office, 1984.

See also: Clark, Mark W.; Joint Chiefs of Staff (JCS); Kŏje-do Prisoner-of-War Uprising; Lloyd, John Selwyn; P'anmunjŏn Truce Talks; United Kingdom (UK); United Nations Command (UNC).

Allison, John M.
(1905–1978)

U.S. Department of State official closely involved with the making of Korean policy as chief of the State Department Division of Northeast Asian Affairs (1947–1950); special assistant to Secretary of State John Foster Dulles (1950–1951); and assistant secretary of state for Far Eastern Affairs (1952–1953).

Born on 7 April 1905, in Holton, Kansas, John M. Allison was educated at the University of Nebraska. After three years of teaching English in Japan, he joined the Foreign Service in 1930. As an Asian expert, during the next eleven years he was posted alternately in China and Japan. After the Japanese attack on Pearl Harbor, he was interned in Japan for six months.

After serving in economic positions in London during and after the Second World War, Allison returned to Washington in 1947 to head the Division of Northeast Asian Affairs. His responsibilities included Korea, which since the war had been under occupation by both U.S. and Soviet forces. With the deepening Cold War, negotiations between the two powers regarding Korea had reached an impasse. In 1947 Allison, as the steering member of the State-War-Navy Coordinating Committee's (SWNCC's) ad hoc subcommittee on Korea, was instrumental in devising SWNCC 176/30. This was a plan whereby Harry Truman's administration tried to reach agreement with the Soviet Union, Britain, and the Republic of China on elections for a unified Korean government and, when this approach failed, turned the issue over to the United Nations (UN). On 14 November 1947 that body, in turn, passed a U.S.-sponsored resolution calling for the withdrawal of foreign troops from Korea and the holding of unified national elections no later than 31 March 1948. Soviet occupation forces, however, denied UN officials access to the North, and the subsequent elections of 10 May 1948 were confined to the southern portion of the country. This laid the groundwork for the creation of two separate, ideologically opposed and mutually antagonistic Korean states on the peninsula, each a client state of one of the two major Cold War protagonists.

When North Korean forces invaded the South in June 1950, Allison was serving as assistant to Dulles in ongoing Japanese Peace Treaty negotiations in Tokyo. From 15 to 20 June, immediately before the outbreak of war, the two men visited South Korea, affirming Washington's commitment to South Korean President Syngman Rhee's regime and stating that threats from the North would come through domestic subversion rather than direct military attack.

Dulles and Allison were in Tokyo when the North Koreans invaded the South. They then cabled Washington to urge that, if necessary, the United States employ military force to prevent a Communist takeover of South Korea. Allison returned to Washington that summer and figured prominently in the debate as to whether U.S. forces should cross the 38th parallel, an issue on which he took an equally hard line, arguing that permanent peace in Korea was unattainable while the peninsula remained divided. He characterized North Korea as an illegitimate puppet state, the establishment of which violated UN resolutions. He also minimized the probability of intervention in Korea by the People's Republic of China. As acting assistant and then assistant secretary for Far Eastern Affairs until 1953, he remained actively involved in the making of Korean policy, albeit during a period largely characterized by stalemate. Allison remained in the Foreign Service until his retirement in 1960, serving successively as ambassador to Japan, Indonesia, and Czechoslovakia. He died in Honolulu on 28 October 1978.

—Priscilla Roberts

References:

Allison, John M. *Ambassador from the Prairie, or Allison Wonderland*. Boston: Houghton Mifflin, 1973.

Foot, Rosemary J. *The Wrong War: American Policy and the Dimensions of the Korean Conflict, 1950–1953*. Ithaca, NY: Cornell University Press, 1985.

Matray, James I. *The Reluctant Crusade: American Foreign Policy in Korea, 1941–1950*. Honolulu: University of Hawaii Press, 1985.

Pruessen, Ronald M. *John Foster Dulles: The Road to Power*. New York: Free Press, 1982.

Stueck, William W., Jr. *The Road to Confrontation: American Policy toward China and Korea, 1947–1950*. Chapel Hill: University of North Carolina Press, 1981.

See also: Dulles, John Foster; Dulles's Trip to Korea.

Almond, Edward Mallory
(1892–1979)

U.S. Army lieutenant general, Far East Command (FEC) chief of staff, and commander of X Corps during the Korean War. Born on 12 December 1892 in Luray, Virginia, Edward "Ned" Mallory Almond graduated from the Virginia Military Institute in 1915. During World War I, he commanded the 12th Machine Gun Battalion of the 4th Infantry Division in France. He fought in the Aisne-Marne and Meuse-Argonne offensives, was wounded in action, and was awarded the Silver Star for gallantry.

In the interwar years Almond was groomed for high command. After serving as an instructor at the Infantry School at Fort Benning, Georgia, he attended the Army Command and General Staff College, the Army War College, the Air Corps Tactical School, and the Naval War College. During 1930–1933 he commanded a battalion in the Philippines. When the United States entered World War II in December 1941, Almond was the assistant chief of staff for operations and training of VI Corps, headquartered in Providence, Rhode Island. Shortly thereafter he became the corps chief of staff.

In March 1942 Almond was promoted to brigadier general and assigned as the assistant commander of the 93d Infantry Division (Colored), then in the process of activating at Fort Huachuca, Arizona. In July 1942 U.S. Army Chief of Staff General George C. Marshall personally selected Almond to command the 92d Infantry Division (Colored). It was to be one of Marshall's most controversial decisions of World War II. Almond was promoted to major general in September 1942.

Almond trained the 92d in Alabama and Arizona, and he commanded it in Italy in 1944 and 1945. The 92d was the only all-black division that fought as a complete division in World War II. Despite the dedication and bravery of its soldiers, the 92d experienced serious problems in both training and combat. To a large degree, this was the result of the general low quality of the white officers assigned to the army's segregated black units. Although Almond himself harbored strong and well-known prejudices against minority soldiers, he ultimately was not held responsible for the shortcomings of his division.

After World War II Almond joined General Douglas MacArthur's Armed Forces Pacific Command, later designated Far East Command, as assistant chief of staff for personnel. Almond quickly became an insider on MacArthur's staff, becoming deputy chief of staff in November 1946 and chief of staff in February 1949. MacArthur, who hated staff meetings and administrative procedures, relied heavily on Almond to oversee the day-to-day running of the command. Having served in Europe in World War II rather than in the Pacific, Almond was unique among MacArthur's inner circle.

On 24 July 1950, Almond became dual-hatted as chief of staff of the United Nations Command (UNC). This was not at all an unusual arrangement, considering that MacArthur served as both UN and U.S. FEC commander in chief and both command headquarters were virtually the same organization. On 26 August 1950, however, MacArthur took the highly unusual step of triple-hatting Almond by designating him commander of the newly formed X Corps—along with his chief of staff duties. This resulted in an almost unprecedented concentration of command and staff responsibilities under a single officer.

X Corps was the force designated to make the landings at Inch'ŏn and was at the time far in the Korean People's Army (KPA, North Korean) operational rear. X Corps initially consisted of the U.S. Army 7th Infantry Division and the 1st Marine Division. Most Marine Corps officers chaffed at the idea of being commanded by a U.S. Army officer for an amphibious assault. During the planning and the conduct of the assault, Almond repeatedly clashed with 1st Marine Division Commander Major General Oliver P. Smith.

MacArthur further compounded the already complicated command structure by making X Corps directly subordinate to FEC headquarters in Japan, rather than subordinate to Lieutenant General Walton H. Walker's Eighth Army in Korea. Military analysts and historians widely regard this as a flagrant violation of the principle of unity of command.

Even after Eighth Army broke out from the Pusan perimeter and linked up with X Corps, MacArthur continued to keep Almond's command directly subordinate to FEC. X Corps was sent around to Korea's east coast for another landing operation at Wŏnsan. Still independent of Eighth Army, Almond led X Corps in its advance to the Yalu River and in the following Changjin (Chosin) Reservoir campaign. After the Chinese military intervention forced the UN forces back down the Korean peninsula, Almond conducted a skillful withdrawal to the port of Hŭngnam and from there evacuated his command by sea.

X Corps returned to the Pusan area, and on 26 December 1950, it finally became an integral part of the Eighth Army. Simultaneously, Almond relinquished his positions as FEC and UNC chief of staff. He received his third star in February 1951, partially in recognition for his handling of the Hŭngnam evacuation.

During the first half of 1951, X Corps operated against KPA and Chinese People's Volunteer Army (Chinese Communist) forces in central Korea, participating in the battles of Wŭnju, Chip'yŏng-ni, the Soyang River, and the Chinese Spring Offensive. During Operation ROUNDUP in February, Almond ignored intelligence reports that X Corps would be in the center of a major Chinese counterattack. When the attack did come, it destroyed two Republic of Korea Army (ROKA, South Korean) divisions under his command.

Almond is one of the most controversial commanders in a war with no shortage of such figures. Often described as "brilliant" and "a human dynamo," he was also dictatorial and blindly loyal to MacArthur's flawed strategic vision. Almond repeatedly clashed with Walker and with most of the U.S. Marine and ROKA officers under his command. His handling of the still-segregated black and Puerto Rican units under his command has resulted in historian Clay Blair branding him a blatant racist. Yet Almond could be a skillful—if uneven—and brave battlefield commander.

In July 1951 Almond returned to the United States to serve as the commandant of the U.S. Army War College at Carlisle Barracks, Pennsylvania. He retired from the U.S. Army in January 1953. After retirement he worked for an insurance company in Alabama, and from 1961 to 1968 he served as the president of the Board of Visitors of the Virginia Military Institute. Almond died on 11 June 1979.

—*David T. Zabecki*

References:

Appleman, Roy E. *South to the Naktong, North to the Yalu.* Washington, DC: Office of the Chief of Military History, 1961.

Blair, Clay. *The Forgotten War: America in Korea, 1950–1953.* New York: Times Books, 1987.

Lee, Ulysses. *The U.S. Army in World War II: The Employment of Negro Troops.* Washington, DC: U.S. Government Printing Office, 1966.

Mossman, Billy C. *U.S. Army in the Korean War: Ebb and Flow, November 1950–July 1951.* Washington, DC: U.S. Army Center of Military History, 1990.

Stanton, Shelby. *America's Tenth Legion: X Corps in Korea.* Novato, CA: Presidio Press, 1989.

See also: Changjin (Chosin) Reservoir Campaign; Hŭngnam Evacuation; Inch'ŏn Landings: Operation CHROMITE; MacArthur, Douglas; Marshall, George C.; ROUNDUP, Operation; Smith, Oliver Prince; Tenth Corps; Walker, Walton Harris.

Amphibious Force Far East (Task Force 90)

U.S. Navy command that played an important role in the Korean War. In June 1950, Amphibious Force Far East (Task Force 90) numbered just 25 vessels. By 15 September 1950, it had grown to 112 U.S. and Allied ships: attack transports, cargo ships, minesweepers, landing ships, patrol vessels, and other vessels. Rear Admiral James H. Doyle commanded Amphibious Force Far East, usually known as Task Force 90 (TF 90).

TF 90's first mission of the war came on 15 July 1950, when it sailed from the Tokyo-Yokosuka area of Japan to P'ohang, Korea, with the U.S. 1st Cavalry Division. Its most important mission in the war was undoubtedly its role in the amphibious landing at Inch'ŏn, Operation CHROMITE. TF 90 was responsible for the landing as well as control of close air support and naval gunfire; it then provided support to the landing force ashore.

Doyle had misgivings about CHROMITE but stated that "Inchon is not impossible." He had little time to plan the assault and no time to rehearse the operation, but simply briefed the appropriate commanders aboard the command ship *Mount McKinley*. In all, the operation involved 260 vessels from the United States, United Kingdom, Australia, Canada, New Zealand, France, and the Netherlands. The Inch'ŏn landing was extraordinarily difficult but was an almost flawless operation; for four decades it remained the only unambiguously successful, large-scale U.S. combat operation.

TF 90's next mission was to carry X Corps to Wŏnsan on the eastern coast of North Korea. The assault was to occur on 20 October 1950; it would have gone according to plan save that mines were discovered in the area. TF 90 vessels then spent most of October sweeping the bay for mines, an operation that claimed U.S. Navy minesweepers *Pirate* and *Pledge*.

TF 90's last mission in the war was to evacuate X Corps from the port of Hŭngnam in northeast Korea. United Nations forces commander General Douglas MacArthur issued orders to that effect on 9 December 1950. The operation began the next day and ended on 29 December 1950. The operation had embarked some 105,000 U.S. and Republic of Korea (South Korean) military personnel and 91,000 civilian refugees.

On 12 September 1950, Task Force 95 replaced TF 90 in Korea.

—*Matthew S. Carman*

References:

Cagle, Malcolm W., and Frank A. Manson. *The Sea War in Korea.* Annapolis, MD: Naval Institute Press, 1957.

Heinl, Robert D. *Victory at High Tide: The Inchon-Seoul Campaign.* Philadelphia: J. B. Lippincott, 1968.

Sandier, Stanley, ed. *The Korean War Encyclopedia.* New York: Garland, 1995.

See also: Inch'ŏn Landings: Operation CHROMITE; Wŏnsan Landing.

An Ho-sang
(1902–1999)

First minister of education for the Republic of Korea (ROK, South Korea), August 1948–May 1950, immediately before the Korean War. An was born in Ŭiryŏng, Kyŏngsangnam-do (South Kyŏngsang Province), on 23 January 1902. He studied in China, Japan, and Germany, where he earned a doctorate in philosophy from Jena University. Returning to Korea, he taught at many universities and became the first president of the Korean Association of Philosophy in 1933. He was targeted to be arrested in the 1942 thirty-three–member Chosŏnŏ Hakhoe (Korean Language Society) incident—an infamous Japanese oppression of Korean intellectuals—but he was spared because of his poor health.

After independence, An was an ideologue for the right-wing nationalists. He taught philosophy at Seoul National University and eagerly expressed nationalist sentiments at lectures organized by the right-wing groups. He also worked for the U.S. military government, mainly in education and science.

When the ROK was established, An played a central role in the creation and implementation of President Syngman Rhee's ruling ideology. An was the longest-serving minister in Rhee's first administration. In 1949 Rhee tried persuading his people to come together to oppose communism by espousing his ruling ideology, and An was the individual who initiated and spread that ideology, the so-called *Ilminjuŭi* (one-people ideology).

An strongly emphasized Korean unity by frequently quoting from the legend of Tan'gun concerning the origins of Korea, and he made reference to "Hwarangism," the spirit of fighters of the Silla dynasty in Korean history from the first century B.C. through the tenth century A.D. An also insisted that South Korea should defeat North Korea, following the model of the unification of the peninsula under Silla. An's forceful anti-Communist stance was also part of the *Ilminjuŭi,* Rhee's ruling ideology. An was one of the founders of Rhee's Liberal Party.

An's ideas were reflected in his administrative policies while he was minister of education. On assuming the position in August 1948, he immediately began large-scale persecution of heterodox teachers. In addition he devised plans to censor and monitor teachers in the classroom. In March 1949 he established the Student National Defense Corps in an attempt to bring under government control student movements heretofore dominated by leftists. After retiring from his ministerial post, An chaired the Taehan Youth Corps, which had two million members that ardently supported Syngman Rhee.

During the Korean War, South Korea experienced political strife, yet An ardently supported Rhee and mobilized the Taehan Youth Corps toward that end. He was also active in the national campaign against an armistice. In spite of An's unswerving loyalty to Rhee, Rhee oppressed Yi Pŏm-sŏk's faction (to which An belonged) shortly after his second seizure of political power. An was finally forced out of the Taehan Youth Corps and the Liberal Party. He continued, however, to implement and spread the *Ilminjuŭi.* An was regarded by many as one of the most conservative and extreme nationalists in modern Korean history. He died in Seoul on 21 February 1999.

—*Insook Park*

References:

Cumings, Bruce. The *Origins of the Korean War.* Vol. 2, *The Roaring of the Cataract, 1947–1950.* Princeton, NJ: Princeton University Press, 1990.

Matray, James I., ed. *Historical Dictionary of the Korean War.* Westport, CT: Greenwood Press, 1991.

Park, Myung-Lim. *Han'guk Chŏnjaeng'ŭi Palbal kwa Kiwŏn* [The outbreak and origins of the Korean War]. Vols. 1, 2. Seoul: Nanam Publishing, 1996.

See also: Syngman Rhee; Yi Pŏm-sŏk (Lee Bum Suk).

Antiaircraft Artillery

Despite the advent of jet technology and its widespread application in the Korean War, the traditional role of antiaircraft artillery (AAA) in point defense remained an integral component of aerial defense. Both the United Nations Command (UNC) and forces of the Chinese People's Volunteer Army (CPVA, Chinese Communist) and the Korean People's Army (KPA, North Korea) employed AAA units. In the case of Communist forces, this employment became ubiquitous after 1950 as the U.S. Fifth Air Force gained and, even after Chinese intervention, maintained air superiority.

Inevitably, AAA demonstrated less effectiveness against jets than against piston-engine aircraft, but even against the former it constituted a credible threat. The same technological watershed touching upon aircraft propulsion in the early 1950s affected all aspects of aerial offense and defense; antiaircraft artillery was no exception. Throughout the conflict in Korea, AAA exhibited features of command, control, and operational use that in some respects were clearly reminiscent of World War II. Conversely, other technical refinements, particularly the beginnings of the broad application of radar for target acquisition, tracking, and gun laying, initiated often technically troublesome changes, which in later decades resulted in the gradual elimination of AAA per se and its replacement with antiaircraft missiles.

On the UNC side, deployment of AAA began modestly enough. Batteries of "quad .50s" were used at Suwŏn by the 507th AAA Battalion near Seoul as base-defense weapons in the earliest days of the war. These .50-caliber machine guns, essentially the same as the Browning M2 used between 1941 and 1945, had an effective range of some 1,200 yards and a rate of fire of 800 rounds per minute. As UNC forces retreated from Suwŏn, these same batteries were mounted in vehicles and used as supplemental reinforcement for the U.S. rear guard, a use not unheard of in World War II. Calls went out immediately for increases in the AAA strength of U.S. and UNC forces even as the first elements of Fifth Air Force began operations from bases in Japan. In fact, the first AAA elements of Fifth Air Force arrived in Korea before President Harry S. Truman authorized the use of ground forces there.

From the beginning, AAA at UNC bases fell under operational control of the base's commander; this had previously been the procedure for AAA at U.S. airfields in Japan, even though the artillery itself fell within the purview of the army. By order of Far East Command, however, those nonorganic (i.e., nondivisional) AAA units assigned to Eighth Army and the Tenth AAA Group fell under the operational control of Fifth Air Force in the person of an attached U.S. Air Force (USAF) air-defense commander.

In June 1951, Eighth Army's AAA strength consisted of two battalions of heavy guns and ten automatic-weapons batteries. For high-altitude defense, 90-mm guns were employed. These guns stood at Pusan, Inch'ŏn, and Seoul. For defense of airfields and ports, 40-mm automatic weapons were used. In that same month, Fifth Air Force requested a minimum of three heavy-gun battalions and twenty automatic-weapons batteries. In response to USAF Lieutenant General Frank Everest's order of 25 July 1951 to establish a formal AAA defense network for Fifth Air Force, the minimum requested strength rose again. By October it stood at five gun battalions and thirty-six automatic-weapons batteries, respectively. In Everest's view the full deployment of Fifth Air Force to a geographically small—and thereby congested "target-rich" theater—demanded increased AAA levels, as did the perceived possibility of an all-out Chinese aerial offensive against UNC air bases.

Another factor aggravating the need for increased AAA was Fifth Air Force's admitted inability to track Communist aircraft by radar. This inability applied particularly to jets flying above 40,000 feet and below 1,000 feet. Since most Allied AAA was visually directed in any case, problems with radar's relative

ineffectiveness were vexatious rather than a critical failure. To offset this deficit, in December 1952 searchlights were added to antiaircraft batteries at Suwŏn, Kimpŏ, and at Cho-do Island in the Yellow Sea. Scattered AAA reinforcements continued to arrive in Korea until February 1953. Calls for reequipping these and older UNC forces with the new, radar-directed 75-mm Skysweeper antiaircraft gun came to naught, as the armistice intervened and brought the fighting in Korea to an end.

Despite the increasing levels of strength in AAA for UNC forces, antiaircraft weaponry was always secondary to air-to-air superiority in fact, if not also in theory. Dominating and eliminating KPA and Chinese air forces remained the primary objective of Fifth Air Force. This would allow repeated strikes on Communist airfields to prevent their repair as well as more effective close air support for UNC troops and interdiction of Communist forces afield.

On the Communist side, however, AAA played a major role, precisely because USAF and other UNC pilots proved so adept at effectively contesting the skies over Korea. In September 1950 the KPA employed some seventy heavy guns and approximately 500 automatic weapons as AAA. The North Koreans presumed that there would be no major Republic of Korea (South Korea) or other aerial forces opposing them. Consequently, AAA capability had been neglected. As a result, the KPA's leadership expressed explicit concern about the physical and moral effects of aerial attack after its defeat in the late summer and fall of 1950. It also set about increasing its AAA strength. In June 1951 Communist AAA levels stood at approximately 300 heavy guns. Strength in automatic weapons remained about the same as in late 1950, but large numbers of smaller-caliber machine guns had been added to the inventory. By early 1953 these levels had risen to more than 800 heavy guns and no fewer than 1,000 automatic weapons (estimates vary). These were concentrated particularly around P'yŏngyang's industries and airfields and air bases, bridges, and dams along the Yalu River.

Compared with that in World War II, flak in Korea was weak but still unacceptable. Most heavy AAA guns were Soviet-model 85-mm M-1939 weapons firing 160 rounds per minute to an effective ceiling of 25,000 feet. The principal automatic weapons used as AAA were also Soviet-model pieces, in this case 37-mm M-1939 cannon having a firing rate of 160 rounds per minute up to 4,500 feet. Most of this weaponry was visually directed, although by 1953 KPA and CPVA troops used ever larger numbers of gun-laying radar sets. Communist forces also equipped large numbers of their AAA batteries with searchlights as UNC aircraft, especially FEAF (Far East Air Force) Bomber

Command's B-29s, switched to night raids to avoid not only flak in daylight but also North Korean and Chinese jets. In that case, clear-night illumination by enemy AAA could reach altitudes of 30,000 feet with radar- or sound-directed searchlights catching bombers first. Visually directed units could then follow suit. All of these capabilities increased dramatically with Chinese intervention in October and November 1950 and rose thereafter.

Consequently for UNC air forces, flak suppression became an important mission in itself and in respect to interdiction and strategic bombing. Communist AAA units complicated suppression by moving regularly and by camouflaging batteries in ways that even the UNC admitted was sometimes excellent. Flak-suppression missions also were most effective only when subsequent raids by bombers on their own targets occurred before AAA crews could reorganize and/or replace their equipment. By helping force UNC bombers to fly at least partially at night and to bomb from higher altitudes (witness the repeated B-29 raids on the Yalu bridges in November 1950), Communist AAA affected both interdiction and the results of strategic bombing. While FEAF Bomber Command sometimes rated flak as "not too serious," it nevertheless remained troublesome and could be deadly, especially below 3,000 feet for piston-engine aircraft such as F-51 Mustangs, AD-2 Skyraiders, and B-26 Invader light bombers. Even the B-29 Superfortresses were not immune. During the war Communist antiaircraft artillery shot down some 550 UNC aircraft of all types.

—*David R. Dorondo*

References:

Futrell, Robert F. *The United States Air Force in Korea, 1950–1953.* Rev. ed. Washington, DC: Office of the Chief of Air Force History, 1983.

Kreis, John F. *Air Warfare and Air Base Air Defense, 1914–1973.* Washington, DC: Office of Air Force History, 1988.

Millett, Allan R. "Korea, 1950–1953." In *Case Studies in the Development of Close Air Support,* edited by Benjamin Franklin Cooling. Washington, DC: Office of Air Force History, 1990.

See also: Aircraft (Principal Combat); Truman, Harry S.

Antiwar Sentiment in the United States

Antiwar sentiment in the United States severely handicapped President Harry S. Truman politically in both foreign and domestic affairs, and it contributed to his 1952 decision not to run for the presidency again.

The Korean War quickly became the most unpopular war ever fought in the United States up to that time, and opposition to it was subsequently surpassed only by that to the Vietnam War. According to one poll, in August 1953, shortly after an armistice was concluded, 62 percent of Americans believed that the war had not

been worth fighting. The war had cost the United States approximately $100 billion, with some 37,000 Americans killed and a further 103,000 wounded. Opposition to the war came from both left and right on the political spectrum but soon became particularly strong among Republicans and conservatives.

When Truman made his June 1950 decision to send U.S. troops to Korea, approximately 75 percent of Americans and a majority of those in Congress approved. White House mail ran 10 to 1 in favor of the war, easily overwhelming small leftist protests in New York City. Popular support continued high well into the fall, particularly after General Douglas MacArthur's initial success at Inch'ŏn, when it appeared that the war would probably end by Christmas. Once Chinese Communist troops entered the war in November 1950, transforming it into a conflict of attrition, public enthusiasm swiftly evaporated, a development exacerbated not only by the growing casualty lists but also by the imposition of unpopular economic controls and rising inflation and taxes.

One major reason the public turned against the war was because, rather than being a full-scale crusade for total victory, it was a limited war, the objectives of which were often less than precisely defined. Truman's recall of MacArthur in April 1951, after the general publicly supported aggressive prosecution of the war against China whatever the consequences, further confused Americans. Although Americans failed to agree as to how they ought to end the war, in a negotiated peace settlement or a fight to the finish with the People's Republic of China (Communist China) and the Soviet Union, by early 1951 it was only too apparent that they hoped it would end sooner rather than later. By spring 1951 the war reached a near-stalemate situation, where it rested for the following two years as inconclusive armistice negotiations failed to reach any satisfactory resolution and the human and fiscal costs mounted.

The war divided the left, the civil rights movement, and the pacifist movement. Some radical leftists and Communist publications attacked the war from the beginning as an example of U.S. imperialism, as did such prominent left-wing African-Americans as Paul Robeson and William Z. Foster. Many liberal but anti-Communist intellectuals, by contrast, supported U.S. intervention as morally justified. Numerous African-Americans fought in the war, which boosted progress toward racial integration in the armed services, and such publications as *Ebony* endorsed the war. The fact that intervention occurred under United Nations auspices reconciled many U.S. pacifist groups, including the United World Federalists, socialists, and Wallace Progressives. There was no organized draft resistance movement, and the figures for draft evasion, conscientious objection, and desertion were no higher than during the Second World War.

Initially only dedicated neo-isolationists, a few Communists, and extreme pacifists, such as A. J. Muste, opposed the U.S. commitment, while Norman Thomas, a revered figure in U.S. socialism, defended intervention. Opposition from liberal intellectuals and academics was, moreover, probably muzzled by the rising tide of McCarthyism, which threatened the career of any college professor or teacher rash enough to criticize the war from a radical perspective.

U.S. conservatives, by contrast, suffered no such inhibitions after late 1950, as the Korean War effectively ended the bipartisan foreign policy consensus that had existed since the Second World War. Republicans could combine support in principle for the Korean War with ferocious criticism of the Truman administration. They charged that ill-considered State Department policies—including Secretary of State Dean Acheson's January 1950 National Press Club speech; the administration's failure to indicate that it would, if necessary, defend the Republic of Korea; the administration's concentration upon Europe rather than upon Asia; and its reluctance to prosecute the war toward clear victory—were responsible for the U.S. debacle. Such accusations were often combined with McCarthyist allegations that Communist agents had infested the administration at every level and that its weaknesses must be ascribed to their traitorous activities. The flames were further fanned by members of the China lobby, those politicians, journalists, business people, and others with links to Jiang Jieshi's (Chiang Kai-shek) Nationalist Guomindang regime on Taiwan, who believed that the United States had provided insufficient aid and support to Nationalist China during the civil war.

Opposition to the Truman administration rose to a dramatic peak in spring and summer 1951 after Truman's dismissal of MacArthur. While the aggressive general's reception obviously reflected frustration over the war rather than a belief that it was unjustified in the first place, it served as a focus for dissatisfaction with the president. For the remainder of his term, Truman's popularity ratings remained exceedingly low, hampering his effectiveness in dealing with Congress, while public discontent with the war's prosecution was consistently high. Some Congressional neo-isolationists, such as Senator Robert A. Taft, who had initially suggested that the United States might liquidate many of its overseas commitments, quite possibly including that to Korea, somewhat unscrupulously seized upon and repeated MacArthur's complaints that more forceful prosecution of the war would have brought victory in short order. So did Senator Joseph R. McCarthy and his followers, with the addi-

tional gloss that such deficiencies were primarily a result of Communist penetration of U.S. officialdom. The ability of their Communist captors to persuade or pressure at least some American prisoners of war to renounce their national allegiances and publicly oppose their country's policies also shocked many Americans and further tarnished the war's image, rightly or wrongly suggesting that troops' morale must be low.

The impending presidential election of 1952, which Republican politicians, smarting from five successive defeats since 1932, were determined to win, added yet more fuel to all these existing fires. The intensely vitriolic attacks to which conservatives subjected Truman and his administration, together with the war's broader unpopularity, were almost certainly the most important reasons for Truman's decision, reached in late 1951, that he would not stand for reelection. In their eagerness to regain the White House, prominent Republicans such as Taft, though finding McCarthy's tactics personally distasteful, tolerated and even encouraged his behavior. So, too, did Dwight D. Eisenhower, the eventual Republican candidate, who neither attempted to rein in the junior senator from Wisconsin during the election campaign nor even to refute his accusations against George C. Marshall, Eisenhower's former military superior. Despite Eisenhower's personal initial support for U.S. intervention, neither he nor other Republicans hesitated to attack the Democrats on their record in Korea. As did Richard Nixon in 1968, Eisenhower promised that, if elected, he would bring the war to a speedy end, though he cautiously left it studiously vague whether he would accomplish this through negotiations or a battlefield victory. His successful conclusion of an armistice agreement in June 1953 finally ended the hostilities, though for the rest of the century the United States retained its commitment to South Korea. The war's conclusion effectively restored the antebellum status quo and, although generating no great public celebrations, substantially enhanced Eisenhower's popularity. Recognizing that public support for such entanglements was likely to be extremely low, for the remainder of his presidency Eisenhower deliberately eschewed commitments to lengthy and frustrating limited wars, relying instead upon a combination of massive nuclear deterrence and covert interventions to project U.S. military power.

—*Priscilla Roberts*

References:

Adler, Selig. *The Isolationist Impulse: Its Twentieth Century Reaction.* New York: Abelard, 1957.

Caine, Philip D. "The United States in Korea and Vietnam: A Study in Public Opinion." *Air University Quarterly Review* 20, no. 1 (Spring 1968): 49–58.

DeBenedetti, Charles. *The Peace Reform in American History*. Bloomington: Indiana University Press, 1980.

Hamby, Alonzo L. "Public Opinion: Korea and Vietnam," *The Wilson Quarterly* 2, No. 3 (Fall 1978). 137–141.

———. *Man of the People: A Life of Harry S. Truman*. New York: Oxford University Press, 1995.

Huey, Gary L. "Public Opinion and the Korean War." In *The Korean War: Handbook of the Literature and Research*, edited by Lester H. Brune. Westport, CT: Greenwood Press, 1996, 409–418.

Kaufman, Burton I. *The Korean War: Challenges in Crisis, Credibility, and Command*. New York: Alfred Knopf, 1986.

Mantell, Matthew E. "Opposition to the Korean War: A Study in American Dissent." Ph.D. dissertation, New York University, 1973.

McCullough, David. *Truman*. New York: Simon & Schuster, 1992.

Mueller, John E. *War, Presidents and Public Opinion*. New York: Wiley, 1973.

Paterson, Thomas G., ed. *Cold War Critics: Alternatives to American Foreign Policy in the Truman Years*. Chicago: Quadrangle Books, 1971.

Pierpaoli, Paul G., Jr. *Truman and Korea: The Political Culture of the Early Cold War*. Columbia: University of Missouri Press, 1999.

Roper, Elmo. *You and Your Leaders: Their Actions and Your Reactions*. New York: William Morrow, 1957.

Sandler, Stanley, ed. *The Korean War: An Encyclopedia*. New York: Garland, 1995.

Spanier, John W. *The Truman-MacArthur Controversy and the Korean* War. Cambridge, MA: Belknap Press, 1959.

Wood, Hugh G. "American Reaction to Limited War in Asia: Korea and Vietnam, 1950–1968." Ph.D. dissertation, University of Colorado, 1974.

See also: Acheson, Dean Goodersham; Casualties; Eisenhower, Dwight D.; Jiang Jieshi (Chiang Kai-shek); MacArthur, Douglas; Marshall, George C.; McCarthy, Joseph R.; McCarthyism; Nixon, Richard Milhous; Taft, Robert Alphonso; Truman, Harry S.; Truman's Recall of MacArthur.

ANZUS (Australia–New Zealand–U.S.) Treaty
(1951)

The ANZUS treaty represents a defense alliance involving Australia, New Zealand, and the United States. The treaty, signed in San Francisco on 1 September 1951, went into effect in April 1952. At the initiative of Australia and New Zealand, the three signatories pledged to "maintain and develop their individual and collective capacity to resist attack" in the Pacific area. The alliance provided a framework for cooperation including military exercises, unit exchanges, joint training, standardization and interoperability of equipment and weapons systems, intelligence and personnel exchanges, and regular high-level political exchanges.

At the time of its creation, the ANZUS alliance reflected U.S. concern over deteriorating security conditions in Korea and in East Asia generally. Australia and New Zealand were also anxious for the treaty, which influenced their decisions to send military units to Korea.

Only two days before the ANZUS treaty was concluded, the United States signed a security pact with the Philippines. Both treaties were intended to lessen those countries' anxieties over the Truman administration's objective of rebuilding Japan as a counterweight to Soviet influence in East Asia.

The war in Korea, and the Chinese intervention in particular, inspired U.S. politicians to shorten the timetable for the revival of Japan. Many other Asian nations, however, having just been freed from Japanese occupation, looked with distrust on anything that might strengthen their former antagonist. Therefore, Washington offered a guarantee against a resurgent Japan to Australia and New Zealand, as well as against aggression from other nations. Washington hoped to trade this pledge of U.S. assistance in the Pacific for support from the other two signatories in a possible conflict in the Middle East.

Soon after the signing of the ANZUS Treaty on 1 September 1951, the United States and Japan signed their peace treaty concluding World War II. Shortly after that the two also signed a security treaty. Although all three members of ANZUS participated in the United Nations defense in South Korea, the treaty organization itself did not play a particular role during the war.

—Zsolt Varga

References:

Jones, Howard. *Quest for Security*. New York: McGraw-Hill, 1996.

Stueck, William W., Jr. *The Korean War: An International History*. Princeton, NJ: Princeton University Press, 1995.

U.S. Department of State. *The ANZUS Alliance*. Washington, DC: U.S. Government Printing Office, 1987.

See also: Australia; Japan; New Zealand; Pacific Pact.

Armistice Agreement
(27 July 1953)

Agreement concluding the Korea War between United Nations Command (UNC) and Communist forces by insuring "a complete cessation of hostilities and of all acts of armed force in Korea until a final peaceful settlement" could be achieved. The agreement was signed at P'anmunjŏm by General Nam Il of the Korean People's Army (KPA, North Korean Army) and senior UNC delegate Lieutenant General William K. Harrison. Later, UNC commander General Mark W. Clark, Chinese People's Volunteer Army (CPVA, Communist Chinese) commander General Peng Dehuai, and Democratic People's Republic of Korea (North Korea) leader Kim Il Sung also signed. Interestingly, the document, which took effect on 27

United Nations Command guard at the armistice negotiations building, P'anmunjŏm, 27 July 1953. (National Archives)

July 1953, does not bear the signature of a Republic of Korea Army (South Korean) representative because the South Korean armed forces had been placed under UNC control by President Syngman Rhee.

Negotiations between UNC and Communist representatives began at Kaesŏng on 10 July 1951. By the fall of 1951, the belligerent parties agreed on locating the cease-fire line, the composition of a supervisory commission, and the procedure to transform a truce into a permanent settlement. On 25 October 1951, the talks were moved to the nearby village of P'anmunjŏm. The only issue of these talks was the repatriation of prisoners of war (POWs). The difficulty arose from the unwillingness of thousands of POWs held in South Korea to return to North Korea and China. Talks often broke down and were frequently boycotted by one side or the other.

A breakthrough in the armistice negotiations occurred at the beginning of 1953. In January U.S.

President-elect Dwight D. Eisenhower hinted that he might resort to the use of nuclear weapons if the talks failed. In March, Soviet leader Joseph Stalin died and the new leaders in Moscow showed willingness to ease Soviet-U.S. tensions. Three weeks after Stalin's death, the North Koreans and Chinese accepted the principle of voluntary repatriation. However, the imminent armistice was endangered by Rhee's 18 June 1953, release of 27,000 POWs from South Korean camps. Finally, the Robertson Mission, headed by Assistant Secretary of State for Far Eastern Affairs Walter Robertson, succeeded in getting Rhee's approval to a truce in return for U.S. military and economic assurances to South Korea. Robertson's visit contributed greatly to the signing of the document.

The Armistice Agreement established a line between the two Koreas. The agreement created a four-kilometer-wide demilitarized zone (DMZ) under the control of a Military Armistice Commission

Lieutenant General William K. Harrison, Jr. signing the Armistice Agreement at P'anmunjŏm, 27 July 1953. (Library of Congress)

(MAC) composed of equal numbers of UNC and combined KPA and CPVA representatives. Ten Joint Observer Teams were to assist the MAC's work in the DMZ. A Neutral Nations Supervisory Commission, assisted by twenty Neutral Nations Inspection Teams, exercised supervision, inspection, and observation of the truce throughout the Korean peninsula.

POWs willing to exercise their right to repatriation were to be exchanged in sixty days at P'anmunjŏm under the supervision of a Committee for Repatriation of Prisoners of War, which was assisted by the Joint Red Cross. POWs opposing repatriation were to be interrogated in the DMZ by the two sides under the supervision of the Neutral Nations Repatriation Commission led by India. Any remaining problems were to be solved at a future political conference. Despite the language of the Armistice Agreement, no real peace settlement was ever reached. At the time of this writing, North and South Korea remain technically in a state of war.

—*Zsolt Varga*

References:

Clark, Mark W. *From the Danube to the Yalu*. New York: Harper & Row, 1954.

Hermes, Walter G. *United States Army in the Korean War: Truce Tent and Fighting Front*. Washington, DC: Office of the Chief of Military History, 1966.

Joy, C. Turner. *How Communists Negotiate*. New York: Macmillan, 1955.

Vatcher, William H., Jr. *Panmunjom*. New York: Praeger, 1958.

Whelan, Richard. *Drawing the Line*. Boston: Little, Brown, 1990.

See also: Cease-Fire Negotiations; Kaesŏng Truce Talks; P'anmunjŏm Truce Talks; Repatriation, Voluntary; Robertson Mission; Truce Talks.

Armor (Tanks)

It is a dictum of modern war that armor and infantry be employed as a team in battle. Infantrymen and tanks provide mutual support and protection. Tanks without accompanying infantry are vulnerable to enemy tank-killer weapons; infantry without accompanying tanks is vulnerable to small arms, machine guns, and other direct-fire weapons. Infantrymen protect the tanks from the tank killers and the tanks engage enemy direct-fire weapons. Armor offensive tactics also envision armor employed in large formations, en masse, to overwhelm an enemy and make deep penetrations. Armor in Korea was rarely used in that fashion, especially after the war became one of position and stalemate. The mountainous terrain and often narrow valleys of Korea, and, in the spring and summer, flooded rice paddies, made it difficult to employ more than a few tanks in one location. Attempts to employ them in larger concentrations invariably led to a number of the tanks becoming bogged down.

The Korean Peoples Army (KPA, North Koreans), particularly early in the war, failed to send infantry along with their tanks in the attack. As a result, once the United States and Republic of Korea Army (ROKA, South Koreans) obtained the 3.5-inch bazooka rocket launcher, Communist tank losses soared. This, coupled with heavy armor losses from United Nations Command (UNC) air attack, ended the threat of KPA armor.

Both UNC and Communist tanks were often employed for long-range, pinpoint sniping fire against enemy positions. Worked to the tops of hills, these mobile "pill boxes" could be dug in, and they proved highly effective in that role.

The KPA and Chinese People's Volunteer Army (CPVA, Chinese Communist) Armies in the Korean War employed the Russian-built T-34/85 tank, reputed to be one of the best tanks in World War II. They also utilized the BA-64 armored car. UNC forces employed the U.S. M-24 light tank; the M4A3 (Sherman), with some variants; the M-26 (Pershing); the M-46 (Patton) tanks; and the British Churchill, Centurion, and some Cromwell tanks. Early in the war, South Korean and U.S. forces used a few M-8 (Greyhound) armored cars. The U.S. Army also used the M-29C Weasel cargo carrier, M-39 armored personnel carriers (APCs), and M-20 armored cars.

Because there were a number of models and variants for each of the tanks discussed below, it is difficult to list specifications that are true of each major type of tank. What follows are typical specifications and characteristics and do not necessarily describe mutations resulting from model changes and other variants.

North Korea and China

T-34/85. This model evolved from the T-34/76, which was equipped with a 76-mm gun. The North Korean Army was reported to have 150 T34/85 tanks at the beginning of the Korean War.

Crew: 5 men
Main gun: 85 mm

Machine guns: two 7.62 mm (one in bow and one coaxially with the main gun)
Weight (combat loaded): 35 short tons
Length (not including gun): 19 feet 7 inches
Width (overall): 9 feet 10 inches
Height (to top of turret): 7 feet 11 inches
Armor: turret front, 90 mm; hull front, 47 mm; hull rear, 60 mm
Ammunition carried: 55 rounds for main gun; 2,745 rounds for 7.62
Engine: 12-cylinder diesel, 493 hp
Maximum speed: 31–34 mph
Armor penetration at 500 yards: 114 mm
Range: 86 miles
Fording depth: 4 feet 4 inches
Vertical obstacle: 2 feet 5 inches
Trench crossing: 8 feet 2 inches

United States

M4A3 and M4A3E8 (Sherman). This tank was the mainstay of U.S. armor during World War II. There were many models and variants of the basic design, including dozers, 105-mm howitzers, rocket launchers, retrievers, flamethrowers, etc. M4A3E8 models carried a small metal box affixed to the right rear, containing an EE-8 sound-powered telephone, enabling an infantryman to communicate with the tank commander.

Crew: 5 men
Main gun: 76 mm
Machine guns: two .30 caliber, one of which was mounted in the bow and the other coaxially with the main gun. One .50-caliber antiaircraft gun, mounted on the top of the turret
Weight (combat loaded): 37 tons
Length (not including gun): 24 feet
Width (overall): 9 feet 10 inches
Height (to top of turret): 9 feet 9 inches
Armor: turret front, 2.5 inches, plus a gun shield of 3.5 inches (6 inches overall); hull front, tapered from 2.5 inches at the top to 4.5 inches at the bottom; hull sides and rear, 1.5 inches
Ammunition carried: officially, 71 rounds for main gun; 6,150 rounds for .30 caliber; 600 rounds for .50 caliber
Engine: Ford 500-hp gasoline
Maximum speed: 26 mph
Armor penetration: HVAP (High velocity armor piercing) 5.3 inches at 1000 yards; other ammunition, 3.5 inches at 1,000 yards
Range: 100 miles
Fording depth: 3 feet
Vertical obstacle: 2 feet
Trench crossing: 7 feet 6 inches

An M-46 Patton tank towing another tank. (National Archives)

M-26 (Pershing). The M-26 was developed near the end of World War II and is classified as a heavy tank.

Crew: 5 men

Main gun: 90 mm

Machine guns: two .30 caliber, one in the bow and one coaxially with the main gun. One .50-caliber antiaircraft gun mounted atop the turret

Weight (combat loaded): 46 tons

Length (not including gun): 21 feet 2 inches

Width (overall): 11 feet 6 inches

Height (to top of turret): 9 feet 1 inch

Armor: turret front, 102 mm; minimum elsewhere, 13 mm

Ammunition carried: 70 rounds for the 90-mm gun; 5,000 rounds of .30 caliber; 550 rounds of .50 caliber

Engine: Ford 500-hp gasoline

Maximum speed: 25 mph

Armor penetration: 195 mm at 1,000 yards

Range: 100 miles

Fording depth: 4 feet

Vertical obstacle: 3 feet 10 inches

Trench crossing: 7 feet 11 inches

M-46 (Patton). The M-46, an improved model of the M-26, was developed just after the end of World War II.

Crew: 5 men

Main gun: 90 mm

Machine guns: two .30 caliber, one mounted in the bow, the other coaxially with the main gun; one .50-caliber antiaircraft gun mounted atop the turret

Weight (combat loaded): 48.5 tons

Length (not including gun): 20 feet 10 inches

Width (overall): 11 feet 6 inches

Height (to top of turret): 9 feet 3 inches

Armor: turret front, 102 mm; minimum of 13 mm elsewhere

Ammunition carried: 70 rounds for the 90 mm; 5,000 of .30 caliber and 550 rounds of .50 caliber
Engine: Continental 810-hp gasoline
Maximum speed: 31–37 mph
Armor penetration: 195 mm at 1,000 yards
Range: 80 miles
Fording depth: 4 feet
Vertical obstacle: 3 feet
Trench crossing: 8 feet 6 inches

M-24 (Chaffee). This was a light tank, employed by reconnaissance units. However, in the U.S. Army divisions in Japan before the war, it was the only type of tank available and all of them were in what was supposed to be the divisional heavy tank battalions. Each division had about 15 to 17 M-24 tanks at the time.

Crew: 5 men
Main gun: 75 mm
Machine guns: two .30 caliber, one in the bow, the other mounted coaxially with the main gun. One .50 caliber antiaircraft mounted atop turret
Weight (combat loaded): 20.25 tons
Length (not including gun): 16 feet 6 inches
Width (overall): 9 feet 8 inches
Height (to top of turret): 8 feet 1 inch
Armor: 38 mm turret front; minimum of 10 mm elsewhere
Ammunition carried: 48 rounds for 75 mm; 3,750 rounds for .30 caliber; 440 rounds for .50 caliber
Engine: two Cadillac V-8s, 110 hp, gasoline
Maximum speed: 35 mph
Armor penetration: 70 mm at 500 yards
Range: 110 miles
Fording depth: 3 feet 4 inches
Vertical obstacle: 3 feet
Trench crossing: 8 feet

M-8 Armored Car. This was the heaviest armored vehicle in the ROK Army at the beginning of the war. It had 27 of them. U.S. reconnaissance units also had a few of these cars at the time.

Crew: 4 men
Main gun: 37 mm
Machine guns: one .30-caliber mounted coaxially; one .50-caliber anti-aircraft gun mounted atop the turret
Weight (combat loaded): 8.75 tons
Length: 16 feet 5 inches
Width (overall): 8 feet 4 inches
Height (including machine gun): 7 feet 4½ inches
Armor: 20 mm turret front; minimum of 3 mm elsewhere
Ammunition carried: 80 rounds for 37-mm; approximately 3,000 for .30 caliber and 400 rounds for the .50 caliber

Engine: Hercules 6 cylinder gasoline, 79 hp
Maximum speed: 56 mph
Armor penetration: 48 mm at 500 yards
Range: 300–350 miles
Fording depth: 2 feet 8 inches
Vertical obstacle: 1 foot

British

United Kingdom forces fighting in Korea employed the Churchill Infantry tank and the heavy Centurion. The British also used the A27M Cromwell and A34 Comet tanks in Korea. Canadians brought M10 Achilles 17-pounder self-propelled guns but soon replaced them with U.S. Sherman tanks.

Churchill VII Infantry Tank. Variants included ones mounting a 95-mm howitzer, flamethrower, bridge layer, mortar, and recovery vehicles. Most used in Korea were the Mark III.

Crew: 5 men
Main gun: 75 mm
Machine guns: two light, one mounted forward in the hull, the other coaxially with the main gun
Weight (combat loaded): 44.8 tons
Length (not including gun): 24 feet 5 inches
Width (overall): 9 feet
Height (to top of turret): 11 feet 4 inches
Armor: turret front, 152 mm; minimum 25 mm elsewhere
Ammunition carried: 84 rounds for 75 mm; amount for machine guns unknown
Engine: Bedford twin-six gasoline, 350 hp
Maximum speed: 15.5 mph
Armor penetration: 68 mm at 500 yards
Range: 90 miles
Fording depth: 3 feet 4 inches
Vertical obstacle: 2 feet 6 inches
Trench crossing: 10 feet

Centurion Medium (Cruiser) Mk-5. Variants include 105-mm gun, armored recovery, bridge layer, and 165-mm demolition charge projector engineer. Its heavy weight (58 tons) and width (11 feet) made it too heavy and too wide for most bridges in South Korea.

Crew: 4 men
Main gun: 20 pounder (83.4-mm) gun
Machine guns: two .30 caliber, one on commander's cupola and one coaxially with main gun. In addition this model carried two six-barreled smoke dischargers.
Weight (combat loaded): 58 tons
Length (not including gun): 24 feet 9½ inches
Width (overall): 11 feet 11½ inches
Height (to top of turret): 9 feet 7¾ inches
Armor: 152 mm on turret front

Tanks of the 89th Tank Battalion, U.S. 25th Infantry Division, crossing the Han River and moving north, 7 March 1951.
(National Archives)

Ammunition carried: 64 rounds for 20 pounder;
   4,250 rounds for machine guns
Engine: Rolls Royce Meteor 4B, 12-cylinder gaso-
   line, 650 hp
Maximum speed: 21.5 mph
Armor penetration: approximately 120 mm at 500
   yards
Range: 60 miles
Fording depth: 4 feet 9 inches (could be prepared to
   ford 9 feet)
Vertical obstacle: 3 feet
Trench crossing: 11 feet

Cromwell A27M Reconnaissance. Originally pro-
duced near the end of World War II and outclassed by
German armor from the start of its production, it was
nonetheless very reliable.
   Crew: 5 men
   Main gun: 75 mm
   Machine guns: two light, one firing forward from
      the turret, the other in the bow

Weight: 28 tons
Armor: 76 mm
Engine: Rolls Royce V-12 Meteor, 600 hp
Maximum speed: 40 mph

Comet A34 Heavy Cruiser. The Comet entered serv-
ice immediately after the Cromwell at the end of
World War II.
   Crew: 5 men
   Main gun: 76.2 mm, but known as a 77 mm
   Machine guns: two light, one coaxial and the other
      in the bow
   Weight: 33 tons
   Armor: 101 mm
   Engine: 600 hp
   Maximum speed: 29 mph

—Uzal W. Ent

References:

Appleman, Roy E. *South to the Naktong, North to the Yalu.*
   Washington, DC: Office of the Chief of Military History,
   1961.

Chamberlain, Peter, and Chris Ellis. *British and American Tanks of World War II*. New York: Arco, 1969.

Foss, Christopher F. *Armoured Fighting Vehicles of the World*. New York: Charles Scribner's Sons, 1971.

Hunnicutt, Richard P. *Sherman*. Belmont, CA: Taurus Enterprises, 1978.

Macksey, Kenneth, and John H. Batchelor. *Tank: A History of the Armoured Fighting Vehicle*. New York: Charles Scribner's Sons, 1976.

See also: Bazooka; China, People's Republic of: Army; Korea, Democratic Republic of: Army (Korean People's Army [KPA]); Korea, Republic of: Army (ROKA); United Kingdom (UK); United States: Army.

Armored Vests

The Korean War sped up the development of body armor. Because of the success of helmets in reducing head wounds during World War I and II, researchers sought to provide protection to other areas of the body from shell, mortar, and grenade fragments, by far the greatest killer of infantry.

During World War II, a joint army-navy committee worked to develop body armor and by the end of the conflict had developed an armored vest made of flexible pads of basket-weave nylon with curved overlapping doron plates. The latter were laminated layers of glass cloth filaments, bonded under pressure into a thin, rigid slab, and named in honor of Army Colonel George F. Doriot, one of the directors of the project.

In 1947 the Marines and navy established a ballistics center at Camp Lejeune to develop and test body armor based on the research halted at the end of the war. When the Korean War began, some 500 sets of armored vests that were developed at the end of World War II were available, and these were provided to the 1st Marine Division during the Inch'ŏn-Seoul operation. Although most of these vests were subsequently discarded by individual Marines they did save a number of lives.

By summer 1951 the researchers had developed a new Marine armored vest that combined curved over-

Men of K Company, 157th Regiment, 3d Infantry Division, who were hit by Communist fire while on patrol, and saved from injury by wearing body armor, 6 April 1952. (National Archives)

lapping doron plates with flexible pads of basket-weave nylon. Weighing 8.5 pounds, it could stop a .45-caliber bullet, all the fragments of a U.S. hand grenade at three feet, three-quarters of the fragments of an 81-mm mortar at 10 feet, and the full thrust of a bayonet. Some 40 vests were tested in the field in Korea in the summer of 1951, rotated among two U.S. Marine regiments and one U.S. Army regiment. The vests, although uncomfortable in the heat and unwieldy, won wide acceptance.

Designated the M-1951 armored vest, it went into full production in late 1951. The army produced its own armored vest. Of only basket-weave nylon, it was inferior to the marine version. By Spring 1952 both armored vests were widely available for marine and army combat troops in Korea. Clearly the vests reduced casualties, especially fatalities.

—Spencer C. Tucker

References:

Montross, Lynn, Hubard D. Kuokka, and Norman W. Hicks. *U.S. Marine Operations in Korea, 1950–1953: The East-Central Front.* Vol. 4. Washington, DC: U.S. Marine Corps Historical Branch, 1962.

Summers, Harry G., Jr. *Korean War Almanac.* New York: Facts on File, 1990.

See also: United States: Army; United States: Marines.

Artillery

The advent of nuclear weapons at the end of World War II cast a long shadow on the evolution of military technology and doctrine. For almost ten years after 1945, conventional weapons were thought of as being virtually obsolete. This was especially true in the case of cannon artillery, with its relatively short-range and high-explosive shells that weighed no more than 200 pounds for the biggest of guns. Yet the lessons of World War II had clearly demonstrated the efficacy of massed and coordinated conventional fires. Caught between these two contradictory poles, artillery weapons and tactics became temporarily frozen in time, with the result that artillery systems at the start of the Korean War were identical to those at the end of World War II.

In the early months of the Korean War, aircraft were the principal source of fire support during the fluid and highly mobile operations. As the pace of operations slowed, however, artillery began to play a more prominent role. Artillery's role increased as stagnation set in and turned into strategic deadlock. This situation brought a return to the type of artillery operations not seen since World War I. Far more frequently than in World War II, artillery firing positions—normally several thousand yards behind the front lines—came under direct ground attack.

Gun crews often faced the dual problems of delivering fire support to the maneuver forces while simulta-

neously defending their firing positions from direct attack. The artillerymen reacted by digging in and heavily fortifying their battery positions using World War I entrenchment methods. The stagnant tactical conditions also required the resurrection of many older firing techniques that had been virtually forgotten in World War II. The World War I–era "box barrage" was reincarnated as "flash fire," a three-sided concentration around the front and sides of friendly defensive positions, designed to seal those positions off from enemy attack with a wall of fire.

The ground itself in Korea created problems for artillerymen on both sides. In the flatlands, the ubiquitous rice paddies made poor gun positions. In the summer the ground was too wet and soft to hold the guns firmly in place and absorb their recoil. In winter the water-soaked, frozen ground made it impossible to dig the guns in. At all times of year, rice paddies were too open and exposed to offer much natural protection. The hilly and mountainous ground offered somewhat better protection, but here the problem was one of finding enough flat ground to emplace an entire battery. Quite often the guns of a single battery were positioned at varying heights and angles of cant, making the gunnery solutions even more difficult and complex. Fire direction problems were compounded by a lack of accurate maps for many areas.

United States and the United Nations

Almost all the artillery pieces used in the Korean War were of World War II vintage. At the beginning of the war, Republic of Korea Army (ROKA, South Korean) units had only obsolete U.S. 105-mm howitzers. In 1951 the United States introduced the M-30 mortar, a slightly improved version of the devastatingly effective M-24 4.2-inch heavy mortar. Although intended as an infantry close-support weapon, British units in Korea often employed their 4.2-inch mortars in separate batteries as field guns.

The basic direct-support gun in the U.S. divisions and most United Nations (UN) units was the 105-mm M-2A1 towed, light howitzer. Originally designed after World War I, the M-2A1 was rugged, accurate, and had a high sustained rate of fire. It was the mainstay of U.S. artillery throughout World War II and Korea. Slightly improved in the mid-1950s as the M-101A1, it continued in service through the Vietnam War and into the early 1990s. It was adopted by many Free World armies, and it became one of the most widely exported artillery designs of all times. The Commonwealth Division continued to rely on the British World War II 25-pounder Mk-4 gun/howitzer.

Throughout the war, senior U.S. commanders continually requested Washington to supply more artillery. United Nations Command (UNC) command-

A KMAG advisor observes ROKA troops loading a 105-mm howitzer. (National Archives)

er General Douglas MacArthur became especially frustrated when his forces received only about one-third of the nondivisional artillery that he had requested. The heavier, nondivisional guns were one of the primary means by which corps commanders could influence the outcome of battles. MacArthur's World War II experiences after a series of false starts in the Pacific campaigns had convinced him that a one-to-one ratio of divisional to nondivisional artillery was necessary to overcome determined and well-prepared enemy resistance.

U.S./UN commanders never believed that they had sufficient artillery, and ammunition frequently was in short supply. Even so, they managed to fire massive amounts in comparison with their enemy. Between June 1950 and December 1952, UN forces shot 1,132,000 tons of artillery and mortar shells. That equaled the U.S. ammunition expenditure in World War II in the Pacific and Mediterranean theaters combined. By December 1952, UN artillery was firing

nineteen rounds for every one Communist round. But even these high rates of fire managed to produce only an average of one Communist casualty for every three tons of ammunition fired.

The later stages of the Korean War saw the introduction of many of the artillery tactics and techniques that were standard during the Vietnam War. The most significant innovation in fire-direction methods was the introduction of the target grid, commonly called the "whiz wheel." It was a rotating tissue paper overlay on a firing chart that graphically converted corrections relative to the forward observer's line of sight to the line of aim of the guns.

The target grid drastically decreased the time necessary to compute corrections, and its simple graphic solution eliminated the mathematical errors common to previous methods. In the era before electronic fire direction computers, it was a powerful tool.

Certain categories of targets, such as troops in the open, are more effectively attacked with rounds that

The 204th FA Battalion fires its 155mm guns on Communist positions, 26 April 1951. (National Archives)

produce an air burst, rather than a ground burst. To accomplish this, UN artillery made wide use of the variable time (VT) fuse. The VT fuse was originally developed in World War II for antiaircraft fire. It was first used in a ground-support role by the U.S. Army during the Battle of the Bulge and is still used today. The VT is a proximity fuse with a small radar transmitter, set to produce an air burst 20 meters above the ground. This is the optimal height for fragmentation effect.

Standard mechanical time fuses can be set to burst at any height above the target, but almost always the height of burst must be adjusted by observer corrections. That compromises the element of surprise and greatly reduces the effectiveness of the fire. For that reason, mechanical time fuses were seldom used in Korea. The VT fuse was especially effective when the artillery round was fired directly above friendly

bunkers under direct attack. The shell fragments would sweep Communist troops off the top of the bunker, while UN troops inside remained relatively protected.

Communist bunkers, on the other hand, were especially difficult to destroy with light and medium (105-mm and 155-mm) artillery fire. One technique, also resurrected from World War I, was to use high-angle fire. This dropped the shell with a point-detonating fuse straight down on the roof of the bunker, which usually was much weaker than the front and sides. The heavy 8-inch howitzer quickly became the weapon of choice for "bunker busting." Firing directly into a bunker from close range, the 8-incher used concrete piercing fuses set for delay to allow the shell to penetrate deep into the bunker wall before exploding. Widely regarded as the most accurate field artillery piece ever developed, the 8-inch was capable of putting round after round into the same hole.

Korean women pass a battery of U.S. Marine howitzers, 12 December 1950. (Corbis)

U.S. artillery introduced two important organizational changes during the Korean War. The first of these was the change to the six-gun battery for light and medium artillery. The U.S. Army had used six-gun batteries during the late eighteenth and early nineteenth centuries, but it switched to four-gun batteries shortly after the War of 1812. The four-gun battery remained the standard through the end of World War II. The six-gun battery remained the standard in the U.S. Army through the 1980s, when the eight-gun battery was introduced.

The introduction of the six-gun battery effectively increased divisional firepower by 50 percent. After the conversion the typical U.S. infantry division had seventy-two guns in four battalions. Three battalions were armed with 105-mm howitzers and had the mission of providing direct support to each of the division's three infantry regiments. The fourth battalion was armed with 155-mm howitzers and had the mission of providing general support to the division as a whole. Artillery battalions assigned to corps had the mission of providing general support to the entire corps or of reinforcing the fires of a division for a specific operation.

The second major innovation was the introduction of the fire support coordination center (FSCC). Before World War II, field artillery was the principal and often the sole source of fire support on the battlefield. World War II experience, however, demonstrated a need for a single agency to control and synchronize with the ground maneuver forces the supporting fires of artillery, infantry mortars, ground support aircraft, and even naval gunfire. During the Vietnam War, attack helicopters were added to the complex equation.

The solution to the problem was the FSCC, a staff cell established at every echelon from regiment through corps and run by the senior field artillery officer. Composed of liaison teams from all the fire support agencies involved in any given operation, the FSCC eliminated duplication of effort, ensured that gaps did not occur in the fire plan, and coordinated to make certain that supporting aircraft were not shot down by friendly fire. The FSCC was first tested in Korea and remains a standard fixture today.

Artillery fire is most effective when it is massed. It is not necessary physically possible to group the guns on the ground, but their fire effects must be massed on the target. All three batteries of a battalion firing one simultaneous round at a target produce a far greater effect than a single battery firing three separate volleys. The number of rounds on the target is the same, but the effect of a single large impact is much greater because of the element of surprise that deprives enemy troops at the target of the opportunity to take cover.

During World War II, the U.S. Army developed a technique for delivering surprise massed fire called "time on target" (TOT). In TOT fire, any number of firing units from a battalion (three batteries) to the artillery of an entire corps are given a single target with a single time and point of impact. Because the various batteries are at different positions on the battlefield and at differing ranges from the target, the times of flight of their shells will all be different. That means that firing units have to fire at different times to ensure that their rounds all impact simultaneously. The coordination for such a fire mission is complicated and requires a great deal of practice to perfect. If the initial target data is correct, however, the effect in the target area is devastating. There is no warning and almost no escape for exposed troops.

UN artillery fire produced mixed results in Korea. During the fighting around Bloody Ridge in August and September 1951, the artillery of the U.S. 2d Infantry Division produced only limited results against Communist bunkers, despite firing more than 153,000 rounds. The 15th Field Artillery Battalion alone set a record for U.S. light artillery by firing 14,425 rounds in a 24-hour period, just short of one round every minute for each of the battalion's twelve guns. The World War II average for 105-mm howitzers was 40 rounds per gun per day.

Perhaps the most lethal use of artillery fire during the war came during what later became known as the "Wonju Shoot." On 14 February 1951, the 119th, 120th, 197th, and 198th Chinese People's Volunteer Army (CPVA, Chinese Communist) Divisions massed to attack the U.S. 2d Infantry Division. Attacking in broad daylight, the Communist lead elements were first spotted by aerial observer Lieutenant Lee R. Hartell of the 15th Field Artillery. Initially calling for fire from his own unit, Hartell got the guns of the entire 2d Infantry Division and eventually most of the guns of X Corps. Hartell and his pilot remained in the air for several hours, directing continuous fire on the exposed Chinese troops. The final casualty estimates were 5,000 Chinese dead and at least three times that many wounded. (Six months later at Kobangsan-ni, Hartell won the Medal of Honor in an action during which, mortally wounded, he called flash fire down on his own position.)

Korean People's Army and Chinese People's Volunteer Army

The KPA and CPVA essentially fought the entire war with pre– and very early World War II Soviet guns. Some were supplied directly by the Soviets and others were manufactured locally to Soviet designs. The locally manufactured guns were generally inferior in quality. The Soviet designs, however, were simple, rugged, and often outranged their U.S. counterparts of comparable caliber.

At the start of the war, the KPA had nearly 1,600 guns—three times the number that the South Koreans had. When the Chinese entered the war, their forces were almost entirely composed of infantry. By the spring of 1952, however, the Chinese had almost 900 guns in Korea. In September 1952, Communist gunners were able to fire 45,000 rounds in a single day into UN front-line positions.

The artillery of a North Korean division was organized similarly to that of a Soviet division of early World War II. At the divisional level it had twelve 122-mm towed howitzers, twenty-four 76.2-mm towed guns, twelve SU-76 self-propelled guns, and twelve 45-mm antitank guns. Each of the division's three regiments also had six 120-mm mortars, four 76.2-mm towed howitzers, and six 45-mm antitank guns.

The North Koreans and Chinese used Soviet fire doctrine that held that the maneuver forces (infantry and armor) existed primarily to exploit the effects of artillery fire. Chinese and KPA infantry actually advanced into their own artillery fire, instead of close behind it. Up through the end of the Cold War, Communist military theorists believed that massed artillery fire by itself was capable of taking and holding ground. Most Western armies believed the relationship between fire and maneuver to be the opposite. The difference in the two theories is more than semantic. The Communist approach could work on the battlefield, but only if the logistics system were capable of supplying the guns with an almost unlimited amount of ammunition. This was always a problem in Korea for the Communists because of their primitive transportation system and constant UN air and sea interdiction of their supply lines.

In addition to always having less ammunition, the Communist gunners also lacked the communications systems and the advanced fire direction techniques necessary to mass effectively and to rapidly shift fires. Despite these shortcomings they handled their artillery reasonably well. On occasions, such as at Taejön Airfield on 16 July 1950, they were even able to produce fires approaching World War II densities.

Communist artillery fire accounted for approximately 35 percent of UN troops killed, and 75 percent of those wounded in Korea. According to some intelligence estimates, the Chinese and the North Koreans actually had more artillery tubes in Korea

U.S. and British Artillery Used by UN Forces

Model	Type	Year Introduced	Caliber	Crew Size	Sustained Rate of Projectile Fire (rounds/min)	Gun Weight (lbs)	Max Weight (lbs)	Range (meters)
M-1A1	Pack Howitzer	1927	75 mm	4	10	14	1,339	8,650
Mk-IV	25-pdr Towed Gun/Howitzer	1946	87 mm	6	5	25	3,968	12,250
M-2A1	Towed Howitzer	1940	105 mm	8	8	33	4,980	10,980
M-30	Heavy Mortar	1951	4.2 inch	6	20	25	650	5,420
M-1	Towed Howitzer	1941	155 mm	11	2	95	11,966	14,700
M-1A1	Towed Gun	1938	155 mm	14	1	95	30,600	22,860
M-2	Towed Howitzer	1940	8 inch	14	1	200	31,700	16,660

Note: The United States also had self-propelled versions of the 105-mm and 155-mm howitzers, the 155-mm gun, and the 8-inch howitzer. Aside from the motor carriage mount, the gun and its performance were the same.

Soviet Artillery Used by KPA and CPVA Forces

Model	Type	Year Introduced	Caliber	Crew Size	Sustained Rate of Projectile Fire (rounds/min)	Gun Weight (lbs)	Max Weight (lbs)	Range (meters)
M-1942	Anti-Tank Gun	1942	45 mm	6	20	3	1,250	4,400
ZiS-3	Divisional Gun	1942	76.2 mm	7	20	13.7	2,640	13,290
M-1937	Mortar	1937	82 mm	5	25	9	99	3,050
M-1938	Heavy Mortar	1938	120 mm	6	12	34	1,110	5,850
A-19	Field Gun	1937	122 mm	9	4	55	15,950	20,610
M-30	Howitzer	1938	122 mm	8	6	48	4,960	11,800

Note: The Soviet SU-76 self-propelled gun was a 76.2-mm ZiS-3 divisional gun mounted on a T-70 light tank chassis. Aside from the motor carriage mount, the gun and its performance were the same.

than did the UN forces during the closing months of the war.

After Korea

The Korean War experience convinced the United States that conventional artillery still had a major role to play on the modern battlefield. Immediately after the war, the U.S. Army began emphasizing the development of self-propelled guns. Such systems made it easier for artillery to keep pace with the faster moving maneuver arms and also offered the gun crews limited armored protection.

The need for battery positions to be able to defend themselves from close-in ground attack led directly to the development of the 105-mm antipersonnel round that fired thousands of nail-like fléchettes at point-blank range into any attacking force. Widely used in Vietnam as the "beehive" round, this was actually a variation on the old canister round that fell out of use shortly after the end of the American Civil War.

Thus the Korean War experience reinforced the traditional U.S. reliance on massed firepower. As General Matthew B. Ridgway once noted, "There is a direct relation between piles of shells and piles of [friendly] corpses. The bigger the former, the smaller the latter." Or as the GIs were fond of saying throughout the Korean and Vietnam wars, "bullets, not bodies." In a conventional though limited war as Korea, there is a great deal of merit to this point of view. In an unconventional, counterinsurgency war such as Vietnam, however, the overreliance on artillery fire seriously handicapped U.S. tactical efficiency.

—*David T. Zabecki*

References:

Bailey, Jonathan B. A. *Field Artillery and Fire Power.* Oxford: Military Press, 1989.

Bellamy, Chris. *Red God of War.* London: Brassey's, 1986.

Boatner, Mark M., III. "Countering Communist Artillery." *Combat Forces Journal* (September 1953): 24–25.

Cocklin, Robert F. "Artillery in Korea." *Combat Forces Journal* (August 1951): 22–27.

Comparato, Frank E. *The Age of Great Guns.* Harrisburg, PA: Stackpole, 1964.

Gugeler, Russell A. "Defense of a Battery Position;" "Artillery at Kunu-Ri;" and "Artillery in Perimeter Defense." In *Combat Actions in Korea.* Washington, DC: U.S. Government Printing Office, 1954.

Schaad, Carl W. "Fire Support Coordination." *Combat Forces Journal* (September 1952): 39–41.

See also: MacArthur, Douglas; Ridgway, Matthew Bunker.

Atrocities

During the twentieth century, ideological wars have produced countless examples of brutality and crimes against humanity. The Korean War was no exception. From 1950 to 1953 the armies and governments of both the Democratic People's Republic of Korea (DPRK, North Korea) and the Republic of Korea (ROK, South Korea) committed or encouraged the killing of civilians and prisoners of war (POWs). Ever since, there has been historical debate over the degrees of responsibility on both sides.

U.S. and British troops were appalled by the casual brutality that they observed routinely inflicted on South Koreans by their own government. One British soldier, a Private Duncan, described a typical scene: "40 emaciated and subdued Koreans were…shot while their hands were tied, and also beaten unnecessarily by rifles. The executioners were South Korean military police." Such incidents created great confusion and ill-feeling toward the ROK among Western troops. "We are led to believe that we are fighting against such actions," Duncan wrote, "and I sincerely believe that our troops are wondering which side in Korea is right or wrong."

ROK treatment of Communist prisoners was particularly harsh in the days after the savage and sudden Korean People's Army (KPA, North Korean) occupation of the South. "At least many hundreds [of alleged Communists] have been shot," reported Australian delegate to the United Nations (UN) Commission for Korea John Plimsoll. He related how prisoners had been forced to dig their own graves, then "rather clumsily and inexpertly shot before the eyes of others waiting their own turn." Feelings of bitterness and the desire for revenge after the atrocities committed during the Communist occupation drove South Korean government officials to such retaliatory measures.

But the KPA occupation of much of the South conditioned this. Indeed the widespread cruelty of the Communist occupation of South Korea during the opening months of the conflict set the moral tone for the rest of the war. It also led South Koreans who were lukewarm or opposed to the government of Syngman Rhee to rally to it as far preferable to that of the Communists.

From June to September 1950 some 26,000 South Korean civilians were murdered by the Communists. At one site near Taejŏn alone, 5,000 bodies were discovered after the North Korean retreat. Members of the South Korean government, police, and intelligentsia were systematically rounded up and executed. Sometimes this included entire families. During the liberation of Seoul, one group of U.S. Marines came upon a trench filled with hundreds of dead South Korean men, women, and children. "It was a ghastly sight," Marine Ed Simmons recalled, "The stench was unbearable. For days civilians were coming out from the center of Seoul in the hope of identifying them." The 5th Cavalry Regiment encountered a similar scene where 200 civilians had been executed. "Many of the murdered," Private First Class Victor Fox remem-

One of the four American soldiers of the 21st Infantry found dead, their hands tied behind their backs and shot through the head. Probably captured on 9 July 1950, they were found the next day. (National Archives)

bered, "were professional and business people, educators, artists, politicians, [and] civil servants. The dead appeared to include entire families, from children to the very aged."

Even more shocking to Americans were discoveries of the corpses of American POWs who had been executed by their North Korean captors. Bodies were typically found in roadside ditches or gullies, hands tied behind the backs with barbed wire, and a single bullet wound to the back of the head. One group of a hundred executed American prisoners was found in a railway tunnel during the UN advance into North Korea. Such sights enraged U.S. troops and inspired random acts of revenge killing of North Korean prisoners. One such incident occurred when the 21st Infantry Regiment took a hill along the Naktong River after a brief firefight. The retreating North Koreans had left a wounded officer behind. "Our officers asked for volunteers to carry him off the hill." Sergeant Warren Avery

recalled. "Of course, no one volunteered; we had all heard about atrocities the North Koreans had participated in. After a little bit of argument about what we should do with this wounded officer the platoon leader went over to him and shot him between the eyes with his .45."

The Chinese, unlike their North Korean allies, were eager to take prisoners alive for propaganda purposes. For American prisoners fortunate enough to survive capture, a long, terrible march into captivity awaited them. This was particularly true during the winter of 1950–1951, when hundreds of Americans died of disease and hypothermia or were simply murdered by their guards. The survival rate for wounded soldiers during these marches was particularly dismal, though in fairness to the Chinese, with their primitive medical facilities, their own wounded were not likely to fare much better. "The signal for death was the oxcart following the column," remembered Captain James

Majury. "If you had to be placed upon that, you would freeze to death."

Arrival at POW camps rarely provided any solace for American prisoners. North Korean–administered camps were the worst. The guards made little attempt to keep their prisoners alive. Starvation, disease, beatings, and months of solitary confinement were the lot of many captives. Conditions improved slightly when the Chinese assumed control of the prison camps in the spring of 1951. That summer, conditions improved further when the Chinese determined that live prisoners made better bargaining chips. Thereafter, prisoner deaths declined rapidly. But the final figures tell a stark tale: of 7,190 Americans captured by the Communists, 2,730 died in captivity. Ninety-nine percent of these died in the bitter first year of the war.

After the truce ending the Korean War on 27 July 1953, there were no trials to prosecute war criminals as had been the case at Nuremberg after the Second World War. However there had been discussion, early in the war, over prosecution of war criminals. During the Wake Island conference between U.S. President Harry Truman and his advisors and General Douglas MacArthur in October 1950, MacArthur had outlined a plan whereby those North Koreans who had committed atrocities would be tried by military tribunals. But the Chinese intervention in late November and the resulting stalemate precluded any formal UN attempt to bring war criminals to justice.

—Duane L. Wesolick

References:

Blair, Clay. *The Forgotten War: America in Korea 1950–1953.* New York: Times Books, 1987.

Halliday, Jon, and Cumings, Bruce. *Korea: The Unknown War.* New York: Pantheon, 1988.

Hastings, Max. *The Korean War.* New York: Simon & Schuster, 1987.

James, D. Clayton. *The Years of MacArthur.* Vol. 3. *Triumph and Disaster 1945–1964.* Boston: Houghton Mifflin, 1985.

See also: Nogŭn-n1 Railroad Bridge Incident; MacArthur, Douglas; Prisoner-of-War Administration, Communist; Prisoner-of-War Administration, United Nations Command; South Korea, Occupation by Democratic People's Republic of Korea; Syngman Rhee; Truman, Harry S.; Wake Island Conference; War Crimes Trials.

Attlee, Clement R.
(1883–1967)

British prime minister (1945–1951), a position that gave him a major role in the formulation of British policy toward the Korean War. Clement R. Attlee was born in London on 3 January 1883 into a middle-class professional family and educated at Haileybury College and University College, Oxford, which he left in 1904 after taking second class honors in modern history. He was called to the bar in 1905. Shortly after-

ward, moved by his experiences in a boys' club in the East End of London, he became a socialist and the club's manager. Abandoning his legal career in 1908, Attlee took several ill-paid jobs, which left him ample time for political work. In 1913 he accepted the position of lecturer in social administration at the London School of Economics.

Attlee was deeply committed to the growing labor movement and somewhat unusual among its leaders in that he saw active service in Mesopotamia and France during the First World War. Elected to the House of Commons in 1923, he became leader of the Labour Party in 1935. During the Second World War, he held several cabinet positions and was also deputy prime minister; in August 1945 he led the Labour Party to its landslide postwar (in Europe) victory.

Attlee and his foreign secretary, Ernest Bevin, were strong protagonists of a policy of firm resistance to Soviet expansion in Europe, and both believed that greater U.S. economic and military involvement in European affairs was essential to guarantee that area's security. In the later 1940s, their heartfelt appeals to the United States were instrumental in that country's implementation of the Marshall Plan in 1948 and the establishment of the North Atlantic Treaty Organization (NATO) in 1949.

During the Korean crisis, Attlee played a large role in the making of British policy because of the poor health of Bevin, who resigned as foreign secretary in March 1951 and died the following month. By 1950, major differences existed between the United States and Britain on Asian policy, focusing upon Hong Kong, Indo-China, anticolonialism, and especially upon the new People's Republic of China, with which Britain, unlike the United States, pragmatically opened trade and recognized almost immediately. British leaders perceived the Korean conflict as a means of demonstrating their loyalty to their ally and regaining the international status that Britain's economic problems and the recent devaluation of the pound had eroded. At the urging of British Ambassador to Washington Sir Oliver Franks, in July 1950 Attlee overrode his reluctant chiefs of staff and committed British troops to the U.S.-led United Nations (UN) forces.

British officials welcomed the massive U.S. enhancement of NATO forces that quickly resulted from the Korean conflict. Even so, Attlee was anxious to restrain the United States, fearing that U.S. leaders might escalate the Korean intervention into either war with China or a full-scale global confrontation with the Soviet Union. British leaders were apprehensive that the former eventuality would not only threaten the British colonies of Hong Kong and Malaysia and split the Labour Party and the Commonwealth, alienating

India, but would also divert U.S. forces from more vital concerns in Europe and the Middle East; the second scenario would unleash devastation upon Western Europe. Attlee therefore consciously dissociated Britain from the U.S. decision to neutralize Taiwan.

Attlee's reservations notwithstanding, he supported the UN decision to cross the 38th parallel, believing that neither the Soviets nor the Chinese would intervene. When Chinese forces entered the war in November 1950, British leaders feared the conflict's further expansion, and Truman's indirect public comments that month as to the potential U.S. use of atomic weapons reinforced their anxieties. In early December Attlee flew to Washington, a move designed to reassure the British public, restrain the United States, and reaffirm Britain's status within the Atlantic alliance. Truman and Secretary of State Dean Acheson agreed with Attlee that the UN objective in Korea should be to achieve an acceptable battlefield position in Korea and then to seek an armistice along that line, eschewing total victory in favor of limited war. Attlee was unable, however, to persuade U.S. leaders to offer political concessions to China in exchange for a cease-fire.

On Attlee's return home, he exaggerated his successes, and the belief became widespread that he had prevented further U.S. escalation of the war. Chinese intervention in the Korean War split the Labour Party, with many leftist arguing that the war was misguided and Attlee's government overly deferential to the United States. In October 1951 Attlee left office after an election in which the heavy budgetary strains of the Korean intervention and rearmament, which brought higher taxes, cutbacks in social spending, inflation, and an unfavorable balance of payments, played a major role in the divided Labour Party's defeat. After a second election loss in 1955, Attlee resigned as party leader and entered the House of Lords. He died in London on 8 October 1967.

—Priscilla Roberts

References:
Attlee, Clement. *As It Happened*. London: Heinemann, 1954.

Brookshire, Jerry H. *Clement Attlee*. Manchester: Manchester University Press, 1995.

Burridge, Trevor D. *Clement Attlee: A Political Biography*. London: Cape, 1985.

Butler, Rohan, and M. E. Pelly, eds. *Documents on British Policy Overseas*. Series II, Vol. 4: *Korea, 1950–1951*. London: Her Majesty's Stationery Office, 1995.

Harris, Kenneth. *Attlee*. Rev. ed. London: Weidenfeld & Nicolson, 1995.

Lowe, Peter. *Containing the Cold War in East Asia: British Policies toward Japan, China and Korea, 1948–1953*. Manchester: Manchester University Press, 1997.

MacDonald, Callum A. *Britain and the Korean War*. Oxford: Blackwell, 1990.

Pearce, Robert D. *Attlee*. New York: Longman, 1997.

Tiratsoo, Nick. *The Attlee Years*. New York: Pinter, 1991.

Williams, Francis, ed. *A Prime Minister Remembers*. London: Heinemann, 1961.

See also: Bevin, Ernest; NATO (North Atlantic Treaty Organization); United Kingdom (UK).

Austin, Warren
(1877–1962)

U.S. representative to the United Nations (UN) (1946–1953), a position in which Austin played a major role in advocating his country's Korean policies. Warren Austin was born on 12 November 1877, in Highgate Center, Vermont, to a middle-class family. After he graduated from the University of Vermont, he joined his father's legal practice in St. Albans, Vermont, and took an active role in state Republican politics. From 1916 to 1917 he represented the National City Bank's American International Corporation in Beijing (Peking), negotiating several loans with the Chinese government for railway and canal projects. He returned to practice law in Burlington, Vermont, in mid-1917, and in 1931 he won a special election to the Senate, where he served for the next fifteen years.

One of the less prominent members of his party with no major legislation to his name, Austin nonetheless distinguished himself by belonging to the small group of internationalist Republicans who opposed the neutrality legislation of the 1930s, advocated increases in military budgets, and believed that Washington should adopt a more active foreign policy. After the United States entered the Second World War, Austin called for immediate planning for the postwar world. In 1942 the Franklin D. Roosevelt administration, anxious to ensure bipartisan support for its foreign policy initiatives, invited Austin to join the State Department's newly formed congressional foreign policy advisory group. In this position and as a key member of the Committee of Eight, leading senators who supported the creation of some form of postwar international organizations, Austin played a major role in persuading the Republican Party leadership in its 1944 platform to endorse the creation of an international organization, together with international financial institutions and the UN Relief and Rehabilitation Administration. In 1942 Austin's internationalist stance led to his dismissal as informal Republican minority leader in the Senate, but in 1946 he won his reward when President Harry S. Truman appointed him the first U.S. ambassador to the UN.

Sympathetic to the idea of an organization that would embody the highest universalist moral and legal principles, during the frequent Cold War crises of this period Austin often found himself and his mission

U.S. delegate to the United Nations Warren Austin, holding a Russian-made submachine gun captured by U.S. forces in July 1950. Austin charged the Russians were sending arms to North Korea. (National Archives)

bypassed by more hard-line members of the Truman administration. Austin was in fact forced to defend positions that seemed to conflict with his personal predilections. An eloquent speaker for the highest U.S. and international ideals, Austin was not a close adviser to any of the secretaries of state under whom he served, and he exercised little influence upon policy formulation. Austin's own outlook hardened as the Cold War developed and intensified, a process reinforced by the outbreak of the Korean War.

Austin returned from vacation to push through the 27 June 1950 UN Resolution that authorized military intervention by that organization's member states. In July Austin pressed strongly for a unified command in Korea under U.S. leadership, a stance that irritated his colleagues in some of the allied and neutral delegations. They were also bothered by his tendency to regard the war as a moral crusade in which U.S. and UN interests were indistinguishable.

In August 1950, when the USSR delegation returned to the UN Security Council, Austin resisted USSR attempts to switch the focus from the Korean situation to the question of UN recognition of the People's Republic of China (PRC). He also hinted that the ultimate aim of UN intervention should not be restricted to a restoration of the antebellum status quo but should include the reunification of the Korean peninsula.

Although less prominent in the General Assembly meetings of November 1950, which were dominated by Secretary of State Dean Acheson and the State Department consultant John Foster Dulles, Austin, after the Chinese intervention of late 1950, expressed his country's outrage in the Security Council and rebutted Soviet and Chinese Communist charges of U.S. aggression. Early in 1951 Austin was also prominent in rebutting attempts by U.S. allies and Arab and Asian powers to end the war by concessions to the

PRC over Taiwan and its representation in the UN and in obtaining passage of the 1 February 1951 UN resolution that condemned the Chinese crossing of the 38th parallel. Austin also stood firmly behind President Truman's decisions to replace General Douglas MacArthur as commander in chief of UN forces and keep the war a limited conflict. Later in 1951 and 1952 his own poor health and the secretary of state's personal involvement in dealing with the UN limited Austin's own activities on Korea.

In 1953 Austin retired to Burlington. Now a hardline anti-Communist, he became honorary chairman of the Committee of One Million, designed to exclude the PRC from the UN. He died on 25 December 1962 at Burlington, Vermont.

—Priscilla Roberts

References:

Foot, Rosemary J. *The Wrong War: American Policy and the Dimensions of the Korean Conflict, 1950–1953.* Ithaca, NY: Cornell University Press, 1985.

Mazuzan, George T. *Warren R. Austin at the U.N., 1946–1953.* Kent, OH: Kent State University Press, 1977.

Stueck, William W., Jr. *The Korean War: An International History.* Princeton, NJ: Princeton University Press, 1995.

"Warren Austin." In *Political Profiles: The Truman Years,* edited by Eleanora W. Schoenebaum. New York: Facts on File, 1978.

See also: Acheson, Dean Goodersham; China, People's Republic of: UN Representation Question; Dulles, John Foster; MacArthur, Douglas; Truman, Harry S.; Truman's Recall of MacArthur.

Australia

One of sixteen nations to provide diplomatic and military assistance to the Republic of Korea (ROK, South Korea) during the Korean War. Australia played a more significant role in policy formation than in military operations.

As with the post–World War II Western democracies, Australia considered the Korean conflict part of the worldwide struggle against the spread of communism. Australian diplomats did, however, criticize the U.S.-supported regime of South Korean President Syngman Rhee. In early 1949 Australia joined with other Pacific and Asian leaders in calling for a Pacific security pact, a military alliance to combat communism, provide collective security in the region, and complement the North Atlantic Treaty Organization.

Australian leaders were among the first to condemn the Democratic People's Republic of Korea (DPRK, North Korea) as the aggressor in the Korean War. In response to a United Nations (UN) request, two Australian military officers, Squadron Leader Ronald J. Rankin and Major Francis S. B. Peach, began field observations along the 38th parallel in May 1950. In early June 1950 Arthur B. Jamieson, Australian representative of the UN Commission on Korea (UNCOK)

in Seoul, submitted the Peach-Rankin Report that asserted that the DPRK had started the war. This report helped turn Australian and Western public opinion against North Korea and strongly influenced UN resolutions calling for an international police action.

Despite its regional leadership position, Australia wedded its Korean policy to British initiatives. On 29 June 1950, the United Kingdom pledged Royal Navy vessels for service in Korea, prompting Australia to follow with a commitment of its own. Learning that Britain mobilized its Royal Air Force the next day, the Australian government immediately ordered a fighter squadron of the Royal Australian Air Force (RAAF) into action. The government also delayed its decision to send the 3d Battalion, Royal Australian Regiment (RAR), until the British sent ground troops.

Australian officials coordinated diplomatic efforts and formulated wartime policy during the Korean conflict. Australian Prime Minister Robert G. Menzies, Minister for External Affairs and External Territories Percy C. Spender, Australian Ambassador to the United States Norman J. O. Makin, and Australian representative on the UN Commission for the Unification and Rehabilitation of Korea James Plimsoll were instrumental in forging and maintaining close diplomatic ties with both the ROK and the United States. Prominent Australians also served on several UN committees, including the Additional Measures Committee, the Temporary Commission on Korea, and the UNCOK.

Australian armed forces were at low strength in June 1950, but those units committed made an important contribution to the UN military effort in Korea. Although Australian service contingents generally fell under U.S. and British operational command, Australian Lieutenant General Sir Horace Clement Hugh Robertson served as commander in chief of the British Commonwealth Occupation Force and British Commonwealth Forces in Korea from 1950 to 1951.

Air force pilots were the first Australians to see action. When North Korean forces crossed the 38th parallel on 25 June 1950, the 77th Mustang Fighter Squadron of the Royal Australian Air Force (RAAF) was stationed in Japan. By 29 June, the squadron was fully operational and among the first UNC armed forces to fight in Korea, flying alongside the Fifth Air Force. The Australian force strafed rolling stock, bridges, truck convoys, and lines of communication south of the Yalu River boundary with Manchuria. In August 1950 alone, forty pilots of the 77th Squadron flew more than 800 sorties (1,745 hours) in combat operations. In July and August, RAAF F-51 Mustangs destroyed an estimated 35 North Korean tanks, 226 vehicles, 4 trains, and a sizable quantity of ammunition and fuel dumps. Australian pilots continued to fly interdiction and support missions for the duration of the war, occasionally escorting bombers and, in Meteor-8 Jets, challenging Chinese MiG-15s.

At the outset of the war, Prime Minister Menzies also placed two Royal Australian Navy vessels, the destroyer HMAS *Bataan* and the frigate HMAS *Shoalhaven* at UN Command disposal. The destroyer HMAS *Warramunga* and four more frigates joined the U.S. Naval Forces Far East. In October 1951 Australia sent to Korea its only aircraft carrier, the HMAS *Sydney*, along with the 20th Carrier Air Group: two squadrons of Sea Furies and one of Fireflies. It remained in Korean waters until February 1952.

Australia's contribution of ground forces was modest, but those troops deployed fought with distinction. On 26 July acting Prime Minister Arthur Fadden broadcast the news that Australia would send a brigade to Korea. Recruiting offices in Australia opened the following day but the 3d Battalion, Royal Australian Regiment did not arrive in Korea until 28 September 1950. It fought under the command of the 27th British Commonwealth Brigade and its maximum strength was 2,282 soldiers. Australian infantrymen crossed the 38th parallel on 2 October 1950. They assisted in the capture and defense of Sariwŏn, fought in skirmishes outside Yongju, and secured a bridgehead across the Ch'ŏngch'ŏn River at Sinanju in late October. The latter action was of special strategic importance because it led to the capture of Pakch'ŏn and Chŏngju, towns along the main route from P'yŏngyang to the Manchurian border. The 3d Battalion received its highest accolades when it faced numerically superior Chinese Communist forces at the defense of the Kap'yŏng River valley during 23–25 April 1951. The battalion withstood successive waves of Chinese attacks for three days and helped the 27th British Commonwealth Brigade repulse an entire Chinese division. For its performance at Kap'yŏng, the 3d Battalion earned the U.S. Presidential Citation.

Australian troops were later incorporated into 28th Commonwealth Brigade, one of three infantry brigades to compose the 1st Commonwealth Division, activated on 28 July 1951. The brigade participated in Operation COMMANDO in October 1951, defended against Chinese assaults on their lines around Little Gibraltar, and fought valiantly in the Battles of the Hook from October 1952 through July 1953.

British Commonwealth Forces (Australia, Britain, Canada, and New Zealand) suffered a total of 1,262 killed and another 4,817 wounded in action. Total casualties for Australian armed forces stood at 1,584, with 339 killed. Of the 10,600 Australian army personnel to serve in Korea between August 1950 and July 1953, 277 were killed in action and 1,210 were wounded. After the armistice, 26 Australian prisoners of war were repatriated.

Considering the low number of casualties, the negligible domestic impact of the war, and the urgency with which Australia sought improved regional security, the nation's participation in the conflict constituted a diplomatic victory. For its prompt avowal of military assistance, Australia was rewarded with a $250 million loan from the World Bank and the security pact known as the ANZUS Treaty (named after its member countries Australia, New Zealand, and the United States), signed on 1 September 1951. International loans and the new military alliance guarded against a resurgent Japan, protected against other potential enemies in the region, and provided Australia with stronger diplomatic relations with the United States.

—*Matthew D. Esposito*

References:

Bartlett, Norman. *With the Australians in Korea.* Canberra: Australian War Memorial, 1954.

Carew, Tim. *Korea: The Commonwealth at War.* London: Cassell, 1967.

McCormack, Gavan. *Cold War/Hot War: An Australian Perspective on the Korean War.* Sydney: Hall & Iremonger, 1983.

O'Neill, Robert. *Australia in the Korean War, 1950–1953.* 2 vols. Canberra: Australian War Memorial and Australian Government Publishing Service, 1981, 1985.

See also: ANZUS (Australia–New Zealand–U.S.) Treaty; Jamieson, Arthur B.; Makin, Norman J. O.; Menzies, Robert G.; Pacific Pact; Plimsoll, James; Robertson, Sir Horace C. H.; Spender, Sir Percy C.; Syngman Rhee; United Nations Additional Measures Committee; United Nations Commission for the Unification and Rehabilitation of Korea.

B

Baillie, Hugh
(1890–1966)

Prominent U.S. newspaper correspondent and executive. Hugh Baillie was born in Brooklyn, New York, on 23 October 1890. He attended the University of Southern California, and while there began his journalism career, first for the *Los Angeles Herald* and later for the *Los Angeles Record.*

In 1912 the *Record* loaned Baillie to United Press (UP) to cover the trial of Clarence Darrow. The nature of the trial suggested a long jury deliberation and the other correspondents left, but Baillie remained to go over his notes. The jury returned after only fifteen minutes with a not-guilty verdict and Baillie was able to scoop the others.

In 1915 Baillie joined the UP permanently, first as manager of its San Francisco bureau, then in Los Angeles, Portland, Chicago, New York, and Washington. His coverage of the 1920 Republican Party Convention earned the respect of fellow correspondents. In 1921 he became general news manager of UP and then general manager in 1922, executive vice-president in 1931, and president in 1935.

As president of UP, Baillie started a news service for radio and also continued to travel and send in reports. He spent a great deal of time in Europe and managed to secure interviews with some of Europe's most influential leaders, including Adolf Hitler, Benito Mussolini, Maxim Litvinov, Edouard Herriot, Pierre Laval, and Josef Stalin. Between 1943 and 1945 he interviewed Generals Bernard Montgomery, Dwight Eisenhower, Omar Bradley, and Douglas MacArthur. In 1943 Baillie reported on action in Sicily, where he was wounded in the leg, and in Belgium in 1944. Many of his reports and interviews were front-page material.

In late 1944 as the war in Europe was drawing to a close, Baillie secured assurances from thirteen governments regarding rights for correspondents. This included freedom of news sources and access to transmission facilities. All news media (newspapers, radio, and later television) worldwide were to have access to all possible news sources.

In 1950 Baillie covered the Korean War from the Pusan perimeter. Later he flew with MacArthur to Seoul and was there for ceremonies marking its recapture. He wrote a dispatch describing MacArthur's return of the city to the Republic of Korea. On 15 March 1951 Baillie again interviewed MacArthur. This occurred just three weeks before the general was relieved of command. In that interview MacArthur told Baillie he intended to take the war north of the 38th parallel because it lacked adequate defenses. When Baillie asked MacArthur how many troops would be required to hold the 38th parallel, the general replied that it was his intent not to hold "any line across the peninsula," but "to drive the Chinese Communists back across the Yalu River, hold that river as our future line of defense and proceed…with unification of Korea."

In 1955 Baillie ended his long tenure as president of UP, now known as United Press International or UPI. In 1959 he published *High Tension*, describing much of his journalistic career, including opinions and descriptions of people he had met. Baillie died of heart failure in La Jolla, California, on 2 March 1966.

—*William H. Van Husen*

References:
Baillie, Hugh. *High Tension; The Recollections of Hugh Baillie.* New York: Harper, 1959.
New York Times 16 March 1951; 3 March 1966; 5 March 1966.
Rothe, Anna. *Current Biography, 1946.* New York: H. W. Wilson, 1947.
See also: Bradley, Omar Nelson; MacArthur, Douglas; Stalin, Josef.

Bajpai, Girja S.
(1891–1954)

Secretary-general of India's Ministry of External Affairs (1947–1952) who played a central role in India's Korean War diplomacy. Girja Bajpai was born in Lucknow on 3 April 1891 to an Indian upper-caste family. He was educated at the Muir Central College, Allahabad, and Merton College, Oxford, earning second-class honors in history. In 1914 he entered the Indian Civil Service, where he was regarded as "perhaps the most brilliant younger Indian member during the period between the wars."

A loyal and dependable civil servant, Bajpai was a member of numerous Indian delegations attending various imperial and roundtable conferences. In 1941 he was appointed as India's first agent general in the United States and spent the next six years in Washington, D.C., where he established good relations with members of Franklin Roosevelt's and Harry Truman's administrations and with the U.S. Congress.

His conservative background and his years of service to the British notwithstanding, Bajpai's ability and reputation were such that shortly after India attained independence in 1947 Jawaharlal Nehru named him secretary-general of the Ministry of External Affairs.

In this capacity Bajpai served Nehru loyally while affirming his own dedicated belief in the need to maintain close Indian ties to the British Commonwealth. Bajpai, who had enjoyed long, close, and generally good relations with both British and U.S. leaders, supported Nehru's nonaligned Cold War stance, but overall acted as a moderating force, attempting to soften the prime minister's somewhat provocative utterances condemning colonialism and what Nehru perceived as U.S. Cold War excesses.

Bajpai's most direct involvement in Korean War diplomacy came in autumn 1950. He regularly received reports from Indian Ambassador to the People's Republic of China (PRC) K. M. Panikkar of his conversations with leading Chinese officials. In late September and early October 1950 Bajpai relayed to Britain and the United States communications from PRC Foreign Minister Zhou Enlai to Panikkar to the effect that, should United Nations (UN) forces move north of the 38th parallel, Chinese troops would intervene in the war. In a late September meeting with U.S. Ambassador to India Loy W. Henderson, Bajpai personally endorsed Panikkar's warning.

Panikkar's open support for normalizing diplomatic relations with the PRC had already reduced his credibility with the British and Americans, but Bajpai's good relations with both Western powers gave additional force to his view that China was not bluffing. Bajpai's efforts were ultimately of no avail; British officials were inclined to give them considerable weight, but U.S. leaders, including President Truman, Secretary of State Dean G. Acheson, and General Douglas MacArthur, argued that to hold back at the 38th parallel would be interpreted as evidence of U.S. weakness and indecision.

Until he left office in 1952, Bajpai fully supported the Indian government's policy of encouraging negotiations likely to lead to an armistice and a compromise peace settlement. In 1952 ill health led him to exchange the Ministry of External Affairs for the governorship of Bombay, "in some ways the most dignified post in India." As India's representative, in 1953 he attended the Geneva UN talks on Kashmir. Sir Girja Bajpai died in Bombay on 5 December 1954.

—*Priscilla Roberts*

References:

Brecher, Michael. *Nehru: A Political Biography.* Oxford: Oxford University Press, 1959.

Caroe, Olaf. "Bajpai, Sir Girja Shankar." In *Dictionary of National Biography, 1951–1960,* edited by E. T. Williams and Helen M. Palmer. Oxford: Oxford University Press, 1981.

Gopal, Sarvepalli. *Jawaharlal Nehru: A Biography.* London: Jonathan Cape, 1979.

Kux, Dennis. *Estranged Democracies: India and the United States, 1941–1991.* New Delhi: Sage, 1993.

Stueck, William W., Jr. *The Korean War: An International History.* Princeton, NJ: Princeton University Press, 1995.

Wolpert, Stanley. *Nehru: A Tryst with Destiny.* New York: Oxford University Press, 1996.

See also: Acheson, Dean Goodersham; Henderson, Loy; India; MacArthur, Douglas; Nehru, Jawaharlal; Panikkar, Sardar K. M.; Truman, Harry S.

Baldwin, Hanson W.
(1903–1991)

Prominent U.S. newspaper correspondent and military commentator. Hanson W. Baldwin was born on 22 March 1903, in Baltimore, Maryland, and graduated from the U.S. Naval Academy, Annapolis, in 1924. After three years of navy service, he resigned his commission and began a career in journalism. He worked first as a reporter for the *Baltimore Sun,* where his father was a managing editor. In 1929 he moved to the *New York Times* as a reporter. After eight years as a reporter, in 1937 he became the paper's military correspondent. In 1937 he spent four months in Europe, traveling widely and reporting on what he believed were preparations for a coming war. On his return he wrote extensively on the lack of U.S. military preparedness.

During World War II Baldwin reported from both the Pacific and European theaters of operation. In 1943 he won a Pulitzer Prize for his wartime reports from the South Pacific. That same year he became the military editor for the *New York Times,* a post he held until his retirement in 1968.

Baldwin covered World War II, the Korean War, and the Vietnam War, and he wrote about issues of strategy, tactics, and weapons, often siding with the military chiefs on major strategic issues. For example, he frequently opposed the "gradualism" of political leaders whose constraints denied victory in war. He accepted that the United States was locked in a struggle with an expansionist Communist world, and he advocated U.S. nuclear superiority over the Soviet Union.

During the Korean War, Baldwin had considerable impact in shaping U.S. public opinion about the war. He noted the "unpopularity of the Syngman Rhee government" and "questionable political and military reliability" of the Republic of Korea Army (ROKA) and police as being "the greatest weakness of the defending forces." Baldwin supported President Harry S. Truman and Secretary of State Dean Acheson during the war, but was on occasion critical of administration military policies.

Baldwin opposed the use of atomic weapons in Korea because of the lack of prominent targets and the public reaction that would ensue. In October 1950 he began a series of articles pointing out U.S. military deficiencies in Korea. In December 1950 he discussed the pros and cons of a United Nations forces withdrawal, and in one of these articles he wrote, "Americans face the greatest threat in our history" and "Western Civilization and our American way of life" were in jeopardy "if the danger from the East" was not opposed. Baldwin opposed a widened war and supported Truman's decision to replace MacArthur, believing the general had been guilty of insubordination. Baldwin recommended that the United States aid the Nationalist Chinese government in Taiwan, speed up the rearmament of Japan, and aid other non-Communist countries in Asia, all to prevent the spread of communism in Asia. Baldwin supported the 1953 armistice that ended the war as the best possible result from the stalemate.

Widely read by political and military leaders, Baldwin was himself occasionally the subject of news, as in 1966 when Secretary of Defense Robert McNamara called a news conference to dispute Baldwin's contention that the Vietnam War had overextended the U.S. armed forces.

Baldwin retired from the *New York Times* in 1968. He wrote and edited nineteen books as well as numerous articles. Baldwin died in Roxbury, Connecticut, on 13 November 1991.

—Robert J. Arvin III

References:

Alexander, Bevin. *Korea: The First War We Lost*. New York: Hippocrene Books, 1986.

Baldwin, Hanson. *Strategy for Tomorrow*. New York: Harper & Row, 1970.

Hastings, Max. *The Korean War*. New York: Simon & Schuster, 1987.

New York Times, 14 November 1991.

See also: Acheson, Dean Goodersham; Truman, Harry S.

Barr, David Goodwin
(1895–1970)

U.S. Army general. Born on 16 June 1895 at Nanafalia, Alabama, David Goodwin Barr attended Alabama Presbyterian College for three years and was commissioned a second lieutenant of infantry in the Officer Reserve Corps in November 1917. During World War I he served with the 1st Division in France and in the occupation of Germany until September 1919, when he returned to the United States. A year later he was promoted to first lieutenant.

In the interwar years Barr served as an instructor with the New York National Guard; with the 16th Tank Battalion at Camp Meade, Pennsylvania; and with 22d Infantry Regiment at Camp McClellan, Alabama. During 1926–1927 he was assigned to the office of the U.S. military attaché in Paris and attended the French tank school at Versailles. He subse-

quently served with tank units at Fort Benning, Georgia, and in October 1930 he became adjutant of the newly formed Mechanized Force at Fort Eustis, Virginia. He attended the Army Command and Staff School at Fort Leavenworth, Kansas, graduating in June 1936.

After graduation from the Army War College in June 1939, Barr was assigned briefly in Washington, D.C., before joining the I Armored Corps at Fort Knox, Kentucky. In May 1941 he became corps G-4 and in June 1942 was advanced to brigadier general and reassigned as chief of staff of the Armored Force, in which position he served until July 1943, when he was sent to London to serve as chief of staff of the European Theater. In January 1944 Barr was named chief of staff, Headquarters, North African Theater of Operations. He was promoted to major general in February 1944, and that September he became chief of staff of the U.S. Sixth Army Group in France. He returned to the United States in July 1945 and served as a personnel officer at Headquarters, Army Ground Forces, until January 1948, when he became chief of the Army Advisory Group in Nanjing (Nanking), China. In that position he advised Secretary of Defense James Forrestal in January 1949 to discontinue arms shipments to Jiang Jieshi (Chiang Kai-shek) because they were being intercepted by Mao Zedong's Communist forces.

In May 1949 General Barr assumed command of the 7th Infantry Division in Japan. He took the division to Korea in September 1950 and commanded it during the hard fighting at Inch'ŏn, in the X Corps amphibious landing at Wŏnsan (which he opposed), on the march to the Yalu River and the subsequent withdrawal, and in fighting around the Changjin (Chosin) Reservoir. Barr was an excellent staff officer and well liked by his troops but lacked the drive of the best combat commanders. He was thus frequently at odds with imperious X Corps Commander Lieutenant General Edward M. Almond and Almond's staff. In accordance with the U.S. Army policy of reassigning senior commanders with recent combat experience to training commands, Barr left Korea in January 1951 to become commandant of The Armor School at Fort Knox, Kentucky. He retired from active duty in February 1952 and died on 26 September 1970 in Falls Church, Virginia.

—Charles R. Shrader

References:

Blair, Clay. *The Forgotten War: America in Korea, 1950–1953*. New York: Times Books, 1987.

"Department of Defense Biographical Sketches," *Washington Post*, 28 September 1970.

See also: Almond, Edward Mallory; Jiang Jieshi (Chiang Kai-shek); Mao Zedong.

Battle Fatigue

Also known as shell shock, battle shock, and battle stress. Such adverse reactions to the stress of combat were termed neuropsychiatric cases (NPs). During the early months of the Korean conflict, NPs were common during the retreat when exhaustion, despair, and fear of encirclement shattered the morale of many men and some units. NPs reached a high point in September 1950, precipitated by the heavy North Korean assault.

A variety of factors contributed to the large number of cases. Many veterans of World War II believed that the Korean fighting was more intense than any they had known. The landscape of denuded hills gave a sense of "no place to hide." The process of fighting up one hill only to be confronted with another beyond was psychologically as well as physically wearing. Many of the newcomers to battle faced the stress of battle suddenly and among strangers. As a result, the ratio of NPs to wounded almost doubled the World War II norm.

A lot of mistakes were made in the handling of these types of casualties during the early months of the Korean conflict. Failures by both commanders and medical officers amplified psychiatric losses. The basic lessons learned in World War I and later relearned in World War II, that men suffering from battle fatigue should be held as close as possible to the front line, was, partly from necessity, forgotten.

Men with mild nonpsychotic symptoms were sent by plane or ship to Japan, the worst possible treatment because it took a soldier from the line and taught him the lesson that escape from danger was the reward for this behavior. The result was the loss of many men, who with a few days of rest, a sedative, and a hot meal, could have returned to duty.

With the formation of the Pusan perimeter, the psychiatric admission rate soared, from fifty cases per thousand troops per year in July 1950 to 258 in August. Between July and December 1950, the 8054th Evac Hospital evacuated 85 percent of its NPs and returned only 15 percent to duty. The combination of retreat, poor command decisions, inexperienced doctors, quick evacuation, and lack of bed space contributed to the heavy neuropsychiatric losses in the early days of the war, when personnel losses were critical. An exception to this situation was the Second Division, where an effort was made from the first days of battle to hold NPs at the clearing station level, where most could be dealt with by several days' rest and then returned to duty.

Eventually the lessons of World War II were relearned, but the presence of veteran medical officers was the key to revival of the World War II approach. Individual, not institutional, memory resulted in a better record for combat psychiatry that saw more NPs treated and returned to duty.

An interesting new development in handling the stress of combat was a morale-enhancing program of what might be termed preventive psychotherapy. World War II statistics showed that sharp increases in casualty rates of all types occurred when troops experienced combat for more than 180 days without relief. Hence, the Department of the Army authorized temporary duty in Japan for the purpose of rest and recuperation (R&R); personnel serving in Korea were authorized a five-day R&R period.

—*James H. Willbanks*

References:

Cowdrey, Albert E. *United States Army in the Korean War: The Medics' War.* Washington, DC: U.S. Army Center of Military History, 1987.

Gabriel, Richard A., ed. *Military Psychiatry: A Comparative Perspective.* New York: Greenwood Press, 1986.

See also: Casualties; Military Medicine; Mobile Army Surgical Hospital (MASH); Rest and Recuperation (R&R).

Bazooka

Antitank weapon developed during the Second World War. The bazooka consisted of a rocket and launcher, operated by a two-member crew. The launcher was a tube with a shoulder stock. The hand grip contained a trigger assembly that was an electric generator to send a current along a wire. Each rocket had two wires extending from the nozzle at its rear; when the rocket was packed, the wires were tucked along the body and grounded with a shorting cap. The loader pulled off the shorting cap before he placed the rocket in the rear of the launcher. He then individually tied off the wires against electrical posts at the back of the launch tube. Squeezing the trigger generated an electric current through the wires to ignite the solid fuel in the rocket.

The 2.36-inch rocket had a shaped charge to concentrate the warhead explosion in a small area, generating a superheated jet of gas with the bulk of its energy forward. This burned through the armor. The great velocity and high temperature of the gas transformed the steel of the armor into a liquid state. The size of the hole might vary from a quarter-inch to two inches in diameter; it depended on the type of the armor, stand-off distance, and other factors. Most of the damage was caused by the superheated jet of gas that consumed oxygen, destroyed articles in its path, and set fire to ammunition and fuel, but also molten droplets of armor were propelled into the target vehicle.

The 2.36-inch rocket proved ineffective against Russian-built T-34/85s in the Korean People's Army (KPA, North Korean) invading force, but it had been successful against German tanks that were better armored than the T-34/85. It was most effective when fired from the flank; heavier frontal armor was always more difficult to defeat, and there was often not enough energy left to destroy the tank. The T-34 was vulnerable to shaped-charge warheads, but was diesel powered and was thus less likely to catch fire than the gasoline-powered German tanks.

In the first engagement involving U.S. troops (Task Force Smith) and the KPA at Osan on 5 July 1950, the U.S. troops fired twenty-two 2.36-inch rounds at the thirty-five–ton T-34/85s. None of the rockets did any damage, probably because of the deterioration of the ammunition in storage. Many of the rounds simply bounced off the armor without exploding.

The 3.5-inch bazookas arrived in Korea by mid-July and with them came an increase in kills. With a larger warhead, which put more gas at greater temperature inside a tank, the 3.5-inch bazookas proved effective. Also the ammunition was new and the teams were probably better trained.

Antitank teams armed with the 3.5-inch bazookas scored successes against the T-34s in fighting for Taejŏn on 19 July 1950. General William Dean, commander of the 24th Infantry Division, led one team himself, stalking a tank for an hour before destroying it. The KPA broke through at Taejŏn, but the 3.5-inch bazooka helped to nullify the T-34, the chief KPA advantage in the early phase of the war.

—Spencer C. Tucker

References:

Alphin, Lieutenant Colonel Arthur B. Letter to author, 29 May 1990.

Blair, Clay. *The Forgotten War: America in Korea, 1950–1953.* New York: Times Books, 1987.

Rees, David. *Korea: The Limited War.* New York: St. Martin's Press, 1964.

Tunis, Edwin. *Weapons.* New York: World Publishing, 1954.

See also: Armor (Tanks); Dean, William Frishe; Task Force Smith.

Bebler, Ales
(1907–1981)

Yugoslavia's permanent delegate at the United Nations (UN) and its Security Council representative when the Korean War began. Born on 8 June 1907, in Idrija, Slovenia, then part of the Austro-Hungarian Empire, Ales Bebler was early involved in the movement for Slovenian independence. As a teenager, admiration for the Soviet Union's stance supporting self-determination for small nations helped make Bebler an ardent recruit to the Communist Party. He took courses at the University of Ljubljana in Slovenia's capital, and in 1930 he obtained a doctorate in law from the University of Paris. Warned that he faced arrest if he returned to Yugoslavia, Bebler remained in Europe and visited Moscow frequently. There in 1935 he met Josip Broz, who would become Marshal Tito. Bebler also improved his linguistic skills

and worked for the Communist cause. He fought in the Spanish Civil War, where he was wounded, and then returned to Slovenia, spending a year in prison for subversive activities.

After the 1941 German invasion of Yugoslavia, Bebler quickly joined the resistance and became one of the leading partisan officers. During the internecine struggles among leftist and monarchist Yugoslav guerrillas, he strongly supported Tito, and on the establishment of the Federative People's Republic of Yugoslavia in December 1945 he became deputy foreign minister, representing his country at every major international conference of the later 1940s. He frequently represented Yugoslavia at the UN, and in 1946 and 1947 he fiercely defended Yugoslavia's role in the Communist insurgency in Greece.

After Tito's public break with Stalin in 1948, Yugoslavia had to steer a carefully calibrated course between the Communist and Western powers, and in the UN Bebler no longer automatically cast Yugoslavia's vote behind the Soviets on such issues as Soviet policy in its satellite states. In 1949, with U.S. support, Yugoslavia won a two-year term on the Security Council. At this time Tito also named Bebler Yugoslavia's permanent delegate to the UN. In January 1950 Bebler was the only Security Council delegate to support the Soviet demand for the exclusion of the Nationalist Chinese delegate and his replacement by a Communist Chinese official.

When the Korean War began, the sharp-tongued, witty, but sometimes vitriolic Bebler performed an intricate balancing act. He initially suggested that the Security Council contact the Democratic People's Republic of Korea (North Korea) government to obtain further information on the invasion, a suggestion that was rejected. Unable to block the UN Security Council resolution of 25 June 1950 calling for North Korea's immediate withdrawal from South Korea, Bebler abstained; he cast the only vote against the resolution two days later calling upon member states to contribute forces to the UN command in Korea.

Tito, unwilling to alienate the United States, announced that Bebler had acted on his own initiative and that Yugoslavia would not attempt to block further UN efforts to assist the Republic of Korea (South Korea). In November 1950 Bebler served as president of the Security Council, where his major preoccupation was a fruitless attempt to prevent the war's escalation in consequence of growing participation by the People's Republic of China (PRC, Communist China) in the fighting by persuading Chinese and U.S. representatives to meet at Lake Success to discuss Chinese intentions. Harry Truman's administration refused to engage in such bilateral talks, as did Chinese delegates, who ignored Bebler's advice to be conciliatory and rejected his offer to serve as a mediator. To U.S. chagrin, on 27 November Bebler suggested that Security Council discussions of the Korean situation be coupled with PRC complaints that the United States had invaded Taiwan, a approach that infuriated U.S. officials.

Washington was relieved when Bebler's term as president ended. For the remainder of his time at the UN and as Yugoslav undersecretary of state from 1952 to 1955, Bebler continued to urge the need to reach a negotiated settlement in Korea and he welcomed the beginning of armistice discussions in 1951. Bebler remained active in Yugoslav politics until 1964, a period in which he also served as ambassador to France and later to Indonesia. In his later years he developed a strong interest in environmental issues, on which he frequently spoke publicly. He died at Ljubljana on 12 August 1981.

—Priscilla Roberts

References:

Barros, James. *Trygve Lie and the Cold War: The United Nations Secretary-General Pursues Peace, 1946–1953.* DeKalb: Northern Illinois University Press, 1989.

"Bebler, Ales." In *Biographical Dictionary of the Comintern.* New, revised, and expanded ed., edited by Branko Lazitch and Milorad M. Drachkovitch. Stanford, CA: Hoover Institution Press, 1986.

"Bebler, Ales." In *Current Biography, 1950.* New York: H. W. Wilson, 1951.

Luard, Evan. *A History of the United Nations.* Vol. 1, *The Years of Western Domination, 1945–1955.* London: Macmillan, 1982.

Stueck, William W. *The Korean War: An International History.* Princeton, NJ: Princeton University Press, 1995.

"Bed-Check Charlies"

The Korean People's Air Force (KPAF, North Korea) developed between 1945 and 1950 in the Soviet-occupied northern half of the Korea peninsula. With the establishment of the Democratic People's Republic of Korea (DPRK, North Korea), the KPAF assumed a status equal to that of the North Korean Army and Navy. By the spring of 1950 the KPAF had 178 aircraft, including obsolescent World War II–era Yak fighters and trainers and even older Polikarpov PO-2 biplane trainers. The latter became associated primarily with the "Bed-Check Charlie" raids during the Korean War, although Yak-18 trainers and others also occasionally flew these missions.

For all practical purposes, by late summer 1950, United Nations Command (UNC) air forces destroyed the KPAF as an effective force. Thereafter, Chinese and Soviet aircraft and crew carried the burden of aerial combat on the Communist side until the armistice of 1953. The KPAF, by contrast, limited itself to nuisance attacks, which, because of their nighttime regularity over UNC positions, became known as "Bed-Check Charlies." Designed to harass, disturb the sleep, and impede nighttime missions of UNC air bases and front-line positions, the raids inflicted only limited actual damage. They did, however, possess a certain value as propaganda.

The PO-2 flew at approximately eighty knots and had a fabric-covered fuselage and surfaces offering little purchase for radar used by UNC forces. Hence nighttime detection of the raiders became problematic. Even airborne radar in Allied night-fighters frequently lost the PO-2s to ground "clutter" on screens. PO-2 pilots took advantage of cloud, fog, and ground-hugging flight patterns in valleys to conceal themselves from UNC defenses. The pilots dropped individual bombs or, occasionally, tossed out hand grenades. The PO-2 was highly maneuverable, and pilots used this to sometimes outwit faster, more sophisticated UNC aircraft, especially jets. The UNC subsequently responded by arming several T-6 trainers ("Mosquito" forward air-control aircraft) with .30-caliber machine guns in the attempt to end the strikes. If caught by searchlights or successfully detected by radar, and pursued by a determined pilot, the PO-2s were utterly helpless.

—David R. Dorondo

References:

Bermudez, Joseph S., Jr. "Korean People's (North Korean) Air Force." In *The Korean War: An Encyclopedia,* edited by Stanley Sandler. New York: Garland, 1995.

Futrell, Robert F. *The United States Air Force in Korea, 1950–1953.* Rev. ed. Washington, DC: Office of the Chief of Air Force History, 1983.

Moore, Dennot, and Peter Bagshawe. *South Africa's Flying Cheetahs in Korea.* Johannesburg: Ashanti, 1991.

See also: Aircraft (Principal Combat); Korea, Democratic People's Republic: Air Force (Korean People's Air Force [KPAF]).

Belgium

As the host and an original signatory of the Western European Union defensive alliance (1948) and North Atlantic Treaty Organization (1949), Belgium was keenly aware of the global dimension of post-1945 security. Motivated by the possibility of a European repetition of the June 1950 events in Korea as well as by the political need to be seen as a reliable ally, Brussels deployed a battalion to the United Nations (UN) forces fighting in Korea. Commanded by Lieutenant Colonel A. Crahay, the Belgian contingent and its attached personnel from Luxembourg arrived in Korea on 31 January 1951.

The Belgian battalion joined the U.S. 3d Division. Participating in the UN Command's (UNC's) offensive then in progress, the Belgians helped scour the outskirts of Seoul for Communist troops after the South Korean capital's liberation on 14–15 March 1951. With the opening of the Communist spring

Belgian troops withdrawing from Hill 194 area, April 1951. (National Archives)

offensive on 22 April, Belgian troops found themselves in the thick of the fighting. Formally attached to the United Kingdom's 29th Independent Brigade, the battalion held the right-center of the 3d Division's front with the First Royal Northumberland Fusiliers and the 1st Gloucestershire Regiment (the Glosters) to their south and west. The Belgians held Hill 194, a tactically difficult position on the north bank of the Imjin River. The river ran at their backs, and its banks in the area were steep. Here the Belgians endured heavy Chinese attacks. For all practical purposes, the battalion was cut off from the rest of the brigade, as Chinese troops drove southward into the 29th Brigade's front between the Belgians and the Fusiliers. By the end of 23 April, however, the battalion had not only withdrawn in relatively good order but had also helped cover the retreat of the U.S. 65th Infantry. The Belgians subsequently partici-pated in the 3d Division's ultimately unsuccessful attempt to extricate

the Glosters from their own disastrously untenable positions south of the Imjin on 24–25 April.

The coming of armistice talks settled the Belgian troops into what became the familiar pattern of the rest of the war: relatively small but often violent actions as UN and Communist forces jockeyed on the ground for political advantage at P'anmunjŏm. In October 1951 the battalion fought in the offensive by the U.S. I Corps in the attempt to drive the Chinese Forty-Seventh Army north of the Yŏkgok-ch'ŏn River near the town of Chŏngjamal. Typical of the fighting was the Belgians' attempt, while seconded to the U.S. 1st Cavalry Division, to take an area of great defensive strength, called Hill 346, as part of Operation POLECHARGE. This ultimately successful attempt aimed at establishing a new defensive line called JAMESTOWN.

Under Belgian law, only volunteers could be sent to Korea. Through the fall of 1951, the Belgian government had to offer special pay and other incentives to keep the battalion at its full complement. Although effective, such incentives complicated UN efforts to maintain all forces at their required strength. In their service, Belgian troops, as with their counterparts from the Netherlands and Luxembourg, performed as effectively as their unit size allowed. Some minor difficulties arose between the Belgians and other UN troops. For example, dietary preferences for more potatoes and bread than U.S. troops typically received caused minor logistical problems remedied with different rations (a situation similar to that affecting Dutch and Turkish soldiers). On the whole, such problems were minimal and did not have an impact upon the battalion's combat readiness.

—*David R. Dorondo*

References:

Hermes, Walter G. *United States Army in the Korean War: Truce Tent and Fighting Front.* Washington, DC: Office of the Chief of Military History, 1966.

Mossman, Billy C. *U.S. Army in the Korean War: Ebb and Flow, November 1950–July 1951.* Washington, DC: U.S. Army Center of Military History, 1990.

See also: Imjin River, Battle of; NATO (North Atlantic Treaty Organization).

Bendetsen, Karl R.
(1907–1989)

Undersecretary of the U.S. Army during the Korean War and, from 1950 to 1952, director general of the U.S. railroad system. Born in Aberdeen, Washington, on 11 October 1907, Karl R. Bendetsen earned a law degree at Stanford University in 1932. He returned to his hometown, where he practiced law until 1940, while also serving as a captain in the field artillery branch of the U.S. Army Officer Reserve Corps. In 1940 he joined the office of the judge advocate general at the War Department in Washington, D.C., helping to draft the Soldier and Sailor Civil Relief Act that same year. After serving briefly as the secretary of war's representative to General Douglas MacArthur's command in the Philippines, Bendetsen joined the War Department General Staff in early 1942 to help direct the relocation of Japanese-Americans living on the West Coast and to establish a prisoner-of-war information bureau. Bendetsen then helped organize the Provost Marshal's Office, the U.S. Army Military Police Corps, and the School of Military Government. Bendetsen was instrumental in assisting War Department labor officials in formulating policies concerning the seizure and operation of strike-plagued private industrial facilities producing vital materials for the armed forces during the early war years. Traveling to Europe in 1944, he was part of the combined Allied staff that helped plan and implement the June 1944 Normandy invasion.

After the war Bendetsen resumed his law career in California but returned to government service in 1948 as a special consultant to the Office of the Secretary of Defense. Early in 1950 he became assistant secretary of the army in charge of general management. Based on his findings as a member of the Civilian Components Policy Board, he developed a five-year plan to expand and increase the combat readiness of the U.S. Army Reserve.

Then, in August 1950, railroad workers threatened a nationwide strike after seventeen months of negotiations failed to resolve a dispute with management over wages and hours. To avoid an adverse effect on the war effort in Korea, President Harry S. Truman issued an executive order establishing federal control over all U.S. railroads and he appointed Bendetsen as general director. The railroads remained under Bendetsen's nominal control until May 1952, when there was a settlement of the dispute. Becoming undersecretary of the army that same month, Bendetsen left government service later that year, joining Champion Papers and Fiber Company as general consultant. After service as a general manager and vice-president, he became the chief executive officer in 1957, remaining in this capacity after Champion merged with U.S. Plywood in 1967. Meanwhile in 1956 Bendetsen had undertaken advisory missions to Germany and the Philippines for the U.S. government. From 1950 to 1959 he also was chairman of the board for the Panama Canal Company.

Although Bendetsen retired in 1973, he did return once more to government service as chair of President Ronald Reagan's panel on the Strategic Defense Initiative in the 1980s.

—*Clayton D. Laurie*

References:

Current Biography, 1952. New York: H. W. Wilson, 1953.

International Who's Who, 1988–1989. London: Europa Publications, 1988.

National Cyclopedia of American Biography. Vol. 38. New York: J. T. White, 1953.

New York Times, 30 June 1989.

Who's Who in America. Vol. 27, *1952–1953.* Chicago: A. N. Marquis, 1953.

See also: MacArthur, Douglas; Truman, Harry S.

Berendsen, Sir Carl August
(1890–1973)

New Zealand ambassador to the United States and leader of its delegation to the United Nations (UN) (1948–1952), during which time he strongly supported U.S. actions in Korea. Born in Sydney, Australia, on 16 August 1890, to parents who moved to New

Zealand in 1900, Carl August Berendsen joined the New Zealand civil service in 1906. As a part-time student, he earned bachelor and master of laws degrees from Victoria College, Wellington. A highly competent professional civil servant, Berendsen initially specialized in labor affairs, but from 1926 he concentrated on foreign policy. In an overlapping series of top-level assignments, during 1926–1935 he was imperial affairs officer in the Prime Minister's Department; during 1928–1943, secretary of the External Affairs Department; during 1935–1943, permanent head of the Prime Minister's Department; and during 1939–1943, secretary to the War Cabinet. A brief spell as high commissioner in Australia was followed by his appointment in 1944 as minister to the United States, a position that became an ambassadorship in 1948 when the legation was raised to an embassy.

In the mid-1930s Berendsen had helped to draft New Zealand's proposals for reform of the League of Nations, and he was one of his country's most prominent representatives at the 1945 San Francisco Conference that created the UN. He headed New Zealand's delegation to the UN from its establishment in 1945 and was a strong opponent of the Security Council's effective insistence on unanimity because of the veto power exercised by its five permanent members. An eloquent, forceful, and entertaining speaker, Berendsen was known for giving flamboyant and passionate but highly effective and well-reasoned public performances advocating those policies he and his country favored.

The fiercely anti-Soviet Berendsen, whose international outlook was much affected by his memories of what he considered the deplorable and dangerous appeasement policies of the 1930s, applauded and encouraged the U.S. intervention in Korea. He publicly stated, to the embarrassment of his government, that the Democratic People's Republic of Korea (DPRK, North Korea) was merely a Soviet puppet, an accusation that Washington had carefully avoided voicing.

Berendsen consistently pressed his own government to back U.S. policies on Korea. Believing that U.S. support was essential to New Zealand's security and survival, he suggested that the United States would regard the Korean situation as a litmus test of those Pacific countries that could be counted as genuine supporters and might deserve inclusion in a U.S.-backed Pacific security pact or alliance.

Berendsen applauded New Zealand's decision of 29 June 1950 to send a naval force of two frigates to the UN Korea command and his government's more reluctant decision four weeks later to commit ground forces. At his government's behest Berendsen reluctantly voted in favor of the UN resolution of 1

December 1950 to establish a three-power committee to facilitate a cease-fire. Privately he regarded this move and the Indian-sponsored Arab-Asian peace initiatives later that month as "inexcusable" appeasement of aggressor nations. He urged his country, as it ultimately did, to support the 1 February 1951 UN resolution introduced by the United States condemning the People's Republic of China (PRC, Communist China) as an aggressor in the war.

A consistent hard-liner, Berendsen urged the bombing of Chinese bases north of the Yalu River and deplored the armistice negotiations that began in 1951. He was delighted when the United States decided to conclude the Australia–New Zealand–U.S. (ANZUS) Treaty and believed he could take some credit for persuading leading U.S. officials to do so. At the 1951 San Francisco Conference at which both ANZUS Treaty and the Japanese Peace Treaty were finalized, a jubilant Berendsen signed both on his country's behalf. When he retired in January 1952 he did so in the unhappy belief that "appeasers" among the allies were acting as a brake and preventing the United States from following highly desirable aggressive policies to prosecute and win the war. In retirement Berendsen lectured extensively on the need to avoid appeasing "Communist imperialism" and to reform the UN. Sir Carl Berendsen died at Dunedin, New Zealand, on 12 September 1973.

—*Priscilla Roberts*

References:
McGibbon, Ian C. "Berendsen, Carl August." In *Biographical Dictionary of Internationalists,* edited by Warren F. Kuehl. Westport, CT: Greenwood Press, 1983.
———. *New Zealand and the Korean War.* Auckland: Oxford University Press, 1992.
———, ed. *Undiplomatic Dialogue: Letters between Carl Berendsen and Alister McIntosh, 1943–52.* Auckland: Auckland University Press, 1993.
Stueck, William W. *The Korean War: An International History.* Princeton, NJ: Princeton University Press, 1995.
Trotter, Ann. "New Zealand in World Affairs: Sir Carl Berendsen in Washington, 1944–1952." *International History Review* 12, no. 3 (August 1990): 466–489.
See also: ANZUS (Australia–New Zealand–U.S.) Treaty; New Zealand.

Bevan, Aneurin
(1897–1960)

Influential British politician and cabinet member. When the Korean War began, Bevan was British minister of health and housing; in January 1951 he became minister of labor. Born on 15 November 1897, in Tredegar, Monmouthshire, to a Welsh miner's family, Bevan himself spent some time in the pits. He left school at thirteen and was largely self-educated through voracious reading in the local Workmen's

Library; he also spent two years from 1919 at the Central Labour College in London, though he later characterized this as a waste of time.

Long periods of unemployment in the 1920s made Bevan a radical, a union activist, and an organizer for the Labour Party; and in 1929 he became a member of Parliament for Ebbw Vale, a seat he would retain until his death. Hard work, eloquence, and charm quickly won him a position of influence within the Labour Party, and he never lost that position of influence. His radical, dissenting temperament tended to make him happier in opposition than in power.

Bevan opposed the First World War, but in the later 1930s his decided anti-Fascist convictions led him to support intervention in the Spanish Civil War, and he became a strong critic of Prime Minister Neville Chamberlain's policies. In early 1939 he was expelled from the Labour Party for supporting Sir Stafford Cripps' Popular Front campaign, but he was readmitted in December. During the Second World War Bevan was highly critical of some aspects of Prime Minister Winston Churchill's policies: he distrusted the big-power diplomacy of the wartime conferences for its neglect of smaller countries' interests, and he feared that Britain devoted insufficient attention to the postwar development of a united Europe strong enough to stand up to both the United States and the Soviet Union.

In 1945 Bevan became minister of health and housing in Prime Minister Clement Attlee's government, which was responsible for establishing the National Health Service and providing subsidized government housing for millions of Britons. Although Bevan supported the Marshall Plan and the North Atlantic Treaty Organization, he opposed the U.S. loan of 1946 to Britain, had reservations as to various features of U.S. capitalism, and feared British subservience to the United States.

When the Korean War began, Bevan, in common with most of the Labour Party, supported the principle of collective security, but he soon began to have misgivings as to the social costs of the war, particularly the impact of rearmament upon Britain's welfare programs. After the People's Republic of China (PRC) intervened militarily, he opposed imposition of sanctions upon the PRC and feared that the bellicose General Douglas MacArthur, commander of United Nations (UN) forces, might drag Britain into a broader Asian conflict. In January 1951 he opposed the British vote in favor of a UN resolution condemning the PRC as an aggressor in the conflict, but Bevan lost that battle. In this dispute Bevan took the opposite side to Chancellor of the Exchequer Hugh Gaitskell, his long-time political opponent. In March 1951 Gaitskell introduced a budget designed to demonstrate to Washington Britain's commitment to heavy expenditure on rearmament. This cut the country's domestic welfare spending, in particular by introducing charges for false teeth and spectacles, which the newly created National Health Service had previously provided gratis. Bevan, who had earlier argued that rearmament should not be achieved at the expense of social spending, accused Gaitskell of being obsessively pro–United States and of usurping ailing Foreign Secretary Ernest Bevin's prerogatives.

On 22 April 1951 Bevan resigned over the issue, in the process splitting the Labour Party. This division contributed to the Labour Party's defeat in the October 1951 general election and was the prelude to almost four decades of intraparty dissension over foreign policy. For the remainder of his life Bevan, perennially opposed to his leaders' endorsement of a pro–United States foreign policy and excluded by them from the party's upper echelons, remained an inspiring and much-loved figure to the Labour Party's radical wing. Acknowledged as a parliamentary orator second only to Winston Churchill, Bevan died at Chesham, Buckinghamshire, on 6 July 1960.

—*Priscilla Roberts*

References:

Campbell, John. *Nye Bevan and the Mirage of British Socialism.* London: Weidenfeld & Nicolson, 1987.

Foot, Michael. *Aneurin Bevan: A Biography.* 2 vols. New York: Atheneum, 1963, 1974.

Jenkins, Mark. *Bevanism, Labour's High Tide: The Cold War and the Democratic Mass Movement.* Nottingham: Spokesman, 1979.

Laugharne, Peter, ed. *Aneurin Bevan: A Parliamentary Odyssey.* Liverpool: Manutius Press, 1996.

MacDonald, Callum A. *Britain and the Korean War.* Oxford: Blackwell, 1990.

Morgan, Kenneth O. *Labour in Power, 1945–1951.* Oxford: Clarendon Press, 1985.

See also: Attlee, Clement R.; Churchill, Sir Winston Spencer; MacArthur, Douglas.

Bevin, Ernest
(1881–1951)

British foreign secretary and largely responsible for his country's policy regarding the Korean War. Born on 9 March 1881, Ernest Bevin was the son of a country midwife who died when he was eight. The two most important intellectual influences upon Bevin were the Methodist religion and the British labor movement. He left school at age eleven and became a carter, a job that led him to become a trade union organizer and a socialist. In 1911 Bevin became a full-time official of the Dockers Union; a decade later this union formed part of the labor coalition whose merger created the powerful Transport and General Workers Union. Bevin was its first general secretary, which also ensured him extensive influence in the broader Trade Union Congress.

During the 1920s Bevin won election to parliament as a Labour Party representative; in this capacity his attendance at international labor conferences and his membership (1929–1931) of the Macmillan Committee on finance and industry gave him a good working knowledge of international finance, trade, and economics. Although a socialist, Bevin resisted the temptation of communism; during the First World War he supported the war effort and had little patience with pacifists. Bevin was a major figure in the Labour Party, thanks to his overbearing personality and block union vote. In the 1930s he was a strong supporter of rearmament, an issue on which he eventually carried the party with him. By the late 1930s Bevin, who had visited Canada, Australia, and New Zealand, believed that the British Commonwealth could form the core of a new League of Nations, based on their economic unity. Although Bevin always remained more a trade unionist than a politician, he regained his Commons seat in 1940 and held it until his death. During the Second World War he served as minister of labor and national service.

After the Labour Party's August 1945 electoral landslide, Prime Minister Clement Attlee appointed Bevin foreign secretary, a position in which his forth-rightness, determination to defend British interests, and personal generosity won the somewhat rough and untutored Bevin the affection and respect of his initial-ly horrified subordinates. As a union leader Bevin had fought to eradicate Communist influence from the labor movement, and both he and Attlee distrusted Soviet expansionism in Europe, for which they believed the only real remedy was greater U.S. eco-nomic and military assistance to the West European nations. In January 1947 Bevin asked U.S. officials to take over responsibility for aid to Greece and Turkey, which furnished the occasion for President Harry S. Truman's speech in which Truman verbally commit-ted his country to assisting any nation facing an inter-nal or external Communist threat (a commitment later known as the Truman Doctrine). Bevin's requests, first for economic and then for military aid to the war-weakened West European countries, were instrumen-tal in persuading U.S. leaders to provide Marshall Plan economic assistance in 1948, followed by the North Atlantic Treaty Organization, a mutual security pact, in 1949.

London and Washington remained divided on important Asian policy issues, including the status of Taiwan, recognition of the new People's Republic of China (PRC), French difficulties in Indo-China, and continuing British rule over Hong Kong and Malaya. Nonetheless, Bevin's fundamental belief in Anglo-American partnership against communism impelled him firmly to support U.S. intervention in Korea. Bevin was conscious of Britain's need neither to alien-ate the British Commonwealth countries, especially India, nor to endanger Hong Kong. This caused some differences between him and U.S. officials. Anxious not to provoke China, Bevin frequently dissociated Britain from U.S. policy on Taiwan and attempted without success to win U.S. leaders over to Britain's position. Even so, he always recognized the overriding importance of maintaining good relations with the United States, the mainstay and keystone of Britain's crucial European policies.

Eager to end a conflict that he feared would divert the United States from what he considered higher pri-orities in Europe and the Middle East, Bevin in early July 1950 suggested that the USSR might persuade the North Koreans to withdraw to the 38th parallel. On 7 July he proposed to U.S. Secretary of State Dean Acheson that, in exchange, Washington might make concessions to Beijing concerning Taiwan and its admission to the United Nations (UN), suggestions Acheson sharply rejected.

Anxious to maintain both close relations with the United States and his country's prestige, Bevin sup-ported the decision to commit British troops to the UN forces in Korea. He also endorsed the October 1950 decision to cross the 38th parallel. In late October 1950, when Chinese troops began to appear in North Korea, Bevin suggested the establishment of a demili-tarized buffer zone along the North Korean–Chinese border, a suggestion the U.S. government ignored. After the massive Chinese intervention in late November 1950, Bevin again proposed a broad settle-ment that would meet the PRC's wishes over Taiwan and admission to the UN, a suggestion that Acheson once again contemptuously rejected. The two foreign ministers also disagreed over the introduction of a UN resolution condemning China for aggression in Korea, but when the roll call came on 1 February 1951, alliance solidarity persuaded Bevin to vote in favor of the U.S.-backed resolution. Although he attempted to exercise an essentially restraining influence on U.S. policy, sufficient U.S. determination generally per-suaded Bevin to yield his ground. The greatly enhanced U.S. military commitment to Europe, imple-menting the recommendations of the Policy Planning Staff paper NSC-68, "United States Objectives and Programs for National Security," which was one of the Korean War's more immediate consequences, may also have helped to allay Bevin's worst apprehensions over European defenses. In March 1951 poor health forced Bevin to resign as foreign secretary. He died in London a month later, on 14 April 1951.

—Priscilla Roberts

References:

Bullock, Alan. *Ernest Bevin: Foreign Secretary, 1945–1951.* New York: W. W. Norton, 1983.

Butler, Rohan, and M. E. Pelly, eds. *Documents on British Policy Overseas.* Series II, Vol. 4, *Korea, 1950–1951.* London: Her Majesty's Stationery Office, 1995.

MacDonald, Callum A. *Britain and the Korean War.* Oxford: Blackwell, 1990.

Weiler, Peter. *Ernest Bevin.* Manchester: Manchester University Press, 1993.

See also: Acheson, Dean Goodersham; Attlee, Clement R.; Franks, Oliver; NATO (North Atlantic Treaty Organization; Truman, Harry S.

BIG SWITCH/ LITTLE SWITCH, Operations (1953)

Code names for the two main exchanges of prisoners of war (POWs) before and after the 1953 Armistice Agreement between the People's Republic of China (PRC, Communist China) and Democratic People's Republic of Korea (DPRK, North Korea) on the one side and the United Nations Command (UNC) on the other. Operations LITTLE SWITCH and BIG SWITCH ended more than two years of stalemate regarding POW issues; Operation LITTLE SWITCH, in particular, opened the door to a comprehensive peace settlement.

In December 1952 the UN and the International Red Cross urged an exchange of sick and wounded POWs on both sides as a good-faith peace gesture that would bring about resumption of talks at P'anmunjŏm that halted on 8 October. While Commander in Chief of UNC Forces General Mark W. Clark agreed to the exchange as a humanitarian display, the PRC representative, with backing from the Soviet Union, rejected the exchange outright, largely over the still unresolved issue of POW repatriation.

Later, on 28 March 1953, DPRK leader Kim Il Sung and Chinese Marshal Peng Dehuai abruptly shifted Communist policy and not only agreed to an exchange of sick and wounded prisoners in accordance with provisions of the 1949 Geneva Convention, but publicly declared that such an exchange could open the door to a comprehensive settlement of all POW and cease-fire related issues. Communist negotiators also suggested that plenary sessions at the peace talks should be immediately resumed. This statement was a clear indication to the UNC and to the United States that an end to the Korean War could ultimately result from the renewed talks. This surprising acceptance of the exchange may have resulted from the uncertainty over Soviet policies after the death of Soviet dictator Josef Stalin on 5 March 1953, and a statement by his successor Georgii M. Malenkov ten days later indicating Soviet willingness to see the Korean War end.

On 30 March PRC Foreign Minister Zhou Enlai (Chou En-Lai) endorsed the exchange idea in a Beijing radio broadcast, although at that time and later he rejected any exchange of POWs that left either Chinese or North Korean Communists in UN hands. Instead he proposed that any prisoners who had not yet made up their minds (all POWs having been screened in April 1952) be placed in the hands of a neutral power, either Switzerland or India, for a final determination of status and location of repatriation. Soviet leaders indicated their acceptance of the plan on 1 April. Subsequent agreement with the UNC was quickly reached at P'anmunjŏm on 11 April, much to the surprise of the United States. The exchange, known as Operation LITTLE SWITCH, was scheduled to commence less than three weeks later.

During the actual LITTLE SWITCH operation, carried out under extraordinary security measures at P'anmunjŏm between 20 April and 3 May 1953, the Communists repatriated 684 sick and wounded UN soldiers, including 94 litter cases. This number included 149 Americans, 471 South Koreans, 32 Britons, 15 Turks, 6 Colombians, 5 Australians, 2 Canadians, and 1 prisoner each from the Philippines, the Union of South Africa, Greece, and the Netherlands. The United Nations Command returned 1,030 Chinese and 5,194 North Koreans, along with 446 civilian internees, for a total of 6,670 people, including 357 litter cases.

The exchange went without major incident but was later marked by controversy. Returning Communist prisoners on their way to Freedom Village in P'anmunjŏm tried to embarrass their UN captors by rejecting rations and by destroying or discarding clothing issued to them, while sensational reports appeared in the Western media alleging that UN POWs had been starved and abused physically and psychologically while in captivity. Additional claims were made that those UN prisoners exchanged in LITTLE SWITCH were not true hardship cases, but were actually collaborators who were thought more likely by the Communists to give a favorable rendition of conditions in captivity. The media also alleged that a number of sick and wounded UN POWs were still being held in spite of the exchange agreements.

Although Operation LITTLE SWITCH did break the deadlock, it did nothing to resolve the larger POW issue that had delayed an armistice agreement since July 1951. However, the voluntary repatriation controversy that had caused so much disagreement and delay was resolved on 25 May 1953, when it was agreed that a UN Neutral Nations Repatriations Commission (NNRC), consisting of representatives from Sweden, Switzerland, Czechoslovakia, and Poland and to be chaired by India, would be created to take responsibility for nonrepatriate prisoners within sixty days of the armistice. During a sixty- to ninety-day period after

A wounded UNC soldier and former POW leaves a Communist ambulance for hospital evacuation on 26 April 1953, during Operation LITTLE SWITCH. (National Archives)

Site selected for the exchange of sick and wounded POWs. Delegate and conference tents are in the background, 15 April 1953. (National Archives)

that, the NNRC, with the assistance of 5,000 Indian Army troops commanded by General Kadenera Subayya Thimayya, would maintain order and supervise both Chinese and North Korean prisoners in the camps. If nonrepatriates could not be convinced by their comrades to return home, and if their fate could not be resolved by a postwar Korean political conference called for under Agenda Item 4 of the Armistice Agreement, the NNRC would be dissolved and any remaining POWs would be released. Those prisoners willing to return home would be released in an operation designated BIG SWITCH.

Operation BIG SWITCH took place between 5 August and 23 December 1953. It was the main and final exchange of POWs taking place at Freedom Village in P'anmunjŏm after the signing of the Armistice Agreement in July. Like LITTLE SWITCH, Operation BIG SWITCH was also marked by controversy over voluntary repatriation and, later, by allega-

tions of Communist brainwashing and torture of UN POWs. During the operation itself, the UNC returned 75,823 POWs (70,183 North Koreans and 5,640 Chinese) of the 132,000 Communist POWs it held; the Communists repatriated 12,773 UNC POWs (7,862 South Koreans, 3,597 Americans, 945 British, 229 Turks, 40 Filipinos, 30 Canadians, 22 Colombians, 21 Australians, 12 Frenchmen, 8 South Africans, 2 Greeks, 2 Dutch, and 1 prisoner each from Belgium, New Zealand, and Japan).

After the initial exchanges under BIG SWITCH in August and September 1953, 22,604 Communist-side nonrepatriates, mostly former Chinese Nationalist soldiers impressed into Communist service, were turned over to the Neutral Nations Repatriation Committee. Of this number, only 137 were convinced to return home during the time allotted by the Armistice Agreement. The remaining nonrepatriates were returned to their original custodians, were then designated civilians, and were released in January 1954. Most subsequently settled in South Korea or in the Republic of China on Taiwan. Only 359 UNC prisoners (335 Koreans, 23 Americans, and 1 Briton) indicated a desire to remain with the Communists. Many of the Americans who had initially decided to remain under Communist control subsequently returned to the United States.

—Clayton D. Laurie

References:

Blair, Clay. *The Forgotten War: America in Korea, 1950–1953.* New York: Times Books, 1987.

Fehrenbach, T. R. *This Kind of War: A Study in Unpreparedness.* New York: Macmillan, 1962.

Hastings, Max. *The Korean War.* New York: Simon & Schuster, 1987.

Hermes, Walter G. *United States Army in the Korean War: Truce Tent and Fighting Front.* Washington, DC: Office of the Chief of Military History, 1966.

See also: China, Republic of; Clark, Mark W.; Kim Il Sung; Malenkov, Georgii Maximilianovich; Peng Dehuai (Peng Tehuai); Stalin, Josef; Thimayya, Kadenera Subayya; Zhou Enlai.

Biological Warfare

Biological warfare, also termed germ or bacteriological warfare, has existed for centuries. An early reference can be traced to the siege of Caffa in 1346 in which plague-infected corpses were hurled over the city walls by the Tartars. During World War I, German agents reportedly inoculated horses with glanders and cattle with anthrax, and in World War II the infamous Japanese Unit 731 conducted experiments with plague in Manchuria in the early 1940s.

Initial allegations of U.S. use of biological warfare in East Germany in 1950, using Colorado beetles against potato crops, and in Canada in 1949, using plague against Eskimos, were made in Eastern Bloc documents in 1950 and 1951, respectively. These were followed by Communist press and governmental accusations in 1951 concerning U.S. employment of biological warfare in China and North Korea. No details were given in these communiqués other than the mention of smallpox being allegedly spread. More formal accusations were levied on 22 February 1952 by the foreign minister of the Democratic People's Republic of Korea (DPRK, North Korea) and on 8 March 1952 by the foreign minister of the People's Republic of China (PRC). These charges were supported by the Soviet Union and vigorously denied by the United States.

The employment of biological warfare by the United States would have made even less sense than that of chemical warfare, which the Communists had also alleged was being employed by U.S. forces. World opinion, U.S. adherence to Western laws of war, and the likelihood of such biological agents also affecting U.S. and Allied troops and the South Korean population made the validity of such charges highly improbable. Human diseases said to be spread were anthrax, plague, cholera, encephalitis, and a form of meningitis. Animal and plant diseases were also said to have been employed by U.S. forces. Vectors, or carriers of disease transference, were said to be insects, spiders, ticks, small rodents, infected clams, and calcareous and sectioned "leaflet" bombs.

These accusations were backed by the 1952 *Report of the International Scientific Commission for the Investigation of the Facts Concerning Bacterial Warfare in Korea and China.* The main incidents chronicled in the report were numerous appearances of plague in North Korea, the Kan-Nan plague incident in northeast China, the K'uan-Tien anthrax incident near the Yalu River, the respiratory anthrax incidents in Liaotung and Liaohsi near the Yalu, and the Taedong cholera incident in North Korea. U.S. planes, such as F-86 fighters, were said to have flown overhead during these incidents and dropped bombs containing insects or rodents or objects such as feathers or packets of clams infected with various diseases. Supporting evidence was provided by recovered bomb fragments and containers and by the testimonies of captured U.S. intelligence agents (South Koreans) and U.S. pilots.

The issue of the United States waging biological warfare against North Korea and China resulted from epidemics that broke out in these Communist countries. These epidemics were traced to poor sanitation and health conditions stemming from the war and a lack of effective medical care for the populace. However, Communist leaders used these epidemics as a propaganda tool and as a means to hide the inadequacies of their health care system. The transparency of this propaganda ploy was illustrated by two events. First, on 23 April 1953, as the war was winding down, the United Nations General Assembly created a commission to investigate the accusations of biological warfare. After the Armistice Agreement was signed, however, the Communists dropped the matter and references to these accusations have since disappeared from East European literature. Second, it was later determined after repatriation that the captured U.S. pilots who had signed false statements of U.S. biological warfare activity had been tortured, threatened with mock execution, and brainwashed into doing so.

Interestingly enough, within a decade after the war ended, the United States admitted that it had the capability to wage biological warfare in Korea. In fact Japanese Lieutenant General Shiro Ishii, who was involved with the Manchurian plague experiments, had been given immunity by the United States in return for his help in further developing its program, which began around 1941. However, in January 1959 a sworn statement was signed that stated that the U.S. "bacteriological warfare capability was based upon resources available and retained only within the continental United States."

As more of the U.S. program became public, it turned out that the true weakness of the Communist accusations stemmed from the types of vectors allegedly used for disease transference. U.S. employment of biological agents would not have been based on such primitive methods as insects and clams or the bombs discussed in the 1952 International Scientific Commission report. Rather, to effectively conduct such warfare, infected aerosol droplets containing particles between 1 and 5 microns (1 micron = 10^{4cm}) would have been dispersed by U.S. aircraft. This would have been the best means to achieve disease transmission. Even then, given the need for a biological warfare agent to be produced in large quantities, survive in storage for a few weeks, be virulent, have a quick-acting incapacitating or lethal effect, produce an epidemic, and be highly stable in an aerosol, this form of warfare is not as easy to wage as Communist propaganda suggested.

—Robert J. Bunker

References:

Clarke, Robin. "Biological Warfare." *Science Journal* (November 1966): 2:71–79.

Commission of International Association of Democratic Lawyers. *Report on U.S. Crimes in Korea.* Pyongyang: Democratic People's Republic of Korea, 31 March 1952.

Cowdrey, Albert A. "'Germ Warfare and Public Health in the Korean Conflict." *Journal of the History of Medicine and Allied Sciences* 39, no. 2 (April 1984): 153–172.

Hersh, Seymour M. *Chemical and Biological Warfare: America's Hidden Arsenal.* Indianapolis: Bobbs-Merrill, 1968.

Report of the International Scientific Commission for the Investigation of the Facts Concerning Bacterial Warfare in Korea and China. Beijing: World Council of Peace, 1952.

Stockholm International Peace Research Institute. *The Problem of Chemical and Biological Warfare.* 6 vols. New York: Humanities Press, 1971–1975.

Blair House Meetings
(25 and 26 June 1950)

At 0800 on Sunday 25 June 1950, U.S. Ambassador to the Republic of Korea (ROK, South Korea) John Muccio was awakened in Seoul by an urgent telephone call from his chief deputy with word that at 0400 forces of the Democratic People's Republic of Korea (DPRK, North Korea) had launched a full-scale military invasion of the South.

In Washington, D.C. (it was then still Saturday 24 June) the State Department summoned officials to verify Muccio's report. Secretary of State Dean Acheson and Assistant Secretary of State for Far Eastern Affairs Dean Rusk soon received word that the attack was more than just a minor military mission. Acheson, who called the invasion "an open, clear, direct challenge" to peace and democracy, then phoned President Harry S. Truman, who was in Independence, Missouri, and remained there until the next day.

Commander of U.S. forces in the Far East General Douglas MacArthur in Tokyo told visiting Special Ambassador John Foster Dulles, "this is probably only a reconnaissance force…. I can handle it with one hand tied behind my back."

For the rest of the night, U.S. officials worked on a response. At 0300 on 25 June, the U.S. government charged the DPRK with a "breach of the peace" and officially requested a meeting of the United Nations (UN) Security Council. The United States then had tremendous influence in the UN, and the UN had previously served as a forum for Korean issues. The rest of the day Acheson and other officials worked to formulate an acceptable response. Many believed the invasion marked the start of World War III. Acheson phoned Truman a second time on 25 June and informed him that the UN Security Council was in session.

As Truman flew to Washington he thought about the road to World War II and how the 1938 Munich Conference had worked to Adolf Hitler's advantage. Truman recalled in his memoirs, "Communism was acting in Korea just as Hitler, Mussolini, and the Japanese had acted ten, fifteen, and twenty years earlier." Truman was determined not to follow a similar path of appeasement. The president was also under great domestic pressure. His popularity had declined as a consequence of the 1949 Communist victory in China. In addition, former State Department official Alger Hiss had been convicted of perjury, providing grist for the mill of right-wing anti-Communist critics who charged the Truman administration with having "sold out" to communism. As well, in February Senator Joseph R. McCarthy had begun his Communist witch-hunt, much of which was aimed at the Truman administration and the State Department. Strong decisive action in Korea would disarm Truman's domestic critics. Truman ordered Acheson to summon his principal advisers to a meeting at Blair House, the elegant federal-style building on Pennsylvania Avenue where the Truman's had been living while the White House was being remodeled.

That same day, 25 June, Truman met at Blair House with Acheson, Secretary of Defense Louis Johnson, Chairman of the Joint Chiefs of Staff General Omar Bradley, Chief of Naval Operations Admiral Forrest Sherman, Air Force Chief of Staff Hoyt S. Vandenberg, and other officials. There was no debate on basic issues. All agreed that the Soviet Union had engineered the attack and that aggression could not be tolerated. DPRK leader Kim Il Sung, they concluded, would never have launched his attack without the Kremlin's approval. The relationship between the USSR and DPRK, commented one official, was the same as "between Walt Disney and Donald Duck." But, as one participant later observed, the real basis for the decision over Korea had less to do with Korea and more to do with aggression. The participants agreed that the war in Korea was not a civil war.

Acheson recommended that the United States supply South Korea with arms and other military equipment. He also suggested that during the evacuation of Americans the U.S. Air Force protect Kimpŏ Airport in Seoul by attacking approaching DPRK ground and air forces. Truman then ordered MacArthur to resupply the ROK Army (ROKA) and to use U.S. air power against the Korean People's Army (KPA, North Korean) invaders.

All present at the conference saw the DPRK invasion as a test of American will and moral courage. Truman thought that the Soviet Union was gambling that the United States would not do anything in Korea and the Soviets would therefore win a victory by default. Although intelligence estimates concluded that World War III was not imminent, U.S. officials did speculate that this attack was the first in what would be a series of Communist attacks worldwide.

Truman saw a domino effect when he stated, "If we let Korea down, the Soviet [Union] will keep right on going and swallow up one piece of Asia after another…the Near East would collapse and no telling what would happen in Europe." General Bradley declared that the United States had to draw a line. Chief of Naval Operations Admiral Forrest Sherman concluded that the Russians did not want war but if they did want one they would get it. All agreed, however, that a wider war including the Soviet Union and/or China was undesirable.

At the meeting there was considerable discussion about the Republic of China (Nationalist China) on Formosa and the People's Republic of China (PRC, Communist China) on the mainland. Johnson, who had just returned from meetings in Tokyo with MacArthur, tried to emphasize the importance of Formosa. MacArthur had discussed this, arguing that Formosa had a critical geopolitical location and tremendous potential as a U.S. air base. Its location, MacArthur concluded, was worth ten to twenty aircraft carriers. Truman thought of Formosa differently, and his response was to order the deployment of the Seventh Naval Fleet into the waters between mainland China and Formosa to prevent a wider war between the two rival states.

Administration officials also discussed Japan. The 1949 Communist victory in China had brought about a shift in Washington's policy toward Japan. U.S. offi-

cials concluded that China posed a serious strategic threat to Japan and thus Japan would have to be strengthened. Rusk called the Korean peninsula a dagger pointing at the heart of Japan. Japan was seen as a Western bastion in Asia, especially in the event of a wider war. If U.S. air and naval bases in Japan were to be lost, the loss would threaten the entire U.S. position in the Pacific. The Truman administration also concluded that the United States would have to work to build up the Japanese economy to prevent the spread of communism there. Washington's view of Japan as vital to U.S. security interests had much to do with Truman's decision to intervene in Korea.

At the conclusion of this first Blair House meeting, Truman imposed a gag order on all those present until such time as he had met with congressional leaders. Truman also asked Acheson to study possible moves by the Soviet Union and to draft a report of decisions reached at the meeting for congressional leaders.

On 26 June the situation in South Korea worsened. Truman then ordered an after-dinner meeting at Blair House to discuss the next U.S. moves. General Vandenberg reported that a U.S. Air Force plane had shot down a Russian aircraft and that ROKA defenses were disintegrating. Acheson then made several recommendations, which were all agreed to. Acheson recommended that the U.S. Air Force and Navy should lend support to ROK forces south of the 38th parallel; that the Seventh Fleet should protect Formosa and prevent the Nationalist Chinese from attacking mainland China, sparking a wider war; and, to show Washington's resolve, that U.S. forces in the Philippines be strengthened and that more aid be sent to the French in Indo-China.

The two Blair House meetings showed the determination of the Truman administration to respond to the DPRK invasion and to take those steps considered necessary to repulse what was seen as Communist aggression and the first step in a Soviet master plan of expansion. Yet the administration remained wary of a wider war with China and/or the Soviet Union. Nonetheless, at the Blair House meetings the Truman administration laid the groundwork for U.S. forces to fight a "limited war" in Korea.

—Mark A. T. Esposito

References:

Acheson, Dean. *Present at the Creation: My Years at the State Department.* New York: W. W. Norton, 1969.

Donovan, Robert J. *Tumultuous Years: The Presidency of Harry S. Truman.* New York: W. W. Norton, 1982.

Hamby, Alonzo L. *Man of the People: A Life of Harry S. Truman.* New York: Oxford University Press, 1995.

Paige, Glenn D. *The Korean Decision, June 24–30.* New York: Free Press, 1968.

Truman, Harry S. *Memoirs.* 2 vols. Garden City, NY: Doubleday, 1955–1956.

See also: Acheson, Dean Goodersham; Bradley, Omar Nelson; China, Republic of; Johnson, Louis A.; Kim Il Sung; MacArthur, Douglas; McCarthyism; Muccio, John J.; Rusk, David Dean; Sherman, Forrest P.; Truman, Harry S.; Vandenberg, Hoyt S.

Bloody Ridge, Battle of
(18 August–5 September 1951)

The GI name adopted as the name of the battle for a group of peaks in the central Korean mountain range seventeen miles north of the 38th parallel, some thirty miles east of Kumhwa, which is the southeast apex of the Iron Triangle. The area is southeast of the North Korean city of P'yŏngyang and about five miles south of another group of hills that would come to be known as Heartbreak Ridge.

Bloody Ridge consisted of hills identified on tactical maps as, west to east, 983, 940, and 773. On 12 August 1951, U.S. 2d Infantry Division commander Major General Clark L. Ruffner received word that his division with its attached Republic of Korea Army (ROKA) units were to attack Bloody Ridge and later Heartbreak Ridge. Information gathered on the Communist defenses of the Bloody Ridge hills pointed to an increasing urgency that the heights be captured because they were being used as observation posts from which artillery fire was being directed at the main United Nations Command (UNC) supply route just to the south.

In the days after 15 August, the ROKA 36th Regiment attacked and captured most of the high ground of Bloody Ridge in bitter fighting where on several occasions there was fierce hand-to-hand combat with bayonets and grenades. The 36th Regiment was unable to secure all the high ground, and on 26 August, units of the Korean People's Army (KPA, North Koreans) counterattacked and then surrounded and recaptured Hill 983 and the saddles between it and Hill 940. The U.S. 2d Division's 9th Regiment was assigned the responsibility of retaking the 983-940 hill mass. The 9th Regiment began its attack in the early morning hours of 30 August. It repeatedly failed in its attempts, and by nightfall all of Bloody Ridge remained in Communist hands. But in the early hours of 31 August the 9th Regiment took and held Hill 773.

Weather conditions were poor. During the fighting for the Bloody Ridge peaks, constant rains turned roads and trails leading to the battle area into rivers of mud. Regardless, UNC artillery, armor, and fighter aircraft subjected the Communist positions to intense bombardment. B Company of the 72d Tank Battalion alone fired 3,069 rounds in support of the operations. Resupply in the high ridges was especially challenging and only ingenious and full exploitation of every possible method enabled the attacks to go forward. Rear-echelon personnel and Korean civilians were pressed into service as carriers for the many hours necessary to negotiate the steep, hazardous, and winding trails to the forward positions. These conditions also equally complicated the evacuation of casualties.

By the beginning of September, the 2d Division's 23d Regiment joined in the assault, first on nearby hills and later on the main mass of Bloody Ridge. On 4 September the division's 38th Regiment occupied Hills 754 and 660, immediately north of Bloody Ridge, and thereby weakened Communist resolve to remain on what had by now become untenable ground.

By 1400 hours on the 4th, troops of 9th Infantry were on the crest of Hill 940, the central peak of Bloody Ridge. Those Communist troops remaining could be seen fleeing to escape the trap. Fighting on Bloody Ridge cost the UNC, mostly the 2d Division, some 2,700 casualties. Confirmed enemy dead totaled 1,389, but the UNC estimated that the Communists incurred some 15,000 casualties in the fighting. Hardly had the fighting for Bloody Ridge ended than another epic struggle began for the ragged peaks of Heartbreak Ridge.

At P'anmunjŏm, peace talks, which had been indefinitely recessed, resumed shortly thereafter, perhaps because of heavy Communist losses or setbacks in the Bloody Ridge and Heartbreak Ridge fighting. No final agreement was reached, however, until nearly two years later, largely because of irreconcilable differences concerning the disposition of Communist POWs, many of whom did not want to be forced to return to Communist control.

At one time during the P'anmunjŏm cease-fire talks, the Communist side demanded that Bloody Ridge, Heartbreak Ridge, and another geographical feature known as the Punchbowl be given up as the price of their agreement to end the fighting. The UN side rejected this demand, however. Bloody Ridge remained under UNC control and is today comfortably within the boundaries of the Republic of Korea.

—*Sherman W. Pratt*

References:
Blair, Clay. *The Forgotten War: America in Korea, 1950–1953.* New York: Times Books, 1987.
Munroe, Clark C. *The Second United States Infantry Division in Korea, 1950–1951.* Tokyo: Toppan, n.d.
Stokesberry, James I. *A Short History of the Korean War.* New York: William Morrow, 1989.
See also: Heartbreak Ridge, Battle of.

BLUEHEARTS, Operation
(July 1950)

United Nations Command (UNC) commander General Douglas MacArthur's planned amphibious operation to land U.S. troops behind the main invading Korean People's Army (KPA, North Korean) forces. MacArthur conceived of this operation on Korea's western coast as a means to cut the flow of KPA troops and supplies to the South.

As early as 27 June MacArthur set the tentative date for the landing as 22 July 1950 with the possibility of putting men ashore as early as 20 July. MacArthur originally planned to use the 1st Cavalry Division to land close to the cities of Inch'ŏn and Seoul. Edward Fomey, an expert on amphibious warfare, was to supervise a crash course in amphibious operation for division personnel.

MacArthur planned for an amphibious operation to consist of the 1st Cavalry Division, an amphibious brigade (Army), a Marine regiment, and a regimental combat team (RCT), with a landing as close to Seoul and Inch'ŏn as possible. The goal was to capture the port of Inch'ŏn and then the Republic of Korea (ROK, South Korea) capital of Seoul.

On 5 July 1950, a group headed by Major General Edward K. Wright, MacArthur's assistant chief of staff for operations (G-3), began planning for the 22 July date. Meanwhile, the 1st Cavalry Division in Japan started invasion training along the coast at Chigasaki; however, events in Korea soon altered the original plan. The rapid KPA advance forced MacArthur to commit to the Pusan perimeter fighting units that had been earmarked for the invasion, notably the 1st Cavalry Division. It landed at P'ohang on the southeast Korean coast to seek out KPA units there. The invasion was postponed first to 10 July and then indefinitely.

Although BLUEHEARTS was not put into effect, MacArthur remained committed to such an amphibious operation. BLUEHEARTS became the basis for his highly successful 15 September 1950 amphibious landing at Inch'ŏn, code-named Operation CHROMITE.

—Sean Williams

References:

Matray, James I., ed. *Historical Dictionary of the Korean War.* Westport, CT: Greenwood Press, 1991.

Rees, David. *Korea: The Limited War.* New York: St. Martin's Press, 1964.

Sheldon, Walt J. *Hell or High Water: MacArthur's Landing at Inchon.* New York: Macmillan, 1968.

See also: Inch'ŏn Landings: Operation CHROMITE; MacArthur, Douglas.

Boatner, Haydon Lemaire
(1900–1977)

U.S. Army general and commander of the Pusan Prisoner-of-War (POW) Command in the Korean War. Haydon L. Boatner, scion of a Louisiana family prominent in military affairs, was born in New Orleans on 8 October 1900. He enlisted in the Marine Corps in 1918 and after World War I attended Tulane University before entering the U.S. Military Academy, from which he was graduated and commissioned a second lieutenant of infantry in 1924. After four years at the Infantry School at Fort Benning, Georgia, Boatner was assigned to the 15th Infantry in Tientsin, China. He studied Chinese and served as assistant military attaché from 1930 to 1934. He then attended the Army Command and General Staff School at Fort Leavenworth, Kansas, graduating in 1939. He subsequently served in various routine infantry assignments until May 1941, when he was assigned to the Lend-Lease Section of the War Department General Staff, where he organized the U.S. military mission to China in August 1941.

Boatner accompanied General Joseph W. Stilwell to Burma in February 1942 and subsequently became chief of staff of the Chinese Army in India. Promoted to brigadier general in November 1942, he commanded combat troops in the Ledo Sector in 1943, and in October 1944 he became commander of the Northern Combat Area Command. He later served as deputy commander of the Chinese Combat Command and represented the United States in negotiations that led to the surrender of Japanese forces in China. After the war, Boatner reverted to colonel and served as the Fourth Army assistant chief of staff for personnel at Fort Sam Houston, Texas, from January 1946 to August 1948, when he became the professor of military science and tactics and commandant of cadets at Texas A&M.

Again promoted to brigadier general in July 1951, Boatner became assistant commander of the 2d Infantry Division in Korea in August 1951 and served with the division until May 1952, when he was chosen to take command of the Kŏje-do POW camp after the rebellion of North Korean and Chinese POWs and the capture of camp commander, Brigadier General Francis T. Dodd. Having no sympathy for the Communist prisoners, "Bull" Boatner ordered United Nations (UN) combat troops into the rebellious POW compounds on 10 June 1952. The rebels were quickly subdued by force, ending the riots and the threat of a mass breakout. Two months later General Boatner was named commander of the Pusan POW Command and became responsible for all POWs held by the UN.

Promoted to major general in August 1952, Boatner returned to the United States in September 1952 and became deputy commander of the Fourth Army. He subsequently commanded the 3d Infantry Division during special tests of new doctrine and equipment at Fort Benning and then served as chief of the Joint U.S. Military Aid Group in Greece from November 1955 until named provost marshal general of the army in

November 1957. Boatner retired from active duty in October 1960 and died on 27 May 1977 in San Antonio, Texas.

—*Charles R. Shrader*

References:

Ancell, R. Manning, and Christine M. Miller. *The Biographical Dictionary of World War II. Generals and Flag Officers—The U. S. Armed Forces.* Westport, CT: Greenwood Press, 1996.

Department of Defense biographical sketch.

Hermes, Walter G. *United States Army in the Korean War: Truce Tent and Fighting Front.* Washington, DC: Office of the Chief of Military History, 1966.

Matray, James I., ed. *Historical Dictionary of the Korean War.* Westport, CT: Greenwood Press, 1991.

Shrader, Charles R., ed. *Reference Guide to United States Military History.* Vol. 5, *1945 to the Present.* New York: Facts on File, 1995.

See also: Dodd-Colson Prisoner-of-War Incident; Kŏje-do Prisoner-of-War Uprising; Prisoner-of-War Administration, United Nations Command.

Bohlen, Charles E.
(1904–1974)

U.S. State Department official. As a member of the Policy Planning Staff from 1950 to 1953, Bohlen advised Secretary of State Dean Acheson on the evolution of U.S. policy during the Korean War. Born in Clayton, New York, on 30 August 1904, the son of a banker and grandson of a former ambassador to France, Charles E. Bolen was educated at St. Paul's School, Concord, New Hampshire, and Harvard University. He joined the U.S. Foreign Service in 1929. There, in company with his lifelong friend George F. Kennan, Bohlen became one of the initially small group of U.S. diplomats trained as Soviet specialists. When the United States resumed diplomatic relations with the Soviet Union in 1933 and reopened its Moscow embassy, Bohlen was one of its three Russian-language officers.

After further assignments in Washington and Tokyo, in 1942 Bohlen became assistant chief of the Russian section of the State Department's Division of European Affairs, and in 1944 he rose to become the division's chief. He attended the Moscow Conference of Foreign Ministers in 1943 and the Teheran and Yalta summits of the Allied leaders in 1944 and 1945, respectively. Although later criticized by Senator Joseph McCarthy for his acquiescence in some of the Yalta decisions, particularly the resignation of much of Eastern Europe to Soviet influence, Bohlen in fact had reservations as to the wisdom of U.S. policies in this area. As with Kennan, he was deeply suspicious of Soviet actions and intentions, believing that Soviet ideology demanded the destruction of capitalism and that this made genuine cooperation impossible. Unlike Kennan, who originally recommended acquiescence in the creation of a Soviet sphere of influence, Bohlen advocated the employment of firm diplomatic pressure to attempt to win Soviet concessions in that area.

Appointed political adviser to the secretary of state in 1946 and counselor to the Department of State in 1947, Bohlen attended most of the major conferences of the time as a member of the U.S. delegation and participated in the development of the Cold War containment policy. Among other responsibilities, he helped to draft Secretary of State George C. Marshall's Harvard University address of June 1947, in which Marshall proposed the European economic aid program that would become the Marshall Plan.

Shortly after the Korean crisis began, Bohlen was temporarily recalled for consultations from the Paris embassy, where he had been transferred as minister in June in 1949. Bohlen's reaction to the Korean War was nuanced and on occasion provoked complaints from Secretary of State Dean Acheson that Bohlen and other Soviet experts were hedging their bets. Bohlen supported U.S. intervention in the conflict but urged restraint, arguing that Stalin's aims were limited to the Korean peninsula and that the invasion of the South was not a prelude to further Soviet military attacks elsewhere in the world, particularly in Europe. Yet Bohlen also warned that the United States must always be on its guard against opportunistic Soviet aggression. The Truman administration effectively rejected his interpretation when it quickly moved to strengthen and reinforce militarily the North Atlantic Treaty Organization in anticipation of a possible Soviet move against West Berlin. In October 1950 Bohlen advised against allowing United Nations forces to cross the 38th parallel into North Korea, advice the Truman administration likewise ignored. When this move resulted in Chinese intervention, Bohlen telephoned Kennan from Paris and forcibly argued that U.S. officials should uncompromisingly resist and fight back rather then embark on negotiations with the Chinese or Soviets from a position of weakness.

In 1951 Bohlen resumed his position of counselor in the State Department itself, serving as its senior representative on the National Security Council's Planning Staff. In August 1951 he accompanied Chairman of the Joint Chiefs of Staff General Omar N. Bradley to Korea, Bohlen's first exposure to the sight of actual combat. This visit convinced Bohlen that a military victory in the war was unlikely, perhaps making him even more anxious that negotiations be pursued at a time and place favorable to the United States. His subsequent involvement in the war was largely related to various aspects of disputes over the contentious and protracted prisoners-of-war issue. In retrospect Bohlen regarded the Korean War as the episode that marked the decisive departure from previous U.S. isolationist policies.

Bohlen subsequently served as ambassador to the Soviet Union, the Philippines, and France; special assistant to the secretary of state from 1959 to 1962 (spanning the Eisenhower and Kennedy administrations); and deputy undersecretary of state from 1968 to 1969, when he retired. He died of cancer on 1 January 1974, in Washington, D.C.

—Priscilla Roberts

References:

Bohlen, Charles E. *Witness to History, 1929–69*. New York: W. W. Norton, 1963.

Isaacson, Walter, and Evan Thomas. *The Wise Men: Six Friends Who Changed the World*. New York: Simon & Schuster, 1986.

Ruddy, T. Michael. *The Cautious Diplomat: Charles E. Bohlen and the Soviet Union, 1929–1969*. Kent, OH: Kent State University Press, 1986.

Sapienza, Madeline. "Charles E. Bohlen." In *Dictionary of American Biography*. Suppl. 9, *1971–1975*, edited by Kenneth T. Jackson. New York: Charles Scribner's Sons, 1994.

See also: Bradley, Omar Nelson; Bradley-Bohlen Mission to Korea; Kennan, George F.; Marshall, George C.; McCarthy, Joseph R.

Bolté, Charles Lawrence
(1895–1989)

U.S. Army general and deputy chief of staff for plans during the Korean War. Charles L. Bolté was born in Chicago on 8 May 1895. He attended student officer training camps and was commissioned a reserve officer in 1916. After his graduation from the Armour Institute of Technology in 1917 with a bachelor of science degree in chemical engineering, Bolté obtained a regular army commission as a second lieutenant of infantry. He served in France during World War I and participated in the Aisne-Marne, St. Mihiel, and Meuse-Argonne campaigns.

In the interwar period, Bolté served with the Historical Branch of the War Department General Staff; as aide-de-camp to the U.S. Army chief of staff; and in Tientsin, China. He completed the Infantry School at Fort Benning, Georgia, in 1927; the Army Command and General Staff School at Fort Leavenworth, Kansas, in 1932; and the Army War College in 1937. He also served as an instructor at both the Infantry School and the Army War College. In 1940 he was a member of the War Planning Group at the Army War College, served temporarily in the office of the Chief of the Air Corps, and was assistant chief of staff for training of IV Corps.

In 1941 Bolté was assigned as officer in charge of war plans for the Special Observer Group in London and subsequently became chief of staff of U.S. forces in the United Kingdom. He was promoted to brigadier general in January 1942 and became the first chief of staff of the European theater of operations. He then returned to the United States and served briefly as assistant commander of the 91st Infantry Division before being promoted to major general in April 1943 and assuming command of the newly activated 69th Infantry Division. In July 1944 he returned to Europe to command the 34th Infantry Division in the heavy fighting in northern Italy and the subsequent occupation.

In November 1945 Bolté was assigned as assistant chief of staff for ground plans, Headquarters, Army Ground Forces, at Fort Monroe, Virginia, and in 1946 he became chief of staff of Army Ground Forces. In 1948 he became director of the Special Joint Planning Group in Washington, and the next year he was named director of the Plans and Operations Division of the U.S. Army General Staff. With the reorganization of Army Headquarters in 1950, Bolté became assistant chief of staff for operations. Promoted lieutenant general in February 1951, he became deputy chief of staff for plans. As the Army's chief planner, Bolté was concerned that overcommitment of U.S. forces in Korea would weaken the defense of other, more vital areas against a possible Soviet attack, and he argued that full mobilization and a change in U.S. global strategy would be necessary to achieve a favorable outcome in the conflict in the Far East. Bolté traveled frequently to the Far East to consult with General Douglas MacArthur and other senior commanders and was in Korea discussing plans for the reduction of United Nations (UN) forces when the Chinese People's Volunteer Army (Chinese Communists) intervened in October 1950. He subsequently recommended the evacuation of UN forces from Korea in anticipation of a global war with the Communists.

In mid-1952 Bolté assumed command of the Seventh U.S. Army in Germany, and in 1953 he became commander in chief, U.S. Army Europe. Promoted to general in July 1953, he returned to Washington in October 1953 and became vice-chief of staff of the army. He retired from active service in April 1955. After his retirement, Bolté chaired the ad hoc committee appointed to study the revision of the Officer Personnel Act of 1947 and was president of various army-related organizations. Bolté died at Mount Vernon, Virginia, on 13 February 1989.

—Charles R. Shrader

References:

Ancell, R. Manning, and Christine M. Miller. *The Biographical Dictionary of World War II. Generals and Flag Officers—The U.S. Armed Forces*. Westport, CT: Greenwood Press, 1996.

Matray, James I., ed. *Historical Dictionary of the Korean War*. Westport, CT: Greenwood Press, 1991.

New York Times, 15 February 1989.

Schnabel, James F. *United States Army in the Korean War: Policy and Direction, The First Year*. Washington, DC: Office of the Chief of Military History, Department of the Army, 1972.

See also: MacArthur, Douglas.

Bond, Niles W.
(1916–)

U.S. Foreign Service officer who had charge of the Korea desk in the State Department from 1949 to 1950. Born on 25 February 1916, in Newton, Massachusetts, Niles W. Bond graduated from the University of North Carolina in 1937. He continued his schooling at the Fletcher School of Law of Diplomacy at Medford, Massachusetts, where he received a master's degree in 1938.

Bond then joined the U.S. Foreign Service. His first assignment was as vice-consul in Havana, Cuba, from 1939 to 1940. He was then posted in Tokyo, where he remained until the Japanese attack on Pearl Harbor. Interned by the Japanese at the start of the war, Bond returned to the United States in August 1942.

During 1942–1945 Bond was vice-consul in the U.S. embassy in Madrid. He then became adviser to the U.S. delegation to the Economic and Social Council until 1947. Bond then spent a short period as vice-consul in Bern, Switzerland. In 1949 he was assigned as assistant chief in the Division of Northeast Asian Affairs and was the officer in charge of Korean Affairs.

In late 1949 Bond traveled to the Republic of Korea (ROK) to assess its military requirements. Upon the outbreak of the Korean War, Bond actively supported expanding ROK military capabilities.

In July 1950 Bond became first secretary on the Tokyo staff of William J. Sebald, political advisor to Commander in Chief United Nations Command General Douglas MacArthur. Bond held this position for two years and then became counselor to the U.S. embassy in Tokyo and from 1953 to 1954 held the same position in the U.S. embassy in the ROK.

After his tour in Korea, Bond held a variety of posts, including in Italy and Brazil. He also served as director of the Office of United Nations Political and Security Affairs. After retiring from the Foreign Service, Bond served as secretary of the Board of Trustees of the Corcoran Gallery of Art.

—Richard Z. Groen

References:

Matray, James I., ed. *Historical Dictionary of the Korean War.* Westport, CT: Greenwood Press, 1991.

U.S. Department of State, Bureau of Public Affairs. *Foreign Relations of the United States, 1950.* Vol. 7, *Korea.* Washington, DC: U.S. Government Printing Office, 1976.

Who's Who in America. Vol. 6, *1949–1950.* Chicago: A. N. Marquis, 1950.

See also: Joint Chiefs of Staff (JCS); MacArthur, Douglas; Sebald, William J.

Bonnet, Henri
(1888–1978)

French ambassador to the United States during the Korean War. Henri Bonnet was born on 26 May 1888, at Châteauponsac, France. He earned a doctorate in history from the University of Paris and then studied at the l'École Normale Supérieure, where he acquired academic credentials as a university professor. He then began teaching at the University of Paris in 1912. Bonnet was drafted as a captain in the French Army during World War I and cited for bravery and honored with the title Chevalier of the Legion of Honor. After the war he was foreign editor of *L'Ere Nouvelle* in 1919.

An expert in foreign relations history, Bonnet gained a post in the Secretariat at the League of Nations from 1920 to 1931. Bonnet's knowledge of international affairs resulted in his appointment as head of the cabinet of the Assistant Secretary-General of the League of Nations. Bonnet also served on the permanent conference of the Hautes Études Internationales, was vice-president of the Center for Studies of Foreign Policy, and a member of the Superior Council of Scientific Research. From 1931 to 1940 he managed the League's International Institute of Intellectual Cooperation.

When the Germans invaded France, Bonnet fled first to London, where he became active in the Free French movement, and then relocated to the United States in 1940 when the New School of Social Research invited him to teach there. He was a political science professor at the École Libre des Hautes Etudes in New York City. By 1941 Bonnet was an adviser to the Worlds Citizens' Association in Chicago, a group that promoted awareness of the world community. He was on the editorial board of the Council of the Free World Association's publication, *Free World*. Bonnet was also vice-president of the International League of Rights of Man.

In 1941 Bonnet published a book, *The World's Destiny and the United States.* The next year he published two books, *The United Nations, What They Are, What They May Become* and *United Nations on the Way: Principles and Policies.* In *Outlines of a Free Future* (1943) Bonnet insisted that there "cannot be a return to the patchwork pattern of nations refusing to recognize their patent interdependence."

Bonnet went to Algiers in 1943 as commissioner of information for the French Committee of National Liberation. By 1944 Bonnet joined the provisional government of the French Republic as a minister of information. That year Charles de Gaulle appointed Bonnet as French ambassador to the United States because of his "experience and personality" and qualities of a "quintessential French diplomat." Bonnet signed the United Nations Charter for France in 1945. He also worked to secure economic aid for Europe through the Marshall Plan and helped establish the North Atlantic Treaty Organization.

When the Korean War began, Bonnet insisted that France have a significant role in developing policy concerning the war. He especially wanted the United States to realize the impact of the Korean War on French Indo-China, where the French were fighting the Communist-led Viet Minh. In 1951 Bonnet initiated a tripartite conference to begin Korean War armistice negotiations. At the Korean War Briefing Meetings, he discouraged diplomats from discussing political matters until after a cease-fire and adequate inspection provisions were secured. Bonnet also followed his diplomatic instructions to request that Indo-China be mentioned in the Joint Policy (Greater Sanctions) Statement, stressing that the Korean armistice would not "jeopardize the restoration or the safeguarding of peace in other parts of Asia."

Bonnet served as French ambassador to the United States until 1955. In retirement he served as vice-president of the France-America Friendship Society and wrote books and articles about foreign affairs and culture. Bonnet died on 25 October 1978 in Paris.

—Elizabeth D. Schafer

References:

Current Biography, 1945. New York: H. W. Wilson, 1946.

New York Times, 6 November 1978.

U.S. Department of State, Bureau of Public Affairs. *Foreign Relations of the United States, 1951.* Vol. 7, Korea and China. Washington, DC: U.S. Government Printing Office, 1983.

U.S. Department of State, Bureau of Public Affairs. *Foreign Relations of the United States, 1952–1954.* Vol. 15, *Korea.* Washington, DC: U.S. Government Printing Office, 1984.

Who Was Who in America. Chicago: Marquis Who's Who, 1985.

See also: Armistice Agreement; Cease-Fire Negotiations; France; Indo-China War, Impact on Korea; NATO (North Atlantic Treaty Organization); Tripartite Meetings.

Border Clashes

(May 1949–June 1950)

When at the end of World War II the United States and the Soviet Union divided the Korean peninsula along the 38th parallel for the purpose of the surrender of Japanese forces, they erected checkpoints and barriers. Japanese soldiers and civilians as well as Koreans passed through these checkpoints. Yet border fighting between the North and South flared up along the parallel in May 1948 when the South held elections under United Nations supervision to establish the Republic of Korea (ROK) government.

Ultimately, border conflicts took hundreds of lives and involved thousands of troops on both sides. Major border conflicts involved battalion-size units on each side. At the same time there were numerous minor patrol skirmishes. Recently declassified Soviet documents reveal that Soviet advisors to the Korean People's Army (KPA) of the Democratic People's Republic of Korea (DPRK, North Korea) were often directly involved in the major border conflicts. A survey of the major border incidents reveals their impact on strategic calculations by Soviet Premier Josef Stalin and DPRK leader Kim Il Sung before the decision to invade South Korea.

On 21 May 1949, minor patrol skirmishes touched off a major border conflict involving the DPRK Border Constabulary on the Ongjin peninsula. The Constabulary occupied strategic positions below the parallel, and the ROK began to bring up reinforcements. On 28 May a KPA battalion again attacked Ongjin. Two battalions of the 12th Regiment of the ROK Army (ROKA) left the port of Inch'ŏn on 29 May to bring total ROKA strength on the Ongjin peninsula to 1,150 army troops and 7,500 police. This incident resulted in the death of several dozen men on each side.

Another major border clash occurred when the DPRK launched a major attack on three points on the Ongjin peninsula—Turak Mountain, Ŭndong-ni, and Kuksa Heights—at 0500 on 4 August 1949. In most previous border clashes the North had mobilized fewer than one or two battalions. The 4 August attack, however, involved approximately two regiments, supported by artillery units. The main assault came directly north of the parallel, at Kuksa Heights, mounted by one regiment reinforced by one battalion and supported by 120-mm mortars and 122-mm howitzers. The objective of the main assault was the city of Ongjin. KPA troops reached the outskirts of Ongjin before ROKA units repulsed them. Early in the battle, two ROKA companies were almost completely wiped out. ROKA losses came to 53 dead and 121 wounded. North Korean casualties reportedly totaled 266 killed, 295 wounded, and 1 captured. The ROKA reinforcement departed Inch'ŏn by landing ship tank at 0300 on 5 August, but the tide prohibited their immediate debarkation. The eventual arrival of the reinforcements brought ROKA strength to roughly two infantry regiments and a battery of 105-mm howitzers. After the ROKA succeeded in dislodging KPA troops from two strategic salients, the region was relatively quiet and serious fighting did not again flare up until mid-October 1949.

Ten days after the clash, on 14 August 1949, DPRK leader Kim Il Sung presented to Soviet Ambassador Terentii F. Shtykov a plan to seize the Ongjin region. The earlier North Korean attack was probably designed to demonstrate the military feasibility of KPA troops occupying the Ongjin region. Kim proposed to destroy two ROKA regiments there and also to occupy, if possible, territory east of the Ongjin peninsula, that is, Kaesŏng. If the ROKA became demoralized in the attack, the KPA would push further south. If the ROKA was not demoralized, it was Kim's intention to seal the territory seized, thus shortening defenses along the parallel by about one-third, that is, about eighty miles.

Because Kim's plan had the possibility of unleashing a general war between the two Korean states, Ambassador Shtykov reported this information personally to Stalin in Moscow on 27 August. The Soviet Politburo met on 24 September and concluded that it was impossible to see the Ongjin operation as other than the beginning of a war between the two Koreas, for which the North was not prepared either militarily or politically. Because of this, it rejected Kim's Ongjin plan.

New evidence from Soviet documents reveals that Stalin now sought to impose tight reins on any DPRK provocation that might escalate into a general war with the ROK. Nonetheless, on 14 October the KPA launched a massive attack on strategic Ŭnp'a Mountain along the 38th parallel, and this directly involved Soviet advisors. After this the Soviet Politburo investigated whether Shtykov had carried out its decision of 24 September, which prohibited the North from provoking a major border incident.

Soviet Deputy Foreign Minister Andrei Gromyko repeated the Politburo's warning to Shtykov and informed him that he was prohibited from recommending to P'yŏngyang that it carry out "active operations" without the prior approval of Moscow. Gromyko also instructed Shtykov to provide timely reports on all plans for such actions and events occurring along the 38th parallel. After this message was delivered to Shtykov and Kim Il Sung, no major border fighting along the 38th parallel occurred until the outbreak of the Korean War in June 1950. The only fighting was in the form of minor patrol skirmishes.

This drop in major border incidents was noted in Far East Command (FEC) intelligence reports. From 21 October 1949 to 14 February 1950, General Douglas MacArthur's FEC intelligence reports noted that recent incidents were all of "a minor nature." When Stalin expressed his desire to approve a DPRK invasion of South Korea and sent military advisors to prepare a plan, no other major border incidents occurred. Stalin sought to curtail border conflicts that might flare up into a general war between the North and South before the DPRK was ready.

This disproves the civil war theory that the war originated as an extension of major border clashes. The Korean War began when and where Stalin regarded it as contributing to the pursuit of his global Cold War strategy and struggle with the United States.

—Youngho Kim

References:

Kim, Youngho. *Han'guk Chŏnjaeng ŭi Kiwŏn kwa Chŏngae Kwajŏng* (The origins and development of the Korean War). Seoul: Dure Publications, 1998.

———. "The Origins of the Korean War: Civil War or Stalin's Rollback?" *Diplomacy & Statecraft* X, no. 1 (March 1999): 186–214.

Weathersby, Kathryn. "The Soviet Role in the Early Phase of the Korean War: New Documentary Evidence." *Journal of American–East Asian Relations* 2, no. 4 (Winter 1993): 425–458.

See also: Gromyko, Andrei Andreyevich; Kim Il Sung; MacArthur, Douglas; Shtykov, Terentii Fomich; Stalin, Josef.

Bowles, Chester
(1901–1986)

U.S. diplomat and ambassador to India from 1951 to 1953. Born on 5 April 1901 to a prosperous New England family, Chester Bowles was educated at the Choate School and Yale University. A founder of the advertising agency Benton and Bowles, he was a liberal Democrat who supported Franklin D. Roosevelt's New Deal reform programs. After holding various Connecticut state positions, in 1943 he became director of the Office of Price Administration and soon became one of the administration's leading liberals. A charter member of Americans for Democratic Action established in January 1947, Bowles was initially friendly to the appeals for cooperation with the Soviet Union made by Henry Wallace and the Progressive Citizens of America, but he moved away from them after the latter's failure to condemn the 1948 Communist coup in Czechoslovakia. In 1948 Bowles initially opposed Harry S. Truman's renomination for the presidency, preferring the more liberal Supreme Court Justice William O. Douglas, although he supported the president after the drive to draft Douglas failed. The same year Bowles won a two-year term as governor of Connecticut, where he implemented major reform measures modeled on the New Deal; in 1950 he lost his reelection campaign to John Davis Lodge.

In 1951 Truman appointed Bowles as ambassador to India, a position in which Bowles made every effort to utilize India's diplomatic contacts with the People's Republic of China (PRC) and the Soviet Union to attain his country's objective of a favorable peace settlement. Personally friendly both to India's domestic reforms and to its nonalignment policy, Bowles urged Prime Minister Jawaharlal Nehru to employ his links with the Communist powers to facilitate peace negotiations, an appeal sympathetic to the Indians, who had already made several initiatives toward a negotiated settlement. Believing, as did the Indians, that the Soviets hoped to prolong the war, Bowles warned Nehru that the United States would extend the fighting unless it was offered a satisfactory settlement. Bowles also relayed to his superiors in Washington the Indian view that the PRC was more eager than the Soviets for an armistice, and he advised that the United States should take advantage of their differences. In November 1952 India's United Nations representative,

V. K. Krishna Menon, introduced a compromise resolution on the difficult and emotional prisoners-of-war issue, which the Soviet Union rejected but the United States endorsed. After Stalin's death in March 1953, the Soviet Union accepted the Menon resolution with modifications, leading to the Armistice Agreement in July. While Bowles' activities were not crucial to the settlement, they assisted in its attainment, and many of his views later proved to be accurate.

After leaving office in 1953, Bowles remained a leading liberal Democrat, always particularly interested in aid to underdeveloped nations and with little faith in Cold War orthodoxies. Under John F. Kennedy he served briefly as undersecretary of state. After his forced resignation from that post in November 1961, Bowles became special adviser on Asian, African, and Latin American Affairs before returning in December 1962 as ambassador to India, where he remained until 1969. Bowles died in Essex, Connecticut, on 25 May 1986.

—Priscilla Roberts

References:

Bowles, Chester. *Ambassador's Report.* New York: Harper, 1954.

———. *Promises to Keep: My Years in Public Life.* New York: Harper, 1971.

"Chester Bowles." In *Political Profiles: The Truman Years,* edited by Eleanora W. Schoenebaum. New York: Facts on File, 1978.

Schaffer, Howard B. *Chester Bowles: New Dealer in the Cold War.* Cambridge, MA: Harvard University Press, 1993.

See also: India; Menon, V. K. Krishna; Nehru, Jawaharlal; Truman, Harry S.

Bowling Alley

Name given by U.S. GIs to a one-mile-long straight stretch of road north of Taegu over which fierce battles were fought between U.S. Army units and the Korean People's Army (KPA, North Korean) during 18–25 August 1950.

As strong KPA forces converged on the South Korean city of Taegu, the 27th Infantry Regiment (Wolfhounds), reinforced, was assigned to back up the 1st Division of the Republic of Korea Army (ROKA), which had been slowly giving ground to numerically superior KPA forces. While ROKA troops held the steep (2,400-foot-high) ground, the Wolfhounds deployed across the main valley road three miles north of Tabu-dong, which is twelve miles north of Taegu. For seven nights the North Koreans attacked down the 200-yard-wide valley, firing tank and self-propelled cannon projectiles, which appeared as balls of fire careening down the corridor similar to bowling balls at a bowling alley. Each night the KPA forces were defeated, suffering heavy infantry casualties and losses in vehicles and equipment. Had the important road hub of Taegu fallen, it would have opened a clear shot for

the KPA to Pusan, which if taken would have doomed U.S. forces in Korea.

Later the Wolfhounds were withdrawn and the 8th Cavalry Regiment was stretched so thin that KPA forces were able, on the night of 2 September, to overrun its 2d Battalion. Desperate fighting limited the KPA advance, however, to about ten miles north of Taegu.

—Jack D. Walker

References:

Appleman, Roy E. *South to the Naktong, North to the Yalu.* Washington, DC: Office of the Chief of Military History, 1961.

Blair, Clay. *The Forgotten War, America in Korea 1950–1953.* New York: Times Books, 1987.

Ent, Uzal W. *Fighting on the Brink: Defense of the Pusan Perimeter.* Paducah, KY: Turner, 1996.

See also: Taegu, Defense of.

Bradley, Omar Nelson
(1893–1981)

U.S. Army general and first chairman of the Joint Chiefs of Staff (1949–1953). Born on 12 February 1893 at Clark, Missouri, Omar Bradley graduated from the U.S. Military Academy, West Point, in 1915 and was commissioned a second lieutenant of infantry. He served in several posts in the United States and was promoted to major in 1918. He taught at West Point and in 1925 graduated from the Infantry School at Fort Benning, Georgia. He then served in Hawaii before graduating from the Command and General Staff School at Fort Leavenworth, Kansas. He served as an instructor at the Infantry School before graduating from the Army War College in 1934. He returned to West Point and in 1936 was promoted to lieutenant colonel. He served on the Army General Staff from 1938 to 1941 and was promoted to brigadier general in February 1941. He then commanded the Infantry School before taking command of the 82d Division. He served briefly as aide to General Dwight Eisenhower and then commanded II Corps at the end of the Tunisian campaign and during the Sicily campaign. He commanded the First Army in the June 1944 invasion of France. In August he received command of the Twelfth Army Group and directed the southern wing of the Allied drive across northern France. At its peak, Twelfth Army Group included 1.3 million men, the largest force ever commanded by a U.S. general. Modest, unassuming, and concerned about the welfare of his men, Bradley was regarded as a "soldier's general" and one of the most successful commanders of the Second World War. He was widely respected for his excellent administrative skills and his calmness when under stress.

Promoted to full general in March 1945, Bradley continued in command of Twelfth Army Group until the end of the war. From 1945 to 1947 he headed the Veterans Administration. In February 1948 he succeeded Eisenhower as Army Chief of Staff and in August 1949 he became the first chairman of the Joint Chiefs of Staff, a post he held throughout the Korean War until August 1953. In September 1950 Bradley was promoted to General of the Army (five-star rank). He disagreed with Secretary of State Dean Acheson's January 1950 definition of a U.S. defensive perimeter that excluded Korea.

During the Korean War Bradley participated in President Harry S. Truman's decision to commit U.S. military forces in the defense of the Republic of Korea. A proponent of U.S. military action, Bradley saw this as a chance to draw a line against Communist expansion. During the war Bradley regularly briefed President Truman on the military situation and he accompanied Truman when he went to Wake Island to meet with MacArthur. Bradley twice visited Korea during the conflict. Throughout, Bradley remained the president's most trusted military adviser.

Bradley sought to limit the conflict and avoid direct conflict with the People's Republic of China. For that reason he opposed using Chinese Nationalist troops in Korea; he also believed they were needed in the defense of Formosa. Bradley fought to keep Europe as the top U.S. military priority, something that General Douglas MacArthur could not appreciate. But Bradley also believed in the domino principle and supported U.S. military aid for the French in Indo-China in the belief that if this was not done the other states of Southeast Asia would become Communist. A realist, he believed that, based on "past performances" by the French, there could be no predications regarding the effects of increased U.S. assistance. Bradley supported Truman in his policies, including the president's dismissal of MacArthur. During the U.S. Senate Foreign Relations and Armed Services Committees hearings to inquire into MacArthur's removal from command, Bradley testified against MacArthur's recommendations. Bradley's attitude toward a widened war in Asia is exemplified in his well-known remark that it would be the "wrong war, in the wrong place, at the wrong time, and with the wrong enemy." Bradley's identification with the Truman administration made him the target of some Republican criticism but he continued as JCS chairman under President Dwight Eisenhower until the expiration of his term in August 1953, when he also retired from the army.

In 1968 Bradley advised President Lyndon Johnson against a U.S. withdrawal from Vietnam. He died in Washington, D.C., on 8 April 1981.

—*Spencer C. Tucker*

References:

Arnold, James R. *The First Domino. Eisenhower, the Military, and America's Intervention in Vietnam.* New York: William Morrow, 1991.

Bradley, Omar N. *A Soldier's Story.* New York: Henry Holt, 1951.

Dupuy, Trevor N., Curt Johnson, and David L. Bongard. *The Harper Encyclopedia of Military Biography.* New York: HarperCollins, 1992.

See also: Acheson, Dean Goodersham; Eisenhower, Dwight D.; MacArthur, Douglas; MacArthur Hearings.

Bradley-Bohlen Mission to Korea
(28 September–3 October 1951)

Fact-finding visit undertaken by Chairman of the Joint Chiefs of Staff General Omar N. Bradley and Counselor to the Department of State Charles E. Bohlen. On 23 August 1951, talks between representatives of the United Nations Command (UNC) and their opponents on a possible truce were suspended after People's Republic of China (PRC) representatives charged that a U.S. airplane had bombed neutral areas around Kaesŏng. President Harry S. Truman's administration was determined to resume the talks as soon as possible, a strategy to which UNC Commander General Matthew B. Ridgway expressed serious reservations. Ridgway believed that Chinese People's Volunteer Army (CPVA, Chinese Communist) forces faced a militarily disadvantageous situation and that a resumption of the talks would benefit them more than it would the UNC. Ridgway also objected to Kaesŏng as a venue for the talks. He made it clear that only direct orders would persuade him to return to the talks. The Bradley-Bohlen visit was an attempt to break this impasse. After lengthy discussions with Ridgway, the two men returned to Washington and submitted a report to the Truman administration.

During this visit, Bradley informed Ridgway that the United States was not prepared to commit further divisions to the Korean conflict because this would require a full mobilization in furtherance of an already unpopular and expensive war. This decision precluded any attempt to make total victory the ultimate goal and implied that the United States would be prepared to negotiate with its opponents. At the same time, the two men accepted Ridgway's contention that the existing military situation was unfavorable to Communist forces and that a resumption of talks would disproportionately benefit them rather than the United States. Bohlen also supported Ridgway's demand that the talks be moved from Kaesŏng. Ultimately P'anmunjŏm became, and would remain, the new site for the talks.

Although in his memoirs Bohlen minimized the mission's broader significance to the Korean War, it can perhaps be regarded as marking the definitive acknowledgment and affirmation of the U.S. decision to wage a limited war, the effective goal of which was the restoration of something fairly close to the antebellum status quo, as opposed to the more ambitious objectives of Korean reunification contemplated by U.S. leaders early in the war.

—*Priscilla Roberts*

References:

Bohlen, Charles E. *Witness to History, 1929–69*. New York: W. W. Norton, 1973.

Bradley, Omar N., and Clay Blair. *A General's Life: An Autobiography*. New York: Simon & Schuster, 1983.

Foot, Rosemary. *A Substitute for Victory: The Politics of Peacemaking at the Korean Armistice Talks*. Ithaca, NY: Cornell University Press, 1990.

Ridgway, Matthew B. *The Korean War: History and Tactics*. New York: Doubleday, 1967.

———. *Soldier: The Memoirs of Matthew B. Ridgway*. New York: Harper, 1956.

See also: Bohlen, Charles E.; Bradley, Omar Nelson; Ridgway, Matthew Bunker.

Brainwashing (Senoe; Xinao)

The behavior of U.S. prisoners of war (POWs) during the Korean War led to a bitter and divisive dispute within the U.S. armed forces over the treatment of these captives and the reasons for the degree to which some collaborated with their captors. During their imprisonment, some U.S. POWs made anti-American propaganda statements, twenty-three chose to remain in China or North Korea, and there were reports of a pervasive collapse of morale and will to resist in the prison camps. The U.S. Army tended to take a harsh view of such conduct, a viewpoint encapsulated in the writings of Eugene Kinkaid. The U.S. Air Force was more sympathetic and endorsed the now-accepted view of Albert D. Biderman that such behavior was far less widespread than was often reported, and, moreover, understandable in view of the persistent indoctrination to which prisoners were often subjected.

Sensational and widely credited rumors circulated to the effect that U.S. prisoners were the victims of brainwashing, which the military termed "a prolonged psychological process designed to erase an individual's past beliefs and concepts and to substitute new ones." These allegations, which informed such films as *The Manchurian Candidate*, were much exaggerated. Prisoners were rarely if ever exposed to effective, deliberate, and systematic efforts to remodel their outlook, though those captured by Chinese troops often experienced clumsier and less well-organized attempts at indoctrination, a process the Chinese termed *xinao*. The North Koreans, by contrast, tended to treat prisoners with far greater brutality, but showed little interest in their reeducation.

The Chinese authorities attempted to use the techniques of social control that they employed in China to persuade their captives to embrace communism and reject their past values and beliefs. Prisoners of the Chinese were segregated by rank, race, and nationality and their leaders removed; bonding and group activities were hampered; and collaboration with their captors was encouraged. In the interests of "reeducation" prisoners were also forced to attend lengthy compulsory political lectures and sometimes compelled to write lengthy self-criticisms and confessions. Cold, hunger, and illness further weakened morale, as did direct violence against those who refused to cooperate. The presence of at least some informers among the prisoners also sapped group spirit and created a pervasive atmosphere of distrust.

Such techniques proved most effective in winning over U.S. conscripts, captured early in the war, who had received inadequate training in resisting indoctrination. U.S. Marines taken prisoner, who had volunteered for military service and had received instruction as to how to handle captivity, generally coped better. Although most U.S. POWs cooperated with their jailers, relatively few actively collaborated, and even those who did generally repudiated their conduct once released. By early 1952 the Chinese had decided that their policy of compulsory indoctrination was a failure and abandoned it, denying that it had ever been instituted. Those prisoners regarded as "reactionary" leaders of resistance to *xinao* faced reprisals, and others underwent extensive interrogations.

After the war, the degree to which U.S. POWs had succumbed to indoctrination became a vexing issue within the military. Those unsympathetic to any cooperation whatsoever argued that the readiness of prisoners to provide any information beyond name, rank, and serial number or to work with their captors at all proved that Americans lacked discipline and had grown soft. Others took the more charitable line that this simply demonstrated that U.S. recruits required more effective training in how to handle imprisonment. While it was often alleged that British prisoners had shown more resilience in captivity, studies demonstrated that in practice their record of resistance was little better than the American. Turkish prisoners, another role model often cited, who did prove less susceptible to indoctrination, were helped by the fact that few Chinese were fluent in their language and also by a policy of ruthlessly executing suspected informers.

In the long run, these allegations led to a strengthening of escape and evasion training within the Western alliance's armed forces and attempts to address the pressures to which captured soldiers might be subjected. In 1955 President Dwight D. Eisenhower announced a six-point Code of Conduct for U.S. POWs that remained in force throughout the Vietnam War. In the late 1980s television appearances by captured U.S. and British airmen during the Gulf War once again forcibly reminded the public that, stimulated by violence and fear, even well-trained military personnel could be temporarily persuaded to renounce their loyalties and endorse their opponent's cause.

—*Priscilla Roberts*

References:

Biderman, Albert D. *March to Calumny: The Story of American POWs in the Korean War.* New York: Macmillan, 1963.

Cunningham, Cyril. "The Origins and Development of Communist Prisoner-of-War Policies." *Journal of the Royal United Services Institution* 119, no. 1 (March 1974): 38–43.

Grey, Jeffrey. "Commonwealth Prisoners of War and British Policy during the Korean War. *Journal of the Royal United Services Institution* 133, no. 1 (Spring 1988): 71–77.

Kinkead, Eugene. *In Every War but One.* New York: W. W. Norton, 1959.

Sandler, Stanley, ed. *The Korean War: An Encyclopedia.* New York: Garland, 1995.

White, William L. *Captives of Korea.* New York: Charles Scribner's Sons, 1955.

See also: Eisenhower, Dwight D.; Prisoner-of-War Administration, Communist; Prisoners of War, Rescreening of; Prisoner-of-War Code of Conduct.

Bridgeford, General Sir William
(1894–1971)

Commander of British Commonwealth forces in the Korean War from 1951 to 1953. Born on 28 July 1894, at Ballarat, Australia, General Sir William Bridgeford was educated at Ballarat High School and the Royal Military College, Duntroon. Service in France during World War I won him a Military Cross, and between the wars he filled a variety of staff and training positions in the small Australian Army, as well as took further courses at the Staff College, Quetta, and the Imperial Defence College, London.

By the late 1930s Bridgeford seemed marked for high rank, though advancement and a high command during World War II came more slowly than expected, probably from personal enmities he attracted in the Greek campaign at the beginning of the war. After commanding the 25th Australian Infantry Brigade in Britain and serving in the Middle East and Greece, in 1942 he returned to Australia, serving in New Guinea and commanding the 3d Armoured Division in the Bougainville campaign. After the war, Bridgeford, an excellent administrator, became quartermaster-general of the Australian Military Forces, and in summer 1950 he headed an Australian military mission to Malaya with the aim of making recommendations to the Australian government as to how to support the British anti-insurgency campaign there. The outbreak of the Korean War preempted such plans and diverted Australian assistance to General Douglas MacArthur's United Nations (UN) forces.

In November 1951 Bridgeford, whose undoubted abilities coexisted with an easygoing and genial personality, was sent to Korea to replace Sir Horace Robertson as Commonwealth commander in chief. Robertson's acerbic temperament had strained Australian relations with top British Foreign Office and military personalities and with his own British subordinates. Bridgeford's more congenial style quickly smoothed over the tensions and difficulties that had developed under his predecessor. In May 1952 circumstances forced Bridgeford to tackle one serious rift among the Commonwealth allies, when at the request of UN Command Commander in Chief General Mark W. Clark he approved the transfer of British and Canadian troops to Kŏje-do to guard Chinese and North Korean prisoner-of-war camps. Riots had already occurred among these prisoners, and the U.S. and South Korean troops had suppressed the uprisings by force. Wishing to avoid any potential unpleasantness, the Canadian government claimed that Bridgeford's decision to transfer its troops to the island was unauthorized, and Canada demanded his dismissal. The British and Australian governments stood behind him, and Bridgeford retained his position until February 1953.

This incident apart, Bridgeford's tenure in Korea was uneventful. He retired from the army in 1953 and soon afterwards became chief executive officer of the 1956 Melbourne Olympic Games. Bridgeford retained a strong interest in sports activities until his death in Brisbane on 21 September 1971.

—*Priscilla Roberts*

References:

Grey, Jeffrey. "Bridgeford, Sir William." In *Australian Dictionary of Biography.* Vol. 13, *1940–1980,* edited by John Ritchie and Christopher Duneen. Melbourne: Melbourne University Press, 1993.

———. *The Commonwealth Armies and the Korean War: An Alliance Study.* Manchester: Manchester University Press, 1988.

O'Neill, Robert J. *Australia in the Korean War 1950-1953.* 2 vols. Canberra: Australian War Memorial/Australian Government Publishing Service, 1981, 1985.

Wood, James. *The Forgotten Force: The Australian Military Contribution to the Occupation of Japan, 1945–1952.* St. Leonards, NSW, Australia: Allen & Unwin, 1998.

See also: Australia; Clark, Mark W.; Far East Command (FEC); MacArthur, Douglas; Robertson, Sir Horace C. H.

Briggs, Ellis
(1899–1976)

U.S. diplomat and ambassador to the Republic of Korea (ROK, South Korea), 1952–1959. Born on 1 December 1899, in Watertown, Massachusetts, and raised in Riverdale, New York, Ellis Briggs graduated from Dartmouth in 1921 with a degree in international relations. He then moved to Istanbul and taught at Robert College there for three years.

In 1925 Briggs joined the State Department and served in a variety of minor posts during 1926–1944 in Latin America and in Washington. He was ambassador to the Dominican Republic in 1944, and in 1945 he was minister-counselor in Chongqing (Chungking), the wartime capital of the Republic of China. He then served as director of the Office of American Republic Affairs in Washington. Briggs was subsequently ambassador to Uruguay (1947–1949), Czechoslovakia (1949–1952), South Korea (1952–1955), Peru (1955–1956), Brazil (1956–1959), and Greece (1959–1961).

On 15 November 1952, President Harry S. Truman appointed the staunch anti-Communist Briggs to replace John J. Muccio as ambassador to the ROK. Briggs held the post throughout the remainder of the war. One of his main tasks was to improve the relationship between ROK President Syngman Rhee and the United States. This task proved an arduous one, not only because of Briggs's own views on issues such as the unification of Korea, the ROK Army, and the armistice, but because he, along with General Mark Clark, found it difficult to meet Rhee's demands. Briggs worked hard with Clark to finalize the armistice and to negotiate a $700 million ROK economic aid package, which helped ease Rhee's intransigence.

Briggs left his Korea post in 1959. Promoted in 1960 to the highest rank in the Foreign Service, career ambassador, he was unable to take up the post as ambassador to Spain the next year because of poor health, thus he retired from the State Department. Briggs published several magazine articles and reports on Korea as well as three books: *Shots Heard Round the World* (1957), *Farewell to Foggy Bottom* (1964), and *Anatomy of Diplomacy* (1968). Briggs died in Gainesville, Georgia, on 21 February 1976.

—*Monica Spicer*

References:
Findling, John. *The Dictionary of Diplomatic History.* Westport, CT: Greenwood Press, 1980.
Matray, James I., ed. *Historical Dictionary of the Korean War.* Westport, CT: Greenwood Press, 1991.
New York Times, 23 February 1976.
Who's Who in America. Chicago: Marquis Who's Who, 1976.
See also: Clark, Mark W.; Eisenhower, Dwight D.; Muccio, John J.; Syngman Rhee; Truman, Harry S.

Briscoe, Robert Pierce
(1897–1968)

U.S. Navy admiral and commander of U.S. Naval Forces, Far East (NAVFE), during the Korean War. Born on 19 February 1897, in Centerville, Missouri, Robert P. Briscoe graduated in 1918 from the U.S. Naval Academy, Annapolis, and was assigned to con-

voy duties during World War I. After the war he served as an instructor at the Naval Academy, on the Yangtze River Patrol in China, and then back at the Naval Academy as head of the Chemistry Department.

In 1937 Briscoe became navigation officer aboard the *Mississippi,* after which he was executive officer of the U.S. Naval Research Laboratory. A pioneer in modern naval electronics, he also served as Navy Department liaison officer with the National Defense Research Committee.

In May 1942 Briscoe commanded the Third Fleet repair ship *Prometheus* in the Pacific theater. He then commanded Destroyer Squadron 5. In July 1943 Briscoe assumed command of the cruiser *Denver* in the Solomon Islands. Off Rabaul that November the *Denver* took an aerial torpedo that inflicted serious damage. During the 36-hour battle, the *Denver* shot down seventeen Japanese planes and assisted in sinking five Japanese ships and damaging four others.

In 1945 Briscoe commanded the Operational Development Force of fifty ships that tested new equipment and weapons along the Atlantic coast. In 1950 he commanded the amphibious force of the Atlantic Fleet, and in January 1952 he took command of the Seventh Fleet. On 4 June 1952, when Vice Admiral C. Turner Joy took over armistice negotiations, Vice Admiral Briscoe became commander of NAVFE.

In 1954 Briscoe became Deputy Chief of Naval Operations and during 1956–1959 he commanded North Atlantic Treaty Organization forces in southern Europe. Briscoe retired from active duty in January 1959 and died in Liberty, Mississippi, on 14 October 1968.

—*Spencer C. Tucker*

References:
Cagle, Malcolm W., and Frank A. Manson. *The Sea War in Korea.* Annapolis, MD: Naval Institute Press, 1957.
Field, James A., Jr. History of *United States Naval Operations: Korea.* Washington, DC: U.S. Government Printing Office , 1962.
Hallion, Richard P. *The Naval Air War in Korea.* Baltimore: Nautical and Aviation Publishing Co. of America, 1986.
New York Times, 16 October 1968.
Summers, Harry G., Jr. *Korean War Almanac.* New York: Facts on File, 1990.
See also: Naval Forces Far East (NAVFE), United States: Navy.

"Bug-out Fever"

Term that in its most unsavory meaning meant to run away from the enemy with little or no fighting. Anyone or any unit that hurriedly left a position in withdrawal was often accused of "bugging out." It originated from some unknown soldier in the first days of the Korean War. Used as two words, "bug out," it often indicated that one was leaving a place soon and rapidly, but not necessarily to escape the enemy, for example, "I'm going to bug out of here, if certain things happen, or fail to happen." It was even a song, using the melody from Hank Snow's country and western song, *Movin' On*. Members of one regiment were supposed to have made up a march cadence, including the words, "bugging out." Even historians and writers of military history have used the term. One writer wrongly ascribed the delaying actions fought by U.S. troops in the first week of the war as a "'bugout' war." He did not understand that the mission at the time was not to defend, but to delay, get the enemy to deploy, hold as long as possible, and then withdraw. Other writers have perpetuated the myth of "bug-out fever" with such statements as describing one command as "a bug-out unit," or that another command had "bugged out" of a series of battles.

It is true that some units had more staying power in battle than others, and that some squads, platoons, and on occasion a very few companies did give ground. This was usually determined by the level of leadership within the unit at the time. Soldiers recognize good leaders and obey them. Units with more staying power were usually those that had, and retained, good leaders.

It is also true that occasionally during the delaying stage of the war some withdrawals were quick and disorganized. But there is no evidence that any battalion or larger-sized command pulled out without orders or that companies and smaller units that did abandon positions withdrew just far enough to escape ground, mortar, and/or artillery assaults on their positions. For example, units of the regiment defending Sŏbuk-san Ridge and Old Baldy along the Naktong River often withdrew or were forced from position, but they never abandoned either of these mountains to the enemy. If they had, it would have constituted a "bug out."

That there was anything like a "bug-out fever" among any U.S. troops in the Korean War is a myth, perpetuated by writers ignorant of the facts. If there had been such a malady, the Korean People's Army (KPA, North Koreans) would have been victorious within two months of the beginning of the war.

As it was, the first two months of the Korean War were two of the bloodiest months of the entire thirty-seven month war. That, in itself, attests to the hard and determined fighting by U.S. and Republic of Korea (South Koren) troops, foiling every KPA thrust into the Pusan perimeter.

—*Uzal W. Ent*

References:

Appleman, Roy E. *South to the Naktong, North to the Yalu.* Washington, DC: Office of the Chief of Military History, 1961.

Ent, Uzal W. *Fighting on the Brink: Defense of the Pusan Perimeter.* Paducah, KY: Turner, 1996.

Goulden, Joseph C. *Korea: The Untold Story of the War.* New York: Times Books, 1982.

Hoyt, Edwin P. *The Pusan Perimeter.* New York: Stein & Day, 1984.

See also: Korea, Democratic People's Republic of: Army (Korean People's Army [KPA]); Korea, Republic of: Army (ROKA); United States: Army.

Bunker Hill, Battle of
(16–18 May 1951)

Battle that took place during the Chinese 1951 spring offensives. The Battle of Bunker Hill, 16–18 May, involved the 38th Infantry Regiment of the U.S. 2d Division, a unit belonging to X Corps, Eighth Army, which at the time called the fighting the Battle of the Soyang River.

The Communist offensive began at the west end of the Eighth Army line on 22 April and had as its immediate objective the capture of Seoul and encirclement of United Nations Command (UNC) troops in the area. Once this goal was achieved, Communist forces hoped to continue their drive and push all UN forces from the entire Korean peninsula. The first phase of the offensive, lasting eight days, failed in its immediate objective, but the Chinese then shifted the second phase of their attack to the X Corps area in the center of the peninsula. It was not until the beginning of May 1951 that UN intelligence sources determined that the new Communist attacks would be coming on its new positions, called the No Name Line.

Major General Clark I. Ruffner's 2d Infantry Division occupied the center position of the No Name Line, stretching sixteen miles by air along the crest of a great, rugged hill mass separating the rivers Hongch'ŏn and Soyang. The division's 3d Battalion, 38th Infantry, held four miles of the line and anchored its defense on Hill 800, which they later nicknamed "Bunker Hill."

In preparation for the expected Communist attacks, a series of twenty-three heavily fortified bunkers were constructed on and around Hill 800, protected by 237,000 sandbags, 385 rolls of barbed wire, and 39 55-gallon fougasse drums. The most probable routes of advance were covered, and patrols were sent out to look for signs of Communist activity. By 14 May the positions atop Bunker Hill were among the strongest ever constructed anywhere during the Korean War.

At Bunker Hill the Chinese hoped to pierce the UN main line of resistance during phase two of their spring offensive. Phase two began on the afternoon of 16 May with attacks on Hill 800. To the sounds of whistles and bugles, the Chinese attacked and managed to push the U.S. forces from a portion of the hill. The next day, however, the U.S. troops counterattacked and regained the crest after their initial attacks with further assaults to straighten the line and remove upward of several hundred Chinese still occupying bunkers in a bulge on the Hill 800 position. By the morning of 18 May, Hill 800 was again firmly in U.S. hands.

At daylight on 19 May, the Chinese disengaged and left the area. Because Hill 800 was the northern most point along the entire UN line and formed a salient into Communist-held territory, the decision was made to withdraw the survivors of the 38th Infantry later that same day.

—Clayton D. Laurie

References:

Gugeler, Russell A. Combat Actions in Korea: Infantry, Artillery, Armor. Washington, DC: Combat Forces Press, 1954.

Miller, John, Jr., Owen J. Carroll, and Margaret E. Tackley. Korea, 1951–1953. Washington, DC: U.S. Army Center of Military History, 1989.

Mossman, Billy C. U.S. Army in the Korean War: Ebb and Flow, November 1950–July 1951. Washington, DC: U.S. Army Center of Military History, 1990.

See also: Chinese Military Offensives.

Burke, Arleigh Albert
(1901–1996)

U.S. Navy admiral who during the Korean War worked on the Inch'ŏn landing and was a member of the United Nations (UN) team that negotiated the Armistice Agreement. Born on a farm outside Boulder, Colorado, on 19 October 1901, Arleigh Albert Burke graduated from the U.S. Naval Academy, Annapolis, in 1923. He first attracted national attention during World War II as a destroyer squadron commander, earning the nickname "31-Knot Burke." In 1944 he became deputy chief of staff to Vice Admiral Marc "Pete" Mitscher, commander of U.S. Naval Forces Far East (ComNAVFE), and served in that post until the end of the war.

When the Korean War began, Rear Admiral Burke was serving as the navy member of the Defense Research and Development Board. Burke then became deputy chief of staff to Vice Admiral C. Turner Joy, ComNAVFE, in Tokyo. Burke had charge of operational planning and coordinated naval support for the September 1950 amphibious landing at Inch'ŏn. Burke coordinated activities for the 71,000-man landing force and 230-ship international fleet. After the successful landing, Burke secured Japanese minesweepers to clear the harbor of Wŏnsan before the U.S. landing there on 25 October 1950. Thereafter, Burke repeatedly advised against further troop movements northward toward the Chinese border.

In May 1951 Burke's Tokyo assignment ended. Commander of the Sixth Fleet Admiral Forrest P. Sherman ordered him to command Cruiser Division 5,

tasked with providing gunfire support for U.S. forces ashore. In early July Burke was unexpectedly albeit temporarily detached from Cruiser Division 5 to join the UN Military Armistice Delegation headed by Joy. According to Burke's biographer, E. B. Potter, this was perhaps "the most important mission of his life."

One of the thorniest problems of the truce talks was the location of the dividing line between North and South Korea. To resolve this impasse, the opposing delegations appointed subcommittees, which included Burke on the UN Command side. When these failed to reach agreement, on 23 August the Communist side suspended negotiations for two months, and Burke found the delay frustrating.

Peace talks resumed on 25 October in P'anmunjŏm. Burke and Major General Henry Hodes negotiated the precise demarcation line between Kaesŏng and Kŭmsŏng. During the diplomatic sessions, Washington intervened, ordering the acceptance of a final demarcation line and cease-fire. Stunned at this, Burke and the other members threatened to resign. Eighth Army commander General Matthew B. Ridgway convinced the negotiating team to return to the truce table and settle on the agreed-upon line of 27 November 1951. Burke then requested to be relieved of duty. Afterward, Hodes, the senior subcommittee member, praised Burke's performance and added that if he ever headed another delegation, "I would want Burke first."

Burke returned to the United States in December 1951. He aired his complaints about the conduct of the war and the cease-fire to Chief of Naval Operations (CNO) Admiral William Fechteler and to the Joint Chiefs of Staff. He also briefed President Harry S. Truman and repeated his suspicions of Communist espionage activities during the peace negotiations. He further recommended cancellation of the cease-fire until the Democratic People's Republic of Korea (North Korea) accepted a reasonable exchange of prisoners of war and enforcement of the armistice.

During the war Burke also took interest in the establishment of a navy for the Republic of Korea (ROK). On visiting the new ROK naval academy at Chinhae, he noted that the struggling young school lacked adequate books and penned an appeal, "Books for Korea," published in 1951 in the U.S. Naval Institute Proceedings. U.S. colleges and naval organizations responded by donating more than 20,000 books to the academy's library.

After the war President Dwight D. Eisenhower appointed Burke, then 54, as CNO over ninety-two more-senior naval officers. Burke played a major role in bringing the U.S. Navy into the nuclear age and served an unprecedented three terms as CNO from 1955 to 1961. In 1977 President Gerald Ford conferred on Burke the Medal of Freedom, and in 1989 a new class of guided-missile destroyers was named for him. Burke died on 1 January 1996, at Bethesda, Maryland.

—*Mary L. Kelley*

References:

Blair, Clay. *The Forgotten War: America in Korea, 1950–1953.* New York: Times Books, 1987.

Cagle, Malcolm W., and Frank A. Manson. *The Sea War in Korea.* Annapolis, MD: Naval Institute Press, 1957.

Potter, E. B. *Admiral Arleigh Burke: A Biography.* New York: Random House, 1990.

See also: Armistice Agreement; Cease-Fire Negotiations; Eisenhower, Dwight D.; Fechteler, William; Inch'ŏn Landings: Operation CHROMITE; Joy, Charles Turner; Kaesŏng Truce Talks; Mine Warfare; Naval Forces Far East (NAVFE); Naval Gunfire Support; P'anmunjŏm Truce Talks; Pusan Perimeter and Breakout; Ridgway, Matthew Bunker; Sherman, Forrest P.; Truman, Harry S.; United Nations Cease-Fire Group; Wŏnsan Landing.

C

Cai Chengwen (Tsai Cheng-wen)
(1915–)

People's Republic of China (PRC) diplomat; chargé d'affaires, and interim chief of the Chinese embassy in P'yŏngyang during the Korean War; military liaison officer in the armistice talks, 1951–1953; and member of the Cease-Fire Committee, July 1953–October 1954. Born in Shuiping, Henan Province, China, in 1915, Cai Chengwen joined the Chinese Communist Eighth Route Army in 1937 and was a military intelligence officer during the Chinese Civil War (1946–1949).

In 1950 Cai was among a group of senior military officers who transferred from the military to the Ministry of Foreign Affairs. In May 1950 he was ordered to report to Zhou Enlai in Beijing. His original assignment was to establish a Chinese mission in Berlin, but when he arrived in Beijing, the Korean War had begun. On 30 June, Zhou Enlai gave Cai a new assignment. With Chinese ambassador to the Democratic People's Republic of Korea (DPRK, North Korea) Ni Zhiliang on sick leave in Beijing, Zhou En Lai ordered Cai to go to P'yŏngyang as chargé d'affaires and interim head of the Chinese embassy and establish contact with DPRK leader Kim Il Sung. The People's Liberation Army (PLA) General Staff wanted to send a small group of military observers to P'yŏngyang, but Zhou Enlai insisted that Cai would suffice. After his first meet with Kim Il Sung, Cai established a direct line to talk to the DPRK leader, and he helped Chinese leaders in Beijing to communicate directly with the North Korean leadership. His official title was later changed to counselor for political affairs in the Chinese embassy.

From July 1951 on, Cai was involved in the armistice talks as secretary-general of the Chinese delegation and one of three military liaison officers, the only one from China, in contact with the United Nations side. Cai coordinated negotiation strategies and tactics between the Chinese and DPRK delegations. After the Armistice Agreement was signed, Cai became the Chinese member on the Joint Cease-Fire Committee until October 1954, when the Chinese transferred all negotiation duties to the DPRK.

Cai was then assigned to the PRC legation in Denmark. After his years in Korea and Denmark, Cai returned to the PLA General Staff in 1956 as deputy director of the Military Intelligence Department. He was promoted to major general in 1961. He later became director of Foreign Affairs at the Ministry of National Defense until he retired in 1982.

—*Richard Weixing Hu*

References:
Guo Huaruo et al., eds. *Jiefangjun Junshi Dacidian* [Dictionary of CPLA military history]. Changchun: Jilin People's Press, 1993.
Wu Rugao et al., eds. *Zhongguo Junshi Renwu Dacidian* [Dictionary of Chinese military figures]. Beijing: Xinhua Chubanshe, 1989.
Zhongguo Junshi Dabaike Quanshu [Chinese military encyclopedia]. Military History, Vol. 1. Beijing: Military Science Press, 1997.
Zhongguo Renmin Zhiyuanjun Renwu Zhi [Biographies of CPVA figures]. Nanjing: Jiangsu Renmin Chubanshe, 1993.
See also: China, People's Republic of; Kim Il Sung; Zhou Enlai.

Cairo Declaration
(1 December 1943)

During World War II in the fall of 1943 the United States initiated the Cairo Conference. President Franklin D. Roosevelt wanted a meeting with British Prime Minister Winston Churchill and Republic of China leader Jiang Jieshi (Ching Kai-shek). Roosevelt hoped to raise the prestige of Jiang's regime and strengthen Chinese opposition to Japan's aggression. He also sought to promote his view of post–World War II Far Eastern power relations. Desirous of a powerful China reaffirming its historic interest in preventing a Japanese-dominated Korea, Roosevelt sought Jiang's pledge regarding postwar Korea. He assumed that China wanted some involvement in a trusteeship on the peninsula once Japan surrendered. Although Jiang favored independence for Korea, Roosevelt's ideas influenced developments.

On 1 December 1943 the three leaders issued the Cairo Declaration. In addition to stripping Japan's prewar territorial acquisitions to China, the statement was a strong support for Korean independence: "The aforesaid three great powers, mindful of the enslavement of the people of Korea, are determined that in due course Korea shall become free and independent."

Roosevelt did not confer with the Department of State, and U.S. East Asian specialists played no role in writing the declaration. Thus the clause regarding Korea manifested itself in different versions. A U.S. version of 24 November said that Korea should have self-government "at the earliest possible moment." The following day Roosevelt changed the wording to proclaim "at the proper moment." Ultimately Churchill's phrase "in due course" was accepted by the United States and the USSR.

Koreans hailed the Cairo Declaration's independence pledge but denounced any suggestion of delayed implementation. Understanding the implication that Korea would be unprepared for freedom by World War II's end, Korean patriots recalled comparable Japanese terminology. Indeed, Japanese Premier Hara Kei had employed an expression likewise interpreted as "in due course" when he announced Tokyo's "cultural policy" toward the peninsula after the 1919 March First Movement.Thus the remaining war years saw Korean nationalists and their expatriate newspapers attacking the declaration. Syngman Rhee and Kim Ku censured it, as did the exile journal *The Voice of Korea*. In time, Korean associations in the United States and Hawaii complained to the U.S. Congress.

Korean exiles in China undermined the Cairo Declaration by construing the English expression "in due course" as "immediately" or "within a few days," since there was no Korean language equivalent. Reprints imported secretly into the peninsula aroused the expectations of the Korean people.

—*Rodney J. Ross*

References:

Cumings, Bruce. *The Origins of the Korean War.* Vol. 1, *Liberation and the Emergence of Separate Regimes, 1945–1947.* Princeton, NJ: Princeton University Press, 1981.

Dobbs, Charles M. *The Unwanted Symbol: American Foreign Policy, the Cold War, and Korea, 1945–1950.* Kent, OH: Kent State University Press, 1981.

Liu, Xiaoyuan. *A Partnership for Disorder: China, the United States, and Their Policies for the Postwar Disposition of the Japanese Empire, 1941–1945.* New York: Cambridge University Press, 1996.

See also: Churchill, Sir Winston Spencer; Jiang Jieshi (Chiang Kai-shek); Syngman Rhee.

Canada

Canada not only sent troops to fight in the Korean War but played a role in the formulation of United Nations (UN) policies toward the war. Canada became involved in the Korean War primarily to support the concept of collective security and the viability of the UN to provide it. In the immediate post–World War II era, Canada had also accepted the basic Western anti-Communist views and espoused its containment around the world. The problem was that Canada's focus for this concern had been North American defense and security of Europe through the North Atlantic Treaty Organization (NATO). The Canadian government had not been particularly interested in Asia. However, the Democratic People's Republic of Korea (DPRK, North Korean) invasion of the Republic of Korea (South Korea) forced Canadians to rethink these principles.

During the Korean War, Canadian Secretary of State for External Affairs Lester Pearson often played a pivotal role in the diplomatic evolution of UN resolutions and tactics. He was, for instance, Canada's representative for the UN Cease-Fire Group and in the delicate negotiations over arranging a compromise on the issue of prisoner-of-war (POW) repatriation. Pearson was also president of the UN General Assembly during the end of the war in 1952–1953.

In addition to this activity, the Canadians worked to moderate the dominant U.S. role in the war both by direct diplomacy and, especially, by the use of the UN framework. While they generally agreed in principle with U.S. ideas and ideals, Canadians feared that the United States could, on occasion, become too ideologically driven and too radical in its methods to win the war. The Canadian government wanted to limit the geographical extent of the war to the Korean peninsula and opposed any action that could provoke the Chinese to intervene in the fighting. Canada agreed only reluctantly with the plan to cross north of the 38th parallel to liberate North Korea from the Communists. It was nervous about the movement of UN forces too close to the Chinese border and about UN planes violating Chinese airspace to pursue Communist aircraft and bomb staging areas. Since UN Supreme Commander Douglas MacArthur either did or advocated all of these things, the Canadians were anxious about his power and relieved over his dismissal.

As a result of Canadian diplomatic maneuvering, often in league with the British, the U.S. State Department began to view the Canadians as being surprisingly uncooperative and even untrustworthy. Although the two nations' ideas were not really that far apart, there were, at times, differences in strategies and goals. The Canadian hope for Korea was simply fulfillment of the original UN mandate of throwing back DPRK aggression and returning to the antebellum status quo. Any thought of becoming heavily involved in an Asian war or of liberating Communist nations there was not part of the Canadian agenda. It was Pearson, in particular, who saw the forum of the UN as a mechanism for reining in any U.S. plans that attempted to move beyond these basic UN goals.

When the war began, the Canadian government saw the need to become militarily involved, but it wanted that involvement to be limited to the sending of three destroyers and the provision of an air transport group. The Canadian armed forces, which had cut back drastically at the end of World War II, could not find the resources to commit troops to North America, NATO, and Korea. There were also historical reasons for being reluctant to increase the size of the military to fight a war in Asia. Large segments of the population, particularly in the French-speaking province of

Quebec, would no doubt oppose the use of conscription for overseas service as they had in both world wars. Also, Canadians had once before sent men to an Asian war with disastrous results. In 1941 partially trained Canadian infantry were rushed to the defense of Hong Kong only to be quickly killed or captured by the invading Japanese. It was a memory that was still vivid a decade later.

And yet, despite these factors, the response of the Canadian press and public to the government's contribution to the UN force was one of dismay over its perceived tokenism. This, coupled with growing pressure from the UN and from its U.S. and British allies, finally led Prime Minister Louis St. Laurent to announce in August 1950 the creation of a Canadian Army Special Force. It was to be made up of volunteers and was especially meant to attract veterans of World War II. The call was an overwhelming success, even in Quebec, which supplied nearly one-third of the total number of recruits. In fact, the enthusiasm for joining the unit was so high across the country that military authorities originally could barely cope with the numbers. Because of this, many of the early enlistees were found within the initial seven months to be unfit for service. Most of the men who were accepted appear to have enlisted for an adventure and not because of economic hardship or any ideological imperative to fight communism. As many as 45 percent were veterans of World War II, including no doubt some who had had difficulty readjusting to civilian life after 1945. For whatever reasons these men joined, their actions saved the government from the political turmoil that undoubtedly would have occurred if conscription had been needed to fill the Korean force.

The initial unit sent was the 2d Battalion of the Princess Patricia's Canadian Light Infantry, more than 900 men who arrived at Pusan, Korea, on 18 December 1950. Pushed at first to join the battlefront as quickly as possible, they insisted on further training and did not go forward until February 1951. They were part of the UN forces that blunted a Chinese attack at Kap'yŏng in April 1951. For twenty-four hours the Canadian unit was surrounded; it drove off the Chinese only by calling down an Allied artillery barrage on its own position. The rest of the Canadian brigade had, in the meantime, been trained at Fort Lewis, Washington, and arrived in Korea on 25 May 1951, almost a year after the war had begun. These men fought in the numerous small and violent battles and raids that were the hallmark of the stalemate of the last two years of the war. In addition to ground forces, the Royal Canadian Navy participated in the blockade of Korea's west coast, and a number of Canadian airmen served with the U.S. Air Force over Korea.

From the beginning there was pressure for the Canadian infantry to become part of a Commonwealth unit alongside the soldiers of Britain, Australia, and New Zealand. A number of political groups within Canada and the Commonwealth governments were keen on this either for the cause of imperial unity or for military efficiency. The Canadian government, however, was hesitant to follow this plan, preferring its troops to be identified only as a UN force that would not be subsumed into a Commonwealth designation seen to be British in nature. Also, Canada had moved much closer to U.S. models of military equipment than had any other Commonwealth member, making it less compatible with the British style. In the end, the Canadians agreed to be part of the 1st Commonwealth Division that became operational on 28 July 1951.

This Canadian tilt toward U.S. military practice and weaponry was the natural outcome of the physical and economic closeness of the United States to Canada. Military integration between the two countries had begun during World War II with the 1941 Hyde Park Agreement. The concepts embodied in that pact were resuscitated during the Korean War by the formation of the Joint United States–Canada Industrial Mobilization Planning Committee. The defense production coordination that this created fit well into the urgent need Canada had to rearm. The logical source of much of this rearmament came from the United States. It all went to enhance the economic integration of the northern half of North America throughout the Cold War era and beyond.

This growing economic and military interaction occurred, nevertheless, during the time that the two nations were bickering over the war's strategy. One of the most heated of the Canadian responses to U.S. command decisions came in the spring of 1952. As a result of violent riots and acts of lawlessness by the Chinese prisoners at the UN POW camp at Kŏje-do Island that had been poorly handled by U.S. guard troops, the units of other nations were called in to help quell the disturbances. One of these units was a company of Canadians. This was done without the prior notification of the Canadian government and that, coupled with the uniquely sensitive and notorious nature of the problem, caused Pearson to complain publicly about it. The U.S. commander was disconcerted by this outcry, seeing the orders as being no different than any other UN operational deployment. Although the POW camp was successfully brought under control, the event added a sense of alienation between Canadians and Americans at the end of the war.

Thirty-three Canadians were captured by the Chinese during the war, most in the last phase of the fighting. Their treatment in captivity was relatively not as harsh in comparison with that which had been meted out to the Americans and British. There had been little attempt at political indoctrination, and no Canadians followed the example of some UN POWs of electing to remain in the People's Republic of China after the war.

By war's end, more than 20,000 Canadians had served in Korea. Of those, 11 officers and 298 soldiers of other ranks had been killed; 59 officers and 1,143 soldiers of other ranks had been wounded. The estimated direct cost of the war for Canada was approximately $200 million.

—*Eric Jarvis*

References:

Granatstein, J. L., and Norman Hillmer. *For Better or for Worse, Canada and the United States to the 1990s.* Toronto: Copp Clark Pitman, 1991.

Morton, Desmond. *Canada and War.* Toronto: Butterworth, 1981.

Stairs, Denis. *The Diplomacy of Constraint: Canada, the Korean War and the United States.* Toronto: University of Toronto Press, 1974.

Vance, Jonathan F. *Objects of Concern: Canadian Prisoners of War through the Twentieth Century.* Vancouver: UBC Press, 1994.

Wood, Herbert Fairlie. *Strange Battleground: The Operations in Korea and Their Effects on the Defense Policy of Canada.* Ottawa: Queen's Printer, 1966.

See also: Cease-Fire Negotiations; Defectors; Hot Pursuit; Kap'yŏng, Battle of; Kŏje-do Prisoner-of-War Uprising; MacArthur, Douglas; NATO (North Atlantic Treaty Organization); Pearson, Lester B.; St. Laurent, Louis S.; 38th parallel, Decision to Cross; Truman's Recall of MacArthur; United Kingdom (UK); United Nations Cease-Fire Group; Wrong, Humphrey Hume.

Cassels, Sir Archibald James H.
(1907–1996)

British Army officer and commander of the 1st Commonwealth Division in the Korean War, 1951–1952. Born in Quetta, India, on 28 February 1907, Archibald James H. Cassels attended the Royal Military Academy at Sandhurst and was commissioned into the Seaforth Highlanders in 1926. He rose rapidly in rank and in World War II became one of the youngest major generals in the history of the British Army. His World War II service culminated with command of the 51st Highland Division in the crossing of the Rhine River.

Subsequent to World War II Cassels's other commands included the 6th Airborne Division in Palestine in 1946. In July 1951 General "Gentleman Jim" Cassels took command of the Commonwealth Division in Korea.

Cassels had the difficult task of forging a division comprising three infantry brigades—British, Canadian, and Commonwealth—which reported to five different governments and had different procedures. Surprisingly Cassels had little difficulty meshing the brigades together as a division. Cassels was

widely appreciated for his ability to work effectively with troops of different nationalities and backgrounds. He was also successful in working with the governments involved. Indeed most of Cassels's problems came not from his own troops but from his corps commander Lieutenant General J. W. "Iron Mike" O'Daniel, who was reluctant to grant Cassels the flexibility and independence allowed in the British Army.

Cassels left Korea on his promotion to lieutenant general in August 1952. After his service in Korea, Cassels held such commands as commander of the British I Corps in Germany; director of operations during the Malayan insurgency, 1957–1959; commander of the North American Treaty Organization Northern Army Group, 1960–1963; and chief of the British General Staff, 1965–1968. In 1968 Cassels was promoted to field marshal and retired from active duty in the British Army. He died at Bury St. Edmunds, Suffolk, on 13 December 1996.

—*Richard Z. Groen*

References:

Barclay, C. N. *The First Commonwealth Division: The Story of British Commonwealth Land Forces in Korea, 1950–1953.* Aldershot, UK: Gale & Polden, 1954.

Carew, Tim. *Korea: The Commonwealth at War.* London: Cassell, 1967.

Cassels, A. J. N. "The Commonwealth Division in Korea." *Journal of the Royal United Services Institute* (April 1953): 362–372.

Grey, Jeffrey. *The Commonwealth Armies and the Korean War: An Alliance Study.* Manchester: Manchester University Press, 1988.

Matray, James I., ed. *Historical Dictionary of the Korean War.* Westport, CT: Greenwood Press, 1991.

See also: Australia; Canada; New Zealand; United Kingdom (UK).

Casualties

There are no complete, definitive casualty figures for military and civilian losses in the Korean War. A war in a country with little governmental or private apparatus for record keeping and involving secretive belligerents, the Korean War defied counting. This condition characterizes many casualty estimates for World War I and II and the First and Second Indochina Wars as well. Casualty figures are also complicated by postwar attempts by the belligerents to exaggerate their enemies' loses and mask their own, although for the United States a simple error and misleading counting rules have confused historians. Many Americans still believe that 54,246 U.S. servicemen died in the Korean War from all causes. The Department of Defense finally went back to original records and concluded that the real figure is 36,914 American warrelated deaths from all causes.

The 54,246 or 54,000 figure, which routinely appears on monuments and in textbooks, became the received wisdom through its use in the *Statistical History of the United States,* a compilation that has

A U.S. soldier comforts a grief-stricken infantryman whose buddy had been killed in action. In the background a corpsman methodically fills out casualty tags, Haktong-ni area, 28 August 1950. (National Archives)

appeared in various editions since 1945 under the sponsorship of the U.S. Bureau of the Census and the Social Science Research Council. Until 1990 the same figure appeared in the official publications of the Department of Defense.

U.S. casualty statistics are confusing because of two counting errors perpetuated by the Department of the Army or the Census Bureau. During the war, for an American soldier to be counted as killed in action (KIA) or died of wounds (DOW), his body had to be recovered and processed or he had to have been seen by two other soldiers as a corpse. Unidentified remains became "Unknown" KIAs. Using such counting rules, the number of battlefield deaths was 19,585 with another 4,544 identified men DOW either in friendly or enemy hands.

Thus, the armed forces had 24,129 identified battlefield deaths, yet eventually settled on the number 33,667 as total battle-related deaths. Where did the additional war-related 9,538 deaths come from? These servicemen were listed missing in action (MIA), and this figure could not be compiled with any accuracy until after the exchange of prisoners of war (POWs) in 1953. POWs identified by name as dying in captivity (all causes) was 2,730 but this figure may not cover all deaths *before* assignment to POW camps. The Department of Defense (reflecting its dependence upon U.S. Army estimates) declared the deceased POWs and remaining MIAs as combat-related deaths, thus raising the figure to 33,667. The Department of Defense still carries the MIA figure as 8,177, but these MIAs are included in the total of war-related deaths.

The difficulty in assessing Korean War deaths is complicated by the category "other deaths," which entered the conventional historical wisdom by 1960 as 20,617. Someone should have been suspicious because

Casualties, U.S. Forces

	Served	KIA/DOW/MIA	Deaths, other	WIA
Army	2,834,000	27,709	2,452	77,596
Navy	1,177,000	493	160	1,576
Marines	424,000	4,267	339	23,744
Air Force	1,285,000	1,198	298	368
Total	5,720,000	33,667	3,249	103,284

this figure would have come close to returning to pre–World War II patterns for the U.S. armed forces, which was that "other deaths" outnumbered battlefield deaths. Yet the service personnel in the Korean War did not endure a major epidemic (like the Spanish flu of 1918–1919) nor did they suffer thousands of deaths, as in Vietnam, from helicopter crashes. When the Department of the Army went back to the Surgeon General's records in the 1990s, it determined that its "other deaths" were actually 2,452. The other services' figures had been too small (797) and consistent to be an issue. Thus "other deaths" figure was really 3,249. How does one explain a differential of more than 17,000 lives? It appears that two things happened: (1) the MIA, including those who died from diseases as POWs, were double-counted and (2) the U.S. Army's figure for "other deaths" included *all* noncombat deaths throughout the army, worldwide, during the Korean War *era* and was reported by the Surgeon General as 10,220. The official casualty figure (all causes) for the U.S. armed forces in the Korean War is now 36,914.

For the non-American contingents of United Nations Command (UNC), the casualty figures are reasonably precise, largely because the units themselves were comparatively small and more careful about recovering and counting their dead and wounded comrades. The thirteen allied nations that contributed ground combat troops, ranging from a division provided by the British Commonwealth to a platoon from Luxembourg, suffered virtually all the UNC casualties (non–United States, non–Republic of Korea [ROK, South Korea]), although airmen from the United Kingdom, Australia, and South Africa died also. The allies lost 3,960 dead, 281 of whom were aviation personnel, and 11,528 wounded.

The statistics for Korean casualties have their own confusions, largely because of the incomplete record keeping by the governments of the ROK and the Democratic People's Republic of Korea (DPRK, North Korea) and the very nature of a civil war that mixed and divided a common population between two

Casualties, United Nations Forces (Non-ROK, Non-U.S.)

Country	Deaths	Wounded
Great Britain	1,078	2,674
Turkey	889	2,111
Canada	309	1,202
Australia	272	1,034
France	271	1,008
Colombia	210	610
Greece	194	459
Thailand	136	469
Netherlands	120	645
Ethiopia	122	566
The Philippines	128	299
Belgium and Luxembourg	104	350
New Zealand	22	79
South Africa	34	0

Note: Figures include all services; deaths include those from all causes and include MIAs.

armies and two sets of authorities. Some twenty years after the war's end, the ROK estimated that its armed services had lost 184,573 KIA/DOW/MIA and 717,083 wounded. Another authoritative source later put the total military deaths at 257,000, which is probably more accurate, given the primitive state of the ROK Army (ROKA) medical service. A widely used U.S. Korean War almanac puts South Korean losses at 415,000 dead and 429,000 wounded in action, which probably confuses "deaths" with "casualties" in the first place and also mixes civilian deaths and/or casualties in the totals. The ROK government in 1974 placed civilian "losses" of all kinds at around 990,968, which indicates the magnitude of suffering in South Korea, but is not helpful in more discriminating analysis. The definitive social history of the Republic of Korea, written by Dr. Andrew C. Nahm, estimates that civilian deaths in South Korea numbered around 244,000 of whom 129,000 were massacred by the Korean People's Army (KPA, North Korea), which means that an almost equal number were killed by "friendly fire" by UNC or by the ROKA and the Korean national police in counterinsurgency operations. Disease, exposure, and starvation deaths probably equaled violent deaths and may be included in Nahm's 244,000 deaths figure, but UN officials think 900,000 deaths not unreasonable.

After June 1950 another 300,000 South Koreans disappeared and remain statistically missing. However, an estimated 200,000 of these Koreans were impressed into the KPA (or joined voluntarily) and then became "North Korean" casualties. Of this category of "missing," Nahm includes an estimated 84,000 South Koreans who were "taken" north into "captivity" in September–October 1950 either to be killed, impressed in the labor force of the DPRK or, in the case of dedicated southern Communists, assimilated into the KPA or the government.

The DPRK government does not admit to any established set of casualty figures. The ROK government claims that the KPA lost 294,931 in dead alone, but makes no effort to account for military wounded and civilian casualties of any kind. Western historians sympathetic to North Korea estimate 2.5 million North Korean *deaths*, a figure that is hard to accept on a historical, comparative basis, but might be acceptable if it refers to all casualties and includes disease deaths as well as those inflicted by direct enemy action. The DPRK government is more interested in telling its citizens as they walk through the Victorious Fatherland Liberation War Museum in P'yŏngyang that the KPA inflicted 405,498 casualties on the U.S. armed forces, 1.1 million casualties on the "puppet" forces and people, and 30,665 casualties on the U.S.'s erstwhile UN allies.

The People's Republic of China (PRC) government and the People's Liberation Army (PLA) are almost as vague and celebratory in their casualty estimates. The U.S. armed forces after the war produced estimates that put Chinese military casualties at more than a million with no confident guess at the relationship of dead to wounded except that deaths alone probably exceeded 500,000. The South Koreans put Chinese deaths at 184,128. The Chinese put their total casualties at 370,000 with 152,400 combat deaths. Other responsible independent estimators put total Chinese *deaths* at around one million, which might be accurate if it includes all deaths (civilian and military) from exposure, disease, and untreatable wounds and includes noncombat deaths in Manchuria, a war zone of sorts.

One last complication on Korean War casualties remains: when does one start counting losses? Most published compilations assume that the war began on 25 June 1950, but a strong case might be made that the war began with the Cheju-do revolt of April 1948 because some guerrilla warfare existed in South Korea from that date until the "official" war commenced. The Republic of Korea War Memorial in Seoul displays plaques for the "war dead" of the armed forces and various national police agencies, and these plaques start with deaths in the line of duty from violence as early as 1945. How does one count the guerrillas and the general population that died in the "unofficial" war? The deaths alone within South Korea, 1945–1950, are variously estimated at between 30,000 and 100,000.

—*Allan R. Millett*

References:

Cole, Paul. *POW/MIA Issues*. Vol. 1, *The Korean War*. Santa Monica, CA: The RAND Corporation for the National Defense Research Institute, 1994.

Democratic People's Republic of Korea, Ministry of Defense. *The Victorious Fatherland Liberation War Museum*. P'yŏngyang, DPRK: Foreign Languages Publishing House, 1979.

Nahm, Andrew C. *Korea, Tradition and Transformation: A History of the Korean People*. Elizabeth, NJ: Hollym International, 1988.

Reister, Frank A. *Battle Casualties and Medical Statistics: U.S. Army Experience in the Korean War*. Washington, DC: Surgeon General, Department of the Army, 1973.

Republic of Korea, Korean Overseas Information Service. "Summary of Damage Caused by North Korea during the Korean War." 6 March 1974, File 620.008, U.S. Eighth Army Historical Files, Eighth Army History Office, Yongsan, Seoul.

Republic of Korea, Ministry of National Defense. *History of the United Nations Forces in Korea*. 6 vols. Seoul: 1967–1970.

U.S. Department of Defense, American Services Information Service. *Defense 97 Almanac*. Alexandria, VA: U.S. Government Printing Office, 1998.

U.S. Department of Defense, Office of Public Information. "Report of U.S. Killed, Wounded, and Missing in Action." 5 November 1954, Summary no. 160, U.S. Eighth Army Historical Files, Eighth Army History Office, Yongsan, Seoul.

See also: Military Medicine; Missing in Action.

Cates, Clifton B.
(1893–1970)

U.S. Marine Corps general. Born at Tiptonville, Tennessee, on 31 August 1893, Clifton Bledsoe Cates graduated from the University of Tennessee in 1916 with a degree in law. In June 1917 he was a second lieutenant in the Marine Corps Reserve and was later called to active duty. He left for France in January 1918 with the 6th Marine Regiment, part of the Army's 2d Infantry Division. Much decorated in the war, Cates fought in the Meuse-Argonne and St. Mihiel Offensives and was wounded in action.

Cates returned to the United States in September 1919 and assumed various positions, most notably aide to President Woodrow Wilson and commander of the Marine Corps detachment on board the battleship *California* in 1923. He served in numerous Marine Corps barracks, including Shanghai during 1929–1932 and 1937–1939. He attended the Army Industrial College in 1932 and the Marine Corps School in 1934. In 1940 he graduated from the Army War College. A colonel in World War II, Cates commanded the 1st Marine Regiment during the landing at Guadalcanal. During 1943–1944 as a brigadier general he was named commandant of Marine Corps Schools at Quantico, Virginia. Promoted to major general, he commanded the 4th Marine Division at Tinian, Saipan, and Iwo Jima.

In June 1946 Cates was commander of the Marine Corps barracks at Quantico, and in January 1948 he became commandant of the Marine Corps and was advanced to four-star rank. As commandant, Cates opposed unification of the armed forces and attempts to diminish the strength of the Marine Corps. Cates was still commandant when the Korean War began. Here he struggled to retain the Marine Corps air arm, while overseeing significant expansion of the Marine Corps during the war.

In January 1952 Cates's tour as Marine Corps commandant came to an end, and he was replaced by General Lemuel C. Sheperd. Because of a rare legal technicality, Cates could not retire and reverted to the rank of lieutenant general, once again serving as commandant of the Marine Corps Schools. In June 1954 he retired with the restored rank of full general. Cates died in Annapolis, Maryland, on 4 June 1970.

—Monica Spicer

References:
Webster's American Military Biographies. Springfield, MA: G & C Merriam, 1978.
See also: Joint Chiefs of Staff (JCS); Shepherd, Lemuel Cornick, Jr.

Cease-Fire Negotiations

After the Communist offensive in the spring of 1951, combat activities slowed and the battle line stabilized along the 38th parallel, where the war originally began. Prospects for a quick military decision seemed unlikely as both sides dug in. Successful campaigns could not be concluded without high cost in casualties. In this situation, a continued stalemate or a negotiated settlement seemed the only alternative.

On 23 June 1951 Soviet United Nations (UN) Delegate Yakov A. Malik advocated a Korean cease-fire and armistice during a UN radio broadcast. He proposed, "as the first step, discussions should be started between the belligerents for a cease-fire and an armistice providing for mutual withdrawal of forces from the 38th parallel." Malik's proposal contained a series of concessions, whereas the earlier Communist stand had demanded the withdrawal of all foreign forces, the settlement of Korean affairs by Koreans, U.S. withdrawal of protection for Formosa, and admission of Communist China to the UN.

The timing was most appropriate for the Communists to initiate negotiations. General James A. Van Fleet's Eighth U.S. Army was on the offensive, and Communist forces had little hope to reach the 38th parallel in the near future. The spectacular recall of General Douglas MacArthur made quite plain that the United Nations Command (UNC) did not intend to broaden the scope of the war. Moreover, U.S. Secretary of State Dean G. Acheson during a 7 June 1951 hearing declared that the UN forces in Korea would agree to a reliable armistice on the 38th parallel, which had long been the core of the Communist proposal. A further Communist hope was to split Republic of Korea (ROK) President Syngman Rhee and the UNC over the conditions of the cease-fire. On 30 June, as expected, Rhee protested the Communist proposal. He made it clear that a demarcation line at the 38th parallel was unacceptable and that only a unified Korea was a feasible solution.

UNC Commander in Chief General Matthew B. Ridgway, nevertheless, responded to Malik's radio statement and proposed the Danish hospital ship *Jutlandia* as a neutral site for negotiations. The Communists, however, insisted that meetings be held at Kaesŏng, the old capital of Korea, just south of the 38th parallel. Kaesŏng had symbolic significance; its location signaled the Communist desire to establish the truce line along the 38th parallel. And, because the city was occupied by Chinese forces, it gave the impression that the UNC had sought the truce. The U.S. press hurriedly published the first direct appeal for talks, which also helped strengthen Communist propaganda.

Liaison officers met at Kaesŏng on 8 July, and two days later regular plenary sessions began. Vice Admiral C. Turner Joy headed the UNC truce team. The other four members were U.S. Air Force Major General Lawrence C. Craigie, U.S. Army Major General Henry I. Hodes, U.S. Navy Rear Admiral Arleigh A. Burke, and ROK Army (ROKA) Major General Paek Sŏn-yŏp. All were military professionals and had little formal political and diplomatic experience. Across the table, however, the Communists lined up experienced negotiators. The chief delegate and nominal leader was Democratic People's Republic of Korea (DPRK, North Korea) Vice Premier and Korean People's Army (KPA) Chief of Staff General Nam Il. The real power during the negotiations seemed to be Major General Hsieh Fang, chief of propaganda of the Northeast Military District of China. Other members of the Communist team included KPA Major General Yi Sang-jo, KPA Major General Chang P'yŏng-san, and Chinese People's Volunteer Army (CPVA, Communist China) General Deng Hua.

The UNC commission was authorized to discuss only military matters, whereas the Communists strove to take the negotiations to political ground. General Nam Il insisted that a demarcation line established on the 38th parallel with a ten-kilometer buffer on either side as a demilitarized zone was a basic condition for the cessation of hostilities. The Communists also demanded the withdrawal of all armed forces of foreign countries from Korea, concrete arrangements for the realization of a cease-fire and armistice, and arrangements relating to the prisoner-of-war (POW) issue. It took two weeks to hammer out the agenda of negotiations, which finally included four items of discussion: establishment of a military demarcation line and a demilitarized zone; arrangements for the supervision to make sure that the terms of the truce were carried out; provisions related to the POWs; and recommendations to governments of countries concerned on both sides.

The Communist delegates were hard bargainers but, above all, were sensitive to preserve face. When UNC delegates, for instance, placed a UN flag on the negotiating table, their counterparts responded with a larger flag and stand. In several other instances, Communists insulted the UNC commission either by deeds or words.

Having established the agenda, the two parties had great difficulties in determining the demarcation line. The UNC did not want to propose a specific border other than the line of contact between ground forces. This would enable the Eighth Army to maintain pressure on Communists to conclude the armistice in a short period of time. The Communist delegation, however, stuck to establishing a specific truce line on the 38th parallel because that would prevent any UNC offensive and expected huge losses. The UNC opposition to the Communist position was based on the argument that the 38th parallel did not reflect military realities. Admiral Joy wanted to bargain and requested ground compensation for UNC aerial and naval advantages that were to be given up once a demarcation line was established. Moreover, the UNC delegates did not hurry to establish such a line, as they feared that their enemies might feel safe and not want to reach a prompt agreement on the other items of the agenda.

Joy's bargaining position soon collapsed when Washington instructed the UNC commission to settle on a temporary demarcation line. On 17 November Joy proposed that the present line of contact of ground forces should constitute the provisional military demarcation line, provided the Armistice Agreement was signed within thirty days. The Communists gladly accepted the proposal on 23 November. They agreed that the actual line of contact would form a temporary demarcation line, from which both sides would withdraw two kilometers to establish a demilitarized zone. If the military Armistice Agreement was not signed in thirty days, the belligerents would return to the positions they held before signing the cease-fire agreement.

On 26 November, staff officers completed the agreement on the line of contact. The next day both sides formally ratified agenda item 2. General Ridgway's concerns soon became reality: the Communists took advantage of the agreement to build an impregnable defense line. With this physical barrier to support them, they could delay the meetings as long as they pleased.

—*Zsolt Varga*

References:

Joy, C. Turner. *How Communists Negotiate*. New York: Macmillan, 1955.

Vatcher, William H., Jr. *Panmunjom*. New York: Praeger, 1958.

Whelan, Richard. *Drawing the Line*. Boston: Little, Brown, 1990.

See also: Acheson, Dean Goodersham; Agenda Controversy; Armistice Agreement; Burke, Arleigh Albert; Kaesŏng Truce Talks; MacArthur, Douglas; Nam Il; Paek Sŏn-yŏp; P'anmunjŏm Truce Talks; Repatriation, Voluntary; Ridgway, Matthew Bunker; Syngman Rhee; Truce Talks; Van Fleet, James Alward.

Central Intelligence Agency (CIA)

Principal U.S. collection and analytical agency for foreign intelligence, created in 1947. The Central Intelligence Agency (CIA) failed to predict the 25 June 1950 North Korean invasion of South Korea and the Chinese military intervention later that same year.

The CIA grew out of the World War II Office of Strategic Services (OSS) headed by William Donovan. The OSS was a quasi-military organization that had unconventional warfare as its specialty. The weakness of the OSS was in clandestine intelligence collection and this legacy was passed on to the CIA.

The 1947 and 1949 National Security Acts organized all U.S. intelligence resources under the umbrella of the new U.S. intelligence community, headed by the director of central intelligence (DCI). The CIA had as its principal mission providing the United States and its allies with warning of attack. The CIA would centralize collection of information and be responsible for its analysis, producing the finished intelligence and intelligence estimates that would then be distributed to policymakers and other analysts. The DCI himself presented comprehensive and finished intelligence products to the president. The DCI served as the chief intelligence advisor to the president, the coordinator of the intelligence community, and the CIA director.

A number of factors contributed to the CIA failure in Korea. The agency was only three years old, its resources were severely limited, intelligence gathering was dissipated with competition between the CIA and military intelligence services, and the CIA neglected other areas of the world in favor of concentrating on the Soviet Union, the chief threat to U.S. security. CIA operations in Asia were meager at best. In part because of General Douglas MacArthur's hostility, it was not until May 1950 that the CIA was able to establish a small field station in Tokyo.

Although on 14 June 1950 the CIA concluded that the North Koreans had built up their military strength to the point that they could invade South Korea and capture Seoul within ten days, this estimate of capability was not news. Certainly the CIA failed to predict intent, and this failure led to the replacement of CIA Director Admiral Roscoe H. Hillenkoetter. On the strong recommendation of General of the Army George C. Marshall, in September 1950 President Truman named Army Lieutenant General Walter Bedell Smith as the new DCI. Smith's reputation as an outstanding bureaucrat and staunch anti-Communist and his excellent record as U.S. ambassador to the Soviet Union all helped to deflect further criticism of the CIA. It also enhanced congressional support for the significant expansion of the agency over the next few years. Under Smith the CIA nonetheless wrongly predicted that China would not intervene in the Korean conflict, and it also failed to anticipate assorted coups in Latin America.

Smith centralized and coordinated CIA activities, and he persuaded General MacArthur not only to allow the agency to operate in Korea but to utilize its intelligence. The Korea field station was headed by former World War II U.S. Army paratroop commander Ben Vandervoort and later by ex–Federal Bureau of Investigation agent Al Haney. Haney's deputy station chief was Army Lieutenant Colonel Jack Singlaub, who during World War II had served in the OSS and volunteered for Korea in the hopes of securing a battalion command.

Intelligence operations for Korea fell under the Joint Advisory Commission, Korea (JACK), which was, in turn, part of the Combined Command Research and Activities in Korea (CCRAK) under MacArthur's chief of intelligence Major General Charles A. Willoughby in Tokyo. Despite this chain of command, the CIA succeeded to a considerable degree in maintaining its independence of CCRAK.

Strict orders prohibited any Americans from being sent into North Korea as agents, but the Korean station, which rapidly expanded to more than 100 personnel, trained thousands of South Korean agents on Yŏng-do, an island off the southern coast of Korea. Virtually all Korean agents sent into the North were killed or taken prisoner and then forced to work for the Democratic People's Republic of Korea. North Korea, the CIA learned, was too small and too tightly controlled to allow success in covert missions.

In absolute terms, the CIA contributed little to the overall U.S. Korean War effort, yet it was a chief beneficiary of the war in terms of resources. At the end of the conflict, the CIA had a network of bases in Japan and Korea and throughout Asia. The war also led to the development of new techniques and skills, such as psychological warfare and the training and recruitment of agents. Experience in psychological operations and agent handling in combat conditions proved useful during the Vietnam War.

—Spencer C. Tucker

References:

Hastings, Max. The Korean War. New York: Simon & Schuster, 1987.
Karalekas, Ann. History of the Central Intelligence Agency. Laguna Hills, CA: Aegean Park Press, 1977.
Kirkpatrick, Lymann B., Jr. The Real CIA. New York: Macmillan, 1968.
Marchetti, Victor, and John D. Marks. The CIA and the Cult of Intelligence. New York: Alfred A. Knopf, 1974.
Prados, John. Presidents' Secret Wars. New York: William Morrow, 1986.
Ranelagh, John. The Agency: The Rise and Decline of the CIA. New York: Simon & Schuster, 1986.
Summers, Harry G., Jr. Korean War Almanac. New York: Facts on File, 1990.
Tully, Andrew. The CIA: The Inside Story. New York: William Morrow, 1962.

See also: MacArthur, Douglas; Marshall, George C.; Military Intelligence; Smith, Walter Bedell; Truman, Harry S.

Ch'ae Pyŏng-dŏk
(1914–1950)

Chief of staff of the Republic of Korea Army (ROKA, South Korea) at the beginning of the Korean War. Born in P'yŏngyang on 17 April 1914, Ch'ae Pyŏng-dŏk graduated from the Japanese military academy in 1935. During World War II he was a Japanese Army officer but he never commanded troops on the battlefield. At the time of the liberation of Korea in 1945, Ch'ae was a major in command of Pup'yŏng Arsenal. After the war, he graduated from the Military English-Language School opened for potential Korean officers, and in January 1946 he was commissioned a captain in the Korean constabulary. Ch'ae held various positions in the constabulary. After its transformation into the ROKA with the establishment of the ROK government in August 1948, he rose rapidly in position, the consequence of President Syngman Rhee's patronage rather than from the respect of Korean military professionals.

In May 1949 Ch'ae became chief of staff of the ROKA as a major general. After an early retirement in

October 1949, the consequence of a feud with Kim Sŏk-wŏn, in April 1950 he returned to the position of chief of staff. Although an outstanding chief of staff could not have offset the Korean People's Army (KPA, North Korean) superiority in artillery, tanks, and planes, Ch'ae bore heavy responsibility for the poor preparation of the ROK for the war and its direction at the beginning of the fighting.

In response to the North Korean invasion, Ch'ae ordered all ROKA reserves, including the 2d Division at Taejŏn, the 3d at Taegu, and the 5th at Kwangju, north of Seoul to engage the KPA in the narrow Ŭijŏngbu corridor. But most of these units were too distant to reach the battlefield on time, and when they did arrive Ch'ae ordered elements to attack piecemeal. Ch'ae dismissed from his post commander of the 2d Division General Yi Hyŏng-kŭn, who strongly objected to Ch'ae's order. Ch'ae's strategy of piecemeal counterattacks sped up the defeat of the ROKA before the fall of Seoul. Ch'ae also ordered the Han River bridges blown prematurely, which brought military disaster for the ROKA. Although the main body of the ROKA, then still north of the river, was able to cross in small boats and rafts in disorganized groups, it had to abandon most of its equipment and supplies.

President Rhee believed that Ch'ae had discredited his position of chief of staff, and, in the course of his inspection trip to Korea on 29 June, General Douglas MacArthur had suggested to Rhee that he remove Ch'ae. U.S. officers in the Korean Military Advisory Group supported this decision because they had not been consulted on the important decision of the blowing up of the Han River bridges.

On 30 June, only five days after the outbreak of the war, Ch'ae was removed as chief of staff and placed in charge of recruitment and training. Ch'ae died in the Battle of Hadong in South Kyŏngsang Province on 26 July 1950.

—*To-Woong Chung*

References:
Appleman, Roy E. *South to the Naktong, North to the Yalu.* Washington, DC: Office of the Chief of Military History, 1961.
Noble, Harold J. *Embassy at War.* Seattle: University of Washington Press, 1975.
Republic of Korea, War History Compilation Committee. *Han'guk Chŏnjaeng sa* [History of the Korean War]. Vol. 2. Seoul: Ministry of National Defense, 1968.
See also: Kim Sŏk-wŏn; Syngman Rhee; Yi Hyŏng-kŭn.

Chang, John Myŏn
(1899–1966)

Republic of Korea (ROK, South Korean) ambassador to the United States during the Korean War. Born at Inch'ŏn in 1899, John M. Chang studied at the Seoul Young Men's Christian Association English School in 1919. The following year he went to the United States and studied Liberal Arts at Manhattan Catholic College. A devout Catholic, Chang on his return to Korea worked as a layman in the P'yŏngyang Diocese. In 1931 he began teaching at Tongsŏng Commercial School and served as its president from 1936 until independence in 1945.

Chang plunged into politics in 1946, and two years he later was elected to the Constitutional Assembly. That same year, along with Cho Pyŏng-ok and Chang Ki-yŏng, Chang went to Paris to the third United Nations (UN) conference, which ended in UN recognition of the ROK as the only legitimate government in the Korean peninsula.

While serving as the first Korean ambassador during 1949–1951, Chang tried to secure U.S. military assistance. When U.S. Secretary of State Dean G. Acheson excluded Korea from the U.S. defense perimeter in his famous National Press Club speech six months before the start of the Korean War, Chang requested that the State Department explain its reasons for this, and he personally appealed to President Harry S. Truman for military assistance, pointing out the weakness of the ROK Army (ROKA). In the course of a dinner in Washington on 10 June 1950, Chang told John Foster Dulles, Dean Rusk, and other high-ranking State Department officials that his regime was in crisis. He asked Dulles, then an adviser to President Truman, to visit Korea when he next traveled to the region to see General Douglas MacArthur in Japan. As a result, Dulles traveled to Korea on 18 June, and many Koreans took this as a signal of U.S. support for the ROK. When the Korean War broke out, Chang immediately conveyed to Truman President Syngman Rhee's appeal for assistance.

As a consequence of Chang's dealings with U.S. government officials, many of the latter came to regard Chang amicably. Most U.S. documents describe him as intelligent, capable, reasonable, and docile. However, some Koreans have regarded him as too pro–United States and lacking in the strong nationalism characterizing many other contemporary Korean political leaders.

Appointed prime minister in November 1950, Chang returned to Korea in January 1951. However, Rhee began to suspect that Chang was conspiring to be the next president, and this resulted in some political problems. In November 1951 Chang participated in the Sixth UN General Assembly session held in Paris with other Korean representatives. At this time Rhee was busy attempting to revise the constitution to facilitate his second forcible seizure of power in 1952. This precipitated a political crisis. On returning to Korea at this critical time, Chang resigned to travel to the United States for medical treatment. Although Chang insisted that his resignation was solely for reasons of health, many suspected that the real reason was political disagreement between himself and Rhee.

In fact, Chang broke politically with Rhee by becoming the leader of the opposition Democratic Party, which he formed with Sin Ik-hŭi, Cho Pyŏng-ok, and others in 1955. The next year, Chang ran for the vice-presidency with Sin Ik-hŭi as his running mate for the presidency. Though Sin died just before the election, Chang was elected vice-president. In the 1960 election he again was the vice-presidential candidate together with Cho as the presidential candidate, but he was defeated.

After the collapse of Rhee's government as a consequence of the 1960 April Student Revolution, Chang seized political power and, after four months of interim government, was inaugurated as prime minister of the Second Republic in August 1960. However, Park Chung Hee's 16 May 1961 coup d'état spelled the end of Chang's government only nine months after its establishment. Chang's was the first and last government in Korean history based upon a parliamentary system. Thereafter, Park prohibited Chang's political activities and briefly had him imprisoned. Upon his release, Chang concentrated on religious activities. He died of hepatitis on 4 June 1966.

—*Insook Park*

References:
Cumings, Bruce. *Korea's Place in the Sun: A Modern History.* New York: W. W. Norton, 1997.
———. *The Origins of the Korean War.* Vol. 2, *The Roaring of the Cataract, 1947–1950.* Princeton, NJ: Princeton University Press, 1990.
Matray, James I., ed. *Historical Dictionary of the Korean War.* Westport, CT: Greenwood Press, 1991.
See also: Acheson, Dean Goodersham; Cho Pyŏng-ok; Dulles, John Foster; MacArthur, Douglas; Rusk, David Dean; Sin Ik-hŭi; Truman, Harry S.

Chang T'aek-sang
(1893–1969)

Republic of Korea (ROK, South Korean) politician who served briefly both as foreign minister and prime minister. Chang T'aek-sang was born in Ch'ilgok, North Kyŏngsang Province, on 22 October 1893. He studied at both Waseda University and Edinburgh University. After returning to Japanese-controlled Korea in 1921, he chaired the Ch'ŏnggu Club, organized by Korean nationalist intellectuals.

Chang was imprisoned by the Japanese for his nationalist activities in May 1938, but steadfastly refused to cooperate with them. After the defeat of Japan, Chang became chief of the Seoul metropolitan police in January 1946, a capacity in which he played a major role in weakening Communist power in South Korea in the liberation period of 1945–1948. Liberal U.S. diplomatic representatives in Korea hated Chang

for his antidemocratic practices and slavish support of Syngman Rhee.

In the first ROK government, Rhee appointed Chang the foreign minister. He was unhappy with the position, as he claimed he had been promised the home ministry, and he resigned after three months in office. He angered U.S. officials by his advocacy of a military invasion of the North and forcible reunification of Korea. Later Chang became ROK representative to the United Nations General Assembly, a post he held until 1951.

Chang was elected to the ROK National Assembly in the 1952 elections and was selected as one of its vice chairmen. Rhee appointed him prime minister in April 1952. Undoubtedly, Rhee had appointed Chang to resolve the political crisis in his favor. As prime minister, Chang played a key role in carrying out the covert directive of Rhee's coup d'état against the Assembly, although the president abandoned him after the incident.

As a four-times-elected assemblyman, Chang was conservative and staunchly anti-Communist. In 1958 he became chairman of the Committee for Fighting against Communism, and he was sent to Geneva to deter the repatriation of Korean Japanese to North Korea in 1959. He acted as a leader of the opposition party after the May 1961 military coup d'état led by Major General Park Chung Hee. Chang died in Seoul on 1 August 1969.

—*Choosuk Suh*

References:
Chang, Pyŏng-hye. *Sangnok ŭi Chayuhon* [The evergreen soul of freedom]. Seoul: Ch'angnang Chang T'aek-sang Kinyŏm Saŏp-hoe, 1992.
Matray, James I., ed. *Historical Dictionary of the Korean War.* Westport, CT: Greenwood Press, 1991.
See also: Korea, Republic of: 1952 Political Crisis; Syngman Rhee.

Changjin (Chosin) Reservoir Campaign
(October–December 1950)

After X Corps' successful landing at the port of Inch'ŏn and recapture of Seoul and after Eighth Army's breakout from the Pusan perimeter, United Nations Command (UNC) forces invaded North Korea. For the invasion, UNC commander General Douglas MacArthur ordered X Corps transferred by sea from the west to Wŏnsan on the east coast, while Eighth Army remained on the west coast for the drive into northwest Korea. This decision tied up the port of Inch'ŏn for weeks and created a delay in the supply of Eighth Army from which it had not fully recovered by the time the Chinese military intervened in the war. Eighth Army commander Lieutenant General Walton H. Walker had no control over this; X Corps was not under his authority but rather responsible only to

An aerial photograph of the north end of the Changjin (Chosin) Reservoir. (National Archives)

MacArthur in Tokyo. MacArthur also removed the Republic of Korea Army (ROKA, South Korean) I Corps from Walker and placed it under General Edward M. Almond's X Corps, in effect raising X Corps on a par with Eighth Army.

On 17 October MacArthur issued UN Operations Order No. 4 to initiate what he hoped would be the final phase of the war. In what MacArthur expected to be the final UNC drive to the Yalu River, the boundary between Eighth Army and the reinforced X Corps had the two commands separated by a gap of between twenty and fifty miles, well beyond supporting distance. MacArthur assumed, wrongly as it turned out, that the terrain in the gap was too rough to permit Communist forces to carry out large-scale operations. Both Eighth Army and X Corps would be forced to divert strong formations to safeguard their open flanks. MacArthur's decision was protested by three staff major generals and Eighth Army commander Walker, but MacArthur justified it on the basis of geography.

The T'aebaek Range, the spine of southern and central Korea, ran north and south and made an advance on two axes the only practical means of overcoming the geographical difficulty.

X Corps began embarking at Inch'ŏn 7 October. It arrived off Wŏnsan on 19 October but had to wait a week aboard ship until the navy cleared mines from the port, which meanwhile had been taken by ROKA forces by land. Although it is impossible to assess the impact of the delay, occasioned by MacArthur's repositioning of forces, in resuming the offensive after the fall of Seoul, the delay certainly allowed the Korean People's Army (KPA, North Korea) to regroup and the Chinese to bring troops into North Korea.

MacArthur's Operations Order No. 4 originally assigned X Corps the objective of a line through P'yŏngwŏn-P'ungsan-Sŏngjin. This was later changed, as was the case of Eighth Army's objective, to occupation of all North Korea. Almond's plan of operations called for the ROKA I Corps to continue its drive up the

The march southward begins from Kot'o-ri in a snowstorm as a Marine infantry battalion attacks northward from Chinhŭng-ni to open up the Main Supply Route, 9 December 1950. (National Archives)

coast to the USSR's Siberian border. The U.S. 7th Division, commanded by Major General David W. Barr, would advance from Iwŏn via P'ungsan to Hyesanjin. The 1st Marine Division would remain in the Wŏnsan-Hŭngnam area to protect X Corps' rear area and its lines of communication until relieved by the 3d Infantry Division from Japan. Once the 3d Division was in place, the 1st Marine Division was to move from Hamhŭng to the Changjin Reservoir (known as the Chosin Reservoir on Japanese maps). From there it would continue northward to the frontier with Manchuria, depending on the tactical situation.

On 24 October MacArthur ordered his commanders to "drive forward with all speed and full utilization of their forces." Victory seemed imminent; the KPA seemed to have all but dissolved. In the west Eighth Army's columns crossed the Ch'ŏngch'ŏn River. In the east X Corps also advanced. The ROKA I Corps started the 26th Regiment of its 3d Division up the road to the Changjin Reservoir without waiting for the 1st Marine Division.

On 25 October, leading battalions of the 26th Regiment about halfway to the Changjin Reservoir encountered Chinese People's Volunteer Army (CPVA, Communist Chinese) troops. A Chinese prisoner reported 3,000 to 4,000 Chinese in the vicinity, troops of the 124th Division. The 26th continued its advance until stopped by CPVA troops supported by KPA tanks. The regiment then took up defensive positions, although it did manage to capture a number of prisoners who were later questioned by Almond, who then sent a personal message to MacArthur confirming the presence of Chinese troops in Korea. As in the west, the Chinese suddenly halted operations and broke contact.

Despite the confirmation of Chinese troops, X Corps continued its advance. The ROKA Capital Division moved northeast along the coast road supported by U.S. naval gunfire against heavy opposition from the KPA 42d Division. On 26 November the Capital Division captured the industrial center of Ch'ŏngjin, only sixty-five miles from the Siberian border. In less than two months since crossing the 38th parallel, the ROKA I Corps had moved by foot and vehicle 425 miles, fighting most of the way.

To the west of the ROKA I Corps on 1 November the U.S. 17th Infantry Regiment of the U.S. 7th Division drove off a strong KPA attack. To its left the 31st Infantry Regiment, which had landed at Iwŏn on 3–4 November, advanced into the mountains toward the Pujŏn Reservoir. On the 8th it ran into a battalion of the CPVA 126th Division on the eastern slopes of Paeksan, a tall peak at the southern end of the reservoir. This was the first encounter of U.S. troops in X Corps with the CPVA.

On 12 November X Corps headquarters ordered the 7th Division to continue its drive northward. General Barr directed his 17th Regiment to take Kapsan and then move up to Hyesanjin on the Yalu River; the 31st Regiment would be to its left, while the 32d Regiment was to secure the southeast shore of the Pujŏn Reservoir. In seven degrees-below-zero weather the 17th took Kapsan on the 14th. It entered Hyesanjin on the 21st. Neither Barr, Almond, nor MacArthur seemed overly concerned that five days earlier a patrol of the 31st had encountered several hundred Chinese at the north end of the reservoir. After leaving strong detachments to hold the mountain passes east of the reservoir leading to the areas to the rear of his division, Barr did take steps to consolidate his division in the area of Hyesanjin-Samsu-Kapsan.

At the same time, the 3d Infantry Division arrived in North Korea at Wŏnsan and proceeded to set up a 100-mile defensive perimeter extending from south of Wŏnsan to north of Hamhŭng. This freed up the 1st Marine Division, and on 30 October Almond ordered it to relieve ROKA I Corps troops on the road to the Changjin Reservoir. The 60-mile-long road from Hamhŭng to Changjin climbs some 4,000 feet. At the beginning of the steepest stretch of road, near Sudong, the Chinese located their initial blocking position.

The 1st Marine Division set out on 1 November, spearheaded by its 7th Regiment, commanded by Colonel Homer Litzenberg. The following morning the 7th relieved the ROKA troops and then promptly ran into the Chinese blocking position. The regiment then bivouacked for the night with its battalions in column. Shortly after midnight on 3 November the CPVA 124th Division struck the 7th Regiment. By daylight the Chinese had secured a dominating position over-

looking a bridge separating two of the three battalions. The 1st Marine Division called in air support, which, combined with determined ground action and artillery fire, drove the Chinese from their positions, killing about 700 and wounding many more. After this there was little Chinese resistance and on 4 November the 7th Regiment took Sudong. On 10 November it moved through the pass to Kot'o-ri, only seven miles from its objective of Hagaru-ri.

The weather now turned bitter cold. On the night of 10–11 November, 35-mile winds and eight-degree-below-zero temperatures hit the plateau. Some 200 men collapsed from cold over the next days. In these circumstances Litzenberg and 1st Marine Division commander Major General Oliver P. Smith were in no hurry to push on to Hagaru-ri. Smith was so concerned that he communicated to Marine Commandant General Clifton B. Cates in Washington his doubts about the wisdom of a campaign in a Korean winter with his division scattered along one road from Hŭngnam to the Yalu. Smith was especially concerned about the nearly 100-mile-wide gap between his own division, which formed the left flank of X Corps, and the bulk of Eighth Army. For a Marine Corps general in the field to counsel caution in carrying out the orders of a supreme commander took great courage. Meanwhile Smith worked to improve and secure his supply line through the pass and to concentrate his division in the Hagaru-ri area before pushing on to the Yalu.

The 1st Marines took the bombed out shell of Hagaru-ri on 14 November. Some 3,000 Chinese troops who had been in occupation there had moved out three days before. That night the temperature dropped to fifteen degrees below zero and snow covered the roads. The 7th Regiment took up defensive positions around Hagaru-ri, and on 19 November work began on an airstrip at Hagaru-ri to supplement supply by road and provide a means of evacuating sick and wounded. Engineers also improved the road, making the pass available for trucks. Smith now concentrated his division at Hagaru-ri. A battalion of Lieutenant Colonel Raymond L. Murray's 5th Marine Regiment arrived at Kot'o-ri on 16 November. The 7th Marines took over responsibility for maintaining the supply line to Hamhŭng. Colonel Lewis B. Puller's 1st Marine Regiment was still in the vicinity of Hamhŭng. It protected the division's rear from harassment by Communist guerrillas. Smith deliberately delayed compliance with X Corps orders to push on to the Yalu as quickly as possible. He did order the 7th Regiment to start out to secure a blocking position at Yudam-ni, some 15 miles from Hagaru-ri over a high mountain pass. Also in accordance with orders, he also pushed the 5th Regiment up the east side of the reservoir toward the Manchurian border. But these moves were deliberately slowed. Smith halted Litzenberg's 7th Regiment on the Hagaru-ri side of the pass until he could close Puller's 1st Regiment into a supporting position. Smith's caution undoubtedly saved his division from annihilation in the weeks to follow.

MacArthur appeared not to notice the warnings from his commanders and saw the advance by Eighth Army and X Corps as little more than an occupation rather than an offensive. He believed that if the Chinese did intervene in force they would be destroyed by UNC artillery fire and bombing. X Corps at least was in better shape logistically than Eighth Army. It was supplied through the nearby ports of Wŏnsan, Hŭngnam, and Iwŏn. Tank landing ships (LSTs) were also directly supplying the ROKA I Corps over the beaches. However, this became more difficult as regiments of the 1st Marine and the 7th Army Division advanced inland and their supply lines lengthened to more than 100 miles over steep and narrow mountain roads.

The Joint Chiefs of Staff (JCS) was concerned about the initial Chinese intervention and the separation between Eighth Army and X Corps, but hesitated to impose changes on their field commander. Brigadier General Erwin Wright, assistant chief of staff for operations in the Far East Command, and his planning group were less inhibited. If X Corps continued to drive northeast of the T'aebaek Mountains, it could render no assistance to Eighth Army. They now suggested it shift its attack to the northwest, threatening the flank and rear of any Chinese units that might try to turn the east flank of Eighth Army. X Corps's objective should be to secure the reservoir and town of Changjin and then drive northwest with two divisions to cut the Chinese Manpojin-Kanggye-Mup'yŏng-ni supply route. MacArthur approved the plan, and on 15 November he directed Almond to reorient his attack to the westward after reaching Changjin. Meanwhile, MacArthur's intelligence chief, Major General Charles A. Willoughby reported a Chinese buildup of the equivalent of four divisions in the Changjin-Pujŏn reservoir area. In a telegram to Washington on 17 November, Willoughby indicated the vulnerability of X Corps' western flank and the supply route from Hŭngnam to the Changjin Reservoir.

Almond, meanwhile, in accordance with MacArthur's instructions, redirected X Corps' attack to the northeast. The 1st Marine Division would attack along the Hagaru-ri-Mup'yŏng-ni axis. The 7th Division would protect the 1st Marine's right flank by assigning a regimental combat team to take Changjin. Almond set the advance to begin at 0800 on 27 November. This new directive, which would send X Corps northwest across the T'aebaek range to assist

Eighth Army with no decrease in its original tasks was well beyond its means to accomplish. General Smith's reaction was contained in his log: "Our line of communications will be very tenuous."

Nevertheless, to Washington and Tokyo, victory seemed at hand when MacArthur announced on 24 November the final drive to the northernmost limit of the Korean peninsula. He envisioned a giant pincer movement with Eighth Army and X Corps crushing between them what remained of Communist forces. But within twenty-four hours of the resumption of Eighth Army's offensive, the situation changed with devastating suddenness. On the night of the 25th, the Chinese struck in force. On the 26th the three divisions of the ROKA 2d Corps disintegrated under Chinese attack, leaving Eighth Army's right flank open and vulnerable. Six Chinese armies (eighteen divisions) poured into this gap to smash Walker's open flank and force its withdrawal. This caught X Corps exposed and vulnerable; its southernmost element, the 7th Regiment at Yudam-ni, was almost 90 miles northeast of the bulk of Eighth Army near Kunu-ri. Nonetheless General Wright in Tokyo considered a plan to send its 3d Division west across the T'aebaek range to shore up the right flank of Eighth Army. Almond strongly objected, pointing out that the road across the T'aebaek shown on the map did not in fact exist on the ground. The weather and terrain would make resupply of the division tenuous at best. MacArthur agreed with Almond that his first task should be to extricate the 1st Marine Division and the two battalions of the 7th Division cut off in the Changjin Reservoir area. MacArthur ordered Almond to withdraw as far as was necessary to protect his command from being flanked and to concentrate his command in the Hamhŭng-Hŭngnam area.

In Washington the JCS, with Truman's concurrence, approved of MacArthur shifting over to the defensive. Once again the chiefs questioned MacArthur's division of command between Eighth Army and X Corps. But MacArthur said that X Corps "geographically threatened" the Chinese attacking Eighth Army, despite the T'aebaek range and that the Chinese had cut the main X Corps supply line and had isolated some elements of the 7th Division. The chiefs authorized MacArthur to ignore the entire northwest of Korea in favor of concentrating on such operations necessary for the security of his command.

Almond now had to extract his exposed and isolated units. With the bulk of the 7th Division well to the north, Almond placed under General Smith's command the 31st Regimental Combat Team, also known as Task Force MacLean for its commander Lieutenant Colonel Allan D. MacLean. It consisted of the 1st Battalion of the 32nd Regiment and 3d Battalion of the

31st Regiment and supporting artillery, all east of the reservoir. After MacLean's capture on 29 November, Lieutenant Colonel Don C. Faith, Jr. headed the task force, which then became known as Task Force Faith.

Almond ordered Smith to withdraw his 5th and 7th Marine Regiments from Yudam-ni, and, working with Barr, to arrange to rescue Task Force Faith. The assembled units would then fight their way out down the Hagaru-ri-Kot'o-ri supply roue to Hŭngnam. The ROKA 3d Division, the farthest north of the ROKA I Corps, would concentrate on the coast at Sŏngjin and there be lifted off by the U.S. Navy to Hŭngnam. The ROKA Capital Division would withdraw back down the coastal road. Supplies in the Wŏnsan area would be lifted off and that port abandoned. The U.S. 3d Division would cover the concentration of X Corps in the Yŏnp'o-Hŭngnam-Hamhŭng area.

Generals Barr and Smith agreed that no relief force could reach the retreating Marines and Task Force Faith until they reached Smith's headquarters at Hagaru-ri, which was being held by only the 3d Battalion, 1st Marine Regiment, and a mix of Marine and army service troops. Smith feared that Task Force Faith could not hold out until he could concentrate at Hagaru-ri and he ordered Faith to fight his way out, promising Marine close air support for the attempt. At the same time, the 5th Marines would withdraw from Yudam-ni to Hagaru-ri.

The thirteen-day retreat of nearly eighty miles began on 1 December. The Marines came out in an orderly single column, despite Chinese resistance, movement over difficult, narrow snow-covered roads, and below-zero weather. Two days later they reached the top of the pass, and the trip downhill to Hagaru-ri was much easier. The Marines made it to Hagaru-ri largely intact with minimum loss in equipment, and bringing out some 1,500 casualties.

Task Force Faith had more difficulty. It had been weakened by two days of attacks by the CPVA 80th Division. Before starting out, Faith had ordered the 57th Field Artillery Battalion's 105-mm guns destroyed, along with excess supplies, and all but twenty-two vehicles, just enough to carry the wounded, who then totaled 600 men. They immediately encountered expected Chinese resistance, but what happened next was not anticipated. U.S. pilots, miscalculating their bomb runs, dropped napalm on the front of the column, and scattered its leading companies. Faith got the column moving again, but he was mortally wounded leading a flanking attack to break past a Chinese roadblock. Task Force Faith now began to disintegrate. Many of the trucks broke down and Faith's successor, Major Robert E. Jones, had to make the difficult decision to leave behind, with guards, many of the wounded.

That night the remnants reached Hudong-ni, halfway to Hagaru-ri, but the Chinese were in control of the village and efforts to dislodge them failed. Jones then tried to run the vehicles with the wounded through but the Chinese shot the drivers in the leading vehicles and raked the remainder. Those men who remained now scattered, most of them toward the frozen reservoir. A small task force of army troops accompanied by tanks tried to break through from Hagaru-ri to Hudong-ni without success. The Chinese did not make a strong effort to pursue the escaping troops across the ice, and they did administer aid to the wounded in Hudong-ni. Of 2,500 men in Task Force Faith, only slightly more than 1,000 made it to Hagaru-ri and only 385 of them were fit to fight. They were reequipped from Marine stocks and, with other army units there, were formed into a provisional battalion. The airstrip at Hagaru-ri was vital, enabling the evacuation of 4,316 casualties and the flying in of 537 replacements.

To the south, attempts to open the road between First Marine Regiment's base at Kot'o-ri and Hagaru-ri suffered a serious setback. The 41st Commando Battalion of the British Royal Marines, commanded by Lieutenant Colonel Douglas S. Drysdale, had recently arrived in Korea and had yet to see combat. Ordered to join the U.S. Marines, it was beefed up with thirty tanks and the Army's B Company of the 1st Battalion, 31st Infantry Regiment. Known as Task Force Drysdale, the 900-man force set out for Hagaru-ri, enjoined to get there "at all costs." On 29 November it ran into well dug-in Chinese troops in an area that came to be known as Hell Fire Valley. About 300 men of the task force were captured, including B Company commander Captain Charles L. Peckham; many more were wounded, including Drysdale. Only 300 made it to Hagaru-ri. The remaining survivors fell back on Kot'o-ri.

Fortunately, the UNC controlled the air and Chinese ground formations were devastated in air strikes. When correspondents met General Smith at Hagaru-ri and queried him about the withdrawal, he told them, "Gentlemen, we are not retreating. We are merely advancing in another direction."

The next stage of the withdrawal, to Kot'o-ri, began on 6 December. It took a day and a half to cover 11 miles through snow under incessant Chinese attack. Smith again regrouped his forces for the 10 additional miles to Chinhŭng-ni, now held by units of the 3d Division, which had freed up the 1st Battalion of the 1st Marine Regiment, enabling it to strike north and aid the Marine column coming from Kot'o-ri. On 8 December the advance continued, but a bridge over the gorge in Hwangch'oryŏng Pass had been destroyed, blocking the Marines. Special prefabricated bridge-building equipment was then dropped by parachute into Kot'o-ri and laid by engineers across the gorge. On 9 December the advance resumed.

In the afternoon of 11 December, the last elements of Smith's command passed through the 3d Division perimeter around the Hamhŭng-Hŭngnam area. The withdrawal must be considered one of the most masterly operations of its kind in the history of war, fought against heavy odds. The campaign had been fought at high cost. During the period 26 October–11 December 1950, the 1st Marine Division suffered 704 killed in action or died of wounds, 187 missing, and 3,489 wounded in action, for a total of 4,380 battle casualties. This was double the number for the Seoul-Inch'ŏn campaign. In addition there were 6,000 nonbattle casualties, most from frostbite. The airstrips at Hagaru-ri and one at Kot'o-ri were vital, enabling Smith to evacuate his wounded. Marines remember the withdrawal with pride; the Chinese, with the admission that in the campaign they came to understand what modern automatic weapons, artillery, and air power could do.

During its campaign in North Korea, X Corps suffered some 11,500 casualties, of which nearly half were killed in action or missing in action. The campaign did tie down the 120,000 men of the twelve divisions of the Chinese Ninth Army Group, which otherwise could have been used against Eighth Army.

MacArthur ordered Almond to redeploy his forces to the Pusan area in the far south and report to the Eighth Army. The evacuation, covered by substantial naval air assets, had already begun when the Marines reached the Hŭngnam staging area. On 10 December Wŏnsan was evacuated. At Hŭngnam, units of the 3d Division ran the perimeter defenses and were the last to be evacuated. In all, 87,000 U.S. and ROKA troops were lifted off, along with some 86,000 Korean refugees who did not want to be left behind, in an operation involving more than 100 ships. When the evacuation was completed on Christmas Eve, engineers blew up the port's waterfront with explosive charges. North Korea, half empty and devastated by the fighting, was left to the Communists.

—*Spencer C. Tucker*

References:

Appleman, Roy E. *East of Chosin: Entrapment and Breakout in Korea*. College Station, TX: Texas A&M Press, 1987.

Collins, J. Lawton. *War in Peacetime: The History and Lessons of Korea*. Boston: Houghton Mifflin, 1969.

Hopkins, William B. *One Bugle, No Drums: The Marines at Chosin Reservoir*. Chapel Hill, NC: Algonquin Books, 1986.

Meid, Pat, and James M. Yingling. *U.S. Marine Operations in Korea, 1950–1953*. Vol. 5, *Operations in West Korea*. Washington, DC: U.S. Marine Corps Historical Branch, 1972.

Montross, Lynn, and Nicholas A. Canzona. *U.S. Marine Operations in Korea, 1950–1953: The Chosin Reservoir Campaign*. Washington, DC: U.S. Marine Corps Historical Branch, 1957.

Russ, Martin. *The Chosin Reservoir Campaign, Korea, 1950*. New York: From International, 1999.

Schnabel, James F. *United States Army in the Korean War: Policy and Direction, the First Year*. Washington, DC: Office of the Chief of Military History, Department of the Army, 1972.

See also: Almond, Edward Mallory; Cates, Clifton B.; Eighth United States Army; Hŭngnam Evacuation; Joint Chiefs of Staff (JCS); MacArthur, Douglas; Puller, Lewis Burwell; Smith, Oliver Prince; Tenth Corps; Walker, Walton Harris; Willoughby, Charles A.

Chauvel, Jean M. H.
(1897–1979)

France's permanent delegate on the United Nations (UN) Security Council, 1949–1952. Jean M. H. Chauvel was born in Paris on 16 April 1897 and educated at the École Gerson, the Lycée Janson-de-Sailly, and the University of Paris, where he earned a law degree in 1921. He then joined the French Foreign Service as a professional diplomat, holding various positions in Beijing, Syria, and Vienna during the 1920s and 1930s. In 1938 he was recalled to Paris, where he became subdirector for Asia-Oceania at the Quai d'Orsay.

After the German invasion of France in 1940, Chauvel spent two years working in the Vichy government as chief of the Foreign Ministry's Far Eastern Division. On 11 November 1942, he resigned to join the French Resistance when the Germans took over previously unoccupied France. In spring 1944 he made his way to Algiers to join the Free French government in exile. In January 1945 he became secretary-general of the Ministry of Foreign Affairs in General Charles de Gaulle's provisional government, and that same month he was also given the permanent, nonpartisan rank of ambassador, which he held until taking up his UN appointment.

In these capacities over the subsequent four years, Chauvel was deeply involved in the negotiations that led to the establishment of the Marshall Plan, the Western European Union, and the North Atlantic Treaty Organization.

As French permanent representative at the UN, Chauvel acquired the reputation of a "scholarly diplomat who gives tightly reasoned arguments replete with detail and documentation." He participated in the four-power discussions with British, U.S., and Soviet representatives that in May 1949 brought about the end of the Berlin blockade; he also supported international control of atomic energy. Although he deplored the January 1950 Soviet decision not to attend Security Council meetings after that body had refused immediately to replace the Nationalist Chinese representative with a People's Republic of China (PRC, Communist China) counterpart, in late June 1950 Chauvel hinted that France was considering recognizing the PRC government. Clearly, France's veto power as a permanent member of the Security Council meant that the United States had to exercise some caution to not offend French sensibilities.

On 27 June 1950 Chauvel stated his "unreserved support" for the U.S. resolution calling for UN military intervention in Korea, and he voted for this the following day. He and his British counterpart Sir Alexander Cadogan cosponsored the 7 July 1950 Security Council Resolution that established the UN Command for its military forces in Korea, although they failed to win U.S. approval for the creation of a separate UN committee to obtain, coordinate, and supervise military contributions by different countries to this force. On 2 August Chauvel publicly stated the French position that, before the UN considered the question of Chinese recognition, North Korean forces must be withdrawn from South Korea. The following day he did, however, reserve France's position on the ultimate recognition of the PRC. Later that month, he disputed Soviet claims that Republic of Korea (South Korean) forces had invaded the North and the contentions of Soviet Ambassador Jacob Malik that, because of his own absence from the Security Council on that occasion, the UN decision to intervene in Korea was invalid.

Despite France's loyal support of its U.S. ally, one of Chauvel's major anxieties during the Korean War was that, should the United States become overly embroiled militarily in Korea, this would reduce the amount of assistance the United States could furnish to France in Indo-China. On the contrary, the Korean conflict substantially enhanced U.S. aid to France for this purpose.

Chauvel attempted to moderate U.S. policies toward China. When the extent of Chinese military intervention in the war became known, Chauvel feared that U.S. aerial bombing raids on Chinese hydroelectric plants on the Yalu River might lead China to broaden its operations to include Indo-China. He therefore pressed the United States to eschew any such military actions. He opposed any UN condemnation of the PRC as an aggressor in Korea and urged the United States to seek a negotiated peace settlement with the PRC and Democratic People's Republic of Korea (North Korea). The PRC refusal to deal with the UN Cease-Fire Group persuaded Chauvel to back the UN Resolution of 1 February 1951, condemning the Chinese as aggressors in the war, but he still remained a strong and vocal advocate of a negotiated cease-fire.

In 1952 Chauvel became French ambassador to Switzerland, and in 1954 he also served on the French delegation at the 1954 Geneva Conference, which was supposed to settle outstanding diplomatic issues in Asia, including the liquidation of France's position in Indo-China. Chauvel later served as France's high commissioner in Austria, ambassador to Great Britain, and permanent representative to the Western European Union, ending his career as diplomatic counselor to the French government. After retiring in 1963, Chauvel wrote several volumes of memoirs. He died in Paris on 31 May 1979.

—*Priscilla Roberts*

References:

"Chauvel, Jean (Michel Henri)." In *Current Biography, 1950*. New York: H. W. Wilson, 1951.

Chauvel, Jean. *Commentaire: d'Alger à Berne (1944–1952)*. Paris: Fayard, 1972.

———. *Commentaire: de Berne à Paris (1952–1962)*. Paris: Fayard, 1973.

Stueck, William W., Jr. *The Korean War: An International History*. Princeton, NJ: Princeton University Press, 1995.

Yoo, Tae Ho. *The Korean War and the United Nations*. Louvain, Belgium: Librairie Desbarax, 1964.

See also: France; Malik, Jacob (Iakov) Alexandrovich.

Cheju-do Prisoner-of-War Uprising (1 October 1952)

While North Korean prisoners derived considerable propaganda value from prisoner-of-war (POW) riots, Chinese Communist prisoners were docile and played only a relatively small role in POW incidents during the first two years of the Korean War. The Chinese then decided that they too should exploit available propaganda weapons, and they began a campaign of POW violence, which did not end until repatriation at the end of the war.

In July 1952, after the transfer of a number of Chinese POWs to Camp 3A near Cheju City on Cheju-do, their leaders began an indoctrination program, conducted secret meetings, and openly confronted U.S. guards. These steps were designed to arouse the remainder of prisoners against their captors. Camp authorities responded with increased security measures. Unannounced shakedown inspections in the camps uncovered flags, as well as daggers, ropes, and other potential weapons. Overt acts of defiance and provocation by prisoners on occasion led to the use of firearms and the death or injury of the individuals involved.

On 21 August 1952, Chinese POWs attacked and inflicted minor injuries on a compound commander and two assistants who had entered the compound to secure tent remnants left by a recent typhoon. Further incidents of increasing violence in August and September led to a complete investigation and replacement of the camp commander. Colonel Richard D. Boerem replaced him.

The first real test of Boerem's authority came on 1 October 1952, when the Chinese prisoners began demonstrations to commemorate the anniversary of the establishment of the People's Republic of China. This came only two days after Boerem assumed command. The principal disturbance occurred at Compound No. 7 where 5,000 die-hard Chinese Communist POWs were housed. The prisoners challenged U.S. authorities by displaying Communist banners, singing Communist songs, demonstrating, and refusing to report for work. They also attacked guards with stones, sharpened tent poles, and wire-wrapped staves.

Using a loudspeaker, Boerem ordered the demonstration to stop and said he would employ force if it did not. When the POWs refused to obey this order, Boerem sent two platoons of the 1st Battalion, 35th Infantry Regiment and 15 members of the Military Police Service Company into the compounds. When unfavorable winds rendered the use of tear gas impractical, the guards used their rifles. Order was restored in half an hour, during which time 56 prisoners were killed and 120 injured, most of these by bullets. Nine United Nations Command (UNC) personnel suffered minor cuts or bruises in the rioting.

Communist leaders and much of world opinion expressed surprise at the number of POWs killed. Nevertheless, the UNC insisted that the proper amount of force had been used. Later it was revealed that the UNC had been forewarned about the demonstration. An informant had revealed POW plans for a mass breakout and the murder of the camp commander. As such riots were designed for propaganda purposes to be used at the armistice negotiations at P'anmunjŏm, the UNC camp authorities should have taken the proper precautions in advance to avert bloodshed.

—*Sunghun Cho*

References:

Cho, Sunghun. "Han'guk Chŏnjaeng Chung UN Kun ŭi P'oro Chŏngch'aek e Kwanhan Yŏn'gu" [UN Forces POW policies during the Korean War]. Ph.D. dissertation, Academy of Korean Studies, Seoul, 1999.

Headquarters U.S. Army Pacific. "The Handling of Prisoners of War during the Korean War," 1960. Unpublished document.

Office of the Assistant Chief of Staff G2, Intelligence, Headquarters, U.S. Army Forces, Far East. "Communist Utilization of Prisoner of War," 1953. Unpublished document.

See also: Prisoner-of-War Administration, United Nations Command.

Cheju-do Rebellion
(1948–1949)

Rebellion in South Korea during 1948–1949. After Korean liberation from Japanese occupation on 15 August 1945, control of Cheju Island was assumed by People's Committees and Committees for the Preparation of Korean Independence. These ideologically progressive committees were particularly effec-

tive in influencing the poor, closely knit local communities. One reason for this was that there were relatively few tenant farmers on Cheju Island; thus, most farmers were not subject to strict landlord control. The establishment of the U.S. Military Government in Korea (USAMGIK) on Cheju occurred slightly later, on 27 October 1945. In the autumn of 1946, the USAMGIK attempted to strengthen its presence on Cheju through the reorganization and enlargement of police units and the founding of the 9th Regiment of Constabulary Units. Meanwhile, the People's Committees continued to develop their local influence in more subtle ways.

In anticipation of the 1947 memorial day for the March First Movement, extra police were dispatched from the mainland. Still sensitive from the Taegu insurrection a few months earlier, the police fired on demonstration spectators, resulting in six deaths and six wounded. In a separate incident on the same day, police fired at pedestrians, resulting in two deaths and six wounded. In protest against these violent attacks, the people of Cheju staged a general strike that placed the People's Committees at odds with the USAMGIK.

This strike and the ensuing unrest resulted in the arrest of 2,500 people over the following year. Also additional police and right-wing activists were assigned to Cheju from the mainland. This had a significantly negative affect on the local population, and in March 1948 the unrest was further compounded by three deaths caused by mainlanders. During this time many people started to leave the island or became involved in secret preparations for armed opposition. The Cheju-do Rebellion of 3 April 1948 was staged to resist police and right-wing oppression, protest U.S. occupation policy, and obstruct a vote on the establishment of a divided government in South Korea.

Socioeconomic reasons were also involved because, during the Japanese occupation, the Cheju economy was heavily reliant on trade with Japan. After liberation, all regular passenger ships to and from Japan were stopped and trade was strictly controlled. These changes had serious implications for Cheju. Basic necessities became short in supply, and the Cheju people therefore used their fishing boats for the illegal transportation of repatriates and goods from Japan. Consequently, the police and right-wing activists constantly harassed the local people on the pretense of controlling smuggling. Police, USAMGIK administrators, and members of right-wing organizations, including Northwest Youth, were all involved in such activities. Members of the Northwest Youth assigned to Cheju were mostly North Koreans who had been expelled by the Communists. They worked as volunteers and were attached to police substations. Because they received no official income, they used their positions to extort money from the local community. They would arrest people on suspicion of smuggling and then torture them until their families paid to have them released. Inevitably the police and right-wing groups were generally despised, not merely for their ideology, but rather for their immoral and corrupt behavior.

The main group responsible for the uprising on 3 April 1948 was the Cheju-do Committee of the South Korean Worker's Party. It utilized the strained relations between the local people and the mainlander police and right-wing organizations to obstruct the 10 May elections.

The uprising began at dawn on 3 April 1948, with the lighting of beacons on the hills surrounding Mount Halla. Eleven of the twenty-four police offices on the island were simultaneously attacked. The residences of Northwest Youth members and leaders of right-wing organizations including the National Society for the Rapid Realization of Korean Independence and the Taedong Youth Corps were also raided. This resulted in the deaths of four police officers, eight right-wing activists, and three insurgents. Twenty-seven people were wounded, two disappeared, and one insurgent was arrested.

In response, 1,700 police officers were sent from the mainland to quell the resistance and the 9th Regiment of Constabulary Units was ordered to move out. On the initiative of regimental commander Lieutenant Colonel Kim Ik-yŏl, a peaceful settlement was reached with the rebels on 28 April 1948; however, USAMGIK authorities in Seoul rejected this. They classified the revolt as a Communist insurgency linked to the Comintern, and to them a negotiated settlement was unacceptable. Complete repression was the only viable solution, which also conveniently fell in line with U.S. interests to avoid criticism from the Soviet Union and produced a cover-up for the Korean police and right-wing organizations on Cheju.

The uprising caused the elections held on 10 May to be declared invalid. Leadership changes and security reinforcements ensued, aimed at taking a tighter control over the island. Such steps, however, merely incited further rebellion, resulting in the assassination of Colonel Pak Chin-gyŏng, the newly appointed commander of the 9th Regiment. In early September another attack was launched against the rebels; meanwhile the South Korean government transformed the existing constabulary units into army units. The situation, however, took an unexpected turn when the 14th Regiment, reassigned to Cheju, rebelled in Yŏsu and Sunch'ŏn.

From 20 October the government authorities initiated the use of scorched-earth tactics. The coastline was blockaded and all mountain areas five kilometers from the shore were declared "enemy zones." The govern-ment ordered all civilians to evacuate these areas and many villages were burned to the ground. The 2d Regiment replaced the 9th Regiment and army-air-naval joint operations were launched. The government ordered walls built around every coastal village to keep out the rebels. As a result, many innocent people were ruthlessly and needlessly massacred by government troops. One such incident was the Pukch'on village massacre.

The situation finally turned around with the visit of President Syngman Rhee to Cheju Island in April 1949 and the holding of elections the following May. Some 50,000 civilian guards (*Minbodan*) were assigned to hunt down the rebel troops hiding in the mountains. In the end, most insurgents, including their leader Yi Tŏk-gu, were killed.

By August 1949 the Cheju-do Rebellion had ended, yet the bloodshed was not over. Those who had been sympathizers or who had played minor roles in the rebellion were released and forced to join the National Guidance Alliance. However, when the Korean War broke out, those with prior records of subversive activities were rearrested, along with the families of known rebels, and most were executed. Rebels who had been imprisoned on the mainland were also summarily executed. On 21 September 1954, six and a half years after the initial uprising, Mount Halla was finally declared a "free zone." The total population of Cheju Island before the uprising was 276,148 people. Initially the rebels numbered around 500 hard-core militants along with 1,000 to 3,000 supporters; later this number dramatically increased as a result of the government's scorched-earth tactics. The exact toll in human lives is still unknown and researchers have given varying estimates ranging from 20,000 to 80,000 people. The official death toll is 27,719, yet the governor of Cheju stated that almost 60,000 people had been killed and about 40,000 had fled to Japan. National records indicate that 39,285 houses were demolished, whereas in reality this figure is likely to have been much higher. According to the local governor, most of the houses built in the hills were leveled, and 230 of 400 villages were completely destroyed.

The Cheju Island Rebellion certainly highlighted the frail legitimacy and raw inexperience of the new Republic of Korea (ROK) government. It is possible that this incident also played a significant role in encouraging North Korean leaders to initiate the Korean War.

—*Man-Ho Heo*

References:

Cheju 4.3 yŏn'gu-so [Research Center on the April 3 Cheju Rebellion]. *Ijesa Malhaemsuda* [Now, I would like to say…]. Vols. 1, 2. Seoul: Hanul, 1989.

Chemin Ilbo 4.3 Ch'uijeban [Chemin Ilbo Reporters on the April 3 Cheju Rebellion]. *4.3 ŭn Malhanda* [The April 3 Cheju Rebellion Says]. Vols. 1, 2. Seoul: Chŏnyewŏn, 1994.

Cumings, Bruce. *The Origins of the Korean War.* Vol. 2, *The Roaring of the Cataract 1947–1950.* Princeton, NJ: Princeton University Press, 1990.

Meade, E. Grant. *American Military Government in Korea.* New York: King's Crown Press, 1952.

Merril, John. "The Cheju-do Rebellion." *Journal of Korean Studies* 2 (1980): 139–197.

See also: Yŏsu-Sunch'ŏn Rebellion.

Chemical Warfare

Chemical warfare is based on the employment of incapacitating, choking, blistering, and nerve- and blood-damaging agents. Examples of such casualty-producing agents are BZ (a lysergic acid diethylamide [LSD] derivative), chlorine gas, AC (hydrogen cyanide), L (lewisite), and GA (tabun). In Korea, some U.S. front-line commanders pressed for the use of chemical agents against Communist troops. These forceful appeals were echoed domestically and the topic was even debated in the *Armed Forces Chemical Journal*, but did not gain any popular or political support. As a result, contrary to Communist propaganda, chemical warfare did not occur in the Korean War.

Although the United States had a sizable stockpile of chemical agents, enjoyed air superiority, and possessed superior chemical defenses over Korean and Chinese forces, initiating chemical warfare was not politically or militarily advantageous. The United Nations (UN) coalition might have been endangered by unilateral U.S. use of chemical weapons, which were viewed with great international antipathy. The Soviet Union could also have provided the Democratic People's Republic of Korea (North Korea) with its own chemical arsenal for retaliatory purposes, and the contamination of confined terrain, such as the Pusan perimeter or the Inch'ŏn landing site, by chemical agents would have been potentially disastrous for UN forces.

Communist allegations of chemical agent use first arose on Beijing radio on 5 March 1951. These allegations were followed by further alleged attacks reported in a Chinese Red Cross publication dated 6 December 1951 and by a commission of the International Association of Democratic Lawyers in its 1952 *Report on U.S. Crimes in Korea.*

At least five alleged incidents were claimed to have taken place based on the U.S. employment of choking and blistering agents. The first alleged incident was on 23 February 1951 when "poison gas of an asphyxiating type" was dropped by two U.S. aircraft against Korean People's Army (KPA, North Korean) positions twenty miles southeast of Seoul on the Han River. The second, and largest, alleged incident took place on 6 May 1951 against Namp'o. Three B-29 bombers were said to have dropped gas bombs, producing a chlorine-like smell, which suffocated 480 people and caused 899 other casualties. The third alleged incident, of 6 July 1951, took place against the village of P'ungp'ae-ri south of Wŏnsan. Two U.S. jets were said to have flown over the village and spread either gas or some other chemical product over an open area 200 meters east of the village. Two farmers on their way to their field were caught in the cloud and suffered blistering of the skin.

The fourth alleged incident took place on 1 August 1951 when a bomb was dropped on the village of Yŏnsan-ni and another on Wŏnch'on-ni in Hwanghae Province. The four deaths and 36 casualities that occurred were attributed to a yellow-green cloud of chlorine-like gas. The fifth alleged incident of 9 January 1952 took place against the small mountain village of Haksŏng-ni north of Wŏnsan. Two U.S. jets were said to have bombarded the village with what again was alluded to as a chlorine-like gas, with the end result of 83 casualties.

The alleged incidents of chemical warfare undertaken by U.S. forces were part of a broader propaganda campaign to influence international opinion. To break up the U.S.-led coalition of UN members against the Communist forces, the *Report on U.S. Crimes in Korea* also chronicled alleged instances of biological and germ (bacteriological) warfare, murders, massacres, air attacks on civilians, and other atrocities and war crimes conducted by U.S. forces.

—*Robert J. Bunker*

References:

Commission of International Association of Democratic Lawyers. *Report on U.S. Crimes in Korea.* P'yŏngyang: Democratic People's Republic of Korea, 1952.

Stockholm International Peace Research Institute. *The Problem of Chemical and Biological Warfare.* 6 vols. New York: Humanities Press, 1971–1975.

Utgoff, Victor A. *The Challenge of Chemical Weapons: An American Perspective.* New York: St. Martin's Press, 1991.

See also: Biological Warfare.

Chen Yi
(1901–1972)

Mayor of Shanghai in the People's Republic of China during the Korean War and later foreign minister. Born in Luozhi in Sichuan province on 26 August 1901, Chen Yi became a Chinese Communist Party (CCP) member in 1923 and joined the Northern Expedition three years later. After Jiang Jieshi's (Chiang Kai-shek's) purge of the Communists in spring 1927, Chen participated in the Nanchang Uprising, the first large-scale CCP military endeavor, later that year. By the early 1930s, Chen had reached the apex of party leadership, after having survived the many vicissitudes of the CCP.

When the Red Army embarked on the Long March in 1934, Chen was left behind in the south to carry out guerrilla warfare against the Guomindang (Nationalists). Chen's contribution to the survival and then rise of the CCP until 1949 was chiefly military in nature. His victory in the important Battle of Huaihai clinched the final outcome of the 1946–1949 civil war.

When the Korean War began, Chen Yi was mayor of Shanghai and was holding other important posts as well. During the war he sent about half a million troops of whom he had control to fight in Korea, although he was not directly involved in military planning or the actual fighting. As mayor of perhaps the most developed Chinese city, he gave full support to the tremendous effort and contributions by Shanghai to the Korean War. In fact, he was vital in the frenzied activities to raise funds, to manufacture and collect war materiel to send to Korea, and to organize groups to go to the front to convey greetings and appreciation to the Chinese soldiers there. In short, Shanghai under Chen Yi played a key role in sustaining the supply lines to the Korean battlefront.

For much of the Korean War, the Chinese People's Resist America Aid Korea Movement ran alongside the "Three Antis" and "Five Antis" Campaigns. Chen Yi played a key role in directing these three campaigns, which fed on one another.

Chen Yi's career changed course at the end of the 1950s when he replaced Zhou Enlai as the foreign minister, although Zhou still retained the overriding say in foreign affairs. Immediately after assuming the new post in February 1958, Chen accompanied Zhou to P'yŏngyang to negotiate the withdrawal of the vast number of Chinese soldiers still stationed in Korea after the cessation of hostilities.

In the Cultural Revolution, Lin Biao, second only to Mao Zedong in influence, targeted Chen as a key enemy. Mao evidently remembered Chen's past contributions, and Chen was spared the most extreme political persecution and suffering. He had the satisfaction of witnessing the fall and death of Lin Biao less than four months before he himself died of cancer on 6 January 1972 in Beijing.

—*Chan Lau Kit-ching*

References:

Kan Yaoji, Lo Yingcai, and Tie Zhuwei, eds. *Zhongguo Yuanshuai Xilie Congshu* [Series of studies of Chinese marshals]. Beijing: Zhonggong Zhongyang Dangxiao Chubanshe, 1996.

Klein, Donald W., and Anne B. Clark. *Biographic Dictionary of Chinese Communism, 1921–1965.* Cambridge, MA: Harvard University Press, 1971.

Matray, James I., ed. *Historical Dictionary of the Korean War.* Westport, CT: Greenwood Press, 1991.

Zhonggong Shanghai Shiwei Dangshi Yanjiushi [Research Institute for Party History, Shanghai City Committee of the Chinese Communist Party]. *Zhongguo Gongchandang Zai Shanghai, 1921–1991* [Chinese Communist Party in Shanghai, 1921–1991]. Shanghai: Shanghai Renmin Chubanshe, 1991.

Zhu Minyan, ed. *Zhonggong Danshi Renwu Yanjiu Huiczii* [Research Bulletin of Chinese Communist Party Members]. Shanghai: Fudan Daxue Chubanshe, 1992.

See also: China, People's Republic of; Lin Biao; Mao Zedong; Zhou Enlai.

China Lobby

Informal grouping of fiercely anti-Communist Americans—business people, publishers, missionaries, politicians, and others—who advocated unstinting support of Jiang Jieshi (Chiang Kai-shek) and the Nationalist Guomindang. Its supporters generally strongly endorsed U.S. intervention in Korea but found the Truman administration insufficiently pro-Jiang and wished to extend the U.S. commitment to include wideranging assistance for Taiwan and possibly the Republic of China's participation in the Korean War.

The China lobby included several influential members of the U.S. Congress, including Senators William F. Knowland of California (later nicknamed "the Senator for Formosa"), Styles Bridges of New Hampshire, and to some extent Richard M. Nixon of California, who formed within the Senate a China bloc that generally lobbied and voted for U.S. assistance of every kind for Nationalist China. They did so in collaboration with private pro-China Americans, prominent among whom were Henry R. Luce, the publisher of *Time*; the newspaper magnate William Randolph Hearst; the industrialist Alfred Kohlberg; the flier Claire Chennault, who organized China's World War II Flying Tigers air force; military men, including Douglas MacArthur; and missionaries. The China lobby had close ties to Guomindang officials, the most notable of whom were members of the Soong family, including Jiang's wife, Soong Meiling; her brother, T. V. Soong; and China's finance minister, their brother-in-law H. H. Kung.

Until the Korean War began, the China lobby concentrated its efforts upon obtaining U.S. military and economic assistance for the Nationalist government and denying similar resources to the Chinese Communists. By 1948 U.S. President Harry S. Truman, appalled by the extensive corruption within the Guomindang regime, wished to halt all such aid, but China lobby supporters succeeded in inserting substantial amounts for China into both the 1948 Marshall Plan and the 1950 Korean Assistance Act as a condition of support for their passage. After the Communist takeover of mainland China in 1949 the Guomindang government fled to Taiwan, and Truman and Secretary of State Dean Acheson contemplated the cessation of U.S. aid to the Nationalists, eventual recognition of the People's Republic of China, and acquiescence in a

Chinese Communist takeover of Taiwan. The China lobby reacted with outrage to the State Department's 1950 publication of *The China White Paper*, which placed the responsibility for the "loss" of China to communism squarely upon Guomindang corruption, incompetence, and unpopularity. Senator Joseph R. McCarthy and the China lobby, by contrast, blamed Jiang's downfall upon the efforts of what they described as traitorous pro-Communist officials within the State Department.

Historians have argued that by 1950 public support for the China lobby was waning, even though Douglas MacArthur, who headed the Japanese occupation forces, visited Taiwan and expressed his unwavering backing for Jiang Jieshi and the cause of international anti-communism. The unexpected North Korean invasion converted the Republic of China on Taiwan into an anti-Communist Asian redoubt and ally that deserved support at all costs, a development greatly enhanced by the November 1950 Chinese intervention in the Korean conflict. The China lobby demanded that, as part of the postinvasion global enhancement of U.S. military commitments, Taiwan be protected. The U.S. Seventh Fleet was transferred to the Taiwan Strait, to prevent a potential Communist invasion, and aid to the Guomindang increased dramatically. Charges that the pro-Communist sympathies of State Department officials had facilitated both the Chinese Communist victory and North Korea's invasion won new public credibility, ending the diplomatic careers of assorted China experts, including O. Edmund Clubb, John Paton Davies, Owen Lattimore, John Stewart Service, and John Carter Vincent. McCarthy's broader allegations that Communist agents and their supporters had infiltrated the entire government also found a more receptive audience.

Although U.S. officials refused Jiang's offers of troops for the Korean conflict, fearing that sending Guomindang soldiers into action against Chinese People's Volunteer Army (Communist Chinese) forces might prove overly provocative, they found themselves tied to an ally that they had previously hoped to jettison.

Despite this new posture, throughout the Korean War members of the China lobby ferociously attacked the Truman administration, which they characterized as soft on communism and deplorably heedless of the demands of national security. They particularly deplored Truman's recall of MacArthur and the president's reluctance to expand the war further by using nuclear weapons against mainland China or bombing Manchurian cities, tactics which they hoped might also lead to a restoration of Guomindang rule. The China lobby also condemned past U.S. policy toward China. Until the late 1960s, fears of attracting similar criticism from the still powerful lobby deterred subsequent administrations from making any serious effort to reopen relations with the People's Republic of China.

—*Priscilla Roberts*

References:

Bachrack, Stanley D. *The Committee of One Million: "China Lobby" Politics, 1953–1971*. New York: Columbia University Press, 1976.

Caridi, Ronald J. *The Korean War and American Politics: The Republican Party As a Case Study*. Philadelphia: University of Pennsylvania Press, 1968.

Caute, David. *The Great Fear: The Anti-Communist Purge under Truman and Eisenhower*. New York: Simon & Schuster, 1978.

Cotton, James. *Asian Frontier Nationalism: Owen Lattimore and the American Foreign Policy Debate*. Atlantic Highlands, NJ: Humanities Press International, 1989.

Davies, John Paton. *Dragon by the Tail: American, British, Japanese, and Russian Encounters with China and One Another*. New York: W. W. Norton, 1972.

Dobbs, Charles M. *The Unwanted Symbol: American Foreign Policy, the Cold War, and Korea, 1945–1950*. Kent, OH: Kent State University Press, 1981.

Fried, Richard M. *Nightmare in Red: The McCarthy Era in Perspective*. New York: Oxford University Press, 1990.

Graebner, Norman A. *The New Isolationism: A Study in Politics and Foreign Policy Since 1950*. New York: Ronald Press, 1956.

See also: Acheson, Dean Goodersham; Knowland, William Fife; MacArthur, Douglas; McCarthy, Joseph R.; Nixon, Richard Milhous; Truman, Harry S.

China, People's Republic of

"We, the four hundred and seventy-five million people of China, have now stood up." So declared Mao Zedong on 1 October 1949, when he and his senior comrades in the Chinese Communist leadership stood atop Tiananmen (Heavenly Peace Gate) in the heart of Beijing and ceremonially proclaimed the establishment of the People's Republic of China. Mao's words reflected an important aspect of his long, violent struggle for power: it was not only, perhaps not even primarily, about following Marxist ideology or creating a Communist political and economic system. Mao's revolution was also propelled by a powerful urge to recapture national pride and to restore China's stature as a great nation—in its own eyes and those of the world—after more than a century of humiliating weakness.

When war broke out in Korea less than nine months later, Mao and his colleagues were by no means eager to send their army into action beyond China's borders. After years of war, Japanese occupation, famine, and civil conflict, China's new leaders faced a vast job of reconstruction. Militarily, their attention was fixed not on Korea but on the island province of Taiwan, now the last bastion of the vanquished Nationalist government led by Jiang Jieshi (Chiang Kai-shek). Communist commanders were keenly aware that their army was in many respects poorly prepared to fight a modern, well-equipped opponent in Korea—or Taiwan, for that matter.

Yet Chinese leaders could not passively ignore Korean events, whatever their misgivings. If China were to act as a great power, as Mao and his colleagues were determined it would, it needed to respond to any threat approaching its borders. Nor could it accept the loss of prestige if it stood by and let a Communist neighbor go down to defeat. Accordingly, China warned in the fall of 1950 that it would join the war if U.S. forces entered North Korean territory. When the warning was ignored, China made good on its threat.

For China, intervening in Korea had profound and long-lasting consequences. The war froze U.S.-Chinese relations in implacable hostility for a generation and helped spur China's drive to develop nuclear weapons. The Korean War also damaged China's alliance with the Soviet Union, which promised but failed to deliver air support for Chinese troops. Mao would never forget or forgive that last-minute betrayal, as he saw it, which contributed to the bitter final break between the two Communist giants a decade later. The war also intensified Mao's obsessions about hidden enemies at home. Hundreds of thousands of Chinese were persecuted as spies or counterrevolutionaries in the first of the mass witch-hunts that would characterize Mao's rule.

Communist Road to Power

The Communist revolution in China was part of a larger upheaval that convulsed the country for decades after the fall of the last emperor in 1911. With no effective central government in control, regional warlords had vied for power while life for ordinary Chinese grew increasingly desperate. The struggle to create a strong, modern national government began to coalesce around the Guomindang, or Nationalist Party (KMT), organized and led by the long-time republican revolutionary Sun Yat-sen. The ferment of the time gave birth to the Communist Party, which held its first party congress in Shanghai in 1921.

While developing their own base of support among peasants and industrial workers, the Communists supported Sun's national government, based in the southern city of Canton (now Guangzhou). In 1925, shortly after Sun's death, the Communists joined forces with the KMT to mount the Northern Expedition, a military campaign to defeat the warlords and unify China under a Nationalist government. As Northern Expedition forces neared Shanghai in March 1927, Communist-led revolutionaries seized control of the city and handed it over to the arriving troops.

Days later, however, Jiang Jieshi (Chiang Kai-shek), the new Guomindang leader, turned on his Communist allies. Paramilitaries, backed by Jiang's troops and organized by a loose alliance of Shanghai gangsters, anti-Communist bankers and industrialists, and foreign business interests, struck on 12 April, seizing Communist labor union headquarters, dispersing the workers' militia units, and hunting down party leaders. Hundreds were arrested and shot. Street protests were put down with gunfire, with many deaths. Surviving party leaders, among them future Prime Minister Zhou Enlai, slipped away to try to rebuild their shattered movement.

In the following years the Communists regrouped in rural areas. A mountainous region in Jiangxi Province became their most important base, grandly known as the Jiangxi Soviet Republic. There the Communists held out until, in October 1934 with Nationalist troops closing in, the party leadership decided to evacuate. Their retreat, enshrined in Communist legend as the Long March, wound some 6,000 miles through some of the world's most remote and harshest terrain before ending more than a year later in Shaanxi Province, the revolutionaries' new base until they returned to conquer all of China fourteen years later.

The Long March also marked Mao Zedong's emergence as the supreme Communist leader. Outranked by rivals when the march started, Mao assumed command along the route. In January 1935 a party conference in the city of Zunyi confirmed Mao's leadership, which he never relinquished.

Soon after the Long March ended, Japan, which had seized Manchuria in 1931, invaded China proper. After occupying Beijing, the Japanese quickly captured Shanghai and other coastal cities, then pushed inland. Facing a common enemy, the Nationalists and Communists once again formed an alliance. But it was a hostile and suspicious partnership, with both sides preparing to resume their struggle even while they were still fighting the Japanese.

After Japan's surrender in August 1945, civil war resumed. Chiang, with aid and logistical support from the United States, sought to reestablish his rule over all of China. But corruption and incompetent leadership drained away his government's popular support. Mao's forces, meanwhile, had gained in size, skill, and confidence during years of guerrilla war against the Japanese. By the fall of 1949 the Guomindang army was being driven out of its last footholds on the Chinese mainland. Mao proclaimed the People's Republic from the top of the Heavenly Peace Gate in Beijing on 1 October. Ten weeks later, Jiang fled with the remnants of his government and army to the island of Taiwan off the southern Chinese coast.

China Enters the Korean War

Despite their success in the civil war, Chinese commanders had reservations in the summer of 1950 as

China's new leaders debated whether to send troops to Korea. The Red Army had spent years developing its skill in guerrilla warfare but had only relatively brief and hurried experience fielding larger units in a conventional conflict. Its equipment, mostly captured from the Japanese or the Nationalists, was worn out and obsolete. A large number of its more than 5 million troops had joined only in the civil war's last stages and had little experience or training. Many were former Nationalist soldiers who had switched sides as Jiang's decrepit army retreated.

Shortly before the Korean fighting began, Mao approved large-scale demobilization plans and publicly announced that the revolution's "military phase" was over. Once the war in Korea started, however, China began preparing for a possible response. In early July Mao ordered a major military buildup in the border region. Formal orders issued by the Central Military Commission on 13 July established the Northeast Border Defense Army, initially made up of the Thirty-eighth, Thirty-ninth, Fortieth, and Forty-second Field Armies, along with artillery, air defense units, and supporting troops. By late July 255,000 troops were in place along the border.

The Chinese buildup continued while, General Douglas MacArthur's United Nations (UN) forces carried out the successful landing at Inch'ŏn, recaptured Seoul, and pursued the disintegrating Korean People's Army (North Korea) northward toward the 38th parallel. On the last day of September, Democratic People's Republic of Korea (DPRK, North Korean) leader Kim Il Sung formally requested Chinese troops. Almost certainly the request was made with reluctance. Kim's regime, regarding the Soviet Union as its principal sponsor and ally, had maintained a distant, chilly relationship with the Chinese Communists. But with his own army facing destruction, Kim now had no alternative to seeking China's help.

There was reluctance on the Chinese side, as well, but Mao did not believe he had any choice either. Defeat of the DPRK would bring hostile foreign forces to China's northeastern border and might encourage Chiang Kai-shek to send his forces back across the Taiwan Strait to reopen the civil war on the mainland. Mao's associates still had doubts. Army chief Lin Biao refused to take command of a Korean campaign, claiming poor health. But Mao decided, according to Chinese documents, possibly as early as 2 October, that war was inevitable and necessary. To lead the Chinese effort, once Lin had bowed out, Mao turned to Peng Dehuai, one of the creators of the Red Army and vice-chairman of the Central Military Commission.

On 8 October Mao issued the official directive: "It has been ordered that the Northeast Border Defense Army be turned into the Chinese People's Volunteers"

(the name was a fig leaf, a transparent device for China to go to war with the United States without formally avowing it) "and that the Chinese People's Volunteers move immediately into the territory of Korea to assist the Korean comrades in their struggle." The same day, Mao dispatched Zhou Enlai to the Soviet Union to iron out details of Soviet support. But instead of confirming earlier promises to provide air cover for Chinese troops, Soviet leader Joseph Stalin told Zhou that air support would not be provided, at least not initially. Stalin's last-minute reversal came as an unwelcome shock in Beijing. Mao briefly halted military preparations but then ordered Peng to proceed.

China explicitly warned the United States of its intention. Prime Minister Zhou called on Indian ambassador to Beijing K. M. Panikkar to relay the message that China would enter the war if U.S. troops entered North Korean territory. Washington chose to regard the message a bluff. MacArthur and his staff belittled the threat ("Scared of a bunch of Chinese laundrymen?" one of MacArthur's top commanders sneered at a worried subordinate) and ordered UN forces to continue their advance. But the Chinese were not bluffing. In mid-October the first Chinese troops crossed the Yalu River. Within a month, ten field armies with approximately 300,000 "volunteers" were on Korean territory.

Korean War and Afterward

Chinese troops fought in Korea for more than two and a half years, paying a heavy price. Western estimates state that nearly a million Chinese soldiers were killed or wounded. Among the dead was Mao's oldest son, Anying. On the home front, Mao used the war to harness Chinese patriotism more closely to Communist Party rule. A nationwide propaganda crusade, dubbed the "great movement of resisting America and assisting Korea," preached hatred of U.S. "imperialists." In a related campaign to "suppress reactionaries," authorities arrested huge numbers of suspects—as many as two and a half million, by one count—for real or imagined opposition to the Communist regime. Many of these were executed, more than 28,000, according to official records, in Guangdong Province alone.

Even while the fighting in Korea continued, the early 1950s was a period of rebuilding and, for most Chinese, a time of relative order after many years of violent turmoil. After the war, the leadership concentrated on reconstructing the national economy. Significant gains in industrial production occurred under the Soviet-style First Five-Year Plan, initiated in 1953. The Soviet Union sent machinery, equipment, and thousands of technical advisers, and it provided some financial support, though on a disappointingly modest scale, in Chinese eyes. Soviet credits were only

4 percent of China's total industrial investment during the plan period. The Soviets also helped rebuild and modernize the Chinese armed forces.

Early in 1958 Mao launched a new policy, the Great Leap Forward. Promising a new life of wealth and comfort, party leaders announced ludicrously unrealistic targets for industrial and agricultural growth. Plenty of technicians and economists could have warned that the plan was a fantasy, but unhappily for China, the Leap came on the heels of a nationwide "anti-rightist" campaign, in which hundreds of thousands were sent to prison or labor camps. Intellectuals had been subject to particularly harsh persecution. As a result, specialists in industry or government bureaus who might have spoken out were frightened into silence instead.

Rather than instant prosperity, the Great Leap brought economic devastation. Millions died of hunger as a direct result of disastrously mistaken agricultural policies. Among the top leaders, only Peng Dehuai had the courage to confront Mao about the famine. For his honesty, Peng was demoted from the leadership (he would later be imprisoned, tortured, and killed). After Peng's downfall, all his senior colleagues, including Zhou Enlai and Deng Xiaoping, the two leaders most widely praised in the West in later years, were cowed into silence. Their failure to speak condemned China's peasantry to two more years of horror before Mao grudgingly allowed some modification of the Great Leap program. China has never disclosed the number of deaths; a study by American demographer Judith Banister estimated that a staggering 30 million Chinese died before the famine finally ended.

In the midst of the Leap, the Soviet-Chinese alliance splintered. Soviet technical advisers were called home and the two Communist powers openly denounced each other's leaders, doctrines, ambitions, and policies. Before long, the Soviet Union had supplanted the United States as China's most dangerous and demonized enemy.

Barely five years after the Great Leap ended, Mao unleashed the Great Proletarian Cultural Revolution—simultaneously a power play against senior leaders, whom Mao now saw as political enemies, and a gigantic effort to recreate a revolutionary spirit in a new generation of Chinese. At the top of the party hierarchy, the supple Zhou Enlai survived, but many of Mao's oldest and closest associates were struck down, while power passed into the hands of Mao's vindictive wife, Jiang Qing, and a small group of other leaders under her patronage. Prominent victims included head of state Liu Shaoqi, who died in prison in 1969, and Deng Xiaoping, who survived to become China's leader after Mao's death.

Across China, youthful Red Guards engaged in a frenzy of persecution. The turmoil shut down schools and paralyzed factories and government offices. The chaos continued for two years until, beginning in late 1968, military officials took direct charge of many enterprises and government bureaus. The Red Guards were ordered to disband, and a draconian new policy sent most young people from cities and towns out to work as field laborers in rural villages.

Mao's last years saw a dramatic realignment in China's foreign relations. Conflict with the Soviet Union turned bloody in 1969 when Chinese and Soviet troops clashed in disputed areas along the northeastern border. The Soviet threat spurred China's leaders to seek improved relations with the United States, and in February 1972 Mao welcomed U.S. President Richard Nixon to Beijing. Nixon's visit ended the long freeze between the two countries, though full diplomatic relations were restored only in 1979.

Post-Mao Era

Mao Zedong died in September 1976 and was officially mourned as a great and heroic leader. But his successors almost immediately abandoned his policies and launched China onto a dramatically different course. Mao's widow Jiang Qing and her closest associates, the group identified with the Cultural Revolution, were arrested and charged with treason less than a month after Mao died. Mao's nominal successor was the colorless functionary Hua Guofeng, but behind the scenes, the veteran Deng Xiaoping, twice the victim of Mao's purges, became the most powerful Chinese leader. By late 1978, though Hua would remain for a few more years as a figurehead, Deng was publicly functioning as China's paramount ruler.

Under Deng far-reaching economic reforms dismantled rural communes and permitted a wide range of free-market enterprise, while also opening China to foreign investment. The economic results were stunning. Rural incomes soared and, for the first time in China's long history, hunger was only a memory for the vast majority of Chinese peasants. Private businesses flourished, creating a new consumer culture. Rock music, imported movies and television programs, and other previously forbidden forms of popular entertainment captured huge audiences.

Reforms brought new problems, however. The gap between rich and poor widened dramatically (after a decade of reform, incomes were more unequal in supposedly socialist China than in capitalist Taiwan or South Korea). Crime, drug addiction, and prostitution reappeared in Chinese cities. Corruption became a widespread problem at all levels of government. And though Deng's China was far more open than Mao's, growing freedom paradoxically produced growing discontent with the repressive, arbitrary power still wielded by the Communist Party and its officials.

In the spring of 1989 student-led demonstrators in Beijing occupied Tiananmen Square, calling for democratic reforms. As the protesters used the word, democracy did not necessarily mean a political system based on popular rule but a disparate mix of ideas: greater freedoms of personal choice and expression; a cleaner, more accountable government; a fairer, less arbitrary system of authority. Those goals commanded wide popular support, but to Deng, a Communist Party member for sixty-five years, giving in to antiparty protests would have meant an unthinkable loss of prestige and authority. On the night of 3–4 June, tanks and troops of the People's Liberation Army stormed into the center of Beijing and reoccupied the square. Hundreds of civilians died in the assault. Some student leaders slipped out of the country, eluding a massive dragnet by Chinese security agencies, but other movement leaders and sympathizers were hunted down, arrested, and sentenced to long prison terms.

In the aftermath of the crackdown, many inside and outside China wondered if the party leadership would try to roll back all the changes of the previous decade. But despite his resistance to political change, Deng remained committed to economic reforms. Nearing ninety, Deng gradually relinquished an active leadership role, but before exiting the political stage for good, he made sure that reform policies would continue under his successors. By Deng's death in February 1995, China's economy was again booming. Tiananmen Square was not forgotten; yet there was little open dissent, as most Chinese seemed ready for the time being to leave political issues aside and enjoy the personal freedoms brought by prosperity.

—*Arnold R. Isaacs*

References:

Becker, Jasper. *Hungry Ghosts: Mao's Secret Famine*. New York: Free Press, 1996.

Chen, Jian. *China's Road to the Korean War: The Making of the Sino-American Confrontation*. New York: Columbia University Press, 1994.

Goncharov, Sergei N., John W. Lewis, and Xue Litai. *Uncertain Partners: Stalin, Mao, and the Korean War*. Stanford, CA: Stanford University Press, 1993.

Salisbury, Harrison E. *The New Emperors: China in the Era of Mao and Deng*. Boston: Little, Brown, 1992

Spence, Jonathan. *The Search for Modern China*. New York: W. W. Norton, 1990.

Spurr, Russell. *Enter the Dragon: China's Undeclared War against the U.S. in Korea, 1950-1951*. New York: Henry Holt, 1988

See also: Kim Il Sung; Lin Biao; Mao Zedong; Panikkar, Sardar K. M.; Peng Dehuai (Peng Te-huai); Stalin, Josef; Zhou Enlai

China, People's Republic of: Air Force

People's Republic of China (PRC) Air Force operations during the Korean War proved important but not decisive in the conflict. Before its October–November 1950 intervention to attack United Nations (UN) forces in North Korea, the PRC deployed several squadrons of its 650 first-line combat aircraft to airfields just north of the Manchurian–North Korean border. Some squadrons flew older World War II–vintage piston-driven aircraft; others piloted the most advanced Soviet-built jet fighters. These modern jets, flown by China's best aviators, outperformed U.S. fighters, significantly affecting the air war over Korea. The PRC, however, never based substantial numbers of its aircraft south of the Yalu River and thus never adequately supported the Chinese People's Volunteer Army (CPVA), the Chinese forces fighting the ground war in Korea.

The Chinese stationed considerable numbers of aircraft of various types in Manchuria, but seldom forayed south of the Yalu River. Some of the older aircraft included the Soviet-built Il-2 Sturmovik, an armored attack aircraft, famous for its effectiveness against German panzers during World War II. Although the Il-2 was seldom used for its designed purpose in Korea, CPVA pilots flying Il-2s occasionally strafed UN troops during the winter of 1950–1951. On 14 October 1950, two aircraft sneaked through UN defenses and bombed Kimpŏ Airfield, but did no damage. Other squadrons flew similar missions with Lavochkin La-9, the last Soviet piston-engine fighter. Occasionally a few "Bed-Check Charlies" harassed UN troops at night, sometimes they flew Polikarpov PO-2 biplanes from another era. U.S. air superiority precluded many such attacks.

After China entered the conflict, the U.S. Fifth Air Force ruled the skies and pounded the long Chinese supply lines that the PRC Air Force could not protect. Bitter recriminations emanated from the Chinese high command, where some ground commanders believed that their air force had left them in the lurch and that, had they been properly supported, they could have driven UN forces into the sea. Certainly the PRC Air Force remained conspicuously absent over Chinese ground troops throughout the war.

The real challenge for the Korean skies began with Chinese introduction of jet fighters that eclipsed the best U.S. fighters deployed in the Far East. A few Chinese and North Korean squadrons were equipped with La-11 jet fighters, but the swept-wing Mikoyan and Gurevich MiG-15 proved to be the bane of UN fighter pilots. First introduced by the Soviet Union in 1948, the MiG-15 was powered by imported British Rolls Royce engines. Before 1950 Soviet engineers replaced the engine with a more powerful version copied from the British import. This variant substantially outperformed the U.S. F-80 Shooting Star and F-84 Thunderjet, even after designers modified it with swept wings and renamed it Thunderstreak.

Chinese MiGs first appeared in Korea on 1 November 1950. A flight of U.S. F-51s sighted a flight of the swept-winged fighters in a diving attack from across the Yalu River. The P-51s turned away in evasive maneuvers and managed to escape without loss. A few days later, a U.S. F-80 managed to shoot down the first MiG, but the Americans realized they confronted a vastly superior aircraft. During the first weeks of November, Chinese MiGs also shot down an RB-29 and a B-29 and damaged several others on bombing missions. Far East Command suspended B-29 missions until more fighter escorts arrived to accompany the bombers.

The Pentagon immediately dispatched the new North American F-86 Sabre to Korea in the hopes of matching the MiG's performance. On 17 December four F-86s tangled with four Chinese MiG-15s south of the Yalu in an area soon dubbed MiG Alley by U.S. pilots. In the fray the Americans downed a MiG without loss. On 22 December in a dogfight reminiscent of World War II, a MiG shot down an F-86, but U.S. pilots claimed six MiGs destroyed. Despite these initial successes, the MiG obviously had a higher service ceiling, outclimbed, and was faster than the U.S. jets.

UN restrictions allowed PRC pilots to put these advantages to their best use. United Nations commander General Douglas MacArthur and the Joint Chiefs of Staff believed that the air threat could be eliminated by attacking Chinese airfields in Manchuria. Both U.S. President Harry S. Truman and other Western leaders believed that such bombings might widen the "limited war" in Korea. As a result, Truman restricted U.S. air operations south of the Yalu. Even if in hot pursuit, U.S. Air Force (USAF) pilots could not venture more than six to eight miles into Manchuria. On 24 November 1950, reacting to negative UN reactions and the collapse of UN ground operations in North Korea, the USAF prohibited hot pursuit across the Yalu.

Realizing that they enjoyed a sanctuary from U.S. attacks, Chinese pilots followed the tactic of climbing to a great altitude advantage and then diving across the river to attack patrolling U.S. aircraft. In July 1951 as many as ninety Chinese MiGs crossed the Yalu to attack U.S. aircraft. Formations and tactics varied, apparently at the whim of the flight leader. Chinese MiGs used every tactic from trail formations to the Lufbery Circle. In some instances Chinese pilots copied Luftwaffe tactics used to attack bomber formations in World War II and flew in line abreast to fire on one F-86. In most aerial encounters the Chinese outnumbered UN planes by three to one, but they seldom chose to engage in extended dogfights. Usually after a firing pass or two, the Chinese pilots, utilizing the MiG's superior airspeed, fled back to safety north of the Yalu.

Until his relief in April 1951, General MacArthur railed against this mandated refuge for PRC aircraft, saying that unless corrective measures were promptly taken the air problem "could assume major proportions." No amount of complaints from the Pentagon changed Truman's mind and the Communist pilots enjoyed their haven until the armistice in 1953.

One of the principal factors affecting Truman's decision was the possibility of Chinese counterattacks to air strikes on their territory. Such attacks posed consequential threats to U.S. sanctuaries of aircraft carriers and bases in South Korea and Japan. After Chinese intervention in the ground war, the PRC Air Force sent Ilyushin Il-28 medium bombers to Manchuria. The Il-28, the first Soviet jet bomber, possessed the speed and range to reach UN bases anywhere in the theater. Chinese Il-28s were also equipped with PSB-N radar for bomb aiming, making these tactical bombers even more lethal. USSR engineers had copied the APQ23 radar from B-29s acquired from the United States and installed them in the Ilyushin bombers, providing the Communists with a night and all-weather bombing capability. Additionally, both the Soviets and PRC operated Tupolev Tu-2 bombers capable of carrying two 1,760-pound aerial torpedoes, a verifiable threat to UN carriers steaming off North Korea's shores.

Both the PRC and USAF employed the skies over Korea as a training ground for their pilots, rotating large numbers of aviators through combat tours. The United States, however, enjoyed an initial advantage. Many USAF pilots were experienced combat veterans of World War II and, in many cases, better training compensated for the inferiority of their fighters. Only the F-86E approached the MiG-15 performance above 30,000 feet, which demonstrated one characteristic that overwhelmed unskilled MiG pilots. The MiG tended to stall in some violent high-speed maneuvers and drop into an unrecoverable spin. During the winter of 1952 American pilots observed thirty-two MiGs that spun out of control with only eight pilots bailing out.

The USSR attempted to increase the effectiveness of the PRC Air Force during 1952–1953. As early as 1950 a Sino-Soviet agreement had visualized the "reconstruction" of the PRC Air Force, promising to sell China 3,000 training and combat aircraft. In June 1951 the PRC had approximately 445 jet aircraft, a year later it boasted well over 1,000. UN intelligence estimates placed 1,485 aircraft of all types in Manchuria, including 950 jet fighters, 165 conventional fighters, 100 Il-28s, 115 ground-attack planes, and 90 transports. Soviet manufacturers shipped increasing numbers of jet fighters to China, including the MiG-17. Faster and more capable, it increased the effectiveness of the Chinese Air Force. The MiG-15, mounting 2 x 23-mm cannon, had a top speed of 664 mph and a ceiling of 50,000 feet. MiG-17s boasted an additional cannon, increased airspeed to 711 mph, and a ceiling of nearly 55,000 feet, but they did not see service in Korea. Intelligence analysts monitoring Chinese Air Force radio frequencies confirmed that, to build morale and gain experience against U.S. pilots, Chinese pilots were accompanied by Soviet instructors on some PRC fighter sweeps south of the Yalu.

During the last few weeks of fighting before the armistice, UN intelligence officers discovered increased numbers of MiG fighters at Antung and more medium bombers on other Manchurian bases. Chinese engineers also began construction of airfields in North Korea, possibly with the intent of launching a major contest for control of the air over Korea. In the last full month of air battles, some of the most intensive combat occurred over Korea, and the United States claimed 74 MiGs destroyed. During the entire conflict, U.S. pilots claimed 976 enemy aircraft destroyed (815 MiG-15s) and another 915 damaged, while losing 1,986 aircraft (224 F-86s), about half of these to enemy action.

MiG performance so baffled U.S. military tacticians and engineers that the U.S. Air Force offered $100,000 to any pilot who delivered a MiG to the Americans. Although they finally acquired the coveted fighter, U.S. Air Force officers did not have an opportunity to evaluate the jet until after the armistice and, to their surprise, discovered that the money failed to influence procurement of the MiG. On 21 September 1953 a North Korean defector flew his MiG-15 to Kimpŏ Airfield outside Seoul. After confiscating the aircraft and interrogating the pilot, air force officers learned he had not heard of the offered money.

—*Stanley S. McGowen*

References:
Blair, Clay. *The Forgotten War: America in Korea, 1950–1953.* New York: Times Books, 1987.
Futrell, Robert F. *The United States Air Force in Korea 1950–1953.* Rev. ed. Washington, DC: Office of the Chief of Air Force History, 1983.
Mondey, David, ed. *The International Encyclopedia of Aviation.* New York: Crown, 1977.
No, Kum-Sok, with J. Roger Osterholm. *A MiG-15 to Freedom.* Jefferson, NC: McFarland, 1996.
Nowarra, Heinz J., and G. R. Duval. *Russian Civil and Military Aircraft, 1884–1969,* translated by Allen Myers. London: Fountain Press, 1971.
See also: Aerial Combat; Aircraft (Principal Combat); "Bed-Check Charlies"; Jet Aircraft, First Clash in History; Joint Chiefs of Staff (JCS); MacArthur, Douglas; MiG Alley; MiG, Operation; Soviet Air War In Korea; Truman, Harry S.

China, People's Republic of: Army

The People's Liberation Army (PLA) of the People's Republic of China provided the forces for Chinese military intervention in North Korea. Known as the Chinese People's Volunteers (CPV) (*Zhongguo Renmin Zhiyuanjun*) in the War to Resist U.S. Aggression and Aid Korea [*Kangmei Yuanchao Zhan Shi*], the Chinese People's Volunteer Army (CPVA) was in North Korea from October 1950 until October 1958. At the time of the intervention, CPVA forces were primarily infantry units drawn from the PLA Fourth Field Army. Peng Dehuai commanded the CPVA during the Korean War. At the time, U.S. and United Nations (UN) forces referred to the CPVA as the Chinese Communist Forces in Korea. Another term of reference was Chinese Volunteers (CV).

The PLA was founded on 1 August 1927, during the Nanchang Uprising led by Zhou Enlai, Zhu De, and He Long. During the final stages of the Civil War (1945–1949), the PLA employed both traditional guerrilla (people's war) and conventional tactics to defeat the Nationalist forces.

At the time of the outbreak of the Korean War, PLA forces were composed of experienced Red Army veterans and former Nationalist units that had been integrated into the PLA. It consisted of the First, Second, Third, and Fourth Field Armies under the command of Zhu De, a figurehead who played no role in Korea. In addition, the North China (Fifth) Field Army, which was officially deactivated in October 1949, played a significant leadership role in Korea after the First Campaign of October 1950.

The First Field Army, commanded by Peng Dehuai, occupied northwestern China (Xinjiang Province), where (as with other PLA forces) it was responsible for civil and military administration. When the Korean War began, two of its corps, the I and III, were reorganized into a new I Corps, which eventually participated in the Korean War. By 1954 all units of the First Field Army were deactivated and either assigned as replacement units to Korea or redesignated as production and construction units in Xinjiang.

The Second Field Army participated in the Huai Hai Campaign (6 November 1948 to 10 January 1949), one of three (in addition to the Shen-ning and Ping-jin Campaigns) decisive campaigns of the Chinese Civil War. The Second Field Army, under the leadership of Liu Bocheng, Deng Xiaoping, and He Long, was responsible for Southwestern China and "liberated" Tibet. The XII, XI, XVI, and LV Corps, which all eventually served in Korea, were led by many of the best commanders of the Second Field Army.

During the Civil War, the Third Field Army participated with the Second Field Army in the Huai Hai Campaign. By the time of the Korean War, the Third Field Army was positioned in East China. Some of its units were moved into Shandong Province (across the Yellow Sea from Seoul) to prevent a U.S. invasion.

More than one-half of the regular forces of the Third Field Army eventually fought in Korea.

The best of the Third Field Army's units and commanders were included in its initial contingent of XX, XXVI, and XXVII Corps (reinforced), which were added to the order of battle between 25 November 1950 and 8 January 1951, under the command of Song Shilun. Song had fought against U.S.-trained and equipped Nationalist forces in the Huai Hai Campaign, effectively using swift marches and envelopment tactics. In Korea he was shocked by the high casualties inflicted by U.S. airpower and the coordination of tactical air assets with accurate ground firepower, which devastated personnel and equipment and disrupted supply lines.

As Chinese personnel losses increased, especially during the Fifth Campaign in 1951, replacement units from the Third Field Army were brought in to Korea. In September 1952 the main strength of the XXI, XXIII, XXIV, and XXV Corps was reassigned to Korea.

At the end of the Civil War the Fourth Field Army, commanded by Lin Biao, was split between northeast and southern China. As the Korean War wore on, the Fourth Field Army moved additional forces into northeast China. At the outbreak of the Korean War, however, the majority of Fourth Field Army units were in southern China, where they had expelled or defeated remaining Nationalist forces. The Fourth Field Army provided the main force for the CPV, and its units were among the best in terms of training and combat experience.

Although the North China (Fifth) Field Army had been deactivated, most key leaders took their units into Korea. Its leadership continued to hold key positions within the PLA up until the eve of the Cultural Revolution (1966–1976). During the initial phase of the Korean War, only the Sixty-sixth Corps of the North China Army moved north.

Later the Nineteenth Army Group commanded by Yang Dechi moved from Shanxi to Shandong Province, where it received new Russian equipment and several months of training before it was sent to Korea in February 1951. Yang Dechi concurrently became the second deputy commander of the CPV and eventually replaced Deng as commander of the CPV.

Yang's unit participated in the Fifth Campaign, during which the Nineteenth Army Group crossed the Imjin River, struck the South Korean 1st Division and the British 29th Brigade, destroyed the 1st Battalion of the Gloucester Regiment, and then pushed toward Seoul. The Nineteenth Army Group suffered heavy losses in the UN counterattack at the Iron Triangle and was forced to withdraw. It was reorganized with Fifth Field Army replacements from the LXIX and XVII, Twentieth Army Group. In June 1951, the LXVII and

LXVIII Corps of the Twentieth Army were assigned to Korea. These units defended at Heartbreak Ridge.

The final decision to intervene militarily in Korea was reached by early October 1950. Mao Zedong feared a potential U.S. encroachment into Chinese soil, but he also saw an opportunity to confront and deter U.S. forces indirectly outside Chinese territory in a preemptive strike. Preparations to support the Chinese decision to intervene began several months before the actual intervention. In July 1950, units from the Fourth Field Army were stationed in northeast China to establish the Northeast Border Defense Forces.

Peng Dehuai arrived in northeast China on 4 September 1950 to prepare to lead intervention forces. On 8 October 1950, Peng Dehuai, then Commander of the Northwest First Field Army forces, became commander and commissar of the CPV. Zhou Enlai reportedly suggested the term "volunteers" in order to reduce the risk of direct war with the United States.

The Central Military Commission (CMC) officially issued the order to send Chinese combat troops into North Korea to assist the Korean People's Army on 8 October 1950. Peng sent vanguard units across the Yalu River by the 18th.

At the top of the command and control structure of the CPVA were Mao Zedong, Chairman of the CMC, and Zhou Enlai, who reported directly to Mao and maintained liaison with Kim Il Sung. Zhou was vice-chairman in charge of daily operations, CMC. Below Zhou were two lines of command: operations, headed by Nie Rongzhen (acting chief of staff); and logistics, headed by Gao Gang, commander, Northeast Military Region.

Peng Dehuai reported directly to Nie Rongzhen as the Commander of the CPV. Subordinate to him were Deng Hua, Commander, Thirteenth Army; Zeng Zesheng, Commander, L Corps; and Xiao Xinhuai, Commander, LXVI Corps. Subordinate to Gao Gang were Li Fuchun, deputy secretary, Chinese Communist Party, Northeast Bureau, and, below him, Li Jukui, head, Logistics Department, Northeast Military Region.

Key members of Peng's staff included Deputy Commanders Hong Xuezhi, Deng Hua, and Han Xianchu, and Chief of Staff Xie Fang, who would later play a key role in the initial armistice negotiations. Deng Hua concurrently commanded the Thirteenth Army.

Based on the publication of Chinese materials since the 1980s, the argument that Commander of the Fourth Field Army Lin Biao initially commanded the CPVA appears to be false. Questions remain, however, about Lin's reported refusal to command the forces, fearing war with the United States, and his subsequent illness and hospitalization in the Soviet Union during 1951–1953. Chinese materials (primary sources and memoirs) identify Peng as the CPVA commander from at least early October 1950.

The initial CPVA consisted primarily of infantry. From 19 October to 5 November 1950, the CPV order of battle included six infantry corps (consisting of eighteen divisions)—the XXVIII, XXXIX, XL, XLII, L, and LX from the Thirteenth Army, Fourth Field Army, under the command of Li Tianyu. In addition the CPV had three artillery divisions, the 1st, 2nd, and 8th.

Estimates of the strength of initial CPV forces vary. Chinese sources claim more than 250,000 personnel, whereas U.S. intelligence reports of the time put the figure at more than 400,000. With poor logistics support stretched over supply lines that reached back to northeast China, the Chinese also relied on about 500,000 laborers (some estimates are as high as 700,000) under the command of Fu Qiudao.

Between 25 November 1950 and 8 January 1951, the Ninth Army, consisting of the XX, the XXVI, and XXX Corps, was added from the Third Field Army commanded by Song Shilun. In addition four engineer regiments and three railway engineer regiments were added. The order of battle increased significantly between 27 January and 21 April 1951, when two additional armies, the Third and Nineteenth, were added. The total strength included forty-eight divisions. Artillery units were augmented with three rocket and four antiaircraft divisions.

Between 22 April and 10 June 1951, the number of infantry armies was reduced slightly to forty-two divisions, while the artillery force was increased slightly from ten to eleven divisions. Four tank regiments were also added. In addition, eight air force divisions were finally ready for combat.

From 11 June 1951, to August 1952, the CPVA reached fifty divisions, nine artillery divisions, five tank regiments, and twelve air force divisions. In addition to the Artillery Force and Air Force commands, the CPV was divided between the East Coast Command (Ninth Army), West Coast Command (Third, Nineteenth, Twentieth, and Twenty-Third Armies), and those units directly under CPV command, including the XXXVIII, XXXIX, XL, XLII, XLVII, and L Corps.

Beginning in September 1952, CPVA units began to rotate back to China. Peak CPVA strength occurred between 18 September and 25 November 1952, when it consisted of sixty-three infantry divisions, ten artillery divisions, and ten air force divisions.

Between 18 December 1952 and 27 July 1953, the CPV stabilized at sixty infantry divisions, ten artillery divisions, four tank regiments, and ten air force divisions. Withdrawal of the CPVA began in May 1953 and lasted until October 1958.

The Chinese divide their intervention in the Korean War into five major offensives: the First Campaign,

beginning on 18 October 1950, when Peng Dehuai crossed the Yalu River with vanguard units, until 25 October 1950; the Second Campaign, which began in mid-November 1950, when the CPV launched an attack against advancing U.S./UN forces on 20 November; the Third Campaign, beginning on 31 December 1950; the Fourth Campaign beginning in January 1951; and the Fifth Campaign beginning in March 1951.

CPVA forces, however, continued to attack until the signing of the armistice. Peng notes that the last battle in which CPV forces stormed UN positions took place in late July 1953. He praised it as an example of how the Chinese forces, despite being poorly equipped, could effectively fight employing the "new tactic" of active defense and positional warfare.

Peng Dehuai commanded the CPV until the Armistice Agreement was signed in 1953. He spent much of 1952–1953, however, in Beijing. Deng Hua, who had been acting commander from August 1953, succeeded Peng for one month. He was replaced by Yang Dechi, who commanded the forces from October 1954 until March 1955. Yang Yun commanded the Chinese forces during the completion of the withdrawal from North Korea in 1958.

—*Susan M. Puska*

References:

Appleman, Roy E. *South to the Naktong, North to the Yalu.* Washington, DC: Office of the Chief of Military History, 1961.

Peng, Dehuai. *Memoirs of a Chinese Marshal: The Autobiographical Notes of Peng Dehuai (1989–1974).* Beijing: Foreign Language Press, 1984.

Whitson, William W., with Chen-Hsia Huang. *The Chinese High Command: A History of Communist Military Politics, 1927-71.* New York: Praeger, 1973.

Zhang, Shu Guang. *Mao's Military Romanticism: China and the Korean War, 1950–1953.* Lawrence: University Press of Kansas, 1995.

See also: China, People's Republic of: Air Force; China, People's Republic of: Navy; Chinese Military Offensives; Deng Hua (Teng Hua); Gao Gang (Kao Kang); Heartbreak Ridge, Battle of; Imjin River, Battle of; Kim Il Sung; Lin Biao; Mao Zedong; Peng Dehuai (Peng Te-huai); Xie Fang (Hsieh Fang); Zhou Enlai.

China, People's Republic of: Navy

The Chinese People's Liberation Army Navy (PLAN) played only an indirect role in the Korean War. In June 1950 the focus of the newly formed PLAN was on coastal defense and amphibious support to the ground forces. The People's Republic of China (PRC), proclaimed by Mao Zedong (Mao Tse-tung) in October 1949, was still in a state of war with the Republic of China (ROC, Nationalist China) regime of Jiang Jieshi (Chiang Kai-shek) that had established itself on Taiwan in Summer 1949.

Throughout 1949 and into the 1950s the People's Liberation Army (PLA) continued military operations against the Nationalists in several of China's eastern and southern coastal provinces. These operations were designed to respond to attacks and raids, consolidate seized territory, eliminate remaining Nationalist enclaves, and prepare for amphibious operations against the Fujian offshore islands as a prelude to an attack on Taiwan itself.

Cognizant of the PRC's naval inferiority to both the United States and to the Nationalists, Mao in early 1949 assigned senior PLA General Zhang Aiping the task of creating the naval component of the PLA. Despite Mao's desire to capture Taiwan and eliminate the Nationalist threat, the priority of military development for the new PRC armed forces was on reorganizing the ground forces and building a modern air component. The task of organizing, equipping, and staffing a sea-going navy, equipped with major capital ships and able to counter U.S. and Nationalist capabilities, was a distant third.

To counter the continuing threat of Nationalist attacks, potentially aided by strong U.S. forces, large PLA ground formations were upgraded and deployed in the vicinity of critical coastal cities (Tianjin, Shanghai, and Guangzhou) and opposite Taiwan. This strategy was based on the PLA's only major strength, its large and experienced although lightly armed conventional ground forces. With coastal defense shored up by the ground forces, the newly formed PLAN began to accumulate ships from a wide variety of sources and to organize and train its naval arm.

In the early 1950s the PLAN consisted of predominately smaller warships (frigates, destroyer escorts, and gunboats), patrol craft, transports, and small numbers of landing craft from a variety of sources. To supplement its troop-carrying and patrol craft inventory, the PRC seized and converted civilian fishing and commercial transport ships, many of which were no more than motorized junks (small wooden coastal craft). It also undertook salvaging ships, including Nationalist warships, sunk in the Yangtze River during the war with Japan (1937–1945) and the Civil War (1945–1949). This included a light cruiser, probably the largest warship in its inventory. The PLAN also bought older World War II military vessels from Britain, which continued to hold Hong Kong and which officially recognized the PRC in 1950. However, the largest number and the most modern vessels included U.S.-, British-, and Japanese-built destroyers, escorts, and coastal patrol and amphibious craft that were either captured or whose crews defected from the Nationalist navy during the Civil War. The PRC also began a program to build smaller craft for the PLAN.

Nationalist naval personnel who were captured or defected provided the bulk of the well-trained and experienced PLAN officers and seamen. Since the PLA had no senior naval officers, Army Corps Commander Xiao Jinguang became the first commander of the PLAN on its official formation in May 1950. As with the rest of the PLA in the early 1950s, the Soviets began to provide greater amounts of more modern equipment and advisors to assist in the modernization program. However, at this time the assistance provided was limited, and the navy was forced to put together its own training program and curriculum predominantly using the expertise of Nationalist naval personnel under the careful eye of politically reliable former ground force commanders and political commissars. Later the PLAN did receive more help from the Soviets, and the groundwork was laid to build a submarine and torpedo boat capability and to enhance PLAN'S coastal artillery with more modern Soviet-supplied artillery.

Despite the assistance provided by the Soviets in the early 1950s, the PLAN was clearly outmatched, even in coastal waters, by the naval and air superiority of the United States and Nationalists in the East and South China Seas. The PLAN concentrated on coastal operations and continued to build a capability to challenge the Nationalists in offshore operations and to complement the land and air forces pending an amphibious assault to liberate Taiwan.

The outbreak of the Korean War and U.S. President Harry S. Truman's subsequent deployment in June 1950 of the U.S. Seventh Fleet to the Taiwan Strait threw off Mao's timetable for the "liberation" of Taiwan. For the PRC this deployment not only provided for the sea and air defense of Taiwan, but was also a concrete manifestation of the link between events on the Korean Peninsula and the continuing conflict between the PRC and the ROC. The United States began to implement a containment policy in East Asia, and the U.S. Navy became the guarantor not only of Taiwan's defense but also of the ROC's political survival. There was in fact little the PRC or its navy could do about it.

The PLAN conducted no major military operations against U.S. or Republic of Korea armed forces during the Korean War. What few actions that did take place between U.S. and PLA naval elements occurred in the area of the Taiwan Strait.

During the early 1950s, U.S. Navy Task Force 72, based in Taiwan, and U.S. naval air elements subordinate to the U.S. Seventh Fleet patrolled and conducted reconnaissance operations that included flights over PRC territory. U.S. ships were fired upon and several U.S. aircraft were shot down. While this effort diverted U.S. naval assets from Korea, it sent a clear message to the PRC of U.S. resolve to thwart any attempt to seize Taiwan. The fact that Nationalist forces continued to conduct attacks and raids against mainland targets periodically heightened tensions in the area, but, even after Chinese ground forces entered the conflict on the Korean Peninsula, there were no major actions between the PLAN and U.S. forces in the East China Sea.

—J. G. D. Babb

References:

Blackman, Raymond V. B., ed. *Jane's Fighting Ships: 1950–51, 1951–52, 1952–53,* and *1953–54.* New York: McGraw-Hill, 1950–1953.

Goncharov, Sergei N., John W. Lewis, and Xue Litai. *Uncertain Partners: Stalin, Mao, and the Korean War.* Stanford, CA: Stanford University Press, 1993.

Hanrahan, Gene I. "Report on Red China's New Navy," *United States Naval Proceedings* 79, no. 8 (August 1953): 847–854.

Jarrell, H. T. Comment on "Report on Red China's New Navy," *United States Naval Proceedings* 89, no. 8 (August 1954): 930–931.

Jian, Chen. *China's Road to the Korean War: The Making of the Sino-American Confrontation.* New York: Columbia University Press, 1994.

Zhang, Shu Guang. *Mao's Military Romanticism: China and the Korean War, 1950–1953.* Lawrence: University Press of Kansas, 1995.

See also: China, People's Republic of; China, Republic of; Jiang Jieshi (Chiang Kai-shek); Mao Zedong; Taiwan, Neutralization of; Truman, Harry S.

China, People's Republic of: UN Representation Question
(1950–1971)

The People's Republic of China (PRC) United Nations (UN) representation issue was put on hold because of the outbreak of the Korean War. In early 1950 it seemed a foregone conclusion that representatives of the PRC would replace those of Nationalist China (Taiwan) in the UN. Mao Zedong's forces controlled the Chinese mainland and were waiting only for good weather to seize the last Nationalist stronghold in Formosa. On 7 January 1950, UN Secretary-General Trygve Lie declared that the question of Chinese representation could be decided on an individual basis by the organs of the UN. Five of the eleven nations in the UN Security Council, including Great Britain, recognized the PRC as the official government of China, with France and Egypt ready to follow suit. Even the United States, the most adamant opponent of recognition, declared it would not veto the entry of the PRC in the Security Council but accept the majority decision. The only impediment appeared to be that Taiwan chaired the Security Council in January 1950.

On 13 January, when a Soviet resolution demanding the expulsion of the Taiwanese representative met with a 6–3 defeat in the Security Council (Britain and Norway abstained), however, the Soviet representative walked out in protest. The USSR had withdrawn its representative from the UN General Assembly and other organs beginning on 8 January. This Soviet walkout severely damaged the chances of the PRC gaining admission to the UN and likely was intended to do so. The longer the PRC remained outside the UN, the more dependent it would be upon Soviet support.

The PRC continued to request admission to the UN and hoped that its planned July invasion of Formosa would force the issue. Instead of using the UN as a propaganda platform, however, Soviet representatives maintained their boycott until 1 August, when the USSR assumed the chair of the Security Council. By then it was too late.

The North Korean attack of 25 June brought the U.S. Seventh Fleet to the Taiwan Strait and forestalled the invasion. It also stirred notions of a coordinated Communist aggression and put the question of Chinese representation on the back burner. A resolution introduced by Soviet representative to the UN Security Council Jakob Malik on 1 August, declaring Taiwan's participation illegal, met defeat in a 8–3 vote.

The entry of the PRC in the Korean War on 16 October 1950 brought the issue of representation again to the fore. The UN repeatedly invited representatives of the PRC to participate in discussions of the war and their intervention. Western diplomats believed that the admission of the PRC to the UN would split the Communist bloc and possibly end Chinese intervention. Since the United States and the PRC did not maintain diplomatic relations, the UN would provide a forum for discussion. British Prime Minister Clement Attlee declared at the end of November that the PRC belonged in the UN, and U.S. Deputy Undersecretary of State Dean Rusk agreed. Representatives of the PRC, however, insisted that representation be considered in conjunction with other issues, including the U.S. defense of Formosa.

As it became clear that the PRC linked developments in Korea with those in Formosa and a seat in the UN, U.S. political leaders reversed their position. Whereas Attlee proposed "returning" Formosa to China and seating the PRC in the UN in January 1951, the U.S. Congress accused the PRC of attempting to shoot its way into the organization. Despite warnings that it would forestall any talks regarding the Korean War, the United States successfully pushed a resolution through the UN branding the PRC as an "aggressor." By May 1951, separation of the two issues had become a linchpin of U.S. policy. Despite its belief that the PRC formed the legitimate government of China, the British government agreed to a moratorium on the question of UN representation for China, and the UN General Assembly postponed any discussion of the issue until October 1952. The PRC did not gain UN representation until 1971.

—*Timothy C. Dowling*

References:

Bailey, Sydney D. *The Korean Armistice.* New York: St. Martin's Press, 1992.

Goncharev, Sergei N., John W. Lewis, and Xue Litai. *Uncertain Partners: Stalin, Mao, and the Korean War.* Stanford, CA: Stanford University Press, 1993.

Simmons, Robert R. *The Strained Alliance: Peking, P'yongyang, Moscow, and the Politics of the Korean Civil War.* New York: Free Press, 1975.

See also: Attlee, Clement R.; Lie, Trygve; Malik, Jakob (Iakov) Alexandrovich; Mao Zedong; Rusk, David Dean; Sino-Soviet Treaty of Friendship and Alliance; Soviet Security Council Boycott; Taiwan, Neutralization of.

China, Republic of

The Republic of China (ROC) was formed as a result of the successful 1911 Revolution, ending thousands of years of dynastic rule in China. However, from its very beginnings the ROC was politically unstable and was never really able to assert secure control over all, or even most, of China. From its formation under the aegis of Sun Yat sen in 1912 and its almost immediate takeover by the militarist Yuan Shi-kai, through the turbulent warlord period of the 1920s, to the victory in the Northern Expedition by Jiang Jieshi (Chiang Kaishek), the ROC struggled politically and militarily. In the late 1920s and 1930s both the Chinese Communists and the Japanese vied with the ROC, now firmly headed by Jiang, for control of China or at least significant portions of its territory and population.

After the Japanese surrender in August 1945, Jiang's Nationalists threw all of their efforts into a renewed civil war against the Communists, led by Mao Zedong (Mao Tse-tung). From 1945 through 1949 the ROC, initially with significant material support from the United States, fought against the forces of the Communist People's Liberation Army (PLA). The imminent military defeat of the Nationalists in mid-1949 forced Jiang to relocate major elements of his military, government, and supporting economic infrastructure, in addition to many followers and families, to the island of Taiwan.

Taiwan, as part of the terms of the Japanese capitulation, was returned to Chinese sovereignty and occupied by Nationalist forces in late 1945. This large island, about eighty miles off the coast of Mainland China, was then inhabited by some 8 million people including a small aboriginal population. Also known as Formosa (the name given to the island by the Portuguese in the 1500s), Taiwan had been a Japanese colony since the end of the 1894–1895 Sino-Japanese War and the Treaty of Shimonoseki. When the ROC

relocated to Taiwan, it added approximately 2 million people to the population and created a Chinese government-in-exile intent on returning to the mainland.

The Nationalists initially also controlled many of the strategically located and militarily important islands off the Chinese coast, several of these within artillery range of the mainland. The largest and most important of these was Hainan in southern China, which was lost in spring 1950. From Taiwan and several of these islands, the Nationalists continued to launch military raids and air strikes against the mainland. Military clashes between the Communists and the Nationalists continued after the inauguration of the People's Republic of China (PRC, Communist China) by Mao in October 1949 in Beijing (Peking).

For the United States the ROC presented both opportunities and vulnerabilities. Called an unsinkable aircraft carrier by General Douglas MacArthur, Taiwan offered the possibility of a location for several excellent air and naval bases and a potential "second front" from which to launch air strikes against the mainland if China entered the Korean War. Certainly the ROC leadership saw great potential for a wider war between the United States and the PRC. A major war might allow the ROC, this time in concert with major U.S. military forces, to conduct amphibious assaults on the mainland, militarily defeat the Communists, and reestablish ROC control over all China.

Almost immediately after the North Korean invasion of the South, U.S. President Harry S. Truman ordered the U.S. Seventh Fleet into Taiwan Strait as a precautionary measure and a warning to Beijing. The ROC also offered 33,000 ground troops for use on the Korea peninsula, but the Truman administration declined the offer, although it sent General MacArthur and several diplomats to discuss security-related issues with Jiang. Truman's refusal of ROC troops was a controversial and politically sensitive issue in the United States. The Republicans sought a hard-line policy against the Communists and a strong military alliance with the ROC, whereas Truman was trying to limit the war in Korea and did not want to provide an excuse for the PRC to enter the war. In addition, given the recent Nationalist military defeats, the value of ROC forces was suspect. Certainly another good reason to refuse Nationalist troops was that they would be needed to protect Taiwan and the occupied offshore islands, specifically Quemoy (Jinmen) and Matsu.

Military and diplomatic support for the ROC and debate over "who lost China" became key issues in U.S. politics and with U.S. allies, including the United Kingdom. Military action against China, specifically in concert with Nationalist forces on Taiwan, was one of the most contentious issues between MacArthur and Truman. Even unilateral military actions by the ROC without U.S. sanction or support might expand the Korean War. This issue became more critical when Chinese People's Volunteer Army (CPVA, Chinese Communist) ground forces entered the Korean War and policy differences between Truman and MacArthur escalated.

The Taiwan issue remains a key area of contention between the United States and the PRC. In 1954, and again in 1958, China's military actions in and around Taiwan Strait precipitated crises that came close to war. After the Korean War and throughout the 1950s and 1960s, the United States maintained a large security assistance organization and had access to major bases in Taiwan. U.S. normalization of relations with the mainland that began in the early 1970s called for the United States to agree to provisions that Mao had called for in the late 1940s. Critical for Taiwan were PRC demands that the United States recognize that there was only one China and cease its military support to the ROC.

In 1979 Washington agreed to remove all U.S. military personnel from Taiwan and begin a program to reduce arms sales to the ROC. The United States also agreed that there is but "one China," but the status of the ROC and Taiwan remains politically contentious. In 1979 Congress passed the Taiwan Relations Act that demanded that the PRC guarantee the peaceful unification of China and Taiwan. For its part, the PRC refused to give up its sovereign right to use force in what it sees as a purely domestic issue but has repeatedly indicated that peaceful unification is also the goal of the Beijing government.

Nevertheless, in the spring of 1996 democratic elections in Taiwan served as an excuse for the PLA to flex its military muscle. The PRC commenced amphibious warfare exercises in the vicinity of the island and test-fired ballistic missiles into the adjacent waters, a not too subtle warning to Taiwan of the limits of its sovereignty. The United States reacted to these provocative exercises by sending two carrier battle groups to the area.

Despite U.S. diplomatic recognition of the PRC and the long-term trend of warming relations between the two countries, the ROC undoubtedly will continue to be a contentious issue in U.S.-China relations. This is in part a legacy of the Korean War and the decision by President Truman to defend Taiwan with the Seventh Fleet in June 1950.

—*J. G. D. Babb*

References:

Eastman, Lloyd E., Jerome Chen, Suzanne Pepper, and Lyman P. Van Slyke. *The Nationalist Era in China, 1927–1949*. New York: Cambridge University Press, 1991.

Fairbank, John K. *China: A New History*. Cambridge, MA: Harvard University Press, 1992.

Finkelstein, David M. *Washington's Taiwan Dilemma, 1949–1950: From Abandonment to Salvation*. Fairfax, VA: George Mason University Press, 1993.

Spanier, John W. *The Truman-MacArthur Controversy and the Korean War*. Cambridge, MA: Belknap Press, 1965.

Spence, Jonathan D. *The Search for Modern China*. New York: W. W. Norton, 1990.

See also: China, People's Republic of; Jiang Jieshi (Chiang Kai-shek); MacArthur, Douglas; Mao Zedong; Truman, Harry S.

Chinese Military Offensives

During the first year of the war, the Chinese conducted six major offensives against the United Nations Command (UNC). Of these, their second and third offensives were the most destructive and raised many questions about the U.S. role in Korea. As a result of these two sudden Chinese victories, the UN decided to remain in Korea, build up its forces, and not let the Chinese be victorious. From January through May 1951, the Chinese conducted four offensives against the UNC, but still could not drive it from Korea. The failure of the Chinese military (Chinese People's Volunteer Army [CPVA], Communist Chinese) to win decisive victories in these last four offensives convinced the leadership that China could not win the war. This led to a military stalemate over the course of the years before an armistice could be arranged between the opposing forces.

Chinese First Offensive (6 October 1950–May 1951)

The entrance of the People's Republic of China (PRC) into the war in Korea was sudden and unexpected in Washington. Through 26 October 1950, the first fighting in North Korea with the CPVA occurred between Republic of Korea Army (ROKA, South Korean) units and what was first thought of as "Chinese Volunteers."

U.S. military intelligence at first thought that the Chinese in Korea would "avoid any overt intervention" against U.S. forces. By 1 November, U.S. commanders had come to realize that the CPVA was not in Korea just to handle supplies for the Korean People's Army (KPA, North Korea), but were trained combat veterans intent on major military activities.

From the beginning of the war, both North Korean and Chinese leaders had been confused over the policy and intentions of the U.S. government. Both North Korea and China believed that the UNC would stop at the 38th parallel. Thus, the UNC crossing of the 38th parallel on 9 October 1950 surprised the governments of both the Democratic People's Republic of Korea (DPRK, North Korea) and the PRC. Beijing now decided to intervene militarily and on 18 October Chinese troops began crossing the Yalu River into North Korea. By the end of October, Marshal Peng

Chinese People's Volunteer Army soldiers, now POWs. Note the fleece-lined caps and quilted uniforms, 4th or 5th November 1950. (National Archives)

Dehuai had six CPVA armies, eighteen divisions in all, in the high mountains of central North Korea.

Reacting to the sudden Chinese entrance into the war, U.S. Eighth Army Commander General Walton H. Walker ordered the 1st Cavalry Division to block the Chinese force that had overrun ROKA forces and was attacking toward Unsan. On the evening of 1 November, the 1st and 2nd Battalions of the 8th Cavalry Regiment had hardly taken up defensive positions north and west of Unsan when they were assaulted by two divisions of the Chinese Thirty-ninth Army. Swarms of Chinese infantry engulfed the U.S. positions.

The remainder of the 8th Cavalry Regiment was soon overrun by the rapid Chinese assault. By midmorning on 2 November, little fighting ability remained in the regiments as small units retreated on foot toward the rear. In spite of a counterattack by the 5th Cavalry Regiment, the Chinese assault could not be stopped and the 8th Cavalry Regiment was almost destroyed.

The sudden attack by the CPVA created a period of confusion throughout Eighth Army's chain of command. Steps were immediately taken to withdraw I Corps below the Ch'ŏngch'ŏn River. Elements of the 19th Infantry Regiment of the 24th Division, along with the 27th British Commonwealth Brigade, were rushed into positions north of the river to protect bridges and tank fords over the river.

The boundary between I Corps and the withdrawing ROKA units crossed the Ch'ŏngch'ŏn on a north-south line at Kunu ri. On 3 November, the 5th Regimental Combat Team (RCT) of the U.S. 24th Division took a defensive position at Kunu-ri behind withdrawing ROKA II Corps. The next morning, the Chinese broke through the ROKA positions, forcing ROKA units to retreat through the 5th RCT. Chinese soldiers soon mixed with the South Koreans, making distinctions between Communist and UN units difficult. Some Chinese even appeared in South Korean uniforms. In the confusion some South Korean soldiers became casualties from U.S. fire. In spite of this turmoil, Colonel John R. Throckmorton's 5th RCT held Kunu-ri and successfully protected the right flank of Eighth Army.

North of the river, the 19th Infantry was fighting for its life as the Chinese moved to positions in its rear. Some units of the regiment were forced to withdraw south of the river and abandon a number of their vehicles. But many of the regiment's positions north of the river were restored, thanks to a counterattack by the 21st Regiment of the 24th Division.

On the western side of the bridgehead on 4–5 November the Chinese struck with equal force against the 27th British Brigade at Pakch'ŏn. The U.S. 61st Field Artillery Battalion (FAB), supporting the British, was partially overrun as it used direct fire by its 105-mm howitzers against the attacking Chinese. Elements of the Argyl and Sutherland Highlanders and the Australians rushed to their rescue, and by 6 November the position was stabilized.

On 6 November, Chinese units surrounding U.S. forces suddenly vanished. To this day there are no clear answers as to why the CPVA suddenly withdrew. Some have speculated that the first engagements were a warning to Allied forces to withdraw from North Korea. Others believe that the CPVA had run out of food and ammunition and needed to regroup and resupply before beginning any new offensive.

—Daniel R. Beirne

References:

Blair, Clay. *The Forgotten War: America in Korea, 1950–1953.* New York: Times Books, 1987.

Hoyt, Edwin P. *The Day the Chinese Attacked: Korea 1950.* New York: Paragon House, 1993.

Spurr, Russell. *Enter the Dragon: China's Undeclared War against the U.S. in Korea, 1950–1951.* New York: Henry Holt, 1988.

Summers, Harry G., Jr. *Korean War Almanac.* New York: Facts on File, 1990.

Toland, John. *In Mortal Combat: Korea, 1950–1953.* New York: William Morrow, 1991.

See also: Unsan, Battle of; Walker, Walton Harris.

Chinese Military Disengagement (November 1950)

The Chinese military disengagement began on 6 November 1950 after the October Battle of Unsan. The sudden withdrawal of the CPVA came as a complete surprise to Eighth Army headquarters. U.S. military intelligence was confused and believed that the allies had been fighting only Chinese "volunteers." The intelligence estimate of Chinese strength was only a third of its actual size. In addition to these faulty estimates, U.S. military intelligence was not aware that new Chinese units were arriving across the Yalu River. East of the high Myohyang Mountains, the Chinese Third Field Army, twelve divisions totalling 120,000 troops, had been assembling since late October. In the west in early November, the eighteen-division, 210,000-man Fourth Field Army had withdrawn after the Battle of Unsan with Eighth U.S. Army to the high Nangnim Range just south of the Yalu River.

Eighth Army commander General Walton H. Walker disagreed with UNC commander General Douglas MacArthur, who wanted an immediate resumption of the offensive. Walker delayed the resumption for two weeks to build up his supplies and his strength to three corps. In the west, I Corps consisted of the U.S. 24th Division, the ROKA 1st Division, and the British Commonwealth Brigade. In the center was the U.S. 25th and 2d Divisions and the newly arrived 5,200-man Turkish Brigade formed IX Corps. The ROKA II Corps of three divisions held the east flank of Eighth Army, extending to the western slopes of the Myohyang Mountains. In reserve were the 1st Cavalry Division, the 187th Airborne RCT, the British 29th Brigade, and battalion-sized units from Belgium, Thailand, and the Philippines.

In Northeast Korea since late October, the UNC X Corps, consisting of the 1st Marine and the U.S. Army 3d and 7th Divisions and ROKA I Corps of two divisions had been moving rapidly into the mountains toward Manchuria. Opposing them were CPVA units, the activities of which were similar to those opposing Eighth Army. In spite of several sharp encounters with the 7th ROKA Regiment and the 7th Marines in early November, these Chinese forces suddenly melted away as did those at Unsan.

Although MacArthur and his staff in Japan were confused about Chinese intentions, they were still convinced that the Chinese soldiers were volunteers and limited in number. At the same time, the sudden Chinese disengagement gave Eighth Army and X Corps time to regroup. Discussions now ensued between MacArthur and the Joint Chiefs of Staff over possible changes of policy now that China had entered the war. MacArthur believed that it was important to complete the UN mission to occupy all North Korea and install a democratic system there.

An attack north had been planned to kick off on 15 November, but logistics forced a delay until 24 November. It had been estimated that 4,000 tons of supplies were needed to begin the offensive operation, and this figure was not reached until 24 November. Some 2,000 tons had to come by rail, 1,000 tons by sea through the port of Chinnamp'o, and 1,000 tons by air.

However, the weather was turning cold and many UNC units still did not have their full allotment of winter clothing.

The sudden appearance of Chinese forces caused a precipitous drop in morale in UNC units. No longer could American servicemen anticipate being home for Christmas. To help boost morale, General Walker insisted that every soldier receive a complete Thanksgiving meal. Cooks baked all night of 22 November to prepare for the enormous feast the next day. For most men it was to be their best meal in Korea. Most forgot the war and its hardships, if only briefly.

For most of November the Chinese troops remained concealed. Often their forces would pull back just when they were attacked by UNC forces. Uncontrovertible evidence left by withdrawing Chinese in the North Korean villages reinforced the front-line American soldiers' belief that they faced major combat forces and not simply volunteers sent from China to help the North Koreans. Most U.S. troops found the situation too quiet, and there was an ominous air.

Eighth Army and X Corps resumed the offensive by pushing slowly into North Korea, in spite of a fifty-mile gap between these two commands. The terrain in the gap consisted of high, rugged mountains with few roads and trails that discouraged vehicular movement between the two commands. At the same time it was favorable to foot movement of nonmechanized forces, which was characteristic of the Chinese forces. Movement at night, thick forests, and a shortage of trained photo reconnaissance interpreters prevented the UNC command from spotting Chinese troop movements in the mountains.

The Korea peninsula, narrow in the center, is at its widest point adjacent to China. As UNC forces moved north, units tended to spread and leave wider gaps, and the flanks of major units were often left unprotected. Thus the ROKA II Corps and the U.S. IX Corps became vulnerable to any major attack on their right flanks from significant CPVA or Korean People's Army (KPA, North Korean) units moving through the Myohyang Mountains.

By 25 November UNC forces were poised to attack and secure the rest of North Korea. Waiting in the mountains between Eighth Army and X Corps were the Chinese Third and Fourth Armies. The stage was thus set for one of the most decisive battles in the Korean War.

—*Daniel R. Beirne*

References:

Alexander, Bevin. *Korea: The First War We Lost.* New York: Hippocrene Books, 1986.

Appleman, Roy E. *Disaster in Korea: The Chinese Confront MacArthur.* College Station, TX: Texas A&M Press, 1989.

————. *East of Chosin: Entrapment and Breakout in Korea.* College Station, TX: Texas A&M Press, 1987.

Blair, Clay. *The Forgotten War: America in Korea, 1950–1953.* New York: Times Books, 1987.

Spurr, Russell. *Enter the Dragon: China's Undeclared War against the U.S. in Korea, 1950–1951.* New York: Henry Holt, 1988.

See also: Eighth United States Army; Joint Chiefs of Staff (JCS); MacArthur, Douglas; Tenth Corps; Walker, Walton Harris.

Chinese Second Offensive (25 November–December 1950)

The second Chinese offensive in Korea took place in late November 1950. The Chinese People's Volunteer Army (CPVA, Communist Chinese) had concentrated in the high mountains of central North Korea during the month of November. Although the Chinese had first entered North Korea in late October 1950 and made limited contact with Allied Forces, they then withdrew back into the mountains to build up their forces. Then in late November two Chinese army groups, the Thirteenth in the west against Eighth Army and the Ninth in the east against X Corps, entered the conflict. This campaign consisted of two separate battles, Ch'ŏngch'ŏn River (25–30 November 1950) and Changjin Reservoir and that with forces to the east (October–December 1950).

In the west the CPVA Thirteenth Army Group of eighteen divisions attacked Eighth Army directly. The weight of the Chinese attack was against the right flank of Eighth Army. Here the Chinese crushed the ROK II Corps and tried to outflank the U.S. IX Corps. The weight of the CPVA attack fell on the 2d and 25th Divisions. The route of withdrawal of the 2d Division was blocked by Chinese road blocks that caused heavy U.S. casualties. Other Eighth Army units along the Ch'ŏngch'ŏn River west of IX Corps near Anju were able to hold back the Chinese assaults long enough for most of Eighth Army to withdraw. CPVA movement was slow, allowing Eighth Army to maintain a deliberate, orderly withdrawal back into South Korea.

CPVA activities against X Corps in northeast Korea in late October were a mirror image of their activities against Eighth Army. In spite of total destruction of the 7th ROK Regiment near Sudong and fierce fighting with the 7th Marine Regiment in early November near Chinhŭng-ni, Chinese forces suddenly melted away as they had at Unsan. As in the west, Chinese forces concentrated in the high mountains of central North Korea and awaited new actions by X Corps.

Instead of linking up with Eighth Army in the west, X Corps received orders to attack north toward the Yalu River. Under this new plan the 1st Marine Division pushed north up a very steep and difficult sixty-four-mile-long road from Hŭngnam to the

Troops of the 1st U.S. Cavalry Division, withdrawing to the south, 3 December 1951. (National Archives)

Changjin Reservoir. The 7th Division was widely dispersed, while the 32d Regiments attacked northwest to link up with the Marines. As a result, a gap of eighty miles extended between the 17th Infantry and the other two regiments.

On 28 November the CPVA mounted its first big assault on 7th Division forces east of the Changjin Reservoir. The Twenty-seventh Chinese Army attacked the dispersed U.S. units. 31st RCT fell back to the 1st Marine Division perimeter at Hagaru-ri, on the southern tip of the Changjin Reservoir.

Meanwhile, the 5th and 7th Marine Regiments attacked west of the reservoir to Yudam-ni. The 1st Marine Regiment had the mission of keeping open the main supply route from Hagaru-ri to Hŭngnam. All during this period of bitter cold weather the Chinese kept attacking the extended Marines and attempted to cut them off from their base of supply. The 5th and 7th Marines were cut off at Yudam-ni when the Chinese secured the Tŏkdong Pass in their rear on the route to Hagaru-ri. The two regiments by-passed the roadblock by moving overland to Hagaru-ri.

The decision for X Corps to withdraw was slow in coming. The size of the Chinese units caused major changes in X Corps commander Major General Edward M. Almond's plans. His corps was widely dispersed with isolated units vulnerable to renewed Chinese attacks. Now his mission was to preserve X Corps while conducting an orderly withdrawal. The first phase of the withdrawal was completed when Marine and army units withdrew from both sides of the Changjin Reservoir into Hagaru-ri. X Corps' withdrawal is considered one of the most masterly in military history.

In spite of heavy losses by U.S. forces, those sustained by the CPVA in northeast Korea in November and December 1950 amounted to a disaster. The CPVA Third Field Army started with twelve divisions of 120,000 men. Marine Corps studies estimate that in these divisions both battle and nonbattle casualties amounted to some 72,000 men.

—Daniel R. Beirne

While the U.S. Far East Air Forces Combat Cargo Command made an all-out effort to aid embattled units of the 1st Marine Division and 7th Infantry Division, the soldiers were trying desperately to link up. This marine is shown just as he reached the crest of the ridge at the link-up point. Wet, stinging snow made the operation most difficult, as hordes of Communist troops charged again and again into UNC forces, December 1951. (National Archives)

References:

Appleman, Roy E. *Disaster in Korea: The Chinese Confront MacArthur.* College Station, TX: Texas A&M Press, 1989.

———. *East of Chosin: Entrapment and Breakout in Korea.* College Station, TX: Texas A&M Press, 1987.

———. *Escaping the Trap: The US Army X Corps in Northeast Korea, 1950.* College Station, TX: Texas A&M Press, 1990.

———. *South to the Naktong, North to the Yalu.* Washington, DC: Office of the Chief of Military History, 1961.

Blair, Clay. *The Forgotten War: America in Korea, 1950–1953.* New York: Times Books, 1987.

Stanton, Shelby. *America's Tenth Legion: X Corps in Korea.* Novato, CA: Presidio Press, 1989.

Toland, John. *In Mortal Combat: Korea, 1950–1953.* New York: William Morrow, 1991.

See also: Ch'ŏngch'ŏn River, Battle of; Eighth United States Army; Tenth Corps; Walker, Walton Harris.

Chinese Third Offensive and Withdrawal from Seoul (31 December 1950–14 January 1951)

On New Year's eve 1950 the CPVA crossed the 38th parallel and invaded South Korea. Their forces consisted of four armies: the Thirty-eighth, Thirty-ninth, Fortieth, and Forty-second. The main weight of the attack fell on the U.S. I and IX Corps defending in western Korea directly north of Seoul. In addition to this attack, the Chinese Sixty-sixth Army and KPA forces attacked across the parallel in the center and east of the Korean peninsula. This last thrust threatened to envelop the ROKA III Corps, struggling to hold back the Chinese thrust in central Korea.

The Chinese attack occurred at night and was preceded by massive artillery and mortar fire. After this artillery barrage came thousands of foot soldiers accompanied by the blowing of bugles. The U.S. 24th and 25th Divisions bore the brunt of the attack. In spite of heavy U.S. counter battery fire, the Chinese continued to attack and take heavy casualties.

By daylight on 1 January 1951, CPVA forces had driven a wedge between the two U.S. divisions, attacking through the weakened ROK 1st and 6th Divisions defending the area between the Americans. Another Chinese force penetrated the UNC defense east of Seoul and threatened to envelop the city. General Matthew B. Ridgway, who had taken command of Eighth Army on 26 December after Walker's death in a jeep accident, ordered the U.S. I and IX Corps to fall back into a bridgehead around Seoul.

UNC commander General Douglas MacArthur had given Ridgway instructions not to risk the destruction of Eighth Army. As a result, Eighth Army established lines upon which withdrawing UNC elements could coordinate their movements. Line C passed along the south bank of the Han River, except for the bridgehead around Seoul. At Yangp'yŏng it extended across the Korean peninsula to the east

coast. Forty miles south of this, another line, D, passed from the west coast at P'yŏngt'aek northeast to the east coast at Wŏnp'o-ri.

By 2 January both I and IX U.S. Corps had formed a bridgehead of ten infantry regiments around Seoul. Several hundred tanks and fifteen artillery battalions of 105-mm, 155-mm, and 8-inch howitzers supported the infantry. Reinforcing these were offshore naval gunfire and close air support.

The defense of Seoul was thwarted, however, when ROK units on the central front collapsed. The CPVA was able to push around Seoul to the east of the city and outflank Eighth Army. Rather than risk the destruction of Eighth Army, Ridgway ordered a slow withdrawal from Seoul to Line C along the south bank of the Han River.

In spite of Chinese pressure, the U.S. I and IX Corps conducted an orderly withdrawal from Seoul. The only incident in the withdrawal took place as the British 29th Brigade was withdrawing. Elements of the Chinese Thirty-ninth Army overran two companies of the Royal Ulster Rifles. Counterattacks by infantry and tanks to recapture the lost positions cost 300 casualties, but the Chinese were forced to disengage. By 4 January the last UNC units in Seoul crossed over the Han River and took up defensive positions along Line C.

Indeed the major problem in the evacuation of the two U.S. corps from Seoul was a flood of South Korean refugees who clogged the roads and river crossings by the thousands. Cold weather added to their suffering as they herded in masses just ahead of the slow-moving CPVA. U.S. engineers worried about the integrity of the Han River bridges and whether they could support U.S. Army heavy equipment as well as the thousands of Korean refugees. In spite of much confusion, a large number of refugees were able to board trains south of the river and travel directly to Pusan.

In the meantime the CPVA continued its drive, shifting its thrust to central South Korea. This move threatened to envelop the U.S. I and IX Corps now defending along Line C. To prevent this from occurring, Ridgway ordered the withdrawal of all UNC forces back to Line D. On 6 January, Eighth Army began its move to the new line, accomplishing it in several days without incident.

Once the army was stabilized on Line D, Ridgway ordered aggressive patrolling. The bitter cold winter was having its effect on Chinese forces and drastically slowed their movement. Gaps as wide as twenty miles appeared between the attacking Chinese and Eighth Army defenders on Line C. In these circumstance Ridgway planned a counterattack to regain the territory recently lost by Eighth Army.

By 11 February the U.S. I and IX Corps had begun the counterattack and were slowly progressing north to

A Korean man carries his father across the icy Han River at Ch'unju, in flight from advancing Communist troops, 14 January 1951. (National Archives)

Pfc. Preston McKnight of the 19th Infantry Regiment uses his poncho to get protection from the biting wind and cold during a break in the action against Chinese forces, 10 January 1951. (National Archives)

the Han River. X Corps, evacuated from Hŭngnam to Pusan at the end of December, was now preparing to move up to Line D to join Eighth Army. Tenth Corps was still composed of the U.S. Army 7th and 3d Divisions and the 1st Marine Division. Added to this was the U.S. Army 2d Division, recovering from its losses in North Korea.

During 7–22 January, X Corps moved up to Line D in central South Korea. In this movement it encountered the KPA II and V Corps, which were pushing into South Korea directly to the east of the Chinese.

—*Daniel R. Beirne*

References:

Blair, Clay. *The Forgotten War: America in Korea, 1950–1953.* New York: Times Books, 1987.

Mossman, Billy C. *U.S. Army in the Korean War: Ebb and Flow, November 1950–July 1951.* Washington, DC: U.S. Army Center of Military History, 1990.

Spurr, Russell. *Enter the Dragon: China's Undeclared War against the U.S. in Korea, 1950–1951.* New York: Henry Holt, 1988.

Toland, John. *In Mortal Combat: Korea, 1950–1953.* New York: William Morrow, 1991.

See also: Eighth United States Army; MacArthur, Douglas; Ridgway, Matthew Bunker; Tenth Corps; Walker, Walton Harris.

Chinese Fourth Offensive (11–18 February 1951)

On the night of 11–12 February 1951, elements of the Fortieth and Sixty-sixth Armies of the CPVA and II and V Corps of the KPA mounted a massive attack on the ROKA III Corps near Hongch'ŏn. The ROKA 8th Division was annihilated, creating a salient in the UNC front. The U.S. 2d Division and the U.S. 187th Airborne RCT supporting the ROKA I Corps struggled to block the Communist penetration.

By 14 February four CPVA divisions assaulted Wŏnju. U.S. artillery wreaked havoc on these Chinese forces as they tried to swarm over the U.S. positions. The Communist assault divisions were shattered in this "Wŏnju Shoot" and the attack came to a halt.

To the east, CPVA units attacked the 23d Regiment and the French Battalion at Chip'yŏng-ni. These two UNC units formed a defensive perimeter around the town and refused to yield this strategic road junction. Eighth Army commander Lieutenant General Matthew B. Ridgway believed that this was a key junction and ordered the defenders to hold it against an estimated 25,000 Chinese attackers. For two days the Chinese mounted attack after attack against the UNC positions, but the defenders refused to surrender. Finally the encircled defenders were saved by the arrival of elements of the 1st Cavalry Division. Unable to break through this Eighth Army line in central Korea while trying to hold back an Eighth Army drive west of the penetration, the CPVA withdrew to regroup at the former KPA defensive position just north of the 38th parallel.

—*Daniel R. Beirne*

References:

Alexander, Bevin. *Korea: The First War We Lost.* New York: Hippocrene Books, 1986.

Appleman, Roy E. *Ridgway Duels for Korea.* College Station, TX: Texas A&M Press, 1990.

Blair, Clay. *The Forgotten War: America in Korea, 1950–1953.* New York: Times Books, 1987.

Ridgway, Matthew B. *The Korean War.* Garden City, NY: Doubleday, 1967.

Toland, John. *In Mortal Combat: Korea, 1950–1953.* New York: William Morrow, 1991.

See also: Chip'yŏng-ni, Battle of; Hoengsŏng, Battle of; Wŏnju, Battle of.

Chinese Fifth (Spring) Offensive (22–30 April 1951)

At 2200 on 22 April 1951, the CPVA attacked Eighth Army across a forty-mile front. The Chinese committed nine armies of about 250,000 men in the attack. Six Chinese armies struck directly at Eighth Army's I Corps above Seoul, while three armies attacked down the center of the peninsula toward X Corps. The Sixty-third Army struck the ROKA 1st Division and the British 29th Brigade defending the left (west) end of I Corps. Although the ROKA 1st Division put up a strong defense, it was forced back several miles, leaving the left flank of the British Brigade exposed. It was eventually overrun by the massive Chinese attack, but not before a brilliant defense that produced enormous Chinese casualties.

Eighth Army units to the right of the British 29th Brigade put up a strong defense directly north of Seoul. To their right, however, the U.S. IX Corps was thinly disposed. Here the CPVA concentrated on the ROKA 6th Division, which fled and left a gaping ten-mile hole in Eighth Army's front. Through this poured thousands of Chinese, who overran many artillery units supporting Eighth Army. The gap was finally plugged when the British Commonwealth Brigade set up a blocking position at Kap'yŏng.

At the same time, the 1st Marine Division to the right of the gap shifted its position to slow down the penetration. Slowly Eighth Army withdrew to form a new position around Seoul, known as the No Name Line. The eight days of combat after 22 April marked the largest single battle of the Korean War. It saved Seoul and inflicted some 70,000 casualties on the Communists.

—*Daniel R. Beirne*

References:

Appleman, Roy E. *Disaster in Korea: The Chinese Confront MacArthur*. College Station, TX: Texas A&M Press, 1989.

Blair, Clay. *The Forgotten War: America in Korea, 1950–1953*. New York: Times Books, 1987.

Fehrenbach, T. R. *This Kind of War: A Study in Unpreparedness*. New York: Macmillan, 1962.

Mossman, Billy C. *U.S. Army in the Korean War: Ebb and Flow, November 1950–July 1951*. Washington, DC: U.S. Army Center of Military History, 1990.

See also: Eighth United States Army; Gloucester (Gloster) Hill, Battle of; Hoge, William M.; Imjin River, Battle of; Kap'yŏng, Battle of; No Name Line, Battle of; Tenth Corps; Van Fleet, James Alward.

Chinese Sixth Offensive (16–23 May 1951)

On the evening of 16 May 1951, the Chinese began their Sixth Offensive. Twenty Communist divisions—

Troops crossing a burned bridge after driving Communist forces from their positions on the East Central Front, 28 May 1951. (National Archives)

fifteen CPVA and five KPA—in all 175,000 men, suddenly attacked the U.S. X Corps and ROKA III Corps, the five divisions of which extended to the east coast. The main weight of the Communist attack fell against Eighth Army's weak right flank. Eighth Army commander Lieutenant General James A. Van Fleet had anticipated that the major attack would be against the heavily defended west flank of Eighth Army protecting the ROK capital of Seoul.

The shock of the Chinese attack caused panic in ROKA units, many of which abandoned their defensive positions and fell back. A huge gap opened up on X Corps' right flank, exposing the rear of the Eighth Army's defense along No Name Line. Six CPVA divisions of 60,000 men struck the U.S. 2d Division to the west of the salient, but it managed to hold its ground and even pushed into the flank of the attacking Communist forces as air and artillery pounded the densely concentrated CPVA units. Simultaneously the U.S. 3d Division was dispatched from the Seoul area to block further CPVA movement into the salient.

Although Eighth Army was severely tested, I and IX Corps units around Seoul held. ROKA units to the right of the salient and the U.S. 2d Division to the left of the salient also held firm. In addition to the U.S. 3d Division, the 187th Airborne RCT was rushed in to block the farthest point of the CPVA penetration and complete the encirclement of the salient. Communist forces could go no further.

The CPVA offensive cost the Communists 90,000 casualties. After five days, the determined Eighth Army stand, coupled with UNC artillery, air power, mines, and barbed wire, brought the Communist Sixth Offensive to a halt.

—*Daniel R. Beirne*

References:

Blair, Clay. *The Forgotten War: America in Korea, 1950–1953.* New York: Times Books, 1987.

Fehrenbach, T. R. *This Kind of War: A Study in Unpreparedness.* New York: Macmillan, 1962.

Mossman, Billy C. *U.S. Army in the Korean War: Ebb and Flow.* Washington, DC: U.S. Army, Center of Military History, 1990.

Ridgway, Matthew B. *The Korean War.* Garden City, NY: Doubleday, 1967.

See also: Bunker Hill, Battle of; Van Fleet, James Alward.

Chinese Summer Offensives (1953)

In the final week of May 1953, after a lull of several months, the CPVA conducted regimental-sized attacks against the UNC in the sector held by the Eighth Army's IX Corps, hitting both the ROKA 9th and Capital Divisions. Although the CPVA was unable to overrun these units, the attacks did signal a two-month long increase in activity all along the front of an intensity not seen since April 1951.

On 28 May, Communist forces struck the U.S. I Corps, hitting five outposts of troops of the U.S. 25th Division and guarding the approaches to Eighth Army's western positions. These outposts, 1,000 yards forward of the main line, were defended by troops from the division's Turkish Brigade. The four days of intense fighting that ensued often included hand-to-hand combat. Although the Chinese eventually took three of the five outposts, they suffered more than 3,200 casualties. The action ended only when the Turks were ordered to abandon the final two outposts. The Turks reported losses of 104 killed in action, 324 wounded in action, and 47 missing in action.

By the first of June it appeared to Eighth Army intelligence officers that the Chinese planned a major blow soon. Their failure immediately to follow up the May attacks against I Corps seemed to indicate that these were diversionary efforts to screen their real intention of pushing the line southward. This was prompted by agenda item 2 of the Armistice Agreement, which called for the demarcation line and demilitarized zone to follow the final battle line. Although the first week of June passed quietly, the continued movement of Communist troops kept UN forces on alert.

The Communist offensive opened on the night of 10 June as the P'anmunjŏm negotiators began to draw the final armistice line. UNC leaders determined that the Communist objective was to achieve a more southerly line or, at the very least, the propaganda value of a symbolic victory at the end of the war. The initial probe, which turned into a general offensive, began as two Chinese divisions moved down both sides of the Pukhan River to attack the ROKA II Corps near Kŭmsŏng. Intense pressure resulted in the loss of Hill 973 by the ROKA 5th Division, which failed either to retake the hill or stem the drive. The hard-pressed ROKA units continued to withdraw south approximately three miles along an eight-mile front until 15 June, when they formed a new line.

The UN situation was just as critical in the corps center, especially after 12 June, when another Chinese division struck the ROKA 8th Division, forcing it to withdraw. The failure of the two ROKA divisions to hold prompted UN commander General Maxwell D. Taylor to shift the boundary between the ROKA II and U.S. X Corps and to commit two ROKA divisions, the 7th and 3d, then in reserve, to the battle.

While Communist forces concentrated their main efforts against the ROKA II Corps, they delivered other attacks on the line. Two outpost positions in front of the ROKA First Division of the U.S. I Corps fell at the end of June after prolonged attacks. Farther east in IX Corps sector, the Chinese employed battalion-strength forces against the U.S. 3d and ROKA 9th

Divisions. In the eastern sector of the Eighth Army's front, North Korean attacks forced a readjustment of the main line positions on the X Corps' right wing. At the same time, Communist forces were successful in seizing Hill 351, the northern anchor of the ROKA First Corps line.

By 18 June the attacks had subsided, allowing General Taylor to stabilize the front and begin relieving the ROKA 5th and 7th Divisions. Beginning on 21 June 1953, he received reinforcements from Japan in the form of the U.S. 187th Airborne Regimental Combat Team and the 34th Regimental Combat Team of the 24th Division.

The Communist side made no further attacks during June or during the first week of July 1953. Measured in terms of ground gained, their effort had been successful. Yet both sides had lost heavily; the Chinese suffered about 6,600 casualties and the ROKA II Corps alone reported losses of more than 7,300 men.

Meanwhile, by 18 June the terms of an armistice agreement were all but complete. On this date, however, South Korean President Syngman Rhee unilaterally ordered the release of 27,000 prisoners of war. To protest, the Communist delegates denounced it as a serious breach of faith and delayed the final agreement for another month.

On 6 July there was another Chinese attack against ROKA forces near the Iron Triangle that inflicted heavy casualties on the South Koreans, as well as a resumption of Communist attacks on Pork Chop Hill, a scene of heavy fighting in March. After an artillery and mortar barrage, a succession of Chinese infantry units assaulted Pork Chop Hill. The attackers far outnumbered the defenders of the U.S. 7th Division, and the situation became chaotic as both sides fed companies, battalions, and then regiments into the battle. Chinese determination may be judged by the fact that they matched each new U.S. company with a battalion. Meanwhile, both sides continued to pound the hill with artillery and mortar barrages. By the morning of 11 July, five U.S. battalions had been committed to holding a company-sized outpost against a full Chinese division. Faced with the prospect of sending additional units into the battle at a time when the armistice was near, Taylor decided to withdraw. Consequently, on 11 July, U.S. units withdrew from Pork Chop Hill.

Elsewhere, on the night of 13 July the Chinese launched a three-division attack against the left flank of the ROKA II Corps in the Kŭmsŏg area and a one-division attack against the right flank of the U.S. IX Corps. Five Chinese divisions broke through the lines, causing the collapse of the ROKA Capital and 3d Divisions, as well as weakening three other ROKA divisions amid great confusion in both corps areas.

Setting a monthly record for artillery rounds fired, the Communists inflicted 14,000 casualties on the South Koreans. Taylor reacted quickly and directed commanders of the U.S. IX and ROKA II Corps to establish and hold a new main line along the south bank of the Kŭmsŏng River. As many ROKA soldiers continue to flee south, Taylor ordered the U.S. 2d and 3d Divisions to extend their sectors to cover gaps created by retreating units while he moved the newly arrived 187th Airborne RCT and the 34th RCT from Pusan to the front. The additional commitment of two units then in reserve, the U.S. 45th Division and ROKA 11th Division, greatly strengthened UN forces.

After the reorganization of UN forces, on 17 July the ROKA II Corps counterattacked with three divisions and managed, by 20 July, to retake the high ground along the Kŭmsŏng River and to establish a new line six miles south of the original line. Although U.S. Secretary of State John Foster Dulles voiced opposition to allowing the Chinese to finish the war with a victory, no attempt was made to restore the original line. With the armistice to be signed at any time, both Generals Taylor and Mark Clark, supported by Army Chief of Staff General J. Lawton Collins, thought it unnecessary to expend lives for terrain not essential to the security of the Eighth Army's front.

This final Communist offensive caused enormous casualties at the end of the war. UN forces estimated that the Chinese had lost more than 72,000 men, more than 25,000 of whom were killed. Of the five Chinese armies that had been identified in the attacks against the ROKA II and U.S. IX Corps, the Chinese lost the equivalent of seven divisions.

Once the United States made plain its refusal to respond in kind, the Communists moved quickly to complete the truce talks. By 19 July the negotiators had reached an accord on all points. Details were worked out within a week and the Korean Armistice Agreement was signed at 1000 hours, 27 July 1953.

—Clayton D. Laurie

References:

Hermes, Walter G. *United States Army in the Korean War: Truce Tent and Fighting Front.* Washington, DC: Office of the Chief of Military History, 1966.

MacDonald, Callum. *Korea: The War Before Vietnam.* New York: Free Press, 1987.

Marshall, S. L. A. *Pork Chop Hill: The American Fighting Man in Action, Korea, Spring, 1953.* New York: William Morrow, 1956.

Miller, John, Jr., Owen J. Carroll, and Margaret E. Tackley. *Korea, 1951–1953.* Washington, DC: U.S. Army Center of Military History, 1997.

See also: Clark, Mark W.; Collins, Joseph Lawton; Dulles, John Foster; Pork Chop Hill, Battle of; Syngman Rhee; Syngman Rhee's Release of North Korean Prisoners of War; Taylor, Maxwell Davenport; Turkey.

Chinese People's Volunteer Army (CPVA)
(See China, People's Republic of: Army)

Chip'yŏng-ni, Battle of
(February 1951)

Mid-February 1951 perimeter defense engagement involving the 23d Infantry Regimental Combat Team (RCT) of the 2d Infantry Division and the Chinese People's Volunteer Army (CPVA, Chinese Communists) in and around the small village of Chip'yŏng-ni about fifty miles east of Seoul. This engagement, together with another at Wŏnju to the east, is described by some writers as the "Gettysburg," or high water mark for the CPVA in Korea. The battle was a major turning point in the Korean War in that it marked the end of the CPVA holding the initiative.

In the weeks after the late November 1950 massive entrance of Chinese forces into the fighting, there was considerable uncertainty over CPVA capabilities and intentions. UN forces had pulled back below the 38th parallel and given up the South Korean capital of Seoul. Large stocks of supplies had been destroyed to prevent their capture, and the UN command had even prepared plans for the total evacuation of the peninsula.

Fighting at Chip'yŏng-ni by the 23d RCT and at Wŏnju by the 2d Division's other two regiments—the 9th and 38th—settled the question of whether U.S. and UN forces could prevail against the CPVA. Completely surrounded and cut off from friendly forces during 13–15 February in almost constant fighting from a perimeter defense formation, the 23d RCT held off a numerically superior enemy force, inflicted staggering casualties on it while incurring only slight casualties in its own companies, save in the counterattacking reserve company.

The Chip'yŏng-ni fighting also signaled a change in U.S. battlefield tactics in Korea. Before it and the Wŏnju engagements, United Nations Command (UNC) forces had followed the practice of "rolling with the punch" when attacked. Instead of "standing and fighting," units would withdraw to avoid anticipated encirclement.

Commanded by Colonel Paul L. Freeman, the 23d RCT included the regiment's three infantry battalions, the French Infantry Battalion, a Ranger Company, and attached artillery, tank, and engineer elements. In early February the 23d RCT was in position in and around the transportation hub village of Chip'yŏng-ni, the juncture of several roads and transversed by a railroad line. On 11–12 February two Chinese armies and a Korean People's Army (KPA, North Korean) corps struck the central UN front, scattered three Republic of Korea Army (ROKA) divisions, and forced other UN troops in the sector to withdraw southward. The Communists aimed their attack at the communication centers of Wŏnju and Chip'yŏng-ni. Colonel Freeman soon received word of the withdrawal of friendly units on his flanks and noted the ominous build up of several divisions of enemy forces to his front. Knowing that he was greatly outnumbered, he asked Division Commander Major General Nick Ruffner when he too could begin a withdrawal. To Freeman's surprise, Ruffner refused permission. Instead, he informed Freeman that new Eighth Army commander Matthew B. Ridgway wanted a test of strengths; Chip'yŏng-ni and Wŏnju were to be defended and held. Freeman was ordered to form a tight perimeter defense pocket, to dig in deeply, and to lay in supplies of food, ammunition, and other items. He was told that if he were attacked and surrounded, he would be resupplied by air drops and a relief column by the 5th Cavalry Regiment of the 1st Cavalry Division driving up from Yŏju to the south.

Freemen promptly began to comply with those instructions, while at the same time carrying out vigorous patrols for up to three miles in front of all forward positions. His battalions were displaced as follows: 1st Battalion to the north sector of the perimeter, 3d to the east, 2d to the south, and the French Battalion to the south and southwest. Freeman held his B Company and the Ranger Company in reserve in the center of the perimeter near his regimental command post (CP).

Shortly after dusk on 13 February, Communist forces began to shell the perimeter center and some forward positions with artillery and mortar fire. Whistles, bugles, and other noise-making devices could be heard in the darkness in front of most perimeter positions. Around midnight, companies of the 1st Battalion came under attack. This spread until by daylight the entire perimeter was under assault, which continued unabated for most of the next three days. Freeman's forward companies held off the Chinese efforts to overrun the town and killed thousands of the attackers. Freeman himself was lightly wounded in the leg by a shell fragment but refused to be evacuated while fighting continued.

Around 0315 hours on the morning of 14 February a large number of Communist troops forced most of F and G Companies of the 2d Battalion from their positions on the southern rim of the perimeter, and occupied high ground there. This was a serious threat to the very existence of the perimeter. It exposed the flank of the remainder of the 2d Battalion to the east and the French Battalion to the west, and gave Communist forces full and unobstructed observation of, and allowed direct fire on, the entire center of the perimeter. The CPVA also held a pathway through which forces could be channeled into the perimeter.

Freeman recognized that the gap in his perimeter must be closed at all costs if his command was to survive. He immediately ordered a counterattack by the Ranger Company and surviving elements of F and G Companies. This commenced at daylight on 14 February but was repulsed with heavy losses.

Freeman then ordered B Company, his regimental reserve, to retake the ground lost and restore the integrity of the perimeter. B Company launched its attack around 1200 on 15 February. The attack occurred across open ground on a sunny day, in full view of Communist forces. The company advanced under intense Communist fire. Mortar and machine-gun fire rained on the attacking troops and men fell on all sides. By 1600, with help from a napalm air strike and Communists forces apparently aware that an armored relief column was approaching from the south, B Company finally routed the enemy and closed the breach in the perimeter. Fighting ended when the perimeter was secured. In its attack, B Company had suffered more than 50 percent casualties and all of its platoon sergeants had been killed or wounded. These casualties are in sharp contrast with the half dozen or so casualties incurred by other on-line companies of the regiment, which had the advantage of being in skillfully prepared, well-protected, deeply dug, text-book-designed and -constructed positions.

By late afternoon on the 15th, elements of the 5th Cavalry Regiment could be seen to the south approaching the perimeter. By dusk, its leading elements entered the perimeter through the road from Yŏju that passed between and marked the boundaries of the 2d and French Battalion positions.

UN casualties in the fighting at Chip'yŏng-ni were 51 killed in action, 250 wounded in action, and 42 missing in action. Confirmed Communist casualties came to 2,000 killed and 3,000 wounded, although their actual losses were assumed to be much higher. The fighting at Chip'yŏng-ni established that UN and U.S. forces could withstand anything and everything that the Communists could throw at them. The CPVA never again held the clear strategic initiative in the war.

—*Sherman W. Pratt*

References:

Blair, Clay. *The Forgotten War: America in Korea, 1950–1953.* New York: Times Books, 1987.

Clodfelter, Michael. *Warfare and Armed Conflicts. A Statistical Reference to Casualty and Other Figures, 1618 1991.* Vol. 2. Jefferson, NC: McFarland, 1992.

Munroe, Clark C. *The Second U. S. Division in Korea, 1950–1951.* Tokyo: Toppan Printing, n.d.

Pratt, Sherman W. *Decisive Battles of the Korean War. An Infantry Company Commander's View of the War's Most Critical Engagements.* New York: Vantage Press, 1992.

Schnabel, James F. *United States Army in the Korean War: Policy and Direction, the First Year.* Washington, DC: Office of the Chief of Military History, Department of the Army, 1972.

U.S. National Archives, 23rd Regiment Command Report, 1–28, February 1951.

See also: China, People's Republic of, Army; Freeman, Paul L., Jr.; Ridgway, Matthew Bunker; Wŏnju, Battle of.

Cho Pyŏng-ok
(1894–1960)

Minister of home affairs in the Republic of Korea (ROK) during the Korean War. Born at Mokch'ŏn (now Ch'ŏnan), South Ch'ungchŏng Province, Cho Pyŏng-ok went to the United States and attended Wyoming High School in Kingston, Pennsylvania, during 1914–1918. After graduation he majored in economics at Columbia University, where he became involved in various Korean overseas independence movement organizations. He earned a B.A. in 1922 and a Ph.D. in 1925 at Columbia.

Returning to Korea, Cho taught at Yŏnhŭi College (now Yŏnsei University) and became deeply involved in the movement for independence. In 1927 Cho was treasurer for Sin'ganhoe, the anti-Japanese nationalist organization. He then worked for a wider movement known as the Unified National Front. During 1929–1932, Cho was imprisoned for his role in the Kwangju Student Movement, a well-known anti-Japanese Korean student effort. Later he was again imprisoned for two years for involvement in an anti-Japanese incident.

In 1945 Cho worked with Kim Sŭng-su and Song Chin-u in setting up the right-wing nationalist Korean Democratic Party. Working with the U.S. military government, Cho played a key role in building up the South Korean National Police. As chief of the Police Bureau he worked to ferret out Communists and maintain public peace. According to U.S. Central Intelligence Agency files, although some Americans in the military government disliked Cho for his harsh and ruthless repression of Korean leftists, most regarded him as a competent administrator.

In 1948, the year of the establishment of the Republic of Korea (ROK), Cho toured friendly countries as President Syngman Rhee's special envoy. He also participated in the United Nations (UN) discussions on Korea and did much to gain international support for the ROK. In June 1950 he was the ROK representative to the UN Security Council when it met to consider the start of the Korean War. The following month he was appointed minister of home affairs.

In the autumn of 1950, with UN forces pushed back into the Pusan Perimeter, things appeared desperate for the ROK. All ministries and the National Assembly had already moved to Pusan, except the ministries of Defense and Home Affairs, which clung to Taegu. U.S. Eighth Army commander Lieutenant General Walton H. Walker ordered that the remaining ministries and Eighth Army also be withdrawn from Taegu. Cho strongly opposed this, insisting that if Taegu were abandoned then Pusan would be lost and the UN would be forced out of Korea. He visited Walker to convince him of his resolve to protect Taegu with the police and, after their meeting, Walker retracted his order. The Ministry of Defense did eventually move to Pusan but the Ministry of Home Affairs did not.

Disappointed by signs of Rhee's dictatorship in May 1951, Cho resigned his ministerial post by submitting a statement that read in part, "as the ROK was born to be a democratic country it should be definitely growing and developing into a democratic country." In 1953 when Rhee ignored the agreement regarding prisoners of war (POWs) reached between the UN and Communist sides by releasing North Korean POWs, Cho publicly condemned Rhee for the resulting international criticism and harm to the ROK's diplomatic position. Arrested for his criticism of Rhee, he was then imprisoned.

On his release from prison, Cho became a leader of the political opposition to Rhee. In 1955 he helped establish the Democratic Party, which opposed Rhee's Liberal Party, and in 1956 Cho was elected its leader. Although he ran as the presidential candidate of his party in the 1960 elections, Cho was forced to go to the United States for medical treatment. He died at Walter Reed Hospital in Washington on 15 February 1960, a month before the election.

—*Insook Park*

References:

Chŏnjaeng Kinyŏm Saŏp-hoe. *Han'guk Chŏnjaeng-sa* [History of the Korean War]. Vol. 1. Seoul: Hanrim Press, 1990.

Matray, James I,, ed. *Historical Dictionary of the Korean War.* Westport, CT: Greenwood Press, 1991.

Park, Myung-Lim. *Han'guk Chŏnjaeng ŭi Palbal Kwa Kiwŏn* [The outbreak and origins of the Korean War]. Vols. 1, 2. Seoul: Nanam Publishing House, 1996.

See also: Kim Sŏng-su; Syngman Rhee; Walker, Walton Harris.

Ch'oe Tŏk-sin
(1914–1989)

Republic of Korea (ROK, South Korea) soldier and diplomat who took political asylum in the Democratic People's Republic of Korea (DPRK, North Korea). In the DPRK he was a politician and a religious leader. Ch'oe Tŏk-sin was born on 17 September 1914 in Ŭiju, North P'yŏngan Province. He graduated from Whampoa, the Chinese military officers' academy, and served as an officer in the Chinese Nationalist Army. He returned to South Korea in 1945 after the end of the war and served as an officer in the ROK Army and as ROK representative to the armistice talks during the Korean War. Based on this military experi-

ence, Ch'oe wrote two books, *My Experience at P'anmunjŏm* (1956) and *Whither the Second P'anmunjŏm?* (1968).

In 1956 Ch'oe retired from the military as commander of I Corps of the ROK Army. In 1961 he became minister of foreign affairs. Two years later he was appointed ROK ambassador to West Germany. In 1967 Ch'oe became the seventh bishop of the Ch'ŏndogyo, an indigenous Korean religion.

Formerly a staunch anti-Communist and zealous supporter of the Park Chung Hee regime, Ch'oe was repelled by government corruption. The government in turn accused Ch'oe of being implicated in a corruption scandal involving the Ch'ŏndogyo. Ch'oe's disagreements with the regime led him to go into exile in the United States in 1976. There he engaged in an anti-ROK government struggle.

An official invitation from the DPRK provided Ch'oe with an opportunity to initiate contacts with high-level North Korean officials. Then in October 1986 he accepted political asylum in North Korea together with his wife and son Ch'oe Hong-hŭi. In the DPRK he served as vice-chairman of the Committee for Peace and Unification of the Fatherland, deputy in the Supreme People's Assembly, chair of the Korean Ch'ŏndogyo Young Friends Party Guidance Committee, chairman of the Central Ch'ŏndogyo Guidance Committee, and president of the Korean Religious People's Association.

Ch'oe was the highest ROK government official to seek refuge in the DPRK and achieved the highest positions among those who took political asylum in the North. He died on 16 November 1989 and is buried at the National Cemetery for the Patriotic Heroes in P'yŏngyang.

—*Jinwung Kim*

References:

Ch'oe, Tŏk-sin. *Che i ŭi P'anmunjŏm ŭn Ŏdiro* [Whither the second P'anmunjŏm?]. Seoul: Ch'ŏng'un Munhwa-sa, 1968.

———. *Nae ga Kyŏkkŭn P'anmunjŏm* [My experience at P'anmunjŏm]. Seoul: Samhong-sa, 1956.

See also: Korea, Democratic People's Republic of: 1953 to the Present.

Ch'oe Yong-gŏn
(1900–1976)

Minister of defense of the Democratic People's Republic of Korea (DPRK), 1948–1976. Ch'oe Yong-gŏn was born in 1900 in T'aech'ŏn, North P'yŏngan Province. Along with Kim Il Sung and Kim Ch'aek, Ch'oe was one of the original inner circle of Manchurian-based Korean leaders selected by the Russians to lead the Korean Workers Party after World War II. In 1946 he was named chairman of the Central Committee of the Chosŏn Democratic Party.

After the establishment of the DPRK in 1948, Ch'oe became minister of defense and held that post until his death in 1976. He was also supreme commander of the Korean People's Army (KPA, North Korea) and a representative at the First People's Congress.

Ch'oe's role in the planning and early execution of the Korean War is shrouded in mystery. In the spring of 1950, Ch'oe appears to have objected to the Soviet-devised plan to invade the South on the grounds that the United States would intervene, and he withdrew from active involvement. Although Kim Il Sung named Ch'oe to the seven-member military council that he established just after the outbreak of the conflict, Ch'oe played no active role until September, when he was named supreme commander of the defense of Seoul.

The evidence for Ch'oe's inactivity before the war lies in the absence of any operational orders issued in his name between late April and August 1950. Before and after this period, until 1976, all operational orders that are available bear his signature. Just before the outbreak of the war, Kim Il Sung was on the verge of purging his long-time colleague, but Ch'oe was spared through USSR leader Josef Stalin's direct intervention. When KPA forces failed to break through the Pusan perimeter defenses in August, Ch'oe resumed command of the Defense Ministry and retained it until his death in September 1976.

—*Richard C. Thornton*

References:

Headquarters, Far East Command. *History of the North Korean Army.* Tokyo: U.S. Army, 1951.

Park, Myong Lim. "North Korea's Inner Leadership and the Decision to Launch the Korean War." *Korea and World Affairs* (Summer 1995): 240–268.

"Yu Song-chol's Testimony Part 9." *Foreign Broadcast Information Service—East Asia Survey* (27 December 1990): 26–27.

See also: Kim Il Sung; Stalin, Josef.

Chŏng Il-kwŏn
(1917–1994)

Republic of Korea Army (ROKA, South Korea) chief of staff, July 1950–July 1951. Chŏng Il-kwŏn was born in Kyŏngwŏn, North Hamgkyŏng Province, North Korea, on 21 November 1917. He transferred from the Japanese Manchurian Military Academy, which he had entered in 1935, to graduate from the Japanese Military Academy in Tokyo in 1940. He then served as a captain in the Japanese Kwantung Army in Manchuria. After his return to Korea, Chŏng graduated from the U.S. military government's Military English-Language School in January 1946 and became the second chief of staff of the Korean Constabulary, predecessor to the ROKA.

When the Korean War began, Chŏng was on a military inspection trip in the United States and was unable to return to Korea until 30 June 1950. Immediately after his arrival, he was promoted to major general to replace Ch'ae Pyŏng-dŏk as ROKA chief of staff on 1 July. South Korean President Syngman Rhee made this change promptly because Ch'ae was a defeated general who had discredited the position of chief of staff.

Although he was its commanding officer, Chŏng lost authority actually to command the ROKA as of 14 July, when President Rhee approved a unified command in Korea and placed the ROK armed forces under authority of United Nations (UN) commander General Douglas MacArthur. Under the command relationship established, Eighth Army commander Lieutenant General Walton H. Walker directed the ROKA through its chief of staff. Although Chŏng followed orders, Walker usually gave him authority in certain matters regarding ROK forces. Chŏng did not direct ROKA military operations in the field, but he did direct planning and he had charge of security operations in rear areas.

Chŏng was highly effective in coordinating activities between the UN Command (UNC) and the ROK government. A prime example of this came at the end of September when UN forces approached the 38th parallel after the successful landing at Inch'ŏn. President Rhee issued secret orders that the ROKA cross the parallel whether or not the UNC decided to advance into North Korea. In fact Rhee admonished Chŏng for not taking such an action immediately. On 29 September, the day before he authorized ROK forces to cross the parallel, Chŏng secured permission from Walker for one company to operate temporarily across the parallel. On 2 October the ROKA 3d and Capital Divisions had already established command posts in Yangyang, eight miles north of the parallel, although General MacArthur made the first official announcement of plans to cross the parallel on that day. Chŏng also cleared all instructions from Eighth Army to ROK corps in the field.

One difficulty Chŏng encountered in his relations with Eighth Army commander came over their different views of the ROKA. Chŏng and President Rhee wanted the United States to provide additional equipment and supplies for their army, whereas the United States regarded the lack of leadership rather than equipment shortages as the most pressing weakness of the ROKA, something that was revealed when the Chinese launched major military offensives.

In July 1951 Chŏng was relieved as chief of staff and went to the United States to enter the Command and General Staff College. On his return to Korea, during July–October 1952 he commanded the ROKA 2d Division. President Rhee, who wanted Chŏng to have battlefield experience to assist him in future high command positions, arranged this unusual appointment of a former chief of staff to command a division. Transferred to the U.S. IX Corps, Chŏng served as deputy commanding officer for another three months. In February 1953 he became commanding general of the ROKA II Corps, a post he held until the end of the war. In 1954 he returned as ROKA chief of staff, and in 1956 he became chairman of the ROK Joint Chiefs of Staff. Retiring from the army the next year, he filled various government posts, including ambassador to France, Turkey, and the United States; prime minister; minister of foreign affairs; and speaker of the National Assembly. He died in Hawaii while on a visit there on 18 January 1994.

—To-Woong Chung

References:

Appleman, Roy E. *South to the Naktong, North to the Yalu.* Washington, DC: Office of the Chief of Military History, 1961.

Chŏng, Il-kwŏn. *Chŏng Il-kwŏn Hoegorok* [Memoirs of Chŏng Il-kwŏn]. Seoul: Koryo Sojuk, 1996.

———. *Chŏnjaeng kwa Hyujŏn [War and truce: Memoirs].* Seoul: Tonga Ilbo-sa, 1986.

Noble Harold J. *Embassy at War.* Seattle: University of Washington Press, 1975.

See also: Ch'ae Pyŏng-dŏk; MacArthur, Douglas; Syngman Rhee; Walker, Walton Harris.

Ch'ŏngch'ŏn River

A 124-mile-long river that flows into the Yellow Sea, dividing the old P'yŏngan Province into North and South P'yŏngan Provinces. The east-west direction of the river provided a physical barrier against many northern invaders in Korean history.

On 25 October 1950 the Chinese People's Volunteer Army (CPVA) suddenly attacked Republic of Korea Army (ROKA) troops in the Unsan area. In twelve days ROKA troops were forced to retreat from areas close to the Yalu River to the Ch'ŏngch'ŏn River. On 28 November, under increasing CPVA pressure, Eighth Army commander general Lieutenant General Walton H. Walker ordered United Nations (UN) forces to withdraw below the Chŏngch'ŏn River. UN Command commander General Douglas MacArthur's Home-by-Christmas offensive, launched on 24 November, had ended in failure.

—Jinwung Kim

References:

Blair, Clay. *The Forgotten War: America in Korea, 1950–1953.* New York: Times Books, 1987.

MacDonald, Callum. *Korea: The War Before Vietnam.* New York: Free Press, 1986.

Matray, James I., ed. *Historical Dictionary of the Korean War.* Westport, CT: Greenwood Press, 1991.

See also: Home-by-Christmas Offensive; MacArthur, Douglas; Walker, Walton Harris.

Ch'ŏngch'ŏn River, Battle of
(25–30 November 1950)

In western Korea the Chinese People's Volunteer Army (CPVA, Chinese Communist) Thirteenth Army Group of eighteen divisions opposed Lieutenant General Walton H. Walker's Eighth Army. The Chinese planned to attack the Republic of Korea Army (ROKA) II Corps in the high mountains on Eighth Army's right flank and overrun it. The Chinese would then move eastward to the Yellow Sea to trap Eighth Army against the Ch'ŏngch'ŏn River. Meanwhile, the U.S. I and IX Corps would be fixed in place by other CPVA units. In this way Eighth Army would be destroyed and United Nations Command (UNC) forces driven from northwestern Korea.

On the night of 25–26 November 1950, the Chinese attacked along the Eighth Army front. The ROKA II Corps and the U.S. IX Corps bore the initial brunt of the attack. In Ninth Corps, two U.S. divisions, the 25th on the left and the 2d on the right, had been progressing slowly toward the Yalu River when they suddenly ran head-on into CPVA units. Task Force Dolvin and the 24th Regiment of the 25th Division were overwhelmed by waves of attacking Chinese. The 27th (Wolfhound) Regiment of the division was rushed in behind the 24th to cover gaps between units. The Chinese, however, managed to move around the 27th and establish roadblocks. There was heavy fighting with high casualties before others overran the Chinese roadblocks and allowed the division to withdraw.

The U.S. 2d Division bore the brunt of the Chinese attack. It caught the full force of three attacking Chinese armies. Six CPVA divisions attacked the 2d Division directly, while six more poured through the ROKA II Corps and made a wide envelopment around the U.S. IX Corps. The result was one of the worst disasters incurred by any U.S. division in the war.

When the ROKA II Corps on the right flank of Eighth Army collapsed, this allowed six Chinese divisions to make a wide envelopment and block the 2d Division's escape route to Tŏkch'ŏn. The only remaining withdrawal route for the division was back along the Ch'ŏngch'ŏn River to Kunu-ri. Here the main route of withdrawal continued south along the river to Anju. Kunu-ri was a key road junction. A secondary road led from the river road through a gap in the mountains to Sunch'ŏn. The river road, which was much longer than the eighteen-mile mountain road, would cause the 2d Division to become involved with traffic from the withdrawing U.S. 25th Division and I Corps.

As the 2d Division's 23d and 38th Regiments became heavily engaged while withdrawing down the Ch'ŏngch'ŏn River, ROKA units on their right had fallen back to Tŏkch'ŏn. This allowed the CPVA to envelop Eighth Army's right flank. To block this, IX

Corps rushed in the newly arrived Turkish Brigade of 5,000 men. Its mission was to push east on the Kunu-ri-Tŏkch'ŏn Road and slow the Chinese advance. Eight miles outside of Kunu-ri the Turks met advancing Chinese forces. The Turks fought bravely but suffered many casualties and were forced to withdraw to Kunu-ri.

On 28 November General Walker ordered the withdrawal of the entire Eighth Army. At this point 2d Division commander Major General Laurence B. Keiser was faced with a difficult decision of withdrawing by either the short route through the mountain pass to Sunch'ŏn or the longer route along the Ch'ŏngch'ŏn River to Anju. In spite of reports of roadblocks along the mountain road to Sunch'ŏn, Keiser decided to risk the shorter route.

On 30 November the 2d Division moved down the mountain road. It had moved barely a mile before lead units ran into heavy Chinese small arms and mortar fire. Unknown to Keiser, an entire Chinese division stretched along both sides of the road for a distance of seven miles. The 2d Division withdrawal route soon became an avenue of death.

U.S. Air Force aircraft assisted the division in its slow movement through the gauntlet. All day aircraft flew up and down the route, strafing suspicious Chinese positions. When the planes were strafing, CPVA fire stopped. When the planes departed, it would begin again. Aided by the air strikes and by fire from the artillery's twin 40-mm guns, the division inched slowly forward.

Disabled vehicles blocked the road and had to be pushed aside. Wounded were loaded on vehicles that could move. The division, overloaded and burdened with heavy equipment belonging to the artillery and engineers, had great difficulty moving through the narrow, winding, mountain road into Sunch'ŏn.

The actions of Keiser and his staff during this battle were unique. When his bodyguard was killed, Keiser leapt from his jeep, fired his rifle at the Chinese, and shouted encouragement to the men around him. None could fault him and his staff for not personally participating in the common struggle.

The 23d Infantry Regiment protected the rear of the column. As the day wore on, fearful that his unit might be cut off, regimental commander Colonel Paul L. Freeman requested and received permission to withdraw along the Ch'ŏngch'ŏn River to Anju. This left the rear of the column vulnerable to extensive Chinese fire and, as a result, a number of units suffered high losses in men and equipment. The 2d Engineer Battalion lost 711 of its original 977 men, along with more than 95 percent of its equipment.

During the withdrawal, the 2d Division sustained such high casualties and equipment losses that it was out of action for several months. Only the arrival of the 1st Cavalry Division at Sunch'ŏn saved the 2d Division from total annihilation.

Meanwhile, in bitter cold weather, ragtag survivors of the U.S. XI and I Corps along with the remnants of the ROKA II Corps poured across the Ch'ŏngch'ŏn River bridges at Anju. All were heading south in a hurry. Trucks of all sizes, tanks, jeeps, self-propelled howitzers, and other wheeled vehicles were loaded down with frightened men, many without helmets or weapons, as they passed across the bridges and headed south. These haggard and bearded men, fearful of being left behind, personified the defeated Eighth Army as it pulled back into South Korea.

—*Daniel R. Beirne*

References:

Blair, Clay. *The Forgotten War: America in Korea, 1950–1953.* New York: Times Books, 1987.

Mossman, Billy C. *U.S. Army in the Korean War: Ebb and Flow, November 1950–July 1951.* Washington, DC: U.S. Army Center of Military History, 1990.

Spurr, Russell. *Enter the Dragon: China's Undeclared War against the U.S. in Korea 1950-51.* New York: Henry Holt, 1988.

See also: Eighth United States Army; Freeman, Paul L., Jr.; Keiser, Laurence B.; Tenth Corps; Walker, Walton Harris.

Church, John H.
(1892–1953)

U.S. Army general who headed the initial survey party dispatched to Korea immediately after the 25 June 1950 Korean People's Army (KPA, North Korean) invasion of South Korea; later commander of the 24th Infantry Division during July 1950–January 1951.

Born in Glen Iron, Pennsylvania, on 28 June 1892, John Huston Church attended New York University during 1915–1917. Entering the U.S. Army during World War I, he was commissioned a second lieutenant and was twice wounded while leading infantry units in combat. Church determined to make the army his career and after the war he served in a variety of assignments. He was an instructor for the National Guard and he had a tour of duty in the Philippines. During World War II, Church was first the assistant commander of the 45th and then the 84th Infantry Divisions. In 1942 he became chief of staff of the 45th Infantry Division and participated with the division in landings at Sicily, Salerno, Anzio, and in Southern France. In September 1944 he became assistant division commander of the 84th Infantry Division during fighting in Germany. His unit was one of the first to reach the Elbe River.

In June 1946 Church commanded the Infantry Replacement Training Center at Fort McClellan, Alabama. Later he served in a similar post at Fort

Jackson, South Carolina, where he also commanded the 5th Division. During 1948–1949 he was stationed at Fort Monroe, Virginia, as deputy chief of army field forces. At the start of the Korean War, Brigadier General Church was serving in the general headquarters, Far East Command, Tokyo.

On 26 June 1950, commander of U.S. Forces in the Far East General Douglas MacArthur named Church to head a survey team to assess the situation in the Republic of Korea (ROK, South Korea). When the team arrived on the evening of 27 June 1950, they found chaos. Church took charge, corralling stragglers in an attempt to form a defensive line at the Han River just south of Seoul. The capital fell late on the 28th. In a radio message to MacArthur, Church advised that only U.S. troops could contain the invasion. After a personal trip to Korea the next day, MacArthur concurred in this assessment. Church then headed the Korean Military Assistance Group.

On 22 July 1950, Church received command of the 24th Infantry Division. Its previous commander, Major General William F. Dean, had been captured by KPA forces when they overran Taejŏn. When Church took command, the 24th Division was exhausted and no longer combat effective. The first U.S. division to arrive in Korea (its Task Force Smith had engaged the enemy on 5 July), it had fought delaying actions for two and a half weeks, but had found itself continually outnumbered, outgunned, and outflanked. It lost almost 50 percent of its strength, most all of its artillery, and some 60 to 70 percent of its other equipment. The toll on senior commanders was high. In addition to its commanding officer (CO), the division had lost—as killed, captured, wounded and evacuated, or relieved—three regimental COs, one regimental executive officer, two staff officers, and seven battalion COs.

On 22 July the 1st Cavalry Division relieved the 24th, which was to be given a period of rest, receive replacements, and reequip. Two days later, however, Eighth Army commander General Walton H. Walker, with his entire left flank exposed, was forced to order the 24th back into the line. The division deployed around Chinju in the southwest.

The fresh KPA 6th Division steadily forced back Church's weakened 24th. Reinforced by another regiment, however, Church was able to contain the KPA advance just west of Masan, the back door to Pusan. By 6 August an entire KPA division crossed the Naktong River into the area known as the "Naktong Bulge" where Church's division was defending. Although the 24th attacked by day, the KPA took back at night the ground gained. Church's division held for eleven days but was not strong enough to eject the penetration. However, the addition of the 1st Marine

Provisional Brigade to his command enabled him to push the KPA back across the river, destroying the crack KPA 4th Division.

Reassigned to the P'ohang area to the east, Church's reinforced 24th Division then contained and defeated a series of furious KPA attacks. Church continued in command of the 24th during the Pusan perimeter breakout and the invasion of North Korea.

Church left Korea in January 1951 and became commandant of the Infantry School at Fort Benning, Georgia. He retired the next year and died on 3 November 1953 in Washington, D.C.

—Jack D. Walker

References:

Appleman, Roy E. *South to the Naktong, North to the Yalu.* Washington, DC: Office of the Chief of Military History, 1992.

Blair, Clay. *The Forgotten War, America in Korea, 1950–1953.* New York: Times Books, 1987.

Ent, Uzal W. *Fighting on the Brink: Defense of the Pusan Perimeter.* Paducah, KY: Turner, 1996.

Fehrenback, T. R. *This Kind of War: A Study in Unpreparedness.* New York: Bantam Books, 1991.

See also: Church Survey Mission to Korea; Dean, William Frishe; MacArthur, Douglas; Walker, Walton Harris.

Church Survey Mission to Korea
(27 June 1950)

Mission undertaken by Brigadier General John H. Church, on 26 June 1950, the day after the North Korean forces crossed the 38th parallel in their invasion of South Korea. In the first hours of the border crossing, Far East Commander General Douglas MacArthur told State Department Special Representative John Foster Dulles, in Tokyo working on the Japanese peace treaty, that the North Korean attack "was not an all-out effort" and that the South Korean Army "would gain victory." In response to a four-point directive from Washington, MacArthur had ordered ammunition sent to Korea, alerted his air and naval forces to provide protection in evacuating Americans from Seoul, and awaited arrival of the Seventh Fleet for further assistance. The dispatch of General Church to Korea would fulfill the remaining item of the directive: that he send a "survey party" to South Korea to find out what was going on there and determine the needs of the Republic of Korea Army (ROKA).

General Church was a staff chief in the general headquarters (GHQ) section of General MacArthur's Far East Command. When called on to head the survey mission to Korea, Church was just shy of his fifty-eighth birthday, frail, and racked with pain from arthritis.

On its way to Kimp'o Airfield at Seoul, the Church party, composed of twelve officers and two enlisted men, was warned that Kimp'o might be in enemy hands, whereupon the pilot changed his destination to

Suwŏn Airfield, twenty miles south of Seoul. The plane landed there in the early evening of 27 June. By then, the U.S. Joint Chiefs of Staff had designated MacArthur as commander of all forces in Korea, and Church's party was given the more imposing title of "GHQ Advance Command (ADCOM)."

Upon arriving at Suwŏn, General Church found confusion bordering on chaos. The South Korean government had fled from Seoul and President Syngman Rhee was in Suwŏn preparing to withdraw to Taejŏn, sixty-five miles further south. The U.S. Korean Military Assistance Advisory Group (KMAG) had disintegrated, its personnel fleeing with the civilians or straggling all over Korea. Thousands of ROKA soldiers and refugees jammed the roads south. The bridge over the Han River had been blown at Seoul, leaving thousands of soldiers with their heavy weapons, transport, and supplies trapped on the north bank.

Church believed that he had been misled about the quality of the ROKA and was greatly surprised to find it in total rout. He attributed the collapse to lack of leadership and not from fear. He noted that most of the ROKA officer corps, never strong and experienced to begin with, had just melted away. He wrote that many of the ROKA soldiers were eager to stand and fight, but without leaders, they did not know how or where to do so.

Church had gone to South Korea merely to gather facts, but the circumstances that developed overtook him, and his role was drastically upgraded. In effect, he assumed command of the tattered ROKA and the defense of South Korea. Within hours he reported to MacArthur that the restoration of the status quo was not within the capability of the ROKA and that if Seoul was to be recaptured "it would be necessary to employ American ground forces."

Church's role and authority in Korea steadily declined with the U.S. decision to commit significant ground forces to the fighting in Korea, especially with the arrival of the 24th Infantry Division in the first few days of July. General Church returned to Tokyo on 14 July. Promoted to major general four days later, on 23 July he became commanding general of the 24th Division.

—Sherman W. Pratt

References:
Blair, Clay. *The Forgotten War: America in Korea, 1950–1953.* New York: Times Books, 1987.
Ent, Uzal W. *Fighting on the Brink: Defense of the Pusan Perimeter.* Paducah, KY: Turner, 1996.
Schnabel, James F. *United States Army in the Korean War: Policy and Direction, the First Year.* Washington, DC: Office of the Chief of Military History, Department of the Army, 1971.
See also: Church, John H.; Dulles, John Foster; Korea Military Advisory Group (KMAG); MacArthur, Douglas; Syngman Rhee.

Churchill, Sir Winston Spencer
(1874–1965)

Prime Minister of Great Britain who led his country in the Korean War from October 1951 onward. Born at Blenheim Palace in Oxfordshire, England, on 30 November 1874, Winston Spencer Churchill, followed his father into a political career. In 1900 he became a Conservative member of Parliament. His tumultuous career culminated in his appointment as prime minister in 1940 for the duration of World War II.

Churchill lost the general election of 1945, but continued as leader of the Conservative Party and spoke out against Soviet expansion in the postwar world. World leaders viewed his "Iron Curtain" speech at Fulton, Missouri, in March 1946 as a call to arms against Communist aggression, and he was consequently branded by some as a warmonger. Churchill, however, did not desire another world war, but believed that the Western powers could negotiate with the Soviets only from a position of military strength. His views revolved around three basic tenants: a balance of power, the defense of British interests, and strong alliances to achieve these ends. The principle of containment fulfilled these goals, and Churchill became an ardent supporter of it after the Berlin airlift crisis of 1948–1949.

The pledge of British Prime Minister Clement Attlee's Labor government to support the United Nations (UN) in Korea on 25 June 1950 had the immediate support of Churchill and the Conservative Party. This support, however, vanished in the proceeding months because of the poor state of Britain's military. Churchill increasingly attacked the Labor government for its unwillingness to rearm for the struggle against Communist expansion. In truth, Labor did increase defense spending, but the results were slight and at great cost. The burdensome program was one of the major reasons for the defeat of Labor by the Conservatives in the 1951 general election that returned Churchill as prime minister.

One of the greatest of Churchill's goals in office was to relax the tension between the West and the Soviet Union in order to achieve his dream of a wideranging summit between the West and the Communists. He therefore sought a swift end to hostilities in Korea.

Throughout the war Churchill completely supported the U.S.-dominated UN effort. He particularly championed the "special relationship" between the United States and Britain. This support, however, hinged on the war not spreading outside Korean borders, which would have the potential of starting a wider conflict with the Communists and wrecking his hope for peace through strength. Churchill also did not favor a greater British role in the war. Washington's suggestion of a

British deputy chief of staff in Korea met only tacit approval. Churchill sought only constant consultation with the United States in order to offer suggestions to end the war. He also wanted to influence U.S. foreign policy in Asia. He disagreed on numerous occasions with this foreign policy. Two of the most contentious issues were U.S. suggestions of increasing force against the Chinese and the prisoner of war (POW) issue. Churchill supported the voluntary repatriation of POWs, but when negotiations stalled he solicited help from India. Although this tactic worked, the move greatly angered the Americans because they did not trust the Indians and viewed Churchill's actions as a betrayal of trust.

The fiercest opposition to Churchill's policies came from within his own government. Some officials, including Anthony Eden, opposed British involvement in Korea and believed that London should focus on strengthening Europe against the Soviets, rather than pursuing a summit. The death of Soviet Premier Josef Stalin in March 1953, however, spurred Churchill's efforts for an armistice and summit talks. Although his summit dream did not become reality until years after the war, the end of the Korean War and the change in Soviet leadership created the potential for future agreements based on his principles. For Churchill, the lasting legacy of the war was the rearmament of the United States and the potential of peace through strength.

After losing the general election of 1955, Churchill continued as a Conservative member of Parliament until failing health forced his retirement. He suffered a stroke on 10 January 1965 and died fourteen days later in London.

—*Eric W. Osborne*

References:

Gilbert, Martin. *Winston S. Churchill*. Vol. 7, *Never Despair, 1945–1965*. Boston: Houghton Mifflin, 1988.

Pelling, Henry. *Churchill's Peacetime Ministry, 1951–1955*. New York: St. Martin's Press, 1997.

Young, John W. *Winston Churchill's Last Campaign: Britain and the Cold War, 1951-5*. Oxford: Clarendon Press, 1996.

See also: Attlee, Clement R.; Defectors; Eden, Anthony; Repatriation, Voluntary; United Kingdom (UK).

Civilian Internee Issue

The issue of civilians interned by the United Nations Command (UNC). Many civilian internees (CIs), although not in the uniform of the Korean People's Army (KPA, North Korea) when taken, had volunteered to serve with the KPA. Others had been forced to serve when they had been taken. Also, because there were no civil assistance personnel to evaluate refugees from combat areas early in the war, many innocent civilians had wrongly been classified as prisoners of war (POWs). Included also were those taken into cus-

tody as security risks. This net was drawn widely in part because in the early days of the Korean War the KPA commonly dressed soldiers in civilian clothes to infiltrate UNC positions. CIs were of both North and South Korean origin and, as with POWs, they were both Communists and anti-Communists.

In all, some 50,000 CIs were held during the war. They were segregated in camps apart from the POWs but were given the same care and rights. In November 1950, Republic of Korea (ROK, South Korean) government officials began investigating the South Korean CIs. If cleared, they were released. The UNC ordered that POWs who had resided south of the 38th parallel before 25 June 1950 also be screened with the intention of reclassifying and releasing many. But there were long delays in carrying out this order. This, coupled with the fact that many were transferred to camps on Kŏje-do, caused a number of CIs to become Communists.

When the armistice negotiations began, the United States took the position that under no circumstances should CIs forcibly impressed into the KPA be returned to the Communists. As a result, their names were not included on the list of POWs turned over to the Communist delegates at P'anmunjŏm on 18 December 1951. But a certain number of these internees asked to be returned to North Korea after the armistice. The detaining authorities then decided to question them.

In November 1951, Eighth Army requested that all CIs be rescreened by a new Korean Civilian Central Screening Committee and by representatives of the U.S. and ROK military, intelligence services, and the ROK National Police. The screening process disclosed that many CIs had been incorrectly detained.

On 18 February 1952, during the rescreening, a demonstration occurred among CIs in Compound 62 of the Kŏje-do POW Camp. U.S. guards had to use bayonets and concussion grenades to break up a threatened attack by some 1,500 prisoners. In the process, 55 POWs were killed and another 159 severely wounded, 23 of whom later died in the prison hospital. Of U.S. personnel, 1 enlisted man was killed, another wounded, and 22 suffered minor injuries.

As a result of the rescreening, the UNC reclassified 41,000 South Koreans from POW to CI status, and some 37,500 POWs of the reclassified CIs were then segregated in separate compounds. These names were then released to the Red Cross.

The ROK government often requested the release of CIs. But UNC commander Lieutenant General Matthew B. Ridgway opposed this on security grounds and because he wished to avoid charges of bad faith from the Communist side that would inevitably follow any such release before the completion of an armistice. This would also give the Communists a pretense to delay or deny the return of UNC, especially Korean, POWs.

As armistice negotiations deadlocked over the repatriation issue, the UNC changed its policy toward CIs and utilized their release as a means of pressuring the Communists. The UNC took the position that their disposition was an internal matter, not subject to the purview of negotiators at P'anmunjŏm. Most of the internees in question were ROK citizens. They were gradually released to return to their homes after a thorough rescreening carried out jointly by ROK and UNC authorities to make certain that none of these individuals posed a threat to UNC security.

Under Operation SCATTER on 29 June 1952, Eighth Army released to the ROK approximately 27,000 CIs who had convinced screening personnel that they would resist repatriation. This left in detention approximately 9,600 CIs who stated that they wanted repatriation. By the end of July, Operation HOMECOMING released 18,746 CIs. By the end of September, a total of 26,574 eligible CIs had been released.

Later, after further investigation, an additional 11,000 of approximately 16,000 South Korean POWs were reclassified as CIs. Thorough screening and investigation of each of these individuals established that many had been improperly classified as POWs. These personnel consisted of ex-ROK soldiers, South Korean civilians who had been impressed by the KPA, and other South Koreans swept up in the UNC security dragnet. They were not among the 83,000 POWs whom the UNC had reported to the Communists for repatriation. These POWs had voiced their determination to resist returning to Communist control and then were subsequently moved to the non-repatriate POW Camp 7 at Masan. The UNC recommended that consideration be given to the release of these internees. Such action would impress Communist negotiators at P'anmunjŏm with the firmness of the UNC stand. Washington approved, and Operation THANKSGIVING, the release plan, was completed on 4 December 1952.

Although the Communists lodged a strong protest over the release of people they considered to be POWs, the UNC held firmly to the position that the individuals concerned were loyal nationals of the ROK and that, as such, the Communists had no claim on their disposition. The UNC considered it a negligible risk that the release of CIs might cause the Communist side to retaliate by holding UNC POWs; but it did cause North Korea to retain many South Korean POWs.

Some 38,000 civilian internees returned to their areas of residence throughout South Korea. Each released CI was given a thirty-day supply of rations, a blanket, a shirt, a pair of trousers, underwear, shoes, two pairs of socks, a hat or cap, and a rain coat. In all, more than 400 CIs died from disease and other causes during imprisonment.

—*Sunghun Cho*

References:

Cho, Sunghun. "Han'guk Chŏnjaeng Chung Min'ganin ŏkryuja ŭi Ch'ŏri e Kwanhan Yŏn'gu" [A study of the treatment of CIs during the Korean War], *Kunsa* [Military history]. Vol. 32. Seoul: Korean Institute of Military History, 1966, 283–312.

Headquarters U.S. Army Pacific. "The Handling of Prisoners of War during the Korean War, 1960." Unpublished document.

See also: Kŏje-do; Prisoner-of-War Administration, United Nations Command; Repatriation, Voluntary; Ridgway, Matthew Bunker; SCATTER, Operation; Truce Talks.

CLAM-UP, Operation
(10–15 February 1952)

United Nations Command (UNC) plan to secure large numbers of Communist troops. By 1952 the Korean War was a stalemate with only limited gains on either side. Between 10 and 15 February 1952 the UNC implemented Operation CLAM-UP, a plan to lure large numbers of Chinese People's Volunteer Army (CPVA, Chinese Communist) and Korean People's Army (KPA, North Korean) troops into the open, where they could be ambushed and captured.

CLAM-UP began on 10 February, when all UN offensive action across the length of the front ceased. No UNC patrols were sent out, no attacks scheduled, and no artillery bombardments were executed. No bombing or close air support was to occur within 20,000 yards of the front. UN troops were ordered to keep a low profile and not to provoke the Communists into action.

The intent of the plan was to make Communist forces believe that UN troops had withdrawn. Communist patrols sent to investigate the sudden silence of the UN forces would be ambushed and captured. The hope was that the sudden mass capture of these troops would break the stalemate.

Communist forces did not fall for this ruse and took the opportunity provided by the lull to move up supplies and reinforcements and to strengthen their defensive positions. As a result, after five days of very limited contact, the UNC abandoned the plan and resumed previous military activity. The failure of Operation CLAM-UP not only caused UN troops to face rejuvenated Communist forces but also showed the extent the UNC would go to break the stalemate of the war.

—*Clint Mundinger*

References:

Hermes, Walter G. *United States Army in the Korean War: Truce Tent and Fighting Front.* Washington, DC: Office of the Chief of Military History, 1966.

Matray, James I., ed. *Historical Dictionary of the Korean War.* Westport, CT: Greenwood Press, 1991.

See also: Active Defense Strategy.

Clark, Joseph James "Jocko"
(1893–1971)

U.S. Navy admiral. Born one-eighth Cherokee on 12 November 1893 in Pryor, Oklahoma, Joseph James "Jocko" Clark graduated in 1917 from the U.S. Naval Academy with the class of 1918. After sea duty on destroyers, he earned his aviator's wings at Pensacola in 1925, thereafter engaging in a variety of aviation duties. During World War II, Clark commissioned carriers *Suwanee* and the second *Yorktown* before leading carrier formations as a rear admiral in the major campaigns off Saipan, Iwo Jima, and Okinawa.

A series of postwar aviation assignments at sea and ashore followed. On 19 September 1951, Clark boarded the carrier *Bon Homme Richard* off Korea as commander of Task Force 77, which he would lead for three short stints until the end of November 1951. Promoted to vice admiral in March 1952, Clark took over the First Fleet and then on 20 May 1952 the Navy's premier combat command, the Seventh Fleet.

Flying his flag on battleships *Iowa*, *Missouri*, or *New Jersey*, Clark organized the planning for the October 1952 Kojo amphibious feint (Operation DECOY) by joint amphibious Task Force 7. In prosecuting the air offensive, Clark worked well with Lieutenant General Glenn O. Barcus, commander of the Fifth Air Force; the two devised the strike of June 1952 against the hydroelectric plant at Sup'ung (Suiho). Clark also won permission from United Nations Command (UNC) commander General Mark W. Clark for naval aircraft to hit the Aoji oil refinery on 1 September 1952. Vice Admiral Clark also pushed the navy to effective operations against the night-flying "Bed-Check Charlies."

Disappointed with the results of the interdiction campaign (Operations STRANGLE/SATURATE), which Clark labeled "a failure," he pressed instead for aerial attacks against Communist supplies stockpiled just out of reach of UN artillery. Unlike close air support techniques, these "Cherokee strikes," named in honor of Clark, were preplanned missions. Begun on 9 October 1952, they consumed about 50 percent of the aerial effort of Task Force 77 and were effective enough to be continued until the end of the war.

Certain naval analysts have retrospectively faulted Clark for paying too little attention to the gunfire capabilities of the Seventh Fleet battleships and cruisers. For instance, he failed to assign to those vessels dedicated spotter aircraft. More controversial among top strategists was Clark's proposal to force the Communists to terms by dropping an atomic bomb in

North Korea; he did manage to win General Mark Clark's approval to assign nuclear weapons to navy carriers during the emergency of mid-July 1953.

Throughout his career Vice Admiral Clark had earned the reputation as a "can-do" type of leader; at one point, General Clark commented, "If I were to order my friend Jocko Clark to take his flagship USS *Missouri* up the Yalu River the answer would be: 'Aye aye, sir!'" On 1 December 1953, Clark stepped down as commander of the Seventh Fleet and retired on the basis of combat awards with the rank of admiral. He had served in the U.S. Navy for forty years.

In retirement, Clark went into business and, with historian Clark Reynolds, published in 1967 his autobiography, *Carrier Admiral*. Clark died in New York City on 13 July 1971.

—*Malcolm Muir, Jr.*

References:

Cagle, Malcolm W., and Frank A. Manson. *The Sea War in Korea.* Annapolis, MD: Naval Institute Press, 1957.

Clark, J. J., and Clark G. Reynolds. *Carrier Admiral.* New York: David McKay, 1967.

Reynolds, Clark G. *Famous American Admirals.* New York: Van Nostrand, 1978.

See also: "Bed-Check Charlies"; Clark, Mark W.; Dam Raids of 1953; Nuclear Warfare; SATURATE, Operation; STRANGLE, Operation; Sup'ung (Suiho) and the Korean Electric Power Plant Campaign.

Clark, Mark W.
(1896–1984)

U.S. Army officer and commander of United Nations (UN) forces in the Korean War, 1952–1953. Born at Madison Barracks (Sackets Harbor), New York, on 1 May 1896, Mark Wayne Clark graduated from the U.S. Military Academy, West Point, in April 1917. He served as an infantry officer in World War I and was wounded. After recovering, he participated with the Third Army in the St. Mihiel and Muese-Argonne offensives.

Clark returned to the United States in November 1919 and was promoted captain shortly thereafter. After the war he served in a variety of posts. He graduated from the Infantry School in Fort Benning, Georgia, in 1925. Promoted major in 1933, he graduated from the Command and General Staff School at Fort Leavenworth, Kansas, in 1935 and from the Army War College in 1937. He then served on the staff of the 3d Infantry Division before returning to the Army War College in 1940 as an instructor. Clark was promoted to brigadier general in August 1941 and to major general in April 1942.

In May 1942 Clark became chief of staff of Army Ground Forces and, a month later, commanding general of II Corps. In October, shortly before the Allied invasion of North Africa, Clark led a covert mission to Vichy-held North Africa to meet with French leaders.

Promoted to lieutenant general in November 1942, Clark commanded land forces in North Africa under General Dwight D. Eisenhower. Beginning in September 1943 Clark led the U.S. Fifth Army during its protracted march up the Italian peninsula. Fifth Army occupied Rome in June 1944 and soon pushed north. In early December 1944, Clark became commander of the Fifteenth Army Group, which consisted of all Allied forces fighting in the Mediterranean theater. The campaign concluded with the surrender of 258,000 German troops in April and May 1945.

Clark's leadership during the Italian offensive remains controversial. Some have criticized him for the Anzio landings, the bombing of Monte Casino, his determination to liberate Rome at the expense of bagging retreating German forces, and "careless" tactics that they say cost thousands of lives. Clark's supporters have argued that difficult terrain, poor weather, and a fanatical German defense caused the casualties and that Clark did as well as possible.

After the war, Clark commanded the Allied occupation of Austria. In 1949 he became commander of U.S. Army Field Forces, Fort Monroe, Virginia, with responsibility for training U.S. combat forces. When the Korean War began, Clark was concerned that this training be realistic. In February 1951 he traveled to Korea to inspect conditions and analyze tactics for use in training.

Clark returned to Korea on 12 May 1952, to replace General Matthew B. Ridgway as U.S. commander in chief (CINC) Far East and United Nations' CINC. Clark arrived to find the ground war stalemated. The most significant combat occurred between F-86s and MiG-15s in the skies over an area of northwestern Korea known as MiG Alley.

Concurrently, armistice negotiations at P'anmunjŏm appeared hopelessly deadlocked over agenda item 4, the exchange of prisoners of war (POWs). The Communist side wanted all prisoners forcibly repatriated, whereas the UN Command (UNC) insisted that only those who wished to return should do so.

On 7 May 1952, Clark learned that enemy POWs in Compound 76 at the Kŏje-do Island POW camp had begun an uprising that ended in the capture of camp commander Brigadier General Francis T. Dodd. Dodd's deputy, Brigadier General Charles F. Colson, primarily concerned with saving Dodd's life, signed a misleading and humiliating statement that proved a propaganda advantage for the Communist side.

After Dodd's release, Clark discovered, as suspected, that the instigators were agents who allowed themselves to be captured. Throughout May and June, new

U.S. Army Lieutenant General Mark W. Clark. (Library of Congress)

camp commander Brigadier General Hayden L. Boatner reported continual unrest and several incidents. This culminated with another uprising on 10 June. This time, Clark ordered a crackdown. In a bloody one-hour clash, guards killed or wounded 150 prisoners; one American died and 13 Americans were wounded. This ended the POW defiance, and methods of identifying agents were soon implemented.

Another problem facing Clark was the behavior of Republic of Korea (ROK, South Korean) President Syngman Rhee, who continually tried to sabotage truce talks. While Clark agreed with Rhee's anti-Communist position, he was angered by his dictatorial methods and his lack of understanding of basic military tactics. Clark even drew up a secret contingency plan known as Operation EVERREADY designed to replace Rhee as president.

Ultimately, Clark, although obedient to President Harry S. Truman's desire to limit the war, agreed with former UN commander General of the Army Douglas MacArthur's belief in total victory. Clark also believed that the Communists would relent to the outstanding armistice issues only if the UNC kept up military pressure. Ground action was a potential problem because it could cause significant casualties. Thus Clark used his air assets to cut Communist communications and supply lines, hit airfields, and destroy dams and reservoirs. The air campaign proved successful.

Throughout his tenure, Clark, like MacArthur, chaffed at restrictions that prevented him from ordering direct attacks on Communist airfields and industrial centers in Manchuria. He drafted a secret contingency operations plan (OPLAN 8-52) that called for a drive to the Yalu River using tactical nuclear weapons and ground forces from Jiang Jieshi's (Chiang Kai-shek's) Republic of China on Taiwan.

Clark had hoped that former General-of-the-Army Dwight D. Eisenhower's election as president in November 1952 would allow him to take the offensive. After Eisenhower's trip to Korea, Clark realized that the new president, like Truman, was anxious to end the war quickly through negotiations. On 27 July 1953, a reluctant and, as he later described, "heavy hearted" Mark Clark signed the Armistice Agreement ending the Korean War. Clark returned to the United States in October 1953.

Clark retired from the army in Spring 1954 and then served as president of the Citadel (1954–1966). He wrote two volumes of memoirs, *Calculated Risk* (1950) and *From the Danube to the Yalu* (1954). In these he made no secret of his sadness over being what he called "the only American commander to end a war short of victory." He also decried what he viewed as Communist sympathizers at home. Clark generally sided with conservative causes and anti-Communist political leaders and movements during his civilian years. Later he would publicly argue that the events in Vietnam were the natural outgrowth of compromise and "appeasement" in Korea.

Clark spent his last years quietly in South Carolina. He died in Charleston, South Carolina, on 17 April 1984.

—William Head and Dean Corey

References:

Blumenson, Martin. *Mark Clark*. New York: Congdon & Weed, 1985.

Clark, Mark W. *From the Danube to the Yalu*. New York: Harper & Row, 1954.

New York Times, 17 April 1984.

Toland, John R. *In Mortal Combat: Korea, 1950–1953*. New York: William Morrow, 1991.

Whelan, Richard. *Drawing the Line: The Korean War*. Boston: Little, Brown, 1990.

See also: Dodd-Colson Prisoner-of-War Incident; Eisenhower, Dwight D.; Jiang Jieshi (Chiang Kai-shek); MacArthur, Douglas; Ridgway, Matthew Bunker; Syngman Rhee; Truman, Harry S.

CLEANUP I and II, Operations
(17 September–3 October 1951)

United Nations Command (UNC) military operations in the Iron Triangle, the traditional invasion route to Seoul. The UNC secured the southernmost apexes of the triangle, Kimhwa in the east and Ch'ŏrwŏn in the west, in June 1951, but the northernmost apex of the triangle, P'yŏnggang, remained in Communist control. The objective of Operations CLEANUP I and II was to secure a five-hill complex 8,000 meters west of Ch'ŏrwŏn. The operations were part of Lieutenant General Matthew B. Ridgway's strategy of "limited objectives."

Rains throughout the spring and summer kept U.S. Army engineers busy repairing military supply routes to the front lines, but monsoons in August washed out many routes through mountainous terrain and threatened to cut the flow of supplies to UNC forces across the entire peninsula. The rail line between Kimhwa and Ch'ŏrwŏn was thus vital to UNC operations in the central part of the front, but it was also within range of Communist artillery fire. Meanwhile Chinese and North Korean troops used the three months since the initiation of the peace talks to dig a network of trenches joining their bunkers along ridgelines all across the front.

Control of the area known as the Bloody Angle became a UNC tactical imperative. CLEANUP's goal was to seize and occupy the ridge line running west of Hill 487 west of Ch'ŏrwŏn, disrupt Communist supply and communications lines, inflict casualties, and knock out artillery and mortar positions. One arm of Hill 487, the apex of Bloody Angle, ran north to Hill 292; another arm ran west along a ridgeline to Hill 477. Engagements were also fought on the western approaches to Hill 477 and the Twin Peaks northeast of Hill 487. CLEANUP fell to the Eighth Army's 3d Infantry Division.

The 3d Reconnaissance Company, 15th Infantry Regiment, 3d Infantry Division, and the 7th Infantry Regiment deployed patrol troops north of Ch'ŏrwŏn. This was a ruse to draw attention from the actual attack to the west. On 17 September, while the 9th and 10th Field Artillery Battalions and 58th Armored Field Artillery Battalion moved into support positions, components of the 7th and 15th easily seized their objectives. Meanwhile the 65th Infantry and 64th Heavy Tank Battalion moved into assembly areas. Despite all preparations, the coordinated attempt on 18 September to take heavily fortified Hill 487 failed. Delays in the attack, occasioned by rain and fog, permitted the Communist defenders to recognize the threat and rush reinforcements to the five-hill complex.

CLEANUP II, which began on 29 September, was an assault on the entire five-hill complex. It was preceded by a nine-day softening up of the heavily fortified objectives; more than 45,000 rounds of artillery and mortar fire pounded the hills. Much of this was from U.S. tanks maneuvered into position so that their gunners could shoot directly into the Communist bunkers.

The 0200 29 September assault by A and B Companies of the 1st Battalion with Company E of the 2d Battalion of the 15th Regiment on Hill 487 began a seven-day battle. Although Companies A and B were able to reach their intermediate objectives without major resistance, they were temporarily halted by accurate Communist artillery fire from the reverse slopes. A Company resumed its assault, but was again halted within seventy-five yards of the crest by grenade and mortar fire. Captain Frank B. Tucker, A Company's commander, was killed in the final assault.

E Company was the first to secure its objective on the southern summit. It too encountered strongly entrenched Communist troops, but managed to fight its way to within a short distance of the bunkers, where the attacking infantry exchanged grenades with the Communist defenders.

The 2d Battalion, 15th Infantry, having accomplished its mission, then had to hold Hill 487 against sustained mortar and artillery fire, fending off three Communist assaults. Rain and fog grounded UNC aircraft. The foul weather also aided the defenders as advancing infantry slipped about in the greasy muck on the steep slopes almost devoid of vegetation, and vehicular traffic slowed to a snail's pace; even tanks found the going difficult.

Meanwhile the 3d Battalion of the 65th Regiment encountered heavy resistance on the Twin Peaks, the two unnumbered hills in the complex. Having secured a foothold on the eastern hill, they were unable to wrest the western one from the Communists. On 30 September, in spite of heavy rain, the 65th continued its assault on the second of the Twin Peaks. Failing in dogged attempts to dislodge Communist forces, G Company of the 15th moved off Hill 487 to support the 65th's attack. The additional support enabled the 3d Battalion of the 65th to take the second hill by midafternoon. G Company then returned to Hill 487.

Doomed by poor weather, CLEANUP II was only partially successful. In early October it fused into Operation COMMANDO, which was to extend what had been gained during CLEANUP II. The advancement of all I Corps components north from Line Wyoming to Line Jamestown guaranteed security of the vitally important Kimhwa to Ch'ŏrwŏn rail line.

—*Richard E. Coate*

References:

Dolcater, Max W. *History of the 3rd Infantry Division in Korea.* San Francisco: U.S. Army Third Infantry Division, 1953. Reprint, Paducah, KY: Turner, 1998.

15th Infantry Regiment Command Report no. 13, 1–31 October 1951; Unit Reports no. 264 and 275, October 1951. Suitland, MD: National Archives.

See also: COMMANDO, Operation; Iron Triangle; Ridgway, Matthew Bunker.

Close Air Support

Close air support (CAS) is the means by which aircraft provide direct fire support to ground troops. During the Korean War, the Korean People's Army (KPA, North Koreans) and Chinese People's Volunteer Army (Chinese Communists) had virtually no close air support.

U.S. close air support was provided by the U.S. Air Force, Navy, and Marine Corps. Specific U.S. units flying CAS were the Fifth Air Force, the 1st Marine Air Wing, and Task Force 77 of the Navy's Seventh Fleet. Air units of other countries, including Australia, South Africa, South Korea, and the United Kingdom, fought under the supervision of the Fifth Air Force or Task Force 77. For these fighter-bomber units, CAS was only one of their missions; others included air superiority, interdiction of the battlefield, and reconnaissance.

CAS helped save United Nations (UN) troops from annihilation in 1950 and 1951. The first occasion was during the retreat into the Pusan defensive perimeter during June–September 1950. The battlefield was very fluid, and artillery units were inadequate for fire support. CAS took the place of heavy artillery and blunted the KPA attacks. The second occasion was after the massive appearance of Chinese forces in November 1950. Adequate artillery could not be brought to bear as UN troops withdrew southward, and CAS blunted many Chinese attacks.

After UN forces began to receive more heavy (155-mm and larger) artillery, ground troops depended less on CAS. Also in 1951 as the front lines became more stabilized and the battlefield less fluid, there was less need for CAS. The threat of Chinese jet aircraft and the rapid movement of Chinese troops southward shifted resources to air superiority and interdiction missions. The success of CAS by 1951 was a remarkable achievement in the face of adverse operating conditions and interservice conflict over doctrine.

In early June 1950, the Fifth Air Force was based in Japan and had no presence in Korea. Its CAS aircraft consisted of F-80 Shooting Stars. These jets could not operate from dirt airstrips in Korea because their engines were subject to damage from loose debris. Having to fly from Japan, the F-80s had only limited time over the target. This problem was solved by providing jury-rigged wing tanks to give the F-80s longer range and using propeller-powered F-51s that could fly from primitive strips in Korea. B-26s were also used for CAS, especially night attacks. As Seoul and the area southward became secure during 1951, improved airfields accommodated F-84 Thunderjets and F-86 Sabres.

U.S. Marines move forward after effective close air support flushes out the Communist forces from their hillside entrenchments. Billows of smoke rise skyward from the target area, Hagaru-ri, 26 December 1950. (National Archives)

Air force doctrine for CAS called for the army to initiate strike requests and approve them up to corps level. The requests then went to a joint operations center where army and air force staff could approve the strikes, unless aircraft were needed for air superiority or interdiction missions or artillery could serve the need. If approved, the air force then provided and controlled attacks. Aircraft were not supposed to attack inside a "bombline" five to eight miles forward of the front lines without direction from air force controllers on the ground.

In 1950 the doctrine did not always work this way because troops were retreating or advancing rapidly, radios were inadequate in types or numbers, and the air force and army lacked adequate personnel to run the system. The air force adopted many expedients, the most significant being to place forward air controllers (FACs) in T-6 Texan aircraft to control strikes. Called

Mosquito flights, these airborne controllers located targets and directed attack aircraft to them. This system proved workable for highly mobile warfare. Not until the army and air force trained additional personnel and secured better radios in late 1950 was the CAS system more congruent with air force doctrine.

The U.S. Army in Korea became discontented with U.S. Air Force CAS doctrine and practice. X Corps commander General Edward M. Almond was the most vocal critic. Having a Marine Corps division in X Corps, Almond also had attached and available for CAS the 1st Marine Air Wing.

The Marines and navy operated under a different CAS doctrine than the air force. During amphibious landings, navy and Marine aircraft were on immediate call as a substitute for heavy artillery. FACs on the ground had only to call an air direction center for the CAS needed. Circling fighter-bombers could respond

This photograph was taken a split second after two napalm fire bombs were released over North Korea, from shackles underneath the wing of an F-51 Mustang of the Fifth Air Force's veteran 18th Fighter Bomb Wing. A sister plane at the far left will follow up with the same type of destructive bombs on this industrial military target. (National Archives)

in ten minutes or less and attack within fifty yards of the front lines. This contrasted with an air force response time of forty minutes at best and aircraft that did not attack closer than five miles to the front lines unless directed by a ground controller. Having pilots with World War II experience, the Marines were more proficient than the air force at this type of CAS.

The army preferred the type of CAS provided by General Ellwood R. Quesada's Ninth Tactical Air Force in Europe during the war. Quesada operated in a manner similar to that of the Marines. Almond's complaints, with which the army staff concurred, found their way into the press.

In response, the air force proposed establishing a joint army–air force board in Korea to recommend improvements in doctrine and practices. Army General John J. Burns presided over the board and reported in March 1951 that, although air force doctrine was "sound and adequate," improvements were needed in the system. The army wanted more Mosquito controllers and the air force wanted the army

to establish strike-request radio nets and sufficient officers to operate them around the clock. These and other improvements were made.

Another problem with CAS was the need to coordinate the aircraft of different services, a role claimed by the air force for itself. On 15 July 1950, Far East Air Force commander General George E. Stratemeyer secured an agreement that the air force would coordinate and control navy and Marine aircraft in the Korean theater. This proved impractical, however, because weather dictated launching schedules for aircraft carriers, and navy aircraft flooded controllers with target requests. There were other problems, including inadequate air force radios, too few FACs, and the use of different maps by the navy and air force. The two services did agree on a physical separation of their areas of operations, the navy in the east and the air force in the west. The service also carried out a few joint operations. In 1952 the navy and air force exchanged liaison officers to bring about greater cooperation in operations. But the air force never controlled naval aviation. After the battle lines were stabilized near the 38th parallel in 1951, the air force succeeded in bringing Marine aircraft under its general control. Marine ground units pressed for Marine aviation to be their exclusive support, and the air force granted this request when possible.

The military learned much about CAS during the Korean War. Jet aircraft could find and attack ground targets at high speed, and the jets were faster to return to targets after rearming and easier than piston-engine aircraft to maintain. Proximity-fused bombs proved lethal against personnel in the open, and napalm bombs were effective against personnel and many other targets. Strikes controlled by radar were also useful at night and in bad weather. The services discovered a need to develop doctrine for the control of all aviation in theater operations.

—*John L. Bell*

References:

Cooling, Benjamin Franklin, ed. *Case Studies in the Development of Close Air Support.* Washington, DC: Office of Air Force History, 1990.

Futrell, Robert F. *The United States Air Force in Korea, 1950–1953.* Rev. ed. Washington, DC: Office of the Chief of Air Force History, 1983.

Hallion, Richard P. *The Naval Air War in Korea.* Baltimore: Nautical and Aviation Publishing Co. of America, 1986.

Hughes, Thomas Alexander. *Over Lord: General Pete Quesada and the Triumph of Tactical Air Power in World War II.* New York: Free Press, 1995.

Momeyer, William. *Air Power in Three Wars: WWII, Korea, Vietnam.* Washington, DC: Department of the Air Force, 1978.

See also: Aircraft (Principal Combat); Almond, Edward Mallory; Quesada, Ellwood R.; Stratemeyer, George E.; United States Air Force (USAF).

Clubb, Oliver Edmund
(1909–1989)

Director of the U.S. State Department's Office of Chinese Affairs, 1950–1951. Born on 16 February 1901 in South Park, Minnesota, Oliver Edmund Clubb graduated from the University of Minnesota in 1928, whereupon he joined the U.S. Foreign Service. He chose to specialize particularly in Chinese politics and more broadly in East Asia, spending the bulk of his diplomatic career in that region, beginning with two years' Chinese and Russian language study in Peking (Beijing) from 1929 to 1931, followed by further assignments in Hankow, Nanjing, and the capital.

Early studies of China's situation in the late 1920s and early 1930s quickly convinced Clubb that major social change and disruption of the existing political system were inevitable. Even in 1931 his suggestions that official corruption posed a major problem to China led one Foreign Service officer at Shanghai to characterize Clubb as a "Red." In 1932 he wrote the

earliest U.S. study of Chinese communism, a 124-page memorandum that was coldly received by the Department of State, and in 1934 his superiors refused him permission to publish it. He continued to submit reports pointing out the weaknesses of Jiang Jieshi's government. Posted to Hanoi in 1941, on 7 December of that year he was captured by Japanese troops and spent the next eight months in an internment camp.

Upon his release, Clubb volunteered to return immediately to China, and from late 1942 until early 1950 he served successively in Chongqing, Lanzhou, Tihwa (Xinjiang), Vladivostok, Shenyang, Changchun, and Beijing. He predicted the impending Communist victory, the likelihood of which his years in Manchuria in the late 1940s made particularly apparent to him.

Upon the establishment of the People's Republic of China (PRC), an event that Clubb witnessed in Beijing on 1 October 1949, he recommended that the United States "temporarily maintain a noncommittal position but early show interest in the new regime's policies, let the Communists for their part get a glimpse of the benefits to be obtained through commerce and good relations with non-Communist countries." He suggested that Washington move to recognize the PRC once its leaders had "indicated a readiness to follow accepted standards of international behavior." He opposed further U.S. backing for the Guomindang (Nationalist) government on the mainland or in Taiwan and supported the maintenance of Western and Japanese trading links with China.

In his later years, Clubb would continue to argue that in 1949 greater flexibility on both sides might have preserved relatively good relations between the United States and the PRC. Such hopes were stymied by China's requisition on 6 January 1950 of U.S. diplomatic premises and the consequent State Department withdrawal of its personnel from China. By this time Clubb had at least temporarily lost faith in the potential for a rapprochement, and in April 1950 he argued that the Communists had "attached China to the Soviet chariot" and that the United States should prepare for war with the PRC.

Clubb returned to the United States by way of Japan and South Korea. On 16 June 1950 he warned of the potential threat to Korea. Upon learning of North Korea's invasion of the South, he left immediately for Washington, and on 6 July became chief of the State Department's Office of Chinese Affairs. Together with John Paton Davies of the Policy Planning Staff, he was one of the Truman administration's major sources of expertise on China during the Korean War.

Clubb opposed the decision to send United Nations forces across the 38th parallel and was the only senior U.S. official who consistently warned that Zhou

Enlai's 2–3 October 1950 statement that China would intervene militarily was not mere bluff. When his advice was ignored and China sent ground forces to Korea, Clubb was less firm in his opposition to General Douglas MacArthur's Home-by-Christmas offensive, since he believed that the United States must stand firm in Korea to divert China from other objectives such as Taiwan. He did, however, continue to oppose extending the war to Chinese territory, fearing that this would lead the Soviets to implement the Sino-Soviet Treaty of Friendship and Alliance and enter the war.

In April 1952 Clubb took early retirement from the Foreign Service. His decision was a consequence of McCarthyite allegations that he possessed pro-Communist sympathies and over many years had systematically undermined Jiang Jieshi's government. In December 1951 a Loyalty Review Board investigation, which lasted for a year and brought interrogations by the Federal Bureau of Investigation and a subpoena to appear before the House Un-American Activities Committee, characterized Clubb as a "poor security risk." Clubb appealed this decision and won reinstatement, but for political reasons, Secretary of State Dean G. Acheson offered him only a low-ranking position in the Division of Historical Research. Clubb turned this down and returned to private life in New York. Clubb held part-time teaching positions at New York University, Brooklyn College, and Columbia University, and he then became a research associate at Columbia's East Asian Institute. During these years he published several books and numerous articles on China, including an account of his State Department years and their termination. Clubb died on 9 May 1989 in New York City.

—*Priscilla Roberts*

References:

Clubb, O. Edmund. *The Witness and I*. New York: Columbia University Press, 1974.

Cohen, Warren I. "Consul General O. Edmund Clubb on the 'Inevitability' of Conflict between the United States and the People's Republic of China, 1949–50." *Diplomatic History* 5, no. 2 (Spring 1981): 165–168.

Kahn, E. J., Jr. *The China Hands: America's Foreign Service Officers and What Befell Them*. New York: Viking Press, 1975.

Lauren, Paul Gordon, ed. *The China Hands' Legacy. Ethics and Diplomacy*. Boulder, CO: Westview Press, 1987.

Schaller, Michael. "Consul General O. Edmund Clubb, John P. Davies, and the 'Inevitability' of Conflict Between the United States and China, 1949–50: A Comment and New Documentation." *Diplomatic History* 9, no. 2 (Spring 1985). 149–160.

See also: Acheson, Dean Goodersham; Davies, John Paton; Jiang Jieshi (Chiang Kai-shek); MacArthur, Douglas; McCarthyism; Zhou Enlai.

Cold War, Origins to 1950

The deadlock between East and West is the single most momentous development of the post–World War II period. Bernard Baruch coined the phrase "Cold War" in the course of a speech in 1947. The Cold War was the rivalry that developed between the two superpowers of the Soviet Union and the United States as each sought to fill the power vacuum left by the defeat of Germany and Japan. Leaders on both sides believed they were forced to expand their national hegemony by the "aggressive" actions of the other. Animosity between the two grew until it became the Cold War.

At the end of World War II, Washington and Moscow each had different views of the world. The United States sought a system based on the rule of law. Ironically the United Nations (UN), which the United States strongly supported, closely resembled the League of Nations, the organization that President Woodrow Wilson had championed at the Paris Peace Conference after World War I and which the United States had then refused to join.

During World War II, President Franklin Roosevelt had not greatly concerned himself with postwar political problems on the assumption that the UN could resolve them later. Washington had been preoccupied with winning the war as quickly as possible and at the least cost in American lives. This was much to the frustration of British Prime Minister Winston Churchill, who, like his Soviet counterpart Josef Stalin, sought to establish spheres of influence. U.S. leaders held to the Wilsonian position that a balance of power and spheres of influence were both outdated and immoral.

A power vacuum existed throughout much of the world at the end of the war. In defeating Germany and Japan, the United States had destroyed traditional bulwarks against Communist expansion. In Europe there was not a single strong continental state to bar Soviet expansion. In the Far East there was only China, which Roosevelt had counted to be one of the great powers and guarantor of a peace settlement, but it was weakened by the long war with Japan and in any case was about to plunge into full-scale civil war.

Americans assumed that wars ended with the shooting, and domestic political considerations compelled the rapid demobilization of the armed forces before the situation abroad had stabilized. Although the Soviet Union was much weaker in 1945 than was assumed at the time, Churchill expressed the view that only the U.S. nuclear monopoly prevented the USSR from overrunning Western Europe.

Although for different reasons, President Roosevelt shared with Premier Stalin a strong antipathy toward European colonialism, and Washington encouraged the disintegration of the European colonial empires.

While idealistic, this reduced the strength of U.S. allies such as Britain, France, and the Netherlands and helped ensure that ultimately the United States would have to carry most of the burden of defense of the non-Communist world.

In 1945 the Soviet Union had just emerged from a desperate struggle for survival. The German and Soviet armies had fought back and forth across and laid waste to vast stretches of the western USSR. Twenty-five million people were left homeless and perhaps one-quarter of the total property value of the country had been lost. The human costs were staggering, with as many as 27 million dead. The effects of all this upon the Russian people could scarcely be comprehended. For the indefinite future, whatever government held power in Moscow would be obsessed with security. This, rather than expansion, was the Kremlin's paramount concern in the immediate postwar years.

Despite all the destruction, the Russians emerged from the war in the most powerful international position in their history. The shattering of Axis military might and the weakness of the Western European powers seemed to open the way to Soviet political domination over much of Eurasia.

Stalin, who had seen the Western powers after World War I erect a *cordon sanitaire* in the form of a string of buffer states against communism, now sought to erect a *cordon sanitaire* in reverse—to keep the West out. This was for security reasons—three times since 1812 Russia had been attacked across the plains of Poland—but it was also to prevent against the spread of Western ideas and political notions. To Western leaders the Kremlin seemed to have reverted to nineteenth-century diplomacy, establishing spheres of influence, bargaining for territory, and disregarding the UN. Western leaders did not appreciate the extent to which security demands drove this policy.

Roosevelt gambled his place in history in part on the assumption that he could arrange a détente with the Soviet Union; but his optimism regarding Stalin was ill-founded. By mid-March 1945 it was all too obvious, even to Roosevelt, that the Soviets were taking over Poland and Rumania and violating at least the spirit of the Yalta agreements regarding multiparty systems and free elections.

Finally there was ideology. Although its leaders had soft-pedaled it during the Second World War, the Soviet Union had never abandoned its goal of furthering international communism. Irrespective of security concerns, the Kremlin was ideologically committed to combating capitalism. It is thus inconceivable that Stalin would not seek to take full advantage of the opportunity that presented itself at the end of the war.

As with that of the United States, Soviet foreign policy was closely tied to domestic needs. The Cold War would aid in enforcing authority and cooperation at home. The Communist world had to appear to be threatened by encircling enemies so that its peoples, who now expected a better life, would close ranks behind the Soviet leadership. Intense national feeling was a tool whereby the government could mobilize public effort and suffocate dissent.

Roosevelt died in April 1945. His successor Harry S. Truman insisted, despite Churchill's protests over mounting evidence that the Soviets were not keeping their pledges, that U.S. forces withdraw from areas that they had occupied deep inside the Soviet zone of Germany. Public opinion polls clearly showed that the American public did not want confrontation and a global economic and political-military struggle with the Soviet Union. Americans were limited internationalists, who merely wanted to enjoy their economic prosperity.

The Soviets were angry over Washington's abrupt termination of Lend-Lease on 21 August 1945, regardless of the terms of the original law. Russian ill will was also generated by the usually smooth cooperation of the Anglo-Saxon powers and Moscow's belief that the two constantly combined against the Soviet Union. The U.S. monopoly of the atomic bomb also aroused fear in the Soviet Union as a small but vocal group of Americans demanded preventive war. Soviet concerns increased when the United States retained bomber bases within striking distance of Russia's industrial areas and undertook naval maneuvers in the Mediterranean.

The USSR, however, rejected a plan put forth by the United States to bring nuclear weapons under international control; instead, they proceeded with their own atomic research and, aided by espionage, exploded their own bomb in September 1949. The atomic arms race thus began.

Certainly U.S. and British attitudes toward Russian activity in Eastern Europe and the Balkans exasperated Moscow. Having accepted Soviet hegemony there, why did the West criticize? Initially Moscow permitted political parties other than the Communists, and now it seemed to the suspicious leaders in the Kremlin as though the West was encouraging these parties against Soviet interests. At a minimum, the USSR required security, while the United States wanted democratic parties in a Western type of democracy. In only one country, Finland, did the Soviet Union and the West achieve the sort of compromise implicit in the Yalta agreements. In countries such as Poland and Hungary, non-Communist parties were highly un-likely to ensure the Soviet Union the security it desired, and Western encouragement of these groups seemed to Moscow to be a threat.

On the U.S. side, the Russian moves kindled exasperation and then alarm as the Soviet Union interfered in the democratic processes of one Eastern European country after another. Not only that, but the UN seemed paralyzed as the Soviet Union, in order to protect its interests when the majority was consistently against it, made increasing use of its Security Council veto. Despite this, Western pressure in the UN did help secure a Soviet withdrawal from northern Iran, in what was the first major test for the international body.

This does not mean that the West was unified. In Britain left-wing Labourites criticized U.S. capitalism and wanted to work with the Russian Communists. The French, especially Charles De Gaulle, made vigorous efforts to build a third force in Europe as a counterbalance to the Anglo-Saxon powers and the Soviet Union. It is thus tempting to conclude that only Moscow could have driven the West to the unity achieved by 1949. As Belgian Paul-Henri Spaak put it, Stalin was the real founder of the North Atlantic Treaty Organization (NATO).

The British bore the brunt of the initial defense against Communism. Foreign Minister Ernest Bevin took up Churchill's role as a voice of Western democracy against totalitarianism and fought many verbal duels with Soviet Foreign Minister Viacheslav M. Molotov in the Council of Foreign Ministers. But for a variety of reasons, chiefly financial, Britain had to abandon its role as the world policeman.

Churchill sounded the alarm regarding the Soviet Union in a March 1946 speech in Fulton, Missouri. With President Truman at his side, Churchill said that "From Stettin in the Baltic to Trieste in the Adriatic, an iron curtain has descended across the continent." The peril would not be surmounted by ignoring it or following a policy of appeasement. Churchill called for a "special relationship" between Britain and the United States to meet the challenge. Americans were not enthusiastic. Ten days later U.S. Secretary of State James Byrnes declared that the United States was no more interested in an alliance with Britain against the USSR than one with the Soviet Union against Britain.

Germany was the principal tinderbox of the Cold War, and by September 1946 the collision of interests there led Byrnes to tell an audience of military government officials and Germans in Stuttgart that the Americans would not withdraw from Germany under pressure, and that the Germans would soon be receiving additional self-government. In early 1947 when peace treaties were finally signed in Paris with other states, the time arrived to begin work on peace arrangements for Austria and Germany, but talks soon deadlocked.

By the spring of 1947 East and West were approaching a complete break over the German question. The Russians never had lived up to the Potsdam agreement to ship food and raw materials to the Western zones in return for reparations. Lacking Soviet cooperation, the British and Americans merged their zones into Bizonia at the beginning of 1947. New Secretary of State George C. Marshall's first appearance as secretary of state at a major conference marked a hardening U.S. reaction, as Washington reached the conclusion that the Soviet Union's actions were aggressive and not defensive.

In addition to its pressure on Iran, Moscow had leaned on Turkey to return land lost by Russia at the end of the First World War and also to permit the USSR a share in the defense of the Straits. There was also trouble in Greece, where Communist guerrillas were at war against the royal government. The civil war began because of a rightist victory in the Greek elections, the return of unpopular King George II, and intransigence on both sides. Fighting flared at the end of 1946 as the Greek Communists secured supplies from Yugoslavia, Bulgaria, and Albania. The Communists seized control of large portions of the north, and Athens appealed to the UN, but the Soviet Union vetoed a Security Council resolution based on an investigative commission's report of evidence of support from the neighboring Communist states.

In February 1947 the British government informed the United States that it could no longer afford to support the Greek government. This came as a shock and surprise to Washington. But on 12 March 1947, President Truman addressed a joint session of Congress and announced what came to be known as the Truman Doctrine. Stating that "We must assist free peoples to work out their own destinies in their own way," he promised that the United States would "support free peoples who are resisting attempted subjugation by armed minorities or by outside pressures." The United States now took up the burden as world policeman.

In a remarkably short time, Congress appropriated $400 million for Greece and Turkey, somewhat over half of this in military aid. This U.S. attempt to draw a line against Communist expansion was successful, helped along by Yugoslav leader Tito's break with Moscow, which cut off most of the aid to the Communist rebels; by the end of 1949 the Greek insurrection was contained.

There was trepidation in the United States about the Truman Doctrine, but the alternative of giving in seemed far more perilous. Nonetheless, the Truman Doctrine was a momentous step; it led to the Marshall Plan and NATO.

By the spring of 1947, the United States had distributed about $16 billion in emergency relief, most of it to European states, but no general recovery had taken place. In fact, Britain, France, and Italy were still in serious distress. The winter of 1946–1947 had been a particularly severe one, and strikes were widespread, particularly in France and Italy. In France the Communists controlled the huge General Confederation of Labor and threatened to bring the country to a standstill and perhaps seize power. If Italy and France, with large Communist parties, could be taken, then perhaps all Europe would fall under Soviet influence.

To prevent this from occurring, a more sustained and better organized effort was needed, and the result was the Marshall Plan. On 5 June 1947, Secretary of State Marshall announced the plan in a speech at Harvard University. He said that the United States would undertake financial assistance to Europe, but only if the nations of Europe got together, devised long-range assistance plans for economic recovery, and concentrated on self-help and mutual assistance. Behind this initiative lay the fear that continued economic troubles would weaken the resistance of the surviving Western nations to communism, but of course future U.S. prosperity was also tied to European economic revival.

The Marshall Plan was sketched out by a State Department planning group headed by George F. Kennan. It was announced as open to all, but the plan was devised so that the Soviet Union would reject it and thus ensure congressional passage. Without the Russians, its success would also be greatly enhanced. The plan called for a joint effort by the countries concerned and a strict accounting of aid to ensure that it would go not only to alleviate distress but for constructive measures to restore economic stability. Molotov insisted on bilateral agreements in which the United States would give money to each country separately, with sums determined according to proportionate share in helping to defeat Germany. He claimed that U.S. oversight of spending constituted interference in internal matters of the countries concerned. The Soviet Union feared that economic aid to the satellite countries might draw them to the West and for that reason did not permit them to participate.

That December Congress passed an Interim Act for $522 million in aid; the following April (1948), it approved the Foreign Assistance Act and appropriated $6.8 billion for the first fifteen months of a program slated to run four years. This came just in time to influence crucial elections in Italy, where the Communists were making a bid for power; with U.S. aid a reality, on 18 April 1948, the Christian Democrats won an absolute majority.

On 16 April 1948, sixteen non-Communist European states signed a convention establishing the Organization for European Economic Cooperation (OEEC). In four years Congress appropriated $13.15 billion in aid, plus an additional amount for Asia, to bring the total to $14.2 billion; Marshall Plan aid was almost completely nonmilitary. Through 1949 the United States spent $20.5 billion on nonmilitary aid and only $1.2 billion in military aid. The big watershed was the Korean War. From 1950 through 1954 the United States spent $14.1 billion on nonmilitary aid and $10.9 billion on military assistance.

Whatever the motives behind these developments in U.S. policy, the Marshall Plan made the recovery of Western Europe possible and began the process of spectacular growth that characterized the West European economies over the next two decades. It was also a strong impetus to economic unification; it pushed the momentum for European economic cooperation and led to the European Common Market.

Both the Truman Doctrine and the Marshall Plan were early manifestations of a so-called "containment policy" against Communist expansion. Writing in an unsigned ("Mr. X") article in the July 1947 issue of the influential *Journal of Foreign Affairs*, George Kennan stated that U.S. policy "must be that of a long-term, patient but firm and vigilant containment of Russian expansive tendencies." Even Kennan did not visualize as total an implementation as occurred.

Communist reaction to the Marshall Plan went beyond rejecting it for Eastern Europe. A wave of Communist-inspired strikes hit western European countries in protest against the Marshall Plan and because Communist ministers had been dropped from both the French and Italian cabinets in May 1947. The Soviet Union also rearmed.

In October 1947 the Russians established the nine-nation Communist Information Bureau, known as the Cominform. It took the place of the Comintern, which had been abolished in 1943 in order to show solidarity with Russia's allies. The new agency had as its goal the propagation of communism throughout the world.

In January 1949 Moscow established the Council for Economic Mutual Assistance, or COMECON. It was intended as an organization parallel to the OEEC for integrating the national economies of the satellite nations with that of the Soviet Union. The Kremlin also announced its own program of economic assistance, known as the Molotov Plan, but under it the Soviet Union received more than it gave, as raw materials were exchanged for shoddy and undesired Russian products.

In late November and early December 1947, the Council of Foreign Ministers made a final attempt at resolving the deadlock over Germany. It ended in total impasse. By this date the lines had hardened, and the Russians tightened the controls in the satellite states. One by one, surviving opposition leaders were purged. Then in February 1948 Czechoslovakia fell to a Communist coup d'état. This sent a shock wave through Western Europe but was also the zenith of Communist expansion in Europe.

In early 1948 the three Western powers began discussing the establishment of a German government for their combined zones. In these circumstances Berlin seemed vulnerable. The Western zones of the city were an island deep within the Soviet zone of Germany. The Kremlin reasoned that if it could seize West Berlin it could dishearten and intimidate the West. It might also discourage U.S. adventures on the European side of the Atlantic. Beginning on 1 April 1948, little by little the Soviets cut off surface access to the city. A week later, the Western governments introduced the new currency for their zones. This was the signal for the blockade to begin in earnest. By early August it was complete.

Direction of this first major battle of the Cold War fell to U.S. Military Governor in Germany General Lucius Clay. He informed Washington: "If we withdraw, our position in Europe is threatened, and Communism will run rampant." Clay said there were three alternatives: to withdraw from Berlin, to attempt to push an armored column up the autobahn, and to organize an airlift to try to supply the city by air. Truman's reaction was, "We shall stay, period." He opted for the third choice as least likely to lead to a shooting war with the Soviet Union. It would not be hard to supply Allied personnel by air but providing for more than 2 million Germans in the Western zones of Berlin seemed impossible. What the Americans called "Operation Vittles" went on for 320 days and transported 1,736,000 tons of supplies in 212,000 flights.

The Russians expected to push the West out of Berlin without war, and, despite numerous threats, never did challenge the aerial supply system. Both sides in effect drew back from a shooting war. By early 1949, however, the Russians were forced to conclude that the blockade was a failure. A counterblockade of East Germany by the West deprived it of essential goods, and this put pressure on the Russians. Soviet representative on the Security Council Jacob Malik finally dropped a hint to his U.S. counterpart Philip Jessup that the Russians were prepared to end the blockade. On 12 May 1949, land traffic to Berlin resumed. During the blockade the new Basic Law (constitution) for the West German Republic was approved.

By its pressure the USSR had forced the West Europeans to face up to the necessity of greater unity among themselves. This led to a whole series of treaties and organizations, such as the Council of Europe and the European Common Market. Militarily the emergency quickly brought about the Brussels Pact and the formation of NATO.

In March 1947 France and Great Britain had already signed a military alliance at Dunkirk. A year later these two countries, as well as Belgium, Luxembourg, and the Netherlands joined forces in the Treaty of Brussels. An agreement for social, economic, and cultural collaboration, it also was a military alliance of the five nations, which inevitably took on the character of a defensive alliance against the Russians. Because the Brussels Pact countries would obviously not be able to defend themselves without U.S. assistance, discussions were soon under way for a broader alliance.

In June 1948 there was a significant break with tradition in U.S. foreign policy. Senator Arthur Vandenburg, Republican and chairman of the powerful Senate Foreign Relations Committee, drafted a resolution that was ultimately approved by the Senate in June 1948. It reaffirmed U.S. policy to work with the UN. It was the sense of the Senate that the veto should be removed from all questions involving international disputes and the admission of new members. It also associated the United States "with such regional and other collective arrangements as are based on continuous and effective self-help and mutual aid, as affect the national security." This ran counter to George Washington's admonition against "entangling alliances," which had been heeded since 1796.

Talks began between the Western European allies and the United States, and on 4 April 1949, the North Atlantic Pact was signed in Washington by the United States, Canada, Britain, France, the three Benelux states, Norway, Denmark, Iceland, Portugal, and Italy. By this treaty, the twelve nations declared that "an armed attack against one or more…shall be considered an attack against them all" and each would assist the attacked in whatever fashion it deemed best, including by armed force. The resultant NATO would be headed by a Council and a defense committee; Supreme Headquarters (SHAPE) was ultimately set up outside of Paris. The treaty went into effect, after ratification, on 24 August 1949, for a twenty-year period. As one pundit put it, "NATO was created to keep the Americans in, the Russians out, and the Germans down." It could be argued, however, that the new U.S. policies, so far removed from the public mood in 1945, were more the result of perceived Soviet pressure than any initiative from Washington.

Thus the first round of the Cold War ended in stalemate, with each side entrenched in its half of the continent. For the time being, however, Europe had a breathing spell. In 1949 the Communists were victorious in China, and on 25 June 1950 war broke out in Korea.

—*Spencer C. Tucker*

References:

Acheson, Dean. *Present at the Creation: My Years at the State Department.* New York: W. W. Norton, 1969.

Bullock, Alan. *Ernest Bevin, Foreign Secretary*. London: Heinemann, 1983.

Byrnes, James F. *Speaking Frankly*. New York: Harper & Brothers, 1947.

Chace, James. *Acheson: The Secretary of State Who Created the American World*. New York: Simon & Schuster, 1998.

Feis, Herbert. *Between War and Peace: The Potsdam Conference*. Princeton, NJ: Princeton University Press, 1957.

Fontaine, Andre. *History of the Cold War, 1917–1966*. 2 vols. New York: Pantheon, 1968.

Gaddis, John. L. *We Now Know: Rethinking Cold War History*. New York: Oxford University Press, 1997.

Kennan, George F. *Memoirs, 1925–1950*. Boston: Little, Brown, 1967.

Kuniholm, Bruce R. *The Origins of the Cold War: Great Power Conflict and Diplomacy in Iran, Turkey and Greece*. Princeton, NJ: Princeton University Press, 1994.

Seton-Watson, Hugh. *Neither War nor Peace: The Struggle for Power in the Postwar World*. New York: Praeger, 1960.

Thomas, Hugh. *Armed Truce: The Beginnings of the Cold War, 1945–1946*. New York: Atheneum, 1987.

Yergin, Daniel H. *Shattered Peace: The Origins of the Cold War*. New York: Penguin Books, 1990.

See also: Acheson, Dean Goodersham; Bevin, Ernest; Churchill, Sir Winston Spencer; Jessup, Philip C.; Kennan, George F.; Malik, Jacob (Iakov) Alexandrovich; Marshall, George C.; Molotov, Viacheslav Mikhailovich; NATO (North Atlantic Treaty Organization); Potsdam Conference; Truman, Harry S.

Collins, Joseph Lawton
(1896–1987)

U.S. Army general and chief of staff of the army, 1949–1953. Born in New Orleans, Louisiana, on 1 May 1896, J. Lawton Collins graduated from the U.S. Military Academy, West Point, in 1917, and was commissioned a second lieutenant. He served with U.S. occupation forces in Germany in 1919, and during 1921–1925 he taught chemistry at West Point. He then attended and served as instructor at various service schools before being assigned to the Philippines during 1933–1936. Collins graduated from both the Industrial War College and the Army War College before serving as an instructor at the latter during 1938–1940. After a short assignment with the Army General Staff, Collins became chief of staff of VII Corps. After the Japanese attack on Pearl Harbor, he was assigned to the Hawaiian Department as chief of staff.

During World War II Collins served with distinction in the Pacific and European theaters, earning the nickname "Lightning Joe" for his role in the defeat of Japanese forces on Guadalcanal. He commanded VII Army Corps in the June 1944 invasion of Normandy and during the December 1944 German Ardennes Offensive. In 1947 Collins became deputy chief of staff of the army under General Dwight D. Eisenhower. In 1948 Collins was promoted to full general, and during 1949–1953 he was army chief of staff.

After the formation of the North Atlantic Treaty Organization (NATO) that same year, Collins became the Joint Chiefs of Staff (JCS) liaison with NATO.

Before the Korean War, Collins concurred with other members of the JCS that Korea lacked the strategic importance to be included in the U.S. defensive perimeter in Asia. In the first few days of the Korean War, General Collins communicated directly with General Douglas MacArthur by teletype and telephone, relaying information to President Harry Truman. Collins then recommended, without consulting other members of the JCS, the immediate deployment of a regimental combat team to Korea.

In early July 1950, Collins flew to Korea with Air Force Chief of Staff General Hoyt S. Vandenberg to discuss means by which the North Korean advance might be slowed and to assess MacArthur's requirements. After a second visit with MacArthur in late August, this time accompanied by Chief of Naval Operations Admiral Forrest P. Sherman, Collins expressed to President Truman his "serious misgivings" about MacArthur's planned amphibious landing at Inch'ŏn. He did, however, support MacArthur's position that the Korean People's Army (North Korean Army) had to be completely defeated by crossing of the 38th parallel in order to prevent the threat of future invasion.

Ultimately the JCS approved the Inch'ŏn operation (Operation CHROMITE). Its great success made it difficult for Collins and the remainder of the JCS to challenge MacArthur's subsequent operational plans and decisions. For example, the JCS accepted MacArthur's explanation for his violation of their order not to allow non-Korean (principally U.S.) forces to approach the Manchurian border. MacArthur claimed that Republic of Korea Army (ROKA, South Korean) forces lacked the strength and "experienced leadership" to seize and hold critical border areas. Collins admitted in his autobiography that the JCS should have given MacArthur greater direction and less discretion in sensitive areas where it was known that its field commander held independent views.

After the withdrawal of United Nations forces from North Korea after the massive People's Republic of China (Communist China) military intervention, in January 1951 Collins and Vandenberg again flew to Tokyo and also visited the battlefront in Korea. Collins found the situation serious, but questioned MacArthur's assertion that U.S. forces should be withdrawn in the event he did not receive "substantial reinforcements," although he did not directly challenge MacArthur on this issue. Collins's report upon his return did much to lessen pressure for consideration of a hasty withdrawal or other drastic initiatives and diminished the impact of General MacArthur's pessimistic appraisal in order to secure support for a wider war. Collins supported Truman's decision to relieve MacArthur.

As with Secretary of Defense George C. Marshall, Collins was by the spring of 1953 sufficiently frustrated by the war's high cost and inconclusive nature to support the use of atomic weapons in an effort to end the war. Collins worked hard to meet the manpower needs of the war and to ensure that the troops were adequately trained and supplied. Less than three weeks after the signing of the armistice, in August 1953 Collins stepped down as chief of staff. Collins should be remembered for his efforts during the Korean War to racially integrate U.S. Army units.

At President Dwight D. Eisenhower's request, General Collins remained on active duty as U.S. representative on the Military Committee and Standing Group of NATO. This assignment was but brief, as Eisenhower sent Collins to Vietnam in November 1954 as his special envoy to assess the situation there and make recommendations as to how the Ngo Dinh Diem government could be strengthened. Collins intervened to forestall the possibility of a coup against Diem by General Nguyen Van Hinh, but he ultimately recommended that the United States consider "alternatives" to Diem. Collins left Vietnam in May 1954 to return to his NATO post.

Collins retired from the U.S. Army in March 1956, and the next year he went to work for the pharmaceutical firm of Chas. Pfizer & Co., retiring from there in 1969. He died in Washington, D.C., on 12 September 1987.

—*Claude R. Sasso*

References:

Blair, Clay. *The Forgotten War: America in Korea, 1950–1953.* New York: Times Books, 1987.

Collins, J. Lawton. *Lightning Joe: An Autobiography.* Baton Rouge: Louisiana State University Press, 1979.

Pogue, Forrest C. *George C. Marshall, Statesman, 1945–1959.* New York: Viking Press, 1987.

See also: Bradley, Omar Nelson; Collins-Sherman Visit to Tokyo; Collins-Vandenberg Visit to Tokyo; Eisenhower, Dwight D.; Inch'ŏn Landings: Operation CHROMITE; Joint Chiefs of Staff (JCS); MacArthur, Douglas; Marshall, George C.; Ridgway, Matthew Bunker; Sherman, Forrest P.; Truman, Harry S.; Truman's Recall of MacArthur; Vandenberg, Hoyt S.

Collins's Visit to Tokyo
(4–8 December 1950)

Visit by Army Chief of Staff J. Lawton Collins to Tokyo to assess the military situation in Korea and to confer with United Nations Command (UNC) commander in chief General Douglas MacArthur regarding U.S. policy as expressed in the Joint Chiefs of Staff (JCS) directive of 1 and 4 December 1950.

After the massive intervention by the Chinese People's Volunteer Army (CPVA, Chinese Communist) at the end of November 1950, U.S. military and political leaders in Washington had serious concerns over the widened war and MacArthur's conduct of it. On 1 December the JCS expressed opposition to MacArthur's division of command between Eighth Army and X Corps. The JCS informed MacArthur that his first task was to extract the marines and units of the Army's 7th Division east of the Changjin Reservoir, and they authorized him to ignore the entire northwest of Korea in favor of concentrating on such operations necessary for the security of his command. MacArthur disagreed with these recommendations. On 4 December the chiefs, with President Harry S. Truman's approval, again informed MacArthur that they believed that the security of his command should have top priority and approved consolidation of UNC forces into beachheads, X Corps on Hŭngman and Wŏnsan and the Eighth Army on Inch'ŏn and Pusan.

While these exchanges were occurring, there were alarming newspaper reports of possible precipitate actions by MacArthur that might lead to a widened war with the People's Republic of China. To have a clearer picture of the situation and secure MacArthur's views about a possible cease-fire, Collins was sent to the Far East to confer with both MacArthur and his principal field commanders.

Accompanied by a small staff, Collins arrived in Tokyo on 4 December. After a brief meeting with MacArthur, Collins flew on to Seoul to meet with Eighth Army commander Lieutenant General Walton H. Walker. That evening Walker briefed Collins, informing him that he did not believe that his forces could hold very long. He feared that Chinese forces would pour into the gap on his right flank left by the Republic of Korea Army Second Corps. If he were required to hold Seoul and the area north of the Han River, his entire army might be encircled. Collins and Walker agreed that a forced evacuation from Inch'ŏn would be costly in terms of troops and equipment, but Walker said he could indefinitely hold Pusan and a perimeter around it.

On the 5th, Collins and Walker visited Lieutenant General Frank Milburn's I Corps headquarters and the command post of the 25th Division. They also made an aerial reconnaissance of Eighth Army's delaying positions. The next day Collins flew from Seoul to Yŏnp'o-ri airstrip south of Hŭngnam. X Corps commander Major General Edward M. Almond met him there, and the two men conferred at Almond's Hŭngnam headquarters. After a briefing they visited the headquarters of the 3d Division and the 7th Division. They then made an aerial reconnaissance of the Hŭngnam defenses and part of the 1st Marine

Division's escape route. Almond expressed optimism that the 1st Marine Division, then fighting its way back from Hagaru-ri, would be free without heavy loss in the next few days and that he could hold the Hŏngnam-Hamhŭng area for a considerable period, extracting his forces when necessary without great difficulty. Collins concurred with this assessment.

Collins returned to Tokyo on the 6th and met with Generals MacArthur, George E. Stratemeyer, Doyle O. Hickey, and Charles A. Willoughby, and Admiral C. Turner Joy for a review of possible military options. They considered three possible scenarios. The first two regarded a continuation of an all-out Chinese attack and the third was to deal with a Chinese decision not to advance south of the 38th parallel.

The first case assumed no bombing of Manchuria, no blockade of China, no reinforcements for the UNC from Nationalist China, and no major U.S. ground reinforcements until April 1951, when four National Guard divisions might become available for deployment. It did assume possible use of atomic bombs in North Korea. MacArthur expressed strong disapproval of these conditions as tantamount to surrender because UNC forces would have to be withdrawn from Korea.

The second situation assumed a naval blockade and bombing of mainland China, the use of Chinese Nationalist troops, and employment of the atomic bomb if tactically appropriate. MacArthur said that under these conditions he would try to hold as far north in Korea as possible and would move X Corps overland to joint Eighth Army in the Pusan bridgehead.

In the third case MacArthur expressed the view that should the Chinese decide not to cross the 38th parallel the UN should accept an armistice in which Korean People's Army (North Korean) troops and guerrillas as well as units of the CPVA would agree to remain north of the parallel. A UN commission could oversee the armistice. Barring the second choice, MacArthur favored the third option. In any event, he believed that Nationalist China should immediately send troops to Korea and other participating UN states should increase their own troop contributions to at least 75,000 men. MacArthur stated that, unless substantial reinforcements were sent immediately, the UNC should pull out of Korea.

Although Collins did not at the time express this viewpoint to MacArthur, he believed that, even with the limitations placed on it, the UNC could hold against the Chinese. He based his assessment on conversations with Almond and Walker.

Collins left Tokyo on 8 December. Besieged by the press on his arrival in Washington, Collins said he believed that the UNC should be able to take care of itself without further serious loss. After Collins reported to the JCS, he and Chairman of the Joint Chiefs of

Staff General Omar N. Bradley briefed President Truman and British Prime Minister Clement R. Attlee, as well as U.S. Secretary of State Dean G. Acheson and Defense Secretary George C. Marshall and other officials. Collins informed them that if the Chinese continued their all-out attacks it would not be possible to hold the Seoul-Inch'ŏn area, but that Walker was confident he could hold a perimeter around Pusan, especially if reinforced by X Corps, to which transfer MacArthur had by then agreed. Collins concluded that the situation in Korea, while serious, was no longer critical.

—*Spencer C. Tucker*

References:

Collins, J. Lawton. *War in Peacetime: The History and Lessons of Korea.* Boston: Houghton Mifflin, 1969.

Schnabel, James F. *United States Army in the Korean War: Policy and Direction, the First Year.* Washington, DC: Office of the Chief of Military History, Department of the Army, 1972.

Schnabel, James F., and Robert J. Watson. *The History of the Joint Chiefs of Staff: The Joint Chiefs of Staff and National Policy.* Vol. 3, *The Korean War.* Wilmington, DE: Michael Glazier, 1979.

See also: Acheson, Dean Goodersham; Attlee, Clement R.; Bradley, Omar Nelson; Collins, Joseph Lawton; Marshall, George C.; Milburn, Frank William; Truman, Harry S.; Walker, Walton Harris.

Collins-Sherman Visit to Tokyo
(19–25 August 1950)

August 1950 visit by Army Chief of Staff J. Lawton Collins and Chief of Naval Operations Admiral Forrest P. Sherman to confer with United Nations Command (UNC) commander in chief General Douglas MacArthur to assess the military situation in Korea. In mid-August the Joint Chiefs of Staff (JCS) designated Collins and Sherman to go to Tokyo and discuss plans with MacArthur for an amphibious landing at Inch'ŏn. The trip to Korea was prompted by the threatening situation facing the UNC along the Pusan perimeter. This had produced congressional concerns that led a member of the House Armed Services Committee to declare that Eighth Army might have to evacuate Korea within seventy-two hours. Collins took advantage of the trip to investigate in person and make his own estimate of the situation.

Collins and Sherman arrived in Tokyo on 21 August and were met at the airport by MacArthur and his staff. The next morning Collins and Sherman flew to Korea for a briefing by Eighth Army commander Lieutenant General Walton H. Walker. In his assessment Walker was confident that Eighth Army could hold the perimeter. After the briefing, the U.S. Navy and Air Force representatives traveled to sites of interest to them while Collins and Walker visited all U.S. divisions along the Pusan perimeter.

The delegation then returned to Tokyo and met with MacArthur and his staff concerning Operation

CHROMITE, the planned landing at Inch'ŏn. During the meetings Collins and Sherman expressed their serious reservations over MacArthur's choice for the amphibious operation, pointing out the problems posed by the narrow channel and high tides, but MacArthur overrode all objections. He said that precisely because of the difficulties pointed out the North Koreans would not expect a landing there. He concluded, "We shall land at Inch'ŏn and I shall crush them."

Collins and Sherman agreed with MacArthur on the necessity to invade North Korea. Unless the Korean People's Army (North Korea) was destroyed, the invasion could occur again. MacArthur expressed confidence that the Soviet Union would not intervene in the conflict.

On their return to Washington, Collins and Sherman briefed the JCS and Truman. On 28 August the president approved Operation CHROMITE and instructed his advisors to begin planning for the invasion of North Korea and reunification of the peninsula.

—*Spencer C. Tucker*

References:
Collins, J. Lawton. *War in Peacetime: The History and Lessons of Korea.* Boston: Houghton Mifflin, 1969.
Heinl, Robert D. *Victory at High Tide: The Inchon-Seoul Campaign.* Philadelphia: J. B. Lippincott, 1968.
Langley, Michael. *Inchon Landing: MacArthur's Last Triumph.* New York. Times Books, 1979.
Schnabel, James F. *United States Army in the Korean War: Policy and Direction, the First Year.* Washington, DC: Office of the Chief of Military History, Department of the Army, 1972.
Schnabel, James F., and Robert J. Watson. *The History of the Joint Chiefs of Staff: The Joint Chiefs of Staff and National Policy.* Vol. 3, *The Korean War.* Wilmington, DE: Michael Glazier, 1979.
See also: Collins, Joseph Lawton; Inch'ŏn Landings: Operation CHROMITE; Joint Chiefs of Staff (JCS); MacArthur, Douglas; Pusan Perimeter and Breakout; Sherman, Forrest P.; Walker, Walton Harris.

Collins-Vandenberg Discussions in Tokyo
(13–14 July 1950)

In the immediate aftermath of his decision to commit U.S. forces to Korea, on 10 July President Harry S. Truman ordered the Joint Chiefs of Staff (JCS) to send two representatives to the Far East to assess the situation. The JCS chose Army Chief of Staff J. Lawton Collins and Air Force Chief of Staff Hoyt S. Vandenberg to confer in Tokyo with Commander in Chief of the United Nations Command (CINCUNC) General Douglas MacArthur. They were to determine MacArthur's military requirements and discuss strategic considerations that would set future military strategy. The JCS was especially concerned that, as MacArthur's requirements mounted, the United States would be able to retain sufficient military assets to meet its worldwide obligations, especially a Soviet threat against Western Europe.

Accompanied by two U.S. Army and two U.S. Air Force staff officers, Collins and Vandenberg arrived in Tokyo in the early morning of 13 July and met with MacArthur at his headquarters later that morning. Joining them were Eighth Army commander Lieutenant General Walton H. Walker, MacArthur's chief of staff Major General Edward M. Almond, and other key staff officers. Commander in Chief of the U.S. Pacific Fleet Admiral Arthur W. Radford arrived during the conference.

U.S. and Republic of Korea (ROK, South Korean) forces were still retreating and the Pusan perimeter was not yet established. Nonetheless, a cool and poised MacArthur exuded optimism, stating that the front would soon be stabilized. He expected that he would be able to take the offensive, but the timing of the latter would depend on the reinforcements granted and how soon they reached him.

Although he acknowledged the importance of JCS requirements elsewhere, MacArthur stressed the primacy of Korea and the need to win there to counter Communist expansion everywhere. He was already pushing for the reunification of Korea, something ROK President Syngman Rhee had already requested of President Truman. MacArthur's military counterstroke would smash the Korean People's Army (KPA, North Korea), and the problem would then be to "compose and unite Korea."

Vandenberg asked MacArthur about the possibility of Chinese or Soviet intervention. MacArthur said he thought it unlikely that they would go to war, although they would certainly seek to aid the North Koreans. Medium bombers striking supply routes out of Manchuria would end that, and in that connection he even mentioned the possibility of employing atomic weapons, a thought that was not pursued. In response to a question from Vandenberg, MacArthur said that if the Chinese did intervene in the war he would cut off troop reinforcements in North Korea rather than in Manchuria. He believed that thirty B-29 daily bombing attacks would be sufficient to isolate North Korea.

MacArthur urged there be no delay in meeting his requirements. "To hell with the concept of doing business as usual," he said. MacArthur concluded the conference with the statement that the situation should not be clouded with questions of priorities: "We win here or lose everywhere; if we win here, we improve the chances of winning everywhere."

Collins then traveled to Korea to meet with Eighth Army commander Lieutenant General Walton H. Walker at Taegu and assess the situation on the ground. Vandenberg visited the headquarters of the

Far East Air Force to discuss air force requirements. Collins returned to Tokyo early on the 14th and met later that morning with MacArthur, to whom he presented the United Nations (UN) flag that UN Secretary-General Trygve Lie had requested be flown over the headquarters of the CINCUNC. Collins also told MacArthur that he thought he could count on the 2d Infantry Division, the 1st Marine Division, the 5th and 29th Regimental Combat Teams, and a regimental combat team from the 11th Airborne Division.

Collins then joined the staff talks in progress discussing troop requirements, especially service units, and plans for an amphibious assault behind KPA lines to cut its communications and supply lines southward. Collins questioned the selection of Inch'ŏn and he also stressed the necessity of constructing fighter airstrips in Korea to provide more time in tactical air support.

Collins and Vandenberg left Tokyo on the afternoon of the 14th. They arrived in Washington the same day and briefed the JCS and Secretary of Defense Louis A. Johnson before meeting with Truman. Although they expressed confidence that Eighth Army could hold a bridgehead around Pusan, they urged the prompt dispatch of reinforcements.

—Spencer C. Tucker

References:

Collins, J. Lawton. *War in Peacetime: The History and Lessons of Korea.* Boston: Houghton Mifflin, 1969.

Schnabel, James F. *United States Army in the Korean War: Policy and Direction, the First Year.* Washington, DC: Office of the Chief of Military History, Department of the Army, 1972.

Schnabel, James F., and Robert J. Watson. *The History of the Joint Chiefs of Staff: The Joint Chiefs of Staff and National Policy.* Vol. 3, *The Korean War.* Wilmington, DE: Michael Glazier, 1979.

See also: Almond, Edward Mallory; Collins, Joseph Lawton; Inch'ŏn Landings: Operation CHROMITE; Johnson, Louis A.; Joint Chiefs of Staff (JCS); Lie, Trygve; Radford, Arthur W.; Syngman Rhee; Truman, Harry S.; Vandenberg, Hoyt S.; Walker, Walton Harris.

Collins-Vandenberg Visit to Tokyo
(15–19 January 1951)

Visit by Army Chief of Staff J. Lawton Collins and Air Force Chief of Staff Hoyt S. Vandenberg to Tokyo in January 1951 to confer with United Nations Command (UNC) commander in chief General Douglas MacArthur and to inspect the situation in Korea.

The trip to the Far East was occasioned by the withdrawal of UNC forces from North Korea after military intervention by the Chinese People's Volunteer Army (CPVA, Communist China) and MacArthur's disagreement with the assessment of President Harry S. Truman and the Joint Chiefs of Staff (JCS) that UNC forces could hold in Korea. MacArthur had stated that without major steps the UNC would be driven off the peninsula, or at least suffer massive casualties. His pronouncements were much more pessimistic than those of new Eighth Army commander Lieutenant General Matthew B. Ridgway, who wrote to Collins on 3 January: "Everything is going fine. We shall be in for some difficult days but I am completely confident of the ability of the Eighth Army to accomplish every mission assigned." Truman called a special session of the National Security Council on 12 January to consider MacArthur's message.

At the meeting Truman said he doubted that MacArthur had actually seen many of the JCS and presidential statements, and so he decided on a personal letter to the general, which he described not as a directive but a statement of views. He affirmed the necessity to stand against aggression in Korea and the need to "deflate the dangerously exaggerated political and military prestige of Communist China." Nonetheless, U.S. policy must secure the support of the great majority of UN member states, which would be necessary were the Soviet Union to attack in Europe. Until a buildup of its forces could be effected, the United States would have to "act with great prudence insofar as extending the area of hostilities is concerned." In making a final decision about Korea, his overriding consideration would be the main threat of the Soviet Union. He concluded with praise for MacArthur and UNC troops.

The JCS did not change their 30 December directive. Although they acknowledged that the UNC could not hold off for any length of time a sustained CPVA drive, the chiefs stated that it would be in the U.S. national interest to do so for as long as possible to permit diplomatic consultations with other UN member states, to maintain U.S. prestige, and to sustain confidence in the UN and in the North Atlantic Treaty Organization. Truman and the chiefs were concerned that MacArthur understand this, and they selected Generals Collins and Vandenberg to carry the message to him as well as to assess the situation in Korea with U.S. field commanders.

Collins and Vandenberg arrived in Tokyo on 15 January. That same day Eighth Army commander Ridgway launched Operation WOLFHOUND, a limited attack by I Corps. MacArthur, clearly upset with the news that it would be some time before reinforcements would be available to him, continued to stress the possibility of a forced UNC withdrawal from Korea, which he said would surely lead to the loss of Hong Kong, Indo-China, and the remainder of Southeast Asia. He also declared that his command should not be held responsible for the defense of Japan while required to hold in Korea. He urged that four mobilized National Guard divisions be sent to Japan at once to help protect it against possible Soviet attack.

After their brief meeting in Tokyo with MacArthur,

Collins and Vandenberg flew to Korea. For the next two days Vandenberg visited ar force installations and Collins toured the front with Ridgway. Collins could sense the "improved spirit" Ridgway had already imparted and left Korea convinced that Eighth Army could take care of itself, which on his return to Tokyo he immediately communicated to Chairman of the JCS General Omar N. Bradley.

Before leaving Tokyo for Washington on 19 January, Collins and Vandenberg again met with MacArthur and his staff. Collins shared with MacArthur his optimistic report to Bradley, and Vandenberg stated that he was pleased with what he had seen in Korea. MacArthur then said he thought that UN forces could hold a beachhead in Korea indefinitely. He also again urged that reinforcements be sent to Japan and stated that he would be satisfied with two National Guard divisions. He also said that he was proceeding with efforts to train Japanese police forces and soon would have four light Japanese divisions.

Upon their return to Washington, Collins and Vandenberg briefed the JCS and then President Truman. This did much to lessen pressure for consideration of a hasty withdrawal from Korea or other drastic initiatives and diminished the impact of General MacArthur's efforts to secure support for a wider war. For the first time since November, Washington was no longer pessimistic about being driven out of Korea. As Collins put it in his memoirs, "General Ridgway alone was responsible for this dramatic change."

—Spencer C. Tucker

References:

Collins, J. Lawton. *War in Peacetime: The History and Lessons of Korea.* Boston: Houghton Mifflin, 1969.

Schnabel, James F. *United States Army in the Korean War: Policy and Direction, the First Year.* Washington, DC: Office of the Chief of Military History, Department of the Army, 1972.

Schnabel, James F., and Robert J. Watson. *The History of the Joint Chiefs of Staff: The Joint Chiefs of Staff and National Policy.* Vol. 3, *The Korean War.* Wilmington, DE: Michael Glazier, 1979.

See also: Bradley, Omar Nelson; Collins, Joseph Lawton; National Security Council (NSC); Ridgway, Matthew Bunker; Vandenberg, Hoyt S.; WOLFHOUND, Operation.

Colombia

Colombia was the only Latin American nation to participate militarily in the Korean War. Colombia had been a strong supporter of the United Nations (UN) from its inception. When the UN asked for troop contributions after the June 1950 Democratic People's Republic of Korea (North Korean) invasion of the Republic of Korea (South Korea), Colombia offered to provide an infantry battalion consisting of 1,000 enlisted personnel and 83 officers. Plans originally called for the battalion to be trained in Puerto Rico, but all training took place in Colombia. The battalion departed Colombia on 12 May 1951 on a U.S. transport and arrived in Korea on 16 June 1951.

Throughout its service in Korea, the battalion fought as part of a U.S. division, originally the 24th Infantry Division and later with the 7th Infantry Division. Colombia made several offers to provide additional troops if the UN would assist with training and arms, including the offer of an entire division with arms purchased from the United States.

Although the Colombian battalion did not arrive until the war was essentially stalemated, it still saw significant action, most notably in the Kŭmsan offensive and the Battle of Old Baldy. A total of 3,089 men served in the battalion in Korea, with 131 killed and 448 wounded in combat. In addition, the battalion incurred 10 noncombat deaths and 162 noncombat injuries. Sixty-nine members of the battalion were listed as missing in action. The U.S. government awarded the battalion a Presidential Unit Citation and individual Colombian soldiers a total of eighteen Silver Stars and twenty-five Bronze Stars for valor.

Colombia also made a limited naval contribution to the war. The frigate *Almirante Padilla* preceded the infantry battalion to Korea and was involved in patrol duties on Korea's west coast, serving with British, Canadian, and U.S. warships. It returned to Colombia in Spring 1952 and was replaced by the *Capitán Tono*, which was in turn followed by the *Almirante Brión*, the last of three Colombian frigates to see service during the war.

The Korean War had a long-term impact on Colombia. Veterans of the conflict played a prominent role in Colombian military and political affairs well into the 1980s. Colonel Alberto Ruiz Novoa, second commander of the battalion, went on to become general, commander of the army, and finally minister of defense in the 1960s. Another Korean veteran, General Fernando Landazábal Reyes, followed a similar career path, becoming commander of the army and minister of defense in the 1980s. General Gustavo Rojas Pinilla, who had also served in Korea, in 1953 led a successful coup, which placed him in the presidency, but he was ousted in 1957 by a group in which other Korean veterans played a prominent role.

Korean veterans constituted an elite force within the Colombian military and applied their combat experience to Colombia's rural civil war. Colombia's involvement in Korea also led to closer ties with the United States. With U.S. help, Colombia became the site of the first Latin American counterinsurgency training school. Many Colombian military personnel were trained in the United States or at U.S. military facilities. Colombia was also a major recipient of U.S.

military aid to Latin America and became a showcase for the Alliance for Progress program in the 1960s, thanks in part to its contributions in the Korean War.

—*Don M. Coerver*

References:

Bushnell, David. *The Making of Modern Colombia: A Nation in Spite of Itself.* Berkeley: University of California Press, 1993.

Danley, Mark H. "Colombian Navy in the Korean War." *The American Neptune* 58, no. 3 (Summer 1998): 243–261.

Helguera, J. León. "The Changing Role of the Military in Colombia." *Journal of Inter-American Studies* 3 (July 1961): 351–358.

Pearce, Jenny. *Colombia: Inside the Labyrinth.* London: Latin American Bureau, 1990.

Ramsey, Russell W. "The Colombian Battalion in Korea and Suez." *Journal of Inter-American Studies* 9 (October 1967): 541–560.

See also: Latin America; Mexico; Old Baldy, Battle of; Order of Battle: United Nations, North Korea, and People's Republic of China; Peruvian Prisoner-of-War Settlement Proposal.

COMMANDO, Operation
(3–8 October 1951)

United Nations Command (UNC) military operation on Eighth Army's left flank to secure hill positions near Yŏnch'ŏn and to advance UN defensive positions some six miles from Line Wyoming to Line Jamestown to shield the key Seoul-Ch'ŏrwŏn-Kimhwa railroad line from Chinese artillery fire. Lieutenant General J. W. "Iron Mike" O'Daniel's U.S. I Corps conducted the operation, and five UNC divisions participated: the Republic of Korea Army (South Korea) 1st, the newly created British Commonwealth, the 1st Cavalry, and the 3d and 25th Infantry.

Operation COMMANDO began at dawn on 3 October 1951. The right and left flank divisions advanced to Line Jamestown without undue casualties or difficulty, but in the center the I Cavalry Division encountered the dug-in Chinese Forty-seventh Army, and heavy hand-to-hand combat ensued on hills dominated by Old Baldy. It took sixteen days for the 1st Cavalry Division to reach Line Jamestown, during which the divisional artillery fired 380,856 rounds.

COMMANDO inflicted heavy casualties on Communist forces, but 1st Corps had also sustained some 4,000 casualties, 2,900 of which were from the 1st Cavalry Division. After Line Jamestown was secured, General O'Daniel ordered the corps to dig in and hold the line. In December the 45th Infantry Division replaced the I Cavalry Division, which was withdrawn from the line and returned to Japan, its sixteen months of fighting in Korea at an end.

Although UN operations during August–October inflicted heavy casualties on the Communist forces (Eighth Army Commander General James Van Fleet put them at 234,000), UNC forces had also suffered

60,000 casualties, of which 22,000 were Americans. The August–October fighting shocked the American public and resulted in a further loss of support for the war. A poll in October found that only 33 percent disagreed with the proposition that Korea was "an utterly useless war." This loss of public support intensified Washington's efforts to secure an armistice and helped limit future UN operations to the maintenance of existing positions.

—*Spencer C. Tucker*

References:

Barclay, C. N. *The First Commonwealth Division: The Story of British Commonwealth Land Forces in Korea, 1950–1953.* Aldershot, UK: Gale & Polden, 1954.

Blair, Clay. *The Forgotten War: America in Korea, 1950–1953.* New York: Times Books, 1987.

O'Neill, Robert J. *Australia in the Korean War, 1950–1953.* Vol. 2, *Combat Operations.* Canberra: Australian War Memorial, 1985.

See also: Australia; Canada; United Kingdom (UK); Van Fleet, James Alward.

Connally, Thomas T.
(1877–1963)

U.S. Senator and chairman of the Senate Foreign Relations Committee, 1949–1953. Connally played a central role in winning congressional support for President Harry Truman's administration's policies. Thomas T. Connally was born on a farm in McLellan County, Texas, on 19 August 1877. He held various state offices before he won election to the U.S. House of Representatives in 1917; in 1928 he was elected to the Senate. Military service in the First World War and his deep admiration for President Woodrow Wilson gave Connally a lifelong interest in foreign policy, demonstrated by his unsuccessful support for U.S. membership in the League of Nations and World Court, his representation of the United States at various international conferences in the 1920s, and his committee assignments in international affairs.

Tom Connally supported U.S. intervention in the Second World War and even helped to draft President Franklin D. Roosevelt's declaration of war against the Axis powers. As chairman of the Senate Foreign Relations Committee, 1941–1947, and as its ranking Democrat, 1947–1949, Connally was instrumental in persuading conservative Democrats in the Senate to support their country's newly internationalist policies, including the creation of the United Nations (UN) and the containment of the Soviet Union through such mechanisms as the Marshall Plan and the North Atlantic Treaty Organization.

Initially Connally was not strongly committed to Korea. In May 1950, even before the Democratic People's Republic of Korea (DPRK, North Korea)

invaded the South, he publicly stated that the fall of the Republic of Korea (ROK, South Korea) was inevitable. Because the ROK was "not absolutely essential" to U.S. security, Connally stated that his country should be prepared to abandon the peninsula. Critics later blamed his pronouncement, together with Secretary of State Dean Acheson's National Press Club speech earlier that year, for encouraging the DPRK invasion. Upon the outbreak of war, however, Connally, in consultation with Truman administration officials, recommended a swift response to this challenge. Connally was prepared to accept the administration's preliminary stance of committing no troops to the South and limiting U.S. aid to the provision of equipment, but once the decision to send U.S. forces had been taken, Connally enthusiastically endorsed it.

Despite his understandable anxiety to safeguard congressional prerogatives, Connally suggested that the administration not seek a declaration of war, lest this be obstructed by hostile Republicans, a strategy which he later thought mistaken. He continually emphasized the importance of working with the UN. In 1951 Connally urged the administration to relieve General Douglas MacArthur, whose behavior he considered insubordinate. Although unable to prevent joint hearings by the Foreign Relations and Armed Services Committees into MacArthur's recall, Connally helped to mitigate their political impact by insisting on closed sessions with public release only of nonsensitive testimony. In 1952 he decided not to run for reelection, spending his retirement practicing law in Washington, D.C., and writing his rather disappointing memoirs. He died in Washington on 28 October 1963.

—*Priscilla Roberts*

References:

Connally, Tom. *My Name Is Tom Connally*. New York: Crowell, 1951.

Gould, Lewis L. "Thomas Terry ('Tom') Connally." In *Dictionary of American Biography, Supplement Seven, 1961–1965*, edited by John A. Garraty. New York: Charles Scribner's Sons, 1981.

Green, George N. *The Establishment in Texas Politics: The Primitive Years, 1938–1957*. Westport, CT: Greenwood Press, 1979.

"Tom Connally," In *Political Profiles: The Truman Years*, edited by Eleanora W. Schoenebaum. New York: Facts on File, 1978.

See also: Acheson, Dean Goodersham; Blair House Meetings; MacArthur, Douglas; NATO (North Atlantic Treaty Organization); Truman's Recall of MacArthur.

Controlled Materials Plan (CMP)

U.S. government plan designed to secure an adequate supply-demand balance during the Korean War of three crucial industrial materials: steel, aluminum, and copper. Because of growing raw materials shortages and the resultant industrial bottlenecks in military production, the Office of Defense Mobilization decided to implement the Controlled Materials Plan (CMP), which had operated during World War II with considerable success. The plan began formal operations on 1 July 1951. The CMP was a vertically integrated control system, decentralized in structure, that simultaneously acted as an allocator of materials and as a planner of production.

Mobilization officials selected the three controlled materials because they are the fundamental components of practically all industrial end-items. By controlling steel, aluminum, and copper, materials shortages as well as production planning, programming, and delivery of defense and civilian items could be handled at once.

At the top of the CMP management pyramid was the Requirements Committee of the Defense Production Administration. Its job was to gather all requests for the controlled materials from the various Industry Divisions of the National Production Authority, which laid claim to specific areas of the industrial economy. The Requirements Committee would then match the available supply of the controlled materials against the claims of the Industry Divisions and would apportion the materials to the claimants based upon military priorities and, of course, the aggregate supply.

During the CMP's first year of operations, material requests routinely exceeded the aggregate supply; however, by 1952 the CMP had managed to bring demand and supply in balance. In spring 1953 President Dwight D. Eisenhower liquidated the CMP.

—*Paul G. Pierpaoli, Jr.*

References:

Hogan, Michael J. *A Cross of Iron: Harry S. Truman and the Origins of the National Security State, 1945–1954*. Cambridge, UK: Cambridge University Press, 1998.

Pierpaoli, Paul G., Jr. *Truman and Korea: The Political Culture of the Early Cold War*. Columbia: University of Missouri Press, 1999.

Vawter, Roderick W. *Industrial Mobilization: The Relevant History*. Washington, DC: National Defense University Press, 1983.

See also: Eisenhower, Dwight D.; Mobilization; Office of Defense Mobilization (ODM); United States: Home Front.

Cordier, Andrew W.
(1901–1975)

United Nations (UN) official. As executive assistant to the UN secretary-general during 1946–1962, and also as UN special representative to Korea during the most intensive years of the war, 1950–1952, Cordier was deeply involved in both the making and the implementation of UN policy toward the conflict and its resolution. Andrew Cordier was born on 3 March 1901, near Canton, Ohio. He obtained a B.A. degree from

Manchester College, Indiana, and M.A. and Ph.D. degrees in history from the University of Chicago. From 1927 to 1944 he chaired the Department of History and Political Science at Manchester, where he built up a solid reputation as a foreign policy expert. In 1944 he joined the State Department as adviser on international security, drafting early versions of the UN Charter; serving on the U.S. delegation to the April 1945 San Francisco Conference and the Preparatory Commission for the UN, which met in London; and advising Senator Arthur Vandenberg, ranking Republican on the Senate Foreign Relations Committee, on UN issues.

In March 1946 Cordier became executive assistant to the first UN Secretary-General Trygve Lie. Holding the rank of undersecretary, Cordier retained the position until 1962, serving under both Lie and his charismatic successor, Dag Hammarskjöld. Known as a "demon parliamentarian" who demonstrated a mastery of detail, procedure, and precedents, Cordier advised sixteen successive General Assembly leaders on protocol and technical procedure, prepared agenda and meetings, supervised UN personnel, and endeavored to mediate disputes between delegates, a skill in which he was particularly adept. His influence was particularly strong under Lie, who relied on him to initiate as well as execute policy; under Hammarskjöld, Cordier was restricted more to the second function, although he described his time with Hammarskjöld as his "richest personal experience." After Hammarskjöld's sudden and unexpected death, Cordier played a major role in keeping the UN functioning, although under Soviet pressure in 1961 he resigned his position to become temporary undersecretary in charge of the General Assembly's daily workings. In 1962 he left the UN to become dean of the School of International Affairs of Columbia University.

Before and during the Korean War and after the armistice, Cordier supervised UN missions in that country. The objective of the first of these, the UN Commission on Korea, established in the wake of the UN resolution of 14 November 1947, was to try to implement Korean reunification. Cordier also directed and supervised the unsuccessful 1947–1948 attempt to bring about withdrawal of all the occupying forces and unite the entire country under one government. When this failed, the UN Membership Committee recommended recognition of the Republic of Korea (ROK, South Korea), established with U.S. support in the southern part of the country. The Soviet Union vetoed this. By contrast, the UN refused to consider the application for separate membership for the Democratic People's Republic of Korea (DPRK, North Korea). Although the UN Commission on Korea submitted a September 1949 report critical of both Soviet and U.S.

intractability over Korean reunification, and of Syngman Rhee as an authoritarian leader, its report on the North Korean attack of 1950 provided evidence justifying the Security Council resolution of 27 June 1950, under which the UN condemned and took action against the DPRK invasion of the ROK.

During the Korean War, Cordier's skills were employed to build an international coalition and support for the policies spearheaded by the United States of using UN forces to defend the ROK and repel the North Korean attack. Among the measures that the UN initiated were appeals in 1951 for additional troops from countries not yet involved in the fighting and the May 1951 official endorsement of additional sanctions upon the DPRK and its allies.

While still strictly speaking a UN functionary, Cordier, in pushing for the passage of such measures and their implementation, was in a sense using his official position to further policies favored by his native country. Even so, UN policy was by no means entirely satisfactory to the United States. For example, the UN Commission for the Unification and Rehabilitation of Korea, established in October 1950, on several occasions from 1950 to 1952 submitted reports highly critical of the Rhee government's authoritarian practices, particularly its summary execution or imprisonment of any Korean suspected of Communist sympathies. During the 1952 South Korean political crisis, it also acted vigorously to restrain Rhee and, despite his opposition, it survived until 1972 from U.S. insistence on preserving the appearance of UN interest in Korean affairs. Until he left the UN, Cordier supervised its activities, together with those of the shorter-lived UN Korean Reconstruction Agency, established in 1951, and the UN Civil Assistance Command, Korea. All were bodies that, besides their other functions, helped to express the continuing unease of both the UN and the United States with many aspects of the Rhee regime they were supporting.

During 1968 student demonstrations, Cordier reluctantly became temporary president of Columbia University, his mission being to restore peace, order, and cooperation to the campus, an endeavor in which his well-honed diplomatic skills brought success. He held this post until 1970, when he resumed his duties as dean. In 1972 Cordier suggested that the United States offer a "Marshall Plan" package of aid to Vietnam, an unsuccessful scheme that remained stillborn.

Cordier retired from Columbia in 1972, after which he chaired a UN panel on establishing a World University, helped to edit two volumes on Dag Hammarskjöld and eight volumes of the papers of the UN secretaries-general, and worked on his memoirs. He died in Great Neck, Long Island, on 11 July 1975.

—Priscilla Roberts

References:

"Andrew W. Cordier," In *Political Profiles: The Kennedy Years,* edited by Nelson Lichtenstein. New York: Facts on File, 1976.

Barros, James. *Trygve Lie and the Cold War: The United Nations Secretary-General Pursues Peace, 1946–1953.* DeKalb: Northern Illinois University Press, 1989.

Lankevich, George J. "Andrew W. Cordier." In *Dictionary of American Biography, Supplement Nine, 1971–1975,* edited by Kenneth T. Jackson. New York: Charles Scribner's Sons, 1994.

Luard, Evan. *A History of the United Nations.* Vol. 1, *The Years of Western Domination, 1945–1955.* London: Macmillan, 1982.

Stueck, William W. Jr. *The Korean War: An International History.* Princeton, NJ: Princeton University Press, 1995.

Yoo, Tae-Ho. *The Korean War and the United Nations.* Louvain, Belgium: Librairie Desbarax, 1964.

See also: Hammarskjöld, Dag; Lie, Trygve; United Nations Commission for the Unification and Rehabilitation of Korea.

Cory, Thomas J.
(1914–1965)

U.S. diplomat and second secretary at the embassy in Seoul, 1949–1950; adviser to the U.S. United Nations (UN) delegation, 1950–1953. Born in San Francisco on 15 June 1914, Thomas J. Cory earned a bachelor's degree from the University of California at Los Angeles in 1935. Joining the U.S. Foreign Service in 1940, he held a variety of junior positions in Canada, Spain, Venezuela, Moscow, Vladivostok, and Nanjing, China. In the last of these postings, during 1948–1949, Cory was responsible for helping to organize the evacuation of American nationals from China as Communist forces there drew ever closer to victory in China's civil war. As second secretary at the U.S. embassy in Seoul, he performed similar functions in 1950 after the North Korean invasion, when he assisted with the emergency 28 June airlift of some 100 U.S. citizens from Kimpŏ Airfield.

In late 1950 Cory was transferred to the UN to advise the U.S. delegation on East European and East Asian issues. Although relatively junior, Cory was in this capacity involved in discussions covering every aspect of U.S. policies toward Korea, particularly those related to the UN and the lengthy and convoluted efforts to reach a peace settlement. In May 1951 he and another U.S. diplomat, Frank Corrigan, shared a limousine ride into Manhattan with Soviet ambassador to the UN Jacob Malik. In conversation with Cory, Malik suggested that, if the United States genuinely desired peace, American and Soviet officials should begin serious talks on the subject. He then inquired as to the current whereabouts of various U.S. diplomats who were Soviet specialists, including George F. Kennan, Charles E. Bohlen, Elbridge Durbrow, and Charles Thayer. Cory and Corrigan promptly reported this conversation to Washington, and Cory was then commissioned to arrange two secret and unofficial

meetings between Malik and Kennan, who was at that time taking a year's sabbatical leave and could therefore be regarded as a private citizen. The two men's conversations broke the impasse between the Soviet Union and the United States on cease-fire negotiations and seems to have been directly responsible for the opening of the Kaesŏng truce talks later that summer. In early 1953 Cory was also responsible for conveying his country's official condolences on the death of Josef Stalin to the Soviet mission at the UN. At a UN General Assembly session in March 1953, he was the indirect recipient of Soviet confidences that the Chinese were indeed in earnest in seeking a peace settlement.

Later that year Cory transferred to the U.S. embassy in Vienna as first secretary. Two years later he left the Foreign Service to work for the Standard Vacuum-Oil Company. He utilized his numerous official contacts to interact with the U.S. government on his employer's behalf on trade issues, licensing matters, and research and development. On several occasions in the early 1960s Cory served as an adviser to the U.S. government at international conferences dealing with oil and mineral rights. He died in a car accident on 14 September 1965, in Cleveland, Ohio.

—*Priscilla Roberts*

References:

Foot, Rosemary J. *A Substitute for Victory: The Politics of Peacemaking at the Korean Armistice Talks.* Ithaca, NY: Cornell University Press, 1990.

Stueck, William W., Jr. *The Korean War: An International History.* Princeton, NJ: Princeton University Press, 1995.

Yoo, Tae-Ho. *The Korean War and the United Nations.* Louvain, Belgium: Librairie Desbarax, 1964.

See also: Bohlen, Charles E.; Kennan, George F.; Kennan-Malik Conversations; Malik, Jacob (Iakov) Alexandrovich.

Coulter, John Breitling
(1891–1983)

U.S. Army general. Born on 27 April 1891, in San Antonio, Texas, John Breitling Coulter graduated from the West Texas Military Academy in San Antonio in 1911 and was commissioned a second lieutenant the next year. He served with the 14th Cavalry on the Mexican border for four years and participated in the 1916 Pershing expedition. Coulter was in Washington, D.C., as a National Guard instructor in 1917 when the United States declared war against Germany. In France he was an aide to the commander of the 42d "Rainbow" Division and later served as a battalion commander in the St. Mihiel Offensive.

Returning to the United States after the war, Coulter was employed in the personnel branch of the War Department General Staff. He then commanded the 2d Squadron of the 14th Cavalry at Fort Des Moines,

Iowa. He graduated from the Cavalry School in 1922 and the Command and General Staff School five years later. Coulter was squadron commander of the 8th Cavalry and training officer for the 1st Cavalry in Fort Bliss, Texas. He graduated from the Army War College in 1933 and Naval War College in 1934 and worked for the U.S. Army military intelligence division headquarters in Washington, D.C., before becoming executive officer of the 4th Cavalry Regiment in 1935. He took command of the regiment in December 1940.

Promoted to brigadier general in October 1941, Coulter commanded the 3d Cavalry Brigade when the United States entered World War II. He then commanded the 2d Infantry Division at Fort Riley, Kansas. In July 1942 he was assistant division commander (later its commander) of the 85th Infantry Division, the first all-draftee division to fight in Italy. Coulter became a major general in March 1943. After training his division in the United States and North Africa, he led it in fighting in Italy from Anzio to the attack on Rome in 1944 and then in securing the strategic Brenner Pass. Coulter's Italian experiences resulted in his being considered an expert on mountain warfare, which would prove useful in the Korean War.

Coulter was commander of the Infantry Replacement Training Center at Fort McClellan, Alabama, in 1945. In January 1948 he commanded the 7th Infantry Division in Korea, and by August 1948 he was deputy to Lieutenant General John R. Hodge, commanding officer of the U.S. Occupation Forces in Korea (USAFIK). Coulter became USAFIK commander when Hodge and Republic of Korea (ROK, South Korean) President Syngman Rhee disagreed about policies. Coulter stayed in Korea until January 1949.

After one year as commander of I Corps in Japan, Coulter returned to the United States as deputy commander of Fifth Army headquarters in Chicago, Illinois. When the Democratic People's Republic of Korea (North Koreans) invaded the ROK, commander of United Nations (UN) forces in Korea General Douglas MacArthur asked Coulter to command I Corps. Coulter may have received his appointment because he had fought in Italy with Major General Edward M. Almond, MacArthur's chief of staff.

Coulter trained his unit at Fort Bragg, North Carolina, and arrived in Korea with his command staff on 13 August 1950. Eighth Army commander Lieutenant General Walton H. Walker did not trust Almond, and he transferred Coulter to IX Corps.

Coulter commanded a weak portion of the South Korean front on the east coast. In charge of Task Force Jackson, consisting of ROK Army (ROKA) I Corps and other U.S. forces, Coulter removed the commander of ROKA I Corps and a ROKA division commander to bring order to what he considered an "hysterical"

ROKA command. Coulter also asked Walker for additional U.S. units to halt the North Korean advance.

Although Walker admired Coulter's ability to motivate ROKA troops, he was unhappy with his overall military leadership and found fault with Coulter's dispositions of his regiments. Walker was also antagonized by Coulter's "insistent and frequent" pleas for help when he was desperately seeking troops to fill gaps in the perimeter. Walker also did not believe that Coulter was the right man to lead the breakout from the perimeter, and on 11 September he gave command of I Corps to Major General Frank W. Milburn.

Walker then gave Coulter command of IX Corps, which was not operational until a week after I Corps had begun the Pusan perimeter breakout. In mid-September Coulter's forces focused principally on securing supply lines and finding and eliminating pockets of bypassed Korean People's Army (North Korean) troops isolated to the rear of the UN Command advance. IX Corps continued this activity after October when Eighth Army crossed the 38th parallel into North Korea. At the Battle of the Ch'ŏngch'ŏn River at the end of November 1950, Coulter's IX Corps and the ROKA II Corps bore the brunt of Chinese attacks against Eighth Army by Chinese People's Volunteer Army (CPVA, Chinese Communist) forces.

Coulter initially underestimated the Chinese threat and believed that the Turkish Brigade would be able to protect Eighth Army's right flank if ROKA forces gave way. On 30 November when the U.S. 2d Infantry Division was forced to abandon its positions, Coulter had already moved his headquarters and was in the rear at P'yŏngyang. Poorly informed of the dangerous situation at the front, he failed to send reserves to assist in 2d Division's withdrawal; nor did he order a less-dangerous withdrawal route from Kunu-ri. As a result of Coulter's indifferent leadership, 2d Division suffered disaster.

Despite his reputation for poor strategic leadership, in February 1951 Coulter was promoted to lieutenant general and deputy commander of Eighth Army by Walker's replacement, Lieutenant General Matthew B. Ridgway. Later Ridgway named Coulter as his liaison officer to the UN Commission for the Unification and Rehabilitation of Korea. This was a wise choice as Coulter got along well with ROKA generals and President Rhee, whom he had known during his prewar service in Korea.

In late 1951 Coulter returned to the United States, and he retired from the army in January 1952. His experiences in Korea led UN Secretary-General Dag Hammarskjöld to appoint Coulter as director of the UN Korean Reconstruction Agency (UNKRA) in May 1953. Coulter served in this post for two years and helped reconstruct war-torn South Korea. He was responsible for such long-term projects as restoring medical facilities and educational institutions as well as reconstructing the agricultural, forestry, and fishing industries and boosting the economy. Coulter also oversaw the building of roads and industries. During 1954 UNKRA received $130 million in U.S. aid.

After the 1956 Suez crisis, Coulter served as Hammarskjöld's adviser regarding peacekeeping forces in the Middle East. The ROK government recognized Coulter's reconstruction work by erecting a statue of him in Seoul in 1959. Coulter died in Washington, D.C., on 6 March 1983.

—Elizabeth D. Schafer

References:

Appleman, Roy E. *Disaster in Korea: The Chinese Confront MacArthur*. College Station, TX: Texas A&M Press, 1989.

———. *South to the Naktong, North to the Yalu*. Washington, DC: Office of the Chief of Military History, 1961.

Blair, Clay. *The Forgotten War: America in Korea, 1950–1953*. New York: Times Books, 1987.

Current Biography, 1954. New York: H. W. Wilson, 1954.

Hoyt, Edwin P. *The Pusan Perimeter*. New York: Stein & Day, 1984.

See also: Almond, Edward Mallory; China, People's Republic of: Army; Chinese Military Offensives; Ch'ŏngch'ŏn River, Battle of; Eighth United States Army; Hammarskjöld, Dag; Hodge, John R.; Korea, Republic of: Army (ROKA); MacArthur, Douglas; Milburn, Frank William; Pusan Perimeter and Breakout; Ridgway, Matthew Bunker; Syngman Rhee; Turkey; United Nations Commission for the Unification and Rehabilitation of Korea; United Nations Korean Reconstruction Agency (UNKRA); United States Army; Walker, Walton Harris.

COURAGEOUS, Operation
(22 March–31 March 1951)

United Nations (UN) Command hasty attack by the U.S. Army I Corps supplementing Operation RIPPER designed to trap and destroy a large number of North

Troops of the 15th Regiment, 30th Infantry Division, move up a hill to attack dug-in Communist troops north of Ŭijŏngbu, March 1951. (National Archives)

Korean troops south of the Imjin River and to bring I Corps in line with the rest of Eighth Army. Operation COURAGEOUS was part of Eighth Army commander Lieutenant General Matthew B. Ridgway's early 1951 campaign to take the initiative away from Chinese People's Volunteer Army (CPVA, Communist Chinese) forces as UN troops fought their way back to the 38th parallel.

Ridgway launched Operation COURAGEOUS on 22 March 1951, intending to trap and destroy Communist forces opposing the U.S. I Corps south of the Imjin River and to exploit the Chinese withdrawal in the wake of the Eighth Army's series of attacks that winter. Operation COURAGEOUS was also a transitory operation marking the Eighth Army's change from counterattacks focused on destroying Communist units to active defense in preparation for the upcoming Communist spring offensive. A part of Operation RIPPER, Operation COURAGEOUS acquired its name after U.S. State Department officials objected to the aggressive connotations of Ridgway's names for his previous attacks.

The primary purpose of Operation COURAGEOUS was to trap and destroy approximately 60,000 Korean People's Army (KPA, North Korean) troops south of the Imjin River while also positioning I Corps along the 38th parallel. Operation COURAGEOUS was to begin with the 187th Airborne Regimental Combat Team (RCT) parachuting into Munsan-ni, a city on the Imjin River twenty miles north of Seoul. The paratroopers were to block the retreat northward of Communist forces. Meanwhile two armored task forces (Task Force Growden and Task Force Hawkins) would attack north, linking up with the paratroopers and acting as the anvil against which the hammer of the Republic of Korea Army (ROKA) 1st Division and the U.S. 3d Infantry Division would attack and destroy the Communist forces.

Operation COURAGEOUS did not go off as planned. By the time the 187th RCT seized Munsan-ni, KPA forces opposing the ROKA 1st Division had already retreated. Ridgway ordered the 187th RCT to attack east toward Ŭijŏngbu in hopes of trapping any KPA forces still opposing the 3d Infantry Division attack. However, the KPA units managed to avoid the 187th RCT again and escaped to the north. Throughout the attack, ROKA and U.S. units advanced steadily north against moderate opposition and acquired their terrain objectives despite difficult weather conditions.

Ridgway considered Operation COURAGEOUS a "qualified success." By 1 April 1951, in conjunction with Operation RIPPER, all twelve of Eighth Army's divisions were in the vicinity of the 38th parallel, having largely cleared South Korea of Communist forces along the way. However, Operation COURAGEOUS had failed to trap and destroy the large numbers of Communist troops for which the attack had been planned. Nevertheless, Operation COURAGEOUS completed the Eighth Army's advance to the 38th parallel and cleared most of the remaining CPVA and North Korean forces from South Korea, thus accomplishing the UN's fundamental objective for the war of maintaining a free and independent ROK.

—*Robert B. Richards and Kelly C. Jordan*

References:

Blair, Clay. *The Forgotten War: America in Korea, 1950–1953.* New York: Times Books, 1987.

Mossman, Billy C. *U.S. Army in the Korean War: Ebb and Flow, November 1950–July 1951.* Washington, DC: U.S. Army Center of Military History, 1990.

Ridgway, Matthew B. *The Korean War.* Garden City, NY: Doubleday, 1967.

See also: Eighth United States Army; Ridgway, Matthew Bunker; RIPPER, Operation.

Cutler, Robert
(1895–1974)

U.S. special assistant to the president for National Security Affairs, 1953–1955, who supervised the formulation and implementation of U.S. policy on Korea during the early part of President Dwight D. Eisenhower's administration and the final months of the Korean War. Robert Cutler was born on 12 June 1895, in Brookline, Massachusetts. A member of an old Boston Brahmin family, Cutler obtained his bachelor's and law degrees from Harvard University and Harvard Law School, where he edited the *Harvard Law Review*. During the First World War, he served as a lieutenant in the American Expeditionary Force. He then practiced law as a partner in the Boston firm of Herrick, Smith, Donald & Farley, specializing in corporate law. Politically he was closely associated with Henry Cabot Lodge, Jr., who became U.S. Senator for Massachusetts in 1936.

During the Second World War, Cutler became a senior colonel of the Officer Procurement Service. As a special assistant in the Department of War, in 1944 he helped to devise the legislation that allowed servicemen to vote in the forthcoming election, and he carried out other special assignments for Secretary of War Henry L. Stimson and Army Chief of Staff George C. Marshall.

Although he returned to private life when the war ended, Cutler carried out intermittent public assignments, in particular directing the preparatory work for the military's successful 1948 effort to lobby the U.S. Senate and obtain a substantial supplementary defense budget appropriation. In 1951 he also served briefly as deputy director of the Psychological Strategy Board, part of the new Cold War security apparatus.

In 1952 Cutler joined his old friend Lodge in organizing the effort to nominate their old friend General Dwight D. Eisenhower as the Republican candidate for the presidency. Once elected, Eisenhower asked Cutler to undertake a study of the National Security Council, which had been created in 1947 to coordinate U.S. policymaking on international affairs. Cutler recommended the establishment of the position of special assistant to the president for National Security Affairs, a post Eisenhower offered to him in 1953.

Under Cutler the National Security Council played a more central role in formulating defense and foreign policy than it did under President Harry S. Truman; as assistant, Cutler chaired the Policy Planning Board, prepared the agenda for the weekly meetings, briefed the president on papers and issues, recorded decisions, and supervised their implementation. Unlike later national security advisers, Cutler conceived his role primarily as that of coordinator and facilitator rather than policymaker. In this capacity he coordinated the negotiations and deliberations that led to the ending of the Korean War, including the release of North Korean prisoners of war by Syngman Rhee's South Korean government, and in 1953 also helped to handle the U.S. response to the death of Josef Stalin, for which no preparation had been made. Cutler unsuccessfully urged Eisenhower to take a stronger line against McCarthyism, on the grounds that its excesses were destroying U.S. international prestige. Leaving the Eisenhower administration in 1955, Cutler resumed the same post in 1957, resigning again in 1958. His last government assignment, during 1959–1962, was as U.S. representative on the Inter-American Development Bank. Cutler died in Boston on 8 May 1974.

—Priscilla Roberts

References:

Bowie, Robert R., and Richard H. Immerman. *Waging Peace: How Eisenhower Shaped an Enduring Cold War Strategy.* New York: Oxford University Press, 1998.

Cutler, Robert. *No Time for Rest.* Boston: Little, Brown, 1966.

Gentile, Richard H. "Robert Cutler." In *Dictionary of American Biography, Supplement Nine, 1971–1975,* edited by Kenneth T. Jackson. New York: Charles Scribner's Sons, 1994.

Henderson, Philip G. *Managing the Presidency: The Eisenhower Legacy—From Kennedy to Reagan.* Boulder, CO: Westview Press, 1988.

Nelson, Anna Kasten. "The Importance of Foreign Policy Process: Eisenhower and the National Security Council." In *Eisenhower: A Centenary Assessment,* edited by Günter Bischof and Stephen E. Ambrose. Baton Rouge: Louisiana State University Press, 1995: 111–125.

———. "'The Top of the Hill': President Eisenhower and the National Security Council." *Diplomatic History* 7, no. 4 (Fall 1983): 307–326.

Prados, John. *Keepers of the Keys: A History of the National Security Council from Truman to Bush.* New York: William Morrow, 1991.

See also: Eisenhower, Dwight D.; Marshall, George C.; McCarthyism; National Security Council (NSC); Stalin, Josef; Truman, Harry S.

D

Dam Raids of 1953

When armistice negotiations to end the Korean War renewed on 26 April 1953, Communist and United Nations (UN) negotiators disagreed on the format for the repatriation of prisoners of war (POWs). The Communists wanted all POWs returned even if they did not wish to return. With peace blocked again, commander of the Far East Command (FEC) General Mark Clark ordered renewed attacks on the Sup'ung (Suiho) hydroelectric generating facility and the Yangsi electric complex.

On 10 May, eight F-84s of the 58th Fighter Interceptor Wing (FIW) dropped delayed-action ordnance on Suiho in spite of the "most intense flak in all of North Korea." The raid caused no major damage and two generators were still in operation. On the night of 10–11 May, thirty-nine B-29s destroyed 63 percent of Yangsi. During follow-up raids of 18–19 May, B-29s finished the job.

On 13 May, UN mediators proposed allowing a neutral nation to act as a repatriation agent so POWs could return in stages. The Communist side rejected this proposal. UN negotiators recessed talks on the 16th. To pressure the Communists into a settlement, United Nations Command (UNC) planners turned their attention to twenty northern irrigation dams. They decided that, because the Communists had built fortifications near the Kuisang Reservoir, it was no longer immune to attack. Only a few days earlier Clark had warned that, if the impasse continued, the UN might release POWs who did not wish to return and launch a new ground offensive. On 22 May, President Dwight D. Eisenhower, during a visit to Washington by Indian Prime Minister Jawaharlal Nehru, repeated Clark's threat and added that the United States was ready to attack targets in Manchuria unless the Chinese relented on the repatriation issue.

The major UNC concern over attacking the dams was the potential worldwide condemnation for destroying the North Korean rice crop (a civilian target) and causing nationwide starvation. Intelligence revealed the presence of thousands of Communist troops in Hwanghae and South P'yŏngan Provinces cultivating and guarding the rice crop. This made the rice a military target. Far East Air Force (FEAF) leaders noted that these 422,000 acres annually produced 283,162 tons of rice. As this was being used solely for Communist troops, FEAF decided to attack the surrounding reservoirs in order to destroy the rice.

In April FEAF commander General Otto P. Weyland was uncertain that these were good targets. But intelligence reports in May convinced both him and General Clark to use these targets as a trump card to force an end to the conflict. The flooding would destroy not only the rice crop but also Communist lines of communications.

The first test raid was aimed at Tŏksan Dam, 20 miles north of P'yŏngyang along the Pot'ong River. On 13 May, fifty-nine F-84s of the 58th FIW attacked the 2,300-foot earth/stone dam in four waves. At first, it appeared that the dam had survived direct hits by the 1,000-pound bombs, but that night the water broke through, causing damage even greater than anticipated. Six rail bridges of the "Georgia" line were washed away. The main north-south highway was destroyed along with 700 buildings and the Sunan Airfield.

Weyland was so pleased that he planned two more raids, one to be executed by the Fifth Air Force (5AF) against the Chasan Dam and another to be flown by FEAF Bomber Command against the Kuwŏn River Dam. On the afternoon of 15 May, thirty-six F-84s of the 58th FIW dive-bombed Chasan using 1,000-pound bombs. There was little damage. The next day, ninety sorties were flown in three waves. The last wave clustered five direct hits and broke the dam. This washed away three rail bridges on the "Fox" line and destroyed hundreds of acres of rice and miles of secondary roads.

On 21–22 May seven Bomber Command B-29s dropped fifty-six 2,000-pound bombs on Kuwŏn River Dam, scoring four direct hits but failing to breach the dam. During this raid the Communists discovered that by lowering the water level in the reservoir they reduced the strain on the dam's walls and reduced the chance of a break.

On 29 May, fourteen B-29s attacked Kuwŏn River Dam again with 2,000-pound bombs. In spite of five direct hits, the dam did not break. Even so, the damage was so great that the Communists had to drain the reservoir completely to make repairs. By the end of the month, most rail and road damage was repaired by labor cadres, but just to repair Tŏksan necessitated the diversion of 4,000 workers at a cost of 200,000 hours of work. The psychological effect of destroying thousands of tons of rice was devastating to the civilian population.

At the same time these raids were being flown, additional B-29 raids on storage warehouses in northwest Korea and F-84/F-86 raids on Sup'ung (Suiho) pushed the North Koreans to the breaking point. This pressure and threats of attacks on highly vulnerable

Hwach'ŏn Dam, under attack by U.S. Navy AD-2 Skyraider aircraft employing torpedoes. (National Archives)

Manchurian targets caused Communist negotiators on 25 May to relent on the repatriation issue and sign an agreement on 8 June.

In spite of objections by South Korean leader Syngman Rhee and two Communist ground offensives designed to grab territory, FEAF close air support and raids on enemy airfields maintained UN control in Korea and finally led to a cessation of hostilities on 27 July 1953.

The dam raids and the threat of extending the war into Manchuria forced the Communist side to finalize the repatriation settlement, the last hurdle to the armistice. The dam raids were then, and continue to be, controversial because some denounced them as attacks on innocent civilians. The counterargument can be made that the rice was a valid military target because it was used by Communist troops. It could also be argued that ending the war more quickly in effect saved lives.

—*William Head*

References:

Futrell, Robert F. *The United States Air Force in Korea, 1950–1953.* Rev. ed. Washington, DC: Office of the Chief of Air Force History, 1983.

Thompson, Wayne. "The Air War over Korea." In *Winged Shield, Wing Sword: A History of the United States Air Force,* edited by Bernard C. Nalty. Washington, DC: United States Air Force History and Museum Program, 1997: 3–52.

See also: Aircraft (Principal Combat); Clark, Mark W.; Eisenhower, Dwight D.; Far East Air Force (FEAF); Far East Command (FEC); Syngman Rhee; United States Air Force (USAF); Weyland, Otto P.

DAUNTLESS, Operation
(11–22 April 1951)

United Nations Command (UNC) offensive military operation. Operation DAUNTLESS occurred in April 1951, coinciding with the dismissal of General Douglas MacArthur. General Matthew B. Ridgway became Far East Commander and General James A. Van Fleet commanded the Eighth Army during Operation DAUNTLESS.

DAUNTLESS followed the successful completion of Operation RUGGED, in which Eighth Army troops reached Line Kansas above the 38th parallel and south of the Hwach'ŏn Reservoir. DAUNTLESS was an attempt by I and IX Corps to establish a 25-

mile bulge toward the crucial Iron Triangle. Two phases were planned: troops would first reach Line Utah and then they would secure Line Wyoming, where they would dig in.

DAUNTLESS began at dawn on 11 April when Lieutenant General Frank W. Milburn's I Corps, consisting of the Republic of Korea Army (ROKA) 1st Division and the U.S. 3d, 24th, and 25th divisions, left the Imjin River line and began the assault. The Hant'an River's steep banks hindered crossing, and Communist snipers fired on the attackers climbing a sheer cliff. Some of the 24th Division units had to delay their advance until the next day, but other units were able to move north into the Iron Triangle.

After reaching Line Utah, on 21 April UNC troops began the second step of Operation DAUNTLESS. I Corps slowly advanced toward Line Wyoming, encountering minimal resistance. In support, Lieutenant General William M. Hoge led his IX Corps in an effort to move from Line Kansas to Line Quantico above the Hwach'ŏn Reservoir. Communist soldiers lit brush fires and the resultant smoky haze obscured vision and concealed their movements. However, a captured Chinese People's Volunteer Army (CPVA) officer revealed that a Chinese counterattack was planned for that night.

The ensuing CPVA Spring Offensive, totaling eight days of combat, was the largest battle in the Korean War. Although UNC troops were forced from their positions gained above the 38th parallel during Operation DAUNTLESS, they repulsed the Chinese offensive and successfully defended Seoul.

—*Elizabeth D. Schafer*

References:

Blair, Clay. *The Forgotten War: America in Korea, 1950–1953.* New York: Times Books, 1987.

Mossman, Billy C. *U.S. Army in the Korean War: Ebb and Flow, November 1950–July 1951.* Washington, DC: U.S. Army Center of Military History, 1990.

Schnabel, James F. *United States Army in the Korean War: Policy and Direction, the First Year.* Washington, DC: Office of the Chief of Military History, Department of the Army, 1972.

See also: Chinese Military Offensives (Chinese Fifth [Spring] Offensive [22–30 April 1951]); Hoge, William M.; Imjin River; Iron Triangle; Kansas-Wyoming Line; MacArthur, Douglas; Milburn, Frank William; Ridgway, Matthew Bunker; RUGGED, Operation; Van Fleet, James Alward.

Davidson, Garrison Holt
(1904–1992)

U.S. Army general and during the Korean War architect of the so-called Davidson Line, a defensive position he laid out within the Pusan perimeter in the summer of 1950.

Garrison "Gar" Holt Davidson was born on 24 April 1904 in the Bronx, New York, and attended the prestigious Stuyvesant High School in lower Manhattan. Appointed to the U.S. Military Academy, West Point, Davidson graduated in the top 10 percent of his class in 1927. Commissioned a second lieutenant of Engineers, Davidson was assigned as assistant football coach at West Point while commanding an Engineer platoon at Fort Dupont, Delaware, and then Fort Dix, New Jersey. In 1930 he became an instructor in the Academy's Department of Natural and Experimental Philosophy. From 1932 to 1937 Davidson was head coach of West Point's football team.

From 1938 to 1940 Davidson served in Hawaii with the Engineer Battalion and then as Hawaiian Division G-4. In 1940 he was assigned as the air base engineer, Hamilton Field, California, and in December 1941 he was transferred to the Construction Division, Office, Chief of Engineers, Washington, D.C., where he supervised construction funds.

During World War II, Davidson was Lieutenant General George S. Patton's engineer in the North African and Sicilian campaigns and then Lieutenant General Alexander Patch's Seventh Army Engineer. As such, he helped plan the invasion of southern France.

In July 1945 Davidson conducted the first mass war crimes trial in Darmstadt, Germany, before the Nuremberg trials. He then became Engineer of the Theater Board, European Theater of Operations, and in 1946 he was assigned as Sixth Army Engineer, Presidio of San Francisco, and then chief of staff, Sixth Army.

In August 1950 he was assigned to the Eighth Army in Korea and given the task of establishing a defensive line behind the Pusan perimeter. This line (never needed), became known as the Davidson Line. He was then appointed assistant commander of the 24th Infantry Division. After the Chinese intervened, Eighth Army commander Lieutenant General Matthew B. Ridgway tapped Davidson to prepare what proved to be very effective defenses around Seoul. Afterward, Davidson became acting commander of the Korea Military Advisory Group (KMAG).

Returning to the United States in July 1950, Davidson was appointed senior U.S. Army member of the Weapons Systems Evaluation Group under the Secretary of Defense. In 1954 he became commandant of the Army Command and General Staff College, where he established a special group to analyze and study combined arms and services doctrine, a forerunner of the Combat Developments Command. He then became superintendent of the U.S. Military Academy, West Point, where he laid the groundwork for academic reform. Promoted to lieutenant general in 1957, he commanded the Seventh Army in Germany in 1960 and then the First Army in New York in 1962. He retired from the Army in May 1964.

Subsequently he was assistant vice-president of the University of California, Berkeley, then resident executive director of the Embarcadero Project in San Francisco. Later, Governor Ronald Reagan named him chairman of the board of trustees of the California Maritime Academy. Davidson was also a member of the National Council of the Boy Scouts of America. Davidson died in Oakland, California, on 25 December 1992.

—Uzal W. Ent

References:

Assembly. Association of Graduates, U.S. Military Academy, West Point, NY (July 1993).

Pointer View. U.S. Military Academy, West Point, NY. 49, no. 6 (12 February 1993).

See also: Davidson Line; Korea Military Advisory Group (KMAG); Ridgway, Matthew Bunker; Walker, Walton Harris.

Davidson Line

United Nations Command (UNC) defensive line north of Pusan and named for Brigadier General Garrison "Gar" H. Davidson. An engineer officer, Davidson established this secondary defense line in the Pusan perimeter in August 1950. General Douglas MacArthur instructed Eighth Army commander Lieutenant General Walton H. Walker to build a defense line closer to Pusan than the Naktong River line in case UNC forces could not stop Korean People's Army (North Korean) forces at the Naktong.

On 11 August, Walker ordered Davidson to lay out this secondary defense line. After surveying the terrain, Davidson told Walker that to achieve better defense of the area the line should be built closer to Pusan than MacArthur stipulated. Walker insisted that Davidson establish the line where MacArthur ordered.

Davidson began laying out the defense line with assistance from Brigadier General Crump Garvin's Second Logistical Command at Pusan and the 2d and 25th Divisions, as well as Korean laborers. Walker refused to approval Davidson's suggestion to remove houses in front of the line. Davidson did clear other natural and human-made obstacles, dig fox holes, string barbed wire, lay mine fields, and erect fortifications along the line.

The Davidson Line stretched 68 miles from Sŏdong-ni on the east coast, starting approximately eight miles north of Ulsan, and continued on high ground to northeast of Miryang and then down the ridge east of Muan-ni and south across the Naktong River to an area northeast of Masan. Eighth Army was prepared to move immediately to the Davidson Line if Soviet forces entered the war and Pusan needed to be protected for evacuation of troops. As it turned out, the Davidson Line did not have to be used.

—Elizabeth D. Schafer

References:

Appleman, Roy E. *Disaster in Korea: The Chinese Confront MacArthur*. College Station, TX: Texas A&M Press, 1989.

———. *South to the Naktong, North to the Yalu*. Washington, DC: Office of the Chief of Military History, 1961.

Blair, Clay. *The Forgotten War: America in Korea, 1950–1953*. New York: Times Books, 1987.

Hoyt, Edwin P. *The Pusan Perimeter*. New York: Stein & Day, 1984.

See also: Davidson, Garrison Holt; MacArthur, Douglas; Pusan Perimeter and Breakout; Walker, Walton Harris.

Davies, John Paton
(1908–)

U.S. State Department official and from 1950 to 1951 the leading China expert on its policy planning staff. Born on 6 April 1908, in Koating, China, to a Baptist missionary's family, John Paton Davies was educated at the University of Wisconsin, Yenching University, and Columbia University. He received a bachelor's degree from Columbia in 1931. Davies then joined the U.S. Foreign Service as a China expert.

During the Second World War, Davies served in China as an adviser to U.S. Military Attaché Lieutenant General Joseph W. Stilwell and Ambassador Patrick Hurley. Davies's reports from China anticipated a Communist victory over the Nationalist (Guomindang) forces of Jiang Jieshi (Chiang Kai-shek) and commented on the existing regime's corruption and inability to win the loyalty of the Chinese people. Davies also suggested that, once in power, the Chinese Communists were likely to develop similar faults, and he argued that the Chinese civil war was a conflict incomprehensible to foreigners and in which the United States should avoid any deep involvement.

In late 1944 Davies assisted with Hurley's attempt to bring about a truce and a coalition government comprising both Chinese Nationalists and Communists. When this failed, he recommended continued U.S. aid to the Nationalists, but he also recommended that if, as he expected, the Chinese Communists eventually attained power the United States should be prepared to cooperate with them in the interests of preventing a Sino-Soviet alliance. Hurley interpreted this position as evidence of Davies's pro-Communist sympathies, and from 1945 onward Davies became a target of the growing China lobby, which repeatedly demanded his dismissal for disloyalty and pro-Communism. As a result, between 1950 and 1953 Davies was subjected to eight separate security investigations, each of which cleared him yet failed to extinguish the residual suspicions as to his potential guilt nurtured by the lobby, which attempted to ascribe to him at least partial responsibility for the October 1949 Communist victory in China.

Davies left China in 1947 to become first secretary at the U.S. embassy in Moscow. In 1950 he was transferred to the Policy Planning Staff, where, perhaps in reaction to the persistent charges against him, his advice on China tended to be relatively militant. Although he favored U.S. recognition of the People's Republic of China, he often condemned Mao Zedong's regime for its close ties to the Soviets.

After the Korean War began in June 1950, the Truman administration depended heavily upon Davies's assessments of the Asian situation and in particular of Chinese Communist intentions. In July 1950 he warned that there existed a serious possibility of Chinese intervention in the conflict and suggested that the United States inform the Red Chinese government that, should this occur, U.S. officials would mount a major bombing campaign against Chinese territory. After the brief Chinese military disengagement of 6 November 1950, Davies argued that the United States should continue its offensive, on the grounds that a failure to do so would invite further Communist advances and U.S. humiliation. The massive Chinese military intervention that followed U.S. adoption of this strategy led a somewhat chastened Davies to endorse British proposals to establish a demilitarized buffer zone between China and North Korea. In late spring 1951, after United Nations (UN) forces had rebuffed the Chinese spring offensives and once more crossed the 38th parallel, Davies helped to arrange unofficial Soviet-U.S. conversations on the subject of a potential cease-fire. Held on 31 May and 5 June, these discussions between U.S. Soviet expert George F. Kennan, at that time on leave of absence at Princeton University, and Soviet Ambassador to the UN Jacob Malik helped to bring about the opening of the Kaesŏng truce talks later that summer.

In 1951 Davies joined the U.S. High Commission in Germany as director of political affairs at the mission in Bonn. In 1953 the Eisenhower administration, fearful of McCarthyism but unable to force the stubborn Davies to resign, exiled him to an obscure diplomatic position in Peru. In 1954 a ninth security investigation, relying in part upon testimony from Hurley, characterized Davies as disloyal, whereupon Secretary of State John Foster Dulles dismissed him. Davies, virtually unemployable in the prevailing political climate, left the United States to run a furniture business in Peru. During the early 1960s, political considerations led President John F. Kennedy and Secretary of State Dean Rusk to refuse appeals from influential Democrats to clear Davies' name. He was not rehabilitated until 1969, when the Massachusetts Institute of Technology employed him on a contract originating from the Arms Control and Disarmament Agency. Later Davies moved to Spain.

—*Priscilla Roberts*

References:

Davies, John Paton. *Dragon by the Tail: American, British, Japanese, and Russian Encounters with China and One Another.* New York: W. W. Norton, 1972.

Foot, Rosemary J. *A Substitute for Victory: The Politics of Peacemaking at the Korean Armistice Talks.* Ithaca, NY: Cornell University Press, 1990.

"John Paton Davies." In *Political Profiles: The Truman Years,* edited by Eleanora W. Schoenebaum. New York: Facts on File, 1978.

Kahn, Ely Jacques. *The China Hands: America's Foreign Service Officers and What Befell Them.* New York: Viking Press, 1975.

Lauren, Paul Gordon. *The China Hands' Legacy: Ethics and Diplomacy.* Boulder, CO: Westview Press, 1987.

See also: China Lobby; Dulles, John Foster; Jiang Jieshi (Chiang Kai-shek); Kennan, George F.; Malik, Jacob (Iakov) Alexandrovich; Mao Zedong; McCarthy, Joseph R.; McCarthyism; Rusk, David Dean.

Dean, Arthur H.
(1898–1987)

U.S. negotiator at the P'anmunjŏm peace talks and special U.S. ambassador to Korea from 1953 to 1954. Born in Ithaca, New York, on 16 October 1898, Arthur H. Dean completed a law degree at Cornell University and in 1923 he joined the leading New York international law firm, Sullivan and Cromwell. During the 1920s and 1930s he performed much work for German and Japanese businesses. His colleagues included John Foster Dulles, whom he succeeded as senior partner in 1949. Dean followed the firm's tradition of devoting much attention to international relations, serving as a director of the Council on Foreign Relations and a member of both the Asia Society and the Institute of Pacific Relations.

In October 1953 Dulles, then secretary of state, sent Dean to Korea with ambassadorial rank to head the U.S. delegation at the P'anmunjŏm postarmistice peace negotiations with the Communist side. As U.S. negotiator, Dean was trapped between intransigent South Koreans, led by President Syngman Rhee, who demanded reunification of all Korean territory under their own control, and the equally obdurate delegates from the Democratic People's Republic of Korea (North Korea) and People's Republic of China (PRC, Communist China). Dean firmly opposed suggestions from the Communist delegates that neutral nations uninvolved in the fighting, effectively the Soviet Union and nonaligned Asian nations who might lean toward the Communist bloc, should be represented in the negotiations. Dean emphasized that only belligerent countries were entitled to be seated, but he offered the Soviets inclusion should they wish to concede their belligerent status. In December 1953 Dean temporarily suspended talks after the Communist Chinese accused the United States of bad faith in permitting

South Korea to relinquish 21,000 non-Communist North Korean and Communist Chinese prisoners of war to United Nations custody, as opposed to returning them to their native countries.

Early in 1954 Dean fell victim to the still strong forces of McCarthyism and the China lobby, whose ire was aroused by press reports that he supported U.S. recognition of the PRC. Senator Herman Welker (Republican, Idaho) not only accused Dean of collaboration with mainland China and "appeasement" but also brought up the issue of Dean's early 1950s membership in the Institute of Pacific Relations (IPR), alleging that Dean had served as its "official spokesman." Dean had resigned from this organization in 1952, after a Senate investigation into IPR involvement in leaking confidential State Department papers to the publication *Amerasia* characterized the IPR as a body that effectively "served Communist interests." Even so, in the prevailing anti-Communist climate, these charges made Dean a political liability to Dulles, who in March 1954 requested that he resign his position. As a mark of his continuing confidence in his former partner, Dulles then promptly sent Dean to Korea as a U.S. emissary to Rhee to review the situation before the opening of negotiations at Geneva in April 1954.

Throughout the 1950s and 1960s Dean continued to urge U.S. recognition of the PRC. Respected by both political parties as an elder statesman, in 1958 he represented his country at an eighty-seven–nation conference in Geneva on the Law of the Sea. In the 1960s he served as an adviser on disarmament to President John F. Kennedy and represented the United States at the Geneva talks on ending nuclear weapons tests. In early 1968, as a member of the Senior Advisory Group on Vietnam, which considered the military's post–Tet Offensive request for 200,000 additional troops, he joined the majority in recommending U.S. withdrawal from the conflict. He died in New York on 30 November 1987.

—*Priscilla Roberts*

References:
"Arthur H. Dean." In *Political Profiles: The Eisenhower Years,* edited by Eleanora W. Schoenebaum. New York: Facts on File, 1977.

Foot, Rosemary J. *A Substitute for Victory: The Politics of Peacemaking at the Korean Armistice Talks.* Ithaca, NY: Cornell University Press, 1990.

Lisagor, Nancy, and Frank Lipsius. *A Law Unto Itself: The Untold Story of the Law Firm of Sullivan & Cromwell.* New York: William Morrow, 1988.

U.S. Department of State, Bureau of Public Affairs. *Foreign Relations of the United States, 1952–1954.* Vol. 15, *Korea.* Washington, DC: U.S. Government Printing Office, 1984.

See also: Dulles, John Foster; Eisenhower, Dwight D.; P'anmunjŏm Truce Talks; Syngman Rhee.

Dean, William Frishe
(1899–1981)

U.S. Army general and commander of the 24th Infantry Division during the Korean War. William Frishe Dean was born in Carlyle, Illinois, on 1 August 1899. He failed to gain admission to West Point and enrolled at the University of California at Berkeley, graduating in 1922. Dean had secured a reserve commission in May 1921, but in October 1923 he was granted a regular army commission as a second lieutenant of infantry.

Dean served with the 38th Infantry Regiment at Fort Douglas, Utah, during 1923–1926. He then saw service in Panama with the 42d and 33d Infantry Regiments. In 1929 he rejoined the 38th Infantry, and in 1934 he was assigned to the 30th Infantry Regiment at the Presidio of San Francisco, California. During 1935–1936 Dean attended the Army Command and General Staff School at Fort Leavenworth, Kansas. After a tour with the 19th Infantry Regiment at Schofield Barracks, Hawaii, he returned to the United States and attended the Army Industrial College in Washington, graduating in June 1939. He served briefly at the Chemical Warfare School at Edgewood Arsenal, Maryland, before returning to Washington that September to attend the Army War College, from which he was graduated in June 1940. He then served in the Operations and Training Division of the War Department General Staff and was appointed assistant to the secretary of the General Staff in January 1941.

In March 1942 Dean was reassigned to Headquarters, Army Ground Forces, where he served as assistant chief, then chief, of the Requirements Section. He was promoted to brigadier general in December 1942, and in February 1944 he became assistant commander of the 44th Infantry Division in Louisiana. He moved with the division to Camp Phillips, Kansas, and from there to southern France in August 1944. He remained with the 44th Infantry Division throughout its campaigns in southern France and Germany. Named to command the division in December 1944, he was promoted to major general in March 1945, and in July 1945 he redeployed the division to the United States in preparation for its reassignment to the Pacific Theater.

In September 1945 General Dean joined the faculty of the Army Command and General Staff School at Fort Leavenworth; he became assistant commandant of the School in June 1946. In October 1947 he was reassigned as military governor of South Korea. He supervised the first free elections there and the inauguration of the Republic of Korea in August 1948. Dean then assumed command of the 7th Infantry Division in Korea and took it to Japan in January 1949. The following June he became chief of staff of the Eighth

U.S. Army in Japan. In October 1949 he was reassigned to command the 24th Infantry Division which subsequently became the first U.S. ground combat unit to respond to the North Korean invasion of South Korea on 25 June 1950. General Dean arrived at Taejŏn Airfield on 3 July 1950 and immediately assumed command of all U.S. forces in Korea.

Striving to stem the North Korean advance, Dean personally led his division in the bitter defense of Taejŏn on 19–20 July, on one occasion attacking a Korean People's Army (KPA, North Korean) tank with only a hand grenade and his .45-caliber pistol. Given the near total disintegration of his division under heavy KPA attack and the lack of communications, Dean's actions can only be characterized as leading by example in desperate circumstances.

Separated from the rest of his command in the confused withdrawal from Taejŏn, Dean wandered alone and injured in the hills until he was betrayed by two South Koreans on 25 August 1950. He thus became the highest ranking United Nations Command officer taken prisoner by the Communists. Dean's courageous conduct in captivity was equal to his bravery at Taejŏn, for which he was awarded the Medal of Honor in February 1951. He was released from captivity on 3 September 1953 and returned a hero, although he was criticized later for his defense of those U.S. prisoners of war who had cooperated with the Communists.

In December 1953 Dean became deputy commander of the Sixth U.S. Army at the Presidio. When he retired from active duty in October 1955, he was awarded the coveted Combat Infantryman's Badge by Army Chief of Staff General Maxwell D. Taylor, thus becoming only the second general officer, after General Joseph W. Stilwell, to be so honored. Dean died at Berkeley, California, on 26 August 1981.

—*Charles R. Shrader*

References:

Ancell, R. Manning, and Christine M. Miller. *The Biographical Dictionary of World War II. Generals and Flag Officers—The U. S. Armed Forces.* Westport, CT: Greenwood Press, 1996.

Appleman, Roy E. *South to the Naktong, North to the Yalu.* Washington, DC: Office of the Chief of Military History, 1961.

Dean, William F., with William L. Worden. *General Dean's Story.* New York: Viking Press, 1954.

Department of Defense biographical sketch.

Matray, James I., ed. *Historical Dictionary of the Korean War.* Westport, CT: Greenwood Press, 1991.

Shrader, Charles R., ed. *Reference Guide to United States Military History.* Vol. 5, *1945 to the Present.* New York: Facts on File, 1995.

See also: Taejŏn, Defense of.

Defectors

Biggest obstacle to armistice negotiations during the Korean War. By February 1952 only the repatriation of prisoners of war (POWs) prevented peace. President Harry S. Truman wanted to concede nothing, in hopes of winning a moral victory through the defection of large numbers of POWs. He believed their nonrepatriation would also undermine the authority of Communist governments. For the same reasons, the Communists were equally intransigent in their demand for repatriation of all POWs.

On 2 April 1952 the Communist delegation at the P'anmunjŏm truce talks demanded lists of all POWs willing to repatriate. The results were shocking for both sides. Of 132,000 Communist POWs, only 70,000 desired repatriation. This was completely unacceptable to the Communist side, which maintained that there must be full repatriation. The problem worsened as a result of the Communist accusation that the United Nations (UN) had used force at the POW camps at Kŏje-do to influence repatriation. This and the resulting Dodd-Colson incident of 7–11 May 1952 damaged negotiations.

A break came in December 1952 with a Red Cross suggestion that all sick and wounded POWs be exchanged as a gesture of peace. On 28 March 1953, North Korean premier Kim Il Sung announced his approval. He also stated that it should serve as a foundation for the settlement of the POW question and a ceasefire. On 30 March, Chinese Foreign Minister Zhou Enlai gave his tacit support. He also proposed that any POW wishing to defect be put in the hands of a neutral state for investigation. On 1 April, Soviet Foreign Minister V. M. Molotov gave his government's approval.

Final negotiations followed an Indian proposal, supported by the British, that a single neutral power would screen all would-be defectors within ninety days in Korea. This went forward despite an attempt by South Korean President Syngman Rhee to sabotage it, whereby 25,000 POWs were released from their camps. The 22,604 POWs who remained after the repatriation of the others in Operations BIG SWITCH and LITTLE SWITCH were turned over to the Neutral Nations Repatriation Commission (NNRC) and an Indian custodial force. The NNRC finally dissolved on 20 January 1954 with the repatriation of only 137 of the POWs. The remainder settled in South Korea or Formosa.

The mass defections on the Communist side dwarfed those of the UN. There were, however, 335 Koreans, 23 Americans, and a Briton who elected not to return home. The Western governments claimed a moral victory, but the issue of defectors prolonged the war and resulted in additional war losses.

—*Eric W. Osborne*

References:

Hastings, Max. *The Korean War.* New York: Simon & Schuster, 1987.

MacDonald, Callum. *Korea: The War Before Vietnam*. New York: Free Press, 1986.

Toland, John. *In Mortal Combat: Korea, 1950–1953*. New York: William Morrow, 1991.

See also: BIG SWITCH/LITTLE SWITCH, Operations; Churchill, Sir Winston Spencer; Dodd-Colson Prisoner-of-War Incident; Eden, Anthony; Eisenhower, Dwight D.; Kim Il Sung; Kŏje-do; Kŏje-do Prisoner-of-War Uprising; Menon, V. K. Krishna; Molotov, Viacheslav Mikhailovich; Repatriation, Voluntary; Truman, Harry S.; Zhou Enlai.

Defense Production Act
(8 September 1950)

Law signed by President Harry S. Truman on 8 September 1950. This important piece of wartime legislation was cast to accomplish two primary goals. First, Congress designed the Defense Production Act to empower the president with specific authority to mobilize U.S. industry and resources for the Korean War. Second, and perhaps more critical, the act enabled the executive branch to build—and maintain at perpetual readiness—U.S. industrial and military mobilization bases in case of an all-out war with the Soviet Union. Thus, the Defense Production Act was in reality the enabling legislation that allowed the nation to arm fully for the protracted Cold War that lay ahead. It ensured the full implementation of NSC-68, "United States Objectives and Programs for National Security."

Included in the specific powers granted the president was the authority to establish production priorities and materials allocations systems, to requisition personal property for defense purposes, to expand productive capacity, to increase the extraction and processing of strategic materials, and to invoke wage, price, and credit controls. Most of the Korean War era mobilization agencies sprang directly from this sweeping piece of legislation.

During the Korean War, the U.S. Congress closely monitored the implementation of the Defense Production Act, modifying it substantially in the summer of 1951. In the summer of 1952, Congress again modified the legislation, although less radically than the year before. As the Korean War dragged on and became increasingly unpopular, Congress used the act as a vote of no confidence against Truman, twice trimming the powers granted to him under the original legislation. Although never again invoked fully after the end of the Korean War, the Defense Production Act remained in force throughout much of the Cold War.

—*Paul G. Pierpaoli, Jr.*

References:

Hogan, Michael J. *A Cross of Iron: Harry S. Truman and the Origins of the National Security State, 1945–1954*. Cambridge, UK: Cambridge University Press, 1998.

Pierpaoli, Paul G., Jr. *Truman and Korea: The Political Culture of the Early Cold War*. Columbia: University of Missouri Press, 1999.

Vawter, Roderick W. *Industrial Mobilization: The Relevant History*. Washington, DC: National Defense University Press, 1983.

See also: Mobilization; Truman, Harry S.; United States: Home Front.

Delaying the North Korean Offensive
(5 July–4 August 1950)

As soon as President Harry S. Truman made the decision to send ground combat troops to Korea, General Douglas MacArthur went into action. Major General William F. Dean's 24th Division was the first division to go to Korea and Dean assumed command of all U.S. Army forces there. His mission was to delay the Korean People's Army (KPA, North Korean) advance as long as possible until substantial U.S. reinforcements could be sent to Korea. Dean immediately formed a task force headed by Lieutenant Colonel Charles B. Smith, which would fly to Korea and move into blocking positions north of Osan. Task Force Smith, as it came to be known, consisted of two reinforced rifle companies and a field artillery battery. In the meantime the rest of the division was assembled to move to Pusan by ship and thence to the front.

Task Force Smith took up position south of Suwŏn where the main highway to Seoul passed through a low saddle in a small ridge. Its first contact with the KPA came about 0745 on 5 July 1950 when a tank column approached. When the tanks got within 700 yards of the dug-in U.S. infantry, they were taken under fire by recoilless rifles and 2.36-inch rocket launchers. These weapons were not effective in stopping the tanks. U.S. 105-mm howitzer fire did, however, knock out two lead tanks, but thirty tanks behind them kept moving around and through the U.S. troops. Later, KPA infantry arrived and outflanked the U.S. position. By early afternoon the U.S. defensive position became untenable. Colonel Smith, fearful of being cut off, then withdrew his men.

The success of this first KPA contact with the U.S. Army made time even more important for United Nations forces. Other U.S. units would now have to make sacrifices to delay the KPA until sufficient resources could be put together to stop the North Korean drive. Geography acquired importance, and rivers became excellent obstacles to slow KPA tanks. General Dean and his planners selected important terrain features where U.S. forces would fight. Places such as Ch'ŏnan, Taejŏn, P'yŏngt'aek, and the Kŭm River were points where U.S. forces would try to block the KPA advance.

The next U.S. unit positioned to block the KPA advance was the 34th Infantry Regiment of the 24th Division. At Ansŏng and Ch'ŏnan, however, battalions of the regiment were outflanked and became disorganized. Again the 2.36-inch rocket proved incapable of knocking out North Korean tanks, and regimental commander Colonel Robert Martin died trying to stop a tank with a rocket launcher. Infiltrating KPA infantry produced both casualties and confusion among U.S. troops.

General Dean decided on the Kŭm River as his next line of defense, with the 34th and 21st Regiments to defend this line. By 12 July the 34th Regiment had blown the Kŭm River bridges and withdrawn behind the river. Here the first real defense in the war occurred. The dogged defense of the Kŭm River line by two battalions of the 21st delayed two of the best North Korean divisions for three days. In spite of this determined defense, the 16th KPA Regiment made a night crossing through gaps in the division position, surprising and overrunning the 63d Field Artillery Battalion, and by the 16th the KPA was poised to attack Taejŏn from the west.

During the early days of the war, bad weather had limited the use of U.S. air power. Not only did heavy rain delay air strikes, but early morning fog provided cover for attacking North Koreans. On 9 and 10 July the skies cleared, and the Fifth Air Force carried out heavy strikes on KPA columns. Massive U.S. air strikes proved highly effective in destroying KPA tanks, artillery, and vehicles.

On 13 July General Walton H. Walker arrived in Korea to take over command of the defense and build up U.S. forces, now known as Eighth Army. At the same time, two new divisions, the 25th and 1st Cavalry, arrived from Japan. Walker needed two additional days to deploy these divisions in defensive positions. To secure this time, Walker ordered General Dean's 24th Division to make a stand at Taejŏn. It was important that Dean be there to keep up the morale of his troops as well as to set an example for leaders of the Republic of Korea Army (South Korea).

On 20 July the North Koreans assaulted Taejŏn by crashing into the defenders and then flanking them in the rear. In the midst of this Dean suddenly found himself fighting as part of an antitank team. New 3.5-inch rocket launchers had just been airlifted from the United States, and with this new weapon Dean was able to knock out several KPA tanks. In spite of this brief success, by late afternoon of 20 July the overall situation for the 24th Division in Taejŏn was hopeless. Despite mass confusion, most U.S. units were able to withdraw from the city, and more than 75 percent of the troops involved survived.

The last ten days in July and the first week in August were crucial in U.S. efforts to delay the KPA long enough for Eighth Army to establish a foothold. Both sides were racing against the clock as the North Koreans made an all-out effort to complete their conquest of the South before the U.S. forces could complete their buildup. At the same time the United States rushed in every available man in an effort to stem the North Korean tide.

On 22 July the 24th Division turned over its frontline positions at Yŏngdong to the newly arrived 1st Cavalry Division. To the right of this division at Sangju was the recently arrived 25th Division. Both these divisions engaged in fierce struggles with KPA units west of the Naktong River. Over the next week the U.S. divisions slowly withdrew to the east side of the river. General Walker had decided that Eighth Army would make a final defensive stand behind the Naktong. Despite taking heavy casualties, KPA units were able to infiltrate between the two U.S. divisions. With their defensive positions untenable, both U.S. divisions made preparations to withdraw. Walker, an aggressive combat leader in Europe under General George S. Patton, was furious with this, and on 29 July he issued his famous "stand or die" order.

Some have criticized this order because KPA success was more a result of the paucity of numbers of defenders rather than to weaknesses in their fighting ability. In any case, Walker needed to build up the morale of Eighth Army. Certainly one of Walker's greatest contributions in the Korean War was his tenacious and brilliant military defense in the early days of fighting.

While most of Eighth Army concentrated on blocking KPA forces north and northeast of Taegu, KPA 6th Division carried out a rapid and wide envelopment south to the Strait of Korea and then east to outflank the U.S. troops and drive toward the port of Pusan, the major access point for U.S. forces into Korea. KPA leaders understood the terrain well and knew that a dash along the coast from the west would avoid the obstacle posed by the Naktong River until just outside Pusan. By 25 July the KPA 6th Division was at Sunch'ŏn, poised to take Chinju, only 55 miles from Pusan.

When General Walker realized the KPA 6th Division goal, he quickly moved the understrength, exhausted 24th Division to block the envelopment. By 26 July the 24th Division, minus its 21st Regiment, held a 30-mile defensive front from Kŏch'ang to Chinju.

The situation was critical. Newly arriving units were immediately sent to help cover this broad front. Among those arriving were the 1st and 3d Infantry Battalions of the 29th Regiment from Okinawa with 400 brand-new recruits who had never trained with the regiment. Both battalions were immediately sent to the front to face two attacking KPA divisions. The 3d Battalion, attached to the 35th Infantry Regiment of the 25th Infantry Division, ran head first into the North Korean 6th Division; most of 3d Batallion's officers were killed in the ensuing fighting and the unit as a whole suffered 50 percent casualties. At the same time, the 1st Battalion was attached to the 27th Infantry Regiment of the 25th Infantry Division. It encountered the KPA 4th Division and suffered many casualties. In two days of fighting during 26–27 July, the two battalions suffered a combined 618 casualties. In September 1950 these two battalions were absorbed into the regiments to which they were attached and ceased to function as units of the 29th Regiment.

Eighth Army had at last reached a point where it could no longer continue to withdraw and still retain a foothold on the Korean peninsula. Walker shifted other units south to meet the onslaught, such as the 27th (Wolfhound) Regiment. Bitter fighting in which U.S. units incurred heavy casualties finally slowed down the attacking KPA 4th and 6th Divisions. As new units arrived, Walker rushed them into the line. These included the 5th Marine Brigade from California and the 5th Regimental Combat Team from Hawaii. At this point Walker was willing to concede to the KPA all of Korea except the area east of the Naktong River, known as the Pusan perimeter. Eighth Army would spend the next forty-five days in costly fighting to defend this area of some 5,000 square miles.

—*Daniel R. Beirne*

References:

Appleman, Roy E. *South to the Naktong, North to the Yalu.* Washington, DC: Office of the Chief of Military History, 1961.

Blair, Clay. *The Forgotten War: America in Korea, 1950–1953.* New York: Times Books, 1987.

Fehrenbach, T. R. *This Kind of War: A Study in Unpreparedness.* New York: Macmillan, 1962.

Leckie, Robert. *Conflict: The History of the Korean War, 1950–1953.* New York: Putnam, 1962.

Toland, John. *In Mortal Combat: Korea, 1950–1953.* New York: William Morrow, 1991.

See also: Dean, William Frishe; MacArthur, Douglas; Task Force Smith; Truman, Harry S.; Walker, Walton Harris.

Demilitarized Zone (DMZ)

The Korean Armistice Agreement provided for a demilitarized zone (DMZ) extending for two kilometers on either side of a mutually agreed upon military demarcation line (MDL). The location of the MDL was a matter of intense negotiations as Agenda Item 2 of the truce talks. Korean People's Army/Chinese People's Volunteer Army (KPA/CPVA) negotiators sought to restore the 38th parallel, whereas the United Nations Command (UNC) side argued for a line considerably to the north. On 27 November 1951, the two sides finally agreed on an MDL running approximately along the line of ground contact between the military forces at that time. Subsequent fighting required some adjustments, but the line was relatively unchanged when the Armistice Agreement was signed

on 27 July 1953. The DMZ itself was established when both sides withdrew their forces, weapons, and equipment two kilometers from the MDL.

The MDL is approximately 150 miles long. It begins in the west, 10 miles south of the 38th parallel and a few miles north of the point where the Imjin River joins the Han River to form the Han River Estuary (HRE). The Armistice Agreement declares the entire HRE open to civil shipping of both sides, although very little "civil shipping" has passed through it since the war. From the HRE, the MDL runs north to P'anmunjŏm, then northeast to the East Sea (Sea of Japan) coast about forty-two miles north of the 38th parallel.

Although the Armistice Agreement uses no such term, both sides make use of the concept of the "MDL extended" to delineate the boundary between their territorial waters on the east coast. These "territorial waters" are not defined by the Armistice Agreement because during the negotiations the UNC side claimed a three-mile and the KPA/CPVA side a twelve-mile limit.

The Armistice Agreement allows each side to have 1,000 "civil police" in the DMZ and 24 in the HRE at any one time for "civil administration and relief." Others may enter with the approval of both sides. Under the provisions of a subsequent agreement, the civil police may be military police armed with nonautomatic weapons. Civilians who previously lived in the area that became the DMZ were permitted to return after the cease-fire, and both sides maintain small farming villages inside the DMZ in the vicinity of P'anmunjŏm.

The Military Armistice Commission (MAC) P'anmunjŏm conference site, roughly 800 meters in diameter and straddling the MDL, is called the Joint Security Area (JSA). A subsequent agreement established a Military Armistice Commission Headquarters Area (MACHA) consisting of the JSA and a corridor along the access roads through the DMZ. Each side is allowed to have 100 civil police in the MACHA at any one time. Of these, 5 officers and 30 enlisted men are permitted inside the JSA to provide security. Initially the guard forces of the two sides could move freely within the JSA, but after a fight on 18 August 1976 that resulted in the death of two UNC officers, a subsequent agreement of 6 September 1976 divided the JSA along the MDL, separating the guard forces.

The Headquarters of both the MAC and the Neutral Nations Supervisory Commission (NNSC) are in the JSA. Overall responsibility for supervising the armistice and for conducting inspections inside the DMZ rests with the MAC, whereas the mission of the NNSC was to monitor the introduction of military personnel and equipment at ports of entry outside the DMZ. Although the NNSC inspection mission has been defunct since 1956 and the North Koreans have refused to deal with the MAC since 1995, the Swiss and Swedish NNSC delegations still maintain a camp in the UNC portion of the MACHA. The North Koreans withdrew from the MAC in 1994, but they still maintain a presence in the JSA under the title "KPA P'anmunjŏm Mission" and continue to recognize the DMZ.

The nature of the DMZ has changed significantly since the Armistice Agreement was signed. The signs marking the MDL have deteriorated and many are now missing. Both sides have encroached on the DMZ and have emplaced mines, fences, fortifications, and other obstacles in violation of the Armistice Agreement prohibition on hazards to movement. Both sides have greatly exceeded the authorized number of personnel permitted in the DMZ and the so-called civil police are actually infantry soldiers armed with automatic assault rifles. Although the introduction of armored fighting vehicles and artillery is rare, the DMZ forces of both sides are known to have crew-served weapons, usually kept out of sight. Despite these changes, the DMZ still provides a buffer—however narrowed, attenuated, and violated it may be—between the military forces of the two sides.

—Donald W. Boose, Jr.

References:

Armistice Agreement of 27 July 1953 and subsequent agreements.

Bailey, Sydney D. *The Korean Armistice.* New York: St Martin's Press, 1992.

Hermes, Walter G. *United States Army in the Korean War: Truce Tent and Fighting Front.* Washington, DC: Office of the Chief of Military History, 1966.

U.S. Department of State, Bureau of Public Affairs. *Foreign Relations of the United States, 1951.* Vol. 7, *China and Korea.* Washington, DC: U.S. Government Printing Office, 1983.

———. *Foreign Relations of the United States, 1952–1954.* Vol. 15, *Korea.* Washington, DC: U.S. Government Printing Office, 1984.

See also: Armistice Agreement; Kaesŏng Truce Talks; Military Armistice Commission; Neutral Nations Supervisory Commission (NNSC); P'anmunjŏm Truce Talks; Truce Talks.

Deng Hua (Teng Hua)
(1910–1980)

Deputy commander and deputy political commissar of the Chinese People's Volunteer Army (CPVA). Born in Guiyang County, Hunan Province, in 1910, Deng Hua joined the Chinese Communist Party (CCP) in 1927. He was a Long March (1935) veteran with years of both combat and political commissar experience. Deng was closely associated with Peng Dehuai from at least 1928, and Deng was a strong supporter of regularization and modernization of the Chinese military. He was also associated with Lin Biao from the early 1940s. In January 1949 Deng formed the Eastern Task Group, which fought in the Pingjin Campaign, one of the three decisive campaigns of the Chinese Civil War (1945–1949). Deng's Fifteenth Army (composed of the XLIII, XLIV, XLV, and, later, the XLVIII Corps) took over the Second Field Army's mission in Jiangxi Province during June–July 1949. Deng was primarily responsible for the early administration of Guangdong Province and Guangzhou, the provincial capital. He supervised the attack on Hainan Island and temporarily administered it. He returned to the mainland in 1950 and became the chief of staff of the South China Military Region.

On 13 July 1950, Mao Zedong signed the "Resolution on Defending the Northeast Border Security," in which Deng was tasked to form a front command at Andong (Dandong) in Northeast China. Deng's Fifteenth Army was among the best of Lin Biao's forces in Guangdong Province.

Deng, who was assisted by Xie Fang, failed to exercise effective control over his forces, even though these were drawn primarily from Lin Biao's Fourth Field Army. Deng requested that Hong Xuezhi assist him, and Mao Zedong approved. Hong arrived in Shenyang on 15 August 1950 and was put in charge of training. On 30 August at a meeting in northeastern China, convened by Gao Gang, Deng gave his views on strategy and tactics for operations in Korea. Although Deng thought that U.S. firepower was well organized and effective, he believed that U.S. troops feared being cut off from their communication lines. He thought the U.S. forces could be defeated because they were politically unmotivated; inferior in night fighting, close combat, and bayonet charges; tactically inflexible; and could not endure hardship.

Deng believed that U.S. forces would have greater logistical problems than the Chinese forces because the U.S. troops were fighting far away from home. Nonetheless, he ruled out frontal assault against U.S. defensive positions. Rather, Deng concluded that Chinese forces must concentrate on the tactics of "a determined and audacious penetration," "close-combat tactics," and "night operations."

Peng Dehuai named Deng one of his deputy commanders and deputy political commissars. Deng was entrusted with crossing the Yalu River, while Peng went on ahead into North Korea because of the deteriorating situation for Korean People's Army (KPA) North Korean forces. On 21 October 1950, Mao Zedong ordered Deng Hua immediately to move the XIII Army Corps from Andong into North Korea and to link up with Peng Dehuai to establish effective command and control. At a command meeting on 22 January 1951, in preparation for the spring offensive, Deng promoted a strategy of mobile defense in which CPVA forces would abandon a position when attacked and counterattack whenever forces were ready.

In February 1951 Deng Hua led the attack on Hoensŏng, routing the entire Republic of Korea Army (ROKA) 8th Division, but his follow-on action at Chip'yŏng-ni proved ill-advised. Lacking effective intelligence, Deng underestimated his enemy strength. He believed that the U.S./UN forces at Wŏnju would continue to retreat and would not reinforce Chip'yŏng-ni; therefore, it could not withstand an attack. Deng ordered an immediate attack, hoping to displace his enemy quickly, but the operation failed.

Between 10 July and October 1951 Deng served as the first senior Chinese delegate to the negotiation team for the Armistice negotiations from 10 July 1951 to 27 July 1953. The team that Deng headed also included Bian Zhangwu, Ding Guoyu, Xie Fang, and Chai Chengwen. Deng was personally selected by Zhou Enlai and the central leadership to match U.S. Navy Admiral C. Turner Joy in rank. The negotiation team was assisted by a team of hand-picked diplomatic specialists headed by Li Kenong, first deputy foreign minister and Central Military Commission (CMC) intelligence director, and Qian Guanhua, two of Zhou Enlai's top aides. Deng left the negotiations when it became apparent that a quick settlement would not be possible.

In late spring 1953 Deng argued that Chinese forces should adopt a retaliatory (*zhenfeng xiangdui*) strategy and launch offensive operations, rather than continue to wait in the defense. Although the CMC endorsed Deng's proposal on 3 April 1953, Mao Zedong intervened and delayed the operation until the armistice talks stalled. In the meantime, Chinese offensive plans were shifted to the South Korean forces, with a surprise attack on 10 June.

Deng believed that the Korean War had provided an invaluable lesson in how a weak military could defeat a strong military in modern warfare. He argued that "an army's political quality will still play a decisive role, no matter how important material and technological conditions may be." Although he called political work the army's "magic weapon," Deng also recognized the importance of "correct strategic thinking" and shrewd "execution of campaign or battle plans."

In 1956 Deng became a full member (of 91) of the Eighth Central Committee. He was one of the six officers with Fourth Field Army affiliations to achieve full-member status. Subsequently, he commanded the Shenyang Military Region until 1959, when he was removed in conjunction with the purge of Peng Dehuai. Demoted, he was reassigned as vice-governor of Sichuan Province. Deng was one of the few generals who spoke out on Peng Dehuai's behalf in August 1959 when he was first criticized.

Deng survived the 1966–1976 Cultural Revolution. After Mao Zedong's death in 1976, Deng was one of the first of Peng Dehuai's associates to be rehabilitated. He became the vice-president of the Academy of Military Science in Beijing and was appointed an alternate member of the Ninth Central Committee. Deng died in 1980.

—*Susan M. Puska*

References:

Klein, Donald W., and Anne B. Clark. *Biographic Dictionary of Chinese Communism, 1921–1965.* Vol. 2, *Lo Jui-ch'ing–Yun T'ai-ying.* Cambridge, MA: Harvard University Press, 1971.

MacFarquahar, Roderick. *The Origins of the Cultural Revolution.* Vol. 2, *The Great Leap Forward, 1958–60.* New York: Columbia University Press, 1983.

Wilhelm, Alfred D. *The Chinese at the Negotiating Table: Style and Characteristics.* Washington, DC: National Defense University Press, 1994.

Zhang, Shu Guang. *Mao's Military Romanticism: China and the Korean War, 1950–1953.* Lawrence: University Press of Kansas, 1995.

See also: China, People's Republic of: Army; Gao Gang (Kao Kang); Peng Dehuai (Peng Te-huai); Xie Fang (Hsieh Fang).

Detachment 2

U.S. Air Force reconnaissance unit. The onset of hostilities in Korea caught the U.S. Air Force unprepared for large-scale reconnaissance operations. Initially, only a handful of marginally obsolete Boeing RB-29s and RB-50s were deployed in Japan to support military operations. Partly to offset this condition, in July 1950 the Strategic Air Command elected to dispatch three of its modern North American RB-45C Tornados to the Far East Air Force. This four-jet design was then the world's most capable photographic aircraft. Its twelve cameras and trimetrogon lenses could map 30,000 square miles from 45,000 feet. However, because the Tornado had only been in service for three months, there were no qualified SAC personnel available to operate them. Volunteers were secured from the Tactical Air Command's 84th Light Bombardment Squadron (363rd Tactical Reconnaissance Wing) based at Langley AFB, Virginia. It had operated the B-45A bomber version since 1948. The crews received several weeks of additional training in RB-45Cs at Barksdale AFB, Louisiana before being shipped to Yokota, Japan by late summer.

Given the nature of their mission and equipment, the three RB-45Cs were known only as Detachment A. The planes commenced photographic missions in November 1950, with several sweeps along the Yalu River. They soon demonstrated the viability of jet-powered aerial reconnaissance.

On 4 December 1950, however, an RB-45C piloted by Captain Charles McDonough, was intercepted by Russian MiG-15s and shot down near Sinuiju in the world's first jet bomber interception. However, the remaining two aircraft continued to fly successfully for several more months, and in the spring of 1951 they began the first regular incursions into Chinese and Soviet airspace.

In May 1950, the need for better planning and facilities led to Detachment A being transferred to the 91st Strategic Reconnaissance Wing at Yokota, where it was renamed Detachment 2. As before, its three RB-45Cs maintained a steady stream of overflights into Communist-controlled areas that were too dangerous for the slower RB-29s and RB-50s. These included Sakhalin Island, Vladivostok, Manchuria, and several points along the China coast. The Soviet and Chinese air forces made several determined attempts to intercept these overflights, but were largely unsuccessful because of careful monitoring by nearby ferret aircraft and the Tornado's flying capabilities.

Aviation history was also made on 14 July 1951, when an RB-45C linked up with a KB-29 tanker in the world's first air-to-air refueling of a combat mission. Detachment 2 remained in operation throughout the duration of the Korean War, having successfully completed 315 combat missions and a minimum of 12 Top Secret flights. A handful of CIA-sponsored projects, unrecorded in Air Force records, were apparently also conducted. After 1 December 1953, the surviving aircraft were subsequently channeled into a new formation, designated 6091st Flight, which continued secret surveillance of Soviet installations for an indeterminate number of months. That same year the unheralded, hard-working RB-45C, which did so much to advance the state of aerial espionage, was dropped from the SAC inventory in favor of Boeing's RB-47 Stratojet.

—*John C. Fredriksen*

References:

Fredriksen, John C. "Detachment 2 Goes to War: RB-45C Reconnaissance Activity in Korea, 1950-1953," *American Aviation Historical Society Journal* Vol. 41 (Winter, 1996): 282-287.

Jolidon, Lawrence. *Last Seen Alive*. Washington, DC: Ink Slinger Press, 1995.

Lashmar, Paul. *Spy Flights of the Cold War*. Annapolis, MD: Naval Institute Press, 1996.

See also: Aircraft; Reconnaissance.

Dodd-Colson Prisoner-of-War Incident
(May 1952)

An uprising by Communist prisoners of war (POWs) at the Kŏje-do camp in May 1952. By the beginning of 1952, the United Nations Command (UNC) delegation at the P'anmunjŏm truce talks had taken a stand on the principle of voluntary repatriation, and the Communists needed a strong showing in favor of forcible repatriation to strengthen their hand at the bargaining table. Beginning in 1952 the Communists

allowed trained agents to be captured as POWs. They were instructed to organize the Communist POWs and foment riots and other disturbances inside UN POW compounds for the purpose of incurring UN punitive countermeasures, which the Communists could then exploit at the peace talks.

On 18 February and 13 March 1952, riots occurred in several UNC POW compounds. In attempting to quell these disturbances, UNC guards fired into the POWs, killing a total of 89 and wounding 166. The Communist side at the truce talks then denounced the UN for "barbarous massacres" and "atrocities." On 28 April 1952, the Communists broke off the peace talks and the POW riots intensified.

On 7 May 1952, during a riot at a camp at Kŏje-do, a small island twenty miles southwest of Pusan, Communist POWs seized U.S. camp commander Brigadier General Francis T. Dodd. The POWs announced that Dodd would not be released until certain demands were met and if there were any attempts to use force he would be killed.

Eighth Army Commander General James A. Van Fleet appointed Brigadier General Charles F. Colson the new camp commander and sent him to Kŏje-do to free Dodd by military force, if necessary. Colson received an ultimatum from the prisoners stipulating a number of conditions upon which Dodd's safe release depended. To obtain Dodd's release, Colson signed a statement conceding that numerous POWs had been killed and wounded by UNC guards, and stating: "I do admit that there has [sic] been instances of bloodshed where many PW [sic] have been killed and wounded by UN forces." Colson promised that he would do all within his power "to eliminate further violence and bloodshed." He guaranteed "humane treatment" of UNC POWs in accordance with the principles of international law and agreed that there would be "no more forcible screening of any remaining POWs in camp."

Dodd was released unharmed, but the Communists exploited Colson's statement as further proof of UNC atrocities, humiliating the United States and Eighth Army and raising serious questions worldwide over the validity of the voluntary repatriation doctrine. Both Dodd's capture and Colson's statement were major international news and had a devastating impact on the UNC's international image.

A subsequent U.S. Army investigating board found both generals blameless, but General Van Fleet and UNC Commander in Chief General Mark W. Clark were outraged and convened another board of inquiry. This board reversed the original decision and both generals were reduced in rank and retired from the army.

General Clark assigned a new camp commander and told Brigadier General Haydon L. Boatner to clean out the compounds and restore order and UN authority. On 10 June, Boatner sent in paratroopers backed by six M-47 Patton tanks and, after a battle of over an hour in which more than 150 prisoners were killed, the situation was brought under control. There was another public outcry but, although there was other sporadic trouble in the prison camps, it was never the magnitude of that over Kŏje-do.

—*James H. Willbanks*

References:

Alexander, Bevin. *Korea: The First War We Lost.* New York: Hippocrene Books, 1986.

Blair, Clay. *The Forgotten War: America in Korea, 1950–1953.* New York: Times Books, 1987.

Fehrenbach, T. R. *This Kind of War: A Study in Unpreparedness.* New York: Macmillan, 1962.

Hermes, Walter G. *United States Army in the Korean War: Truce Tent and Fighting Front.* Washington, DC: Office of the Chief of Military History, 1966.

Vetter, Harold J. *Mutiny on Koje Island.* Rutland, VT: Charles E. Tuttle, 1965.

See also: Boatner, Haydon Lemaire; Clark, Mark W.; P'anmunjŏm Truce Talks; Repatriation, Voluntary; Van Fleet, James Alward.

Doyle, James H.
(1897–1981)

U.S. Navy rear admiral. James Henry Doyle was born on 29 August 1897, in Jamaica, New York, on Long Island. He graduated from the U.S. Naval Academy, Annapolis, in 1920. Commissioned an ensign in the U.S. Navy, he earned a law degree from George Washington University in 1929 and was assigned to the office of the navy's Judge Advocate General in Washington, D.C., from 1932 to 1935. During World War II, Doyle was an operations officer and staff commander of Amphibious Forces South Pacific, serving in the Guadalcanal and Solomons Islands campaigns. He commanded the cruiser *Pasadena* and advanced to rear admiral by 1947.

Doyle was in charge of submarine demolition at Coronado, California, when the Korean War began. Ordered to Japan at the behest of General Douglas MacArthur, who recognized his expertise and experience with amphibious tactics, Doyle commanded the U.S. Amphibious Forces Far East (Task Force 90). His first mission was to move men and supplies from Japan to Korea. The 1st Cavalry Division landed at P'ohang in July 1950, and army and navy officers praised Doyle and his staff for this rapid deployment.

Doyle next participated in the planning for the Inch'ŏn landing. Naval officers, including Doyle, were at first skeptical of MacArthur's plan because the port of Inch'ŏn had narrow channels, strong currents, and dangerous tides that could leave ships stuck in mud flats, making them vulnerable to enemy gunfire. Aware of these hazards, Doyle told MacArthur at a briefing, "General, I have not been asked nor have I volunteered my opinion about this landing. If I were asked, however, the best I can say is that Inchon is not impossible." MacArthur said that he would withdraw the landing force if enemy resistance was too great, but Doyle exclaimed, "No, General, we don't know how to do that. Once we start ashore we'll keep going!"

As the date for the invasion neared, Doyle also expressed concern about an approaching typhoon, but MacArthur insisted that invasion preparations continue. Doyle participated in strategy and planning sessions on board the battleship *Missouri* with Seventh Fleet commander Vice Admiral Arthur D. Struble and 1st Marine Division commander Major General Oliver P. Smith.

Commanding the attack force from aboard his flagship, the *Mount McKinley*, on 15 September 1950, Doyle ordered that the flag signaling "Land the Landing Force" be raised before sunrise. The resulting Inch'ŏn landing was a success and led to the recapture of the Republic of Korea (ROK) capital of Seoul.

Doyle's next mission was to reload X Corps troops at Inch'ŏn in early October and transport them by sea to Korea's east coast for an amphibious landing at Wŏnsan. Delayed until minesweepers cleared navigable channels to the port, Doyle's attack force began landing without resistance on 25 October.

After Chinese forces entered the war, Doyle commanded the reverse amphibious operation, evacuating soldiers and civilians in frigid December weather from Hŭngnam and other North Korean east coast ports. Over the span of 14 days, 105,000 military personnel, 17,500 vehicles, 350,000 tons of cargo, and 91,000 Korean refugees were evacuated. Doyle also arranged for ships' bakeries to prepare bread and rice for refugees remaining in Hŭngnam. From the deck of the *Mount McKinley*, Doyle watched the last U.S. troops blow up militarily valuable buildings and materials in Hŭngnam. "As we pulled out with all friendly troops embarked, [Major General Edward M.] Almond and I, through our binoculars, saw Chinese Communist troops coming over the ridge behind Hŭngnam, only three or four miles away," Doyle remembered.

Leaving Korea, Doyle became president of the Navy Board of Inspection and Survey in Washington, D.C., and then chairman of the Joint Amphibious Board at Norfolk, Virginia. He retired from the navy in 1953 and practiced law first in Austin, Texas, and then in San Francisco, California. He was active in civic affairs in both cities. Doyle died in Oakland, California, on 9 February 1981.

—*Elizabeth D. Schafer*

References:

Cagle, Malcolm W., and Frank A. Manson. *The Sea War in Korea.* New York: Arno Press, 1980.

New York Times, 11 February 1981.

Washington Post, 13 February 1981.

Who's Who in America, 1954–1955. Vol. 28, *1955.* Chicago: A. N. Marquis, 1955.

See also: Amphibious Force Far East (Task Force Ninety); Hŭngnam Evacuation; Inch'ŏn Landings: Operation CHROMITE; MacArthur, Douglas; Smith, Oliver Prince; Struble, Arthur D.; Tenth Corps; United States Navy; Wŏnsan Landing.

Draft

Selective service, known informally as the draft, was the primary and essential means of personnel procurement during the Korean War. In 1940 the United States adopted the first peacetime draft in its history with the passage of the Selective Training and Selective Service Act. The draft law was renewed during and immediately after World War II. Believing that volunteers would generate sufficient personnel, President Harry S. Truman's administration did not press for renewal in March 1947, and selective service was allowed to lapse. At the time, the administration was focusing on universal military training (UMT), six months of military training for all able-bodied 18-year-old men who would serve as a trained reserve component in the event of a military crises.

However, after the Czechoslovakian coup in February 1948, the U.S. Congress revived selective service in June 1948. The main thrust of the 1948 draft law was to spur volunteers rather than be the primary means of acquiring personnel, as the draft had been in World War II. The law was successful. Enough volunteers responded that by early 1950 almost no one was being drafted. Truman's State of the Union Message in 1950 requested another extension of selective service. While the House and Senate worked out differences in their separate bills, the Korean War erupted. Congress responded with an immediate one-year extension.

Still, the United States entered the Korean War with a very small regular military, little active reserve component, and an almost moribund procurement system. Although U.S. Far East Commander General Douglas MacArthur called for additional personnel in Korea to stem the Communist invasion, Army Chief of Staff General Omar N. Bradley was not willing to jeopardize requirements in Europe to funnel more troops to Korea. While waiting for the new draft to procure men who then had to be trained, reserve units of World War II veterans filled the void. By 1 September 1950, more than 600 reserve units were recalled; however, most were inactive units not ready for combat. Also, families complained about recalling the veterans who had already served their time. As the draft began to produce soldiers, the Department of Defense issued calls for 50,000 inductees in September and in October, 70,000 for November, and 40,000 for December 1950.

When MacArthur demanded more personnel during the Chinese intervention in Korea in late November 1950, draft calls jumped to 80,000 per month for the first three months of 1951. However, when the army exceeded its authorized strength, draft numbers decreased in the spring. In fiscal year 1951, more than 587,000 men were drafted and the Defense Department related that most of the 630,000 volunteers who entered during this period were draft motivated. The United States could not have fought the war without the draft. Although only the army employed the draft, the threat of involuntary induction generated enough volunteers to fill navy and air force needs.

In 1951 Truman authorized deferments for college students, which in effect allowed many to escape the war. Labor unions complained bitterly and unsuccessfully about this class bias. Fathers also enjoyed exemptions, and farm workers received more generous deferment consideration than did those in other sectors of the economy. Despite some controversy over deferment policies, public opinion surveys demonstrated that most Americans viewed the draft favorably.

In 1951 Congress passed the Universal Military Training and Service Act, which extended selective service until 1955. It also provided for a universal military training option to fill the Reserves; however, Congress had to vote specific authorization to implement this provision. The new law authorized the creation of a National Security Training Commission to submit recommendations concerning UMT implementation to Congress. Truman appointed a five-member commission, which returned a report in October 1951. Hearings on the commission's report in early 1952 came to an abrupt end when the House voted to recommit its UMT implementation bill to committee and a Senate bill also failed.

By 1953 the armed forces stood at 3.5 million men, 1.5 million of whom were inducted through selective service. Although the Korean War military was not demobilized as rapidly as that after World War II, President Dwight D. Eisenhower's administration reduced the armed forces to 2.47 million by the end of the decade; the Army was reduced sharply from 1.5 million to 860,000 men. The draft was retained with generous deferments for education, various occupations, and dependency. With annual induction calls below 100,000, the draft had minimal impact on the lives of U.S. youth in the post–Korean War decade.

—Joe P. Dunn

References:

Flynn, George Q. *The Draft, 1940–1973.* Lawrence: University Press of Kansas, 1993.

Gerhardt, James M. *The Draft and Public Policy: Issues in Military Manpower Procurement, 1945–1970.* Columbus: Ohio State University Press, 1971.

See also: Bradley, Omar Nelson; MacArthur, Douglas; Truman, Harry S.; United States Army.

Drumright, Everett Francis
(1906–)

U.S. diplomat and embassy counselor in Seoul during the Korean War. Born in Drumright, Oklahoma, on 15 September 1906, Everett Francis Drumright attended the Oklahoma Agricultural and Mechanical College during 1925–1926 and then earned a bachelor's degree from the University of Oklahoma in 1929.

Drumright entered the U.S. Foreign Service in 1931. His first posting was at Ciudad Juarez, Mexico, as vice-consul. He then was posted to Hankow, China, and was a language officer in Beijing (Peking) during 1932–1933. Drumright was a vice-consul at Shanghai from 1934 to 1937 and served as third and second secretary in the U.S. embassy at Nanjing (Nanking) from 1938 to 1941. Before returning to the United States in 1944, he was a counselor and first secretary at Chongqing (Chungking), the wartime capital of the Republic of China.

Employed by the Department of State in Washington from 1944 to 1946, Drumright held posts in U.S. embassies in London, Tokyo, and Seoul after World War II. When U.S. Ambassador to Korea John J. Muccio visited the United States, Drumright, his assistant, was in charge of the embassy's concerns in the Republic of Korea (ROK). He wrote most of the official cable dispatches from Seoul to Washington because Muccio did not like this task. Drumright often assumed the authority to send telegrams without clearing them with Muccio. Colleague Harold Noble, who worked with Drumright in Seoul, praised him as being "hard-driving, energetic, and dogmatic." Noble noted that Drumright reviewed every document sent from or to the embassy and was aware of all of the embassy's activities, ranging from motor pool assignments to requests for air power. Drumright's fluency in Chinese was helpful because some Korean government officials had been exiled in China when the Japanese occupied Korea.

Drumright focused on strengthening the ROK, but he experienced resistance from President Syngman Rhee who was unsure of U.S. intentions. Drumright, as many of his peers, did not envision a full-scale Democratic People's Republic of Korea (North Korea) invasion of the ROK. On 23 June 1950, he sent a cable to the State Department claiming, "The [South] Korean Army, in particular, has made enormous progress during the past year." Two days later, when he received news of the invasion, Drumright thought it was probably just a limited attack and sought confirmation before notifying the State Department. He was the first person in the embassy to learn about the invasion. Once he had received verification of the intensity of the assault, Drumright called Muccio to initiate policy decisions regarding evacuation of embassy staff. The men met at the embassy, where Muccio stat-

ed that he did not want to leave Seoul, but Drumright insisted that the U.S. embassy staff move south with the ROK government.

Riding in his Buick, Drumright joined the procession of official vehicles heading to Taejŏn to regroup with the ROK leaders. While he worked in Taejŏn, Drumright actively sought U.S. military support to appease President Rhee, who angrily complained about the lack of sufficient troops to defend South Korea. Drumright also helped move the ROK leaders to safety at Taegu in mid-July when Korean People's Army (KPA, North Korean) forces approached Taejŏn. From July to September 1950 Drumright wrote detailed letters to State Department official John M. Allison, providing factual information and his opinions of political and military events in Korea. Drumright often accompanied military attaché Colonel Bob Edwards to battlefields because Drumright believed that to make informed decisions embassy officers should not isolate themselves from the realities of combat. Drumright's reports in which he stated that only reunification would end the Korean War may have inspired Allison to support troops crossing the 38th parallel.

When Seoul was restored to ROK control in September 1950, Drumright returned to the embassy with his colleagues. He complained to Allison that his knowledge of military events was often limited to radio and newspaper reports. That fall he cabled intelligence information to the State Department regarding the possibility of People's Republic of China (PRC) forces entering the war. Drumright's messages reveal an underestimation of PRC intentions, as when he cabled: "Eighth Army intelligence is of view, with which Embassy inclined to concur, Sino Communists will avoid overt intervention."

In 1951 Drumright left Korea and went to India, serving in embassies at New Delhi and Bombay. Two years later he transferred to the State Department Office of Far Eastern Affairs. Drumright worked four years in Hong Kong and then concluded his diplomatic career as ambassador to the Republic of China on Taiwan from 1958 to 1962. Drumright was named a trustee of the China Foundation for Promotion of Education and Culture and received the Cordon of Brilliant Star from the Republic of China for his services.

—*Elizabeth D. Schafer*

References:

Noble, Harold J. *Embassy at War*. Seattle: University of Washington Press, 1975.

U.S. Department of State, Bureau of Public Affairs. *Foreign Relations of the United States, 1950*. Vol. 7, *Korea*. Washington, DC: U.S. Government Printing Office, 1976.

Who's Who in America, 1966–1967. Chicago: Marquis Who's Who, 1967.

See also: Allison, John M.; Delaying the North Korean Offensive; Korea, Democratic People's Republic of, Invasion of the

Dulles, John Foster
(1888–1959)

U.S. secretary of state, 1953–1959. Born on 25 February 1888, in Watertown, New York, John Foster Dulles was the oldest of five children. Because his father was a Presbyterian minister and Dulles was raised in a conservative, church-oriented home, many of his later foreign policy pronouncements reflected a high degree of religiosity.

Dulles attended public schools in Watertown before attending Princeton University, where he graduated with honors. His interest in diplomacy began at an early age. His grandfather John Watson Foster was President Benjamin Harrison's secretary of state and his uncle Robert Lansing would later be President Woodrow Wilson's secretary of state. The influence of his forbears was great and opened many doors for him throughout his life.

Dulles's exposure to formal diplomacy began while he was still in college; in 1907 he was granted leave from Princeton to attend the Second Hague Conference as a secretary for the Imperial Government of China, a position his grandfather had secured for him. At the end of the conference Dulles studied at the University of Paris for a year; there he encountered the philosopher Henri Bergson, whose teachings influenced him during his early career.

On his return to the United States, Dulles completed his degree at Princeton and entered law school at George Washington University. Dulles never formally completed his law degree, but passed the New York State Bar exams in 1911. He then took a position as a lawyer with Sullivan and Cromwell.

Dulles nonetheless kept up his interest in diplomacy. When World War I began, Robert Lansing, then secretary of state, sent Dulles on a tour of Latin America to lobby support for the United States. Dulles spent the remainder of the war as a lawyer for the War Industries Board before Lansing invited him to the Paris Peace Conference to work for the U.S. delegation.

During the 1920s and 1930s Dulles continued work for Sullivan and Cromwell, rising to senior partner while maintaining an active interest in foreign affairs. He avoided partisan politics and confined himself to writing about diplomacy. In 1937 Dulles became involved in politics in a direct way when he assisted Thomas Dewey in becoming district attorney in New York. Like Dewey, Dulles became associated with the moderate wing of the Republican Party.

Throughout the 1940s Dulles continued to be viewed with suspicion by the Republican right-wing, especially as he served as President Harry S. Truman's delegate to the United Nations from 1946 until 1948. His own turn at office came in 1949 when then New York Governor Dewey appointed him to serve out the rest of Robert Wagner's U.S. Senate term. Although Dulles was rapidly being viewed as a foreign policy expert by both parties, Republican suspicions were again raised in 1950 when President Truman named him to be his special ambassador to Japan for negotiations on a Japanese peace treaty.

By this time Dulles had grown increasingly worried over Soviet intentions in the Cold War. Events in Europe and Asia convinced him that the Soviets were determined and aggressive, willing even to risk war to achieve their objectives. The Korean War confirmed his fears.

Dulles believed that the Soviet Union was behind the 1950 Democratic People's Republic (North Korea) invasion of the Republic of Korea (ROK, South Korea), and he convinced himself that Beijing and Moscow were preparing for conflict on a world scale. He came to view the Truman administration as too cautious and unwilling to confront communism with the determination required. As soon as Senate ratification of the Japanese Peace Treaty was complete, Dulles resigned from his special position in the State Department to began working on the foreign policy plank of the Republican Party for the 1952 presidential election.

Dwight D. Eisenhower had been a reluctant candidate for the presidency, but, once committed, he became a formidable challenger. Campaigning on the slogan known as K1C2 (Korea, Communism, and corruption), he exploited the public perception that the Democrats and their standard bearer Adlai A. Stevenson were soft on Cold War issues and were failing to contain the spread of communism.

Perhaps even more damaging to the Democrats was the growing unpopularity of the Korean War. Truman had not been able to break the stalemate and a settlement seemed distant. Eisenhower capitalized on his image as a war hero to offer strong, expert leadership when he made his pledge that if elected, he would "go to Korea." Although he offered few specifics, the promise that he would go to Korea gave hope that his military expertise would result in an end to the conflict.

Dulles's role in the Eisenhower presidential campaign was to act as foreign policy advisor. His involvement in the campaign began in May 1952, when he and Eisenhower met in Paris to begin an on-going dialogue over foreign policy. He continued this after Eisenhower's victory when the new president named him his secretary of state. Eisenhower, who was concerned over the growing costs of the Cold War, was impressed with Dulles's views; together they fashioned a policy that was popularly known as Massive Retaliation and later as the New Look. It was also known as "more bang for a buck."

The essence of Massive Retaliation was that the United States would scale back costly, conventional armaments and maintain its security through reliance on nuclear weapons. Dulles frequently implied publicly that, if U.S. interests were threatened, the use of nuclear weapons would be considered. Massive Retaliation was tested when Eisenhower set about trying to resolve the Korean impasse almost immediately after taking office.

Within weeks of his inauguration, President-elect Eisenhower did in fact go to Korea to confer with United Nations commander Lieutenant General Mark Clark and ROK President Syngman Rhee. Upon returning home to consider his options, in mid-May 1953 Eisenhower instructed Dulles, then on a trip to India, to let it be known that the United States was prepared to consider employing nuclear weapons to break the deadlock in the peace talks. Although there is still debate over the impact of Dulles's threat in ending the deadlock, the Armistice Agreement was signed in July 1953.

Dulles remained as secretary of state until his death from cancer in 1959. During his six years as secretary, Dulles was always the chief spokesman for Eisenhower's foreign policy, of which Massive Retaliation remained the center piece. Seemingly, the value of this was confirmed in the armistice ending fighting in Korea. In the years afterward, Dulles and Eisenhower elaborated on their Massive Retaliation doctrine. They also sought to "roll back" Communism. After providing encouragement to Communist regimes in Eastern Europe to rebel, the Eisenhower administration provided scant tangible support when that actually happened in Hungary in 1956. Critics also saw Massive Retaliation as unnecessarily dangerous and provocative. Dulles rather than Eisenhower drew most of the criticism for this. Dulles died in Washington, D.C., on 24 May 1959.

—*Phillip A. Cantrell II*

References:

Guhin, Michael A. *John Foster Dulles: A Statesman and His Times*. New York: Columbia University Press, 1972.

Hoopes, Townsend. *The Devil and John Foster Dulles*. Boston: Little, Brown, 1973.

Pruessen, Ronald W. *John Foster Dulles: The Road to Power*. New York: Macmillan, 1982.

See also: Clark, Mark W.; Dulles's Trip to Korea; Eisenhower, Dwight D.; Japanese Peace Treaty; Stevenson, Adlai E.; Syngman Rhee; Truman, Harry S.

Dulles's Trip to Korea
(15–20 June 1950)

By mid-January 1950 the Truman administration had made it clear that both Formosa and Korea were outside the geographic area that the United States was prepared to defend militarily. However, as President Harry S. Truman prepared to send his special representative John Foster Dulles to the Far East to begin talks with Japan over a peace treaty, anger and criticism were mounting in the U.S. Congress over what was perceived as the president's reluctance to take a stronger stance against communism in Asia.

When Dulles stopped in Korea on 15 June 1950 on his way to Japan, he sought to reassure Republic of Korea (ROK) President Syngman Rhee. In an address before the Korean National Assembly on the 19th and against the backdrop of border clashes, Dulles told Koreans that the United States supported them in their struggle against North Korean "aggression." Although Dulles offered no specifics or guarantees of U.S. support for the ROK, he implied assistance from the West. To many observers at the time, it appeared as if Dulles's remarks were phrased in part to rectify the damage caused by earlier statements by Truman and Secretary of State Dean Acheson that had excluded the ROK from the U.S. defensive perimeter. Dulles also journeyed to the 38th parallel and was photographed in the company of Republic of Korea Army (ROKA) officers glaring into North Korea.

When the Democratic People's Republic of Korea (DPRK, North Korea) invaded the South on 25 June, Dulles and his entourage were in Japan. Dulles was deeply troubled by the news. China and the Soviet Union had signed a mutual defense treaty in February and he saw the DPRK invasion as a sign of greater hostilities to come. He also assumed that the invasion was directed and supported by China and the Soviet Union and that Japan would be next if the aggression were not halted in Korea. He consequently recommended that the United States intervene with force to prevent a ROK defeat.

Dulles also advocated swift action on the Japanese Peace Treaty. He soon returned to Washington to finalize the details, convinced more than ever that Japan represented vital U.S. security interests in Asia. If the ROK fell, communism would be virtually unchallenged on the Asian continent and Japan would be the only bulwark against further aggression. Dulles thus sought to negotiate a treaty that would enhance Japan's economy and strength. He originally hoped that Japanese Prime Minister Yoshida Shigeru could be persuaded to accept rearmament of his country.

After negotiations on this point stalled, Dulles settled for an agreement that allowed U.S. troops to be permanently stationed in Japan.

The Korean invasion contributed to a hardening in Dulles's personal attitude toward Communist expansion. Before and during his June 1950 visit to Korea, Dulles had harbored the belief that the Soviet Union and China would not risk open aggression and instead rely on subversion. The DPRK invasion confirmed his worst fears that the Cold War was entering a new and potentially more dangerous stage. The United States would have to defend its interests with greater vigor.

—Phillip A. Cantrell II

References:

Finn, Richard B. *Winners in Peace: MacArthur, Yoshida and Postwar Japan.* Berkeley: University of California Press, 1992.

Hoopes, Townsend. *The Devil and John Foster Dulles.* Boston: Little, Brown, 1973.

Pruessen, Ronald W. *John Foster Dulles: The Road to Power.* New York: Macmillan, 1982.

See also: Dulles, John Foster; Japanese Peace Treaty; Syngman Rhee; Truman, Harry S.

E

Economic Stabilization Agency (ESA)

U.S. government agency created by executive order on 9 September 1950 to carry out the mandates of the Defense Production Act. This executive order also enumerated the two key operational agencies under the aegis of the ESA: the Wage Stabilization Board and the Office of Price Stabilization. The main responsibility of the ESA was to control inflation through macroeconomic stabilization, primarily by the use of price and wage controls. The Truman administration designed the ESA along the same lines as the Office of Defense Mobilization, that is, the ESA was to be a policymaking and coordinating office only; actual price and wage controls would be administered through the appropriate constituent agencies.

The agency's other major responsibility was to serve as a clearinghouse of information, both public and administrative. Thus the director of the ESA served as the main liaison between the economic stabilization offices and the various industrial mobilization agencies. The director also provided the American public with reports, news, and other information dealing with the policies and implementation of wage and price controls throughout the Korean War.

As with the other stabilization and mobilization agencies of the war, the ESA used advisory committees representing a diverse cross-section of industries and interest groups. These committees kept key sectors of the economy working together on issues relating to price and wage controls. They also provided the ESA with statistical information and data that were used to establish and modify price and wage controls.

During its existence, the ESA was under the direction of several different administrators, including Alan Valentine, Eric Johnston, Roger Lowell Putnam, and Michael V. DiSalle. President Dwight D. Eisenhower liquidated the ESA, along with its constituent agencies, in the spring of 1953, just weeks before the Armistice Agreement was signed. No advocate of economic controls, and in light of easing inflation and materials shortages, Eisenhower chose to bring a formal end to wage and price controls in the United States. He effected this by closing all of the stabilization agencies, including the ESA.

—*Paul G. Pierpaoli, Jr.*

References:

Hogan, Michael J. *A Cross of Iron: Harry S. Truman and the Origins of the National Security State, 1945–1954.* Cambridge, UK: Cambridge University Press, 1998.

Pierpaoli, Paul G., Jr. *Truman and Korea: The Political Culture of the Early Cold War.* Columbia: University of Missouri Press, 1999.

Rockoff, Hugh. *Drastic Measures: History of Wage and Price Controls in the United States.* New York: Cambridge University Press, 1984.

See also: Defense Production Act; Eisenhower, Dwight D.; Mobilization; Office of Defense Mobilization (ODM); Office of Price Stabilization (OPS); United States: Home Front; Wage Stabilization Board (WSB).

Eden, Anthony
(1897–1977)

British foreign secretary during the Korean War. Born on 12 June 1897, on the family estate in County Durham, Robert Anthony Eden attended Eton between 1911 and 1915. He volunteered for military service in World War I, becoming an infantry lieutenant in the King's Royal Rifle Corps. During two years' service on the western front, Eden rose to the rank of captain and won the Military Cross for gallantry. In 1918, at age 20, he became the youngest brigade major in the British Army.

At Oxford University between 1919 and 1922 Eden studied oriental languages and graduated with honors. The next year he was elected as a Conservative member of Parliament and served until 1925. Independently wealthy, Eden traveled abroad for many years. During 1931–1934, he was undersecretary for foreign affairs, specializing in defense, colonial, and Middle East issues. In June 1935 he was elevated to cabinet rank as lord privy seal and became minister of League of Nations affairs. That October he became the youngest secretary of state for foreign affairs in 100 years under Prime Minister Stanley Baldwin, and he continued in that position under later Prime Minister Neville Chamberlain. Eden opposed Chamberlain's appeasement of Nazi Germany and Fascist Italy, however, resigning his position in protest in February 1938.

When Britain declared war on Germany in September 1939, Eden accepted Chamberlain's call to become secretary of state for dominion affairs. The following May, when Winston Churchill became prime minister, he appointed the high-principled, hardworking, and well-organized Eden to the post of secretary of state for war. Six months later, in October 1940, Churchill made Eden his foreign secretary. Eden advised the prime minister on matters of diplomacy during World War II and was thought extremely influential in Allied decision making. He aided in the formulation of the Atlantic Charter, lend-lease agreements, and alliances with the United States and Soviet Union. He also played a key role at the Teheran, Cairo, Yalta, and Potsdam Conferences. Eden led the British delegation to the San Francisco Conference establishing the United Nations in April 1945.

Although a close friend and advisor to Churchill, Eden often disagreed with Churchill's hard-line views toward communism, although he later came to share them. Eden left office when Churchill was voted from power in July 1945, but he supported British foreign policies that favored the Truman Doctrine, the Marshall Plan, the Berlin Airlift, and the North Atlantic Treaty Organization (NATO). After the general election of October 1951, Eden agreed to return as foreign secretary and deputy prime minister when Churchill again became prime minister.

Although the British government supported the U.S. decision to intervene in Korea and sent troops to the United Nations (UN) Command, Eden and Labour Prime Minister Clement R. Attlee differed significantly with the Americans, especially Secretary of State John Foster Dulles, about the nature of communism and People's Republic of China (PRC, Chinese Communist) participation in the war. Whereas the Americans viewed the Chinese military intervention as part of a Soviet-orchestrated, Communist quest for world domination, Eden saw PRC behavior as one of defending national interests. He feared that U.S. exaggerations of the threat, and resulting irrational conclusions, would lead to a wider war. Although Eden would have liked to increase Britain's military commitment to the fighting in Korea to improve its bargaining position, Britain's weakened postwar economic and military posture would not allow this move.

In December 1951, to speed up the cease-fire negotiations, Eden agreed to a U.S. proposal for issuing a joint policy (called Greater Sanctions) statement threatening the PRC with retaliation in the event of any postarmistice aggression. Eden was unwilling, however, to specify the kind of measures Britain would support and in fact opposed any form of blockade, citing London's familiar concerns over Hong Kong and the possibility of clashes with the Soviet Union. Eden was worried by the impasse that developed at P'anmunjŏm in the spring of 1952 over the agenda item regarding prisoners of war (POWs), especially after the Sup'ung (Suiho) bombing operation, which the United States had mounted without consulting Britain, a political embarrassment for him personally. Eden attempted to find a compromise on the POW issue that would avert the risk of further U.S. escalation of the war. Although unwilling to endorse forcible repatriation, he believed that the United States was unnecessarily rigid in order to embarrass the PRC and to avoid political criticism in an election year.

At the UN General Assembly in November 1952, Eden supported the POW settlement proposal that was put forth by India's V. K. Krishna Menon and that U.S. Secretary of State Dean Acheson opposed. Although Acheson eventually accepted the UN resolution in modified form, the relationship between Acheson and Eden ended on a sour note. In his relations with the new Eisenhower administration, Eden was suspicious of the influence of the Republican Party right wing and had little faith in the judgment of Secretary of State John Foster Dulles. Eden was openly critical of President Dwight Eisenhower's February 1953 threats to unleash Nationalist Chinese forces on Taiwan against the Chinese mainland. In talks with Dulles, Eden insisted on prior consultation in the event of any move to escalate the war in Korea. After the truce talks resumed in April 1953, Eden, who had continued his efforts to promote a cease-fire, was worried because the United States seemed more concerned with appeasing Republic of Korea (ROK, South Korea) President Syngman Rhee and Republican hard-liners than with reaching a settlement. In this situation, Eden pressed strongly for a compromise and went so far as to threaten withdrawal of British approval for the Greater Sanctions statement.

In 1954 Eden became Lord Avon. He continued to support foreign policies promoting the concept of European unity, albeit without significant British participation. Eden, like Churchill, opposed British membership in the European Defense Community and the European Coal and Steel Community, the predecessor entity to the European Economic Community. Eden did propose expanding the Brussels Pact of 1948 to include the Federal Republic of Germany in NATO, while guaranteeing the French that rearmament posed no threat because 50,000 British troops would remain in West Germany. In 1954 he introduced the Eden Plan for German Reunification, one of the last attempts during the Cold War to bring about a unified Germany through diplomatic means. The Soviet Union rejected the plan.

Eden's standing in U.S. government circles further diminished in April 1954 when he refused to support U.S. efforts to aid beleaguered French Union Forces besieged by Communist forces at Dien Bien Phu in northern Vietnam. In the attempt to repair this rift in the Western Alliance, Eden endorsed the 1954 Geneva Conference on Indo-China and Korea.

In April 1955 Eden succeeded Churchill as prime minister and immediately set out to improve Britain's relations with the Soviet Union and United States. Yet Eden's efforts to take back the Suez Canal by military force in November 1956 severely set back these efforts. Britain capitulated to U.S. demands to withdraw from Egypt, and the entire affair underscored in Eden's eyes how far Great Britain had declined as a major power. Eden's health was poor during the crisis and on 21 November 1956 he was advised by his physicians to go on holiday. Citing continuing poor health, Eden resigned as prime minister on 9 January 1957.

Eden's health never improved and, after his departure from public life, he retired to his country home of Alvediston in Wiltshire. Here he wrote three volumes of memoirs: *Full Circle* (1960), *Facing the Dictators* (1962), and *The Reckoning* (1965). A fourth book, *Another World, 1897–1917* (1976), described his early life. Taken ill during a visit to his friend W. Averell Harriman in Florida, Eden died at his home in England on 14 January 1977. He was one of the most influential British statesmen of the twentieth century.

—Clayton D. Laurie

References:

Aster, Sidney. *Anthony Eden*. London: Weidenfeld & Nicholson, 1976.

Campbell-Johnson, Alan. *Eden: The Making of a Statesman*. New York: Washburn, 1955. Reprint, Westport, CN: Greenwood Press, 1976.

Carlton, David. *Anthony Eden: A Biography*. London: A. Lane, 1981.

Dutton, David. *Anthony Eden: A Life and Reputation*. New York: Arnold, 1997.

James, Robert Rhodes. *Anthony Eden*. New York: McGraw-Hill, 1987.

Rothwell, Victor. *Anthony Eden: A Political Biography, 1931–1957*. New York: St. Martin's Press, 1992.

See also: Acheson, Dean Goodersham; Attlee, Clement R.; Churchill, Sir Winston Spencer; Dulles, John Foster; Eisenhower, Dwight D.; Harriman, William Averell; Menon, V. K. Krishna; Sup'ung (Suiho) and the Korean Electric Power Plant Campaign; Syngman Rhee; United Kingdom (UK).

Eighth United States Army
(1944 to the present)

Main United Nations Command (UNC) ground combat force in Korea during the war. Activated in 1944 as a part of General Douglas MacArthur's Southwest Pacific Area, the Eighth U.S. Army was the U.S. Army's only active field army between 1946 and 1950. Because it was the major army headquarters in Japan at the outbreak of the Korean War, it became and remained the base element for the UNC. Forces assigned to it, in addition to U.S. forces, initially consisted of only the Republic of Korea Army (ROKA), but it eventually grew to include units from nineteen separate nations. Sixteen countries provided ground forces (ranging in size from a sixty-personnel detachment to a brigade), including Australia, Belgium, Canada, Colombia, Ethiopia, France, Greece, Luxembourg, the Netherlands, New Zealand, the Philippines, the Republic of Korea, Thailand, Turkey, the United Kingdom, and the United States; India, Italy, Norway, and Sweden provided medical detachments.

Beginning with a strength of approximately 83,000 soldiers, at its peak in July 1953 Eighth Army numbered around 933,000 soldiers (split roughly in half between ROK troops and forces from other countries, the largest contingent coming from the United States), making it the largest and most diverse field army ever commanded by a U.S. general.

Before the beginning of hostilities in Korea, the Eighth Army conducted the occupation of Japan. Lieutenant General Robert L. Eichleberger, its World War II leader, commanded it until 15 September 1948, when Lieutenant General Walton H. Walker assumed command. Consisting of four of the Army's ten combat divisions, Eighth Army included the 7th Infantry Division, the 1st Cavalry Division, the 25th Infantry Division, and the 24th Infantry Division. By the late 1940s, Eighth Army had no active corps headquarters, and each of its combat divisions lacked nearly 7,000 soldiers, one-fourth of its authorized field artillery and antiaircraft batteries, and most of its armor assets, while most of its infantry regiments were short an infantry battalion. In June 1950 Eighth Army had a total strength of approximately 83,000 soldiers, and it lacked over 30 percent of the strength necessary to be an effective fighting force. It was also, with few exceptions, poorly trained, equipped, staffed, and led.

Responding to the Korean People's Army attack, on 30 June 1950 U.S. President Harry S. Truman authorized the use of U.S. forces in Korea. With the routing of Task Force Smith on 5 July 1950, U.S. and ROKA units continued their withdrawal south, ultimately occupying a 150-mile perimeter around the ROK southern port of Pusan by 4 August 1950. In the meantime, Walker arrived in Korea on 13 July 1950 and activated the Eighth U.S. Army in Korea (EUSAK) to control all UN ground forces in Korea. EUSAK, further bolstered by the arrival of additional units and exercising command authority over all ROKA troops, stubbornly held the Pusan perimeter for more than forty days while MacArthur planned an amphibious turning movement at Inch'ŏn using a corps not under EUSAK's control.

In conjunction with the U.S. Army's X Corps landing at Inch'ŏn (Operation CHROMITE), the Eighth Army launched a penetration on 16 September 1950 designed to break out of the Pusan perimeter and link up with X Corps units south of Seoul. After a week of hard fighting, EUSAK succeeded and launched a pursuit of the KPA units to the north, making contact with elements of the U.S. X Corps on the morning of 27 September 1950. During this period, the Eighth Army acquired the rudiments of an effective field army structure, activating the U.S. I and IX Corps, respectively, on 13 and 23 September 1950.

Eighth Army crossed the 38th parallel on 9 October 1950 (ROKA forces had already crossed on 1 October

Eighth Army commander Lieutenant General James Van Fleet (2nd from left) visits a command post of the 65th regiment of the 3d Infantry Division, 17 April 1951. Standing with Van Fleet are (L to R): Chief of Staff of Eighth Army Major General Leven A. Allen, 3d Division commander Major General Robert H. Sohle, and I Corps commander Lieutenant General Frank W. Milburn. (National Archives)

1950) with the mission of not only destroying the retreating North Koreans but also unifying the Korean peninsula, if practicable. After capturing the North Korean capital of P'yŏngyang on 19 October 1950, Walker continued his advance north until reaching the Yalu River on 26 October 1950. EUSAK launched MacArthur's ill-fated Home-by-Christmas Offensive on 24 November 1950, but the intervention of approximately 300,000 soldiers of the Chinese People's Volunteer Army (CPVA, Chinese Communist) stopped Walker's attack on 25 November 1950 and sent Eighth Army reeling back below the Ch'ŏngch'ŏn River by 29 November 1950. Over the next three weeks, Walker withdrew Eighth Army farther and farther south, abandoning P'yŏngyang and establishing a strong defensive line north of the 38th parallel and Seoul.

On 23 December 1950, Walker died in a jeep accident. His replacement, Lieutenant General Matthew B.

Ridgway, commanded the unit until he replaced General MacArthur as UNC commander in April 1951. Lieutenant General James A. Van Fleet succeeded Ridgway, and both he and Ridgway remained in their commands until replaced by Lieutenant Generals Maxwell D. Taylor and Mark W. Clark, respectively. Clark and Taylor retained their commands until the war's end in July 1953.

Ridgway immediately incorporated the X Corps into the Eighth Army and began planning to resume the offensive. After withdrawing from Seoul in response to the CPVA's Third Phase Offensive in early 1951, Ridgway launched a series of attacks throughout the winter and spring of 1951 using the "meat grinder" strategy, which allowed EUSAK to recapture Seoul and, under the command of James A. Van Fleet, to occupy positions north of the 38th parallel. After a period of intense fighting in fall 1951,

EUSAK assumed the active defense on 12 November 1951, essentially ending its large-scale offensive operations. As a result, limited objective attacks planned at battalion, regiment, division, and corps to regain ground lost to the Communists and to inflict maximum casualties on the enemy became the order of the day for most of EUSAK. During winter 1951–1952, two National Guard divisions, the 40th and 45th Infantry, replaced the 24th Infantry Division and the 1st Cavalry Division, respectively. In February 1953 General Taylor, the new commander of Eighth Army, removed "Korea" from its title. Eighth Army remained in Korea until the end of the fighting on 27 July 1953, and it continues to be the major U.S. ground forces headquarters in Korea.

—Kelly C. Jordan

References:

Alexander, Bevin. *Korea: The First War We Lost.* New York: Hippocrene Books, 1986.

Appleman, Roy E. *South to the Naktong, North to the Yalu.* Washington, DC: Office of the Chief of Military History, 1961.

Blair, Clay. *The Forgotten War: America in Korea, 1950–1953.* New York: Times Books, 1987.

Ridgway, Matthew B. *The Korean War.* Garden City, NY: Doubleday, 1967.

See also: Clark, Mark W.; Home-by-Christmas Offensive; Inch'ŏn Landings: Operation CHROMITE; MacArthur, Douglas; Ridgway, Matthew Bunker; Task Force Smith; Taylor, Maxwell Davenport; 38th parallel, Decision to Cross; Truman, Harry S.; United Nations Command (UNC); United States Army; Van Fleet, James Alward; Walker, Walton Harris.

Eisenhower, Dwight D.
(1890–1969)

President of the United States, 1953–1961. Born in Denison, Texas, on 14 October 1890, Dwight David Eisenhower grew up in modest circumstances in Abilene, Texas, acquiring a love of history at Abilene High School, from which he was graduated in 1909. In 1915 he graduated from the U.S. Military Academy, West Point. He served in a variety of training assignments until in 1918 he was posted to the U.S. Expeditionary Force in France, but World War I ended before his arrival. Postings during the 1920s to the Panama Canal Zone and Paris and staff courses at Fort Leavenworth and the Army War College, where Eisenhower excelled, led to five years in Washington, where during 1930–1935 Eisenhower served in the War Department. In 1936 he reluctantly accompanied outgoing Army Chief of Staff General Douglas MacArthur to the Philippines to train the new Commonwealth's army, but on the outbreak of European war in 1939 Eisenhower insisted upon returning to the United States. During these years the two men developed the personal animosity that would persist for the remainder of their careers.

As the United States began to raise the military forces that would ultimately win the Second World War, Eisenhower initially served as chief of staff to the new Third Army. Transferred to the War Department in Washington after the Japanese attack on Pearl Harbor, he held various increasingly responsible staff jobs, working in the War Plans Divisions, where he helped to elaborate the Europe-first strategy. Promoted to major general in April 1942, Eisenhower that June transferred to London as commander of the European Theater of Operations and commander of U.S. forces in Europe. In November 1942 he commanded the Allied invasion of North Africa, and in 1943 he launched the invasion first of Sicily and then Italy. In December 1943 U.S. President Franklin D. Roosevelt informed the general of his selection as commander of the Allied Expeditionary Force to invade Western Europe. Eisenhower commanded this force through the end of the war in Europe. In December 1944 he was promoted to general of the army, and by the end of the war he was a national hero.

By this time, Eisenhower apparently already cherished hopes of eventually translating his fame into a political career even though he had never voted and had no party affiliation. From May to November 1945, Eisenhower commanded Allied occupation forces in Germany. He then returned to Washington to serve as chief of staff of the army, serving in that capacity until his retirement in February 1948. Eisenhower then became president of Columbia University, a post he held until the summer of 1952. During this time he participated prominently in study groups at the Council on Foreign Relations and spent at least one or two days a week in Washington, informally chairing the Joint Chiefs of Staff during Admiral William D. Leahy's illness. Eisenhower strongly endorsed the Truman administration's developing Cold War policies, including intervention in Korea. His major focus, however, remained the European situation and the Soviet-American rivalry.

On 1 January 1951, Eisenhower took leave from Columbia to strengthen the infant North Atlantic Treaty Organization (NATO), which U.S. officials feared the Korean War might jeopardize. Eisenhower became the First Supreme Allied Commander Europe and organized NATO headquarters in Paris.

In 1952 the Republican Party, desperate to choose a candidate who would bring it the presidency, turned to Eisenhower. Internationalist Republicans were equally determined to ensure that their party's nominee would effectively endorse and continue the Truman administration's Cold War policies, and therefore swung their weight against the broadly isolationist Senator Robert A. Taft, Eisenhower's strongest rival.

Resigning his NATO post, Eisenhower campaigned hard for victory, though he tended to leave his running mate, Senator Richard M. Nixon of California, and Senator Joseph R. McCarthy to mount the more aggressive attacks on his former colleagues within the Truman administration's military and diplomatic circles. In a campaign marked by vicious rhetoric and accusations, Republicans criticized the administration strongly for mishandling the war in Korea and blamed the administration's failure to give specific security guarantees to the Republic of Korea. They also assailed the Democrats' tactics in fighting and mobilizing for the war, especially the recall of former United Nations (UN) commander General MacArthur, and suggested that these weaknesses were the result of the presence of Communist spies, agents, and their associates within the administration.

McCarthy in particular characterized Truman, Secretary of State Dean G. Acheson, and Secretary of Defense George C. Marshall, Eisenhower's former military superior, as pro-Communist in outlook. Many senior Republican politicians found McCarthy's tactics personally distasteful but tolerated them in the interests of electoral victory. Although Eisenhower initially intended to refute McCarthy's charges by publicly defending Marshall, political considerations finally persuaded him to remain silent and effectively acquiesce in them, a decision which many regard as a lasting stain upon his own reputation.

During the campaign, Eisenhower promised that, if elected, he would pay a personal visit to Korea, which he secretly did in early December 1952 as president-elect. This trip confirmed his existing suspicions that a major new United Nations Command (UNC) military offensive was not feasible and that the United States should therefore seek to bring the lengthy armistice negotiations, deadlocked after two years on the question of repatriation of prisoners of war, to a speedy conclusion. This emphasis was reinforced by his personal desire to reduce military spending and balance the budget, preoccupations that characterized his entire presidency.

After meeting with Acheson and Truman in November 1952, Eisenhower effectively endorsed the administration's stance that prisoners should undergo only voluntary repatriation. In December 1952 he also rejected recommendations from MacArthur that the ground war should be expanded. Eisenhower also demurred from suggestions by Commander in Chief Pacific Fleet Admiral Arthur H. Radford and his secretary of defense designate, Charles E. Wilson, that the United States should follow an Asia-first policy. Eisenhower emphasized that NATO must remain the linchpin of U.S. global strategy.

Once inaugurated, Eisenhower moved quickly to end the war. He did so in part through a strategy of cal-

culated escalation. In an effort to pressure the People's Republic of China (PRC) to negotiate seriously and resume stalled armistice talks, in February 1953 the President announced that the United States would "unleash" Taiwan's Guomindang leader Jiang Jieshi (Chiang Kai-shek) and permit him to attack the Chinese mainland. The same month, the National Security Council decided that, were an armistice not concluded in the near future, UN forces should bomb Chinese bases and supply camps in Manchuria, impose a blockade upon the mainland, and possibly employ tactical nuclear weapons. These decisions were deliberately conveyed to PRC leaders through the agency of Jawharlal Nehru, India's prime minister, and Eisenhower believed that they were responsible for persuading China to open serious bargaining. The death of Stalin in March 1953 and the subsequent power vacuum in Russia were almost certainly contributing factors and may have been even more significant than Eisenhower's threats because the Soviet leader, primarily interested in leaving the United States embroiled in an expensive conflict, always pressed China to continue hostilities.

In early 1953 China announced its readiness to resume serious armistice talks, an offer that Eisenhower, ignoring the contrary advice of Secretary of State John Foster Dulles that further fighting might enhance the U.S. position on the ground, quickly accepted. By June 1953 a compromise settlement had been reached on all points, including the vexing issue of the repatriation of prisoners of war. President of the Republic of Korea (ROK) Syngman Rhee, desperate to prolong the war in the hope of implementing Korea's ultimate reunification, unsuccessfully tried several different tactics designed to sabotage the negotiations, but, if anything, they hardened the resolve of both Americans and Chinese to reach a workable settlement.

Eisenhower rejected suggestions that the Central Intelligence Agency should arrange for Rhee's assassination. Instead, on 12 July 1953, as peace talks resumed, he dispatched Assistant Secretary of State Walter Robertson to Seoul to persuade Rhee to cease his obstructionism. After two weeks Eisenhower finally extorted Rhee's pledge to accept a cease-fire, which was signed immediately, on 27 July 1953. In return, Rhee was promised a U.S.–ROK mutual security treaty, which was quickly concluded, on 8 August 1953; $200 million in immediate economic aid, only the first installment of a long-term aid program; and U.S. assistance in expanding the ROK Army to twenty divisions was guaranteed.

In the United States there was a prevailing sense of relief that the war was finally over. Even though a final peace treaty has yet to be signed, the United States has maintained a substantial military presence in South Korea ever since, and serious tensions still characterize North Korea's relationship with both the South and the United States.

In 1954 Eisenhower firmly rejected suggestions by the ever bellicose and hopeful Rhee that their two countries should embark on nuclear action against North Korea. Eisenhower's stand reflected his broad disinclination to use nuclear weapons in any circumstances, even as his defense policy relied increasingly upon a nuclear deterrent. Rhee's suggestions were ostensibly prompted by the Chinese and North Korean failure to hold further talks to address outstanding issues still unresolved. About the same time, Eisenhower quietly supported the ultimately successful campaign to destroy McCarthy, whose hysterically anti-Communist tactics had become a major embarrassment to the administration, the Republican Party, and the country's international image.

Eisenhower was easily reelected president in 1956 and remained in office until he retired in 1961. His final act in office was to express his strong antipathy toward the growth of the military-industrial complex, over the development of which he had largely presided. In retirement Eisenhower lived on his cherished farm in Gettysburg, Pennsylvania, but was occasionally consulted by Presidents John F. Kennedy and Lyndon B. Johnson, whose foreign policies he was generally prepared publicly to endorse, when necessary. He died in Washington, D.C., on 28 March 1969.

In recent years historians have lauded the relative moderation and restraint of his foreign policy, yet Eisenhower must also be held at least partially responsible for the initial development of the U.S. commitment to Vietnam, a commitment that would bedevil the United States for more than a decade after he left office, having exhorted his successor to hold the line in Indo-China. Although his policies were undoubtedly more restrained than the more extreme suggestions advocated by such figures as Dulles and Radford, overall Eisenhower subscribed to the prevailing Cold War orthodoxy and helped to ensure its general acceptance.

—*Priscilla Roberts*

References:
Ambrose, Stephen E. *Eisenhower.* 2 vols. New York: Simon & Schuster, 1983–1984.
Bailey, Sydney D. *The Korean Armistice.* London: Macmillan, 1992.
Bowie, Robert R., and Richard H. Immerman. *Waging Peace: How Eisenhower Shaped an Enduring Cold War Strategy.* New York: Oxford University Press, 1998.
Broadwater, Jeff. *Eisenhower and the Anti-Communist Crusade.* Chapel Hill: University of North Carolina Press, 1992.
Caridi, Ronald J. *The Korean War and American Politics: The Republican Party As a Case Study.* Philadelphia: University of Pennsylvania Press, 1968.
Chandler, Alfred D., Jr., and Louis Galambos, eds. *The Papers of Dwight D. Eisenhower.* 17 vols. to date. Baltimore: Johns Hopkins University Press, 1970–.
Divine, Robert A. *Foreign Policy and U.S. Presidential Elections, 1952–1960.* New York: New Viewpoints, 1974.
Eisenhower, Dwight D. *Mandate for Change, 1953–1956.* Garden City, NY: Doubleday, 1963.
Foot, Rosemary J. *A Substitute for Victory: The Politics of Peacemaking at the Korean Armistice Talks.* Ithaca, NY: Cornell University Press, 1990.
Medhurst, Martin J., ed. *Eisenhower's War of Words: Rhetoric and Leadership.* East Lansing: Michigan State University Press, 1994.
Melanson, Richard A., and David Mayers. *Reevaluating Eisenhower: American Foreign Policy in the 1950s.* Urbana: University of Illinois Press, 1986.
See also: Acheson, Dean Goodersham; Armistice Agreement; Dulles, John Foster; Eisenhower's Trip to Korea; Joint Chiefs of Staff (JCS); Marshall, George C.; McCarthy, Joseph R.; McCarthyism; National Security Council (NSC); NATO (North Atlantic Treaty Organization); Nehru, Jawharlal; Nixon, Richard Milhous; P'anmunjŏm Truce Talks; Radford, Arthur W.; Robertson Mission; Robertson, Walter Spencer; Taft, Robert Alphonso; Truman-Eisenhower Transition Meeting; United States–Republic of Korea Mutual Defense Treaty; U.S. Policy toward Korea: 1950–1953; Wilson, Charles Edward.

Eisenhower's Trip to Korea
(2–5 December 1952)

Dwight D. Eisenhower's visit to Korea, undertaken in strict secrecy in the interregnum between Eisenhower's winning the presidential election of 1952 and assuming office in January 1953, reinforced the president-elect's existing conviction that total victory in the Korean War was unattainable and a negotiated settlement was therefore desirable, if not essential.

On 24 October 1952, during the presidential election campaign, Republican candidate Eisenhower announced in Detroit that, if successful in this contest, he would personally "go to Korea." His rationale was that only by doing so could he "learn how best to serve the American people in the cause of peace" and "bring the war to an honorable end." With deliberate ambiguity he failed to specify precisely what he envisaged to be. Eisenhower's pledge therefore won an enthusiastic response from both those Americans who desired peace above all and those who still hoped that the Second World War commander in chief could devise a means of bringing about a sweeping victory to conclude the conflict.

On 29 November 1952, Eisenhower left the United States en route for Korea. He was accompanied by Chairman of the Joint Chiefs of Staff General Omar N. Bradley, Secretary of Defense–Designate Charles E. Wilson; Attorney General–Designate Herbert Brownell; and Commander in Chief of the Pacific Fleet Admiral Arthur H. Radford.

President-elect Dwight D. Eisenhower (left) and commander of the 2d Infantry Division Major General James C. Fry (right), during Eisenhower's visit to United Nations Command units, 4 December 1952. (National Archives)

Arriving in Seoul on 2 December 1952, Eisenhower spent little time with Republic of Korea (ROK) President Syngman Rhee, who was anxious to convince him to mount a full-scale invasion of North Korea and unify the country under Rhee's leadership. In two separate meetings the president-elect spent a total of approximately one hour with Rhee, and he declined Rhee's invitations to join with him in a large public military review or to address the National Assembly, denying Rhee the prestigious association for which he had hoped and the opportunity to present his military plans. Eisenhower likewise refused to allow United Nations Commander in Chief Lieutenant General Mark W. Clark to present his own proposal for a new offensive intended to drive the Chinese back to the Yalu River and unite both Koreas.

Instead, bundled in heavy winter clothes, Eisenhower and his companions devoted most of the three-day visit to trips to the bitterly cold front, inspecting military units and talking at length with commanders and their men. These first-hand experiences succeeded in convincing the already skeptical Eisenhower that the grandiose schemes Rhee and Clark cherished were unrealistic, and that, as he had long suspected, a negotiated settlement restoring something close to the antebellum status quo would provide the least costly and most practicable end to the war. "My conclusion as I left Korea," Eisenhower wrote later, "was that we could not stand forever on a static front and continue to accept casualties without any visible results."

Although his election campaign had criticized the Truman administration's containment policies and called for the rollback of communism, Eisenhower decided to bear whatever political costs he might incur in pushing for an armistice settlement and acquiescing to the continued existence of the North Korean state. Almost certainly, he was also motivated by the calculation that the detrimental political effects implicit in a lengthy continuation of the Korean War would far outweigh those incumbent in implementing peace. Once inaugurated as president, Eisenhower therefore authorized a renewed and even aggressive effort at the ongoing P'anmunjŏm talks to reach a diplomatic settlement, which eventually resulted in the Armistice Agreement, which was signed on 27 July 1953.

—Priscilla Roberts

References:

Ambrose, Stephen E. *Eisenhower.* 2 vols. New York: Simon & Schuster, 1983–1984.

Bailey, Sydney D. *The Korean Armistice.* London: Macmillan, 1992.

Caridi, Ronald J. *The Korean War and American Politics: The Republican Party As a Case Study.* Philadelphia: University of Pennsylvania Press, 1968.

Divine, Robert A. *Foreign Policy and U.S. Presidential Elections, 1952–1960.* New York: New Viewpoints, 1974.

Eisenhower, Dwight D. *Mandate for Change, 1953–1956.* Garden City, NY: Doubleday, 1963.

Foot, Rosemary J. *A Substitute for Victory: The Politics of Peacemaking at the Korean Armistice Talks.* Ithaca, NY: Cornell University Press, 1990.

Stueck, William W., Jr. *The Korean War: An International History.* Princeton, NJ: Princeton University Press, 1995.

See also: Armistice Agreement; Bradley, Omar Nelson; Clark, Mark W.; Eisenhower, Dwight D.; Radford, Arthur W.; Syngman Rhee; Wilson, Charles Edward.

Elsey, George M.
(1918–)

Administrative assistant to President Harry S. Truman and, as such, present at many high-level discussions on the Korean War. Born in Palo Alto, California, on 5 February 1918, George M. Elsey graduated from Princeton in 1939 and earned a master's degree in U.S. history from Harvard University in 1940. After active duty with the U.S. Naval Reserve, in 1946 Elsey, in company with Clark Clifford, was assigned as assistant naval aide to President Truman in the White House Map Room. Elsey's duties soon grew to encompass those of a civilian administrative assistant and speech writer. His editorial skills and well-honed, balanced, and incisive use of language made his services much in demand.

In 1946 Elsey and Clifford wrote a report, "American Relations with the Soviet Union," that went far beyond the president's original request for a list of Soviet violations in agreements with the United States. It suggested that the Soviet Union had pursued an expansionist policy throughout Europe, that its leaders were not to be trusted and would observe or ignore international agreements as best suited their own ends, and that the Soviets were actively promoting Communist takeovers in Turkey, Greece, and China. The report, which echoed Soviet expert George

F. Kennan's famous "Long Telegram" and "X Article," urged that the United States ensure itself of adequate military strength "to confine Soviet influence" and continue to develop more sophisticated weapons. Fearing that the memorandum was too outspoken and controversial, Truman chose not to distribute it among his staff. Elsey and Clifford also contributed to the final draft of the Truman Doctrine speech of 12 March 1947, which called upon the United States to oppose the spread of communism throughout the world. In this case, however, the Department of State was responsible for the sweeping rhetoric, which Elsey considered rather exaggerated.

In 1947 Elsey replaced Clifford as special counsel to the president, and from 1949 to 1952 he served as the president's administrative assistant. Although Elsey was a spectator rather than a policymaker on Korea, his own outlook helped to reinforce the assertive outlook of other members of the Truman administration concerning the conflict.

After leaving the White House, Elsey joined the American Red Cross and served from 1958 to 1961 as its vice-president. He became its president in 1970. During the 1960s he served as an adviser to both large corporations and public interest groups.

—Priscilla Roberts

References:

Clifford, Clark, with Richard Holbrooke. *Counsel to the President: A Memoir.* New York: Random House, 1991.

"Elsey, George M." In *Political Profiles: The Truman Years,* edited by Eleanora W. Schoenebaum. New York: Facts on File, 1978.

Hamby, Alonzo L. *Man of the People: A Life of Harry S. Truman.* New York: Oxford University Press, 1995.

McCullough, David. *Truman.* New York: Simon & Schuster, 1992.

See also: Cold War, Origins to 1950; Kennan, George F.

Emmons, Arthur B., III
(1910–1962)

U.S. Foreign Service officer who served as vice-consul in Seoul during 1940–1941, consul in 1946, and officer in charge of Korean affairs at the Department of State during 1950–1952. Emmons was privy to the making of his country's policy toward Korea, but did not exercise a major influence upon Korean War diplomacy. Born on 30 August 1910 into a Boston Brahmin family, Arthur B. Emmons III graduated from St. Paul's Harvard University in 1933. He spent most of the rest of the decade on strenuous mountain climbing expeditions in the Himalayas, mapping previously unexplored regions, before joining the Foreign Service in 1939.

Emmons was stationed in Montreal and Hangzhou, China, and then spent a year as vice-consul in Seoul. After the bombing of Pearl Harbor, he spent several months in a Japanese internment camp and returned to the United States with other diplomats in 1942. His most important influence on U.S. policy toward Korea came at this time, when he submitted a report emphasizing that Korea's economic backwardness and exploitation under Japanese rule had created widespread political apathy among average Koreans and that the Japanese had suppressed most potential political leaders. Emmons also warned that after the war Korea's strategic location as a neighbor of China, Russia, and Japan might well cause it again to become the focus of international rivalries. Emmons's discouraging report was a major factor in the State Department's wartime decision to attempt to establish a postwar United Nations (UN) trusteeship over Korea.

Emmons returned to Asia in 1945 to work on General Douglas MacArthur's political advisory staff in Tokyo. In 1946 he was briefly posted to Seoul as consul before moving to the embassy in Madrid for four years. As one of the few Foreign Service officials with substantial Korean experience, in July 1950 he was recalled to Washington to serve as the State Department officer in charge of Korean affairs. Although Emmons was privy to the detailed debates and discussions on policy, important decisions were generally made by his superiors, and his influence on the making as opposed to the implementation of policy was marginal. He did have the principal responsibility for devising detailed U.S. proposals for war crimes trials, an issue that factored in the peace negotiations.

In 1952 Emmons twice served as a member of the U.S. delegation to UN meetings in Paris and New York. He subsequently held various diplomatic positions in U.S. embassies in Australia, Ireland, and Malaya, and in 1959 he returned to Washington as special assistant for Southeast Asia Treaty Organization Affairs in the State Department's Bureau of Far Eastern Affairs. Emmons died in Washington on 22 August 1962.

—*Priscilla Roberts*

References:

Cumings, Bruce. *Child of Conflict: The Korean-American Relationship, 1943–1953.* Seattle: University of Washington Press, 1983.

Foot, Rosemary J. *A Substitute for Victory: The Politics of Peacemaking at the Korean Armistice Talks.* Ithaca, NY: Cornell University Press, 1990.

Matray, James I. *The Reluctant Crusade: American Foreign Policy in Korea, 1941–1950.* Honolulu: University of Hawaii Press, 1985.

Stueck, William W., Jr. *The Korean War: An International History.* Princeton, NJ: Princeton University Press, 1995.

———. *The Road to Confrontation: American Policy toward China and Korea, 1947–1950.* Chapel Hill: University of North Carolina Press, 1981.

See also: MacArthur, Douglas; U.S. Policy toward Korea before 1950.

Entezam, Nasrollah
(1900–)

Iran's permanent delegate to the United Nations (UN) during 1947–1952 and 1953–1956; concurrently from 1950 his country's ambassador to the United States; and during 1950–1951 president of the UN General Assembly. Born on 16 February 1900 in Teheran to an aristocratic family, Nasrollah Entezam was educated at the University of Teheran and the University of Paris. In 1918 Entezam took up his family's traditional career of foreign service by entering the Ministry of Foreign Affairs, and between the wars he served in relatively junior capacities at his country's Paris, Warsaw, London, and Berne embassies, as well as at the League of Nations in Geneva.

Returning to Iran in 1938, for four years he was director of the political department of the Ministry of Foreign Affairs, and in 1943 he held several cabinet ministries in quick succession before becoming minister of state for foreign affairs in 1944. After representing his country at the 1945 San Francisco Conference, in 1946 he attended the UN General Assembly's First Session, protesting the continuing presence in Iran of Soviet wartime occupation forces, which were withdrawn shortly afterward.

The next year Entezam became Iran's permanent delegate to the UN and, after fulfilling various committee assignments, in 1949 he served "with distinction" as chairman of the Assembly's special political committee. Deploring harsh personal attacks and similar behavior, he won a reputation for low-key efficiency, competence, and tact and in 1949 was a candidate for president of the UN General Assembly, though in the interests of Asian unity he withdrew in favor of Carlos P. Romulo of the Philippines.

A year later, in September 1950, the UN General Assembly presidency went to Entezam. His one-year term coincided with bewilderingly rapid changes of fortune in Korea, whose conflict he unsuccessfully attempted to mediate. Because Iran hoped to receive U.S. economic aid while improving its relations with the Soviet Union, he had to tread a delicate path while maintaining a judicious appearance of fairness to all, a feat he performed rather skillfully without alienating either of the rivals. Under his guidance the UN General Assembly set up a committee to consider the question of People's Republic of China (PRC, Communist China) membership and passed a resolution guaranteeing Korea's postwar freedom, unity, and independence.

Entezam welcomed the UN action on Korea as making a reality of collective security in the defense of peace. In December 1950, attempting to facilitate the efforts of a group of thirteen Arab and Asian nations to bring about an armistice, Entezam chaired an ad hoc cease-fire group that tried to discuss ways and means of ending the fighting with the United States and PRC. When this effort failed, Entezam encouraged the formation of the UN Good Offices Committee, established under a resolution of 1 February 1951. He then chaired this committee during its efforts to open negotiations with the PRC. Although this venture was unsuccessful, it postponed until May the U.S. demands to impose "additional measures," primarily economic sanctions, upon China.

In later years Entezam served during 1957–1962 as Iran's ambassador to France and then for a year as minister without portfolio. His conciliatory skills were called upon once more during 1966–1969, when he served as a judge upon the Indo-Pakistan Western Boundary Case Tribunal.

—Priscilla Roberts

References:

Barros, James. *Trygve Lie and the Cold War: The United Nations Secretary-General Pursues Peace, 1946–1953*. DeKalb: Northern Illinois University Press, 1989.

"Entezam, Nasrollah." In *Current Biography, 1950*. New York: H. W. Wilson, 1951.

Luard, Evan. *A History of the United Nations*. Vol. 1, *The Years of Western Domination, 1945–1955*. London: Macmillan, 1982.

Stueck, William W., Jr. *The Korean War: An International History*. Princeton, NJ: Princeton University Press, 1995.

Yoo, Tae-Ho. *The Korean War and the United Nations*. Louvain, Belgium: Librairie Desbarax, 1964.

See also: United Nations Cease-Fire Group.

Ethiopia

The only African nation to send infantry to fight in the Korean War. Ethiopia, of all countries, knew of the consequences that could follow the failure of international collective security, having experienced the inability of the League of Nations to protect its independence against Italian fascist aggression in 1935. However, Ethiopian Emperor Haile Selassie brought his country into the Korean War primarily to gain the attention and influence that such a gesture would win in the eyes of the Western alliance.

An Ethiopian battalion arrived in Korea in March 1951 and was attached to the U.S. 7th Infantry Division. Unlike the Americans, the Ethiopians rotated their serving battalion every 12 months so that fresh troops could replace their war-weary predecessors. At peak strength, approximately 1,277 Ethiopian soldiers served in Korea.

The Ethiopian Battalion was an excellent fighting force that never left its dead or wounded on the battlefield or had a soldier captured. The Ethiopians became renowned on both sides for their ability to conduct patrols, particularly at night, a form of combat that became standard during the last two years of the stalemate in Korea.

By sending ground troops, Haile Selassie succeeded in gaining U.S. diplomatic support and military aid for the future. This action helped to identify Ethiopia with the anti-Communist bloc and to gain favor for the government's goals of controlling the rebellious province of Eritrea and of dominating neighboring Somaliland. Thus, for Ethiopia, Korea proved to be a very successful war.

—Eric Jarvis

References:

Hermes, Walter G. *United States Army in the Korean War: Truce Tent and Fighting Front*. Washington, DC: Office of the Chief of Military History, 1966.

Marcus, Harold G. *Ethiopia, Great Britain and the United States, 1941–1974: The Politics of Empire*. Berkeley: University of California Press, 1983.

Marshall, S. L. A. *Pork Chop Hill: The American Fighting Man in Action, Korea, Spring, 1953*. New York: William Morrow, 1956.

Stueck, William W., Jr. *The Korean War: An International History*. Princeton, NJ: Princeton University Press, 1995.

See also: Old Baldy, Battle of; Rotation of Troops System.

EVERREADY, Operation

Contingency plan developed by the United States to remove Republic of Korea (ROK) President Syngman Rhee. With the resumption of peace talks at P'anmunjŏm in April 1953 after a six-month recess, United Nations Command (UNC) and Communist negotiators came within reach of a peace settlement that would bring an end to the three years of fighting. Only one major obstacle remained, ROK President Syngman Rhee.

Outraged at the proposed settlement, Rhee publicly announced that his government would never consent to any agreement that did not completely disarm the Democratic People's Republic of Korea (North Korea), remove all Chinese military forces from Korea, and reunify the peninsula under a single democratic government. Rhee mobilized South Koreans to oppose the armistice and threatened to fight on without the aid of the UNC should the Communist Chinese be allowed to remain south of the Yalu River. U.S. leaders saw Rhee's rhetoric as not only a hindrance to the peace effort but as possibly making the ROK dangerously susceptible to being overrun militarily by the Communists.

Fearful that three years of sacrifice might be thrown away, the United States sought to counter Rhee through a series of contingency plans. The most extreme of these was Operation EVERREADY. Prepared by Eighth Army, it called for specific plans to be made, the severity of which were dependent on Rhee's defiance of the UN. The first plan would be implemented if ROK troops failed to obey UN directives, and the second would be implemented if the ROK government pursued an independent course. In either of the latter instances, Eighth Army would disarm ROK forces and restrict the movement of its military and civilian populations. A third plan was prepared to deal with the ROK should it actually threaten UN forces. If the latter were to occur, then Eighth Army would execute a coup d'etat and remove President Rhee from power while establishing martial law to secure the armistice.

Commander of Eighth Army Lieutenant General Mark Clark was hesitant to follow through on the third scenario. He did not have the personnel for a coup or a subsequent military occupation of South Korea, in part because of commitment of his forces at Kŏje-do. A successful coup was also unlikely because there was no one who had Rhee's stature. Removing the popular Rhee would probably only create more chaos and be regarded as an insult to Korean nationalism. An unstable republic would be more vulnerable to Communist invasion.

Not wanting to invest in such a risky operation, U.S. policy never went beyond threats and psychological warfare. Even today, it is not clear whether Operation EVERREADY was merely a precaution for a worse-case scenario or a legitimate plan of action serious considered.

—*Bradford A. Wineman*

References:

Blair, Clay. *The Forgotten War: America in Korea, 1950–1953.* New York: Times Books, 1987.

Goulden, Joseph C. *Korea: The Untold Story of the War.* New York: Times Books, 1982.

Park, Suin Yup. *From Pusan to Panmunjom.* Washington, DC: Brassey's, 1992.

Whelan, Richard. *Drawing the Line: The Korean War, 1950–1953.* Boston: Little, Brown, 1990.

See also: Clark, Mark W.; Syngman Rhee.

F

Far East Air Force (FEAF)

Primary U.S. Air Force component serving in Korea during the Korean War. The primary responsibility of Far East Air Force (FEAF, pronounced as a word that rhymes with "leaf") was to support the Far East Command (FEC) in defending Japan, Korea, and other U.S. and United Nations (UN) interests in East Asia. The overall UN theater commander was also the overall FEC commander. In order, the commanders were General of the Army Douglas MacArthur, Lieutenant General Matthew B. Ridgway, and Lieutenant General Mark W. Clark. The FEAF commander served on the FEC commander's staff. During the Korean conflict, there were three FEAF commanders: Lieutenant General George E. Stratemeyer (25 June 1950–21 May 1951), Lieutenant General Earle E. Partridge (21 May–10 July 1951), and General Otto P. Weyland (10 July 1951–31 July 1953).

Being the primary U.S. air power organization in Korea, FEAF also came under U.S. Air Force administrative supervision pursuant to the acquisition and deployment of weapon systems, munitions, supplies, pilots, and crews. In this regard, it served two masters—the overall theater commander and Chief of Staff of the Air Force (CSAF) General Hoyt S. Vandenberg.

The primary subordinate units included Fifth Air Force (5AF), FEAF Bomber Command, and FEAF Combat Cargo Command (Provisional)/315th Air Division (Combat Cargo). Other subordinate units included the Twelfth Air Force (12AF), Thirteenth Air Force (13AF), FEAM (Far East Air Material) Command, FEA Log Force, and 314th Air Division/Japan Defense Force. The 5AF oversaw tactical combat missions employing a myriad of tactical air assets such as the propeller-driven F-51 Mustang and F-82 Twin Mustang. Some light bombardment squadrons employed the World War II Douglas Aircraft version of the twin-engine B-26 light bomber. 5AF airmen also flew jet fighters and fighter-bombers such as the F-80 Shooting Star, F-84 Thunderjet, and, later, various models of the F-86 Sabrejet.

Commanders of the 5AF were Lieutenant General Earle E. Partridge (25 June 1950–21 May 1951), Major General Edward Timberlake (21 May–1 June 1951), Lieutenant General Frank F. Everest (1 June 1951–30 May 1952), Lieutenant General Glenn O. Barcus (30 May 1952–31 May 1953), and Lieutenant General Samuel E. Anderson (31 May–31 July 1953). Tactical units under 5AF were Tactical Air Wing/Third Bombardment Wing (BW); 4th Fighter Interceptor Wing (FIW), commanded by jet air ace Colonel Harrison R. Thyng, 1 November 1951–20 October 1952; 8th Fighter Bomber Wing (FBW); 17BW; 18FBW; 27th Fighter-Escort Wing (FEW); 35FIW, commanded by World War II ace Colonel Fred C. Gray, 1 December 1950–7 February 1951; 49FBW; 51FIW, commanded by jet air ace Colonel Francis S. Gabreski, 6 November 1951–13 June 1952; 58FBW; 67th Tactical Reconnaissance Wing; 136FBW; 452BW; 474FBW; as well as the 6002d, 6131st, 6133d, 6149th, and 6150th Tactical Support Wings.

FEAF's primary strategic bombing force was Bomber Command, headed during the early months of the war by Major General Emmett O'Donnell. It flew World War II–era B-29s, which were designated medium bombers in Korea. Subordinate units included Medium Bomber Command (later the 19th Bomb Group [BG]); 22BG; 92BG; 98BG (later the 98th Bomb Wing); and the 307BG (later the 307BW).

FEAF cargo/transport operations fell under Major General William H. Tunner's Combat Cargo Command and included the 1st, 61st, 314th, and 315th Troop Carrier Groups (TCGs) and the 374th, 403d, 437th, and 483d Troop Carrier Wings (TCWs).

At the beginning of the war, General Stratemeyer had about 400 combat aircraft and 250 cargo/transport planes in East Asia, most of them in Japan. The 5AF had eight squadrons of F-80s, two squadrons of B-26s, and three squadrons of F-82s. In many ways FEAF's inventory mirrored the overall problems that the Air Force had in convincing U.S. leadership to supply funds to upgrade its air assets, especially new jet bombers and fighters. The 1950s witnessed a growing inclination in both U.S. political parties that emphasized a solely nuclear strategic role for the air force and major cuts in expensive conventional forces. As General Vandenberg remarked, it was a "shoestring air force."

The first FEAF bombers over Korea were twelve B-26 Invaders on the morning of 28 June, followed by four B-29s that afternoon. The first air encounters of the war came during 27–28 June 1950, with bombing raids by B-29s and aerial fighter dogfights. At 1200 on the 28th, five F-82s, escorting the evacuation of U.S. citizens from Seoul's Kimpŏ Airfield, engaged five Yak fighters, shooting down three. Around 1600 that same day, eight North Korean Il-10s tried to strafe Kimpŏ. Four F-80s, at extreme range, brought down four of them.

Throughout the Korean War, FEAF played a critical role in preserving South Korean sovereignty.

The raid at Sorye Dong: LTVAs leaving the well of *Fort Marion* with the Royal Marines, April 1951.

Whether defending the Pusan perimeter, supporting the Inch'ŏn landing, covering the late 1950s retreat, or attacking industrial, supply/communication, and logistics targets during the long stalemated phase of the war, FEAF fighters, bombers, and cargo aircraft participated in all United Nations Command operations. Operations such as the hydroelectric raids, SATURATE, STRANGLE, and even the dogfights over MiG Alley were all part of FEAF's mission during the Korean War.

In the course of the war, U.S. aircraft dropped 500,000 tons of bombs on Korea; the FEAF accounted for two-thirds of this total. These bombs killed an estimated 150,000–200,000 Communist troops and destroyed nearly 1,000 aircraft, 800 bridges, 1,100 tanks, 800 locomotives, 9,000 railcars, 70,000 motor vehicles, and 80,000 buildings. But the price was not cheap. Nearly 1,200 FEAF personnel died in Korea, and 750 aircraft were destroyed. The Military Air Transport Service (MATS), Air Rescue Squadron (ARS), rescued 170 downed crewmen and MATS's aeromedical evacuation system transported thousands of critically injured Allied personnel.

In many ways, FEAF's successful employment of new aircraft, such as the F-86, and institutionalization of a myriad of policy, organizational, and even psychological lessons learned during the Korean conflict served as the foundation of today's modern U.S. Air Force.

—*William Head*

References:

Futrell, Robert F. *The United States Air Force in Korea, 1950–1953.* Rev. ed. Washington, DC: Office of the Chief of Air Force History, 1983.

Thompson, Wayne. "The Air War over Korea." In *Winged Shield, Wing Sword: A History of the United States Air Force,* edited by Bernard C. Nalty. Washington, DC: U.S. Air Force History and Museum Program, 1997: 3–52.

Tunner, William H. *Over the Hump.* Washington, DC: Office of Air Force History, 1985. Reprint.

See also: Clark, Mark W.; MacArthur, Douglas; MIG Alley; Partridge; Earle Everard; Ridgway, Matthew Bunker; Stratemeyer, George E.; Vandenberg, Hoyt S.; Weyland, Otto P.

Far East Command (FEC)

Command effectively created on 1 January 1947 with the selection of General of the Army Douglas MacArthur to head it. The operational area of responsibility of Far East Command (FEC) included more than 265,000 square miles and nearly 100 million people. Although FEC was not clearly defined, Japan, the Ryukyu Islands, the Philippines, the Marianas, the Bonin Islands, and Korea all fell within its defensive perimeter. Most U.S. troops within the command were in occupation duty in Japan.

With such a large area to defend, General MacArthur requested substantial troop levels, but Washington did not provide them. On 1 January 1947, FEC numbered more than 300,000 personnel, including some 42,000 in the army air forces. By 1 January 1948, these levels had fallen to only 142,000 men. At this time MacArthur was also tasked to keep 30,000 troops in Korea until elections were held there. By April 1948, FEC strength was at its lowest point, with Eighth Army having only 45,561 men of an authorized strength of 87,215 and only 26,494 of these in combat units. The latter were distributed among five divisions and an antiaircraft artillery group.

MacArthur continued to complain to the Joint Chiefs of Staff (JCS) that if reductions continued he would not be in position to meet all tasks assigned to his command. The JCS informed him on 9 November 1948 that he should expect a further reduction in Far East Air Forces (FEAF) strength in 1949 and that FEC troop levels would shrink to only 120,000 men by 1 July 1949. During visits to Japan by JCS members and Secretary of the Army Frank Pace, Jr. in 1949, MacArthur argued that his troop levels should be increased rather than decreased. He held that Europe was getting an unfair percentage of troop allocations. MacArthur was informed that troop levels were below authorized strength in all commands because of force reductions and low enlistment rates. FEC troop strength continued to decline; by 25 June 1950, it had dropped to only 108,500 men.

All U.S. occupation forces were withdrawn from Korea by 30 June 1949. The JCS considered Korea to be outside the U.S. defense perimeter and hence FEC's zone of responsibility. No contingency plan was prepared to deal with a Democratic People's Republic of Korea (North Korea) invasion of the Republic of Korea (South Korea). This was in line with the 4 April 1948 policy, approved by President Harry S. Truman, stating that the United States should not become entangled in the defense of Korea. In a 12 January 1950 speech, Secretary of State Dean Acheson did not include Korea and Formosa in the U.S. defense perimeter.

MacArthur wanted a minimum force of five full-strength infantry divisions and one separate Regimental Combat Team in the Far East to deal with any possible problems. In June 1950 he had only four understrength divisions stationed at various points in

Japan. They were the 1st Cavalry Division and the 7th, 24th, and 25th Infantry Divisions. These four divisions composed Eighth Army, which was at only about 70 percent of its combat strength.

Each of Eighth Army's divisions lacked nearly 7,000 soldiers and was woefully short of equipment. Eighth Army had only one-fourth of its authorized field artillery and antiaircraft batteries; it also lacked most of its armor assets. In mid-1950 ammunition stocks were perilously low, and Eighth Army had only 21 recoilless rifles of 226 authorized for its combat units.

Most FEC troops were not combat trained. To attract enlistees the U.S. Army had allowed soldiers to choose their job specialty and, as a result, in June 1950 there were many more support than combat troops within FEC. Many replacements arriving in the Far East also were not fully trained and were of questionable quality; many were in Class IV and V on the Army General Classification Test. These factors, combined with the occupation duties, limited the units from conducting large training exercises. This was a concern for many commanders in FEC, and MacArthur ordered that a timetable be implemented starting on 10 June 1949 and ending by 31 December 1950, allowing for coordinated air-ground training. Within this time frame, units were to complete company, battalion, regimental, and finally division training cycles; yet by 25 June 1950, units had completed only the battalion phase of the cycle.

Compounding these problems, FEC suffered from supply shortages and relied on World War II equipment, much of which was in poor condition. FEC had received no new tanks, vehicles, or other equipment since 1945, and 90 percent of its armament and 75 percent of its vehicle stocks were supplied by local rebuild programs. Such problems existed throughout the U.S. Army. Fewer than 900 serviceable M-24 light tanks were at bases in the continental United States and 2,557 M-24s were unserviceable. The situation for medium M4A3 tanks was only slightly better with 1,826 serviceable and 1,376 unserviceable tanks, but none of these was allocated to FEC. U.S. forces in the Far East were thus in a poor state of combat readiness when the uneasy peace in Korea was shattered in the predawn hours of 25 June 1950.

—*Ronald Fiocca*

References:

Far East Operations Plan 1-50, General Headquarters, Far East Command, Vol. 1 (1 February 1950), in G-3, FEC files. Washington, DC: Office of the Chief of Military History.

Schnabel, James F. *United States Army in the Korean War: Policy and Direction, the First Year.* Washington, DC: Office of the Chief of Military History, Department of the Army, 1972.

See also: Acheson, Dean Goodersham; MacArthur, Douglas; Truman, Harry S.

Fechteler, William
(1896–1967)

U.S. Navy admiral. William Fechteler, the son of Admiral Augustus Fechteler, was born on 6 March 1896 in San Rafael, California. He attended the U.S. Naval Academy, Annapolis, graduating in 1916. During World War I he served as an aide to the Atlantic Fleet commander on the battleship *Pennsylvania*. Sea tours, duty in Washington, and service as an instructor at the Naval Academy followed.

At the beginning of World War II, Fechteler was operations officer for the U.S. Navy Destroyer Command. From 1941 to 1943 he was assistant director of the Navy's Personnel Bureau, and in August 1943 he assumed command of the battleship *Indiana* in the Pacific. Promoted to rear admiral in January 1944, Fechteler assumed command of Amphibious Group 8, Seventh Fleet Amphibious Force. He then directed amphibious operations in New Guinea. In early 1945 during the Philippines campaign, he directed landings on Luzon and Palawan.

In 1946, after staff duty in Washington, Fechteler was promoted to vice admiral. He then commanded battleships and cruisers in the Atlantic Fleet. During 1947–1950 he was deputy chief for personnel, in which capacity he appeared before Congress to push for wage increases. In February 1950 he was promoted to full admiral and assumed command of the Atlantic Fleet. He was serving in that position when the Korean War began.

On 16 August 1951, President Harry Truman appointed Fechteler chief of naval operations (CNO), succeeding Admiral Forrest P. Sherman, who died of a heart attack while in office. Before Fechteler became CNO, the Korean War had reached stalemate. Fechteler's principal task as CNO was to maintain US naval strength and to oversee the blockade of North Korea and mainland China. Although his involvement in the war was limited, Fechteler did speak out against concessions to the Communists at the P'anmunjŏm armistice talks.

Fechteler left his post as CNO in August 1953, and during 1953–1956 he commanded North Atlantic Treaty Forces in southern Europe. He retired from the Navy in July 1956. Later he was an executive with the General Electric Company. Fechteler died at Bethesda Naval Hospital on 4 July 1967.

—*Monica Spicer*

References:
Matray, James I., ed. *Historical Dictionary of the Korean War.* Westport, CT: Greenwood Press, 1991.
Summers, Harry G., Jr. *Korean War Almanac.* New York: Facts on File, 1990.
Webster's American Military Biographies. Springfield, MA: G & C Merriam, 1978.
See also: Sherman, Forrest P.; Truman, Harry S.

Film and Literature of the Korean War

That the Korean conflict is America's forgotten war may be attributed at least in part to the reluctance of book publishers and movie makers to exploit the war in the pursuits of enlightenment and entertainment. In what might later be described as a Catch-22 situation, the book and movie people shunned the Korean War because it was not popular, and the war remained unpopular without the cheerleading and propaganda benefits the popular arts could provide.

Ironically, books and movies tended to give Americans a more unfavorable disposition toward the Korean War than the later Vietnam War because much that was written and shown cast a negative light on U.S. involvement in Indo-China. By contrast, the Second World War against Nazi Germany and imperial Japan continued to inspire major works in the performing literary arts for years afterward, including during the three-year span of the Korean War.

So many movies and books were focused on the Second World War that readers and moviegoers tired of them before the victorious conclusion for the Allies; but after only a few years World War II was again deemed commercially safe, with such high-visibility films as *Twelve O'Clock High* and *Battleground* and best-selling novels such as *From Here to Eternity* (James Jones) and *The Caine Mutiny* (Herman Wouk), both of which also had blockbuster success on film after the Korean War had heated up.

The modest first wave of movies that focused on the Korean conflict were medium- to low-budget flag-wavers with emphasis on action and without political or ideological substance. Although they appear fitfully on television and are available mostly on video, these minor efforts with easily interchangeable titles are essentially forgotten, examples being *Battle Taxi*, *Battle Zone*, and *Mission Over Korea*, all arriving before 1952.

Two movies directed by Samuel Fuller—*The Steel Helmet* and *Fixed Bayonets*—were at least well-made, earning praise for their realistic battle creations in a Korea filmed in the Ventura Hills near Hollywood. *Fixed Bayonets* now has trivia value because one of its soldiers is James Dean in a virtually nonspeaking role. Joseph Lewis's similarly constituted *Retreat, Hell!* had documentary-like authority in depicting the U.S. Marine withdrawal from Korea's Changjin Reservoir in the wake of a massive Chinese offensive. Such entries appeared to have little impact on the public, however.

Tay Garnett's *One Minute to Zero* (Robert Mitchum, Ann Blyth) and Richard Brooks's *Battle Circus* (Humphrey Bogart, June Allyson) were two major studio projects that boasted established directors and popular stars of the period, but were torn to ribbons by the critics. *Battle Circus* was essentially remade without attribution many years later, drastically revised to its everlasting benefit, as *M*A*S*H*, which in turn spawned the long-running, well-liked television sitcom of the same name.

An outstanding Korean War movie, filmed before the war's end but released in 1954 after its conclusion, was *The Bridges at Toko-Ri,* directed by Mark Robson and based on James Michener's novel, one of the more eloquent Korean War–based fictions. This film contained two splendid performances, one by William Holden, as an officer recalled from the Naval Reserve, and the other by Fredric March, as an admiral who, reflecting at the film's conclusion on the Holden character's supreme sacrifice, asks "Where do we find such men?"

Some years later, before Vietnam and while the Korean War was already on its way to becoming forgotten, some notable films dealing with various aspects of the fracas appeared spasmodically. *Pork Chop Hill* (1959), with Gregory Peck leading a solid all-male cast, was a visual triumph for veteran director Lewis Milestone—who, 29 years earlier, had directed *All Quiet on the Western Front*, a great war movie that was also America's first great talking picture. Hall Bartlett's *All the Young Men* (1960) was mediocre at best, but, as an Alan Ladd-Sidney Poitier story, it offered valuable comment on race relations among Korean War troops. John Frankenheimer's *The Manchurian Candidate* (1962) is a much-admired melodrama without military action or other scenic trappings of war, but it offers a provocative examination of psychological aftereffects of the Korean War; it also contains Frank Sinatra's finest straight acting on film. As late as 1977, Joseph Sargent's *MacArthur*, with Gregory Peck in the controversial title role, devoted much of its footage to General Douglas MacArthur's flamboyance during the Korean War, climaxing with his dismissal by President Harry Truman.

Today's moviemakers often focus on Vietnam, from time to time on World War II, and occasionally on the Great War of 1914–1918, but they have essentially abandoned the Korean War. This is not true of the historians. In the early 1980s the war was rediscovered simultaneously by a battery of authors and scholars exercising the benefit of a distanced perspective. Clay Blair's *The Forgotten War* received perhaps the strongest critical endorsement, although most entries were accorded respect. However, a prevailing thought is that the great comprehensive book on the Korean War has not yet appeared. A possibly cynical afterthought is that when it does appear, not enough people will take notice.

—*Larry Swindell*

References:

Alkoate, Jack, ed. *Film Daily Year Book.* New York; Film Daily. Annual vols. 1952-1962.

Sarris, Andrew. *The American Cinema: Directors and Directions, 1929-1968.* New York: E.P. Dution, 1968.

Shipmon, David. *Cinema: The First Hundred Years.* New York: St. Martin's, 1993.

See also: Historiography of the Korean War; MacArthur, Douglas; Poetry of the Korean War; Truman's Recall of MacArthur.

Finletter, Thomas K.
(1893–1980)

U.S. secretary of the air force during 1950–1953. Born on 11 November 1893, to a socially prominent Philadelphia family, Thomas K. Finletter did his undergraduate work at the University of Pennsylvania and then entered that institution's law school. His legal studies were interrupted by military service in the First World War. Although he was a lawyer, as were his father and grandfather before him, he broke with family tradition by leaving Philadelphia and joining the New York law firm of Cravath and Henderson. He then became a partner at Coudert Brothers. Another departure from his forebears' practice was his decision, after the United States failed to join the League of Nations, to eschew the Republican Party and become a Democrat.

In 1941 Finletter became special assistant to the secretary of state and two years later was appointed executive director of the Office of Foreign Economic Coordination, a post in which he was responsible for the acquisition of strategic materials from abroad and their denial to the Axis powers. Although Finletter left the State Department in 1944 to return to his law practice, in May 1945 he served as a consultant to the U.S. delegation to the United Nations Conference. In July 1947 President Harry S. Truman named him chairman of an Air Policy Commission to investigate all aspects of military and civil aviation in the light of the developing Cold War. The commission's report, "Survival in the Air Age," recommended the swift and massive expansion of the air force over a five-year period to enable the United States to meet a potential Soviet air attack. It also recommended development of a hydrogen bomb. In May 1948 Finletter became head of the Economic Cooperation Administration in Great Britain, where he remained until June 1949.

In April 1950 Truman appointed Finletter secretary of the air force. He succeeded Stuart Symington, an outspoken advocate of a greatly expanded air force. Finletter shared his predecessor's sympathies, though he was more tactful in expressing them. He was initially subject to severe budgetary constraints imposed by his superior, Secretary of Defense Louis Johnson and by the Truman administration's eagerness to reduce military spending. The outbreak of the Korean War in June 1950 removed both these obstacles to expansionist defense policies. Johnson was replaced, first by

George C. Marshall and then by Robert A. Lovett, and defense expenditures increased nearly fourfold.

By the time Finletter left office in 1953, the air force, which benefited disproportionately from enhanced military spending, had grown well beyond the size envisaged in his earlier report. Finletter, whose position was much subordinate to that of the secretary of defense, exercised little direct influence on Korean War policies. At the first Blair House meeting in June 1950, Finletter spoke against the commitment of ground troops, and he recommended tact and moderation during the events that led to the recall of General Douglas MacArthur.

After 1953 Finletter returned to private life and his law practice, but remained deeply involved in public affairs as an adviser to the prominent Democratic politicians W. Averell Harriman and Adlai Stevenson. Finletter's 1954 book, *Power and Policy*, reiterated his belief that nuclear supremacy was essential to deterrence and that defense must have a higher priority than national economy. In the late 1950s he argued the existence of a "missile gap" with the Soviet Union. Perhaps paradoxically, as a founder of the United World Federalists in the late 1940s, Finletter also continued to explore means of curbing international aggression through the development of peaceful, legal means of mediation.

From 1961 to 1965 Finletter served as U.S. ambassador to the North Atlantic Treaty Organization, where during the Cuban missile crisis he played a key role in gaining European support for U.S. policies. He also wrote extensively on international affairs and U.S. policy, publishing the books *Foreign Policy* (1958) and *Interim Report* (1968). Finletter died in New York City on 24 April 1980.

—*Priscilla Roberts*

References:

Borklund, Carl W. *Men of the Pentagon: From Forrestal to McNamara*. New York: Praeger, 1966.

Condit, Doris M. *History of the Office of the Secretary of Defense*. Vol. 2, *The Test of War, 1950–1953*. Washington, DC: Office of the Secretary of Defense, 1988.

Futrell, Robert F. *The United States Air Force in Korea, 1950–1953*. Washington, DC: U.S. Government Printing Office, 1961.

O'Sullivan, John. "Thomas Knight Finletter." In *Dictionary of American Biography: Supplement Ten, 1976–1980*, edited by Kenneth T. Jackson. New York: Charles Scribner's Sons, 1995.

Rearden, Steven L. *History of the Office of the Secretary of Defense*. Vol. 1, *The Formative Years, 1947–1950*. Washington, DC: Historical Office, Office of the Secretary of Defense, 1984.

"Thomas K. Finletter." In *Political Profiles: The Truman Years*, edited by Eleanora W. Schoenebaum. New York: Facts on File, 1978.

See also: Harriman, William Averell; Johnson, Louis A; Lovett, Robert A.; Marshall, George C.; Stevenson, Adlai E.; Truman, Harry S.; Truman's Recall of MacArthur.

Forward Air Controllers (FACs)

Airborne coordinators between ground troops and tactical fighter-bombers, developed from a concept pioneered by the U.S. Marines in the Pacific and the U.S. Air Force in Italy during World War II. After intense debate concerning air force autonomy, in April 1950 U.S. senior officers of the Fifth Air Force, Far East Air Forces, recognized the necessity of close army–air force tactical cooperation. As a result, in early July 1950 the army and air force established a Joint Operations Center (JOC), code-named Angelo, at Taejŏn.

In accordance with accepted air-ground operations doctrine, the air force assigned Tactical Air-Control Parties (TACPs) to the new center. Each TACP consisted of an experienced flight officer serving as the ground-based forward air controller and the airmen who operated the TACP jeep and AN/ARC-1 radio equipment.

The first TACP deployment with the 24th Infantry Division in July 1950 exposed serious deficiencies in both equipment and procedures, however. Advancing north from Taejŏn, the six TACPs of Detachment 1, 620th Aircraft Control and Warning Squadron, quickly found their World War II–vintage equipment both fragile and awkward to transport. More seriously, their AN/ARC-1 radio units required line-of-sight transmission. TACP crews thus found themselves forced to expose their unarmored jeeps to Communist fire to make close observations. By 11 July only three Detachment 1 jeeps remained operational.

Detachment 1's failure prompted JOC planners to improvise an alternate to ground-based forward observation. World War II experience had proven the effectiveness of liaison pilots directing fighter-bomber attacks against ground targets. On 9 July Lieutenants James A. Bryant and Frank G. Mitchell reported to Taejŏn with two L-5G liaison planes equipped with four-channel very high frequency (VHF) radios.

Upon their arrival Bryant and Mitchell found their equipment inoperative, however. Undaunted, they quickly commandeered two 24th Division L-17 aircraft, code-naming themselves Angelo Fox and Angelo George. So successful was their first mission—they each coordinated approximately ten F-80 ground attack flights—that the JOC commander proclaimed 9 July "the best day in Fifth Air Force history."

After 11 July, FAC observers replaced their slower liaison aircraft with T-6 "Texan" trainers. Although unarmed, the T-6 was both faster and more maneuverable than other available options and could accommodate the more versatile eight-channel AN/ARC radio sets. Later improvements during the summer of 1951 included the installation of SCR-300 infantry radio sets, which enabled direct communication with ground troops and expanded VHF-channel capacity linking the Mosquitoes, the airborne and ground controllers of close air support. Technicians further enhanced the T-6's capabilities by installing 2.25-inch subcaliber aircraft rockets to mark Communist positions. To overcome the line-of-sight radio transmission problem, the 6147th Tactical Air Control Squadron introduced C-47 Dakota transports equipped with radio sets capable of handling twenty channels of VHF radio traffic. Flying some twenty miles behind the front lines, the C-47s, code-named Mellow, acted as relays between the FACs and fighter-bombers.

By early 1951, Mosquito controllers based close to the front lines could manage multiple ground-attack flights for up to three hours. They played key roles in the success of such major offensives as Operations THUNDERBOLT and KILLER.

—Jeff Kinard

References:

Cleveland, W. M. *Mosquitos in Korea.* Portsmouth, NH: Peter E. Randall, 1991.

Futrell, Robert F. *The United States Air Force in Korea, 1950–1953.* Rev. ed. Washington, DC: Office of the Chief of Air Force History, 1983.

Proctor, Richard T. *Radio Jeeps in the Korean War.* Gibsons, British Columbia: n.p., 1984.

Toland, John. *In Mortal Combat: Korea, 1950–1953.* New York: William Morris, 1991.

See also: Airborne Operations; Aircraft (Principal Combat); Close Air Support; Jet Aircraft, First Clash in History; KILLER, Operation; THUNDERBOLT, Operation.

France

When the Korean War began in June 1950 French forces had been fighting for three and a half years in Indo-China. Despite its heavy commitment to the Indo-China War (1946–1954), France, the oldest military ally of the United States, sent military and naval assistance to United Nations forces in Korea. On the seas this took the form of the frigate *La Grandière*, which participated in patrol and blockade duties off the Korean coast. On land the French provided the *Battalion de Corée*, the Korea Battalion, also known as the French Battalion. At peak strength it numbered 1,185 men. Ralph Monclar, the *nom de guerre* of French Foreign Legionnaire Magrin Vernerrey, who had risen to lieutenant general, reverted to lieutenant colonel to command the battalion in Korea. Its men were volunteers, recruited from a variety of sources in Metropolitan France and overseas.

The Korea Battalion trained at Camp d'Avours in the Sarthe Department of France during September-October 1950. This base continued to train replacements, which were then sent to Korea every two months.

The battalion arrived in Korea by sea at the end of November and spent some time familiarizing itself with American weapons and equipment. The Korea Battalion was usually attached to the 2d Infantry Division and saw heavy fighting beginning in January 1951.

The French, who advocated bayonet charges, soon established an enviable military reputation. The battalion won three U.S. Presidential Unit Citations in fighting at the Twin Tunnels, in the Battle of Chip'yŏng-ni, and at Hongch'ŏn. It also fought in the September-October 1951 Battle of Heartbreak Ridge. The entire battalion rotated out of Korea that winter and was replaced by another unit with the same designation from France.

In the entire war France suffered 271 killed and 1,008 wounded. Twelve French POWs were repatriated at the end of the conflict. Following the armistice the Korea Battalion was sent to Indo-China where it was first known as the Korea Regiment. Reinforced, it became *Groupement Mobile* 100. GM 100 was largely destroyed in a series of battles in July 1954 just before the end of the Indo-China War.

The Korean War had a considerable effect on the French military effort in Indo-China in that it induced the Truman administration to extend direct military aid and increase assistance there. On 27 June 1950, in his statement on Korea, President Harry S. Truman announced an "acceleration" in U.S. military assistance to Indo-China. Especially after the massive Chinese military intervention in Korea, Paris stressed the interdependency of the two fronts of Indo-China and Korea in opposing the spread of Communism, as did Washington. Thus the French were somewhat bitter when the United States pushed for an armistice in Korea in 1953 after it had pressured France not to conclude an arrangement in 1952 with the Viet Minh, which would have been on better terms that those ultimately worked out in 1954.

Within France, public opinion became ambivalent on the war following the Chinese intervention. The left-wing press tended to blame General Douglas MacArthur's aggressiveness for the Chinese entry into the war. The Korean War did have an important impact on France in that it forced a shift in emphasis in Western Europe and France from economic recovery to rearmament. With U.S. manpower committed to Korea and French troops in Indo-China, there was a shortage of manpower to defend against a possible attack by the Soviet Union on Western Europe. The United States put heavy pressure on France to allow the Federal Republic of Germany (West Germany) to rearm. Paris, seeking to avoid an independent West German army, proposed the Pleven Plan that led to the European Defense Community (EDC). This ultimately failed when the French National Assembly rejected it in August 1954, but West Germany was then allowed to rearm within the framework of NATO.

—Spencer C. Tucker

References:

Blair, Clay. *The Forgotten War: America in Korea, 1950-1953.* New York: Times Books, 1987.

Republic of Korea, Ministry of National Defense. *The History of the United Nations Forces in the Korean War.* 6 vols. Seoul: War History Compilation Commission, 1967-1975.

Sandler, Stanley, editor. *The Korean War: An Encyclopedia.* New York: Garland, 1995.

Summers, Harry G., Jr. *Korean War Almanac.* New York: Facts on File, 1990.

See also: Chinese Fourth Offensive; Chip'yŏng-ni, Battle of; Heartbreak Ridge; Indo-China War, impact on Korea; Order of Battle.

Franks, Oliver
(1905–1992)

British ambassador to the United States, 1948–1952. Born near Bristol on 16 February 1905 into a clerical family, Oliver Franks was educated at Bristol Grammar School and Queen's College, Oxford, where he obtained a first-class honors degree. Until 1939 Franks taught philosophy at Oxford and Glasgow Universities, holding a chair at the latter institution. On the outbreak of the Second World War he joined the Ministry of Supply as a temporary civil servant, and in 1945 he became that ministry's permanent secretary.

From 1946 to 1948 Franks resumed the academic life as provost of Queen's College, Oxford, returning to public life in 1947 to chair the sixteen-nation Conference on European Economic Cooperation (CEEC), which prepared the report that laid the groundwork for the Marshall Plan. This job completed, Franks received the mission of persuading U.S. officials and the American public to support this blueprint, as they would be providing the greater part of the funding for this enterprise. He led a CEEC delegation to the United States and traveled throughout the country, speaking to Chambers of Commerce, Rotary Clubs, and other organizations. He also worked closely with Truman administration officials. Although Congress reduced the total sum of aid recommended in the report from $22.4 billion to $17 billion over four years, both European and British officials considered this overall result satisfactory. Franks's rapport with the United States led Prime Minister Clement Attlee and Foreign Secretary Ernest Bevin in the spring of 1948 to offer him the position of ambassador to the United States. Franks soon developed a close relationship with U.S. Secretary of State Dean Acheson; approximately once a week the two men would meet for lengthy, unofficial, off-the-record discussions of world events. Franks could take at least some of the credit for the disproportionately large share of Marshall Plan aid that Britain received in the late 1940s and for Washington's decision to establish and join the North Atlantic Treaty Organization, which came into being in 1949.

During the Korean War, Franks's friendship with Acheson helped to mend rifts in the Anglo-American relationship caused by Britain's tendency to urge restraint and caution upon its ally, particularly when dealing with the People's Republic of China (PRC). As soon as the fighting began, Franks conveyed Britain's strong endorsement of the U.S. position and its contribution of naval forces to the common cause. He was also, however, obliged to make it clear that Britain differed with the United States on the Taiwan issue. On 7 July 1950, when Franks delivered a message from Bevin suggesting that proposed peace terms extended to the Democratic People's Republic of Korea (North Korea) should include concessions on Taiwan to the newly established PRC, as well as its admission to the United Nations, Acheson sharply demurred.

Franks fervently believed that Britain had to send ground troops to the Korean conflict as proof of its solidarity with the United States. On 15 July he wrote an uncharacteristically emotional personal letter to Attlee pleading this cause, which influenced Britain's cabinet decision of 25 July to override the dissenting Joint Chiefs of Staff and commit two British brigades to Korea. Although this force was relatively small and Americans tended to discount the British military contribution, Franks believed that the symbolic gesture of U.S. and British troops fighting shoulder to shoulder as comrades was a valuable mechanism to defuse tensions over policy matters that might arise between the two countries.

In Franks's remaining years as ambassador, Korea gave rise to numerous Anglo-American incidents that tested this hypothesis and demanded all his diplomatic skills. In general, these disputes were the fruit of Britain's greater readiness to contemplate concessions to the PRC in exchange for peace in Korea, tactics that were political anathema to the Truman administration, which was then suffering fierce attacks from the Republican right over its allegedly weak and insufficiently anti-Communist, if not downright traitorous, China policies.

Anglo-American tensions were provoked by a British proposal of November 1950 that a demilitarized buffer zone be established on the North Korean–Chinese border as a means of allaying China's fears of invasion or capitalist contamination; by President Truman's public comments of November 1950 that appeared to contemplate the use of nuclear weapons; by British proposals of December 1950 and January 1951 that, as earlier, envisaged concessions to China on Taiwan and United Nations (UN) membership as the price of peace in Korea; by U.S. insistence that the British support the UN resolution of 1 February 1951, condemning China as an aggressor; and by frequent U.S. criticisms of Britain's continuing trade with China. During the Korean War, Britain was subjected to substantial U.S. pressure to undertake a massive rearmament program, which it did; however, in combination with the ending of Marshall Plan aid in 1951, this precipitated a serious financial crisis in Britain. Franks's economic expertise and ingenuity in suggesting solutions to aid and supply problems—for example, through offshore purchasing and increased charges for services at U.S. bases in Britain—helped to alleviate this situation's worst effects, thereby improving what were often decidedly stormy Anglo-American relations.

Despite requests from Foreign Secretary Anthony Eden to stay on, Franks resigned his post and returned to Britain in December 1952. He served as chairman of Lloyds Bank from 1954 to 1962, after which he returned to academic life as provost of Worcester College, Oxford, a position he retained until 1976. On several occasions Franks chaired government committees charged with investigating and reporting on matters of public interest, including the security services, Oxford University, and the Falklands War. In 1962 he was awarded a life peerage. Sir Oliver Franks died in Oxford on 25 October 1992.

—*Priscilla Roberts*

References:

Boyle, Peter G. "Oliver Franks and the Washington Embassy, 1948–1952." *British Officials and British Foreign Policy, 1945–1950,* edited by John Zametica. Leicester: Leicester University Press, 1990.

Butler, Rohan, and M. E. Pelly, eds. *Documents on British Policy Overseas.* Series II, Vol. 4, *Korea, 1950–1951.* London: Her Majesty's Stationery Office, 1995.

Danchev, Alex. *Oliver Franks: Founding Father.* New York: Oxford University Press, 1993.

MacDonald, Callum A. *Britain and the Korean War.* Oxford: Blackwell, 1990.

Stueck, William W., Jr. *The Korean War: An International History.* Princeton, NJ: Princeton University Press, 1995.

See also: Acheson, Dean Goodersham; Attlee, Clement R.; Bevin, Ernest; Churchill, Sir Winston Spencer; Eden, Anthony; Morrison, Herbert S.; NATO (North Atlantic Treaty Organization).

Freeman, Paul L., Jr.
(1907–1988)

U.S. Army officer and, during the Korean War, commander of the 23d Infantry Regiment of the 2d Infantry "Indianhead" Division from the regiment's arrival in Pusan on 4 August 1950 until he was wounded and

evacuated during the fighting at Chip'yŏng-ni in mid-February 1951.

Freeman was born on 29 June 1907 in Manila, where his father, an army colonel, was stationed. Freeman graduated from the U.S. Military Academy, West Point, in 1929. Before World War II, Freeman served with the 2d Infantry Division at Fort Sam Houston, Texas, and at Fort Benning, Georgia; with the 15th Infantry in Tianjin (Tientsen), China; in the Sino-Japanese War as an observer; and as a military attaché in Chongqing (Chungking), China.

During World War II Freeman served in China, India, and in Burma as assistant chief of staff for Stilwell's Chinese-American Force. He organized a special combat team later known as Merrill's Marauders, and he advised and accompanied General George C. Marshall on trips to Quebec, London, and elsewhere. During the Korean War Freeman commanded the 23d Infantry Regiment as it went into position on the Naktong River in the Pusan perimeter; in the breakout in September; on the push northward across the 38th parallel to the Ch'ŏngch'ŏn River valley north of Kunu-ri, where the Chinese intervened; in the blocking rearguard action at Kunu-ri; in the withdrawal of United Nations forces to positions south of the 38th parallel; and finally in the February engagements at the Twin Tunnels and at Chip'yŏng-ni.

Freeman's unit was the last 2d Division regiment to withdraw from the northernmost positions and thus held back the Chinese so that the remainder of the Eighth Army could safely relocate to the south. His decision to withdraw from Kunu-ri on a west road to Anju instead of southward to Sunch'ŏn, where the Division's other two regiments, the 9th and 38th, were being massacred in a gauntlet, became controversial. It was said that he disobeyed orders and that had he followed the other regiments south, he might have prevented their destruction. Freeman insisted that he did have authority from Assistant Division Commander Brigadier General Joseph S. Bradley to change his escape route and that, had he followed the other regiments, the 23d would have merely met the same fate.

At Chip'yŏng-ni, Freeman led his regiment in a three-day victorious perimeter defense, inflicted crushing casualties on many Communist divisions, and established for the first time that a U.S. regiment, employing schoolbook techniques and tactics, could prevail against anything thrown at it. When he was wounded in the leg by a shell fragment, Freeman refused evacuation even though his replacement had arrived and the helicopter waiting to carry him out had to leave without him. He agreed to leave only at the end of the fighting.

Ultimately promoted to full (four-star) general, Freeman served as commanding general of U.S. Army, Europe, for three years before his retirement in 1967. He died on 17 April 1988 in Carmel, California.

—*Sherman W. Pratt*

References:

Blair, Clay. *The Forgotten War: America in Korea, 1950–1953.* New York: Times Books, 1987.

Monroe, Clark C. *The Second United States Infantry Division in Korea, 1950–1951.* Tokyo: Tappan, n.d.

Pratt, Sherman W. *Decisive Battles of the Korean War. An Infantry Company Commander's View of the War's Most Critical Engagements.* New York: Vantage Press, 1992.

Washington Post, 20 April 1988.

See also: Chip'yŏng-ni, Battle of; Marshall, George C.

G

Gao Gang (Kao Kang)
(1902–1954)

Chinese People's Volunteer Army (CPVA) general; commander and political commissar of the Northeast Military Region, responsible for logistics support. Born in Heng-shan, Shaanxi Province, around 1902, Gao Gang was a key leader of Communist forces in Shaanxi during the early 1930s. Gao served as the political commissar of the Shaanxi and Gansu Provinces guerrilla forces in 1931. Between 1933 and 1934 he was political commissar of the Shaanxi-Gansu Military Committee. Gao helped develop the Soviet area in Yenan that would provide sanctuary to the survivors of the Long March (1935) and to Mao Zedong, who arrived there on 19 October 1935. Gao was trained at the Xi'an Military Academy. He remained in Yenan until 1945, when he was transferred to the northeastern region of China (Manchuria).

In May 1949 Gao was sent on a secret mission of top Chinese leaders to Moscow. Along with Liu Shaoqi, Gao headed the Chinese committee to handle Soviet loans and material assistance. On 2 November 1949 when the People's Liberation Army (PLA) entered Shenyang and established the Chinese Communist Party (CCP) Northeast Bureau, Gao Gang was named the secretary. Gao was especially powerful in the region because he held all major posts of the military, Communist Party, and government. He maintained close ties to senior government and military leaders in the USSR, as well as Russian railway and resource interests in Manchuria.

On 4 August 1950, a Politburo meeting convened in Beijing to discuss accelerating preparations to assist the Democratic People's Republic of Korea (North Korea). On 5 August 1950, Mao Zedong ordered Gao to mobilize the Northeast Border Defense Force (NBDF) to prepare for intervention in Korea by late August. With preparations ineffective, on 15 August Gao sent a telegram to Mao suggesting that mobilization be postponed. Mao responded by informing Gao that preparations must be completed no later than 30 September. As commander and political commissar of the Northeast Military Region, Gao was ordered to "take full charge of coordinating and guaranteeing all requisitions of supplies from the rear base, as well as for assistance provided to Korean comrades."

During late August, Beijing increased pressure on Gao to complete mobilization for the possible intervention. Gao is reported to have opposed intervention at a 4 October 1950 meeting, primarily on the basis of economic concerns, arguing that the new republic could not support a war and the people would be "disenchanted." Other reports contradict this, claiming that Gao supported Mao's decision to intervene in Korea. In any case, on 5 October 1950, Mao's decision to intervene prevailed. In the formal order of 8 October, the NBDF was renamed Chinese People's Volunteers, with Gao in charge of supplies, transportation, and other rear services.

In the early summer of 1951, Mao sent PLA Chief of Staff Xu Xiangqian to Moscow to secure munitions and military technology. Gao later was sent to assist, but the Soviets hesitated, fearing war with the United States and being distrustful of China.

As a regional commander Gao commanded all PLA ground, navy, and air forces as well as the Public Security forces (including the border guards). He was responsible for training, recruiting, organizing, and arming all forces. He also commanded the militia and served as the custodian of its arms and ammunition. Gao also supervised support to specialized units, such as air defense, railway, airborne, and amphibious units within northeast China. Gao operated the local military schools and training centers, and he handled all inductions and separations. He was also responsible for the maintenance of law and order, including the arrest of "counterrevolutionaries, bandits, and enemy agents."

From late 1953 to early 1954, Gao was the target of the first major purge within the CCP leadership since the founding of the People's Republic of China. Both Gao and Rao Shushi, political commissar of Shanghai, were accused of building "independent kingdoms" and following erroneous economic policies. Gao, for example, had established one-man management within factories, an innovation Mao Zedong hated, rather than relying on the cumbersome revolutionary factory management committees. Rao and Gao were accused of trying to seize power from Zhou Enlai and Liu Shaoqi to assume the senior positions next to Mao. Gao's close links to the Soviet Union may also have been a factor in his downfall.

Gao disappeared in early 1954 without explanation. His last known public appearance was on 20 January 1954. For his alleged crimes, Gao was deprived of all his posts and expelled from the party. Deng Xiaoping later announced that Gao Gang had been guilty of the ultimate treason by committing suicide in 1954.

—*Susan M. Puska*

References:

Chen, Jian. *China's Road to the Korean War: The Making of the Sino-American Confrontation.* New York: Columbia University Press, 1994.

Rice, Edward E. *Mao's Way.* Berkeley: University of California Press, 1974.

Spence, Jonathan D. *The Search for Modern China.* New York: W. W. Norton, 1990.

Zhang, Shu Guang. *Mao's Military Romanticism: China and the Korean War, 1950–1953.* Lawrence: University Press of Kansas, 1995.

See also: China, People's Republic of: Army; Deng Hua (Teng Hua); Mao Zedong; Peng Dehuai (Peng Te-huai); Xie Fang (Hsieh Fang).

Gay, Hobart Raymond
(1894–1983)

U.S. Army general and commander of the 1st Cavalry Division in the Korean War. Born in Rockport, Illinois, on 16 May 1894, Hobart R. "Hap" Gay graduated from Knox College in 1917. That same year he was commissioned a second lieutenant of cavalry in the regular army. During and immediately after World War I, he served with the 12th and 7th Cavalry Regiments on the Mexican border. During 1923–1925 he was a student at the Cavalry School at Fort Riley, Kansas, where he remained as an instructor until 1929. Then, having lost an eye in a polo match, he was transferred to the Quartermaster Corps and assigned to the Quartermaster Depot and Remount Purchasing Headquarters at Fort Reno, Oklahoma. He commanded that organization from 1934 to 1936, when he was ordered to Fort Clayton in the Panama Canal Zone to serve as post quartermaster. He graduated from the Quartermaster School in Philadelphia in 1939. After a brief assignment as post quartermaster at Fort Myer, Virginia, Gay graduated from the Army Industrial College in Washington, D.C., in 1940. From January 1941 to February 1942 Gay served successively as division quartermaster and commander of the 14th Quartermaster Battalion in the 2d Armored Division and as quartermaster of the I Armored Corps at Fort Benning, Georgia.

In July 1942 Gay became chief of staff of the I Armored Corps. Later he was chief of staff, Western Task Force, at Camp Young and Camp A. P. Hill, Virginia. In November 1942 he deployed with I Corps to North Africa. He was promoted to brigadier general in June 1943, and in July he became chief of staff of the Seventh Army, with which he served in Sicily.

In February 1944 Gay became chief of staff of the Third Army serving in Britain, France, and Germany. Promoted to major general in March 1945, he became chief of staff of the Fifteenth Army in Germany in October 1945. General Gay survived the automobile accident in which General George S. Patton, Jr. was killed, and in January 1946 he assumed command of the Fifteenth Army. The next month he was reassigned to command the 1st Armored Division. The following April, Gay became commander of the 2d Constabulary Brigade, in which post he served until August 1947.

General Gay returned to the United States to command the Military District of Washington during 1947–1949, when he assumed command of the 1st Cavalry Division in Osaka, Japan. When the Korean War began, Gay led the 1st Cavalry Division to Korea, where it entered action on 19 July 1950. It subsequently took part in the defense of the Pusan perimeter, the breakout and drive north to the Yalu River, and the hard-fought withdrawal from North Korea during November–December 1950. As 1st Cavalry Division commander, Gay made several extremely difficult decisions, among them blowing the bridge across the Naktong River on 3 August 1950, which resulted in the death of a number of Korean refugees. He also decided to withdraw the 5th Cavalry Regiment, leaving the 8th Cavalry Regiment to its fate in the October 1950 battle near Unsan.

General Gay relinquished command of the 1st Cavalry Division in February 1951 and was reassigned as deputy commander of the Fourth Army at Fort Sam Houston, Texas. He later commanded the VI Corps at Camp Atterbury, Indiana, from July 1952 to April 1953 and the III Corps at Fort MacArthur, California, and Fort Hood, Texas, from April 1953 to September 1954. Promoted to lieutenant general in September 1954, Gay then commanded the Fifth Army at Fort Sheridan, Illinois. Gay retired from active duty in August 1955 and became superintendent of the New Mexico Military Institute. He died on 19 August 1983 and is buried at Fort Bliss, Texas.

—*Charles R. Shrader*

References:

Ancell, R. Manning, and Christine M. Miller. *The Biographical Dictionary of World War II. Generals and Flag Officers—The U. S. Armed Forces.* Westport, CT: Greenwood Press, 1996.

Appleman, Roy E. *South to the Naktong, North to the Yalu.* Washington, DC: Office of the Chief of Military History, 1961.

Shrader, Charles R., ed. *Reference Guide to United States Military History.* Vol. 5, *1945 to the Present.* New York: Facts on File, 1995.

U.S. Department of Defense biographical sketch.

See also: Eighth Army; Naktong Bulge, First Battle of; Unsan, Battle of.

Geneva Conference of 1954
(26 April–15 June 1954)

Conference, commonly associated with the Indo-China War, that was called to deal with a range of Far East problems, but primarily to find a peaceful resolution for the issue of Korean reunification. During the 1953 Korean War armistice discussions at

P'anmunjŏm, United Nations Command (UNC) and Communist delegates tacitly agreed that a political conference should be called to resolve the issue of reunification. U.S. representatives concurred in this, but preparations for the conference were delayed. Democratic People's Republic of Korea (DPRK, North Korea) representatives insisted that the Soviet Union and India be represented, a demand that the United States initially would not accept. A relaxation in tension between the United States and USSR after the death of Soviet Premier Josef Stalin eased U.S. opposition on this issue.

During the 25 January–18 February 1954 Four-Power Berlin Conference involving representatives of the United States, Britain, France, and the Soviet Union, the major powers agreed to hold a conference that would meet in Geneva on 26 April "for the purpose of reaching a peaceful settlement of the Korean question." This would include representatives of the United States, Britain, France, the Soviet Union, the People's Republic of China, the two Koreas, "and other countries the armed forces of which participated in the hostilities in Korea."

On 26 February 1954, the U.S. State Department invited those powers that had participated on the UN side in the Korean War. The Soviet Union invited North Korea and mainland China. Thus, Australia, Canada, Colombia, Ethiopia, Greece, Luxembourg, the Netherlands, New Zealand, the Philippines, Thailand, and Turkey joined the others at Geneva. A total of fifteen meetings were held, spread over the seven-weeks between 26 April and 15 June 1954.

In early meetings the United States and its allies agreed upon two basic principles: first, the reunification of North and South Korea had to be based upon free, democratic elections; and second, the Communist side had to affirm the authority of the UN to supervise elections. Thus U.S. Secretary of State John Foster Dulles requested the removal of Chinese troops from Korea so that the proposed elections could follow. The Communist side rejected this request and also rebuffed the idea that elections be monitored only in the North; they insisted on peninsula-wide monitoring. Chinese Foreign Minister Zhou Enlai demanded Korea-wide elections with no foreign intervention. His implication was that UN troops also should leave South Korea. Ultimately Dulles left Geneva, frustrated with the course of the talks and realizing that the Communist side would not agree to UN demands. Undersecretary of State Walter Bedell Smith then took charge of the U.S. delegation.

There was no agreement during the seven-week-long conference over how the Korean elections should be held. The U.S. side wanted the United Nations to play a large role. The Communist side, however, offered no proposals that included the UN in either the electoral or reunification process. On 3 May 1954, Smith objected to a Communist attempt to dominate the electoral commission. British Foreign Minister Anthony Eden later complained that the Communist proposals "impose conditions which would enable elections to be held after only a long and complicated series of delays." On 22 May, DPRK representative Nam Il proposed a plan calling for the creation of social organizations based upon population to supervise the elections. Smith objected, citing that the DPRK would maintain a veto power over the process and could limit representation to Communist-dominated organizations.

Both sides drifted further apart on the issue of elections and the role of the UN. Even by 15 June, the last day of the conference, the two sides were unable to agree on any single substantive issue regarding Korea. Despite requests by the Communist side that discussions continue, the U.S.-led side issued a final statement. Entitled "Declaration by the Sixteen," it stated that the Communists would not accept the two basic tenets of free elections and UN supervision. For that reason the United States and its allies agreed that it was fruitless to continue discussions at Geneva. They concluded by reaffirming the right and responsibility of the UN to settle the Korean question. The Communist side then charged the U.S.-dominated group with prematurely ending discussions. Zhou Enlai personally charged the United States with blocking the reunification of Korea.

To date, the UN upholds the legitimacy of the Republic of Korea (South Korean) government because its delegates monitor elections there. North Korea continues to refuse UN representatives to monitor its elections.

—Mark A. T. Esposito

References:

Brands, H. W. "The Dwight D. Eisenhower Administration, Syngman Rhee and the 'Other' Geneva Conference of 1954." *Pacific Historical Review* 61 (February 1987): 78–99.

Randle, Robert. *Geneva, 1954. The Settlement of the Indochinese War.* Princeton, NJ: Princeton University Press, 1969.

Reitzel, William, Morton A. Kaplan, and Constance G. Coblenz. *United States Foreign Policy, 1945–1955.* Washington, DC: Brookings Institution, 1956.

See also: Armistice Agreement; Dulles, John Foster; Eden, Anthony; Smith, Walter Bedell; Zhou Enlai.

Geneva Convention of 1949

The Geneva Convention of 1949 was an enlarged version of the Geneva Convention of 1929, which it replaced. During the Korean War, controversy centered on the 1949 document's Convention IV, covering the treatment of prisoners of war (POWs), specifically their right to repatriation. The Communists stuck to the literal interpretation of Article 118 of the 1949 convention. Article 118 stated that "Prisoners of War shall be released and repatriated without delay after the cessation of active hostilities." The United Nations Command (UNC), on the other hand, favored a looser interpretation of the accords and proposed nonforcible repatriation. This difference was present not only during the armistice negotiations but also in the General Assembly of the UN. The United States emphasized that the 1949 document was to defend the individual, whereas the Communist side argued that the document was meant to ensure the rights of the countries to which the POWs belonged.

The U.S. stand arose in part from World War II, during which millions had escaped from the Communist sphere of influence to Western Europe only to be returned and punished. Washington did not wish to suffer such a political defeat again. Another reason for the UNC stand was that there were about 150,000 Communist POWs, whereas only 10,000 UNC prisoners were held by the Communists in their POW camps. Thus, compulsory repatriation would have yielded excessive advantage to the Communist forces.

Interestingly, the United States, although among the signatory powers of the 1949 Geneva Convention, never ratified the document. And neither the People's Republic of China nor North Korea had signed the convention. Still, both sides professed their intention to adhere to its principles and spirit, although on occasion the Communists articulated that because they had not signed the document they were not bound by its terms.

The Geneva Convention of 1949 required that adequate information regarding the number, location, and general situation of prisoners of war be forwarded to the Red Cross. The Communists repeatedly failed to provide this information, in spite of UNC protests. The Chinese held that the return of POWs should be more important than information about them. Because they were not among the Geneva Convention signatory powers, the Chinese took the position that they were not bound by its terms.

The Geneva Convention of 1949 also called for marking POW and civilian internee camps. Yet most Communist camps were unmarked, and the loss of prisoner lives during UNC aerial attacks always presented the Communists with a good opportunity for propaganda. POW camps in North Korea were often in close proximity to potential UNC targets. Indeed, UNC POWs were held as human shields against UNC air strikes.

Communist propaganda did not fail to exploit the underlying opportunities in having masses of Chinese and North Korean prisoners in South Korea. Defying the terms of the Geneva Convention, Communist lead-

ers encouraged riots in UNC camps. One infamous example was the Kŏje-do POW uprising of May–June 1953. In the Communist-controlled camps, the Chinese also launched a massive program of indoctrination. In their camps, compulsory political lessons were held every day to prove the superiority of the Communist system and indoctrinate the prisoners for propaganda purposes. To a lesser extent, the United States introduced an educational program for Communist POWs to demonstrate the supremacy of capitalism and Western values.

After the most divisive issue of the talks had delayed the armistice by over a year, the first steps toward a compromise came in early 1953 when, in Operation LITTLE SWITCH, under Article 109 of the Geneva Convention, both sides agreed to an exchange of sick and wounded POWs.

—*Zsolt Varga*

References:
Clark, Mark W. *From the Danube to the Yalu.* New York: Harper & Row, 1954.
The Geneva Conventions of August 12, 1949. Geneva: International Committee of the Red Cross, 1949.
Hastings, Max. *The Korean War.* New York: Simon & Schuster, 1987.
Vatcher, William H., Jr. *Panmunjom.* New York: Praeger, 1958.
See also: BIG SWITCH/LITTLE SWITCH, Operations; Brainwashing (*Senoe; Xinao*); Kŏje-do Prisoner-of-War Uprising; Neutral Nations Repatriation Commission; P'anmunjŏm Truce Talks; Prisoner-of-War Code of Conduct; Repatriation, Voluntary.

Germany, Federal Republic of

The Korean War had significant influence on the Federal Republic of Germany (FRG). As a consequence of the war, the FRG moved to rearmament and participation in the European Defense Community (EDC) and the North Atlantic Treaty Organization (NATO).

In 1949 U.S. Secretary of State Dean Acheson testified before Congress that the FRG would never be included in NATO. Most Europeans, including a majority in the FRG, agreed with contemporary British popular opinion that any rearming of Germany was "sinister and repugnant." FRG Chancellor Konrad Adenauer stood virtually alone in favoring German rearmament. The Korean War changed all that.

Coming after the Communist takeover of Czechoslovakia in 1948, the 1948–1949 Berlin blockade, and the successful Communist revolution in China, the North Korean invasion of South Korea reinforced the notion of a coordinated Communist plan for global revolution. Many people believed that it signaled a new willingness to engage in a "hot war" and saw the FRG as the next target. Others compared it to Czechoslovakia in 1938, when Nazi Germany usurped an entire state after part had been ceded. Adenauer noted that the socialist German Democratic Republic (GDR, East Germany) had 50,000 men under arms in addition to a sizable Soviet military presence in that country and that East German leaders boasted of a "fifth column" inside the FRG. Western policymakers concluded that the defense of Europe and of the FRG needed strengthening.

Adenauer exploited the situation. In separate memoranda to the High Commission of the Council of Europe, he first offered the services of a German military contingent in any European army formed and then asked, without stating it as a quid pro quo, that the state of war between the Allied powers and the FRG be terminated and the occupation replaced with an alliance. He followed up in August 1950, suggesting that a force of 50,000–80,000 German volunteers serve as a counterweight to the forces in the GDR, thus freeing U.S. troops for duty elsewhere.

Advised by U.S. General Omar Bradley and John J. McCloy, the U.S. High Commissioner in Germany, that German rearmament was essential to the defense of Europe, Acheson reversed his position. In September 1950, he proposed that a ten-division German army be included in NATO. European leaders neither endorsed nor rejected the idea totally. The French advocated the acceptance of German troops in a European army, but not in Germany. The situation in Korea, however, made German rearmament a goal of U.S. defense policy. The February 1952 Lisbon Accords solidified the German contribution to and membership in the soon-to-be-created (May 1952) EDC. The FRG would contribute twelve army divisions as well as air force and navy contingents. It would not be a member of NATO; that happened in 1955. A second agreement replacing the Occupation Statute of 1949 with a "Contractual Agreement" officially ending Allied controls in the FRG was ratified in conjunction with the EDC treaty.

—Timothy C. Dowling

References:

Crawley, Aidan. *The Rise of Western Germany, 1945–1972.* London: Collins, 1973.

Kaufman, Burton I. *The Korean War: Challenges in Crisis, Credibility, and Command.* Philadelphia: Temple University Press, 1986.

See also: Acheson, Dean Goodersham; Bradley, Omar Nelson; Cold War, Origins to 1950; France; NATO (North Atlantic Treaty Organization).

Gloucester (Gloster) Hill, Battle of
(22–25 April 1951)

Key battle during the Chinese Fifth (Spring) Offensive named after the 1st Battalion, Gloucestershire Regiment, 29th British Brigade; also known as the Battle of Hill 235. In April 1951 United Nations Command (UNC) ground forces had established positions along the waist of the Korean peninsula and had launched a series of successful attacks to secure the dominant terrain north of the 38th parallel. In an effort to halt this advance, Chinese People's Volunteer Army (CPVA, Chinese Communist) forces prepared their Fifth, or Spring, Offensive.

On 30 March 1951, the 29th British Brigade was attached to the U.S. 3d Infantry Division defending positions along the Imjin River. The 29th's area of responsibility began near Chŏksŏng village and extended east to the junction of the Imjin and Hant'an Rivers. The 1st Battalion, Gloucestershire Regiment (hereafter, the Glosters) had the brigade's left flank between Chŏksŏng and Sŏlma-ri. The Royal Northumberland Fusiliers held the center and the Belgian battalion secured the right flank on the far side of the Imjin River. A two-mile gap of unoccupied hills spread the distance between the Glosters and Fusiliers. To the left, a mile gap existed between the Glosters and the Republic of Korea Army 1st Infantry Division's 12th Regiment.

On 22 April twenty-seven CPVA divisions attacked the UNC 40-mile front. At midnight on 22 April, probing patrols from the CPVA Sixty-Third Army's 187th Division approached the 29th British Brigade's front line, slipping between the Belgian Battalion and Fusiliers. That night the Glosters fought a difficult and costly battle, requiring their commander, Lieutenant Colonel James P. Carne, to pull his forward companies back and tighten his position on and around Hill 235.

At 0830 on 23 April aerial reconnaissance reported CPVA forces entering the gap between the Glosters and Fusiliers. Throughout the day, several divisions of the Chinese 64th Army pushed across the Imjin and through the gaps to the left and right of the Glosters' position. That night, probing attacks developed into full assaults on the Glosters. Although completely surrounded, outnumbered, and weakened from increasing casualties and diminishing ammunition, the British inflicted heavy casualties on the attacking Chinese and managed to hold Hill 235.

By dawn on 24 April the Glosters's situation was critical. Throughout that day, units from the 3d Infantry Division tried to cut through to rescue them, but all attempts failed. On the morning of 25 April, Colonel Carne attempted to withdraw what remained of his battalion from Hill 235 and fight his way back to 3d Division lines.

On 22 April the Glosters' strength had been 35 officers and 738 enlisted men. Only 4 officers and 36 enlisted men, all from the battalion's D Company, managed to break through to friendly lines. Only a handful of the battalion's other officers and enlisted personnel was subsequently rescued.

By holding Hill 235 as long as it did, the Glosters prevented the Chinese from pushing into I Corps' rear area. For its bravery the battalion was awarded a U.S. Presidential Unit Citation.

—*Mark R. Franklin*

References:

Appleman, Roy E. *Ridgway Duels for Korea.* College Station, TX: Texas A&M Press, 1990.

Farrar-Hockley, Sir Anthony. *The British Part in the Korean War.* Vol. 2, *An Honourable Discharge.* London: Her Majesty's Stationery Office, 1994.

————. *The Edge of The Sword.* London: Frederick Muller, 1954.

Mossman, Billy C. *U.S. Army in the Korean War: Ebb and Flow, November 1950–July 1951.* Washington, DC: U.S. Army Center of Military History, 1990.

Summers, Harry G., Jr. *Korean War Almanac.* New York: Facts on File, 1990.

See also: Chinese Military Offensives; KILLER, Operation; RUGGED, Operation; THUNDERBOLT, Operation.

Grafström, Sven
(1902–1955)

Leader of the Swedish delegation to the United Nations (UN) who served on its Good Offices Committee and the Neutral Nations Supervisory Commission during and after the Korean War. Born in Stockholm on 2 November 1902, Sven Grafström obtained a degree from the Stockholm School of Economics in 1923. He entered the Swedish Foreign Service in 1928, serving successively in Oslo, London, Moscow, Tehran, Ankara, and Warsaw; in 1939 he returned to Sweden after evacuating Swedish nationals from Poland. After nine years in various foreign office positions in Stockholm, in 1948 he was appointed leader of the Swedish delegation at the UN.

Although described in an obituary as "strongly pro-Allied" during the Korean War, Grafström also believed that relatively conciliatory tactics toward the Communist countries were most likely to succeed. He thought it essential that the UN act to check North Korea's invasion of the South, but he held it counterproductive publicly to blame the Soviet Union for the war. Throughout the war Grafström remained a committed advocate of a negotiated settlement.

In December 1950 Grafström unsuccessfully suggested the dispatch of a small UN delegation to Beijing to negotiate with the Chinese leadership over the war, but also to emphasize UN support for South Korea. In early 1951 Grafström agreed to serve as the Swedish representative on the UN Good Offices Committee, the principal objective of which was to open talks with the People's Republic of China (PRC) in the hope of facilitating a negotiated peace settlement, which he and others thought now depended principally upon China's acquiescence. Because Sweden still maintained its representation in Beijing, UN diplomats believed that the Swedes offered a potentially excellent conduit through which to pursue this objective.

Grafström also maintained close contact with U.S. officials because no such settlement could be achieved without U.S. goodwill. After three months the Good Offices Committee had made no headway, and the UN moved to impose further sanctions on the PRC. In May 1951 the Swedish government sent Grafström a message that it had received feelers suggesting that the Soviets were ready to reopen negotiations with the West, one of several such episodes that led to the Kennan-Malik conversations and the subsequent reopening of armistice negotiations.

In 1953 Grafström was named president of the four-member Neutral Nations Supervisory Commission that oversaw the implementation of the Armistice Agreement; this position carried the special rank of major general. In 1954 he was appointed Swedish minister to Mexico. Grafström died on 3 January 1955 in an accidental fall from the Côte d'Azur–Paris express.

—*Priscilla Roberts*

References:

Grafström, Sven. *Anteckningar,* edited by Stig Ekman. 2 vols. Stockholm: Samfundet för utgivande av handskrifter rörande Skandinaviens historia, 1989.

Hanhimaki, Jussi M. *Scandinavia and the United States: An Insecure Friendship.* New York: Twayne, 1997.

Stueck, William W., Jr. *The Korean War: An International History.* Princeton, NJ: Princeton University Press, 1995.

Utrikespolitiska Institutet. *Sweden and the United Nations: Report by a Special Study Group of the Swedish Institute of International Affairs.* New York: Manhattan Publishing, 1956.

Yoo, Tae-Ho. *The Korean War and the United Nations.* Louvain, Belgium: Librairie Desbarax, 1964.

See also: Kennan-Malik Conversations; Neutral Nations Supervisory Commission; United Nations Good Offices Committee.

Graves Registration

Mission of the U.S. Army Quartermaster Corps to collect, evacuate, and identify the military dead; also known as mortuary affairs. The care given the American battle deaths in the Korean War often was extended to other nationalities caught up in the fighting.

The Korean conflict was the first instance in which all American dead were not temporarily interred in foreign soil until the end of fighting to be transported home. Instead, a policy evolved in which the deceased were quickly moved back from battle lines to a Quartermaster graves registration unit such as the 148th QMGR Company headquartered at Wŏnju. From there they were flown to a central QM facility in Japan, to be shipped onward to the United States, often

Replacement of temporary headboards with crosses, U.S. 1st Cavalry Division temporary cemetery, Taegu, 25 August 1950. (National Archives)

arriving within thirty days of the soldier's death. Thanks in part to the Korean experience, in the Vietnam War this procedure was refined so that, on average, only seven days elapsed from the time of death to receipt of the remains by the next of kin.

Historically this efficiency was a long time in coming. The antecedents of today's mortuary affairs duties originated in the American Civil War, in which roughly 42 percent of all who died were not identified. In the Mexican-American War (1846–1847) few of the dead were ever identified or their graves located. Only in 1917 did the War Department begin requiring combat soldiers to wear dog tags for identification purposes. In World War II more than 250,000 Americans died and were buried in overseas temporary or permanent cemeteries.

Because the graves registration mission had always been considered a wartime service, the World War II QMGR units were disbanded in peacetime. When the Korean War commenced in June 1950, there existed a single 30-member unit, the 108th QMGR Platoon, in Yokohama, Japan, for deployment to Korea.

In the first days of the conflict, the dead were buried in eleven small division-level cemeteries immediately behind the fluctuating battle lines. The fluid tactical situation in fall 1950 forced closure of those cemeteries and evacuation of 5,000 bodies to Kokura, Japan. This was the first time in U.S. history that a mass disinterment of combat dead occurred while hostilities were in progress.

During the war and during the armistice since, QMGR search and recover teams have scoured the battleground looking for missing-in-action personnel. This work could be dangerous with the uncovering of live grenades and small-arms ammunition, but more than 97 percent of recovered American dead in the Korean War have been identified.

Today the 54th Quartermaster Company at Fort Lee, Virginia, is the only active mortuary affairs unit in the U.S. Army. Individuals from that company provided assistance after the 1995 bombing of the federal building in downtown Oklahoma City, Oklahoma.

—*Richard A. Garver*

References:

Alexander, Bevin R. "Quartermaster Field Service Platoon in Action." U.S. Army Center of Military History, Historical Manuscripts Collection, no. 8-5. 1A BA 60.

Anders, Steven E. "With All Due Honors." *Quartermaster Professional Bulletin* (September 1988): 21–25.

Martz, John D. Jr. "Homeward Bound." *Quartermaster Review* (May–June 1954): 14–15, 144–149.

See also: Casualties.

Great Britain (See United Kingdom)

Greece

One of nineteen members of the United Nations (UN) providing combat and other support for the United Nations Command (UNC) during the Korean War. The Greeks provided an infantry battalion of volunteers that served with and became, in effect, an integral part of the 7th Regiment of the 1st Cavalry Division. Many of the members of the Greek Battalion were not newcomers in the fight to contain Communism because during 1945–1949 Greece had been involved in its own struggle to overcome internal civil war and external invasion by Communist forces. Clay Blair noted in *The Forgotten War* that the 1949 victory by the Greek Army was a "'landmark victory' for the Truman Doctrine and a great personal triumph for [General James A.] Van Fleet who was lionized in Athens and elsewhere."

The Greek Battalion arrived in Korea in November 1950 and was promptly committed just as the Chinese were intervening. Most of the Greek officers were hand picked and spoke English. Battalion commander Lieutenant Colonel Dionyssios G. Arbouzis had been in combat on and off since 1940, fighting Italians, Germans, and then Communist guerrillas. (In 1974, as a four-star general, he became commander in chief of Greek armed forces.)

The 7th Regiment warmly embraced the Greeks; the Americans regarded the Greek Battalion as a superior outfit with excellent fighters and leaders. It fought with distinction throughout most of the war with the 1st Cavalry Division. Typical of its many instances of heroism was an action near Wŏnju, on Hill 381, occupied by the Greek Battalion on 28 January 1951. The 7th Cavalry regimental history noted (quoted in Clay Blair, *The Forgotten War*, p. 661):

> Fierce and bitter fighting raged throughout the night as three times the enemy reached the crest of Hill 381 only to be driven off by the ferocious counter-attacks of the brave Greek company

holding the top of the hill. The fighting on this hill—hand to hand with grenades, rifle butts and bayonets—saw many examples of heroism as the tenacious Greek soldiers entered their first major action as part of the United Nations Forces. The hilltop on which they fought was vital to the security of the regiment.... Those who ran out of ammunition fought with their bare hands to retain this important hill.

The Greeks also provided air support in the 13th Hellenic Flight (squadron) of seven C-47 Dakota transport planes. This squadron arrived at the same time as the infantry battalion and served with the 21st, and later the 6461st, U.S. Transport Squadrons. At peak strength in 1952, more than 1,200 Greek soldiers were serving with the UNC in Korea.

During the Korean War the Greeks sustained a total of 199 dead and 610 wounded.

—*Sherman W. Pratt*

References:

Blair, Clay. *The Forgotten War: America in Korea, 1950–1953.* New York: Times Books, 1987.

Mastryoyannis, D. I. "The 13th Hellenic Flight: Greeks in the Korean War." *Graybeards* 7, no. 4 (June 1993): 49.

Pratt, Sherman W. *Decisive Battles of the Korean War. An Infantry Company Commander's View of the War's Most Critical Engagements.* New York: Vantage Press, 1992.

See also: Van Fleet, James Alward.

Grenades

Various forms of grenades were employed by United Nations and Communist forces in the Korean War. The basic United Nations Command (UNC) defensive hand grenade was the MkII fragmentation "pineapple" grenade that had seen service in World War II and was originally based on the British Mills pattern. It had a serrated cast-iron body, was olive drab, and was filled with 2 ounces of flaked trinitrotoluene (TNT). The M26 fragmentation grenade superseded the MkII later in the war. This egg-shaped grenade was lighter, could be thrown farther, and had a better fragmentation pattern than the older MkII. The basic UNC offensive grenade was the MkIIIA1, which was can-shaped, black with a yellow band, and filled with 8 ounces of flaked TNT.

Other UNC hand grenades included the M6 irritant gas (adamsite) grenade filled with CN-DM (chloroacetophenone and diphenylaminechlorarsine) and the M7(M7A1) tear gas and M25(M25A1) riot-control grenades filled with CN. More specialized hand-grenade types were the AN-M14 incendiary grenade filled with thermite used for materiel destruction, the M15 smoke grenade filled with white phosphorus used to screen small unit actions and for harassment, and the

M18 colored smoke and AN-M3 red smoke grenades used for signaling.

UNC rifle grenades consisted of bursting, pyrotechnic signal, and smoke signal classes. The first class consisted of the M9A1 high-explosive antitank (HEAT) rifle grenade that was able to penetrate 3 inches of armor plate, the MkII fragmentation hand grenade launched with a projection adapter (M1), and the M19A1 white phosphorus smoke rifle grenade. The second class consisted of star signal parachute and cluster devices in white (M17A1/M18A1), green (M19A1/M20A1), amber (M21A1/M22A1), and red (M51A1/M52A1). The third class consisted of the M22 colored smoke rifle grenade and M23 colored smoke streamer rifle grenade series that came in red, violet, yellow, and green colors.

Communist forces employed both antipersonnel and antitank hand grenades in Korea. Because no color-coding system was used, standardized grenade body and fuse colors varied. The older Soviet defensive fragmentation grenade was the TNT-filled F1 (Chinese Type 1/M33 PRC) that was akin to the cast-iron U.S. pineapple grenade. It saw limited use presumably because it had been upgraded to the lighter RG42 (also known as RTD-1942) economy version. This version consisted of a tin canister, fragmentation sleeve, TNT filler, and F1 igniter and lever system. The Chinese equivalent device was called the Type 42 PRC. Also seeing limited service was the older Soviet RGD33, a dual-use offensive and defensive stick grenade, which came with a removable fragmentation sleeve. Less sophisticated Chinese stick grenades were also used. Grenade quality ranged from good to crude. A metal casing containing TNT or picric acid was attached to a wooden stick and was activated by a cord-initiated pull-friction fuze.

Soviet antitank hand grenades were based on the RPG40, RPG43, and RPG6 models that dated back to World War II. These TNT-filled grenades could be thrown only about twenty meters. All of these grenades used fabric streamers for stabilization once thrown. While the RPG40 is a crude area-blast device that is more effective against lightly armored vehicles, the RPG43 and RPG6 models were built around a shaped charge that could penetrate 75 mm and 100 mm of armor plate, respectively.

—*Robert J. Bunker*

References:

U.S. Department of the Army. *Hand and Rifle Grenades.* FM 23-30. Washington, DC: U.S. Government Printing Office, 1949.

U.S. Department of the Army. *Miscellaneous Chemical Munitions.* TM 3-300. Washington, DC: U.S. Government Printing Office, 1950.

U.S. Marine Corps Base, Quantico. *Vietcong Mine Warfare.* Quantico, VA: Department of the Navy, 1966.

Weber, Mike. *Grenades!* Ontario, Canada: Unit Nine, 1979.

See also: Small Arms (Pistols, Rifles, Submachine Guns, Automatic Weapons).

Gromyko, Andrei Andreyevich (1909–1989)

Leading Soviet diplomat; who served the Soviet Union for almost fifty years as ambassador, deputy foreign minister, foreign minister, and finally its president. Andrei Andreyevich Gromyko was born in the village of Old Gromyki, near Minsk, on 18 July 1909. He earned a doctorate in economics at Moscow University and rose to prominence as a Soviet diplomat during World War II. In 1943 he replaced Maxim Litvinov as ambassador to the United States.

Gromyko played a prominent role at Soviet Premier Josef Stalin's side during the July–August 1945 Potsdam Conference and when Stalin first met Mao Zedong (Mao Tse-Tung) in December 1949. Gromyko was the USSR's permanent representative to the United Nations (UN) from 1946 until he was named ambassador to the United Kingdom in 1952.

The always-proper Gromyko made it clear in his memoirs that he advised against absenting Soviet UN delegate Jakob A. Malik from his post on the eve of the U.S. effort to secure UN condemnation of the Democratic People's Republic of Korea (DPRK, North Korean) invasion of the Republic of Korea (ROK, South Korea). Gromyko warned Stalin of the possible consequences, but failed to dissuade him from this decision, which kept faith with the Chinese Communists, whose absence from the Security Council was the ostensible reason for the Soviet protest.

On 4 December 1950, Deputy Foreign Minister Gromyko, no doubt on Stalin's order, urged Chinese Ambassador Wang Jiaxiang to have his government order the Chinese People's Volunteer Army (CPVA) across the 38th parallel to pursue retreating UN Command (UNC) forces. By April 1951, after the unsuccessful CPVA offensive, Gromyko indicated Soviet interest in a diplomatic solution to the war. He had already informed UN Secretary-General Trygve Lie and the governments of Great Britain and India that the Soviet Union desired peace in Korea; he now informed U.S. Ambassador to Moscow Admiral Alan G. Kirk that UN delegate Malik's speech represented official Soviet policy. Gromyko urged that the combatants commence peace talks, limiting themselves to military matters to the exclusion of "political or territorial" considerations. Leaving political matters unresolved would, of course, protect the DPRK. U.S. Secretary of State Dean G. Acheson accepted this as the basis for talks, and the long and frustrating negotiations then commenced.

Gromyko subsequently became the longest-serving Soviet foreign minister, holding that post from 1957 to 1985. Gromyko claimed in his memoirs that Mao Zedong hoped to lure U.S. ground forces onto the Chinese mainland during the 1958 dispute with Taiwan (Formosa) over the offshore islands and then have the Soviets employ nuclear weapons to destroy them. Gromyko rejected the scheme and withdrew the Soviet offer to provide the Chinese with atomic weapons.

During the 1958 Berlin crisis, Gromyko warned that, should fighting break out, "modern military technology" (i.e., Soviet intercontinental ballistic missiles) would spread the flames of war to the United States; but after the 1962 Cuban missile crisis, he was among those calling for renewed friendly relations with the United States. Gromyko subsequently played a role in negotiating a number of arms reductions agreements with the United States.

In 1985 Gromyko was "kicked upstairs" to the largely honorific position of chairman of the Supreme Soviet (nominal president of the USSR). He retired from public life in September 1988 and died in Moscow on 2 July 1989.

—*Claude R. Sasso*

References:

Gaddis, John Lewis. *Russia, the Soviet Union and the United States: An Interpretive History.* New York: McGraw-Hill, 1978.

Gromyko, Andrei. *Memoirs.* New York: Doubleday, 1989.

Kennedy-Pipe, Caroline. *Stalin's Cold War: Soviet Strategies in Europe, 1943 to 1956.* Manchester: Manchester University Press, 1995.

See also: Acheson, Dean Goodersham; Kirk, Alan Goodrich; Lie, Trygve; Malik, Jacob (Iakov) Alexandrovich; Mao Zedong; Potsdam Conference; Stalin, Josef.

Gross, Ernest Arnold
(1906–)

U.S. delegate (ambassador) to the United Nations (UN), 1949–1953. Ernest Arnold Gross was born in Brooklyn, New York, on 23 September 1906. He attended New York public schools, and in 1927 he graduated from Harvard University. After spending a year at Oxford University, he returned to Harvard, completing his law degree in 1931. He then became a legal advisor in the State Department. In 1933 he was admitted to the bar and spent the next year with the National Recovery Administration. From 1934 to 1938 he worked in the private sector, but he returned to government service to work with the National Labor Relations Board until 1943, when he was commissioned a U.S. Army captain. In 1946, having risen to lieutenant colonel, Gross returned to the State Department, heading various departments as an assistant secretary of state.

In October 1949 Secretary of State Dean Acheson selected Gross as deputy delegate to the UN under chief delegate Warren Austin. Two months later Austin took an extended leave of absence, making Gross acting chief of the delegation.

When North Korea invaded the South on 25 June 1950, Gross called on UN Secretary-General Trygve Lie to convene the Security Council under Article 99 of the UN Charter. Gross sponsored a resolution calling the invasion a "breach of the peace" and called on "authorities of North Korea to withdraw their armed forces to the 38th parallel." He pointed out that Article 2 of the UN Charter imposed upon the organization a duty to "ensure that States which are not members of the United Nations act in accordance with these principles so far as may be necessary for the maintenance of international peace and security." Failing a withdrawal, all member states were "to render every assistance to the United Nations in the carrying out of this resolution." The resolution went on that such an attack "strikes at the fundamental purposes of the United Nations." Openly defying UN interest and authority, such an attack thus "concerns the vital interest which all the Member nations have in the Organization." With the USSR then boycotting the Security Council, the resolution carried.

On 27 June 1950 Lie and Gross approached Soviet Ambassador Jacob Malik, inviting him to the next Security Council session. Malik declined to attend. Later Lie and Gross agreed that had he attended he would have vetoed any further assistance to Korea, perhaps jeopardizing the UN role in repelling the North Korean invasion.

In December 1950 Gross was part of a three-member UN committee designed to establish a cease-fire plan for Korea. The People's Republic of China was invited to participate and initially the Chinese delegation, led by General Wu Xiuquan, appeared enthusiastic. This soon changed. The Chinese sought to tie any peace plan in Korea to other issues in Asia, most notably the future of Taiwan, which they saw as a province of mainland China. Although the UN cease-fire plan failed, Gross was pleased that the Western nations remained united. In July 1951 he stated that there would be no UN surrender in Korea and that the ultimate goal remained a peaceful and unified Korea. Gross recommended that any truce in Korea be worked out by military delegations in the field, not by high-level bureaucrats with political agendas. Field commanders had a better perspective of tactics and conditions, he said.

In February 1953 Gross officially became the U.S. delegate to the UN. Two months later he resigned. From 1954 to 1979 he was partner in the law firm of Curtis, Mallet-Prevost, Colt, and Mosle. Since 1979 he has chaired the UN Development Corporation. Gross lives in New York City.

—*William H. Van Husen*

References:

Gross, Ernest A. *The United Nations: Structure for Peace.* New York: Harper & Brothers, 1962.

Lie, Trygve. *In the Cause of Peace.* New York: Macmillan, 1954.

New York Times, 26 June 1950, 14 July 1951, 3 January 1952, 9 January 1952.

Rothe, Anna. *Current Biography, 1951.* New York: H. W. Wilson, 1952.

See also: Acheson, Dean Goodersham; Austin, Warren; Lie, Trygve; Malik, Jacob (Iakov) Alexandrovich; Wu Xiuquan (Hsiu-Ch'uan).

Guo Moruo
(1892–1978)

Chinese writer and People's Republic of China (PRC, Communist China) diplomat. Born in the county of Loshan of the prefecture of Jiading in the province of Sichuan, China, probably on 16 November 1892, Guo Moruo was, apart from his political involvement in the Chinese Communist Movement, a major literary and scholarly figure in the cultural history of twentieth-century China. It is, therefore, not surprising that Guo became the foremost proponent and propagandist of the Communist cause over a long time both before and after the establishment of the PRC. During his lifetime many came to distrust Guo's personal and political integrity. After his death the motives behind his unfailing ideological support of the Communist position have increasingly been called in question, even by scholars in Communist China.

In August 1950, shortly before the PRC entered the Korean War, Guo Moruo, with Li Lisan as his deputy, led a congratulatory mission to P'yŏngyang on the occasion of the fifth anniversary of Korea's liberation from Japanese rule. After the war began, Guo churned out articles, speeches, and songs glorifying Chinese soldiers fighting at the front and to arouse and sustain support for China's war effort.

At the Second World Peace Congress held in Warsaw in mid-November 1950, Guo headed the Chinese delegation that stressed transgressions by U.S. "imperialism" and China's desire for a peaceful solution to the Korean problem. Guo must have impressed the other delegates sufficiently because he was elected a vice-chairman of the World Peace Council at the congress. This set the pattern of his activities during the remainder of the war: writing and speaking in China in support of the country's wartime role and touring many places to explain China's position and expose U.S. "atrocities," including the alleged use of biological warfare. In addition, Guo was closely involved with the work of the national committee of the Chinese People's Resist America Aid Korea Movement. In May 1950 he was awarded the highest medal by Democratic People's Republic of Korea (North Korean) authorities for his wartime contributions.

For many years after the Korean War, Guo Moruo received favor after favor from PRC leaders. Guo was not persecuted during the Cultural Revolution, when so many Communist leaders, who had sacrificed much and contributed greatly to the Communist cause, were subject to torture and suffering and even execution. He was apparently protected by Mao Zedong himself. Guo Moruo died a peaceful death on 12 June 1978.

—*Chan Lau Kit-ching*

References:

Gong Jimin and Fang Rennian. *Guo Moruo Nianpu.* 3 vols. Tianjin: Tianjin Renmin Chubanshe, 1983.

———. "Guo Moruo Zhuan." In *Zhongguo Xiandai Zuojia Zhuanji Congshu.* Beijing: Beijing Shiyue Wenyi Chubanshe, 1988.

Wang Jiquam and Ton Weigang, eds. *Guo Moruo Nianpu.* Vol. 2. n.p.: Jiangsu Renmin Chubanshe, 1983.

Yan Jiaqi and Gao Gao. *Turbulent Decade: A History of the Cultural Revolution,* translated by D. W. Y. Kwok. Honolulu: University of Hawaii Press, 1996.

See also: China: People's Republic of; Mao Zedong.

H

Haman Breakthrough
(31 August–9 September 1950)

North Korean breakthrough 25th Division lines that threatened the entire southern flank of the Pusan perimeter. On the night of 31 August 1950, the Korean People's Army (KPA, North Korean) 6th and 7th Divisions struck into the lines of the U.S. 24th and 35th Infantry Regiments.

On the eve of this attack, the 25th Division was deployed as follows: Colonel Henry Fisher's 35th Regiment was in the north from a point where the Naktong River turns to flow eastward, southward 26,000 yards to the right flank of Colonel Arthur Champeny's 24th Regiment, which took the line southward along ever-higher and rugged ridges, including Battle Mountain and P'ilbong to a point near the top of Sŏbuk-san Mountain.

The front was 12,000 yards wide, with all three rifle companies of Lieutenant Colonel Paul F. Roberts's 2d Battalion of the 24th Regiment (2d/24th) occupying 6,000 yards on lower hills just south of the 35th Regiment. Lieutenant Colonel John L. Throckmorton's 5th Regimental Combat Team carried the line on descending but rugged hills to the valley near the southern seacoast. Republic of Korea Army (ROKA, South Korean) troops carried the line across the valley to the sea.

On the night of 31 August, elements of the KPA 7th Division drove through a force of 300 ROK police deployed near the center of the 35th's line and headed for the position of Battery B, 64th Field Artillery Battalion (FAB) to the rear. Simultaneously, up to two regiments of the KPA 6th Division attacked along the border between the 35th and 24th Regiments and overran the 24th command post (CP) in Haman. Artillery there successfully withdrew to new positions and the regimental CP displaced about two miles to the rear along recently constructed Engineer Road. A counterattack by the regimental reserve, Lieutenant Colonel Gerald Miller's 1st Battalion of the 24th Infantry (minus Company B), failed to halt the KPA advance.

Major General William B. Kean, commanding the 25th Division, then asked Eighth Army commander General Walton H. Walker for the entire 27th Infantry Regiment of the 25th Division, then in Eighth Army reserve. Walker authorized release of only Lieutenant Colonel Gilbert Check's 1st Battalion. On the afternoon of 1 September, this battalion attacked along Engineer Road and recaptured Haman. But large numbers of KPA troops in the rear of the 35th Infantry threatened to overrun four artillery batteries. General Walker could not be reached, so on his own initiative General Kean directed Lieutenant Colonel Gordon E. Murch's 2d Batallion of the 27th Regiment out of reserve to counterattack behind the 35th. This counterattack began about 1700 and lasted most of the night against stubborn KPA resistance.

The 1st Battalion's attack on 2 September virtually restored 2d Batallion of the 24th's lines, but at some cost in casualties. Meanwhile, once the two battalions of the 27th had begun their counterattacks, strong KPA forces threatened the new 24th Infantry CP and a number of artillery positions. Again on his own initiative, General Kean pulled Lieutenant Colonel George DeChow's 3d battalion of the 29th out of reserve and committed it. The 2d Batallion of the 27th Infantry pressed its counterattack behind the 35th Infantry front through 5 September, when it was ordered to halt and prepare to attack toward 1st Battalion 27th.

On 3 September the 27th's 3d Battalion battled several hundred North Korean troops over high and rugged terrain west of a segment of the main supply route known as "the Horseshoe" for a deep, long curve resembling a horseshoe. Plagued by persistent KPA small-arms fire, all three firing batteries of Lieutenant Colonel Walter Preston's 159th Field Artillery Battery (FAB) eventually displaced into the Horseshoe area, where they were sheltered from the KPA fire.

On 3 September, the 3d Battalion suffered heavy casualties when a thousand KPA troops suddenly counterattacked. The situation behind the 35th became so serious that on 5 September, the 1st Batallion of the 27th Infantry was relieved on the line by elements of the 24th Infantry and sent to aid the 2d Battalion of the 27th.

In the early hours of 6 September, the KPA made a determined effort to seize the 1st Battalion of the 27th Infantry assembly area, the CP of Lieutenant Colonel John L. Wilkins's 2d Batallion of the 35th Infantry, and three nearby artillery batteries. U.S. infantry and artillery met the attack with heavy fire, including direct fire from the guns of Company C, 64th FAB, a battery newly arrived from the United States. After the battle, more than sixty KPA bodies littered the paddies in front of the battery. KPA dead were hauled away by the truck load.

The KPA 6th and 7th Divisions suffered heavy casualties in their failed attack. In the first seven days of September, the 25th Division buried more than 2,000 KPA dead behind its lines. For its stand during the battle, the 35th Infantry was awarded a Distinguished Unit Citation.

While these battles were taking place, Lieutenant Grady M. Vickery's 1st Platoon, Company F, 35th Infantry, reinforced by a 75-mm recoilless rifle, a 105-mm howitzer, a tank platoon, engineer squad, and twenty-five to thirty ROKA soldiers, defended a bridge over the Nam River on the 35th's extreme right flank.

On the nights of 5–8 September KPA troops attempted to take the bridge. On the first night, about seventy-five of them were killed. Each night, the KPA attackers came in from a different direction, but were each time turned back with heavy losses. However, early on the morning of 9 September a lone U.S. airplane bombed the bridge, dropping the center span.

The defeat of the KPA 6th and 7th Divisions by the 25th Division in the 31 August–9 September 1950 Haman breakthrough, coupled with the virtual destruction of the KPA 2d and 9th Divisions by the 2d Division and Marine Brigade to the north, dealt the KPA a severe setback.

—Uzal W. Ent

References:
Appleman, Roy E. *South to the Naktong, North to the Yalu.* Washington DC: Office of the Chief of Military History, 1961.
Bowers, William T., William M. Hammond, and George L. MacGarrigle. *Black Soldier, White Army.* Washington, DC: U.S. Army Center of Military History, 1996.
Ent, Uzal W. *Fighting on the Brink: Defense of the Pusan Perimeter.* Paducah, KY: Turner, 1996.

See also: Naktong Bulge, Second Battle of; P'ohang, Battle of; Taegu, Defense of; Walker, Walton Harris; Yŏngch'ŏn, Battle of.

Hammarskjöld, Dag
(1905–1961)

Secretary-General of the United Nations (UN), 1953–1961. Dag Hjalmar Agne Carl Hammarskjöld, a descendant from a long line of government and military leaders, was born in Jonkoping, Sweden, on 29 July 1905. He attended Uppsala University, where he received a bachelor's degree in 1925, a master's degree in 1928, a degree in law in 1930, and a doctorate in political economy in 1934. While studying for his doctorate, Hammarskjöld was appointed secretary of the Swedish government committee on unemployment and in 1933 associate professor of political economics at the University of Stockholm.

In 1935 Hammarskjöld was secretary of the Bank of Sweden. The following year he was undersecretary of the Department of Finance for the Swedish government, a post that he held until 1945. From 1941 until 1948 he was chairman of the board of governors for the Bank of Sweden. Hammarskjöld entered diplomatic service in 1946 as a specialist in finance. In 1947 he was Sweden's delegate for the organization of the Marshall Plan. In 1948 he was Sweden's chief delegate to the Organization for European Economic Cooperation and served as its vice chairman until 1949. In 1951 he was appointed deputy foreign minister and a member of the Swedish cabinet. In the fall of 1952 he became vice chairman of the Swedish delegation to the UN; and in February 1953, its chairman.

In the summer of 1950 when North Korea invaded South Korea, secretary-general of the UN Trygve Lie helped organize UN support for South Korea. The Soviets then labeled Lie as "an abettor of American aggression who, having finally discarded his mask, has given up all pretense of respecting the [UN] Charter." The Soviet delegation was unrelenting in its criticism of Lie, and, as a result, in early 1953 Lie made it known that, if a suitable successor were found, he would step down as secretary-general. A short list of candidates was presented to the Security Council, but each candidate was rejected by the Soviets as being too friendly to the United States.

On 31 March 1953, in consultation with France and Great Britain, U.S. Ambassador Henry Cabot Lodge proposed Hammarskjöld as Lie's successor. Although diplomatic notes signed by Hammarskjöld protesting the Soviet downing of Swedish planes in the Baltic Sea had been passed to Moscow only one year before, the Soviets nevertheless found Hammarskjöld acceptable. On 7 April the General Assembly elected him by a 57–3 vote, and he was inaugurated on 10 April.

On 18 June 1953, just before the armistice went into effect, South Korean President Syngman Rhee released (allowed to escape) some 25,000 anti-Communist North Korean prisoners of war. Western and Asian leaders criticized Rhee; Hammarskjöld, who feared the incident would cause a disruption in the armistice talks, called this unilateral action "irresponsible." Had the North Koreans called off truce talks, the UN General Assembly would have met in a special session presumably to criticize or even levy sanctions on South Korea. Previously the General Assembly had resolved to hold off on any further sessions dealing with Korea until after the establishment of a cease-fire. For his actions, Rhee believed that repatriating non-Communists back to North Korea would be a detriment to their safety and well being.

After the cease-fire went into effect in July 1953, an exchange of prisoners took place. However, fifteen U.S. airmen were still held in the People's Republic of China (PRC). In December 1954 the General Assembly passed a resolution requesting the secretary-general to bring about their release, the first "leave it to Dag" resolution. In January 1955 Hammarskjöld traveled to Beijing, where he was received by Premier Zhou En-lai. Hammarskjöld did not go to China armed with a UN resolution. Because the PRC was not a member of the UN, it had no obligation to honor any such resolution. What Hammarskjöld did use as leverage was the Charter itself, signed in San Francisco in 1945 by a bipartisan Chinese delegation made up of Communist and Nationalist delegates. Chinese and Western representatives held several meetings, although these accomplished little in bringing about the release of the captives. Six months later on 29 July, Hammarskjöld's 50th birthday, the Beijing government released eleven of the captives. Given the nature and specific date of the release, this was viewed as a triumph for Hammarskjöld's diplomacy.

With the end of hostilities on the Korean peninsula and the death of Stalin and subsequent denunciation of Stalinism by the Soviet government, Hammarskjöld encouraged dialogue between East and West. Many influential leaders in the United States, most notably Senator William Knowland, criticized Hammarskjöld; they viewed negotiations as appeasement, a mistake made in 1938 when dealing with Adolf Hitler. Hammarskjöld argued that one could negotiate with an adversary; one did not have to like or approve of the adversary, and it was not necessary to sell out one's principles.

On 19 September 1961, Dag Hammarskjöld died in a plane crash near Ndola, Northern Rhodesia, at age 56. He was en route to a meeting with President Moise Tshombe of the breakaway Katanga Province. UN forces were sent at the request of the Congolese central government to wrest control away from Tshombe and unify the Congo. As a result of his efforts in the Congo, his handling of the 1956 Middle East crisis, and the release of the captive airmen from the Korean War, Hammarskjöld was posthumously awarded the Nobel Peace Prize in October 1961.

—William H. Van Husen

References:

Boyd, Andrew. *United Nations: Piety, Myth, and Truth.* Baltimore: Pelican Books, 1964.
Candee, Marjorie Dent. *Current Biography, 1953.* New York: H. W. Wilson, 1954.
Kelen, Emery. *Hammarskjold.* New York: Putnam, 1966.
Lash, Joseph P. *Dag Hammarskjold, Custodian of the Brushfire Peace.* Garden City, NY: Doubleday, 1961.
New York Times, 8 April 1953, 11 April 1953, 13 January 1955, 19 September 1961.
See also: Knowland, William Fife; Lie, Trygve; Stalin, Josef; Zhou Enlai.

Han P'yo-uk
(1916–)

Republic of Korea (ROK, South Korean) diplomat. Han P'yo-uk was born in Pukch'ŏng county, South Hamgyŏng Province, North Korea, on 20 May 1916, into a middle-class farming family. He graduated from Yŏnhŭi Junior College, the predecessor of present-day Yonsei University, and then from Syracuse University in 1941. Han then worked for the Korean independence leader Syngman Rhee, in Washington, D.C. In 1947 Han received his master's degree in political science from Harvard University. The next year, on the establishment of the Republic of Korea (ROK) with Rhee as its first president, Han became first secretary of its embassy in Washington.

At 9:00 P.M., 24 June 1950, Han received a phone call from the United Press Washington Bureau, informing him that the Democratic People's Republic of Korea (DPRK, North Korea) had just attacked the ROK. Han and Ambassador John M. Chang arrived at the U.S. State Department around 10:40 P.M. Assistant Secretary Dean Rusk told him that the State Department had just received a telegram from the U.S. Embassy at Seoul reporting the DPRK invasion of the ROK. Soon Chang and Han received Rhee's instructions by telephone to ask the United States for immediate military assistance.

When the emergency session of the United Nations (UN) Security Council invited Ambassador Chang to appear on 28 June, Han drafted Chang's speech that stressed the unprovoked DPRK attack as "a crime against humanity." On the afternoon of 27 June, Han accompanied Chang to the White House for a meeting with U.S. President Harry S. Truman. The president assured the ROK diplomats of strong U.S. commitment.

In November 1950 Chang became ROK prime minister. In March 1951, when Yang Yu-ch'an became Chang's successor, Han was promoted to councilor. In that capacity he prepared many memoranda for the truce talks and for the September–October 1953 talks between President Rhee and U.S. Secretary of State John Foster Dulles that led to the mutual defense treaty, signed on 1 October 1953, between the ROK and the United States.

During the three-year period of the Korean War, the ROK Foreign Ministry debated whether it should concentrate its primary effort on the U.S. State or Defense Departments. Han strongly argued for the primacy of the State Department.

During April–June 1954, when Ambassador Yang participated in the Geneva Conference, Han as minister and chargé d'affaires prepared many position papers for both Yang and Rhee. In July 1954, when Rhee visited Washington and strongly recommended to President Dwight Eisenhower's administration a hard-line policy toward Communist states, Han disappointed him by reporting cautiously that U.S. public opinion was opposed to such a stand. Throughout the entire period of his service in Washington, Han was also involved in the ROK-Japanese negotiations through conversations with State Department officials handling that issue.

Han maintained his position in the interim government led by Hŏ Chŏng after the collapse of the Rhee government in April 1960. But with the advent of President John Kennedy's administration in the United States, in August 1960 he resigned his post and taught at George Washington University. In 1964 he received a doctorate in political science from the University of Michigan. Han's dissertation was "The Problem of Korean Unification: A Study of the Unification Policy of the Republic of Korea, 1948–1960."

The ROK Pak Chung Hee government subsequently appointed Han to serve as ambassador to Switzerland, Thailand, the UN, and then the United Kingdom. Retired from foreign service in 1981, Han is currently professor emeritus of Kyŏnghŭi University in Seoul.

—*Hakjoon Kim*

References:

Han P'yo-uk. *Hanmi Oegyo Yoramgi* [The Cradle Period of the Korean-American Diplomacy]. Seoul: Chung'ang Ilbo-sa, 1984.

————. *The Republic of Korea and the United States: A Diplomat's Plea for Korea: Selection of Ambassador Pyo Wook Han's Speeches*. Seoul: Institute of Foreign Affairs and National Security, Ministry of Foreign Affairs, 1987.

See also: Chang, John Myŏn; Dulles, John Foster; Rusk, David Dean; Syngman Rhee; Truman, Harry S.

Han River Operations
(29 June–3 July 1950)

The 25 June 1950 attack by the 135,000-member Korean People's Army (KPA, North Korea) took the smaller Republic of Korea Army (ROKA, South Korea) by surprise. Efforts by four ROKA divisions— the 1st, 7th, 6th, and 8th, as well as the 17th Regiment on the Ongjin Peninsula—stretched from west to east along the 38th parallel, failed to stem the advance by KPA armor columns and infantry, most notably at Ŭijŏngbu north of Seoul, the last line of defense for the capital.

Within 72 hours the KPA had taken Seoul, the ROK government had fled to Suwŏn, and masses of troops and terrified civilians jammed roads south. Panicked by the speed of the KPA onslaught, ROKA commanders prematurely destroyed the Han River bridges early on 28 June, killing more than 1,000 soldiers and civilians in the process and trapping 44,000 ROKA troops with their heavy equipment north of the river. By nightfall on 28 June only 6,200 soldiers of the ROKA 1st and 7th Divisions had managed to cross the Han. By that same date, the ROKA could account for only 22,000 of the 100,000 soldiers on its rolls when the invasion began.

No significant U.S. combat units were in Korea when the invasion started, although U.S. military personnel were stationed in the country as part of the Korean Military Advisory Group. The only major U.S. military force in the region was the Eighth Army in Japan, consisting of four relatively undertrained and underequipped divisions totaling approximately 106,000 men under General Douglas MacArthur.

MacArthur visited Suwŏn on 29 June and quickly concluded that only U.S. forces could halt the KPA and reorganize the thoroughly demoralized ROKA. To accomplish this objective, he sought to establish a defensive line along the Han River using a U.S. regimental combat team to be followed at the earliest possible date by two combat divisions. MacArthur's decision was a major reversal of his own and U.S. military thinking, which had sought to avoid committing U.S. forces to a ground war on the Asian continent.

Initial U.S. support of the proposed defensive system, however, was limited to minor air and naval strikes against North Korean airfields, port facilities, and ground forces. On 29 June alone, for example, the 350 aircraft of the U.S. Far East Air Force (FEAF) flew 172 sorties, while the light cruiser *Juneau* shelled Democratic People's Republic of Korea (North Korea) ports along the east coast. Air support at the Han River line was meager and did little to slow the attack. After the KPA captured Kimpŏ Airfield near Seoul on 28 June, FEAF had to use Suwŏn Airfield. Two days later as advance Communist forces neared Suwŏn, U.S. units were forced to evacuate that strip as well.

The KPA did not pause after capturing Seoul but immediately pressed ROKA defenses along the Han. While the main attack was directed at the industrial center of Yŏngdŭngp'o immediately across the Han from Seoul, on 1 July other KPA units began crossing the river en mass. Because most of the bridges had already been destroyed, the KPA left its tanks on the northern shore and its troops swam or rafted across the river. The hastily regrouped, lightly armed ROKA 1st and 7th Divisions were able to slow the advance for only forty-eight hours before Inch'ŏn and Yŏngdŭngp'o fell and the main Han bridges were repaired sufficiently to allow KPA armored units to again storm south down the Seoul-Suwŏn-Osan-Taejŏn corridor. The last remnants of the ROKA, disorganized, leaderless, and short of weapons and ammunition, finally withdrew from the Han on 3 July.

One of the immediate results of the collapse of the Han River defenses was that MacArthur had to reassess his needs. Initially he had stated that two U.S. divisions would be adequate to stabilize the situation, but after the Han defenses collapsed, he warned the U.S. Joint Chiefs of Staff that at least four divisions, plus support units, would be required. He was just beginning to grasp the true nature of the situation when the first U.S. ground force, Task Force Smith, consisting of one-half of a battalion from the 21st Infantry Regiment, 24th Infantry Division, arrived in Pusan by air on 1–2 July. This small force moved north by truck to Osan, where it encountered the KPA on 5 July.

As the tactical situation grew increasingly grim, the remainder of the U.S. 24th Infantry Division, along with the 25th Infantry and the 1st Cavalry Divisions, hastily began preparations to move from Japan to Pusan, South Korea, where a center of resistance was being prepared.

—*Clayton D. Laurie*

References:
Blair, Clay. *The Forgotten War: America in Korea, 1950–1953.* New York: Times Books, 1987.
Fehrenbach, T. R. *This Kind of War: A Study in Unpreparedness.* New York: Macmillan, 1963.
Hastings, Max. *The Korean War.* New York: Simon & Schuster, 1987.
Miller, John Jr., Owen J. Carroll, and Margaret E. Tackley. *Korea, 1951–1953.* Washington, DC: U.S. Army Center of Military History, 1989. Reprint, 1997.
Schnabel, James F. *United States Army in the Korean War: Policy and Direction, the First Year.* Washington, DC: Office of the Chief of Military History, Department of the Army, 1972.
See also: Eighth United States Army; MacArthur, Douglas; Osan, Battle of; Pusan; Task Force Smith.

Harriman, William Averell
(1891–1986)
Influential U.S. diplomat and foreign policy advisor. Born on 15 November 1891, in New York City, W. Averell Harriman was the son of railroad magnate E. H. Harriman. He graduated from Groton preparatory school in 1908 and from Yale University in 1913. Harriman inherited his father's massive fortune and in 1916 bought a shipyard. During 1917–1925, as head of the Merchant Shipping Corporation, he controlled one of the largest merchant fleets in the world.

In the 1930s Harriman served President Franklin Roosevelt in various capacities with the National Recovery Administration, the Business Advisory Council of the Department of Commerce, and the Office of Production Management. In the latter capacity, Harriman was chief of the raw materials branch and, as Roosevelt's special envoy, coordinated Lend-Lease aid to Britain and the USSR during 1941–1943. In 1943 Roosevelt appointed him U.S. ambassador to Moscow.

Harriman served President Harry S. Truman in turn as secretary of commerce (1946–1948), director of economic aid to Europe under the Marshall Plan (1948–1950), and U.S. representative on the North Atlantic Treaty Organization (NATO) commission studying Western defenses in 1951.

When the Korean War began in June 1950, Harriman arranged his early return from Europe with a phone call to Truman, informing the president that Europeans were "gravely concerned lest we fail to meet the challenge in Europe." Harriman took up residence in the Executive Office Building, a blow to his ego because he fully expected to be at Truman's side as a special assistant to the president for national security affairs and with his own staff.

Harriman's principal task was to keep Secretary of State Dean G. Acheson and Secretary of Defense Louis A. Johnson from coming to blows, but he persuaded Truman to let him join a delegation led by Deputy Army Chief of Staff General Matthew Ridgway to Tokyo to confer with General Douglas MacArthur. Harriman's role was to assure MacArthur that Truman was trying to meet his troop requirements, while impressing on him the administration's concern that committing too many divisions in Asia would leave Europe vulnerable to Soviet attack, and to impress on MacArthur that Jiang Jieshi (Chiang Kai-shek) must not be encouraged to initiate a war with the People's Republic of China (PRC, Communist China). Harriman returned to Washington a supporter of MacArthur's bold plan for an amphibious operation at Inch'ŏn and with the general's assurance that neither the Chinese nor Russians would intervene in Korea.

Harriman played an important role when the war turned against the United Nations (UN) forces after the massive PRC military intervention. At a critical National Security Council meeting on 28 November 1950, Harriman challenged Truman to assert his leadership. Truman responded by accelerating NSC-68, "United States Objectives and Programs for National Security," recommendations for vastly expanding U.S. defense spending and rearmament.

Harriman, along with Secretaries Acheson and Johnson, influenced Truman's decision to direct MacArthur to issue a disclaimer of views he had expressed with regard to Nationalist China in an August 1950 speech to the Veterans of Foreign Wars. MacArthur had done so despite a pledge to Harriman in their Tokyo meeting that he would refrain from making statements that might be misconstrued as Truman administration policy.

In October, after the successful Inch'ŏn landing, Harriman, political advisor Charles Murphy, and Truman flew to Wake Island for a face-to-face meeting with MacArthur. Harriman believed the hour and a half meeting largely resolved misunderstandings between the president and his field commander.

Harriman also played a prominent role in Truman's decision to fire Secretary of Defense Johnson. Johnson mistakenly believed Harriman sided with him in his differences with Acheson, but, as it turned out,

Harriman reported to Truman Johnson's effort to enlist his assistance to secure Acheson's dismissal. Harriman greatly admired Johnson's successor, General of the Army George C. Marshall.

Harriman was the author of the presidential order aimed at curbing MacArthur's public criticism of the Truman administration's war policies by requiring all policy statements to be approved in advance by the administration. MacArthur's subsequent letter to Republican House Minority Leader Joseph Martin, made public on 5 April 1951, led to Truman's meeting with Harriman, Acheson, Marshall, and Chairman of the Joint Chiefs of Staff General Omar Bradley. Harriman advised that MacArthur be fired immediately, but Truman hesitated. After further consultation Truman agreed, and Harriman drafted the dismissal announcement. This concluded Harriman's role in the Korean War.

Truman soon sent Harriman on a special mission to Iran. He then became the primary link between Truman and newly appointed Supreme Commander of NATO General Dwight D. Eisenhower. Harriman's work with NATO led to his 1951 appointment to head the newly created Mutual Security Administration, a post he held until 1953. In 1954 he was elected governor of New York, but was defeated for reelection in 1958 by Nelson A. Rockefeller.

In 1961 President John F. Kennedy appointed Harriman undersecretary of state for Far Eastern Affairs, the number-three position at the State Department. In this capacity Harriman negotiated several key agreements, including the 1962 Laos Accords. He actively sought the removal of Republic of Vietnam President Ngo Dinh Diem and helped draft the telegram to U.S. Ambassador Henry Cabot Lodge that implied U.S. support for a coup against him.

Harriman was not close to President Lyndon B. Johnson. In March 1964 he was given charge of African affairs at the Department of State; the next year he was appointed ambassador at large. Although he publicly supported the president's Vietnam policies, privately Harriman worked to change them, especially in the matter of negotiating with the Democratic Republic of Vietnam. In 1968 Johnson appointed Harriman as the U.S. representative at the Paris Peace Talks. Harriman retired from public life on the election of President Richard Nixon in 1969. Harriman died in New York on 26 July 1986.

—*Claude R. Sasso*

References:
Abramson, Ruby. *Spanning the Century: The Life of W. Averell Harriman, 1891–1986.* New York: William Morrow, 1992.
McCullough, David. *Truman.* New York: Simon & Schuster, 1992.
Truman, Harry S. *Memoirs.* Vol. 2, *Years of Trial and Hope.* Garden City, NY: Doubleday, 1956.

See also: Acheson, Dean Goodersham; Bradley, Omar Nelson; Eisenhower, Dwight D.; Jiang Jieshi (Chiang Kai-shek); Johnson, Louis A.; MacArthur, Douglas; Marshall, George C.; Martin, Joseph W.; NATO (North Atlantic Treaty Organization); Ridgway, Matthew Bunker; Truman, Harry, S.

Harrison, William Kelly, Jr.
(1895–1987)

U.S. Army general and chief United Nations (UN) negotiator in armistice talks at P'anmunjŏm. Born in Washington, D.C., on 7 September 1895, William K. Harrison, Jr. was a direct descendant of President William Henry Harrison. He graduated from the U.S. Military Academy, West Point, in 1917 and was commissioned a second lieutenant of cavalry. He served with the 1st Cavalry Regiment in California and Arizona until August 1918, when he was assigned to West Point. He studied languages in France and Spain during 1919–1920 and taught at the Military Academy until August 1922. He then attended the Cavalry School at Fort Riley, Kansas, graduating in May 1923.

After a tour with the 7th Cavalry Regiment at Fort Bliss, Texas, he was assigned to the 26th Cavalry School at Camp Stotsenburg in the Philippine Islands. In 1927 he was reassigned to the 2d Cavalry Regiment at Fort Riley and subsequently attended the advanced course at the Cavalry School, graduating there in 1929. He then served with the 9th Cavalry and the Cavalry Board until 1932. Harrison then attended the two-year course at the Army Command and Staff School at Fort Leavenworth, Kansas, and remained there as an instructor until 1937, when he entered the Army War College. Upon graduation from the War College the next year, he was assigned to the 6th Cavalry Regiment at Fort Oglethorpe, Georgia. In July 1939 he was reassigned to the War Plans Division of the War Department General Staff, and in March 1942 he became deputy chief of the Strategic Plans and Policy Group. On 23 June 1942 Harrison was promoted to brigadier general and became assistant commander of the 78th Infantry Division at Camp Butner, North Carolina. He was reassigned as assistant commander of the 30th Infantry Division in October 1942 and deployed to Europe with the division in February 1944, participating in operations in Normandy, the drive across France, and the push into Germany. In June 1945 General Harrison assumed command of the 2d Infantry Division in Czechoslovakia and returned with the division to the United States.

After a brief period in command of the 38th Regimental Combat Team at Camp Carson, Colorado, Harrison was assigned to duty in Japan in August 1946. That November he was appointed executive for administrative affairs and reparations with the General Headquarters, Supreme Commander of the Allied

Powers, in Tokyo. He became Chief of the Reparations Section in May 1948. In February 1949 he returned to the United States to become chief of the Army–Air Force Troop Information and Education Division. He was promoted to major general that March. In September 1950 he assumed command of the 9th Infantry Division at Fort Dix, New Jersey.

In December 1951 Harrison became deputy commander of the Eighth U.S. Army in Korea, and the following month he assumed additional duties as a member of the UN Command (UNC) Korean Armistice Delegation. On 19 May 1952, Harrison succeeded Admiral C. Turner Joy as head of the UNC delegation at P'anmunjŏm. Harrison was promoted lieutenant general in September 1952. A tough negotiator, he led the contorted and often frustrating negotiations that eventually led to a cease-fire ending the Korean War on 27 July 1953. The most difficult issue he faced was that of voluntary repatriation of prisoners of war (POWs) held by the UNC. Communist negotiators insisted that all North Korean and Chinese POWs be returned to their control, but Republic of Korea (ROK) President Syngman Rhee and some UN leaders demanded that the POWs be given the right to choose whether or not to be repatriated to Communist control. When the Communist side became obstinate on the POW issue, General Harrison unilaterally suspended the talks on 8 October 1952. They were not resumed until the Communist attitude changed in March 1953.

While heading the Korean armistice talks, Harrison was assigned successively as deputy commander of U.S. Army Forces Far East in October 1952 and Chief of Staff, Far East Command, in April 1953. After the Korean Armistice Agreement was signed in July 1953, Harrison served as commander in chief of the newly formed U.S. Army Caribbean Command with headquarters at Quarry Heights in the Panama Canal Zone. He retired from active service in February 1957. A Baptist lay evangelist, Harrison was active in fundamentalist religious affairs until his death on 25 May 1987 in Springfield, Pennsylvania.

—*Charles R. Shrader*

References:

Ancell, R. Manning, and Christine M. Miller. *The Biographical Dictionary of World War II. Generals and Flag Officers—The U.S. Armed Forces.* Westport, CT: Greenwood Press, 1996.

Hermes, Walter G. *United States Army in the Korean War: Truce Tent and Fighting Front.* Washington, DC: Office of the Chief of Military History, 1966.

Matray, James I., ed. *Historical Dictionary of the Korean War.* Westport, CT: Greenwood Press, 1991.

Shrader, Charles R., ed. *Reference Guide to United States Military History.* Vol. 5, *1945 to the Present.* New York: Facts on File, 1995.

U.S. Department of Defense biographical sketch.

See also: P'anmunjŏm Truce Talks.

Heartbreak Ridge, Battle of
(13 September–15 October 1951)

One of the savage battles fought for control of ridgelines during the period of stalemate in the Korean War and the last major United Nations (UN) offensive of the war. During three weeks of brutal fighting in late August and early September 1951, U.S. and Republic of Korea Army (ROKA, South Korean) forces suffered more than 2,700 casualties in taking Bloody Ridge. When forces of the Korean People's Army (KPA, North Koreans) withdrew from Bloody Ridge, they dug in along the ridge just to the north, soon dubbed Heartbreak Ridge. General Kim Hong commanded the KPA 6th Division, reinforced by the 12th Division. KPA troops soon prepared bunkers, trenches, and gun positions as fortified and camouflaged as those on Bloody Ridge.

In early September, Eighth U.S. Army Commander Lieutenant General James Van Fleet ordered U.S. forces to take this heavily armed stronghold. The assault began on 13 September with an artillery barrage. Brigadier General Thomas E. de Shazo, acting commander of the 2d Division, chose to employ a single regiment, the 23d, as the assault force. The 9th would provide limited support and the 38th Regiment, with the French Battalion, would be in reserve. De Shazo planned to approach Heartbreak Ridge between the middle peak (Hill 931) and southern peak (Hill 894). The 3d Battalion would turn north along the ridgeline and take the northern peak (Hill 851), while the 2d Battalion took Hills 931 and 894. After Hill 894 fell, the 9th Regiment would then advance on a hill a mile west and slightly south of Hill 894.

A forty-five–minute initial artillery barrage against the entrenched defenders had little effect, and in its initial advance the 23d sustained heavy casualties from North Korean artillery and mortar fire and encountered an entrenched regiment embedded in bunkers. With his men pinned down on the lower slopes, de Shazo ordered the 9th Regiment to change its mission and advance on the southern peak of Hill 894. The next day the regiment took the crest of the hill. The 9th suffered heavy casualties during the following days from repeated KPA counterattacks. However, the success of the 9th Regiment did not help the beleaguered 23d. On 16 September, the 23d's commander, Colonel James Y. Adams, ordered his other two battalions to attack abreast on either side of the pinned-down battalion. Withering casualties and a battle of attrition resulted.

Over the next weeks the attackers opened up a number of new fronts in flanking movements to try to divert some of the entrenched KPA forces. Casualties were high. The first U.S. and French attempt to relieve the 23d Regiment failed. A new plan to employ tank-

An aerial view of Heartbreak Ridge. (National Archives)

supported infantry west of Heartbreak Ridge proved more successful. During the first week of October, the attackers gradually secured the peaks along the ridgeline, although KPA forces fought well and refused to surrender under heavy United Nations Command (UNC) artillery fire. At daybreak on 13 October, the French and U.S. troops stormed the last pinnacle; after thirty days of vicious fighting, Heartbreak Ridge was securely in UNC hands. In support of the operation, the Fifth Air Force had dropped 250 tons of bombs. Although the KPA attempted to retake Heartbreak Ridge in early November, the attack failed. The UNC retained the ridge until war's end.

Both sides had fought well in what was reminiscent of World War I trench warfare, but at immense cost. The 2d Division suffered more than 3,700 casualties (1,832 of them from the French Battalion), while the UNC estimated Chinese and KPA casualties at approximately 25,000. A small piece of relatively worthless real estate was acquired, but behind

Heartbreak Ridge was yet another Communist-held mountain.

From July 1951, when cease-fire talks began, until November 1951, when the war settled into a stalemate, UN forces had sustained 60,000 casualties, 22,000 of them U.S. casualties, along a single line of battle. Many of these casualties occurred during the bloody months of September and October. The carnage during this period can be better understood when compared with the 28,000 U.S. casualties from the beginning of the war in June 1950 until the massive Chinese intervention that November, a period in which the war was fought over virtually the entire Korean peninsula. Estimated Communist losses during the July–November 1951 period were almost 234,000 men.

By the end of October 1951, it was obvious to the UNC that the losses sustained in this kind of fighting could hardly be justified. Battle lines changed little from this point on until the final armistice in July 1953. Today the Battle of Heartbreak Ridge remains one of

Soldiers of the 27th Infantry Regiment, near Heartbreak Ridge, take advantage of cover and concealment in tunnel positions, 40 yards from Communist forces, 10 August 1952. (National Archives)

the best-remembered examples and symbols of the brutal and inconclusive combat of the Korean War.

—*Joe P. Dunn*

References:

Alexander, Bevin. *Korea: The First War We Lost*. New York: Hippocrene Books, 1986.

Appleman, Roy E. *Disaster in Korea: The Chinese Confront MacArthur*. College Station, TX: Texas A&M Press, 1989.

Blair, Clay. *The Forgotten War: America in Korea, 1950–1953*. New York: Times Books, 1987.

Knox, Donald. *The Korean War: An Oral History*. Vol. 2. San Diego: Harcourt Brace Jovanovich, 1988.

See also: Bloody Ridge, Battle of; Van Fleet, James Alward.

Helicopter Employment

During the Korean War, U.S. military planners were only beginning to comprehend, and to a limited extent utilize, the unique versatility and capabilities helicopters brought to the battlefield. High-ranking officers first regarded rotary-wing aircraft as little more than an odd-looking gadget. Before the Korean War, one general commented that to make the helicopter really useful it needed powered wheels so that "you could drive it right up to field headquarters." By the end of the war, United Nations (UN) forces employed helicopters to evacuate wounded, rescue downed aviators, ferry troops and supplies, adjust artillery fires, fly aerial reconnaissance missions, and fulfill missions performed by light fixed-wing liaison aircraft.

In April 1944 the first helicopter rescue of a downed airman took place in Burma, where a Tenth Air Force pilot flew a Sikorsky R-4B into a landing area cut into the jungle and brought the injured pilot back to a hospital within ten minutes. U.S. Air Force (USAF) and U.S. Navy (USN) planners recognized the significance of rescuing downed aircrews and quickly returning them to combat, not to mention the effect that swift rescues had on the morale of their pilots and crew

members. With the Korean War, the USAF had activated several Sikorsky H-5 helicopter-equipped air
rescue squadrons. On 4 September 1950, a USAF H-5,
covered by a rescue air combat patrol, performed the
first rescue of a downed aviator from behind
Communist lines in Korea.

To extend the range of air rescue units, the USAF
stationed helicopters on islands off the coast of North
Korea. Dubbed "Angels" by carrier pilots, USN helicopter crews, flying Sikorsky R-3s, R-4s, and R-5s,
stood ready during carrier operations to pluck downed
flyers from the ocean or, if necessary, from behind
enemy lines.

Shortly after the outbreak of the Korean War, U.S.
Army officers realized that many severely wounded
soldiers could not survive a long, overland ambulance
ride to field hospitals, especially in the confusion of a
mass retreat down the Korean peninsula. Thus came
the innovation of using helicopters as air ambulances.
During July 1950, U.S. Army units requested 3d Air
Rescue Squadron, Fifth Air Force, to evacuate critically wounded men from forward aid stations.
Equipped with Sikorsky H-5s, air force pilots exploited their aircraft's ability to fly low and operate from
confined landing areas to extract numerous wounded
soldiers who would otherwise not have survived. As a
result of the squadron's success, the U.S. Army formally adopted helicopters for medical evacuation.

On 22 November 1950, the U.S. Army 2d Helicopter
Detachment, the first of four such units scheduled for
Korean deployment, arrived from the United States
after two months' accelerated training. Equipped with
Bell H-13s, the unit was attached to the 8055th Mobile
Army Surgical Hospital (MASH). As Chinese People's
Volunteer Army (CPVA, Chinese Communist) forces
flowed southward in their winter offensive, many UN
units found themselves cut off from support. The
wounded suffered terribly from the cold and became a
burden to their comrades, who had to carry the injured.
During November 1950–February 1951, air force,
army, and Marine helicopters flew through high winds
and snow storms to carry in ammunition, blood plasma,
gasoline, and other critical supplies. Braving enemy
ground fire, the pilots then took the most seriously
wounded back to advanced hospitals.

MASH units located well forward and rapid helicopter evacuation allowed surgeons to treat life-threat-
ening injuries within minutes, drastically reducing the
death rate of critically wounded troops. The death rate
was 4.5 percent in World War II, but in Korea it
reached a new low of 2.5 percent. As a result of initial
successes, the U.S. Army ordered 500 H-13Es,
equipped with two external litters and specifically
designed as air ambulances. Incomplete records indicated that helicopters from all services may have res-

cued as many as 25,000 people in Korea, both
wounded troops and Korean civilians.

Some U.S. commanders promptly recognized the
helicopter as a means to swiftly overcome rugged terrain and influence combat situations. During the Battle
of the Changjin Reservoir, 27–29 November 1950,
Major General Edward M. Almond used a helicopter
to visit several subordinate headquarters and shore up
his crumbling defenses. Subsequently, consistent with
availability, commanders employed "choppers," the
popular term in Korea, personally to observe battlefields and convey crucial orders to remote positions.

The 1st Marine Division was the first to use helicopters to insert significant numbers of troops into
combat situations in the hilly Korean terrain. On 30
August 1951, Marine Transport Squadron 161 arrived
at Pusan equipped with fifteen Sikorsky HRS-1s,
which the 1st Marine Division used to ferry troops and
supplies as well as evacuate wounded. Navy carriers
ranging up and down the Korean coast also carried
marine helicopters of the same type and the Marines
employed the Sikorsky aircraft to reinforce or resupply
their troops ashore.

Imaginative military tacticians and strategists promptly perceived the effect that helicopters might have by
multiplying combat power. In 1951 Lieutenant General
Matthew B. Ridgway urged the army to add helicopter
companies to its transportation battalions. He believed
that the army could destroy large numbers of Chinese
forces if the military had the capability to rapidly deploy
and extract troops at will in the difficult Korean topography. Ridgway also regarded helicopter resupply of isolated units more effective and economical than that by
parachute. When the larger Sikorsky H-19 helicopters
began arriving in Korea in 1952, army operations officers immediately incorporated them into combat operations. The H-19 carried up to ten personnel and a much
larger cargo load than Bell H-13s or Hiller H-23s. In
May 1953 the U.S. Army's 6th Transportation Company
(Helicopter), flying 12 H-19s, resupplied three front-line
infantry regiments for three days.

Along with its capabilities, the helicopter possessed
several drawbacks and limitations. The early machines
suffered from underpowered engines, resulting in
inadequate cargo capacity. Even when later models
arrived, equipped with upgraded engines and transmis-
sions, only limited amounts of supplies and personnel
could be transported by a single aircraft. Occasionally
crews carried rifles and light machine guns for self-
protection, but weight restrictions usually precluded
the luxury of hauling such weapons and ammunition.
Inclement weather also affected helicopter missions;
high winds, turbulence around hilltops, dense fog,
blowing rain, sleet, snow, and high ambient temperatures restricted or prohibited pilots from flying into

isolated landing areas. A few attempts at inserting or extracting clandestine intelligence teams behind Communist lines proved unsuccessful; the noise from engines and rotor blades alerted Communist troops of the landing locations. Intense small arms and artillery fire limited missions because choppers were vulnerable to combat damage (Korean War models lacked the armor and self-sealing fuel tanks of later versions). Despite their shortcomings, helicopters proved their worth in the Korean War .

—*Stanley S. McGowen*

References:

Brown, David A. *The Bell Helicopter Textron Story: Changing the Way the World Flies*. Arlington, TX: Aerofax, 1995.

Futrell, Robert F. *The United States Air Force in Korea 1950–1953*. Washington, DC: Office of Air Force History, United States Air Force, 1983.

McGuire, Francis G. *Helicopters, 1948–1998*. Alexandria, VA: Helicopter Association International, 1998.

Mossman, Billy C. *Ebb and Flow: November 1950–July 1951*. Washington, DC: U.S. Army Center of Military History, 1990.

See also: Changjin (Chosin) Reservoir Campaign; Logistics in the Korean War; Military Medicine; Mobile Army Surgical Hospital (MASH); Ridgway, Matthew Bunker.

Helicopter Types and Nomenclature

United Nations forces, mainly those of the United States, employed several types of helicopters in the Korea War. Produced by several aviation firms, these rotary wing aircraft filled many roles and gained celebrity in rescuing downed airmen and rapidly ferrying critically wounded soldiers to field hospitals.

The Bell Aircraft Corporation's Model 47, designated H-13 by the U.S. Army, became the most recognizable helicopter associated with the Korean War, perhaps because of its identification with the movie and popular TV series *M*A*S*H*. Many H-13s performed in war as they did on screen, ferrying injured soldiers to advanced Mobile Army Surgical Hospitals (MASH units) waiting to receive battlefield casualties.

USAF H-19 Chickasaw helicopter of the 3d Air Rescue Group rescuing a downed airman. (National Archives)

U.S. Marine Sikorsky HRS-2 Chickasaw helicopter delivering supplies to a forward position. (National Archives)

On 8 May 1946, the Bell Model 47, designed by Arthur M. Young, became the first commercially certificated helicopter and was immediately evaluated by the U.S. Navy for antisubmarine patrols and by the U.S. Air Force for the rescue of downed airmen. In 1948 the U.S. Amy ordered 65 H-13s and officially nicknamed it the Sioux. Large numbers of H-13s began arriving in Korea shortly after hostilities began in June 1950. The first models, H-13Bs, had side-by-side seating for two personnel inside a Plexiglas bubble cockpit, but in many situations, power limitations demanded flying with less than full fuel tanks in order to lift two men.

By 1951 army commanders began to comprehend the vast capabilities of helicopters on the battlefield and ordered more powerful models. In 1950 the H-13s had a four-wheel landing gear, which was replaced with lighter and more versatile skid gear in 1951. Bell engineers equipped the new H-13E with two sets of controls, a 200-horsepower Franklin engine, and a redesigned tail boom. The H-13E carried two personnel along with the pilot. The army ordered 500 H-13Es with two externally mounted litter supports; this type became the first helicopter specifically designed as an air ambulance.

The U.S. Army also ordered significant numbers of Stanley Hiller Jr.'s Model 360, officially the H-23 Raven. To fulfill its government contracts, Hiller Aircraft procured Bell Aircraft's surplus 200-horsepower Franklin engines for the H-23A. The H-23 design incorporated a three-passenger bench seat inside an enclosed Plexiglas cabin. The H-23's unique rotor control system allowed the pilot to fly the helicopter using a subrotor paddle-blade system mounted at right angles to the main rotors. Several H-23s arrived in Korea with externally mounted medevac panniers (litters) and were attached to MASH units, but, as with most early helicopters, they lacked sufficient power for all situations. The H-23 became a standard training aircraft for U.S. military services.

Igor Sikorsky, who fled Russia during the Bolshevik revolution, may justifiably be considered the father of modern helicopters. He established his own aircraft engineering firm in the United States in 1923. On 14 September 1939, he flew the Vought-Sikorsky VS-300, the world's first direct-lift aircraft. During World War II, Sikorsky produced the R-4, which introduced the standard main rotor and anti-torque tail rotor design that was followed by most U.S. helicopter manufacturers. The R-4 had severe limitations in lift and maneuvering capabilities and was followed by the R-5 and R-6. The R-6 Hoverfly was an all-metal, streamlined two-seat design of the R-4, incorporating a molded fiberglass forward cabin and lighter magnesium in its structure. Powered by a 180-horsepower engine, it remained underpowered but proved a serious search and rescue machine used effectively by both the navy and air force.

The R-5 (H-5) became one of the best known helicopters of the Korean War. The navy's version of the R-5, the HO3 Dragonfly, modified with a larger cabin and three-passenger bench seat, incorporated a more powerful engine and a rescue hoist. The Sikorsky helicopters, dubbed "Angels" by navy pilots, quickly reached downed aircrews, hovered over them, and picked them up with a hoist, whereas fixed-wing aircraft could only drop rafts or small lifeboats.

Responding to a U.S. Army requirement for a ten-passenger utility transport helicopter, Sikorsky Aircraft designed the S-55 in 1948. Driven by the impetus of the Korean War, the S-55 quickly went into production as the H-19 Chickasaw and in 1951 was adopted by the U.S. Army, Air Force, Navy, Marines, and Coast Guard. The H-19 layout, incorporating a separate fuselage/cabin and tail boom, established the principal of separating the crew compartment, engine, and passenger cabin.

More powerful, faster, and rugged than previous helicopters, the H-19's increased performance capabilities made it one of the most significant rotary wing aircraft of the Korean War. While the H-5, H-13, and H-23 normally carried a pilot and technician and two personnel or litters, the H-19 increased this capacity to a crew of three and eight litters or ten personnel. Its 120-mile combat radius overshadowed smaller helicopters' range of 80–90 miles. Equipped with floats, air-sea rescue versions could land alongside airmen downed at sea, but most rescues were usually accomplished with a hoist. As more H-19s became available, they replaced older Sikorsky models that had worn out or were lost in combat. Commercial designs of the H-19 (S-55) found their way into Warsaw Pact countries and were copied by Soviet engineers, whose designs became the mainstay of helicopters for Soviet armed forces.

During most of the Korean War, all helicopter units struggled with shortages of trained mechanics and spare parts. Spark plugs, fouled from poor quality fuel, and rotating components deteriorated more quickly than anticipated under combat conditions. Helicopters arrived in the theater faster than military schools could supply trained mechanics, resulting in decreased availability of aircraft. Late in the war, military logisticians finally conceived a plan for scheduled maintenance and spare part replacement that significantly increased the number of operational aircraft.

The helicopter came into its own in the Korean War. Techniques and tactics begun here reached fruition in the later Vietnam War.

—*Stanley S. McGowen*

References:

Brown, David A. *The Bell Helicopter Textron Story: Changing the Way the World Flies.* Arlington, TX: Aerofax, 1995.

Futrell, Robert F. *The United States Air Force in Korea, 1950–1953.* Washington, DC: Office of Air Force History, United States Air Force, 1983.

McGuire, Francis G. *Helicopters, 1948–1998.* Alexandria, VA: Helicopter Association International, 1998.

Mossman, Billy C. *U.S. Army in the Korean War: Ebb and Flow, November 1950–July 1951.* Washington, DC: U.S. Army Center of Military History, 1990.

Simpson, R. W. *Airlife's Helicopters and Rotorcraft.* Shrewsbury, England: Airlife, 1998.

See also: Mobile Army Surgical Hospital (MASH).

Henderson, Loy
(1892–1986)

U.S. diplomat. Born near Rogers, Arkansas, on 28 June 1892, Loy Henderson graduated from Northwestern University in 1915 and afterward attended Denver Law School. During World War I, he was in France with the Red Cross and became a member of the Inter-Allied Commission to Germany, in repatriation and prison camp inspection duties. He remained with the Red Cross until 1921.

In 1922 Henderson joined the U.S. Foreign Service, serving at a series of posts in Dublin, Queenstown, Washington, Riga, Kaunas, Tallinn, and Moscow. He was in Moscow as second secretary during 1934–1936 and first secretary during 1936–1938. He was then chief of the Division of East European Affairs. Subsequently Henderson returned to Moscow as counselor of the U.S. embassy. During World War II, he was the U.S. representative at a meeting between British Prime Minister Winston Churchill and Soviet Premier Josef Stalin. In 1943, because of his reputation for not compromising with the Communists, Henderson was sent by U.S. President Franklin Roosevelt's administration to Iraq.

On his return to Washington in 1945, Henderson became chief of the Division of Near Eastern and African Affairs. In August 1947 he traveled to Greece in an attempt to convince that government to expand its political base and to oversee the aid given Greece under the Truman Doctrine. Henderson remained in Washington until 1948, during which time he also served as advisor to U.S. Ambassador to the United Nations (UN) Warren Austin.

During 1948–1951 Henderson was U.S. ambassador to India and minister to Nepal. It was in his role as ambassador to India that Henderson became a prominent figure in the Korean War. Because there were no diplomatic relations between the United States and the People's Republic of China (PRC), Henderson often relayed messages back and forth to his Washington counterpart, Indian Ambassador Sardar K. M. Panikkar. Henderson also attempted to make clear to Washington the Indian government's firm stance on neutrality and its wish to find a resolution to the conflict before it spread.

Henderson helped persuade Indian Prime Minister Jawaharlal Nehru to instruct the Indian UN delegate to vote for the 27 June UN resolution concerning Korea. He also acted as liaison for talks on the July 1950 Indian cease-fire plan and the Indian request that the PRC receive a Security Council seat.

Henderson was one of the officials to warn Washington that, if U.S. troops crossed the 38th parallel, China would enter the war. These warnings were in vain, as the U.S. President Harry Truman's administration did not take them seriously.

From 1951 to 1953 Henderson was ambassador to Iran. In 1955 he was an assistant secretary of state. Later that year he became a deputy undersecretary of state. In that position he was a member of the Suez Commission, attending the conferences in 1956 as well as leading a group arranging for the opening of diplomatic relations between the U.S. and several new African nations in 1960.

After his retirement from the State Department, Henderson was a professor at American University; he was also associated with the Washington Institute of Foreign Affairs. Henderson died in 1986.

—*Monica Spicer*

References:

Findling, John. *Dictionary of American Diplomatic History.* Westport, CT: Greenwood Press, 1980.

Matray, James, ed. *Historical Dictionary of the Korean War.* Westport, CT: Greenwood Press, 1991.

See also: Austin, Warren; China, People's Republic of; Churchill, Sir Winston Spencer; India; Nehru, Jawaharlal; Panikkar, Sardar K. M.; Stalin, Josef.

Hickerson, John D.
(1898–1989)

U.S. Foreign Service officer and assistant secretary of state for United Nations (UN) Affairs, 1949–1953. Born in Crawford, Texas, on 26 January 1898, John

Dewey Hickerson was educated at the University of Texas, but his studies there were interrupted by military service in World War I. In September 1920 he joined the U.S. Consular Service, transferring to the Foreign Service in 1924. Early postings in Latin America were followed by assignment to the State Department in Washington, where he specialized in Western European affairs. He became assistant chief of the Division of European Affairs in 1930 and chief of the British Commonwealth Division of the Office of European Affairs in 1944.

Hickerson served as an adviser to the U.S. delegation at the 1945 San Francisco Conference that established the UN. Appointed director of the Office of European Affairs in 1946, he served as political adviser to the secretary of state at subsequent meetings of European foreign ministers. Hickerson was one of the principal architects of the North Atlantic Treaty Organization, chairing the group of senior foreign ministry officials that drafted the 1949 treaty. Strongly anti-Soviet, he blamed Soviet obstructionism for the inability to reach postwar international agreement on the control of atomic energy.

In 1949 Hickerson was appointed assistant secretary of state for UN affairs, a position he held for the next four years. One of the earliest participants in the top-level State Department discussions that began on the evening of 24 June 1950 (Washington time), Hickerson, as soon as news of North Korea's invasion of the South reached him, immediately recommended that the United States follow the contingency plans drawn up for this eventuality and take the matter to the UN. He prepared the draft resolution that the United States later placed before the UN and was heavily involved in arranging for an emergency session of the international organization.

Hickerson was one of those present at the two Blair House meetings of 25 and 26 June, when President Harry S. Truman met with his top diplomatic and military officials to discuss policy toward Korea and took the decision to intervene. At the second meeting, Hickerson laid before those assembled the draft of the resolution that the United States submitted and that the UN adopted the following day. This called upon member states to contribute military forces to the effort to drive North Korean forces from the South.

Throughout the war, Hickerson played a significant role in drafting the resolutions on Korea that his country submitted to the UN, and he acted as a coordinator and liaison between State Department officials in Washington and the U.S. delegation at the UN. He also dealt with allied and neutral nations, particularly the European countries, attempting to win their support for U.S. conduct of the war. Early in 1951 when the ongoing stalemate and U.S. intransigence toward the

People's Republic of China generated intense Allied dissatisfaction, he began to attend the Korean War briefing meetings of Allied ambassadors, essentially serving as a reinforcement to Assistant Secretary of State for Far Eastern Affairs Dean Rusk. The two men shared a deep conviction, the product of their memories of what they viewed as the disastrous appeasement policies of the 1930s, that the United States must, whatever the cost, resist the forcible expansion of communism. After Rusk's resignation in late 1951, Hickerson took over primary responsibility for presenting the U.S. position at these sessions, though he was generally believed to be less effective than his predecessor in allaying Allied apprehensions. Lacking Rusk's Asian expertise, Hickerson was also less influential in the detailed formulation of policy toward Korea.

After the July 1953 armistice, Hickerson spent two years teaching at the National War College. He served as U.S. ambassador to Finland, 1955–1959, and the Philippines, 1959–1962, after which he retired from the Foreign Service. He died in Bethesda, Maryland, on 18 January 1989.

—*Priscilla Roberts*

References:
Barros, James. *Trygve Lie and the Cold War: The United Nations Secretary-General Pursues Peace, 1946–1953.* DeKalb: Northern Illinois University Press, 1989.
"Hickerson, John D(ewey)." In *Current Biography 1950.* New York: H. W. Wilson Co., 1951.
Luard, Evan. *A History of the United Nations.* Vol 1, *The Years of Western Domination, 1945–1955.* London: Macmillan, 1982.
Stueck, William W. *The Korean War: An International History.* Princeton, NJ: Princeton University Press, 1995.
Yoo, Tae-Ho. *The Korean War and the United Nations.* Louvain, Belgium: Librairie Desbarax, 1965.
See also: Blair House Meetings; Truman, Harry S.

Hickey, Doyle O.
(1892–1961)

U.S. Army general. Born in Rector, Arkansas, in 1892, Doyle O. Hickey graduated from Hendrix College in 1912. Shortly afterward, he moved to Memphis, Tennessee, where he worked for a lumber company. Hickey joined the U.S. Army in 1917 and received officer training before leaving for France, where he served at the end of the war. Hickey continued in the army after the war and served with the 1st Artillery Regiment at Fort Sill, Oklahoma. He graduated from the Field Artillery School in 1924. Later he served with the 3d and 10th Field Artillery Regiments as well as in the Philippines with the 24th Field Artillery Regiment during 1927–1930.

After spending time with the 7th Artillery Regiment, Hickey was named chief of the U.S. Army Protection Division, with responsibility for park police and building guards in Washington, D.C. He graduated from the Command and General Staff School in 1936.

During 1938–1940 Hickey served in the Philippines. He then served with the 9th Field Artillery Regiment at Fort Bragg, North Carolina. After this he became executive officer at the Field Artillery Replacement Training Center, a post in which he was serving when the United States entered World War II. Hickey was then assigned to Fort Knox, Kentucky. In 1944, then a brigadier general, Hickey commanded the 3d Armored Division in France, a unit that was instrumental in stopping German forces in the Battle of the Bulge.

After World War II Hickey served with both the U.S. Army Ground Forces and Army Field Forces. In 1949 Major General Hickey became deputy chief of staff for the Far East Command in Tokyo and was serving in that post at the outbreak of the Korean War. In September 1950 Hickey became acting chief of staff to General Douglas MacArthur when the latter assigned Major General Edward M. Almond as commander of X Corps. Hickey played an important role in planning United Nations Command (UNC) operations, and he also helped convince MacArthur not to resign after Washington had rejected his early November 1950 proposal to bomb the Yalu bridges.

When President Harry S. Truman dismissed MacArthur in April 1951, Hickey, now a lieutenant general, was acting commander of the UNC until the arrival of General Matthew B. Ridgway. For the remainder of the Korean War, Hickey served as Ridgway's chief of staff. In 1953 Hickey retired from the army. He died at Pass Christian, Mississippi, on 20 October 1961.

—*Monica Spicer*

References:
Matray, James I., ed. *Historical Dictionary of the Korean War.* Westport, CT: Greenwood Press, 1991.
New York Times, 21 October 1961.
See also: Almond, Edward Mallory; Far East Command (FEC); MacArthur, Douglas; Ridgway, Matthew Bunker; Truman, Harry S.

Higgins, Marguerite
(1920–1966)

U.S. war correspondent renowned for her reporting from the front in Korea. Born on 3 September 1920 in Hong Kong and educated in France and Britain, Marguerite Higgins graduated from the University of California at Berkeley in 1941. The following year she earned a master's degree from Columbia University's School of Journalism.

Higgins had already been a campus reporter for the *New York Herald Tribune* and went to work for the newspaper full time after leaving the Columbia University. Initially assigned to the city staff, she was more interested in obtaining an assignment overseas to report on World War II. After much campaigning, she finally received the assignment she so desperately wanted. In 1944 she went by sea to Southampton. After a brief period in London, she moved to Paris, later joining the Seventh U.S. Army's advance into Germany and filing battlefield reports along the way. By 1945 she was chief of the Berlin bureau for the *Herald Tribune* and covered the Allied liberations of the concentration camps at Buchenwald and Dachau.

In April 1950 Higgins went to Tokyo as chief of the *New York Herald Tribune*'s Tokyo Bureau. She was thus one of the first reporters to arrive in Seoul after the 25 June 1950 North Korean invasion of South Korea. She fled the city with other U.S. nationals on 27 June and returned to Tokyo. However, she quickly went back to South Korea and was in Suwŏn when General Douglas MacArthur visited there on 29 June 1950. She flew back to Tokyo with the general aboard his aircraft, the *Bataan*. During an exclusive interview, MacArthur told Higgins that the Republic of Korea Army (ROKA) was in good condition but lacked effective leadership, and he therefore intended to recommend the commitment of U.S. ground forces.

Higgins was the only female war correspondent in Korea and many in authority did not appreciate her presence in the theater. In July 1950 Eighth Army Commander Lieutenant General Walton W. Walker barred women from combat zones, but Higgins appealed to MacArthur, who lifted the ban.

Higgins reported from the front and was the first correspondent to note the inadequacy of the 2.36-inch bazooka against Korean People's Army (KPA, North Korean) tanks. She also accompanied the U.S. Marines at the landing at Inch'ŏn. In 1951 she won a Pulitzer Prize for her war-front reports, and that same year she published a book, *War in Korea: Report of a Woman Combat Correspondent*, which became a bestseller. By all accounts Higgins was tough and courageous, and she was credited with helping to save the lives of many wounded soldiers and Marines, earning much respect in the process.

After the Korean War she stayed in Asia until 1958, when she returned to Washington as a diplomatic correspondent for the *Herald Tribune*. Higgins died on 3 January 1966 of a rare tropical disease she had contracted during a tour of Vietnam, Pakistan, and India. She was buried in Arlington National Cemetery under a simple stone engraved with the following words: "And now she is with her boys again."

—*James H. Willbanks*

References:
Blair, Clay. *The Forgotten War.* New York: Times Books, 1987.
Higgins, Marguerite. *War in Korea: Report of a Woman Combat Correspondent.* Garden City, NY: Doubleday, 1951.
May, Antoinette. *Witness to War: A Biography of Marguerite Higgins.* New York: Beaufort Book, 1983.
See also: Bazooka; Inch'ŏn Landings: Operation CHROMITE; MacArthur, Douglas; Walker, Walton Harris; Women in the Military.

Historiography of the Korean War

(This review essay on the literature of the Korean War by Allan R. Millett appeared in the July 1997 issue of *The Journal of Military History* under the title, "A Reader's Guide to the Korean War." It is here reproduced in revised form with the gracious permission of Professor Millett, editor Dr. Henry Bausum, and the Society for Military History.)

Just which Korean War one reads about depends on what lessons the author intends to communicate, for the history of the war reeks with almost as much didacticism as blood. For an indictment of American and United Nations intentions and the conduct of the war, see Jon Halliday and Bruce Cumings, *The Unknown War* (New York: Pantheon, 1988). Their sympathy for the plight of Korea is admirable, but their bias toward the Communists is less appealing. In his new book, *Korea's Place in the Sun: A Modern History* (New York: W. W. Norton, 1997), Cumings does not relent much from his position that the Communists had a slight edge in legitimacy and popularity and that America's conduct of the war was worse than a North Korean victory. British authors have written significant books: David Rees, *Korea: The Limited War* (London: Macmillan, 1964); Callum A. MacDonald, *Korea: The War before Vietnam* (New York: Free Press, 1986); Peter Lowe, *The Origins of the Korean War* (London: Longman, 1986); and Max Hastings, *The Korean War* (New York: Simon and Schuster, 1987). These authors give short shrift to American politics, but offer historical perspective and emotional distance. After publishing his book, however, MacDonald drifted into the Halliday-Cumings camp of anti-American criticism in his subsequent articles. William J. Stueck, Jr., *The Korean War: An International History* (Princeton, N.J.: Princeton University Press, 1995) provides the definitive history of the war as a test of the United Nations and postwar diplomatic deftness. Expanding in the anti-imperialist critique of the Peter Lowe genre is the interesting but overwrought Steven Hugh Lee, *Outposts of Empire: Korea, Vietnam and the Origins of the Cold War in Asia, 1949–1954* (Montreal and Kingston: McGill-Queen's University Press, 1995).

John Toland and Clay Blair, two of America's most popular (in both senses of the term) military historians, have few reservations about the legitimacy of intervention or the Republic of Korea's right of self-defense. They are more interested in assessing U.S.

military performance, however, individual as well as collective. Although Toland integrates South Korean and Chinese interviews to good effect, his focus is on the American effort. Blair's strengths are his knowledge of the Eighth Army and a keen eye for operational matters and sharp characterization of U.S. Army leaders. The two books in question are John Toland, *In Mortal Combat: Korea, 1950–1953* (New York: Morrow, 1991), and Clay Blair, *The Forgotten War. America in Korea, 1950–1953* (New York: Times Books, 1987).

Works by disgruntled critics of America, the Truman administration, and the Army have a place in a Korean War library. The key political jeremiad is I. F. Stone, *The Hidden History of the Korean War, 1950–1951* (Boston: Little, Brown, 1952), which portrays Truman as the dupe of the sinister Asia First partisans at home and abroad, led by John Foster Dulles and Jiang Jieshi (Chiang Kai-shek). The military counterpoint to Stone is T. R. Fehrenbach, *This Kind of War: A Study of Unpreparedness* (New York: Macmillan, 1963), a sharp critique of American culture's weakening effect on soldiers and politics, a book reprinted by the Army in 1993 with its errors and misrepresentations intact. More recent books in the same genre are Bevin Alexander, *Korea: The First War We Lost* (New York: Hippocrene, 1986), and Joseph Goulden, *Korea: The Untold Story* (New York: Times Books, 1982), both short on original information and insight. Robert Leckie's *Conflict: The History of the Korean War* (New York: Putnam, 1962) reflects an admiration for the American infantryman and supports the war. Burton I. Kaufman, *The Korean War: Challenges in Crisis, Credibility, and Command* (Philadelphia: Temple University Press, 1986) is a measured study of the Truman administration's conduct of the war. A new effort to look at the war's domestic context is Lisle A. Rose, *The Cold War Comes to Main Street: America in 1950* (Lawrence: University Press of Kansas, 1999).

Anthologies of informed, scholarly essays (sometimes mixed with good oral history) offer easy entrée to the issues. The best of a full field are Francis H. Heller, ed., *The Korean War. A 25-Year Perspective* (Lawrence: Regent's Press of Kansas for the Harry S. Truman Library, 1977); Bruce Cumings, ed., *Child of Conflict: The Korean-American Relationship, 1943–1953* (Seattle: University of Washington Press, 1983); Frank Baldwin, ed., *Without Parallel: The American-Korean Relationship since 1945* (New York: Random House, 1973); William J. Williams, ed., *A Revolutionary War: Korea and the Transformation of the Postwar World* (Chicago: Imprint Publications, 1993); James I. Matray and Kim Chull-Baum, ed., *Korea and the Cold War* (Clare-

mont, Calif.: Regina Books, 1993); Nagai Yonosuke and Akira Iriye, ed., *The Origins of the Cold War in Asia* (New York: Columbia University Press, 1977); Korean War Research Committee, War Memorial Service-Korea, *The Historical Reillumi-nation of the Korean War* (Seoul: War Memorial Service, 1990); and James Cotton and Ian Neary, eds., *The Korean War in History* (Atlantic Highlands, N.J.: Humanities Press, 1989).

Causes of the War

A civil war—as Korea surely was—has internal and international dynamics and its own shifting set of political actors, all of whom have agendas of their own. The Korean War is no exception. It was one of many such wars in this century in which the "great powers" chose to make a smaller nation a battleground. Of course, small nations (often plagued with politicians with large ambitions and imaginations) are perfectly capable of enticing larger nations to help sway the local political balance against domestic rivals or other great powers. The Chosŏn dynasty in Korea, for example, struggled to maintain its isolation and independence by playing the Chinese off against the Japanese, then appealed to Czarist Russia and the United States to protect it from its patrons. This too-clever but desperate bit of diplomacy resulted in two wars, the annexation of Korea by Japan in 1910, and thirty-five years of misery.

Just how much background one seeks is a matter of taste and time. There is ample reading: Carter J. Eckert, Lee Ki-Baik, Young Ick Lew, Michael Robinson, and Edward W. Wagner, *Korea: Old and New* (Seoul: Ilchokak, Publishers for the Korea Institute, Harvard University, 1990); George M. McCune and Arthur L. Grey, *Korea Today* (Cambridge, Mass.: Harvard University Press, 1950); Choi Bong-Youn, *Korea—A History* (Rutland, Vt.: C. E. Tuttle Co., 1971); Donald Stone Macdonald, *The Koreans* (Boulder, Colo.: Westview Press, 1988); and Andrew C. Nahm, *Korea, Tradition and Transformation: A History of the Korean People* (Elizabeth, N.J.: Hollym International, 1988).

Literature on Korean-American relations before 1950 stands as a monument to the power of after-the-fact wisdom. Nevertheless, the idea of a Communist plot, orchestrated by Moscow, that fell on an innocent South Korea basking in peace and prosperity, belongs in the dustbin of history. Ravaged by forced participation in World War II, with an elite compromised by two generations which survived under Japanese rule, Korea was divided by more than occupying armies and the 38th parallel. It was caught between two modernizing movements, tainted legitimacy, authoritarian instincts, romantic economic dreams, and a dedication to political victory and control over a unified Korea. Kim Il Sung or Syngman Rhee would have felt comfortable on the throne of the kings of Unified Silla at Kyŏngju. For perspective on the conflicts before 1950, see Kwak Tae-Han, John Chay, Cho Soon-Sung, and Shannon McCune, eds., *U.S.-Korean Relations, 1882–1982* (Seoul: Institute for Far Eastern Studies, Kyungnam University, 1982).

Works notable for their successful effort to link U.S. foreign policy with Korean political history include James I. Matray, *The Reluctant Crusade: American Foreign Policy in Korea, 1941–1950* (Honolulu: University of Hawaii Press, 1985); Gregory Henderson, *Korea: The Politics of the Vortex* (Cambridge, Mass.: Harvard University Press, 1968); James Merrill, *Korea: The Peninsular Origins of the War* (Newark: University of Delaware Press, 1989); William J. Stueck, Jr., *The Road to Confrontation: American Policy Toward China and Korea, 1947–1950* (Chapel Hill: University of North Carolina Press, 1981); Charles M. Dobbs, *The Unwanted Symbol: American Foreign Policy, the Cold War, and Korea, 1945–1950* (Kent, Ohio: Kent State University Press, 1981); and Lisle Rose, *Roots of Tragedy: The United States and the Struggle for Asia, 1945–1953* (Westport, Conn.: Greenwood Press, 1976). For a more comprehensive and fresh look at the politics of Korean War mobilization and its effects on American domestic policy, see Paul G. Pierpaoli, Jr., *Truman and Korea: The Political Culture of the Early Cold War* (Columbia: University of Missouri Press, 1999).

Whether regarded with awe or dismay (or both), an inquiry that stands alone for its ability to define the causes of the conflict is Bruce Cumings, *The Origins of the Korean War*, vol. 1, *Liberation and the Emergence of Separate Regimes, 1945–1947* (Princeton, N.J.: Princeton University Press, 1981), and vol. 2, *The Roaring of the Cataract, 1947–1950* (Princeton, N.J.: Princeton University Press, 1990). While Cumings may see wheels within wheels where none exist and be a master of inference, he knows Korean politics and recoils from the cant of American politicians, generals, and diplomats. He is no admirer of the Communists and especially Kim Il Sung, but his political bias prevents him from seeing any legitimacy in the non-Communist leadership in South Korea, and he ignores the power of organized Christianity in the struggle for the soul of Korea. Also, Cumings has a limited understanding of the armed forces, so he often finds a malevolent purpose in simple bungling. While he writes too much, most of it is required reading.

The convoluted course of American diplomacy did not change in 1950. Arguments on the political direction of the war are found in Rosemary Foot, *The Wrong War: American Policy and the Dimensions of the Korean Conflict* (Ithaca, N.Y.: Cornell University Press, 1985), as well as in *A Substitute for Victory: The Politics of Peacemaking at the Korean Armistice Talks* (Ithaca, N.Y.: Cornell University Press, 1990).

A major work by a Japanese scholar-journalist, Ryo Hagiwara, who covered North Korean politics for a Japanese Communist newspaper, places the onus for initiating the 1950 invasion on Kim Il Sung. In *The Korean War: The Conspiracies by Kim Il Sung and MacArthur* (Tokyo: Bungei Shunju Press, 1993), he concluded that P'yŏngyang pursued a course of risky opportunism that assumed reluctant support from China and Russia.

Assessments of the literature are found in Rosemary Foot, "Making Known the Unknown War: Policy Analysis of the Korean Conflict in the Last Decade," *Diplomatic History* 15 (Summer 1991): 411–431, and Judith Munro-Leighton, "A Postrevisionist Scrutiny of America's Role in the Cold War in Asia, 1945–1950," *Journal of American–East Asian Relations* 1 (Spring 1992): 73–98. In addition, see Keith D. McFarland, *The Korean War: An Annotated Bibliography* (New York: Garland, 1986). Other valuable references are James I. Matray, ed., *Historical Dictionary of the Korean War* (Westport, Conn.: Greenwood Press, 1991); Harry G. Summers, *Korean War Almanac* (New York: Facts-on-File, 1990); Lester Brune, ed., *The Korean War. Handbook of the Literature and Research* (Westport, Conn.: Greenwood Press, 1994); Stanley Sandler, ed., *The Korean War: An Encyclopedia* (New York: Garland, 1995); and three finding aids of films, the Inchon landing, and the defense of the Pusan Perimeter, all edited by Paul M. Edwards and published by Greenwood Press. Professor Edwards compiled a comprehensive bibliography, *The Korean War* (Westport, Conn.: Greenwood Press, 1998). The Brune anthology is especially useful since it provides a series of essays that review the scholarship and historiography of a wide-range of Cold War subjects. The bibliographical listing of essays and articles is the most comprehensive one now available, a rival to the electronic bibliography that can be provided by the Air University Library for serious researchers.

U.S. Political Direction

After presiding over the end of World War II as an accidental president, Harry S. Truman certainly did not need another war but got one. His version of events is found in his two-volume *Memoirs* (Garden City, N.Y.: Doubleday, 1955–1956), a selective but vital account to understanding problems at home and abroad. Truman biographies abound in uneven quality: David McCullough, *Truman* (New York: Simon and Schuster, 1992); Robert Donovan, *Tumultuous Years:*

The Presidency of Harry S. Truman (New York: Norton, 1982); Richard F. Haynes, *The Awesome Power: Harry S. Truman as Commander in Chief* (Baton Rouge: Louisiana State University Press, 1973); Robert H. Ferrell, *Harry S. Truman and the Modern American Presidency* (Boston: Little, Brown, 1983); Donald R. McCoy, *The Presidency of Harry S. Truman* (Lawrence: University Press of Kansas, 1984); Bert Cochran, *Harry Truman and the Crisis Presidency* (New York: Funk and Wagnalls, 1973); William E. Pemberton, *Harry S. Truman: Fair Dealer and Cold Warrior* (Boston: Twayne Publishers, 1989), and Alonzo L. Hamby, *Man of the People: The Life of Harry S. Truman* (New York: Oxford University Press, 1995).

Secretary of State Dean Acheson provided a personal interpretation of the war in *Present at the Creation* (New York: Norton, 1969) and in an abridged account, *The Korean War* (New York: Norton, 1971). The standard biographies of Acheson are Gaddis Smith, *Dean Acheson* (New York: Cooper Square, 1971), vol. 16 in the American Secretaries of State and Their Diplomacy series and James Chace's *Acheson; the Secretary of State Who Created the Modern World* (New York: Simon and Schuster, 1998); see also Ronald L. McGlothlen, *Controlling the Waves: Dean Acheson and U.S. Foreign Policy in Asia* (New York: Norton, 1993), and Douglas Brinkley, ed., *Dean Acheson and the Making of U.S. Foreign Policy* (New York: St. Martin's Press, 1993).

Accounts by other participants include U. Alexis Johnson and J. Olivarius McAllister, *The Right Hand of Power* (Englewood Cliffs, N.J.: Prentice-Hall, 1984), and Harold J. Noble, *Embassy at War* (Seattle: University of Washington Press, 1975). The institutional participation of the Department of State must be gleaned from documents published in *The Foreign Relations of the United States*, a standard though controversial publications program; volumes covering the period 1950 to 1953 total twenty-nine and were published between 1976 and 1984. National Security Council documents are also available in the National Security Archive, George Washington University.

The basic study on American intervention is Glenn D. Paige, *The Korean Decision, June 24–30* (New York: Free Press, 1968). Distressed by postwar Korean politics, Paige later denounced the book as too sympathetic to Truman and Acheson, but it remains a good work.

Koreans on the War

Treatments of the war written by Koreans and translated into English reflect a wide range of perspectives—except, of course, in official (there is no other) accounts by North Korea. Among the South Korean sources, however, one can find various degrees of outrage over intervention, remorse over the role of the Koreans themselves in encouraging foreign intervention, deep sadness over the consequences of the war, pride and contempt over the military performance of Koreans, a tendency to see conspiracy everywhere, and a yearning for eventual unification, peace, economic well-being, and social justice. There is no consensus on how to accomplish these goals, only the certainty that the war ruined the hope of a better Korea for the balance of the century. The literature also reflects a search for innate order and the rule of law, against a pessimistic conclusion that politics knows no moral order. Among the more scholarly and insightful works by Korean scholars are Kim Myung-Ki, *The Korean War and International Law* (Clairmont, Calif.: Paige Press, 1991); Pak Chi-Young, *Political Opposition in Korea, 1945–1960* (Seoul: Scoul National University Press, 1980); Cheong Sung-Hwa, "Japanese-South Korean Relations under the American Occupation, 1945–1950" (doctoral dissertation, University of Iowa, 1988); Kim Chum-Kon, *The Korean War, 1950–1953* (Seoul: Kwangmyong, 1980); Kim Joung-Won, *Divided Korea: The Politics of Development, 1945–1972* (Cambridge, Mass.: Harvard University Press, 1975); Kim Gye-Dong, *Foreign Intervention in Korea* (Aldershot, U.K.: Dartmouth Publishing, 1993); Cho Soon-Sung, *Korea in World Politics, 1940–1950* (Berkeley: University of California Press, 1967); and, in Korean, Kim Yang-Myong, *The History of the Korean War* (Seoul: Ilshin-sa, 1976).

Syngman Rhee is mythic in the depth of his failure and the height of his success, including keeping America involved in Korea, more or less on his terms. He succeeded where Jiang Jieshi, Ferdinand Marcos, and Ngo Dinh Diem failed. Robert T. Oliver, Rhee's American advisor and information agent, wrote two admiring books noted for their conversations and speeches: Robert T. Oliver, *Syngman Rhee: The Man Behind the Myth* (New York: Dodd, Mead, 1955) and *Syngman Rhee and American Involvement in Korea, 1942–1960* (Seoul: Panmun Books, 1978). A less sympathetic view is found in Richard C. Allen, *Korea's Syngman Rhee: An Unauthorized Portrait* (Rutland, Vt.: Tuttle, 1960). Rhee's political contemporaries, who often shifted between being rivals and supporters, left extensive but untranslated memoirs. An exception is Louise Yim, *My Forty Year Fight for Korea* (London: Gollancz, 1952). Collective portraits of Korea's civilian and military leaders are found in Lee Chong-Sik, *The Politics of Korean Nationalism* (Berkeley: University of California Press, 1963), and Kim Se-Jin, *The Politics of the Military Revolution in Korea* (Chapel Hill: University of North Carolina Press, 1971).

The Democratic People's Republic of Korea's account is *The U.S. Imperialists Started the Korean War* (Pyongyang: Foreign Language Publishing House, 1977). For general background, see Robert A. Scalapino and Lee Chong-Sik, *Communism in Korea*, 2 vols. (Berkeley: University of California Press, 1973), and Suh Dae-Sook, *The Korean Communist Movement, 1918–1948* (Princeton, N.J.: Princeton University Press, 1967). For a biography of the late Great Supreme Leader, see Suh Dae-Sook, *Kim Il Sung: The North Korean Leader* (New York: Columbia University Press, 1988), which is rich in data and insight. Expatriate North Korean officers discuss the war in Kim Chull Baum, ed., *The Truth About the Korean War* (Seoul: Eulyoo Publishing, 1991), along with Russian and Chinese participants.

Military Allies, Political Doubters

The study of political and military relations between the United States and the Republic of Korea is not exactly a "black hole" in Korean War historiography, but it is certainly a gray crevice. Activities of the Military Advisory Group Korea (KMAG) are described in very measured terms by Robert K. Sawyer, *KMAG in War and Peace* (Washington: Office of the Chief of Military History, 1962), which is largely silent on atrocities, corruption, nepotism, and incompetence in the ROKA officer corps. Little of the work deals with the 1950–1953 period, and it ignores the impressive fighting ability of some ROKA units and the professionalism of some of its officers. Sawyer is also less than frank in discussing U.S. Army policies that crippled the ability of the ROKA to resist the Korean People's Army invasion from the North. How, for example, could a ROKA division manage with no tanks and only one battalion of limited-range 105-mm howitzers? Some of these problems receive attention in Paek Sŏn-Yŏp, *From Pusan to Panmunjom* (Washington: Brassey's, 1992), the memoirs of an outstanding corps and division commander. Paek, however, and his brother General Paek In-Yŏp, are quiet on their past in the Japanese army and their dogged pursuit of the Communist guerrillas in the South, 1948–1950. The late Chŏng Il-Kwŏn, another ROKA officer, left extensive but untranslated memoirs. Frustrations over nation-building are more directly addressed in Gene M. Lyons, *Military Policy and Economic Aid: The Korean Case, 1950–1953* (Columbus: Ohio State University Press, 1961).

The American military of 1950–1953, absorbed with its own problems of survival, showed little understanding of the greater agony of Korea, including a much-maligned South Korean army. But there is no longer any excuse for such insensitivity. A novel by Richard Kim, *The Martyred* (New York: George

Braziller, 1964) and Donald K. Chung, *The Three Day Promise* (Tallahassee, Fla.: Father and Son Publishing, 1989), an autobiography, both relate heart-rending stories of family separation and ravaged dreams. The war is summarized in a work published by the Korean Ministry of National Defense, *The Brief History of ROK Armed Forces* (Seoul: Troop Information and Education Bureau, 1986). Soldiers of the Eighth Army could not avoid dealing with Koreans since many served in American units under the Korean Augmentation to the U.S. Army (KATUSA) program, still in effect today, but often a haven for affluent conscripts who speak some English. An official history of the KATUSA program prepared by Richard Weinert and later revised by David C. Skaggs was published as "The KATUSA Experiment: The Integration of Korean Nationals into the U.S. Army, 1950–1965," *Military Affairs* 38 (April 1974): 53–58. For an interesting Korean perspective on the American war effort, see Bill Shinn, *The Forgotten War Remembered, Korea: 1950–1953* (Elizabeth, N.J.: Hollym International, 1996), the memoir of a Korean-American newspaper correspondent.

The Armed Forces

The body of literature on the strategic and operational performance of the armed forces in the Korean War is substantial and dependable, at least for operational concerns. Building on its commitment to a critical history in World War II, the military establishment worked with the same stubborn conviction that both the public and future generations deserved to know what happened in Korea and why. The products are generally admirable. For a big picture, start with Doris Condit, *The Test of War, 1950–1953* (Washington: Historical Office, Office of the Secretary of Defense, 1988), the second volume in the "History of the Office of the Secretary of Defense" series. For the perspective on the Joint Chiefs, see James F. Schnabel and Robert J. Watson, *The Joint Chiefs of Staff and National Policy*, vol. 3, *The Korean War* (Wilmington, Del.: Michael Glazier, 1979), reissued in 1998 by the JCS Joint History Office in a more polished format.

The Department of the Army went to work with a vengeance on the history of the Korean War, but faded in the stretch. It produced an important policy volume: James F. Schnabel, *United States Army in the Korean War: Policy and Direction: The First Year* (Washington: Office of the Chief of Military History, 1972). It published two theater-level operational titles: Roy E. Appleman, *South to the Naktong, North to the Yalu* (1961), which covered the Eighth Army and X Corps from June until late November 1950, and Walter Hermes, Jr., *Truce Tent and Fighting Front* (1966), on the "stalemate" period from October 1951 to July

1953. A much-delayed third volume by Billy Mossman, *Ebb and Flow* (1990), plugged the chronological gap from November 1950 to July 1951. The candor void is filled by Roy Appleman who dedicated his later years to writing tough-minded critiques, all published by the Texas A&M University Press: *East of Chosin: Entrapment and Breakout in Korea* (1987); *Escaping the Trap: The U.S. Army in Northeast Korea, 1950* (1987); *Disaster in Korea: The Chinese Confront MacArthur* (1989); and *Ridgway Duels for Korea* (1990). His work is required reading for anyone interested in tactical expertise on cold weather and night operations. While Appleman does not quite supersede S. L. A. Marshall, *The River and the Gauntlet* (New York: Morrow, 1953) or *Pork Chop Hill* (New York: Morrow, 1956), he shares the battlefield. So does Shelby Stanton with *America's Tenth Legion: X Corps in Korea, 1950* (Novato, Calif.: Presidio Press, 1989), which resurrects the reputation of U.S. Army Lieutenant General Edward M. Almond, a commander endowed with intelligence and skill yet cursed by a wretched personality. Battle books of the coffee-table variety abound. For a detached analysis, see Russell A. Gugeler, *Combat Actions in Korea* (Washington: Office of the Chief of Military History, 1954; reissued in 1970 and 1987).

The official Marine history is Lynn Montross et al., *History of U.S. Marine Operations in Korea, 1950–1953*, 5 vols. (Washington: Historical Branch, G-3, Headquarters, Marine Corps, 1954–1972), which covers the experience of the 1st Marine Division and 1st Marine Aircraft Wing, Fleet Marine Force Pacific. Of other semiofficial Marine Corps books, the best is Robert D. Heinl, *Victory at High Tide: The Inchon-Seoul Campaign* (Philadelphia: Lippincott, 1968), and Lynn Montross, *Cavalry of the Sky: The Story of U.S. Marine Combat Helicopters* (New York: Harper and Brothers, 1954).

The Navy published a one-volume official history: James A. Field, Jr., *History of United States Naval Operations Korea* (Washington: Director of Naval History, 1962); but two officers with line experience in World War II produced an earlier and livelier account: Malcolm W. Cagle and Frank A. Manson, *The Sea War in Korea* (Annapolis: Naval Institute Press, 1957). Walter Karig, Malcolm W. Cagle, and Frank Manson, *Battle Report, The War in Korea* (New York: Rinehart, 1952) is Navy journalism and instant history at its finest, strong on immediacy and short on perspective. Naval aviation receives special treatment in Richard P. Hallion, *The Naval Air War in Korea* (Baltimore: Nautical and Aviation Publishing, 1986).

The Air Force published one large monograph on the Korean War, the literary equivalent of a one-megaton blast with endless fallout: Robert F. Futrell, *The United States Air Force in Korea, 1950–1953*, rev. ed. (Washington: Office of the Chief of Air Force History, 1983), which is encyclopedic on the Air Force's effort to win the war alone and too coy about the actual results. Recent anthologies from the Office of Air Force History on the uses of combat aviation include essays on air superiority, strategic bombing, and close air support in Korea. Their modification of Futrell will be slow, but will start with Conrad C. Crane's history of the Korean air war, *A Rather Bizarre War: American Airpower Strategy in Korea, 1950–1953* (University Press of Kansas, 1999).

Convinced of the value of their historical programs during and after World War II, the American armed forces mounted programs of field history and interviewing that served as documentary and internal-use histories as well as the grist for the official history publications series and unsponsored histories by private authors. Scholarly Resources has published on microfilm four sets of documents: (1) U.S. Army historical studies and supporting documents done during the war over virtually every aspect of the conflict; (2) the interim evaluation reports done as periodic operational reports done for the Commander Pacific Fleet (1950–1953) as periodic operational reports prepared by the Seventh Fleet and the Marine division and aircraft wing; (3) documents and reports preserved by the Department of State on Korea, 1950–1954; and (4) the documents created and stored by the United Nations armistice commission, 1951–1953. University Publications of America has produced a similar collection on microfiche of unpublished histories and after-action reports collected during and shortly after the war by the Far East Command's military history detachment. The sources of these studies are largely the participants themselves, the interviews then supplemented with Army records. The studies not only reconstruct operations from the division to the platoon level, but they also deal with a wide range of topical subjects.

Books by or about senior American leaders are generally well done and show how wedded these officers were to World War II norms. Two Army officers of high repute wrote histories of the war: J. Lawton Collins, *War in Peacetime* (Boston: Houghton Mifflin, 1969), and Matthew B. Ridgway, *The Korean War* (Garden City, N.Y.: Doubleday, 1967). But larger shadows blur the Collins-Ridgway war: Forrest C. Pogue, *George C. Marshall, Statesman, 1945–1959* (New York: Viking, 1987); D. Clayton James, *The Years of MacArthur: Triumph and Disaster, 1945–1964* (Boston: Houghton Mifflin, 1985); and Omar N. Bradley and Clay Blair, *A General's Life* (New York: Simon and Schuster, 1983). D. Clayton James with Anne Sharp Wells, *Refighting the Last*

War: Command and Crises in Korea, 1950–1953 (New York: Free Press, 1993), argues that World War II spoiled generals and distorted understanding of such concepts as proportionality and the relationship between ends and means. Limited war did not suit the high commanders of the 1950s, but only MacArthur challenged Truman's policy. This cautionary tale remains best told in John W. Spanier, *The Truman-MacArthur Controversy and the Korean War* (Cambridge, Mass.: Belknap Press, 1959). For naval leaders, see Robert W. Love, Jr., ed., *The Chiefs of Naval Operations* (Annapolis, Md.: Naval Institute Press, 1980). The view from the top of the Air Force is found in Phillip S. Meilinger, *Hoyt S. Vandenberg* (Bloomington: Indiana University Press, 1989). For the use of Army reserve forces, see William Berebitsky, *A Very Long Weekend: The Army National Guard in Korea* (Shippensburg, Pa.: White Mane Press, 1996).

Logistics and Coalition Warfare

Korea provided an early test of whether the U.S. armed forces could support a limited war, coalition expeditionary force, and extemporize a regional, long-term base system at the same time. The answer, with many qualifications, was yes. The global picture (for one service) is described in James A. Huston, *Outposts and Allies: U.S. Army Logistics in the Cold War, 1945–1953* (Selinsgrove, Pa.: Susquehanna University Press, 1988). A more detailed account of the combat theater by the same author is *Guns and Butter, Powder and Rice: U.S. Army Logistics in the Korean War* (Selinsgrove, Pa.: Susquehanna University Press, 1989). An earlier study is John G. Westover, *Combat Support in Korea* (Washington: Office of the Chief of Military History, 1955). The best place to start the study of Korean War manpower and matériel mobilization is Terrence J. Gough, *U.S. Army Mobilization and Logistics in the Korean War* (Washington: U.S. Army Center for Military History, 1987). The medical experience may be found in Alfred E. Cowdrey, *The Medic's War* (Washington: U.S. Army Center of Military History, 1987), another volume in the "United States Army in the Korean War" series. There are no comparable separate logistical histories for the other services, whose historians dealt with such matters as part of their operational histories.

The Allies

The political environment on Korean affairs at the United Nations is found in the works of Stueck (see above); Yoo Tae-Hoo, *The Korean War and the United Nations* (Louvain, Belgium: Librairie Desbarax, 1965); and Leon Gordenker, *The United Nations and the Peaceful Unification of Korea: The Politics of Field Operations, 1947–1950* (The Hague: Martinus Nijhoff, 1959).

At the height of the war, the U.N. Command included ground forces from fourteen countries, excluding the United States. Nineteen nations offered to send ground combat units as part of the U.S. Eighth Army, but four proposed contributions were too little, too late. Three infantry divisions offered by the Chinese Nationalist government fell into another category: too large, too controversial. The largest non-U.S. contribution was the 1st Commonwealth Division, organized in 1951 from British army battalions and similar units from Canada, Australia, and New Zealand. The smallest was a platoon from Luxembourg. The ground forces included a Canadian brigade, Turkish brigade, New Zealand field artillery regiment, and battalions from France, Thailand, Ethiopia, Greece, the Philippines, Belgium, Australia, Colombia, and the Netherlands. The force reveals a careful political and geographical balance: contingents from Europe, Latin America, Africa, and Asia. Air and naval forces were similarly reinforced. Eight navies and four air arms deployed combat elements while eight nations sent air and sea transport. Five nations sent only medical units: Denmark, India, Italy, Norway, and Sweden.

Since the limited size of non-U.S. and non-ROKA contingents precluded them from having a great impact on the operational course of the war, their participation has been largely ignored in the United States. The exception is the dramatic participation of one or other units in a specific battle, for example, 1st Battalion, Gloucestershire Regiment, which fought to the last bullet and trumpet call on the Imjin River in April 1951. This approach overlooks the potential lessons about coalition warfare represented in U.N. Command. It also ignores the useful exercise of seeing one's military practices through the eyes of allies, in this case nations that sent their best and toughest soldiers to Korea for experience. To honor them, Korea published short accounts in English of these national military contingents: Republic of Korea, Ministry of National Defense, *The History of the United Nations Forces in the Korean War*, 6 vols. (Seoul: War History Compilation Commission, 1975). The battlefields of Korea also have excellent monuments (most erected by Korea) to U.N. forces. The United States has made no comparable effort to recognize these forces, many of which were more effective than comparable American units. (For example, the most vulnerable corridor into the Han River Valley was defended in 1952 and 1953 by the 1st Marine Division and 1st Commonwealth Division.) Most American treatments of foreign contributions, however modest, are incorporated in U.S. organizational histories.

The 1st Commonwealth Division experience provides the most accessible account of service with the Eighth Army and only muted criticism of the high command. The British history was written by a member of 1st Glosters, an esteemed general, and able historian, Sir Anthony Farrar-Hockley. His books are *The British Part in the Korean War*, vol. 1, *A Distant Obligation* (London: HMSO, 1990), and vol. 2, *An Honourable Discharge* (London: HMSO, 1994). They supersede C. N. Barclay's *The First Commonwealth Division: The Story of British Commonwealth Land Forces in Korea, 1950–1953* (Aldershot, U.K.: Gale and Polden, 1954). Other accounts include Norman Bartlett, *With the Australians in Korea* (Canberra: Australian War Memorial, 1954); Robert O'Neill, *Australia in the Korean War*, 2 vols. (Canberra: Australian War Memorial, 1981 and 1985); Herbert Fairlie Wood, *Strange Battleground: The Official History of the Canadian Army in Korea* (Ottawa: Queen's Printer, 1966); Historical Section, General Staff, Canadian Army, *Canada's Army in Korea* (Ottawa: Queens Printer, 1956); and Tim Carew, *Korea: The Commonwealth at War* (London: Cassell, 1967). For an insightful review, see Jeffrey Grey, *The Commonwealth Armies and the Korean War* (Manchester: Manchester University Press, 1988). An ambitious effort to integrate national history and the war is Ian McGibbon's *New Zealand and the Korean War*, vol. 1, *Politics and Diplomacy* (Auckland: Oxford University Press, 1992) and vol. 2, *Combat Operations* (Auckland: Oxford University Press, 1996). Denis Stairs, *The Diplomacy of Constraint: Canada, the Korean War and the United States* (Toronto: University of Toronto Press, 1974) is a comparable work. On naval cooperation, see Thor Thorgrimsson and E. C. Russell, *Canadian Naval Operations in Korean Waters, 1950–1953* (Ottawa: Queens Printer, 1965). See also Adrian Walker, *A Barren Place: National Servicemen in Korea, 1950–1954* (London: Leo Cooper, 1994).

Special Operations

The story of United Nations Command (UNC) special operations is full of sound, fury, and secrecy, signifying more promise than performance. Much of the story remains unexplored and, perhaps, classified, as in the case of communications intelligence and cryptography. It is not easy, for example, to trace the story of Combined Command for Reconnaissance Activities Korea (CCRAK), Major Don Nichols's Detachment 2, 6004th Air Intelligence Service Squadron, and the international commandos of the Special Activities Group (SAG). The most "exposed" UNC special operations are those that involved UNC-ROKA partisan forces (eventually the United Nations Partisan Forces Korea) and U.S. Army airborne ranger companies.

These units are the central characters in Ed Evanhoe, *Dark Moon: Eighth Army Special Operations in the Korean War* (Annapolis, Md.: Naval Institute Press, 1995), and William B. Breuer, *Shadow Warriors: The Covert War in Korea* (New York: John Wiley, 1996), with a good advisor's memoir, Col. Ben S. Malcom, *White Tigers: My Secret War in North Korea* (Washington: Brassey's, 1996). Air Force special operations are described in Colonel Michael E. Haas, *Apollo's Warriors: United States Air Force Special Operations during the Cold War* (Montgomery, AL: Air University Press, 1997).

Russia and the War

From the beginning there were the Soviets—until they were written out of the history of the Korean War by their own hand and by those Western historians who could not identify a bear even if he was eating out of one's garbage can. The Soviet Union may not have started the war, but it certainly gave it a big bear hug and embraced it past Stalin's death and a period of détente in the mid-1950s. The collapse of the Soviet Union has reopened the issue of Russian connivance and collaboration, bolstered by tantalizing glimpses of Communist internally oriented histories and supporting documents. Retired Russian generals and diplomats have become regular participants in Korean War conferences, but Russian official histories are not translated or widely available to Western scholars with the requisite language skills. Nevertheless, the Russian role as sponsor continues to receive clarification and is not diminished. Early plans emerge in Eric Van Ree, *Socialism in One Zone: Stalin's Policy in Korea, 1945–1947* (Oxford: Oxford University Press, 1988). Most recent admissions and revelations come from Soviet veterans who have talked to the media or participated in international conferences, including pilots and air defense specialists. Documentary evidence has come primarily from Communist Party and foreign ministry archives. Material from the armed forces and KGB has been limited. Few documents have been translated and published, although Kathryn Weathersby—a Russian historian at the Woodrow Wilson Center for Scholars in Washington, D.C.—has taken up the grail of translation and interpretation through the *Bulletin* of the Cold War International History Project and the working papers issued by the Wilson Center. The British scholar Jon Halliday has also been active in interviewing Russian veterans.

Much of Moscow's involvement is found in works on Sino-Soviet relations primarily interpreted from a Chinese perspective. Two titles in this genre are Robert R. Simmons, *The Strained Alliance: Peking, Pyongyang, Moscow, and the Politics of the Korean War* (New York: Columbia University Press, 1975), and

Sergei N. Goncharov, John W. Lewis, and Xue Litai, *Uncertain Partners: Stalin, Mao and the Korean War* (Stanford, Calif.: Stanford University Press, 1993).

Closer to the Russian sources are Vladislav Zubok and Constantine Pleshakov, *Inside the Kremlin's Cold War: From Stalin to Khrushchev* (Cambridge, Mass.: Harvard University Press, 1996), and Mark A. O'Neil, "The Other Side of the Yalu: Soviet Pilots in the Korean War, Phase One, 1 November 1950–12 April 1951" (Ph.D. diss., Florida State University, 1996).

China and the War

The recent release or leakage of Chinese sources, especially the wartime correspondence of Mao Zedong, has resulted in a new wave of scholarship by Hao Zrifan, Zhai Zhihai, Zhang Shu-gang, Chen Jian, and Michael Hunt in both article and essay form. These scholars add texture to such earlier works as Joseph Camilleri, *Chinese Foreign Policy: The Maoist Era and Its Aftermath* (Oxford: Martin Robertson, 1980); Tang Tsou, *America's Failure in China: 1941–1950* (Chicago: University of Chicago Press, 1963); and Melvin Gurtov and Byoong-Mo Hwang, *China Under Threat: The Politics of Strategy and Diplomacy* (Baltimore: Johns Hopkins University Press, 1980).

The continued complexity of Sino-American relations (with Korean history subsumed in this fatal and enduring attraction) continues to draw serious scholars to issues intricate and elusive: Thomas Christensen, *Useful Adversaries: Grand Strategy, Domestic Mobilization and Sino-American Conflict, 1947–1958* (Princeton, N.J.: Princeton University Press, 1996); Alfred D. Wilhelm, Jr., *The Chinese at the Negotiating Table* (Washington, D.C.: National Defense University Press, 1994); and Stephen Endicott and Edward Hagerman, *The United States and Biological Warfare* (Bloomington, Ind.: Indiana University Press, 1998). The latter work will attract special attention since the principal scholars at the Cold War International History Project, The Woodrow Wilson Center, announced in November 1998 that they had found Russian documents that proved that the Chinese and North Korean germ warfare charges were a hoax. The documents were then published in the CWIHP *Bulletin* (Winter, 1998/1999).

One result of international collaboration on exploring the conflict between the United States and China is Harry Harding and Yuan Ming, eds., *Sino-American Relations, 1945–1955* (Wilmington, Del.: Scholarly Resources, 1989). A critical view of the People's Liberation Army is found in Zhang Shu-gang, *Mao's Military Romanticism: China and the Korean War, 1950–1953* (Lawrence: University Press of Kansas, 1995), based largely on a self-assessment, but this work should be matched with Chen Jian, *China's Road to the Korean War: The Making of the Sino-American Confrontation* (New York: Columbia University Press, 1994), on China's intervention and also based on Chinese sources. Unfortunately, the People's Liberation Army's official history, Shen Zonghong and Meng Zhaohui et al., *Zhongguo renmin Zhiguanjun Kangmei yuanchao zhanshi* [A history of the war to resist America and assist Korea by the Chinese People's Volunteers] (Beijing: Military Science Press, 1988), remains untranslated—at least for public use. Three Western works of lasting value are Alexander L. George, *The Chinese Communist Army in Action: The Korean War and Its Aftermath* (New York: Columbia University Press, 1967); Allen S. Whiting, *China Crosses the Yalu: The Decision to Enter the Korean War* (New York: Macmillan, 1960); and Walter A. Zelman, *Chinese Intervention in the Korean War* (Los Angeles: University of California Press, 1967). For a face-of-battle account of People's Liberation Army struggles in the winter of 1950–1951, see Russell Spurr, *Enter the Dragon: China's Undeclared War Against the U.S. in Korea, 1950–1951* (New York: Henry Holt, 1988), which is based on interviews with veterans. Charles R. Shrader, *Communist Logistics in the Korean War* (Westport, Conn.: Greenwood Press, 1995), provides an able introduction to a critical subject on Sino-Korean operational limitations.

Aftermath

Finally, the impact of the war is discussed with care in the anthologies by Heller and Williams cited earlier. Also see the work edited by Lee Chae-Jin, *The Korean War: A 40-Year Perspective* (Claremont, Calif.: Keck Center for International and Strategic Studies, 1991). One beneficiary of the war was Japan—or at least those Japanese political groups allied to America, capitalism, and the social status quo. War-fueled prosperity and the diminished ardor for social reform is captured in Howard B. Schonberger, *Aftermath of War. Americans and the Remaking of Japan, 1945–1952* (Kent, Ohio: Kent State University Press, 1989), and Michael Schaller, *The American Occupation of Japan: The Origins of the Cold War* (New York: Oxford University Press, 1985). *The Journal of American–East Asian Relations* 2 (Spring 1993), is dedicated to "The Impact of the Korean War" with essays on Korea, China, Japan, and the United States. An especially interesting and stimulating effort at comparative, cross-cultural analysis of the effects of the Korean and Vietnam Wars is Philip West, Steven I. Levine, and Jackie Hiltz, eds., *America's Wars in Asia: A Cultural Approach to History and Memory* (Armonk, N.Y.: M. E. Sharpe, 1998), which is an anthology of essays produced by a conference held in

1995 at the University of Montana's Mansfield Center. Although the authors, especially the Asians, offer stimulating interpretations of the war's effects, they are ill-informed about the military events upon which some of their analysis rests.

The publishing event of the fiftieth anniversary will be the appearance of an English-language translation of the War History Compilation Committee, Ministry of National Defense, Republic of Korea, *Han'guk Chŏnjaeng-sa* (1966–1977) in six volumes. *The Korean War*, of which one (1977) volume of three has appeared, is much more than an abridged version of the original series. Organized by professional historians of the new Korea Institute of Military History, physically located at the War Memorial, Yongsan, Seoul, the *Korean War* is a major revision that incorporates the most recent Soviet documents and Chinese writing on the war, enhanced by extensive interviews with ROK Army veterans. The direction of the project is Colonel (Doctor) Chae Han Kook, chief of the Institute's new history department.

—Allan R. Millett

Hodge, John R.
(1893–1963)

U.S. Army general who headed the military government in southern Korea after the Japanese surrender in 1945. John R. Hodge was born on 12 June 1893, in Golconda, Illinois. In May 1917 he began officer training with the U.S. Army Infantry Reserve at Fort Sheridan, Illinois, and was commissioned a second lieutenant in October. During World War I, he served with the 61st Infantry in France during the St. Mihiel and Meuse-Argonne offensives.

After that war, Hodge in 1921 transferred to the Mississippi Agricultural and Mechanical College. He spent four years there as assistant professor of military science and tactics, rising to the rank of captain. From 1925 to 1926 he attended the Army's Infantry School in Fort Benning, Georgia. In 1926 he was assigned to the 27th Infantry at Schofield Barracks, Hawaii. Between 1927 and 1931 he served with the 22d Infantry Brigade, later transferring to the 18th Infantry at Fort Hamilton, New York.

Between 1932 and 1936 Hodge completed training at the Chemical Warfare School at Edgewood, Maryland, completed a two-year course of study at the Army's Command and Staff School, Fort Leavenworth, Kansas, finished another two-year course at the Army War College, Washington D.C., and completed his formal military training at the Air Corps Tactical School, Maxwell Field, Alabama.

In 1936, having been promoted to major, Hodge was assigned to the 23d Infantry, Fort Sam Houston, Texas. Late that same year he returned to Washington,

D.C., where he was assigned to the Operations and Training Division (G-3) of the War Department General Staff. Besides being promoted to lieutenant colonel during his five years on the G-3 staff, Hodge prepared plans that were used when the United States entered World War II.

In 1941 Hodge was assigned to the Army's VII Corps as its organization and training officer. Shortly after the attack on Pearl Harbor, he became chief of staff, VII Corps and transferred to San Jose, California. In 1942 he was appointed the assistant division commander of the 25th Division and participated in the Guadalcanal campaign.

In June 1943 Hodge took command of the Americal Division, a composite division of U.S. and New Caledonian forces. A month later he assumed temporary command of the 43d Division. Before his arrival, thirty days of continuous fighting had failed to remove the enemy from New Georgia Island. His leadership helped bring the rapid defeat of the Japanese. During his tour in the Solomon Islands, Hodge was wounded on Bougainville. He soon recovered and in April 1944 received command of the forming XXVII Corps. Hodge led the Corps during its assault on Japanese-held islands, including Leyte and Okinawa.

After Japan's surrender General Douglas MacArthur selected Lieutenant General Hodge to command U.S. Army Forces in Korea (USAFIK). They were responsible for civil control and daily operations in Korea south of the 38th parallel. Hodge appointed 7th Division commander Major General Archibald V. Arnold to handle civil affairs as head of the U.S. Army Military Government. This included such basic functions as running utilities and forming a security force. Occupation tasks were often difficult because few Koreans had any experience in self-government, Korea having been annexed by Japan in 1910.

During this period, opposition from the local populace arose when Hodge announced a plan to retain some Japanese officials in their former positions. Subsequently USAFIK appointed a board of ten U.S. officers to examine political and military conditions to determine if a national defense program was needed. Hodge approved the board's plan for a South Korean army but MacArthur disagreed. In the fall and winter 1947–1948, MacArthur's belief that the Koreans needed only a constabulary force eventually won out. In the spring of 1948, army officials ordered Hodge to develop plans to withdraw U.S. forces by the end of the year.

In May 1948, South Korean citizens elected the Republic of Korea's (ROK) first national assembly. The assembly chose Syngman Rhee to be ROK's first president. On 15 August he was inaugurated, and 24 August Hodge and Rhee signed an agreement to transfer control of the nation's security forces to the new government. Three days later Hodge returned to the United States.

Hodge served in various posts until 1952, when President Harry S. Truman appointed him chief of Army Field Forces, a position he held until his retirement in 1953. Hodge died on 12 November 1963 in Washington, D.C.

—Dean Corey and William Head

References:

Matray, James I., ed. *Historical Dictionary of the Korean War.* Westport, CT: Greenwood Press, 1991.

National Cyclopedia of American Biography. Vol. 1. New York: James T. White, 1969.

New York Times, 13 November 1963.

Sawyer, Robert K. *KMAG in War and Peace.* Washington, DC: Office of the Chief of Military History, U.S. Army, 1962.

See also: MacArthur, Douglas; Syngman Rhee.

Hoengsŏng, Battle of
(January 1951)

Engagements that occurred in early January 1951 in conjunction with the launching of the Third Chinese Offensive. The battle took place around the town of Hoengsŏng (a.k.a. Hoensong) in central Korea, 29 miles south of the 38th parallel, on the Hongch'ŏn-Hoengsŏng-Wŏnju "highway." Although scarcely more than a narrow third-class mountain trail, it was the main and vital north-south link for these important centers. The United Nations Command considered retention of Hoengsŏng vital to the defense of Wŏnju some ten miles to the south, which, in turn, was considered the key to holding South Korea in the early days of Chinese intervention.

On 1 January 1951, units of the Chinese People's Volunteer Army (CPVA, Communist China) crossed the 38th parallel in the central highlands of Korea. Temperatures fell to twenty-five degrees below zero as howling blizzards swept through the mountain passes. Roads were snow and ice-covered, treacherous, and nearly impassable for artillery tractors and other heavy gear. The area abounded with Communist guerrillas who roved the mountains, set up road blocks, and assisted regular unit attacks.

As the CPVA assault rolled into South Korea and headed toward Hoengsŏng, Republic of Korea Army (South Korean) divisions on line in the Ch'unch'ŏn-Han'gye areas, just below the parallel, disintegrated. On 2 January Major General Robert McClure's U.S. 2d Infantry Division began an attack northward from the Wŏnju area into the teeth of the onrushing Chinese. Leading the attack, and quickly locked in fierce battle, was Colonel Paul Freeman's 23d Regiment with its French Battalion. As the fighting intensified, new Eighth Army commander Lieutenant General Mat-

thew B. Ridgway arrived and met with the regimental and battalion commanders, impressing on them the absolute necessity of blocking the Communist advance on the vital road hub of Wŏnju.

The 23d stopped the Chinese advance on Hoengsŏng and then eliminated a roadblock north of the town. It then immediately established blocking positions of its own, which it maintained until 5 January. As the regiment was digging in and consolidating its positions, orders to continue the advance to Hongch'ŏn, the next town north, were canceled. New orders were received attaching the 2d Division to X Corps, with instructions to establish a new defense line. These orders were simultaneous with, and apparently a consequence of, Ridgway's 3 January order for Eighth Army to withdraw from Seoul.

In the days to follow, the 2d Division's regiments remained in the Hoengsŏng-Wŏnju area with the 23d north of Hoengsŏng, the 38th well entrenched in the town, and the 9th farther south in the vicinity of Wŏnju. The division's position remained precarious because of the continued withdrawal of Republic of Korea Army (ROKA, South Korean) units on its flanks. This left it exposed on three sides to Korean People's Army (KPA, North Korean) attack.

On 5 January the 23d was ordered to pull back to Wŏnju and blow the bridges as it withdrew. On the previous day Ridgway had issued a directive rescinding previous Army Commander Lieutenant General Walton H. Walker's scorched earth policy and declaring that demolitions would be limited to those that would "combine maximum hurt to the enemy with minimum harm to civilian populations." Bridges would be blown with an eye to "substantial delay to the enemy without imposing undue hardship on the population." The bridges blown by the 23d appeared to meet that criteria.

With this move by the 23d in conjunction with the rest of the division, fighting shifted from the Hoengsŏng area to positions farther south and concentrated in the Wŏnju and Chip'yŏng-ni areas where intense and decisive engagements took place in mid-February.

—Sherman Pratt

References:

Blair, Clay. *The Forgotten War: America in Korea, 1950–1953.* New York: Times Books, 1987.

Munroe, Clark C. *The Second United States Infantry Division in Korea, 1950–1951.* Tokyo: Toppan Printing, nd.

Pratt, Sherman W. *Decisive Battles of the Korean War. An Infantry Company Commander's View of the War's Most Critical Engagements.* New York: Vantage Press, 1992.

Schnabel, James F. *United States Army in the Korean War: Policy and Direction, the First Year.* Washington, DC: Office of the Chief of Military History, Department of the Army, 1972.

See also: Freeman, Paul L., Jr.; McClure, Robert A.; Ridgway, Matthew Bunker; Walker, Walton Harris.

IX Corps commander Lieutenant General William M. Hoge, along with Major General Blackshear M. Bryan, Lieutenant General James Van Fleet, and Lieutenant General Matthew B. Ridgway. (National Archives)

Hoge, William M.
(1894–1979)

U.S. Army general and commander of IX Corps in Korea, February–November 1951. Born on 13 January 1894, in Booneville, Missouri, where his father was principal of Kemper Military School, William M. Hoge moved with his family when he was eight to Lexington, Missouri, where his father became the co-owner of Wentworth Military Academy. Hoge graduated from Wentworth in 1911 and went from there to West Point. Upon graduation in 1916, he was commissioned in the Corps of Engineers.

Hoge's first assignment was with the 1st Engineers on the Mexican border. In 1917 he assumed command of a company in the 7th Engineers at Fort Leavenworh, Kansas. In February 1918, the regiment departed for France, where Hoge was promoted to major and took command of a battalion and fought in the St. Mihiel and Meuse-Argonne offensives. He was presented the Distinguished Service Cross by General John Joseph Pershing personally and was also awarded the Silver Star for bravery.

Between the wars Hoge graduated from the Massachusetts Institute of Technology with a degree in civil engineering. He also graduated in 1928 from the Command and General Staff College at Fort Leavenworth, Kansas. In 1935 he went to the Philippines to command the 14th Engineer Battalion, Philippine Scouts. When General Douglas MacArthur activated the Philippine Army, he requested Hoge serve as chief of engineers of the new force.

In February 1942 Hoge received the mission of constructing a military road across Northwest Canada to Alaska, the ALCAN highway. By September 1942 he and his engineers had cut 1,030 miles of road through virgin forest over uncharted land, and convoys were moving supplies to Alaska.

After leaving Alaska, Hoge served briefly with the 9th Armored Division before he was sent to Britain to command the Provisional Engineer Special Brigade

Group, which participated in the D-day assault on the Normandy beaches, specifically on what was code-named Omaha Beach. In October 1944 he returned to the 9th Armored Division as the commander of Combat Command B and led it through tough fighting around Saint-Vith in the Battle of the Bulge. In March 1945 his troops seized the railway bridge across the Rhine River at Remagen, providing the Allies with their first bridgehead east of that river. By the end of the war he had been promoted to major general and was commanding the 4th Armored Division, which had spearheaded the U.S. Third Army's drive across Germany into Czechoslovakia.

After World War II, Hoge commanded the Engineer Center at Fort Belvoir and later commanded U.S. troops in Trieste. In February 1951 Major General Bryant E. Moore, commander of IX Corps in Korea, died suddenly, and Eighth Army commander Lieutenant General Matthew B. Ridgway, an old and close friend, summoned Hoge to Korea as Moore's replacement.

As commander of IX Corps until November 1951, Hoge directed his troops in the critical battles in central Korea that resulted in the stabilization of the fighting near the 38th parallel. In Operations RUGGED, DAUNTLESS, PILEDRIVER, and COMMANDO, Hoge demonstrated the tenacity and aggressiveness that had made him famous during World War II.

After leaving Korea, Hoge commanded the Fourth Army in San Antonio and the Seventh Army in Germany and served as commander in chief of U.S. Army forces in Europe. After retiring from the Army in 1955 as a four-star general, Hoge served as chairman of the board for Interlake Iron Company in Cleveland, Ohio. He died at Fort Leavenworth, Kansas, on 29 October 1979.

—James H. Willbanks

References:

Blair, Clay. *The Forgotten War: America in Korea, 1950–1953.* New York: Times Books, 1987.

MacDonald, Charles B. *A Time for Trumpets.* New York: William Morrow, 1985.

Middleton, Harry J. *The Compact History of the Korean War.* New York: Hawthorn Books, 1965.

See also: COMMANDO, Operation; DAUNTLESS, Operation; MacArthur, Douglas; PILEDRIVER, Operation; Ridgway, Matthew Bunker; RUGGED, Operation.

Home-by-Christmas Offensive
(24 November 1950)

Offensive launched on 24 November 1950 after the United Nations Command (UNC) forces had crossed the 38th parallel and were securing North Korea. The Home-by-Christmas Offensive received its name from a remark by Supreme Commander of UN Forces General Douglas MacArthur to reporters during a trip to the front. He proclaimed that the offensive would consolidate control over all of North Korea, and he assured victory and announced that his troops would be "home by Christmas." The statement was unfortunate as both the goal and its timetable were unrealistic. Nevertheless, the news media seized this phrase and it became the popular name for the UNC offensive that began on 24 November.

Chinese forces had already intervened once in the fighting. By 24 October, there were nearly 200,000 Chinese troops in North Korea, but MacArthur depreciated their presence, even after Chinese troops decimated South Korean forces in several encounters south of the Yalu River and after U.S. troops had their first encounter with Chinese troops on 1 November. On 2 November MacArthur had informed the Joint Chiefs of Staff (JCS) that he estimated that there were only 16,500 Chinese troops in North Korea. Recognizing the new realities, Eighth U.S. Army commander Lieutenant General Walton H. Walker on the same day ordered his troops to retreat to the Ch'ŏngch'ŏn River. By mid-month they had dug in there and could have established a permanent boundary at this location. However, MacArthur wished to launch a new offensive to unify Korea and conclude the war on his terms. Throughout November he sparred with Washington over restrictions on his conduct of the war, and he continued to drastically underestimate the numbers of Chinese in North Korea, a figure that continued to grow. When his late November offensive began, MacArthur estimated that 40,000–80,000 Chinese troops were in Korea. The actual number was between 300,000 and 340,000.

On 24 November MacArthur announced the resumption of the offensive and dismissed the possibility of further Chinese intervention. Actually, the offensive had begun in the eastern part of Korea weeks earlier. On 21 November the 17th Regiment of the 7th U.S. Division reached Hyesanjin on the Yalu River. On 29 November a portion of the 32d Regiment of the 7th Division also reached the Yalu at Singalp'ajin about 20 miles downstream from Hyesanjin. These would be the only U.S. troops to reach the Yalu.

Walker, who had delayed the resumption until he thought Eighth Army was ready, resumed the advance on 24 November. The Chinese soon responded, and within three days Walker realized that his forces were in serious trouble. Eighth Army began its withdrawal on 28 November, with the U.S. 2d Division holding the Chinese long enough to allow the withdrawal of the remainder of Walker's forces in western Korea. On 29 November the 2d Division began its own withdrawal, but suffered more than 3,000 casualties and lost much of its equipment. Eighth Army withdrew

Thanksgiving Day services for U.S. troops in North Korea near the Yalu River, 23 November 1950. (National Archives)

120 miles in only ten days. It evacuated P'yŏngyang on 5 December and continued down to the 38th parallel, where it established defensive positions.

In the eastern sector of North Korea, the 25,000-man 1st Marine Division had on 27 November begun its own advance along a primitive dirt track that ran northwestward from the western side of the Changjin (Chosin) Reservoir. However, on the first night of the advance 30,000 Chinese attacked the Marines. Some 50,000 Chinese were positioned along the road and another 40,000 were in reserve. MacArthur telegraphed the Pentagon that evening, stating that the intervention of massive numbers of Chinese had created an entirely new war.

The Marines west of the reservoir began fighting their way southward along the barren terrain to Hagaru-ri at the Changjin Reservoir's southern tip. On 3 December they linked up with survivors of two battalions of the 7th U.S. Infantry Division, which had been overrun to the northeast. Of 2,500 men in the battalions,

only 1,000 made it to Hagaru-ri alive, and of those more than 600 were wounded. During the initial advance, Marine Major General Oliver P. Smith had been concerned about potential massive Chinese intervention. He had expressed these reservations to the Marine Corps commandant and proceeded cautiously, leaving detachments of men and stockpiles of supplies along the route of advance. These caches proved vital when his retreating forces had to fight their way back against overwhelming Chinese forces. Had he been less cautious, his forces could have been surrounded and destroyed. After a week of courageous fighting, the Marines finally reached relative safety. The cost had been high, with 700 Marines killed and 3,500 wounded. The UNC estimated Chinese deaths at 15,000 killed by the Marines and another 10,000 by air strikes.

Only a month after proclaiming that the troops would be home by Christmas, MacArthur had presided over a 275-mile retreat, the longest in U.S. military history. Although he had underestimated and depreciated his enemy, MacArthur blamed his failures on timid and irresolute policies of President Harry S. Truman. Unrepentant and undaunted, MacArthur during the next weeks decidedly increased the tensions between himself and the Truman administration and JCS. Thus the failed offensive that intended to win the war widened the conflict and set in motion the circumstances that led to MacArthur's dismissal from command.

—Joe P. Dunn

References:

Alexander, Bevin. *Korea: The First War We Lost*. New York: Hippocrene Books, 1986.

Appleman, Roy E. *Disaster in Korea: The Chinese Confront MacArthur*. College Station, TX: Texas A&M Press, 1989.

Blair, Clay. *The Forgotten War: America in Korea, 1950–1953*. New York: Times Books, 1987.

Knox, Donald, and Albert Coppel. *The Korean War: An Oral History*. 2 vols. San Diego: Harcourt Brace Jovanovich, 1885–1988.

See also: Changjin (Chosin) Reservoir Campaign; Joint Chiefs of Staff (JCS); Smith, Oliver Prince; Walker, Walton Harris.

Hong Kong, British Crown Colony of

When hostilities began in Korea, Hong Kong was a British colony, as it would remain until 1997. Until the Communist takeover of mainland China in 1949, U.S. officials viewed British control of Hong Kong as an embarrassing anomaly that conflicted with the overtly anticolonial U.S. stance. During the Second World War, U.S. President Franklin D. Roosevelt unsuccessfully suggested that, after its liberation from Japan, Hong Kong should be restored to Chinese rule. In 1949 the United States turned down a British request for U.S. military assistance should Hong Kong be attacked by another power, a decision recommended by the Joint Chiefs of Staff and the Department of State and enshrined in the NSC-55 ("Implications of a Possible Chinese Communist Attack on Foreign Colonies in South China"), the department's policy planning staff.

During the Korean War, Britain's concern to retain Hong Kong was one of the factors impelling the British to try to persuade the United States to adopt a relatively conciliatory line toward the People's Republic of China (PRC) and to open negotiations to end active hostilities. U.S. leaders tended to disregard or even resent Britain's diligent efforts to safeguard Hong Kong's interests and viability. U.S. military leaders and officials continued to assume that Hong Kong was indefensible and that its takeover by the PRC was virtually inevitable. A particular point of contention in the Anglo-American relationship was the degree to which Hong Kong continued to trade with the PRC. The United States imposed a commercial embargo in 1950 on that trade, and the trading was also subjected to broad United Nations (UN) censure and sanctions in 1951. Despite British arguments that Hong Kong depended on trade with China for many of its daily necessities and that to cut off commerce might well lead to a complete Sino-British break and a Communist takeover, the colony experienced determined though only partially successful pressure from the United States to cease to supply the mainland with goods that might assist the Chinese in their fighting against UN forces in Korea.

During and after the Korean War, both private U.S. organizations and the U.S. government provided assistance to those refugees from the mainland who entered the colony by tens of thousands in the late 1940s and early 1950s. Hong Kong also began to function as a useful intelligence-gathering center for U.S. spies and diplomats who were excluded from the Chinese mainland, and it continued to play that role at least until the 1980s. Not until the late 1950s, however, did President Dwight D. Eisenhower's administration quietly assume an unpublicized commitment to Hong Kong's defense.

—Priscilla Roberts

References:

Clayton, David. *Imperialism Revisited: Political and Economic Relations between Britain and China, 1950–54*. London: Macmillan, 1987.

Law, Debbie Yuk Fun. "Uneasy Accommodation: U.S. Hong Kong Policy, 1949–60." Ph.D. dissertation, University of Hong Kong, forthcoming.

Lowe, Peter. *Containing the Cold War in East Asia: British Policies towards Japan, China and Korea, 1948–1953*. Manchester: Manchester University Press, 1997.

Tang, James T. H. *Britain's Encounter with Revolutionary China, 1949–54*. Basingstoke, UK: Macmillan, 1992.

Tsang, Steve. *A Modern History of Hong Kong, 1941–1997*. London: I. B. Tauris, 1997.

Tucker, Nancy Bernkopf. *Uncertain Friendships: Taiwan, Hong Kong, and the United States, 1945–1992*. New York: Twayne, 1994.

Welsh, Frank. *Borrowed Place: A History of Hong Kong*. Rev. ed. New York: Kodansha, 1997.

See also: Attlee, Clement R.; Bevin, Ernest; United Kingdom (UK).

Hook, Battles of the
(26 October 1952–27 July 1953)

Series of battles fought between Chinese People's Volunteer Army (CPVA, Chinese Communist) forces and elements of the U.S. 7th Marine Regiment and later various units of the 29th Brigade of the Commonwealth Division. On the western portion of the peninsula, south of the 38th parallel and north of Seoul, the Hook is a J-shaped, or fishing hook–shaped, hill that dominates the Sami-ch'ŏn valley, a vital approach to the Republic of Korea (South Korean) capital. Depicted as a feature that was so daunting in its appearance as to be "indescribably sinister," the

Hook, or the "bloody Hook" as it was called by members of the Commonwealth Division, was the site of near continuous small-unit fighting during the latter stages of the war.

The first United Nations troops to weather the onslaught of Communist forces intent on seizing the Hook were the men of the 1st Battalion, 7th Marines. In savage fighting during 26–27 October, the two sides battled in a manner characteristic of the trench warfare on the Western Front of World War I. After days of gradually intensifying artillery preparations, the Chinese mounted a concerted effort on the 26th to wrest control of the hill. The CPVA attack was strong enough that at one point on the afternoon of the 27th the Chinese drove the Marines off the Hook. However, with determination and supporting fires from artillery, armor, and aircraft, the Marines retook the hill later that day.

Although the Marines were relieved on 4 November by men of the British Army's 1st Battalion, the Black Watch, the rotation was not indicative of any reduction in the perceived value of the Hook. Aware of its importance, the hill's new keepers, with the assistance of combat engineers and laborers from the Korean Service Corps, set about strengthening the defenses left by the Marines.

With their more comprehensive fortifications, the soldiers of the Black Watch were well disposed to fend off another major assault of Communist forces on 18 November. Attacking under cover of darkness, approximately 500 Chinese soldiers infiltrated and assaulted the British positions. In fighting between small units and scattered individuals, the Black Watch retained control of the Hook while suffering 107 casualties, of which 16 were killed in action. Communist loses were more severe; more than 100 of their dead were left on the battlefield.

Although Chinese pressure on the hill was unrelenting, it was not until May that the largest of the Hook battles took place. On 28–29 May the 1st Battalion, the Duke of Wellington's Regiment, was embroiled in a desperate defensive action. After the familiar prescription of days marked by gradually intensifying artillery bombardments, the Chinese unleashed three battalions of their 133d Division in a dramatic night assault. Inflicting approximately 1,000 casualties on the attackers in fighting at extremely close range, the British managed to keep the hill at a cost of 148 casualties.

Despite further days of shelling and numerous night assaults, including fighting mere hours before the cease-fire, the Hook remained in the hands of the Commonwealth Division until the end of the Korean War.

—*Charles A. Steele*

References:
Carew, Tim. *The Commonwealth at War*. London: Cassell, 1967.
Farrar-Hockley, Sir Anthony. *The Official History of the British Part in the Korean War*. London: Her Majesty's Stationery Office, 1995.
Grey, Jeffrey. *The Commonwealth Armies and the Korean War: An Alliance Study*. Manchester: Manchester University Press, 1988.
Macdonald, John. *Great Battlefields of the World*. New York: Macmillan, 1985.
Meid, Pat, and James M. Yingling. *U.S. Marine Operations in Korea, 1950–1953*. Vol. V, *Operations in West Korea*. Washington, DC: U.S. Marine Corps Historical Branch, 1972.
See also: United Kingdom (UK).

Hospital Ships

Seven ships formally served as floating hospitals or patient transports during the Korean War. As the war progressed, their role changed dramatically from what was originally envisioned.

The *U.S. New Haven* class vessels were dedicated 500-foot hospital ships first built during World War II. The *Consolation* was in commission in 1950 and made a rapid trip from the eastern United States to Korea when hostilities broke out. The rest of the class were in the reserve fleet in San Francisco. The *Benevolence* and *Repose* were activated, but *Benevolence* sank in the Golden Gate channel on its way to Korea. The *New Haven* was activated in its place and joined the *Consolation* and the *Repose* in Korean waters by mid-October.

Almost from the outset the ships were used as stationary floating hospitals. They were initially berthed at Pusan but moved north along both the east and west coasts of Korea after the United Nations Command breakout from the Pusan perimeter.

In the hectic early days of the war (before organized air evacuation from Korea to Japan was in place), the U.S. troop ships *Sgt. George D. Keathley* and *Sgt. Andrew Miller* were pressed into service to move wounded to rear area hospitals. Early on, even these resources were overwhelmed and local ferries were pressed into service.

The Royal Navy furnished its *Maine*, a captured Italian liner that was present in Far Eastern waters in June 1950. The ship was ill suited for medical duties, however; it was overcrowded and had only a single air-conditioning unit, which allowed lower deck temperatures to exceed 100 degrees. The Danish ship *Jutlandia* also served in the early part of the war. It was a converted passenger and cargo vessel staffed with volunteers that made two trips from the Pacific to Europe to return wounded United Nations troops to their home countries.

As helicopter and fixed-wing transport became available, the role of the hospital ships changed dramatically. C-47s and C-54s assumed essentially all transport duties, and the ships were moored close to appropriate areas to serve as fixed base hospitals. At first, flat-topped barges were moored next to the ships to allow helicopter access. Later, formal "helo" decks were added so that patients could be brought directly on board. At various times, the ships were also moored directly to piers and served as both floating hospitals and outpatient clinics. The upper three decks housed up to 800 in-patients, whereas the lower three decks were administrative and clinic spaces.

By September 1952 the U.S. Navy hospital ships had admitted 40,662 patients; about 35 percent were battle casualties and the rest were diseases and nonbattle injuries.

—*Jack McCallum*

References:

Cowdrey, Alfred E. *United States Army in the Korean War: The Medic's War.* Washington, DC: Center for Military History, 1987.

Coyl, E. B. "Hospital Ships in Korea." *Military Surgeon* 112 (1953): 342–344.

See also: Aeromedical Evacuation; Military Medicine; Mobile Army Surgical Hospital (MASH).

Hot Pursuit

Pursuit by United Nations Command (UNC) aircraft of attacking Communist aircraft into Manchurian airspace. Throughout the Korean War, UNC air operations were limited to repelling Communist aircraft engaged in offensive missions into Korea. The matter of air counteraction against targets in Manchuria first arose in early November 1950 when Soviet and Chinese planes operating from bases northwest of the Yalu River began appearing in increasing numbers. At the 26 June 1950 National Security Council (NSC) meeting, U.S. President Harry S. Truman approved air cover for the evacuation of American dependents and support for Republic of Korea Army (South Korean) troops. He confined such operations to south of the 38th parallel; however, faced with the imminent loss of Seoul, Washington began to reevaluate restrictions on the 38th parallel.

As a result of the 29 June 1950 NSC meeting, U.S. Commander in the Far East General Douglas MacArthur was permitted to conduct air operations into North Korea against military targets, including air bases. Yet he was instructed to take special care to keep these well clear of the frontiers with Manchuria and the Soviet Union. Strict regulations on the scope of UN air operations were intended to restrict the war to the Korean peninsula.

On 7 November 1950 General MacArthur stated that the restrictions provided a complete sanctuary for hostile aircraft upon their crossing of the Manchurian border. He further stated that unless corrective measures were promptly taken this factor could assume decisive proportions, and he requested instructions for dealing with this new threat. In response to MacArthur's request the U.S. Joint Chiefs of Staff began seriously to consider permitting hot pursuit of attacking Communist aircraft across the Yalu River and Manchuria.

U.S. allies reacted unfavorably to hot pursuit because they were concerned about the possibility of a widened war. These governments raised the question whether the United States should hold consultations before undertaking any military action over Manchuria and whether the U.S. cosponsorship of the 10 November Security Council Resolution referring to holding inviolate the Sino-Korean frontier would be interpreted by the United States as authorizing action against Manchuria beyond that of hot pursuit. Finally, Washington agreed to consult with its allies with as much advance notice as possible.

MacArthur did not request authority to undertake hot pursuit after Washington decided not to push the matter and made the frontiers of Manchuria and the Soviet Union inviolate. Yet the United States made clear that the UNC reserved the right to protect forces under its command. In event of a large-scale air attack against UN troops from Manchurian bases, the UNC would be free to bomb airfields from which such air attacks originated, or, if Chinese Communist forces, in support of their forces in Korea, attacked UN forces outside Korea, the UNC would be free to counteract.

Washington did, however, authorize pursuit by UNC aircraft of attacking Communist aircraft up to two or three minutes flying time into Manchurian airspace. In April 1952, F-86s struck Dandong (Antung) Airfield in Manchuria, and from this point much of the Manchurian sanctuary was lost to Communist aircraft.

—*Youngho Kim*

References:

No Kom-Sok, with J. Roger Osterholm. *A MiG-15 to Freedom. Memoir of the Wartime North Korean Defector Who First Delivered the Secret Fighter Jet to the Americans in 1953.* Jefferson City, NC: McFarland, 1996.

U.S. Department of State, Bureau of Public Affairs. *Foreign Relations of the United States, 1950.* Vol. 7, *Korea.* Washington, DC: U.S. Government Printing Office, 1976.

See also: Joint Chiefs of Staff (JCS); MacArthur, Douglas; Truman, Harry S.

HUDSON HARBOR, Exercise
(August–October 1951)

Exercise to determine the feasibility of tactical use of atomic weapons in Korea. Its roots can be traced to increasing debate among U.S. leaders in April 1951 concerning the use of atomic weapons. Signs of

Chinese air and ground preparations for a spring offensive and a corresponding buildup of Soviet forces in the Far East alarmed U.S. President Harry S. Truman sufficiently that he ordered nuclear weapons and more Strategic Air Command (SAC) bombers to bases on Okinawa. Commander of SAC General Curtis LeMay was informed of Truman's intentions on 5 April 1951, and on the 7th he met with U.S. Air Force Chief of Staff General Hoyt Vandenberg to finalize plans. The two decided to deploy the 9th Bomb Wing from Travis Air Force Base, California to Guam on a training mission and then to maneuver it to Okinawa "for a possible action against retardation targets." (Retardation targets are those attacked to slow an enemy ground advance.)

On 11 April the Joint Chiefs of Staff (JCS) issued LeMay a directive to prepare plans "against targets listed and targets of opportunity in the Far East." After the aircraft were deployed with the nuclear cores to complete nine bombs, LeMay sent his deputy, General Thomas Power, to the Far East to coordinate with the new commander in chief in the Far East (CINCFE), General Matthew Ridgway, and to direct any atomic operations. This mission was so sensitive that when the U.S. Air Force Staff in Washington found out that a congressional committee was heading for Guam at the same time, they directed that General Power "be missing" during their visit. Though the nuclear-capable SAC B-29s, and sometimes B-50s, never moved to Okinawa, the deployment to Guam continued until the end of the war. LeMay complained on numerous occasions that the need for frequent squadron rotation kept "one of our atomic wings in a constant state of disruption."

This incident raised many issues about atomic operations in Korea for both SAC and the JCS. LeMay was concerned about retaining control of such missions and designated General Power as "Deputy Commanding General, SAC X-RAY" with that responsibility. These arrangements were finalized in a 2 May meeting between Power, Far East Air Forces Commander Lieutenant General George Stratemeyer, and Major General Doyle Hickey of Ridgway's staff. The conference also produced a memorandum on planning for SAC "atomic retardation operations" in the Far East. When Power returned to the United States, atomic responsibility in the theater passed to the chief of Far East Air Force (FEAF) Bomber Command, which meant that Power still took orders from FEAF for conventional operations but answered to SAC on nuclear issues.

Ground commanders in the theater feared that SAC would rather hit the Soviet homeland than support them. Before he was relieved of command, General Douglas MacArthur, supreme commander of United Nations forces, had asked for his own atomic capability for the early stages of an expanded war on two occasions: in December 1950, for thirty-four bombs primarily for retardation targets; and in March 1951, to hit enemy airfields on D-day if hostilities expanded. Inspired by a series of alarming messages warning of possible Soviet reaction to the approaching completion of a peace treaty between Japan and the United States, Ridgway renewed the requests in May 1951, bolstered by his new agreements with SAC. Two army staff studies conducted at about that time complained that SAC considered only strategic use of the bomb and had no appreciation of tactical strike capabilities. Planning, intelligence, command relationships, and training in SAC and Far East Command were inadequate to support Ridgway's ground operations with nuclear weapons. When the JCS discussed one of these studies in August, it directed CINCFE to test atomic delivery procedures by conducting simulated strikes in Korea after coordination with SAC and the commander in chief, Pacific, since the navy also had some carrier-based nuclear capability. At the same time, Ridgway was asking for just such tactical support to be available to him.

The JCS action resulted in Exercise HUDSON HARBOR, four practice missions conducted by SAC X-RAY (under the temporary command of SAC's Major General Emmett "Rosie" O'Donnell, who was supposedly on "a normal overseas inspection trip") on tactical targets chosen by CINCFE. For security, the operations were covered as conventional strikes in support of front-line troops and would have appeared that way to observers where the ordnance was delivered. Single B-29s were often used for strikes relatively close to the front lines. However, the missions were conducted as close to actual nuclear procedures as possible, to include waiting three and a half hours to get simulated presidential permission to release the weapons for a first strike. Contrary to the assertions of historians such as Bruce Cumings, there is no indication that these operations were designed to send any message to the enemy, and it seems unlikely from the cover story and flight paths that the Communists could have presumed the missions' intent.

By the time tests concluded in October 1951, HUDSON HARBOR demonstrated that the evaluation of potential tactical atomic targets was inadequate and the delay between selection and delivery was too long. Objectives such as troop concentrations that appeared lucrative enough for a nuclear strike had dispersed or dug in by the time exercise aircraft reached their location. In addition, CINCFE and SAC disagreed on the best way to pick objectives. Ridgway wanted to base choices on each unique battlefield situation, whereas LeMay favored standard "yardsticks." As far as the

Air Staff was concerned, the exercise failed to establish that there were any suitable targets for atomic bombs in Korea. Instead of increasing the chances that nuclear weapons would be used there, the results of the exercise bolstered the arguments of those in SAC and the JCS who believed that there was no tactical role for such weapons in the theater.

—*Conrad C. Crane*

References:

Crane, Conrad C. *American Air Power Strategy in Korea, 1950–1953.* Lawrence: University Press of Kansas, 1999.

MacDonald, Callum. *Korea: The War Before Vietnam.* New York: Free Press, 1986.

Schnabel, James F., and Robert J. Watson. *The History of the Joint Chiefs of Staff: The Joint Chiefs of Staff and National Policy.* Vol. 3, *The Korean War, Part II.* Wilmington, DE: Michael Glazier, 1979.

See also: Aircraft (Principal Combat); Hickey, Doyle O.; MacArthur, Douglas; O'Donnell, Emmett; Ridgway, Matthew Bunker; Stratemeyer, George E.; Truman, Harry S.; Vandenberg, Hoyt S.

Hull, John E.
(1895–1975)

U.S. Army general and commander in chief of both the United Nations Command (UNC) in Korea and the U.S. Far East Command, 1953–1955. John E. Hull was born on 26 May 1895, in Greenfield, Ohio. He attended Miami University in Oxford, Ohio, where he was a noted football player. Military service in the First World War, including six months of active duty in France, led him to abandon his initial plans of becoming a physician and make the military his profession. Like most U.S. Army officers of the time, Hull spent the interwar years in a variety of posts around the United States and Hawaii, including several assignments as an assistant professor in military science and tactics. He also attended staff courses at Fort Benning, Fort Leavenworth, and the Army War College.

During World War II, Hull was assigned to the War Department's General Staff rather than the combat service he would have preferred. An excellent staff officer and low-key in style, he worked mostly behind the scenes; he won recognition from military insiders but was little known to the public. In 1944 he was promoted to assistant chief of staff in charge of the operations division, and the following year he rose to brigadier general.

As commanding general of the U.S. Armed Forces in the Pacific, 1946–1948, Hull supervised the 1947 atomic tests on Eniwetok. Returning to Washington, during 1949–1951 he served as director of the weapons system evaluation group, where his responsibilities included testing the new and controversial B-36 bomber and assessing its place in overall U.S. defenses. Promoted to deputy chief of staff for opera-

tions and administration in 1951, later that year he became vice-chief of staff of the army and a four-star general.

On 7 October 1953, Hull took over General Mark W. Clark's position as commander in chief of the UNC and of the U.S. Far East Command, which comprised the entire Pacific area. His major responsibility was to implement the terms of the recently concluded armistice, and in particular to cooperate with the Neutral Nations Repatriation Commission (NNRC) to solve the problem of unrepatriated prisoners of war (POWs).

Hull made conscious efforts to build up the morale of the U.S.'s Asian allies. In his first speech in Tokyo in October 1953 he spoke of his desire to contribute to peace in the Far East and urged Japan to build up its strength "against Communist aggression." He took a firm line on the still-contentious POW issue. Under the terms of the armistice, 22,000 still unrepatriated POWs from Communist countries who had refused to return to their homelands were to be held in custody by Indian troops for 120 days. When this period expired on 22 January 1954, Hull insisted that they be released, and he refused to accept the ruling of the NNRC's Indian chairman, General K. S. Thimayya, that the prisoners should remain in custody until an international political conference should convene to decide their ultimate fate. Hull stated publicly, "For the United Nations Command now to agree to further and indefinitely prolonged captivity of these prisoners of war would negate the very principle of human rights for which so many men of this command have fought and died." A compromise was reached whereby between 20 and 22 January the prisoners were initially returned to their original captors, and Hull proceeded to declare them free civilians.

Hull presided over the drawdown of U.S. forces in Korea. In 1954 he announced that, although "for the present we will have to maintain our combat strength" in Korea, two U.S. divisions were to be withdrawn from Korea and replaced by Republic of Korea Army (South Korean) troops. Overall, Hull's tenure as commander in chief was a relatively trouble-free period of retrenchment and consolidation, when outstanding war-related issues were resolved and the situation on the Korean peninsula began to settle into the pattern it would continue to follow until the late twentieth century. At least some of the credit for this was the result of Hull's relaxed, self-confident, and modest style of leadership.

Hull retired from the army in 1955 and was replaced by General Maxwell D. Taylor. Shortly after his return to the United States, Hull was elected president of the Manufacturing Chemists Association. He died in Washington, D.C., on 10 June 1975.

—*Priscilla Roberts*

References:

Bailey, Sydney D. *The Korean Armistice.* New York: St. Martin's Press, 1992.

Hermes, Walter G. *United States Army in the Korean War: Truce Tent and Fighting Front.* Washington, DC: Office of the Chief of Military History, 1966.

"Hull, John E(dwin)." In *Current Biography, 1954.* New York: H. W. Wilson, 1955.

See also: Neutral Nations Repatriation Commission; Repatriation, Voluntary; Taylor, Maxwell Davenport; Thimayya, Kadenera Subayya.

Human Wave Attacks

Communist Chinese offensive tactic. Lacking air superiority, mechanization, and advanced weaponry, Chinese strategists exploited their few advantages, notably numbers and morale, to achieve military goals. Both for psychological effect and to avoid United Nations Command (UNC) aircraft, a typical assault began under cover of night. Preceded by infiltration of enemy defenses and a mortar barrage, Chinese troops then surged forward in successive waves to overwhelm their better-armed opponents and capture their weapons.

Chinese troops initially deployed in Korea were far from the suicidal "drug-crazed fanatics," stereotyped in the Western press. They were more typically idealistic veterans of World War II and China's civil war, willing to sustain heavy casualties for objectives. Although poorly armed, these troops were highly indoctrinated in Mao Zedong's (Mao Tse-tung) revolutionary guerrilla theories and saw themselves as Korea's liberators. The human wave attack was thus the practical application of Mao's tenet of "man over weapons." Their earlier successes operating in the vast expanses of their homeland amid a sympathetic population had seemingly proven the validity of Mao's teachings.

Early human wave attacks initially achieved dramatic success against unprepared United Nations (UN) and Republic of Korea Army (ROKA, South Korean) troops. The night attacks, accompanied by a cacophony of bugle calls, drums, and shouts, often produced panic among surprised defenders. Isolated in freezing foxholes along thinly armed defensive lines, many bolted for the rear or surrendered. The Chinese success in their offensive at the end of 1950 and the large stores of modern weaponry that consequently fell into their hands convinced most Communist troops of the efficacy of human wave tactics.

Yet as the Chinese pushed farther south, the effectiveness of Maoist indoctrination and military theory weakened dramatically. The war in Korea presented new, unexpected challenges to what was essentially a guerilla army trained in the fluid tactics of infiltration and encirclement. Lacking air cover and mechanization, supply lines became increasingly tenuous as the Chinese moved farther from their home bases. Also, as UNC opposition stiffened into stubbornly defended fixed positions, its enemy weapons found their way into the invaders' hands. As with the UN forces, the Chinese too found themselves operating in a hostile, alien environment. Many poorly clothed troops suffered from frostbite or froze to death during the harsh Korean winters. Moreover, morale steadily eroded as the Communists, accustomed to perceiving themselves as freedom fighters, found the South Koreans hostile to their presence and unwilling to provide food and assistance.

UN forces also recovered from their initial shock more rapidly than anticipated. They soon strengthened their positions with extensive mine fields and fully exploited their superiority in artillery and air power. U.S. troops developed effective new defensive countermeasures to the human wave assaults. Such innovations as antiaircraft searchlights teamed with quad-mounted caliber .50 machine guns accounted for staggering numbers of casualties. Attrition eventually claimed tens of thousands of the more ideologically motivated and battle-tested Chinese veterans. They in turn were replaced with less effective conscripts. By the time of the peace talks, the human wave campaign had effectively run its course.

—Jeff Kinard

References:

Blair, Clay. *The Forgotten War: America in Korea, 1950–1953.* New York: Times Books, 1987.

George, Alexander L. *The Chinese Communist Army in Action: The Korean War and Its Aftermath.* New York: Columbia University Press, 1967.

Hastings, Max. *The Korean War.* New York: Simon & Schuster, 1987.

Ridgway, Matthew B. *The Korean War.* Garden City, NY: Doubleday, 1967.

Toland, John. *In Mortal Combat: Korea, 1950–1953.* New York: William Morrow, 1991.

See also: Mao Zedong.

Hŭngnam Evacuation
(9–24 December 1950)

Evacuation by the U.S. Navy from North Korea of troops under the U.S. X Corps, including the U.S. 1st Marine Division, 7th Infantry Division, and 3d Infantry Division, and the Republic of Korea Army (ROKA, South Korean) I Corps, including the 3d and Capital Infantry Divisions. When the People's Republic of China massively intervened in the Korean War in late November 1950, its 250,000 ground forces threatened to cut off and destroy United Nations (UN) units operating in the mountains of North Korea. To prevent that catastrophe and to concentrate UN units in more easily defended terrain farther south, on 9

December Commander in Chief, United Nations Command (UNC) General Douglas MacArthur ordered evacuation by sea of X Corps.

Commander U.S. Naval Forces, Far East Vice Admiral C. Turner Joy had already alerted his command on 28 November to prepare for such a contingency, and he now began deploying naval forces to waters off Hŭngnam on the east coast of North Korea. Turner also dispatched other units under Rear Admiral Lyman A. Thackrey to Korea's west coast to handle evacuation from Chinnamp'o and Inch'ŏn, in company with British, Australian, and Canadian ships, of the Eighth U.S. Army and other UNC forces. The mission at Chinnamp'o was accomplished between 4 and 6 December, although most of the Allied forces made their way south in vehicles or on foot. In addition, during December and early January 1951, Thackrey's ships pulled 69,000 military personnel, 64,000 refugees, 1,000 vehicles, and more than 55,000 tons of cargo out of Inch'ŏn.

As the Marines and soldiers in biting cold and wind fought their way out of encirclement at the Changjin (Chosin) Reservoir and elsewhere in northeast Korea during December, several hundred navy and Marine aircraft operating from airfields ashore and from the ships of Task Force 77 (aircraft carriers *Philippine Sea*, *Leyte*, *Princeton*, and *Valley Forge*, light carrier *Bataan*, and escort carriers *Sicily* and *Baedong Strait*) pummeled Communist ground troops. Other U.S. planes airdropped supplies. Conducting round-the-clock air operations from snow- and wind-swept carrier decks and from unimproved airstrips ashore demanded the most of sailors and Marines working feverishly to help bring their comrades out of the frozen hills of North Korea.

When UN ground units began moving into the defensive perimeter around Hŭngnam, cruisers *St. Paul* and *Rochester*, six destroyers, and three rocket ships of Rear Admiral Roscoe H. Hillenkoetter's gunfire support group (Task Group 70.8) stood by to

U.S. 7th Division troops embarking aboard a landing craft, Hŭngnam, 14 December 1950. (National Archives)

Refugees on Green Beach. (National Archives)

put a ring of fire between the troops and the Communists. On 23 December the battleship *Missouri* steamed in and added shells from its 16-inch guns to the gunfire-support mission. Between 7 and 24 December, these combatants fired 18,637 5-inch, 2,932 8-inch, 162 16-inch, 71 3-inch, and 185 40-mm rounds and 1,462 rockets in the direction of already bloodied Chinese forces, which wisely chose not to contest the evacuation.

In an orderly fashion on 10 December, ships under Commander Amphibious Force, Far East (Task Force 90) Rear Admiral James H. Doyle began embarking the withdrawing ground troops and their equipment from Hŭngnam (and some ROKA 3d Division troops from Wŏnsan further to the south). The Marines, who had endured the hardest fighting, were the first to board the evacuation ships. They were followed by the ROKA units on the 17th and by the U.S. Army divi-

sions during the third week of December. By 24 December 1950, Task Force 90 had embarked 105,000 military personnel, 17,500 tanks and other vehicles, 350,000 measurement tons of cargo, and 91,000 Korean civilians. Marine and air force transports airlifted out another 3,600 troops, 196 vehicles, and 1,300 tons of cargo.

Navy underwater demolition team personnel ensured that little of military value would be left behind. As the fleet steamed away from Hŭngnam on 24 December, thunderous explosions rocked the waterfront, raised an enormous cloud of dust, and reduced piers, cranes, warehouses, and other port facilities to twisted rubble. Although U.S. troops would not be home for Christmas, as General MacArthur had anticipated earlier, they would at least enjoy the relative safety and comfort of ships steaming in a sea controlled by the U.S. Navy and its allies.

In a classic demonstration of the flexibility and mobility of sea power, soon after evacuating these ground troops from North Korea, the UN fleet disembarked them at secure ports in South Korea. In a matter of weeks these U.S. and Korean troops were back on the fighting front defending the Republic of Korea against the Communist forces.

—*Edward J. Marolda*

References:

Cagle, Malcolm W., and Frank A. Manson. *The Sea War in Korea*. Annapolis, MD: U.S. Naval Institute Press, 1957.

Field, James A., Jr. *History of United States Naval Operations: Korea*. Washington, DC: U.S. Government Printing Office, 1962.

Schnabel, James F. *United States Army in the Korean War: Policy and Direction, the First Year*. Washington, DC: Office of the Chief of Military History, Department of the Army, 1972.

See also: Amphibious Force Far East (Task Force Ninety); Joy, Charles Turner; MacArthur, Douglas; Tenth Corps.

I

Imjin River

A 159-mile-long river that flows through the central part of the Korean peninsula from east to west into the Yellow Sea. Because of its geographical conditions, the basin of the river became one of the most important territories that the old three kingdoms of Silla, Koguryŏ, and Paekche tried to possess in the sixth century. Kaesŏng and P'anmunjŏm, where the truce talks were held, are just north of the river. Presently, the mouth of the river constitutes a part of the demarcation line between North and South Korea.

During the Korean War the Imjin River was an important defensive line for South Korea and United Nations Command (UNC) forces and a scene of battle. When the Korean People's Army (KPA, North Korean) invaded the South on 25 June 1950, the Republic of Korea 1st Division, which held along the Imjin River, fought for the following two days there in a vain attempt to hold back the KPA forces.

After General Douglas MacArthur's Home-by-Christmas Offensive ended in failure, in mid-December the Eighth U.S. Army abandoned all of North Korea above the 38th parallel and conducted a hasty, deep withdrawal to the Imjin River. There the army began shaping the defensive position known as Line B. On New Year's Eve 1950, Chinese People's Volunteer Army (CPVA, Chinese Communist) forces crossed the 38th parallel and invaded South Korea, and the Eighth Army was forced to abandon Line B. CPVA forces occupied Seoul on 4 January 1951. The Eighth Army regained the river during its spring 1951 advance northward. In April the CPVA launched its Fifth Offensive, the main object of which was to capture Seoul, retaken by UN forces on 14 March. In the Battle of the Imjin River (22–25 April 1951), the 29th British Infantry Brigade inflicted heavy losses on the CPVA and frustrated CPVA attempts to break through to Seoul.

—*Jinwung Kim*

References:
Blair, Clay. *The Forgotten War: America in Korea, 1950–1953.* New York: Times Books, 1987.
MacDonald, Callum. *Korea: The War Before Vietnam.* New York: Free Press, 1986.
Stueck, William W., Jr. *The Korean War: An International History.* Princeton, NJ: Princeton University Press, 1995.
See also: Chinese Military Offensives; Imjin River, Battle of.

Imjin River, Battle of
(22–25 April 1951)

Intense fighting that took place near the mouth of the Imjin River at and northeast of its confluence with the Han River about 30 miles north of Seoul as part of the Chinese People's Volunteer Army (CPVA, Chinese Communist) Fifth Offensive, launched on 21 April 1951 with the objective, among others, of recapturing Seoul.

Between Republic of Korea Army (ROKA, South Korean) units at the mouth of the river and the 6th ROKA and U.S. 1st Marine Divisions north of Kap'yŏng, from west to east the British Division and U.S. 3d, 25th, and 24th Divisions, along with the ROKA 6th Division, were in position on a line running northeast to Yŏch'ŏn, about ten miles north of the 38th parallel and then east. Only a week earlier, General James A. Van Fleet had assumed command of Eighth U.S. Army and ordered that step two of Operation DAUNTLESS be launched with the objective, on the west in I Corps area, of advancing the United Nations Command (UNC) front from Line Utah, where troops were then located, to Line Wyoming at the Iron Triangle, an area lying roughly between the North Korean towns of Ch'ŏrwŏn, P'yŏnggang, and Kimhwa. Van Fleet expected that the second step of DAUNTLESS would provoke a major Chinese Communist Forces counterattack, for which he considered himself fully prepared. UNC Commander General Matthew B. Ridgway had stipulated to Van Fleet that, temporarily at least, real estate was not important; the main task was to kill Communist soldiers.

On the morning of 21 April, I and IX Corps attacked toward Line Wyoming with six infantry regiments abreast. The attack was slow and methodical with generally light or nonexistent Communist resistance, except for that encountered by the 24th Regiment, which met a stubborn pocket of resistance and advanced only a quarter of a mile. The assault continued slowly the next day in clear and crisp weather.

At about 2200 on 22 April, the CPVA, consisting of nine armies of twenty-seven divisions (about 250,000 men) struck Eighth Army across a 40-mile front. The attack was mounted under a full moon with bugles and horns blowing and flares. The main weight of the Chinese Sixty-third Army attack in the west fell on the British Royal Northumberland Fusiliers, Gloucester and British Brigades. The Gloucesters and Fusiliers were on the south bank of the shallow, fordable Imjin and Hant'an Rivers on a nine-mile front and not intact. As the fury of the Chinese attack increased and their forces penetrated and circulated,

The V.S. 25th Infantry Division front north of Ch'ŏrwŏn, 23 April 1951. (National Archives)

the British troops held their ground, demonstrating their reputation for being slow on the offensive but unshakable in the defense.

During the fighting, the besieged Belgian Battalion had to be reinforced by a battalion of the U.S. 7th Infantry Regiment. The Turkish Brigade to the east, known as being good on offense and poor on defense, was shattered and soon fled. Elsewhere all along the front, fierce fighting continued through 23 April, with many units cut off and then rescued and relocated.

During the same period farther to the east, heavy fighting involved the Commonwealth Brigade, the 65th Puerto Rican Regiment, the 1st Cavalry, and the 3d and 7th Infantry Divisions, together with more than a dozen battalions of infantry units from other UN countries operating as components of various U.S. regiments. The UN forces inflicted staggering casualties on the CPVA, but the security of non-Korean units was repeatedly imperiled by the constant collapse and fleeing of ROKA units. The collapse of the ROKA 6th Division left a gaping ten-mile hole in the Eighth Army's central front. Van Fleet was particularly critical of the Koreans and said, "They were just no good and it was useless for us to be getting shot at 5,000 miles from home in our futile effort to help them."

By dawn on 24 April, the Chinese offensive had reached full fury, with battles raging across the front from Munsan to Ch'unch'ŏn. All UNC forces had by then pulled back to Line Kansas, and by the 28th in the west they had pulled back to below the Imjin River mouth almost to the outskirts of Seoul on Line Lincoln (or Golden). Van Fleet then issued a communiqué saying that in the face of enemy "human-wave" tactics, Eighth Army soldiers "had fought with consummate skill and vigor and had inflicted an estimated 70,000 enemy casualties."

—Sherman Pratt

References:

Blair, Clay. *The Forgotten War: America in Korea, 1950–1953.* New York: Times Books, 1987.

Hastings, Max. *The Korean War.* New York: Simon & Schuster, 1987.

Schnabel, James F. *United States Army in the Korean War: Policy and Direction, the First Year.* Washington, DC: Office of the Chief of Military History, Department of the Army, 1972.

See also: DAUNTLESS, Operation; Ridgway, Matthew Bunker; Van Fleet, James Alward.

Inch'ŏn Landing: Operation CHROMITE
(15 September 1950)

Amphibious assault and U.S. General Douglas MacArthur's Korean War masterstroke. Quickly planned despite opposition from Washington, the Inch'ŏn landing was a brilliant strategic coup that turned the tide of the war.

By mid-July 1950, Republic of Korea Army (ROKA, South Korean) and U.S. troops were restricted to the Pusan perimeter. Even as the U.S. forces endeavored to blunt the Korean People's Army (KPA, North Korean) offensive and secure the vital port of Pusan, MacArthur prepared to open a second front, believing that it was preferable to a frontal assault on the Pusan perimeter. An attack elsewhere would present the North Koreans with a two-front war. MacArthur was confident that Eighth Army could hold the perimeter and so began diverting resources for an invasion force.

Inch'ŏn was the point selected. Korea's second largest port, Inch'ŏn was only 15 miles from the ROK capital of Seoul. This area was the most important road and rail hub in Korea and a vital link in the main KPA supply line to their forces on the Pusan perimeter.

Observing the Inch'ŏn landing from the USS *Mount McKinley*, 15 September 1950; Brigadier General Courtney Whitney, Major General Edwin K. Wright, General Douglas MacArthur, and Major General Edmond Almond. (National Archives)

View from Inch'ŏn, Wŏlmi-Do is in the background. (National Archives)

Cutting the line here would starve KPA forces facing Eighth Army. Kimpŏ Airfield near Inch'ŏn was one of the few hard-surface airfields in Korea. The capture of Seoul would be a serious psychological and political blow for the North Koreans, the sort of grand gesture that so appealed to MacArthur. As Major General Charles Willoughby, MacArthur's assistant chief of staff for intelligence, later put it: "MacArthur courageously set his eyes on a greater goal; to salvage the reputation of Allied arms, to bring into sharper focus the colossal threat of imperialist Mongoloid pan-Slavism under the guise of Communism, and to smash its current challenge in one great blow."

MacArthur initially planned to put the 1st Cavalry Division ashore at Inch'ŏn as early as 22 July. Events overtook this, and the operation was abandoned on 10 July. That same day MacArthur met in Tokyo with Lieutenant General Lemuel Shepherd, commander of the Pacific Fleet Marine Force. With Joint Chiefs of Staff (JCS) approval, Shepherd said the whole 1st Marine Division could be in Korea within six weeks and in action by 15 September. MacArthur immediately requested the two remaining regiments of the division. Its 5th Regiment, about to sail from San Diego, was already earmarked for action along the Pusan perimeter, where it would be redesignated the 1st Provisional Marine Brigade. At first the JCS agreed to send only the 1st Regiment, but on 10 August it allowed MacArthur the 7th as well; however, only the 1st and 5th were at Inch'ŏn on D-day.

Planning for the Inch'ŏn invasion, code-named Operation CHROMITE, began on 12 August and was completed in only one month. It was carried out by the interservice Joint Strategic Plans and Operations Group (JSPOG), under control of the Operations Division of the Far East Command. The Special Planning Staff of JSPOG emerged as the nucleus of the staff of X Corps. The corps was activated on 26 August, the same day that MacArthur appointed his chief of staff, Major General Edward M. Almond, to command it. Low morale in Eighth Army may have led MacArthur to divide military authority in Korea; X Corps was entirely separate from Eighth Army, a decision that would have unfortunate subsequent repercussions.

Objectives of Operation CHROMITE were neutralization of Wŏlmi-do, the island controlling access to Inch'ŏn harbor (the Marines regarded this as essential to protect the subsequent assault on Inch'ŏn); the landing at Inch'ŏn and capture of the city; seizure of Kimpŏ Airfield; and, finally, capture of Seoul.

The only real opposition to the idea of a second front came from Eighth Army. Its staff was strongly

LSTs (Landing Ship, Tank) unloading supplies on Red Beach following the Inch'ŏn landing. Note that the LSTs are stranded in mud flats. (National Archives)

opposed to weakening the Pusan perimeter and believed that if reinforcements intended for X Corps were sent to them they could defeat the North Koreans without what appeared to be a risky grandstand play. Apart from Eighth Army, there was general agreement on a second front, but not on the place; only Mac-Arthur favored Inch'ŏn.

The JCS and most of MacArthur's subordinate commanders, including all key Navy and Marine commanders in the Far East, opposed Inch'ŏn. Both the tide and terrain made the operation extremely hazardous. Tidal shifts at Inch'ŏn were sudden and dramatic; the range of spring tides was from an average of 23 feet to a maximum of 33. At ebb tide the harbor turned into mud flats, extending as far as three miles from the shoreline. Although most landing craft drew 23 feet, the tank landing ships (LSTs)—considered vital in getting heavy equipment to the shore

quickly—drew 29 feet. The navy estimated that there was a narrow range around two dates, 15 September and 11 October, when the tides would be high enough to let the LSTs gain Inch'ŏn. Even then, the landing forces would have only a three-hour period on each tide in which to enter or leave the port. This meant that supplies could be landed during only six hours in each 24-hour period.

Flying Fish channel was narrow, winding, and studded with reefs and shoals; its five-knot current was also a problem. One sunken ship there would block all traffic. There were no beaches, only twelve-foot-high sea walls that would have to be scaled. Also, the Marines would have to take Wŏlmi-do eleven hours in advance of the assault on Inch'ŏn. At the landing site in Inch'ŏn itself there were few cargo-handling facilities. Undamaged, Inch'ŏn had a capacity of 6,000 tons a day, only 10 percent that of Pusan. Also, steep hills from the beaches would allow the defenders to fire down on the attackers. All of these conditions precluded a night assembly of the invasion force; the main landing would have to take place in the evening with only two hours of daylight to secure a perimeter ashore.

Suggestions were made for landing either at Kunsan to the south or Chinnamp'o to the north. But Kunsan was too close to the Pusan perimeter; and Chinnamp'o, P'yŏngyang's port, was too far north. P'osŭng-myŏn, 30 miles south of Inch'ŏn, was rejected because of an inadequate road net from its beaches.

On 23 August MacArthur met with his critics in a final dramatic meeting in the Dai-Ichi building in Tokyo. His commanders, Lieutenant General George E. Stratemeyer, Vice Admiral C. Turner Joy, and General Almond were there. Army Chief of Staff General J. Lawton Collins and Chief of Naval Operations Admiral Forrest P. Sherman were on hand from Washington to express the "grave reservations" of the JCS to the operation. The U.S. Navy and Marine Corps contingent included Commander in Chief Pacific Admiral Arthur Radford, Vice Admiral A. D. Struble, and Rear Admiral James H. Doyle; Generals Shepherd and Oliver P. Smith represented the Marine Corps.

Doyle, an expert on amphibious operations, began the meeting by listing navy objections. He concluded his remarks with, "The best I can say is that Inch'ŏn is not impossible." General Collins expressed reservations about withdrawing the Marine Brigade from the Pusan perimeter and the possibility that, once ashore, X Corps might be pinned down at Inch'ŏn. He preferred Kunsan.

Finally MacArthur spoke for about forty-five minutes. He said he recognized the hazards but expressed confidence in the navy and Marines to overcome them. To inject reinforcements on the Pusan perimeter might risk stalemate. An envelopment from a landing at Kunsan would be too narrow. That the North Koreans did not anticipate an assault at Inch'ŏn would help ensure its success: "The very arguments you have made as to the impracticabilities involved will tend to ensure for me the element of surprise. For the enemy commander will reason that no one would be so brash as to make such an attempt…." If the war in Korea was lost the fate of Europe would be jeopardized. He concluded, "I can almost hear the ticking of the second hand of destiny. We must act now or we will die…. We shall land at Inch'ŏn, and I shall crush them."

Although some senior officers at the briefing remained unconvinced, MacArthur's remarks were the turning point in the debate. General Shepherd made one subsequent futile effort to persuade MacArthur to

choose P'osŭng-myŏn, where navy divers had landed and found beach conditions suitable.

On 28 August MacArthur received formal approval from the JCS for the Inch'ŏn landing. The Chiefs took the unusual precaution of securing the written approval of President Harry S. Truman for the operation; this undoubtedly reflected fears that, if the operation were unsuccessful, they would be held responsible. There is no indication that Truman ever believed it might fail.

The major units of X Corps were two divisions: 7th Army and 1st Marine. Support units were the 92d and 96th Field Artillery Battalions (155-mm howitzers); the 50th Antiaircraft Artillery Battalion; the 19th Engineer Combat Group; and the 2d Engineer Special Brigade. The 7th was the one remaining division of Eighth Army not sent to Korea from Japan. Commanded by Major General David G. Barr, the 7th Division was seriously understrength and was augmented by all available reinforcements, including Koreans. More than 8,600 Korean recruits arrived in Japan before the division embarked for Inch'ŏn; approximately 100 were assigned to each rifle company and artillery battery. The 7th Division strength on embarkation was 24,815 men, including Koreans.

The 1st Marine Division, commanded by Major General Oliver P. Smith, was made a heavy division with the addition of the Marine Brigade, redesignated the 5th Marines. On invasion day, the 1st Marine Division numbered 25,040 men, including 2,760 army troops and 2,786 Korean Marines attached; with the addition of the 7th Marine Regiment, organic marine strength increased by 4,000 men. Lieutenant General Walton Walker, commander of Eighth Army, was upset that the brigade would be withdrawn from the line with the North Koreans planning a new assault against the Pusan perimeter in early September. He secured agreement that it would be released only at the last possible moment and that a regiment of the 7th Army Division would be kept in Pusan harbor as long as possible to act as a floating reserve.

The Marine Corps considered it vital that Inch'ŏn be successful. Many influential figures were questioning the Marine Corps's viability. A year before, Cahirman of the Joint Chiefs of Staff General Omar Bradley had observed that large-scale amphibious landings were a thing of the past. As General Shepherd put it, "The Marine Corps was fighting for its very existence."

Over 200 agents inserted into the Inch'ŏn area reported approximately 500 North Korean Army troops on Wŏlmi-do, 1,500 around Inch'ŏn, and another 500 at Kimpŏ Airfield. There were, however, major reinforcements only a few hours away, in the southeast.

The final Inch'ŏn plan was ready by 4 September. On D-day the tides would be at 0659 and 1919 with a

1st Division Marines use scaling ladders to climb over the sea wall in the 15 September 1950 Inch'ŏn invasion. (National Archives)

maximum of 31 feet of water in the evening. A battalion landing team of 5th Marines was to be put ashore on the morning tide at Green Beach on Wŏlmido at 0630. The major landings would be at 1730, at Red Beach, Inch'ŏn's sea front, and at Blue beach, three miles to the southeast, in order to command rail and road lines from Seoul. Eight LSTs would follow the assault force with heavy equipment and landing teams.

Deception to confuse the North Koreans as to the intended landing site included bombarding Chinnamp'o by a British naval task force and unloading a landing party at Kunsan from a British frigate. Miraculously, although the destination of Inch'ŏn was not closely held, no word of it got to the KPA command.

Admiral Struble (on the *Rochester*) commanded Joint Task Force 7, the naval force organized for the Inch'ŏn landings. Rear Admiral Doyle, second in command, was on the *Mount McKinley*. Each of seven sub-

ordinate task forces was assigned specific objectives. More than 230 ships took part in the operation.

The armada of vessels carrying nearly 70,000 men was a makeshift affair. It included ships from Australia, Canada, New Zealand, France, Holland, and Great Britain. Marine aircraft from two escort carriers, naval aircraft from the *Boxer*, and British aircraft from a light British carrier were to provide air support over the landing area. Thirty-seven of forty-seven LSTs in the invasion were hastily recalled from Japanese merchant service and were run by Japanese crews.

Loading was delayed for 36 hours by the 110-mph winds of typhoon Jane on 3 September. There was some damage but deadlines were met. On 13 September the task force, now at sea, was assaulted by typhoon Kezia with 60-mph winds, although no serious damage resulted.

The convoy reached the Inch'ŏn Narrows just before dawn on 15 September, the fifth day of air and naval bombardment of Wŏlmi-do. The naval Gunfire Support Group was made up of four cruisers and six destroyers. At 0633 the 5th Marines went ashore at Wŏlmi-do. MacArthur observing the landing from the bridge of the *Mount McKinley*. Resistance was light; the U.S. flag was raised on Radio Hill at 0655, and Wŏlmi-do and nearby Sowŏlmi-do were both secured by noon. A total of 108 North Koreans were killed and 136 were captured. Approximately 100 more who refused to surrender were sealed in caves by tank dozers. Marine casualties were 17 wounded.

The Marines requested permission to continue their advance across the 400-yard causeway to Inch'ŏn but were refused. The invaders were now cut off from the fleet by a vast sea of mud. There was little KPA fire from Inch'ŏn, and covering aircraft could detect no reinforcements en route.

At 1430 the cruisers and destroyers in the invasion force began a shore bombardment of Inch'ŏn. KPA fire was sporadic and light. At 1645 the first wave of landing craft left the transports for Inch'ŏn, and at 1731 the first Americans climbed up ladders onto the seawall. As on Wŏlmi-do, most of the defenders were still in a state of shock from the bombardment.

The sun was setting and visibility was further inhibited by smoke and drizzle. Careful plans went awry or were forgotten as the landing craft made for the waterfront. Some in the second wave grounded and the men were forced to wade ashore, but within six hours the Marines were firmly lodged in Inch'ŏn. Eight specially loaded LSTs also made it to the seawall, where they disgorged jeeps, trucks, tanks, and supplies.

The Marine landing force sustained casualties on D-day of 20 killed in action, 1 missing, and 174 wounded. On the morning of 16 September, the 1st and 5th regiments linked up ashore and began the drive east to Seoul; the ROK Marines were left behind to mop up Inch'ŏn.

Early on 17 September the 5th Marines ambushed a column of six KPA T-34 tanks and 200 infantry. By the night of the 17th much of Kimpŏ Airfield had been taken; it was completely in Marine hands on the 18th. That same day, the 7th Infantry Division started landing at Inch'ŏn; and on the 21st the remaining Marine Regiment, the 7th, disembarked. By the end of the 19th, 5th Marines had cleared the entire south bank of the Han River on their front; they crossed the river a day later, but were soon slowed by determined KPA resistance. The 1st Regiment encountered difficult fighting with a regiment of the KPA 18th Division on the 22nd, before it too reached the Han.

On 16 September, a day after the Inch'ŏn invasion, General Walker's Eighth Army began its breakout along the Pusan perimeter and drove north. The Inch'ŏn and Pusan forces made contact on 26 September at Osan.

MacArthur and Almond were determined to capture Seoul on 25 September, three months to the day after the North Korean invasion. Almond had made it clear to General Smith that the city must fall by that date. But the U.S. flag, soon to be replaced by that of the United Nations, was not raised at the Capitol Building, by the 5th Marines, until the afternoon of 27 September, although Almond announced just before midnight on the 25th that the city had fallen. On 29 September MacArthur presided over an emotional ceremony in the Capitol Building marking the liberation of Seoul and the return of the Syngman Rhee government.

The victory of the Inch'ŏn-Seoul campaign greatly increased MacArthur's self-confidence—he now tended to dismiss reservations from Washington about his plans. The KPA was so badly beaten that MacArthur was certain the war for Korea had been won and that it was just a matter of mopping up. Certainly MacArthur did not anticipate massive Chinese intervention.

—*Spencer C. Tucker*

References:

Appleman, Roy E. *South to the Naktong, North to the Yalu.* Washington, DC: Office of the Chief of Military History, 1961.

Field, James A., Jr. *History of United States Naval Operations: Korea.* Washington, DC: U.S. Government Printing Office, 1962.

Gugeler, Russell A. *Combat Actions in Korea.* Washington, DC: U.S. Army Center of Military History, 1954.

Montross, Lynn, and Nicholas A. Canzona. *U.S. Marine Operations in Korea.* Vol. 2, *The Inchon-Seoul Operation.* Washington, DC: U.S. Marine Corps Historical Branch, 1954–1957.

Rees, David. *Korea: The Limited War.* New York: St. Martin's Press, 1964.

India

The Republic of India sought to preserve its neutrality during the Korean War while working for an end to the war that would be satisfactory to both sides and prevent the conflict from spreading. India's determination to preserve a neutral stance led to its abstaining from a number of United Nations (UN) votes.

The most probable reason for India's stubborn nonpartisanship was that India had gained independence from Great Britain in 1947 after a century of British rule, and Indians were determined to go their own way, proving their independence to both their former rulers and their friends. Not only were Indians breaking from the past, but they were also attempting to establish their country as a new leader in Asia, and this precluded involvement with either the Communist or Western powers and their respective satellites. India did not distinguish between either side. Although it condemned the Democratic People's

Republic of Korea (DPRK, North Korean) invasion of the Republic of Korea (ROK, South Korea), it was also outspoken in opposing the UN decision to send troops north of the 38th parallel.

On 25 June 1950, in the Security Council, India joined the Republic of China (Nationalist China), Cuba, Ecuador, Egypt, Norway, the United Kingdom, and the United States in voting for the resolution condemning the DPRK for its invasion of the ROK. This resolution called for an immediate cessation of hostilities and for the DPRK to withdraw its forces north of the 38th parallel. It also called on all member states to give necessary assistance to the UN to enforce the resolution and to refrain from providing any assistance to the DPRK.

Shortly thereafter, however, India stressed its nonaligned stance by abstaining from voting for an even stronger UN resolution. Many saw India's abstention as weakening the UN position. India again abstained from voting on a Soviet-sponsored resolution that called on the United States to cease its "aggression" against the People's Republic of China (PRC, Communist China). India also abstained in a vote on a United States–sponsored resolution that called on the PRC to withdraw its armed forces from Korea. Curiously, given India's neutral stance, it did provide assistance to the UN military effort in Korea, but only medical assistance.

India did take a leading role in endeavoring to secure a diplomatic resolution of the conflict. India suggested that a solution to the conflict rested on the UN's admitting the PRC to membership. Although India did criticize the PRC on occasion, for example, regarding its policies on Tibet, it continued to push for PRC admission to the UN, albeit without success.

Additionally, after the six-months' recess of negotiations over the matter of voluntary repatriation of prisoners of war, it was India that initiated the Neutral Nations Repatriation Commission, consisting of Switzerland, Sweden, Czechoslovakia, Poland, and itself. An Indian general chaired the commission, and India supplied troops and support personnel in the form of the Custodial Force India. The PRC and DPRK rejected this arrangement until March 1953, when PRC Foreign Minister Zhou Enlai (Chou En-lai) indicated that China would accept it.

Because the United States and the PRC did not have diplomatic relations with one another, India also served the useful role of mediator and conduit between the two. The United States sought to persuade India to convince the PRC to stay out of the war. Months before Chinese entry, in August 1950 Indian's ambassador to China, Sardar K. M. Panikkar, informed the United States that Chinese leaders claimed that it was highly unlikely that the PRC would intervene.

Washington was suspicious because U.S. intelligence had detected a buildup of Chinese troops in Manchuria. In September, however, Zhou Enlai reported to Panikkar that if U.S. troops crossed the 38th parallel China would definitely intervene and that China would remain passive if it was solely South Korean troops who entered North Korea. Panikkar passed the message to the British and Americans, but Washington refused to heed the warning.

India's neutrality did not come without a price. The subject of Indian participation in the Korean peace conference was decided in August when the UN General Assembly voted against a British plan to invite India to the conference. U.S. Secretary of State John Foster Dulles proclaimed the vote to be the "price" India paid for neutrality.

India steadfastly refused to provide troops to assist the UN forces in Korea. This was in part for diplomatic reasons but also because the Indian Army was small, poorly equipped, and preoccupied with domestic concerns. As a concession to not sending troops, however, India's Prime Minister Jawaharlal Nehru did agree to send the 16th Field Ambulance and Surgical Unit. It arrived in South Korea in November 1950 with 346 enlisted men and 17 officers and supported British Commonwealth forces.

—*Monica Spicer*

References:

Doody, Agnes G. "Words and Deeds: An Analysis of Jawaharlal Nehru's Non-Alignment Policy in the Cold War, 1947–1953." Ph.D. dissertation, Pennsylvania State University, 1961. Unpublished manuscript.

Range, Willard. *Jawaharlal Nehru's World View; a Theory of International Relations.* Athens: University of Georgia Press, 1961.

Sandler, Stanley, ed. *The Korean War: An Encyclopedia.* New York: Garland, 1995.

See also: China, People's Republic of; Dulles, John Foster; Inch'ŏn Landings: Operation CHROMITE; MacArthur, Douglas; Nehru, Jawaharlal; Neutral Nations Repatriation Commission; Panikkar, Sardar K. M.; Repatriation, Voluntary; Zhou Enlai.

Indo-China War, Impact on Korea

Containment of communism and support for anti-Communist resistance and local self-determination were the unifying factors driving U.S. policy in Korea and Indo-China. Before the invasion of Korea, U.S. containment policy focused mainly on Europe and was primarily economic in nature. But when the Communists came to power in China, U.S. President Harry S. Truman and his advisors feared that, if another Asian country fell to communism, all Asia would subsequently come under Communist domination.

The U.S. response to the invasion of the Republic of Korea (ROK, South Korea) by the Democratic

People's Republic of Korea (DPRK, North Korea) crystallized the policy of direct confrontation with the Communist world that characterized both Truman's and President Dwight D. Eisenhower's administrations. Although the State and Defense Departments initially disagreed on the need to increase military and economic assistance to Korea, they did agree on increased assistance to Indo-China. Started before the Korean War, the Indo-China War—fighting between the French and Communist-dominated Viet Minh in Vietnam—began in November 1946. At the same time, the Cold War intensified with the 1948 Communist takeover of Czechoslovakia and the 1948–1949 Berlin blockade. The DPRK invasion of the ROK confirmed the belief held by many in the West that the Communists sought world domination by force.

In Vietnam at the end of 1949, Viet Minh prospects changed dramatically when the Communists won control of China. The long China-Vietnam border allowed the People's Republic of China (PRC) to supply the Viet Minh with arms and equipment and to provide advisers and technicians, as well as sanctuaries where the Viet Minh could train and replenish its troops. On 18 January 1950, the PRC formally recognized North Vietnamese leader Ho Chi Minh's Democratic Republic of Vietnam (DRV) and agreed to furnish it with military assistance. On 30 January the Soviet Union followed suit.

By the end of 1952 more than 40,000 People's Army of Vietnam (PAVN, Viet Minh) enlisted men and 10,000 officers had been trained in China. There was also an abundance of arms available from the substantial stocks of weapons, including artillery that the United States had supplied to the Chinese Nationalists. PRC support of the DRV grew steadily. In 1951 it provided no fewer than 20 tons of military assistance per month; in 1952, 250 tons; in 1953, 600 tons; and in 1954, 4,000 tons per month.

Communist aid to the Viet Minh triggered a change in U.S. policy toward the Indo-China War. Up to this point, Washington had been largely ambivalent toward the conflict. President Truman did not follow the advice of Asian experts in the State Department who urged him to recognize the DRV and encourage the ultimate independence of the region from French rule. The Europeanists, preoccupied by the Soviet military threat to Western Europe and desirous of keeping France in the North Atlantic Treaty Organization, ultimately won the day. With Germany still disarmed, France was the only continental power capable of providing the resources to resist the USSR. To keep French support against the Soviet Union in Europe, the United States tacitly supported French policy in Indo-China.

PRC support of the DRV was the final straw, however. On 7 February 1950, the United States recog-

nized the French-created State of Vietnam (SVN). Few Americans had even heard of Vietnam and, if they had, at this point they were hardly alarmed. In May, Washington agreed to furnish forthwith between $20 and $30 million in direct aid, with more the next fiscal year. The United States also funded the war indirectly because massive amounts of Marshall Plan aid freed up other French resources for Indo-China.

The Korean War solidified the Truman administration's position toward Indo-China. Now containing the spread of communism took priority over anticolonialism. The United States also changed its policy of providing only indirect aid to the war in Indo-China. On 27 June 1950, in his statement on Korea, President Truman announced: "The attack upon Korea makes it plain beyond all doubt that communism had pushed beyond the use of subversion to conquer independent nations and will now use armed invasion and war...." Truman said he had directed "acceleration in the furnishing of military assistance to the forces of France and the associated states in Indo-China" and that he was sending a military mission there "to provide close working relations with those forces."

On 30 June, eight C-47 transports arrived in Saigon with the first direct shipment of U.S. military equipment. U.S. support for the French effort in Indo-China grew steadily. With the establishment of a Military Assistance Advisory Group (MAAG), U.S. military aid rose from $100 million in 1950 to $300 million in 1952, and more than $1 billion in 1954, when it was financing some 80 percent of the French effort. Overall U.S. military assistance amounted to nearly $3 billion, or nearly 60 percent of the cost of the Indo-China War.

The French insisted that all U.S. military assistance be channeled directly to them rather than through the SVN. Although a Vietnamese National Army was established in 1951, it remained firmly under French control.

Both Washington and Paris came to see Korea and Vietnam as mutually dependent theaters in a common Western struggle against communism. Thus Washington brought pressure to bear on France not to conclude peace with the Viet Minh in 1952, when Paris might have had better terms than it did two years later. When the United Nations concluded an armistice in Korea in 1953 at U.S. urging, Paris was understandably upset with Washington.

The PRC's most important strategic goal was to preserve its national security and the security of countries bordering it, especially Korea and Vietnam. Mao Zedong (Mao Tse-tung) saw U.S. military action in Korea as part of a comprehensive plan for eventual U.S. domination of Asia. If the United States succeeded in Korea, then Taiwan, the states of Indo-China, and other countries in the region would follow. An encircled China might have to fight on multiple fronts. The Chinese leadership believed that PRC success in halting U.S. expansion in Asia would encourage anti-colonialism in Asia. Additionally, the Chinese believed that U.S. action in Korea would encourage increased action by the French along the Sino-Vietnam border.

During Korean armistice negotiations, some, such as U.S. Secretary of State John Foster Dulles, preferred to increase pressure on the Chinese and reduce PRC prestige by decisively defeating it on the battle-field. Dulles and the French feared that an armistice in Korea would release Chinese forces to concentrate on Indo-China, which was correct. Once the armistice was signed, Ho Chi Minh intensified Viet Minh activities, and China increased the level of its military assistance to Indo-China.

The Korean armistice convinced many that the Indo-China problems should also be settled. The 1954 Geneva conference did not unify Korea, but it did bring to an end the French phase of the fighting in Indo-China and a de facto partition of Vietnam.

—Carol J. Yee

Troops of the 7th Regiment, U.S. 3rd Infantry Division, in action at the Iron Triangle, 3 July 1951. (National Archives)

References:

Rotter, Andrew J. *The Path to Vietnam: Origins of the American Commitment to Southeast Asia.* Ithaca, NY: Cornell University Press, 1987.

Spector, Ronald H. *Advice and Support. The Early Years: United States Army in Vietnam.* Washington, DC: U.S. Army Center of Military History, 1983.

Stueck, William W., Jr. *The Road to Confrontation: American Policy toward China and Korea, 1947–1950.* Chapel Hill: University of North Carolina Press, 1981.

Zhang, Shu Guang. *Mao's Military Romanticism: China and the Korean War, 1950–1953.* Lawrence: University Press of Kansas, 1995.

See also: Acheson, Dean Goodersham; China, People's Republic of; Cold War; Dulles, John Foster; France; Geneva Conference of 1954; MacArthur, Douglas; Mao Zedong; Truman, Harry S.

Infiltration

In its military context, to pass troops either singly or in small groups through enemy lines. Infiltration was a major problem for the United Nations Command (UNC) early in the Korean War, when the fronts were fluid. Infiltrations usually took place at night or in conditions when visibility was limited. Some Korean People's Army (KPA, North Korean) troops put traditional Korean white robes over their uniforms and attempted to pass through UNC lines unnoticed among the many refugees. Other troops made use of the mountainous and inhospitable Korean terrain to bypass UNC units altogether. During the UNC advance into North Korea, in what he expected to be the final drive to the Yalu River, U.S. General Douglas MacArthur facilitated infiltration by the KPA by continuing the divided command and separating Eighth Army from X Corps by the T'aebaek range. Some special troops were also infiltrated by sea at the beginning of the war.

Once to the rear of UNC positions, infiltrators would regroup and then conduct sabotage operations or attack military positions. Such operations before the Korean War had the effect of dispersing Republic of Korea Army (ROKA) units, forcing them to deploy for guerrilla rather than conventional operations.

KPA infiltrations tactics also produced civilian casualties when UNC troops fired on refugee columns. The problem was largely resolved in the spring of 1951 when the front was stabilized.

—*Spencer C. Tucker*

References:

Bermudez, Joseph S., Jr. *North Korean Special Forces.* 2d ed. Annapolis, MD: Naval Institute Press, 1998.

Summers, Harry G., Jr . *Korean War Almanac.* New York: Facts on File, 1990.

See also: MacArthur, Douglas; Special Operations.

Iron Triangle

Geographical area just north of the 38th parallel and in the central part of the Korean peninsula. This was a traditional invasion route from the North to Seoul and thus hotly contested, especially during the static phase of the Korean War. The Iron Triangle is delineated by three cities: Kimhwa in the east, Ch'ŏrwŏn in the west, and P'yŏnggang in the north.

United Nations Command (UNC) forces took the Iron Triangle in October 1950 during the UN offensive into North Korea; it was lost after the massive Chinese People's Volunteer Army (CPVA, Chinese Communist) offensive late the next month. By June 1951 the first two corners of the triangle were again in UNC hands. Task Force Hawkins reached P'yŏnggang on 13 June 1951, but found no Communist troops there. With the failure of the majority of Task Force Hamilton to reach there in support, Task Force Hawkins was withdrawn and P'yŏnggang remained in control of Communist forces for the remainder of the war. The Chinese demanded that the final armistice line include the two southern cities of the Iron Triangle, but the UNC rejected this and they remain within the Republic of Korea today.

—*Spencer C. Tucker*

References:

Blair, Clay. *The Forgotten War: America in Korea, 1950–1953.* New York: Times Books, 1987.

See also: CLEANUP I and II, Operations; DAUNTLESS, Operation; RUGGED, Operation.

J

Jackson, Charles Douglas "C. D."
(1902–1964)

U.S. President Dwight D. Eisenhower's special assistant for Cold War planning. Born in New York City on 16 March 1902, Charles Douglas "C. D." Jackson was educated at the Hill School in Pottstown, Pennsylvania, and at Princeton University, where he graduated in 1924. Jackson directed his family's marble and stone importing business. He was forced to sell the company in 1931 during the Great Depression. He then became a special assistant to Henry R. Luce, founder of *Time*, *Life*, and *Fortune* magazines.

From 1942 to 1943, Jackson, who was an ardent prewar internationalist and had founded the interventionist Council for Democracy in 1940, was special assistant to Laurence A. Steinhardt, U.S. ambassador to Turkey. From 1943 to 1944, Jackson was deputy chief of the U.S. Office of War Information Overseas Branch and deputy chief of the Psychological Warfare Branch, Allied Force Headquarters. In these capacities, he advised General Dwight Eisenhower and other Allied military leaders on psychological warfare and propaganda in the Mediterranean theater and, after January 1944, in northwest Europe, where he served as deputy chief of the Psychological Warfare Division of Supreme Headquarters, Allied Expeditionary Forces.

By the time Jackson returned to civilian life as vice-president and managing director of *Time*, *Life*, *Fortune* International in July 1945, he was regarded as one of the country's foremost experts on the organization and practice of psychological warfare. During the postwar years, Jackson was closely involved with the National Committee for a Free Europe, Radio Free Europe, the Crusade for Freedom, and other organizations attempting to halt the spread of communism.

In 1952 Jackson began working in Eisenhower's presidential campaign, formulating themes for addresses, drafting speeches, and advising the candidate on political matters. Jackson became so closely involved in the campaign that he was considered by many to be an indispensable member of Eisenhower's unofficial strategy team.

Shortly after he was elected president, Eisenhower appointed Jackson as special assistant for Cold War planning. Jackson's job was to ensure that the administration remained on the offensive when dealing with the Soviets, particularly in propaganda and ideological matters. Jackson considered the Korean conflict, as it had developed by the spring of 1953, to be an obvious field for psychological warfare. He believed that propaganda and covert operations could go far toward winning the Cold War against the Soviet Union and the People's Republic of China (Communist China) and that the Communist states were far ahead of the United States in such areas. In response, Jackson wrote speeches for Eisenhower that called for an honorable settlement and free elections leading to a reunified Korea. He also devised propaganda programs for preventing the demoralization of South Koreans as it became clear that Republic of Korea President Syngman Rhee and his followers would not succeed in liberating the North as a result of the war. These plans sought to encourage compliance with the terms of an armistice and to promote democracy in postwar South Korea.

After the July 1953 armistice, Jackson, one of the few liberals in the conservative Eisenhower administration, continued his anti-Communist activities, especially through Radio Free Europe. Increasingly, however, he came under attack from conservatives for his views supporting clemency for convicted spies Julius and Ethel Rosenberg. Jackson also urged Eisenhower to speak out against anti-Communist witch-hunts conducted by Senator Joseph McCarthy. His attacks on McCarthy were met in kind by the senator and his assistant Roy Cohn, who questioned Jackson's loyalty and described him as a dangerous liberal who was subverting the White House. When Eisenhower refused to be drawn into the imbroglio, in March 1954 Jackson resigned as special assistant and returned to *Time*, Inc.

In later years Jackson remained active with a number of philanthropic causes and organizations, including the International Executive Service Corps. He died of cancer in Washington, D.C., on 19 September 1964.

—*Clayton D. Laurie*

References:

Brands, H. W. *Cold Warriors: Eisenhower's Generation and American Foreign Policy.* New York: Columbia University Press, 1988.

Current Biography. New York: H. W. Wilson, 1952.

Laurie, Clayton D. *The Propaganda Warriors: The American Crusade against Nazi Germany.* Lawrence: University Press of Kansas, 1996.

———. "The U.S. Army and Psychological Warfare Organization and Operations, 1918–1945." Washington, DC: U.S. Army Center of Military History. Unpublished manuscript.

Lichtenstein, Nelson, and Eleanora W. Schoenebaum, eds. *Political Profiles: The Truman Years.* New York: Facts on File, 1978.

Who's Who in America, 1950–1951. Chicago: A. N. Marquis, 1950.

See also: Eisenhower, Dwight D.; McCarthy, Joseph R.; McCarthyism.

Jamieson, Arthur B.
(1910–1991)

Australia's representative successively on the United Nations Temporary Commission on Korea (UNTCOK) and the UN Commission on Korea (UNCOK), 1948–1950. Born on 2 July 1910 in Ballarat, Victoria, and educated at the University of Melbourne, 1933–1935, Jamieson studied Japanese at Bunrik University, Tokyo, and during 1937–1940 he lectured in Japan at Nihon University and the Tokyo University of Commerce. After serving in the Royal Australian Navy during World War II, Jamieson joined the Department of External Affairs in 1947, and shortly afterwards he was transferred to the Tokyo embassy. In 1948 he was concurrently appointed as Australia's representative on UNTCOK, the establishment of which was authorized by the UN resolution of 12 November 1947. UNTCOK metamorphosed into UNCOK, by direction of a 12 December 1949 resolution.

As Australia's representative on UNCOK, Jamieson publicly articulated his country's policy toward Korea. Until North Korea invaded the South, this was by no means always consonant with U.S. policy. A junior diplomat, Jamieson implemented and served as a spokesman for Australian policy rather than initiating it, but his views and reports did exercise some influence on the attitudes of more senior Australian officials toward the Korean situation.

Australia initially opposed UNTCOK's May 1948 endorsement of elections restricted to Korea's southern portion, taking the line that the UN objective should be to establish a unified national government for all of Korea, not to divide the country. When Australia's protests on this matter were rejected by the UN General Assembly's Interim Committee, the Australian government acquiesced in the elections, but Jamieson's superiors instructed him to absent himself from the country in August 1948, when the southern Republic of Korea was inaugurated.

In 1949 Jamieson frequently sent to the Department of External Affairs reports highly critical of the often harsh and brutal means that new President of the Republic of Korea (ROK, South Korea) Syngman Rhee was employing to consolidate his rule and eradicate his political opponents. Although this information was one reason for the Australian government's protests against Rhee's tactics, such condemnation had little or no practical impact.

In June 1950 Jamieson not only signed the UNCOK report of 24 June 1950, which provided evidence that the Democratic People's Republic of Korea (DPRK, North Korea) had begun the war, but he personally endorsed its conclusions in reports to Canberra. Because he was by no means an uncritical admirer of Rhee's government, Jamieson's testimony carried particularly heavy weight in persuading his own and other governments that the conflict was indeed the result of DPRK aggression.

During the war, Jamieson's dispatches continued to characterize the Rhee administration as brutal, reactionary, oppressive, and undemocratic. Accepting this view of the ROK government, Australian statements deliberately emphasized the necessity for the UN to maintain collective security in the face of outright aggression, but quite consciously failed to suggest that Rhee's regime deserved such support on its own merits.

In September 1950 Jamieson left UNCOK, and the following year the Department of External Affairs recalled him from Korea to Canberra, where he held various positions that utilized his Asian expertise. His later career also included several further assignments at the Tokyo embassy and service in Jakarta, Rome, and Milan. His final posting was as consul general in Osaka. Jamieson retired in 1975 and died near Canberra on 12 December 1991.

—*Priscilla Roberts*

References:

Luard, Evan. *A History of the United Nations.* Vol 1, *The Years of Western Domination, 1945–1955.* London: Macmillan, 1982.

McCormack, Gavan. *Cold War, Hot War: An Australian Perspective on the Korean War.* Sydney: Hale & Iremonger, 1983.

O'Neill, Robert J. *Australia in the Korean War, 1950–1953.* 2 vols. Canberra: Australian War Memorial/Australian Government Publication Service, 1981, 1985.

Stueck, William W., Jr. *The Korean War: An International History.* Princeton, NJ: Princeton University Press, 1995.

Yoo, Tae-Ho. *The Korean War and the United Nations.* Louvain, Belgium: Librairie Desbarax, 1964.

See also: Australia; Syngman Rhee.

Japan

Japan played an indirect yet significant role during the Korean War. When the war broke out in June 1950, Japan was still under the Allied occupation with General Douglas MacArthur as its supreme commander. The United States soon transferred some 80,000 troops to Korea from its air and naval bases in Japan. With the Korean peninsula only about 165 nautical miles away, U.S. military bases and logistic facilities in Japan were of critical importance to the prosecution of the war. As a repair and supply shop, Japan produced under procurement demands such items as ammunition, barbed wire, trucks, tires, communications equipment, coal, and textiles. It also provided a number of hospitals for wounded U.S. soldiers. Although the United Nations Command did not request that Japan make a major military contribution, Japan did operate minesweepers to clear Korean waters and ships to carry soldiers and supplies. Throughout the war, one Japanese sailor was killed off Wŏnsan and eight others were wounded.

The Korean War immensely affected the political economy of postwar Japan. Perhaps most important, it facilitated the nation's rearmament. Soon after the war broke out, MacArthur altered his earlier decision to demilitarize Japan permanently and ordered creation of a rudimentary army to replace the U.S. ground troops that were sent to Korea. One month later, the National Police Reserve (NPR) of 75,000 men was established. In 1952 the NPR was expanded to a National Safety Force with a small naval component. In 1954 it further evolved into Land, Sea, and Air Self-Defense Forces with 250,000 men. The Korean War and the threat of Communist expansionism made the gradual rearmament more acceptable to the Japanese people.

Many officers of Japan's nascent armed forces were recruited from those individuals who had been purged from public life for roles they had played in World War II. The number of Japanese who had been purged reached around 200,000. Although depurging began as early as 1949, in light of the growing Communist threat, the Korean War accelerated the process. The first big release of purgees came in October 1950. After establishing an appeals board to review the purges on the petition of Prime Minister Shigeru Yoshida, MacArthur approved all 10,094 recommendations for release.

Economically the Korean War contributed greatly to Japan's postwar recovery. During the war, Japanese companies received a great many special orders for goods and services for U.S. troops in Korea. These war procurement expenditures, which amounted to between $2.4 and $3.6 billion, raised domestic production and efficiency, improved business profits, encouraged capital investment, and increased foreign exchange earnings. The war procurement was a blessing for the Japanese economy; the country had suffered deep recession and high unemployment from austerity measures imposed earlier by the government to contain hyperinflation. The Japanese economy picked up speed after the war, passed its prewar peak in the mid-1950s, and continued a 10 percent per year growth rate in the next two decades. Although the Korean War alone would not have caused Japan's economic recovery, the "special procurement" created an export boom and helped restore the Japanese economy.

The Korean War also affected the timing and content of the Japanese peace treaty signed in September 1951. By the time the war broke out, the Allied occupation of Japan had lasted nearly five years, but the U.S. government was divided over when to end the occupation and how to conclude peace with Japan. The Pentagon insisted, among other things, on the Soviets signing the peace treaty. It maintained that excluding the Soviet Union from the peace settlement would provide Moscow with an excuse for hostile action

against Japan after the treaty was signed. The State Department, on the other hand, advocated an early peace settlement, even without Soviet participation. It argued that a prolonged occupation would antagonize the Japanese people and harm, rather than serve, U.S. interests. The outbreak of the Korean War ended the debate: the Pentagon dropped its demand for a Soviet signing of the treaty and agreed to an early peace settlement, and the State Department accepted the Pentagon's request for Japanese rearmament.

Another major controversy was over Japanese trade with China, although this debate took place in large part between Washington and Tokyo. Although initially divided, U.S. government advisors sought to curtail trade between Japan and the People's Republic of China after the 1949 Communist victory in China and the conclusion of the Sino-Soviet Friendship Treaty in early 1950. Instead, they sought to promote Southeast Asia as Japan's new source for food and raw materials imports and exports. Japanese leaders strongly doubted that Southeast Asia could replace China, the largest trading partner of prewar Japan. Tokyo argued that Beijing and Moscow were not monolithic and that Japanese trade with China would moderate Communist behavior and help precipitate a Sino-Soviet split. This debate, too, came to an end with the outbreak of the Korean War. The United States virtually banned Japan's trade with China. Ironically, however, it was the United States, not Southeast Asia, that replaced China as Japan's major trading partner in subsequent years. The war contributed to a shift of Japanese interest in foreign markets to the United States, marking the beginning of a dynamic and often tempestuous trade relationship.

—*Akitoshi Miyashita*

References:

Dingman, Roger. "The Dagger and the Gift: The Impact of the Korean War on Japan." *Journal of American-East Asian Relations* 1, no. 1 (1993): 29–55.

Finn, Richard B. *Winners in Peace: MacArthur, Yoshida, and Postwar Japan.* Berkeley: University of California Press, 1992.

Schaller, Michael. *The American Occupation of Japan: The Origins of the Cold War in Asia.* New York: Oxford University Press, 1985.

See also: Japan Logistical Command; Japanese Peace Treaty; MacArthur, Douglas.

Japan Logistical Command

Before the outbreak of the Korean War in June 1950, ports, depots, hospitals, and other logistical installations providing support for U.S. occupation troops in Japan were under the control of Headquarters, Eighth U.S. Army. The Japan Logistical Command (JLC) was created on 24 August 1950 to assume the logistical support responsibilities of Headquarters, Eighth U.S.

Army Rear, which was ordered to Korea. Commanded by Major General Walter L. Weible and with headquarters in Yokohama, the JLC had two main functions: to support U.S. Army forces in Japan and Korea and to carry out the U.S. Army's responsibilities for the occupation of Japan. Accordingly, the JLC processed supply requisitions submitted by the Eighth Army in Korea, maintained theater stock records, and ordered supplies from the United States for direct shipment to forces in Korea or to restock U.S. depots in Japan. The JLC also shipped materiel from depots in Japan to Korea and supervised the operation of all ports, depots, and other support facilities in Japan not assigned to General Headquarters of the U.S. Far East Command, the U.S. Navy, the U.S. Air Force, or other United Nations (UN) forces.

The JLC carried out its functions through three subordinate area commands. The Central Command was colocated with JLC headquarters in Yokohama and was responsible for support operations and facilities in central and southern Honshu. The Northern Command was established on 28 August 1950 with headquarters at Sapporo and was commanded by Brigadier General Edwin W. Piburn. The Northern Command was responsible for support operations and facilities on Hokkaido and in Northern Honshu. On 19 September 1950, the Southwestern Command was established with headquarters in Osaka. Commanded by Brigadier General Carter W. Clarke, it was responsible for support operations on the islands of Shikoku and Kyushu and all logistical facilities in southwestern Japan. With its creation on 1 October 1952, the Headquarters, U.S. Army Forces Far East, absorbed the JLC and became the primary U.S. Army administrative headquarters in Japan. The Northern Command was eliminated, but the Central and Southwestern Commands were continued until after the Korean War ended.

The JLC was organized under a Table of Distribution rather than the usual Table of Organization and Equipment in order to reduce its requirements for military personnel. In general, U.S. military personnel assigned to the JLC acted as supervisors for local Japanese laborers or oversaw the work of Japanese civilian contractors.

Although during its twenty-five months of existence the JLC provided essential logistical support for UN forces in Korea and U.S. occupation forces in Japan, it also played a key role in the economic development of Japan. Contracts let and supervised by the JLC during the Korean War, particularly those for the rebuilding of tracked and wheeled vehicles and the manufacturing of other military supplies and equipment, were in large part responsible for initiating the amazing post–World War II Japanese economic boom.

—*Charles R. Shrader*

References:
Hermes, Walter G. *United States Army in the Korean War: Truce Tent and Fighting Front.* Washington, DC: Office of the Chief of Military History, 1966.
Huston, James A. *The Sinews of War: Army Logistics, 1775–1953.* Washington, DC: Office of the Chief of Military History, U.S. Army, 1966.
Logistical Problems and Their Solutions. APO 301: Headquarters, Eighth United States Army Korea, Historical Section and Eighth Army Historical Service Detachment (Provisional), 1952.
Schnabel, James F. *United States Army in the Korean War: Policy and Direction, the First Year.* Washington, DC: Office of the Chief of Military History, Department of the Army, 1972.
See also: Logistics in the Korean War.

Japanese Peace Treaty
(8 September 1951)

The June 1950 Democratic People's Republic of Korea (DPRK, North Korean) invasion of the Republic of Korea (ROK, South Korea) generated sufficient alarm in the United States that President Harry S. Truman's administration moved to end the post–World War II U.S. occupation of Japan. Although the occupation, headed by General Douglas MacArthur, had proceeded relatively smoothly, by 1950 several considerations caused Truman to begin negotiations for bringing the occupation to an end. Chief among these was that Cold War tensions between the United States and the Soviet Union had escalated dramatically since the end of World War II. Several crises around the globe between the United States and the USSR, as well as Russia's successful detonation of an atomic bomb in 1949, strengthened Truman's resolve to contain communism. Moreover, that same year Mao Zedong's Communist forces defeated the Nationalists in China. But it was the outbreak of hostilities in Korea in 1950 that caused the administration to take immediate steps toward ending the occupation.

Assuming that Moscow was behind the DPRK invasion of the ROK, leaders in Washington feared the potential loss of all of Asia to Communist aggression. They believed that Japan must be turned into a strong U.S. ally and bulwark to communism in the Far East. On 18 May 1950, President Truman selected John Foster Dulles to be his special representative to Japan to negotiate an end to the occupation. Dulles embarked on his trip to Japan on 14 June to begin formal discussions with Japanese Prime Minister Yoshida Shigeru. He stopped first in South Korea.

Yoshida's immediate objectives in the treaty talks were to secure Japanese independence and an end to the U.S. occupation. Beyond that, Yoshida wanted a permanent guarantee of U.S. security support. Dulles, reflecting fears in Washington that Communist aggression was imminent in all of Asia, originally sought rapid Japanese rearmament, but Yoshida wanted Japan to be able to concentrate on economic growth with minimal expenditure for rearmament. Yoshida's solution was to offer permanent U.S. bases in Japan while committing his country to only a minimal rearmament.

While negotiations went forward in Japan, the Truman administration arranged for an international conference in San Francisco to sign the treaty. By September 1951, with negotiations complete between Dulles and Yoshida, the Japanese delegation traveled to San Francisco. On 8 September, after little more than a week of international debate, Japan signed a peace treaty with forty-eight nations. A bilateral security arrangement with the United States allowing U.S. troops to remain in Japan indefinitely was signed separately.

While the Soviet Union and its Communist-bloc allies attended the conference, they abstained from signing the treaty. The USSR professed outrage that Japan was absolved from paying any war reparations but also free to rearm if it so desired. Regardless, U.S. Secretary of State Dean Acheson, who presided at the conference, allowed no debate on the treaty before the signing took place, and Russian objections were thus ignored. However, many Pacific nations would not sign the treaty until the United States agreed to sign separate security pacts with them. These included the Philippines, Australia, and New Zealand. The final agreement permitting the United States to maintain defensive military bases in Japan was not signed until February 1952. Although historians have debated its merits, the Japanese Peace Treaty has generally been seen as an admirable, nonrestrictive agreement. Even though its foreign policy was linked to U.S. expectations for many years, Japan had regained its national sovereignty and suffered few punitive measures for its part in the Pacific War.

The Korean War provided not only the impetus for a Japanese peace treaty, but also a market for Japanese manufactured goods; Japan supplied war materials to the U.S. military for the remainder of the hostilities. Under the umbrella of U.S. military protection, Japan was freed from large military expenditures of its own and was able to concentrate on postwar economic growth. It has been the chief ally of the United States in Asia ever since.

—Phillip A. Cantrell II

References:

Dower, J. W. *Empire and Aftermath: Yoshida Shigeru and the Japanese Experience, 1878–1954.* Cambridge, MA: Harvard University Press, 1979.

Finn, Richard B. *Winners in Peace: MacArthur, Yoshida and Postwar Japan.* Berkeley: University of California Press, 1992.

Yoshitsu, Michael M. *Japan and the San Francisco Peace Settlement.* New York: Columbia University Press, 1983.

See also: Acheson, Dean Goodersham; Dulles, John Foster; Japan; MacArthur, Douglas; Mao Zedong.

Jebb, Sir Hubert Miles Gladwyn
(1900–1996)

Permanent British representative to the United Nations (UN) during the Korean War. Hubert Miles Gladwyn Jebb was born on 25 April 1900 at Firbeck Hall near Rotheram in Yorkshire and educated at Eton and Magdalen College, Oxford, earning first class honors in history. He joined the Foreign Service in 1924 and in the next fifteen years spent several terms in the nonpolitical civil service positions of parliamentary undersecretary and secretary of state in the Foreign Office. These terms spanned the governments of Ramsay MacDonald, Stanley Baldwin, and Neville Chamberlain.

A polished and unassuming man, Jebb was considered hard working and intellectually acute. In 1940 he became assistant undersecretary in the Ministry of Economic Warfare and, after demonstrating excellent organizational abilities, in 1942 was promoted to head of the Foreign Office's economic and reconstruction department. He accompanied Prime Minister Winston Churchill, Foreign Minister Anthony Eden, and other British politicians to discussions and conferences in Washington, Quebec, Cairo, Tehran, Dumbarton Oaks, Yalta, and Potsdam, and he was a member of the British delegation at the 1945 San Francisco Conference that created the UN.

At the first UN General Assembly session, held in London in 1946, Jebb served as acting secretary-general and there forcefully supported international controls over atomic energy. In 1946 he became assistant undersecretary of state in charge of UN affairs. He gained personal ambassadorial rank in 1948 when he represented Britain on the Brussels Treaty Commission that created the military Western European Union, a precursor of the North Atlantic Treaty Organization. In 1949 he was appointed to the British UN delegation, and in 1950 he became Britain's permanent representative to that body.

During the Korean War, Jebb's bureaucratic skills were directed to the forceful representation of British interests; he played a prominent part in drafting crucial resolutions on the war. As president of the UN Security Council in September 1950, he was instrumental in ensuring that the Republic of Korea continued to maintain its independent UN representation, a key move in retaining its status as a separate national entity. Acting on instructions from Prime Minister Clement Attlee and Foreign Secretary Ernest Bevin, when evidence of sporadic Chinese military intervention began to emerge in October 1950, Jebb advocated direct negotiations with the People's Republic of China, a tactic the United States rejected.

Although his position obliged him publicly to endorse his country's firm support for the United States, Jebb was concerned that increased military commitments in Asia would weaken European defenses. Instead, the Korean War led to the rapid implementation of a major enhancement of U.S. military commitments to Western Europe, as recommended in the Policy Planning Staff paper NSC-68, "United States Objectives and Programs for National Security." Following his superiors' instructions and his own instincts, as Britain's representative on the UN Collective Measures Committee Jebb opposed actions likely to widen or prolong the war.

In 1954 Jebb became British ambassador to France, where he and his wife replaced the popular Duff and Lady Diana Cooper. Jebb remained in this post until his retirement in 1960, when he was ennobled as Lord Gladwyn of Jebb. From 1965 to 1988 Gladwyn served as the Liberal Party's deputy leader in the House of Lords, from 1966 to 1973 as a member of parliamentary delegations to the Council of Europe and the Western European Union, and from 1973 to 1976 as a Member of the European Parliament. He devoted much effort to the cause of European unity, at various times serving as president of both the European Movement and the Atlantic Treaty Association and chairman of the Campaign for the European Political Community. He wrote several books dealing with European issues as well as his memoirs. Jebb died on 26 October 1996 at his home at Halesworth.

—*Priscilla Roberts*

References:

Butler, Rohan, and M. E. Pelly, eds. *Documents on British Foreign Policy Overseas.* Series II, Vol. 4, *Korea, 1950–1951.* London: Her Majesty's Stationery Office, 1995.

Gladwyn, Cynthia. *The Diaries of Cynthia Gladwyn,* edited by Miles Jebb. London: Constable, 1995.

Gladwyn, H. M. G. J. *The Memoirs of Lord Gladwyn.* London: Weidenfeld & Nicolson, 1972.

MacDonald, Callum A. *Britain and the Korean War.* Oxford: Blackwell, 1990.

Stueck, William W., Jr. *The Korean War: An International History.* Princeton, NJ: Princeton University Press, 1990.

See also: Attlee, Clement R.; Bevin, Ernest; Churchill, Sir Winston Spencer; Eden, Anthony; Franks, Oliver.

Jessup, Philip C.
(1897–1986)

U.S. representative to the United Nations (UN) General Assembly during 1948–1952 and ambassador-at-large, 1949–1953. Philip C. Jessup was born in New York City on 5 January 1897. He obtained a bachelor's degree from Hamilton College and pursued further studies in law at Yale and Columbia Universities. During the 1920s and 1930s he taught international law at the latter institution and was widely recognized as the foremost U.S. expert on the subject, often representing his country at international diplomatic meetings on legal issues. In the later 1940s, Jessup held several UN positions, culminating in his appointment in 1948 as deputy to U.S. Ambassador to the UN Warren R. Austin.

In 1949 President Harry S. Truman nominated Jessup as ambassador-at-large, a post in which he won the permanent opprobrium of the China lobby by editing the famous "White Paper" on China Policy, which the State Department published in 1949. This report, ascribing the impending Communist victory in China to the corruption of Jiang Jieshi's (Chiang Kai-shek's) Guomindang (Nationalist) regime, was an analysis that Jiang Jieshi's U.S. supporters fiercely resented. In 1950 Jessup was named by Senator Joseph R. McCarthy as one of various State Department official with "an affinity for Communist causes." McCarthy elaborated these charges in hearings before the Tydings Committee, which was established to investigate McCarthy's allegations of Communist infiltration of the U.S. foreign policy apparatus. McCarthy alleged that Jessup had belonged to six supposedly Communist-front organizations, the most heinous being the Institute of Pacific Relations, which was implicated in the passing of classified State Department information to the Soviet Union. Alfred Kohlberg, head of the China lobby, claimed that Jessup had launched a smear campaign against the Chinese Nationalists and was the author of the claim that the Chinese Communists were merely agrarian reformers. In July 1950 the Tydings Committee cleared Jessup of all these charges, but he remained a target of McCarthyite suspicions and of further rumors that he had recommended that the United States cut off aid to the Nationalists on Taiwan and recognize Communist China. As a result, in 1951 the appropriate Senate subcommittee voted three to two against Truman's appointment of Jessup as a delegate to a forthcoming UN General Assembly meeting in Paris, though Truman circumvented this decision by giving Jessup a recess appointment.

Jessup's UN responsibilities frequently resulted in verbal clashes with Soviet Minister of Foreign Affairs Andrei Y. Vyshinskii over Korea. In spring 1948 Jessup persuaded the UN Interim Committee to permit the UN Temporary Commission on Korea to supervise the elections that were to take place in Korea's southern occupation zone on 10 May 1948. In January 1950 Jessup visited the Republic of Korea in an attempt to encourage greater political democracy and economic reform. That June he was present at both Blair House meetings of U.S. officials on Korea and prepared the minutes for each. Jessup also accompanied Truman on his 15 October 1950 Wake Island meeting with General Douglas MacArthur, and he was privy to the president's subsequent decision to recall his field commander. Continuing political attacks on his loyalty made Jessup something of a liability to the Truman administration. In late 1952 he left government service to resume his former teaching career at Columbia University and his interests in international law and foreign policy. From 1961 to 1970 he served as a judge on the International Court of Justice in Geneva, and, even after giving up this post, continued to pursue lecturing, research, and writing in international law. Jessup died in Norfolk, Connecticut, on 31 January 1986.

—*Priscilla Roberts*

References:

Klehr, Harvy, and Radosh, Ronald. *The Amerasia Spy Case: Prelude to McCarthyism.* Chapel Hill: University of North Carolina Press, 1996.

Oshinsky, David M. *A Conspiracy So Immense: The World of Joe McCarthy.* New York: Free Press, 1983.

"Philip C. Jessup." In *Political Profiles: The Truman Years,* edited by Eleanora W. Schoenebaum. New York: Facts on File, 1978.

Thomas, John N. *The Institute of Pacific Relations: Asian Scholars and American Politics.* Seattle: University of Washington Press, 1974.

See also: Austin, Warren; China Lobby; Jiang Jieshi (Chiang Kaishek); MacArthur, Douglas; McCarthy, Joseph R.; McCarthyism; Truman, Harry S.; Truman's Recall of MacArthur; Vyshinskii, Andrei Ianuarovich.

Jet Aircraft, First Clash in History
(8 November 1950)

Action in MiG Alley between U.S. Fifth Air Force Lockheed F80-C Shooting Star and Soviet-built MiG-15. In early 1950 the U.S. Far East Air Forces (FEAF) targeted two railroad bridges spanning the Yalu River on the Sino-Korean border as a major route for supplies and troops entering North Korea. Subsequent U.S. airstrikes against the bridges, connecting the Manchurian city of Dandong (Antung) and the provisional North Korean capital of Sinŭiju, prompted the People's Republic of China to establish a major air base at Antung to protect the vital supply line.

On 8 November 1950, U.S. FEAF Bomber Command B-29s mounted attacks on the two bridges. Antung-based MiG-15s rose to intercept and engaged U.S. fighters of the 51st Fighter Interceptor Wing flying top cover for the bombers. Although their propeller-driven F-51 Mustangs and F-80 Shooting Star jet fighters were outclassed by the MiGs, the better-trained U.S. pilots proved superior to their probably Chinese opponents. A dogfight ensued between a MiG pilot and Lieutenant Russell J. Brown, piloting an obsolete F-80C. The MiG pilot's inexperience mismatched with Brown's skill enabled Brown to exploit his plane's single advantage over the MiG. Attempting to evade Brown, the MiG pilot dove, allowing Brown's heavier aircraft the speed to overtake and down the faster, more maneuverable,

Communist jet. This action was the first clash between jet aircraft in history.

—*Jeff Kinard*

References:

Futrell, Robert F. *The United States Air Force in Korea, 1950–1953.* Rev. ed. Washington, DC: Office of the Chief of Air Force History, 1983.

Gunston, Bill, ed. *The Illustrated History of Fighters.* New York: Exeter Books, 1981.

Toland, John. *In Mortal Combat: Korea, 1950–1953.* New York: William Morrow, 1991.

See also: Aircraft (Principal Combat); MiG Alley.

Jiang Jieshi (Chiang Kai-shek)
(1887–1975)

Born on 30 October 1887, at Xikou, in Fenghua County, Zhejiang Province in eastern China, Jiang Jieshi (Chiang Kai-shek) was from a farming family, but his father, who died when Jiang was a young boy, was a salt merchant. Raised without a father in difficult economic and political times, Jiang's formal education did not begin until he was in his teens, when he was tutored in the traditional Chinese classics. In 1905 after several months in a middle school, he went to Japan planning to begin military studies. Because he was not sponsored by the Chinese government, he was not allowed to enroll and returned to China. Determined to become a military officer, Jiang passed the competitive entrance examinations and began his military instruction in 1906 at China's prestigious Paoting Military Academy. Because of his hard work and potential, he was then selected by the faculty to go to Japan to attend the Preparatory Military Academy in Tokyo.

Although Jiang did well, he did not go on to Japan's Military University to complete his training. While in Tokyo, he met several key members of China's revolutionary party, the Dongmenghui (Alliance Society), and began to foster the political and military associations that would involve him over the next several years in the intrigues of the founding and consolidation of the Republic of China (ROC) in the aftermath of the 1911 revolution. His military prowess and political savvy eventually led to his leadership role in the military arm of the Nationalist Party (Guomindang).

In the early 1920s, Jiang rose to prominence as a close ally and supporter of the ROC's first president, Sun Yat-sen, whose primary base of power was in southern China. Sun selected Jiang to serve as commandant of the Whampoa Military Academy in Guangzhou (Canton). He also sent him to the Soviet Union to negotiate for military assistance. The Soviets, and later the Germans and the Japanese, supplied arms and advisors to support Sun's efforts at the officers' training school at Whampoa. During this time, the Chinese Nationalists and Communists were working together to consolidate power over a divided nation and build a united China that included a modern, professional military establishment. Jiang's deputy at Whampoa was Zhou Enlai (Chou En-lai) who would later serve as Mao Zedong's (Mao Tsetung) deputy for much of his tenure as the leader of China. After 1949, Zhou was the second most powerful leader in the People's Republic of China (PRC) until his death in 1976.

In 1925 Sun died and a power struggle ensued within the Nationalist Party. The united effort with the Communists became problematic for Jiang and his faction. Over the next three years, Jiang prevailed in his quest for party leadership. He also began to purge the Communists from the Nationalist Party, a purge that culminated in the 1927 Shanghai Massacre. Beginning in 1926, Jiang conducted a set of military campaigns, known as the Northern Expedition, first in the south and then in the north against a weak government in Beijing (Peking) and various warlords. Jiang was now firmly in charge and established a national capital at Nanjing (Nanking) in 1928.

From 1928 until 1937, when the declared war between China and Japan began, Jiang worked to consolidate political power, defeat regional warlords opposed to a China united under the Nationalist flag, and eliminate the Communists. Jiang's Nationalist armies conducted five unsuccessful extermination campaigns against Mao and the Red Army, later named the People's Liberation Army (PLA). One of these campaigns resulted in the Long March, which took on great symbolic significance for the Communist Chinese movement. Although it was a series of military defeats and strategic retreats with only a few tactical victories for the Communists, Mao and the leadership cadre of the Chinese Communist Party survived and began to rebuild the party and the army in Yenan in north-central China.

In 1936, while visiting northern China to supervise further military actions against the Communists, Jiang was kidnapped by several of his own officers and handed over to the Communists in what is known as the Xian (Sian) incident. In the ensuing negotiations, Jiang, who was widely recognized as the leader of China, was freed under the condition that he accept a second united front between the Nationalists and the Communists to oppose the Japanese occupation of Chinese territory. Although this effort soon fell apart in reality, the fiction of this combined, patriotic front to fight the Japanese lasted until 1945.

With the Japanese surrender, the Chinese Civil War began anew as both the Communists and the Nationalists moved quickly to consolidate territory formerly occupied by the Japanese. Jiang and the Nationalists received significant amounts of U.S. mil-

itary assistance and some direct naval, Marine, and air support to protect key areas and transport Nationalist forces. The Nationalists enjoyed a clear superiority in equipment and numbers, but the Communists had developed significant support among the peasant population, an experienced and competent military and political cadre, and a highly mobile and effective conventional army that had a secure base of operations in north China. The U.S. attempt to mediate a cessation of hostilities and a negotiated peace was seen by the Communists as favoring Jiang and the Nationalists. The Communists sought the total defeat of the Nationalist forces and complete political control of China, aims that U.S. General George C. Marshall found out were not negotiable.

By 1948, Jiang's hold on the Chinese mainland was tenuous, and the United States found itself in a difficult position. The Communists controlled more territory and had gained the upper hand militarily, and, significantly for the United States, Mao, despite some key differences with Soviet Premier Josef Stalin, began the "lean to one side" policy toward the Soviets. Strategically, faced with problems with the Soviets in Europe and in the Middle East, the United States did not want to intervene directly with military forces in an attempt to save Jiang. As the Communist victory increasingly appeared to be inevitable, U.S. President Harry S. Truman's administration reduced material support to the Nationalist effort and attempted to distance itself from Jiang. Opposing this, a large and influential element of the Republican Party wanted to support the Nationalists as part of a more confrontational China policy as the Cold War strategy of the global containment of communism began to emerge.

In the summer of 1949, Jiang, as the leader of the ROC, moved the Nationalist government and the remnants of his military to Taiwan and other offshore island enclaves. The PLA under the direction of Mao then mopped up Nationalist units still defending in several outlying areas. The PLA also began to build up units and conduct preliminary operations against the offshore islands necessary for an amphibious attack on Taiwan itself. The very survival of Jiang's regime seemed in doubt until North Korea attacked South Korea in June 1950. With the outbreak of the war and Chinese and Soviet support for North Korea, Nationalist China became a major regional player under Jiang's leadership.

Despite his military defeat, Jiang continued to be the senior political and military authority for the Nationalists now consolidating power on Taiwan. He was in a position to be a major factor in U.S. East Asian policy debate and in strategic decision making vis-à-vis Communist China during the Korean War. His stated primary goal was the reunification of China under the Nationalist banner, impossible without significant U.S. assistance. Jiang's diplomatic efforts to reinvigorate an alliance with the United States and his direction of military actions by ROC forces against Mao's PLA, launched from Taiwan, significantly complicated Truman's attempts to limit the war to the Korean peninsula and avoid a wider confrontation in Asia with the PRC. Jiang fully understood the dynamics of the strategic security debate in the United States and was experienced in the game of domestic factionalism and with the political-military nature of international relations.

At the outbreak of the Korean War, Jiang offered the United States several ROC ground divisions (33,000 troops) to fight as part of the United Nations (UN) forces in Korea. This controversial offer was diplomatically rejected by the Truman administration. As a precautionary measure, however, the U.S. Seventh Fleet was sent to the Taiwan Straits. This move was indicative of an emerging, if somewhat reluctant, U.S. commitment to defend the Nationalist government on Taiwan in the face of Chinese support for North Korea. Jiang also met with commander of UN forces in Korea General Douglas MacArthur, who supported increased aid to the Nationalists, in order to discuss military cooperation. There followed a series of controversial diplomatic missions from the Truman administration to determine the parameters of ROC-U.S. cooperation designed to limit ROC involvement.

While Truman wanted to limit the war to the Korean peninsula, the developing situation in East Asia provided a significant opportunity for Jiang to pursue his political and military goals. The direct involvement of Communist Chinese ground forces in Korea may very well have ensured the survival of the Nationalist regime.

Jiang's diplomatic maneuvering during both Truman's and President Dwight D. Eisenhower's administrations eventually led to a formal military alliance between the ROC and the United States. The United States established a large military advisory mission to Taiwan, provided significant amounts of arms and equipment, and had access to bases and facilities. This alliance relationship did not begin to unravel until President Richard M. Nixon's administration's negotiations with the PRC during 1971–1972 that ultimately led to the U.S. one-China policy and the ROC being replaced by the PRC in the United Nations. However, it was not until 1979 during President Jimmy Carter's administration that the treaty relationship ended. The formal alliance was replaced by the Taiwan Relations Act, but the U.S.-ROC relationship had fundamentally changed in the 1970s.

In the midst of this turbulent period, while still president of the ROC, Jiang died on 5 April 1975 in Taibei

(Taipei). He was replaced as Nationalist leader by his son, Jiang Jingguo (Chiang Ching-kuo), then premier and head of the Guomindang. The younger Jiang had begun the process of democratizing the island and oversaw the truly spectacular economic development of Taiwan.

—*J. G. D. Babb*

References:
Chiang Kai-shek. *China's Destiny and Chinese Economic Theory.* New York: Roy, 1947.
Crozier, Brian. *The Man Who Lost China: The First Full Biography of Chiang Kai-Shek.* New York: Charles Scribner's Sons, 1976.
Eastman, Lloyd, Jerome Chen, Suzanne Pepper, and Lyman Van Slyke. *The Nationalist Era in China, 1927–1949.* New York: Cambridge University Press, 1991.
Fairbank, John K. *China: A New History.* Cambridge, MA: Harvard University Press, 1992.
Finkelstein, David M. *Washington's Taiwan Dilemma, 1949–1950.* Lanham, MD: George Mason University Press, 1993.
Gittings, John. *The World and China, 1922–1972.* New York: Harper & Row, 1974.
Liu, F. F. *A Military History of Modern China, 1924–1949.* Princeton, NJ: Princeton University Press, 1956.
Schaller, Michael. *The United States and China in the Twentieth Century.* New York: Oxford University Press, 1979.
Spence, Jonathan D. *The Search for Modern China.* New York: W. W. Norton, 1990.

See also: China, Republic of; China Lobby; MacArthur, Douglas; Mao Zedong; Marshall, George C.; Truman, Harry S.; Zhou Enlai.

Johnson, Louis A.
(1891–1966)

U.S. secretary of defense, 1949–1950. Born on 10 January 1891, in Roanoke, Virginia, Louis Arthur Johnson graduated from the University of Virginia in 1912. He then moved to Clarksburg, West Virginia, where he practiced law. Elected to the West Virginia House of Delegates as a Democrat in 1917, Johnson was selected party floor leader. He served with the American Expeditionary Force in France during World War I as a captain in the 80th Infantry Division. Discharged in 1919, Johnson was a colonel in the reserves.

Active in Democratic Party politics, Johnson was a delegate and chairman of the veterans' advisory committee at the Democratic National Convention. He participated in the founding of the American Legion, a veterans' group, of which he was elected national commander in 1932. The American Legion offered him opportunities to learn about national defense topics and meet politically influential people such as future president Harry S. Truman. Johnson assisted President Franklin D. Roosevelt in communicating with veterans' groups that protested administrative cuts of veterans' pensions. To reward him for this work, Roosevelt appointed Johnson assistant secretary of war in 1937.

Aggressive and hardworking, Johnson often seemed at odds with Secretary of War Harry H. Woodring about how the War Department should be managed. Johnson wanted to modernize and increase the size of the U.S. Army, and he was credited for preparing it for mobilization in World War II. Johnson wanted to be secretary of war, but, as Roosevelt was campaigning for his third term in 1940, the threat of war necessitated a bipartisan administration and Roosevelt selected Republican Henry L. Stimson, who named his own assistant secretary, forcing Johnson to resign.

Johnson became president of the General Dyestuff Corporation (of I. G. Farben), managed property, and acted as Roosevelt's personal representative in India. Johnson supported sending military aid to non-Communist countries and was the first chairman of the North Atlantic Defense Committee in the North Atlantic Treaty Organization (NATO) at the beginning of the Cold War.

When Truman campaigned against Thomas E. Dewey in 1948, public opinion polls predicted that Truman would lose. Johnson agreed to head the Democratic finance committee, personally giving $250,000 to the fund and raising some $1.5 million. After his reelection, Truman appointed Johnson as secretary of defense.

The position of secretary of defense was created in 1947 when the Army and Navy Departments and new Department of the Air Force merged into one group. The secretary of defense was a member of the president's cabinet and the National Security Council. Johnson replaced first Secretary of Defense James V. Forrestal on 28 March 1949. When he was sworn into office, Johnson promised to continue unification of the armed forces and to maintain military strength while reducing spending. Johnson soon closed military installations and cut back on training.

Johnson's most immediate problem was interservice strife that hindered cooperation between the three armed forces branches. He considered his most crucial decision to be delineating air force and navy roles in air warfare. He promoted land-based strategic air power, sparking the "revolt of the admirals." Based on recommendations from the Joint Chiefs of Staff (JCS), Johnson canceled construction of the U.S. Navy supercarrier *United States* in April 1949. Secretary of the Navy John L. Sullivan resigned, and the admirals, protesting Johnson's policies to the House Armed Services Committee, suggested that he was trying to destroy the navy. Truman expressed anger at Johnson for interfering in other departments, explaining "Louis began to show an inordinate ego-

tistical desire to run the whole government." Many thought Johnson's political posturing was an effort to secure the 1952 Democratic presidential nomination. While Johnson's enemies thought him arrogant and unqualified, his supporters believed him to be dynamic and capable. Blunt and determined, Johnson cut wasteful expenditures in the Department of Defense; later his detractors would blame him for the lack of U.S. military preparedness for the Korean War.

Because of congressional pressure to freeze spending and the Truman administration's economizing, the U.S. military found itself with depleted supplies and unprepared to wage war. In June 1950, Johnson and JCS Chairman General Omar N. Bradley spent two weeks in the Far East touring military installations and meeting with commanders. Returning to Washington on 24 June, Johnson believed that things were going well in the Pacific. At ten o'clock that night, a reporter asked Johnson if he had heard that the Democratic People's Republic of Korea (DPRK, North Korea) had attacked the Republic of Korea (ROK, South Korea). Johnson received a report about the invasion from a Pentagon duty officer but was unsure of its accuracy because Far East briefings had not suggested that such an attack was imminent. Johnson gave Secretary of the Army Frank Pace authority to delegate the situation and went to bed. Based on Truman administration pronouncements, Johnson did not envision sending U.S. forces to defend the ROK.

On 25 June, Johnson met Truman at the airport with Secretary of State Dean G. Acheson and Undersecretary of State James E. Webb, reassuring Truman, who wanted to stop the DPRK invasion, "I'm with you, Mr. President." Meeting with Truman and the service secretaries at Blair House that evening, Johnson opposed sending troops to Korea, but agreed to issue military supplies to support United Nations (UN) efforts in halting the Korean People's Army (KPA, North Korean) invasion. He seemed more concerned with U.S. relations with Formosa (Taiwan) than with Korea.

When the KPA invasion intensified the next day, Johnson supported the State Department's recommendation that U.S. air and naval assets be employed. He stressed that, if Chinese or Soviet troops entered the war, the United States should withdraw to avoid escalating the conflict. By 29 June, Johnson agreed with the JCS recommendation that ground troops be sent to South Korea because if the Communists were successful in Korea then other countries such as Formosa and Japan would be at risk.

After the United States entered the war, Johnson's duties included overseeing the procurement of vital supplies, increasing troop strength, establishing NATO forces, and conducting public relations. Many of his tasks were the same as before the war, but securing additional appropriations added to those. New duties included creating the UN military command and securing Allied support for UN operations. Johnson ensured that, although the conflict was officially a UN action, U.S. leaders were in charge. He attempted to meet Truman's desire that as many UN nations be represented as possible, while appeasing the JCS that only forces that could contribute militarily were welcomed. Ironically, Johnson spent the summer of 1950 building up the very military forces he had assiduously downsized during the previous fifteen months. He supervised the calling up of reserves and National Guard units and secured $12 billion in supplemental appropriations.

During the war, Johnson met with Truman daily to share his opinions and the viewpoints of the JCS. Johnson had operational command of the armed services. The chain of command during the Korean War ran: president, secretary of defense, JCS, and UN Command/Far East commander. At times Johnson supported actions such as the Inch'ŏn landing, which the JCS initially opposed. Realizing that he was not a talented military thinker, Johnson usually accepted JCS views and then communicated them to Truman.

On the other hand, Johnson waged a personal war with Secretary of State Acheson, attacking his Asian policies, specifically regarding Formosa. Acheson wanted to distance U.S. relations with the Chinese Nationalists, whereas Johnson wanted closer ties with Jiang Jieshi (Chiang Kai-Shek) and his regime on Formosa, including having Nationalist Chinese troops serve in Korea. Johnson manipulated situations to discredit Acheson and the State Department while emphasizing his own strengths. This feud with Acheson hurt important policy decisions, such as in early 1950, when Acheson invited Johnson and JCS chairman General Omar N. Bradley to talk about aspects of U.S. national security policy.

As the Korean War expanded in July and August 1950, Johnson's problems worsened as criticism increased about the poor military performance and high casualties of U.S. troops in Korea. Congress and the press made Johnson a scapegoat and demanded that Truman fire him. During his last months in office, Johnson became more irrational, and rumors circulated that he was divulging secret information to Republicans for their use in the fall elections. Johnson also delayed obeying Truman's order for him to ask that MacArthur omit his demand for use of Formosa as a military base in East Asia in his published message to the Veterans of Foreign Wars convention. MacArthur complied, but a transcript was released with the incriminating comments. Truman's

opponents used that publication to attack his credibility. Johnson also publicly hinted that Truman had changed his mind about supporting Formosa. Angry that Johnson indiscriminately voiced his opinion and perpetuated the feud with Acheson, Truman wrote in his diary that Johnson was "the most ego maniac[*sic*] I've ever come in contact with—and I've seen a lot." Acheson believed that Johnson was mentally unbalanced and should not have power over international policy. Finally on 12 September, Truman called Johnson to the White House to demand his resignation. Johnson resigned a week later on the 19th. George C. Marshall, former U.S. Army chief of staff and secretary of state, succeeded him as secretary of defense.

In a farewell speech presented to the American and Canadian Bar Association, Johnson expressed confidence in a UN victory in the Korean War and warned of the financial and humanitarian costs of war. "When the hurly-burly is done and the battle is won," Johnson concluded, "I trust that the historian will find my record of performance creditable, my service honest and faithful, commensurate with the trust that was placed in me and in the best interests of peace and our national defense."

After his resignation, Johnson had a brain tumor removed; this may indeed have caused his irrational behavior. He continued working as a senior partner in the Washington law firm of Steptoe and Johnson. He died on 24 April 1966 in Washington, D.C.

—*Elizabeth D. Schafer*

References:

Acheson, Dean. *Present at the Creation: My Years at the State Department.* New York: W. W. Norton, 1969.

Condit, Doris M. *History of the Office of the Secretary of Defense.* Vol. 2, *The Test of War, 1950–1953.* Washington, DC: Office of the Secretary of Defense, 1988.

Kinnard, Douglas. *The Secretaries of Defense.* Lexington: University of Kentucky Press, 1980.

New York Times, 25 April 1966.

Rearden, Steve L. *History of the Office of the Secretary of Defense.* Vol. 1, *The Formative Years, 1947–1950.* Washington, DC: Historical Office, Office of the Secretary of Defense, 1984.

Schnabel, James F., and Robert J. Watson. *The History of the Joint Chiefs of Staff: The Joint Chiefs of Staff and National Policy.* Vol. 3, *The Korean War.* Wilmington, DE: Michael Glazier, 1979.

See also: Acheson, Dean Goodersham; Antiwar Sentiment in the United States; Blair House Meetings; Bradley, Omar Nelson; China, Republic of; Inch'ŏn Landings: Operation CHROMITE; Jiang Jieshi (Chiang Kai-shek); Korea, Democratic People's Republic of, Invasion of the Republic of Korea; MacArthur, Douglas; Marshall, George C.; National Security Council (NSC); Pace, Frank, Jr.; Taiwan, Neutralization of; Truman, Harry S.; Truman's Domestic Agenda and the Korean War; United States Air Force (USAF); United States Army; United States Navy; Webb, James E.

Johnson, U. Alexis
(1908–1997)

U.S. State Department deputy assistant secretary of state for Far Eastern Affairs, 1951–1953. Born on 17 October 1908, in Falun, Kansas, U. Alexis Johnson graduated from Occidental College in 1931. He then attended the Georgetown School of Foreign Service for a year and joined the Foreign Service in 1935. An Asian specialist, in his early career Johnson held minor positions in Tokyo, Seoul, Tientsin, and Mukden, and he was interned by the Japanese for several months after the attack on Pearl Harbor. While vice-consul in Seoul in the 1930s, he encountered Syngman Rhee, whom he considered "a hopeless idealist," ill-fitted for power.

After assignments in Brazil and Chicago, in 1945 Johnson returned to Asia, where he served briefly in Manila and for four years in Yokohama. In 1945 Johnson was responsible for briefing General John R. Hodge, newly appointed head of U.S. occupation forces in Korea, on that country's politics and culture. During his years in Japan, where he was the first postwar State Department representative, Johnson's Korean expertise meant that in practice he spent much of his time in Korea advising Hodge and U.S. occupation forces.

Recalled to Washington in 1949 to be assistant deputy director in the State Department's Office of Northeast Asian Affairs, Johnson was in that position when the war began, and Assistant Secretary of State Dean Rusk gave him primary operational responsibility for Korea. Johnson was involved in many of the major deliberations on the war and in late fall 1950 contributed to discussions as to whether the victorious United Nations (UN) forces should be content with restoring the antebellum status quo or cross the 38th parallel into North Korean territory and attempt to reunify the country. Johnson supported the latter, more aggressive strategy. Unlike other U.S. officials, such as Rusk, John M. Allison—then Johnson's immediate superior—and John Paton Davies, Johnson was one of several State Department officials, among them Livingston T. Merchant and O. Edmund Clubb, who argued unsuccessfully that Chinese threats to enter the conflict should UN forces cross the boundary were genuine, and thus only Republic of Korea Army (ROKA, South Korean) troops should be used beyond that point.

In early 1951 Johnson supported President Harry S. Truman's recall of General Douglas MacArthur as commander in chief of the UN forces and argued against the recalcitrant general's resumption of his previous position heading the Japanese occupation government on the grounds that his dismissal had compromised his prestige and credibility too severely for this to be desirable. Johnson drafted much of Secretary of State Dean Acheson's testimony for the subsequent senate hearings on MacArthur's dismissal. In 1952 Johnson, now deputy assistant secretary of state for Far Eastern Affairs, tried with little success to solve the deadlock at the P'anmunjŏm truce talks over the contentious issue of the repatriation of prisoners of war (POWs) captured by the UN forces. He visited several POW camps in Korea and reported that these were violent, dangerous, and in practice had become largely independent of UN control. Johnson agreed with Matthew B. Ridgway, the new Commander of UN forces, that prisoners unwilling to return to their own countries should not be forcibly repatriated. His reports of these findings led Truman seriously to contemplate implementing his own earlier proposal for the unilateral release of UN POWs.

Appointed ambassador to Czechoslovakia in 1953, Johnson coordinated U.S. arrangements for the 1954 Geneva summit conference, ensuring compliance with Secretary of State John Foster Dulles's demands that the U.S. delegation not be seated next to any Communist representatives. At the 1955 Geneva summit conference Johnson held talks with Chinese Communist officials. Subsequently, Johnson served as ambassador to Thailand and Japan, U.S. representative to the Southeast Asia Treaty Organization, deputy undersecretary of state under Presidents John F. Kennedy and Lyndon B. Johnson, undersecretary of state under President Richard M. Nixon, and, in the mid-1960s, deputy ambassador to the Republic of Vietnam. In 1973 he was named an ambassador-at-large, and until 1977 he served as chief U.S. delegate at the Strategic Arms Limitation Talks. Even after his retirement, Johnson remained a State Department consultant. He died in Raleigh, North Carolina, on 24 March 1997.

—*Priscilla Roberts*

References:

Foot, Rosemary J. *A Substitute for Victory: The Politics of Peacemaking at the Korean Armistice Talks.* Ithaca, NY: Cornell University Press, 1990.

———. *The Wrong War: American Policy and the Dimensions of the Korean Conflict, 1950–1953.* Ithaca, NY: Cornell University Press, 1985.

Johnson, U. Alexis, with J. Olivarius McAllister. *The Right Hand of Power.* Englewood Cliffs, NJ: Prentice-Hall, 1984.

Matray, James I. *The Reluctant Crusade: American Foreign Policy in Korea, 1941–1950.* Honolulu: University of Hawaii Press, 1985.

Stueck, William W., Jr. *The Road to Confrontation: American Policy toward China and Korea, 1947–1950.* Chapel Hill: University of North Carolina Press, 1981.

See also: Acheson, Dean Goodersham; Allison, John M.; Clubb, Oliver Edmund; Dulles, John Foster; Hodge, John R.; MacArthur, Douglas; Merchant, Livingston; P'anmunjŏm

Truce Talks; Prisoner-of-War Administration, United Nations Command; Ridgway, Matthew Bunker; Rusk, David Dean; Syngman Rhee; Truman, Harry S.; Truman's Recall of MacArthur.

Joint Chiefs of Staff (JCS)

Organization embracing the heads of the U.S. armed services. Formalized by the 1947 National Security Act, the Joint Chiefs of Staff (JCS) originally consisted of only the chiefs of staff of both the U.S. Army and Navy and the chief of naval operations. The 1949 National Security Act created the position of chairman, with the individual being selected from one of the armed services to preside over JCS deliberations. The commandant of the Marine Corps was not a member of the JCS, but in 1952 was permitted to sit in on JCS deliberations in matters involving the Marine Corps.

On the outbreak of the Korean War, Army General Omar N. Bradley was the chairman of the JCS. The first to hold that post, he served a four-year term as chairman until August 1953, when he also retired from the army. Both Army Chief of Staff General J. Lawton Collins and Air Force Chief of Staff General Hoyt S. Vandenberg served all but the last month of the war. Chief of Naval Operations Admiral Forrest P. Sherman died in office in August 1951; Admiral William M. Fechteler replaced him. Marine Corps General Clifton B. Cates completed his four-year tour as commandant in December 1951; General Lemuel C. Shepherd, Jr. followed him.

An advisory body only, the JCS had no command authority. It served as a transmitting agent for orders from the president (commander in chief of the armed forces) and the secretary of defense to commanders in the field, during the Korean War the commander in

The Joint Chiefs of Staff (L to R): Chief of Naval operations Admiral Forrest P. Sherman, Chairman of the Joint Chiefs of Staff General Omar N. Bradley, Air Force Chief of Staff General Hoyt S. Vanderberg, and Army Chief of Staff J. Lawton Collins, 29 November 1949. (National Archives)

chief, Far East Command, in Tokyo. It also developed recommendations to present to the president through the secretary of defense regarding defense policies. The JCS had little influence on the conduct of the war and often saw General Douglas MacArthur flout its directives; however, President Harry Truman took the precaution of getting JCS concurrence before he relieved MacArthur of his command.

—*Spencer C. Tucker*

References:

Korb, Lawrence J. *The Joint Chiefs of Staff: The First Twenty-Five Years.* Bloomington: Indiana University Press, 1976.

Schnabel, James F., and Robert J. Watson. *The History of the Joint Chiefs of Staff: The Joint Chiefs of Staff and National Policy.* Vol. 3, *The Korean War.* Wilmington, DE: Michael Glazier, 1979.

Summers, Harry G., Jr. *Korean War Almanac.* New York: Facts on File, 1990.

See also: Bradley, Omar Nelson; Cates, Clifton B.; Collins, Joseph Lawton; Fechteler, William; MacArthur, Douglas; Sherman, Forrest P.; Truman, Harry S.; Vandenberg, Hoyt S.

Jooste, Gerhardus Petrus
(1904–1990)

South African ambassador to the United States, 1950–1954 and permanent representative to the United Nations (UN), 1949–1954. Gerhardus P. Jooste was born on a sheep farm at Winburg, South Africa, on 5 May 1904. He was educated at Grey College at Bloemfontein before majoring in political science at the University of Pretoria in the Transvaal. After five years in the civil service, in 1929 he became private secretary to Nicolaas Christiaan Havenga, South Africa's finance minister and a leading National Party figure. Jooste accompanied Havenga to several major international imperial and economic conferences and League of Nations meetings. Jooste was regarded as an able representative of the interests, views, and outlook of the Afrikaaners; he defended apartheid and advocated South Africa's complete separation from Great Britain.

In 1934 Jooste earned a master's degree in political science from the University of Pretoria and joined the Union of South Africa's Department of External Affairs. Between 1937 and 1941 he served in Belgium, Paris, and London, before returning to Pretoria, where he successively headed the Department of External Affairs' Economic Division and, in 1946, its Political and Diplomatic Division.

In 1948 a National-Afrikaaner coalition government headed by Daniel F. Malan took power in South Africa, with Jooste's former patron Havenga once again finance minister. Jooste quickly took on the responsibility of defending South Africa's racial policies and its claims to a trusteeship over the former German colony of South-West Africa in the UN, initially as an alternate delegate in late 1948, the next

year as a full-time delegate. In 1949 he was concurrently appointed ambassador to the United States, a tribute to his forceful and vigorous personality; this position was perceived as demanding a diplomat of the highest ability and an astute defender of South African policies on apartheid. In November the same year, Jooste dramatically walked out of the fifty-nine–member Trusteeship Committee and refused to return for the remainder of the session after that body had permitted the hearing of testimony on internal conditions in South-West Africa.

South Africa's determination to continue to administer South-West Africa without UN constraint and its hope to obtain U.S. acquiescence in this and in its increasingly harsh apartheid policies was largely responsible for its attitude toward the Korean War. Initially Jooste stated in the UN that South Africa's government had "never regarded the Far East as falling within its sphere of military responsibility in preserving peace." Yet, hoping to win U.S. endorsement of South Africa's control of South-West Africa, which in December 1950 would become the subject of a five-nation investigative committee, in July 1950 South Africa responded to U.S. demands for Allied support and contributed a fighter squadron and ground troops to UN forces in Korea.

Jooste attended and was one of the more active and influential contributors at the Korean War briefing meetings. These somewhat sporadic Washington gatherings of representatives from the principal countries contributing to the UN forces in Korea were intended to promote Allied unity and ensure that all the nations involved were fully informed on the course of the fighting and of negotiations. After the late 1950 military intervention by the People's Republic of China (Communist China), South Africa's reluctance to assume the burdens of a lengthy conflict led Jooste consistently to advocate relatively conciliatory policies likely to facilitate an early cease-fire.

In 1954 Jooste became his country's high commissioner in London, returning to South Africa in 1956 to spend the next ten years as secretary for external affairs. After 1968 he retained his influence, serving as special adviser to the prime minister and also as chairman of the state procurement board (1968–1971). In retirement he lived in Pretoria, the focus of his entire working life, where he died in June 1990.

—*Priscilla Roberts*

References:

Barber, James P., and John Barratt. *South Africa's Foreign Policy: The Search for Status and Security, 1945–1988.* New York: Cambridge University Press, 1990.

Borstelmann, Thomas. *Apartheid's Reluctant Uncle: The United States and Southern Africa in the Early Cold War.* New York: Oxford University Press, 1993.

"Jooste, Gerhardus Petrus." *Current Biography, 1951*. New York: H. W. Wilson, 1952.

Stueck, William W., Jr. *The Korean War: An International History*. Princeton, NJ: Princeton University Press, 1995.

See also: South Africa, Union of.

Joy, Charles Turner
(1895–1956)

U.S. Navy admiral, senior United Nations (UN) delegate to the Korean Armistice Conference at Kaesŏng and later P'anmunjŏm (July 1951–May 1952), and commander U.S. Naval Forces, Far East (COMNAVFE) (1949–1952). Born on 17 February 1895 in St. Louis, Missouri, C. Turner Joy attended private schools in Missouri, New York, and Pennsylvania before accepting an appointment to the U.S. Naval Academy, Annapolis, in 1912.

After graduation and commissioning as an officer in the U.S. Navy in 1916, Joy served on the battleship *Pennsylvania*, flagship of the Atlantic Fleet. After World War I he was chosen for postgraduate education in ordnance engineering and in 1923 earned a master of science degree from the University of Michigan. For the next nineteen years Joy served in the navy's Yangtze Patrol in China, with commander destroyers, battle force, and on board the destroyer *Pope* and battleship *California*. In May 1933 he took command of the destroyer *Litchfield*. Shore duty included ordnance and gunnery-related billets in the Bureau of Ordnance in Washington, D.C., the Naval Mine Depot at Yorktown, Virginia, and the U.S. Naval Academy.

During the first two years of World War II in the Pacific, while serving as a staff officer on board the cruiser *Indianapolis* and then carrier *Lexington*, Joy helped plan successful naval operations against Japanese forces in the Solomon and Aleutian Islands. He capped that tour with command of cruiser *Louisville*. After heading the Pacific Plans Division in

Admiral C. Turner Joy, commander of U.S. Naval Forces, Far East, and chief UNC delegate to the Korean Armistice Conference, seen in his quarters at the UNC base camp at Musan-ni. (National Archives)

the navy's Washington headquarters from August 1943 to May 1944, now Rear Admiral Joy rejoined the U.S. Pacific Fleet. Cruiser and amphibious commands under his leadership performed with skill and valor in the Marianas, Philippines, Iwo Jima, and Okinawa campaigns.

During the immediate postwar period, Joy led U.S. naval forces operating on the Yangtze River and along China's coast. He also oversaw the politically sensitive task of transporting troops of Nationalist Chinese leader Jiang Jieshi (Chiang Kai-shek) from south to north China and Manchuria, then invested by Communist forces under Mao Zedong (Mao Tsetung). Joy then had a three-year tour as commander of the Naval Proving Ground in Dahlgren, Virginia.

In August 1949 Joy was promoted to vice admiral and selected as COMNAVFE. From his headquarters in Tokyo, Vice Admiral Joy organized and directed U.S. and allied naval forces that fought desperately to stop and then turn back the Korean People's Army (KPA, North Korean) offensive that swept south into the Republic of Korea (South Korea) during the summer of 1950. Surface and air units under his command bombed and shelled advancing KPA troops, road and railway bridges, and supply depots. His combat fleet quickly established its presence in the Yellow Sea and the East Sea (Sea of Japan) to discourage Soviet and Chinese military action and to protect the seagoing reinforcement and resupply of UN forces holding the vital port of Pusan.

Naval Forces, Far East carriers, cruisers, destroyers, and amphibious ships, along with allied warships, carried out the bold amphibious assault at Inch'ŏn, which deployed strong U.S. and South Korean ground units ashore in the rear of the KPA. Then Joy's naval forces successfully evacuated Marine, army, and South Korean troops, refugees, and equipment from the port of Hŭngnam in December 1950, when Chinese armies swept down from the hills of North Korea and threatened to destroy the UN command. Allied naval units under Joy helped stop the spring 1951 Communist offensive.

Joy's obvious leadership qualities, ability to function well under pressure, and understanding of U.S. goals in the Far East, led to his selection in June 1951 as the senior UN delegate to the newly convened Korean Armistice Conference. Many observers noted that during the cease-fire negotiations with his Chinese and North Korean opposites, who seemed unconcerned with the lack of progress, Joy usually exuded self-confidence, firmness, and patience. On a few occasions, however, the admiral publicly criticized the rigid negotiating posture and uncooperative manner of the Communist side. The Chinese and North Korean delegates, however, only carried out the dictates of the political leaders in Moscow, Beijing, and P'yŏngyang, who were not inclined to compromise on key issues. Joy also bemoaned the periodic changes in the UN's basic policy positions. Exasperated by the lack of progress in the negotiations, he asked to be replaced.

In May 1952, Joy was called home and named superintendent of the U.S. Naval Academy. Even though diagnosed with leukemia soon afterward, Joy did not retired from active service until July 1954, at the end of his tour. The following year, Macmillan published his *How Communists Negotiate*, which detailed the exasperations of the P'anmunjŏm negotiations. Vice Admiral Joy died of cancer at the Naval Hospital in San Diego, California, on 6 June 1956.

—*Edward J. Marolda*

References:

Field, James A., Jr. *History of United States Naval Operations: Korea.* Washington, DC: U.S. Government Printing Office, 1962.

Goodman, Allan E., ed. *Negotiating While Fighting: The Diary of Admiral C. Turner Joy at the Korean Armistice Conference.* Stanford, CA: Stanford University Press, 1978.

Joy, C. Turner. *How Communists Negotiate.* New York: Macmillan, 1955.

U.S. Navy Biographical Files, Operational Archives, Naval Historical Center, Washington, D.C.

See also: Hŭngnam Evacuation; Inch'ŏn Landings: Operation CHROMITE; Jiang Jieshi (Chiang Kai-shek); Mao Zedong.

K

K1C2 (Korea, Communism, Corruption)

Political slogan for the Republican Party in the United States during the 1952 election campaign. In the presidential campaign, the Republican Party hammered away at perceived mistakes by the Truman administration during the previous four years. The Republicans were quick to point out the three areas that most directly affected U.S. citizens: Korea, communism, and corruption. As the 1952 campaign continued, the Republicans abbreviated their attack on the Democratic Party to "K1C2."

The "K" in K1C2 stood for Korea. The Republicans emphasized the lack of success of the Truman administration in winning the Korean War. The war was supposed to be over quickly, but it had become mired in stalemate after the People's Republic of China (PRC) entry, and it remained so in 1952. Furthermore, in April 1951 President Harry S. Truman had relieved national icon General Douglas MacArthur from command in Korea. The Republican Party tried to convince the American people that the Democratic Party was unwilling to fight to win the war in Korea. Republican presidential hopeful Dwight Eisenhower pledged that, if elected, he would personally go to Korea. This implied that he would bring about a favorable outcome to the war.

The first "C" in K1C2 stood for communism. Republicans emphasized not only the battle against Communist forces in Korea but the expansion of Communist power throughout the world. Republican campaigners blamed Democrats for the 1949 "loss of China." That same year also the Russians had exploded an atomic bomb. Republicans used these two events to convince Americans that the Communist world was gaining on the United States and the Free World.

The second "C" in K1C2 stood for corruption. While the Democratic administration was dealing with problems in foreign affairs, Republicans sought to capitalize on domestic problems. They charged that the Democrats in Washington were corrupt. Democratic Party presidential hopeful Adlai E. Stevenson helped the Republican cause when he pledge to "clean up the mess in Washington." Republican vice-presidential candidate Richard M. Nixon also charged mismanagement of government agencies under the Democrats, citing the Alger Hiss case as an example.

Overall, K1C2 benefited the Republican Party in its bid for the presidency in 1952. Although Eisenhower's reputation as a war hero and problem solver certainly helped him win the election, the K1C2 program further convinced many Americans that the Democrats were weak on Korea, communism, and corruption.

—David R. Buck

References:

Divine, Robert. *Foreign Policy and U.S. Presidential Elections.* Vol. 2. New York: New Viewpoints, 1974.

McCullough, David. *Truman.* New York: Simon & Schuster, 1992.

Reichard, Gary W. *Politics As Usual: The Age of Truman and Eisenhower.* Arlington Heights, IL: Harlan Davidson, 1988.

See also: Eisenhower, Dwight D.; MacArthur, Douglas; Nixon, Richard Milhous; Stevenson, Adlai E.; Truman, Harry S.; Truman's Recall of MacArthur.

Kaesŏng

South Korean city and capital of the old Koryŏ Kingdom (918–1392), known as Songak or Kaegyŏng at that time. Kaesŏng lies just south of the 38th parallel and 35 miles northwest of Seoul. When the North Koreans invaded the South on 25 June 1950, within a few hours they seized this key town, on the main railroad line leading to Seoul.

From June 1951, both the United Nations (UN) side and the Communist side sought to end the fighting in Korea through a political settlement or an armistice. But these negotiations proved difficult from the beginning, and there was an immediate dispute over the neutrality of the conference site. The Communists suggested Kaesŏng, which lay actually within territory they controlled. Washington accepted this as demonstration of sincerity to expedite a settlement.

As a negotiating site, Kaesŏng possessed considerable propaganda value for the Communist side. Moving their troops to surround the city before discussions began on 10 July, the Communists used their control of access to portray the UN as a defeated enemy suing for peace. After the suspension of truce talks on 23 August, the UN side insisted on a new site for the armistice negotiations. Finally, with the resumption of truce talks on 25 October, P'anmunjŏm, where neutrality could be better guaranteed, became the new site of the talks.

Presently, because of its strategic location, Kaesŏng is an important city in the Democratic People's Republic of Korea (DPRK, North Korea). It is a city under the direct control of the central DPRK government, along with Ch'ŏngjin.

—Jinwung Kim

References:

Blair, Clay. *The Forgotten War: America in Korea, 1950–1953.* New York: Times Books, 1987.

MacDonald, Callum. *Korea: The War Before Vietnam*. New York: Free Press, 1986.

Matray, James I., ed. *Historical Dictionary of the Korean War*. Westport, CT: Greenwood Press, 1991.

Stueck, William W., Jr. *The Korean War: An International History*. Princeton, NJ: Princeton University Press, 1995.

See also: Kaesŏng Truce Talks; Kansas-Wyoming Line.

Kaesŏng Bombing Proposal

Kaesŏng, original site of the Korean truce talks, was also a transportation hub and depot area. When the talks moved to P'anmunjŏm in October 1951, the Korean People's Army/Chinese People's Volunteer Army (KPA [North Korean]/CPVA [Chinese Communist]) delegation continued to use Kaesŏng as their support base. Kaesŏng, the United Nations Command (UNC) support base at Munsan, the P'anmunjŏm negotiation site, and the roads from Kaesŏng and Munsan to P'anmunjŏm were designated as neutral zones under the 22 October 1951 P'anmunjŏm Security Agreement. By a separate agreement of 24 November 1951, the UNC gave safe conduct to two daily KPA/CPVA convoys between P'yŏngyang and Kaesŏng.

On 3 January 1953, UNC Commander in Chief Lieutenant General Mark W. Clark notified the U.S. Joint Chiefs of Staff (JCS) that he had reliable intelligence that the Chinese and North Koreans were taking advantage of the security agreements, including the convoy safe conduct, to stockpile supplies at Kaesŏng. The truce talks were then in indefinite recess, stalled over the prisoner-of-war repatriation issue. Clark saw no need for daily convoys to support the KPA/CPV delegation and submitted a plan to terminate the convoy immunity until the talks resumed. To reduce KPA/CPVA propaganda exploitation of the move, the JCS recommended that Clark limit the convoys to one a week rather than end the safe conduct entirely. Accordingly, the UNC informed the KPA/CPVA on 23 January 1953 that they would henceforth be permitted to send only one weekly convoy each way so long as the truce talks were in recess.

On 7 February 1953, Clark informed the JCS that he had reason to believe that the KPA/CPV had transformed the 28–square mile Kaesŏng neutral zone into a major advanced military base and espionage center. He therefore requested authority to abrogate the security agreements and bomb Kaesŏng if a Communist attack appeared imminent. On 9 February, Clark told the JCS that an offensive from Kaesŏng was likely to be supported by large-scale air attacks from Manchurian bases and asked for advance approval to strike those bases if the scale of KPA/CPV air operations threatened UNC security.

The National Security Council (NSC) debated these proposals on 11 February. The members of the NSC agreed that the "Kaesŏng sanctuary" should be ended, but concurred with U.S. Secretary of State John Foster Dulles that previous support of the UN allies was essential. President Dwight D. Eisenhower noted that Kaesŏng provided a good target for tactical atomic weapons, but questioned the validity of Clark's information about an imminent KPA/CPV offensive and opposed giving Clark advance approval to attack Manchurian bases.

In an interim response on 13 February, the JCS advised Clark that a division-sized or larger attack from Kaesŏng would constitute KPA/CPV abrogation of the security agreement and under those circumstances Clark could attack Kaesŏng. Absent such an attack, Clark could not unilaterally abrogate the agreement but he could announce a future date after which the UNC would no longer consider Kaesŏng and Munsan immune from attack. The JCS argued that this would give Clark the ability to deal with the military threat while reducing any negative political impact. On 18 February, Clark submitted a letter along those lines for JCS approval, but he postponed taking action because of indications that the truce talks might resume. No KPA/CPVA offensive from Kaesŏng ever materialized.

The issue arose once more in May 1953 when Clark outlined to the JCS a plan for increased military pressure, including an attack on Kaesŏng, if the truce talks stalled again. Subsequent progress in the negotiations forestalled any requirement to implement the plan.

—*Donald W. Boose, Jr.*

References:

Hermes, Walter G. *United States Army in the Korean War: Truce Tent and Fighting Front*. Washington, DC: Office of the Chief of Military History, 1966.

Schnabel, James F., and Robert J. Watson. *The History of the Joint Chiefs of Staff: The Joint Chiefs of Staff and National Policy*. Vol. 3, *1951–1953, The Korean War, Part 2*. Washington, DC: Office of Joint History, Office of the Chairman of the Joint Chiefs of Staff, 1998.

U.S. Department of State, Bureau of Public Affairs. *Foreign Relations of the United States, 1952–1954*. Vol. 15, *Korea. Part 1*. Washington, DC: U.S. Government Printing Office, 1984.

See also: Clark, Mark W.; Dulles, John Foster; Eisenhower, Dwight D.; Kaesŏng; P'anmunjŏm Security Agreement; P'anmunjŏm Truce Talks; Truce Talks.

Kaesŏng Neutral Zone Controversy

Controversy over the site of early negotiations between the United Nations Command (UNC) and the Korean Peoples Army (KPA, North Korea) and Chinese People's Volunteer Army (CPVA, Chinese Communists). A broadcast by UNC commander Lieutenant General Matthew B. Ridgway offering to discuss an armistice initiated the talks. Ridgway suggested negotiating aboard a Danish Hospital Ship in

Wŏnsan harbor. The Chinese suggested talks at Kaesŏng on the 38th parallel. Kaesŏng was the location of the ancient capital of Korea and only 35 miles northwest of Seoul, but it was in Communist-controlled territory. Washington accepted the proposed site over Ridgway's strenuous objections.

Although the Communists designated Kaesŏng a neutral zone, in reality armed Communist troops surrounded the area, and from the beginning the Communists used the location of the talks to their advantage. At the preliminary meeting on 8 July when liaison officers arrived by helicopter, heavily armed guards surrounded them. Negotiations that day resulted in agreement that the UNC convoy would display white flags and drive up the road to ensure that there would be no fighting. On 10 July when the UNC delegates arrived, Communist newsmen photographed the convoy and used the white flags to insinuate that the UN side was surrendering. Ridgway noted in his memoirs that when the talks began there was "no atmosphere of neutrality at all." Kaesŏng was controlled by the Communists and their armed guards were posted everywhere. "Red soldiers with Tommy guns gruffly ordered our envoys about."

UNC chief negotiator Vice Admiral C. Turner Joy protested these arrangements and having to pass through Communist checkpoints to reach the conference site. The UN delegation refused to return to the negotiating table until the Communist side removed the armed soldiers from the site and allowed UN press members access to the talks. He also demanded that UNC convoys have free access to the site from Seoul during daylight hours.

Negotiations resumed after the Communists removed the armed soldiers and allowed the UN press inside on 15 July at a third session. Admiral Joy, however, insisted on a circular 5-mile security zone around Kaesŏng and a ban on armed troops within a half mile of the negotiating site.

Despite Communist agreement on these conditions, violations continued. On 4 August, the Chinese allowed a company of armed soldiers to march past the UNC delegation site in the negotiating area. Again Ridgway called off the talks in protest. On 8 August, the Communist side accused the UN of ambushing a KPA patrol near the neutral zone. The leader of the patrol was killed and several wounded, causing the Koreans to demand an apology. However, guerrillas had carried out the ambush and the UNC refused to apologize for an incident over which it had no control. On the same day, the Communists also charged the UNC with having bombed a truck inside the truce area. The UNC investigating officer found what he believed to be a faked bombing site. The UNC also denied any responsibility.

On 10 August, the talks resumed only to stop again upon a Communist claim that UNC aircraft had bombed within the Kaesŏng neutral zone. This time the UNC delegation refused to return to the site and insisted on holding negotiations in P'anmunjŏm, a truly neutral site between the front lines and subject to joint policing. Washington endorsed this stand. The talks did not resume, at P'anmunjŏm, until 25 October 1951.

—*William Robert O'Neal, Jr.*

References:

Alexander, Bevin. *Korea: The First War We Lost.* New York: Hippocrene Books, 1986.

Blair, Clay. *The Forgotten War: America in Korea, 1950–1953.* New York: Times Books, 1987.

Matray, James I., ed. *Historical Dictionary of the Korean War.* Westport, CT: Greenwood Press, 1991.

Ridgway, Matthew B. *The Korean War.* Garden City, NY: Doubleday, 1967.

See also: Joy, Charles Turner; Kaesŏng Truce Talks; P'anmunjŏm Truce Talks; Ridgway, Matthew Bunker.

Kaesŏng Truce Talks
(10 July–24 October 1951)

The first phase of the Korean War truce talks, including a long recess from 23 August to 24 October 1951, took place at Kaesŏng, about 35 miles north of the South Korean capital of Seoul. Commander in Chief of United Nations Command Lieutenant General Matthew B. Ridgway had proposed that the talks take place aboard a Danish hospital ship anchored in Wŏnsan harbor. Kim Il Sung, supreme commander of the Korean People's Army (KPA, North Korea), and Peng Dehuai, commander of the Chinese People's Volunteer Army (CPVA, Chinese Communists), counterproposed Kaesŏng as the conference site and the United Nations Command (UNC) accepted. After a preliminary meeting by liaison officers on 8 July 1951, talks began there on 10 July.

The chief KPA/CPVA negotiator was Lieutenant General Nam Il, KPA chief of staff and vice foreign minister of the Democratic People's Republic of Korea (DPRK, North Korea). He was assisted by Major General Yi Sang-jo, chief of the KPA Reconnaissance Bureau, and Major General Chang P'yŏng-san, chief of staff of the KPA 1 Corps. The Chinese delegation consisted of CPVA Deputy Commander Lieutenant General Deng Hua and CPV Chief of Staff Major General Xie Fang. UNC chief negotiator, Vice Admiral C. Turner Joy, commander of U.S. Naval Forces Far East, was assisted by Major General Henry I. Hodes, chief of staff of Eighth U.S. Army; Major General Laurence C. Craigie, vice commander of Far East Air Forces; Rear Admiral Arleigh A. Burke, Joy's deputy chief of staff; and Major General Paek Sŏn-yŏp, commanding general of the

United Nations Command delegates to the armistice negotiations, Kaesong, 13 August 1951. Admiral C. Turner Joy is in the center with General Paik Sŏn-yŏp of the South Korean Army on his left. (Imperial War Museum)

Republic of Korea (ROK, South Korean) Army I Corps. Both the UNC and the KPA/CPVA teams stayed the same throughout the Kaesŏng talks.

During the first meeting, the two sides established their initial positions. The UNC insisted that the talks be limited to Korea-related military matters, requested arrangements for International Red Cross visits to prisoner-of-war (POW) camps, and proposed a joint armistice supervisory mechanism with authority to conduct inspections. The KPA/CPVA side called for an immediate cease-fire, a 20-kilometer-wide demilitarized zone (DMZ) along the 38th parallel, and withdrawal of foreign troops from Korea.

The two sides then exchanged proposed agendas, but before they could begin substantive discussions they had to deal with UNC concerns about access and security at the conference site. Kaesŏng had been unoccupied at the time of the initial overtures but, before the talks started, Chinese forces moved into the town. During the first meeting, the KPA/CPVA took advantage of their control of the conference setting to portray themselves as hosts and the UNC as defeated supplicants. They also refused access to Kaesŏng by journalists accompanying the UNC delegation, causing the UNC to halt the plenary talks until the KPA/CPVA agreed to the establishment of a Kaesŏng neutral zone to which both sides would have free access.

The negotiators then turned to the agenda. The two most intractable issues were KPA/CPVA insistence on a 38th parallel truce line and on the withdrawal of foreign troops from Korea. These reflected fundamental differences in objectives that would eventually take months of negotiation to resolve, but by 26 July the two sides found ways to sidestep these issues and agree to a five-point agenda: (1) adoption of the agenda; (2) fixing a military demarcation line between both sides to establish a demilitarized zone as a basic condition for a cessation of hostilities in Korea; (3) concrete arrangements for the realization of a cease-fire

Delegates from the Korean People's Army and the Chinese People's Volunteer at the preliminary meeting of the Kaesong armistice talks, 8 July 1951. (Imperial War Museum)

and armistice in Korea, including the composition, authority, and functioning of a supervising organization for carrying out the terms of a cease-fire and armistice; (4) arrangements relating to POWs; and (5) recommendations to the governments of the countries concerned on both sides.

Having agreed on the agenda, the negotiators immediately began discussion of item 2, the location and nature of the military demarcation line (MDL) and DMZ. The KPA/CPVA side insisted on an MDL along the 38th parallel. The UNC argued that the MDL location should reflect its air and naval superiority and, having already crossed the 38th parallel, proposed an MDL considerably north of the line of ground contact. After two weeks of fruitless debate, Admiral Joy proposed on 15 August that a subcommittee be formed to discuss item 2 in a less formal atmosphere. These "subdelegation" meetings of two negotiators plus assistants from each side became a regular and often helpful feature of the talks and would eventually be applied to all of the agenda items. By 22 August, differences had narrowed. The UNC had acknowledged

that the ground line of contact might represent the sum of all air, naval, and ground combat power, and the KPA/CPVA had softened its insistence on using the 38th parallel as the truce line.

On 23 August, with agreement on item 2 in sight, the KPA/CPVA side unilaterally called an indefinite recess, ostensibly to protest alleged UNC air attacks against the conference site, but probably to provide time to reassess their strategy. The UNC, which had been dissatisfied with the Kaesŏng conference site from the beginning, took this opportunity to seek a change of venue for the talks. When the KPA/CPVA indicated a willingness to resume negotiations, the UNC proposed moving the conference site to P'anmunjŏm, six miles to the east. Several weeks of staff officer negotiations ensued.

Meanwhile, military activity continued. KPA/CPVA forces generally remained on the defensive during the Kaesŏng talks, but UNC air and naval forces continued attacks against KPA/CPVA lines of communication and installations. These included a major air attack against the DPRK capital of P'yŏngyang on 30 July 1951 and

Jeep drivers wait outside the Kaesŏng teahouse as negotiations get underway, 10 July 1951. (National Archives)

another on 25 August against the port of Najin (Rashin) near the Soviet border. UNC ground forces also conducted substantial limited objective attacks all along the front from 18 August to 23 October, pushing the line of contact north by about 10 miles.

On 22 October, the staff officer discussions came to a successful close when the two sides agreed to resume the talks on 25 October. The truce negotiations now entered a new phase at P'anmunjŏm.

—<i>Donald W. Boose, Jr.</i>

References:

Chen, Jian. "China's Strategies to End the Korean War." In <i>Mao's China in the Cold War: Inquiries and Reinterpretations.</i> Chapel Hill: University of North Carolina Press, in press.

Goodman, Allan E., ed. <i>Negotiating while Fighting: The Diary of Admiral C. Turner Joy at the Korean Armistice Conference.</i> Stanford, CA: Hoover Institute Press, 1978.

Hermes, Walter G. <i>United States Army in the Korean War: Truce Tent and Fighting Front.</i> Washington, DC: Office of the Chief of Military History, 1966.

U.S. Department of State, Bureau of Public Affairs. <i>Foreign Relations of the United States, 1951.</i> Vol. 7, <i>China and Korea.</i> Washington, DC: U.S. Government Printing Office, 1983.

Wilhelm, Alfred D., Jr. <i>The Chinese at the Negotiating Table: Style and Characteristics.</i> Washington, DC: National Defense University Press, 1991.

See also: Agenda Controversy; Burke, Arleigh Albert; Cease-Fire Negotiations; Joy, Charles Turner; Kaesŏng; Kaesŏng Neutral Zone Controversy; Li Kenong (Li K'e-nung); Nam Il; Paek Sŏn-yŏp; P'anmunjŏm Security Agreement; P'anmunjŏm Truce Talks; Ridgway, Matthew Bunker; Truce Talks; Xie Fang (Hsieh Fang).

Kang Kŏn
(1918–1950)

Korean People's Army (KPA, North Korean) general. Kang Kŏn, whose original name was Kang Sin-t'ae, was born into a poor peasant family in Sanju, North Kyŏngsang Province, South Korea, in 1918. Together with Kim Il Sung, he joined the anti-Japanese struggle in Manchuria in 1932. Kang joined at only fourteen and participated in battles from the age of fifteen. When Japanese oppression intensified in the early 1940s, Kang fled with Kim Il Sung to the Soviet territories. Just before the end of the war, Kang was serving as an officer of the Independent 88th Brigade, a unit of Chinese and Koreans attached to the Red Army's Far Eastern Front.

After the end of the Second World War, Kang stayed in Manchuria. He returned to North Korea in the summer of 1946 to help establish the KPA and played a key role in it. In September 1949, Kang became chief of the General Staff of the KPA. As such, he played an important role in preparing for the Korean War and in the initial stage of the conflict. Only thirty-two when the war broke out, he could already draw on eighteen years of military experience. Indeed most of the high-ranking KPA officers of the time were young like Kang Kŏn and shared the military experience of the anti-Japanese struggle.

Kang Kŏn was killed in action by a land mine on 8 September 1950, just before the Inch'ŏn landing. At the time, he was chief of the General Staff of the KPA. Lieutenant General Nam Il succeeded him as chief of the General Staff and Kim Ch'aek became KPA frontline commander. The Democratic People's Republic of Korea (DPRK) government honored Kang Kŏn with a statue, park, and the Kang Kŏn Military Officers' Academy. He was buried at the Mount Taesŏng National Cemetery for the Revolutionary Heroes in P'yŏngyang, which is reserved for those who played critical roles in the anti-Japanese struggle and the establishment of the DPRK.

—Jinwung Kim

References:

Chungang Ilbo, ed. *Pukhan Inmyŏng Sajŏn.* Seoul: Chungang Ilbo-sa, 1981.

Scalapino, Robert A., and Lee Chong-Sik. *Communism in Korea.* 2 vols. Berkeley: University of California Press, 1973.

See also: Kim Ch'aek; Kim Il Sung; Nam Il.

Kansas-Wyoming Line

After the United Nations (UN) forces pushed Chinese People's Volunteer Army (CPVA, Chinese Communist) and Korean People's Army (KPA, North Korean) forces back to the 38th parallel in late March 1951, Eighth U.S. Army commander Lieutenant General Matthew B. Ridgway determined that his forces should adopt the objective of seizing and fortifying positions along terrain features that favored the defense and offered better security.

The first such objective was to be named Line Kansas. On high ground north of the 38th parallel, it began at the junction of the Han and Imjin rivers and ran northeastward and eastward 115 miles to Yang-yang. The new line would include 14 miles of tidal water on the left flank and the 10-mile water barrier of the Hwach'ŏn Dam Reservoir in the center.

Once Line Kansas was achieved, Ridgway intended to drive another 20 miles further north, into North Korea, and establish a similar belt named Line Wyoming. From these positions he intended to maintain contact with Communist forces through heavily armed patrols. If the Communist side should counterattack, as Ridgway expected, then Eighth Army was to resist along Line Wyoming and, while causing heavy casualties, fall back if and when necessary to the better fortified Line Kansas.

In the face of a Communist buildup that spring, on 5 April Ridgway opened Operation RUGGED, a general advance toward Line Kansas. By 9 April the U.S. I and IX Corps and the Republic of Korea Army (ROKA, South Korean) I Corps on the east coast had reached the new line. The U.S. X and ROKA III Corps in the center and central-east sectors were also drawing up to the line, although hampered by terrain and a lack of supply routes. The I and IX Corps continued to advance thereafter, attacking Ch'ŏrwŏn with the intention of seizing a line designated Utah, an outward bulge of Line Kansas, to be in a position to strike at the Communist-held Iron Triangle.

By early April, all U.S. and ROKA units were at or near their assigned positions. As UN forces were edging toward Line Wyoming, on 12 April Ridgway replaced General Douglas MacArthur as commander in chief United Nations Command, and Lieutenant General James A. Van Fleet took command of Eighth Army.

Meanwhile, UN forces continued to edge forward. The Hwach'ŏn Dam was taken on 16 April. On the east coast, South Korean forces captured Taep'o-ri. Other ROKA units north of Seoul sent patrols across the Imjin River and to the northeast. By 17 April, UN units could no longer find their enemy, and thereafter the advance toward Line Utah was virtually unopposed. Even as the advance continued, however, evidence of Communist preparations for a counterattack were apparent.

By 19 April 1951, all U.S. I and IX Corps units were in positions along Line Utah, preparing for the next phase, the advance to Line Wyoming. But during the daylight hours of 22 April, Communist activity across the whole front sharply increased, and the UN offensive halted abruptly, short of Line Wyoming. Communist lines became alive with movement as their forces moved boldly into the attack.

Under heavy pressure, Eighth Army grudgingly withdrew to Line Kansas and ultimately to within 5 miles of Seoul, while inflicting heavy casualties on the attackers. By mid-May Eighth Army launched its own counteroffensive, catching the Communists by surprise, and by mid-June it was back at the Kansas-Wyoming Line. Van Fleet's instructions were to fortify Line Kansas and to continue reconnaissance in force and limited attacks to keep the Communist side off balance.

At this point several factors influenced development of the defensive lines. First, Ridgway knew that he could expect no reinforcements from either U.S. or UN sources. Second, U.S. military leaders were aware that an armistice might materialize if the advance into North Korea was modest; however, if the advance was too deep, it would likely prevent negotiations. Third, each additional mile of territory taken would negatively alter the logistical balance, which now favored UN forces. And finally, U.S. military and political leaders were reluctant to accept the casualties that would result from further offensive actions.

Realizing that any postarmistice demarcation line would be determined by the positions of the contending armies, Ridgway and Van Fleet agreed that Line Kansas must be held because it offered excellent defensive positions. Although Ridgway had hoped to push units out some 20 miles further north to Line Wyoming, he and Van Fleet concluded that such an advance would cost too many lives. By mid-summer 1951, Eighth Army had established its positions by blending the Kansas and Wyoming lines into a new UN main line of resistance. Much bloody fighting lay ahead, but the Kansas-Wyoming Line would remain the Main Line of Resistance (MLR) with modest revisions, throughout the armistice negotiations and remaining two years of war.

—*Clayton D. Laurie*

References:

Hermes, Walter G. *United States Army in the Korean War: Truce Tent and Fighting Front*. Washington, DC: Office of the Chief of Military History, 1966.

Miller, John, Jr., Owen J. Carroll, and Margaret E. Tackley. *Korea, 1951–1953*. Washington, DC: U.S. Army Center of Military History, 1997.

Mossman, Billy C. *U.S. Army in the Korean War: Ebb and Flow, November 1950–July 1951*. Washington, DC: U.S. Army Center of Military History, 1990.

Schnabel, James F. *United States Army in the Korean War: Policy and Direction, the First Year*. Washington, DC: Office of the Chief of Military History, Department of the Army, 1972.

See also: MacArthur, Douglas; Ridgway, Matthew Bunker; Van Fleet, James Alward.

Kap'yŏng, Battle of
(24–27 April 1951)

Critical battle that took place during 24–27 April 1951, in and around the town of Kap'yŏng on the Kap'yŏng and Pukhan rivers, about 30 miles northeast of Seoul and 10 miles southwest of Ch'unch'ŏn, Korea. U.S. IX Corps units, including the 1st Marine Division, the 3d and 24th Infantry, and the 1st Cavalry Divisions, were in position along Line Kansas in the central sector. The 27th British Commonwealth Brigade was in and around Kap'yŏng. The 27th consisted of the 1st Battalion, Middlesex Regiment; 1st Battalion, Argyll and Sutherland Highlanders Regiment; and 3d Battalion, Royal Australian Regiment. It was supported by the 16th Field Regiment, Royal New Zealand Artillery. Also supporting the 27th was Company A of the 2d Division's 72d Tank Battalion. On 22 April the 28th British Commonwealth Brigade began the process of relieving the 27th British Commonwealth Brigade. The 28th included the 1st Battalion, King's Own Scottish Borderers Regiment; and the 2d Battalion, Princess Patricia Canadian Light Infantry Regiment. After the battle the 3d Battalion, Royal Australian Regiment remained with the 28th Brigade, as did the New Zealand artillery unit.

On 23 April the Chinese People's Volunteer Army (CPVA, Chinese Communists) launched its Fifth Offensive, with the main thrust concentrated in the Kap'yŏng River valley extending northward from the town of Kap'yŏng. United Nations Command (UNC) Commander Lieutenant General Matthew B. Ridgway and Eighth Army Commander Lieutenant General James A. Van Fleet considered the retention of Kap'yŏng essential, in that whoever held Kap'yŏng would control the entire central sector of the Korean front. Its loss could enable Communist forces to swing eastward and behind, and cut off, the 3d and 1st Marine Divisions and numerous Republic of Korea Army (ROKA, South Korean) units on line.

On the morning of the 24th, the CPVA offensive reached its full fury. ROKA divisions in position north of Kap'yŏng fled in panic, whereupon the New Zealanders and Middlesex battalions, on line with the ROKA divisions, were compelled to pull back to the Kap'yŏng area. As the Chinese neared Kap'yŏng, tanks of the 2d Division, and the Princess Pats and Australian battalions in the hills around the tankers found themselves in the path of the Communist drive and the only barrier to a successful penetration and split of the Eighth Army front.

By midnight on the 23rd the tankers were surrounded but, with Australian and Canadian troops in the high ground on either side, they stood firm while the tide of battle engulfed them. Fighting raged through the night and into the morning of the 24th and for three days and nights thereafter with the U.S. force cut off but still intact. During the fighting, tanks fought their way back through Communist road blocks with loads of wounded and returned along the flaming corridor to the beleaguered position, transporting rations and ammunition to the defending infantry.

The stand by the troops at Kap'yŏng enabled the flanking divisions to pull back in an orderly manner and set up new defense lines. When the positions at Kap'yŏng could be relinquished without further danger to the divisions holding the shoulders of the penetration, on 25 April the Kap'yŏng forces withdrew in a fighting rearguard action as part of a general Eighth Army retirement from Line Kansas. U.S. casualties numbered some 5,000, of whom 923 were killed in action.

An irony of the Kap'yŏng battle was that some of the fiercest fighting took place on 25 April, a day celebrated in Australia and New Zealand as Anzac Day, a national holiday commemorating the 1915 commitment of their forces in the Battle of Gallipoli in World War I. The Anzac veterans of the Kap'yŏng fighting were granted special permission as fighting died down to celebrate their "double holiday" with extra rations of beer and stronger "spirits."

—*Sherman W. Pratt*

References:

Blair, Clay. *The Forgotten War: America in Korea, 1950–1953.* New York: Times Books, 1987.

Clodfelter, Michael. *Warfare and Armed Conflicts. A Statistical Reference to Casualty and Other Figures, 1618–1991.* Vol. 2. Jefferson, NC: McFarland, 1992.

Munroe, Clark C. *The Second United States Infantry Division in Korea, 1950–1951.* Tokyo: Tappan Printing, n.d.

Pratt, Sherman W. *Decisive Battles of the Korean War. An Infantry Company Commander's View of the War's Most Critical Engagements.* New York: Vantage Press, 1992.

See also: Australia; Ridgway, Matthew Bunker; Van Fleet, James Alward.

Katzin, Alfred G.
(1906–1989)

Personal representative of the United Nations (UN) secretary-general in Korea, 1950–1953. Alfred G. Katzin was born on 1 February 1906, in Cape Town, South Africa. During 1926–1939, he engaged in various private businesses in Cape Town, and for the final three years of this period he also served as a member of the Executive Board of the South African Federation of Chambers of Industry and as vice-president of the Cape Chamber of Industries. Five years of military service with the British and South African armies, culminating in a year, 1944–1945, spent as economic adviser and chief of civilian supplies planning at the Balkan Military Headquarters won him the rank of colonel. His war service was followed by two years with the London and Washington offices of the newly created United Nations Relief and Rehabilitation Administration. Katzin spent the remainder of his career from 1948 onward attached to the UN in one capacity or another, initially as special counsel to the secretary-general and then as United Nations Children's Fund fund-raising coordinator.

On the outbreak of the Korean War, UN Secretary-General Trygve Lie appointed Katzin as his personal representative in Korea, and Katzin arrived in Korea on 6 July 1950, less than two weeks after the war began. He was expected to liaise between Lie and the UN Command, the Republic of Korea (ROK, South Korea), and all other military forces in Korea under UN auspices. Katzin's military credentials, general competence, and diplomatic skills immediately won him the respect of General Douglas MacArthur, the notoriously temperamental UN commander in chief, and also of John J. Muccio, the U.S. ambassador to the ROK.

Katzin's relations with most U.S. officials cooled, however, after the military intervention in late 1950 by the People's Republic of China (PRC, Communist China). He strongly supported granting the PRC a seat in the UN if this would persuade its government to negotiate a cease-fire, a position Katzin continued to favor throughout the war.

From 1951 to 1952, Katzin also served on the twelve-nation United Nations Collective Measures Committee, which was intended to study methods of strengthening UN power to protect international peace and security, if necessary by means of force. Heavily weighted in favor of the Allies, in February 1951 this committee evolved into the Additional Measures Committee, its purpose to decide upon further sanctions against the aggressors in Korea. In May 1951 the new committee recommended the imposition of harsh economic sanctions on the PRC and the Democratic People's Republic of Korea (North Korea). Although more conciliatory than U.S. officials would ideally have preferred, essentially Katzin supported a decidedly pro-Ally line, and his diplomatic and negotiating skills helped to push this through the complicated UN bureaucracy.

After the Korean War, Katzin remained with the UN in a variety of positions, a model of the international civil servant who ultimately rose to the rank of assistant secretary-general. In 1954 he became the organization's personnel director, and he was deputy undersecretary of the Department of Public Information during 1956–1957 and acting head of its Office of Public Information from 1958 to 1960. In 1956 he supervised the Suez Canal clearance operations, and from 1958 to 1961 he was also attached to the United Nations Special Assignments Unit. In the early 1960s, Katzin helped the UN in organizing conferences on world energy resources and science and technology.

In his later years Katzin remained a consultant to the UN. After some years in Geneva, Switzerland, he retired to Weybridge, England, where he died on 15 May 1989.

—*Priscilla Roberts*

References:

Barros, James. *Trygve Lie and the Cold War: The United Nations Secretary-General Pursues Peace, 1946–1953.* DeKalb: Northern Illinois University Press, 1989.

Lie, Trygve. *In the Cause of Peace: Seven Years with the United Nations.* New York: Macmillan, 1954.

Luard, Evan. *A History of the United Nations.* Vol. 1, *The Years of Western Domination, 1945–1955.* London: Macmillan, 1982.

Stueck, William W., Jr. *The Korean War: An International History.* Princeton, NJ: Princeton University Press, 1995.

U.S. Department of State, Bureau of Public Affairs. *Foreign Relations of the United States, 1950.* Vol. 7, *Korea.* Washington, DC: U.S. Government Printing Office, 1976.

Yoo, Tae-Ho. *The Korean War and the United Nations.* Louvain, Belgium: Librairie Desbarax, 1964.

See also: Lie, Trygve; MacArthur, Douglas; Muccio, John J.

Kean, William Benjamin
(1897–1981)

U.S. Army officer, regarded by many as the most effective division commander among those who first entered Korea. Born on 9 July 1897, in Buffalo, New York, William B. (Bill) Kean entered the U.S. Military Academy, West Point, in June 1917. His class graduated under a crash program on November 1918. In December, he and his classmates were returned to the academy as "student officers" and regraduated in June 1919.

Kean's peacetime career was routine, promising little in meaningful advancement. Although he was eventually selected to attend the Command and General Staff College, he was not chosen for the Army War College. However, in 1939 Kean was assigned to the personnel section of the U.S. Army's chief of infantry Lieutenant Colonel Omar N. Bradley. In his memoirs Bradley recalled Kean "as a hard taskmaster and a perfectionist, curt and abrasive with his underlings, but an able, professional infantryman."

Shortly after the entry of the United States into World War II, Bradley was given command of a recently activated National Guard division and chose Bill Kean, whom he jokingly called "Captain Bligh," as his chief of staff.

As Bradley advanced rapidly to corps and army command, Kean went with him as his chief of staff. In 1944, when Bradley became commander of the Twelfth Army Group, he left Kean, then a brigadier general, as First Army chief of staff, reportedly to stiffen the resolve of General Courtney Hodges, reputedly low-key and conservative.

After the German surrender, First Army was selected as part of General Douglas MacArthur's force to invade Japan, and Hodges and Kean led a small planning staff to Manila to plan the operation, when Kean first met MacArthur. Japan's surrender obviated the planned invasion. During 1947–1948, Kean commanded the 5th Infantry Division. In September 1948, Army Chief of Staff Bradley appointed Kean to command the 25th Infantry Division in Japan. This coincided with Lieutenant General Walton H. Walker's arrival in Japan to assume command of the U.S. Eighth Army.

After the outbreak of the Korean War, the 25th Infantry Division was deployed early in July 1950 to Korea, where it performed well. Brigadier General George Bittman Barth, Kean's division artillery commander, wrote that Kean was "highly competent professionally and endowed with sound judgement, unswerving determination and tireless energy…[a] strong commander." Barth also recalled that Kean's personal courage was "of the highest order."

William W. Dick, who retired as a lieutenant general, was then Barth's artillery executive officer in Korea. He wrote that "Kean was a superb commander in every respect…. A brilliant tactician, excellent manager and absolutely tireless." Kean was a no-nonsense but fair commander, whose workday "would have crushed nine out of ten younger men." Dick had served under five different division commanders in his career and rated Kean at the top.

In Korea, Kean was admired not only by his staff but was held in high esteem by his superiors as well. He was so highly regarded that he was the last of the division commanders who brought their divisions to Korea from Japan to be reassigned.

In February 1951, Kean returned to the United States to assume command of III Corps. In this capacity he conducted the first maneuver by U.S. troops under actual atomic blast conditions. In July 1952 Lieutenant General Kean commanded the Fifth Army, which position he held until his retirement in 1954.

Kean accepted the post of executive director of the Chicago Housing Authority, a position he held until July 1957. He died on 18 March 1981 in Altemonte Springs, Florida.

—Uzal W. Ent

References:

Assembly (West Point, NY: Association of Graduates), March 1982.

Barth, George B. "Tropic Lightning and Taro Leaf in Korea July '50–May '51." (typewritten monograph, June 1951).

Blair, Clay. *The Forgotten War: America in Korea, 1950–1953.* New York: Time Books, 1987.

Bradley, Omar N., and Clay Blair. *A General's Life: An Autobiography.* New York: Simon & Schuster, 1983.

Register of Graduates and Former Cadets, 1802–1988 United States Military Academy. West Point, NY: Association of Graduates, 1988.

See also: Bradley, Omar Nelson; MacArthur, Douglas; Walker, Walton Harris.

Keiser, Laurence B.

(1895–1969)

U.S. Army officer and commander of the 2d Infantry Division in the Korean War from 8 July through 6 December 1950. His tenure as commander of the division witnessed its virtual destruction during the Chinese onslaught of late November 1950.

Born in Philadelphia, Pennsylvania, on 1 June 1895, Laurence Bolton "Dutch" Keiser graduated from the U.S. Military Academy, West Point in 1917 as an infantry officer in the same class with J. Lawton Collins, Matthew B. Ridgway, and Mark W. Clark. He was one of the few members of his class to see combat in World War I, and he won the Silver Star for actions during the Romagne operation. Rising steadily through the ranks after World War I, during World War II he served as a corps chief of staff in Italy and as an army chief of staff in Texas. Keiser became a brigadier general in January 1944, and he became a major general in 1950 and assumed command of the 2d Infantry Division at Fort Lewis, Washington, on 8 July 1950.

With his unit alerted for combat almost immediately after the outbreak of the Korean War, Keiser had his division consolidated in the Pusan perimeter by 19 August 1950. Occupying the critical Naktong Bulge area, on 16 September 1950 the 2d Division repulsed a determined North Korean attack and assumed the offensive. Two days later, the 2d Division broke out from the perimeter and advanced northward as a part of the newly activated U.S. IX Corps. After conducting mop-up operations in southwestern Korea, Keiser's unit crossed the 38th parallel and moved north.

On 25 November 1950, attacking Chinese People's Volunteer Army (CPVA, Chinese Communist) forces provided Keiser with his greatest battlefield challenge. Responding to the desperate battlefield situation, he fought a difficult holding action at Kunu-ri on 29 November 1950 to cover Eighth Army's withdrawal, joining the fighting himself on several occasions. Rejecting advice to take a different route, Keiser withdrew his division through a six-mile gauntlet of Chinese forces, exposing the majority of his unit to murderous Chinese fire throughout.

By 1 December 1950, Keiser was completely exhausted and his division shattered. Over the preceding two days the 2d Division had lost almost 5,000 men and a majority of its equipment. As a result, on 6 December 1950, Eighth U.S. Army commander Lieutenant General Walton H. Walker relieved Keiser of command and replaced him with Robert B. McClure.

Returning to the United States, Keiser assumed command of the 5th Infantry Division. He retired from active duty as a permanent major general in 1954.

Dutch Keiser will not be remembered as one of the U.S. Army's foremost generals, but he was able to provide the 2d Infantry Division with competent leadership during the critical period of the Pusan perimeter fighting. He died on 20 October 1969, in San Francisco, California.

—*Jeffrey M. Colvin and Kelly C. Jordan*

References:

Blair, Clay. *The Forgotten War: America in Korea, 1950–1953.* New York: Times Books, 1987.

Marshall, S. L. A. *The River and the Gauntlet: Defeat of the Eighth Army by the Chinese Communist Forces, November 1950, in the Battle of the Chongchon River, Korea.* New York: William Morrow, 1953.

See also: "Bug-out Fever"; Chinese Military Offensives; Ch'ŏngch'ŏn River; Coulter, John Breitling; Freeman, Paul L., Jr.; Kunu-ri, Battle of; Marshall, Samuel Lyman Atwood; Naktong Bulge, Second Battle of; Pusan Perimeter and Breakout; Walker, Walton Harris.

Kelly Hill, Battle of (17–24 September 1952)

Battalion-sized engagement, lost by U.S. forces, that was typical of a number of outpost struggles with Chinese forces in the period from 1952 to 1953. In mid-September 1952 the Chinese probed for soft spots in the United Nations Command (UNC) lines.

In the U.S. 3d Division sector of the Jamestown Line, a series of small lightly held outposts was scattered in front of the main line of resistance (MLR). Kelly was one such outpost. Located in the west sector of the Eighth Army front, it was about one mile west of the double horseshoe bend of the Imjun River and eight miles northwest of Yŏngch'ŏn.

In September 1952, OP Kelly was held by C Company, 2d Battalion, 65th Infantry Regiment. The position had a waist-deep circular trench that ringed its military crest and four bunkers. Facing Kelly were the 2d and 3d Battalions of the 348th Regiment, 116th Division, of the thirty-ninth Chinese People's Volunteer Army (CPVA).

On the night of 17 September an estimated company of the Chinese 2d Battalion probed Kelly's defenses. Early on the 18th, the commander of the U.S. 65th Regiment, Colonel Juan C. Cordero, sent B Company to relieve C Company on Kelly. Chinese mortar fire on Kelly continued during the day, and that evening an estimated two companies from the Chinese 2d Battalion attacked the outpost from three directions. One of these attacks broke through. That night communications were lost with the defenders, but reports of Chinese herding American prisoners down the slopes of Kelly indicated the position had been taken.

A reconnaissance of Kelly early on the 19th by a platoon from E Company soon ran into Chinese machine gun and rifle grenade fire. 2nd Battalion commander Lt. Col. Carlos Betance-Ramirez then ordered two platoons from his E company to advance on Kelly on the morning of the 20th. One platoon fought its way to the top but the Chinese immediately sent reinforcements. Under mounting Chinese pressure, the U.S. platoons withdrew.

In the meantime, Major Albert C. Davies's 1st Battalion had moved into position to counterattack through 2d Battalion's positions. Its attack began on the evening of the 20th, but the Chinese opened up a highly effective mortar and artillery fire as the companies of the 1st Battalion began their advance across the valley floor en route to Kelly. B Company was soon reduced to only 26 men, forcing its withdrawal. Meanwhile, Chinese fire also took its toll on A and C Companies. Air-burst, time-fuzed artillery fire was particularly effective in demoralizing the attackers and reduced them to about 120 men. The Chinese held Kelly with perhaps 100 men but were able to reinforce it at will.

Early on the morning of the 21st, UNC artillery fire pounded Kelly, but when the remnants of A and C Companies attempted to resume their advance, they encountered Chinese hand grenades and small arms fire. By noon, two squads from C Company had almost reached the summit, when first Chinese mortar fire and then a counterattack forced them to withdraw. In the early afternoon, with his battalion having taken more than 70 casualties in the fight for Kelly, Davies ordered A, B, and C Companies to return to their staging areas. That night the 3d Battalion relieved the 1st Battalion.

The action then slowed for several days. Commander of the 3d Battalion Lt. Col. Lloyd E. Wills and his staff now prepared to retake Kelly. Wills received permission to use his three rifle companies in the attack. K Company would attack from the East and L from the West; I Company would remain in reserve.

The attack opened at 0520 on 24 September with 30 minutes of fire from 105mm guns of the 58th Field Artillery Battalion. A platoon of tanks from the 64th Tank Battalion also came up. In all, the artillery and tanks fired 25,000 rounds in support of the attackers. The infantry assault began at 0610 and the Chinese replied with accurate small arms, machine gun, mortar, and artillery fire that soon pinned down K Company. With his men suffering heavy losses, K Company Commander Captain William C. English requested permission to pull back and reorganize, which Colonel Cordero refused. Contact was then lost with K Company, although the artillery observer reported 10 men were with him. Cordero ordered this small force to continue the attack.

To the west, a squad from K Company reached the top of Kelly at 0720 against heavy Chinese resistance. The squad requested tank fire, but radio contact with it

was soon lost. Colonel Cordero then ordered I Company forward to take up A Company's zone. Accurate Chinese artillery fire soon scored direct hits on I Company, however, and contact with it was also lost. Its men then began to straggle back to the MLR without weapons or equipment.

At 1000 Wills telephoned 3d Division Assistant Division Commander Brig. Gen. Charles L. Dasher, Jr. to inform him that the battalion had only two platoons available for combat. Dasher ordered Wills to cease the attack. In all, 3d Battalion had sustained 141 casualties in the action. 3d Division commander Major General Robert L. Dulaney then decided the regiment should not renew the attack.

During 17–24 September, in the Battle for Outpost Kelly and surrounding outposts, the 65th Regiment sustained 350 casualties, or almost 10 percent of its strength. In his command report, Colonel Cordero blamed the poor performance of the 65th on the rotation system, which had claimed many experienced platoon sergeants and corporals. During January–September 1952, 8,700 men had rotated from the unit, of whom nearly 1,500 were noncommissioned officers. Only 435 non-coms had been received to replace these losses, leaving privates to hold many leadership positions in rifle platoons. Also a great many enlisted men in the regiment spoke only Spanish, creating a serious communications barrier with their English-speaking officers. Determined Chinese resistance was also a factor in the 65th's failure to retake OP Kelly.

On the night of 24 September, 3d Battalion went into reserve while the 65th Regiment confined itself to patrolling. On 30 September the Republic of Korea (ROK) 1st Division relieved the 3d Division.

—*Spencer C. Tucker*

References:
Hermes, Walter G. *United States Army in the Korean War: Truce Tent and Fighting Front.* Washington, DC: Office of the Chief of Military History, 1966.

Kennan, George F.
(1904–)

U.S. diplomat and Korean War policy adviser. Born on 16 February 1904 in Milwaukee, Wisconsin, George F. Kennan graduated from Princeton University in 1925 and the following year attended Foreign Service School. An acknowledged authority on Russia, he received postings in numerous European capitals including Moscow. Kennan authored the so-called Long Telegram of 1946, an 8,000-word analysis and critique of Soviet behavior. In it Kennan held that the Soviet Union was motivated by Communist ideology and historic Russian insecurity. The message was well received in Washington and contributed to Kennan's reputation as a Soviet expert. In July 1947, *Foreign*

Affairs published Kennan's essay, "The Sources of Soviet Conduct." It appeared under the pseudonym "Mr. X," although it was soon known that Kennan was the author. This "X article," as it came to be known, restated points of the Long Telegram and advocated "patient but firm and vigilant containment of Russian expansive tendencies." Soon Kennan became known as the originator of the doctrine of containment.

By 1947 Kennan chaired the Policy Planning Staff in the State Department, where he fashioned the containment doctrine and provided crucial insights for the Truman Doctrine and the Marshall Plan. In the early 1950s he joined the Institute for Advanced Study at Princeton.

Before the Korean War, Kennan gave scant attention to the peninsula. In 1946 he pressed the State Department to quit collaboration with the Soviets in Korea and to back nationalists Syngman Rhee and Kim Kuo. The next year, perceiving South Koreas as then unimportant strategically, Kennan urged the United States to disengage with minimal embarrassment. In early 1948 he urged a policy of realism, believing that policymakers needed to appreciate developing nationalism and Asian consciousness. By August, Kennan suggested a restored obligation to the peninsula as a symbol of U.S. resolution to withstand Soviet threats. He defended the Korean Aid Bill of 1949, admitted a bleak outlook, and conceded the possibility of an invasion from the North. While endorsing economic aid for South Korea, he confirmed that no administration plan existed to employ combat units. That year when Kennan met with General Douglas MacArthur in Japan, both agreed on the desirability of a sovereign South Korea yet a limited U.S. role.

Surprised by the outbreak of war in Korea in mid-1950, Kennan put off a State Department leave of absence and counseled President Harry S. Truman about Soviet involvement. Assuming that the invasion had occurred with Moscow's blessing, Kennan approved of a vigorous reply to the Korean People's Army (KPA, North Korean) invasion of the South and advised Truman to oppose the invaders militarily to compel their retreat above the 38th parallel. Kennan, focusing on the war's general implications, believed a Communist conquest of South Korea to be harmful to Washington's reputation and an incitement to future aggression. Kennan also believed that the United States needed to demonstrate its pledge to protect Japan and to ensure that Formosa remained free of Communist control. Thus Kennan supported deployment of the Seventh Fleet to the Taiwan Strait, but he questioned Truman's use of the United Nations (UN) as the instrument to implement Korean policy. With occupying forces in Japan and responsibility for South

Korean stability, he argued that the United States had full authority to act unilaterally, given the absence of a Japanese peace treaty.

Kennan favored a limited war in Korea. He cautioned against an advance beyond the 38th parallel, coupled with efforts to reunify the peninsula, as contrary to Soviet interests. Indeed, considering Korea's secondary significance and a need to allocate U.S. assets elsewhere, Kennan suggested that Moscow be assigned a primary role in the country. Before the People's Republic of China (PRC) intervened in late 1950, he doubted any Chinese influence on Communist policy in Korea and wondered whether China's leadership held any real goals in the war.

Alarmed when China entered the conflict, Kennan became preoccupied with the emergency and advised Truman to ready the United States for a military disaster. To avoid a disorderly UN retreat from the peninsula, he advocated measures to contain the Chinese in Korea as well as economic sanctions against the PRC. Kennan was convinced that neither action would result in military confrontation with the Soviets.

Worried about public impatience and congressional calls for disengagement or total war, Kennan advocated negotiations with Moscow. He supported Truman's recall of General MacArthur and, when designated by the State Department to contact Russian UN Ambassador Jacob Malik about Korea, he conducted amicable conversations with the latter in 1951, leading to cease-fire negotiations in the spring of that year.

Kennan later served as ambassador to the Soviet Union and Yugoslavia. Living well into his ninth decade, he still produces scholarly literature.

—*Rodney J. Ross*

References:

Kennan, George F. *Memoirs: 1950–1963.* Vol. 2. Boston: Little, Brown, 1972.

Mayers, David. *George Kennan and the Dilemmas of U.S. Foreign Policy.* New York: Oxford University Press, 1988.

Miscamble, Wilson D. *George F. Kennan and the Making of American Foreign Policy, 1947–1950.* Princeton, NJ: Princeton University Press, 1992.

See also: Kennan-Malik Conversations; MacArthur, Douglas; Syngman Rhee; Truman, Harry S.

Kennan-Malik Conversations
(31 May 1951 and 5 June 1951)

These secret conversations were initiated by U.S. President Harry Truman's administration to explore the possibility of a cease-fire after United Nations (UN) forces had repelled the 1951 Chinese spring offensive and recrossed the 38th parallel. This situation offered the prospect of a peace that would restore something close to the antebellum status quo and end an increasingly unpopular and costly U.S. military commitment.

Washington decided to approach Moscow, using as an intermediary George F. Kennan, the Foreign Service Soviet specialist who headed the Policy Planning Staff until a difference of views between him and Secretary of State Dean Acheson had led to Kennan's resignation in 1949. In 1951 Kennan was at Princeton University on a year's leave of absence from the Foreign Service, so he could be conveniently characterized as a private citizen with no official status. The Soviet functionary with whom the United States initiated contact was Soviet Ambassador to the United Nations Jacob Malik, whose vehement public defenses of his country's policies were somewhat notorious.

After Malik agreed to meet Kennan, they had two encounters, five days apart, in the Soviet UN compound at Glen Cove on Long Island. They spoke in Russian. At the first meeting, Kennan made it clear that no progress toward a cease-fire would be possible unless the Soviet Union and the United States could agree on procedural guidelines acceptable to both. Speaking as a private individual in order to avoid binding his government, Kennan suggested that an armistice be declared on existing battle positions and a supervisory commission be established to prevent renewal of hostilities. Although Malik repeatedly raised the question of outstanding disputes between the United States and the People's Republic of China (PRC), including the status of Taiwan and PRC representation in the UN, Kennan clearly stated that the United States would not tie a cease-fire to wider issues of this nature. The reiterated references to China caused Kennan to believe that the Soviet relationship with the PRC inhibited the Russians in discussing a cease-fire.

Although Malik contended that Kennan's statements regarding a cease-fire could in no way be construed as a new departure, he also indicated that his country would be interested in listening to more detailed proposals; Kennan in turn responded that this would be pointless unless the Soviets indicated that a cease-fire was in principle desirable. Kennan also suggested that they arrange another meeting, which was set for 5 June.

At the second meeting, it was apparent that Malik's superiors in Moscow had sent him instructions. Malik stated that the Soviet Union sought the earliest possible peaceful solution to the Korean conflict. He reminded Kennan that, because Soviet forces were not involved in the fighting, the USSR could not itself participate in discussions on a potential cease-fire, but he also proffered his supposedly personal opinion that the United States should initiate contacts with the Chinese and North Koreans on the subject. Kennan regarded Malik's statement as a hopeful sign, particularly

because Malik made no attempt to link a Korean cease-fire with a wider East Asian political settlement of outstanding issues, a strategy on which the Chinese had previously always insisted. Kennan believed that without Soviet support the Chinese would soon find themselves unable to maintain this position. Kennan's hopes were justified when, on 25 June 1951, Malik made a public radio address in which he officially set forth the Soviet position regarding a cease-fire. This cleared the way to opening the Kaesŏng truce talks.

—*Priscilla Roberts*

References:

Foot, Rosemary J. *A Substitute for Victory: The Politics of Peacemaking at the Korean Armistice Talks.* Ithaca, NY: Cornell University Press, 1990.

Hixson, Walter L. *George F. Kennan: Cold War Iconoclast.* New York: Columbia University Press, 1989.

Kennan, George F. *Memoirs.* 2 vols. Boston: Little, Brown, 1967, 1972.

Stueck, William W., Jr. *The Korean War: An International History.* Princeton, NJ: Princeton University Press, 1995.

See also: Acheson, Dean Goodersham; Kaesŏng Truce Talks; Kennan, George F.; Malik, Jacob (Iakov) Alexandrovich.

KILLER, Operation
(21 February–6 March 1951)

United Nations Command (UNC) operation from 21 February to 6 March 1951. Heavy fighting marked the first two weeks of February 1951, resulting in a Korean People's Army (KPA, North Korean) salient into UN lines to near Chech'ŏn. U.S. IX Corps Commander Lieutenant General Edward M. Almond recommended to U.S. Eighth Commander Lieutenant General Matthew B. Ridgway that the IX and X Corps attack to envelop and destroy this salient. Ridgway concurred, issuing operations orders on 19 February for what he called Operation KILLER.

The boundary between the IX and X Corps was shifted eastward effective on the date of the attack, 21 February, as was that between the X Corps and the Republic of Korea Army (ROKA, South Korean) II Corps, farther east. KILLER's objective was to destroy Communist forces east of the Han River and south of Line Arizona, which ran generally eastward from near Chip'yŏng-ni, across the IX and X Corps fronts, to the boundary between the U.S. X and ROKA III Corps.

The plan called for the 1st Marine Division (attached to IX Corps) to make KILLER's main attack north and northeast through the 2d Division and along Route 29, beginning at 1000 on 21 February. At the same time, the British Commonwealth Brigade and the U.S. 1st Cavalry and 24th Infantry Divisions (balance of IX Corps, west of the Marine Division) would attack north from Yŏju and Chip'yŏng-ni. The 7th Infantry Division (in the eastern sector of X Corps) would attack north to Pangnim-ni, then turn west toward the 1st Marine Division. Once the 1st Marine Division passed through it, the 2d Division was to shift positions to the western flank of X Corps and on 22 February attack north, pushing Communist forces, which would then be caught in a three-sided attack. The 187th Airborne Regiment, which had been on line with the 2d Division, was designated as the corps reserve. The ROKA 5th Infantry Division was to attack abreast of the U.S. 2d Division while the ROKA III Corps would protect the attackers' right flank.

From its start, the offensive bogged down because of heavy rains, mud, swollen streams, swept-away bridges, and caved-in railroad tunnels. At night the ground froze, but daytime warming turned it into mud. It was often necessary to air drop supplies to front-line troops. On the 23rd the weather cleared enough to allow tactical air to attack the Communist forces.

On the 24th, IX Corps commander Major General Bryant E. Moore died of a heart attack shortly after incurring minor injuries in a helicopter crash. Ridgway then temporarily appointed Major General Oliver P. Smith, the 1st Marine Division commander, to lead IX Corps.

The 1st Marine Division reached Hoengsŏng, just south of Line Arizona, on the 23rd and their portion of that line on 2 March. By 6 March all elements of IX Corps attained the line. The X Corps, meeting tough North Korean resistance, closed on Line Arizona the next day.

Because the bulk of Communist soldiers withdrew from the salient by the second day, KILLER did not live up to its name, although IX Corps reported 7,819 Communist dead, 1,469 wounded, and 208 captured. Yet it did restore and strengthen the battle line that Communist forces had breached and provided Eighth Army engineers with valuable experience in coping with bad weather. This paid dividends during the forthcoming rainy season.

—*Uzal W. Ent*

References:

Appleman, Roy E. *Ridgway Duels for Korea.* College Station, TX: Texas A&M Press, 1990.

Blair, Clay. *The Forgotten War: America in Korea, 1950–1953.* New York: Times Books, 1987.

Mossman, Billy C. *U.S. Army in the Korean War: Ebb and Flow, November 1950–July 1951.* Washington, DC: U.S. Army Center of Military History, 1990.

See also: Almond, Edward Mallory; Ridgway, Matthew Bunker; Smith, Oliver Prince.

Kim Ch'aek
(1903–1951)

Key deputy to Democratic People's Republic of Korea (DPRK) leader Kim Il Sung; Korean People's Army (KPA, North Korean) front-line commander from September 1950 to his death in January 1951. Born in North Hamgyŏng Province, the northernmost part of the Korean peninsula, in 1903, Kim Ch'aek went to Manchuria and joined the Chinese Communist Party there in 1925. Kim Ch'aek had a typical Kapsan (Soviet exile) faction background in North Korean politics and epitomized the type of leader who came to the fore under Kim Il Sung.

Kim Ch'aek participated in the 1930s anti-Japanese guerrilla movement in eastern Manchuria. In 1941 the Japanese forced him, Kim Il Sung, and others into the Maritime Province of Siberia. In August 1939 the Japanese had mobilized six battalions of the Kwantung Army and 20,000 men of the Manchukuo Army and police in a six-month antiguerrilla campaign, the main target being the Kim Il Sung–led guerrillas. In September 1940 the Japanese mounted an even larger counterinsurgency campaign, which lasted more than two years. Thousands of Korean and Chinese guerrillas were killed, but future North Korean leaders Kim Il Sung and Kim Ch'aek survived.

Trained by the Russians in Soviet territory, Kim Ch'aek returned to Korea with the Soviet army in August 1945. Just before the Manchurian guerrillas departed for Korea, the top Korean Communist leaders, including Kim Il Sung, Kim Ch'aek, Ch'oe Hyŏn, and Ch'oe Yong-gŏn, agreed among themselves to promote Kim Il Sung as the maximum figure because of his wider reputation and personal strength. They supported him after the guerrilla group returned to Korea and with unstinting loyalty for the rest of their lives. Along with other Manchurian guerrillas, they became the core of the North Korean hierarchy.

As a Kim Il Sung stalwart, Kim Ch'aek was the primary organizer and tactician of Kim's Kapsan faction. When the P'yŏngyang Military Academy opened in October 1945 to train Poandae (peace maintenance corps) officers, Kim Ch'aek headed it. Kim Il Sung's forces established themselves in the Poandae, and merged with other anti-Japanese forces associated with Yenan (Yan'an) under Mu Chŏng, Kim Tu-bong, and others to form the North Korean Army. In August 1946, Kim Ch'aek was named a member of the thirteen-member presidium in the North Korean Worker's Party. When the Second Congress of the North Korean Worker's Party met in P'yŏngyang in March 1948, Kim was included among the seven members of the political committee. At the time of the creation of the DPRK in early September 1948, he became a vice-premier, along with Pak Hŏn-yŏng and Hong Myŏng-hŭi, under Premier Kim Il Sung. Kim Ch'aek also held the key cabinet position of minister of industry. With the merger between the North and South Korean Worker's parties in mid-1949, he became one of the members of the all-important eight-member political committee.

On 25 June 1949, the old Democratic National United Front was renamed the Democratic Front for the Unification of the Fatherland. Key leaders of the Korean Worker's Party totally dominated this new organization and Kim was a member of the leadership committee. On 26 June 1950, the presidium of the Supreme People's Assembly issued an extraordinary decree giving the military committee of the party responsibility for prosecuting the war. Kim was a member of that seven-member committee under Chairman Kim Il Sung.

In mid-July 1950, Kim Ch'aek issued an appeal to Korean People's Army (KPA, North Korean) soldiers in which he stated that the war would already have been won had it not been for U.S. intervention, and he again stressed North Korean confidence in final DPRK victory. In September he succeeded Kang Kŏn, killed in action by a land mine, as KPA front-line commander. In late 1950 he organized some 10,000 guerrillas from retreating KPA units in the area between Ch'unch'ŏn and Wŏnsan and mounted continuous guerrilla attacks against the United Nations forces. Behind Allied lines, his guerrillas coordinated their actions with the Sino–North Korean offensive.

An extremely effective "number two man" in Kim Il Sung's circle, Kim Ch'aek was killed in a U.S. bombing raid in January 1951. After the Korean War, the North Korean city of Sŏngjin was renamed Kim Ch'aek City for him. A DPRK engineering university is also named for him.

—Jinwung Kim

References:

Cumings, Bruce. *Korea's Place in the Sun: A Modern History.* New York: W. W. Norton, 1997.

Matray, James I., ed. *Historical Dictionary of the Korean War.* Westport, CT: Greenwood Press, 1991.

Scalapino, Robert A., and Lee Chong-Sik. *Communism in Korea.* 2 vols. Berkeley: University of California Press, 1973.

See also: Kang Kŏn; Kim Il Sung.

Kim Chong-wŏn
(1922–1964)

Republic of Korea Army (ROKA, South Korean) officer, intensely loyal to South Korean President Syngman Rhee's government. Born in Kyŏngsan, North Kyŏngsang Province, in 1922, Kim Chong-wŏn joined the Japanese army in World War II, eventually obtaining the rank of sergeant. The defeat of Japan led him to join the South Korean Constabulary force on its founding in 1946, and he graduated from the first class of the Constabulary· Academy as an officer. Kim led forces against the October 1948 Yŏsu-Sunch'ŏn Rebellion as well as against Communist guerillas in South Korea during 1948 and 1949. His intensely authoritarian nature during these operations brought

grudging respect from his own troops and his enemies. It also gave him the nickname of *Paektusan* ("Tiger") for the cruelty he exhibited.

Kim's role in the Korean War exhibited the hard nature of his prewar service. He commanded the 17th Regiment of the ROKA on the outbreak of war. Although the claim had never been proven, some maintained that the Korean War began with an invasion of North Korea by Kim's regiment rather than the popularly held view that the Communist North Koreans attacked first. Kim's regiment was stationed at the 38th parallel on 25 June 1950 and consequently was one of the first to engage the invading Korean People's Army (KPA, North Korean) forces. The Communist onslaught destroyed Kim's regiment and led the ROKA command to transfer him to the 23d Regiment. In July 1950, Kim lost his command in an incident in which he executed a platoon leader and an enlisted man for giving ground to the KPA.

Kim's dismissal did not signal the end of his military career. Syngman Rhee and his subordinates recognized the Tiger's unswerving loyalty to the South Korean regime. In October 1950, Kim received command of the military police in P'yŏngyang, the capital of the Democratic People's Republic of Korea (DPRK, North Korea), during its occupation by United Nations forces. In 1951 he was also appointed to the South Kyŏngsang District Martial Law Command as chief of the Civil Affairs Department. Command of this force included jurisdiction over Pusan, which for a time in 1951 was the temporary capital for Syngman Rhee's government. Kim's loyalty and strong-arm tactics certainly gained the favor of Syngman Rhee. Kim's loyalty made him immune from attacks against his cruelty. The Kŏch'ang incident of February 1951, however, clearly showed that Syngman Rhee's government could not ignore public sentiment. In the incident, ROKA troops killed hundreds of villagers within the county of Kŏch'ang on the largely unproven charge that they were Communist collaborators. The ROK National Assembly launched an investigation of the incident and sent an investigating group to the area. Upon their arrival, these individuals were attacked by ROKA forces, ordered to do so by Kim. The Tiger blatantly used his authority in an attempt to protect Syngman Rhee's regime from embarrassment. Ultimately Rhee had to yield to public indignation. Court-martialed, Kim was sentenced to jail for three years.

Although Rhee could not stop Kim's trial, he was able to procure amnesty for him after he had served only three months of his sentence. Rhee also secured a position for Kim as chief of police in various areas of the ROK and, in May 1956, as the head of the national police. In September 1956, however, Kim lost his position of influence after being implicated in an assassination attempt on John M. Chang, vice-president of the ROK and a leading member of the opposition against Rhee. Protracted trials finally convicted Kim in July 1961. The Tiger received a fifteen-year prison term. He died in 1964 while serving his sentence.

—*Eric W. Osborne*

References:

Allen, Richard C. *Korea's Syngman Rhee: An Unauthorized Portrait*. Rutland, VT: Charles E. Tuttle, 1960.

Han, Sungjoo. *The Failure of Democracy in South Korea*. Berkeley: University of California Press, 1974.

Ilbosa, Tonga. *Pihwa Cheil Konghwaguk*. Vols. 2 and 5. Seoul: Hongja Chulpansa, 1975.

See also: Chang, John Myŏn; Kŏch'ang Incident; Syngman Rhee; Yŏsu-Sunch'ŏn Rebellion.

Kim Il Sung
(1912–1994)

President of the Democratic People's Republic of Korea (DPRK) and general secretary of the Committee of the Korean Workers Party. Born into a peasant family in the village of Mangyŏndae, southwest of P'yŏngyang, on 15 April 1912, Kim was the eldest of three sons. His original name was Kim Sŏng-ju, but he later adopted the name Kim Il Sung, a legendary hero of the Korean independence movement. When Kim was seven, his family immigrated to Manchuria, China, where he attended school. Japan had annexed Korea in 1910, and from an early age Kim was involved in anti-Japanese endeavors. In 1929 he was expelled from school and jailed for activities against Japanese expansion into northeastern China. At age nineteen he joined the underground Chinese Communist Youth League, and by 1932 he was leading Korean guerillas on raids against Japanese outposts in northern Korea. Fleeing the Japanese crackdown on guerillas in the region, Kim and his followers went to the Far Eastern areas of Siberia in the Soviet Union in 1941. Little is known about his relationship with the Soviets during this period.

In August 1945 Kim surfaced as a major in the Soviet Red Army that took the Japanese surrender in the northern half of Korea above the 38th parallel. The Soviets designated him to establish a provisional administrative system in the North. After eliminating numerous potential other Communist and nationalist opponents, in February 1946 Kim founded and headed the Soviet-sponsored North Korea Provisional People's Committee. In July the North Korean Worker's Party was organized with Kim Il Sung as vice-chairman but actually in charge. Kim also organized the Korean People's Army (KPA). Under Soviet sponsorship, Kim led the communization of North Korea through people's committees founded at the local, county, and provincial levels. In February 1947 the North Korean People's Assembly replaced the People's Committee, and Kim headed the executive branch of the government.

When the North Koreans and Soviets refused to participate in nationwide elections, in May 1948 United Nations (UN)–sponsored elections were held in the southern portion of the country. After this, the UN recognized the Republic of Korea (South Korea) as the only legitimate government in Korea. North Korea held its own elections in August 1948 and in September proclaimed the DPRK as the legitimate government of all Korea.

Kim was elected premier and he dedicated himself to unifying the country. After subversion efforts in the south failed and supported by the northern Communist leadership, Kim ordered a military invasion of the South, which began on 25 June 1950. Kim believed unrealistically that the invasion would trigger an uprising in the South that would bring certain victory. Although North Korea's "Fatherland Liberation War" initially enjoyed success, the U.S./UN intervention turned the tide. Kim himself led his troops in the early months of the war and was wounded in a battle near Hamhŏng. Faced with the unexpected UN forces, Kim panicked and his army disintegrated. The intervention of the People's Republic of China in November 1950 saved North Korea; however, China took over management of the war. Peng Dehuai, commander of the Chinese forces, allegedly proclaimed that the war was between General Douglas MacArthur and himself and that Kim had no part in it.

In December 1950, after Chinese forces regained P'yŏngyang, Kim issued a diatribe at the third joint plenum of the Central Committee meeting in which he blamed virtually all Koreans who had played any part in the war. He publically admonished government officials, and removed numerous individuals from authority and expelled them from the party. However, as the fortunes of the war improved Kim reinstated most of them. During 1951 Kim engaged in a confrontation with First Secretary of the Party Hŏ Ka-i. This led to Hŏ's expulsion from the party in November 1951 and his suicide in 1953. In 1952 a group of leading party members plotted against Kim and attempted a military coup against him in early 1953. When it failed, they were arrested and most were executed.

The brutal three-year-long Korean War was destructive for North Korea. Besides suffering estimated battlefield deaths of some 295,000 and many more civilians killed, the North was physically devastated. Chinese forces did not withdraw until 1958 and the alliance between South Korea and the United States rendered hope of victory over the southern regime virtually impossible. The demilitarized zone (DMZ)

Democratic People's Republic of Korea leader Kim Il Sung with the commander of the Chinese People's Volunteer Army, General Peng Dehuai. (Xinhua News Agency)

between the two countries became one of the most heavily fortified areas in the world.

In the wake of the war, Kim focused on consolidating power and rebuilding his country's industrial and military power. Following a classic Stalinist model, Kim purged Communists and all potential opponents. Executions, imprisonment, and forced exile were rampant. The DPRK shut itself off from the world, maintaining diplomatic relations only with Communist bloc countries. As Kim endeavored to balance his country between the two adversaries in the growing Sino-Soviet conflict, North Korea became one of the most xenophobic regimes on the globe.

In January 1968, after a P'yŏngyang-sponsored assassination attempt of President of the Republic of Korea Park Chung Hea, the DPRK triggered a major confrontation with the United States when it seized the USS *Pueblo* in international waters off its coast. Finally, after two decades of isolation, Kim in the 1970s attempted to join the world community. Low-level talks with the South began, and Kim tried to

establish himself as a leader in the Third World and so-called Non-Aligned Nations. In 1973 North Korea secured observer status in the UN, and by 1976 it had established diplomatic relations with 130 countries. North Korea also became a major arms supplier to guerrilla movements and radical states in the Third World and a supporter of international terrorism.

Possible rapprochement with South Korea was shattered in 1976 when North Korean troops killed two U.S. officers at P'anmunjŏm. Then in July 1977 an unarmed U.S. helicopter was shot down. Several North Korean spy rings and underground actions in South Korean were uncovered in the late 1970s and early 1980s, including a plan to assassinate South Korean President Chun Doo Hwan in 1982 and an actual attempt in Rangoon, Burma, in October 1983. A North Korean ship dispatched to destroy a South Korean nuclear power plant was destroyed in 1982, and in 1984 South Korea discovered a series of underground invasion tunnels under the DMZ. In 1986, North Korea threatened to disrupt the 1988 Summer

Olympic Games in Seoul, and in November 1987, terrorists linked to North Korea brought down a South Korean airliner, killing 115 people.

As Communist regimes collapsed in Eastern Europe in the 1990s, the absolute dictator Kim remained among the last of the world's Stalinist holdouts. He consolidated his powers as the "Supreme Leader," and he developed his own political philosophy, known as *Chuch'e* (self-reliance), which included political independence, insofar as this was possible, from both the USSR and China. This appealed to deep-rooted Korean resistance to foreign control. Kim referred to *Chuch'e* as "a creative application of Marxism-Leninism."

In his last years, dealings with South Korea once again intensified. In September 1990 the prime ministers of the two Koreas conducted the first high-level talks between the countries since the end of the Korean War.

Kim Il Sung died of heart failure on 8 July 1994, at his villa at Myonhyang-san Mountain about a hundred miles north of P'yŏngyang. He was succeeded by his son, Kim Jong Il.

—Joe P. Dunn

References:

Bai, Bong. *Kim Il Sung: A Political Biography.* 3 vols. New York: Guardian Books, 1970.

Cumings, Bruce. *The Origins of the Korean War:* Vol 1, *Liberation and the Emergence of Separate Regimes, 1945–1947,* and Vol 2, *The Roaring of the Cataract.* Princeton, NJ: Princeton University Press, 1981, 1990.

Suh, Dae-Sook. *Kim Il Sung: The North Korean Leader.* New York: Columbia University Press, 1988.

———. *Korean Communism, 1945–1980.* Honolulu: University of Hawaii Press, 1981.

See also: Peng Dehuai (Peng Te-huai).

Kim Jong Il
(1942–)

Eldest son of Democratic People's Republic of Korea (DPRK, North Korean) leader Kim Il Sung and his eventual political heir and successor. Today the North Korean regime claims that Kim Jong Il was born in a log cabin on the slopes of Mount Paekdu, the legendary birthplace of Tan'gun, mythic father of the Korean people. In fact he was born on 16 February 1942 in a Soviet military camp near Khabarovsk in the Maritime Province of Siberia, where his father's guerrilla band had been forced to take refuge from the Japanese. After the Japanese surrender in 1945, Kim Jong Il moved to Korea with his father. In the late 1940s, he lost his mother, Kim Chŏng-suk, a guerrilla activist, who died while giving birth to a stillborn child. Kim was evacuated to China during the Korean War. His father Kim Il Sung remarried, to Kim Sŏng-ae, in the early 1960s.

Kim graduated from Kim Il Sung University in 1964 and went to work in the Central Committee of the North Korean Worker's Party, with special responsibility for films, theater, and art, which became his lifetime passion. In that capacity, he kidnapped a South Korean actress and her former husband, a film director, separately from Hong Kong in 1978. They quoted him as saying that he ordered their forcible abduction to improve North Korea's unprofessional film industry. The pair made motion pictures for Kim Jong Il in the North, and Kim treated them as his "special guests" until their escape in Vienna in 1986.

Kim Il Sung had early on chosen his son to be his political heir. He wanted to avoid the years of confusion and the ultimate repudiation that followed the deaths of his Russian and Chinese contemporaries. Throughout the 1970s the ground was carefully laid for Kim's succession of his father. The North Korean top leadership, including Pak Sŏng-ch'ŏl, O Chin u, Kim Yŏng-nam, Yi Chong-ok, Chŏn Mun-sŏp, and Sŏ Ch'ŏl, supported the succession. In preparation for this eventuality, North Korean authorities went to extraordinary lengths to glorify Kim Jong Il and his accomplishments. North Korean people began placing his portraits along with those of his father in their homes, offices, and workplaces. In September 1973 Kim became a secretary of the Central Committee of the Worker's Party and, the following year, a member of its Politburo. By then, songs were being sung about him among party cadres, which carried special notebooks to record his instructions. And a slogan came into being: "Let's give our fealty from generation to generation."

Despite his prominence in the Worker's Party, Kim's rise to power and selection as his father's successor were unacknowledged for several years, and his activities were masked under the mysterious Tang Chung'ang (Party Center), who was given credit for wise guidance and great deeds. This veil was lifted at the Sixth Congress of the Worker's Party in October 1980 when Kim was publicly named to the Presidium of the Politburo, the Secretariat of the Central Committee, and the Military Commission. In other words, he was openly designated successor to his father.

Kim received the title of Dear Leader, close to that of Kim Il Sung's Great Leader. Both Kims were addressed and referred to in specific honorific terms that were not used for anyone else. As with his father's 15 April birthday, Kim's 16 February birthday came to be celebrated as a national holiday. In December 1991 Kim was named supreme commander of the North Korean armed forces. By the time of his father's death in July 1994, Kim Jong Il had come to be ranked second in the leadership, behind his father and ahead of his father's old comrade-in-arms, O Chin-u, who died of cancer in early 1995.

Since succeeding his father in July 1994, the junior Kim has virtually been in command but remained officially in the shadows. He has not taken up all of his father's posts and he continues to be called *yŏngdoja*, or leader. This less-than-charismatic successor has ruled the North in accordance with the teachings of the departed leader, or *yuhun*. Kim Il Sung was omnipresent in death as well as in life, but he also left his son an economy on the verge of collapse. Under Kim Jong Il's rule, North Korea's economy has continued to deteriorate and the government has been unable to feed its people.

—Jinwung Kim

References:
Chosŏn Ilbo [Chosŏn daily], 8 July 1997.
Chung'ang Ilbo [Chung'ang daily], 8 July 1997.
Cumings, Bruce. *Korea's Place in the Sun: A Modern History.* New York: W. W. Norton, 1997.
Oberdorfer, Don. *The Two Koreas: A Contemporary History.* Reading, MA: Addison-Wesley, 1997.
See also: Kim Il Sung.

Kim Paek-il
(1917–1951)

Republic of Korea Army (ROKA, South Korean) general and commander of its I Corps from September 1950 to March 1951. Born in Yŏn'gil (Yanji), Manchuria, on 30 January 1917, Kim graduated from the Japanese Manchurian Military Academy in 1938 and served as a junior officer in Manchuria during Japanese rule until the liberation of Korea. Upon his return to Korea in 1945, he entered the English Language School, which the U.S. Army military government opened in Seoul to assist in the possible creation of a ROKA.

Kim was serving as the ROKA deputy chief of staff on the outbreak of the Korean War. When ROKA forces were shattered at the 38th parallel, Kim assisted Chief of Staff Major General Ch'ae Pyŏng-dŏk in planning the retreat. Kim wanted to remove troops and equipment to the south side of the Han River, but he failed to dissuade Ch'ae from an overly hasty order to blow the bridges over the river. As a result, about 70 percent of the ROKA forces were stranded north of the river when Seoul fell on 28 June 1950.

Promoted to brigadier general in July 1950, Kim was appointed commander of I Corps in September. Commanding the Capital Division and 3d Division, he fought bloody battles at P'ohang, Kigye, and An'gang, and his forces helped stabilized the North Korean threat to the eastern corridor along the Pusan perimeter.

On 1 October Kim's troops crossed the 38th parallel without pause, while United Nations (UN) forces were waiting for directives authorizing their movement into North Korea. In a surprisingly rapid advance, Kim's troops entered Wŏnsan on 10 October. The two divisions, which were in competition with each other, entered the city at the same time and secured it the next day. Major General Edward M. Almond's X Corps landed by sea several weeks after Wŏnsan had been secured by Kim's ROKA forces. Kim was promoted to major general in October 1950.

After securing Wŏnsan, the ROKA I Corps continued its rapid advance northward. The Capital Division occupied Ch'ŏngjin on 26 November and planned to turn to Hoeryŏng at the Manchurian border. But the Chinese large-scale offensive at the Changjin Reservoir turned the tide completely, causing UN forces to go from the offensive to the defensive. X Corps and ROKA I Corps forces were withdrawn toward Hŭngnam and then extracted by ship to Pusan. Some 105,000 troops and 91,000 Korean refugees were evacuated from Hŭngnam. Kim was in large part responsible for the decision to take the refugees. He persuaded General Almond to include them in the evacuation despite a shortage of ships. Kim told Almond that the ROKA forces would take ground routes for withdrawal and give vessels allotted for them to the refugees.

Kim died on 28 March 1951, killed in a helicopter crash in the T'aebaek Mountains while returning to his command post at Kangnŭng. Paek Sŏn-yŏp succeeded him.

—To-Woong Chung

References:
Appleman, Roy E. *South to the Naktong, North to the Yalu.* Washington, DC: Office of the Chief of Military History, 1961.
Han, Pŏn-ung. *Yŏngungdŭl ŭi Hangjin* [The march of the heroes]. Seoul: Ulchi, 1986.
Mossman, Billy C. *U.S. Army in the Korean War: Ebb and Flow, November 1950–July 1951.* Washington, DC: U.S. Army Center of Military History, 1990.
See also: Almond, Edward Mallory; Hŭngnam Evacuation; Paek Sŏn-yŏp; Tenth Corps.

Kim Sae-sun
(1901–1989)

Chargé d'affaires at the Republic of Korea's (ROK's, South Korea's) Washington embassy, 1948–1950, and counselor. Born at Ch'ŏrwŏn, Kangwŏn Province, in 1901, Kim Sae-sun graduated from Waseda University in Tokyo in 1925, and from Northwestern and Columbia Universities in the United States, earning his M.A. in political science from the latter in 1933. A Korean nationalist, Kim remained in the United States, and, when the United States and Japan went to war in December 1941, he obtained a position in the State Department as a translator of Japanese materials. In

1942 Kim moved to the Board of Economic Warfare as a researcher on the Japanese economy, and some years later he went to the Department of Justice as an expert on Japan. He also became a close friend and supporter of the exiled Korean nationalist leader Syngman Rhee and undertook assignments for the Korean Commission, which Rhee established in the United States to work for Korea's independence from Japanese domination.

When the ROK was established in 1948, Kim became chargé d'affaires at his country's embassy in Washington. Well aware of the need to win the support of Republicans and Congress for Korea, he developed a particularly close relationship with John Foster Dulles, then an adviser to the Department of State on East Asian affairs and the Japanese Peace Treaty. Kim advised Dulles on his "you are not alone" speech, which, with retrospectively exquisite timing, the future secretary of state delivered before the ROK National Assembly on 19 June 1950. After the Democratic People's Republic of Korea (North Korea) invasion of 25 June 1950, Kim and his ambassador, John M. Chang, made desperate efforts to line up administration and congressional support for their country, frantically lobbying every influential figure or group they could.

After President Harry Truman's administration decided to intervene, Kim worked vigorously to obtain both private and governmental U.S. economic assistance for his country, especially aid for refugees and for rehabilitation. His personal popularity helped to smooth over the perennial tensions and conflicts that characterized and disturbed the relationship between the United States and its client, the ROK. From the time the Kaesŏng armistice talks began in July 1951, Kim, after his government's stated policy of opposing any peace settlement that failed to bring about Korea's unification under the ROK, maneuvered determinedly but ultimately unsuccessfully to sabotage all negotiations that attained less than this objective.

Kim Sae-sun died in 1989.

—*Priscilla Roberts*

References:

Matray, James I., ed. *Historical Dictionary of the Korean War.* Westport, CT: Greenwood Press, 1991.

Oliver, Robert T. *Syngman Rhee and American Involvement in Korea, 1942–1960: A Personal Narrative.* Seoul: Panmun Books, 1978.

Pruessen, Ronald W. *John Foster Dulles: The Path to Power.* New York: Free Press, 1982.

U.S. Department of State, Bureau of Public Affairs. *Foreign Relations of the United States, 1950.* Vol. 7, *Korea.* Washington, DC: U.S. Government Printing Office, 1976.

———. *Foreign Relations of the United States, 1951.* Vol. 7, *Korea and China.* Washington, DC: U.S. Government Printing Office, 1983.

———. *Foreign Relations of the United States, 1952–1954.* Vol. 15, *Korea.* Washington, DC: U.S. Government Printing Office, 1984.

See also: Chang, John Myŏn; Dulles, John Foster; Syngman Rhee.

Kim Sŏk-wŏn
(1893–1978)

Republic of Korea Army (ROKA, South Korea) officer and commander of the Capital Division in July 1950 and the 3d Division in August. Born in Seoul on 29 September 1893, Kim Sŏk-wŏn graduated from the Japanese Military Academy in 1916. He served in the Japanese Army and rose to the rank of full colonel. Kim gained a reputation as an excellent combat leader during the 1931 Japanese invasion of Manchuria and in subsequent fighting against the Chinese Army. He preferred the attack and led from the front. In 1937 his two companies defeated a Chinese division, and Japanese Emperor Hirohito personally decorated him for bravery.

During the period of the U.S. military government after the liberation of Korea, Kim did not attend the Military English-Language School opened for potential Korean officers. He was considered too old for the school, which accepted mostly former junior officers in their twenties and thirties. In 1945 Kim founded Sŏngnam High School in Seoul and began a new career as its principal.

In January 1949, after the establishment of the ROK, Kim returned to the military and was appointed commander of the 1st Division at Kaesŏng at the 38th parallel. Kim was forced to retire that October when he charged ROKA Chief of Staff General Ch'ae Pyŏng-dŏk with incompetence. Kim returned to service after the Democratic People's Republic of Korea (DPRK, North Korea) invasion of the ROK. On 7 July, South Korean President Syngman Rhee, who took Kim's past war experiences into consideration, appointed him to command the Capital Division. During the first half of July, Kim had success in battles at Ch'unch'ŏn and Ch'ungju in the central mountains of South Korea and delayed the Korean People's Army (KPA, North Korean) attack from the side toward Taejŏn for about ten days. At the end of the month, however, Kim made a critical mistake in the Battle of Andong. Failing to understand the timing in U.S. Eighth Army Commander Lieutenant General Walton H. Walker's directive to withdraw to the Naktong perimeter, Kim failed to coordinate with the neighboring divisions. As a result, his division and the ROKA 8th Division suffered heavy casualties before withdrawing from Andong. Both ROKA Chief of Staff Chŏng Il-kwŏn and I Corps Commander Kim Hong-il had difficulties in exercising their command responsibilities with Kim because he was so much older than they were; Kim also was uncomfortable about his superiors.

Although transferred to command III Corps in August, Kim was relieved of the post the next month. Thereafter, as he put in his memoirs, he became a "useless old soldier." After his retirement in 1956, Kim returned to his post as principal of Sŏngnam High School. He died on 7 August 1978 in Seoul.

—*To-Woong Chung*

References:

Kim, Sŏk-wŏn. *Nobyŏng ŭi Han* [An old soldier's remorse: memoirs]. Seoul: Yukbŏp-sa, 1977.

Republic of Korea, War History Compilation Committee. *Han'guk Chŏnjaeng-sa*. Vol. 2. Seoul: Ministry of National Defense, 1968.

See also: Ch'ae Pyŏng-dŏk; Syngman Rhee; Walker, Walton Harris.

Kim Sŏng-su
(1891–1955)

Vice-president of the Republic of Korea (ROK, South Korea), May 1951–June 1952. Kim Sŏng-su was born in Koch'ang, North Chŏlla Province, on 18 October 1891. His father owned considerable property with land in Honam in southwestern Korea. Thanks to this property, Kim became the most eminent of those from Honam who played an important role in Korea after World War II.

In 1908 Kim went to Japan in pursuit of a modern education, and during 1910–1914 he studied on the Faculty of Politics and Economics at Waseda University. Upon graduation he returned to Korea and took over Chung'ang High School, which had been in financial difficulty, and ultimately became its principal in 1917. Kim believed that a nationalistic educational institution could further the cause of Korean independence.

In 1920 he founded a newspaper, *Tonga Ilbo* (East Asia Daily), which has grown into one of the largest media organizations in Korea. In the hope of instituting a higher educational academy, he finally took over Posŏng College (now Korea University) and became president of that school in 1932. Kim was a moderate nationalist who dedicated himself to promoting education for the younger generation before independence.

Kim was also a major businessman and wealthy landowner. He founded Kyŏngsŏng Textile Company in 1919, which became the largest Korean-owned company in Korea during the Japanese colonial period. The company and his extensive land holdings were important sources of his wealth, all of which made for him one of Korea's first *Chaebŏl* (conglomerates). At this time, it was almost impossible to achieve significant prosperity without the assistance of the Japanese, so Kim must have compromised with them to a degree.

After the Second World War, South Korea came under the control of a U.S. military government, and Kim worked for it as chief counselor. In 1945 he joined with rightists and his old friend Song Chin-u to form the conservative Korean Democratic Party and became the leader of the party. That same year Kim also became vice-president of a right-wing organization of which Syngman Rhee was the head, and in 1947 Kim became vice-chairman of the Association for Fighting Against Trusteeship.

When the ROK was established in 1948, Kim supported Rhee's opinion that it would be necessary to establish a South Korean government distinct from that of North Korea. However, he disagreed with Rhee's insistence on a presidential system. Kim supported a British parliamentary system; thus he gradually began to oppose Rhee. Although elected second vice-president of the ROK on 15 May 1951 during the Korean War, Kim resigned that office in an attempt to resist Rhee's dictatorship and his oppression of the National Assembly. In 1952 when Rhee schemed to revise the constitution in a new seizure of political power by force, Kim tried to oppose Rhee and protect the constitution.

Returning to Seoul from Pusan (which had been the temporary capital) in 1953, and despite that he was seriously ill and confined to bed, Kim urged anti-Rhee groups to unite. His health did not improve, however, and he died on 18 February 1955 in Seoul.

—*Insook Park*

References:

Cumings, Bruce. *Korea's Place in the Sun: A Modern History.* New York: W. W. Norton, 1997.

Kim, Hakjoon. *Haebang Kong'gan ŭi Chuyŏkdŭl* [The principal actors of the liberation period]. Seoul: Tonga Ilbo-sa, 1996.

Matray, James I., ed. *Historical Dictionary of the Korean* War. Westport, CT: Greenwood Press, 1991.

See also: Syngman Rhee.

Kim Tu-bong
(1889–1961?)

Chairman of the Supreme People's Assembly, the legislative body of the Democratic People's Republic of Korea (DPRK, North Korea) and a member of the DPRK Politburo during the Korean War. Born in southeast Korea in 1889, Kim Tu-bong was an ardent nationalist who supported a unified, Communist Korea. During World War II, Kim Tu-bong, in concert with Ch'oe Ch'ang-ik and Mu Chŏng, led the Yenan (Yan'an) faction. This group, supported by the Chinese Communists, was based in China and comprised revolutionary Koreans who fought against the Japanese occupying Korea.

Returning to Korea after the war, Kim Tu-bong's faction competed for national power. Its greatest opponent was the group led by veteran Communist Kim Il Sung. On 30 March 1946 the Yenan faction organized into the Sinmin-dang, or New People's

Party, with Kim Tu-bong as the chairman. The party enjoyed widespread popularity, and Kim Il Sung, despite Soviet support, could not dispose of Kim Tu-bong. Kim Il Sung consequently opted, five months after the creation of the Sinmin-dang to merge the two parties into the North Korean Worker's Party (NKWP). Kim Tu-bong accepted this arrangement and became chairman of the party.

Kim Tu-bong's triumph was short-lived because of the demise of the NKWP's counterpart organization in the south, the South Korean Worker's Party (SKWP) in June 1949. Its end marked the birth of the Korean Worker's Party (KWP), headed by Kim Il Sung. Kim Tu-bong shared the position of vice chairman with Pak Hŏn-yŏng and became chairman of the Supreme People's Assembly. He served in this capacity throughout the Korean War and firmly supported the unification of Korea, by force if necessary.

Discontent over Kim Il Sung's dictatorship sparked a revolt after the war that led to Kim Tu-bong's demise. In August 1956 a group that included members of the Yenan faction tried to organize a coalition calling for democratic party management and collective leadership to replace Kim Il Sung's dictatorship. They claimed that the interests of the people were being neglected in favor of policies that supported heavy industry and unfairly high salaries to army officers. Kim Il Sung's supporters crushed the revolt and, over the next two years, disposed of those responsible. The Yenan faction was destroyed, which allowed Kim Il Sung to strengthen his power. In August 1957 Kim Tu-bong was stripped of his chairmanship and in March 1958 he was expelled from the KWP. It is believed that he died a political outcast in 1961 while working in an agricultural cooperative.

—*Eric W. Osborne*

References:

Koh, Byung Chul. *The Foreign Policy of North Korea*. New York: Praeger, 1969.

McCune, George M., and Arthur L. Grey. *Korea Today*. Cambridge, MA: Harvard University Press, 1950.

Nam, K. *The North Korean Communist Leadership, 1945–1965: A Study of Factionalism and Political Consolidation*. Tuscaloosa: University of Alabama Press, 1974.

See also: Kim Il Sung; Korea, Democratic People's Republic of, 1945–1953; Korea, Democratic People's Republic of, 1953 to the Present; Mu Chŏng (Kim Mu-chŏng); Pak Hŏn-yŏng.

Kim Ung
(?–?)

General of the Korean People's Army (KPA, North Korea). Born in the early twentieth century, Kim Ung was a staunch Korean nationalist. He fled to China to escape Japanese oppression, and in the late 1920s or early 1930s he received military training at the Whampoa Military Academy in China. While in China, Kim became a dedicated Communist, and in 1934 he probably accompanied members of the Chinese Communist Party on their Long March to Yenan (Yan'an).

During the late 1930s and 1940s, Kim served with the Communist Eighth Route Army in North China during the Civil War, reputedly reaching the rank of brigade or division commander. Soviet officials apparently advised Kim and other North Korean military men, who went under the name of the Korean Volunteer Army, to remain attached to Communist Chinese units even after Korea's liberation from Japanese rule in 1945, on the grounds that this would enable Korean Communists to gain valuable fighting experience that they could later utilize in their own country. In North Korea's internal politics Kim was regarded as a member of the China-oriented "Yenan faction," which some believed was not entirely sympathetic to North Korea's leader, Kim Il Sung.

A harsh disciplinarian and demanding leader whose men respected rather than loved him, in the Korean War Kim won the reputation of being "the hardest and ablest of Communist field generals." Lieutenant General Kim Ung served as commander of the KPA's I Corps during the initial North Korean assault. In September 1950 he succeeded Lieutenant General Kang Kŏn, who died in action, as chief of staff to the front-line commander General Kim Ch'aek, whose position Kim Ung apparently took over some time in 1951 and held for the remainder of the war. From late 1950 onward, his previous military experience fighting with People's Liberation Army (PLA, Communist Chinese) forces was undoubtedly advantageous to him when dealing with his mainland Chinese allies. After the Korean War ended, Kim served as the Democratic People's Republic of Korea (DPRK, North Korean) vice-minister of defense, but in 1958 Kim Il Sung purged him along with numerous other adherents of the country's "Yenan" and "Soviet" political factions. Rehabilitated many years later, from 1973 to 1978 Kim served as the DPRK ambassador to South Yemen. He was purged once more in 1978, and nothing is known of his subsequent career.

—*Priscilla Roberts*

References:

Appleman, Roy E. *South to the Naktong, North to the Yalu*. Washington, DC: Office of the Chief of Military History, 1961.

Cumings, Bruce. *The Origins of the Korean War*. 2 vols. Princeton, NJ: Princeton University Press, 1981, 1990.

Hermes, Walter G. *United States Army in the Korean War: Truce Tent and Fighting Front*. Washington, DC: Office of the Chief of Military History, 1966.

Kim, Joungwoon A. *Divided Korea: The Politics of Development, 1945–1972*. Cambridge, MA: Harvard University Press, 1975.

Lim, Un. *The Founding of a Dynasty in North Korea: An Authentic Biography of Kim Il-Sung*. Tokyo: Jiyu-sha, 1992.

Matray, James I., ed. *Historical Dictionary of the Korean War.* New York: Greenwood Press, 1991.

Merrill, John. *Korea: The Peninsular Origins of the War.* Newark: University of Delaware Press, 1989.

Simmons, Robert R. *The Strained Alliance: Peking, Pyongyang, Moscow, and the Politics of the Korean Civil War.* New York: Free Press, 1975.

See also: Kim Ch'aek; Kim Il Sung; Korea, Democratic People's Republic of: Army (Korean People's Army [KPA]).

Kimpŏ Airfield

Strategic transportation site for supplies and troops. During the Korean War Kimpŏ Airfield, on the northwest edge of Seoul, was crucial. Improved during the post–World War II U.S. occupation, Kimpŏ was the most modern airfield in Korea and capable of serving jet aircraft.

On 25 June 1950, while hundreds of U.S. personnel and dependents were being evacuated from Seoul at Kimpŏ, Korean People's Air Force (PAF, North Korean) aircraft strafed the field. In the attack, fuel pumps, the control tower, and a transport plane were all damaged. The U.S. Air Force 8th Fighter Wing protected the field while remaining civilians were airlifted to Japan. On 27 June, Fifth Air Force jet fighters shot down seven North Korean Air Force fighters at Kimpŏ.

Kimpŏ Airfield changed hands several times in the war. After the Korean People's Army (KPA, North Koreans) captured Kimpŏ, United Nations Command (UNC) aircraft strafed aircraft on the ground and bombed runways to impede Korean People's Air Force operations there. The UNC regained the airfield in September 1950 after the Inch'ŏn landing. Supplies were flown to Kimpŏ by cargo planes, and the airfield was also used by fighter-bomber groups, including jets flying two hundred miles north to the Yalu River.

The Communists again secured Kimpŏ on 5 January 1951, when Chinese People's Volunteer Army (CPVA, Chinese Communist) forces pushed Eighth U.S. Army south of Seoul. In February 1951 the Allies recaptured Kimpŏ. Engineers then restored Kimpŏ's runways and facilities, and the airfield supported UNC forces for the remainder of the war.

Kimpŏ was the site of airlifts of orphans out of Korea as well as a transportation center for soldiers flying to and from Japan on leave. Despite radar, Communist aircraft occasionally flew over Kimpŏ undetected and dropped bombs and propaganda leaflets. One month after the armistice, a North Korean pilot defected by landing his MiG-15 at Kimpŏ. After the war the Republic of Korea used Kimpŏ both as a military base and civilian airport. Today Kimpŏ is the largest international airfield in the ROK.

—*Elizabeth D. Schafer*

References:

Futrell, Robert F. *The United States Air Force in Korea, 1950–1953.* Rev. ed. Washington, DC: Office of the Chief of Air Force History, 1983.

No, Kum-Sok, with J. Roger Osterholm. *A MiG-15 to Freedom: Memoir of the Wartime North Korean Defector Who First Delivered the Secret Fighter Jet to the Americans in 1953.* Jefferson, NC: McFarland, 1996.

Thompson, Annis G. *The Greatest Airlift: The Story of Combat Cargo.* Tokyo: Dai-Nippon Printing Co., 1954.

See also: Chinese Military Offensives; Inch'ŏn Landings: Operation CHROMITE; Korea, Democratic People's Republic of: Air Force (Korean People's Air Force [KPAF]); Rest and Recuperation (R&R); Seoul; Seoul, Fall of; Seoul, Recapture of; Strategic and Tactical Airlift in the Korean War; United States: Air Force (USAF).

Kingsley, J. Donald
(1908–1972)

First agent general of the United Nations Korean Reconstruction Agency (UNKRA), 1951–1953. Born in Cambridge, New York, on 25 March 1908, John Donald Kingsley by 1933 had earned a B.A., an M.A., and a Ph.D. in public affairs from Syracuse University. Marked for academic distinction, he immediately became a professor at Antioch College, where he coauthored the book *Public Personnel Administration* (1936). He spent 1935–1937 as a postdoctoral fellow at the London School of Economics. Kingsley soon had the opportunity to gain practical experience in public affairs, a career change that became permanent. During World War II, he joined the War Manpower Commission, holding several positions there until 1945, when he moved to the Office of War Mobilization and Reconversion. In 1946 President Harry S. Truman named Kingsley his liaison officer with the Commission on Higher Education, and in 1947 the president appointed him executive secretary of the Scientific Research Council.

Broader horizons beckoned, and that same year Kingsley moved to Geneva, Switzerland, to work for the International Labor Office. Two years later he was appointed director general of the International Refugee Organization (IRO), charged with caring for, resettling, and repatriating approximately 1,500,000 displaced persons whom war had left stateless. Kingsley had overall responsibility for refugee camps and assembly centers, and he devoted special energy to persuading nations to relax immigration restrictions and to accept elderly, ill, or blind refugees as well as the able bodied. The IRO wound up its operations in 1951, when Kingsley's international reputation as a humanitarian and an expert in public administration led the UN to offer him the position of UNKRA's first agent general.

Initially Kingsley's skills in bureaucratic infighting were tested to their limits in a series of clashes with the

UN Command in Korea over the extent of his authority. Eventually, he succeeded in winning the military's respect, however grudgingly bestowed, and, as the battlefield situation stabilized from mid-1951 onward, was able to make substantial progress toward the economic and social rehabilitation of the Republic of Korea (ROK, South Korea). At least some of the credit for the ROK's postwar recovery was due to Kingsley's wartime efforts.

Kingsley spent the remainder of his career in further high-level philanthropic endeavors. In 1953 he returned to the United States as executive director of the Community Council of Greater New York. In 1958 he joined the Ford Foundation, directing its Middle Eastern and African programs from 1963 to 1972. Kingsley died in Greenwich, Connecticut, on 1 June 1972.

—*Priscilla Roberts*

References:

Cumings, Bruce. *Korea's Place in the Sun: A Modern History.* New York: W. W. Norton, 1997.

Holborne, Louise Wilhelmine. *The International Refugee Organization, a Specialized Agency of the United Nations: Its History and Work, 1946–1952.* New York: Oxford University Press, 1956.

"Kingsley, J(ohn) Donald." In *Current Biography, 1950.* New York: H. W. Wilson, 1951.

Stueck, William W., Jr. *The Korean War: An International History.* Princeton, NJ: Princeton University Press, 1995.

Yoo, Tae-Ho. *The Korean War and the United Nations.* Louvain, Belgium: Librairie Desbarax, 1964.

See also: Refugees; Truman, Harry S.; United Nations Korean Reconstruction Agency (UNKRA).

Kirk, Alan Goodrich
(1888–1963)

U.S. ambassador to Moscow, 1949–1951. Born 30 October 1888 in Philadelphia, Pennsylvania, Alan Goodrich Kirk graduated from the U.S. Naval Academy, Annapolis, in 1909. While serving in Canton, China, Ensign Kirk witnessed the 1911 Chinese Revolution, led by Sun Yat-sen, which brought an end to the Ch'ing dynasty. In the early 1920s Kirk became executive officer and navigator of the presidential yacht *Mayflower* under Presidents Woodrow Wilson and Warren Harding, as well as a naval aide to the White House. After several promotions and numerous shipboard and staff assignments, then Captain Kirk went to London in June 1939 as U.S. naval attaché under Ambassador Joseph P. Kennedy. Kirk later served as director of Naval Intelligence and chief of staff to the commander of U.S. naval forces in Europe, Admiral Harold Stark. Returning to sea duty, in 1943 Rear Admiral Kirk headed the Atlantic Fleet's Amphibious Force, which participated in the Allied landing in Sicily that July.

Kirk then commanded the Western Task Force in the 6 June 1944 D-day landing at Normandy. The massive amphibious assault was the high point of his military career.

After retiring from the Navy a full admiral in February 1946, Kirk served as ambassador to Belgium and minister to Luxembourg for three years. In July 1949 he was appointed U.S. ambassador to the Soviet Union, a post he held through October 1951.

Kirk had few opportunities to exercise his diplomatic talents in the USSR. Cold War tensions and Kirk's staunch anti-Soviet sentiments led to Kirk's being treated with suspicion and hostility. Although frustrated by the hostility of Soviet Foreign Minister Andrei Vyshinskii and his government, Kirk persisted in finding ways to make himself useful. He traveled more than 10,000 miles in an attempt to learn as much as possible about the USSR. His Soviet hosts kept him diplomatically isolated, inviting him to the Kremlin a mere two times during his term of service, including only one audience with Soviet Premier Josef Stalin. When the Korean War began in June 1950, Kirk blamed Stalin for the Democratic People's Republic of Korea (DPRK, North Korean) invasion. Kirk strongly supported U.S. military intervention to assist the Republic of Korea (ROK, South Korea), under the assumption that more aggression would follow if the invasion was not deterred by force.

Kirk's reports to Washington echoed views held by President Harry S. Truman and his top advisors. Despite his hawkish stance, Kirk played the role of dove in the Korean War. Responding to Soviet United Nations (UN) representative Jacob Malik's vague cease-fire proposal in a 23 June 1951 radio address, Truman instructed Kirk to obtain details from the Soviets. Vyshinskii suggested that a military armistice might be worked out, with political and territorial questions to be discussed later. On this basis Truman ordered UN commander in Korea Lieutenant General Matthew B. Ridgway to attempt to open negotiations with the Communist forces. The result was the Kaesŏng truce talks, which began on 10 July and were suspended on 23 August 1951. Six weeks later, as he was preparing to end his service in Moscow, Alan Kirk requested a farewell meeting with Stalin. Because the Soviet dictator was on vacation, Kirk met with Vyshinskii on 5 October. This meeting may have helped break an impasse in the negotiations. Under instructions from Washington, Kirk delicately expressed his fear that the Korean conflict might spread and he hoped that Stalin might use his influence with the Chinese and North Koreans to convince them to rejoin the stalled truce negotiations. The Soviet government, after the face-saving maneuver of blaming Ridgway for the collapse of the talks, agreed to speak with its two East Asian allies. Soon thereafter the DPRK agreed to a change in location, and negotiations resumed on 25 October 1951 in P'anmunjŏm.

After returning to the United States, Kirk headed two prominent anti-Soviet groups, the Psychological Strategy Board (the National Security Council's attempt to counter Communist propaganda) and the American Committee for the Liberation of the Peoples of Russia. In addition, he directed two businesses that had interests in Belgium and Africa. President John F. Kennedy recalled Kirk to diplomatic service as ambassador to the Republic of China (Taiwan) in May 1962. Kirk resigned in poor health the following April and died in New York City on 15 October 1963.

—*Edward Sharp*

References:

Current Biography, 1944. New York: H. W. Wilson, 1945.

Garraty, John A., ed. *Dictionary of American Biography. Supplement Seven, 1961–1965.* New York: Charles Scribner's Sons, 1981.

New York Times, 16 October 1963.

Who's Who in America, 1952–53. Vol. 27. Chicago: Marquis, 1952.

See also: Cease-Fire Negotiations; Cold War, Origins to 1950; Kaesŏng Truce Talks; Malik, Jacob (Iakov) Alexandrovich; P'anmunjŏm Truce Talks; Ridgway, Matthew Bunker; Stalin, Josef; Truman, Harry S.; Union of Soviet Socialist Republics; Vyshinskii, Andrei Ianuarovich.

Knowland, William Fife
(1908–1974)

U.S. Senator from California, leading member of the China lobby, and one of the strongest critics of the Truman administration's Asian policies. William Fife Knowland was born in Alameda, California, on 26 June 1908, of a family that was both wealthy and politically prominent. In 1914 Knowland's father, Joseph Russell Knowland, bought the *Oakland Tribune,* which gave both father and son a strong power base in the California Republican Party. From an early age, William Knowland was determined to become president of the United States, an ambition that his family did not discourage.

In 1929 Knowland obtained a degree in political science from the University of California at Berkeley. In 1932 at age 24 he was elected to the California State Assembly, and in 1933 he became assistant publisher of the *Oakland Tribune,* a position that he used to enhance his political career. In rapid succession Knowland became state senator (1934), a member of the Republican National Committee (1938), and chairman of its executive committee (1941).

During the Second World War, Knowland saw military service, rising from private to major. At his father's urging, in August 1945 Governor Earl Warren of California appointed Knowland to the U.S. Senate

to fill the vacancy created by the death of Hiram W. Johnson. A popular choice, Knowland won the two following elections, 1946 and 1952, by large majorities, and in 1952 was nominated on both the Democratic and Republican tickets. Initially regarded as a moderate Republican, Knowland soon aligned himself with the right, fiercely challenging Democratic New Deal policies. In 1948 he was defeated when he ran against the domestically somewhat more liberal Robert A. Taft for the post of Senate floor leader.

Knowland supported the Truman administration's European Cold War policies but argued that the administration's handling of Asian issues was deplorable. As early as 1946 he warned that a hostile Asian regime headed by "a twentieth-century Genghis Khan" might well "come forth…to jeopardize…the security of this nation." Aligning himself with the China lobby, Knowland became identified with the interests of Jiang Jieshi's Nationalist Guomindang government. In the 1950s, winning the nickname "the Senator for Formosa," Knowland disagreed strongly with the China White Paper's conclusions that Guomindang corruption and inefficiency were responsible for the Communist victory in China. He derided the document as a "whitewash" and blamed the Communist victory on what he characterized as defeatism within the State Department.

After visiting Chongqing (Chungking) in 1949 one day before it fell to Communist troops, Knowland became obsessed with the need to defeat communism in Asia and to support Jiang Jieshi. He strongly supported Senator Joseph R. McCarthy's witch-hunts and attempts to purge the administration and American life of Communists. Before the Korean War began, Knowland called for unstinting U.S. economic and military aid to Jiang Jieshi's rump Guomindang regime on Taiwan, and during the war he unsuccessfully demanded that the U.S. government "unleash Chiang Kai-shek" and allow Guomindang troops to join the United Nations forces.

Knowland consistently called for the use of much tougher and more provocative military tactics against the People's Republic of China (PRC, Communist China) and the Democratic People's Republic of (DPRK, North Korea). He supported suggestions put forward by General Douglas MacArthur that atomic weapons be used against mainland China and vehemently opposed President Truman's recall of MacArthur in spring 1951. Judging all U.S. foreign policies by their impact upon the Republic of China, Knowland remained harshly critical of U.S. policies even after the Republican Dwight D. Eisenhower assumed the presidency in 1953.

Replacing the dying Taft as Republican majority leader in 1953, a position he held for six years—the last four as head of the minority—the clumsy Knowland was repeatedly outmaneuvered by his wilier Democratic counterpart, Lyndon B. Johnson. Knowland remained a hard-liner in foreign affairs, advocating a naval blockade of mainland China and the withdrawal of U.S. economic aid from nations that remained neutral in the Cold War. In the mid-1950s he set in motion the legislative machinery that brought down McCarthy, although Knowland personally refused to vote for his colleague's censure. He was also a strong supporter of the unsuccessful Bricker constitutional amendment, which would have required Senate approval of all executive agreements.

In 1958 Knowland campaigned unsuccessfully for governor of California. Upon his father's death in 1966, Knowland succeeded him as editor and publisher of the *Oakland Tribune* and became a political power broker; he was widely and correctly regarded as the real boss of Oakland. A strong supporter of Barry Goldwater in 1964, Knowland was instrumental in Ronald Reagan's rise to national prominence as governor of California. Heavily in debt and with nearly $1 million in loans coming due, on 23 February 1974 Knowland shot himself fatally at his retreat near Monte Rio in Sonoma County, California.

—*Priscilla Roberts*

References:

Caridi, Ronald J. *The Korean War and American Politics: The Republican Party As a Case Study.* Philadelphia: University of Pennsylvania Press, 1968.

Dictionary of American Biography: Supplement Nine, 1971–1975, edited by Kenneth T. Jackson. New York: Charles Scribner's Sons, 1994.

Kepley, David R. *The Collapse of the Middle Way: Senate Republicans and the Bipartisan Foreign Policy, 1948–1952.* New York: Greenwood Press, 1982.

Koen, Ross Y. *The China Lobby in American Politics.* New York: Harper & Row, 1974.

Montgomery, Gayle B., and James W. Johnson. *One Step from the White House: The Rise and Fall of Senator William F. Knowland.* Berkeley: University of California Press, 1998.

Reinhard, David W. *The Republican Right Since 1945.* Lexington: University Press of Kentucky, 1983.

Tananbaum, Duane. *The Bricker Amendment Controversy: A Test of Eisenhower's Political Leadership.* Ithaca, NY: Cornell University Press, 1988.

See also: China Lobby; China, Republic of; Dulles, John Foster; Eisenhower, Dwight D.; Jiang Jieshi (Chiang Kai-shek); MacArthur, Douglas; McCarthy, Joseph R.; Taft, Robert Alphonso; Truman, Harry S.; Truman's Recall of MacArthur.

Kŏch'ang Incident
(10–11 February 1951)

Infamous incident in which Republic of Korea Army (ROKA) soldiers massacred civilians at Sinwŏn-myŏn, Kŏch'ang-kun in South Kyŏngsang Province.

Some 719 people, 75 percent of them children and the elderly, were slaughtered on 10 and 11 February 1951 by Major Han Tong-sŏk's 3d Battalion of Colonel O Ik-gyŏng's 9th Regiment in Brigadier General Ch'oe Tŏk-sin's 11th Division.

The 11th Division of some 10,000 men had been created on 2 October 1950 to wipe out North Korean People's Army stragglers and Communist Chiri-san (Mt. Chiri) guerrillas. This force, estimated at about 40,000, had been quite active.

Suppression of the guerrillas was not easy. A succession of battles occurred between ROKA forces and the guerrillas, and there were areas where ROKA forces dominated in the daytime and the guerrillas dominated at night. Sinwŏn-myŏn was one such area. In early December 1950, a force of some 400–500 guerrillas attacked the town and killed many policemen. The 9th Regiment was assigned the task of sweeping up the guerrillas in the southern part of the Chiri-san area.

When the 3d Battalion of the regiment advanced on Sinwŏn-myŏn on 7 February 1951, the guerrillas had already fled. When the army left, the guerrillas returned and joined battle with the police. The 3d Battalion, which advanced on Sinwŏn-myŏn again, first assembled about 1,000 inhabitants at Sinwŏn Elementary School and singled out and released family members of the army, police, government officials, and other influential citizens. Then the remaining people were accused of having betrayed the country to the Communists. They were given death sentences at a summary trial of a military tribunal, with Major Han as presiding judge. These civilians were taken to a mountain valley and executed, their bodies burned to destroy the evidence.

Sin Chung-mok, an ROK National Assemblyman from Kŏch'ang-kun, first made public the atrocity on 29 March 1951. Since reports by the ministers of defense, home affairs, and justice on the incident conflicted, the National Assembly then dispatched an investigation committee. But this team failed to reach the scene because Deputy Provost Marshal Kim Chong-wŏn disguised a platoon of ROKA soldiers as Communist guerrillas and ordered them to attack the investigators on 7 April.

Subsequently, the National Assembly adopted a resolution censuring the government on this matter. As a result, the three ministers resigned, and the investigation resumed in early June 1951 on the special instruction of South Korean President Syngman Rhee. The provost marshal headquarters then arrested O Ik-gyŏng, Han Tong-sŏk, Kim Chong-wŏn, and an intelligence officer in the 3d Battalion, Second Lieutenant Yi Chong-dae. These four were ordered to stand trial by court-martial. Yi Chong-dae was found not guilty;

the others were convicted. O Ik-gyŏng received life imprisonment, Han Tong-sŏk was given ten years in prison, and Kim Chong-wŏn was sentenced to a three-year prison term. Before long, however, the three officers were released on a special amnesty from President Rhee. Even today, the real truth of the tragedy has not been fully disclosed.

—*Jinwung Kim*

References:
Matray, James I., ed. *Historical Dictionary of the Korean War.* Westport, CT: Greenwood Press, 1991.
Wŏlgan Chosŏn [Chosŏn monthly], September 1988.
Yŏrum Publishing Co., ed. *Han'guk Hyŏndae Sahoe Undong Sajŏn* (A dictionary of the contemporary Korean social movement, 1880–1972). Seoul: Yŏrum, 1988.
See also: Ch'oe Tŏk-sin; Kim Chong-wŏn; Syngman Rhee.

Kŏje-do

A 146-square-mile island, Korea's second largest, off the south coast of the Korean peninsula some thirty air miles from Pusan. During the Korean War, the bulk of United Nations Command (UNC) prisoner-of-war (POW) camps were on Kŏje-do.

When China intervened in the Korean fighting at the end of November 1950, the UNC gave greater attention to the control of POWs. In February 1951 Lieutenant General Matthew B. Ridgway, commander of the Eighth Army, launched Operation ALBANY, evacuating all POWs to Kŏje-do. At that time, secure territory, well removed from the battlefield, was at a premium. On Kŏje-do, prisoners suffered from overcrowded conditions and poor sanitation.

The POW problem on Kŏje-do grew more serious. By May 1951, the camp command was accepting 2,000 new prisoners every day, the majority of them Chinese captured in the spring offensives. The shortage of adequate staff and expertise forced the camp command to rely upon prisoner cooperation. Compound representatives maintained discipline, distributed supplies, and served as liaisons with the camp administration. Guards rarely entered the POW enclosures.

Behind the barbed wire, however, camp life was shaped not by military discipline but by political struggle. Both Korean and Chinese prisoners were divided into anti-Communists and Communists and these were in conflict with each other. When the UNC took a stand on the principle of voluntary repatriation and set out to conduct screening of prisoners, it met with violent resistance. During May and June 1952, Communist POWs began rioting, which resulted in many deaths. After the disturbances, nonrepatriates were removed from Kŏje-do: the Chinese went to Cheju-do; the Koreans, to the mainland.

—*Jinwung Kim*

References:
Blair, Clay. *The Forgotten War: America in Korea, 1950–1953.* New York: Times Books, 1987.
MacDonald, Callum. *Korea: The War Before Vietnam.* New York: Free Press, 1986.
Stueck, William W., Jr. *The Korean War: An International History.* Princeton, NJ: Princeton University Press, 1995.
See also: Kŏje-do Prisoner-of-War Uprising.

Kŏje-do Prisoner-of-War Uprising (7 May–10 June 1952)

Communist prisoner-of-war (POW) riot that occurred at Compound 76 on Kŏje-do, an island off the south coast of the Korean peninsula. The incident considerably delayed settlement of the outstanding issue in the P'anmunjŏm truce talks, agenda item 4, POW repatriation.

When China intervened in the Korean fighting in November 1950, the United Nations Command (UNC) paid greater attention to control of Communist POWs. In February 1951, Eighth Army Lieutenant General Commander Matthew B. Ridgway launched Operation ALBANY, which evacuated all POWs to Kŏje-do, which was far removed from the battlefield and regarded as secure territory. On the island, however, U.S. forces had difficulty in supervising the POWs because of the lack of sufficient manpower and scant experience in such affairs.

On the POW repatriation issue, the UNC delegation at the P'anmunjŏm truce talks took a stand on the principle of voluntary repatriation and to this end set out to conduct prisoner screenings. At first Ridgway entered discussions on agenda item 4 without any indication of Washington's final position on repatriation. On 15 January 1952, Washington authorized him to agree to an all-for-all exchange, provided that no forcible return would be required. But Ridgway was warned that this was not necessarily an irrevocable stand. A final position was not worked out until the end of February.

On 2 February, U.S. Assistant Secretary of State for Far Eastern Affairs U. Alexis Johnson proposed the screening of the POWs. This involved interviewing the prisoners and segregating them into repatriates and nonrepatriates. The latter would be removed from the POW lists and the Communist side offered an all-for-all exchange of the remainder. On 27 February, the Johnson plan was approved by President Harry S. Truman as the final and irrevocable U.S. position at the P'anmunjŏm talks.

Washington assumed that screening would take place in an atmosphere that guaranteed each POW freedom of choice. But this was far from the case. There was violent resistance among POWs, reportedly on direct orders from the Communist high command,

A portrait of Josef Stalin displayed by Communist POWs during a demonstration on Kŏje-do. (National Archives)

against screening. Apparently the Communist leaders wanted a strong showing in favor of forcible repatriation to strengthen their hands at the bargaining table.

The first serious violent incident occurred on 18 February 1952 between a battalion of the U.S. 27th Infantry Regiment and Communist POWs. After the incident, Eighth Army commander Lieutenant General James A. Van Fleet, hoping to improve discipline, appointed Brigadier General Francis T. Dodd as the camp commander. Yet Dodd had little experience in Asia and knew neither Korean nor Chinese. In the meantime, specially trained Communist agents were instructed to be captured at the front to gain access to the UN stockade on Kŏje-do. These agents conveyed to "loyal" prisoners the latest orders for creating disturbances by all available means. In a well-planned operation, on 7 May Communist POWs kidnapped Dodd and announced that in return for his release certain demands had to be met. The terms were directed to Brigadier General Charles F. Colson, next in command at the camps. Colson's main concern was to save

Dodd's life. He also feared that a military operation might produce high casualties on both sides, and thus he agreed to accept many of the conditions. He was forced to sign a humiliating statement in which he admitted that the UN forces killed and wounded many POWs. He assured the prisoners that, after Dodd was released unharmed, "in the future POWs can expect humane treatment in this camp" and there would be "no more forcible" screening undertaken. The statement was obtained under coercion to save Dodd's life, but its effect was devastating to the UNC's international image. The Communist delegation at P'anmunjŏm used Colson's admission as a propaganda weapon to disrupt armistice negotiations. In the West, news of the incident produced a deluge of criticism aimed at the United States.

The infamous Dodd-Colson incident coincided with the transfer of General Ridgway as supreme military commander to the North Atlantic Treaty Organization and the arrival of Lieutenant General Mark W. Clark as UNC commander. Clark was a militant anti-

A Republic of Korea Army sergeant stands beside a display of weapons taken from Chinese POWs in Compound 72, Kŏje-do, South Korea. (National Archives)

Communist, who had been convinced by his experiences with the Russians in postwar Austria that the Communists understood only force. His immediate response to the Dodd-Colson affair was to take firm measures to restore order. Washington, embarrassed by the whole incident, strongly supported this.

Clark sent combat troops to Kŏje-do, and both Dodd and Colson were court-martialed and reduced in rank to colonel. A new POW command was established, and a new camp commander, Brigadier General Haydon L. Boatner, a tough-minded combat commander fluent in Chinese, was dispatched to bring the compounds under control. At the end of May, Operation REMOVAL cleared refugees from the vicinity of the camps to prevent communication between the POWs and the Communist high command.

Meanwhile the Communists attempted to squeeze more advantage out of the situation on Kŏje-do. At one point they contemplated a major breakout from the Communist POW–held compounds. But Clark was determined to impose discipline, and Boatner took swift and effective steps to recover firm control.

The Communist POWs tried to resist Boatner's efforts to dilute their strength. When Operation BREAKUP dispersed the Communist compounds into smaller units, on 10 June there was a serious bloody clash. After more than an hour of fighting, Boatner's troops broke the Communist resistance. More than 150 prisoners were killed or injured. One U.S. soldier died and thirteen were wounded.

Thereafter, despite sporadic violence and acts of defiance, the POW camps were under control. The nonrepatriates were then removed from Kŏje-do, the Chinese to the island of Cheju-do and the Koreans to the mainland.

—Jinwung Kim

References:

MacDonald, Callum. *Korea: The War Before Vietnam.* New York: Free Press, 1986.

Matray, James I., ed. *Historical Dictionary of the Korean War.* Westport, CT: Greenwood Press, 1991.

Stueck, William W., Jr. *The Korean War: An International History.* Princeton, NJ: Princeton University Press, 1995.

See also: Boatner, Haydon Lemaire; Clark, Mark W.; Dodd-Colson Prisoner-of-War Incident; Johnson, U. Alexis; Prisoners of War, Rescreening of; Ridgway, Matthew Bunker; Van Fleet, James Alward.

Korea Aid Bill, 1947

The abortive Korea Aid Bill of 1947 envisaged the provision of more than $500 million in U.S. economic assistance to South Korea. Its strategy was to establish large-scale fertilizer plants with the objective of restoring and enhancing Korean rice production. The ultimate intention was to export the surplus

to Japan, the main pre–Second World War market for Korea's grain. The bill's foremost architect, Undersecretary of State Dean G. Acheson, believed that this measure would play a key part in Northeast Asia's economic recovery. Not only would it enable Japan to end its dependence on expensive food aid from the United States, a substantial budgetary drain on the occupying power, but the restoration of Japanese-Korean trade would also revive southern Korea as a potential market for Japan's industrial production, thereby rebuilding Japan's own economy. This in turn would strengthen both South Korea itself and Japan's ability to serve as a key U.S. ally in Northeast Asia.

The Korea Aid Bill originated in a January 1947 proposal by State Department Director of Far Eastern Affairs John Carter Vincent to provide South Korea with a $50 million development grant to supplement existing aid provided by the War Department. Acheson, who had broad responsibility for State Department policy planning, was eager to enlarge this relatively modest scheme so that it would encompass what he perceived to be the interlinked economic revival of Japan and South Korea. The following month, a joint mission to Korea from the Departments of War, State, and Agriculture, and a special interdepartmental committee dominated by Acheson, both recommended an expansion of the plan into a three-year, $600 million economic rehabilitation program. Acheson went even further and linked this aid program to the concurrent $400 million Truman Doctrine commitment to Greece and Turkey announced in March 1947, a scheme that he largely devised. He specifically informed Congress that Korea was another country where U.S. aid could prove vital in enabling its citizens to resist the expansion of communism, which the Truman Doctrine had declared to be a global objective of U.S. foreign policy.

To obtain approval from the Bureau of the Budget, Acheson reduced the overall cost to $540 million. The War Department, though eager to reduce if not liquidate the U.S. commitment to Korea, reluctantly endorsed the revised package, which was christened the Korea Aid Bill. Initially, the bill was submitted to the Senate and House Armed Services Committees, but the latter claimed to have insufficient time to consider the bill. Senator Arthur H. Vandenberg, the influential chairman of the Senate Committee on Foreign Relations, had already expended substantial political capital to obtain passage of aid to Greece and Turkey. When Acheson requested that he consider the bill, he refused to do so before 1948. Acheson left the State Department on 30 June 1947 and the Korea Aid Bill lost its most determined advocate. On 4 August 1947, the State, Navy, and War Departments announced a new policy of minimizing U.S. military and financial commitments in Korea, with a view to ultimate complete withdrawal. In autumn 1947, the State Department withdrew the Korea Aid Bill. Only when Acheson returned to the Department as Secretary in 1949 did he revive the program, winning congressional approval for a similar bill in early 1950.

—Priscilla Roberts

References:

Chace, James. *Acheson: The Secretary of State Who Created the American World.* New York: Simon & Schuster, 1998.

Dobbs, Charles M. *The Unwanted Symbol: American Foreign Policy, the Cold War, and Korea, 1945–1950.* Kent, OH: Kent State University Press, 1981.

Matray, James I. *The Reluctant Crusade: American Foreign Policy in Korea, 1941–1950.* Honolulu: University of Hawaii Press, 1985.

McGlothlen, Ronald. "Acheson, Economics, and the American Commitment in Korea, 1947–1950." *Pacific Historical Review* 58, no. 1 (February 1989): 23–54.

———. *Controlling the Waves: Dean Acheson and U.S. Foreign Policy in Asia.* New York: W. W. Norton, 1993.

Stueck, William W., Jr. *The Road to Confrontation: American Policy toward China and Korea, 1947–1950.* Chapel Hill: University of North Carolina Press, 1981.

See also: Acheson, Dean Goodersham; Cold War, Origins to 1950; Korea Aid Bill of 1950.

Korea Aid Bill of 1950

The Korea Assistance Bill of 1949, which evolved into the Far Eastern Economic Assistance Act of 1950, committed the United States to providing aid not just to the Republic of Korea but also to the rump regime of Jiang Jieshi's Guomindang government on Taiwan. The State Department had withdrawn a similar economic rehabilitation program that Dean Acheson, then undersecretary of state, proposed in 1947. In spring 1948 the policy planning paper NSC-8 recommended the "liquidation of the U.S. commitment of men and money in Korea," a policy whose implementation began as soon as the Republic of Korea was established in August 1948, when U.S. troops were withdrawn.

As the Cold War intensified, the State Department, unlike the Joint Chiefs of Staff, was nonetheless unwilling to contemplate the new regime's collapse or to surrender southern Korea to a potential Communist takeover. The hope was that economic recovery and development would stabilize the new republic and enable it to resist both potential Northern attacks and internal subversion. By early 1949 the State Department had begun to formulate a three-year economic development plan for the new republic, a scheme based on the abandoned Korea Aid Bill of 1947. Returning to the department as secretary in January 1949, Acheson quickly threw himself behind

this proposal, which he submitted to Congress in June 1949. The revised bill recommended a systematic three-year economic recovery plan costing from $350 to $385 million and focusing upon improving output of coal, electrical power, fertilizer, and fishing. As with its predecessor, the new proposal envisaged an integrated economic partnership between industrialized Japan and then largely agricultural South Korea, under which the Republic of Korea (ROK) would provide Japan with the bulk of its rice, which would in turn enable Korea to purchase industrial goods from Japan. One collateral benefit would be the elimination of U.S. food aid to Japan; at this time the United States still provided occupied Japan with 25 percent of its food supplies, at an annual cost of $400 million (an increase from $330 million in 1947).

Initially the Korea Assistance Act, for which Acheson and other officials lobbied heavily, failed to win passage in Congress. Despite military assurances that a North Korean invasion was unlikely, some congressional representatives characterized the ROK as too unstable to survive, while supporters of Jiang Jieshi assailed Truman's administration's readiness to aid South Korean President Syngman Rhee's regime while denying economic assistance to the Guomindang on Taiwan. On 19 January 1950, one week after Acheson's National Press Club speech excluding Korea from the U.S. defense perimeter, the House of Representatives defeated the bill by a vote of 192 to 191.

Arguing that its rejection would have "disastrous" consequences for U.S. foreign policy, Acheson and President Truman resubmitted a revised bill, the Far Eastern Economic Assistance Bill. Besides mounting a sustained public relations effort on its behalf, they reduced the cost of the scheme's first year to $100 million. To attract support from the Republican China lobby, the bill now included limited economic aid for the Republic of China. In mid-February 1950, Congress approved the act, and in June, Acheson obtained congressional consent to another bill that appropriated $100 million for the plan's second year.

Historians have condemned the act as being passed for making the ROK into an unnecessary symbol of U.S. resolve to resist communism while simultaneously committing the United States to Jiang Jieshi's regime on Taiwan. Some have also suggested that Congress's initial rejection of the Korea Assistance Bill emboldened Kim Il Sung to take the decision to invade. It is difficult to prove that, even though the State Department may have originally intended to promote South Korean self-sufficiency. As Cold War lines hardened in Asia, one consequence of the Korea Aid Bill was to identify U.S. prestige more strongly with the ROK's survival.

—Priscilla Roberts

References:

Chace, James. *Acheson: The Secretary of State Who Created the American World.* New York: Simon & Schuster, 1998.

Dobbs, Charles M. "Limiting Room to Maneuver: The Korean Assistance Act of 1949." *Historian* 48, no. 4 (November 1986): 525–538.

———. *The Unwanted Symbol: American Foreign Policy, the Cold War, and Korea, 1945–1950.* Kent, OH: Kent State University Press, 1981.

Matray, James I. *The Reluctant Crusade: American Foreign Policy in Korea, 1941–1950.* Honolulu: University of Hawaii Press, 1985.

McGlothlen, Ronald. "Acheson, Economics, and the American Commitment in Korea, 1947–1950." *Pacific Historical Review* 58, no. 1 (February 1989): 23–54.

———. *Controlling the Waves: Dean Acheson and U.S. Foreign Policy in Asia.* New York: W. W. Norton, 1993.

Stueck, William W., Jr. *The Road to Confrontation: American Policy toward China and Korea, 1947–1950.* Chapel Hill: University of North Carolina Press, 1981.

See also: Acheson, Dean Goodersham; Jiang Jieshi (Chiang Kai-shek); Kim Il Sung; Korea Aid Bill of 1947; Truman, Harry S.

Korea, Democratic People's Republic of: 1945–1953

Soviet Far Eastern Army troops occupied both North Korea and Manchuria in August 1945. Before the occupation, Moscow had no concrete plans regarding government in the northern part of the Korean peninsula. When the Soviet Army entered North Korea, it encountered self-governing People's Committees in all the regions. Between the Japanese surrender and the Soviet occupation, the Korean people had already taken over government of the North themselves. The Soviet Army recognized these People's Committees throughout the northern half of Korea.

Stalin wanted to establish a pro-Soviet power base in North Korea by occupying it as soon as possible, but he did not try to establish a Communist regime directly. Stalin ordered the Twenty-fifth Army commander in North Korea to set up a United Front of parties in which the Communists would dominate, a practice similar to that used by Stalin in Eastern Europe. The Soviets sought to use Christian nationalist Cho Man-sik as a figurehead leader of the coalition government that would bridge the Left and the Right. The Soviet goal, however, was eventually to secure hegemony by the Left.

North Korean Communist leader Kim Il Sung returned to Wŏnsan as a major in the Soviet Twenty-fifth Army. On 14 October 1945, the Russians presented him to the North Korean people as a national hero. Kim had been a leader of a Chinese Communist guerrilla unit during 1932–1940 and had participated in the Korean national liberation movement as a member of the Chinese Communist Party. The area in which he had fought was in the vicinity of the north-eastern border region between Korea and China, and he had become well known as a guerrilla leader inside Korea fighting the Japanese until the end of the 1930s. Kim Il Sung escaped a Japanese sweep in 1940, and his faction of guerrillas joined the Twenty-fifth Army and received Soviet military ranks.

Kim's political identity was complicated. At the end of the war, however, he and his followers reorganized the Korean Communist Party, which had been dismantled by the Communist International (Comintern) in 1929. With the Soviet occupation of North Korea, the political Left included Kim Il Sung and his allies; a leftist group of Koreans from Chinese Yenan (Yan'an); Koreans from Soviet Central Asia; and a substantial number of Korean leftists and Communists who had remained in Korea during the colonial period.

These groups competed with the Communist group in the South, led by Pak Hŏn-yŏng, which had established a Korean Communist Party headquarters in Seoul in September 1945. The Soviet Army and the Kim Il Sung group sought to make P'yŏngyang the political center and cut the linkage with the party center in Seoul. However, the Pak Hŏn-yŏng group resisted such a transfer. But thanks in large part to the Soviet Army, in October 1945 Kim Il Sung and his followers established the North Korean bureau of the Korean Communist Party in P'yŏngyang and reached a compromise with Pak Hŏn-yŏng. In October 1945, Korean leaders in the North organized the Bureau of Five Provinces Administration, a loose administrative body coordinating widespread People's Committees.

Until the end of 1945, a coalition regime of leftists and right nationalists controlled the political arena in North Korea. The Russians did allow organization of some political parties, which carried out political activities. In February 1946, the North Korean Provisional People's Committee was established as a response to the Moscow Conference of December 1945, which had called for the creation of a Korean Interim Government for five years during a trusteeship of the Allied powers. Nationalist leader Cho Man-sik opposed that decision because of the trusteeship. The Soviets and leftists supported it because they emphasized creation of the interim government. The Soviets then ousted the right nationalists from participation in politics.

The Provisional People's Committee constituted the first central government in the North and immediately initiated socialist policies. In March 1946, land reform was begun and dispossessed landlords without compensation. In June, major industries, which had been owned mostly by the Japanese, were nationalized. The social revolution was relatively peaceful, without any massive purge of class enemies. The new regime, in fact, encouraged landlords and capitalists to flee south. At the same time, pro-Japanese Koreans were removed from positions of influence in the North. Through these processes, the Communist Bureau in the North declared its independence from the Communist Party in the South.

In August 1946, the North Korean Worker's Party (NKWP) was inaugurated; it came to dominate northern politics. After this the outward political pluralism in the North disappeared. Kim Il Sung became the absolute leader of the North Korean regime and the Korean Communist movement. In November, elections for the provincial people's committees were held throughout the North. This led to the formation of the North Korean People's Assembly as a legislature and the People's Committee as an executive power. The Soviet Army then transferred power to that government.

During this time the military situation in Manchuria greatly influenced events in North Korea. In the early period of the Chinese Civil War, North Korea was a refuge for defeated elements of the Chinese Communist army. Partly in response to the situation in Manchuria, from the fall of 1946 the North began organizing its own military force. At the same time in the South, a military organization appeared under the tutelage of the American Military Government. At that point, the so-called party-state regime came into being, closely modeled after that of the USSR. Although the united front remained in being, in effect there was one-party rule by NKWP, which controlled the other small political parties and the social organizations.

Despite this, the socialist transformation of all society, including the collectivization of agriculture, was not yet on the political agenda. The Democratic People's Republic of Korea (DPRK) remained at the stage of a Communist people's democracy until the mid-1940s. The agricultural sector was based on private ownership of small farms. Privately owned businesses dominated the commercial sector and small capitalist enterprises were allowed.

Within party politics of the North, there were several Communist factions: the Manchurian faction, led by Kim Il Sung; the Yenan faction; the Soviet faction; and the domestic faction. These served to keep a power balance, but Kim Il Sung was the dominant figure in North Korean politics. Kim presided over the executive machine and his faction controlled the military, but Soviet-returned Hŏ Ka-i controlled the party machinery. Externally, Yenan-returned Kim Tu-bong played the role of nominal chief of state.

There were power struggles over party management. For instance, in 1947 leaders of the Yenan faction insisted that the party follow Maoist ideology and propaganda lines. They criticized the imitation of the Soviet style and supported one more appropriate for Korean conditions. This led to the Soviet faction, which had been strengthened by the beginning of the

Cominform in the fall of 1947, to repress some of the Yenan faction. But there was no bloody purge in the NKWP at this time.

In early 1947 North Korea began an economic program on a central planning model, placing priority on heavy industry. During the colonial era, the Japanese had developed a heavy chemical industry in the northern part of Korea to support attacks against mainland China. From 1947 to the beginning of the Korean War, the North Korean economy expanded rapidly under a centrally organized mobilization system. This later enabled the DPRK to accumulate the comprehensive capabilities to initiate the Korean War.

From March 1946 on, a joint U.S. and USSR Commission struggled to settle the question of a unified Korean government as called for at the December 1945 Moscow Conference. The Soviet delegates demanded that those groups (mainly rightists) that had opposed trusteeship be excluded from consultation. The United States, however, supported the rightist groups that refused to accept the Moscow decision, and therefore the first Joint Commission failed to reach agreement. The Joint Commission met again in May 1947, but it achieved nothing toward a unified Korea and resigned indefinitely on 6 May. From July 1946 on, throughout the entire Korean peninsula, right-left confrontation became acute.

Internationally, from autumn 1947 on, the Cold War prevented any compromise between the U.S. and USSR. Only in the South, on 10 May 1948, did the general elections called for by the United Nations (UN) take place. On 15 August 1948, the Republic of Korea (ROK) was officially inaugurated under U.S. auspices.

The North, meanwhile, opposed the separate elections in the South and sought a unified government based on other than popular elections. Some Southern rightists and centrists, such as Kim Ku and Kim Kyu-sik, as well as leftists, resisted the separate election process. Kim Ku and Kim Kyu-sik had a dialogue with the Kim Il Sung regime in May 1948 in P'yŏngyang. They opposed the establishment of two states and urged unification of the Korean peninsula under one government. This did not prevent separate governments from emerging in both the South and North.

Some Southern rightist and many leftist dissidents participated in the creation of the government in the North. Under the facade of universal suffrage throughout all Korea, on 25 August the North held an election for the Supreme People's Assembly.

On 9 September, the DPRK was proclaimed, with its capital in P'yŏngyang, and Kim Il Sung became premier. The DPRK was the co-product of the NKWP and the South Korean Worker's Party (SKWP), led by Pak Hŏn-yŏng. The two parties were united into the Korea Worker's Party (KWP) in September 1949, as the strategy of resorting to military force to achieve unification began to find acceptance. In short, the KWP was very much an amalgam of different Communist groups.

Although the Korean War resulted from North Korea's preemptive military invasion of the South, it was an inevitable collision of the two states, each of which sought sole legitimacy over the Korean peninsula. At the beginning of the war, North Korean political, economic, and military strength, assisted by the Soviet Union and China, was superior to that of South Korea. As a result, the Korean People's Army (KPA, North Korean Army) was able to occupy the entirety of South Korea, save the Pusan perimeter in the southwestern corner of the peninsula, for almost three months. During that period of occupation, North Korean officials tried to transplant the North Korean politicoeconomic order in South Korea through the means of land reform and election processes identical to those in North Korea.

But with the participation of the United States and other UN forces, the military situation was soon reversed. Indeed, North Korea was almost absorbed by the Republic of Korea Army and U.S. and other UN forces. Only massive military support from the People's Republic of China enabled the DPRK to escape defeat.

After the Chinese People's Volunteer Army (CPVA, Chinese Communists) and KPA recaptured the areas of North Korea occupied by UN forces, the DPRK took several measures. Its governmental system changed in the aftermath of the war. At the end of 1952, the administrative system was reorganized; the four levels of province, county, township, and village (To-Kun-Myŏn-Ri) were reduced to three: province, county, and village (To-Kun-Ri). Central authority could now easily reach into the countryside. Peasant autonomy virtually disappeared and agricultural labor was regimented, partly in the interest of more effective production. In the frontier regions, some collective farms were created.

This collectivization had germinated during the Korean War. The war also enabled Kim Il Sung to consolidate his power base. He stigmatized the most powerful figure in the Soviet faction, Hŏ Ka-i; isolated, Hŏ is said to have committed suicide. An influential figure in the Yenan faction, Pak Il-u (then incumbent interior minister), was demoted to a minor post. Kim Il Sung's strongest rival, Pak Hŏn-yŏng, was purged as a U.S. spy, along with principal members of the former SKWP. Kim Il Sung made Pak and his faction the scapegoats for the North Korean military failure during the war.

—*Dong-man Suh*

References:
Suh, Dae-Sook. *Kim Il Sung: The North Korean Leader.* New York: Columbia University Press, 1988.
Suh, Dong-man. "Kita Chosen ni Okeru Shakaishugi no Seiritsu, 1945–1961" [The formation of the socialist system in North Korea]. Doctoral dissertation, Department of International Relations, University of Tokyo, 1995. Unpublished manuscript.
Wada, Haruki. *Kita Chosen: Yugekitai Gokka no Genzai* [North Korea: the present guerrilla state]. Tokyo: Iwanami Shoten, 1998.
Yi, Chong-sŏk. *Chosŏn Nodongdang Yŏn'gu* [A study of the Korean Worker's Party]. Seoul: Yŏksa Pip'yŏng-sa, 1995.

See also: China, People's Republic of; Kim Il Sung; Korea, Republic of: History 1947–1953; Union of Soviet Socialist Republics; U.S. Policy toward Korea before 1950; U.S. Policy toward Korea: 1950–1953.

Korea, Democratic People's Republic of: 1953 to the Present

The Korean War brought the near total destruction of the economic and industrial bases of the Democratic People's Republic of Korea (DPRK). Consequently, during 1953–1956 the DPRK leadership embarked on postwar reconstruction and development programs. In 1954 the government launched an agricultural cooperative movement as the means of restructuring rural society. By the end of 1956, thanks to massive economic and technical assistance provided by the Soviet Union, the People's Republic of China (PRC), and the Communist East European states, the DPRK was able to restore its economy to the level of the prewar year of 1949.

In general the DPRK has given priority in economic policy to the development of heavy industry. The government also inaugurated the radical policy of collectivization in agriculture. It spanned the period 1954–1958, moving Chinese style through three types of cooperatives. There were increasing degrees of cooperatives, ranging from the pooling of labor and some collective use of implements and animals to the distribution of income based solely on work contribution. But from the early period, the third category was pushed predominantly. By August 1958 the entire peasant population had joined agricultural cooperatives. At the same time, industry and commerce were completely socialized. By 1958 the economic system had been entirely transformed into a socialist economy.

During this period, the party leadership consisted of two contending groups. The majority group was centered around Kim Il Sung, advocating the policy orientation toward heavy industry and radical collectivization. The minority group, consisting of the Soviet faction and the Yenan faction, supported a policy favoring light industry and gradual collectivization. At the end of 1955, Kim Il Sung resolved the differences by enunciating the *Chuch'e* (self-reliance) ideal in thought and propaganda. *Chuch'e* included political independence, as much as was possible, from both the USSR and China. This appealed to deep-rooted

Korean resistance to foreign control. Kim referred to *Chuch'e* as "a creative application of Marxism-Leninism." But the de-Stalinization policy of Soviet leader Nikita Khrushchev after the 1956 Twentieth Congress of the Communist Party of the Soviet Union encouraged criticism of Kim Il Sung in North Korea.

In August 1956, at the party plenum of the Korean Workers' Party (KWP), some leaders of the Yenan faction and the Soviet faction attacked Kim Il Sung, challenging his one-person rule and pressing for liberalization of economic and social control. But the dissident group was too weak to defeat Kim, and his majority group succeeded in expelling some leaders of the opposition group from KWP membership.

The USSR and PRC also interfered in the power struggle within North Korea, and Kim Il Sung accepted the request of Nikita Khrushchev and Mao Zedong to restore party membership to the purged Soviet and Yenan faction members. The rebirth of Stalinism in the Soviet Union, flowing from the failed October 1956 Hungarian revolt, however, allowed Kim Il Sung to recover his leadership within the KWP. Beginning in early 1957, he ruthlessly purged leaders of the Yenan and Soviet factions from the party and the government. The so-called August Factional Incident was the most serious political power struggle in North Korea since the beginning of the Communist regime there.

By the time of the First Party Conference in March 1958, Kim Il Sung had eliminated the opposition group completely from the party leadership elected by the Third Party Congress in April 1956. Kim's loyal supporters now began to take complete control of the party leadership. By the Fourth Party Congress in 1961, all factions other than those loyal to Kim Il Sung had been eliminated.

At the 1958 Party Conference, the government announced its first five-year economic plan, and the policy of emphasizing heavy industry was restored to dominant position. Beginning in 1957, Soviet economic aid to North Korea decreased sharply. The DPRK then embarked on production based on mass mobilization of people inspired by other than material incentives. Similar to the PRC's Great Leap Forward, in 1959 it was named the *Ch'ŏllima* (flying horse) Movement.

From 1959 to 1962 the ruling system changed. All aspects of government came to be dominated by party committees. In local administration, the so-called Ch'ŏngsan-ni Method was introduced in 1960. As in other Communist countries, the party was superior to the government at all administrative levels. Until this time, the administrative system had operated under the dual control of the party committee and the people's committee. From 1961 the Taean Work System was applied in the management of industrial enterprises.

Individual companies came to be run by factory party committees rather than by industrial managers. About the time of the September 1961 Fourth Party Congress, the basic socialist system of North Korea was completed. Officially this system continues to the present.

In the Sino-Soviet dispute, which became acute in the 1960s, the DPRK supported the PRC rather than the USSR. As the Soviet–North Korean relationship grew strained, the DPRK leadership began to criticize the Soviet Union overtly, and the Soviets then halted economic and military aid. As a result, the DPRK embarked on an independent policy line. A new *Chuch'e* line was announced: summarized as independence in politics, self-reliance in the economy, and self-defense in military affairs. At the same time, Park Chung Hee's Republic of Korea (ROK) military government, established by a coup d'état in May 1961, pushed with U.S. backing for normalization talks with Japan in order to receive economic aid from that country. North Korea feared this new "southern triangle" of the ROK, Japan, and United States as a tripartite military alliance directed against it.

The DPRK followed the twin goals of economic construction on the one hand and military augmentation on the other. At the same time, Kim Il Sung took a militant posture toward South Korea and the United States, increasing defense expenditures at the expense of economic development. In fact, the completion date of the first seven-year economic plan (1961–1967) had to be postponed to 1970.

In 1965 the United States began bombing North Vietnam and sent ground troops to South Vietnam. South Korea decided to dispatch its own military units to South Vietnam. Although North Korea did not match the commitment of South Korea to the fighting in Vietnam, it did send some pilots to North Vietnam. As the Vietnam War escalated, military tensions on the Korean peninsula also increased.

During the period of the Cultural Revolution in China, Beijing asked the DPRK to initiate the same policies. This strained Sino–North Korean relations. North Korean leaders worried that Maoism, which was exalted during the Cultural Revolution, might have a strong influence on North Korea. The personality cult of Kim Il Sung was strengthened from competition with Mao. *Chuch'e* thought was hailed as "Kimilsungism." In 1967 the movement for consolidation of the "Unitary Ideological System" was organized to heighten Kimilsungism to the monolithic ideology of the KWP. Kim Il Sung purged some dissidents who opposed this movement. These included those who had fought with him in Kapsan and Manchuria against the Japanese.

The dissidents' independent attitude was combined with a milder line toward unification and economic policy. Until this time, no one who belonged to the Kim Il Sung faction had been purged from the party and government. Kim's role continued to be exalted, and he was presented as having had a predominant place over his followers and colleagues in the long struggle against Japan.

Kim Il Sung was held up as the supreme leader, a great warrior, and the head of the government and party bureaucracy. The revolutionary thought and tradition of Kim's fight against the Japanese was inculcated into the entire population so that all the North Korean people might live and work like guerrilla fighters in Manchuria. Kim Il Sung was reconfirmed as the *Suryŏng* (Great or Maximum Leader), and the whole tradition of anti-Japanese guerrilla struggle in Manchuria was transformed into Kim's personal activities. The history of the anti-Japanese guerrilla struggles in Manchuria became state mythology.

A new state structure came into being during the period 1967–1972. It was based on the previous state socialist system begun before 1961. The new regime was institutionalized in the 1972 constitution. In it the *Suryŏng*'s position was defined as the *Chusŏk* (president). The new constitution concentrated political power in the person and office of *Chusŏk*. The *Suryŏng* would have direct communication with his people through on-the-spot "guidance," such as visits to villages and factories.

Notwithstanding difficulties with its external relations, the North Korean economy recorded a high growth rate until the early 1970s. At one time, North Korean economy was styled as the model for "Third-World Socialism." But from that point, the North Korean economy stagnated, confronted by the inherent stagnation in the contradictions of a state socialist system. To overcome its problems, the DPRK secured billions of dollars in loans from Western countries at the beginning of its second Six-Year Plan (1971–1976), but the rapid escalation of oil prices in the early 1970s forced North Korea into default on repayment of its foreign loans. The DPRK chose the path of closing doors to a capitalist market economy. Foreign economic relations were restricted to Communist states.

The succession of power from Kim Il Sung to his son Kim Jong Il began during this time. At first, Kim Jong Il's career was concentrated in policy and propaganda. From 1968 to 1971, his activities were conspicuous in cinema and opera. He won the confidence of his father and top leaders through his successful production of operas, the subjects of which were the guerrilla activities against the Japanese. When he became a party secretary in 1973 and a member of the Politburo in 1974, Kim Jong Il was the second most powerful figure within the party and the heir to his father's position. Although some loyal followers of Kim Il Sung resisted

Kim Jong Il's ascendancy to power, they were soon ousted from the party and government. His succession was formalized in the Sixth Party Congress in October 1980. No later than 1980, the DPRK had moved from the one-person rule of Kim Il Sung to the two-person rule of Kim Il Sung and Kim Jong Il.

Kim Jong Il controlled the party organization and ideology. He took the leading role in forming the DPRK state image. In the 1970s, he formulated a number of slogans closely tied to the nationalist struggle against Japan. In the early 1980s, this took the form of the slogan, "the Party as Mother." This followed "the Suryŏng as Parent." These put forward the image of a "Family State." In 1986, the image of "an Organic Whole of Socio-political Life" was proclaimed, in which the Suryŏng was "the brains of this organic whole of socio-political life." The party was "the nerve center" of this organic whole. This state was described as a human body. In these images, Confucianist traditions and the organic notion of the state were intermingled. The only independent force in the state was the leader (Suryŏng), and the people became dependent upon him. The *Chuch'e* ideal was turned on its head.

From the 1980s, Asian socialist countries, including China and Vietnam, began to undertake economic reforms and a more open-door policy toward the West. The spectacular economic development of such Asian states as the ROK, Singapore, Taiwan, and Hong Kong had a strong influence on these socialist countries. In 1984 the DPRK initiated moves to open its doors as well when it enacted a joint-venture law. But this was unsuccessful because the DPRK leadership shrank from the necessary reforms that the PRC was carrying out; the rigid *Chuch'e* DPRK ideal was a barrier to bold changes in policy. And a new Cold War situation in northeast Asia brought about by the Soviet invasion of Afghanistan prevented Kim Il Sung and Kim Jong Il from changing the existing policy line. The confrontation between the United States and the Soviet Union intensified and the United States took a hard line toward the DPRK. For North Korea, the Sino-U.S. reconciliation was not as important as the Soviet-U.S. antagonism. In the 1980s, the USSR stepped up its economic and military aid to the DPRK.

The drastic reform politics of the socialist camp, which originated from Soviet leader Mikhail Gorbachev's *glasnost* (openness) and *perestroika* (restructuring) after 1985, was an enormous shock to the North Korean leadership. Another blow came from the 1988 Seoul Olympics, in which Soviet and East European countries participated. This led Soviet-bloc countries to normalize their diplomatic relations with the ROK in the early 1990s. In 1992 the PRC also established diplomatic relations with the ROK.

To ward off external isolation, the DPRK joined the United Nations (UN) in 1991 simultaneously with the ROK. The DPRK signed accords with the ROK regarding denuclearization and reconciliation, and in 1990 it began normalization talks with Japan. But diplomatic normalization between the USSR and ROK meant the removal of the Soviet nuclear umbrella for North Korea. The DPRK's response to the Soviet action was that it would consider independent steps to offset the U.S. nuclear umbrella over the ROK. This greatly upset the United States, which called for the inspection of DPRK nuclear weapons development.

The confrontation between the United States and the DPRK over the latter's nuclear weapons program reached a crisis point in 1994. This ended in an agreement worked out with the intervention of ex–U.S. President Jimmy Carter for a summit meeting between DPRK President Kim Il Sung and ROK President King Young Sam, but this was aborted by Kim Il Sung's sudden death.

In 1995, however, the United States and the DPRK agreed that Washington would lead a consortium to supervise and finance the construction of two light-water nuclear reactors in North Korea. In return, the DPRK agreed to discontinue its alleged nuclear weapons program and to allow international inspections.

In 1996 there was another crisis when the DPRK declared that it would no longer honor the 1953 Korean War Armistice Agreement. To answer this, the United States and the ROK proposed four-party peace talks involving the DPRK, ROK, United States, and PRC. These talks have not gone well.

The collapse of the Soviet Union and communism in Eastern Europe in the early 1990s dealt a fatal blow to the North Korean economy because the Soviet Union and Eastern Europe states had been North Korea's major trading partners. Factory output decreased dramatically because of the deficient supply of energy and raw materials. To overcome this adverse situation, in the early 1990s the DPRK resumed the open-door policy. In 1991 it declared the Najin-Sŏnbong district a free-trade zone. At the end of 1993, North Korea signaled a more active change that placed priority on agricultural production, light industry, and trade, all in a three-year economic plan. But after the abrupt death of Kim Il Sung on 8 July 1994, the North has kept silent on its plan. The DPRK in fact has registered negative economic growth in real terms since 1990. After 1995, poor weather conditions contributed to successive poor harvests and a resultant severe famine.

In addition to unfavorable natural conditions for farming, the inflexible Chuch'e position has aggravated food production. Responding to urgent North Korean appeals, the international community extended enormous food aid to the North. Although it is impossible to put together an accurate picture of conditions in the North, many North Koreans have fled the North and its famine conditions. Certainly, the central rationing system for food and daily necessities broke down. In rural and urban areas, farmer and citizen markets are spreading rapidly. In 1996 the DPRK modified the system of collective farms in order to raise agricultural productivity. Farmers were allowed to dispose of a larger portion of their surplus production on the open market.

For more than three years after the July 1994 death of Kim Il Sung, Kim Jong Il ruled the North solely as the supreme commander of the People's Army. Amid persistent reports of socioeconomic unrest since Kim Il Sung's death, the military took the initiative even in economic activities. After the end of his father's 48-year rule, Kim Jong Il has used the military to maintain order. In a crisis-management regime, Kim used the slogan of "March Through Distress" to represent the difficulties during this era. The term harkened back to the most difficult period of the anti-Japanese guerrilla war in Manchuria during 1938–1939. Kim also stressed a "Revolutionary Military Spirit" tied to the army. The Korean People's Army is regarded as the pillar of the revolution and main force for Chuch'e in official ideology. Based on the state socialist system, the DPRK moved from a party state to a party-military state.

The Kim Jong Il regime was inaugurated officially in September 1998. Retaining his position as chairman of the National Defense Commission, Kim Jong Il formalized his succession to power. In October 1997 he had already assumed the post of general secretary of the Central Committee of the Worker's Party. A constitutional amendment provided that the chairman of the Presidium of the Supreme People's Assembly represent the DPRK in its relations with foreign countries, but there is no doubt that Kim Jong Il is the supreme leader of the DPRK and KWP.

The new constitution legalized a change in the agricultural production system and in markets in the cities and the countryside. It also introduced the concept of cost-benefit into economic management. The changes in the economic articles in the new constitution are comparable to those of the 1982 constitution of the PRC. Although the DPRK is not at the level of the socialist market economy of China, obviously it is undergoing economic change. At the same time, the military ensures the regime's survival.

The DPRK has yet to normalize diplomatic relations with the United States and Japan, and since 1992 it has rejected dialogue with the ROK. Besides continuing friendly relations with the PRC, diplomatic normalization with Washington and Tokyo is an important external condition for survival of the North Korean regime. In 1999, South Korean President Kim Dae Jung appealed for diplomatic normalization between the DPRK and the United States and Japan in return for eliminating the DPRK's nuclear and missile threats. Clearly, the future direction and survival of the DPRK depends to a considerable extent on favorable external relations with the United States, Japan, and the ROK and economic assistance from them.

—*Dong-man Suh*

References:

Suh, Dae-sook. *Kim Il Sung: The North Korean Leader.* New York: Columbia University Press, 1988

Suh, Dong-man. "Kita Chosen ni Okeru Shakaishugi no Seiritsu, 1945–1961" [The formation of the socialist system in North Korea]. Doctoral dissertation, Department of International Relations, University of Tokyo, 1995. Unpublished manuscript.

Wada, Haruki. *Kita Chosen: Yugekitai Gokka no Genzai* [North Korea: the present guerrilla state]. Tokyo: Iwanami Shoten, 1998.

Yi, Chong-sŏk. *Chosŏn Nodongdang Yŏn'gu* [A study of the Korean Worker's Party]. Seoul: Yŏksa Pip'yong-sa, 1995.

See also: China, People's Republic of; Japan; Kim Il Sung; Kim Jong Il; Korea, Republic of: History, 1953 to the Present; Mao Zedong; Stalin, Josef; U.S. Policy toward Korea: 1953 to the Present.

Korea, Democratic People's Republic of: Air Force (Korean People's Air Force [KPAF])

During August–September 1945, the Korean Aviation Society was established as the first flying organization in North Korea. At Sinŭiju Airfield, it was headed by Colonel Yi Ha-wal, a Korean who served in the Japanese Air Force during World War II. That October a pilot-training program was begun, supervised by Soviet advisors. In 1946 the program became part of the military and was moved to P'yŏngyang as part of the Korean People's Army Military Academy. In November 1948, it became the Korean Air Regiment, and in January 1950, it expanded into a division.

The North Korean Air Division consisted of three regiments. The first was a fighter regiment of three battalions; the second was a ground-attack regiment, also with three battalions; the third regiment was the training regiment, consisting of fighter training at P'yŏngyang Air Base, and ground-attack training and maintenance and communications training at Yŏnp'o Airfield (where the ground-attack regiment was also based). Two technical battalions were stationed at P'yŏngyang Air Base. These had both administrative and supply functions at the division level headquarters.

In April 1950, the North Korean Air Division numbered some 1,675 officers and enlisted men: 76 pilot officers, 364 nonrated officers who took on support roles, 875 enlisted men, and 360 cadets. On 15 April 1950, the Soviet Air Force gave the North Koreans 63

planes, which raised the number of their working aircraft from 115 to 178.

In June 1950, the Korean People's Air Force (KPAF) consisted of forty World War II–era Yakolev (Yak) propeller-driven fighters, sixty Yak trainers, seventy Ilyushin Sturmovik Il-10 and Lavochkin La-9 fighter-bombers, and ten Polikarpov PO-2 biplanes, 25-year-old reconnaissance aircraft. General Wang Yong, a Soviet Air Academy graduate and World War II bomber pilot, commanded the KPAF.

The KPAF was far superior to the Republic of Korea Air Force (ROKAF, South Korea). Early in the Korean War, the KPAF carried out attacks on South Korea in support of the Korean People's Army (KPA's) invasion. For example, on 29 and 30 June there were two strafing attacks by six fighters and four attack bombers on Suwŏn Airfield in South Korea. Four Yak-9s also attacked two U.S. Air Force (USAF) F-80s and a Yak made a run at a B-29. In July the KPAF carried out several small, insignificant air strikes. On 2 July, ten KPAF planes strafed and dropped leaflets on Suwŏn Airfield. On 6 July, four Yak-9s strafed Osan. On 7 July, an unknown number of aircraft dropped eight bombs on Hapch'ŏn. Three days later, several Yak-9 fighters strafed Kimpŏ Airfield and also hit the U.S. Army 19th Infantry Regiment at Ch'ŏngju. On 11 July, three KPAF Yak fighters attacked a flight of U.S. F-80s and shot down a B-29 bomber. On 12 July, two KPAF aircraft shot down a L-4 liaison plane. On 15 July, KPAF planes attacked four B-26 bombers, forcing one to make an emergency landing. Finally on 17 July, Yak-9s carried out air attacks and a leaflet drop on Taejŏn.

The United Nations Command (UNC) soon struck back in the air. Heavy and well-coordinated attacks led principally by the aircraft from the U.S. Fifth Air Force and Navy Task Force 77 produced UNC domination of the skies by 20 July 1950. Bombing attacks on North Korean airfields early in the war had a lasting effect, limiting the force that the North Koreans could use at one certain time. This is why the North Koreans could not make the most efficient use of their substantial force. At least 152 North Korean planes were destroyed on the ground between the beginning of the war and September 1950. The principal North Korean airfield at P'yŏngyang was rendered useless by one bombing raid in August, forcing the North Koreans to move their facilities underground.

Apart from small, sporadic air attacks by the KPAF after the end of July, the remainder of air resistance came from the Chinese People's Volunteer Air Force (Chinese Communist). After the People's Republic of China intervened in the war, the KPAF used air bases in Manchuria. KPAF planes were rebuilt with Soviet help, and 1,400 personnel from the KPAF were trained as pilots outside of Korea. Major North Korean activity in China was at Harbin and Jirin Airfields.

Later in the war, the KPAF did use night harassing attacks with PO-2 aircraft, known to GIs as "Bed-Check Charlies," but these raids had little effect on UNC operations. With the signing of the Armistice Agreement in July 1953, the KPAF moved back into North Korea.

—*Brian A. Arnold II*

References:

Futrell, Robert F. *The United States Air Force in Korea, 1950–1953*. Rev. ed. Washington, DC: Office of the Chief of Air Force History, 1983.

Hallion, Richard P. *The Naval Air War in Korea*. Baltimore: Nautical and Aviation Publishing Co. of America, 1986.

Sandler, Stanley, ed. *The Korean War: An Encyclopedia*. New York: Garland, 1995.

Summers, Harry G., Jr. *Korean War Almanac*. New York: Facts on File, 1990.

See also: "Bed-Check Charlies"; Korea, Republic of: Air Force (ROKAF); United States Air Force (USAF).

Korea, Democratic People's Republic of: Army (Korean People's Army [KPA])

The army of the Democratic People's Republic of Korea (DPRK, North Korea), the Korean People's Army (KPA, also known as the North Korean People's Army [NKPA] or North Korean Army [NKA]) was a well-balanced and well-trained army at the beginning of the Korean War, easily dominating the Republic of Korea Army (ROKA, South Korea). Although somewhat larger than the ROKA when the war began, at the end of the conflict the KPA was less than half the strength of the resurgent South Korean Army.

At the end of World War II, the Soviets arrived in what would become North Korea. Soon afterward, local Communist security formations sprang up, such as the People's Guards and the Red Guards. These were soon replaced by the Peace Guardians, a province-level police force under the centralized control of the Department of Public Safety. On 25 September 1945, Kim Il Sung and a number of other Soviet-trained Koreans landed at Wŏnsan. These former guerrillas had fought against the Japanese and they became advisors to provincial governments, supervising provisional police bureaus.

The Communist Party's control of the police was tightened by the Central Party School of Police Officials, begun in January 1946. The P'yŏngyang Military Academy was organized in 1945 to provide officers for the Constabulary. Three additional and similar schools were established, and the four academies produced officers for the Peace Preservation Officers' Training Schools. These "schools" were a front for the North Korean armed forces.

In 1946 North Korea organized a Railway Constabulary, independent of the Department of Public Safety, with the mission of receiving officers and men of the Volunteer Army and new recruits. Shortly thereafter both the Peace Preservation Officers' Training Schools and the Railway Constabulary became part of the security forces under the Department of Public Safety (later the Department of Internal Affairs). Also in that year, officers and enlisted men who had been members of the Korean Volunteer Army in Manchuria were released to enroll in the Korean Railway Constabulary.

In December 1946, the Russians began arming North Korean forces, including with equipment from Soviet troops returning home. In 1947 Russia began trading arms for foodstuffs from North Korea. The Soviet Army also provided the early training. By December 1946, North Korean training units had permanently assigned Soviet officer advisors. Nearby Russian army garrisons also supplied special training cadres.

In 1946 a major armed forces recruiting campaign was launched. Former members of the Korean Volunteer Force and of other Chinese Communist–trained forces were all inducted into the armed forces, as were former members of the Japanese Army, or those who had been trained by the Japanese as policemen. Police force volunteers were all transferred into North Korea's new "security" formations, and members of the North Korean Labor Party were urged to enlist. Men between the ages of 18 and 35 were subject to a general conscription.

Arrangements were made for Soviet-trained North Korean troops to be employed in the Chinese Communist Army. Under this program, in March and April 1947, more than 30,000 North Korean troops, equipped with Soviet arms, were sent to Manchuria for training.

The true mission of the Peace Preservation Officers' Schools was to organize, equip, and train a national army. In September 1947, this was revealed with the organization of the Department of Military Affairs. Coincidentally the First, Second, and Third Peace Preservation Officers' Training Centers became the People's Army's 1st and 2d Division and the Independent Infantry Brigade. But the North Korean government did not announce activation of an armed force known as the "People's Army" until 8 February 1948, the same year that the Department of Military Affairs became the Ministry of National Defense. The People's Army at the time numbered about 30,000 men, with an additional 170,000 trainees, including members of the Police Constabulary, Fire Brigades, and Coast Guard.

The 3d Division was formed from the Independent Mixed Brigade in October 1948. The 4th Division was formed in late 1949, while the Chinese Communist 164th and 166th Divisions, made up of Koreans, became the nucleus of the 5th and 6th Divisions in July and August. The 7th, later redesignated the 12th, was composed of veterans of the Chinese Communist 15th and 156th Divisions. A tank battalion was organized in the fall of 1948 and expanded into a regiment by May 1949. This regiment eventually became the 105th Armored Division. The 10th and 15th Divisions were formed in March 1950 and the 13th in June of that year.

In late June 1950, just before the war's outbreak, the KPA, or Inmingun, numbered between 150,000 and 180,000 troops. Right after the beginning of hostilities, the 1st and 3d Border Constabulary brigades, which had been follow-up troops in the invasion of South Korea, were redesignated the 8th and 9th Divisions, respectively. North Korea also had Soviet-trained pilots, aircraft mechanics, tankers, and tank maintenance personnel.

The typical North Korean infantry division was authorized 12,092 personnel, including three infantry regiments, an artillery regiment (two 76-mm howitzer battalions, a 122-mm mortar battalion, and a battalion of self-propelled 76-mm guns), an antitank battalion, signal battalion, engineer and medical battalions, an information and training battalion, a reconnaissance company, and a transportation company.

In June 1950, North Korea had 150 T-34 tanks, 120 of them in the 105th Armored Brigade. The brigade had three tank regiments, each with 40 tanks. Each battalion had 13 tanks and each tank company four tanks. Company, battalion, and regimental commanders each had a personal tank. Tank crews had five men. At the end of June 1950, the brigade was expanded to the 105th Armored Division.

The Russian-built T-34, with a low silhouette, good armor, a wide tread and good gun, was one of the better tanks to come out of World War II. The South had no weapon to oppose it.

Estimated Strength of the NKPA at the Beginning of the Korean War:

1st Division (2d, 3d, 14th Regiments)	11,000
766th Independent Infantry Unit	3,000
2d Division (4th, 6th, 17th Regiments)	10,838
12th Motorcycle Regiment	2,000
3d Division (7th, 8th, 9th Regiments)	11,000
105th Armored Brigade (107th, 109d, 203d Armored Regiments; 206th Mechanized Infantry Regiment	6,000
4th Division (5th, 16th, 18th Regiments)	11,000
5th Division (10th, 11th, 12th Regiments)	11,000
1st Brigade, Border Constabulary	5,000
6th Division (1st, 13th, 15th Regiments)	11,000
2d Brigade, Border Constabulary	2,600

7th Division (1st, 2d, 3d Regiments; 18 June 1950, redesignated 12th Division (30th, 31st, 32d Regiments)	12,000
3d Brigade, Border Constabulary	4,000
5th Brigade, Border Constabulary	3,000
10th Division (25th, 27th, 29th Regiments)	6,000
7th Brigade, Border Constabulary (helped form 7th Division July 1950)	4,000
13th Division (19th, 21st, 23d Regiments)	6,000
Army, First and Second Corps	6,000–7,000
Total	125,438–126,438
Plus (probably under Army command):	
122-mm Artillery Regiment	1,300
603d (83d) Motorcycle Reconnaissance Battalion	3,500
Engineer Brigade	2,500
Signal Regiment	1,000
Guerrilla Command	2,500
Total	10,800
Grand total	136,238–137,238

In June 1950, the North Korean Air Force numbered 2,000 men and some 180 aircraft. The Coast Guard numbered 13,700 men, the marines 9,000, and the internal security force 34,000.

During the drive into South Korea and the subsequent long and bloody struggle along the Pusan perimeter, the KPA suffered horrendous casualties. The recruitment, training, and transportation of replacements from North Korea was almost impossible. As a result, the North Koreans impressed thousands of South Korean young men into their army. In later interrogation of prisoners of war from the KPA, 40,000 of them claimed to be South Koreans forced into the KPA as replacements for losses around the Pusan perimeter.

In early August 1950, in addition to troops in North Korea, the front-line KPA consisted of two corps: I Corps including 3d, 4th, and 6th Divisions (later also the 2d, 7th, 9th, and 10th Divisions); and II Corps including 1st, 5th, 8th, 12th, 13th, and 15th Divisions and the 766th Independent Infantry Regiment. The 4th Division was destroyed during the First Battle of the Naktong Bulge later in August 1950. The 4th was not reconstituted until after the Chinese entered the war in late 1950.

The KPA activated the 45th (89th, 90th, and 91st Regiments), 46th (93d, 94th, and 95th Regiments), and 47th (2d, 3d, and 4th Regiments) Divisions during August 1950; the 37th Division (74th, 75th, and 76th Regiments) about September; and the 27th Division (7th, 14th, and 32d Regiments) in late November or early December. Other commands formed just before the outbreak of the war, or shortly thereafter, included the 956th Independent Marine Regiment (July 1949), which was redesignated the 23d (239th) Marine Brigade. In 1951 this brigade was engaged in defending the west coast. In late May 1951, the KPA 36th Division was inactivated and its 63d Regiment was integrated into the brigade. In October 1951, the brigade was redesignated a mechanized artillery brigade, then, in June 1952, again the 23d Brigade. It continued, however, to be a coastal defense organization.

The 24th Mechanized Artillery Brigade was organized in August 1950 and reorganized into the 24th Division about November of that year. The 25th Mechanized Artillery Brigade is believed to have been formed from the 25th Coastal Defense Brigade (activated in August 1950) in October 1951. The 26th Brigade, organized in August 1950, was converted to the 25th Mechanized Artillery Brigade, also in October 1951.

During the invasion of Inch'ŏn and subsequent fighting in the vicinity of Yŏngdŭngp'o and in Seoul, U.S. troops were opposed by troops from the North Korean 17th, 18th (Seoul), and 31st Divisions, the 22d, 70th, and 89th Regiments; 78th Independent Regiment; 42d Mechanized Brigade; 107th and 111th Security Regiments; 918th Coast Artillery Regiment; 19th Antiaircraft Regiment; 10th Railroad Regiment; and at Kimpŏ Airfield, the 1st Air Force Division, which had the mission of operating the airfield, and the 877th Air Force Unit.

The foregoing indicates that the KPA was a diverse and viable organization, at least until the Inch'ŏn landing. From that point on, the army disintegrated and its principal major commands attempted to escape from the Pusan perimeter and back into North Korea. The official U.S. Army history of that period of the war claims that only 25,000–30,000 disorganized KPA soldiers escaped back into North Korea.

However by 23 November 1950, the KPA had the I through V Corps in North Korea and the VI, VII, and VIII Corps in Manchuria. The corps in North Korea included the 1st through 10th, 12th, 15th, 17th, 24th, 27th, 31st, 38th, 41st, 43d, and 47th Infantry Divisions and the 105th Armored Division. Those in Manchuria contained the 13th, 18th, 19th, 32d, 36th, 37th, 42d, 45th, and 46th Divisions. During January and February 1951, the KPA underwent reorganization. In I Corps, which included the 8th, 17th, and 47th Divisions, the 17th was converted to a mechanized unit containing about twenty tanks. In the II Corps, the 31st Division was deactivated and its personnel distributed among the three other corps divisions: the 2d, 9th, and 27th. II Corps also controlled the much-reduced 10th Division, then operating as a guerrilla force behind United Nations Command (UNC) lines. The 38th and 43d Divisions were deactivated in the North Korean V Corps and their personnel distributed among the remaining 6th, 7th, and 12th Divisions.

These deactivations to obtain personnel to replace losses indicate that the North Koreans were experiencing extreme difficulty in replacing battle losses.

To strengthen forces opposing the UN in January 1951, the KPA brought the VI, VII, and VIII Corps from Manchuria. The VI Corps assembled in mid-February just northwest of Seoul. The VII Corps closed into assembly areas near Wŏnsan on the east coast later that month. The 42d and 46th Divisions of VIII Corps were positioned near Hŭngnam, while the 45th Division went on to become part of II Corps, just north of the 38th parallel in eastern Korea.

Fighting in Korea slowed down in June and July 1951, allowing the Chinese and North Koreans to maintain a higher flow of replacements. However, as the following chart shows, three of the North Korean's seven corps were only about half strength, and another at about two-thirds. Only the III, VI, and VII Corps were close to being full strength.

U.S. Eighth Army's estimate of KPA opposing strength as of 1 July 1951:

I Corps (8th, 19th, 47th Division)	15,800
II Corps (2d, 13th, 27th Division)	18,700
III Corps (1st, 15th, 45th Division)	30,400
IV Corps (4th, 5th, 105th Armed Division; 26th Brigade)	29,200
V Corps (6th, 12th, 32d Division)	14,300
VI Corps (9th, 17th Mechanized, 18th, 23d Division)	35,500
VII Corps (3d, 24th, 37th, 46th Division; 63d Brigade)	35,500
Other forces	31,700
NK guerrillas in South Korea	7,500
Total KPA	218,600

All seven North Korean corps were on the front, three in the west and four in the east. During the last months of 1951, North Korean strength remained about 225,000 troops.

By November 1952, only two North Korean corps (49,700 troops) were on line. Four other corps (140,000 troops) were in reserve. Chinese forces on line numbered 166,000 and more than 350,000 in immediate reserve. In the last four months of the war, March–July 1953, North Korean ground forces numbered some 260,000 troops. By contrast, South Korea had over 500,000 troops in ground forces, including marines.

—*Uzal W. Ent*

References:

Appleman, Roy E. *South to the Naktong, North to the Yalu.* Washington, DC: Office of the Chief of Military History, 1961.

Ent, Uzal W. *Fighting on the Brink: Defense of the Pusan Perimeter.* Paducah, KY: Turner, 1996.

Heinl, Robert D. *Victory at High Tide: The Inchon-Seoul Campaign.* Philadelphia: J. B. Lippincott, 1968.

Hermes, Walter G. *United States Army in the Korean War: Truce Tent and Fighting Front*. Washington, DC: Office of the Chief of Military History, 1966.

History of the North Korean Army. Military Intelligence Section, HQ. U.S. Far East Command, Tokyo, Japan, 31 July 1952.

Montross, Lynn, and Nicholas A. Canzona. *U.S. Marine Operations in Korea, 1950–1953*. Vol. 2, *The Inchon-Seoul Operation*. Washington, DC: U.S. Marine Corps Historical Branch, 1955.

See also: Kim Il Sung; Korea, Democratic People's Republic of: Navy (Korean People's Navy [KPN]); Korea, Republic of: Army (ROKA); Order of Battle: United Nations, North Korea, and People's Republic of China.

Korea, Democratic People's Republic of, Invasion of the Republic of Korea
(25 June 1950)

Recently declassified Soviet documents reveal that Democratic People's Republic of Korea (DPRK, North Korea) leader Kim Il Sung on many occasions asked Soviet leader Josef Stalin to support a DPRK invasion of the Republic of Korca (ROK, South Korea). During the 5 March 1949 Kim-Stalin meeting in Moscow, Kim inquired whether the Soviet Union would support an invasion. Stalin replied that the DPRK must not attack the ROK until such time as it had absolute military superiority. Stalin also emphasized that the division of the Korean peninsula along the 38th parallel resulted from the agreement between the U.S. and USSR and thus the parallel was the internationally recognized boundary. During the same meeting, Stalin told Kim that the DPRK could attack the South only if the ROK attacked first.

After the withdrawal of U.S. forces from the South in June 1949 (Soviet occupation forces had departed the North in December 1948), Kim Il Sung reported to Soviet Ambassador to the DPRK Terentii F. Shtykov on 12 August 1949 that the ROK did not intend to attack the DPRK and that the South had decided to build a defensive line along the parallel. Kim complained that the North had lost the chance for a counterattack against the South because of ROK defensive policies. Kim said that the only alternative left to the North was to launch the attack against the South; massive insurrections by South Koreans in support of the North would be followed by an invasion. Shtykov repeated the Soviet position established by Stalin during the Kim-Stalin meeting the previous March.

After the Communist victory in China and the establishment of the People's Republic of China (PRC), Kim reopened the issue of a DPRK invasion of the ROK in a conversation with Shtykov on 17 January 1950. Kim stated that the liberation of South Koreans was next in line after the liberation of China and that he was unable to sleep at night over how to resolve the Korean reunification question. Stalin had authorized the North to go on the offensive if there should be an attack by the South, but ROK President Syngman Rhee was not instigating an attack and, as a result, the liberation of the southern part of Korea was being prolonged. Nonetheless, Kim said that he could not initiate an invasion because he was a Communist and a disciplined person, and for him Stalin's orders were law. He informed Shtykov that he needed to visit with Stalin to secure approval for an invasion. After receipt of Shtykov's report on this conversation, on 30 January 1950, Stalin cabled Shtykov: "He [Kim Il Sung] must understand that such a large matter in regard to South Korea such as he wants to undertake needs extensive preparation. The matter must be organized so that there would not be too great a risk. If he wants to discuss this matter with me, then I will always be ready to receive him and discuss with him. Transmit all this to Kim Il Sung and tell that I am ready to help him in this matter."

In April 1950, Kim met with Stalin in Moscow to discuss the invasion. In the course of the meeting, Stalin approved the invasion with one condition: "the question [of the North Korean invasion] must be decided finally by the Chinese and Korean comrades together, and in case of a disagreement by the Chinese comrades, the resolution of the question must be put off until there is a new discussion." After the Moscow meeting with Stalin, on 13 May Kim met in Beijing with Mao Zedong. He conveyed Stalin's statements to Mao, but the PRC leader wanted confirmation directly from Stalin. Thus on 14 May 1950, Soviet Ambassador to China N. V. Roshchin delivered a message from Stalin in which the Soviet leader repeated what he had said to Kim. After reviewing Stalin's telegram, Mao agreed to the DPRK invasion of the ROK.

On 4 February 1950, Kim Il Sung had asked Stalin to provide the DPRK with military equipment for three army divisions, thus increasing the Korean People's Army (KPA) to ten divisions. In return, the DPRK promised to send 9 tons of gold, 40 tons of lead, and 15,000 tons of monazite to the Soviet Union. The KPA was reorganized with Soviet weapons and ready in late May to launch the invasion. At the beginning of the invasion, the DPRK mobilized seven divisions and one armored brigade.

Newly released Soviet documents show that Stalin dispatched a group of Soviet military advisors, including Lieutenant General Vasiliev to prepare the invasion plan in February 1950 before the secret Stalin-Kim meeting in Moscow in April. As part of the propaganda campaign, the DPRK issued an appeal to the South for peaceful unification, but meantime, KPA troops were concentrated along the 38th parallel.

The KPA operational plan envisioned that its troops would advance 10–13 miles per day and would in the main complete military activity within 22–27 days. Following the invasion plan, on 12 June North Korean troops began to move to their advanced positions near the 38th parallel. They completed this on 23 June. Operational planning at the divisional level and area reconnaissance was carried out with the participation of Soviet advisors. All preparatory measures for the invasion were completed by 24 June.

On 24 June divisional commanders were issued orders with the precise timing of the attack. A defense ministry statement was read to the troops to the effect that the ROK Army (ROKA) had provoked a military attack by violating the 38th parallel and that the DPRK government had ordered the KPA to counterattack. Shtykov reported to Stalin on 26 June that the order was met with great enthusiasm by the soldiers and officers of the KPA.

According to the report prepared in early June by chief military advisor to the KPA Lieutenant General Vasiliev, North Korean troops numbered 130,000, including air force personnel. The KPA had 80,000 rifles, 4,000 submachine guns, and 793 heavy machine guns. It was equipped with 151 tanks. There were 239 Soviet advisors and instructors.

The KPA troops were in their starting positions by 2400 hours on June 24. Military operations began at 0440 on the 25th. Artillery preparation was accompanied in the course of 20–40 minutes by direct fire and a 10-minute artillery barrage.

The North deployed its 1st and 6th Divisions along the Kaesŏng-Munsan-Seoul corridor, the 4th Division along the Tongduch'ŏn-Ŭijŏngbu-Seoul corridor, and the 3d Division along the P'och'ŏn-Ŭijŏngbu-Seoul corridor to capture the city of Seoul. The KPA 2d and 7th Divisions were to occupy Ch'unch'ŏn and then quickly move to the southern area of the Han River. The KPA deployed the 3d Border Constabulary Brigade and the 14th Regiment of the 6th Division commanded by General Pang Ho-san on the Ongjin peninsula. The 5th Division and the 766th Independent Unit were on the East Coast.

Initial KPA operations were designed to avoid flanking attacks by ROKA troops on the Ongjin peninsula and the East Coast. These KPA troop dispositions can be construed as holding actions to hold ROKA flank forces in place while the main shock troops, roughly five KPA divisions and an armored brigade, moved on Seoul. If the North tried to move its forces along the Kaesŏng-Munsan corridor with ROKA troops left on the Ongjin peninsula, the flanking of Northern troops by South Korean forces through Haeju and Kaesŏng would disrupt the initial KPA operational plans

The KPA also sought to surround ROKA troop dispositions north of the Han River by quickly dispatch-

ing the 2d and 7th Divisions to the Suwŏn area after they had captured Ch'unch'ŏn. Northern intentions are clearly shown in a captured map of the invasion plan. Actual KPA operations in the Ch'unch'ŏn area did not proceed as expected because of valiant resistance on the part of the ROKA 6th Division deployed there. After a KPA soldier had defected, Lieutenant Colonel Yim Pu-t'aek of the ROKA 6th Division ordered a reconnaissance team near the parallel to survey movements of KPA troops and the advance deployment of tanks. As a result of this, the ROKA 6th Division was prepared, a sharp contrast with the lack of readiness of other ROKA divisions. Stubborn counterattacks by the ROKA 6th Division prevented the KPA from capturing the city of Ch'unch'ŏn for three days and inflicted heavy losses on the KPA 2d Division. This also disrupted the original KPA operational plans.

The ROKA 1st, 7th, and Capital Divisions were deployed in the northern part of Seoul and bore the main brunt of the KPA shock troops at the beginning of the war. The ROKA 2d, 3d, and 5th Divisions, deployed in the rear area as a reserve, then moved north of the Han River and on 27 June engaged the KPA troops. This ROKA troop deployment shows that all principal ROKA divisions would have been cut off north of the Han River had the KPA 2d and 7th Divisions been able to move quickly on the Suwŏn area after capturing Ch'unch'ŏn. Thus the successful resistance by the ROKA 6th Division on the Ch'unch'ŏn front allowed the ROKA to regroup and erect the Han River defensive line, which in turn allowed it to delay the KPA offensive until U.S. and other United Nations forces arrived.

Despite heroic ROKA resistance, the KPA, spearheaded by tanks, continued to bear down on Seoul. During the night of 27 June, the KPA 3d Division entered the city. The next day all of Seoul fell.

After the capture of Seoul, KPA troops regrouped there for three days until they began to cross the Han River on 1 July. This delay was one of the fatal strategic errors committed by DPRK strategists and their Soviet advisors during the war. One reason for the delay was the lack of logistical equipment to cross the Han River. Stalin did not understand why the KPA had halted its advance after the capture of Seoul. On 1 July he cabled Shtykov to order the KPA troops to continue the advance because the sooner the South was conquered the less chance there was of U.S. intervention. Task Force Smith of the U.S. 24th Division, the first U.S. fighting unit, arrived in South Korea as KPA troops began to cross the Han River. On 5 July the U.S. 24th Division was fully deployed in the South and ready to meet the KPA troops along with the reorganized ROKA.

—Youngho Kim

References:

Kim, Youngho. *Han'guk Chŏnjaeng ŭi Kiwŏn gwa Chŏngae Kwajŏng* (The origins and development of the Korean War). Seoul: Dure, 1998.

———. "The Origins of the Korean War: Civil War or Stalin's Rollback?" *Diplomacy & Statecraft* X, no. 1 (March 1999): 186–214.

Weathersby, Kathryn. "New Russian Documents on the Korean War." *Cold War International History Project Bulletin* nos. 6–7 (Winter 1995–1996): 30–84.

———. "To Attack, or Not to Attack? Stalin, Kim Il Sung, and the Prelude to War." *Cold War International History Project Bulletin* no. 5 (Spring 1995): 1–9.

———. "The Soviet Role in the Early Phase of the Korean War: New Documentary Evidence." *Journal of American–East Asian Relations* 2, no. 4 (Winter 1993): 425–458.

See also: Kim Il Sung; Mao Zedong; Shtykov, Terentii Fomich; Stalin, Josef; Syngman Rhee; Task Force Smith.

Korea, Democratic People's Republic of: Navy (Korean People's Navy [KPN])

Navy of the Democratic People's Republic of Korea (DPRK, North Korea), formed in 1948 along with the Korean People's Army (KPA). KPN combatants consisted mainly of Soviet-built P-4 motor torpedo boats, some ex-Japanese minesweepers, and small former U.S. Navy vessels left in North Korean waters at the end of World War II.

The KPN had its beginnings as a coastal defense force shortly after Soviet troops occupied the northern half of the Korean peninsula in August 1945. In 1946 the coastal defense force was reorganized and renamed the Korean Coast Guard. In February 1948, it was designated the Korean People's Navy even though it lacked any large surface units.

In June 1950, the KPN had three squadrons of attack craft stationed at three ports: Ch'ŏngjin (1st Squadron), Wŏnsan (2d Squadron), and Chinnamp'o (3d Squadron). From these locations the KPN mounted raids against both coasts of the Republic of Korea (ROK, South Korea). The most successful operation undertaken by KPN forces occurred in the days immediately after the 25 June 1950 invasion of South Korea when it landed the 766th Independent Unit at Kangnŭng and Samch'ŏk on the central east coast of Korea.

Shortly thereafter the KPN was almost totally destroyed. Early on 2 July 1950, four KPN P-4 motor torpedo boats were escorting ten small freighters from Wŏnsan to Chumunjin when they encountered a force of U.S. Navy and other United Nations Command warships. The KPN force was destroyed before any of the motor torpedo boats could even launch a torpedo; the only known KPN naval battle of the war was over before it began. After this action, the KPN sought protection for its few remaining naval assets at ports in the People's Republic of China (Communist China) and the Soviet Union.

The KPN was more successful in defensive operations. It deployed minefields to protect its port cities of Wŏnsan, Ch'ŏngjin, Hamhŭng, and Chinnamp'o. This was the only notable KPN success of the war.

—*Ronald A. Fiocca*

References:

Cagle, Malcolm W., and Frank A. Manson. *The Sea War in Korea.* Annapolis, MD: Naval Institute Press, 1957.

Field, James A., Jr. *History of United States Naval Operations: Korea.* Washington, DC: U.S. Government Printing Office, 1962.

See also: Naval Battles; United States Navy.

Korea, Geography and History to 1945

Korea and its long history have remained largely unknown to Americans, except for the period since 1950 when the United States and the United Nations were engaged in fighting there. Koreans know their country as "the Land of the Morning Calm." The Korean peninsula, on the East Asian Pacific coast, is about one hundred miles wide and almost a thousand miles long at its extremities. To the west is the Yellow Sea and to the east is the East Sea (Sea of Japan). To its north Korea has a common frontier of several hundred miles with the Chinese province of Manchuria and with Russia for about a dozen miles just south of the port of Vladivostok. Japan lies to the southeast across the narrow Strait of Tsushima. Korea's southern and western coasts have ice-free ports distinguished by some of the most extreme tidal variations in the world. The eastern shore has few adequate harbors other than Pusan, P'ohang, Wŏnsan, and Hŭngnam. Although Korea lies mostly in a temperate zone, it has harsh winters in the wind-swept north next to Manchuria and dusty, sweltering harsh summers in the south.

Much of Korea consists of rugged mountains terraced with rice paddies and interlaced with countless valleys dotted with towns and villages. It has been described as a harsh land inhabited by a hardy, harassed people who rarely if ever had been completely free. The main theme in most of Korean history has been war and tragedy. Suppression and mistreatment have been the heritage of its long-suffering people. Still, it is a land of striking beauty with numerous temples and other historical structures that have managed to survive the ravages of war.

The Korean people are a Tungusic branch of the Ural-Altaic family, which migrated into the area from the northwestern regions of Asia. Koreans are racially and linguistically homogeneous, with no sizable indigenous minorities, except for Chinese and Japanese—a consequence of periodic foreign invasions. The Korean language is a Uralic language, remotely related to Japanese, Hungarian, Finnish, and Mongolian. Shamanism and Buddhism are the traditional religions, but in the late nineteenth century Christian missionaries arrived and founded schools, hospitals, and other institutions. Millions of Koreans converted to Christianity. Korea has also had an estimated 4 million adherents of Ch'ŏndogyo, a native religion founded in the mid-nineteenth century fusing elements of Confucianism and Christianity.

Throughout most of history, Korea has played a relatively quiet and obscure role on the world stage. There have been several instances, however, when developments in Korea involved the outside world, including the United States. As the nexus of three powerful states—China, Russia, and Japan—Korea was destined for a stormy history. The country has long been overshadowed by its more powerful neighbor of China and has been more or less dominated or controlled by that country. The Korean peninsula has been said to "point like a dagger" at the heart of Japan. Japanese leaders saw control of Korea as a necessary step to dominating Manchuria and China.

Korean legend has it that in 2333 B.C. the Heavenly Ruler's son, Hwanung, on a visit to earth found a beautiful young woman, who had just been transformed from a bear, sitting under a tree. He breathed on her and she gave birth to Tan'gun, who became Korea's first king. The bear and forest motif is seen as revealing the northern Asiatic origin of the Korean people.

In the following millennia various peoples from China, Manchuria, Japan, or elsewhere moved into the Korean peninsula, resulting in a mixture of various cultural elements. The earliest known Korean state was Old Chosŏn, in present-day northwestern Korea and southern Manchuria. In 108 B.C. the Chinese invaded and occupied Old Chosŏn. This coexisted with the Korean kingdom of Koguryŏ, founded in the first century B.C. Further south, the kingdoms of Paekche and Silla emerged in the third or fourth century A.D. On the southern coast a fourth Korean state, Kaya, also emerged. Unlike the others, it had a close relationship with Japan.

Initially Koguryŏ was the most powerful of the Korean states. By the fifth century it controlled most of the peninsula and Manchuria. In the mid-sixth century, Silla conquered Kaya and took the area around Seoul in the Han River valley. By 668 Silla, having formed an alliance with the Tang dynasty in China, conquered the other Korean states and established the first unified Korean state. This inaugurated a period of prosperity and cultural flowering in which Chinese cultural influences were important but a distinctly Korean state was established.

In the ninth century, Silla's central power declined in the face of quarrels among the nobility, and during 890 to 935 the three former kingdoms reemerged. This time the northern state of Koryŏ (from Koguryŏ) brought all the peninsula as far north as the Yalu River under its control. Koryŏ gave its name to modern Korea. The Koryŏ period dated from 918 to 1392.

From 993 to 1018 Koryŏ fought a series of wars with the Khitan Liao rulers of Manchuria. Koryŏ maintained its position, agreeing to a peace in 1022 that accepted Liao suzerainty but secured Koryŏ territorial gains.

Under a strong central government a period of cultural flowering soon followed. Buddhism spread and influenced the arts. The Koreans also came to produce exquisitely distinctive ceramics. In the twelfth century, however, central power eroded as the nobles again became restless and the Jurchen Chin dynasty added external pressure. In 1170 military leaders took power, turning the kings into puppet rulers.

Koryŏ independent rule ended with the Mongol invasions. These began in 1231 and led to Mongol conquest of Koryŏ in 1259. The Koryŏ kings reasserted their influence under Mongol control, taking Mongol princesses for wives. Court life also followed Mongol patterns.

A notable event in Korean history occurred during the Mongol period when the "Golden Horde" of Ghengis Kahn and his successor Khublai Kahn reached the country. In 1267, having conquered Korea, the Mongols attempted to cross the East Sea and invade Japan. That attempt failed because of a sudden and ferocious storm at sea known to the Japanese as the *kamikaze,* or divine wind, a term reapplied centuries later during World War II to Japanese suicide pilots. Since the Mongols advanced as far eastward as Korea but no farther, Korea has the distinction of constituting the high-water mark of the Mongol invasions to the East.

Mongol power gradually dissipated and Korea became part of a revitalized China, adopting many aspects of Chinese culture. Confucianism also spread. In 1392 the Chosŏn (Yi) dynasty came to power in Korea and remained the ruling dynasty until Japan annexed the country in 1910.

In the early years of the Chosŏn dynasty the country flourished intellectually and economically. Buddhism was replaced by the Confucian ethical system. Widespread advances occurred in medicine, astronomy, geography, and agriculture. Skilled artisans, inventors, philosophers, and scholars raised Korean civilization to heights similar to those of the Chinese.

Progress, however, was retarded or suspended by a series of foreign invasions. At the end of the sixteenth century, in 1592 and 1597, Japanese forces again invaded, under Toyotomi Hideyoshi. These troops defeated the Korean army as part of an abortive attempt to attack China and conquer East Asia as far as India. The war ended marauding raids on Korean coasts by Japanese pirates, but it struck a heavy blow to the Chosŏn structure. Government, the economy, and the whole societal structure disintegrated.

In 1627 and 1636, before the country had recovered from the Japanese invasions, the Manchus invaded Korea. The Manchu invasions were an outgrowth of their struggle for power to control China. The invasions further weakened Korea.

After these catastrophic foreign invasions, which underlined its weakness and inability to maintain its independence and identity, Korea entered a 200-year period during which it refused all contacts with the outside world. During this period Korea became known as "the Hermit Kingdom."

The 1840s and 1850s began a period of heightened Western interest and activity in the Far East. The United States was among the nations interested in the region, and in 1852 Commodore Matthew C. Perry sailed a squadron to Japan and took the first steps toward "opening up" that country to the West and to international trade.

In the summer of 1866 the U.S. merchant ship *General Sherman* sailed up the Taedong River to P'yŏngyang. Granted shore leave, many of its crew got drunk, committed riotous acts of looting, and insulted Korean women. The indignant local population then killed and imprisoned many of the crew and attacked and burned the ship.

Five years later in 1871, a U.S. Navy flotilla arrived in Korean waters to retaliate for this incident. In June it shelled Korean forts and landed Marines to seize several of them. The invaders were repulsed by Taewŏngun (1820–1898), father of the boy-king Kojong (1852–1919). Eventually, in the 1880s, Korea and the United States signed a treaty that opened Korea to foreign trade when in 1882 American Commodore Robert W. Shufeldt, with the reluctant help of the Chinese imperial government, negotiated a treaty that provided for limited commerce and trade under a most-favored nation arrangement for the United States. It also provided for the exchange of diplomats, protection of navigation, and extraterritoriality for U.S. citizens. The treaty could have given the United States great influence in Korea had it been enacted more quickly. The Koreans requested U.S. diplomats and military advisors, but the matter dragged on for several years and advisors did not reach Korea until 1888 when the Japanese were steadily increasing their presence and influence in the country.

Japan defeated China in a war in 1894–1895 and, by the end of the nineteenth century, Russia and Japan were the dominant powers in the region. Each sought to control Manchuria and Korea, and leaders of both countries were eager for a war to resolve the issue. As a consequence of the Russo-Japanese War (1904–1905), Japan took over Korea. From 1905 until the end of World War II, Japan occupied and controlled the country. The United States raised no objection; President Theodore Roosevelt even remarked, "We cannot possibly interfere for the Koreans against Japan....They could not strike one blow in their own defense." Indeed the 1905 Treaty of Portsmouth, brokered by the United States, recognized the undisputed supremacy of Japan in Korea. Washington even negotiated a secret "agreed memorandum" with Tokyo that approved Japan's "suzerainty" over Korea in return for its pledge not to interfere with U.S. interests in the Philippine Islands. Korean King Kojong's appeal for U.S. assistance under the "good offices" of the Shufeldt Treaty thus fell on deaf ears.

Japanese rule in Korea was oppressive and exploitive. The period 1905–1910 was in particular a time of uprisings and rebellions, all of which the Japanese savagely crushed. And the Koreans had few modern weapons. According to Japanese statistics, 14,566 Korean "rebels" were killed between July 1907 and December 1908. In 1910 Japan formally annexed Korea with little or no resistance from either the Korean people or the world at large.

The ensuing 35 years of Japanese rule were marked by complete suppression and exploitation of the Korean people and their land. Although the Japanese did build highways, railroads, dams, and factories, such projects were principally designed for military use and to consolidate Japan's position. The port of Pusan, for example, was constructed with military purposes in mind, as was the rail line running from Pusan north to the Manchurian border. Japan also integrated Korean industry into its own economy. Korea became completely dependent upon Japan for most manufactured products, repair parts, and markets.

Koreans were again disappointed by the West at the end of World War I. U.S. President Woodrow Wilson's Fourteen Points included "self determination of peoples," and nationalist leaders everywhere took heart from this. Korean nationalists such as Syngman Rhee, the post–World War II president of the Republic of Korea (ROK), were unaware of the subtlety of the president's remarks and considered this concept as applying to Koreans as well as to Czechs, Poles, and other European peoples.

The Koreans soon again rose in revolt and as many as two million Koreans demonstrated against the Japanese occupiers. On 1 March 1919, in the course of a great rally in Keijo (Seoul), demonstrators read a declaration of independence. Many Koreans assumed that the Americans would come to their support, but this did not occur. Japan had been an ally during the war and Wilson's remarks were intended for European peoples, not those of Africa and Asia.

Chinese nationalists in the matter of the Shandong (Shantung) peninsula, Vietnamese nationalists such as Ho Chi Minh, and Koreans all learned that "self-determination," at least as far as U.S. policy was concerned, did not apply to them.

The Japanese response to the Korean demonstrations was both swift and brutal. They ended the demonstrations by killing thousands of Koreans and arresting almost 50,000, and the ruthless and exploitive nature of Tokyo's colonial policy continued unabated. The Japanese controlled key government and economic functions and banned Koreans from responsible government and administrative posts and from educational opportunities. Nearly 80 percent of the Korean people could neither read nor write. Although they were only 3 percent of the population of Korea, the Japanese there were the absolute masters of the country.

As Japan continued its tight control of Korea, nationalist leaders fled abroad to continue their political activity and to set up a government in exile. On 10 April 1919, some of them met in Shanghai and established a Korean provisional government. Dr. Syngman Rhee headed the group as premier. The nationalist exiles sought complete independence for Korea. They also sought to establish themselves as the official Korean government, but they never could agree on how their goals should be realized, and frequent clashes and personality conflicts developed. Two men, Rhee and Kim Ku, both of whom were revered by the Korean people, emerged as the most important figures in the exile government, and in the mid-1930s Kim became its premier. Many Koreans in the United States, China, and elsewhere supported the provisional government. There was also support, albeit secret and passive, from Koreans inside Korea.

The year 1925 saw the beginnings of Communist activity in Korea. In that year a strong Korean Communist movement was formally organized. The movement grew steadily among the well-organized anti-Japanese underground. The Korean Communists were in contact with the Russian Communists through the Far Eastern Division of the Communist International (Comintern). Because of a secret agreement with Tokyo, however, Moscow abstained from greatly encouraging the Korean Communists during the Japanese occupation. Many Korean Communists, however, took refuge during this period in Manchuria, China, and Russia. In 1931 Japan invaded and annexed Manchuria, renaming it Manchukuo. Nominally independent, Manchukuo was in fact completely controlled by the Japanese.

During World War II, the Japanese ruined much of the Korean industrial plant by overworking machinery without adequate maintenance. Japan's expropriation of almost all chemical products, especially nitrogen, for their war effort caused near total soil depletion in Korea.

Korea became a matter for Allied attention as World War II was coming to an end in Europe. At the December 1943 Cairo Conference involving leaders of the United States, Great Britain, and China, a joint statement was released regarding Korea that read as follows: "The aforesaid three great powers, mindful of the enslavement of the people of Korea, are determined that in due course Korea shall become free and independent." As one of many countries being freed from German or Japanese control, Korea was destined to become a focal point for clashing U.S.-Soviet interests.

The United States attached little importance to Korea as a strategic area, but Washington did recognize that, if at some future date Korea fell into unfriendly hands, it could hamper the forthcoming U.S. occupation of Japan and restrict U.S. freedom of movement in the area. And U.S. leaders knew that the USSR maintained its traditional interest in Korea.

At the February 1945 Yalta Conference, President Franklin D. Roosevelt and Premier Josef V. Stalin touched on the postwar status of Korea. Roosevelt advocated a twenty- to thirty-year trusteeship there administered by the United States, the Soviet Union, and China. Stalin suggested that Great Britain should also be a trustee. At Yalta, Stalin agreed to bring the Soviet Union into the war against Japan "two to three months" after the end of the war in Europe. After Roosevelt's death in April 1945, Stalin told President Harry S. Truman's special envoy Harry Hopkins that Russia was committed to a four-power trusteeship for Korea.

Agreement regarding the extent of advancement into Korea of Soviet and U.S. military forces were not to be reached until the July 1945 Potsdam Conference of the Great Powers after the end of fighting in Europe and before the August declaration of war against Japan by the Soviets.

—Sherman Pratt

References:

Goodrich, Leland Matthew. *Korea: A Study of U. S. Policy in the United Nations.* New York: Council of Foreign Relations, 1956.

Korea, Its Lands, People and Culture of All Ages. Seoul: Hakwŏn-sa, 1960.

McCune, George M. *Korea Today.* Cambridge, MA: Harvard University Press, 1950.

Republic of Korea, Ministry of National Defense. *The History of the United Nations Forces in the Korean War.* Vol. 1. Seoul: War History Compilation Commission, 1967.

Schnabel, James F. *United States Army in the Korean War: Policy and Direction, the First Year.* Washington, DC: Office of the Chief of Military History, Department of the Army, 1972.

U.S. Department of State, Bureau of Public Affairs. *Background Notes, South Korea.* Washington, DC: U.S. Government Printing Office, 1991.

The World and Its People: Japan and Korea. New York: Greystone Press, 1963.

See also: China, People's Republic of; Japan; Stalin, Josef; Syngman Rhee; Union of Soviet Socialist Republics; U.S. Policy toward Korea before 1950.

Korea: History, 1945–1947

At the November 1943 Cairo Conference, Allied leaders issued a declaration calling for in due course a "free and independent" Korea. However, the Allied leaders did not elaborate on how this was to be accomplished. At the February 1945 Yalta Conference, U.S. President Franklin D. Roosevelt advocated a twenty- to thirty-year trusteeship for Korea to be administered by the United States, the Soviet Union, and China. Soviet leader Josef Stalin suggested that Great Britain also be a trustee.

The July 1945 Potsdam Conference after the end of the war in Europe dealt in part with the Japanese surrender in Korea and that country's occupation and administration. At Yalta, the Soviet Union had agreed to enter the war against Japan "two to three months" after the end of the war in Europe. In a briefing and information paper, Lieutenant Colonel Claire Hutchin of the U.S. Army's Operations Division of the War Department General Staff pointed out the implications of quadripartite trusteeship. Hutchin noted that Korea's location gave the Soviet Union a vital interest in that country. He argued that the USSR would "probably want to occupy both Manchuria and Korea" and that it was "militarily capable of effecting this occupation before it would be possible for U.S. military forces to occupy those areas." Hutchin reasoned that the Soviet Union "would even await a time when U.S. efforts will have practically destroyed Japan and then seize Korea at a slight cost."

This analysis by Colonel Hutchin, who was to become a battalion commander of the 23d Infantry Regiment in the first year of the Korean War, highlighted the importance of a complete prior understanding with the Soviet Union, particularly with respect to a line of demarcation specifying the occupation zones for the purposes of the Japanese surrender. He concluded that the United States would not be in a position to force the independence of Korea by bringing pressure on the USSR in the Far East and, therefore, U.S. aims there "must be negotiated."

Hutchin reasoned that, if both the Russians and the Americans occupied Korea, it would be essential to determine precisely how much of the country each would occupy. A line needed to be drawn for the benefit of military commanders but also for political reasons. It would designate respective military zones to avoid a military clash between Russian and U.S. forces. There was also a need to establish quickly a land boundary in Korea if Russian occupation of the entire peninsula was to be prevented.

The determination of such a line of demarcation became the subject of intense and urgent staff activity in the weeks after the Potsdam Conference. Discussions between Russian Marshal Alexsey Antonov and U.S. General George C. Marshall resulted in agreements on a boundary line for U.S. and Russian naval and air operations in the Pacific and the East Sea (Sea of Japan). In the west the boundary line ended on the Korean east coast at the 38th parallel. State-War-Navy Coordinating Committee members Colonels Dean Rusk and Charles Bonesteel entered into somewhat frenzied consideration of such a line. They proposed the 40th parallel or as far north as possible. Rusk favored the narrow neck of the peninsula that ran approximately parallel with Wŏnsan at the 39th parallel, but there was doubt that the Russians would agree to a line so far north. Rusk and Bonesteel decided on the 39th parallel as a proposed dividing line, with the 38th parallel as a final position. A line at least at the 38th parallel would have the advantage of giving U.S. forces the port and communications area of Keijo (Seoul). In the end, Washington merely suggested the 38th parallel to Moscow, which surprisingly accepted it.

On 9 August 1945, the USSR formally entered the war against Japan and two days later Soviet troops invaded Korea, landing on the northeast coast near Najin (Rashin). Several days later they were on the 38th parallel, well before the first U.S. troops arrived in Korea. Although it appears clear that neither the Soviet Union nor the United States contemplated the 38th parallel as anything other than a tactical boundary for the benefit of field military commanders to avoid confusion on the battlefield during the Japanese surrender, this line, modified by the 1953-established demilitarized zone, became a permanent boundary (at least to the year 2000) between two separate, hostile states: the Democratic People's Republic of Korea (DPRK, North Korea) in the North and the Republic of Korea (ROK) in the South.

The arrival of U.S. troops in Korea came at a time when the country was in the throes of demobilization. The United States was thrust into a remote part of the world about which it knew little and where it had no long-range strategic interests. It also came at a time when the United States was preoccupied with conditions and problems elsewhere, especially in countries it had just defeated and that lay in shambles.

Against this background, commander of the U.S. XXIV Corps General John R. Hodge landed troops at Kimpŏ Airfield near Seoul on 4 September 1945 and four days later at the port of Inch'ŏn. XXIV Corps consisted of the 6th, 7th, and 40th Infantry Divisions (the 40th was shortly thereafter deactivated). Hodge's mission was to accept the surrender of Japanese troops in South Korea, to establish a civilian government composed of Koreans, to establish and train a national defense organization and civilian police force or constabulary, and to provide security internally and along the 38th parallel border.

Hodge's troops were mostly either fresh from U.S. basic training camps or battle weary from the Pacific campaigns. They were not happy to arrive in an unknown land rather than being sent home. Hodge himself had conflicting instructions governing relations with the Korean population. He was told to treat the Koreans as "liberated people" or as "semi-friendly." But he proceeded to brief his officers to treat the Koreans as "enemies of the United States." Guidance from U.S. Commander in the Far East General Douglas MacArthur was scant. When Hodge requested instructions he was told, "use your own judgment."

Under those circumstances, mistakes and misjudgments piled upon each other. Perhaps among the greatest of these, to the intense irritation of the Korean people, was the U.S. reliance on, and continued use of, Japanese officials in key administrative posts during the early days of the occupation. With the end of the war and the defeat of Japan, the Koreans had expected to be relieved of their hated Japanese oppressors. On the contrary, the Japanese secret police and its Korean allies continued to mistreat and oppress the Korean population. The United States also made other missteps that further alienated the Korean people. With the advent of the Cold War and U.S. preoccupation with the perceived threat of Communist activity around the world, the United States tended to support only the more conservative Korean political movements. This politically excluded large numbers of Koreans who were not Communists but were also not disposed toward conservatism, which they related to the period of Japanese control. An additional cause of friction was U.S. support for the return of self-proclaimed independence leader Syngman Rhee, who had lived in the United States for many years, but was not well known or liked by a large number of Koreans.

Political activity in South Korea in the early post–World War II years was concentrated in two groups, the Korean People's Republic (KPR) and the Korean Democratic Party (KDP). U.S. authorities regarded the KDP as more conservative and anti-Communist. Hodge's attitude was that the more liberal KPR should be eliminated. On 10 November 1945, U.S. authorities shut down the most prominent Seoul newspaper sympathetic to the KPR, allegedly for accounting irregularities.

The U.S. military government in Korea, initially under General Hodge and later under Major General Archibald Arnold, had little success in controlling affairs south of the 38th parallel. In October 1945, the United States created an eleven-member Korean "Advisory Council" to assist the military governor. Although its membership was supposed to be broadly representative, only one person, Yŏ Un-hyŏng, was drawn from the left. At first he declined to have anything to do with the council, claiming that it reversed the roles of who was host and who was guest in Korea. When he finally agreed, at Hodge's request, to attend a council meeting, he took one look around and walked out.

The council was doomed from the start. It reminded Koreans too vividly of their recent colonial experience. Indeed, its chairman had been a member of the Japanese government advisory body and had supported the Japanese war effort. Hodge was convinced that the best course was to work with the conservative KDP, which he believed was trusted by much of the population.

Throughout the winter of 1945–1946, the U.S. authorities supported a campaign to suppress both the KPR and labor unions, which were widely viewed as tools for Communist subversion. As this struggle was taking place, another controversy developed. A well-intentioned U.S. effort to ease landholding for peasants and create a free market for rice backfired. Instituted measures unleashed a wave of speculation, hoarding, and profiteering on an unprecedented scale. Officials made fortunes in rice smuggling and speculation. In February 1946 the U.S. authorities were forced to end the free market and institute rigid rationing.

By the spring of 1946, U.S. officials were well aware that they had made little progress in creating an orderly and democratic society in South Korea. Rather, they saw clear signs of a seething, discontented population on the brink of major disorder. The more regulated and controlled but ruthless policies taking place north of the 38th parallel were in sharp contrast to the drifting and uncertain policies of the U.S. military government in the South.

On 16 December, Hodge submitted to MacArthur a grim report that subsequently reached the desk of President Harry S. Truman. Hodge wrote, "Under present conditions with no corrective action forthcoming, I would go so far as to recommend we give serious consideration to an agreement with Russia that both the U.S. and Russia withdraw forces from Korea simultaneously and leave Korea to its own devices and an internal upheaval for its self-purification." Hodge blamed difficulties in South Korea on the Russians and their skillful manipulation of political groups. Relations between Americans and Koreans were strained also by the enthusiasm in Korea for national unification that Hodge and his colleagues opposed as unrealistic.

On 27 December 1945, the Foreign Ministers' Conference in Moscow ended with the Russians accepting a U.S. proposal for a five-year, four-power "International Trusteeship" for Korea. This was seen as a concession by Moscow, reflecting the Russian belief that the political left in Korea was sufficiently strong to ensure its ultimate triumph no matter the political arrangement. It also indicated Moscow's willingness to appease the West in the Far East in expectation of a freer hand in Europe.

Also in December 1946 in South Korea a Korean Provisional Legislature, the membership of which was dominated by the political Right, held its first meeting. Most of the members boycotted the meetings in protest against what was seen by Koreans as U.S. intervention in the elections. A growing body of "rightist" Korean officials were coming to control the central bureaucracy of the Interim Government. In 1947, 70 of 115 of these officials had held office during the Japanese occupation. Only 11 had any record of anti-Japanese activity. The first chief of staff of the South Korean Army was a former colonel in the Japanese Army.

Meanwhile the 6th and 7th U.S. Divisions were carrying out varied missions throughout South Korea. In Taegu the 6th ran a weapons school; in Chinhae, a cannon school. In Seoul the 7th established a cannon school for the Constabulary and both divisions provided advisors. There was also what became known as the Korean Military Advisory Group. The 7th Division's 32d Infantry Regiment took up position along the 38th parallel, facing Soviet troops to the north. Initially, contacts with the Russians were cordial, but gradually the 38th parallel became a hostile and armed miniature "iron curtain."

In February 1947 Ferris Miller, a U.S. Navy officer in the September 1945 Inch'ŏn landing party returned to Korea and was dismayed at what he found. Historian Max Hastings recorded his observations: "Nothing worked—the pipes were frozen, the electricity kept going off. The corruption was there for anyone to see. A lot of genuine patriots in the South were being seduced by the North....there were Korean exiles coming home from everywhere....everyone was struggling—even the Americans....Most of our own people hated the country. There were Koreans wearing clothes made of army blankets; orphans hanging around the railway stations; people chopping wood on the hills above Seoul, the transport system crumbling. It was a pretty bad time."

North of the 38th parallel the Communist Party, known as the Korean Workers' Party, became the dominant political organization and actual source of power. Under the leadership of Kim Il Sung, the North Korean Communists spent their first year under Soviet occupation consolidating their political standing by setting up people's committees and carrying out massive land reform. The class of landholder peasants suddenly had a vested interest in the survival of the regime that had given them small plots of land. On the other hand, wealthy landlords, proprietors of nationalized businesses, or others who felt threatened by the new regime often fled south, creating nearly a million refugees. The Communists won a series of rigged local and regional elections in November 1946 and formed a provisional government that lasted for two years. On the international socialist holiday of 1 May in 1948, a new Soviet-inspired constitution was announced and a permanent government set up soon thereafter. Kim Il Sung, who ended up ruling the Democratic People's Republic of Korea (DPRK) for its first forty-six years, had received training and military experience while in the USSR during World War II, and he owed his political ascendancy to Stalin. The North Korean dictator maintained cordial relations with the Soviet Union until it dissolved in 1991, but he showed greater independence each year that he remained in power.

In the DPRK, executive power came to be vested in a president, the head of state and of the government. The constitution provided for a unicameral legislature known as the Supreme People's Assembly, and a judicial system consisting of a central court and provincial or people's courts. Kim soon eliminated opposition within his own party by purging moderate and right-wing elements. He also suppressed religious and most other sectarian groups, took over land and other wealth held by the Japanese or others considered enemies of the regime, and initiated socialist economic programs.

In the years immediately after the end of World War II, relations between U.S. and Soviet authorities in Korea centered around the Joint Soviet-American Commission. Earlier attempts to establish a four-power trusteeship for the country, as mentioned at the Yalta and Potsdam conferences, had failed; and at the December 1945 Moscow Conference of Foreign Ministers, U.S. Secretary of State James Byrnes and Soviet Foreign Minister V. M. Molotov reached agreement on the establishment of a Joint Commission to govern Korea. The task of the commission was to work out measures to assist in the political, economic, and social progress of the Korean people and the development of democratic self-government and national independence.

The Joint Commission never had much chance of success. In January 1946 the Russian press began attacking certain Korean leaders as conservatives and labeling them "reactionaries." The Soviet news agency Tass claimed that the United States excessively favored the conservatives and professed astonishment at the behavior of the U.S. command in Korea. It charged the United States with inspiring reactionary demonstrations against the decisions of the Moscow conference. Meanwhile the U.S. delegation to the Joint Commission held conferences in Seoul to discuss positions to take to counter Soviets arguments at the forthcoming initial meeting of the commission.

The Joint Commission held its first meeting at the Tŏksu Palace in Seoul on 20 March 1946. After opening ceremonies, as anticipated the Russian delegation announced its position that only Korean parties or organizations that had not opposed the trusteeship should be eligible to participate with the commission in forming a new government. Because virtually all Koreans except the Communists favored immediate independence and opposed the trusteeship concept, this would have meant that only Communists would be consulted in the formation of a unified government. The United States rejected this position at the first meeting and in twenty-four fruitless sessions thereafter. On 6 May the commission adjourned sine die, and on 15 May the Russians blamed the United States for the failure of the Joint Commission. The first major effort to unify Korea had ended in failure, although commission meetings were continued without results through the summer and fall of 1947.

On 28 August 1947, the U.S. State Department proposed to Soviet Minister Molotov that a four-power conference be convened in Washington to discuss Korean issues and that early elections in both zones be held to choose representatives to a national provisional legislature to form a united Korea. The Russians rejected the proposal on the grounds that the Joint Commission had not exhausted its work. The Americans believed that the Russians merely wanted to prolong the deadlock and blame them for the commission's failure.

Washington then decided to refer the entire Korean independence problem to the United Nations (UN) General Assembly for its consideration. On 17 September 1947, over Moscow's objection, U.S. Secretary of State George C. Marshall appeared before the General Assembly and argued that further attempts to solve the Korean problem by bilateral negotiations would only delay establishment of an independent, united Korea and that the time had come for impartial judgment by other UN members. From the Russians' viewpoint, the U.S. plan was the worst thing that could happen because it would bring the international body into the picture and probably frustrate permanently Russia's efforts to gain control of the country. Nor did the Soviets want the UN to hold elections that would have added to the prestige of that organization and probably resulted in the defeat of Communist candidates.

The Soviet response was a proposal, similar to that advanced by Hodge earlier, that both parties withdraw and let the Koreans determine their own destiny. It was clear that Moscow believed that leftist forces both North and South would prevail. Washington, apparently believing the same, rejected the proposal. The U.S. government instead proposed that there be UN-supervised elections throughout Korea, followed by independence and the withdrawal of all foreign forces. The UN General Assembly approved this plan in a vote of 46 to 0 with the Eastern bloc abstaining.

As 1947 drew to a close, the United Nations Temporary Commission on Korea announced that it would hold its first meeting in Seoul in January 1948. This was followed by increasing internal unrest in the South, now run mostly by Koreans. There were also frequent border clashes along the 38th parallel, the blame for which should be divided between the North and South. Syngman Rhee managed to win the UN-sponsored 1948 election held only in the South, which was boycotted by the Left, including the Communists. His regime was widely characterized as dictatorial, ruthless, and repressive. It was friendly to the United States, however, and received U.S. military and economic assistance.

The first years of Korean history after World War II had been far from peaceful, effective, and productive. As the 1940s drew to a close, it was clear that tensions were increasing between North and South.

—*Sherman Pratt*

References:

Berger, Carl. *The Korean Knot: A Military and Political History.* Philadelphia: University of Pennsylvania Press, 1957.

Goodrich, Leland Matthew. *Korea: A Study of U.S. Policy in the United Nations.* New York: Council on Foreign Relations, 1956.

McCune, George M., with Arthur L. Grey. *Korea Today.* Cambridge, MA: Harvard University Press, 1950.

Republic of Korea, Ministry of National Defense. *The History of the United Nations Forces in the Korean War.* Seoul: War History Compilation Commission, 1972.

Sandusky, Michael C. *America's Parallel.* Alexandria, VA: Old Dominion Press, 1983.

See also: Hodge, John R.; Korea Military Advisory Group (KMAG); MacArthur, Douglas; Marshall, George C.; Molotov, Viacheslav Mikhailovich; Potsdam Conference; Rusk, David Dean; Stalin, Josef; Syngman Rhee; Truman, Harry S.

Korea Military Advisory Group (KMAG)

U.S. military advisors aiding the Republic of Korea Army (ROKA) in the period before the Korean War. Officially established on 1 July 1949, the Korea Military Advisory Group (KMAG) assumed the functions of some 100 men in provisional military advisory teams that had been operating as part of the U.S. military occupation force in Korea since January 1946. At that time, 18 lieutenants in the deactivating 40th

A KMAG instructor assists in training a ROKA soldier in the use of the Browning automatic rifle (BAR), 16 June 1951. (National Archives)

Infantry Division had been detached as advisors to assist in the organization of eight Korean Constabulary Regiments, which had been conceived as having a police function. In March 1948, the Constabulary was expanded to 50,000 men. KMAG's mission was "to advise the government of the Republic of Korea in the continued development of the Security Forces of that government." KMAG personnel helped train these personnel in the use of light weapons and artillery. In December 1948, the Constabulary became the ROKA.

By March 1949, there were approximately 114,000 ROKA troops: 65,000 in the army, 4,000 in the Coast Guard, and 45,000 in the police force. Brigadier General W. L. Roberts had charge of KMAG advisors, and Brigadier General Francis W. Farrell was chief of KMAG. KMAG fell under the overall authority of U.S. Ambassador John J. Muccio, although in purely military matters KMAG coordinated directly with the Department of the Army. The original KMAG detach-

ment had 482 military advisors; they were the only U.S. military personnel in Korea after the departure of U.S. occupation troops in June 1949.

KMAG advisors were dispersed among the ROKA divisions. Primarily involved in military training, they also worked to try to improve conditions in the ROKA, where mistreatment of soldiers was endemic and arbitrary execution was a standard disciplinary action for unacceptable behavior. KMAG was also involved in the establishment of the ROK military schools system, including the Korean Military Academy, which entered its first class of cadets on 6 June 1950. KMAG also helped select ROKA officer personnel for training in the United States.

Occasionally KMAG personnel were involved in combat. Two years before troops of General Douglas MacArthur's Far East Command (FEC) battled the Korean People's Army (KPA, North Korean) troops on the peninsula, KMAG officers and men were involved in border clashes in places such as Sunch'ŏn and Posŏng. These actions resulted in at least two advisors being captured, but both managed to escape.

As advisors to Korean forces, KMAG officers were often commanders in all but name. KMAG also helped the ROKA set up various military schools in addition to the military academy, and they helped train liaison and observation pilots of the ROK Air Force. Training of fighter pilots did not begin until after the outbreak of the Korean War, when this was taken over by the Far East Air Force (FEAF). Also, fifteen U.S. Coast Guard personnel helped to train the ROK Coast Guard, although these personnel were withdrawn in August 1948, when they were replaced by civilian technicians. In August 1950, the commander of U.S. Naval Forces in the Far East assumed responsibility for training the ROK Coast Guard and navy advisory functions.

After the start of the Korean War and the desperate need for combat troops, KMAG was attached to Lieutenant General Walton H. Walker's Eighth Army. KMAG personnel fought effectively enough that the commander of the 1st Cavalry Division, to which they were attached, did not want to let them go.

After the North Korean invasion of 25 June 1950 and subsequent rapid expansion of the ROKA into ten divisions and three corps headquarters, MacArthur ordered a comparable expansion of KMAG. Its wartime strength grew to 1,308 men, two-thirds of whom were enlisted personnel. It also provided advisors to the ROKA down to the battalion level.

KMAG personnel played a vital role in training the ROK armed forces, often in difficult circumstances and with cultural and language barriers to overcome. They also provided important leadership to the ROKA as it underwent its battlefield travails and as it quintupled in size during the war.

—Colin P. Mahle

References:

Hastings, Max. *The Korean War*. New York: Simon & Schuster, 1987.

Sandler, Stanley, ed. *The Korean War: An Encyclopedia*. New York: Garland, 1995.

Sawyer, Robert K. *Military Advisors in Korea: KMAG in Peace and War*. Washington, DC: Office of the Chief of Military History, U.S. Army, 1962.

Summers, Harry G., Jr. *Korean War Almanac*. New York: Facts on File, 1990.

Toland, John. *In Mortal Combat: Korea, 1950–1953*. New York: William Morrow, 1991

See also: Border Clashes; Far East Command (FEC); MacArthur, Douglas.

Korea, Republic of: 1952 Political Crisis

The 1952 Republic of Korea (ROK, South Korean) political crisis began on 25 May when President Syngman Rhee declared martial law in Pusan to force the ROK legislature to pass constitutional amendments that would ensure Rhee's reelection. This action alarmed and angered South Korea's United Nations (UN) allies, who had sought to describe the Korean War as a conflict between democracy and communism. In the end, however, the principal ally, the United States, acquiesced in Rhee's action.

The 1948 ROK constitution provided for a popularly elected National Assembly, the members of which elected the president for a four-year term. Rhee aggravated the institutional tension between the president and the legislature by refusing to share power with the assemblymen and by using the national security apparatus to intimidate his opponents. By 1952 Rhee had lost much of his support in the National Assembly and his reelection was in doubt. In an attempt to retain power and weaken the National Assembly, Rhee proposed constitutional amendments providing for direct popular election of the president and a bicameral legislature. In January 1952, the National Assembly overwhelmingly rejected the proposed amendments. Rhee then instituted a campaign of political harassment and demonstrations against his opponents. When the legislators held firm, Rhee declared martial law in Pusan, the temporary ROK capital, and the surrounding regions effective 25 May 1952 and jailed more than fifty opposition politicians. Most were soon released, but seven were charged with participating in a Communist conspiracy and several others then went into hiding.

These actions caused great concern among South Korea's allies. Rhee's tactics shattered the image of the ROK as a country moving toward democracy and jeopardized international support for the U.S.-led war effort. U.S. Embassy officials and members of the UN Commission for the Unification and Rehabilitation of Korea (UNCURK), the principal UN agency in Korea, tried without success to persuade Rhee to end martial law and release the jailed politicians. U.S. President Harry S. Truman sent a personal letter that may have prevented Rhee from dissolving the National Assembly, but had no other impact. At the urging of U.S. chargé d'affaires Allan Lightner in Pusan, and Australian member of UNCURK James Plimsoll, the U.S. government considered stronger action, including support of a coup by ROK military officers and direct military intervention by the UN Command (UNC). Ultimately, however, the United States and its UN allies confined their efforts to admonitions and encouragement of a political compromise.

The United States has been criticized for its failure to intervene in the crisis, but such an action carried its own risks. A coup could have led to civil war or a mil-

itary dictatorship. U.S. intervention could have resulted in fighting between U.S. and ROK forces. But although both Rhee and his opponents couched their arguments in Western political and cultural terms, the crisis was not a clear-cut issue of dictatorship versus democracy. In the words of the UNCURK report, "the moves in the political struggle were greatly influenced by personalities and by competition for power and patronage."

The senior U.S. military leaders in Tokyo and Korea—UNC Commander in Chief Lieutenant General Mark W. Clark and Eighth U.S. Army Commander Lieutenant General James A. Van Fleet—were also reluctant to intervene in what they saw as primarily a ROK internal political issue. At the direction of the U.S. Joint Chiefs of Staff, both generals reluctantly supported the embassy and UNCURK overtures. Although Clark developed a contingency plan for UNC intervention (Operation EVERREADY), he insisted that it should be undertaken only if the situation deteriorated to the point of jeopardizing military operations. He argued that the UNC did not have sufficient forces to resist a possible Communist military offensive, suppress the ongoing Kŏje-do prisoner-of-war uprising, and deal with civil disturbances at the same time.

The crisis ended in early July when Rhee's police rounded up all the legislators and confined them in the National Assembly building until they passed compromise legislation giving Rhee his amendments but also providing for a limited degree of Cabinet responsibility to the National Assembly. Elections were set for 5 August 1952, providing the opposition little time for campaigning. Rhee easily won another presidential term, none of the charges against the opposition assemblymen was sustained, and an uneasy peace returned to the ROK political scene. Civil war and political chaos had been averted, but the National Assembly was weakened and excluded from any effective policy making role. Rhee's political power had been greatly strengthened at the expense of the international and, ultimately, domestic legitimacy of his government.

—Donald W. Boose, Jr.

References:
Henderson, Gregory. *Korea: The Politics of the Vortex.* Cambridge, MA: Harvard University Press, 1968.
Keefer, Edward C. "The Truman Administration and the South Korean Political Crisis of 1952: Democracy's Failure?" *Pacific Historical Review* 60, no. 2 (May 1991): 145–168.
O'Neill, Robert J. *Australia in the Korean War, 1950–1953.* Vol. 1, *Strategy and Diplomacy.* Canberra: Australian War Memorial/Australian Government Publishing Service, 1981.
United Nations. *Report of the United Nations Commission for the Unification and Rehabilitation of Korea.* General Assembly Official Records: Seventh Session. Supplement 14 (A/2181). New York: United Nations, 1952.
U.S. Department of State, Bureau of Public Affairs. *Foreign Relations of the United States, 1952–1954.* Vol. 15, *Korea.* Washington, DC: U.S. Government Printing Office, 1984.

See also: Clark, Mark W.; EVERREADY, Operation; Kŏje-do Prisoner-of-War Uprising; Korea, Republic of: History, 1947–1953; Lightner, Edwin Allan, Jr.; Plimsoll, James; Syngman Rhee; Truman, Harry S.; United Nations Commission for the Unification and Rehabilitation of Korea; Van Fleet, James Alward.

Korea, Republic of: Air Force (ROKAF)

The Republic of Korea Air Force (ROKAF) began the Korean War with only twenty-two aircraft, all trainers. Thirty years later, in 1982, it began producing its own aircraft, the F5F Chegong (Air Mastery).

In August 1946, a number of civilians formed the Association to Establish a Korean Air Force. Three years later, in part because of their efforts, an Army Air Unit began. On 13 September 1948, the Army Air Unit received ten Piper L-4 training planes from the United States. A derivative of the famous Piper Cub, these were used for flight training, which was begun at an air base at Yŏido. On 15 September, the ten L-4s, flown in formation by civilian pilots, made an exhibition flight over the Republic of Korea (ROK, South Korean) capital of Seoul. In October 1948, the United States provided the ROK with ten L-5s, and these became the foundation of the air force.

In October 1948, the Army Air Unit assisted in putting down the Yŏsu-Sunch'ŏn Rebellion by providing transportation for commanders, observation, leaflet drops, and liaison among ground units. In 1949 the Army Air Unit was again mobilized to help quell riots on Cheju Island. It also participated in the May 1948 border clashes between ROK and KPA (Korean People's Army, North Korean) troops in the Ongjin area.

The Army Air Unit had been subordinate to the Army, but on 1 October 1949, the ROKAF became a separate service branch. At that time it numbered just 1,600 personnel and twenty liaison aircraft. The Army Aviation Officer's School also became the Aviation Officer's School.

After the Yŏsu-Sunch'ŏn rebellions and border clashes with the KPA, the ROKAF sought to obtain fighter-bomber aircraft, but the United States rejected the ROK request. Washington was reluctant to provide the ROK with weapons that it thought might be used in an invasion of North Korea, sparking a war that might involve the United States.

Thanks to a national subscription campaign, the ROK was able in March 1950 to obtain funds to purchase ten North American T-6 aircraft from Canada. To thank the people of Korea, the T-6s were christened

"Kŏn'guk (nation founding) Aircraft" on 14 May 1950, at Yŏido Air Force Base.

At the time of the Democratic People's Republic of Korea (DPRK, North Korean) invasion of the ROK, the DPRK had some 200 aircraft, including fighters and twin-engine bombers. The ROKAF was only a fraction of its size and consisted of only 22 aircraft: the 12 unarmed light aircraft (eight L-4s and four L-5s) transferred from the United States and the 10 T-6s contributed by the people of Korea. These aircraft were stationed at Taejŏn, Taegu, Kwangju, Kunsan, and Cheju Air Bases.

Within the first two days of the invasion, the ROK stockpile of 274 15-kg (33-pound) bombs and a number of hand grenades dropped from the L-4s and L-5s had all been used up, and ROKAF aircraft were restricted solely to reconnaissance missions. Most of the aircraft were soon destroyed.

On 2 July 1950, the U.S. Air Force (USAF) transferred to the ROKAF ten F-51 fighter-bombers. The next day, Colonel Yi Kŭn-sŏk led a formation of four of these to attack KPA troops, tanks, vehicles, and supplies in the Sihŭng area. The ROKAF flew close ground support and interdiction missions during the remainder of the war. Of ROKAF accomplishments, the most notable were the 15 January 1951 destruction of the Sŭngho-ri Railroad Bridge near P'yŏngyang and strikes on the DPRK capital of P'yŏngyang on 29 August 1952. During the war, the ROKAF claimed to have made 8,726 cuts in Communist supply lines. It also conducted missions against Communist guerrillas operating in the Chiri Mountain area and at Kangnŭng. During the war, thirty-nine ROKAF pilots flew more than 100 sorties each; twenty-seven were killed over Communist-controlled territory. Colonel Kim Jŏng-yŏl was chief of staff of the ROKAF at the beginning and throughout most of the war (1 October 1949–1 December 1952), and he was succeeded by Major General Ch'oe Yong-dŏk (1 December 1952–1 December 1954).

In August 1955, the ROKAF received fourteen F-86Fs and nine T-33s from the United States, and the next year the USAF provided an additional sixty-eight F-86Fs. The ROKAF also conducted joint training exercises with the USAF. The ROKAF also took over all U.S.-operated radar sites. When North Korea introduced the MiG-19, the ROKAF received U.S. F-5s. The January 1968 *Pueblo* incident led the United States to provide to the ROKAF the F-4 Phantom, which provided the ROKAF for the first time with supersonic capabilities.

—*Matthew V. Martin*

References:
Futrell, Robert F. *The United States Air Force in Korea, 1950–1953*. Rev. ed. Washington, DC: Office of the Chief of Air Force History, 1983.

Republic of Korea, Ministry of National Defense. *The Brief History of ROK Armed Forces*. Seoul, Troop Information and Education Bureau, 1986.
See also: Aircraft (Principal Combat); United Nations Command Air Forces; United States Air Force (USAF); Yŏsu-Sunch'ŏn Rebellion.

Korea, Republic of: Army (ROKA)

Badly outgunned at the outset of the Korean War, and battered repeatedly by enemy offensives throughout, the Republic of Korea Army (ROKA) emerged as a strong force at the end of the conflict.

On 13 November 1945, the U.S. military government in South Korea established the Office of the Director of National Defense. This directorate had jurisdiction over the Bureau of Police and a new Bureau of Armed Forces. The bureau was to supervise the Army and Navy Departments. The army was originally envisioned to consist of one corps of three divisions, supported by air components of one transport and two fighter squadrons, with a total complement of 45,000 men. Until an army could be formed, national security would be enforced by a national police force, originally intended to number 25,000 men. However the U.S. State-War-Navy Coordinating Committee in Washington, fearing the Soviets might misinterpret this, recommended delaying implementation of the plan until after a joint U.S.-USSR commission on establishing a unified government could meet.

An alternate plan, BAMBOO, establishing a 2,500-man police reserve, was then adopted. It called for one company of six officers and 225 enlisted men to be stationed in each province. The company would actually be an infantry company, without mortars and the like. Teams of two U.S. officers and four enlisted men were sent to each province to begin recruiting, organizing, and training the companies. Gradually, the single company in each province was to expand into a battalion and then into a regiment. By April 1946, this national constabulary force numbered just over 2,000 men, armed principally with World War II Japanese rifles. U.S. advisors and demonstration teams from U.S. occupation troops helped train the constabulary. Training often included actual experience in quelling disorders and battling guerrillas.

By May 1947, the United States and Soviet Union had failed to agree on reunifying Korea under a single government. That month the U.S. military government set up an interim South Korean government. On 8 February 1948, North Korea announced the establishment of the North Korean People's Army, and in March the United States announced support for a 50,000-man South Korean Constabulary. On 8 April, the U.S. Department of the Army ordered that a South Korean armed force be organized, equipped, and trained for internal defense and security. However,

Republic of Korea Army (ROKA) 6th Division troops prepared for inspection, 21 July 1949. (National Archives)

fearful that the South Koreans might use this to attack the North and embroil it in a war, the United States restricted the armament of the new army, depriving its divisions of adequate antiaircraft, antitank, and artillery and denying any armor at all. As a result, in 1950 the ROKA was pitifully armed when the Korean People's Army (KPA, North Korean Army) invaded the South. At that time, about the only weapons with which some of the ROKA troops were proficient were U.S. machine guns, 60- and 81-mm mortars, 57-mm antitank guns, and obsolete U.S. 105-mm howitzers.

In 1948 South Korea expanded its Constabulary from nine to fifteen regiments in five brigades. U.S. troops left South Korea in late 1948 and early 1949, turning over some of their equipment to the ROK military.

On 19 October 1948, Communist agents within the ROKA 14th Regiment fomented a mutiny. The planned revolt was prematurely set off when the regiment was suddenly ordered to Cheju-do to quell disorders there. The regiment had been issued U.S. M1

rifles, but had retained its old Japanese rifles as well. The mutineers, some regimental noncommissioned officers (NCOs), had planned to use the extra rifles to arm sympathetic people in nearby villages. These NCOs fomented antipolice sentiment among the troops of the 14th, who attacked to seize the nearest town. However, loyal troops and their U.S. advisors rushed to the scene. Within six days, two of them spent in savage fighting, the Cheju-do Rebellion was quelled. Many of the mutineers slipped off into the nearby mountains to become guerrillas.

As a result of the Cheju-do Rebellion, more than 1,500 Communists were identified within and purged from the Constabulary. The 14th Regiment was abolished and its colors burned. All units having the number four, either alone or in combination with other numbers, were redesignated and that number was forbidden to be used from that point on.

On 5 December 1948, the ROK government created the Departments of National Defense, Army, and

Korean People's Army flag captured by a Republic of Korea unit, 28 August 1950. (National Archives)

Navy. Simultaneously, all Constabulary brigades were redesignated army divisions, and fourteen army branches were created. By March 1949, the ROKA totaled 65,000 men.

On 1 July 1949, the United States organized the Korean Military Advisory Group (KMAG) to train and advise the South Korean military. Hampered by the requirement to keep troops deployed along the 38th parallel, lack of proper training areas, and cultural and language problems, the men of KMAG struggled to perform their mission.

When the Korean War began in June 1950, the ROKA numbered 98,000 men. Of this, 65,000 were combat troops with the balance in headquarters and service units. The army had eighty-nine serviceable (but obsolete), short-ranged 105-mm howitzers; 114 57-mm antitank guns (useless against the KPA's T-34 tanks); twenty-two M-8 armored cars equipped with 37-mm guns, and fifteen half-tracks.

The ROKA infantry division was authorized 10,948 men, organized into three infantry regiments, an engineer and an artillery battalion (ten 105-mm howitzers), and one company each of antitank, signal, ordnance, quartermaster, and medical troops. (The comparable North Korean infantry division numbered 12,092 men, with sixty mortars and artillery pieces outranging the heaviest artillery in the ROK division.)

ROKA major organizations and strengths are listed below. (Three divisions had but two regiments, and another had only two regiments and one battalion.)

Organization of the South Korean Army, June 1950:

1st Division (11th, 12th, 13th Regiments)	9,715
6th Division (7th, 8th, 19th Regiments)	9,112
2d Division (5th, 16th, 25th Regiments)	7,910
7th Division (1st, 3d, 9th Regiments)	9,698
3d Division (22d, 23d Regiments)	7,059
8th Division (10th, 21st Regiments)	6,866

Capital Division (2d, 12th Regiments)	7,061
17th Regiment	2,500
5th Division (15th, 20th Regiments and 1st Separate Battalion)	7,276

When North Korea invaded the South on 25 June 1950, the ROKA had deployed along the 38th parallel elements of the 17th Infantry Regiment, the 1st, 7th, and 6th Divisions and the 10th Regiment, 8th Division. These elements equated to but four regiments and a battalion and they were strung the length of that line. In the ensuing retrograde action, ROKA units suffered terrible losses.

On 26 June 1950, the ROKA was reorganized as follows:

ROKA headquarters	3,000
Replacement Training Command	9,016
Chonju Training Command	8,699
Kwangju Training Command	6,244
Pusan Training Command	5,256
3d Division (1st Cavalry, 22d, 23d Regiments)	8,829
ROKA nondivisional troops	11,881
I Corps (activated 5 July 1950)	3,014
Capital Division (1st, 17th, 18th Regiments)	6,644
8th Division (10th, 16th, 21st Regiments)	8,864
II Corps (activated about 15 July 1950)	976
1st Division (11th, 12th, 15th Regiments)	7,601
6th Division (2d, 7th, 19th Regiments)	5,727
Total assigned	94,570
Wounded/nonbattle casualties	8,699
Total effectives	85,871
Total in divisions	37,670

The ROKA faced serious problems of bringing the surviving divisions to full strength and securing more troops, while at the same time opposing the KPA. In the long term, it planned to build up forces to drive the KPA back north.

The ROKA opened a series of training centers and schools for replacements and officers. The first center was opened at Taegu on 14 July 1950 as the First Replacement Training Center. It operated on a 10-day schedule, receiving and sending out 1,000 recruits daily. Three more replacement training centers opened in August: one at Kimhae, northwest of Pusan; another at Kup'o-ri, also near Pusan, and a third at Samnangjin, also northwest of Pusan. Kimhae and Kup'o-ri each had a daily capacity of 500 men; Samnangjin, 200 men daily. A fifth center was opened in September on Chejudo Island; it was capable of producing 750 replacements daily. In addition to providing replacements for the ROKA, these centers also supplied Korean recruits for the Korean Augmentation to U.S. Army (KATUSA) program, whereby Korean soldiers were attached to

U.S. units as replacements. In mid-August the ROKA opened the Ground General School at Tongnae near Pusan. It was principally to train infantry second lieutenants and had a normal capacity of 250 candidates per week. The first class reported on 23 August.

Based on a staff study, United Nations Command (UNC) commander General Douglas MacArthur had concluded in late July or early August that for the foreseeable future the South Koreans could field and support no more than four divisions. But U.S. Ambassador to South Korea John J. Muccio and Eighth Army commander Lieutenant General Walton H. Walker disagreed. Finally persuaded, on 9 August MacArthur authorized Walker to "at once" increase the strength of the ROKA to whatever level he believed advisable and practicable.

Soon afterward Walker unveiled a plan to increase the ROKA to ten divisions, along with necessary supporting corps and army troops. The plan called for one division to be activated by 10 September and an additional division by the 10th of each following month until five new divisions had been formed. Supporting units would be activated to coincide with the new divisions as equipment availability dictated. MacArthur approved the plan, and on 2 September the Department of the Army agreed to supply minimum initial equipment, except certain items of heavy engineer, signal, and ordnance equipment, beginning on 10 November.

Korean Military Advisors quickly drew up Tables of Organization and Equipment for the new divisions, based on the World War II U.S. infantry division, omitting most of the heavy equipment. MacArthur provided some additional equipment from his stocks, and some other nonstandard items were procured locally. Within six weeks, three new ROKA divisions, the 7th, 11th, and 5th, were activated and partially outfitted. At the same time, activation of the 9th and 2d Divisions was begun.

Activation of these new divisions was accomplished in unorthodox ways. Activation of the ROKA 2d Division, although not typical, provides insight into the draconian methods utilized in quickly forming these new divisions. In early November 1950, Assistant G-3 Advisor with KMAG Major Thomas B. Ross was given one day to form the ROKA 2d Division. He visited each of the ROK training centers near Seoul where recruits were assembled before being processed. At each he requested the Koreans in charge to line up the recruits in groups of 200. He designated each group as a company, formed these into battalions, and designated each center as a regiment. Ross selected the most intelligent-looking men in each group to be company noncommissioned and commissioned officers. ROKA headquarters provided the battalion, regimental, and division commanders and staffs. KMAG scraped together a divisional advisor group, and a few days later the 2d Division left on its first mission to engage and destroy large groups of guerrillas in the mountains of northeastern South Korea. As each recruit boarded a truck, he was issued a weapon. Most received M1 rifles; some received an automatic rifle or a machine gun. On the way to the guerrilla area, the 2d Division devoted about one-quarter of each day to training. In spite of this haphazard beginning, the 2d eventually became an effective division.

On 23 September 1950, about the time of the breakout from the Pusan perimeter, the ROKA still had the same five combat divisions. Its estimated strength was then 75,000 men.

On 23 November 1950, the principal elements of the ROKA were organized as follows:
I Corps: Capital Division, 3d Division
   (less 26th Regiment), 8th Division
II Corps: 6th Division, 7th Division, 9th Division
III Corps: 2d Division, 5th Division, 11th Division

The ROKA 1st Division was attached to the U.S. I Corps, and the 26th Regiment and the 3d Division was attached to the U.S. 3d Infantry Division. The ROKA 8th Division was destroyed during a Communist offensive during 11–13 February 1951. Its remnants were removed from the front and used in the rear to reconstitute a new 8th Division.

By 1 July 1951, the ROKA had but one active combat corps, I Corps, commanded by Major General Paek Sŏ-yŏp, commander of the ROKA 1st Division at the start of the war. This corps included the ROKA Capital, 3d, and 11th Divisions. The ROKA 1st and 9th Divisions were attached to the U.S. I Corps; the ROKA 2d and 6th Divisions, to the U.S. IX Corps; and the 5th, 7th, and 8th Divisions, to the U.S. X Corps. The 5th ROK Marine Battalion was attached to the U.S. I Corps and the ROKA 1st Marine Regiment was attached to the U.S. 1st Marine Division, then part of X Corps.

At the end of June 1951, the ROKA numbered 260,548 "troops." This figure may have included Marines. There is no breakdown, although an additional 12,718 soldiers were still attached to U.S. units (KATUSAs).

From the outset, ROKA divisions had no armor, primarily because an earlier KMAG commanding officer reported that South Korea was not suitable tank country. The 105-mm howitzer battalion per division was also inadequate. Over the remaining period of the war, these two deficiencies were made up, with varying success, by attaching U.S. artillery and armor battalions to ROKA divisions. Sometimes, as in the case of the ROKA 1st Division, the supporting artillery was somewhat unusual. About the time of the Pusan

perimeter breakout, an artillery group, consisting of a 90-mm gun battalion, a 105-mm howitzer battalion, and a heavy (4.2-inch) mortar battalion was attached to the ROKA 1st Division. The gun battalion was unusual, because guns, unlike howitzers, have a fairly flat trajectory. Howitzers, because of the extremely mountainous terrain of Korea, were far more effective than guns.

In spring 1951, the United States decided to provide each ROKA division with one tank company along with maintenance personnel to keep the tanks operational. In April, therefore, KMAG personnel began training armored troops at the ROKA Infantry School. Two tank companies were activated in October 1951. Equipped with M39 armored vehicles mounting 90-mm guns, one company that month joined the ROKA I Corps. A shortage of tanks prevented the second company from completing its training. It was not until spring 1952, when some M-24 tanks arrived from the United States, that additional tank companies could be formed. By October, one Marine and four ROKA tank companies had been formed, but three others were awaiting their equipment, en route from the United States.

Steps were also taken to provide ROKA divisions with more artillery. In September 1951, UNC commander Lieutenant General Matthew B. Ridgway authorized activation of four 105-mm howitzer battalions before the end of the year. In November three headquarters batteries and six 105-mm firing batteries were also authorized. They began training in January 1952. ROKA officers were sent to the United States for training.

Ridgway then proposed a program designed to organize and train sufficient 105- and 155-mm artillery battalions to provide each of the ten ROKA divisions with a full complement of three 105-mm battalions and one 155-mm battalion. The Department of the Army granted his request in May 1952. By October, sixteen 105-mm artillery battalions were ready for duty, and another four were scheduled to join the ROKA by year's end. In the meantime, cadres of six ROK 155-mm battalions had undergone training with U.S. divisional artillery. By November, they were ready for their battalion firing tests.

The U.S. shortsightedness in failing to provide ROKA divisions with adequate artillery and armor when they were being organized and trained in 1949 certainly had cost untold lives and subjected ROKA divisions to severe punishment, and sometimes defeat, because they were outgunned by the KPA. It was only in late 1952 that some of this was redressed, although the M-24 tank, with which the U.S. armed some ROKA tank units, was obsolete at the outset of the Korean War and virtually worthless on the battlefield in 1952.

In October 1952, U.S. President Harry S. Truman authorized expansion of the ROKA to twelve divisions. Shortly afterward, the ROK 12th and 15th Divisions were activated, along with six separate regiments. The 12th Division and three regiments were ready by the end of December, and the 15th Division and the other three regiments were operational in January 1953. In November 1952, the ROKA had 415,120 men, the KATUSA had 28,000, and the ROK Marines had 19,800.

On 1 November 1952, U.S. Far East Command and UNC commander General Mark W. Clark submitted a plan to increase the ROKA to twenty divisions by August 1953 and increase the number of ROKA corps from two to six to handle the additional divisions. He envisioned that for every two ROKA divisions organized, equipped, and trained one U.S. or other UN division could be placed in reserve, and by May 1953 he would be able to release four U.S. divisions and two corps headquarters for deployment elsewhere.

Although Clark's plan was not implemented, President Truman did approve expansion of the ROKA to fourteen divisions and six separate regiments. On 31 January 1953, Clark instructed U.S. Eighth Army commander Lieutenant General James A. Van Fleet to commence forming the ROKA 20th and 21st Divisions. On 9 February Van Fleet activated the new divisions. The new strength ceiling for the ROKA, including KATUSAs and Marines, was raised to 507,880 men.

As 1953 opened, the ROKA was a steadily improving fighting force, growing larger and stronger with each passing month. Its training centers were more than meeting the requirements for replacements and men for newly activated commands. When the ceasefire was signed ending hostilities, the South Koreans possessed a large, new, and strong army of which they could be proud.

—*Uzal W. Ent*

References:

Appleman, Roy E. *South to the Naktong, North to the Yalu.* Washington, DC: Office of the Chief of Military History, 1961.

Ent, Uzal W. *Fighting on the Brink: Defense of the Pusan Perimeter.* Paducah, KY: Turner, 1996.

Hermes, Walter G. *United States Army in the Korean War: Truce Tent and Fighting Front.* Washington, DC: Office of the Chief of Military History, 1966.

Mossman, Billy C. *U.S. Army in the Korean War: Ebb and Flow, November 1950–July 1951.* Washington, DC: U.S. Army Center of Military History, 1990.

Sawyer, Robert K. *Military Advisors in Korea: KMAG in Peace and War.* Washington, DC: Office of the Chief of Military History, U.S. Army, 1962.

See also: Cheju-do Rebellion; Clark, Mark W.; Collins, Joseph Lawton; Korea, Democratic People's Republic of: Army (Korean People's Army [KPA]); Korea, Republic of: Air Force (ROKAF); Korea, Republic of: Marines; Korea, Republic of: Navy (ROKN); Korean Augmentation to the United States Army (KATUSA); MacArthur, Douglas; Muccio, John J.; Order of Battle: United Nations, North Korea, and People's Republic of China; Paek, Sŏn-yŏp; Ridgway, Matthew Bunker; Truman, Harry S.; Van Fleet, James Alward; Walker, Walton Harris.

Korea, Republic of: History, 1947–1953

The history of South Korea after the liberation in August 1945 through the end of the Korean War in July 1953 was marked by two complicated and interactive events: a state-building process with a variety of conflicting forces, and the emergence of the Cold War rivalry between the United States and the Soviet Union; the two were intertwined and aggravated each other. The year 1947 saw the failure both of state building among competing political groups in Korea and negotiations between the United States and the Soviet Union. State building was then transferred to the United Nations (UN), and a process of divided nation-building began.

From August–September 1945, when troops of the Soviet Union and the United States occupied Korea north and south, respectively, of the 38th parallel to accept the Japanese surrender, to August 1947, when the Second Session of the U.S.-Soviet Joint Commission ended without result, all efforts to establish a unified independent state by domestic political groups and via international negotiations failed.

In the North a Soviet-style government came into operation under Kim Il Sung with Soviet guidance. However, in the South, the issue of state building was more complicated. U.S. Army troops led by Lieutenant General John R. Hodge entered the South on 8 September 1945, but the United States refused to recognize either the People's Republic hurriedly set up by Yŏ Un-hyŏng or the provisional government in exile led by Kim Ku that had fought against Japanese rule in China. The United States proposed an international trusteeship for a limited time that would lead to a unified and independent Korean government. Most Korean political groups opposed this plan, except those on the left. Indeed Washington was embarrassed that the trusteeship plan was strongly resisted by pro-U.S. rightist groups while it was supported by pro-Soviet leftist groups.

U.S.-Soviet wartime cooperation abruptly ended, and by early 1947 the Cold War had solidified. The Soviet Union had already set up Communist satellite states in Eastern Europe, and the United States responded with its containment policy. Under these circumstances, although it met in March 1946 and May 1947, the U.S.-Soviet Joint Commission, which was to decide on an appropriate mechanism for establishing an interim Korean government, was deadlocked.

Domestic political groups could not reach agreement on state building either. Four major political groups, each with distinctive political ideas and different styles of government, vied for influence. Syngman Rhee and the Korean Democratic Party (KDP) believed in strong anti-communism and favored divided state-building in Korea to a unified Communist state. At the other extreme, Pak Hŏn-yŏng led the South Korean Labor Party (SKLP) and sought a revolutionary Communist state in connection with the North. On the center-right, Kim Ku and Kim Kyu-sik favored a strong nationalist stance with unification at any cost. On center-left, Yŏ Un-hyŏng sought a socialist unified government. The emerging Cold War precluded both the center-right and center-left solutions, and the American Military Government (AMG, 1945–1948) suppressed the SKLP. Rhee and the KDP fit with the Cold War and prevailed with U.S. support.

Because the U.S.-Soviet Joint Commission was stalemated, on 17 September 1947 the United States brought the Korean issue before the UN. On 14 November, the UN General Assembly passed a resolution over Soviet opposition based on the U.S. proposal that a UN Temporary Commission on Korea (UNTCOK) be established to observe the election of a Korean legislative body empowered to form a Korean government. The UNTCOK delegation arrived in Seoul in early January 1948, but the Soviet Union denied it access to the North. Under U.S. pressure, in February 1948 UNTCOK called for "elections in that part of Korea accessible to the Commission."

Against the backdrop of an election in the South alone and the possible division of Korea, a North-South Political Leaders' Coalition Conference was held in P'yŏngyang in April but without result. In spite of widespread opposition, the election took place on 10 May 1948. A total of 198 legislators were elected, with the KDP in the majority. The new legislature promulgated a constitution on 17 July and elected Syngman Rhee as the first president of the republic. On 15 August, the government of the Republic of Korea (ROK) was officially inaugurated, and on 12 December, the UN declared the ROK as the only legitimate government in Korea.

At the same time, the North proceeded with its own state building. As early as the November 1947 UN resolution, the North Korean People's Congress established a constitutional committee. It adopted a constitution on 10 July 1948, elected representatives to a Supreme People's Congress on 25 August, and declared the Democratic People's Republic of Korea (DPRK) with Kim Il Sung as premier on 9 September.

Thus by September 1948 two separate regimes on each side of the 38th parallel had been established, each claiming legitimacy over all Korea and threatening to unify the country by force. Soviet occupation forces withdrew from the North in December 1948 and the U.S. forces from the South in June 1949. However, in the South since early 1948 there had been a number of insurgencies against the division. These led to guerrilla struggles that lasted until the eve of the Korean War. On 7 February 1948, the Pak Hŏn-yŏng's SKLP staged a general strike. On 3 April 1948, in the Cheju-do Rebellion, Communist guerrilla units and supporters occupied most towns on Cheju Island and disrupted the 10 May general elections there. On 19 October, in the Yŏsu-Sunch'ŏn Rebellion, 2,500 troops rebelled at the port of Yŏsu under SKLP instigation. The ROK government was able to end most of this by late October. These rebellions were followed by numerous small guerrilla actions designed to topple the Rhee government, but most of these had been ended by May 1950. On the other hand, during 1949, border conflicts escalated along the 38th parallel.

On 25 June 1950, Korean People's Army (KPA, North Korean) forces crossed the 38th parallel and invaded South Korea. The next day, the UN Security Council adopted a U.S. resolution that confirmed an armed attack upon the ROK by forces from North Korea. On 27 June, U.S. President Harry S. Truman ordered U.S. air and naval forces to resist Communist aggression in Korea. That same day, the UN Security Council ratified Truman's decision and passed a second resolution calling on UN members to assist in repelling the armed attack and to restore peace and security in the region. Seoul fell on 28 June. Two days later, Truman ordered U.S. ground forces in Japan to Korea. The UN created a unified command to be led by an American. Truman appointed General Douglas MacArthur to that position. Sixteen UN member states provided troops to the United Nations Command (UNC), but U.S. and South Korean troops bore the brunt of the fighting.

The North Korean troops continued to advance even with the presence of U.S. troops in the field. In early August 1950, the UNC forces had been driven into the so-called Pusan perimeter along the Naktong River. Then, on 15 September UNC forces conducted a daring amphibious landing at Inch'ŏn. At the same time, troops along the Pusan perimeter broke out. The KPA was then caught in the convergence of the Allied forces from north and south, and more than 125,000 prisoners were taken.

Allied forces recovered Seoul on 28 September and passed the 38th parallel on 1 October. Meanwhile Rhee and Truman ordered the Allied forces into the north, and on 7 October the UN General Assembly adopted a U.S. resolution to establish a unified, democratic Korea. On 20 October, UNC forces entered P'yŏngyang and then headed north for the Yalu River, the border with the People's Republic of China (PRC). However, the PRC then sent troops (the Chinese People's Volunteer Army, CPVA) across the Yalu River into North Korea. The Soviet Union also entered the war secretly, providing air cover to CPVA and KPA forces operating in the northern part of North Korea. By 15 December, after bitter winter fighting, sheer CPVA numbers forced the UNC troops back below the 38th parallel. Seoul was reevacuated on 4 January 1951, but Communist forces were halted about 30 miles south of Seoul, and a UNC counteroffensive began in late January. By 31 March, Allied forces had recaptured Seoul and regained the 38th parallel. The battle line then stabilized slightly north of that line.

On 11 April 1951, Truman replaced the insubordinate MacArthur with Eighth Army Commander Lieutenant General Matthew B. Ridgway. From this time on, Truman sought to limit the fighting, in spite of strong opposition from Rhee. On 10 July 1951, truce negotiations began between the UN and the Communist commanders at Kaesŏng and were later resumed at P'anmunjŏm. Negotiations centered on two issues: the location of the cease-fire line and terms for exchange of prisoners. From the beginning, Rhee opposed negotiations that would leave Korea divided; he demanded that a military offensive be resumed. A final agreement had to wait until after the inauguration of U.S. President Dwight D. Eisenhower in January 1953 and the death of Soviet Premier Josef Stalin in March 1953.

On 27 July 1953, the Korean Armistice Agreement was signed by PRC, DPRK, and U.S. representatives. Rhee refused to sign. Although the Communists had argued for the restoration of the 38th parallel, the military line became the armistice line, with a demilitarized zone created to extend 2 kilometers along each side of it. The Military Armistice Commission and the Neutral Nations Supervisory Commission were created to enforce the armistice. A Neutral Nations Repatriation Commission was entrusted with the repatriation of prisoners, 21,809 of whom (7,582 Korean and 14,227 Chinese) chose to stay in South Korea or go to Taiwan.

The Korean War resulted in tremendous human casualties and material destruction. The ROK government estimates that its armed services lost 184,573 dead, died of wounds, and missing in action and 717,083 wounded. Another source gives total ROK military deaths at 257,000. Civilian casualties in South Korea are estimated at up to 900,000 civilians dead of all causes and another 300,000 missing (perhaps 200,000 of these disappeared into the KPA, either pressed or joined voluntarily and then became KPA casualties). The physical destruction of the war was also enormous. Two-fifths of Korea's industrial facilities and one-third of its houses were destroyed.

Politically, the First Republic (1948–1960) had digressed gradually toward authoritarian rule. The AMG took over administrative, police, and military organizations that had been created by the Japanese colonial government. Rhee also depended heavily on the bureaucracy and police to secure political support under weakly developed representative institutions. Immediately after the inauguration of the first government in 1948, the National Assembly, dominated by the Korean Democratic Party, attempted to oust Rhee by replacing the presidential system with a parliamentary system. Rhee then forced the National Assembly to amend the constitution for a popular election of the president in July 1952. In August 1952, he was reelected, and he continued in power until he was ousted in 1960.

In 1945 sharecropping tenancy was the predominant form of land tenure. Of the total cultivated land, 65 percent was in tenancy arrangements. Of rural households, 85 percent were in full or part tenancy. Considering that most South Koreans were subsistence farmers, land reform emerged as one of the most urgent issues. The North had completed a sweeping socialist land reform of expropriation and redistribution as early as March 1946. In reaction to this and under pressure from the peasants, the South also undertook land reform, which proceeded in two stages. In March 1948, the AMG distributed formerly Japanese-owned lands—some 12.3 percent of the lands in cultivation farmed by 29.3 percent of the total rural households. This was of great benefit to the rightist political group in the May 1948 general election. The new ROK government also undertook major land reform. In April 1949, the National Assembly passed a land reform act; by April 1950, the government had completed distribution of land. Some 91.9 percent of the total land and 80.7 percent of total rural households were by then owned by those who worked the land. This reform reduced the threat of peasant revolutionary movements and promoted political stability in the ROK.

—*Hochul Lee*

References:

Committee on National History Recording. *Taehan Minguk-sa* [History of the Republic of Korea]. Seoul: T'amgu-dang, 1988.

Cumings, Bruce. *The Origins of the Korean War: Liberation and the Emergence of Separate Regimes, 1945–1947.* Princeton, NJ: Princeton University Press, 1981.

———. *The Origins of the Korean War: The Roaring of the Cataract, 1947–1950.* Princeton, NJ: Princeton University Press, 1990.

Halliday, Jon, and Bruce Cumings. *Korea, The Unknown War.* New York: Pantheon, 1988.

Han, Woo-Keun. *The History of Korea.* Seoul: Eul-Yoo, 1970.

Hart-Landsberg, Martin. *Korea: Division, Reunification, and U.S. Foreign Policy.* New York: Monthly Review Press, 1998.

Institute of National Defense and Military History. *Hankuk Chŏnjaeng* [The Korean War]. 3 vols. Seoul: Institute of National Defense and Military History, 1995–1997.

Kim, Hak-jun. *Han'guk Chŏnjaeng: Kiwŏn, Kwajŏng, Hyujŏn, Yŏnghyang* [The Korean War: origins, processes, armistice, and impact]. Seoul: Pakyŏng-sa, 1989.

———. *Han'guk Munje wa Kukje Chŏngch'i* [The Korean issue and international politics]. Seoul: Pakyŏng-sa, 1976.

Lee, Hochul. "Political Economy of Land Reform: A Historical Institutional Explanation." Ph.D. dissertation, Rutgers University, 1993.

Lee, Ki-baik. *A New History of Korea.* Cambridge, MA: Harvard University Press, 1984.

Merrill, John. *Korea: The Peninsular Origins of the War.* Newark: University of Delaware Press, 1989.

Song, Kŏn-ho, Man-gil Kang, Hyŏn-ch'ae Pak, Chang-jip Ch'oe, et al. *Haebang Chŏnhu ŭi Insik* [Perspectives on the period before and after the liberation]. 4 vols. Seoul: Hangil-sa, 1979–1989.

See also: Border Clashes; Casualties; Cheju-do Rebellion; Cold War, Origins to 1950; Eisenhower, Dwight D.; Hodge, John R.; Inch'ŏn Landings: Operation CHROMITE; Kim Il Sung; MacArthur, Douglas; Neutral Nations Repatriation Commission; Neutral Nations Supervisory Commission (NNSC); Pusan Perimeter and Breakout; Ridgway, Matthew Bunker; Stalin, Josef; Syngman Rhee; Truman, Harry S.; Yŏsu-Sunch'ŏn Rebellion.

Korea, Republic of: History, 1953 to the Present

In the spring of 1953, as armistice talks entered their final stage, the situation in South Korea was grim. The Republic of Korea (ROK) had been devastated by war; its infrastructure was hard hit, and it had suffered millions of military and civilian casualties. Throughout the war, ROK President Syngman Rhee had pushed for the reunification of Korea by military force. This was clearly impossible without massive U.S. assistance, which U.S. President Dwight D. Eisenhower would not provide. While he remained a strong advocate of reunification, Rhee recognized the limits of U.S. assistance and in the end reluctantly agreed to the armistice terms.

Rhee received assurances that the United States would not abandon the ROK, and a formal Mutual Defense Treaty between the two nations came into force in late 1954. This provided for the continued stationing of U.S. troops in the ROK. In addition to agreeing to underwrite expansion and improvement of ROK military forces, the United States, along with its allies and the United Nations (UN), agreed to provide economic and humanitarian assistance to rebuild the South. The United States was by far the major contributor in this effort, giving over $1 billion in aid from 1954 to 1960.

In terms of domestic politics during the immediate postwar period, the autocratic and increasingly corrupt Rhee administration soon lost popular support as it changed laws and rigged elections to remain in power. The enormous task of rebuilding a nation devastated by war took a back seat to survival of Rhee's regime, and the South's economy struggled accordingly, despite significant amounts of foreign assistance.

Rhee tried to build the ROK economy using a system of commodity exchange and import substitution and was able to make some gains in the areas of education and urban development. This was in fact the beginning of a rural-to-urban migration in South Korea that would continue through the 1990s. During this period, the military also began to play a critical role in national development.

In April 1960, after a series of antigovernment demonstrations and increasing political opposition within his own party, Rhee resigned the presidency and went into exile in the United States. Foreign minister Hŏ Chŏng assumed executive authority. July elections resulted in a coalition government under Yun Po-sŏn as figurehead president and Chang Myŏn (John M. Chang) as premier. Over the next year moderate elements sought to institute sweeping economic and political reforms. A lack of progress and increasing opposition violence opened the door for an internal military solution.

On 16 May 1961, Major General Park Chung Hee and a small group of younger officers mounted a successful coup and seized power. The ROK military quickly backed Park, who kept President Yun as a figurehead during a ten-month transition period. Park focused on eliminating governmental corruption and developing economic self-sufficiency. By 1963 Park had fully consolidated his political power. He resigned from the military and gained a measure of legitimacy by narrowly winning a popular election for the presidency.

Park's major themes were building Korean pride and nationalism, and his regime began an extended period of political stability and economic development for the ROK. Park shifted the economy from import substitution to support for heavy industry and export-driven growth, largely under the control of *chaebŏls*, financial, industrial, and business conglomerates similar to the Japanese *zaibatsu*. The economy came under the supervision of trained economists in a newly instituted central planning body, the Economic Planning Board. To protect farmers and the agricultural sector,

Park initiated a comprehensive rural development program known as the *saemaŭl undong* (New Village Movement). During this period, he also sought and received substantial foreign investment.

Park, as Rhee before him, still worried about the U.S. commitment to the security of South Korea. Understanding the geopolitical significance of U.S. efforts to internationalize the war in Vietnam, Park sent 45,000 ROK troops to Southeast Asia in 1965. Korean troops in Vietnam expanded the ROK's value as a U.S. ally, and in return Washington provided millions of dollars to South Korea in additional military and humanitarian assistance. This aid enabled the ROK to modernize its armed forces and significantly boosted its domestic economy. This resulted in greater opportunities for a nascent middle class to start small, independent businesses that expanded and helped to diversify the economy.

Three major incidents during 1968–1969 identified limitations in the U.S. commitment to South Korea. The North Korean capture of the USS *Pueblo*, the attempt to assassinate Park at the presidential official residence, and the shooting down of a U.S. EC-121 intelligence collection and command and control aircraft demanded a strong U.S.-ROK reaction. Yet in all three incidents the primary response was a heightened state of alert for both ROK and U.S. forces, but no retaliatory military action. This lack of any decisive military response by the United States, and its failure to support any unilateral retaliation by the ROK armed forces, greatly disappointed the South Korean leadership.

In the early 1970s, Park was losing popular support and becoming increasingly dictatorial in his efforts to retain power at the same time as the Korean economy experienced a major downturn, accelerated by the U.S. pullout from Vietnam and the Middle East oil crisis. South Koreans were also disappointed with Park's failed efforts at rapprochement with the Democratic People's Republic of Korea (DPRK, North Korea). After a period of popular and hopeful negotiations spurred on by improved Sino-U.S. relations, ROK efforts at détente with the North deteriorated. The leaders of both Koreas stepped back from a policy of improved relations, for which neither side was ready to cede sovereignty.

Park's domestic problems were exacerbated by U.S. President Jimmy Carter's announced plan to withdraw U.S. forces from South Korea. This immediately set off alarm bells in Seoul as South Koreans feared abandonment by their ally. The deteriorating security relationship, coupled with Carter's condemnation of Park's human rights abuses, seriously undermined the ROK president's internal political legitimacy. Escalating civil protests led Park to expand his

executive powers and increase suppression of popular dissent.

The political situation changed abruptly on 26 October 1979, when President Park was assassinated by Kim Chae-gyu, director of the Korea Central Intelligence Agency (KCIA). Over the next two months political and military factions vied for power. Students, workers, and opposition parties all conducted major demonstrations that often resulted in violence. In early December, Ch'oe Kyu-ha, then prime minister, was elected the new president by the National Conference for Unification. Ch'oe promised popular elections and a new constitution within a year, and he also released political prisoners. In response, on 12 December 1979, Lieutenant General Chun Doo Hwan seized control of the military. Over the next few months, he gained control of the KCIA, and with his strong support in the army, on 17 May 1980, he was able to seize complete control of the government in a military coup.

Areas of traditional opposition erupted in protest. Chun responded by arresting key political opponents (including future presidents Kim Yong Sam and Kim Dae Jung), censoring the press, establishing political reeducation programs, and using loyal military units to crush demonstrators. From 18 through 27 May, Chun deployed Special Forces and elite airborne units to quell the Kwangju uprising in southwestern Korea. During this action, thousands of Koreans were killed or wounded, despite government denials to the contrary. Although there is no evidence of U.S. assistance or complicity in this, Korean popular opinion was shaped by the perception of a U.S. failure to intervene or subsequently to condemn Chun's actions.

Despite his brutal methods and widespread opposition, Chun stabilized the situation, and in August 1980 he "won" election as the new ROK president. He then began a major program of economic initiatives aimed at quieting critics at home and abroad. Focusing on stabilization, Chun shifted the economy to labor-intensive light industries, lifted import restrictions, and reduced foreign borrowing. Like Park before him, Chun continued to use the *chaebŏls* as the primary driver of the economy.

In foreign relations Chun fostered close ties with U.S. President Ronald Reagan, despite among certain sectors of the populace the emergence of anti-Americanism rooted in the U.S. response to the Kwangju massacre. Chun expanded relations with the Japanese that led to large government-to-government loans to support the ROK regime. He also initiated informal contacts with the People's Republic of China (PRC) and the Soviet Union in an attempt to drive a wedge between the North and its traditional allies. Chun's successful handling of foreign policy and the economy gained him a measure of legitimacy and political acceptance.

However, two major incidents in 1983 severely tested the Chun regime. In September the Soviets shot down a civilian airliner, Korean Airlines (KAL) Flight 007 that the USSR claimed had violated its airspace over Sakhalin Island in route to Korea. This incident was a major setback for Chun's policy and resulted in the suspension of ROK-Soviet relations for five years. A month later in Rangoon, Burma (Myanmar), an attempt by DPRK agents to assassinate Chun resulted in the deaths of several senior ROK cabinet members. Fearing that this was part of a larger North Korean operation against the South, ROK forces went on alert, and additional U.S. forces were immediately deployed to the region. These events stunned governments around the world, and international opinion very much sided with South Korea, but the regional and international environment was also rapidly changing.

U.S. support for the removal of President Ferdinand Marcos in the Philippines was an obvious example of changing U.S. policy toward military dictatorships in Asia. Early in his administration, Chun had promised an end to military rule, and he now sought to oversee a peaceful transition before the 1988 Summer Olympics in Seoul. He had been in office eight years and according to the constitution could not run for another term. Student protests, which were joined by a cross section of the Korean populace, made it clear that there would be strong opposition to any attempt by Chun to remain in power. Faced with overwhelming popular dissent, Chun turned over executive power to another army general, Roh Tae Woo. To defuse the volatile domestic situation, on 29 June 1987, Roh declared that free, popular elections would be held, political prisoners released, basic civil rights would be guaranteed, and freedom of the press granted.

In December 1987, in a three-way race, Roh Tae Woo triumphed over two major opposition party figures in the first truly popular election for president of Korea since 1971. The election of a military officer over two civilian candidates who had both suffered at the hands of the military during the Park and Chun eras was unexpected. However, the three-way race split the reformist vote and allowed Roh to win with a plurality. The two opposition candidates, Kim Yong Sam and Kim Dae Jung, both later won presidential elections and served as the first two elected civilian leaders of Korea since President Syngman Rhee.

The 1988 Seoul Olympics were a great success. The games were attended by virtually all of North Korea's Communist allies and were a major embarrassment for the DPRK. The Seoul Olympics signaled the ROK's rise to prominence and maturity as a regional Asian power. This was dramatically shown by the ROK's

great restraint when the DPRK perpetrated another major terrorist incident, the bombing of KAL Flight 858. The ROK was a major economic success story, had conducted a peaceful and democratic transition of government, and was now in a position to conduct a more independent foreign policy.

President Roh, with the backing of the United States, and taking advantage of the end of the Cold War, began to implement a policy of "*nordpolitik*" that had its roots in the Chun era with initiatives toward the PRC and the USSR. Roh expanded diplomatic initiatives into Eastern Europe, starting with Hungary and Poland. His policy also included efforts to normalize relations with North Korea and a continued improvement of relations with China and Russia. Roh's policies achieved dramatic results, including a cancellation of Soviet economic and military support for the DPRK and closer ROK political and economic relations with China. In 1991, under the urging of the major powers, the DPRK withdrew its long-time opposition, and the two Koreas became members of the UN. The ROK was now seen more as an equal partner than client state by the United States and as a rising independent actor by the regional states.

Nonetheless, a state of war continued in Korea. Despite the Cold War having ended in Europe, two of the world's largest and best equipped military forces still confronted each other along the demilitarized zone near the 38th parallel. Violent incidents at sea and along the common border between the DPRK and ROK continued all too frequently. Nevertheless, in the early 1990s concrete steps were taken to reduce tensions between the two Koreas. In 1992 a program was established under the aegis of the UN's International Atomic Energy Agency (IAEA) to inspect nuclear facilities in the North.

In the midst of another round of negotiations with the DPRK, the first civilian leader of the South since Syngman Rhee, former political dissident Kim Young Sam, was elected president. In a shrewd political maneuver, Kim had joined Roh's ruling party to carry the election. Kim immediately moved to reorganize the government, to fight corruption, and to bring the military under firm civilian control. Former presidents Chun and Roh were arrested, tried, and convicted of crimes related to their abuses of power while in office. Their death and life sentences, respectively, were later commuted and eventually both were granted pardons. The sweeping changes in the South, including the successful transition to civilian rule, an economy that was significantly outperforming that of the North, a major military modernization program, and successful diplomatic initiatives toward China and Russia, all put the DPRK and its aging leader Kim Il Sung at a major disadvantage.

Once again ROK-DPRK relations began to deteriorate. The North found new ways to reestablish a crisis environment on the peninsula. The DPRK rejected the nuclear inspection regime, embarked on the possible production of nuclear weapons, worked to develop new missile technology, and sold arms to the volatile Middle East. This brought about a joint ROK and U.S. effort to oppose a DPRK weakened by the loss of its traditional Chinese and Russian supporters.

U.S. President William Clinton's first official foreign visit was to South Korea, where he specifically warned the North of dire consequences were it to use nuclear or chemical weapons against the ROK. At this time, the ROK began to play a more critical role in negotiations with the DPRK over strategic issues. The ROK leadership convinced the United States to pursue multilateral approaches in negotiations with the DPRK. Although progress was slow, the effort seemed to be gaining momentum, when Kim Il Sung died unexpectedly in July 1994. His son, Kim Jong Il, took over the running of the government, although the official process of replacing his father, who had become a cult figure in the North, continued for some time. In subsequent years, Kim Jong Il appeared to be solidly in control of the party apparatus, the military, and the government.

Despite this transition in the DPRK leadership, in October 1994 the DPRK signed the Framework Agreement. This pact called for an extensive inspection regime to be carried out by the IAEA and the closing of certain nuclear-related facilities. The DPRK was promised two light-water reactors to replace its current heavy-water plants and was to receive a supply of oil in the interim until the new power plants came on line.

After the agreement was signed, there were indications that the DPRK might not be fully living up to all the terms of the agreement, but it is difficult to determine the status of various claims and counterclaims. Over the past several years, the DPRK's political and security situation has been complicated by a sharply declining economy and widespread famine. UN humanitarian relief organizations and independent nongovernmental organizations were granted unprecedented access to the North and reported that millions are malnourished and hundreds of thousands may have died. The UN, the United States, the ROK, and the international community shipped tons of foodstuffs to alleviate the suffering in the North. This did not, however, prevent the DPRK from continuing its military provocations against the ROK.

Just before the December 1997 election, the economy of South Korea failed. The value of the Korean currency dropped by more than half, several major *chaebŏls* declared bankruptcy, and large-scale unemployment put the country in turmoil. This economic crisis was blamed on the government-*chaebŏl* relationship that restricted free market competition and allowed high-risk borrowing. The new South Korean leader would inherit the worst economic situation in the country since the Korean War.

In 1997 another civilian and former political dissident, Kim Dae Jung, was elected president of the ROK. He instituted the Sunshine Policy, yet another attempt to bring about a peaceful transition and unification of the peninsula. However, in the midst of this latest set of initiatives by the South and increased economic interaction, the DPRK continued its military provocations. During 1997–1998 the North attempted several infiltrations of the ROK by submarine and small surface craft and developed and launched a multistage rocket that could reach all of the Japanese Islands, thus precipitating another period of major crisis.

The DPRK continues to use warlike rhetoric to threaten the South and calls for the immediate withdrawal of U.S. forces. Perhaps more ominous for the future of Korea are reports that the 1994 Framework Agreement is also in trouble and that the DPRK has restarted its nuclear weapons program, particularly at Kŭmch'ang-ni. It is clear that the Cold War has not ended in Korea and that continued tensions on the peninsula are not likely be resolved easily or quickly, barring a catastrophic collapse of the DPRK.

At the same time, economic problems continue in Asia and in South Korea. In this evolving crisis environment, questions have arisen about the best path to reunification, Korea's role in the region, and appropriate levels of defense spending. It remains to be seen whether or not the ROK can regain its position in the world's economic structure and return to its heady days as one of the Asian tigers.

The ROK maintains a modern, well-equipped force of over half a million troops that stands ready to defend the ROK against DPRK aggression. At the same time, the ROK struggles to regain economic stability and to further develop its democratic political institutions. The DPRK maintains a force of over a million troops in an aggressive forward-deployed posture. The North's economy continues to decline precipitously, and its political institutions remain rooted in a repressive, socialist, cultist "Kimilsungism." Although neither the PRC nor Russia, historic patrons of the DPRK, appear willing to support an invasion of the South or the development of nuclear weapons and missile technology, the Korean peninsula remains a flash point.

—*J. G. D. Babb*

References:

Barnds, William J., ed. *The Two Koreas in East Asian Affairs.* New York: New York University Press, 1976.

Bok, Lee Suk. *The Impact of US Forces in Korea*. Washington, DC: National Defense University Press, 1987.

Bunge, Frederica M., ed. *North Korea: A Country Study (DA Pam 550-81)*. Washington, DC: U.S. Government Printing Office, 1989.

Clough, Ralph N. *Embattled Korea: Rivalry for International Support*. Boulder, CO: Westview Press, 1987.

Cumings, Bruce. *Korea's Place in the Sun: A Modern History*. New York: W. W. Norton, 1997.

Hermes, Walter G. *United States Army in the Korean War: Truce Tent and Fighting Front*. Washington, DC: Office of the Chief of Military History, 1966.

Keon, Michael. *Korean Phoenix: A Nation from the Ashes*. Englewood, NJ: Prentice-Hall International, 1977.

Kihl, Young Whan, ed. *Korea and the World: Beyond the Cold War*. Boulder, CO: Westview Press, 1994.

Oberdorfer, Don. *The Two Koreas: A Contemporary History*. Reading, MA: Addison-Wesley, 1997.

Savada, Andrea M., and William Shaw, eds. *South Korea: A Country Study* (DA Pam 550-41). Washington, DC: U.S. Government Printing Office, 1990.

See also: Eisenhower, Dwight D.; Syngman Rhee; U.S. Policy toward Korea, 1950–1953; U.S. Policy toward Korea: 1953 to the Present.

Korea, Republic of: Korean Service Corps (KSC)

The Korean Service Corps (KSC) provided personnel to carry critically needed ammunition, medical supplies, food, water, and other supplies to front-line United Nations Command (UNC) troops. The KSC grew out of ad hoc groups of South Korean men and boys who, early in the war, were pressed into service to carry supplies of all kinds to front-line UN forces. Often, these carriers were the only means to resupply the front with ammunition, food, water, and other much-needed supplies and to evacuate critically wounded and the dead. In the beginning, the carriers were recruited locally or from refugee camps and usually were paid for their serv-

Republic of Korea National Guard recruits receive their first issue of clothing and equipment, Taegu, 20 April 1951. (National Archives)

Korean porters transporting supplies to the front. (National Archives)

ices in food, or a pittance of money, and a place to sleep.

In the beginning such workers were known as "Choggie" or "Chiggie" for the Korean word *chige* (carrying frame or carrier). The bearers used back carriers, which GIs dubbed "A-frames" because the device resembled the capital letter A. The outer legs of the carrier were wide-spread at the bottom and came close together at the top. These two legs were held apart by a series of wooden slats, with the bottom-most slat resembling the horizontal line of the letter A. A wooden bar or slat was placed at more or less right angles from each leg of the A, upon which the load could be rested and lashed to the uprights of the frame. A bearer often could carry his own weight on his A-frame. However, for sustained operations or long hauls, 50 pounds per porter was the norm. On a daily basis, a bearer could carry 50 pounds for up to 10 miles.

As the KSC was formalized, some personnel were drawn from refugee camps, but most came from the ROK National Guard. By 1 April 1952, the U.S. Eighth Army was supported by 65 KSC companies, each with 240 porters.

The size of the corps slowly increased, but control and discipline were not uniform. In November 1951, UNC commander Lieutenant General Matthew B. Ridgway authorized U.S. Eighth Army commander Lieutenant General James A. Van Fleet to increase the corps to 60,000 men. Simultaneously, all laborers and carriers in the combat zone were organized and brought under tighter control and discipline. This would ensure combat troops of more reliable service support. Shortly thereafter, the KSC was increased to 75,000 men. Term of service in the KSC was six months. In mid-September 1952, Van Fleet asked the Republic of Korea Army (South Korea) to increase the

Korean Service Corps to 100,000 men. The additional personnel allowed him to form six new carrier regiments and bring the existing regiments up to strength.

Untold numbers of KSC members were killed or wounded during the war. Unheralded and unsung, their story never told, these bearers contributed immeasurably to the success of UN troops during the Korean War.

—*Uzal W. Ent*

References:

Ent, Uzal W. *Fighting on the Brink: Defense of the Pusan Perimeter.* Paducah, KY: Turner, 1996.

Hermes, Walter G. *United States Army in the Korean War: Truce Tent and Fighting Front.* Washington, DC: Office of the Chief of Military History, 1966.

Mossman, Billy C. *U.S. Army in the Korean War: Ebb and Flow, November 1950–July 1951.* Washington, DC: U.S. Army Center of Military History, 1990.

Sawyer, Robert K. *Military Advisors in Korea: KMAG in Peace and War.* Washington, DC: Office of the Chief of Military History, U.S. Army, 1962.

See also: Korea, Republic of: National Guard (Fifth Reserve Corps); Ridgway, Matthew Bunker; Van Fleet, James Alward.

Korea, Republic of: Marines

Republic of Korea (ROK, South Korean) Marines fought under the operational command of the U.S. 1st Marine Division. The Korean Marine Corps was organized on 15 April 1949 by the transfer of 80 officers and men from the ROK Navy, plus an additional 300 recruits. Among the officers transferred from the Korean Navy was Captain Sin Hyŏn-jun, who became the first commandant of the newly founded Corps.

The initial 380 officers and men were equipped with only small quantities of rifles left by the Japanese at the end of World War II, and the new Corps was initially housed in worn-out aviation sheds at the Tŏksan Airfield, near Chinhae. The newly formed unit was organized into an infantry battalion consisting of two rifle companies. After an intensive five-month training program, the two rifle companies were sent to the southwestern part of South Kyŏngsang Province to quell disturbances created by Communist partisans. In December 1949, the ROK Marine Corps, expanded to two battalions (strength of 1,200 men), was ordered to Cheju Island to provide internal security.

When the North Koreans invaded South Korea on 25 June 1950, ROK Marines were ordered to join the ROK Army (ROKA) in trying to stem the advance of Korean People's Army (KPA, North Korean) troops. During the period 20 July to 3 August 1950, the Korean Marines took part in delaying actions at Kunsan, Yŏsu, Namwŏn, Chinju, and Masan and acquitted themselves well. As a consequence, ROK President Syngman Rhee promoted all Korean Marines who participated in these battles to the next higher grade.

By 1 September 1950, the Korean Marine Corps was expanded to one regiment plus one battalion. The first major independent action conducted by the young Marine Corps occurred at the battle of T'ongyŏng during 23 August–15 September 1950. The South Koreans attacked and defeated a North Korean force preparing to invade Kŏje-do.

On 5 September 1950, operational control of the Korean Marine Corps Regiment was assigned to the 1st U.S. Marine Division. On 15 September, the Korean Marine Regiment participated in the Inch'ŏn landing with the U.S. Marines and also in the subsequent assault on Seoul, which was retaken on 28 September 1950.

Upon completion of the battle for Seoul, the Korean Marines boarded tank landing ships (LSTs) and proceeded to Wŏnsan, landing there on 28 October 1950. They were attached to U.S. X Corps and were assigned the mission of maintaining security along the main supply route in the Kosŏng-Wŏnsan area. Later, during the withdrawal from the Wŏnsan area, Korean Marine Corps battalions occupied a portion of the perimeter defense. On 7 and 9 December, the 1st and 3d Battalions were withdrawn from Wŏnsan to Chinhae by LST, and on 15 December the 2d and 5th Battalions were evacuated from Hamhŭng by air.

For the next six weeks the Korean Marine Corps units underwent extensive training and reorganization. On 24 January 1951, the 1st Marine Corps Regiment and the 5th Korean Marine Corps Battalion departed for the Andong-Yŏngdŏk area. There they joined the U.S. 1st Marine Division, engaging and defeating the 10th KPA Division, which had infiltrated the main line of resistance by moving along the T'aebaek Mountains and which had been wreaking havoc on the United Nations (UN) supply lines and rear installations. By 12 February, all organized Communist resistance in the area had been eliminated.

During the second landing at Inch'ŏn on 15 February the 5th Korean Marine Battalion made an unopposed landing and occupied Inch'ŏn while other UN forces were occupying Seoul. After completing this action, the Korean Marines were ordered to the Kimpŏ peninsula to maintain defensive positions.

On 22 May 1951, the U.S. 1st Marine Division with the 1st Korean Marine Corps Regiment attached, went into the attack as part of the operation to seize the Punchbowl area. After fifteen days of bitter fighting, the Korean Marines secured their objective, the Tuscol Ridge. In July, after 148 days on the line, the U.S. and Korean Marines were withdrawn and went into X Corps reserve. During the remainder of July and most of August 1951, while it was in reserve, the Korean Marine Corps Regiment underwent an extensive training program. During this time, a U.S. Marine Corps Advisory Team of one officer, one noncommissioned officer, and an interpreter was assigned to each Korean Marine company.

On 30 August 1951, the U.S. 1st Marine Division and the 1st Korean Marine Regiment again went into attack. They were assigned the mission of seizing the northern vein of the Punchbowl. All objectives were secured by 5 September. For the rest of the year, the U.S. 1st Marine Division, with attached Korean Marine units, defended a 12-mile sector, making occasional tank-infantry raids into Communist-controlled territory.

Although there were no major actions during this period, the Korean Marine Corps was busy. An artillery battalion was organized and trained, an engineer platoon was activated, and a tank company was organized and trained. By this time the Korean Marine Corps had grown to over 4,000 officers and men.

During the remainder of the hostilities, the majority of the Korean Marine Corps units remained under the operational control of the U.S. 1st Marine Division and defended their assigned main battle positions until the signing of the Korean Armistice Agreement. On 14 September 1953, the 2d Korean Marine Corps Regiment was formed with the 5th, 6th, and 7th Battalions. It was also attached to the U.S. 1st Marine Division for operational control. On 1 March 1954, the 1st Korean Marine Corps Brigade was formed, with Headquarters assuming administrative responsibility for all Korean Marine Corps elements assigned to the U.S. 1st Marine Division. On 15 January 1955, the 1st Korean Marine Corps Division was authorized and activated by ROK presidential order.

The Korean Marines played a significant role during the bitter fighting of the Korean War. From those beginnings, the Republic of Korea Marine Corps grew to become the world's second largest amphibious corps behind only the U.S. Marine Corps.

—*James H. Willbanks*

References:

Montross, Lynn, and Nicholas A. Canzona. *U.S. Marine Operations in Korea, 1950–1953.* Vol. 1, *The Pusan Perimeter.* Washington, DC: U.S. Marine Corps Historical Branch, 1954.

———. *U.S. Marine Operations in Korea, 1950–1953,* Vol. 2, *The Inchon-Seoul Operations.* Washington, DC: U.S. Marine Corps Historical Branch, 1955.

See also: Border Clashes; Inch'ŏn Landings: Operation CHROMITE; Infiltration; Kimpŏ Airfield; Punchbowl; Pusan Perimeter and Breakout; Syngman Rhee; Tenth Corps; United States: Marines; Wŏnsan Landing.

Korea, Republic of: National Guard (V Reserve Corps)

The Republic of Korea (ROK, South Korean) National Guard, later known as V Reserve Corps, performed many vital services for the ROK Army (ROKA) and the United Nations Command. The ROKA reserves were originally known as the National (or Korean) Youth Corps. This organization then became the National Guard, and finally V Reserve Corps.

The National Guard provided most of the personnel for the Korean Service Corps (KSC). The KSC came into being to provide porter and other service to front-line troops. When the National Guard became the V Reserve Corps, its officers were selected from the cadres of regulars and armed primarily from ROK sources. It ran ROKA induction stations and provided internal security against guerrillas. Personnel sent to the KSC from V Reserve Corps also helped construct field fortifications, string barbed wire, and lay mines. For example, in early June 1952 a KSC contingent helped the U.S. 45th Division troops fortify the hill known as Old Baldy.

Because the National Guard/V Reserve Corps and the Korean Service Corps were so closely related, their histories overlap.

—*Uzal W. Ent*

References:

Hermes, Walter G. *United States Army in the Korean War: Truce Tent and Fighting Front.* Washington, DC: Office of the Chief of Military History, 1966.

Mossman, Billy C. *U.S. Army in the Korean War: Ebb and Flow, November 1950–July 1951.* Washington, DC: U.S. Army Center of Military History, 1990.

See also: Korea, Republic of: Korean Service Corps (KSC); Korea, Republic of: National Guard Scandal.

Korea, Republic of: National Guard Scandal (1951)

Incident in which top leaders of the Republic of Korea (ROK, South Korean) National Guard misappropriated for themselves government money and goods apportioned to the organization. As a result, more than 1,000 enlisted guardsmen died of starvation, illness, and cold.

After the Chinese intervention in the Korean fighting in October–November 1950, President Syngman Rhee's ROK government enacted the National Guard Act. Passed on 11 December 1950, this law authorized training of reservists and their prompt mobilization in time of national emergency. According to the law, men ages 17–40, except soldiers, police, and other public servants, were to be enlisted in the equivalent of second-class reserve forces. Reservists other than students were to be "voluntarily" assigned to the National Guard. The chief of staff of the ROK Army (ROKA) was to command and supervise the National Guard on the instruction of the minister of defense.

Immediately after promulgation of the law on 16 December 1950, President Rhee reorganized the

Taehan Youth Corps, regarded as his personal army, into the National Guard and appointed Corps leaders to key posts in the newly formed organization. Kim Yun-gŭn, head of the Taehan Youth Corps, became commander, Yun Ik-hŏn was made deputy commander, and Pak Kyŏng-gu became chief of staff.

The Taehan Youth Corps had been formed in December 1949 to absorb all the rightist youth groups active in anti-leftist political repression in South Korea below the 38th parallel after the Second World War. Shortly after the ROK was established under U.S. auspices in mid-August 1948, President Rhee, principal leader of the Korean Right, ordered all rightist youth organizations to be unified. Under his instruction, more than twelve youth groups combined to form the Taehan Youth Corps.

When United Nations forces were in a headlong retreat southward after the Chinese offensive in January 1951, those men who were enlisted in the National Guard were sent to North Kyŏngsang Province on foot, where they were scheduled to be trained. The leaders of the National Guard seized this occasion to embezzle a large sum of public funds and materials. The consequent serious shortage of supplies brought about the death of many enlisted men while others fell seriously ill. The budget for the National Guard of an estimated 500,000 members for the three-month period of January–March 1951 amounted to 20.9 billion won ($8.7 million). From the budget, however, only 13 billion won ($5.4 million) was actually expended. A close investigation after the scandal revealed that 2.4 billion won ($1 million) of government money and 52,000 sŏk (8,300 tons) of grain were illegally diverted by National Guard leaders. In addition, a large amount of medical supplies and subsidiary food were also illegally seized.

When the South Korean National Assembly learned about the scandal, on 30 April 1951 it passed a bill to dissolve the National Guard. It was finally disbanded on 12 May. Minister of Defense Sin Sŏng-mo, who had attempted to conceal the incident, was removed on 7 May and, ten days later, new Defense Minister Yi Ki-bung announced the arrest of National Guard Commander Kim Yun-gŭn. The provost marshal headquarters of the ROKA investigated the scandal and on 15 June brought eleven leaders of the National Guard, including Kim Yun-gŭn and Yun Ik-hŏn, before a military tribunal. On 19 July, the court-martial sentenced five individuals, including Kim and Yun, to death. The scandal ended with their execution on 13 August 1951 near Taegu, provincial capital of North Kyŏngsang Province. But questions still remain whether money expropriated by them might have gone into the coffers of high-ranking government leaders, including President Rhee.

The National Guard scandal demonstrated the undemocratic inclination of the Syngman Rhee regime, whose authority depended upon powerful private organizations to maintain Rhee's power.

—*Jinwung Kim*

References:

Kukbang-bu p'yŏnch'an wiwŏn-hoe. *Han'guk Chŏngjaeng-sa.* [History of the Korean War]. Seoul: Kukbang-bu p'yŏnch'an wiwŏn-hoe, 1968.

Matray, James I., ed. *Historical Dictionary of the Korean War.* Westport, CT: Greenwood Press, 1991.

Yŏrum Publishing Co., ed. *Han'guk Hyŏndae Sahoe Undong Sajŏn* [A dictionary of contemporary Korean social movements, 1880–1972]. Seoul: Yŏrum, 1988.

See also: Korea, Republic of: National Guard (Fifth Reserve Corps); Syngman Rhee.

Korea, Republic of: Navy (ROKN)

Perhaps the most aggressive and effective, if smallest, member of the Republic of Korea (ROK, South Korean) armed services during the first year of the Korean War. At the outset of the conflict, the ROK Navy (ROKN) had 6,956 men and seventy-one naval vessels of various types, largely ex-U.S. and ex-Japanese minesweepers and picket boats. The largest ROKN vessel was a frigate, the *Paektusan.* The ROKN was based at Inch'ŏn, Kunsan, Mokp'o, Yŏsu, Pusan, P'ohang, and Mukho. Its service installations were at Chinhae.

The ROKN was outnumbered by the 13,700 men and 110 naval vessels of the Korean People's Navy (KPN, North Korea). The concentration of ROKN units at western and southern ports on 25 June also enabled the North Koreans to land ground forces at a few locations along the east coast as far south as Samch'ŏk and send a 1,000-ton freighter loaded with 600 troops toward the port of Pusan.

The ROKN and its United Nations (UN) allies, however, soon drove not only KPN combatants but reinforcement and resupply vessels from the seas that touch the shores of the Republic of Korea. The first night of the war, submarine chaser *PC 701* sortied from Pusan, made contact with a North Korean freighter, and sank it. The North Korean ship's embarked troops would no longer pose a threat to the vital port of Pusan. On 2 July, just south of the 38th parallel in the East Sea (Sea of Japan), U.S. cruiser *Juneau*, British cruiser *Jamaica*, and British frigate *Black Swan* sank three torpedo boats and two motor gunboats of the KPN. This was the first and last time during the war that KPN forces elected to fight the UN navies for control of the sea. Also on 2 July, the ROKN's Naval Base Detachment at P'ohang wiped out a North Korean landing force. The next day, minesweeper *YMS 513* destroyed three Communist supply vessels near Chulp'o on the southwestern coast.

Despite these initial successes, the result of action by resourceful local naval commanders, the ROKN suffered from lack of central direction in the early weeks of the war. This was in large part a result of the absence of ROKN Chief of Naval Operations Admiral Son Wŏn-il, who was in the United States to take delivery of three former U.S. Navy submarine chasers, and the capture by the Korean People's Army (KPA, North Korea) of the ROKN naval headquarters in Seoul.

Consequently, Commander U.S. Naval Forces, Far East, Vice Admiral C. Turner Joy, with the consent of South Korean authorities, designated Commander Michael J. Luosey as deputy commander, Naval Forces, Far East, and directed him to take operational control of the ROKN. With an American staff of one other officer and five enlisted sailors, the young officer assumed operational control of the ROKN at Pusan on 9 July. The other navies of the UN coalition also followed the operational direction of the U.S. Navy during the Korean War.

Luosey spent the first few weeks coordinating with the other United Nations Command (UNC) forces and arranging for logistic support of his ships and men. He also set up inshore patrol sectors along the coasts of South Korea and directed the ROKN's one tank landing ship (LST) to move 600 South Korean Marines to Kunsan on the southwestern coast. The small contingent was unable to stop the advancing KPA, so a few days later the Marines were reembarked. During the next two weeks, the ROKN used the naval infantry in short-duration landing operations in the same area.

The tide began to turn when Admiral Son reached South Korea with the newly acquired submarine chasers, and the ROKN helped slow the KPA offensive push toward Pusan. On 22 July, *YMS 513* destroyed a trio of Communist supply vessels near Chulp'o. Less than a week later, *PC 702* and *PC 703* caught a group of North Korean sampans carrying ammunition west of Inch'ŏn and sank twelve of them.

There was no respite for the ROKN as KPA efforts to crush UN ground forces holding the Pusan perimeter approached a climax in August. With UNC air forces making travel on South Korean roads increasingly lethal for KPA logistic units, the Communists looked to the sea to ease their supply and reinforcement problems.

On the west coast during the first week of August, *YMS 302* and other ROKN vessels eliminated motor and sail boats and junks carrying supplies. Five times during the period 13–20 August the ROKN made contact with Communist vessels, on one occasion sinking fifteen of them and capturing another thirty.

PC 702 and four motor minesweepers sank numerous North Korean craft, which went down with their embarked troops, and seized many more. To extend the ROKN's reach further north along the west coast, on 9 August the LST established an advanced logistic support base on Ŏch'ŏng Island near Kunsan. During this same period, the ROKN disrupted a North Korean effort to capture P'ohang with troops landed by sea. The ROKN played an important, if small part, in the overall UNC effort that defeated the North Korean attempt to crush the Pusan perimeter and push the allies into the sea.

Like other UN forces, the ROKN carried out operations during late August and early September to prepare the way for the amphibious assault against Inch'ŏn, Operation CHROMITE, which would change the course of the war. Understanding the ability of naval forces to range far and wide on the KPA's flanks, Commander Luosey directed the ROKN to occupy islands on Korea's Yellow Sea coast to divert North Korean attention from the impending amphibious assault and to use the islands as bases of operation for gathering intelligence, landing guerrilla parties, and conducting coastal raids. On 17 and 18 August, in Operation LEE, named for the commanding officer of *PC 702*, that submarine chaser and two minesweepers landed a 110 guerrilla troops on Tŏkjŏk Island southwest of Inch'ŏn. The next day, troops were landed on Yŏnghŭng Island in the approaches to the port. Then, on 8 September, to divert North Korean attention from Inch'ŏn, Lee's units landed guerrillas on an island to the north.

In this period the UNC discovered that the North Koreans were laying sea mines in the approaches to the western coast. Confirming this worrisome development, on 10 September *PC 703* sank a KPN mine-laying vessel off Haeju. Even though UNC warships spotted and destroyed other North Korean mines as they steamed toward Inch'ŏn on 13 and 14 September to open Operation CHROMITE, the fearsome weapons did not prevent accomplishment of the amphibious assault. Soon UNC ground forces captured Seoul, ended the siege of Pusan, and forced the badly bloodied KPA to flee to the north. Simultaneously, the ROKN recaptured islands in the south lost earlier, took control of other islands off North Korea, and established forward bases at Chinnamp'o on the west coast and Changjŏn on the east coast.

As UNC ground forces, supported by air forces, pursued the KPA and occupied almost all of North Korea during October and November, Communist mines sank and damaged UNC naval vessels. Sea mines manufactured in the Soviet Union and deployed under the direction of Russian advisors in the waters off the Korean peninsula, took their first victims in late September. Among UNC vessels sunk or damaged was *YMS 509.*

Mines not only prevented the 250 ships of Vice Admiral Arthur D. Struble's task force from landing troops of the U.S. X Corps and the South Korean I Corps at Wŏnsan in mid-October, but they sank and damaged UNC ships and killed and wounded many sailors. On 12 September, while clearing lanes through the 3,000 mines laid in the approaches to Wŏnsan, U.S. minesweepers *Pirate* and *Pledge* hit mines and quickly sank, with great loss of life. Six days later, ROKN *YMS 516* virtually disappeared from the explosion of an influence mine. Half of the minesweeper's crew went down.

The UNC fared better in the clearance of the western port of Chinnamp'o between 28 October and 6 November. Involved in that operation were ten U.S. ships, thirteen Japanese-crewed minesweepers, and ROKN *YMS 502, YMS 306, YMS 513,* and *YMS 503.* To ensure that the approach lane was free of the more than 300 mines laid by the North Koreans, on 6 November the Korean crew of a tug sailed their vessel through the passage from Chinnamp'o to the Yellow Sea. The sailors of *YMS 503* then brought their minesweeper into the port from offshore waters.

For the remainder of the Korean War, the crews and ships of the ROKN operated in harm's way all around the peninsula. The ROKN not only continued to clear mines from coastal waters, in the process losing minesweeper *JMS 306* and *PC 704,* but raided North Korean–held islands, landed special warfare units and guerrillas behind the lines, fired on targets ashore, maintained a tight coastal blockade, and assisted other UNC navies in the movement of troops, equipment, and refugees. Through hard fighting and the development of professional skills, by 27 July 1953 the ROKN had become a respected and valued member of the UNC team.

—Edward J. Marolda

References:
Field, James A., Jr. *History of United States Naval Operations: Korea.* Washington, DC: U.S. Government Printing Office, 1962.
Republic of Korea, Ministry of National Defense. "Activity of the Republic of Korea Navy." In *The History of the United Nations Forces in the Korean War.* Vol. 1. Seoul: War History Compilation Commission, 1972.
See also: Inch'ŏn Landings: Operation CHROMITE; Joy, Charles Turner; Korea, Democratic People's Republic of: Navy (Korean People's Navy [KPN]); Son Wŏn-il; United States Navy.

Korean Augmentation to the United States Army (KATUSA)

The first U.S. ground troops saw battle on 5 July 1950. By mid-August, U.S. casualties had been so

great that the replacement flow was unable to keep pace. Clearly, some extraordinary measure was required. That measure was the utilization of Korean recruits as replacements in U.S. units—a radical and controversial action.

Once the decision was made, the Far East Command planned to attach between 30,000 and 40,000 Republic of Korea Army (ROKA, South Korean) recruits to the four U.S. divisions in Korea and the 7th Infantry Division in Japan. The program was officially dubbed Korean Augmentation to the United States Army (KATUSA), and the attached Korean soldiers were known as KATUSAs. The Far East Command envisioned that each KATUSA would be paired with a GI in a buddy system.

On 9 August 1950, General Douglas MacArthur ordered Lieutenant General Walton Walker to fill up each U.S. rifle company and artillery battery with 100 ROKA soldiers. These men would still be members of the ROKA, but attached to U.S. Army units. The South Korean government provided their pay and administration. The U.S. units to which they were attached provided command and control, as well as rations and special service items (tooth paste, shaving cream, etc.). KATUSAs could not be promoted beyond the rank of private first class.

ROKA replacement centers produced about 2,950 recruits daily. Each day, 500 recruits were assigned to the KATUSA program. Although this inhibited the growth of the ROKA, it replaced the critical shortages of personnel in U.S. front-line units.

In a way, the KATUSA program was pioneered by Lieutenant Colonel Peter Clainos Commanding officer of the 1st Battalion, 7th Cavalry Regiment (CO, 1st/7th Cavalry). About 1 August, he unofficially accepted four ROKA officers and 133 enlisted volunteers into his battalion, in exchange for food and weapons. A Lieutenant Chŏng, a Korean trained in Tokyo wearing a Japanese samurai sword, marched his contingent into Clainos's command post. The colonel attached Chŏng to his headquarters, the other officers to Companies A, B, and C, and two Korean enlisted men to each rifle squad in the companies. Nine days later, these soldiers participated in the battle of Triangulation Hill. Two were killed and seven wounded. All the wounded refused evacuation, except one who was unable to walk.

The 7th Division in Japan had been badly depleted by requisitions of replacements placed upon it. As a result, the division received some of the first KATUSAs. Between 16 and 24 August, 8,625 Korean officers and enlisted men were attached to the division (almost half its authorized strength).

Korean recruiting methods were often nothing short of draconian. Men and boys were simply rounded up

Private Yun Ch'an (15) of the ROKA assigned to the U.S. Army 3d Battalion, 19th Regiment, confers with Sergeant Major Clarence Hollis. (National Archives)

and shipped off to post, then on to training centers. Some levies sent to Japan included boys still carrying their school books. One young man, who had gone for medicine for his sick wife, still had the medicine with him when he arrived in Japan.

On 20 August, U.S. divisions in Korea began receiving their Korean recruits, when the 24th and 25th Divisions each received 250 men, and the 2d and 1st Cavalry Divisions received 249 men apiece. For a week thereafter, each division averaged 250 more men each day. On 29 and 30 August, the 1st Cavalry averaged 740 men per day; the 24th Division, 950 each day. Near the end of August, the plan changed so that each division received 400 recruits every fourth day until each had 8,300 Korean recruits.

These Korean recruits were not always paired with GIs, as envisioned. Some commands formed all-Korean platoons—a fifth platoon—in the company, usually led by an American lieutenant, with assistance from a few GIs from the company. Other units formed all-Korean squads in platoons, led by one or two GIs. Still others made them ammunition bearers, laborers, or supply carriers.

During the Japanese occupation of Korea, from the turn of the century until the end of World War II, all Koreans were forced to learn Japanese in Korean schools. As a result, almost every Korean was fluent in the Japanese language. Some U.S. companies had enough men who had come from Japan that the KATUSAs could be more easily integrated into existing squads on a buddy system.

The early KATUSAs had almost no training and were completely ignorant of fighting and battle. A few had barely fired more than eight rounds from an M1 rifle, and none had undergone individual or combat training, nor even an orientation of what to expect. Most were a week or less from a peasant civilian life. They could not understand English and were completely ignorant of western culture. As a result, most were doomed to an early death or injury in their first battle. Troops that had never served in Japan had no common language with which to communicate with their Korean recruits, and the GIs were not interested in learning Japanese or Korean. This led to many needless combat deaths and injuries among these Koreans and the GIs alike.

Another barrier to the effective employment of KATUSAs was racial prejudice by many U.S. soldiers. To them, a Korean was an inferior being and nothing a KATUSA did, or did not do, changed this bias. Cultural, language, and racial barriers inherent in the KATUSA program significantly undermined the efficiency that otherwise might have been possible.

Eventually, 50 percent or more of U.S. rifle companies were KATUSAs. Some became fine soldiers; a few of them won U.S. Bronze Star Medals for bravery.

This was the highest U.S. award that could be given to a KATUSA.

About late October 1950, before the Chinese intervention, most Korean attachments were returned to the ROKA, leaving six or less in U.S. rifle platoons. The ones who remained were selected by the unit concerned to be retained in the company or platoon. Only the 7th Division retained a large KATUSA contingent into 1951. The integration of more than 32,000 young Korean soldiers into U.S. divisions provided the vital numbers needed to achieve victory in the Pusan perimeter.

—*Uzal W. Ent*

References:

Appleman, Roy E. *South to the Naktong, North to the Yalu.* Washington, DC: Office of the Chief of Military History, 1961.

Ent, Uzal W. *Fighting on the Brink: Defense of the Pusan Perimeter.* Paducah, KY: Turner, 1996.

Sawyer, Robert K. *Military Advisors in the Korean War: KMAG in Peace and War.* Washington, DC: Office of the Chief of Military History, U.S. Army, 1962.

Korean Communications Zone

The Korean Communications Zone (KCOMZ) was established on 21 August 1952 to relieve Lieutenant General James A. Van Fleet, commander of the Eighth U.S. Army in Korea (EUSAK), of his logistical and rear-area control responsibilities. In contemporary U.S. Army doctrine, a communications zone was the specified area behind the front lines where supply and administrative facilities could be established and operated to relieve the front-line commander of responsibility for functions not directly related to combat operations. KCOMZ thus assumed responsibility for the lines of communications in Korea; the operation and maintenance of ports, railroads, depots, and other logistical facilities; the operation of prisoner-of-war camps; the coordination of refugee relief and reconstruction efforts; and relations with the government of the Republic of Korea (ROK, South Korea).

KCOMZ, commanded by Major General Thomas W. Herren from headquarters at Taegu, was designed to have 75,000–100,000 personnel and to support a force of about 400,000 men, but because of personnel shortages it actually operated with only about 30,000 assigned personnel and supported more than 800,000 United Nations Command (UNC) and ROK combat troops as well as some 100,000 Communist prisoners of war and civilian internees. The area for which KCOMZ was responsible extended over approximately the southern two-thirds of the ROK, its boundary with EUSAK running roughly along the 37th parallel. As of November 1952, KCOMZ coordinated the work of four separate commands: the Korean Base Section, operated by the 2d Logistical Command; the 3d Military Railway Service, which operated and maintained railroads within the UNC area; the UN Prisoner of War Command; and the UN Civil Assistance Command. Until 1 January 1953, the KCOMZ operated as a major subordinate command of the U.S. Far East Command. However, with the reorganization of the U.S. Far East Command on 1 January 1953, KCOMZ was made a subordinate element of the newly formed U.S. Army Forces Far East.

One of the most difficult tasks undertaken by KCOMZ was the reorganization of the UNC camps for North Korean and Chinese Communist prisoners of war after the riots in the Kŏje-do camps in May and June 1952. The Communist prisoners of war numbered well over 150,000, and their control and repatriation in 1953 were major issues. Another important rear area security task was the hunting down of North Korean guerrillas in South Korea. Major General Herren argued successfully that that task would be performed better by ROK Army troops.

With the creation of KCOMZ in August 1952, the 2d Logistical Command was made a subordinate element of KCOMZ with responsibility for the operation of the Korean Base Section. In theory, KCOMZ was a planning, policymaking, and coordinating headquar-

ters, but because the boundaries of KCOMZ and the Korean Base Section (2d Logistical Command) were coterminous, the distinction between planning/coordination and operational matters was not sharply defined, and the layering of the theater logistical structure led to some inefficiency and duplication of effort in providing support to UN forces in Korea.

—*Charles R. Shrader*

References:

Hermes, Walter G. *U.S. Army in the Korean War: Truce Tent and Fighting Front.* Washington, DC: Office of the Chief of Military History, 1966.

Huston, James A. *Guns and Butter, Powder and Rice: U.S. Army Logistics in the Korean War.* Selinsgrove, PA: Susquehanna University Press, 1989.

———. *The Sinews of War: Army Logistics, 1775–1953.* Washington, DC: Office of the Chief of Military History, 1966.

See also: Eighth U.S. Army; Logistics in the Korean War; Van Fleet, James Alward.

Korean War Veterans Memorial (Dedicated 27 July 1995)

The Korean War Veterans Memorial in Washington, D.C., was dedicated on 27 July 1995, the forty-second

The Korean War Veterans Memorial in Washington, D.C. (Courtesy of the American Battle Monuments Commission)

anniversary of the Korean War armistice. The opening of the memorial represented the culmination of more than eight years of effort by veterans to gain recognition for the sacrifices they and their fallen comrades made during what they had long regarded as a forgotten war.

The dedication ceremonies, attended by U.S. President William Clinton and Republic of Korea (ROK) President Kim Young Sam, were the focal point of a week of commemoration for veterans of the Korean War. Generals Raymond G. Davis, U.S. Marine Corps (Retired) and Richard G. Stilwell, U.S. Army (Retired) were cited by name by President Clinton for their efforts to develop the memorial; both were members of the Korean War Veterans Memorial Advisory Board.

The memorial is on the Mall adjacent to the Lincoln Memorial and across the Reflecting Pool from the Vietnam Veterans Memorial. It has an ensemble of elements including a triangular Field of Service that contains nineteen seven-foot-tall stainless steel statues depicting a poncho-clad combat patrol—fifteen soldiers, two Marines, a sailor, and an airman—moving toward a U.S. flag at the apex of the triangle. Beyond the flag, surrounded by a grove of linden trees, is a 30-foot-diameter Pool of Remembrance. Another key facet is a 164-foot, polished, black granite wall that rises from the pool and extends toward the soldiers. This wall honors the war's noncombatants by presenting etchings of approximately 2,500 of these people based on photographs made during the war. A curb along a walkway lists the twenty-two countries that participated in the United Nations police action.

The memorial has several design features that add layers of meaning for visitors. It recalls everyone who participated in the struggle rather than only the war's dead. The nineteen statues reflecting against the polished wall of etchings create the illusion of thirty-eight soldiers. This is a reference both to the 38th parallel, which divides Korea into two nations, and to the number of months from the outbreak of the war to the armistice. Night lighting gives a soft glow to the mural while pinpoint spotlights illuminate the faces of the soldiers.

Vermont sculptor Frank C. Gaylord executed the poncho-clad soldiers; New York muralist Louis Nelson brought the long wall of etchings to fruition. The $18.1 million cost of the memorial came from numerous small, personal donations and large contributions from U.S. subsidiaries of Korean corporations.

There are few written inscriptions at the memorial. The statement, "Freedom Is Not Free," is inlaid into the granite wall as it emerges from the pool. At the base of the flag pole, to be read as one faces the advancing patrol, is a paraphrase of a statement by

Secretary of Defense Frank Carlucci on the occasion of the thirty-fifth anniversary of the cease-fire:

Our Nation Honors
Her Sons and Daughters
Who Answered the Call
To Defend a Country
They Never Knew
And a People
They Never Met
1950–KOREA–1953

To the west of the memorial is a Kiosk with computers and an accessible database containing information about most of the U.S. soldiers who were killed in action.

The movement to establish this memorial began in 1985 during a trip to Seoul, South Korea, by survivors of the 25th Infantry Division, known to themselves as the "Chosin Few." These men believed that their military service had been largely unappreciated by a nation that was much more focused on World War II and the later Vietnam conflict. This concern was transformed into action the next year when the 15,000-member Korean War Veterans Association, in reaction to the dedication that year of the Vietnam Veterans memorial, approached President Ronald Reagan and Congress for the opportunity to establish a memorial. On 28 October 1986, Congress authorized the American Battle Monuments Commission to develop the memorial.

There were more than 500 entrants in the 1989 competition to determine the best design for the memorial. The requirements for entrants included that they were to design a veterans' rather than a war memorial and that a U.S. flag must be part of the design. The selection committee consisted solely of Korean War veterans who were assisted by professionals in architecture and landscaping. The winning entry, by a team of architects from Pennsylvania State University, envisioned a string of thirty-eight soldiers moving down a walkway in a loose column along a wall toward a U.S. flag. The memorial was designed to involve visitors by giving them the opportunity to join the procession by moving among the marching soldiers.

The identification of the winning design was followed by several years of controversy before the final design could be constructed. The implementing architectural firm of Cooper-Lecky changed the design before submitting it to national commissions for approval, an action that led the creators of the winning design to sue. Although this suit was ultimately unsuccessful, the Commission of Fine Arts required additional alterations before granting final approval for a memorial that does reflect the spirit of the initial winning design.

Ceremonies accompanying the dedication of the memorial stretched across an entire week and gave surviving veterans numerous opportunities to get together with long-lost buddies. At the same time, reminders of events that had helped to shove the Korean experience into the back reaches of national consciousness were present. The dedication occurred midway between the fiftieth anniversaries of the end of World War II in Europe and in Japan. But the veterans present in Washington, D.C., for the dedication and those who have since visited the memorial clearly recognize that they are forgotten no more.

—*David S. Trask*

Reference:
Highsmith, Carol M., and Ted Landphair. *Forgotten No More: The Korean War Veterans Memorial Story.* Washington, DC: Chelsea, 1995.

Kŭm River, Battle of
(14–26 July 1950)

July 1950 battle involving the U.S. 24th Infantry Division and units of the Korean People's Army (KPA, North Korean Army). By 13 July, some 5,500 men in the 19th, 21st, and 34th Regiments of Major General William F. Dean's 24th Infantry Division defended the Kŭm River. From left to right they were the 24th Reconnaissance Company, screening five miles; 3d Battalion, 34th Infantry, on a four-mile front; and the 19th Infantry, less than 2,000 soldiers, stretched along a thirty-mile front. The 1st Battalion of the 34th was in reserve two miles to the rear. The badly battered 21st Regiment (about 1,100 men) was back near Taejŏn. On the night of 13 July, the 40 survivors of Company K of the 34th were evacuated because of extreme combat fatigue.

Between 0800 and 0930 on 14 July, some 500 members of the KPA 16th Regiment of the 4th Division crossed the Kŭm about two miles beyond the 34th Infantry's left flank. On that flank, Company L of the 34th was soon forced to withdraw as a consequence of heavy artillery and mortar fire. Company I, to the right of Company L, remained on position, retiring under orders, about 0930. Commanders of both units later reported being unable to communicate with or find the battalion headquarters all day. Unknown to them, the command post had moved to Nonsan, twenty miles from the river.

About 1340 KPA troops overran the 63d Field Artillery Battalion (FAB), three miles south of the river. The 1st Battalion of the 34th was then ordered to this abandoned artillery position to retrieve equipment, rescue survivors, and return before dark. Although subjected to KPA machine gun and small arms fire, the battalion salvaged some vehicles, rescued a few artillerymen, and withdrew as ordered.

From left to right, 1st Battalion of the 19th defended about four miles of regimental river front, with Companies B, A, and C positioned in platoon and company strong points. Two platoons screened two miles of river some two miles to the left, while Company E had responsibility for about six miles some two miles to the right. The 2d Battalion of the 19th (less Company E) was in reserve a mile behind the regiment's center. The 52d and 13th FABs (105-mm howitzer) and 11th FAB (155-mm howitzer) supported the 19th from positions two miles south of the river.

While the 34th withdrew, the 19th was ordered to defend. On the 15th, the KPA 3d Division probed regimental flanks and, exploiting defensive gaps, launched its main attack at 0300 on 16 July. A counterattack by 19th Infantry reserves momentarily halted and reversed one thrust, but the North Koreans established a strong roadblock in the rear. The 1st Battalion was then forced from its position and into the roadblock. Of 3,401 men in the regiment and its supporting artillery, 650 were lost; half of them from the 1st Battalion.

—*Uzal. W. Ent*

References:
Appleman, Roy E. *South to the Naktong, North to the Yalu.* Washington, DC: Office of the Chief of Military History, 1961.
Blair, Clay. *The Forgotten War: America in Korea, 1950–1953.* New York: Times Books, 1987.
Ent, Uzal W. *Fighting on the Brink: Defense of the Pusan Perimeter.* Paducah, KY: Turner, 1996.
Toland, John. *In Mortal Combat: Korea, 1950–1953.* New York: William Morrow, 1991.
See also: Dean, William Frishe.

Kunu-ri, Battle of
(26 November–1 December 1950)

Fighting in late November 1950 in and around the town of Kunu-ri on the Kaech'ŏn River, about thirty miles inland from the Yellow Sea and approximately midway between the North Korean capital of P'yŏngyang and the Yalu River on the Manchurian border. The engagements involved the U.S. Army 2d, 24th, and 25th Infantry Divisions in the areas around the Ch'ŏngch'ŏn River valley to the north; the 1st Cavalry Division, the 187th Airborne Regiment, and the Turkish and British Brigades to the east and south; and the Republic of Korea Army (ROKA, South Korean) corps and divisions. The battle encompassed the gauntlet ambush and slaughter of the 2d Division's 9th and 38th Regiments on the Kunu-ri to Sunch'ŏn road. In a more narrow sense, however, the battle of Kunu-ri could refer to the fighting mainly by the 23d Infantry Regiment, particularly its Company B, on high ground south of Kunu-ri and the Kaech'ŏn River in the early hours of 30 November, a few days after the massive Chinese People's Volunteer Army (CPVA, Chinese Communist) intervention.

In response to the CPVA drive south, the U.S. Eighth Army began an urgent and rapid withdrawal south of the 38th parallel. The 2d Division was left behind in a rear guard action to cover the withdrawal of the rest of the Eighth Army. It was to be the last division out. Of the division's three regiments, the 23d was to be the last to withdraw and was covering the withdrawal of the 9th and 38th regiments. The 1st Battalion of the 23d was covering the withdrawal of the other battalions and was in position on high ground straddling the road south from Kunu-ri and about a half mile from the Kaech'ŏn River. B Company was on the high ground east of the escape road with C Company opposite on the west side.

Around 0300, B Company's commander was informed that the last of the friendly units had passed through the road below its positions and that any further movements would be those of Communist forces to be resisted. At dawn, hundreds of CPVA troops swarmed around and into B Company's positions. They had crossed the river and the rice paddies far below and silently climbed the forward slopes. Fierce hand-to-hand combat and firefight ensued with the surviving Chinese troops gradually withdrawing back down the forward slopes. Between 300 and 500 Chinese bodies were counted on the hill in and around the company positions. B Company had incurred about 20 casualties: 6 killed and the rest wounded.

During the day, the plateau and flood plain below and in front of B and C Companies became the center of frenzied CPVA activity. Around noon, clusters of men could be seen moving toward the U.S. positions, but in a clearly disorganized and sporadic way. They seemed to be fighting among themselves, some pushing others to the ground or hitting or clubbing others. As they neared 1st Battalion sentries on the road below through the pass, it was learned that some were remnants of the black 3d Battalion of the 25th Division's 24th Regiment. Some of the 24th troopers were seen overpowered, clubbed, and left for dead, or captured and taken away. Those who managed to reach friendly lines were totally spent, disoriented, terrified, and hungry. Most were without arms or equipment. Many were wounded, or had frozen feet and hands.

Throughout the day, planes of the Far East Air Force (FEAF) pounded targets of opportunity in the valley in front of the 23d's positions with napalm, machine gun fire, rockets, and bombs. The FEAF flew an astonishing 287 close air support missions that day. Commanders reported that it was the greatest concentration of aircraft on a single target at any time during the Korean War. Throughout the day, men from B Company carried their dead and wounded off the high ground into the valley behind their position. By late afternoon, the troops on high ground could observe long columns of Chinese troops in the distance moving around the flanks of the 23d's positions and toward their rear. Nervousness increased as the expected permission to withdraw was not forthcoming until dusk. It was almost dark when the awesome shoot of over 3,000 rounds in less than 20 minutes commenced. Because of concerns that in a night withdrawal the howitzers of the 15th Field Artillery Battalion with the 23d might topple on hairpin curves of the narrow and winding escape road and block movement of the entire column, the difficult decision was made to abandon the guns. Artillerymen removed the breech blocks and sights and then blew the guns with thermite grenades after first firing off all their ammunition, rather than leaving it behind or carrying it out in vehicles badly needed for personnel.

The 23d completed its withdrawal, while under near-constant Chinese attack, with far fewer casualties than those of the regiments in the gauntlet; by remaining through the day, it held back the CPVA just long enough to allow time for the safe and orderly withdrawal of the rest of Eighth Army. The 2d Division rear-guard defense had saved the day, but at terrible cost. Division casualties for the six days of fighting at and north of Kunu-ri came to 4,940, or almost one-third of the unit's strength.

—Sherman W. Pratt

References:

Blair, Clay. *The Forgotten War: America in Korea, 1950–1953.* New York: Times Books, 1987.

Clodfelter, Michael. *Warfare and Armed Conflicts. A Statistical Reference to Casualty and Other Figures, 1618–1991.* Vol. 2. Jefferson, NC: McFarland, 1992.

Command Report, 23rd Infantry Regiment, November 1950. National Archives, Suitland MD.

Hastings, Max. *The Korean War.* New York: Simon & Schuster, 1987.

Munroe, Clark C. *The Second U.S. Infantry Division in Korea, 1950–1951.* Tokyo: Toppan Printing, n.d.

Pratt, Sherman W. *Decisive Battles of the Korean War. An Infantry Company Commander's View of the War's Most Critical Engagements.* New York: Vantage Press, 1992.

See also: Close Air Support; Eighth U.S. Army.

L

Latin America

During World War II, cooperation between the United States and Latin America had reached an unprecedented level. The United States was primarily interested in gaining the economic cooperation of the Latin American countries and envisioned a limited military role for the area. Only two countries, Brazil and Mexico, actually furnished combat troops. Brazil sent an expeditionary force of 25,000 that participated in the Italian campaign of 1944–1945; Mexico provided a fighter squadron that served in the Pacific.

In the immediate postwar years, Latin America was much more concerned with economic development than with the growing Cold War between the United States and the Soviet bloc. U.S. emphasis on strategic concerns meant that top priority was given to Europe, Asia, and the Middle East. Even though the Communist threat was seen as minimal in the region, the United States concluded its first postwar regional security agreement with Latin America. At a conference in Rio de Janeiro in August 1947, the United States and the Latin American nations signed the Inter-American Treaty of Reciprocal Assistance that called for a collective response to aggression, whether originating within or outside the Americas. Collective measures included the use of armed force. However, there was disagreement between the United States and the Latin American nations over international organizations. Although the Latin American nations constituted an important group in the United Nations (UN), originally accounting for about 40 percent of the votes in the General Assembly, they wanted the primary emphasis to be on a regional organization, the Organization of American States (OAS), which was established in 1948.

The outbreak of war in Korea in June 1950 posed no immediate threat to Latin America, but the United States, opting for a multilateral response, wanted to maximize Latin American support for U.S. and UN efforts to block Communist expansion. The two Latin American members of the Security Council, Cuba and Ecuador, were crucial in getting the two-thirds vote required for the resolution of 27 June 1950 calling for collective military action.

Efforts by the United States to get Latin American nations to contribute troops to the UN Command (UNC) produced meager results. Whereas the U.S. State Department was eager to broaden the base of support for UN operations, U.S. military officials were concerned about the problems of arming, training, and transporting troops from less-developed countries. Brazil expressed interest in contributing troops, but expected substantial military and economic aid in return; Peru took much the same position. The Bolivian government initially indicated that it would provide troops, but reversed its position in the face of domestic opposition. Chile, Mexico, and Uruguay also declined to contribute troops on the grounds of lack of domestic support for such a move. Argentina had one of the most professional armed forces in Latin America, but had been feuding with the United States politically and economically for almost a decade. Most of the remaining Latin American countries had military establishments that were either so small or so poorly trained and equipped that they would have been considered a military liability, rather than an asset, to UN forces. Only one Latin American nation made a direct military contribution to the war: Colombia provided one infantry battalion and a frigate for Korean service.

The lack of military support from Latin America should not have been a surprise to U.S. officials. The minimum military contribution accepted, one battalion, made it difficult for many of the Latin American countries to supply troops. U.S. expectations of being reimbursed for any assistance in equipping Latin American forces for Korea made it financially difficult for many countries in the region to get involved. Latin America also believed that the United States had neglected the region since 1945, focusing its interest on and putting its aid into other parts of the world. Latin America was particularly disappointed by the lack of economic and financial assistance furnished to it by the United States after World War II, especially when billions of dollars in U.S. aid were flowing to Europe and Asia. Also influencing the unenthusiastic military response of the Latin American countries was their belief that the situation in Korea was a distant conflict that posed no immediate threat to Latin America. There was also no tradition in Latin America of sending troops to other regions of the world; even World War II with its global aspect and greater threat to the region had induced only two nations, Brazil and Mexico, to make direct military contributions. Shifting military fortunes and changing UN goals in the Korean conflict also discouraged military involvement. When the situation facing the UNC in Korea briefly brightened in the fall of 1950, the United States reduced efforts to secure troop contributions. As the war evolved from defense of South Korea to unification of the Korean peninsula to military stalemate, it became increasingly difficult to sell to

Latin American governments and their peoples the idea of supplying troops.

The uncertain U.S. attitude toward Latin America surfaced in its dealings with the OAS. The Council of the OAS had early on given its approval to the UN operation, but it was not until December 1950 that the United States requested a meeting of foreign ministers under the OAS Charter. The meeting finally took place in late March 1951 in Washington, with the UN military situation in Korea improving after the shock of massive intervention by the Chinese Communists. While the United States was primarily interested in gaining political and military cooperation, the Latin American nations insisted that the conference also deal with economic concerns. The conference called for prompt action against international communism and support for the UN, but there were no formal commitments of additional forces for Korea. The conference did recommend that each American republic develop units within its armed forces that would be available for service as UN units. The conference urged all members of the OAS to develop their military capabilities in order to fulfill their commitments under the Inter-American Treaty of Reciprocal Assistance, which did not apply to the Korean situation. The meeting also called for a cooperative effort to deal with the current economic emergency caused by the international situation as well as a long-term commitment to economic development. Even the discussion of economic development was often couched in strategic terms, or the "total concept of Hemisphere defense," as the Final Act of the conference put it. The United States received a Latin American promise to give priority to the production of strategic materials, whereas the United States recognized the need to address the economic problems posed by the current emergency as well as the postwar period. The United States declined to make any specific promises regarding development aid and deferred discussion of most economic matters to a conference to be held after the Korean War was over—even though the economic conference that the United States had promised would be held immediately after World War II had still not taken place.

The United States did succeed in getting the economic support for the Korean War that it wanted from the Latin American nations. As had been the case in World War II, the United States was concerned with maintaining the flow of strategic raw materials and commodities from Latin America. The United States attempted to encourage this flow by linking it to promises of military assistance. Under the 1951 Military Security Act, the United States entered into bilateral agreements with twelve Latin American countries. The United States provided military aid; in return the Latin American country agreed to facilitate the pro-duction and transfer of strategic materials to the United States and to cooperate in restricting trade with nations threatening the security of the Western Hemisphere. This latest program demonstrated again the inherent problems in soliciting Latin American support for the effort in Korea. Less than 1 percent of the funds requested for the program's first year was designated for Latin America. Brazil did not approve an agreement until May 1953 as a result of domestic opposition that saw the program as an effort to pressure Brazil into sending troops to Korea.

Various Latin American nations also became involved in different activities connected with the Korean War. Brazil, Mexico, and Venezuela served on the UN's Additional Measures Committee, which explored economic sanctions against China and which were later approved by the General Assembly. With armistice talks stalled over the issue of repatriation of prisoners of war, both Mexico and Peru put forward proposals to deal with the problem. Although neither of the proposals was actually implemented, they did keep the momentum going toward an eventual resolution of the problem.

From the standpoint of the United States, Latin American involvement in the Korean War produced mixed results. Despite early Latin American promises and later U.S. aid, only Colombia actually provided military forces, a battalion, the lowest level that the UNC would accept. Economic cooperation presented a brighter picture, with the United States successfully gaining access to the Latin American raw materials and commodities needed to prosecute the war. The war produced greater coordination of hemispheric security activities, but highlighted rather than harmonized the basic disagreement in hemispheric priorities between the United States and Latin America.

—Don M. Coerver

References:

Houston, John A. *Latin America in the United Nations.* New York: Carnegie Endowment for International Peace, 1956.

Pan American Union. *Fourth Meeting of Consultation of Ministers of Foreign Affairs, Final Act.* Washington, DC: Pan American Union, 1951.

———. *Fourth Meeting of Consultation of Ministers of Foreign Affairs, Proceedings.* Washington, DC: Pan American Union, 1951.

Stueck, William W., Jr. *The Korean War: An International History.* Princeton, NJ: Princeton University Press, 1995.

See also: Colombia; Mexico; Peruvian Prisoner-of-War Settlement Proposal; Truce Talks.

Lay, James S.
(1911–1987)

Executive secretary to the U.S. National Security Council, 1949–1961. James S. Lay was born in Washington, D.C., on 24 August 1911. He initially pursued a business career. After earning a bachelor of science degree in electrical engineering from Virginia Military Institute and an master's degree in public utilities from Harvard Business School, he joined Stone and Webster in 1935 and from then until 1941 worked for several of that firm's public utilities subsidiaries. In May 1941 Lay, who had already joined the U.S. Field Artillery Reserve, was called up for active duty. He quickly found a niche in intelligence work. In August 1942 he was assigned to the War Department's British empire branch of the military intelligence service. After some time in the London embassy, working in the military attaché's office, in December 1943 Lay became the secretary to the Joint Chiefs of Staff's Joint Intelligence Committee.

As the Cold War developed, the United States began to develop a permanent intelligence establishment, to which Lay gravitated. Although he left the military in October 1945, Lay promptly joined the State Department as a management analyst working under the special assistant for research and intelligence. By the end of the year, he was secretary of the National Intelligence Authority and in 1946 became the division chief of the Central Intelligence Group. In 1947 President Harry S. Truman's administration replaced this body with the new National Security Council (NSC). Its mandate was to supervise the new Central Intelligence Agency (CIA) and to assess and coordinate U.S. diplomatic and defense policies and strategies as a whole, drawing together the often fragmented government apparatus dealing with these issues and providing the president with advice and information on them. Initially Lay served as its assistant executive secretary; twenty-eight months later, when the first executive secretary, Rear Admiral Sidney W. Souers resigned in December 1949, his hand-picked successor Lay took over from him, remaining in the post until the end of President Dwight D. Eisenhower's administration.

Lay's position carried executive as opposed to policymaking responsibilities, and Lay always emphasized that the NSC's functions were purely advisory, to ensure that "all views on security matters are heard, and, if agreement cannot be reached, that the divergent opinions are presented to the President." Lay personally provided both Truman and Eisenhower with daily briefings summarizing all the information that the NSC staff had gathered. In this capacity, the self-effacing Lay was also responsible for drafting all NSC papers, including NSC-68, "United States Objectives and Programs for National Security," and those relating to U.S. policy toward Korea during and after the war. As such, Lay was privy to all of the most confidential material on U.S. foreign affairs during these years.

In 1961 Lay joined the CIA as assistant to the director, a post he held until he retired in 1971, thus providing much-needed continuity in a period when the CIA attracted fierce public and political criticism. From his retirement until his death, Lay remained a consultant to the President's Foreign Intelligence Advisory Board. He died in Falls Church, Virginia, on 28 June 1987.

—Priscilla Roberts

References:

Darling, Arthur B. *The Central Intelligence Agency: An Instrument of Government, to 1950.* University Park: Pennsylvania State University Press, 1990.

"Lay, James S(elden) Jr." In *Current Biography, 1950.* New York: H. W. Wilson, 1951: 329–331.

Nelson, Anna Kasten. "'The Top of the Hill': President Eisenhower and the National Security Council." *Diplomatic History* 7, no. 4 (Fall 1983): 307–326.

Prados, John. *Keepers of the Keys: A History of the National Security Council from Truman to Bush.* New York: William Morrow, 1991.

See also: Central Intelligence Agency (CIA); Eisenhower, Dwight D.; National Security Council (NSC); Truman, Harry S.

Lemnitzer, Lyman Louis
(1899–1988)

U.S. Army general; in the Korean War he led the 7th Infantry Division, 1951–1952. Born in Honesdale, Pennsylvania, on 29 August 1899, Lyman Louis Lemnitzer attended the U.S. Military Academy at West Point during World War I. Graduating in 1920 with a commission as a second lieutenant of artillery, he rose slowly through the ranks to major during the interwar years, serving both in the United States and the Philippines. During this time he attended the Coastal Artillery School, the Command and General Staff School, and the Army War College and also taught on two separate occasions at West Point.

World War II accelerated Lemnitzer's career. After service with the 70th Coast Artillery and 38th Coast Artillery Brigade (1940–1941), he gained valuable experience as a plans and operations officer on the War Department General Staff and at Army Ground Forces Headquarters in 1941 and 1942. After his promotion to brigadier general in June 1942, he commanded the 34th Coast Artillery Brigade and was concurrently plans and operations officer at Allied Force Headquarters in Britain and North Africa, as well as deputy chief of staff of the Fifth Army. Later, between 1943 and 1945, Lemnitzer served first as the assistant chief of staff to Field Marshal Sir Harold Alexander's Fifteenth Army Group in Italy and later held the position of chief of staff to Alexander when the latter became the supreme allied commander, Mediterranean. In these various combat and staff positions, Lemnitzer demonstrated that he could manage people and plans, winning the confidence of his superiors, both British and American.

Lemnitzer's proven ability to deal easily with both military personnel and civilian leaders explains his postwar selection as the senior army representative to the Joint Strategic Survey Committee created by the Joint Chiefs of Staff (JCS) in 1946 and 1947 to develop plans for what would later become the North Atlantic Treaty Organization (NATO). After assignment as deputy commandant at the National War College, 1947–1949, Lemnitzer became the Defense Department's director of the Office of Foreign Military Assistance. The key U.S. military figure in support of such assistance programs, he was as much a lobbyist for such aid in Congress as administrator of the program.

Returning to field command in 1950, Lemnitzer led the 11th Airborne Brigade. He made his first parachute jump at the age of fifty-one. He then commanded the 7th Infantry Division in Korea, during December 1951–July 1952. His return to Washington in 1952 as deputy chief of staff for plans and research did not signify, however, his complete disengagement from East Asian affairs. From 1955 to 1957, General Lemnitzer commanded U.S. Forces, Far East, and the Eighth Army, and was soon promoted to the positions of commander in chief Far East and United Nations Command, as well as governor of the Ryukyu Islands. He was U.S. Army vice-chief of staff, 1957–1959, and U.S. Army chief of staff, 1959–1960. Lemnitzer reached the pinnacle of the military hierarchy when President Dwight Eisenhower named him chairman of the JCS in 1960. After his term as JCS chairman, he commanded U.S. forces in Europe, 1962–1967, and then served as Supreme Allied Commander in Europe, 1967–1969, commanding NATO, which he helped to create.

Even after retirement from the military, Lemnitzer, who resided in Washington, D.C., remained active in government and participated on a panel investigating the domestic activities of the Central Intelligence Agency in 1975. He died in Washington, D.C., on 12 November 1988.

—*Clayton D. Laurie*

References:

Appleman, Roy E. *South to the Naktong, North to the Yalu.* Washington, DC: Office of the Chief of Military History, 1961.

Bell, William Gardner. *Commanding Generals and Chiefs of Staff, 1775–1983.* Washington, DC: U.S. Army Center of Military History, 1983.

Binder, L. James. *Lemnitzer: A Soldier for His Time.* Washington, DC: Brassey's, 1997.

Hermes, Walter G. *United States Army in the Korean War: Truce Tent and Fighting Front.* Washington, DC: Office of the Chief of Military History, 1966.

Lichtenstein, Nelson, and Eleanora W. Schoenebaum, eds. *Political Profiles: The Kennedy Years.* New York: Facts on File, 1978.

See also: Eisenhower, Dwight D.; NATO (North Atlantic Treaty Organization).

Leviero, Anthony H.
(1905–1956)

White House correspondent for the *New York Times.* Born in Brooklyn, New York, on 24 November 1905, Anthony Harry Leviero left school at fourteen and, after several years of working for maritime insurance and shipping concerns, at the age of twenty became a copy boy and night police reporter for the New York *American.* In 1929 he moved to the *New York Times,* simultaneously continuing his education in night classes at Columbia University and the College of the City of New York.

In 1923 Leviero also enrolled in the New York National Guard and then transferred to the U.S. Army Reserve in 1935 as a second lieutenant in the Military Intelligence Reserve. He was called to active duty as an intelligence officer and first lieutenant in March 1941 and saw active service in Europe, rising to the rank of lieutenant colonel. In 1945 he rejoined the *New York Times,* concentrating increasingly on politics, defense, and international affairs, and in 1947 he became its White House correspondent, one of the press pack who accompanied President Harry S. Truman virtually everywhere he went, including the November 1950 Wake Island Conference. Leviero was known as a hard-working, diligent, and dedicated reporter who indulged in none of the classic vices of the journalist's profession. In March 1951 the *New York Times* gave him a roving assignment, leaving him free to concentrate on any issue or story that he considered newsworthy.

After Truman relieved General Douglas MacArthur of his command, Leviero watched the general's televised address to Congress of 19 April 1951, in which he harshly criticized Truman's Asian policies as being "blind to reality." At the Wake Island meeting six months earlier, Truman and others had given Leviero the impression that the general and the president were in fundamental agreement on the war and overall Asian policy. Scenting a story, Leviero approached three administration officials who had been present at the talks and asked for access to the notes of these discussions. One of his sources allowed him to view the stenographic transcripts and other records taken on these occasions that had been collated by Chairman of the Joint Chiefs of Staff General Omar N. Bradley. The source allowed Leviero to take notes from these materials, though not to quote them directly. The next day, 21 April, Leviero's story filled four columns of the *New York Times,* revealing that

MacArthur had assured Truman that victory would be achieved by Thanksgiving, that he was convinced the People's Republic of China (PRC, Communist China) would not intervene in the war, and that, even if this should occur, United Nations forces could easily repel any Chinese attack.

Although MacArthur's congressional supporters and other newspapers hinted that the Truman administration planted this story, Leviero stated that no official had volunteered the information, and that he obtained it "only by asking the right questions at the right time." The Pulitzer Prize awarded him for distinguished reporting on 5 May 1952 specifically cited "his achievement in securing a record" of the Wake Island conversations. After Leviero completed his year on roving assignment, his employers once again made him White House correspondent. He died in Washington of a heart attack on 3 September 1956, while covering that year's presidential campaign.

—Priscilla Roberts

References:

Berger, Meyer. *The Story of the* New York Times: *1851–1951.* New York: Simon & Schuster, 1951.

Berry, Nicholas O. *Foreign Policy and the Press: An Analysis of the* New York Times' *Coverage of Foreign Policy.* New York: Greenwood Press, 1990.

Hamby, Alonzo L. *Man of the People: A Life of Harry S. Truman.* New York: Oxford University Press, 1995.

"Leviero, Anthony H(arry)." In *Current Biography, 1952.* New York: H. W. Wilson, 1953.

McCullough, David. *Truman.* New York: Simon & Schuster, 1992.

Salisbury, Harrison E. *Without Fear or Favor: An Uncompromising Look at the* New York Times. New York: Times Books, 1980.

Schaller, Michael. *Douglas MacArthur: The Far Eastern General.* New York: Oxford University Press, 1989.

See also: Bradley, Omar Nelson; Truman, Harry S.; Truman's Recall of MacArthur; Wake Island Conference.

Li Kenong (Li K'e-nung)
(1899–1962)

Head of the Chinese People's Volunteer Army (CPVA, Chinese Communist) delegation at the Korean War armistice talks, 1951–1953, and chief of the Military Intelligence Department of the Chinese People's Liberation Army (PLA) during the Korean War. Born in Chao Xian, Anhui Province, China, on 15 September 1899, Li Kenong joined the Chinese Communist Party (CCP) in 1926. He worked for CCP underground organizations in Hubei and Shanghai in the late 1920s, and in 1930 he became the Red Army's director of Internal Security Affairs. After the Long March he became the chief intelligence officer of the CCP.

When the Xi'an Event occurred on 12 December 1936, Mao Zedong sent Li to contact General Zhang Xueliang in Xi'an. Li later joined Zhou Enlai in per-

suading General Zhang to release Jiang Jieshi (Chiang Kai-shek) in order to facilitate establishment of a national united front against the Japanese invasion. During the War of Resistance against the Japanese, he was Zhou Enlai's liaison with the Nationalist government. His negotiation skills and intelligence made him a trusted aide to Zhou Enlai and Mao Zedong in dealing with the Nationalists. Li was later promoted to chief of the CCP Intelligence Department. In that capacity, he controlled CCP intelligence operations and was responsible for the security of CCP leaders.

When the Korean War began, Li was director of the Military Intelligence Department, PLA General Staff, where he coordinated all intelligence operations. Foreign Minister Zhou Enlai also made him vice minister of foreign affairs to deal with the international ramifications of the Korean War. From 1951 to 1953 Li Kenong headed the CPVA negotiation team at the armistice negotiations. His team members included Deng Hua (deputy commander of the CPVA), Qiao Guanhua (Ministry of Foreign Affairs), and Ni Zhiliang (Chinese ambassador to the Democratic People's Republic of Korea [North Korea]).

Li was the key figure in formulating negotiation strategies and he was also involved in major battle decisions. Because of his military and intelligence background, the Chinese government gave him full authority to coordinate armistice talks and battlefield strategy. As the central figure in the armistice negotiations, Li reported directly to Mao Zedong and Zhou Enlai in Beijing.

After the war the Chinese government promoted Li to general. He also served for a time as deputy chief of staff of the PLA and director of the CCP Investigation Department. This put him in a critical position in charge of national intelligence operations. But long hours of work brought a deterioration in his health. He died on 9 February 1962.

—Richard Weixing Hu

References:

Guo Huaruo et al., eds. *Jiefangjun Junshi Dacidian* [Dictionary of the CPLA military history]. Changchun: Jilin People's Press, 1993.

Wu Rugao et al., eds. *Zhongguo Junshi Renwu Dacidian* [Dictionary of Chinese military figures]. Beijing: Xinhua Chubanshe, 1989.

Zhongguo Junshi Dabaike Quanshu [Chinese military encyclopedia]. Military History, Vol. 2. Beijing: Military Science Press, 1997.

Zhongguo Renmin Jiefangjun Jiangshuai Miniu [Brief biographies of the CPLA's marshals and generals]. Vols. 1–3. Beijing: PLA Press, 1986, 1987.

See also: China, People's Republic of; Jiang Jieshi (Chiang Kaishek); Mao Zedong; Zhou Enlai.

Lie, Trygve
(1896–1968)

Secretary-General of the United Nations (UN), 1946–1953. Trygve Halvden Lie was born in Oslo,

Norway on 16 July 1896. He joined the Labor Party and at sixteen became president of his political cell. In 1919 he graduated from Oslo University Law School and became secretary in charge of administration for the Labor Party. In 1922 he became legal advisor to the Trade Union Federation. It was here that his diplomatic skills were honed. He acquired a reputation for settling disputes early and fighting test cases in the courts. So effective were his skills that in the period 1930–1935 Norway's economy was entirely strike free.

On 20 March 1935, the Labor Party defeated the Liberal Party and Lie joined the new cabinet as minister of justice. After a cabinet reorganization in June 1939, Lie became minister of commerce. Four months later, shortly after the outbreak of World War II, he took over the new department of Shipping and Supplies, where he was noted for saving considerable stores and a sizable portion of the merchant fleet for Allied use before Norway's June 1940 surrender to Nazi Germany.

In February 1941 Lie became foreign minister of the government-in-exile in London, and in April 1945 he headed the Norwegian delegation to the San Francisco Conference that led to the establishment of the UN. After his government's return to Norway, Lie continued as foreign minister. In January 1946 he headed the Norwegian delegation to the UN, and on 1 February he was elected as the UN's first secretary-general by a unanimous vote in the Security Council and a 46–3 vote in the General Assembly.

With the onset of the Cold War, Lie had no shortage of challenges. These included the Communist insurrection in Greece, Soviet pressure on Turkey, the Berlin blockade, unrest in Palestine, the Communist victory in China, and the Korean War.

The UN provided for "full and unfettered" elections to be held in Korea in May 1948 under the observation of the United Nations Commission on Korea (UNCOK). Authorities in the North refused UN-supervised elections, so elections were held below the 38th parallel only, where two-thirds of the population lived. The result was an overwhelming victory for the government of South Korea and the election of Syngman Rhee as president. In December 1948 the General Assembly recognized the Republic of Korea (South Korea) as the only legitimate government, but, because of the Soviet Union's veto in the Security Council, South Korea was unable to join the international body.

On 21 October 1949, the General Assembly passed Resolution 293 recognizing the Rhee government and charged UNCOK with the duty of peaceful unification of the Korean peninsula. Meanwhile elections were held in the North under Soviet supervision and the People's Democratic Republic of Korea came into being. By the end of 1949, the United States withdrew

its occupation forces from the South and the Soviet Union withdrew its forces from the North, while underwriting a massive arms buildup there.

As tensions built and border skirmishes increased in May 1950, UNCOK increased its observation teams along the 38th parallel. At daybreak, 25 June 1950 (24 June in the Western Hemisphere), North Korean forces invaded the South. Lie immediately invoked Article 99 of the UN Charter and convened the Security Council at 1400 hours on 25 June. Lie held that Korea was a ward of the UN and thus the invasion was an attack against the UN itself. He labeled the North Koreans as aggressors in violation of the principles of the UN Charter, and he called upon the Security Council "to take steps necessary to reestablish peace." The resolution was carried by a vote of 9–0 with Yugoslavia abstaining. The Soviet Union was absent because of its boycott of the Security Council beginning on 10 January 1950 to protest the Council's recognition of the Goumindang Chinese (Taiwan) government as opposed to the Communist government under Mao Zedong.

According to UNCOK, the North's invasion was "well planned, concerted, and full scale." The retreat of South Korean forces quickly turned into a rout, and on 27 June the Security Council passed a resolution calling on member states to "furnish such assistance to the Republic of Korea as may be necessary to repel the armed attack and to restore international peace and security to the area." Earlier that day Lie encouraged Yakov Malik to attend the Security Council meeting, but Malik insisted on maintaining the Soviet boycott.

Soviet Ambassador Andrei Gromyko raised the question of legality of the UN response to Korea, denouncing as illegitimate the Goumindang Chinese government and its seat in the Security Council. Additionally, he proposed that the Soviet boycott of the Security Council was a de facto veto. Lie affirmed that the boycott was in fact not an automatic veto but more of an abstention. Gromyko compared Korea to the American Civil War, an internal matter outside the scope of the UN. Lie countered that Korea had been the special interest of the UN and pointed to the elections on May 1948 and the December 1948 General Assembly recognition of the Republic of Korea. Lie also viewed the conflict as a threat to international peace and thus a matter for the UN.

On 14 July, Lie drafted a cable to all member nations of the General Assembly, requesting any assistance to the UN Command in Korea. Sent by U.S. diplomatic channels, this became known as the fifty-three cables denoting the membership of the General Assembly. By 7 August, forty-one nations had responded, most offering concrete assistance. Besides the United States and Korea, fifteen nations sent troops to

Korea, and other countries, such as Denmark, Norway, Sweden, and India, sent humanitarian aid in the form of field hospitals and ambulance services.

Lie wanted an international committee to direct UN forces, but the United States opposed this because it was providing the bulk of the troops and materiel. As a result, a compromise was reached with a unified command under a U.S. commander to be chosen by U.S. President Harry Truman. The unified command would carry the blue and white UN flag and would send periodic reports to the Security Council.

On 1 December 1950, after the People's Republic of China (PRC) intervention in the war and at Lie's invitation, a PRC delegation arrived at Lake Success, the temporary UN headquarters on Long Island, to discuss both a cease-fire in Korea and the Formosa issue. This was the PRC's first direct contact with the UN, and initially its delegation, led by General Wu Xiuquan, seemed eager for a cease-fire. On 9 December, Lie was prepared to offer cease-fire conditions with demarcation along roughly the same border (38th parallel) as the pre–25 June invasion. When General Wu returned to discussions, however, his enthusiasm had waned, presumably the result of Soviet pressure not to pursue truce talks. Much to Lie's regret, the Chinese delegation left New York on 19 December with no settlement of either the Korean War or the issue of Formosa.

By spring 1951, Chinese and North Korean forces were back above the 38th parallel. On 1 June, Lie called for a cease-fire along the 38th parallel, claiming that the main purposes of the UN mission in Korea were fulfilled. U.S. Secretary of State Dean Acheson supported this notion, but UN field commanders were not enthusiastic, as UN forces were then somewhat north of the 38th parallel. The North Koreans also wanted a cessation of hostilities during truce talks, and UN Commander Lieutenant General Matthew Ridgway believed that this would only bog down negotiations while giving North Korean and Chinese forces time to regroup for a sustained counteroffensive.

In mid-June, Lie circulated among UN delegations a memorandum calling for direct talks with North Korea and a negotiated cease-fire among military commanders in the field. Malik responded favorably to Lie's memo. On 4 July, the PRC and North Korea agreed to talks beginning 10 July. These talks dragged on during two more years of fighting.

Soviet support for Lie plummeted as a result of his actions during the Korean War. The Russians accused him of failing to bring about a cease-fire through peaceful means and of launching aggressive war in a mission of peace. Lie argued that, had he pursued negotiations instead of taking a military stand, the North Koreans would have completed their conquest of the South and any posturing by the world commu-

nity would have been a failure. But the Korean War also undermined Lie's hope of acting as a bridge between East and West.

In October 1950 the Security Council could not agree on a successor to Lie, and the selection process was passed to the General Assembly. The Assembly vote was forty-six for Lie, five against (all Soviet bloc), and eight abstentions. Lie's term was extended for three years, but he did not complete it. Largely as a result of continued Soviet criticism, Lie made it known in early 1953 that, if a suitable successor could be found, he would step down. On 31 March Swedish diplomat Dag Hammarskjöld was nominated, and on 7 April he succeeded Lie as UN secretary-general.

Lie retired to his native Norway on a UN pension. He then wrote several books, including *In the Cause of Peace*, which detailed his seven years as secretary-general. In 1955 he was appointed governor of Oslo and Akershus, a position he held until 1968. From 1963 to 1964 he was minister of industries, and in 1965 he was minister of commerce. Lie received a total of twenty-five honorary doctorates. He died of a heart attack in Geilo, Norway, on 30 December 1968.

—*William H. Van Husen*

References:
Blair, Clay. *The Forgotten War: America in Korea, 1950–1953.* New York: Times Books, 1987.
Lie, Trygve. *In the Cause of Peace.* New York: Macmillan, 1954.
New York Times, 31 December 1968.
Rothe, Anna. *Current Biography, 1946.* New York: H. W. Wilson, 1947.
Whelan, Richard. *Drawing the Line.* Boston: Little, Brown, 1990.
See also: Acheson, David Dean; Gromyko, Andrei Andreyevich; Hammarskjöld, Dag; Inch'ŏn Landings: Operation CHROMITE; Malik, Jacob (Iakov) Alexandrovich; Ridgway, Matthew Bunker; Truman, Harry S.; Wu Xiuquan (Wu Hsiu-Ch'uan).

Lightner, Edwin Allan, Jr.
(1908–1990)

U.S. Foreign Service officer and counselor and later chargé d'affaires of the U.S. embassy in Pusan in March 1951. Born in New York City in 1908, E. Allan Lightner graduated from Princeton University in 1930 and joined the Foreign Service the same year. His early assignments were in Latin America. After World War II, Lightner headed Central European Affairs for the State Department.

On 1 March 1951, Lightner was assigned as counselor to the U.S. embassy in Pusan, Republic of Korea (ROK, South Korea), succeeding Everett I. Drumright. It was Lightner's first posting in Asia. During Ambassador John J. Muccio's absence during May–June 1952, Lightner was chargé d'affaires, and he thus became involved in the struggle then in progress between the ROK National Assembly and ROK President Syngman Rhee.

In the ROK political crisis, Lightner's sympathies were clearly with the Assembly. He was probably the U.S. embassy official most opposed to Rhee, a position Lightner was not reluctant to hide, and he actively worked to involve Washington in supporting the Assembly against Rhee.

Lightner met with Rhee on several occasions, meetings that were often stormy. Lightner found unacceptable Rhee's political practices against his opponents and believed that anyone else would be preferable as president. When some ROK military leaders approached Lightner about securing U.S. support for a coup against Rhee, Lightner reported to Washington that it might not be necessary to have to support this but simply to let it be known that the U.S. government was in conversations with the plotters, but President Harry S. Truman's administration rejected this. Lightner left Korea in February 1953 after Rhee had won reelection as president. As Lightner predicted, Rhee became a virtual dictator.

Lightner's subsequent diplomatic postings took him to Berlin and Libya. As assistant chief of the U.S. mission in Berlin, he was involved in the 1960 spy exchange in Berlin that saw downed American U-2 pilot Francis Gary Powers exchanged for U.S.-based Soviet spymaster Colonel Rudolf I. Abel. Lightner was in Berlin when the Berlin Wall was erected in October 1961 and was twice apprehended by East German authorities for crossing into East Berlin, by which he sought to demonstrate the U.S. right to unrestricted access to all Berlin occupation zones. He was released only when armed U.S. soldiers crossed the border to free him. Lightner was U.S. ambassador to Libya from 1963 to 1965, during which time he negotiated with the Libyan government the use of Wheelus Air Force Base at Tripoli. His last posting, 1967–1970, was as deputy commandant for international affairs at the National War College. Lightner retired to Bayside, Maine, where he died on 15 September 1990.

—Spencer C. Tucker

References:
Matray, James I., ed. *Historical Dictionary of the Korean War.* Westport, CT: Greenwood Press, 1991.
New York Times, 18 September 1990.
See also: Drumright, Everett Francis; Korea, Republic of, History: 1947–1953; Syngman Rhee.

Limb, Ben C. (Yim Pyŏng-jik)
(1893–1979)

Activist for Korean independence and Republic of Korea (ROK, South Korean) minister of foreign affairs, 1949–1951. Born in Puyŏ, South Ch'ungchŏng Province, South Korea, on 16 October 1893, Ben C. Limb studied at the Young Men's Christian Association School in Seoul where Syngman Rhee taught before going into exile in the United States. Limb followed his mentor to the United States and, thanks to Rhee's introduction, entered Ohio State University. As a student at Ohio State, he founded *The Korean Student Review* and became its editor-in-chief. After graduating from the university in 1920, he assisted Rhee's educational work in Hawaii.

In April 1919, shortly after the March 1 Independence Movement took place in Japanese-occupied Korea, Limb organized the Unified Korean Meeting in Philadelphia, which included Rhee and Che-p'il (Jason) Sŏ. During 1920–1921 Limb served the Interim Korean Government as secretary to Rhee, then the president of the government.

In 1941 Limb became an executive member of the American Korean Association. In February 1942 he took charge of public relations as a captain of the Korean Defense Constabulary, then in San Francisco. In 1943 he served as chief secretary of the American Korean Association in Washington, D.C., and the next year he worked at the Office of Strategic Services, assisting its operations in the Far East.

In 1949 ROK President Rhee appointed Limb his foreign minister. In this capacity, as the Democratic People's Republic of Korea (DPRK, North Korea) was rearming, Limb repeatedly sought U.S. military assistance for the ROK. He repeatedly presented evidence of DPRK rearmament with offensive weapons, but his requests received a cold shoulder from U.S. Brigadier General William L. Roberts, chief of the Korean Military Advisory Group. Limb also requested clarification from U.S. Secretary of State Dean G. Acheson when in the course of an important foreign policy address the latter excluded South Korea from the U.S. defense perimeter. Limb continued his efforts for heightened U.S. military assistance even after the war began.

In September 1950 Limb was sent to New York as the chief ROK delegate to the Fifth United Nations (UN) General Assembly. The next year he became ROK ambassador to the UN. This was his last official position in Rhee's administration. After the 1961 military coup d'état, Limb became the chief of the National Movement Center for Reconstruction, set up by the coup's leadership. In 1965 he became ambassador to India, and in 1967 he became ambassador at large. In 1968 he became advisor to the ROK National Unification Board, the government post that had charge of North-South relations. In 1973 he served as a goodwill envoy to African countries, and the next year he became chairman of the Korean Anti-Communist Federation. Ben Limb died in Seoul on 8 February 1979.

—Choo-suk Suh

References:
Matray, James I., ed. *Historical Dictionary of the Korean War.* Westport, CT: Greenwood Press, 1991.

Noble, Harold J. *Embassy at War.* Seattle: University of Washington Press, 1975.

Yim Hyŏn-hŭl. *Taehan Min'guk Chŏngbu-sa* [History of the Korean Provisional Government]. Seoul: Chipmundang, 1982.

See also: Acheson, Dean Goodersham; Korea, Republic of: 1953 to the Present; Roberts, William L.; Syngman Rhee.

Lin Biao
(1907–1971)

Army commander and defense minister of the People's Republic of China (PRC, Communist China). Regarded as one of PRC's most brilliant military leaders, Lin Biao was also one of its greatest traitors—or so it was alleged after Lin died while trying to escape from China in 1971.

Lin, born in Hubei Province on 5 December 1907, began to burnish his military reputation at an early age. After joining the Communist Youth League in Shanghai, he entered the famed Whampoa Military Academy, was commissioned at eighteen, and before his twenty-first birthday had risen to command a regiment in the Northern Expedition, in which the Communists and Jiang Jieshi's (Chiang Kai-shek) Nationalists jointly campaigned against the warlords of northern China.

After Chiang broke with the Communists, Lin held major commands in the Red Army and accompanied Mao on the legendary Long March to the Communists' new base in Yenan (Yan'an). There Lin commanded the Red Army Academy and then led the 115th Division against the invading Japanese. After Japan's surrender, Lin was the architect of some of the most significant Communist victories in the Chinese civil war, including the capture of Beijing.

Lin's ability and experience made him the logical choice to command Chinese forces in the Korean War. But reportedly Lin opposed going to war outside China's borders while the new Communist government still faced tremendous tasks of consolidation and reconstruction inside the country. Claiming poor health, Lin refused to take charge of the Korean effort, and Mao appointed General Peng Dehuai instead.

Lin remained largely out of sight during the Korean War and for several years thereafter. Some historians claim that he fought in the Korean War and may even have been wounded there, although there is no proof of this in Chinese sources. Lin's Fourteenth Army was, however, first to cross the Yalu River into Korea.

In 1955 Lin was elevated to Politburo rank. Four years later, he replaced Peng Dehuai as defense minister. In 1969 the Communist Party's constitution officially designated Lin as Mao's chosen successor, but Mao soon became suspicious that Lin was plotting against him. Their hidden struggle reached its melodramatic climax in 1971 when, according to the official account, Lin, together with his wife, his son, and

key supporters, planned to have Mao killed while the chairman was traveling on his special train. When Mao returned safely to Beijing, Lin realized his plot had failed and tried to escape in an air force plane, apparently bound for the Soviet Union. The plane crashed in Mongolia in the early hours of 13 September 1971, killing Lin and all others on board. The facts of the Lin Biao affair remain murky, and the full truth may never be known with certainty.

—*Arnold R. Isaacs*

References:

Chen, Jian. *China's Road to the Korean War: The Making of the Sino-American Confrontation.* New York: Columbia University Press, 1994.

Klein, Donald W., and Anne B. Clark. *Biographic Dictionary of Chinese Communism, 1921–1965.* Cambridge, MA: Harvard University Press, 1971.

Li Zhisui. *The Private Life of Chairman Mao,* translated by Tai Hung-chao. New York: Random House, 1994.

See also: China, People's Republic of; Jiang Jieshi (Chiang Kai-shek); Peng Dehuai (Peng Te-huai).

Lloyd, John Selwyn
(1904–1978)

British minister of state for foreign affairs during the Korean War. John Selwyn Lloyd was born on 28 July 1904, in West Kirby, Wirral. He was educated at Fettes College, Edinburgh, and Magdalene College, Cambridge. Lloyd was called to the bar in 1930 and in the following years built up both a successful law practice and a solid local government record in Cheshire. During the Second World War, he served in the British Army in the European theater, rising from second lieutenant to brigadier general. In the general election of 1945, Lloyd's war record helped him to victory as member of Parliament for his native area of Wirral, a seat that he held for thirty-five years. From 1948 to 1950 Lloyd combined his parliamentary duties with those of a judge. Although a poor public speaker and somewhat introverted and shy, he won recognition as an expert on financial and economic questions and for his organizational skills.

In 1951 when the Conservative Party regained power, Lloyd was appointed minister of state at the Foreign Office, where his duties included heading the British delegation at meetings of the United Nations (UN) General Assembly. He steadily advocated a firm line in resisting both Chinese and Soviet pressure in Asia; he also insisted that the United States must consult Britain over the conduct of the Korean War. It was largely to ensure British input that in June 1952 he accompanied British Minister of Defense Lord Alexander to Tokyo for discussions with Commander in Chief of UN Forces Lieutenant General Mark Clark. Lloyd deplored the behavior of President of the

Republic of Korea (South Korea) Syngman Rhee, whom Lloyd found dictatorial and unpredictable, and he urged President Harry S. Truman's administration to take more effective measures to pressure Rhee. Lloyd's legal background predisposed him to take an active interest in efforts to find a means to resolve the ongoing impasse at the P'anmunjŏm truce talks over the question of the repatriation of prisoners of war (POW), and he devoted considerable energies to persuading the Truman administration to accept some version of V. K. Krishna Menon's November 1952 POW settlement proposal and the ensuing UN Resolution of 3 December 1952.

Lloyd's influence over foreign affairs increased in 1954, when Foreign Secretary Anthony Eden was absent or ill for long periods and left much of the Foreign Office's routine responsibilities in his hands. In 1954 Lloyd was promoted to minister of defense, and in December 1955 he became foreign secretary. Despite fevered speculation that he would resign and persistent verbal abuse and taunts from the opposition benches, Lloyd survived the 1956 Suez crisis and remained foreign secretary until 1960, when he became chancellor of the exchequer. In "the night of the long knives" of July 1962, Prime Minister Harold Macmillan abruptly dismissed Lloyd, together with a third of his cabinet. In October 1963 Lloyd became leader of the House of Commons, remaining there until the Labour Party victory eleven months later. In 1971 he was elected speaker of the House of Commons, a role that won him general praise for his sedulous fairness to all parties and viewpoints. He died at Preston Crowmarsh, Oxfordshire, on 17 May 1978.

—*Priscilla Roberts*

References:
Lloyd, Selwyn. *Mr. Speaker, Sir*. London: Jonathan Cape, 1976.
Lowe, Peter. "The Settlement of the Korean War." In *The Foreign Policy of Churchill's Peacetime Administration, 1951–1955,* edited by John W. Young. Leicester: Leicester University Press, 1988: 207–231.
MacDonald, Callum A. *Britain and the Korean War*. Oxford: Blackwell, 1990.
Seldon, Anthony. *Churchill's Indian Summer: The Conservative Government, 1951–1955*. London: Hodder & Stoughton, 1981.
Stueck, William W., Jr. *The Korean War: An International History*. Princeton, NJ: Princeton University Press, 1995.
Thorpe, D. R. *Selwyn Lloyd*. London: Jonathan Cape, 1989.
Young, John W. *Winston Churchill's Last Campaign: Britain and the Cold War 1951–5*. Oxford: Clarendon Press, 1996.
See also: Churchill, Sir Winston Spencer; Clark, Mark W.; Eden, Anthony; Menon, V. K. Krishna.

Lodge, Henry Cabot, Jr.
(1902–1985)

Advisor to Republican and Democratic presidents, U.S. senator, and diplomat; Dwight Eisenhower's campaign manager and advisor during the transition from the Truman to the Eisenhower administrations during 1952–1953. Born in Nahant, Massachusetts, on 5 July 1902, Henry Cabot Lodge, Jr. was the grandson of Senator Henry Cabot Lodge. Educated at Harvard University, he began his career as a journalist with the *Boston Evening Transcript* and the *New York Herald Tribune*.

In 1933 Lodge was elected to the Massachusetts House of Representatives and in 1936 to the U.S. Senate. Except for three years' service as a U.S. Army lieutenant colonel in North Africa and Europe during World War II, Lodge remained in the Senate until 1953. During World War II, Lodge met Eisenhower, then supreme commander of the Allied Expeditionary Force, and occasionally served as Eisenhower's French-language translator. Lodge's wartime experiences convinced him of the folly of isolationism, and he thereafter advocated an active foreign policy. After World War II and his return to the Senate, Lodge formed a close partnership with Arthur Vandenberg; together the two men were instrumental in gaining Republican support for the Truman Doctrine, the Marshall Plan, and the North Atlantic Treaty Organization.

Lodge was among those who urged Eisenhower to seek the presidency in 1952, and he helped run the campaign. His work for Eisenhower, however, so distracted him from his own reelection bid that he was narrowly defeated by his Democratic challenger John F. Kennedy. After the presidential transition in late 1952, however, Lodge was appointed U.S. ambassador to the United Nations (UN).

Lodge supported U.S. intervention in Korea. While working on the presidential transition, he found the Korean War the most pressing topic. There was much concern by the outgoing administration that the incoming Republicans would give in to pressures to repatriate Communist prisoners of war in order to reach a settlement and honor campaign promises to end U.S. involvement.

In the spring of 1953, Lodge participated in cabinet and National Security Council meetings, as Eisenhower sought to find ways to achieve a cease-fire and then a strategy to compel Republic of Korea (ROK) President Syngman Rhee to accept it. Although the extent of Lodge's influence on Korean policy is not known, he did much to execute U.S. foreign policies at the UN. He took a hard anti-Communist line throughout, and he was a strong advocate of U.S. positions on the 1956 Hungarian uprising and Suez crisis, as well as the crisis involving Quemoy and Matsu in 1957.

In 1960 Lodge was Vice-President Richard M. Nixon's running mate in the latter's unsuccessful presidential bid. In spite of Lodge's Republican affiliations, however, Democratic President John F.

Kennedy appointed Lodge the U.S. ambassador to the Republic of Vietnam in June 1963. Lodge's experiences during the Korean War undoubtedly influenced his actions in Saigon, especially his support for the ouster of South Vietnamese President Ngo Dinh Diem in November 1963. Although Lodge resigned as ambassador in May 1964 to assist Republican Senator Barry Goldwater's presidential bid, he agreed to again become the U.S. ambassador to South Vietnam at the behest of Democratic President Lyndon B. Johnson in July 1965 and remained in that post until April 1967. From April 1968 until January 1969, Lodge was U.S. ambassador to the Federal Republic of Germany, before accepting Republican President Richard Nixon's invitation to serve as chief U.S. negotiator at the Paris Peace Conference to end the Vietnam War. Frustrated by Communist tactics there and the slow pace of the talks, Lodge left in November 1969. In June 1970 he accepted his final government post, becoming President Nixon's special envoy to the Vatican, serving until 1977. He died in Beverly, Massachusetts, on 27 February 1985.

—*Clayton D. Laurie*

References:

Hatch, Alden. *The Lodges of Massachusetts.* New York: Hawthorn, 1973.

Lodge, Henry Cabot. *As It Was: An Insider View of Politics and Power in the 50s and 60s.* New York: W. W. Norton, 1976.

———. *The Storm Has Many Eyes: A Personal Narrative.* New York: W. W. Norton, 1973.

Miller, William J. *Henry Cabot Lodge.* New York: Heinemann, 1967.

See also: Eisenhower, Dwight D.; Syngman Rhee.

Logistics in the Korean War

Logistics is the procurement, maintenance, and transportation of military materiel, facilities, and personnel. It was a major factor for both sides in the Korean War. Strategic and operational decisions of both the United Nations Command (UNC) and Communist forces were based largely on logistical considerations. The timing and duration of offensives were dictated by logistics, and the operational objectives were themselves often logistical in nature: factories, bases, lines of communications, stockpiles of supplies and equipment, and means of transportation.

Although the rugged terrain and harsh climate of Korea affected both sides equally, each side possessed its own particular set of logistical advantages and disadvantages that shaped its organization and operations. The principal difficulties faced by the UNC, once the personnel and supply shortages of the early months of the war were eliminated, were the complexity and rapid growth of UN forces in the field and a U.S. global strategy that assigned a higher priority to an antici-

pated defensive war in Europe than to the reality of an ongoing war in Korea. The major problem for the Korean People's Army (KPA, North Korea) and the Chinese People's Volunteer Army (CPVA, Chinese Communists) in Korea was more concrete: how to maintain a flow of supplies to the front in the face of an intense UNC air interdiction program. In the end, both sides overcame the major obstacles. Although the Communists were never strong enough logistically to employ their superior numbers to defeat the UN forces and eject them from the Korean peninsula, they were able to maintain a flow of supplies to front-line units sufficient enough to enable them to conduct an almost impenetrable static defense and, in the last months of the war, to mount strong sustained offensive actions.

Impact of Climate and Terrain

The physical environment of the Korean peninsula posed challenges to both sides. The northern mountains restricted access between southern Manchuria and northern Korea, and the central T'aebaek Range severely limited east-west communication in Korea itself. The rugged terrain throughout the country limited the construction and operation of railroads and highways and required numerous tunnels, bridges, defiles, and steep grades. Consequently, the best fixed transportation routes were found in the gentler terrain of the western section of the country. The east-west river systems in Korea acted as obstacles to north-south movement, and the mountains served to channelize north-south communications and limited the degree to which forces operating on one north-south axis could be reinforced or supplied from parallel axes. The overall effect of such restrictions of the lines of communication was to impede military logistical and tactical mobility and flexibility and make movements more vulnerable to ground and air interdiction.

Seasonal weather conditions in Korea limited observation and air operations, but their most important effect on ground operations was to limit trafficability. Snow, ice, and poor visibility in winter and mud and dust in summer inhibited highway operations and complicated the maintenance of both rail lines and highways. Heavy rains from June to September created poor trafficability conditions throughout most low-lying areas. Cross-country mobility was further limited by the extensive rice paddies that were flooded from March to October in the north and from May to October in the south. The most favorable season for cross-country movement was from late September to late November.

As any veteran of the Korean War will attest, the terrain and climate of the Korean peninsula also took their toll on soldiers and materiel. Winter cold and summer heat adversely affected the performance of

U.S. Marines find movement difficult in the rainy season for laden trucks, 25 August 1952. (National Archives)

weapons and vehicles and produced numerous person-nel casualties. In winter, grease in weapons froze, vehi-cles refused to start, and soldiers suffered frostbite, hypothermia, and other cold-related injuries. In sum-mer, dust clogged air filters and eroded weapons; high temperatures and humidity spoiled supplies and pro-duced heat stroke and other heat injuries. The moun-tainous terrain also generally limited the use of motor vehicles and pushed men and animals to the limits of their stamina.

In general terms, the Korean peninsula was one of the least favorable places on earth for conducting mod-ern mechanized warfare. The rugged terrain in partic-ular tended to offset any advantage that a modern, technologically sophisticated army might have over an enemy with few complicated weapons or vehicles, a fact that was demonstrated definitively during the Korean War.

United Nations Command Logistics

The Korean War has been called one of the greatest logistics undertakings in history. Despite an over-whelming superiority in developed natural resources; industrial capacity; armaments stockpiles; and ground, sea, and air transport; the UNC faced a number of dif-ficult logistical challenges. When war erupted on 25 June 1950, both the Republic of Korea (ROK) and its protector, the United States, were unprepared logisti-cally. Industrial production of war materiel had fallen precipitously from World War II highs; existing stock-piles of weapons, vehicles, and other equipment and supplies, particularly ammunition and spare parts, were in short supply and aging; and, as with the com-bat units they were to support, military logistical organizations were understaffed and poorly trained. Moreover, the principal sources of logistical support for the UNC were in the continental United States, far from the theater of operations. Had it not been for stockpiles of surplus World War II equipment and supplies remaining in the Far East, the expansible support base in occupied Japan, and the reservoir of logistical experience remaining in the post–World War II U.S. armed services, the outcome of the North Korean onslaught in June 1950 might have been much different. However, those things were available, and after several months of desperate defensive fighting on the Pusan perimeter, the tremendous logistical potential of the United States and its UN allies began to make itself felt with ever increasing weight as resources of personnel and materiel were mobilized and the overwhelming U.S. superiority in industrial production, transportation, and organizational know-how were brought to bear.

In retrospect, the UN logistical effort in Korea might have been better managed. The "creeping mobilization" of 1950–1953 might have been conducted more systematically and with a greater sense of urgency. The preoccupation with a possible attack by the Soviet Union in Europe that siphoned off funds, personnel, and the lion's share of the best equipment and supplies might have yielded to the reality of the existing situation in the Far East. And the post–World War II parsimony and general sense of euphoria, based in large part on the unfounded belief that the U.S. monopoly of the atomic bomb would solve every military problem, might have been replaced by a more prescient understanding of the coming age of limited war. But such was not the case, and, in any event, UN commanders and logisticians faced a number of more immediate and more concrete problems.

The UNC logistical effort in the first year of the war was plagued by shortages of every kind. Trained logistical personnel were scarce, and spare parts, tanks, water trailers, hot tire patches, combat boots, typewriters, generators, entrenching tools, and rock crushers were just a few of the items in short supply. Ammunition, particularly artillery ammunition and antitank rounds for the newly introduced 3.5-inch rocket launcher, was a special problem, especially after the Chinese Communist intervention in November 1950. Many items were in short supply; others were old, obsolete, or simply unsuited to the situation. Fortunately, most of the pressing materiel shortages were relieved by mid-1951, in part because of the successful ordnance rebuild program in Japan.

Another major challenge for UNC logisticians resulted from the steady growth in the numbers of troops supported and the complex variety of materiel required to support the various ROK and UN contingents. The United States supplied over half of all logistical support for the expanding ROK armed forces and a high percentage of that for the other UN forces, each

of which had different requirements because of differences in national tastes, customs, and religious requirements. Logistical complexity was compounded by sheer numbers. By the end of the war in July 1953, the UNC was supporting 932,539 personnel: 302,483 from the United States, 590,911 from the ROK, and 39,145 from other UN countries.

For the UNC as well as the Communists, the key to the whole logistical effort was transportation. Here the UNC had a decided advantage as far as strategic airlift and sealift were concerned, but land transportation was nearly as great a problem for the UNC as for the KPA and the CPVA. The generally small and poorly equipped South Korean ports were bottlenecks, and the available railroads on which the UNC relied for the bulk of its surface movements were limited in both coverage and capacity in addition to being vulnerable to Communist sabotage and direct attack. Motor transport was also vulnerable, limited by the rugged terrain and hostile climate, and constantly scarce as a result of the lack of trained personnel and maintenance problems stemming from overuse on poor roads and shortage of spare parts. The innovative use of fixed wing transports and helicopters made up only a small part of the overall UNC shortfall in ground transport, a problem that continued throughout the war.

Despite the many deficiencies, UNC logisticians were amazingly successful in supporting their combat forces in the field. During the thirty-seven months of war, some 31.5 million measurement tons of supplies were shipped to Korea from the United States, more than twice the amount shipped to France for the American Expeditionary Force in World War I and 82 percent more than the total amount of supplies shipped to U.S. Army ground forces in the Southwest Pacific theater in World War II. Between the spring of 1950 and the summer of 1953, the ordnance rebuild program in Japan alone turned out some 489,000 small arms, 1,418 artillery pieces, 34,316 fire control items, 743 combat vehicles, and 15,000 general purpose vehicles at a savings of some $9.5 million. By July 1953, UNC forces in Korea were fully, perhaps even lavishly, equipped and supplied, but such support did not come cheap. The total cost of U.S. Army operations in Korea from 27 June 1950 to 30 June 1953 was more than $17.2 billion, including more than $11.7 billion for supplies, more than $1.5 billion for the movement of troops and supplies, more than $1.7 billion for the operation of facilities in the United States and the Far East directly supporting operations in Korea, and more than $2.2 billion in pay and allowances.

Communist Logistics

From the point of view of KPA and CPVA logistical activities, the Korean War can be divided into three

U.S. Marine Sikorsky HRS-2 helicopter delivering supplies to a forward UN position in North Korea. Note the mountainous terrain. Helicopters proved invaluable in such conditions. (National Archives)

main periods. From June 1950 to July 1951, the Communists struggled to keep their forces supplied in the face of intensive UNC air interdiction efforts and aggressive ground operations. Consequently, the KPA and CPVA were unable to exploit their initial operational successes by sustained offensive action. In the second period, from July 1951 through December 1952, the KPA and CPVA reorganized and strengthened their logistical forces and developed effective methods for coping with the UNC air interdiction program. In the final period, from January 1953 through July 1953, KPA/CPVA logistical systems achieved maturity and demonstrated an ability not only to meet the requirements of a strong static defense but to stockpile in forward areas the supplies necessary to sustain prolonged offensive operations.

A number of factors influenced the ability of the KPA and CPVA to support their forces in the field adequately. In the first instance, the logistical require-ments of both the KPA and the CPVA in Korea were extremely low in comparison to those of UNC forces. The minimal provision of food, clothing, and medical support to front-line Communist troops sometimes caused great hardship and suffering, but apparently did not cause a significant deterioration of morale and discipline. Contrary to common opinion, the KPA and CPVA in Korea were dependent on formal, albeit relatively lean, logistical systems. Maximum use was made of captured supplies and items, particularly foodstuffs, requisitioned in areas near the front lines, but in the final analysis the KPA and CPVA relied principally on war materiel obtained through regular channels. The logistical systems of the KPA and CPVA in Korea differed significantly, but the logistical doctrine and methods of both armies were quite flexible and they changed, as did tactical organization, during the course of the war, mostly in the direction of the more rigid but more efficient Soviet model. In

U.S. and ROK troops on a tank, passing through South Korean refugees, 5 January 1951. Movement of men and supplies was made more difficult by the throngs of refugees using the roads. (National Archives)

much the same way, the logistical organizations of the KPA and CPVA also exhibited great internal variation from unit to unit as well as considerable change over time, again in the direction of the Soviet model.

The efficiency of KPA/CPVA logistical support was directly affected by the ebb and flow of combat operations up and down the Korean peninsula. The farther south Communist forces advanced, the longer and more exposed became their lines of supply and the less efficient its overall logistical performance. The same was true, of course, for UNC forces moving in the opposite direction. In view of the extended supply lines required, the KPA/CPVA distribution system was extremely vulnerable and thus the focal point of UNC efforts to degrade Communist combat potential. Again contrary to common opinion, the KPA /CPVA distribution system relied principally on rail movement supplemented by motor transport at intermediate

levels. For the most part, carts, pack animals, and human bearers were used only in the immediate area of the front (regimental level and below), for unit movements, and for supplementary operations in rear areas. However, the lack of KPA/CPVA motor transport at the lower levels was an important defect of the Communist logistical system in that reliance on front-line animal and human-pack transport restricted the tactical mobility and flexibility of the KPA and CPVA in combat operations, particularly their ability to shift forces rapidly or exploit breakthroughs.

The Communists compensated for a low level of logistical mechanization with extensive employment of personnel and extraordinary exertion. The KPA and CPVA in Korea also demonstrated great ingenuity and determination in working around UNC attempts to interdict their lines of communications and destroy their logistical resources. They were particularly adept at passive air defense measures, including camouflage, and in the rapid restoration of destroyed and damaged fixed transport facilities (bridges, rail lines, and highways). Even so, until the last seven months of the war, the KPA/CPVA logistical system was not able to deliver sufficient war materiel to front-line forces to permit them to sustain extended offensive operations. Until early 1953, most Communist offensive operations petered out within six to eight days from exhaustion of available food, ammunition, and other key supplies. However, the KPA and CPVA were able to supply their forces on the front lines with the minimum amounts of essential supplies necessary to a strong static defense against UNC forces, and by early 1953 they were beginning to demonstrate a capability to stockpile sufficient supplies to support sustained offensives as well. By the end of active hostilities in July 1953, the KPA/CPVA had on hand in forward areas sufficient food, fuel, ammunition, and other supplies to support a general offensive of 17–24 days' duration.

The Communist logistical situation at various times would have been complicated significantly by more sustained aggressive action on the part of UNC forces. The failure of UNC forces to maintain a high operational tempo after July 1951, and thus place constant pressure on the Communist forces, permitted the KPA and CPVA to stockpile supplies in periods of reduced combat. Static situations thus favored the KPA/CPVA in that, to be effective, interdiction must be employed against an enemy using supplies at a high rate. In Korea, the KPA/CPVA were allowed to initiate or break off contact at will and thus could rest and build up supplies as they wished. The failure to maintain constant ground pressure on the Communist forces can be attributed to both the political and materiel constraints under which UNC commanders operated, but the potential nemesis of the Communist distribution system, the UNC air interdiction program, was also restrained by the lack of adequate technology for detecting movement at night and under conditions of reduced visibility, as well as by the limited number of suitable aircraft that could be applied to the interdiction effort. The constant improvement of KPA/CPVA antiaircraft artillery coverage further restricted the UNC air interdiction effort. Although often cited as a critical restraint on UNC forces, the existence of a Communist supply base in Manchuria that was immune from attack was a relatively unimportant factor. Had UNC air forces been able to attack the Manchurian bases, the end result of the UNC air interdiction effort would probably not have been materially affected.

The inconclusive outcome of the Korean War reflected, as least in part, the parity in logistical effec-

tiveness of the two opponents. At first glance, the UNC would seem to have had an enormous logistical advantage over the North Korean and Chinese forces. The UNC had more of everything—food, ammunition, gasoline, and transport—as well as the unmatched advantages of plentiful ocean and air transport backed by unchallenged sea control and air superiority. But despite the large numbers of troops supported, the relative dearth of supporting industrial capacity and transportation infrastructure and relatively low level of mechanization, the Communists adapted well to the primitive logistical environment in Korea and were able to maintain a steady flow of supplies to front-line units. Communist logistical requirements were kept relatively low and simple, and personnel were substituted for mechanization. Despite more than one million UNC air sorties directed against their lines of communication, transport equipment, supply installations, and industrial facilities over a period of three years, the KPA and CPVA were stronger than ever when the Armistice Agreement was signed on 27 July 1953. Thus, although UNC and KPA/CPVA logistical systems were very different in terms of available resources, technology, organization, methods, and the demands placed upon them, they were both highly effective. The success of both sides in supplying their forces in the field was a major factor in the operational stalemate in Korea.

—Charles R. Shrader

References:

Huston, James A. *Guns and Butter, Powder and Rice: U.S. Army Logistics in the Korean War.* Selinsgrove, PA: Susquehanna University Press, 1989.

———. *The Sinews of War: Army Logistics, 1775–1953.* Washington, DC: Office of the Chief of Military History, 1966.

Shrader, Charles R. *Communist Logistics in the Korean War.* Westport, CT: Greenwood Press, 1995.

See also: Japan Logistical Command; Korean Communications Zone; Railroads, Korean National; Second Logistical Command; Strategic and Tactical Airlift in the Korean War; Third Logistical Command.

Lovett, Robert A.
(1895–1986)

U.S. undersecretary of state and secretary of defense during the Korean War, who also played an important role in the Marshall Plan and in the creation of the North Atlantic Treaty Organization (NATO). Born on 14 September 1895 in Huntsville, Texas, Robert Abercrombie Lovett attended Yale University. While there, Lovett founded the university unit of the U.S. Naval Reserve Flying Corps, which in 1917 was dispatched for duty with Britain's Royal Naval Air Service. From March 1917 until December 1918, Lovett commanded the first U.S. Naval Air Squadron.

Upon returning home and graduating from Yale University, Lovett entered Harvard law and business schools before joining the Wall Street investment banking firm of Brown Brothers. In 1926 he became a partner, and five years later he orchestrated a merger between Brown Brothers and W. Averell Harriman and Company. During the remaining interwar years, Lovett concentrated on international investment and banking matters.

As a champion of air power, Lovett wrote a study in 1940 on airplane production that caught the attention of Assistant Secretary of War Robert P. Patterson and Secretary of War Henry L. Stimson. In particular, Lovett's recommendations that the United States should be increasing its aircraft production to meet what he saw as the growing German threat led to his appointment as a special assistant to the secretary of war from December 1940 to April 1941 and then assistant secretary of war for air thereafter. Lovett had responsibility for aircraft production and procurement.

Throughout World War II, Lovett had the ear of U.S. Army Chief of Staff General George C. Marshall and probably did more than any other man to bring the United States into the modern age of air power. An advocate of strategic bombing and an independent air force, Lovett organized the U.S. Strategic Bombing Survey to document the effect and importance of air power in the war against Germany and Japan.

After the war, Lovett returned to investment banking, but in 1947 his close friend Secretary of State George C. Marshall recalled him to government service to serve as undersecretary of state. In this position Lovett worked to secure congressional approval for the Marshall Plan, the rehabilitation of Germany, and the creation of NATO. Lovett also helped to plan the Berlin airlift. When Marshall resigned as secretary of state in 1949, Lovett also left government service, returning to his law practice.

During the Korean War, when Louis A. Johnson was replaced as secretary of defense, Lovett rejoined Marshall, Johnson's replacement, as undersecretary of defense in September 1950. While Marshall concerned himself with operational aspects of the war, Lovett concentrated on the Pentagon's internal administration, budgeting, and procurement. His main contribution during the war was to develop plans with industry that would enable a swift conversion from civilian to military production in wartime and to construct a permanent industrial mobilization base.

When Marshall resigned in September 1951 for reasons of ill health, President Harry S. Truman nominated Lovett as Marshall's successor. As secretary of defense from 1951 until 1953, Lovett expanded not only missile development programs but also research into chemical and biological weapons. He was also a strong advocate of conscription and a coordinated defense budget. Even as the war in Korea raged, Lovett continued to prepare for the next war. Known as an independent thinker, he was also one of the harshest Truman administration critics of General Douglas MacArthur, particularly regarding what Lovett thought was the general's reckless plan for victory using air power in Korea. Although a trusted aide of Truman, as secretary of defense Lovett concentrated on administrative and logistics matters, whereas Chairman of the Joint Chiefs of Staff General of the Army Omar N. Bradley became Truman's closest military advisor.

Lovett served as secretary of defense until the end of the Truman administration. After Dwight Eisenhower's inauguration as president in 1953, Lovett returned to banking, became the chief executive officer of the Union Pacific Railroad, and held a seat on the Columbia Broadcasting System's television board of directors. After the 1960 presidential election, President-Elect John F. Kennedy offered Lovett a choice of three cabinet posts—state, defense, or the treasury—but he declined further government service for health reasons. He did, however, act as an unofficial advisor and contact point between Kennedy and former officials of the Truman administration, and he was a member of the inner circle, known as ExCom, that advised Kennedy during the 1962 Cuban missile crisis.

Although his influence declined during the years of Lyndon B. Johnson's presidency, Lovett did contribute to a study of nuclear nonproliferation in 1964, and he advised Johnson on foreign policy issues. Lovett died in Locust Valley, New York, on 7 May 1986.

—*Clayton D. Laurie*

References:

Halberstam, David. *The Best and the Brightest.* New York: Random House, 1972.

Isaacson, Walter, and Evan Thomas. *The Wise Men: Six Friends and the World They Made: Acheson, Bohlen, Harriman, Kennan, Lovett, McCloy.* New York: Simon & Schuster, 1986.

Kinnard, Douglas. *The Secretary of Defense.* Lexington: University Press of Kentucky, 1980.

Lichtenstein, Nelson, and Eleanora W. Schoenebaum, eds. *Political Profiles: The Kennedy Years.* New York: Facts on File, 1978.

Schoenebaum, Eleanora W., ed. *Political Profiles: The Truman Years.* New York: Facts on File, 1978.

Who's Who in America, 1950–1951. Chicago: Marquis, 1950.

See also: Bradley, Omar Nelson; Johnson, Louis A.; MacArthur, Douglas; Marshall, George C.; Truman, Harry S.

Lowe, Frank E.
(1885–1968)

Major general, U.S. Army Reserve, and personal military observer for President Harry S. Truman during the Korean War from August 1950 to April 1951 who wrote long, perceptive letters directly to Truman on every aspect of the war's conduct. Born in Springfield, Massachusetts, on 20 September 1885, Frank E. Lowe graduated from Worcester (Massachusetts) Polytechnic Institute in 1908. A successful engineer and businessman, Lowe left his work as a mining engineer in Texas, Mexico, and Central America to join the U.S. Army in June 1917. He finished World War I as a field artillery captain, with combat experience in France as a III Corps artillery supply and ammunition unit commander. An extrovert and enterprising and imaginative, he returned to New England and founded a successful coal and marine services company in Portland, Maine. Lowe was a Republican. His business success allowed him to be active in the interwar U.S. Army Reserve, the American Legion, the Reserve Officers Association, and the Veterans of Foreign Wars. Among other veterans who shared his interest in army reserve forces policy was Harry S. Truman, also an American Expeditionary Force artilleryman and U.S. senator.

When the United States mobilized for World War II, Lowe volunteered for active duty and became a key assistant of Army Chief of Staff General George C. Marshall in handling matters related to the army reserve components. His work so impressed Marshall that in August 1942 he assigned Lowe as his liaison officer to the Senate Special Committee Investigating the National Defense Program, chaired by Senator Truman. Both Marshall and Truman praised Lowe's ability to handle delicate personal and organizational relationships and to show sound, independent judgment. Lowe returned to civilian status as a reserve major general in September 1946 after helping develop plans for reconstituting the U.S. Army Reserve.

In the first weeks of the Korean War, Truman (now president), probably on the recommendation of his military aide, Major General Harry Vaughan, asked Lowe to return to active duty at age sixty-five and to go to Japan and Korea as his personal observer. Truman's letter of instruction charged Lowe to go anywhere and see anything he chose in order to give the president a personal view of the U.S. armed forces in combat. These letters were routed through Vaughan. Lowe's influence on Truman's views on the war is uncertain, but his reports remain an important source on the United Nations Command.

As U.S. Air Force Major General Earle E. Partridge, Jr. noted at the time, Lowe had an exceptional opportunity to see the war. "With no other responsibility beyond those of observation, he probably has the most extensive knowledge of the Korean operations of anyone in the theater." Nevertheless, Lowe did not have as many admirers in the Eighth Army as he had in the 1st Marine Division, the Far East Air Forces, and the

Seventh Fleet, all of whom he visited on many occasions, including the Inch'ŏn landing. Lowe, for example, reported that the 1st Marine Division was "without a doubt the best fighting unit in Korea today." He praised the courage and the professionalism of all the airmen and sailors he observed. His opinion of the Eighth Army, especially its leadership, was less enthusiastic. "No, Mr. President, the old Army that trained you and trained me, the Army we respected and loved is dead. Make no mistake about it, it is well nigh as extinct as the dodo."

The Eighth Army, with the exception of the 1st Cavalry Division, did not embrace Lowe, but ridiculed his appearance and traveling arrangements. Lowe cut a unique figure in uniform: tall and regal, he preferred a pith helmet to the steel variety, riding britches and high-laced boots to conventional fatigues and combat boots, and a World War I pistol rig. He had two loyal traveling companions, Captain Albert G. Hume, his driver and secretary and a twenty-month veteran of service in the Korean Military Advisory Group, and Sergeant First Class Vincente Diala, a Filipino guerrilla veteran, photographer, and master machine gunner, both of them detached from the Army Counterintelligence Corps to protect Lowe from the Communists and himself since the general had an abundance of energy, courage, and curiosity. Lowe's team moved about with a jeep, bristling with machine guns, and a trailer bulging with camping equipment and fine liquors.

Lowe's hospitality and connections with Truman gave him entrée and insight within Eighth Army, which he found overstaffed, undertrained, undisciplined, and poorly supplied. He was especially critical of army personnel policies, which provided untrained officers and troops in inadequate numbers to army infantry regiments.

By the time he left Korea in April 1951, Lowe had won the admiration of the Eighth Army's second commander, Lieutenant General Matthew B. Ridgway, who awarded him a Distinguished Service Cross for his valor in visiting and inspiring infantry units locked in combat. "He has done a conspicuously fine and useful job here," Ridgway wrote a friend. Lowe had certainly met Ridgway's standards of "fearlessness, physical stamina and determination." Lowe protested when his detractors suggested that his exposure to fire filled a personal, emotional need, insisting in his final report to Truman on 30 April 1951 that he had taken no unnecessary risks and done nothing that did not provide useful operational observations and suggestions for new tactics and training. Truman, with Ridgway's approval, ordered Lowe to receive a Distinguished Service Medal for his Korean mission, awarded in June 1951.

Lowe believed his greatest failing was his inability to reassure Truman that MacArthur was a true military genius who posed no political threat to the administration. Lowe believed that members of the army staff and the State Department interfered with his reports, but a subsequent investigation found no plot to destroy Lowe's credibility.

After his return to civilian life, Lowe, who retained his admiration for both Truman and MacArthur, nursed his frustration with the war's course until he finally granted an interview to Jim Lucas, a former Marine and Scripps-Howard war correspondent. Lucas then wrote a series of exposés in which Lowe charged the Army General Staff with misleading Truman and undermining MacArthur. Lowe's rift with the Pentagon and Harry Vaughan's fall from grace for corruption effectively ended Lowe's public career. He died in Harrison, Maine, on 27 December 1968.

—*Allan R. Millett*

References:

Frank Lowe correspondence file, General George C. Marshall Papers, Marshall Library.

Frank E. Lowe File, President's Secretary's Files, Harry S. Truman Papers, Truman Library.

Lieutenant General M. B. Ridgway to J. R. Beishline, 19 April 1951, General Matthew B. Ridgway Papers, U.S. Army Military History Institute.

Major General Frank E. Lowe service file and biographical data, Reference Division, U.S. Army Center of Military History.

See also: Korea Military Advisory Group (KMAG); Marshall, George C.; Ridgway, Matthew Bunker; Truman, Harry S.

Luxembourg, Grand Duchy of

One of the smallest European nations, covering only 998 square miles, in the later 1940s Luxembourg abandoned its traditional policy of neutrality after enduring German occupation in both world wars. It now looked to an alliance with other Western European nations and the United States to ensure its safety militarily. Luxembourg was a founding member of the Western European Union (1948), the North Atlantic Treaty Organization (NATO) (1949), Benelux (1944), the European Coal and Steel Community (1952), and the European Economic Community (1958).

Like other NATO countries, Luxembourg initially welcomed the June 1950 U.S. decision to support United Nations (UN) intervention in Korea, regarding this as tangible evidence that U.S. military support would be similarly forthcoming in the event of a European crisis. From NATO's initial creation, Luxembourg shared the common anxiety of its European partners that the U.S. military commitment to the alliance was insufficient and that in the event of a European conflict the United States might prove unreliable. Initial fears that the Korean War might divert scarce resources from NATO were allayed by U.S. President Harry S. Truman's increase of U.S. forces permanently stationed in Europe to four divisions, a consequence of the implementation in late 1950 of NSC-68, "United States Objectives and Programs for National Security," which brought a fourfold increase in U.S. defense expenditures and NATO's transformation into a formidably armed defensive organization capable of deterring an attack from the Soviet Union.

Like other U.S. allies, Luxembourg came under pressure to demonstrate Allied solidarity by increasing its own military spending and contributing at least a symbolic number of troops—a requested 100 men—to UN forces fighting in Korea. Luxembourg did so, incorporating its minuscule contingent of one company of troops into the battalion sent by Belgium. From late 1950, Luxembourg joined with its European NATO partners to recommend that the United States follow relatively conciliatory policies in the war, seeking a negotiated peace settlement that would bring hostilities to an end as soon as possible.

—*Priscilla Roberts*

References:

DeVaney, Carl N. "Know Your Allies." *Military Review* 32, no. 12 (December 1953): 11–19.

Hommel, Nicolas. "Luxembourg: From Neutrality to the Atlantic Alliance." *NATO Review* 30, no. 12 (December 1981): 29–33.

Kaplan, Lawrence S. *The United States and NATO: The Formative Years.* Lexington: University Press of Kentucky, 1984.

Newcomer, James. *The Grand Duchy of Luxembourg: The Evolution of Nationhood, 963 A.D. to 1983.* Fort Worth, TX: Texas Christian University Press, 1984.

Trausch, Gilbert. *Le Luxembourg: Emergence d'un État et d'une Nation.* Anvers: Fonds Mercator, 1989.

See also: Belgium; NATO (North Atlantic Treaty Organization); Truman, Harry S.

M

MacArthur, Douglas
(1880–1964)

Supreme commander of United Nations (UN) forces during the Korean War. Douglas MacArthur, son of Civil War hero and career army officer General Arthur MacArthur, was born on 26 January 1880 at Fort Dodge, Arkansas. He spent much of his youth on frontier army posts, where he gained a lifelong love of the military. He attended the U.S. Military Academy at West Point, graduating at the head of his class in 1903. During World War I, MacArthur served in France, where he earned numerous combat decorations and ended the war as a brigadier general commanding an infantry division.

In 1930 MacArthur became army chief of staff. The outbreak of World War II found him in the Philippines where, in 1941, President Franklin Roosevelt appointed him U.S. Far East commander. The news of the Japanese attack on Pearl Harbor stunned MacArthur and sent his command into a stupor. Nine hours after hearing of the sneak attack, his own air force was destroyed on the ground by a Japanese air raid. The Japanese then invaded Luzon, the key island in the Philippine archipelago. MacArthur scrapped the original defense plan, which called for a staged withdrawal to the Bataan peninsula, and spread his command and supply depots over Luzon in order to defend all possible landing sites. This proved a disastrous mistake, as his troops were forced to retreat to Bataan without the large stockpile of supplies originally positioned there. American and Filipino soldiers made a brave but futile stand at Bataan and were eventually overwhelmed by the Japanese. By then MacArthur was in Australia, where Roosevelt had ordered him to take charge of Allied forces in the southwest Pacific. Upon his arrival in Australia, MacArthur electrified the Allied world, then reeling from defeat on all fronts, with his promise to the Filipinos: "The President ordered me to break through enemy lines . . . I came through and I shall return."

During 1943–1944 MacArthur launched a series of coordinated land, sea, and air "tri-phibious" turning movements against Japanese bases in New Guinea. This brilliant campaign, in which his troops suffered very minor casualties in comparison with the bloodletting then going on in the Central Pacific and Europe, brought MacArthur within striking distance of the Philippines. However, President Roosevelt and the Joint Chiefs of Staff (JCS) were not convinced of the need to liberate the Philippines. Some believed that a landing on Formosa would be more profitable as a base for further operations against Japan. But MacArthur convinced Roosevelt that this amounted to an abandonment of the Filipinos and would break America's (actually MacArthur's) solemn vow to return. Roosevelt gave in and MacArthur's forces then landed in and liberated the Philippines. MacArthur presided over the formal Japanese surrender in Tokyo Bay on 2 September 1945.

After the war MacArthur became supreme commander of Allied Powers in Japan. He advocated numerous democratic reforms in the defeated nation and, more than any other individual, created the postwar Japanese state.

When MacArthur took command in Tokyo, he also gained responsibility for the U.S. occupation of South Korea (Korea having been a colony of Japan). Preoccupied with the multitude of problems in postwar Japan, he sent Lieutenant General John Hodge and his XXIV Corps to occupy Korea south of the 38th parallel in accordance with agreements reached with the Russians, who occupied Korea north of the parallel. This decision was made largely because Hodge and his corps were readily available on nearby Okinawa. Unfortunately Hodge, a solid commander in battle, lacked diplomatic skills and had little understanding of Korea or its people. South Korea was plagued with internal turmoil throughout the U.S. occupation, but MacArthur was too busy with Japanese affairs to pay much attention to it, despite repeated pleas from Hodge.

MacArthur's sole trip to Korea during the occupation was on 15 August 1948 to witness the inauguration of the Republic of Korea's (ROK's) first president, Syngman Rhee. After the ceremony, MacArthur assured an anxious Rhee that, in the case of Communist aggression, he would defend Korea "as I would California." This pledge conflicted with later statements made by Truman administration officials in Washington, echoed by MacArthur himself, which excluded Korea from the U.S. defensive perimeter. These public declarations may have given Communist leaders in P'yŏngyang, Beijing, and Moscow the impression that the United States lacked interest in Korea and would not intervene there in the event of a North Korean invasion of South Korea.

In 1948 U.S. occupation troops in South Korea, along with Russian soldiers in the north, withdrew from the peninsula in accordance with a United Nations agreement. The Soviets supplied their North

General Douglas MacArthur addresses a joint session of Congress, 19 April 1951. (National Archives)

Korean allies with an abundance of tanks, heavy artillery, and military aircraft. President Rhee repeatedly pleaded with MacArthur for airplanes and naval vessels, but MacArthur, fearful that they might be used for aggressive purposes, denied the requests. Weapons provided to the ROK military were limited to small arms and light artillery.

By 1950 MacArthur's Far East Command (FEC) was in no shape to fight a war. Drastic cutbacks in the U.S. defense budget had severely reduced its troops and equipment. The four divisions making up the Eighth Army were all severely under strength, each consisting of about 12,800 troops instead of the authorized strength of 18,900. MacArthur had also allowed readiness and training in his command to deteriorate until, after five years of soft occupation duty, it was unfit to engage a determined foe in combat. A U.S. Army study described the FEC on the eve of war as "flabby and soft, still hampered by an infectious lassitude, unready to respond swiftly and decisively to a full-scale emergency."

That emergency came on 25 June 1950 when North Korea launched a full-scale invasion of South Korea. That same day MacArthur dispatched a cargo ship bearing ammunition, with an air and naval escort, to the beleaguered South Koreans, thus establishing U.S. intervention. Two days later President Harry S. Truman approved the use of U.S. air and naval forces south of the 38th parallel, but he gave no authorization for the use of ground troops.

On 29 June MacArthur flew to Korea to view the situation for himself. What he saw there dismayed him. The ROK capital of Seoul had already fallen, and roads were jammed with refugees and troops of the defeated ROK Army (ROKA) heading south. MacArthur observed the fires burning in Seoul to the north and realized that U.S. troops would have to be thrown "into the breach" if South Korea was to be saved. He also envisaged a later amphibious landing, far behind enemy lines, which could offset the enemy's superior numbers and "wrest victory from defeat."

The next day MacArthur, back in Tokyo, received authorization from Washington to utilize limited ground forces to protect the southern port of Pusan, toward which ROK forces were retreating. Washington also authorized MacArthur to use air assets against targets north of the 38th parallel. MacArthur informed Washington that this was not sufficient; U.S. troops would have to be committed in force in order to avert total defeat. President Truman then decided to give MacArthur "full authority to use the ground forces under his command." The United States was now fully committed to war in Asia.

On 8 July Truman formally selected MacArthur to command UN forces in Korea. MacArthur was the obvious candidate for the position, but at least one prescient observer (correspondent James Reston) noted that "diplomacy and a vast concern for the opinions and sensitivities of others are the political qualities essential to his new assignment, and these are precisely the qualities General MacArthur has been accused of lacking in the past."

MacArthur threw Lieutenant General Walton Walker's Eighth Army into battle against the rampaging North Koreans immediately after receiving consent from Washington. Task Force Smith, an ad hoc group of 430 men from the 24th Infantry Division, was rushed to the peninsula ahead of the main U.S. forces in an attempt to slow the North Korean advance. However, the ill-equipped and poorly trained Americans were badly mauled in their first actions against the determined and well-equipped Korean People's Army (KPA, North Korean) and were forced to retreat along with their ROK allies. The Eighth Army was gradually forced back until the only Korean soil under UN control was a perimeter around the vital port of Pusan. Walker was contemplating further withdrawals when, on 27 July, a "grim faced" MacArthur arrived at Eighth Army headquarters and informed Walker and his staff that further retreat would be "unacceptable." Immediately after this conference Walker issued his famous "stand or die" order to the Eighth Army. There would be no American Dunkirk in Korea.

With UN lines stabilized along the Pusan perimeter, the JCS suggested that MacArthur send a senior officer to meet on Formosa with Chinese Nationalist leader Jiang Jieshi (Chiang Kai-shek) to assess Formosa's defenses and inform Jiang that U.S. Navy ships would intercept any Nationalist raids against the People's Republic of China on the mainland. Truman was already concerned about the possibility of Chinese intervention in Korea and was determined not to provoke Beijing over the sensitive issue of Formosa.

The JCS recommended MacArthur not go but left this up to him. MacArthur decide to make the trip himself. A strong advocate of Formosa and convinced of its importance to U.S. defense, MacArthur issued statements following the meeting that seemed to imply Formosan-American military cooperation. Reaction in Washington was swift, as numerous officials made clear to MacArthur the president's intention to keep Formosa neutral.

The matter seemed resolved until, on 20 August, MacArthur sent a letter to the Veterans of Foreign Wars convention in Chicago in which he stridently pleaded the case for U.S. defense of Formosa. Truman, outraged by what he considered to be public defiance of his foreign policy, ordered MacArthur to retract his message. But the damage had already been done. The U.S. press had published the text of the letter amid speculation of a rift between Truman and MacArthur. It was at this time, Truman later recalled, that he first considered relieving the general.

Meanwhile, the situation in Korea remained grave for UN forces, still confined to their defensive positions around Pusan. MacArthur, eschewing a frontal assault to break the stalemate, gave full attention to his scheme for landing U.S. troops deep in the enemy's rear. The plan, christened Operation CHROMITE, called for a two-division (X Corps) amphibious assault on the port of Inch'ŏn, on Korea's west coast twenty miles from Seoul. The invaders would seize the capital, cutting the lines of communication of the KPA, while Eighth Army broke out of the Pusan perimeter. The KPA would be caught and destroyed in a massive pincers movement. But the general had to convince skeptical members of the JCS that the risky plan would work with a minimum of casualties. The plan was bold. Inch'ŏn was less than ideal for an amphibious operation. It had high tides and swift currents and lacked landing beaches (the troops would have to assault the heart of the city over seawalls).

MacArthur acknowledged the difficulties involved and assured his superiors that surprise was guaranteed because the North Koreans would never suspect such a daring operation. "We shall land at Inch'ŏn" he said "and I shall crush them!" The JCS and President Truman finally gave their reluctant approval to Operation CHROMITE, which commenced on 15 September.

MacArthur watched the 1st Marine Division landings from the bridge of the command ship *Mount McKinley*. North Korean resistance was light as the Marines seized Inch'ŏn. MacArthur had been correct; the Koreans were taken by surprise, and U.S. casualties were light. U.S. and ROKA troops then moved to capture Seoul while the bulk of Communist forces, far to the south, disintegrated and fled northward following the breakout of the Eighth Army from the Pusan perimeter. The landings had worked brilliantly, just as

MacArthur had predicted. It was the high point of his career, and a dangerous aura of invincibility now surrounded the general.

On 26 September UN forces recaptured Seoul, and three days later MacArthur presided over the ceremony reinstating President Rhee's government in the capital. MacArthur's forces were now on the 38th parallel, where he held them in check. He favored pursuing KPA troops into North Korea, but the popular myth that he ordered troops across the parallel on his own authority is totally false.

In the wake of military success, Washington and the UN were overly optimistic. President Truman decided, and the UN resolved, that United Nations Command (UNC) forces should enter North Korea, destroy remaining Communist forces, and reunite the peninsula under a democratic government. MacArthur was given this fateful directive by the JCS on 27 September. He was warned, however, not to allow non-ROK forces to enter any of the northern provinces bordering China. On 1 October ROK troops crossed the parallel. Two days later, the Chinese issued a warning, largely ignored in Washington, that U.S. troops entering North Korea would "encounter Chinese resistance." Chinese troops began secretly entering North Korea on 14 October.

Supremely confident, MacArthur unwisely split his forces, sending X Corps to land (unopposed it turned out) on the east coast at Wŏnsan and Iwŏn, while Eighth Army drove north toward P'yŏngyang, which fell on 19 October. The two forces were dangerously divided by the rugged T'aebaek mountains and could not come to each other's aid if an emergency arose.

On 15 October MacArthur met with President Truman (their first and only meeting) on Wake Island. They met with members of the JCS and discussed a wide array of topics. These were seemingly chosen at random, since there was no set agenda for the conference, which lasted less than two hours. MacArthur was asked if he thought Chinese intervention likely. He responded negatively and assured everyone present that even if the Chinese did enter the conflict there would be "the greatest slaughter" of Chinese troops. MacArthur and Truman then departed, smiling for reporters and seemingly in agreement about the progress of the war. Flying back to his headquarters in Tokyo that same day, MacArthur grumbled that the meeting had been a mere political junket in which the president was trying to bask in the reflected glow of the successful general. Paranoid as always, he feared that the Wake meeting had been a political ambush in which his comments would be used against him if things turned sour in Korea.

On 24 October MacArthur, ignoring the JCS directive forbidding non-ROK troops to enter the provinces

along the Yalu River, ordered all his forces north. The JCS remonstrated briefly, then relented. The next day Chinese forces struck several UNC units without warning, inflicting heavy casualties before mysteriously withdrawing back into the rugged mountains. MacArthur chose to ignore this evidence of Chinese intervention, or disregard it as a mere warning from Beijing. He ordered his commanders forward.

Throughout November, UNC forces made contact with numerous Chinese forces, but the general again chose to ignore or downplay the threat. On 24 November he launched the final UNC drive which, he told reporters, would "get the boys home by Christmas." The next day some 180,000 Chinese troops struck the Eighth Army; On 27 November X Corps was attacked by another 120,000. UN forces, divided by the T'aebaek mountains, were forced into full retreat. Troops of X Corps were surrounded near the Changjin (Chosin) Reservoir and compelled to break out southward toward the port of Wŏnsan, suffering heavy casualties in the process. With his forces in full retreat, MacArthur informed Washington that "we face an entirely new war."

This brought another test of wills with Washington. MacArthur demanded that restrictions on the bombing of Yalu bridges be lifted. Washington gave way, but the attacks, restricted to the Korean ends of the bridges, were largely ineffective in stopping the Chinese. MacArthur, stung by press criticism, lashed out at Washington, blaming restrictions placed on his forces as the reason for the UN disaster. On 5 December Truman issued directives, obviously aimed at MacArthur, ordering government officials to use "extreme caution" when making public statements and to have all public statements cleared by Washington before release to the press.

On 29 December MacArthur received a new directive from Washington informing him that the original goal of Korean unification was being scrapped. "Korea," the general was told, "is not the place to fight a major war." MacArthur railed at what he regarded as the loss of fighting spirit in Washington. He responded with his own demands for a naval blockade of China, air and naval bombardment of the Chinese mainland, and utilization of Nationalist troops from Formosa. He informed the JCS that if these demands were turned down, then defeat and evacuation were the only alternatives for UN forces. But MacArthur would be proven wrong again, this time by the new ground commander of the Eighth Army, the resourceful and aggressive Lieutenant General Matthew Ridgway, who had taken command following General Walker's death in a jeep accident. Ridgway stabilized UN lines south of the 38th parallel and even launched counterattacks against the Chinese. No evacuation would be necessary. The luster MacArthur had gathered at Inch'ŏn was now badly tarnished.

Increasingly disturbed by the stalemate in Korea and Washington's restrictions, MacArthur issued a statement that violated Truman's directive, predicting a "savage slaughter" and further stalemate if his methods for waging war were not adopted. The press dubbed it the "Die for Tie" statement. No rebuke came from Washington. On 24 March MacArthur effectively torpedoed a peace initiative from Washington to the Chinese when he insulted the Communists' ability to wage war and called upon the Chinese to admit defeat. This open defiance convinced Truman that the general had to go. As if to seal the decision, MacArthur sent an inflammatory letter to House Minority Leader Joseph Martin in which he again savaged U.S. foreign policy. The policy rift between MacArthur and Truman was now making world headlines. Truman believed he had to act. On 11 April MacArthur, in Tokyo, received the news that he had been relieved of all his commands. He turned to his wife and said simply, "Jeannie, we're going home at last" (he had not been to America in fourteen years).

MacArthur returned to a tumultuous welcome, enjoying ticker-tape parades through cities across America. He addressed a joint session of Congress, but, despite an epic speech, he refused to simply fade away. He testified at the Congressional investigation of his dismissal and there again attacked Truman administration policies in Asia. He toured the country in full uniform, giving shrill, often extremist, speeches at every stop. But gradually he lost his following among the public and a chance at a run for the presidency.

In 1952 MacArthur met with President-Elect Dwight D. Eisenhower and presented a plan for victory in Korea. It called for, among other things, the creation of a radioactive wasteland across the peninsula near the Yalu River to stem the Chinese flow of men and supplies. Eisenhower tucked the plan in his pocket, thanked MacArthur politely, and simply forgot about the odd proposal.

MacArthur spent his remaining years quietly, living with his wife in New York City's Waldorf Hotel. He visited briefly with Presidents John Kennedy and Lyndon Johnson, urging both to avoid war in Asia at all costs. MacArthur died on 3 April 1964 at Walter Reed Hospital in Washington, D.C. He is buried in Norfolk, Virginia.

—Duane L. Wesolick

References:

Blair, Clay. *The Forgotten War: America in Korea, 1950–1953.* New York: Times Books, 1987.

———. *MacArthur.* New York: Times Books, 1977.

Hastings, Max. *The Korean War.* New York: Simon & Schuster, 1987.

James, D. Clayton. *The Years of MacArthur.* Vol. 3, *Triumph and Disaster, 1945–1964.* Boston: Houghton Mifflin, 1985.

MacArthur, Douglas. *Reminiscences.* New York: McGraw-Hill, 1964.

Manchester, William. *American Caesar: Douglas MacArthur, 1880–1964.* Boston: Little, Brown, 1978.

Rovere, Richard, and Arthur Schlesinger. *The General and the President, and the Future of American Foreign Policy.* New York: Farrar, Straus & Young, 1951.

Schaller, Michael. *Douglas MacArthur: Far Eastern General.* New York: Oxford University Press, 1989.

Taafe, Stephen. *MacArthur's Jungle War: The 1944 New Guinea Campaign.* Lawrence: University Press of Kansas, 1998.

See also: China, Republic of; Eighth United States Army; Far East Command (FEC); Hodge, John R.; Inch'ŏn Landings: Operation CHROMITE; Jiang Jieshi (Chiang Kai-shek); Joint Chiefs of Staff (JCS); MacArthur Hearings; Martin, Joseph W.; Pusan Perimeter and Breakout; Ridgway, Matthew Bunker; Syngman Rhee; Task Force Smith; Tenth Corps; 38th parallel, Decision to Cross; Truman, Harry S.; Truman's Cease-Fire Initiative; Truman's Recall of MacArthur; United Nations Command (UNC); Wake Island Conference; Walker, Walton Harris; Yalu Bridges Controversy.

MacArthur Hearings
(3 May–25 June 1951)

Hearings by U.S. Senate Foreign Relations and Armed Services Committees to inquire into General Douglas MacArthur's removal from command and President Harry S. Truman's Far East policy.

MacArthur's removal in April 1951 caused a storm of public outrage in the United States, leading several state legislatures to condemn this action. Longtime critics of President Truman's China policy and old-guard Republicans demanded a congressional investigation. The Democrats, who controlled the Senate, established a joint committee and named Senator Richard B. Russell of Georgia the chairman. Republican senators wanted the hearings broadcast over radio and television, but the Democrats secured closed hearings and the daily issuance of censored transcripts to protect classified information. The twenty-six senators on the two committees were permitted to ask questions in order of their seniority, resulting in the duplication of questions, which produced a hodgepodge of testimony in no particular order.

The first witness on 3 May was General MacArthur himself. He testified for three days. The Democrats treated him with great deference but asked questions to show his variance with administration policy. MacArthur's testimony was an amplification of his 19 April speech to Congress arguing for a complete military victory over China. He stated that his forces could have stopped the Chinese at the end of 1950 had he been allowed to bomb Manchurian bases. He also stated that his proposals of 24 March 1951 would have resulted in the defeat of the Chinese had he been allowed to execute them. These proposals were a naval blockade of China, naval attacks on Chinese coastal industrial sites, dispatch of Chinese Nationalist troops to Korea, and the insertion of Nationalist guerrillas along the coast of mainland China. MacArthur denied that the Soviet Union would enter an expanded war, and he wanted the United States to defeat China despite Allied opposition to such a course.

Senator Brien McMahon of Connecticut told MacArthur that he had been wrong about Chinese intervention in Korea and asked if he could also be wrong about Soviet intervention. If the Soviets intervened, Senator McMahon asked, how could the United States defend itself? MacArthur replied that it was not his responsibility to determine defense needs, as he was only a theater commander. McMahon replied that MacArthur had made the point that he wanted to make: that the president and his advisers had to look at the Korean War from a global viewpoint. McMahon pointed out that MacArthur, as a theater commander, lacked knowledge of worldwide defense needs and was not in a position to know the ramifications of expanding the war into China.

MacArthur professed not to understand why he was relieved or why his 24 March ultimatum to the Chinese, threatening an attack on China proper, would cause problems for Truman while the president was trying to secure a negotiated settlement. He blamed politicians for causing the stalemate by exercising control over strategic decisions, such as bombing Manchuria, that should best be left to military professionals. MacArthur stated that he and the Joint Chiefs of Staff (JCS) were in full agreement on policy, and it was President Truman and his secretary of state who had made it impossible to win the war.

After MacArthur finished testifying, six administration witness refuted his testimony. These included Secretary of Defense George C. Marshall, Chairman of the Joint Chiefs of Staff General Omar N. Bradley, Army Chief of Staff General J. Lawton Collins, Air Force Chief of Staff General Hoyt C. Vandenberg, Chief of Naval Operations Admiral Forrest P. Sherman, Secretary of State Dean G. Acheson, and State Department Legal Counsel Adrian S. Fisher. Marshall testified that MacArthur's policy risked a world war and the loss of Allied support, while Sherman believed that a naval blockade would be difficult to maintain with the British and Soviets controlling three Chinese ports. Vandenberg said the United States would have to double the size of its strategic bombing force to be able to bomb China effectively. But Bradley was the most powerful critic of MacArthur's desire to attack China. He asserted that war with China would be the "wrong war, at the wrong place, at the wrong time, and with the wrong enemy."

On the issue of MacArthur and the JCS agreeing on military policy, all the witnesses contradicted MacArthur's statement that their message of 12 January 1951 supported his desire for total victory. The JCS proposed a naval blockade and aerial reconnaissance of China and removal of restrictions on the Nationalists, contingent on the near-defeat of United Nations forces. This JCS proposal had never been approved as policy.

With regard to MacArthur's insubordination, Marshall cited six occasions when the general had failed to secure approval for public statements as directed by the president. Collins related how MacArthur had disregarded a directive that he send only South Korean troops near the Chinese border along the Yalu River.

Acheson was quizzed mainly on the administration's China policy. Afraid that the senators' questions would not make administration policy clear, Acheson presented a prepared statement. His argument was that the United States did not "lose" China; the corruption of Jiang Jieshi's (Chiang Kai-shek's) administration and the generalissimo's failure to broaden the base of the government caused internal collapse. Acheson argued that there was no connection between the Yalta Agreements and the Communist victory in China.

Last to testify were supporters of Republican critics of Far East policy, but even they opposed MacArthur's desire to expand the war. General Albert C. Wedemeyer remarked that it was better to withdraw from Korea than to broaden the war.

On 17 August 1951 the committee decided to send the transcript of the hearings to the Senate without a majority or minority report but allowed committee members to append their concluding statements if they so desired. Eight old-guard Republican senators stated that MacArthur's removal was not justified and that Truman's foreign policy was disastrous. By this time the political passions aroused by MacArthur's dismissal had subsided.

—*John L. Bell*

References:

Acheson, Dean. *Present at the Creation: My Years at the State Department.* New York: W. W. Norton, 1969.

Bradley, Omar N., and Clay Blair. *A General's Life: An Autobiography.* New York: Simon & Schuster, 1983.

James, D. Clayton. *The Years of MacArthur: Triumph and Disaster, 1945–1964.* Boston: Houghton Mifflin, 1985.

Kaufman, Burton I. *The Korean War: Challenges in Crisis, Credibility, and Command.* Philadelphia: Temple University Press, 1986.

U.S. Senate Committee on Armed Services and the Committee on Foreign Relations. *Inquiry into the Military Situation in the Far East and the Facts Surrounding the Relief of General of the*

Army Douglas MacArthur from His Assignments in That Area. 82d Cong., 1st sess. Washington, DC: U.S. Government Printing Office, 1951.

See also: Acheson, Dean Goodersham; Bradley, Omar Nelson; Collins, Joseph Lawton; Jiang Jieshi (Chiang Kai-shek); Joint Chiefs of Staff (JCS); MacArthur, Douglas; Marshall, George C.; Sherman, Forrest P.; Truman, Harry S.; Vandenberg, Hoyt S.

Machine Guns

Automatic weapons generally classified as "light," one-man weapons issued in standard rifle calibers; "medium," often requiring a crew; and "heavy," fitted to heavier mounts and ranging from rifle calibers to .50 caliber or higher. Both United Nations (UN) and Communist forces issued large numbers of machine guns deployed in a variety of roles: ground, armored, aircraft, and antiaircraft.

No entirely new machine gun designs saw service in Korea. Most were veterans of World War II, and significant numbers of weapons bore World War I–era dates of manufacture. Their Korean War experiences, however, led participant nations to renew machine gun development in the early 1950s. Their efforts led to such innovations as the more versatile, general-purpose machine guns that appeared soon after the war.

Although the various UN contingents (notably the United Kingdom) issued their own weapons, most relied on the United States for the majority of their machine gun issues. The Chinese and North Koreans found it expedient to field examples of virtually any machine guns used prior to 1950. These included Japanese weapons captured by the Soviets in Manchuria and U.S. and Chinese weapons abandoned by the Chinese Nationalists during China's civil war. Communist ordnance stores thus included a bewildering variety of captured U.S. .30- and .50-caliber machine guns, World War II Japanese 6.5-mm, 7.7-mm, 12.7-mm, and 13.2-mm weapons, as well as

Machine guns in action against Communist forces defending the central Korean front, 22 February 1951. (National Archives)

German 7.92-mm MG34s and MG42s. Later in the conflict the Communists also issued thousands of machine guns that were either of Soviet manufacture or Chinese copies of Soviet designs.

U.S. forces and most of their UN allies fielded light and medium company and battalion-level machine guns that used the standard .30-06 U.S. rifle cartridge. The U.S. Browning water-cooled Model 1917Al and air-cooled Models 1919A4 and A6 machine guns saw extensive service in Korea. They were not only the standard U.S. infantry machine gun but were so ubiquitous that they can be considered at least substitute standard for their allies and, when captured, by the Communists as well. Designed by prolific weapons innovator John Browning, all three weapons had won fame in World War II, the M1917Al also claiming World War I service.

Other than their cooling systems, the Brownings are virtually identical in their method of operation. They are recoil-operated, belt-fed weapons, the 1917Al achieving 450–600 rpm; the 1919A4, 400–550 rpm; and the 1919A6, 400–500 rpm. The M1917Al weighs 41 pounds with water and was typically mounted on the 53.15-pound M1917Al tripod. The 31-pound Model 1919A4 served as an antiaircraft weapon and, in fixed mode, aboard tanks and other armored vehicles. Fitted to the 16.22-pound M2 tripod, the M1919A4 joined the M1919A6 as the most widely used Allied infantry machine guns in Korea. The 32.5-pound Model 1919A6 was fitted with a shoulder stock, carrying handle, and bipod for ground use. Belgium's Fabrique Nationale d'Armes de Guerre also manufactured large numbers of the .30-caliber Browning, supplying them to the Belgian government as well as other nations.

Few weapons approach the reputation and versatility of the Browning .50-caliber M2 machine gun series. The basic M2 evolved from a World War I John Browning prototype mated with a Winchester-designed cartridge. Early models were water cooled, but soon after their introduction an air-cooled version appeared for aircraft use. These models were soon joined by a heavier-barreled M2 that was capable of longer sustained fire. The air-cooled M2 weighs 65 pounds, 2 ounces and is capable of 800 rpm, whereas the M2HB (heavy barrel) weighs 84 pounds and fires at 500 rpm.

Very similar in appearance to the .30-caliber Browning, the M2 heavy machine gun proved itself in both aircraft and antiaircraft roles during World War II. The M2 is a recoil-operated, belt-fed weapon that saw service in Korea aboard tanks and other armored vehicles, and aircraft—most notably the F-86 Sabre. It could also be tripod mounted in an infantry role. The antiaircraft M2HB saw considerable success as a heavy ground-support weapon when fired from the

M45 quad mount. Its massive firepower proved a devastating counter to Chinese "human-wave" attacks.

The British Vickers Machine Gun Mark I closely rivals the Browning designs in longevity of service and popularity among the troops who manned it. The Mark I was adopted in 1912 and manufactured in both England and Australia. It served the British Commonwealth until being declared obsolete in 1968. The Mark I, when mounted on the Mark IVB tripod, served as the standard heavy infantry machine gun for Commonwealth troops. It also proved its versatility in naval, aircraft, antiaircraft, tank, and other armored vehicle roles.

The belt-fed, water-cooled Vickers is capable of automatic fire only, achieving a cyclic rate of 450–550 rpm. A modified Maxim design utilizing a gas-assisted recoil system of operation, the Mark I was issued with either smooth or corrugated water jackets. It is chambered for the standard British .303-caliber rimmed rifle cartridge.

Although relatively heavy at 90 pounds (unloaded with tripod), slow firing (450 rpm), and prone to misfeeds owing to its rimmed cartridge, the Vickers nevertheless commanded the loyalty of its crews. Other than its cartridge problems, the weapon itself was well designed and constructed. Most importantly, it was reliable under the harshest conditions.

Commonwealth tank and other armored vehicle machine guns included the U.S. .30-caliber Browning Machine Gun, and the 7.92-mm Besa Machine Gun. The Besa was based on a pre–World War II Czech design and chambers the German 7.92-mm rimless service cartridge. The Besas, in Marks 1, 2, 2*, 3, and 3* are gas-operated, belt-fed weapons featuring adjustable cyclic rates. The Besa was particularly highly regarded by its crews for its high rate of fire (low: 450–550 rpm; high: 750–850 rpm) and long-range accuracy.

Still recovering from World War II, France issued a hodgepodge of domestic and foreign machine guns, primarily U.S. .30-caliber Brownings, but also British Brens and Vickers, as well as World War II German 7.92-mm MG34s and MG42s. The 27.48-pound French 7.5-mm Model 1931A tank and fortress machine gun was developed before World War II. Its design is based on the famous Browning Automatic Rifle; it is gas-operated and capable of automatic fire only. The M1931A achieves an impressive rate of sustained fire at 750 rpm owing to its heavy barrel. After World War II, the M1931A was adapted to either the 32.15-pound French M1945 tripod or the 16.22-pound U.S. M2 tripod for infantry use. It also saw use as a fixed tank and armored vehicle machine gun. The Model 1931A accepts either a box or side-mounted 150-round drum magazine.

Fighting with the 2d Infantry Division north of the Chongchon River, a weapons squad leader points out the North Korean position to his machine gun crew, 20 November 1950. (National Archives)

Communist forces tended to rely heavily on captured U.S. and Japanese ordnance early in the war, later replacing those weapons lost to attrition with Soviet, Soviet-captured, and Chinese copies of Soviet machine guns. In short, as with many armies of guerrilla origin, the Communists used what was available, regardless of condition or quality.

Owing to their ready availability, many types of Japanese machine guns saw Communist service in Korea. These most probably included the 6.5-mm Taisho 3, Taisho 11, Type 91, and Type 96, as well as the 7.7-mm Type 92, Type 97 and Type 99. Other weapons included the 7.92-mm Type 98, a copy of the German MG15 and the .303 Type 89, a copy of the British Vickers. The 13.2-mm Type 93 was the standard Japanese heavy-caliber machine gun—a dramatic contrast to the diminutive reduced-power training machine guns that were also pressed into emergency service.

These Japanese weapons presented a host of logistical liabilities. Although the weapons were relatively plentiful, ammunition proved scarce. Both the Chinese and the North Koreans found it necessary to

manufacture new cartridges for them—a daunting task, considering the wide variety of Japanese service calibers. To compound the ammunition problem, most World War II Japanese machine guns can best be characterized as somewhat eccentric in design.

The Type 92 is representative of most Japanese machine guns. It is a modified French Hotchkiss design and saw wide use in World War II as well as in Korea. The Type 92's advantages—it was well made and was capable of accepting both the 7.7-mm semi-rimless Type 92 round and the Type 99 rimless round—were more than offset by its flaws. The Type 92 weighed a heavy 122 pounds unloaded with tripod and fired at a slow 450-rpm cyclic rate. Furthermore, its strip-fed ammunition required oiling before loading to facilitate extraction—a cause of frequent jamming under dusty or other adverse conditions. Still, expediency dictated the Type 92's continued use throughout the war.

As existing stocks of weapons became depleted, the Soviet Union stepped in to replace them with machine guns from its own considerable stocks of domestic and captured weapons. Early Soviet machine guns were based on Maxim designs. These include the water-cooled Model 1910 Maxim (SPM), the air-cooled Maxim Tokarev, and the Maxim Koleshnikov. All are belt-fed, recoil-operated weapons chambered for the rimmed Russian 7.62-mm rifle cartridge. The Model 1910 was mounted on the Sokolov two-wheeled carriage, and the Tokarev and Koleshnikov were fitted with bipods for infantry use. Their cyclic rate was 500–600 rpm. The 7.62-mm Goryunov SG43 replaced the Maxim M1910 as the Soviet battalion-level and armored vehicle machine gun. It is gas-operated and fed by either a 250-round drum or belt. It has a cyclic rate of 600–700 rpm.

—*Jeff Kinard*

References:

Hobart, F. W. A. *Pictorial History of the Machine Gun.* London: Ian Allan, 1971.

Hogg, Ian, and John Weeks. *Military Small Arms of the Twentieth Century.* Chicago: Follett, 1973.

Smith, W. H. B. *Small Arms of the World.* Harrisburg, PA: Stackpole Books, 1969.

See also: Small Arms (Pistols, Rifles, Submachine Guns, Automatic Weapons).

Makin, Norman J. O.
(1889–1982)

Australian ambassador to the United States, 1946–1951. Born on 31 March 1889, in Petersham, Sydney, Norman J. O. Makin was educated at Broken Hill Public School. In 1919 he entered public life as a member of the federal parliament representing the Australian Labour Party and remained there until 1946. From 1929 he was speaker of the House of Representatives, and from 1941 to 1946 he served in the Australian war cabinet and the advisory war council as minister for the navy and munitions.

In 1946, when Australia's Washington legation was upgraded to an embassy, Makin became his country's first ambassador to the United States. He also led the Australian delegation at the United Nations (UN), was elected to the first UN Security Council in 1946, and served as the latter's first president. Although Australia's Labour government was defeated in the general election of December 1949, the successor Conservative administration of Robert Menzies did not replace Makin until May 1951.

Makin's major contribution during the Korean War was to push for the conclusion of a regional security pact between the United States and Australia, which came to fruition in 1951 with the ANZUS (Australia–New Zealand–U.S.) Treaty. In late June 1950 he reported to his superiors in Canberra that, since U.S. officials were grateful for Australia's speedy support over Korea, this was an appropriate time to press the United States to conclude such an arrangement.

As with other Australian officials, Makin expressed his country's reservations over aspects of U.S. policy on the war. In late 1950 he communicated to U.S. leaders Australian concerns that, in retaliation for the People's Republic of China (PRC, Communist China) intervention in Korea, the United States might respond in such a way as to broaden and escalate the conflict. During and after British Prime Minister Clement Attlee's December 1950 visit to the United States, Makin laid out his own country's reservations on any potential U.S. use of atomic weapons in the war, views that essentially resembled those of Attlee.

In late 1950 Makin discussed with U.S. officials suggestions by Australian Minister for External Affairs Percy C. Spender that the United States might withdraw its recognition of Jiang Jieshi's (Chiang Kai-shek's) Nationalist Guomindang government of Taiwan to obtain a peace settlement with the PRC. In February 1951 Makin also warned the U.S. State Department of Australia's fears that, as the tide of war turned again in Korea, UN forces might repeat their earlier mistake of crossing the 38th parallel and pushing far north into Korea. Although U.S. officials tended to resent and sometimes ignored such warnings and suggestions from their allies, such caveats did exercise a restraining influence on the more extreme U.S. policymakers.

Makin left Washington in May 1951 and returned to politics, sitting in the House of Representatives from 1954 until he retired in 1964. He died in Glenelg on 20 July 1982.

—*Priscilla Roberts*

References:

Barclay, John St. J. *Friends in High Places: Australian-American Diplomatic Relations.* Melbourne: Oxford University Press, 1985.

Bridge, Carl, ed. *Munich to Vietnam: Australia's Relations with Britain and the United States Since the 1930s.* Melbourne: Melbourne University Press, 1991.

Harper, Norman. *A Great and Powerful Friend: A Study of Australian American Relations between 1900 and 1975.* St. Lucia: Queensland University Press, 1987.

McIntyre, W. David. *Background to the Anzus Pact: Policy-Making, Strategy, and Diplomacy, 1945–55.* New York: St. Martin's Press, 1995.

O'Neill, Robert J. *Australia in the Korean War, 1950–1953.* 2 vols. Canberra: Australian War Memorial/Australian Government Publication Service, 1981, 1985.

See also: ANZUS (Australia–New Zealand–U.S.) Treaty; Attlee; Clement R.; Australia; Jiang Jieshi (Chiang Kai-shek); Menzies, Robert G.; Spender, Sir Percy C.

Makins, Sir Roger Mellor
(1904–)

British career diplomat and deputy undersecretary of state for Foreign Affairs, 1948–1952; and British ambassador to the United States, 1953–1956. Born in London on 3 February 1904, Roger Mellor Makins was educated at Christ Church College, Oxford, where he won first-class honors in history. He was called to the bar in 1927 and joined the Foreign Office the following year. His first overseas posting was to Washington, where he married the daughter of Senator Dwight F. Davis and began the earliest of what would be many close ties with numerous influential and prominent Americans.

For the rest of his career Makins remained one of the strongest British advocates of a close Anglo-American relationship, which he considered should be the essential keystone of British foreign policy. This outlook, which he saw as a means of ensuring Britain's status as the "third world power," informed all his subsequent professional activities. During the 1930s Makins also served in Norway and the League of Nations, and in the Second World War he spent 1943 to 1945 in northwest Africa in various staff capacities for the resident minister, Harold Macmillan, who described Makins as "never satisfied with second best." Makins's tireless work, enormous competence, intellectual brilliance, and economic ability all won great respect.

Makins spent 1945–1947 as minister at the British embassy in Washington, focusing particularly on economic issues and atomic energy; he also undertook much public relations work explaining British policies publicly and privately to Americans, an enterprise in which his U.S. connections and knowledge were especially valuable. In 1948 Makins returned to the Foreign Office as deputy undersecretary of state, where he concentrated once more on economic issues, especially the implementation of the European Recovery Plan.

As a career official Makins remained in place when in autumn of 1951 the Conservatives ousted Clement Attlee's Labour government. He gave politicians of both parties advice that consistently reflected his well-matured view—shared by a number of influential senior civil servants—that Britain should remain an important international force, active in Commonwealth, European, and world affairs, and that to do so it needed U.S. support.

Makins' political superiors, whether Labour or Conservative, generally concurred in his arguments that they must persuade inexperienced U.S. officials not to overreact in Korea while neglecting the European interests that he considered a higher priority. Makins accompanied Prime Minister Clement Attlee on his December 1950 visit to the United States, when the prime minister demurred at the use of atomic weapons, suggested U.S. conciliation of China, and urged the speedy opening of armistice talks, points the British continued to put forward for the remainder of the war.

In 1953 Makins replaced Oliver Franks as British ambassador in Washington, when the Korean armistice negotiations were in their final months, and as the settlement's multifarious details were determined, he worked closely with the Eisenhower administration. Throughout his four-year ambassadorship he attempted to alleviate those difficulties in the Anglo-American relationship that were created or at least enhanced by often-tactless U.S. Secretary of State John Foster Dulles.

On returning to Britain in 1956, Makins became joint permanent secretary of the treasury, and on his retirement in 1959 spent five years as chairman of Britain's Atomic Energy Authority. In 1964 Makins was ennobled as Lord Sherfield. From 1966 to 1970 he chaired the Hill Samuel Group, and from 1974 to 1979 he was Warden of Winchester College Oxford. Makins held numerous directorships and served in various capacities on many public bodies.

—*Priscilla Roberts*

References:

Butler, Rohan, and M. E. Pelly, eds. *Documents on British Policy Overseas. Series II,* Vol. 4, *Korea, 1950–1951.* London: Her Majesty's Stationery Office, 1995.

Edwards, Jill. "Roger Makins: 'Mr. Atom.'" In *British Officials and British Foreign Policy, 1945–50,* edited by John Zametica. Leicester: Leicester University Press, 1990.

Lowe, Peter. *Containing the Cold War in East Asia: British Policies toward Japan, China and Korea, 1948–1953.* Manchester: Manchester University Press, 1997.

MacDonald, Callum A. *Britain and the Korean War.* Oxford: Blackwell, 1990.

Stueck, William W., Jr. *The Korean War: An International History.* Princeton, NJ: Princeton University Press, 1990.

See also: Attlee, Clement R.; Bevin, Ernest; Churchill, Sir Winston Spencer; Eden, Anthony; United Kingdom (UK).

Malenkov, Georgii Maximilianovich (1902–1988)

Soviet political leader who initiated diplomatic moves to end the Korean war, 1952–1953, and premier of the USSR, 1953–1955. Born on 8 January 1902 in Orenberg, Georgii Malenkov joined the Bolshevik Party in 1920. After working in the Organizational Bureau (Orgburo) of the Central Committee between 1925 and 1930, Malenkov became secretary of the Moscow Orgburo. Using his control over personnel dossiers, Malenkov established a power base within the Moscow Party organization, and in 1939 he became a member of the Central Committee.

Despite close ties to Soviet Security Ministers Nikolai Yezhov and Lavrentii Beria, and deep involvement in the 1930s "Great Terror," Malenkov was perhaps the most pacific of Stalin's inner circle with regard to foreign policy. After the Soviet dictator died on 5 March 1953, Malenkov emerged at the head of the new "collective leadership" and quickly moved to initiate peace talks in Korea. On 15 March, the Soviet government offered to obtain the release of British and French citizens seized by the Democratic People's Republic of Korea (DPRK, North Korea) at the outset of the conflict. On 28 March, presumably under Soviet prompting, the North Korean regime rendered a favorable response to the United Nations proposal to exchange sick and wounded prisoners of war. Two days later Chinese Foreign Minister Zhou Enlai returned to Beijing after attending Stalin's funeral and proposed truce negotiations.

It is unlikely that this policy of accord was of Malenkov's devising; the Soviet "peace offensive" began in the autumn of 1952. Malenkov presented a commanding front as a politician, yet he followed policy more often than he created it. Ruthless in internal affairs, he was charitable in foreign affairs and is often credited with helping end the Greek civil war in 1948–1949. It was Malenkov who delivered the keynote address at the Nineteenth Communist Party of the Soviet Union (CPSU) Congress in October 1952 that announced the USSR's peaceful diplomatic intentions in Korea.

Ironically, Malenkov probably played a key role in persuading the Chinese to intervene in Korea as well. He met Mao Zedong during the latter's 1949–1950 visit to Moscow, and scholars believe that Malenkov visited Beijing in autumn 1950 regarding the Chinese intervention across the Yalu River.

In his speech at the Nineteenth CPSU Congress, Malenkov spoke of the U.S. "attack on the Korean People's Republic." In 1951 he participated in Stalin's "war cabinet" along with Beria, Andrei Zhdanov, and Viacheslav Molotov—all hard-line Stalinists. Yet as premier of the USSR during 1953–1955, he reduced the defense budget in favor of consumer goods and incentives for collective farmers.

By 1955 Malenkov had lost in the struggle to succeed Stalin. His involvement in the purges of the 1930s and the Leningrad Affair of 1948–1949, his ties to Yezhov and Beria, and his refusal to retreat from Stalinist tactics isolated him in the Soviet Politburo. In June 1957, Malenkov was ousted for plotting, along with Molotov and other hard-liners, to replace Nikita Khrushchev as premier. He became the director of a hydroelectric station in Kazakhstan and retired in 1964. His membership in the CPSU was revoked in 1964. Malenkov died in Moscow, unrepentant, on 14 January 1988.

—*Timothy C. Dowling*

References:
Ebon, Martin. *Malenkov: Stalin's Successor.* New York: McGraw-Hill, 1953.
MacDonald, Callum. *Korea: The War Before Vietnam.* New York: Free Press, 1986.
Medvedev, Roy. *All Stalin's Men.* Garden City, NY: Anchor Press/Doubleday, 1984.
See also: Mao Zedong; Molotov, Viacheslav Mikhailovich; Stalin, Josef; Union of Soviet Socialist Republics; Zhou Enlai.

Malik, Jacob (Iakov) Alexandrovich (1906–1980)

Soviet diplomat and representative to the United Nations (UN) during the first years of the Korean War. Born in 1906 in Kharkov, Jacob (Iakov) Alexandrovich Malik was in 1925 accepted to the Kharkov Institute of Economics. He graduated in 1930 and then continued his studies at the Institute for Diplomatic and Consular Officials. In 1937 he began his diplomatic career as a member of the Press Department of the People's Commissariat for Foreign Affairs. In 1939 Malik was appointed to the Soviet Embassy in Japan, and in 1942 he became Soviet ambassador to Japan. In August 1946 Malik became deputy minister for foreign affairs, and in 1948 he became the representative of the USSR to the UN.

As with other Soviet diplomats, Malik did not have much room to express any personal initiative while at the UN. He was expected to closely follow the orders of Soviet Leader Josef Stalin. Thus on 13 January 1950, on Moscow's orders, Malik walked out of the Security Council to protest the UN refusal to seat the People's Republic of China (PRC, Communist China) in place of Nationalist China on Taiwan. This action indicated that Soviet officials perceived a demonstrative stand in support of China as being more important than their participation in the council's work.

The absence of a Soviet representative on the Security Council definitely played into the hands of Western powers, as it allowed them to control its sessions and made UN intervention in Korea possible. There is little doubt that, had he been present at the council proceedings, Malik would have exercised his right of veto. U.S. Secretary of State Dean G. Acheson later characterized Malik's absence as a "long helpful Russian boycott...."

Moscow finally thought it appropriate to return to the Security Council in August when it was Malik's turn to preside. Earlier that summer the other ten members of the council decided at an informal meeting that if the Soviet boycott continued, they would pass the presidency of the council to the United Kingdom, the next member in alphabetical order. However, on 27 July Malik indicated that he would return to the council on 1 August and preside over its meetings.

Malik's presidency that month made the sessions frustrating and unfruitful. Some of the issues he brought to the Security Council included recognition of the representative of the PRC and "peaceful settlement of the Korean question."

Procedural issues dominated the thirteen Security Council meetings under Malik's presidency. The outspokenly anti-American Malik also condemned the United States for "aggression" in Korea and for making the UN an instrument of U.S. foreign policy.

At the end of May 1951, at the Truman administration's initiative, U.S. diplomat George F. Kennan met with Malik to discuss the possibility of a resolution of the Korean conflict. During their second meeting in early June, Malik spoke of Soviet interest in a ceasefire in Korea, noting that the U.S. should work directly with the Democratic People's Republic of Korea (DPRK, North Korea) and the PRC, as the Soviet Union was not a belligerent. Then, in a UN address on 23 June 1951, Malik suggested that the two warring sides discuss an armistice based on the 38th parallel, but he made no reference to the withdrawal of foreign troops from Korea. In 1952, at a meeting of the UN Disarmament Commission, Malik accused the United States of distributing germ-infested foodstuffs in Korea.

In September 1952 Valerian Zorin replaced Malik as Soviet representative to the UN. In 1953 Malik became ambassador to Great Britain, and from 1960 to 1968 he was deputy foreign minister. In 1968 Malik again returned to the UN as Soviet representative, where he served until 1976. He died in Moscow on 12 February 1980.

—Natalia Petrouchkevitch

References:

Bailey, Sydney D. *The Korean Armistice.* London: Macmillan, 1992.

Hastings, Max. *The Korean War.* New York: Simon & Schuster, 1987.

Lowe, Peter. *The Origins of the Korean War.* New York: Longman House, 1986.

Paige, Glenn D. *The Korean Decision, June 24–30, 1950.* New York: Free Press, 1968.

Stairs, Denis. *The Diplomacy of Constraint: Canada, the Korean War, and the United States.* Toronto: University of Toronto Press, 1974.

See also: Acheson, Dean Goodersham; Biological Warfare; China, People's Republic of: UN Representation Question; Kennan, George F.; Kennan-Malik Conversations; Soviet Security Council Boycott; Stalin, Josef; Union of Soviet Socialist Republics; Zorin, Valerian Alexandrovitch.

Manchuria

Chinese province that played a crucial role in the Korean War. It is the closest Chinese province to Korea and shares the majority of the border with the Democratic People's Republic of Korea (North Korea). Manchuria's border with North Korea mostly follows the Yalu and Tumen rivers. Manchuria is an important raw materials base for China, and leaders of the People's Republic of China (PRC, Communist China) were concerned about having U.S. forces in close proximity to it. Chinese concerns over U.S. forces invading North Korea helped bring about the Chinese decision to intervene militarily in the war.

Russia and Japan had both made efforts to control Manchuria. The Japanese had secured important economic concessions in the province thanks to their defeat of Russia in the Russo-Japanese War of 1904–1905. Then in 1931 the Japanese Kwantung Army took over the entirety of the province and Japan set up the puppet state of Manchukuo. The province reverted back to China following the Second World War, but Nationalist leader Jiang Jieshi's (Chiang Kai-shek's) precipitous efforts to control it brought about an early military defeat at the hands of the Mao Zedong's Communists. Manchuria provided the avenue for the PRC to become involved in the Korean war. It also was the pipeline for much of the Chinese/Soviet logistical effort.

As Korean People's Army (KPA, North Korean) forces were pushed toward their border with the PRC, Chinese troops massed north of it. Following the initial Chinese military intervention, United Nations commander General Douglas MacArthur requested approval from Washington to bomb the bridges across the Yalu River over which supplies passed from Manchuria into North Korea. Although Truman authorized a strike on the Korean side only, many Chinese troops and supplies had already moved into North Korea and the Yalu was soon frozen, allowing the movement of supplies across it without benefit of the bridges.

During the remainder of the Korean War, Manchuria continued to serve as the resource base and conduit for Chinese military and armaments to enter Korea.

—David R. Buck

References:

Appleman, Roy E. *Disaster in Korea: The Chinese Confront MacArthur.* College Station, TX: Texas A&M Press, 1989.

Stueck, William W., Jr. *The Korean War: An International History.* Princeton, NJ: Princeton University Press, 1995.

Whiting, Allen S. *China Crosses the Yalu.* Stanford, CA: Stanford University Press, 1960.

See also: China, People's Republic of; Chinese Military Offensives; Jiang Jieshi (Chiang Kai-shek); Logistics; MacArthur, Douglas; Manchurian Sanctuary; Mao Zedong; Yalu Bridges Controversy.

Manchurian Sanctuary

The term *sanctuary* denotes an area or region enjoying specially favored treatment in view of the belligerent status of its occupiers. After Chinese intervention in the Korean War, Manchuria served as a supply center and air base for Communist forces, including Soviet air forces.

To prevent the conflict from escalating into another world war, United Nations Command (UNC) forces were not permitted to attack or bomb Manchuria. The concept of Manchurian sanctuary was developed to explain the special status of the region during the Korean War. Yet UNC commander General Douglas MacArthur argued that this was not justified from a military point of view.

On 6 November 1950, MacArthur stated that the flow of Chinese troops and supplies over the Yalu River bridges jeopardized UNC forces in Korea. The only way to stop this movement was destruction of the bridges by air attack. MacArthur indicated that he planned to employ ninety B-29 aircraft to strike the international bridge at Sinŭiju over the Yalu. Washington suspended the operation, over MacArthur's strong protests, in the belief that the Communist side might consider it a prelude to an attack on Manchuria. MacArthur replied that the operation was within the scope of the rules of warfare and of resolutions and directives he had received. Washington did authorize MacArthur to proceed with bombing in North Korea near the frontier, including targets at Sinŭiju and the Korean side of the Yalu River bridges.

MacArthur also complained that Washington was refusing to allow aerial reconnaissance beyond the Manchurian border despite the need to gather normal field intelligence. In his 19 April 1951 speech to Congress after he was relieved of his command, MacArthur argued that simple military necessity mandated the removal of restrictions on air reconnaissance of Manchuria.

Nonetheless, Washington's directive to MacArthur of 5 August 1950 authorized aerial reconnaissance of all Korean territory, including coastal waters up to the Yalu River on the west and up to but short of the Korean-Soviet international boundary on the east; these authorizations were subject to the understanding that such operations would be conducted from as far south of the frontiers of Manchuria or the Soviet Union as practical and that in no cases would those frontiers be overflown.

After the massive Chinese military intervention in late November 1950 MacArthur announced the beginning of "an entirely new war." Bombing the Yalu bridges was soon a moot point, as the Yalu froze over, making it impossible for UNC air power to interdict the flow of troops and supplies from Manchuria. As a result, MacArthur advocated doing away with the Manchurian sanctuary altogether. His insistence on removing the sanctuary privilege was tantamount to spreading the area of hostilities into Manchuria.

Chairman of the Joint Chiefs of Staff General Omar N. Bradley dismissed MacArthur's argument that only the Chinese enjoyed the sanctuary privilege. Large-scale Communist air attacks from Manchurian bases could deal a severe blow to crowded airfields in South Korea and Japan. A Communist air attack on Pusan, the well-illuminated UNC supply center, could cripple UNC logistic capabilities. Thus the sanctuary privilege was not a unilateral practice. During the war the Soviet Union provided only air cover for Chinese forces in Manchuria. Its air force was never used to strike behind the UNC front line or to destroy supply ports such as Pusan and Inch'ŏn. This self-imposed Soviet restraint cannot be construed as resulting from Soviet Premier Josef Stalin's goodwill or a desire to minimize bloodshed; it was based on strategic calculations.

As Chinese forces captured Seoul and advanced south, their lines of communications became long enough for UNC forces to cause them serious logistic troubles. The increase in the effectiveness of UNC air attacks on Chinese forces within Korea undermined MacArthur's argument that it was necessary to directly strike Chinese territories to halt Communist advances. The United States then seized the opportunity to hold and stabilize a line in Korea without doing away with the Manchurian sanctuary.

—*Youngho Kim*

References:

U.S. Department of State, Bureau of Public Affairs. *Foreign Relations of the United States, 1950.* Vol. 7, *Korea.* Washington, DC: U.S. Government Printing Office, 1976.

See also: Bradley, Omar Nelson; Joint Chiefs of Staff (JCS); Logistics; MacArthur, Douglas; Stalin, Josef.

Mao Zedong
(1893–1976)

Leader of the People's Republic of China. A great visionary, Mao Zedong was also one of history's deadliest tyrants. A rebel from childhood, Mao helped found the Chinese Communist Party in 1921, took command of the revolution fourteen years later in the midst of the Red Army's epic Long March, fought another fourteen years before the Communists' final victory, and then remained China's supreme ruler for more than a quarter-century until his death at age eighty-two.

The leader of China's Communist revolution was born on 26 December 1893 in a peasant home in Hunan Province. He was educated at his village primary school and subsequently entered high school in Changsha, the provincial capital. Mao was in Changsha when, on 10 October 1911, revolution broke out against the last of the Qing Dynasty emperors. Mao joined the revolutionary army but saw no fighting and returned to his studies after six months as a soldier.

After graduating from the provincial teacher-training college, Mao went to Beijing (Peking), where he worked as an assistant librarian at Beijing University and began to learn about Marxism. In July 1921 he attended the Chinese Communist Party's founding congress in Shanghai. Seeing Marxist theories through a Chinese prism, unlike many of his more orthodox comrades, Mao believed that revolution in China had to begin among peasants, rather than in an embryonic industrial working class. During the 1920s he spent much of his time organizing peasant unions in his native Hunan province.

At the end of the decade, with the Communists fighting for survival against Jiang Jieshi's (Chiang Kai-shek's) Guomindang (Nationalist) government, Mao retreated farther into the countryside instead of joining other Communist leaders in suicidal urban uprisings. By 1934 Mao's base in Jiangxi province was under heavy pressure from Nationalist troops. That October some 86,000 Communists slipped through the Nationalist blockade and began a 6,000-mile retreat that became known as the Long March. Mao, in political eclipse when the march began, became the party's supreme leader during the trek, a role he never relinquished. At the end of the Long March, with only about 4,000 left from the original force, Mao and his comrades established a new base in Yan'an (Yenan) in northern China.

Between 1937 and 1945, Mao and his army fought a new enemy in Japan. In that conflict Mao and his commanders refined the art of "people's war." Mao summed up the strategy in only sixteen Chinese characters: "The enemy advances, we retreat; the enemy camps, we harass; the enemy tires, we attack; the enemy retreats, we pursue."

The Red Army became a political as well as military weapon. Instead of victimizing the peasantry, as Chinese soldiers had done from time immemorial, Mao's troops sought to win over the population to their cause. Instead of looting, raping, and destroying, Communist soldiers were ordered to pay for food, respect women, and help repair war damage. The ideal, and to an extent the reality, was an army that commanded public support and could, in Mao's most famous simile, swim among the people as fish swim in the sea.

Following Japan's defeat, the struggle between Communists and Nationalists resumed, but by now the tide was running strongly in Mao's favor. By the fall of 1949 the Nationalist government and what remained of its army had fled to the island of Taiwan. On 1 October Mao stood under China's new flag, red with five gold stars, and proclaimed the People's Republic of China.

The Communists were not gentle in establishing their regime. "A revolution is not the same thing as inviting people to dinner or writing an essay or painting a picture or embroidering a flower," Mao once

The official portrait of Chinese Communist leader Mao Zedong. (Library of Congress)

wrote. "It cannot be anything so refined, so calm and gentle." In the first years of the People's Republic, hundreds of thousands, perhaps millions, were executed as landlords or capitalist exploiters. Millions more were imprisoned or tortured for real or imaginary crimes against the revolution, or simply for having a privileged background. Rigid ideological controls were imposed on educators, artists, and the press.

Less than a year after he came to power, the outbreak of war in Korea presented Mao with difficult choices. His priority was on consolidating his new government and rebuilding China. But a North Korean defeat would bring hostile foreign forces to China's northeastern border, and, Mao feared, might encourage Jiang Jieshi to send his forces back across the Taiwan Strait to reopen the civil war on the mainland. The key issue for China was whether counterattacking U.S. forces would halt at the 38th parallel in the fall of 1950 or continue their advance into North Korea. If the latter, Mao decided, China had no choice but to enter the war.

On 8 October, the day after the first U.S. troops moved onto North Korean territory, Mao issued the official directive: "It has been ordered that the

Northeast Border Defense Army be turned into the Chinese People's Volunteers" (the name was a figleaf, a transparent device for China to go to war with the United States without formally avowing it) "and that the Chinese People's Volunteers move immediately into the territory of Korea to assist the Korean comrades in their struggle."

Mao's decision to intervene in Korea cost the life of his oldest son. Mao Anying, age twenty-eight, was killed in a U.S. air strike on a Chinese People's Volunteer Army command post in November 1950, just weeks after the intervention began.

For many ordinary Chinese, life gradually improved in the years following 1949. But Mao was impatient for faster progress. Uninformed about economics and technology, and convinced that the sheer muscle power of China's huge population could accomplish any goal if it were just mobilized properly, he began dreaming of a "Great Leap Forward" that would hurl China out of poverty and backwardness and create a modern, prosperous state virtually overnight.

The Great Leap produced numerous follies, but the worst calamity occurred in agriculture. Intoxicated by his own visions and seduced by crackpot theorists (at one point, Chinese "scientists" claimed to have crossed a cotton plant and a tomato plant to produce red cotton!) Mao decreed an overnight transition from family or small cooperative farms to vast People's Communes, while calling for absurdly high increases in grain production. The results were devastating. From 1959 to 1961, as many as 30 million Chinese died as a direct or indirect result of Great Leap policies.

In the wake of the disaster, Mao withdrew from day-to-day administrative details. But he nursed a deep grievance against those who he imagined had sabotaged his plan. In 1966 Mao struck back with the Great Proletarian Cultural Revolution, an event so irrational and bizarre that recorded history shows nothing else quite like it. Proclaiming "rebellion is justified," Mao urged China's youth to rise up against the party bureaucracy and against the "four olds": old habits, old customs, old culture, and old thinking.

At Mao's call, brigades of youthful Red Guards waving the little red book of Mao's thoughts spread out to "make revolution" in schools, factories, and offices throughout China. Within months, the country was in chaos. Red Guard groups splintered into rival mobs, each determined to outdo the other in rooting out enemies and tearing down everything that symbolized incorrect thoughts or China's past. Teachers, managers, intellectuals, and anyone suspected of insufficient revolutionary purity were paraded before howling mobs and forced to confess their misdeeds. Savage beatings were common. Many victims died

under torture; constant physical and mental harassment drove many others to commit suicide.

Among those persecuted were almost all of the old cadres—party workers and Red Army soldiers whose struggle and sacrifice had brought the Communists to power. Meanwhile, the glorification of Mao reached extraordinary heights. His face, with its high-domed forehead, backswept hair tufting over each ear, and the celebrated mole just to the left of the center line of the chin, gazed out from virtually every wall in China. Badges with his image became part of the national dress. Schoolchildren and office workers began every day with bows before Mao's picture.

Not even the frenzy of leader-worship could stem a growing sense that something was wrong, however. In the torrent of slogans and accusations, the movement's goals grew steadily more inexplicable. "The whole nation slid into doublespeak," Jung Chang, then a teenager, recalled in her memoir, *Wild Swans*. "Words became divorced from reality, responsibility, and people's real thoughts. Lies were told with ease because words had lost their meanings—and had ceased to be taken seriously by others."

China paid a heavy price for Mao's mad fantasies: the educational system was shattered for years; economic losses were ruinous; much of China's rich artistic legacy was destroyed; society was fractured; and ideals crumbled. After two years of chaos, order was gradually restored, often at gunpoint by People's Liberation Army units, but a mood of fear and uncertainty persisted through the remaining years of Mao's rule.

The Red Guards were disbanded and millions of young people were sent from towns and cities to work as farm laborers. Out loud, nearly all of them obediently vowed willingness to "serve the people" wherever they were sent. But inwardly, many were confused, disillusioned and hurt.

On 28 July 1976, a disastrous earthquake struck north China. Nearly a quarter-million people were killed and physical destruction was immense, even in Beijing, 100 miles from the epicenter. In Chinese tradition, such disasters were thought to signal the end of a dynasty. The Communist regime officially scorned such superstitions, but to many Chinese the old beliefs were vindicated when, at ten minutes past midnight on 9 September, Mao died.

Believing that sheer willpower and human muscles could overcome any obstacle, Mao had turned China into a gigantic laboratory for his experiments in transforming human society. But when his grandiose dreams failed, instead of recognizing that his policies were flawed, Mao tore China apart in mad witch-hunts for the "demons and monsters" who had frustrated his efforts.

Mao's career was rich in contradictions. He proclaimed Marxism his lifelong faith, but his revolutionary ideas owed little to Marx and much more to ancient Chinese sagas of bandits and peasant rebellions. He preached simplicity and egalitarianism, but had himself glorified as a virtual god-king. He declared war against China's feudal past and its oppressive traditions, but his reign, rife with arbitrary cruelties and constant intrigues, mirrored many of the worst aspects of imperial despotism.

Mao's remains were given a place of high honor in an enormous mausoleum on Tiananmen Square, but his ideas were entombed with him. Less than a month after his death, his widow Jiang Qing and her three closest associates, the "Gang of Four" who had been the chief zealots of the Cultural Revolution, were imprisoned. Deng Xiaoping, whom Mao had twice expelled from the leadership, regained power and within a few years reversed nearly all of Mao's policies. In the end, it was the pragmatic Deng rather than the visionary Mao who laid the groundwork for economic reforms that transformed China in the 1980s and 1990s.

—Arnold R. Isaacs

References:

Chang, Jung. *Wild Swans: Three Daughters of China.* New York: Simon & Schuster, 1991.

Goncharov, Sergei N., John W. Lewis, and Xue Litai. *Uncertain Partners: Stalin, Mao and the Korean War.* Stanford, CA: Stanford University Press, 1993.

Salisbury, Harrison E. *The New Emperors: China in the Era of Mao and Deng.* Boston: Little, Brown, 1992.

Spence, Jonathan. *The Search for Modern China.* New York: W. W. Norton, 1990.

See also: China, People's Republic of; Jiang Jieshi (Chiang Kaishek); Zhou Enlai.

March First Movement
(1 March–30 April 1919)

Independence movement of Koreans against Japanese colonial rule and perhaps the most significant nationalist event in modern Korean history. After Japan annexed Korea in 1910, Koreans began organizing into a variety of groups, whose sole objective was to win Korea's independence. Some members of these nationalist groups were studying in the United States, and they tried to persuade the U.S. government to assist in their fight for independence. Others worked from headquarters in China or at home in Korea.

Inspired by U.S. president Woodrow Wilson's Fourteen Points and concept of "self-determination of peoples," the leaders of several Korean nationalist groups planned to demonstrate against their Japanese colonial rulers. This was spurred by the death of former Chosŏn Dynasty ruler King Kojong in January 1919 and rumors that he had been poisoned by a Japanese doctor. After much discussion the nationalists decided to draft a declaration of independence, which they planned to read at Pagoda Park in Seoul, at 2:00 p.m. on 1 March 1919, two days before the former ruler's funeral. Thirty-three representatives of the nationalist groups signed the declaration of independence and a petition, both of which were sent to the governments of the United States and Japan, and to the Paris Peace Conference. Additionally, organizers had thousands of copies made and distributed to various localities.

Evidence suggests that initially the organizers did not plan to provoke a national uprising. They simply assumed this would be a nonviolent action by a small group of nationalist representatives expressing the desires of the Korean people. As the day drew near, the planners changed the location of the demonstration from Pagoda Park to a restaurant near the park. They feared that the park would give the more radical nationalists the opportunity to transform a dignified occasion into a volatile uprising.

On 1 March residents of Seoul and citizens from local areas began arriving at Pagoda Park to hear the declaration of independence. When none of the nationalist representatives arrived, at 2:00 a schoolteacher stood up and read the declaration to the crowd. When he finished, the crowd joined him in chanting "Long live Korea, Long live Korean independence!" The crowd then moved into the streets and began marching down Chongno, one of Seoul's principal thoroughfares. More and more people joined the march, and by day's end tens of thousands of Korean citizens had participated in the demonstration. Similar events occurred elsewhere in the country; between 500,000 and 2 million Koreans participated in these demonstrations from 1 March until the end of April.

The demonstration was so well coordinated and planned in such secrecy that it caught the Japanese government in Korea completely by surprise. Although the demonstrators conducted themselves peacefully, the Japanese reaction was severe. The Japanese government immediately imposed restrictions on traffic, outlawed assemblies and street demonstrations, and closed several markets. The Japanese searched and destroyed houses, schools, and churches, looking for documents and those individuals responsible. According to one government report, between 1 March and 30 April, 26,713 Koreans were arrested, 553 were killed, and another 1,409 were injured.

The March First Movement was truly a nationwide demonstration, involving every segment of Korean society. Students, teachers, and graduates from the mission schools led the demonstrations in the countryside. Most noteworthy, for the first time in Korean history, several thousand Korean women participated in these demonstrations, establishing their place as partners with men in the struggle for independence.

The events also brought new nationalist leaders to the fore. Many of those involved in the movement fled abroad, and in the Chinese city of Shanghai several of them organized what became the best known Korean nationalist organization, the self-styled Korean Provisional Government. It elected Syngman Rhee as its first president.

The March First Movement did not bring Korea's liberation from Japanese rule, but with the help of American and other foreign missionaries, the events of 1 March 1919 and Korea's struggle against a brutal Japanese colonial government became known to the world. Missionaries serving in Korea did not join the movement, but they were sympathetic to Korea's plight and approved of the nonviolent nature of the demonstrations. More importantly, they witnessed the events and reported in detail what they saw to their respective governments. In doing so, they succeeded in building international outrage against the Japanese for the cruel nature of their rule. This eventually forced the Japanese government to modify and somewhat reform its policy toward Korea after 1919.

—*Mark R. Franklin*

References:

Bark, Dong Suh. "The American-Educated Elite in Korean Society." In *Korea and the United States: A Century of Cooperation,* edited by Young Nok Koo and Dae Sook Suh. Honolulu: University of Hawaii Press, 1984.

Ku, Dae Yeol. *Korea under Colonialism: The March First Movement and Anglo-Japanese Relations.* Seoul: Seoul Computer Press, 1985.

Lee Chong-Sik. *The Politics of Korean Nationalism.* Berkeley: University of California Press, 1963.

Nahm, Andrew C. *Korea, Tradition and Transformation: A History of the Korean People.* Elizabeth, NJ: Hollym International, 1988.

Shin, Young Il. "American Protestant Missions to Korea and the Awakening of Political and Social Consciousness in the Koreans between 1884 and 1941." In *U.S.-Korean Relations,* edited by Tae-Hwan Kwak et al. Seoul: Seoul Computer Press, 1982.

See also: Korea, Geography and History to 1945; Syngman Rhee; U.S. Policy toward Korea before 1950.

Marshall, George C.
(1880–1959)

One of the foremost soldier-statesmen of the twentieth century, U.S. secretary of state, and U.S. secretary of defense during the Korean War. General of the Army George Catlett Marshall, if not America's greatest soldier, was one of the nation's most capable and one of the great men of the twentieth century. Born in Uniontown, Pennsylvania, on 31 December 1880, Marshall graduated from the Virginia Military Institute in 1901. He made his military reputation while serving as a staff officer to General John C.

Pershing in the First World War. Marshall held a variety of posts after the war, including command of the Infantry School at Fort Benning, Georgia. In September 1939 President Franklin D. Roosevelt advanced Marshall over a number of more senior officers to appoint him chief of staff of the army. It proved a wise choice indeed. Known as the "Organizer of Victory," Marshall served in that post throughout the Second World War. He was promoted to general of the Army in December 1944.

On the urging of President Harry S. Truman, Marshall returned to public service as special envoy to China (1945–1947), secretary of state (1947–1949), and president of the American Red Cross (1949–1950). In August 1950 Truman persuaded Marshall to replace Defense Secretary Louis Johnson, who was forced to resign on 12 September 1950.

Truman had been upset by Johnson's feuding with other cabinet members, especially Secretary of State Dean Acheson. Truman decided by late June to remove Johnson but waited to sound out Marshall and see if his views were in accord with his own and those of Acheson regarding Korea. A fierce congressional fight over Marshall's confirmation occurred as a result of hysteria over the Communist victory in China. Marshall met these personal attacks, as with all others, with calm logic.

Marshall's top priority as secretary of defense was more personnel for the armed forces to meet the demands of both Korea and Europe while at the same time maintaining an adequate reserve. He secured the appointment of Anna M. Rosenberg as assistant secretary of defense for manpower and brought Robert A. Lovett back into government service. Marshall also restored harmony between the defense and state departments. Early on he established a good working relationship with the military chiefs. Chairman of the Joint Chiefs of Staff (JCS) General Omar N. Bradley had served under Marshall in the Second World War and the two men worked well together, as was the case with Bradley's successor, General J. Lawton Collins. Marshall respected and worked well with General George E. Stratemeyer and Admiral Forrest P. Sherman.

The Inch'ŏn landing and the Pusan perimeter breakout preceded Marshall's confirmation as secretary of defense, but he participated in the decision authorizing MacArthur to conduct operations north of the 38th parallel. Marshall shared the view held by MacArthur and the JCS that he should follow up his victory. A secret "eyes only" signal from Marshall to MacArthur on 29 September declared Washington's commitment to an advance into North Korea. Marshall put it in these words, "We want you to feel unhampered strategically and tactically to proceed north of the 38th parallel." But he advised MacArthur against advance announcements that might precipitate a new vote in the United Nations.

For some time the top figures in the Truman administration had worried about a clash with China. Despite MacArthur's unbridled confidence at the Wake Island meeting with Truman on 15 October, the Chinese had already begun to move forces into Korea. After the initial Chinese military actions with Republic of Korea and U.S. units at the end of October, neither Marshall nor the Joint Chiefs made any effort to halt MacArthur's advance.

Marshall opposed granting MacArthur permission to bomb the Yalu bridges unless the security of all his forces was directly threatened; but after MacArthur predicted dire results if nothing was done, Truman authorized the strike. Marshall supported the recommendation from the JCS authorizing pursuit of Communist aircraft into Manchurian airspace, but Allied reaction caused the proposal to be dropped. Marshall and the JCS were generally supportive of MacArthur because of traditional Pentagon reluctance to supervise field commanders too closely, and the fact that MacArthur was no ordinary commander.

Following the second, and massive, Chinese military intervention, rather than criticize MacArthur, Marshall and the JCS sought ways to help him. At the meeting of the National Security Council on 28 November, Marshall agreed with the president and the JCS that all-out war with China must be avoided. The United States should continue to work through the United Nations and maintain Allied support for the war. When the JCS instructed MacArthur to withdraw X Corps from its exposed position, Marshall inserted a statement that the region northeast of the waist of Korea was to be avoided except for military operations essential to command security.

In the debate over what to do about the changed military situation in Korea, Marshall opposed a cease-fire with the Chinese. He believed that would represent a "great weakness on our part" and admitted that the United States could not in "all good conscience" abandon the South Koreans. When British Prime Minister Clement Attlee suggested negotiations with the Chinese, Marshall expressed opposition. He pointed out that it was almost impossible to negotiate with the Chinese Communists, and he also expressed fear of the effects on Japan and the Philippines of concessions to the Chinese. At the same time Marshall sought ways to avoid a wider war with China. When many in Congress favored an expanded war with China, Marshall was among administration leaders who in February 1951 stressed the paramount importance to the United States of Western Europe.

In the 6 April meeting between President Truman and his closest advisers to discuss the firing of General MacArthur, Marshall urged caution, pointing out that if MacArthur were recalled Congress might obstruct military appropriations. Later that morning Truman asked Marshall to review all messages between Washington and Tokyo over the past two years. When the five men met again the next morning, Marshall declared that he shared Averell Harriman's view that MacArthur should have been dismissed two years earlier for flouting administration directives over occupation policies in Japan. Given the political risks involved, Marshall and the other men involved in the decision to sack MacArthur exhibited a considerable degree of courage.

In the Senate hearings that followed the general's dismissal, Marshall defended the decision. Long-time rivals, in many ways, Marshall and MacArthur represented different viewpoints: Democrat versus Republican, Europe-first versus concentration on Asia, and limited war versus total war.

Marshall defended the concept of limited war in Korea; he hoped it would "remain limited." He said there was no easy solution to the Cold War short of another world war, the cost of which would be "beyond calculation." As a result, the Truman administration's policy was to contain Communist aggression by different methods in different areas without resort to total war. Such a policy was not "easy or popular." Marshall believed that the Western alliance had to be kept intact, the United States must rearm as quickly as possible, the status quo should be maintained, and Formosa should "never be allowed" to come under Communist control.

By now the Truman administration was under heavy attack. In June 1951, when Senator Joseph McCarthy demanded the resignations of Acheson and Marshall and threatened Truman with impeachment, he all but called Marshall a Communist. The unjust attacks against him may well have confirmed Marshall's decision to step down from a position he had agreed to hold only for six months to a year. In any case McCarthy's attack ended Marshall's usefulness as a nonpartisan member of the administration. At Truman's request he stayed on until 1 September 1951, when he officially resigned. He was replaced by his deputy, Robert A. Lovett. For Marshall it was the end of fifty years of dedicated government service.

Apart from all his other services, as secretary of defense Marshall had restored morale in the armed forces, rebuilt a cordial relationship between the defense and state departments, increased the size and readiness of the armed forces, and assisted Truman in the crisis over the MacArthur firing. These were not inconsiderable achievements. Awarded the Nobel Prize for Peace in 1953, Marshall was the first soldier so honored. Marshall died in Washington D.C., on 16 October 1959.

                                                            —Spencer C. Tucker

References:
Acheson, Dean, *Present at the Creation: My Years in the State Department*. New York: W. W. Norton, 1969.
Pogue, Forrest C. *George C. Marshall, Statesman, 1945–1959*. New York: Viking Press, 1987.
See also: Acheson, Dean Goodersham; Attlee, Clement R.; Bradley, Omar Nelson; Collins, Joseph Lawton; Harriman, William Averell; Johnson, Louis A.; Joint Chiefs of Staff (JCS); Lovett, Robert A.; MacArthur, Douglas; McCarthy, Joseph R.; Sherman, Forrest P.; Stratemeyer, George E.; Truman, Harry S.; Truman's Recall of MacArthur.

Marshall, Samuel Lyman Atwood
(1900–1977)

One of the most influential, albeit controversial, military historians of the twentieth century. Born on 18 July 1900, in Catskill, New York, S. L. A. Marshall, widely known as "Slam" after his initials, gained all of his direct military experience as a reservist, first receiving his commission from the ranks during World War I at age seventeen. For the next sixty years he pursued parallel careers as a reserve officer and as a journalist and writer. As a reporter and a military columnist for the *Detroit News*, he covered many of the world's major conflicts during that period.

During World War II Marshall was the chief historian of the U.S. European Theater of Operations. He recruited many of the historians and initiated the work that led to the widely respected *U.S. Army in World War II* series. Marshall's own books about World War II included *Night Drop* (1962) and *Bastogne: The First Eight Days* (1946).

Marshall pioneered the technique of conducting direct interviews with participants of combat actions as soon as possible after the event. As a result of these interviews, Marshall in 1947 wrote *Men Against Fire*, a penetrating analysis of the U.S. infantryman and small-unit cohesion and effectiveness. Marshall pointed out many problems with U.S. combat performance and offered recommendations to correct them. The U.S. Army adopted many of his recommendations.

As a reserve colonel Marshall served in Korea as a historian and military analyst with the army's Operations Research Office. Despite other negative press stories at the time, Marshall wrote a report praising the combat performance of the 2d Infantry Division's partially integrated 9th Infantry Regiment. This was at a time when the army was still having great difficulty coming to terms with and implementing President Harry S. Truman's 1948 executive order to integrate the armed forces.

During his several trips to Korea, Marshall continued to file stories with his newspaper, write articles for the *Combat Forces Journal* (later titled *ARMY* magazine), and gather material which he used for his books. His Korean War volumes include *The River and the Gauntlet* (1953) and *Pork Chop Hill* (1956), which later became a movie starring Gregory Peck. Marshall also wrote the Medal of Honor recommendation for Captain Lewis Millett, who led his Company E, 27th Infantry in a bayonet charge near Soam-ni in February 1951.

During the Vietnam War, as a retired reserve brigadier general, Marshall made several trips to the war zone under U.S. Army sponsorship. Together with Colonel David H. Hackworth he wrote *Vietnam Primer*, which the army published as *DA Pamphlet 525-2*. Over 2 million copies of the lessons-learned manual were printed. Marshall wrote five other books on Vietnam battles.

During his lifetime Marshall was widely regarded as a great military historian and an astute analyst of combat operations. His close friend Carl Sandburg called him "the greatest of writers on modern war." Marshall himself worked hard to cultivate this image. The army could always count on him to present the organization in its most positive light, and that in turn opened many doors. Marshall delighted in his close associations with the great and the near-great high-ranking commanders of the day.

In the years since his death, a far more mixed opinion of Marshall has emerged. A disillusioned Hackworth once called him "the Howard Cosell of combat" and "the Army's top apologist." But in his 1987 book, *The Korean War*, historian Max Hastings still referred to Marshall as "perhaps America's finest combat historian of the twentieth century."

Some historians have criticized Marshall's work by indicating flaws and inconsistencies in both his data and his much-vaunted interview techniques. Marshall, nonetheless, did have a profound impact on the post–World War II U.S. Army and its training doctrine. Many veterans of infantry combat continue to agree that regardless of the flaws in Marshall's data or data collection methods, his conclusions in *Men Against Fire* were correct.

Marshall died in El Paso, Texas, on 17 December 1977.

                                                            —David T. Zabecki

References:
Marshall, S. L. A. *Bringing up the Rear: A Memoir*. San Raphael, CA: Presidio Press, 1979.
———. *Men against Fire*. New York: William Morrow, 1947.
———. *Pork Chop Hill: The American Fighting Man in Action, Korea, Spring, 1953*. New York: William Morrow, 1952.
———. *The River and the Gauntlet: Defeat of the Eighth Army by the Chinese Communist Forces, November 1950, in the Battle*

of the Chongchon River, Korea. New York: William Morrow, 1953.

Spiller, Roger J. "S. L. A. Marshall and the Ratio of Fire." *Journal of the Royal United Services Institution* 133, no. 4 (Winter 1988): 67–71.

Williams, Frederick D. *SLAM: The Influence of S. L. A. Marshall on the United States Army.* Fort Monroe, VA: U.S. Army Training and Doctrine Command, 1990.

See also: African-Americans and the Korean War; Truman, Harry S.

Martin, Joseph W.
(1884–1968)

Congressman and critic of Korean War policy. Born on 3 November 1884 in North Attleboro, Massachusetts, Joseph W. Martin served in the state legislature and then in 1924 he won election to the U.S. House of Representatives, where he served for over four decades. Martin was assistant floor leader to the Republican minority, chairperson of the GOP Congressional Campaign Committee, and, in 1939, House Republican leader. He received consideration as a possible presidential nominee in the election of 1940. When Republicans won a House majority in 1946, he became speaker. When President Harry S. Truman won an unexpected victory in 1948 and the Democrats gained control of Congress, the isolationist and fiscally conservative Martin reverted to his former role as minority leader.

Representative Martin criticized Truman's Korean War policies as too Eurocentric and unaggressive. In a 12 February 1951 Brooklyn speech, he expressed anxiety about an administration preoccupation with Europe that debilitated America's strength in Asia. He suggested that the Nationalist Chinese army on Formosa should be used to establish a secondary Asian front to ease the strain on the United Nations in Korea. Martin added, "There is good reason to believe that General [Douglas] MacArthur favors such an operation [and] there should be no limitation on force once war was declared." The congressman forwarded a transcript of his address to MacArthur, accompanied by a cover letter requesting the United Nations commander's "views on this point, either on a confidential basis or otherwise."

Responding in a letter on 19 March, MacArthur agreed with Martin. The general concurred with his views on Formosa, assailed the idea of limited war, and declared "There is no substitute for victory." On 5 April Martin read the text of the correspondence to the House. Despite MacArthur's claim that his letter was "merely [a] routine communication as I turn out by the hundred," he had indeed confided to a partisan critic of the Truman administration who employed his comments for political advantage. The general's response to Martin neglected a request of nondisclosure.

Considering previous assertions by MacArthur, President Truman perceived his letter to Martin as the general's final act of open defiance. The president became persuaded that he could no longer disregard MacArthur's challenge to his constitutional powers as commander in chief and architect of foreign policy. The general's letter to Martin, the most recent episode of "rank insubordination," became "the last straw" leading to his 10 April dismissal.

After receiving news of MacArthur's recall, Republican leaders, among them Senators Robert A. Taft and Kenneth S. Wherry, assembled in Martin's office. When they emerged, the minority leader informed the press that a congressional probe of Truman administration military and foreign affairs was in order, and they wanted MacArthur to present his opinions to Congress. Furthermore, Martin said the subject of impeachment came up, suggesting indictments of other administration figures as well as the president.

Martin sought to turn the Korean War issue into an electoral triumph in 1952. When MacArthur returned to the United States, he tendered Martin support for a presidential bid. Martin chaired the Republican National Convention, where the general gave the keynote address. At the convention Martin charged that the Democrats, success at hand, "decided the best way to win was to lose." Later, the joint report on the Democratic Eighty-second Congress, published by Martin and Senate Minority Leader Styles Bridges, alleged that the majority party had no answer for the endless Korean conflict.

As a result of Dwight D. Eisenhower's overwhelming electoral victory in 1952 in which the Republicans regained control of the Congress, Martin became speaker for a second term. He lost the speakership in 1954 once the Democrats regained control of the House and Senate, and, four years later, was removed as Republican floor leader. Thwarted in a renomination bid in the Republican primary for a House seat in 1966, Martin died in Hollywood, Florida, on 7 March 1968.

—*Rodney J. Ross*

References:

Caridi, Ronald J. *The Korean War and American Politics: The Republican Party As a Case Study.* Philadelphia: University of Pennsylvania Press, 1968.

James, D. Clayton. *The Years of MacArthur.* Vol. 3, *Triumph and Disaster, 1945–1964.* Boston: Houghton Mifflin, 1985.

Martin, Joseph. *My First Fifty Years in Politics.* New York: McGraw-Hill, 1960.

See also: MacArthur, Douglas; Taft, Robert Alphonso; Truman, Harry S.; Truman's Recall of MacArthur.

Matthews, Francis P.
(1887–1952)

U.S. secretary of the navy, 1949–1951. Born on 15 March 1887, in Albion, Nebraska, Francis P. Matthews graduated from Creighton University. He was a banker, corporate executive, and attorney in Omaha. He was also a prominent Catholic layman. Matthews became president of the National Thrift Assurance Company, the Securities Investment Corporation, and an Omaha bank. He also served as general counsel for the Reconstruction Finance Corporation. A supporter of President Harry S. Truman in the 1948 campaign, Matthews helped influence the Nebraska delegation in Truman's favor. He was nonetheless surprised when Truman appointed him successor to John L. Sullivan as secretary of the navy.

Taking office on 25 May 1949 during the tumultuous "Revolt of the Admirals," Matthews admitted incautiously to the press that his only qualification for the post was ownership of a small boat on a Minnesota lake. Dubbed "Rowboat Matthews," the new secretary immediately earned the enmity of many sailors by playing a key role in forcing out Chief of Naval Operations Admiral Louis Denfeld during the controversy over the B-36 bomber and the canceled supercarrier *United States*. In the course of the Congressional hearings, Matthews painted such a rosy picture of navy morale that he was literally jeered by officers in the audience.

Matthews deepened this chasm of distrust by enthusiastically supporting Secretary of Defense Louis Johnson in the latter's severe pruning of the navy's budget and by striking at Denfeld's supporters. One of the prominent victims of this purge was Captain Arleigh Burke, who Matthews illegally removed from the promotion list to flag rank. Matthews also attempted to quash criticism within the navy of the sister services. On the positive side, Matthews appointed as Denfeld's successor Admiral Forrest Sherman, who got Burke reinstated and convinced Congress to fund a nuclear submarine and to pay more attention to naval aviation.

Despite the outbreak of the Korean War, Matthews was slow to reverse course from shrinking the navy. He failed, for instance, to push forward the supercarrier project, leaving the task to Congressman Carl Vinson. Worse, in an August 1950 public speech commemorating the sesquicentennial of the Boston Naval Shipyard, Matthews issued a call for preventive war against the Communist bloc, arguing that Americans should become "the first aggressors for peace." Both the State Department and the Oval Office repudiated his remarks. After being dressed down by President Truman for "talking out of turn about foreign policy," Matthews was, in the president's words, "very contrite." Nonetheless his days as secretary of the navy were numbered.

Following a Far Eastern inspection tour, on 28 June 1951, Matthews was named ambassador to Ireland and formally left the secretary's post on 31 July. Dan A. Kimball succeeded him. Matthews cannot be ranked among the effective civilian leaders of the navy. Malcolm Cagle and Frank Manson, in *The Sea War in Korea*, mention him only once in the entire volume. Paolo Coletta's biographical sketch of Matthews concludes, "Completely unversed in the ways of the Navy and of Washington, he broke the chain of competent men James V. Forrestal had trained . . . ." His principal accomplishment was to install Forrest Sherman as chief of naval operations. Matthews died of a heart attack on 19 October 1952 in Omaha.

—*Malcolm Muir, Jr.*

References:

Barlow, Jeffrey G. *Revolt of the Admirals: The Fight for Naval Aviation, 1945–1950*. Washington, DC: Naval Historical Center, 1994.

Cagle, Malcolm W., and Frank A. Manson. *The Sea War in Korea*. Annapolis, MD: Naval Institute Press, 1957.

Coletta, Paolo E., "Francis P. Matthews, 25 May 1949–31 July 1951." In *American Secretaries of the Navy*. Vol. 2, *1913–1972*, edited by Paolo E. Coletta. Annapolis, MD: Naval Institute Press, 1980.

See also: Burke, Arleigh Albert; Johnson, Louis A.; Sherman, Forrest P.; Truman, Harry S.

Matthews, H. Freeman
(1899–1986)

U.S. diplomat during the Korean War. Born in Baltimore, Maryland, on 26 May 1899, Harrison Freeman Matthews graduated from Princeton University in 1921, finishing a master's degree the next year. Matthews completed postgraduate courses at the Ecole Libre de Sciences Politiques in Paris in 1922 and 1923. His first career post with the U.S. Foreign Service was in Budapest in 1923, and he also held posts in Madrid, Havana, and Bogotá. Matthews was the first U.S. representative to the Franco government after the Spanish Civil War. During World War II he worked at the U.S. embassy in Paris, then at Vichy when the Germans occupied France. Relocating to London, Matthews was General Dwight Eisenhower's political adviser and assisted with strategic plans for the 1942 invasion of North Africa.

In the following year, Matthews began work as director of European affairs at the State Department. He became influential in U.S. foreign policy and advised Presidents Franklin D. Roosevelt and Harry S. Truman. Matthews attended wartime conferences at Potsdam, Yalta, and Cairo, as well as postwar foreign ministers' meetings in Moscow and Paris.

Appointed ambassador to Sweden in 1947, Matthews served in that post until 1950, when he became the deputy undersecretary of state to Secretary of State Dean G. Acheson. In this position Matthews participated in discussions about policy making and diplomatic efforts during the Korean War. He acted as a liaison between the state and defense departments, an especially difficult job while temperamental Secretary of Defense Louis A. Johnson was in office. Matthews offered advice regarding the conduct of the Korean War and related diplomatic efforts. He has been credited for providing the initiative that helped efforts in seeking a cease-fire and armistice in May 1951. Throughout his career, Matthews was involved in complex diplomatic situations, calmly deliberating answers to difficult questions.

Aware that during the post–World War II Berlin Crisis communication with the Soviet Union's United Nations (UN) representative had helped resolve issues, Matthews suggested that the spring 1951 stalemate might be ended through informal contact with the Soviet ambassador at the UN. Matthews suggested to Acheson that George F. Kennan should attempt to talk secretly to Jacob A. Malik, the Soviet Union's UN representative, to assess Soviet attitudes toward a cease-fire. Acheson agreed, and Kennan reported that Malik told him on 5 June 1951 that the Soviets wanted peace but that the United States needed to contact the Chinese and North Koreans. During a 23 June 1951 radio address, Malik suggested both sides should withdraw to the 38th parallel and begin cease-fire and armistice talks. Although the armistice did not occur in 1951, Matthews's efforts to begin negotiations were helpful in encouraging future deliberations at the Kaesŏng truce talks.

Working closely with Undersecretary of State James E. Webb during the Korean War, Matthews remained in office until 1953. He began work as ambassador to the Netherlands in 1953 and became ambassador to Austria four years later. While in that post he supervised meetings with U.S. president John F. Kennedy and Soviet Union leader Nikita Khrushchev. Matthews retired from the Foreign Service in May 1962 and was chairman of the United States Section of the Permanent Joint Board on Defense for the United States and Canada for six years. He died on 19 October 1986, in Washington, D.C.

—*Elizabeth D. Schafer*

References:
Acheson, Dean G. *Present at the Creation: My Years in the State Department*. New York: W. W. Norton, 1969.
Current Biography, 1945. New York: H. W. Wilson, 1946.
New York Times, 21 October 1986.
Who's Who in America, 1972–1973. Chicago: Marquis Who's Who, 1972.
See also: Acheson, Dean Goodersham; Cease-Fire Negotiations; Johnson, Louis A.; Kaesŏng Truce Talks; Kennan, George F.; Kennan-Malik Conversations; Malik, Jacob (Iakov) Alexandrovich; Potsdam Conference; Truce Talks; Truman, Harry S.; Webb, James E.

McCarthy, Joseph R.
(1908–1957)

U.S. senator and the best-known exponent of the sweeping charges of domestic Communism that helped to create a political climate of hysteria and suspicion in the United States during the Korean War. Born in Grand Chute, Wisconsin, on 14 November 1908, to a farming family of modest circumstances, Joseph R. McCarthy was educated at Little Wolf High School, Manawa, and Marquette University, where he earned an LL.B. in 1935. He then practiced law in Wisconsin.

An early interest in politics led to McCarthy's 1939 election as judge of the Tenth Judicial Circuit in Wisconsin, a position he left in 1942 to join the military. Although McCarthy's war record was rather undistinguished, he inflated it and ran for the Senate as a Republican. After losing in 1944, he succeeded two years later in defeating the veteran Robert M. La Follette, Jr. During the campaign McCarthy characterized his opponent as "communistically inclined." McCarthy's early years in the Senate were legislatively vacuous and distinguished principally by his persistent disregard for, and violation of, that body's traditions, privileges, and etiquette and his skill in alienating powerful colleagues in both parties.

On 9 February 1950, seeking an issue on which to focus a successful reelection campaign, McCarthy used the occasion of a speech at Wheeling, West Virginia, to state that he possessed a list of names of acknowledged Communists employed by the State Department. Various Republicans had made similar charges against Roosevelt and Truman administration officials ever since the mid-1930s. The distinctive features of McCarthy's allegations were their seeming veracity and his willingness not only to deliberately make numerous untruthful statements but to continue to repeat them even when they were shown to be lies. His timing was opportune in that his speech came three weeks after the conviction of the former State Department official and suspected Soviet agent Alger Hiss for perjury in misstating the extent of his pro-Communist sympathies and contacts during the 1930s and early 1940s. McCarthy was also fortunate in that senior Republican politicians, however distasteful they might have found his tactics, were prepared to tolerate these as a means to achieve what they considered the desirable end of reclaiming the presidency in 1952 for the Republican Party after twenty years of Democratic dominance. Although a congressional investigation chaired by Democratic Senator Millard Tydings of Maryland found no evidence to substantiate McCarthy's charges, he continued to reiterate these and similar allegations against other Democratic officials with undiminished vigor.

The Communist takeover of mainland China in October 1949 and indications that the United States might abandon the rump Guomindang (Nationalist) regime of Jiang Jieshi (Chiang Kai-shek) on Taiwan, won McCarthy favor with the China lobby, those American partisans of Jiang who were determined to ensure continuing U.S. support for him. The unexpected June 1950 outbreak of the Korean War, following earlier suggestions by Secretary of State Dean Acheson in a speech six months earlier at the National Press Club that Korea lay outside the U.S. defensive perimeter, gave new credibility to McCarthy's accusations of traitorous incompetence in the State Department. Thus, it is entirely fair to state that the Korean War fully unleashed McCarthyism. During the Truman administration's remaining years, McCarthy flourished unchecked, subjecting numerous State Department officials, particularly Asian experts such as John Paton Davies, John Stewart Service, and John Carter Vincent, as well as higher officials such as Acheson, President Harry S. Truman, and General George C. Marshall, to generally unsubstantiated but persistent charges that they were either subversive Communist agents or at least naive and unreliable fellow-travelers. Numerous Americans, including government officials, civil servants at all levels, academics, entertainment figures, writers, and many others, likewise became the target of similar allegations, mostly unfounded and undocumented, rarely substantiated, sometimes malicious in origin, but often extremely difficult to disprove and capable of ruining careers and denying numerous opportunities to otherwise well-qualified individuals.

McCarthy's charges hampered the Truman administration's freedom of action in dealing with the Korean War, particularly with respect to the nonrecognition of China and its policies toward Taiwan, and subjected it to intense criticism over such matters as the replacement of General Douglas MacArthur as commander in chief of the United Nations forces in early 1951. China specialists who attracted his opprobrium tended to be shifted from Asian positions to presumably less sensitive assignments in Europe or elsewhere, if they were not dismissed, and within the State Department vast amounts of time and energy were devoted to refuting his charges.

During the 1952 election campaign McCarthy flourished; although Republican candidate Dwight D. Eisenhower disliked the Senator's tactics, political expediency led him to acquiesce in them and implicitly endorse McCarthy's allegations. It was thought particularly disgraceful that Eisenhower failed to publicly defend his World War II commander, General Marshall. The Republican capture of both houses of Congress that year and his own reelection initially seemed to give McCarthy further power; in 1953 he became chairman of both the Senate Committee on Government Operations and its Permanent Subcommittee on Investigations. Ironically, the Repub-

lican victory contained the seeds of McCarthy's own defeat, as the party leaders, no longer shackled by their eagerness to defeat the Democrats, found McCarthy's penchant for bullying, lying, and seeking publicity increasingly embarrassing and sought to dissociate themselves from his excesses.

In 1954 McCarthy extended his investigations to the military, a move the armed forces resisted, and he also launched increasingly harsh attacks on the Eisenhower administration, which eroded his support within his own party. In early 1954 televised hearings on alleged subversive activities in the military exposed all the unattractive aspects of McCarthy's methods to the U.S. public, features deliberately emphasized by respected broadcaster Edward R. Murrow. On 11 July 1954 a fellow Republican, Senator Ralph E. Flanders of Vermont, introduced a resolution calling for McCarthy's censure, and on 2 December after lengthy hearings, the Senate voted 67–22 to condemn him for behavior described as "contemptuous, contumacious, and denunciatory" and obstructive of justice.

Although still a senator, McCarthy spent his final years in relative obscurity, largely ignored by his colleagues, the president, and the press. On 2 May 1957, he died of complications due to alcoholism at the naval hospital in Bethesda, Maryland.

—*Priscilla Roberts*

References:

Kepley, David R. *The Collapse of the Middle Way: Senate Republicans and the Bipartisan Foreign Policy, 1948–1952.* New York: Greenwood Press, 1982.

Landis, Mark. *Joseph McCarthy: The Politics of Chaos.* Selingrove, PA: Susquehanna University Press, 1987.

Oshinsky, Daniel M. *A Conspiracy So Immense: The World of Joe McCarthy.* New York: Free Press, 1983.

Reeves, Thomas C. *The Life and Times of Joe McCarthy: A Biography.* New York: Stein & Day, 1982.

Rovere, Richard H. *Senator Joe McCarthy.* New York: Harper & Row, 1959.

See also: Acheson, Dean Goodersham; China Lobby; Davies, John Paton; Jessup, Philip C.; Jiang Jieshi (Chiang Kai-shek); MacArthur, Douglas; Marshall, George C.; McCarthyism; Nixon, Richard Milhous; Service, John Stewart; Truman, Harry S.; Truman's Recall of MacArthur.

McCarthyism

Militantly anti-Communist American movement of the late 1940s and 1950s, named after its best-known exponent (Republican Senator Joseph R. McCarthy of Wisconsin), which created a climate of often hysterical antiradicalism in the United States, giving rise to often outrageous and far-fetched allegations that many prominent U.S. officials were either Soviet agents or at least "fellow travelers" with dangerously pro-Communist sympathies.

The roots of McCarthyism lay in the long-standing antiforeign tradition of the United States, dating back at least to the mid-nineteenth century, one early manifestation of which was the "Know-Nothing" party, followed later by the Red Scare of 1919 just after the end of the First World War. Conservative opposition to the New Deal during the 1930s and 1940s gave new intensity to this outlook, leading to the establishment during the 1930s of no fewer than three congressional committees to investigate Communist penetration of government, the best known of these being the House Un-American Activities Committee (HUAC).

Set up in 1938 and chaired by Congressman Martin Dies, HUAC investigated charges that Roosevelt and, later, Truman administration figures had radical or pro-Soviet sympathies or connections. Such fears gained new credibility with the development of the Cold War and concomitant growing anxiety in the later 1940s over the Soviet Union and its influence. In 1947 HUAC regained public attention when it probed Communist ties of several leading Hollywood figures.

Historians such as Ronald J. Caridi and Richard M. Freeland have held the Truman administration partially responsible for the increasing plausibility of McCarthyism in the later 1940s. They cite the president's deliberate invocation of the Soviet threat in such foreign policy messages as the Truman doctrine speech of February 1947; the establishment, by Executive Order 9385 of 3 March 1947, of the Federal Loyalty Program, which monitored U.S. government servants; and accusations by Truman supporters during the 1948 election that rival Democratic politician Henry A. Wallace and his Progressive Citizens of America Party were naive in dealing with the Soviets and penetrated by Communist influences.

After 1948, when Republican candidate Thomas E. Dewey unexpectedly lost the presidential election to Truman, leading Republicans such as Robert A. Taft undoubtedly tolerated and encouraged charges that the Truman administration was effectively honeycombed with Communists, regarding such tactics, distasteful though they might be, as a potential means of ending the twenty-year Democratic monopoly of the presidency.

McCarthyism reached a peak, and also found a name for itself, when McCarthy, apparently seeking an issue on which to win reelection to the Senate, charged in a 9 February 1950 speech at Wheeling, West Virginia, that he possessed a list of known Communists currently serving in the State Department. Three weeks earlier, former State Department official and alleged Soviet agent Alger Hiss had been convicted of perjury for having testified to his lack of previous Communist connections; Secretary of State Dean Acheson's public refusal to ostracize his old friend Hiss would make him, in turn, the target of similar allegations. McCarthy's apparently well-documented though in fact ill-founded and exaggerated charges led to the establishment of a congressional investigating committee under Senator Millard Tydings; although it found no evidence to substantiate them, McCarthy continued to repeat these and many other accusations of the same nature against a wide variety of targets. The growing China lobby, eager to ensure continued U.S. support for the unpopular Nationalist regime of Jiang Jieshi (Chiang Kai-shek), which in 1949 Communist forces had ejected from the Chinese mainland to its island redoubt of Taiwan, was also quick to argue that any U.S. official who was less than uncritically committed to Jiang's cause was *ipso facto* a Communist agent.

The unexpected June 1950 eruption of the Korean War, together with several well-publicized contemporaneous espionage cases involving well-placed American, Canadian, and British spies, gave yet more plausibility to claims that the United States was riddled with secret Communist sympathizers. To many, particularly Republicans, Truman's decision early in 1951 to replace the insubordinate but vehemently—and publicly—anti-Communist General Douglas MacArthur, the commander in chief of United Nations forces, seemed to confirm suspicions that Communist influence extended to the highest levels of the U.S. government. Prominent U.S. leaders, among them Truman, Acheson, and Secretary of Defense George C. Marshall, together with numerous more junior State Department and other officials, particularly those responsible for Asian policy, were subjected to charges that they were covertly acting in the interests of the Soviet Union and international communism. Rebutting such allegations was time-consuming and hampered their effectiveness; in some cases promising diplomatic careers, such as those of John Paton Davies, John Stewart Service, and John Carter Vincent, were ended by persistent claims of pro-Communist sympathies, and even those less affected, such as Charles E. Bohlen or Philip C. Jessup, sometimes found confirmation in subsequent appointments difficult. Although in 1953 McCarthy became chairman of both the Senate Committee on Government Operations and its Permanent Subcommittee on Investigations, his influence declined rapidly after Republican president Dwight D. Eisenhower's electoral victory, in part because of the increasing discomfort and embarrassment which his excesses provoked among leading Republicans, whom political expediency had earlier led to endorse many of McCarthy's charges. In 1954 when McCarthy attempted to investigate alleged subversion in the armed forces, he met determined opposition from the military and, after televised hearings in which his aggressive bullying and unabashedly untruthful tactics alienated many Americans as well as his colleagues, he was censured by the Senate and lost virtually all his political influence.

In the long run, McCarthyism contributed to the U.S. commitment during the Korean War to Jiang's Nationalist regime on Taiwan as the only legitimate government of China and the consequent nonrecognition for over twenty years of the Communist People's Republic of China. The persistent attacks on the State Department's Asian specialists, which in most cases led to their resignation, also created a serious long-term deficit of U.S. diplomatic expertise in this area. The legacy of McCarthyism was also apparent in the reluctance of U.S. officials in the 1950s and 1960s to abandon Asian regimes to Communism for fear of the political consequences, an outlook that undoubtedly contributed to the subsequent U.S. involvement in Vietnam.

—*Priscilla Roberts*

References:

Caridi, Ronald J. *The Korean War and American Politics: The Republican Party As a Case Study.* Philadelphia: University of Pennsylvania Press, 1968.

Caute, David. *The Great Fear: The Anti-Communist Purge under Truman and Eisenhower.* New York: Simon & Schuster, 1978.

Freeland, Richard M. *The Truman Doctrine and the Origins of McCarthyism.* New York: Schocken, 1971.

Fried, Richard M. *Nightmare in Red: The McCarthy Era in Perspective.* New York: Oxford University Press, 1990.

Griffith, Robert. *The Politics of Fear: Joseph R. McCarthy and the Senate,* 2d ed. Amherst: University of Massachusetts Press, 1987.

Kepley, David R. *The Collapse of the Middle Way: Senate Republicans and the Bipartisan Foreign Policy, 1948–1952.* New York: Greenwood Press, 1982.

Schrecker, Ellen. *Many Are the Crimes: McCarthyism in America.* Boston: Little, Brown, 1998.

See also: Acheson, Dean Goodersham; Bohlen, Charles E.; China Lobby; Davies, John Paton; Eisenhower, Dwight D.; Jessup, Philip C.; Jiang Jieshi (Chiang Kai-shek); MacArthur, Douglas; Marshall, George C.; McCarthy, Joseph R.; Nixon, Richard Milhous; Service, John Stewart; Taft, Robert Alphonso; Truman, Harry S.; Truman's Recall of MacArthur.

McClure, Robert A.
(1897–1957)

U.S. Army major general, chief of the Psychological Warfare Division during the Korean War, and originator of the idea of voluntary repatriation of prisoners of war (POWs). Born in Matoon, Illinois, on 4 March 1897, Robert A. McClure attended the Kentucky Military Institute (1912–1915). He was commissioned in the U.S. Army in 1916 and served in the Philippine Islands and in China. During the interwar years McClure attended the Infantry and Cavalry Schools, the Command and General Staff School, and the Army War College. He later taught at the Infantry School

and Army War College before becoming the military attaché in London.

In October 1942 McClure was appointed chief of the Psychological Warfare Service attached to the Operation TORCH task force in the invasion of North Africa. Task force commander General Dwight Eisenhower charged him with conducting psychological warfare against Axis forces. Following a reorganization of the Anglo-American Allied Force Headquarters, McClure, now a brigadier general, became chief of the Information, News, and Censorship Division, which included a new Psychological Warfare Branch. He continued in that position through 1943 as Allied forces liberated North Africa and invaded Sicily and Italy.

As one of the highest ranking officers with any experience in psychological warfare, McClure was asked by Eisenhower to join Supreme Headquarters, Allied Expeditionary Force, as chief of the new Psychological Warfare Division in January 1944. Here McClure coordinated Anglo-American civilian and military strategic and tactical propaganda campaigns against Germany.

In July 1945 McClure became director of the Information Control Division of the U.S. military government in Germany; he remained in that post until 1947. Between 1947 and 1950 he was chief of the U.S. Army Civil Affairs Division and commandant of Fort Ord, California.

When the Korean War began in 1950, McClure became head of the Department of the Army's Psychological Warfare Division and played a leading role in promoting the use of psychological warfare in Korea. McClure was a founder of what would become the U.S. Army Special Warfare Center and School at Fort Bragg, North Carolina, and he served as its first director, from April 1952 until March 1953.

McClure was instrumental in persuading army officials and then the Truman administration to adopt a position opposing the forcible repatriation of Communist POWs. On the eve of the truce talks in July 1951 McClure approached U.S. Army Chief of Staff General J. Lawton Collins regarding the possible fate of Chinese prisoners who had fought under the Nationalists in the recent civil war. These individuals, McClure had learned, had been forced to join the Communist cause, and he feared that harsh punishments, or even execution, awaited them on their return. To forestall this possibility, McClure recommended that instead of sending the POWs back to the People's Republic of China (PRC, Communist China) against their will, the United States should undertake to send them to the Nationalist Republic of China (ROC) on Taiwan, a territory still officially considered a part of China. McClure believed that by doing so the United

States could avoid repeating its World War II experience of forcibly repatriating prisoners to the Soviet Union, where many were subsequently executed or sent to labor camps. Such a policy would also enhance United Nations psychological warfare by giving new assurance to Communist soldiers considering surrender that they would not be repatriated against their will. Finally, McClure concluded that the publicity surrounding the announcement that thousands of POWs would choose not to return home would seriously weaken Communism and be a major propaganda triumph for the United States.

Collins submitted McClure's idea to the Joint Chiefs of Staff on 6 July 1951. Shortly thereafter, Washington informed the commander in chief of United Nations Command General Matthew B. Ridgway that he could develop a position based on the principle of voluntary repatriation. The Communist delegations at the truce talks refused to accept this policy and for the next eighteen months rejected out of hand all attempts at compromise concerning this issue. This created an impasse that stalled progress toward a peace settlement or armistice.

In February 1952 McClure proposed a new idea that avoided the term of "voluntary repatriation" altogether. Under his plan, the United Nations would agree to a prisoner exchange, but would exclude those claiming they were impressed into Communist service, those who did not reside in an area controlled by the Communists, or those who claimed political asylum. Men in these categories would be referred to the governments concerned under Item 5 of the proposed armistice agreement. In this manner the issue of repatriation would become a postwar issue separated from the talks seeking an end to the fighting. The POW issue was settled on 26 April 1953, when both sides accepted the idea of voluntary repatriation that included an extensive screening process.

In 1953 McClure became chief of the U.S. military mission to Iran, remaining in that position until his retirement in 1956. He died in Shalimar, Florida, on 1 January 1957.

—*Clayton D. Laurie*

References:

Hermes, Walter G. *United States Army in the Korean War: Truce Tent and Fighting Front*. Washington, DC: Office of the Chief of Military History, 1966.

Laurie, Clayton D. *The Propaganda Warriors: The American Crusade against Nazi Germany*. Military Studies Series. Lawrence: University Press of Kansas, 1996.

———. "The U.S. Army and Psychological Warfare Organization and Operations, 1918–1945," Washington, DC: U.S. Army Center of Military History. Unpublished manuscript.

New York Times, 5 January 1957.

Who Was Who in America, 1951–1960. Chicago: Marquis, 1963.

Who's Who in America, 1950–51. Chicago: Marquis, 1950.

See also: Collins, Joseph Lawton; Eisenhower, Dwight D.; Joint Chiefs of Staff (JCS); Ridgway, Matthew Bunker.

"Meat Grinder" Strategy
(January–June 1951)

An offensive technique used by the U.S. Eighth Army during the first half of 1951 that emphasized deliberate advances supported by firepower. This helped the United Nations Command (UNC) regain the initiative in the Korean War. Although it did not produce operations that achieved decisive results, this method was an ideal complement to the strategy of attrition that focused on inflicting maximum punishment on Communist forces instead of securing terrain objectives pursued by the UNC during the second half of the war's first year. The strengths of this technique included simplicity, control, reduced UNC casualties, and maximum use of firepower; the drawbacks included a deliberate sacrifice of maneuver, little chance for individual initiative, predictability, and a decidedly negative impression on the public.

Eighth Army commander Lieutenant General Matthew B. Ridgway developed this method in early 1951. The Eighth Army continued to use this method under Lieutenant General James A. Van Fleet's leadership until the battlefield situation stabilized in June 1951. Although the U.S. press criticized the technique as excessively brutal and the U.S. State Department viewed the term "meat grinder" as reducing the intent of Eighth Army operations to little more than wanton killing, this technique was one of the main components of the Eighth Army's rebirth in early 1951, and it is largely responsible for the UNC's ability to recapture Seoul and reposition itself along and above the 38th parallel in its final locations.

The Chinese intervention into the Korean War in the fall and winter of 1950 forced the Eighth Army to withdraw well below the 38th parallel by the beginning of January 1951. This and the arrival of General Ridgway to command the Eighth Army in late December 1950 were important precursors to the development of the "meat grinder" technique. The Eighth Army was a beaten unit in the wake of the Chinese intervention, and its leaders had to do something to restore its sagging spirit or risk being driven off the Korea peninsula entirely. Upon his arrival and after assessing the Eighth Army's senior leadership, Ridgway relieved one of three corps commanders and five of six division commanders, and he supported the relief of nineteen of forty-seven regimental commanders during the first six weeks of 1951. The combination of these two events made it imperative for the Eighth Army to take the offensive quickly and to develop plans for offensive actions that would be relatively simple to execute.

The destruction caused by the Meat Grinder strategy was undeniable, but such harsh tactics were essential to the recapture of Seoul. Here, a Marine tank and infantry move along a war-torn street, March 1951. (National Archives)

After conducting his own reconnaissance of the Eighth Army's front and the success of Operations WOLFHOUND, THUNDERBOLT, and ROUNDUP and Task Force Johnson, Ridgway initiated Operation KILLER using the meat grinder technique. Beginning by drawing the I, IX, and X Corps together to eliminate any gaps between units, Ridgway launched his offensive with a number of predetermined phase lines to control the movement of the units involved. Moving methodically from phase line to phase line, Ridgway directed that the attacking units completely destroy all Communist units in their paths, prevent any gaps from developing between units, and adhere precisely to his movement instructions. During the conduct of the operation, Ridgway coordinated massive artillery and close air support with the units' employment of their organic firepower, particularly tanks, machine guns, and mortars. This produced a plodding but unstoppable advancing juggernaut. While preventing units

from exploiting local successes and denying individual commanders any initiative, Operation KILLER was a successful endeavor, and it signaled a dramatic battlefield reversal in favor of the UNC during which the Eighth Army seized the initiative from Communist forces.

Building on the triumph of the method and the operation, Ridgway launched additional operations of similar design to capitalize on his success. Operations RIPPER, COURAGEOUS, RUGGED, and DAUNTLESS followed the basic outline of KILLER: closing gaps between units and then attacking methodically by moving under Ridgway's direction between a series of predetermined phase lines that made maximum use of all available firepower.

Using this technique, the once-beaten Eighth Army of 1950 was attacking in corps strength by the end of January 1951 and in army strength by the middle of February 1951. By March 1951 the UNC had recap-

After completing his assignment as chairman of UNCOK, Menon returned to India as foreign secretary. In 1950 he helped establish full diplomatic relations with the People's Republic of China (PRC, Communist China). This recognition irritated Washington and dampened relations between India and the United States. Menon preferred to steer India's foreign policy similar to that of Yugoslavia by aligning neither with the East nor the West. From 1952 to 1961 he was Indian ambassador to the Soviet Union, Poland, and Hungary. There he established an Indo-Soviet bond that would last decades after his retirement.

Following this tour as ambassador, Menon retired from foreign service and became president of the India-Soviet Cultural Society and chairman of the Indian Institute of Russian Studies. He wrote several books, including his autobiography *Many Worlds*, *The Flying Troika* (extracts from his diary), and *Delhi-Chungking*, which describes a four-month journey he made on foot and on horseback to China during World War II. Menon died of undetermined causes on 21 November 1982, in Ottapalam, India.

—*William H. Van Husen*

References:
Candee, Marjorie Dent, ed. *Current Biography, 1957*. New York: H. W. Wilson, 1952.
Christian Science Monitor, 21 January 1948.
New York Times, 22 November 1982.
See also: China, People's Republic of; India; United Nations Temporary Commission on Korea.

Menon, V. K. Krishna
(1896–1974)

Indian representative to the United Nations in 1952 who played a crucial part in the negotiations that led to the Korean armistice agreement. Born on 3 May 1896, at Calicut (Kozhikode) in the state of Kerala, the son of an Indian lawyer of the Malabar aristocracy, V. K. Krishna Menon graduated from the Madras Presidency College in 1918. He was then attracted to Annie Besant's Theosophical Society and also became active in the movement for Indian home rule. Moving to England, he earned a first-class B.Sc. degree and an M.Sc. in political science from the London School of Economics, and he also worked ardently for the Indian nationalist cause.

Menon became a well-connected member of the British Labour Party, close to such leading lights as Harold Laski, Sir Stafford Cripps, and Aneurin Bevan; and for fourteen years, beginning in 1934, he served on the St. Pancras Borough Council. It was partly from his influence that in 1944 the Labour Party passed a resolution demanding independence for India. Menon was also a close friend of Jawaharlal Nehru, whom he

met in 1927 and with whom he worked for Indian independence. At Nehru's request Menon represented the Indian Congress Party in various international venues, publicizing and furthering the Indian nationalist cause. Both Menon and Nehru, whose political views had received a sympathetic hearing from many British intellectuals, made a distinction between the British government and its policies and the country's people. From 1947 to 1952 Menon served as Indian high commissioner in London, where he was instrumental in keeping India within the British Commonwealth; he then became India's representative to the United Nations (UN), a position he held until 1962.

Sharp-tongued, obsessive, and vain, Menon alienated many U.S. officials, who resented his bitter anticolonial outbursts and his commitment to Indian nonalignment and who wrongly considered him pro-Soviet in outlook. As a leading nonaligned Asian nation with a recent anticolonial history and socialist leanings, India did, however, possess useful contacts with the Soviets and even more with the Chinese.

When he took up his UN position in 1952, Menon followed a policy consonant with the broad objectives of India's nonaligned stance of preventing further escalation of the war while facilitating negotiations among the major belligerents and their allies and patrons. By late 1952 the war was at a stalemate while the P'anmunjŏm truce talks had reached an impasse over the issue of the repatriation of prisoners of war. Menon immediately tried to suggest a compromise, and in November 1952 he formally introduced a prisoners of war (POW) settlement proposal in the United Nations. After significant modifications, this laid the foundation for the eventual agreement on this point, concluded on 8 June 1953. In early 1954, when an anticipated postarmistice Korean political conference intended to deal with this and other matters did not take place, Menon again moved to further the peace process, suggesting that any prisoners still unrepatriated should be returned to their original captors or custodians, who would be left responsible for their release, thereby circumventing a contentious issue.

As India's representative to the UN, Menon later made substantial contributions to resolving crises in Indo-China and Cyprus. He was immensely popular with the Indian general public, who appreciated his strong defense of India's position on Kashmir and Goa in the UN. His anticolonial attacks on Western nations on these issues and over Suez, his strong support for the 1955 Bandung Conference of Afro-Asian nations and a somewhat brief Sino-Indian entente, and his failure to condemn the 1956 Soviet intervention in Hungary, all won him the bitter antagonism of John Foster Dulles and other U.S. officials, as well as conservative Indians. Despite this opposition, Nehru

tured Seoul and recrossed the 38th parallel. Once north of the Han River, the Eighth Army used the meat grinder technique to "elbow forward" and improve its overall defensive position. After absorbing the Chinese Fifth Phase Offensive, Van Fleet used the meat grinder method again in June 1951 during Operation PILEDRIVER to recapture lost territory and move farther north, before halting for the first of many armistice negotiations throughout the war.

Despite the limitations inherent in the meat grinder technique, its greatest strength was that the Eighth Army's new leadership could successfully execute it while undertaking offensive operations that were essential in the transformation of the Eighth Army from a beaten unit to a competent and confident organization. In addition, the methodical advance dictated by the meat grinder approach maximized the Eighth Army's firepower advantage, minimized U.S. casualties, and allowed the soldiers to experience some much-needed battlefield success during the first half of 1951. Although this technique did limit individual initiative and opportunities for exploitation, it helped Ridgway, Van Fleet, and lower-level commanders to control combat operations and ensure that they continued to support the UN's limited political objectives. While the term itself was very unpopular and the technique was not perhaps the most elegant or sophisticated method of making war, the meat grinder strategy was particularly well suited for the situation faced by Eighth Army in the first half of 1951.

—*Kelly C. Jordan*

References:
Appleman, Roy E. *Ridgway Duels for Korea*. College Station, TX: Texas A&M Press, 1990.
Blair, Clay. *The Forgotten War: America in Korea, 1950–1953*. New York: Times Books, 1987.
Hoyt, Edwin P. *The Day the Chinese Attacked*. New York: Paragon House, 1990.
Matray, James I., ed. *Historical Dictionary of the Korean War*. New York: Greenwood Press, 1991.
Mossman, Billy C. *U.S. Army in the Korean War: Ebb and Flow, November 1950–July 1951*. Washington, DC: U.S. Army Center of Military History, 1990.
Ridgway, Matthew B. *The Korean War*. Garden City, NY: Doubleday, 1967.
See also: Close Air Support; COURAGEOUS, Operation; DAUNTLESS, Operation; Eighth United States Army; KILLER, Operation; PILEDRIVER, Operation; Ridgway, Matthew Bunker; RIPPER, Operation; RUGGED, Operation; Van Fleet, James Alward.

Media

The Korean War was the last major conflict covered primarily by print journalism. Stories on the war were run in newspapers, magazines, and wire services by the Associated Press (AP), United Press (UP), and the

International News Service (INS). Improvements in communications technology enabled stories to reach publication just hours after a battle occurred.

Radio was also a key component of Korean War journalism. The number of radio stations in the United States had increased significantly after World War II. In 1945 there were 960 AM radio stations and 50 FM stations in the United States. By 1950 there were 2,300 AM radio stations and 760 FM stations. Included were four national radio networks, of which NBC and CBS were the most popular. Americans listened nightly to reports about the war on these stations and their affiliates.

Television was still a novelty, and satellites were years away. But visual images of the war appeared in regular newsreel footage of the war before feature films in movie theaters. Such newsreel footage took several days to reach the United States, however.

Many of the war correspondents who reported live from Korea were seasoned veterans of war reporting, most having served in a similar capacity during World War II. When the war began there were only five journalists in South Korea, but by September 1950 there were 238 journalists there, and this number would later increase to 270. This was still far fewer than the 419 journalists who would cover the Vietnam War twenty years later.

There were two groups of journalists in the Korean War: those who reported from the front lines where the action was most intense and those who reported from the general safety of Allied headquarters. Journalism was not without risks, especially for those who sought to be close to the action. Over the course of the war, fifteen journalists were killed in action. Jim Becker of AP cynically remarked that it was a contest between the U.S. Air Force and the Communists as to who could kill the most journalists. Death on the battlefield was not the fate of others, however. One, Frank Noel, an AP photographer, was captured by the Chinese in 1951 and held prisoner for the remainder of the war.

From the beginning of the war there was a conflict of interest between the military and the press. Correspondents often encountered problems with military protocol regarding journalists. Ironically, it was the journalists themselves who called for full military censorship at the beginning of the war in order to limit competition among themselves and to reduce the risk of security breaches, as well as to improve the quality of reporting. For example, news of the Inch'ŏn landing appeared in newspapers while the troops were still at sea. Commander of the United Nations Command (UNC) General Douglas MacArthur at first refused to implement censorship of the press. He called on journalists to act responsibly, but at the same time he warned them not to reveal troop movements and the locations of UNC forces. Press censorship was finally imposed on 21 December 1950. Reportedly, this was favored by almost 90 percent of the journalists. Censorship remained in effect until the end of the war.

From the beginning of the war journalists wrote about the many problems facing the UNC during the early months of the war. They questioned UN involvement and whether South Korea was worth saving. Journalists showed the human side of the conflict by picturing soldiers suffering from malaise, disillusionment, homesickness, wounds, the cold, and other problems. Two reporters flew to Japan, where they investigated the lack of preparedness of Allied troops at the beginning of the war and equipment shortages. Military authorities would not allow these journalists to return to Korea because they feared their stories would affect morale. Journalists also covered corruption in the Syngman Rhee government by showing how South Korean police profited from selling army supplies, and how brothels and alcohol were made available to troops.

After censorship went into effect journalists were severely limited in what they were allowed to write. They were always told to report their stories from "Somewhere in Korea" and were forbidden to mention a specific unit by name until that information had been released by official sources; they also had to have permission from the authorities to write about any military action. They could not disclose the nationality of troops and were not allowed to report the number of casualties after a battle.

In January 1951 all journalists covering the United Nations Command were placed under military jurisdiction and given a list of possible punishments if they disobeyed military policies regarding censorship. MacArthur later expelled seventeen journalists who had questioned his policies and had been openly critical of the UNC war effort. The editor of *Stars and Stripes* was fired after he published a photograph of General William Dean in captivity. A few journalists later chose to return to the United States to be able to freely express their views on the war without censorship or fear of reprisal. Official news sources were often slanted. The Public Information Office of the Far East Command released news stories on the war, but these were biased to the point that they became little more than propaganda. Some topics that appealed to journalists but were not given full attention included the possible employment of the atomic bomb, disunity among the different UNC nations, the behavior of Allied troops as prisoners of war, and the P'anmunjŏm peace talks.

At the peace talks, UN correspondents were not allowed to speak with the UNC delegates, and they were denied access to maps and documents used by the military. This angered many reporters, and some turned to Communist reporters for information. The latter were happy to provide information and disinformation to Western reporters, much to the embarrassment of the UNC. UNC commander Lieutenant General Matthew B. Ridgway prohibited contact between Allied reporters and their Communist counterparts to reduce the threat of compromising military security.

Two of the best-known Communist reporters were Alan Winnington of the *London Daily Worker*, and Australian Wilfred Burchett. In earlier wars it would have been considered treason if a member of an Allied nation had reported from the enemy camp, and this was perhaps a first in war journalism. Burchett unleashed a propaganda attack, accusing the UN of employing germ warfare in Korea. He claimed that the UNC had toxic gases in bullets and artillery shells and had released bacterial warfare agents such as lice, ticks, and beetles against the Communist side to spread typhus and bubonic plague. The United States was slow to respond to these charges, and this helped lend credence to the Communist charges, which were later revealed to have been a deliberate propaganda hoax.

Another first in war journalism was Marguerite Higgins, correspondent for the *New York Herald Tribune*. Told several times to leave the battlefield because it was no place for a woman, she helped pioneer the way for future female reporters in later wars.

Journalists played an important role in the Korean War. They provided firsthand coverage from the battlefield and took considerable risks to inform the American public about the war. Several, including Higgins and Keyes Beech, won the Pulitzer Prize for their efforts in covering the war.

—*James R. Mahala*

References:

Beech, Keyes. *Tokyo and Points East.* Garden City, NY: Doubleday, 1964.

Braestrup, Peter. *Battle Lines: Report of the Twentieth Century Fund Task Force on the Military and the Media.* New York: Priority Press, 1985.

Higgins, Marguerite. *War in Korea.* Garden City, NY: Doubleday, 1951.

Kahn, E. J., Jr. *The Peculiar War: Impressions of a Correspondent in Korea.* New York: Random House, 1952.

Mercer, Derrik. *The Fog of War: The Media on the Battlefield.* London: Heinemann, 1987.

Summers, Harry G., Jr. *Korean War Almanac.* New York: Facts on File, 1990.

See also: Biological Warfare; Dean, William Frishe; Film and Literature of the Korean War; Higgins, Marguerite; MacArthur, Douglas; Ridgway, Matthew Bunker; Syngman Rhee.

Medics, Combat

In any armed conflict medical services are extremely important. Korea was no exception to this. In the combat zone, medical treatment started on the battlefield.

Enlisted men of a regimental medical company were called "medics" in the army and "corpsmen" by Marine units. Marine corpsmen were actually navy hospital corpsmen assigned to Marine units as combat medics. In army units one medic was attached to each rifle platoon, with a total of seven medics in a rifle company. Marine units were similarly manned. Most combat patrols included a medic.

These medical personnel had to deal with all manner of wounds and injuries, including those caused by small arms, heavy weapons, mortars, and artillery fire. Depending on the time of year they also dealt with frostbite and heat prostration, as well as various illnesses.

Medics, usually unarmed, carried out their duties in the heat of battle. With only small first-aid kits, they often accomplished medical near-miracles. Once battlefield casualties had been treated, they were evacuated to the battalion aid station by litter bearers. Many of these bearers were men of the Korean Service Corps. Some wounded had to find their own way to the rear if they were judged to be "walking wounded."

Depending on the seriousness of their injuries, the wounded men were then evacuated by jeep, ambulance, or helicopter to the regimental collecting station, the division clearing station, or a Mobile Army Surgical Hospital. Early in the war some fixed-wing liaison aircraft were also used for medical evacuation. Combat soldiers had a high regard for the medics and always felt better when medics were present during an operation.

The valor of the medics is attested to by the awarding of medals for valor. Medics received eight of the 131 Medals of Honor awarded in the Korean War. Of these, four (three posthumous) were awarded to army medics and four (all posthumous) went to navy hospital corpsmen serving with Marine units.

—*Norman R. Zehr*

References:

Apel, Otto F., Jr. *MASH.* Lexington: University Press of Kentucky, 1998.

Cowdrey, Albert E. *United States Army in the Korean War: The Medic's War.* Washington, DC: U.S. Army Center of Military History, 1987.

Jordan, Kenneth N., Sr. *Forgotten Heroes.* Atglen, PA: Schiffer Military/Aviation History, 1995.

Meid, Pat, and James M. Yingling. *U.S. Marine Operations in Korea, 1950–1953.* Vol. 5, *Operations in West Korea.* Washington, DC: U.S. Marine Corps Historical Branch, 1972.

See also: Aeromedical Evacuation; Hospital Ships; Military Medicine; Mobile Army Surgical Hospital (MASH).

Menon, Kumara Padmanabha Sivasankara (1898–1982)

India's ambassador to the People's Republic of China (1947–1948) and then the Union of Soviet Socialist Republics (1952–1961); chairman of the United Nations Temporary Commission on Korea (194? in Kottayam, Kerala State, India, on 18 Octobe? Kumara Padmanabha Sivasankara Menon gra? from Madras Christian College in 1918 and atte Christ Church, Oxford University, in Great Br? earning a master's degree with honors. Menon ? became a career civil servant in India, serving first Madras between 1922 and 1925. From 1925 to 1943 ? worked in the Foreign and Political Department in Ne? Delhi. During World War II Menon was appointe? agent-general to China to promote Sino-Indian cooper-ation in the war effort. After India's independence in 1947, Menon became its first ambassador to China.

In late 1947 the nine-nation United Nations Temporary Commission on Korea (UNCOK) came into being, and in January 1948 Menon became its chairman. The choice of Menon was no accident, as his reputation and success in forming a solid relationship with China was well known. Commission members were also aware that Koreans would identify with the representative of an Asian nation that had recently won independence.

In a 21 January 1948 speech Menon called for free elections throughout the entire Korea peninsula. To insure these elections, he set up three committees: one to study the means for securing a free atmosphere for the forthcoming elections; another to study Korean public opinion; and the third to develop an electoral system for Korea. This last committee was to study existing Korean electoral laws, both North and South, and recommend a mechanism compatible with these and General Assembly requirements. Commission goals were to hold free and unfettered elections; to ensure maximum voter turnout; and to create an atmosphere promoting voter enthusiasm. Not only must electors be free to vote, but there was to be freedom for candidates of all parties, including those of the extreme left and right. Menon believed that both East and West ideologies could coexist. He hoped that Korea might be able to take concepts from both camps and evolve its own system.

North Korea balked at allowing UN-supervised elections, and, as a result, elections were held on 10 May 1948, only south of the 38th parallel. The Soviet Union refused to cooperate and denied Commission members entry into North Korea. Menon feared that electing a national government in the South would "set off a vaster cataclysm in Asia and the world." He wanted any partial-peninsula election to be held for the selection of representatives to consult with UNCOK only and not the establishment of a divided Korea. However, as a result of U.S. pressure on the commission, the Interim Committee agreed to hold elections in as much of Korea as was accessible—namely the portion of the peninsula south of the 38th parallel.

appointed him minister without portfolio in 1956 and minister of defense from 1957 to 1962. In the latter capacity Menon was generally held responsible for the debacle suffered by India in the 1962 Sino-Indian War, a disaster from which his career never recovered. Menon died in New Delhi on 5 October 1974.

—Priscilla Roberts

References:

Brecher, Michael. *India and World Politics: Krishna Menon's View of the World*. London: Oxford University Press, 1968.

Gopal, Sarvepalli. *Jawaharlal Nehru: A Biography*. London: Jonathan Cape, 1979.

Iyer, V. R. Krishna. *Nehru and Krishna Menon*. Delhi: Konark, 1993.

Raychaudhuri, T. "Menon, Vengalil Krishnan Kunji-Krishna." In *Dictionary of National Biography, 1971–1980*, edited by Lord Blake and C. S. Nicholls. Oxford: Oxford University Press, 1986.

Stueck, William W., Jr. *The Korean War: An International History*. Princeton, NJ: Princeton University Press, 1995.

See also: Bevan, Aneurin; Dulles, John Foster; India; Nehru, Jawaharlal.

Menzies, Robert G.
(1894–1978)

Prime minister of Australia throughout the Korean War. Born at Jeparit, Australia, on 20 December 1894, to a storekeeper who later became a member of the Legislative Province of Victoria State, Robert G. Menzies was educated at private schools and at Melbourne University, where he read law and won first-class honors. Menzies proceeded to practice law, specializing in constitutional law. By the late 1920s he had not only won an outstanding professional reputation but was also making a handsome income. Within eleven years of his entry into politics in 1928, Menzies had become leader of the United Australia Party (UAP), and from 1939 to 1941 he served as prime minister. After several years in opposition, during which the politically astute Menzies skillfully reconstituted the elements supporting the UAP as the right-of-center Liberal Party, he was reelected prime minister in 1949.

Prime Minister Menzies consulted with both the British and U.S. governments over Korea, but his own inclination was to follow the British line whenever possible. His government viewed the outbreak of the Korean War as part of a global struggle between communism and democracy, and on 27 June 1950 it responded by sending a squadron of heavy bombers to assist British Commonwealth forces combating the Communist insurgency in Malaya. The Truman administration put considerable pressure on its international allies and supporters, including Australia, to contribute military assistance to United Nations (UN) forces fighting in Korea. On 29 June, after the British sent naval vessels to Korea, Menzies followed suit,

committing an Australian destroyer and a frigate, and the following day, under some pressure from U.S. Far East commander General Douglas MacArthur, Menzies added a fighter squadron of P-51 Mustangs from the Royal Australian Air Force, which was already based in Japan.

Menzies and the British were both initially reluctant to commit ground troops, and discussions Menzies held in London with the British cabinet in July 1950 initially reinforced his predilections on this question. The British changed their minds after Menzies's departure by sea for the United States, and during his absence the Australian cabinet, led by Minister of External Affairs Percy C. Spender, decided to commit the 3d Battalion of the Royal Australian Regiment. Upon his arrival Menzies learned of this about-face and immediately capitalized on it to enhance Australia's prestige in the United States. In Washington he addressed both houses of Congress and secured a World Bank loan of $250 million. Menzies personally doubted whether a security pact with the United States was necessary and thought its American political prospects were poor, but the ANZUS (Australia–New Zealand–U.S.) Treaty, which was negotiated in 1951, was greatly facilitated by the Australian contribution to Korea.

Despite Menzies's firm support for the U.S. position on Korea, he, as with the British, was not totally uncritical of the U.S. stance. Less than anxious to tarnish Australia's advantageous image as a loyal U.S. ally or damage the new Australian-American alliance, he generally expressed Australian misgivings within a Commonwealth framework and left the British, Canadians, or Indians to take the lead in questioning U.S. policies. Menzies shared British concerns that the United States might escalate the war by attacking mainland Chinese territory or that it might employ atomic weapons. He fully endorsed British Prime Minister Clement Attlee's attempt, on his December 1950 visit to the United States, to dissuade Americans from use of their nuclear capabilities. In February 1951, as UN forces regained ground after the first shock of Chinese intervention, Australia expressed its concern that the UN forces might once more push too far into North Korean territory.

Menzies remained prime minister until his retirement in 1966, and throughout that time he remained a loyal ally to both Britain and the United States, joining the Southeast Asia Treaty Organization (SEATO) in 1954, sending Australian troops to assist the United States in Vietnam, and always regarding communism as the greatest international and Asian menace, to be combated at all costs. In retirement he wrote two volumes of memoirs. He died in Melbourne on 15 May 1978.

—Priscilla Roberts

References:

Cain, Frank, ed. *Menzies in War and Peace.* St. Leonards, NSW, Australia: Allen & Unwin, 1997.

Martin, A. W. *Robert Menzies: A Life.* Carlton: Melbourne University Press, 1993.

Menzies, Robert. *Afternoon Light: Some Memories of Men and Events.* London: Cassell, 1967.

———. *The Measure of the Years.* London: Cassell, 1970.

O'Neill, Robert J. *Australia in the Korean War, 1950–1953.* 2 vols. Canberra: Australian War Memorial/Australian Government Publication Service, 1981.

Prasser, Scott, J. R. Nethercote, and John Warthurst, eds. *The Menzies Era: A Reappraisal of Government, Politics and Policy.* Sydney: Hale & Iremonger, 1995.

See also: ANZUS (Australia–New Zealand–U.S.) Treaty; Attlee, Clement R.; Australia; MacArthur, Douglas.

Merchant, Livingston
(1903–1976)

U.S. deputy assistant secretary of state for Far Eastern affairs from 1949 to 1951 and special assistant to the secretary of state on mutual security affairs from 1951 to 1952. Born in Boston, Massachusetts, on 23 November 1903, into a long-established prominent New England family, Livingston Merchant was descended from one of the signers of the Declaration of Independence. After study at Princeton he joined the New York and Boston firm of Scudder, Stevens, and Clark as an investment counselor. In 1942, soon after the United States entered the Second World War, Merchant joined the Department of State, serving as assistant chief of the Division of Defense Materials until 1945, when he became chief of the War Areas Division. Both positions called upon Merchant's special expertise in economic matters, as did his subsequent assignment as counselor for economic affairs in the U.S. embassy in Paris. He formally joined the Foreign Service in 1947, when he was serving as chief of the State Department's Aviation Division. Throughout his long diplomatic career, Merchant was a skilled and able bureaucrat and administrator rather than an innovative thinker or broad strategist.

Merchant's first Asian posting was as counselor of the U.S. embassy in Nanjing from 1948 to 1949. He witnessed first hand the collapse of Jiang Jieshi's (Chiang Kai-shek's) Guomindang (Nationalist) government to the Communists. Disillusioned by the former's corruption and inefficiency, Merchant and other State Department Asian experts favored some form of rapprochement between the United States and Mao Zedong's People's Republic of China as both desirable and inevitable. Serving from 1949 to 1951 as deputy to Assistant Secretary of State for Far Eastern Affairs Dean Rusk, Merchant shared his superior's unassuming personal style and adopted the

posture of a loyal team player, a professional approach Foreign Service personnel generally tended to favor. While both men contributed to sometimes heated debates on U.S. Asia policy, including China, Japan, Korea, and Indo-china, neither was strongly identified with one particular viewpoint or outlook, and both men escaped the worst of the often bitter ensuing recriminations.

As Rusk's deputy, Merchant attended many of the most crucial policy meetings on the Korean War and was privy to the highest policy debates and decisions, although he initially tended to function as an observer rather than a key participant. He handled much of the war's routine diplomacy, and, as his experience grew, over time he became more involved in policy formulation and readier to express his personal views. As special assistant to the secretary of state on mutual security affairs (1951–1952), deputy for political affairs to the U.S. special representative in Europe (1952–1953), and assistant secretary of state for European affairs (1953–1956), Merchant dealt with the war's broader implications for U.S. defense policy. During the new Eisenhower administration, Merchant's European responsibilities also imposed on him the task of representing to his superiors in the State Department, including Secretary John Foster Dulles, the strong conviction of America's European allies that the war should be brought to an early conclusion. Merchant fulfilled this charge conscientiously.

In the later 1950s Merchant rose to become under secretary of state for political affairs, the third-highest position in the State Department. He also served two separate terms as ambassador to Canada, 1956–1958 and 1961–1962. After his retirement in 1962, Merchant became executive director of the World Bank, from 1965 to 1968. He died on 15 May 1976 in Washington, D.C.

—Priscilla Roberts

References:

"Livingston T. Merchant." In *Political Profiles: The Eisenhower Years,* edited by Eleanora W. Schoenebaum. New York: Facts on File, 1977.

McMahon, Robert J. "Livingston T. Merchant." In *Dictionary of American Biography, Supplement Ten, 1976–1980,* edited by Kenneth T. Jackson. New York: Charles Scribner's Sons, 1995.

U.S. Department of State, Bureau of Public Affairs. *Foreign Relations of the United States, 1950.* Vol. 7, *Korea.* Washington, DC: U.S. Government Printing Office, 1976.

———. *Foreign Relations of the United States, 1951.* Vol. 7, *Korea and China.* Washington, DC: U.S. Government Printing Office, 1983.

———. *Foreign Relations of the United States, 1952–1954.* Vol. 15, *Korea.* Washington, DC: U.S. Government Printing Office, 1984.

See also: Dulles, John Foster; Jiang Jieshi (Chiang Kai-shek); Mao Zedong; Rusk, David Dean.

Mexico

Mexico was the most important Latin American nation from the U.S. viewpoint, and Washington was hoping for the same type of support from Mexico during the Korean War that it had received during World War II. Then Mexico had worked closely with the United States economically to provide strategic materials and even labor needed for the U.S. war effort. Mexico was one of only two Latin American nations to furnish combat troops during World War II, a fighter squadron that saw action in the Pacific. Once the war ended, it wanted to maintain the close wartime economic ties to promote the rapid industrialization that government policy was pursuing. Mexico was more reluctant, however, to maintain the close military ties of World War II. Mexico supported the Inter-American Treaty of Reciprocal Assistance signed in Rio in 1947 but was unenthusiastic—if not downright suspicious—of U.S. efforts to create closer military links in the name of hemispheric defense. Like the other Latin American nations, Mexico was disenchanted with the U.S. emphasis on strategic concerns and doubted the seriousness of the Communist threat to the hemisphere in general or to Mexico in particular.

After the North Korean invasion of South Korea, Mexico supported the U.S. position on the major resolutions relating to the war in the United Nations (UN) General Assembly and offered to provide foodstuffs and medical supplies for the conflict. The United States, however, wanted a Mexican troop commitment, hoping that this might encourage contributions from other Latin American countries. In April 1951 U.S. officials made a formal request to a Mexican delegation in Washington headed by Foreign Minister Manuel Tello that Mexico contribute a division to the fighting in Korea. Tello replied that public opinion in Mexico would not support sending Mexican troops outside of Mexican territory and reminded U.S. officials that the U.S. government had earlier agreed with Mexico's view that support for military action in Korea did not obligate Mexico to send troops there. Tello also indicated that Mexico would not be able to bear the cost of supporting a division in the field, since the United States had a policy of requiring reimbursement for any expenses incurred by the U.S. government in equipping, training, transporting, or maintaining troops of other nations in connection with Korean service. Tello in particular emphasized the problem of sending Mexican troops to Korea with presidential elections scheduled in Mexico for July 1952; the Mexican Senate would have to approve any commitment of Mexican forces outside the country, a process that would almost certainly spark a major debate over the constitutionality of such a move as well as raise the volatile question of national sovereignty.

Washington continued to work for a promise of Mexican troops, hoping that the growing economic ties between the two countries might produce a change in Mexico's position. The United States had granted Mexico "most-favored nation" status in trade, even though no trade agreement was in force. The United States also backed loans to Mexico from the U.S. Export-Import Bank and the World Bank, as well as a growing program of technical assistance under the Point IV Program. Washington made a final effort to enlist Mexican military support at a meeting in Mexico City in early 1952. The United States wanted to reach an agreement with Mexico under the U.S. Mutual Security Act of 1951, which provided U.S. military assistance in exchange for a promise from the recipient country to participate in "missions important to the defense of the Western Hemisphere." Mexican officials were so nervous about the appearance of making a military commitment that the joint press release announcing the meeting put the emphasis on improving Mexico's defensive capabilities rather than on hemispheric defense.

When negotiations got under way in February 1952, the Mexican delegation again cited domestic political and constitutional problems that prevented the signing of a standard military assistance agreement. Negotiations quickly reached an impasse, although U.S. negotiators strung out the proceedings, fearing that an abrupt termination of the negotiations might discourage other Latin American nations from signing similar agreements. The end came when the U.S. delegation announced that it would have to return to Washington for consultation and further instructions. Mexico never signed a military assistance pact and never provided troops for UN operations in Korea.

While the United States unsuccessfully attempted to gain Mexico's military support, Mexico continued to provide diplomatic support for U.S. efforts. One of the most important developments in this area was Mexico's proposal in the UN aimed at breaking the deadlock over repatriation of prisoners of war (POWs), which had become the single biggest obstacle to an armistice. On 2 September 1952, Mexico's permanent representative to the UN, Luis Padilla Nervo, presented a letter to UN Secretary-General Trygve Lie containing a proposal from Mexican president Miguel Alemán. His plan was later offered as a draft resolution in the General Assembly on 1 November 1952. Alemán's plan recognized the principle of voluntary repatriation, which had been supported by the United States. The difficult question of what to do with those refusing repatriation would be handled by granting them temporary asylum with any UN member agreeing to the proposal. Those refusing repatriation would be given immigrant status and allowed to seek employment. Those who originally refused repatriation but later changed their minds would be returned to their home countries under UN auspices. The United States originally welcomed the proposal but later backed a proposal by the Indian delegation and suggested to Padilla Nervo that any action be deferred. Alemán's proposal was never voted on by the General Assembly, but its submission did help promote an eventual resolution of the POW controversy.

Although Mexico never provided the kind of military support that the United States thought appropriate, it did provide important economic and diplomatic support for the goals being pursued by the United States and the UN in Korea. It was perhaps unrealistic for U.S. officials to expect that Mexico would make a larger military contribution to the Korean War (a division), a conflict that Mexico considered both distant and nonthreatening, than it had in World War II, when a much more obvious and immediate military threat was present. Mexico had also undergone a lengthy process of reducing military influence in politics; Mexican politicians feared that military involvement in Korea ran the risk of returning the military to politics with a larger portion of the national budget.

—Don M. Coerver

References:

Parkinson, F. *Latin America, the Cold War, and the World Powers, 1945–1973.* Beverly Hills, CA: Sage, 1974.

U.S. Department of State, Bureau of Public Affairs. *Foreign Relations of the United States, 1951.* Vol. 2. Washington, DC: U.S. Government Printing Office.

———. *Foreign Relations of the United States, 1952–1954.* Vols. 4 and 15. Washington, DC: U.S. Government Printing Office, 1984.

See also: Colombia; Latin America; Padilla Nervo, Luis; Peruvian Prisoner-of-War Settlement Proposal; Repatriation, Voluntary.

Meyer, Clarence E.
(1891–1965)

U.S. economic mediator in Korea. Born on 14 August 1891, at East Ashford, New York, Clarence Earle Meyer graduated from Syracuse University in 1913. He began his career with the Standard Oil Company, marketing petroleum products in China. He then worked in the company's Hong Kong office when Standard Oil Company merged with its competitor, the Vacuum Oil Company, to create first the Socony-Vacuum Oil Corporation then, in 1933, the Standard Vacuum Oil Company. The next year Meyer was named general manager of the Standard-Vacuum Oil Company in Japan. He was imprisoned for seven months in solitary confinement after the United States declared war on Japan following the Japanese attack on Pearl Harbor.

After repatriation in 1942, Meyer was the petroleum attaché at the U.S. embassy in London. Three years later he returned to the United States to serve as director of the Standard-Vacuum Oil Company. He was vice-president in charge of the company's business in China and Japan from 1946 to 1950. Meyer was also director of the Far East–American Council of Commerce and Industry from 1945 to 1950. He retired from business in 1950 and began a seven-year U.S. government career, especially assisting the State Department with financial matters. Meyer was chief of missions for the U.S. Economic Cooperation Administration in Vienna, Austria, and for the Mutual Security Agency in the Far East.

During the Korean War Meyer settled currency concerns between the Republic of Korea and the United States. President Harry S. Truman appointed him director of a presidential mission in April and May 1952 to resolve the exchange rate between the U.S. Army and Republic of Korea (ROK). The ROK government had advanced Korea's currency, the wŏn, to the United Nations Command (UNC) to finance military operations during the Korean War. By February 1952 a dispute about the currency exchange rate had escalated into what was called the suspense account controversy.

South Korea suffered extremely high wartime inflation, with prices in early 1952 reaching almost forty times the 1947 level. The ROK government balanced its budget and tightened credit, believing that advancing currency for the use of UN forces was the primary cause of inflation. The Koreans wanted to settle wŏn advances, amounting to $70 million, to prevent hyperinflation. The Korean government hoped to keep the conversion rate at 6,000 wŏn to $1 and expressed disfavor of the UNC's joint control of Korea's foreign reserves. The United States argued that it needed the $70 million of advances to use after the war for rehabilitation of Korea and that the conversion rate should be 10,000 to 1. The ROK did not want to permit the UNC to control Korea's foreign exchange. The ROK government also demanded that all wŏn advances be settled quickly so that Korea would have funds to buy imports to sell to Koreans. The resulting profits would be taken out of circulation in an effort to stop inflation.

Lieutenant General Matthew B. Ridgway was determined to stop UN spending of wŏn and suggested that President Harry S. Truman send a special mission to help improve economic relations between Korea and the United States. Meyer led what became known as the Meyer Mission in the spring of 1952 to negotiate with the ROK. The mission's primary goal was to work with the ROK to stabilize the South Korean economy through improved use of U.S. economic aid and application of antiinflationary measures. The mission also sought decisive debate about how to reimburse the Korean government and establish the rate of exchange regarding advances of wŏn to UN forces.

On 24 May 1952, Meyer secured the Agreement on Economic Coordination, which promised to settle wŏn advances made since January 1952. Claims made during the first eighteen months of the war were delayed for settlement until after 31 March 1953. The UNC promised to repay the ROK all wŏn that had been sold to UN troops from January 1952 to May 1952 at the rate of 6,000 to 1. Outstanding wŏn balances drawn after 1 June 1952 were to be settled at an agreeable conversion rate. The UNC would also pay $4 million monthly to South Korea to apply against the settlement.

These payments helped slow inflation. Meyer and the Korean government representatives created the Combined Economic Board. Consisting of ROK and UNC representatives, this board strove to coordinate South Korean foreign exchange to stabilize finances and reconstruct the postwar Korean economy.

Meyer's expertise in Asian business enabled this successful understanding of financial relationships between the UNC and the ROK. By June 1953 Prime Minister Paek Tu-jin, formerly the ROK finance minister, visited the United States seeking future economic aid. He noted that the Meyer Mission had satisfactorily resolved the currency exchange issue and that it was no longer a problem.

After his Korean War work, Meyer was a member of missions to the Far East for the U.S. International Cooperation Administration. He was director of economic aid and chief of economic affairs at the U.S. embassy in Tokyo through 1957. Meyer also performed economic evaluations for the U.S. Department of State in Taiwan, the Philippines, and Honduras and worked for the Standard Oil Company in Australia. He won awards for public service and was president of the Japan-American Society in 1960. Meyer died on 15 March 1965, in Washington, D.C.

—*Elizabeth D. Schafer*

References:

National Cyclopedia of American Biography. Vol. 51. New York: James T. White, 1969.

New York Times, 17 March 1965.

U.S. Department of State, Bureau of Public Affairs. *Foreign Relations of the United States, 1952–1954.* Vol. 15, *Korea.* Washington, DC: U.S. Government Printing Office, 1984.

Who Was Who in America. Chicago: Marquis Who's Who, 1968.

See also: Korea, Republic of, History, 1947–1953; Meyer Mission; Paek Tu-jin; Truman, Harry S.; U.S. Policy toward Korea: 1950–1953.

Meyer Mission
(10 April–24 May 1952)

U.S. mission to the Republic of Korea (ROK) to deal with financial concerns. On 10 April 1952 President Harry S. Truman appointed Economic Cooperation Administration official Clarence E. Meyer as the head of a special mission to the ROK. The objective of the mission was to reach an agreement with Seoul "on measures which would promote the stability of the Korean economy and facilitate the military operations of the United Nations Command in Korea." Meyer was also to work out appropriate arrangements for control and coordination of the foreign exchange resources in South Korea.

In the general improvement of cooperation, the agreement concluding the Meyer Mission provided for the establishment of a combined economic board composed of one representative each from the ROK and the United Nations Command (UNC). The board's recommendations were directed toward the development of a program designed to provide maximum support to the UNC military effort in Korea, to relieve the hardships of the Korean people, and to develop a stable Korean economy. The board also was to coordinate all foreign currency exchange in South Korea.

In the spring of 1951 South Korea was experiencing massive inflation. The Seoul government saw the advances of its currency, the wŏn, for use by UN forces as the basic cause of inflation. The government recommended immediate and full settlement of outstanding wŏn advances ($70 million) to pay for imports, which could then be sold to Koreans. The ROK was also determined to keep the artificial current conversion rate of wŏn to dollars (6,000 to 1) for future transactions.

U.S. officials thought that the $70 million advance would have been inefficient because of the instability of the Korean economy. Instead of "premature reconstruction and development," they suggested using the amount after the war for basic rehabilitation. In his report to Washington, Meyer emphasized that the ROK should make every effort to utilize its earnings of foreign exchange to achieve the maximum counterinflationary effect.

The agreement also provided for a schedule of monetary adjustments in South Korea. All government experts in Washington agreed that the current wŏn-to-dollar rate of 6,000 to 1 was unrealistic and should be at least be 10,000 to 1. Under the terms of the agreement, the UNC agreed to repay to the ROK all wŏn sold to UN troops at the 6,000-to-1 rate for the period January–May 1952. Thereafter the UNC agreed to pay $4 million per month on account to be applied in settlement for Korean currency used by its forces. In addition, as soon as practicable after 31 March 1953, the UNC was to make full and final settlement at realistic conversion rates for any wŏn used by UNC forces between 1 June 1952 and 31 March 1953.

The ROK government used these foreign exchange payments with some success to curb inflation.

However, while the agreement provided for certain responsibilities of the board in economic coordination and reconstruction, in practice the organization concentrated its efforts primarily on the financial relations between the UNC and the ROK.

—*Zsolt Varga*

Reference:
U.S. Department of State, Bureau of Public Affairs. *Foreign Relations of the United States, 1952–1954.* Vol. 15, *Korea.* Washington, DC: U.S. Government Printing Office, 1984.
See also: Meyer, Clarence E.; Truman, Harry S.; United Nations Korean Reconstruction Agency (UNKRA).

Michaelis, John Hersey
(1912–1985)

U.S. Army officer, during the Korean War commander of the 27th Infantry Regiment. His superb leadership made it the best known U.S. command of the Korean War and earned him two battlefield promotions. Born at the Presidio of San Francisco, California, on 21 August 1912, John Hersey ("Mike") Michaelis attended grammar and high school in Lancaster, Pennsylvania. He then served in the army for a year before being appointed to the United States Military Academy, West Point, from Pennsylvania.

Graduating in the Class of 1936, Michaelis was commissioned in the infantry and assigned to Fort Thomas, Kentucky. Tours of duty in the Philippines and Fort Benning, Georgia, followed. During World War II Michaelis served with the 502d Parachute Infantry Regiment, 101st Airborne Division. When the regimental commander broke his leg and became incapacitated, division commander Major General Maxwell D. Taylor appointed the thirty-two-year-old Michaelis to the command. Michaelis was severely wounded in Holland; after he returned from the hospital, during the Battle of the Bulge, Taylor promoted him to full colonel and made him division chief of staff.

After the war Michaelis, along with a number of other young colonels, was reduced in rank to lieutenant colonel. He recalled that the army believed that they were too young to be full colonels. Michaelis served in the Pentagon from 1945 to 1948, the last two years as senior aide to Chief of Staff general of the Army Dwight D. Eisenhower. Eisenhower rated him as one of four lieutenant colonels "of extraordinary ability."

Michaelis was then assigned to Eighth Army headquarters in Japan. At the beginning of the Korean War he received command of the 27th Infantry Regiment as it arrived in Korea. His leadership of that regiment earned Michaelis and the 27th enviable combat reputations. Known to many in the regiment as "Iron Mike," Michaelis was soon promoted to colonel and, in February 1951, to brigadier general and assistant commander of the 25th Infantry Division. At age thirty-eight, he was the youngest general in the U.S. Army.

In early May 1951 Michaelis left Korea. The next year he became commandant of cadets at West Point. Subsequent assignments included commanding general, U.S. Army Alaska; V Corps; Allied Land Forces, Southeast Europe; and Fifth U.S. Army. From 1969 until his retirement as a four-star general in 1972, Michaelis served as commander in chief, United Nations Command, U.S. Forces, Korea and U.S. Eighth Army.

Michaelis retired to St. Petersburg, Florida. He died on 31 October 1985 of a heart attack at his summer home in Dillard, Georgia.

—*Uzal W. Ent*

References:
Assembly, July 1989. (West Point, NY: Association of Graduates.)
Blair, Clay. *The Forgotten War: America in Korea, 1950–1953.* New York: Times Books, 1987.
See also: Eisenhower, Dwight D.; Taylor, Maxwell Davenport.

MiG Alley

A 6,500-square-mile airspace in northwest Korea, site of the most intense jet aircraft combat throughout the war. In early 1950 the Communists established a MiG-15 base at the Manchurian border city of Dandong (Antung) to guard vital railroad bridges over the adjacent Yalu River. On 8 November 1950 the first jet-versus-jet combat resulted in the downing of a Soviet-built MiG-15 by a U.S. F-80 Shooting Star. MiG Alley quickly evolved as a testing ground for the new jet tactics as U.S., Soviet, and Chinese pilots pitted their skills and aircraft against one another. Russian and Chinese MiG-15 pilots enjoyed a number of advantages over their United Nations (UN) counterparts. The MiG-15 was superior in some respects to the North American F-86 Sabre, the most advanced U.S. fighter. Moreover UN pilots, based below the 38th parallel, were fighting over hostile territory and were severely limited in operational time over the Alley.

Typically, however, U.S. pilots were more aggressive and better trained and had often honed their combat skills in World War II. In contrast, Communist pilots exhibited a wide diversity of combat effectiveness. Skilled MiG pilots, or "honchos" in U.S. pilot parlance, won grudging respect as dangerous opponents, whereas novice Communist pilots, exhibiting little training, earned the derisive label of "nimwit."

As the war progressed, U.S. MiG Combat Air Patrols (MIGCAPS) effectively countered such Communist tactics as southbound "trains" of up to eighty MiGs each. On 22 July 1953, the last jet combat in MiG Alley ended when Sabre pilot Lieutenant Sam P. Young scored his first kill, a MiG-15.

—*Jeff Kinard*

References:

Blair, Clay. *The Forgotten War: America in Korea, 1950–1953.* New York: Times Books, 1987.

Futrell, Robert F. *The United States Air Force in Korea, 1950–1953.* Rev. ed. Washington, DC: Office of the Chief of Air Force History, 1983.

Sherwood, John Darrell. *Officers in Flight Suits: The Story of American Air Force Fighter Pilots in the Korean War.* New York: New York University Press, 1996.

See also: Aircraft (Principal Combat); Jet Aircraft, First Clash in History.

MiG, Operation

United Nations Command (UNC) effort to secure a MiG-15 aircraft. The swept-wing MiG-15, which made its combat debut in Korea in November 1950, quickly demonstrated its superiority over the straight-winged U.S. fighters in action at that time. It was also a match for the F-86 Sabre brought in specifically to counter it.

The MiG not only posed a threat to UNC bombing operations in North Korea but also to U.S. bombers in event of a war with the Soviet Union. Because so little was known in the West about the MiG, efforts were made to try and capture one to study its characteristics. The U.S. Far East Air Force formed a special guerrilla unit specifically to capture MiG parts, which it obtained in crashes. In April 1951 a technical team landed by helicopter to inspect a wreck. They blew it apart with grenades to secure some of the pieces but were soon driven off. The same month U.S. Navy units searched unsuccessfully for a MiG that had crashed at sea near the mouth of the Yalu River.

On 9 July a pilot ejected from a MiG northwest of P'yŏngyang. His aircraft continued out to sea and crashed on a sandbar off Sinmi-do in the Yalu Gulf. Operation MiG was the effort to capture that downed aircraft. It included the British aircraft carrier *Eagle* and cruiser *Birmingham*, Republic of Korea Navy small craft, and a lifting barge procured in Japan. On 20 and 21 July under cover of bombardment, the MiG was lifted off and taken to Pusan. It was then transported for evaluation to Wright-Patterson Air Force Base in Ohio, where it provided information on both engine performance and airframe.

The air force remained anxious to secure an undamaged MiG for combat evaluation and, in Operation MOOLAH, it offered cash incentives toward that end. No MiG was secured, however, until after the armistice, when a North Korean pilot defected with his aircraft to Kimpŏ Airfield. He had not been aware of the financial incentive.

Although the MiG-15 and F-86 aircraft may have been well matched in characteristics, ultimately UNC command pilots made the difference over their Communist counterparts, and F-86 Sabres eventually compiled a 7-to-1 victory ratio over their MiG-15 opponents.

—Spencer C. Tucker

References:

Futrell, Robert F. *The United States Air Force in Korea, 1950–1953.* Rev. ed. Washington, DC: Office of the Chief of Air Force History, 1983.

MacDonald, Callum. *Korea: The War Before Vietnam.* New York: Free Press, 1986.

Matray, James I., ed. *Historical Dictionary of the Korean War.* Westport, CT: Greenwood Press, 1991.

No, Kum-Sok, with J. Roger Osterholm. *A MiG-15 to Freedom: Memoirs of the Wartime North Korean Defector Who Delivered the Secret Fighter Jet to the Americans in 1953.* Jefferson, NC: McFarland, 1996.

Schuetta, Laurence V. *Guerrilla Warfare and Airpower in Korea, 1950–1953.* Montgomery, AL: Aerospace Studies Institute, Air University, 1964.

See also: Aircraft (Principal Combat); MiG Alley; MOOLAH, Operation.

Milburn, Frank William
(1892–1962)

U.S. Army general and commander of the U.S. I Corps during the Korean War. Born on 11 January 1892 in Jasper, Indiana, Frank W. Milburn graduated from the U.S. Military Academy and was commissioned a second lieutenant of infantry in June 1914. Between 1914 and 1918 he served with the 5th, 33d, and 15th Infantry Regiments in the Panama Canal Zone. He then returned to the United States for duty at Camp Beauregard, Louisiana.

In the immediate post–World War I period, Milburn served with the 5th Infantry at Camp Zachary Taylor, Kentucky; with the 28th Infantry at Camp Dix, New Jersey; as a student at the Infantry School; and at the student officer training camp at Plattsburg Barracks, New York. He also served as an instructor at the Infantry School at Fort Benning, Georgia, from 1922 to 1926, after which he was the professor of military science and tactics of the Reserve Officer Training Corps at the University of Montana, where he was also football coach. He then attended the two-year course at the Army Command and General Staff School at Fort Leavenworth, Kansas, graduating in 1933. He was then assigned briefly to Fort Sheridan, Illinois, as post adjutant and executive officer of the 12th Brigade. He subsequently returned to Fort Leavenworth, where he was an instructor at the Command and General Staff School from 1934 to 1938. After service with the 29th Infantry at Fort Benning, in July 1940 Milburn became plans and operations officer of the 8th Infantry Division at Fort Jackson, South Carolina. In May 1941 he was reassigned to duty as a regimental commander with the 6th Infantry Division at Fort Leonard Wood, Missouri.

Having been promoted to brigadier general in February 1942, Milburn assumed command of the 83d Infantry Division at Camp Breckinridge, Kentucky, in August 1942. He was promoted to major general the next month, and in December 1943 he stepped up to command the XXI Corps at Camp Polk, Louisiana. In October 1944 Milburn took XXI Corps to Europe and commanded it in operations there until July 1945, when he became the acting commander of the Seventh U.S. Army. In September 1945 he briefly commanded the XXIII Corps in Europe, and that November he returned to the United States to command the V Corps at Fort Jackson. Milburn returned to Europe in May 1946 as commanding general of the 1st Infantry Division.

After his promotion to lieutenant general, in June 1949 Milburn became acting commander of the U.S. Army Europe (USAREUR), and two months later he was officially assigned as deputy commander of USAREUR, a position in which he served until 1950.

On 10 August 1950 the U.S. IX Corps was activated at Fort Sheridan, Illinois, and Milburn was assigned to command it. With a small group of staff officers he left Fort Sheridan for Korea by air on 5 September 1950. On 11 September commander of the Eighth U.S. Army in Korea General Lieutenant Walton S. Walker reassigned Milburn to command I Corps at Taegu for the breakout from the Pusan perimeter. When Walker was killed in an automobile accident near Ŭijŏngbu on 23 December 1950, Milburn briefly assumed command of the Eighth Army until the arrival of Lieutenant General Matthew B. Ridgway on 25 December. Milburn subsequently commanded I Corps, consisting of the 3d and 24th U.S. Infantry Divisions, the 1st Republic of Korea Army Infantry Division, the Turkish Brigade, and the British 29th Infantry Brigade in the drive north toward the Yalu, the capture of P'yŏngyang, the Battle of Ch'ŏngch'ŏn River, and during the subsequent withdrawal of United Nations forces from North Korea in November–December 1950. He then led the I Corps in the defense against the Communist 1951 spring offensive and the subsequent United Nations counteroffensive.

Milburn retired from active duty in April 1952. He then served as the athletic director at Montana State University in Missoula, Montana, until 1954. He died in Missoula on 25 October 1962.

—*Charles R. Shrader*

References:

Ancell, R. Manning, and Christine M. Miller. *The Biographical Dictionary of World War II. Generals and Flag Officers—The U. S. Armed Forces.* Westport, CT: Greenwood Press, 1996.

Appleman, Roy E. *South to the Naktong, North to the Yalu.* Washington, DC: Office of the Chief of Military History, 1961.

Department of Defense biographical sketch.

Matray, James I., ed. *Historical Dictionary of the Korean War.* Westport, CT: Greenwood Press, 1991.

New York Times, 26 October 1962.

Schnabel, James F. *United States Army in the Korean War: Policy and Direction, the First Year.* Washington, DC: Office of the Chief of Military History, Department of the Army, 1972.

See also: Ridgway, Matthew Bunker; Walker, Walton Harris.

Military Air Transport Service (MATS)

Primary organization furnishing air transportation for U.S. armed forces. The Military Air Transport Service (MATS) was created on 1 June 1948 by a merger of the Air Transport Command (ATC) and the Naval Air Transport Service. MATS was placed under the command and direction of the chief of staff of the U.S. Air Force, with consent of the secretary of defense. The commander was either an air force or navy officer. MATS's primary responsibility was to provide air transportation for all departments and agencies of the Department of Defense and for other government agencies as authorized.

General Henry H. Arnold, then commander of the U.S. Army Air Corps (renamed U.S. Army Air Forces [USAAF] on 22 June 1941), created the first U.S. military air transport unit, the Air Corps Ferrying Command (ACFC) in May 1941, primarily to dispatch lend-lease aircraft to Great Britain. By 1942 it had delivered almost 1,350 aircraft. After the attack on Pearl Harbor, ACFC missions were expanded and air routes to the various theaters of war were developed to systematize the U.S. transport system. At the same time, new models of transport aircraft were purchased, which had more payload and range. These included the C-46, the C-47, and later the C-54.

In July 1942 USAAF officials changed ACFC's designation to ATC. Commanded by then–Major General William H. Tunner, one of ATC's greatest successes was the resupply of China from India beginning in December 1942. This operation was called "Flying the Hump" by pilots because its routes crossed the perilous Himalayan Mountains. ATC aircraft delivered 650,000 tons of supplies to beleaguered Nationalist Chinese forces holed up in Chongqing (Chungking).

After the war in June 1948, when the Department of Defense formed MATS, it charged the new organization to manage all strategic airlifts. To accomplish this, four squadrons were created under MATS: Naval Air Transport Service, the Air Weather Service, the Air Rescue Service, and the Airways and Air Communications Service.

The first big challenge for MATS after the war was the Soviet blockade of Berlin, which began less than a month after MATS was formed. By September 1949 the blockade had been broken by General Tunner and his crews, who flew nearly 1.8 million of the 2.35 million tons of supplies delivered to West Berlin during "Operation Vittles."

Nine months later the Korean War broke out. This time MATS operated a strategic logistics and supply pipeline of nearly 11,000 airline miles from the United States to Japan to Korea. In nearly three years MATS delivered 80,000 tons of cargo and 214,000 combat troops and support personnel to the Korean Theater of Operations. Air Rescue Service personnel saved hundreds of pilots and crews who were able to ditch or parachute off the Korean coast and many who bailed out over land, some in enemy territory. Last but not least, the subsequent aeromedical evacuation airlift returned over 65,000 wounded personnel to the United States.

Major General Tunner commanded in-theater airlift, cargo, and transport assets from 26 August 1950 to 8 February 1951. Officially, he commanded the Far East Air Forces (FEAF) Combat Cargo Command (Provisional) and 315th Air Division (Combat Cargo). He had actually arrived in July 1950 to take charge of airlifting United Nations and U.S. troops and supply assets to Korea with about 250 mostly C-119 Flying Boxcars (some C-46s, C-47s, and C-54s too) scraped together by CSAF General Hoyt Vandenberg to plug the hole through which the enemy was pouring. Among the first units airlifted to Korea were the 187th Airborne Regiment of the 101st Airborne Division and portions of the 1st Marine Division.

One of the biggest early airlift assignments for MATS and FEAF Combat Cargo Command was the evacuation of U.S. citizens (many civilian dependents) out of Korea to Japan. The success of ferrying civilians out and troops in helped solidify the Pusan perimeter and allowed General Douglas MacArthur to execute his daring Inch'ŏn landings. In a very real sense, the ability of MATS and other airlift personnel to rapidly deploy vital men and materials to Korea throughout the war proved decisive in stemming the North Korean advance in 1950 and ultimately preserving the Republic of Korea.

After the Korean War, Tunner and others realized that MATS needed larger and more technologically advanced cargo/transport aircraft. In the 1950s this led to the development and deployment of propeller-driven cargo aircraft such as the C-124, C-130 (mostly for tactical airlift), and C-133. Clearly, the workhorse of this era was the C-124 Globemaster (known to pilots in Korea who flew it as the "Crowd Killer").

The 1960s saw the development of the first strategic jet airlift aircraft, the C-141 Starlifter. Entering the inventory in 1965, the C-141 (modified to be the "B" model in the 1970s and 1980s) and its much larger sister jet "trash hauler," the C-5 Galaxy (in service in 1969), proved particularly effective in providing strategic airlift support to such theaters of operation as Southeast Asia and the Persian Gulf.

In 1966 Congress recognized how important strategic airlift had become. As a result, it redesignated MATS the Military Airlift Command, headquartered at Scott Air Force Base, Illinois. Military Airlift Command was placed on the same level as other air force combat elements such as the Tactical Air Command and Strategic Air Command. In 1992, in the air force's general reorganization, the command's designation was changed to Air Mobility Command.

—*William Head*

References:

Futrell, Robert F. *The United States Air Force in Korea, 1950–1953.* Rev. ed. Washington, DC: Office of the Chief of Air Force History, 1983.

Thompson, Wayne. "The Air War over Korea." In *Winged Shield, Wing Sword: A History of the United States Air Force,* edited by Bernard C. Nalty. Washington, DC: U.S. Air Force History and Museum Program, 1997: 3–52

Tunner, William H. *Over the Hump.* Washington, DC: Office of Air Force History, 1985. Reprint, New York: Duell, Sloan, and Pearce, 1964.

See also: Aircraft (Principal Combat); MacArthur, Douglas; Military Sea Transport Service (MSTS); Vandenberg, Hoyt S.

Military Armistice Commission

Commission to supervise the implementation of the 27 July 1953 Korean Armistice Agreement, to monitor activity and investigate armistice violations inside the demilitarized zone (DMZ) and the Han River Estuary, to negotiate the settlement of armistice violations, and to act as a channel of communication between the two sides. In the months immediately after the signing of the Armistice Agreement, the Military Armistice Commission (MAC) also supervised the activities of the Neutral Nations Repatriation Commission, the Committee for Repatriation of Prisoners of War, and the Committee for Assisting the Return of Displaced Civilians.

During the truce talks both sides quickly agreed on the need for a military armistice commission with equal representation from both sides, but they differed as to the nature and scope of its activities. The United Nations Command (UNC) sought to establish a supervisory mechanism with the power of inspection throughout Korea in order to verify and enforce armistice compliance and prevent a military buildup. The Korean People's Army/Chinese People's Volunteer Army (KPA/CPVA) side accepted the idea of armistice supervision inside the DMZ but rejected the notion of MAC inspections in North Korea outside the DMZ. When, after months of negotiations, the UNC accepted a KPA/CPVA proposal for inspections outside the DMZ by teams of neutral nations, the way was clear for agreement on the composition and functions of the MAC. The commanders of the opposing sides would be solely responsible for enforcement of and compliance with the armistice. The MAC would supervise the armistice inside the DMZ, while the Neutral Nations Supervisory Commission would carry out inspections and conduct investigations outside the DMZ and report its findings to the MAC.

The MAC consisted of five members from each side, at least three of whom had to be general or flag officers. It was a joint organization with no chairman and would meet at the call of either side to discuss charges of armistice violations and other armistice-related matters. Each side's component of the MAC was authorized to have "staff assistants" and a secretariat to perform administrative functions. In addition, the armistice provided for ten Joint Observer Teams (JOTs), reduced to five teams in 1955, each composed of two to three field-grade officers from each side plus additional support personnel. The MAC could dispatch these JOTs to the DMZ or the Han River Estuary to investigate alleged armistice violations.

The commission held its first meeting on 28 July 1953, the day after the Armistice Agreement was signed. Its early work consisted of supervising the withdrawal of military forces from the DMZ, overseeing the repatriation of prisoners of war and the remains of war dead, delineating the MAC Headquarters Area, and establishing procedural rules for the operation of the MAC and its subordinate organizations. These matters were easily settled, but the commission proved totally unable to adjudicate armistice violations. Nor were the JOTs able to reach agreement on the circumstances of the alleged violations they investigated. After 1967 the KPA/CPVA rejected all further UNC proposals for JOT investigations. The last official JOT action ever conducted took place in 1976 to survey and delineate the boundary between the two sides in the P'anmunjŏm conference area following a clash between the guard forces in which two UNC officers were killed by KPA guards.

Although most MAC activity consisted of unproductive allegations and denials, the commission did some useful work. Serious incidents could be defused at MAC meetings; noncontroversial administrative actions, such as the return of remains, were often carried out in a businesslike and nonconfrontational manner; and the commission was a useful channel of communication. Beginning in 1971, the governments of North and South Korea also found it convenient to use the MAC conference facilities to carry out dialogue.

From 1953 to 1991 the UNC senior member was a U.S. officer. When the UNC appointed a Republic of Korea major general as senior member in 1991, the KPA rejected his credentials and refused to attend further MAC meetings. In 1994 the KPA unilaterally withdrew from the MAC, but it continued to maintain a negotiating organization at P'anmunjŏm under the

title "Korean People's Army P'anmunjŏm Mission." Later that year the Chinese government recalled the CPVA MAC delegation.

Despite these changes, much of the administrative and communications work of the MAC continues and talks below the plenary level still take place from time to time. In this manner the last vestiges of the Military Armistice Commission continue to operate.

—*Donald W. Boose, Jr.*

References:

Armistice Agreement, 27 July 1953, and subsequent agreements.

Hermes, Walter G. *United States Army in the Korean War: Truce Tent and Fighting Front.* Washington, DC: Office of the Chief of Military History, 1966.

U.S. Department of State, Bureau of Public Affairs. *Foreign Relations of the United States, 1951.* Vol. 7, *China and Korea.* Washington, DC: U.S. Government Printing Office, 1983.

Wilhelm, Alfred D., Jr. *The Chinese at the Negotiating Table: Style and Characteristics.* Washington, DC: National Defense University Press, 1991.

See also: Agenda Controversy; Armistice Agreement; Demilitarized Zone (DMZ); Kaesŏng Truce Talks; Neutral Nations Repatriation Commission; Neutral Nations Supervisory Commission (NNSC); P'anmunjŏm Truce Talks; Truce Talks.

Military Awards and Decorations

United Nations

The United Nations Service Medal was the first military award established by the United Nations. It was authorized on 12 December 1950 in accordance with Resolution 483(V). Originally it was intended to be a general service medal with bars indicating the operation or the area of service. The reverse of the medal bears the inscription "For service in defence of the principles of the charter of the United Nations." The ribbon consists of seventeen alternating blue and white stripes, representing the United Nations colors. The ribbon is surmounted with a "Korea" bar.

The criterion for the award was thirty days in the Korea area of operations (including support bases in Japan and Okinawa) between 27 June 1950 and 27 July 1954. Military personnel of all nations that provided troops were eligible, subject to the approval of their own national forces. Civilians of international relief agencies, such as the Red Cross, the Salvation Army, the St. John's Ambulance Brigade, and the Young Men's Christian Association also qualified for the award.

This particular medal was never awarded for any action other than Korea, and in 1961 its name was officially changed to the United Nations Korean Medal. The award also was unique among modern medals because it was awarded in ten different official language versions. These include English (2,760,000 awarded), Korean (1,225,000), Amharic (5,650),

Dutch (5,800), French (16,900), Greek (9,000), Italian (135), Spanish (1,300), Thai (10,650), and Turkish (33,700). An unofficial Tagalog version also was issued to Philippine troops.

United States

The first U.S. military decorations for combat in Korea were awarded for actions that took place between 9 and 11 June 1871. Nine U.S. sailors and six Marines received the Medal of Honor when the Asiatic Squadron under Rear Admiral John Rodgers landed a shore party and captured several forts around the Korean capital in retaliation for being fired upon by the forts ten days earlier.

The current system of U.S. military decorations came into being during World War I. Until that time, the only U.S. decoration was the Medal of Honor, first established during the American Civil War. With the establishment of additional decorations in 1918, Congress created the concept of the "Pyramid of Honor." For the first time in U.S. history it was recognized that there were degrees of military service to the nation, each worthy of its own level of recognition.

At the apex of the Pyramid of Honor is the Medal of Honor (often erroneously called the Congressional Medal of Honor). The highest U.S. military award for battlefield heroism, it is awarded by the president in the name of Congress to members of the U.S. Armed Forces who distinguish themselves by gallantry and intrepidity at the risk of their lives above and beyond the call of duty while engaged in combat against an armed enemy of the United States. U.S. troops sometimes irreverently referred to it as the "Big Sticker" or the "Blue Max"—a reference to the old imperial German Pour le Mérite and the Medal of Honor's blue ribbon. One hundred thirty-one Americans received the Medal of Honor (ninety-three posthumously) during the Korean War—seventy-eight soldiers, forty-two marines, seven sailors, and four airmen. The Unknown Soldier of the Korean War also received the Medal of Honor.

Some levels of the Pyramid of Honor have more than one decoration because each branch of the service has its own unique award. In 1950 there were different army and navy designs for the Medal of Honor. At the next level down, the decorations even had slightly different names, but the Distinguished Service Cross and Navy Cross were equivalent. Many decorations, including the Silver Star, Distinguished Flying Cross, Legion of Merit, Bronze Star Medal, Air Medal, and Purple Heart, were and are awarded by all branches of the military. In 1960 the U.S. Air Force introduced the Air Force Cross and its own design for the Medal of Honor and the Distinguished Service Medal. During the Korean War, airmen received army decorations.

The second-highest U.S. awards for combat heroism are the Distinguished Service Cross (DSC) and the Navy Cross. During the Korean War 805 Americans received the DSC and 220 (mostly marines) received the Navy Cross. Fourteen Allied soldiers also received the DSC.

Unlike many European systems of decoration, both officers and enlisted soldiers are eligible for all U.S. military awards. Some, such as the Medal of Honor, the DSC, and Silver Star, are only for combat heroism. Others, such as the Distinguished Service Medal, are only for exceptional service. Some U.S. decorations, such as the Bronze Star or the Army Commendation Medal and Navy Commendation Medal, can be awarded for either service or valor. Awards made for valor are indicated by a bronze "V" device attached to the medal's ribbon.

Most U.S. heroism decorations are for combat actions only. One exception is the Soldier's Medal, which is the highest award for noncombat heroism. The Distinguished Flying Cross is awarded for heroism in flight during either combat or noncombat situations. The Bronze Star is awarded for either heroic or meritorious action. Technically, it can be awarded for noncombat service, but in practice it is almost always awarded for wartime service only.

The Legion of Merit is unique in the U.S. system because it exists in four classes. Originally established in 1942 as a decoration for high-ranking foreigners, the lowest class (Legionnaire) is also awarded to Americans. The Purple Heart, established by George Washington in 1782, was America's first standing military decoration. It lapsed after the Revolutionary War, but it was reestablished in 1932 as a decoration for wounds (including mortal wounds) received in combat. Purple Hearts awarded for Korea numbered 117,315.

In some countries, such as the former Soviet Union, soldiers wear multiple medals or ribbons for subsequent awards of the same decoration. The army and air force designate subsequent awards by affixing a bronze oak leaf cluster to the medal's ribbon. The navy and Marines use a small bronze star device. Fifth subsequent awards are indicated by a silver oak leaf cluster or a silver star device, respectively.

Although not a military decoration in the strictest sense, one of the most highly prized U.S. military awards is the Combat Infantryman Badge (CIB). A silver rifle on a blue bar backed by a silver oak wreath, the CIB was first authorized in World War II to distinguish infantrymen actively engaged in ground combat. A second award of the CIB is indicated by a star at the open top of the oak wreath. An individual can earn only one CIB per war; thus a soldier with a star on his CIB had served as an infantryman in both World War II and Korea. An equally prestigious award is the Combat

Field Medic Badge (CFMB) that distinguishes medics who directly supported infantry units. Both the CIB and the CFMB are unique to the army and are worn on the left breast, above the decorations, service medals, and all other qualification badges.

Among the U.S. military services, the army has a unique way of recognizing overseas service in a combat zone. Every U.S. Army soldier wears the patch of his current unit of assignment on his left shoulder. (The air force, navy, and Marines do not use unit shoulder patches.) A soldier who serves overseas in a combat zone with a unit is entitled to wear that unit's patch permanently on his right shoulder. Often erroneously called a "combat patch," its proper designation is an "overseas service patch." Well into the late 1970s, U.S. Army soldiers could still be seen wearing patches on their right shoulder from Korean service.

Immediately following World War II, U.S. military personnel performed occupation duty in Korea between 3 September 1945 and 29 June 1949. That service was recognized with the Army of Occupation Medal or the Navy Occupation Service Medal. All personnel who served in the U.S. armed forces anywhere in the world during the Korean War period, from 27 June 1950 to 27 July 1954, received the National Defense Service Medal (NDSM). Initially established by Presidential Executive Order 10448, the NDSM was authorized again for service during the Vietnam War and again during the period of the Persian Gulf War, the Bosnia peacekeeping mission and in Kosovo.

Those who actually served in Korea or its contiguous airspace or waters between 27 June 1950 and 27 July 1954 received the Korean Service Medal, established by Presidential Executive Order 110179. As in previous wars, participation in each specific campaign entitled the soldier to wear a small bronze star device on the medal's ribbon. Every fifth campaign was indicated with a small silver star device. Ten campaigns were conducted during the Korean War. A bronze arrowhead device on the Korean Service Medal indicated participation in an assault operation. In addition, paratroopers who participated in a combat jump also were authorized to wear a small gold star affixed to their airborne wings.

Between 1 October 1966 and 30 June 1974 U.S. troops serving in Korea were authorized the Armed Forces Expeditionary Medal. A state of war technically still existed between the two Koreas, and this was a period of high tension, numerous infiltration attempts by the North Koreans, and frequent armed clashes along the demilitarized zone. Some soldiers were awarded the CIB during this period, and U.S. troops did suffer casualties.

In 1956 the U.S. Congress authorized the Merchant Marine Korean Service Ribbon Bar for crew members who served aboard ships flying the American flag in Korean waters. In May 1988 the Congress also authorized the Merchant Marine Korea Service Medal to correspond to the existing campaign ribbon bar. In 1986 Congress authorized the creation of the Prisoner of War Medal, for all U.S. servicemen held captive by an enemy force after 5 April 1917—thus making award of the medal retroactive to World War I.

The United States also recognizes entire units with military decorations. Individuals who are members of the unit at the time the award is won are entitled to wear the unit award permanently on their uniforms. An individual joining a decorated unit at a later time can only wear the unit award while assigned to the unit.

The Distinguished Unit Citation for army and air force units and the Presidential Unit Citation for navy units were established in 1942. In 1957 the Distinguished Unit Citation was redesignated the Presidential Unit Citation (PUC). The PUC is the equivalent of a Distinguished Service Cross for a unit. At the next level down, the Naval Unit Citation is the unit equivalent of an individual Bronze Star. The army Meritorious Unit Citation (MUC), which has stricter criteria, is considered the equivalent of a unit Legion of Merit.

The army unit awards are easily identifiable by the gilt frame around the ribbon. The PUC is a solid blue ribbon in a gilt frame. The MUC originally was an embroidered gold wreath on an olive patch, worn on the lower left sleeve of the uniform. After the Korean War the MUC was converted to a solid red ribbon in a gilt frame. Members of the army wear unit awards over their right pockets. Members of the navy, air force, and Marines wear unit awards over their left pockets, integrated with their individual awards.

Great Britain and the Commonwealth

The British use a composite system of military awards. Some awards are only for officers, some are only for enlisted men, and some are for both. The highest British award for combat valor is the Victoria Cross (VC), established in 1856. The highest British award for noncombat valor is the George Cross (GC), established in 1940. The VC can only be awarded for gallantry in the face of enemy fire, whereas the GC is awarded for acts of noncombat heroism in either peacetime or war.

The criteria for the VC are actually more restrictive than for the U.S. Medal of Honor, which requires courage in the face of the enemy and the threat of loss of one's own life, but not necessarily under direct enemy fire. Thus, U.S. soldiers have been awarded the Medal of Honor for acts of extreme heroism while prisoners of war. British soldiers under the same conditions receive the GC. Both officers and enlisted men are eligible for both the VC and GC, and British civilians in noncombat situations are eligible for the GC. During the Korean War four British soldiers received the VC (two posthumously); and two Britons and one Australian received the GC (all as prisoners of war).

After the VC and GC the next highest British military awards are the first three classes of the Order of the British Empire, the Distinguished Service Order (DSO), and then the last two classes of the Order of the British Empire. Only officers are generally eligible for these awards. Both orders can be given for either exceptional service or for heroism, but the DSO is given only for wartime service. Officers receiving the DSO are considered to have "just missed" the award of the VC. During the Korean War the DSO was awarded to sixty-two British, eleven Australian, ten Canadian, and four New Zealand officers.

The Distinguished Conduct Medal (army and air force) and the Conspicuous Gallantry Medal (navy) are the awards for enlisted men who "just missed" the VC. The Distinguished Service Cross (navy), Military Cross (army), and Distinguished Flying Cross (air force) are combat heroism decorations for officers, although in some cases warrant officers qualify. The enlisted equivalents are the Distinguished Service Medal (navy), Military Medal (army), and Distinguished Flying Medal (air force).

Subsequent awards of British medals and decorations are indicated by a bar affixed to the medal ribbon, or by a heraldic rose device affixed to the ribbon bar. British soldiers who are Mentioned in Dispatches (MID) are authorized to wear an oak leaf device on the appropriate campaign medal. During Korea over 1,300 Commonwealth and 77 Allied soldiers were MID.

During the war, two British soldiers were awarded the U.S. Distinguished Service Cross, and nineteen were awarded the Silver Star. The 1st Battalion, Gloucestershire Regiment, and the Royal Artillery's C Troop, 170th Independent Mortar Battery both received the American Presidential Unit Citation for action at the Imjin River 22–25 April 1951. The American PUC remains a permanent part of the Gloucestershire uniform to this day.

Commonwealth soldiers, including those of Great Britain, New Zealand, Australia, and the Union of South Africa, all received the Korea Medal for service in the Korean War. Canadians received the Korea Volunteer Service Medal, which had a different ribbon and the name "Canada" on the medal beneath the Queen's profile.

France

France's highest decoration is the Légion d'Honneur, instituted by Napoléon Bonaparte in 1802 and awarded to French citizens and foreigners for outstanding services to France, civil or military. In practice it is rarely awarded to enlisted men. For Korean War service, it was awarded in the three lower of its five classes: Commander once, Officer seven times, and Chevalier twice.

The Médaille Militare, instituted by Louis Napoleon in 1852, is France's highest strictly military decoration. It is a most unusual decoration in that it can be awarded only to enlisted men and noncommissioned officers, and to generals and admirals. Officers from the ranks of lieutenant through colonel cannot receive the award. The Médaille Militaire was awarded 193 times for Korean War service.

The Croix de Guerre des Théâtres d'Operations Extérieures was awarded 2,898 times for Korea. Created in 1921 to recognize valor in expeditionary operations, it was similar to the Croix de Guerre of the two world wars. Since all members of the French Battalion in Korea were volunteers, they essentially all received the Croix du Combattant Volontaire. In 1980 a bar for "Corée" was authorized for that decoration.

Finally, all French servicemen in Korea received the French Korean Campaign Medal, the Médaille Commémorative Française des Opérations de l'Organisation des Nations Unis en Corée. The medal was authorized by the French Ministry of Defense on 8 January 1952.

Republic of Korea (ROK)

The highest military decoration of the Republic of Korea is the Order of Military Merit. The order has four classes: T'aegŭk, Ŭlchi, Ch'ungmu, and Hwarang. Each class has three grades, designated by a gold star, a silver star, or no device on the ribbon and ribbon bar. Foreigners are eligible for the Order of Military Merit. After his repatriation as a prisoner of war, the Taeguk Class with Gold Star was awarded to Major General William F. Dean, former commander of the U.S. 24th Infantry Division. Dean also received the U.S. Medal of Honor.

The Defense Medal was the only other South Korean decoration for military service outside of the Order of Military Merit group. South Korea also had a Wound Medal in two classes: First Class for the loss of a limb, loss of sight, or other disabling wound; and Second Class for all other wounds. Families of soldiers killed in action received the Family of Killed in Action Award.

The South Korean War Service Medal is officially called the June 25 Incident Participation Medal. This medal was awarded to many Allied soldiers, but the U.S. government declined the blanket awarding of the War Service Medal to U.S. troops. The United States did, however, allow its units to accept award of the Korean Presidential Unit Citation. As with the

American PUC, the Korean PUC is a ribbon in a gilt frame. U.S. personnel wore it on their uniforms in the same manner as the American unit citations.

Other Allied Nations

Most other Allied nations that sent troops to Korea recognized their service with the creation of Korean service medals or the awarding of existing general service medals with Korea bars. Those nations include Belgium, Colombia, Ethiopia, India, Luxembourg, the Netherlands, Norway, the Philippines, and Thailand. Danish personnel who served on the hospital ship *Jutlandia* received the special Jutlandia Medal.

Greece and Turkey did not institute special medals for Korea service. Their soldiers received only the United Nations Korea Medal. Ironically, most Turkish soldiers either refused to wear the medal or wore it with a plain dark red ribbon—because the ribbon's original colors are also those of Turkey's bitter historical rival, Greece.

Democratic People's Republic of Korea (DPRK)

As with most Communist countries of the Cold War era, the North Korean military awards system was strongly influenced by the system of the former Soviet Union. The highest DPRK decoration is the Gold Star Medal, which carries with it the title of Hero of the Korean DPR. Its purpose is to honor "heroic exploits in war." It is the equivalent of the Hero of the Soviet Union, which it resembles. As in the former Soviet system, the title of Labor Hero of the Korean DPR is a noncombat decoration considered to be of equal status.

The Order of the National Flag exists in three classes. It can be awarded for military valor or for outstanding political, cultural, or economic achievement. The Freedom and Independence Order is a combat award for commanders. The order's First Class is for division and brigade commanders, and the Second Class is for all other commanders. The Soldier's Honor Medal is a combat decoration for enlisted men and second lieutenants. It too is awarded in two classes.

The Military Merit Medal was the closest thing the North Koreans had to a campaign medal at the time of the war. On 25 July 1985, the Fatherland Liberation Commemoration Medal was established in recognition of the fortieth anniversary of the founding of the Korean Workers' Party and to commend those who served in the "Fatherland Liberation War that opposed the American invaders and their tools." Chinese People's Volunteer Army (CPVA, Chinese Communist) troops who served during the war were awarded the Military Merit Medal.

People's Republic of China

The Commemorative Medal for Opposing America in Assisting Korea was the Chinese campaign medal for the Korean War. Since the People's Republic of China was not officially in Korea, Chinese People's Volunteer Army (CPVA) members were awarded this medal by the People's Political Consultative Conference National Committee. The Chinese characters on the medal read, "Oppose America, Aid Korea, Commemorative." Similar commemorative medals were awarded to Chinese troops by some of the Chinese provinces close to the Korean border—Sungjiang and Liaoshi Provinces among them.

The Chinese also issued two very similar-sounding medals in conjunction with the visits to Korea of high-ranking Chinese delegations. The Commemorative Medal for War to Resist U.S. Aggression and Aid Korea was awarded in March 1951 to senior CPVA officers. On 18 September 1952, the Commemorative Badge for the Victory and Peace of the Korean War was issued to all Chinese troops and to DPRK officials.

Ironically, China was the only nation to issue a victory or peace medal in connection with the Korean War. Authorized on 25 October 1953, the Peace Medal reads "Glorious Peace" on its obverse and "War to Resist U.S. Aggression and aid Korea" on its reverse.

Relative Precedence of U.S. Military Decorations
During the Korean War

1. Navy Medal of Honor (1861)

   Army Medal of Honor (1862)

2. Distinguished Service Cross (1918)

   Navy Cross (1919)

3. Army Distinguished Service Medal (1918)

   Navy Distinguished Service Medal (1918)

   Coast Guard Distinguished Service Medal (1949)

4. Silver Star (1918)

5. Legion of Merit (1942)

6. Distinguished Flying Cross (1926)

7. Soldier's Medal (1926)

   Navy and Marine Corps Medal (1942)

8. Bronze Star (1942)

9. Air Medal (1942)

10. Navy Commendation Medal (1944)

    Army Commendation Medal (1945)

    Coast Guard Commendation Medal (1951)

11. Purple Heart (1932) *

---

* Note: After the Vietnam War, the precedence of the Purple Heart was elevated to just beneath the Bronze Star.

Campaigns Authorized for Wearing of the Star Device and
Assaults Authorized for Wearing of the Arrowhead Device
on the U.S. Korean Service Medal

1. UN Defensive	27 Jun 1950–15 Sep 1950
2. UN Offensive	16 Sep 1950–2 Nov 1950
3. Chinese Intervention	3 Nov 1950–24 Jan 1951
4. First UN Counteroffensive	25 Jan 1951–21 Apr 1951
5. Chinese Spring Offensive	22 Apr 1951–8 Jul 1951
6. UN Summer-Fall Offensive	9 Jul 1951–27 Nov 1951
7. Second Korean Winter	28 Nov 1951–30 Apr 1952
8. Korea Summer-Fall	1 May 1952–30 Nov 1952
9. Third Korean Winter	1 Dec 1952–30 Apr 1953
10. Korea Summer-Fall	1 May 1953–27 Jul 1953
Amphibious Assault, Inch'ŏ	15 Sep 1950
Airborne Assault, Sunch'ŏn-Sukch'ŏn	20 Oct 1950
Airborne Assault, Munsan-ni	23 Mar 1951

Relative Precedence of British Orders and Decorations

1. Victoria Cross (VC) (1856)
2. George Cross (GC) (1940)
3. Order of the British Empire, Knight Grand Cross (GBE) (1917)
4. Order of the British Empire, Knight Commander (KBE) (1917)
5. Order of the British Empire, Commander (CBE) (1917)
6. Distinguished Service Order (DSO) (1886)
7. Order of the British Empire, Officer (OBE) (1917)
8. Order of the British Empire, Member (MBE) (1917)
9. Distinguished Service Cross (DSC) (1914)

   Military Cross (MC) (1914)

   Distinguished Flying Cross (DFC) (1918)
10. Air Force Cross (AFC) (1918)
11. Distinguished Conduct Medal (DCM) (1854)

    Conspicuous Gallantry Medal (CGM) (1855)
12. George Medal (GM) (1940)
13. Distinguished Service Medal (DSM) (1914)

    Military Medal (MM) (1916)

    Distinguished Flying Medal (DFM) (1918)
14. Air Force Medal (AFM) (1918)
15. British Empire Medal (BEM) (1917)
16. Mentions in Dispatches

Relative Precedence of Military Decorations of the
Republic of Korea (ROK)

1. Distinguished Military Service Medal—T'aegŭk Class (1948)
2. Distinguished Military Service Medal—Ŭlchi Class (1948)
3. Distinguished Military Service Medal—Ch'ungmu Class (1948)
4. Distinguished Military Service Medal—Hwarang Class (1948)
5. Defense Medal (1950)
6. First Class Special Wound Medal (1950)
7. Second Class Wound Medal (1950)

Relative Precedence of Military Decorations
of the Democratic People's Republic of Korea (DPRK)

1. Title of Hero of the Korean DPR/Gold Star Medal (1950)
2. Title of Labor Hero of the Korean DPR (1951)
3. Order of the National Flag (1951)
4. Freedom and Independence Order (1950)
5. Soldier's Honor Medal (1950)
6. Order of Labor (1950)
7. Military Merit Medal (1949)

Soviet Union

The opening of records and archives since the end of
the Cold War has revealed a significant presence of
Soviet troops in North Korea during the war. These
included advisers and liaison officers, air defense crews
in the vicinity of the Manchurian airfields, and rotating
units of Soviet pilots flying MiG-15s. Although the picture is still incomplete, it appears that more than fourteen Soviet pilots achieved "ace" status in the skies
over Korea. At least twenty-one of these pilots received
the Soviet Union's highest decoration, the Gold Star
Medal and the title of Hero of the Soviet Union.

—David T. Zabecki

References:
Borts, Lawrence H. *United Nations Medals and Missions.*
Fountain Inn, SC: MOA Press, 1998.
Cunningham-Boothe, Ashley. *Marks of Courage.* Royal
Leamington Spa, UK: Korvet, 1991.
Hall, Donald. *British Orders, Decorations and Medals.* St. Ives,
Huntingdon, Great Britain: Balfour, 1973.
Ingraham, Kevin R. *Honors, Medals and Awards of the Korean
War, 1950–1953.* Binghamton, NY: Johnson City, 1993.
Kerrigan, Evans. *American Medals and Decorations.* London:
Apple Press, 1990.
U.S. Senate Committee on Veterans' Affairs, 96th Cong. *Medal of
Honor Recipients 1863–1978.* Washington, DC: U.S.
Government Printing Office, 1979.
See also: Appendix: Medal of Honor Winners.

Military Intelligence

U.S. military intelligence during the Korean War proved to be a roller coaster of triumphs and failures, innovations, and botched opportunities. Most high-ranking U.S. military officers disdained anything resembling unconventional intelligence gathering techniques, which resulted in failures to counter Communist tactics and strategies. General Douglas MacArthur relied on the conventional intelligence estimates of his Far East Command (FEC) G-2, Chief of Intelligence General Charles Willoughby, rather than trust the newly organized Central Intelligence Agency (CIA).

In the late 1940s the fledgling CIA infiltrated agents into China and North Korea who reported preparations for Kim Il Sung's June 1950 invasion of South Korea. U.S. intelligence officers failed to discover the preparations because the Korean People's Army (KPA) delivered orders by courier rather than sending them by radio. When KPA troops moved near the 38th parallel, MacArthur's staff concluded that the increased activity was some type of agricultural project.

Five days before the KPA attacked South Korea, CIA chief Roscoe Hillenkoetter sent intelligence estimates to President Harry S. Truman and his cabinet indicating that the KPA could mount a coordinated attack at any time. Both Washington and MacArthur's FEC ignored the warnings and, as a result, U.S. and Republic of Korea Army (ROKA) troops were totally unprepared for the onslaught that drove them to the brink of disaster.

Preparations for MacArthur's 15 September 1950 amphibious operation at Inch'ŏn necessitated substantial intelligence on the landing beaches. On 1 September a reconnaissance team clandestinely slipped ashore to check the high tides, mud flats, and beach defenses near Inch'ŏn. Critical information from this team allowed the FEC to correct its erroneous tide charts and adjust the landing plan, assisting in a successful operation. The night before the invasion the team infiltrated onto P'almi-do, an island that had an abandoned lighthouse atop a 219-foot peak. The team lit the light to guide the invasion force and then evacuated to waiting ships.

By the end of September United Nations Command (UNC) forces had recaptured Seoul and stood along the 38th parallel. MacArthur sought to free all of Korea from Communist domination, and with UN concurrence he launched a coordinated attack across the parallel, intending to advance north to the Yalu River, the border between North Korea and Chinese Manchuria.

Through People's Republic of China (PRC) radio broadcasts, Beijing warned the UN not to invade North Korea, but U.S. and UN officials ignored these warnings. On 2 October 1950 ROKA divisions attacked across the 38th parallel. PRC Foreign Minister Zhou Enlai then summoned Indian ambassador to China Sardar K. M. Panikkar to a meeting in which Zhou sent a message to the UN that the PRC would intervene militarily if UN forces crossed the 38th parallel. MacArthur ignored the warning and assured President Truman and the Joint Chiefs of Staff that China would not enter the conflict because the People's Liberation Army (PLA) was not prepared for any large assault. Truman regarded the Chinese threat as a "bald attempt to blackmail the UN." MacArthur promised a "great slaughter" if Chinese troops attacked UNC forces.

Again FEC analysis proved faulty because officers ignored agent reports and lacked methods of decrypting PLA radio messages. The PRC used Mandarin dialect and MacArthur's staff lacked trained linguists. Nationalist Chinese analysts easily read Beijing's messages, but U.S. officers distrusted the Nationalists' self-serving transcripts.

The FEC nevertheless had other sources that indicated large numbers of Chinese forces gathering across the Yalu. The 91st Strategic Reconnaissance Squadron, flying missions from Japan, provided some indication of unusual Chinese troop movements in Manchuria. CIA agents confirmed reports of PLA movements, but analysts believed that the Chinese were capable of "intervening effectively but not necessarily decisively."

Between 16 and 19 October three Chinese armies crossed the Yalu into North Korea. UN intelligence failed to understand Chinese march discipline and combat capabilities. These Chinese armies marched 286 miles in sixteen to nineteen days from Manchuria to combat-assembly areas. Marches began after dark and ended before daylight, when all troops were hidden from UN air reconnaissance. PLA officers had authority to shoot anyone who disobeyed orders to remain concealed. By late October over 210,000 Chinese troops had infiltrated into North Korea, literally under the noses of the UN. On 25 October these Chinese forces, known as the Chinese People's Volunteer Army (CPVA), struck the UNC in its drive toward the Yalu. Numerous CPVA prisoners indicated six Chinese armies in two army groups opposed the Eighth Army and X Corps. Both photo reconnaissance in Manchuria and Korean civilians confirmed movements of large formations of CPVA, but MacArthur ignored all indications of intervention and sent UN forces north into a Chinese trap.

On 24 November over 300,000 Chinese troops attacked and, in a sustained drive, forced UNC divisions to retreat south of Seoul. Historian David Rees said that "Inchon was imagination and intuition over sound military logic. The intelligence failure two months later was that too."

When Lieutenant General Matthew B. Ridgway arrived in Korea, his initial intelligence briefing concerning the CPVA was a big "goose egg" on a map with 175,000 scrawled inside it. By early 1951 the UNC actually faced about 400,000 Chinese troops with a few reorganized KPA divisions numbering just under 100,000 men. Ridgway immediately reorganized his intelligence structure and began relying on his own subordinates rather than FEC staff in Japan.

Ridgway also initiated the Li Mi Project to screen Korean refugees for KPA spies. UNC counterintelligence teams discovered hundreds of spies, guerrillas, and saboteurs among the refugees scattered across South Korea.

Poor organization and interservice rivalry inhibited most U.S. intelligence efforts in Korea. Combined Command for Reconnaissance Activities Korea and its supposed subordinate Joint Activities Command Korea (JACK) constantly bickered for funding and scarce assets. The CIA, presumably under JACK, ran numerous, still classified, successful covert operations into North Korea, infiltrating Korean agents by parachute, small boats, and "line crossers." North Koreans, trained by the United States, jumped behind the front lines from high altitude B-26s in a precursor to U.S. Army's High Altitude Low Opening operations. Military intelligence officers ignored much valuable information brought back by these clandestine operatives.

The army, air force, navy, and Marines all ran separate intelligence-gathering systems, including patrols, prisoner snatches, photo reconnaissance, radio interception, and a series of covert operations. Each service shared its information with only its higher headquarters. Agents employed by one service sold information to other services; sometimes one report might be sold four or five times. Because individual services refused to coordinate covert missions, agents sometimes called in air strikes on one another.

On 25 January 1953, the United States dropped a "Green Dragon Team" of ninety-seven men forty miles from P'yŏngyang in an effort to form a popular guerilla resistance in North Korea, but the mission was compromised. When C-119s attempted to resupply the team they met intense antiaircraft fire, and an air strike was called on the area. This was the last attempt to use paramilitary intelligence measures before the armistice in July 1953.

— Stanley S. McGowen

References:

Appleman, Roy E. *Disaster in Korea: The Chinese Confront MacArthur.* College Station, TX: Texas A&M Press, 1989.

Blair, Clay. *The Forgotten War: America in Korea, 1950–1953.* New York: Times Books, 1987.

Breuer, William B. *Shadow Warriors: The Covert War in Korea.* New York: Wiley, 1996.

Evanhoe, Ed. *Dark Moon: Eighth Army Special Operations in the Korean War.* Annapolis, MD: Naval Institute Press, 1995.

Heinl, Robert D. *Victory at High Tide: The Inchon-Seoul Campaign.* Philadelphia: J. B. Lippincott, 1968.

Malcom, Ben S. *White Tigers; My Secret War in North Korea.* Washington, DC: Brassey's, 1996.

Mossman, Billy C. *U.S. Army in the Korean War: Ebb and Flow, November 1950–July 1951.* Washington, DC: U.S. Army Center of Military History, 1990.

Rees, David. *Korea: The Limited War.* New York: St. Martin's Press, 1964.

See also: Central Intelligence Agency (CIA); Joint Chiefs of Staff (JCS); Kim Il Sung; MacArthur, Douglas; Panikkar, Sardar K. M.; Ridgway, Matthew Bunker; Truman, Harry S.; Willoughby, Charles A.; Zhou Enlai.

Military Medicine

Although it began only a half decade after the end of World War II, the Korean conflict engendered signal advances in military medicine, including the refinement of the Mobile Army Surgical Hospital (MASH), helicopter transport of the sick and wounded, and improvements in the treatment of vascular injuries, head injuries, and shock. Many of these techniques ultimately were translated to civilian medicine and have become standards of care.

Military medicine was in a tenuous state when Korean People's Army (KPA, North Korean) forces invaded the Republic of Korea (South Korea) on 25 June 1950; it was, if anything, in a worse situation than the combat arm.

After World War II, in response to both those still in uniform and civilians at home, doctors had been rapidly demobilized. Between June 1945 and June 1950, the Army Medical Corps had lost 86 percent of its officers and 91 percent of its enlisted personnel. In an attempt to replenish the supply, residencies had been opened at a number of army hospitals with the intent that, in return for being paid during postgraduate training, the new specialist physicians would serve for a time in the military. Unfortunately, the program was new, the potential help was still in the process of being trained, and the predicted nadir of physician supply was June 1950.

In addition, there was a relative shortage of civilian physicians, and those in domestic practice were busy, prosperous, and not anxious to volunteer for service in Korea. A specific doctor draft was not instituted until August 1950, and it produced no direct help in Korea until January 1951. Nevertheless, by 1952, 90 percent of physicians serving in Korea were draftees.

The first military medical contingent in Korea was the Advance Command and Liaison Group of fifteen officers and two enlisted men dispatched by the Far East Command on 27 June 1950. Its mission was to care for American refugees fleeing the North Koreans and to begin replenishing supplies lost in the fall of Seoul.

For medical purposes, the war may be divided into three phases: offensive operations, defense against invading forces and withdrawal, and static defensive operations. This distinction is important because the rate and type of injury differ among the three.

For the first time in the history of military medicine, data on each battle casualty and nonbattle casualty (divided into disease and nonbattle injuries) was collected on punch cards and returned to Washington for computer analysis by the Medical Department and the Surgeon General. An entirely separate set of data was collected by the Adjutant General, and the two sets do not uniformly agree. Surgeon General records report 18,769 killed in action, 77,788 wounded in action and admitted to treatment facilities, and 14,575 with wounds not requiring admission. The Adjutant General's records report 19,658 killed in action and 79,526 wounded in action. Only the Surgeon General collected data on disease and nonbattle injury. A total of 443,163 patients were admitted to treatment facilities during the war; this included 365,375 nonbattle admissions (82.4 percent). Of these, 290,210 were for disease and 75,165 were for nonbattle injury. Over the course of the war, 30 of each 1,000 active-duty personnel were killed in action, 121 of each 1,000 were admitted for battle injury, and 570 of each 1,000 were admitted for disease or nonbattle injury. In general all of these incidences declined as the war progressed.

The most common battle injuries were penetrating wounds (57 percent) and fractures (23 percent), although the specific mechanism of injury varied with the type of combat. Average casualties per division per day were 119 in withdrawal, 77 in defense against a main force, and 67 in offense against a main force. In addition, the death rate among casualties was 25.2 percent in defense and only 14.6 percent in offense. Death rates also varied according to the weapon with which the casualty was inflicted: 28.4 percent for small arms, 23.8 percent for mines and booby traps, 18.4 percent for artillery, and 10.8 percent for hand grenades.

Army hospitals in Korea performed 89,974 surgical procedures. Fifty-nine percent of those admitted with battle wounds required some sort of surgery, and the case-fatality rate was 2.5 percent (compared to 4.5 percent for World War II). Many patients required more than one operation, with the average being 1.2 procedures per wounded patient admitted. Surgery in Korea tended to be quick and of the salvage variety, leaving definitive treatment to rear-area hospitals.

One of the most important technical advances during the war was the increased use of whole-blood transfusions in resuscitation of patients in shock. A wounded soldier received an average of 3.3 pints of whole blood, although transfusions of 15 to 30 units were not unusual. This placed a predictable strain on the donation system, with 21,188 pints collected in the United States and 22,099 pints collected in Japan in 1950 alone. It is an interesting sidelight that Caucasian and native Japanese blood was segregated, although it is not known whether this was for medical or racial reasons.

Neurosurgery posed a particularly difficult problem both because of the complexity of the injuries and the extreme shortage of trained personnel. By 1952 a special evacuation path through the 8209th (and later the 8063d) MASH units commanded by Lieutenant Colonel Arnold Meirowsky was established to care for wounds of the head and spinal cord.

Vascular injuries posed another technical challenge. Use of vein grafts to repair arterial injuries was a significant advance, and, by 1951, these repairs resulted in salvage of 85 percent of limbs with major vascular disruptions. Cold injuries were an especially common cause of nonbattle traumatic admissions. During 1950 there were 1,791 cases of cold injury, for an incidence of 34 per 1,000. Medics were particularly hampered in the actions around the Changjin and Pujon reservoirs when it became so cold that medicine, intravenous fluids, and plasma froze and could not be used.

Infectious disease was a persistent problem. Of those treated for nonbattle-related causes and not requiring admission, 90 percent had infectious or parasitic disease. The most common were respiratory disease (20 percent), ill-defined febrile illnesses, and diarrheal disease. The latter was especially severe early in the war when hygienic facilities were lacking. Gastrointestinal disease (especially shigellosis) occurred at a rate of 120 per 1,000 per year in August 1950. Other common infectious problems were encephalitis, polio, hemorrhagic fever, hepatitis, and venereal disease. Malaria and plague were locally endemic but never became a serious problem for United Nations troops.

The third most common disease problem was neuropsychiatric (NP) illness. The frequency of disability from psychiatric illness varied greatly with the stage of the war. Early in the war, young psychiatrists were stationed at the rear. Because they were not close to battle and were inexperienced, they tended to be liberal in sending home soldiers with psychiatric complaints. As the war progressed, physicians were moved closer to the front and became less sympathetic and the rate of psychiatric disability dropped. A second factor was the kind of fighting going on at the time. The rate of "NPs" dropped from 249 per 1,000 before the Pusan breakout to 18.4 per 1,000 during the advance, though it rose again when the winter weather set in.

Wounded soldiers of K Company, 38th Regiment, 2d Infantry Division being treated at a forward aid station near Old Baldy, 19 September 1952. (National Archives)

Deployment of medical facilities proceeded rapidly in the fall of 1950. By November four MASHs, with bed capacity increased from a planned 60 to 150, had been established in Korea, along with three 400-bed semi-mobile evacuation hospitals, four 400-bed field hospitals, one station hospital, and three hospital ships. Two additional MASHs were deployed in 1951, and one of the evacuation hospitals was moved to Japan in December 1950. After the Chinese entered the war, three additional evacuation hospitals were committed, but they functioned as immobile station hospitals. The field hospitals were converted to treat prisoners of war.

The evacuation sequence from facility to facility was from battalion aid station to regimental collecting station to division clearing station to evacuation hospital at Pusan to Korean air fields to 118th Station Hospital at Fukuoka (Kyushu, Japan) to other army hospitals in Japan (Osaka and Tokyo) to Tripler Army Hospital (Hawaii) to Travis Air Force Base (California) or Lackland Air Force Base (Texas) to zone-of-the-interior hospitals. Patients requiring emergency stabilization or surgery could be sent from either the regimental collecting stations or the division clearing stations to the MASH units. From there, the stabilized patients were sent on to either the evacuation hospital at Pusan or directly to Fukuoka. Of admissions for battle injury, 10 percent received final disposition at a forward unit (aid, clearing, or collecting station), 57 percent at army hospitals in the Far East Command, 6 percent at non-army hospitals (navy or air force), and 26 percent at hospitals in the United States. These figures include both discharge and death, although 96 percent of all deaths occurred in one of the

Casualties aboard a U.S. Army hospital evacuation train. (National Archives)

Far East Command hospitals. Eighty percent of division wounded eventually returned to duty.

Transport changed as the war progressed. Because the terrain was difficult, the initial stages were by hand-carried litter, especially when combat units were moving either in advance or retreat. From the aid and clearing stations, transport was primarily by rail. Early in the war, gasoline-powered rail cars ("Doodlebugs") carried patients from the front at Choch'iwŏn to Taejŏn. They held 17 litters or 50 ambulatory patients and traversed the thirty miles in about forty-five minutes. As the front stabilized later in the war, formal rail transport was more frequent. Rail facilities were brought to within 8,000 yards of the front line, and evacuation trains typically comprised eight ward cars, two orderly cars, a kitchen, a dining car, a pharmacy car, an officer personnel car, and a utility car.

Because of both improved transport (both rail and air) and treatment facilities relatively close to the front line, a remarkable 58 percent of soldiers wounded in battle received medical care within two hours of injury and 85 percent were treated within six hours. The median time from wound to first care was ninety minutes, and 55 percent of casualties were hospitalized the same day they were wounded—a number that rose to nearly 100 percent by 1953.

Early in the war evacuation from Pusan to Fukuoka was principally by ship, with hospital ships, troop transports, and even ferries pressed into service. This relatively slow and expensive method of transport was quickly replaced by air evacuation. In the first year of the war, C-47s were used, although, as the war progressed, C-54s became available. The longer range of the C-54s allowed direct transfer to Honshu, and transports were divided 40-40-20 percent between Itazuki Air Base (Fukuoka), Itami Air Base (Osaka), and Tachikawa Air Base (Tokyo).

Because there was an initial shortage of all physicians and a persistent lack of some specialists, a tactical decision was made to substitute triage and transport for personnel. The army realized that the best use could be made of scarce personnel by concentrating them in hospitals in rear areas. Patients who were predicted to recover in fewer than 30 days were kept at Pusan; those expected to recover in 30 to 120 days were kept in Japan; and those anticipated to have prolonged recovery were returned to the United States. A complex of evacuation units grew around the 8054th Evacuation Hospital at Pusan. The 8054th was initially in the Pusan Middle School but grew to several buildings with 1,200 beds that handled up to 12,000 admissions a month. It was assisted by the Swedish Red Cross Hospital, the First Prisoner-of-War Hospital, and several hospital ships and specialized units.

The overall record of army medicine in Korea compares favorably to that of World War II. The case-fatality rate for those wounded in battle in the earlier war was 4.5 percent, dropping to 2.5 percent in the latter. In addition, these rates dropped as the war progressed— that for 1950 is not known, but for 1951 it was 2.1 percent, and by 1952 it was down to 1.8 percent. Of those wounded but not killed in Korea, 87.9 percent returned to duty, 8.5 percent were separated as disabled, and 1.4 percent were separated for administrative reasons. Overall, medical care in Korea was characterized by rapid transport, effective early resuscitation and surgery, and some advances in surgical technique and decline in mortality rates from battle injury.

—Jack McCallum

References:

Apel, Otto F., Jr. *MASH*. Lexington: University Press of Kentucky, 1998.

Cleaver, Frederick. *U.S. Army Battle Casualties in Korea*. Chevy Chase, MD: Operations Research Office, 1956.

Cowdrey, Albert E. *United States Army in the Korean War: The Medic's War*. Washington, DC: U.S. Army Center of Military History, 1987.

Smith, Allen D. "Air Evacuation—Medical Obligation and Military Necessity." *Air University Quarterly* 6 (1953): 98–111.

See also: Aeromedical Evacuation; Hospital Ships; Mobile Army Surgical Hospital (MASH).

Military Sea Transport Service (MSTS)

U.S. unified logistics organization established by the 1947 National Security Act to handle ocean transportation of all the military services. The Military Sea Transport Service (MSTS) actually came into being in October 1949 when it absorbed the Naval Transportation Service and shops and seagoing functions of the Army Transportation Corps. The Korean War broke out as this transfer of army troop ships to MSTS was in progress; it was completed as scheduled on 1 July 1950. Established in the Navy Department,

MSTS was essential to the U.S. war effort. The Military Air Transport Service (MATS) of the U.S. Air Force moved supplies, but most troops and supplies went from the continental United States to Korea by sea.

When the Korean War began, MSTS had fifty transports, forty-eight tankers, twenty-five cargo ships, and fifty-one miscellaneous smaller craft. This was only slightly more than 1.5 million dead-weight tons and could not begin to meet the requirements of U.S. forces in Korea. Chief reliance fell on civilian ships under MSTS charter. MSTS chartered eighty-seven of these, and it also brought out of the reserve mothball fleet a number of World War II vessels. Soon after the start of hostilities MSTS returned to service fifteen of these; and over the next months it reconditioned and returned to service groups of twenty, thirty, forty, and twenty-five ships. Until the latter could be made ready, MSTS chartered thirteen foreign ships. Early in 1951 the Maritime Administration let contracts for a $350 million program to build fifty new, fast cargo ships.

MSTS included chartered vessels, navy-manned (USS) and civil service–manned (USNS) transport and cargo vessels, and oil tankers from the Armed Services Petroleum Purchasing Agency. It also controlled the SCAJAP (Shipping Control Administration Japan) fleet of twelve freighters and thirty-nine tank landing ships (LSTs).

As a consequence of the war, military cargo handled by Japanese ports jumped from 125,000 tons in May 1950 to 1.4 million tons in September. The average thereafter was 1.2 million tons. Two-thirds of the traffic by sea to and from Japan went through the port of Yokohama. Pusan was the only deep-water port in Korea capable of handling a high volume of traffic; an excellent harbor, it could berth up to twenty-nine ocean-going ships at a time. The LSTs proved invaluable, as twelve to fifteen of these could unload at the same time over the beach. Pusan's total discharge potential was 40,000–45,000 tons per day. By late 1952 Pusan and its outports were handling about a million tons of cargo a month; all other South Korean ports, of which Inch'ŏn was the most important, were handling about a third of that total.

By autumn 1950 MSTS had under its control 404 vessels of different kinds, of which 350 were in ocean service, although not all of these vessels were in the Pacific. From June 1950 to June 1953, MSTS moved to, from, and within the Far East some 52,111,299 tons of cargo; 21,828,879 tons of petroleum; and 44,918,919 passengers.

—Spencer C. Tucker

References:

Cagle, Malcolm W., and Frank A. Manson. *The Sea War in Korea*. Annapolis, MD: Naval Institute Press, 1957.

Field, James A., Jr. *History of United States Naval Operations: Korea*. Washington, DC: U.S. Government Printing Office, 1962.

Huston, James A. *Guns and Butter, Powder and Rice: U.S. Army Logistics in the Korean War*. Selinsgrove, PA: Susquehanna University Press, 1989.

Sandler, Stanley, ed. *The Korean War: An Encyclopedia*. New York: Garland, 1995.

Summers, Harry G., Jr. *Korean War Almanac*. New York: Facts on File, 1990.

See also: Japan Logistical Command; Logistics in the Korean War; Military Air Transport Service (MATS); Second Logistical Command; United States Navy.

Mine Warfare

The naval mine has been a mainstay of modern warfare. The North Sea Mine Barrage, a large minefield laid by the U.S. Navy and Royal Navy between Scotland and Norway during World War I inhibited the movement of the German U-boat fleet. Mines released by U.S. Navy submarines and dropped by U.S. Army Air Forces B-29 bombers in the Western Pacific during World War II sank hundreds of Japanese warships, merchant ships, and smaller vessels. Enemy-laid mines also took a high toll of Allied ships in both world wars.

Thus, when President Harry S. Truman ordered U.S. armed forces into action in Korea at the end of June 1950, U.S. naval leaders took steps to deal with the mine threat. In early July, the commander of Naval Forces Far East Vice Admiral C. Turner Joy ordered Mine Squadron Three to clear enemy mines from the approaches to P'ohang on Korea's east coast. The United Nations Command (UNC) was desperate to stop the southward advance of the Korean People's Army and needed troops quickly deployed ashore at P'ohang.

Accordingly, Lieutenant Commander D'arcy V. Shouldice, in command of fleet minesweeper *Pledge* and motor minesweepers *Kite, Chatterer, Redhead, Partridge, Osprey*, and *Mockingbird*, carried out a sweep of the approaches to the port and confirmed that the Communists had not mined those waters. As a result, on 18 July 1950, the U.S. Army's 1st Cavalry Division disembarked and soon added its combat power to that of the units on the Pusan perimeter. Minesweepers also ensured that there were no mines around the essential port of Pusan.

The UNC was fortunate that it did not have to deal with North Korean minefields in the first critical months of the war because the Allied navies did not have adequate mine countermeasure resources. Owing to postwar demobilization and defense budget cuts, the World War II force of 500 mine warfare vessels, manned primarily by naval reserve sailors, had been reduced to a worldwide contingent of two destroyer minesweeper divisions, two fleet minesweeper divisions, and twenty-one smaller craft. During the post-war years the navy devoted much more of its attention and resources to the development of new aircraft carriers, jet aircraft, and shipboard surface-to-air missile systems than mine warfare ships and equipment.

Freedom from North Korean sea mines did not last long. As Allied forces carried out operations in preparation for the large-scale amphibious assault at Inch'ŏn, they discovered minelaying activity. On 4 September crewmen on the U.S. destroyer *McKean* spotted mines in the water near Chinnamp'o, and several days later two British warships destroyed a number of floating mines in the same area. Then on 10 September the crew of Republic of Korea Navy (ROKN) *PC 703*, a former U.S. Navy submarine chaser, caught a North Korean boat dropping mines in the water in the approaches to Inch'ŏn. Commander Yi Hŭng-so's ship dispatched the Communist minelaying vessel with one shot from its deck gun. Allied warships en route to the landing sites at Inch'ŏn on 13 and 14 September also spied mines piled on the shore for laying or already in the water. As they continued their passage up Flying Fish Channel, destroyers *Mansfield, DeHaven, Lyman K. Swenson*, and *Henderson* used their guns to eliminate the mines. The North Koreans had begun their minelaying operation too late to stop General Douglas MacArthur's amphibious landing at Inch'ŏn.

No sooner were UNC ground troops safely ashore at Inch'ŏn, however, than Soviet-made mines began to take a toll on UNC ships along the periphery of the Korea peninsula. On 26 September off North Korea, U.S. destroyer *Brush* struck a mine that killed thirteen sailors, wounded thirty-four more, and put the ship out of action. Two days later *YMS 509* of the ROKN sustained damage from a "floater" on the south coast. The next day *Mansfield*, spared at Inch'ŏn, hit a mine in North Korean waters that sent it to a shipyard in Japan. Then, in one day, 1 October, Communist mines destroyed the wooden-hulled U.S. minesweeper *Magpie*, killing or injuring its entire crew of thirty-three men, and badly damaged ROKN *YMS 504*. Sailors were killed and ships damaged in these separate incidents, but UN operations were not seriously disrupted. This could not be said of the planned Allied landing at Wŏnsan, when an armada of 250 warships and transports, the latter carrying 50,000 Marines and soldiers of the U.S. X Corps, waited idly offshore as minesweepers worked to clear an approach route through waters containing over 3,000 mines laid with the direct assistance of Soviet advisors.

On 10 October Captain Richard C. Spofford's Mine Squadron 3, warned by the helicopter crew from U.S. cruiser *Worcester* that mines were present in the waters off Wŏnsan, began its dangerous clearance mission. During that day and the next two, Spofford's nine vessels, helped by helicopter and PBM seaplane spot-ters, cleared a twelve-mile-long lane toward the landing site. The ships neutralized over thirty mines, while the men of Underwater Demolition Team 3 marked another fifty mines for later destruction. In midmorning of 12 October, however, minesweeper *Pirate* hit a mine and quickly sank, with six of its crewmen, and an hour later *Pledge* and six of its sailors met the same fate. Shore batteries added to the danger and difficulty of the operation. By the 18th, two days before the planned landing, the minesweeping force had almost cleared all moored contact mines from the approach lane to the beach. That day, however, magnetic influence mines destroyed ROKN *YMS 516*; half of its crew was lost. Discovery of these new weapons stalled the operation. Finally, on 25 October the way was clear for X Corps to deploy ashore at Wŏnsan. The operation, however, would be an "administrative landing," since Republic of Korea Army ground units had liberated Wŏnsan on 11 October.

At one point Rear Admiral Allan Smith, in charge of the advance force at Wŏnsan, cabled the navy's Washington headquarters that "we have lost control of the seas to a nation without a navy, using pre–World War I weapons, laid by vessels that were utilized at the time of the birth of Christ." His words and the experience at Wŏnsan energized the navy's mine warfare community.

Allied fortunes improved in the operation to clear mines from the approaches to Chinnamp'o on Korea's west coast. This port served P'yŏngyang, which was occupied by the fast-advancing U.S. Eighth Army on 19 October. The closer UN ground troops got to North Korea's border with the People's Republic of China in late fall 1950, the longer was the supply line from Inch'ŏn, so the ground units needed a port opened farther to the north.

Consequently, even before the Wŏnsan operation was over, Admiral Joy ordered establishment of a new mine clearance force for Chinnamp'o. This ad hoc group included destroyer *Forrest Royal*, destroyer minesweepers *Thompson* and *Carmick*, small minesweepers *Pelican*, *Swallow*, and *Gull* (newly arrived from the United States), ROKN *YMS 502*, *YMS 306*, *YMS 513*, and *YMS 503*, LST *Q-007*, high-speed transport *Horace A. Bass* with Underwater Demolition Team 1 embarked, dock landing ship *Catamount* carrying fourteen minesweeping boats, thirteen Japanese-manned minesweepers, and salvage ship *Bolster*. U.S. Navy PBM seaplanes and helicopters and Royal Navy Sunderland aircraft were used not only to spot mines but to destroy them with their machine guns.

The group began its work on 28 October when aircraft began searching for the more than 300 mines that North Koreans who had been involved in the minelaying operation claimed were in the water. On 6 November, a Korean-manned tug, with U.S. Navy commander Donald N. Clay on board, steamed from Chinnamp'o to the Yellow Sea to prove that the channel was free of mines. Then ROKN *YMS 503* made the passage from the sea to the port. The docking of hospital ship *Repose* in Chinnamp'o on 20 October signaled the opening of the port to seagoing support vessels. Not a man or a ship was lost carrying out the successful mine clearance operation at Chinnamp'o.

The stabilization of the fighting front around the 38th parallel from 1951 to 1953 ushered in a new era in mine warfare. Since the UNC navies had driven Communist combatants from the sea early in the war, Communist forces did what they could to deny the UNC use of the waters off North Korea. They made liberal use of sea mines along both coasts and covered their minefields with shore batteries. They deployed the mines from junks and sampans and released them in rivers that carried them to the sea. On occasion, nature aided the Communists, when fierce Asian typhoons tore mines loose from their moorings and spread them far and wide.

Between 1951 and 1953 the UNC mine clearance force often went in harm's way to threaten amphibious assaults, land guerrillas behind the lines, and open waters close offshore from which warships could bombard targets ashore. Nighttime sweep operations also became more frequent, as did the seizure of Communist minelaying junks and sampans. These operations compelled the Communists to spread their forces and distracted them from concentrating on the ground war, but not without cost. From 1951 to 1953, mines sank U.S. minesweeper *Partridge* and tug *Sarsi* and ROKN ships *JMS 306* and *PC 704*. More than twice that many UNC mine clearance ships were damaged by mines or shore fire.

During the Korean War enemy mines caused 70 percent of all U.S. Navy casualties and sank the only four U.S. naval vessels lost in combat. The Korean War showed clearly that in the future the sea mine would be the weapon of choice for many of the U.S. Navy's adversaries and a fixture of late twentieth century naval warfare.

—*Edward J. Marolda*

References:

Cagle, Malcolm W., and Frank A. Manson. *The Sea War in Korea.* Annapolis, MD: Naval Institute Press, 1957.

Field, James A., Jr. *History of United States Naval Operations: Korea.* Washington, DC: U.S. Government Printing Office, 1962.

Lott, Arnold S. *Most Dangerous Sea: A History of Mine Warfare and an Account of U.S. Navy Mine Warfare Operations in World War II and Korea.* Annapolis, MD: U.S. Naval Institute, 1959.

Melia, Tamara Moser. *"Damn the Torpedoes": A Short History of U.S. Naval Mine Countermeasures, 1777–1991.* Washington, DC: Naval Historical Center, 1991.

See also: Joy, Charles Turner; Korea, Republic of: Navy (ROKN); Truman, Harry S.; United States Navy.

Missing in Action

A tragic and enduring legacy of the Korean War remains the thousands of servicemen categorized as missing in action (MIA). Although statistics vary from nation to nation and from source to source, the most reliable figures of U.S. soldiers missing in action are found in a 1994 report sponsored by the U.S. Department of Defense. This extensive RAND report establishes the total number of U.S. body-not-returned (BNR) cases of the Korean War at 8,140. Of this number, 5,945 BNR cases have been positively verified as dead either by repatriated U.S. soldiers or extensive documentation provided by U.S. forces in Korea. Death cannot be firmly established for the remaining 2,195 cases, mostly soldiers, whose whereabouts remain unknown.

Military officials and historians have offered various explanations for the large numbers of MIAs in the Korean War. In a conflict characterized by the unfettered use of heavy ordnance, bodies of soldiers were often obliterated beyond recognition or recoverability. In the confusion of battle, soldiers were lost in the rugged terrain of densely wooded areas or swampy marshes. Aircraft incidents in which planes went down at sea or in remote mountainous areas also account for some missing servicemen. Defections to the other side help explain the high number of MIAs among North and South Korean forces.

Contributing to the high figures of missing U.S. soldiers was an antiquated U.S. recovery policy that had been practiced during World War II. The United Nations Command (UNC) established temporary cemeteries throughout the Korea peninsula from Pusan to the Yalu River. Bodies were temporarily interred in various sites until the United States adopted a new repatriation policy in December 1950. Consequently, armed service personnel often recovered, buried, exhumed, and reburied the bodies of soldiers several times before repatriation took place. Needless to say, many were simply lost in the process.

MIA cases remain intricately tied to the prisoner of war (POW) issue. During the conflict, Chinese People's Volunteer Army (CPVA, Chinese Communist) forces and the Korean People's Army (KPA, North Korean) forced thousands of POWs to march on foot to the rear. Many UNC servicemen perished during such long death marches. Survivors suffered through the horrible conditions of makeshift POW camps, collection points, and detainment centers. Most U.S. captives were released during the POW exchange following the July 1953 armistice, but 389

Americans who were positively known to be alive in Communist POW camps were not repatriated.

The UNC's Military Armistice Commission repeatedly raised this issue, but KPA and CPVA representatives denied any knowledge of the whereabouts of these missing Americans. To add insult to injury, between 1990 and 1992, the Democratic People's Republic of Korea (DPRK, North Korea) turned over forty-six sets of remains to U.S. authorities, but forensic experts could not authenticate a single set as American.

From October 1991 to April 1993 the U.S. Department of Defense funded two research projects to determine whether any American servicemen and civilians were transported to the Soviet Union or its satellites during Word War II, the early Cold War, and the Korean War, but evidence remains inconclusive. Despite this, the U.S. government and its citizens continue efforts to recover and repatriate the remains of persons missing in action during the Korean War.

—Matthew D. Esposito

References:
Cole, Paul M. *POW/MIA Issues.* Vol. 1, *The Korean War.* Santa Monica, CA: RAND, 1994.
Mossman, Billy C. *U.S. Army in the Korean War: Ebb and Flow, November 1950–July 1951.* Washington, DC: U.S. Army Center of Military History, 1990.
See also: Armistice Agreement; BIG SWITCH/LITTLE SWITCH, Operations; Casualties; P'anmunjŏm Truce Talks; Prisoners of War Administration, Communist and United Nations Command.

Mobile Army Surgical Hospital (MASH)

The idea of mobile hospitals with their tentage, supplies, and personnel able to accompany military units dated to the American Expeditionary Force in World War I. General Douglas MacArthur deployed mobile surgical units in the Pacific during World War II, but with limited success. Between 1948 and 1949 five Mobile Army Surgical Hospitals (MASH units) were created, but none was based in the Pacific. When the Korean War began in 1950, the necessity for such units was evident, and three MASH units were activated: the 8055th on 1 July, the 8063d on 17 July, and the 8076th on 19 July. The 8055th left Sasebo for Pusan on 6 July and proceeded by train directly to Taejŏn. The 8063d left 18 July for P'ohang to support the 1st Cavalry Division. The 8076th arrived in Pusan on 25 July and moved up the Taejŏn-Taegu corridor to support Eighth Army. All three would follow their combat units after the United Nations breakout from the Pusan perimeter and the subsequent invasion of North Korea.

In 1951 the 8225th MASH unit was deployed and an additional unit was organized by the Norwegians and sent to Ŭijŏngbu the same year. Two additional

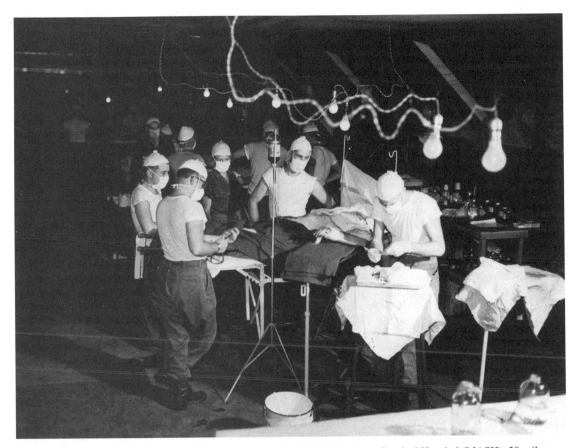

An operation being performed on a wounded soldier at the 8209th Mobile Army Surgical Hospital (MASH), 20 miles from the front line, 4 August 1952. (National Archives)

MASH units, one of which (the 8209th) specialized in caring for neurosurgical cases, were deployed in 1952.

The MASH was initially intended to be a 60-bed unit to provide early treatment and triage. Each was to have a headquarters detachment, a preoperative and shock treatment area, an operating section, a postoperative area, a pharmacy, an x-ray section, and a holding ward. It was to be staffed by fourteen medical officers, twelve nurses, two Medical Service Corps officers, one warrant officer, and ninety-seven enlisted men. One of the medical officers was assigned as commander, and there were two anesthesiologists, one internist, four general medical officers, and five surgeons. The number of beds, mission, and staffing never exactly fit the plan. Because of the excess of wounded over treaters, especially in the early part of the war, the MASH units grew into small evacuation hospitals. At one point, just the holding area of the 8076th had 200 beds.

MASH units received patients (usually by rail or helicopter) from aid or collecting stations. After the patients were stabilized they were transferred either to the evacuation hospitals at Pusan or directly to one of the Far East Command's facilities in Japan.

Early in the war there was a severe shortage of personnel to staff MASH units. Residency programs in the army hospital system were tapped to provide partially trained specialists on temporary duty (TDY). These young physicians and dentists were often asked to perform jobs for which they had little or no training; it was not uncommon for dentists to give anesthesia, psychiatric residents to operate on abdomens, and radiologists to repair fractures.

Both lack of training and high volume led to less than fastidious surgical technique. Open wounds were cleaned but not closed, leaving the definitive surgery to hospitals farther down the chain. A typical abdominal operation involved making a large incision, after which any visible bleeding was controlled. Then the gut was examined for visible perforations, which were clamped and repaired. The abdominal cavity was then rinsed to clean out loose food and parasites (some of which were worms up to a foot long). The viscera were then replaced and the patient closed.

The doctor shortage was eased by the draft of 1950, but a new set of problems arose. Fully 90 percent of military physicians in Korea were drafted, and many had served in World War II as enlisted men. They had only recently completed their medical training and begun busy civilian practices, and they had little enthusiasm for their new predicament and little inclination to cooperate with military rules and discipline. As the war progressed and the lines stabilized, MASH units became fixed hospitals, relatively remote from the front lines and staffed with female nurses with access to a variety of recreational facilities and temptations. Major Kryder van Buskirk ran the 8076th MASH in a way both typical and readily recognized by those familiar with Richard Hooker's (Dr. Richard Hornberger) novel *M*A*S*H*. These men were capable of working or playing for long hours with singular dedication.

Although quirky and often confused, the pattern of care begun in Korea's MASH units joined the helicopter transport model in forming the template for the shock-trauma services now present in virtually every large city in the United States.

—Jack McCallum

References:

Cleaver, Frederick. *U.S. Army Battle Casualties in Korea.* Chevy Chase, MD: Operations Research Office, 1956.

Cowdrey, Albert E. *United States Army in the Korean War: The Medic's War.* Washington, DC: Center of Military History, U.S. Army, 1987.

Reister, Frank. *Battle Casualties and Medical Statistics: U.S. Army Experience in the Korean War.* Washington, DC: Office of the Surgeon General, 1973.

See also: Aeromedical Evacuation; MacArthur, Douglas; Military Medicine.

Mobilization

The rapid calling up of U.S. armed forces was a key factor in staving off defeat in the Korean War. In June 1950 the United States was not ready for war. All branches of the armed services had suffered from Truman administration defense cutbacks, which had wide public support, following World War II.

The three U.S. Army divisions in Japan in General Douglas MacArthur's Far East Command committed to the initial fighting had only two rather than the allotted three battalions each per regiment. Within these there were only two artillery batteries, one antiaircraft artillery battery, and one light tank company, rather than the standard three medium tank companies.

On 30 June 1950, Congress passed the Selective Service Extension Act. This gave the president the authority to call up the National Guard and organized reserves to active service for a period of twenty-one months. The next month the Selective Service issued a call for 50,000 draftees for September who would be ready to be sent to Korea by the end of the year.

The army had to call up the National Guard and the active reserve. The figures were substantial, involving a total of 591,487 regular troops, 324,761 National Guard, and 184,015 active reservists. Also called up were 324,602 inactive volunteer reservists and 91,800 inactive reservists. By 14 August 1950, 1,457 National Guard units had been called for service. During the course of the war the army reserve contributed 244,300 officers and men. Most were from the untrained and unpaid inactive and volunteer reserves rather than from active units.

In June 1950 the Marine Corps had 74,279 officers and men on active duty worldwide. The 1st Marine Division was so short of manpower that other units had to be stripped to bring it up to strength before it could be deployed to Korea. On 19 July the Organized Marine Corps Reserve was called to active duty, and it was followed by the Volunteer Marine Corps Reserve on 15 August 1950. Of all these personnel, 99 percent of the reserve officers and 77.5 percent of the enlisted personnel were World War II veterans. By October 1951 all Marine units had been activated.

The navy had to call up reserves as well. It also recalled some of its mothball reserve fleet of older seagoing vessels. The navy also called up fighter squadrons: twenty-two reserve fighter squadrons were added to the Seventh Fleet Strike Force.

The air force had also suffered from defense cutbacks. From the Air National Guard 145 F-51 Mustangs were placed into active service. Soon afterward, troop carrier wings and fighter-bomber wings were called to service. A total of twenty-two wings of Air National Guard and ten Air Force Reserve wings were called up: some 100,000 personnel.

This military mobilization was vital in enabling the United States to stave off defeat in Korea. Fortunately, despite the defense cutbacks, the reservists were available and, with or without training, many were soon in battle and playing a vital role.

—Sean Williams

References:

Field, James A., Jr. *History of United States Naval Operations: Korea.* Washington, DC: U.S. Government Printing Office, 1962.

Futrell, Robert F. *The United States Air Force in Korea, 1950–1953.* Rev. ed. Washington, DC: Office of the Chief of Air Force History, 1983.

Giusti, Ernest H. *The Mobilization of the Marine Corps Reserve in the Korean Conflict.* Washington, DC: Historical Branch, G-3 Division Headquarters, U.S. Marine Corps, 1967.

Summers, Harry G., Jr.. *Korean War Almanac*. New York: Facts on File, 1990.

See also: Far East Command (FEC); United States: National Guard; United States: Reserve Forces.

Molotov, Viacheslav Mikhailovich (1890–1986)

Soviet foreign commissar and minister from 1939 to 1949 and 1953 to 1956. The dour Molotov played a relatively minor role in the Korean conflict because he was frequently out of favor with Josef Stalin for the last four years of the aging tyrant's life. Stalin, however, did send him to a crucial conference with the Chinese in 1950 and Molotov took part in the armistice negotiations after bring restored as foreign minister in March 1953.

Born V. M. Skriabin in Kukarka, Viatka Province (now Omsk Oblast), Viacheslav Mikhailovich Molotov had been a Bolshevik since 1906 and a staunch supporter of Stalin as early as 1922. This dogged loyalty was rewarded in 1939 when he replaced Maxim Litvinov as foreign commissar. His title was changed to the more traditional "foreign minister" during World War II, when he gained great prominence as Stalin's right-hand man in complex wartime diplomacy. This prominence may have cost him his job in March 1949, when the notoriously jealous and suspicious Stalin replaced him with Andrei Vyshinskii. Although Stalin sent Molotov's wife into exile in Siberia and may have planned to execute him, Molotov continued to serve after 1949 as first deputy chairman of the USSR Council of Ministers, but he did not regain the foreign minister's portfolio until after Stalin's death.

One turning point in the war came in August 1950 when Chinese and Soviet officials met to discuss possible responses in the event that United Nations (UN) forces crossed the 38th parallel. The Soviet delegation, headed by Viacheslav Molotov, wanted to avoid direct conflict with the United States but recognized the unacceptability of a Western overthrow of their client state in North Korea. Both parties apparently agreed that Chinese forces, with indirect Soviet assistance, would be used to support Kim Il Sung's regime, triggered by a crossing of the 38th parallel by UN troops. Stalin may have chosen Molotov for this conference because the former foreign minister favored a relatively hard line stance vis-à-vis the United States.

After Stalin's death on 5 March 1953, Molotov's rhetoric softened abruptly as he took back the position of foreign minister. Part of a new ruling troika with Georgi Malenkov and Lavrenti Beria, Molotov worked to revive the armistice negotiations. He did not play a direct role in the P'anmunjŏm discussions, but he did try to pressure the participants when progress stalled on the issue of prisoner-of-war repatriation.

When Nikita Khrushchev used his position as First Secretary of the Communist Party of the Soviet Union to fight his way to the top of the Soviet hierarchy, Molotov was one of the losers. Removed as foreign minister in May 1956, Molotov joined an ultimately unsuccessful attempt by the "anti-Party group" to depose Khrushchev in 1957. Stripped of his remaining posts, Molotov was given the relatively mild punishment of "exile" in the Mongolian People's Republic as the Soviet ambassador from 1957 to 1960. He never regained prominence in Soviet public life. Molotov spent the last two decades of his life in a modest dacha in Zhukovka, where he died on 8 November 1986.

—Edward Sharp

References:

Beloff, Max. *Soviet Policy in the Far East, 1944–1951*. London: Oxford University Press, 1953.

Chuev, Felix. *Molotov Remembers*. Chicago: Ivan R. Dee, 1993.

MacKenzie, David. *From Messianism to Collapse: Soviet Foreign Policy, 1917–1991*. New York: Harcourt Brace College Publishers, 1994.

Zubok, Vladislav, and Constantine Pleshakov. *Inside the Kremlin's Cold War: From Stalin to Khrushchev*. Cambridge, MA: Harvard University Press, 1996.

See also: China, People's Republic of; Cold War Origins to 1950; Malenkov, Georgii Maximilianovich; Mao Zedong; P'anmunjŏm Truce Talks; Stalin, Iosef; Union of Soviet Socialist Republics; Vyshinskii, Andrei Ianuarovich.

MOOLAH, Operation

Launched in April 1953, during the final stages of the P'anmunjŏm armistice talks, Operation MOOLAH offered $100,000 and political asylum to the first Communist pilot of an undamaged MiG-15 who defected with his airplane to the United Nations Command (UNC) and $50,000 to any subsequent imitators.

Operation MOOLAH's objectives were, first, to acquire a Soviet-built MiG for assessment and evaluation, something the U.S. Air Force had long hoped to accomplish; and second, to subject Communist forces to psychological pressure as truce negotiations reached a critical stage. Lieutenant General Mark W. Clark, commander in chief of UN forces in Korea, was an enthusiastic supporter of the scheme, which according to him was devised over a bottle of brandy in Seoul by United Press correspondent Dick Applegate. Other accounts credit Harvard University's Russian Research Center. On learning of the potential scheme in November 1952, Clark embraced it enthusiastically, although he waited until April 1953 to announce the offer, quite possibly to deprive the outgoing Truman administration of any possible kudos. The air force budgeted $250,000 for the operation.

UNC shortwave radio broadcasts in Korean, Chinese, and Russian—since it was believed correctly

Mig-15 fighter flown to Kimp'o airfield on 21 September 1950 by North Korean Lieutenant No Kŭom-sŏk. (National Archives)

that, despite Soviet claims of neutrality, at least some Russian MiG pilots were flying in Korea—publicized its details, as did almost 2 million leaflets in those languages dropped along the Yalu River and over North Korean airfields.

Operation MOOLAH's effects remain problematic. Clark, an enthusiastic supporter, claimed that it forced the Communists to ground all planes until their pilots had undergone loyalty checks. The Far East Air Force more cautiously suggested that the break in flights probably owed more to bad weather, although the official U.S. Air Force history speculated that, since aircraft bearing Soviet markings scarcely appeared in the skies after the offer, the Soviets in particular might have removed their pilots from combat missions. UNC radio propaganda on the operation in Russian was jammed, whereas broadcasts in Korean and Chinese experienced no such interference. Even before Operation MOOLAH, however, MiG pilots had become decidedly reluctant to venture into battle against the U.S.-made F-86Fs, which had just come into service.

The first Communist pilot to defect did not do so until 21 September 1953, several months after the armistice was concluded. Lieutenant No Kŭom-sŏk of the North Korean Air Force, who landed his MiG-15 at Kimpŏ Airfield, claimed to have been unaware of any reward and to be motivated solely by personal considerations. Although President Dwight D. Eisenhower had approved the original offer, he now found it somewhat embarrassing. The war had ended and, although he believed that the Central Intelligence Agency (CIA) was morally obliged to fulfill its promise, he thought $100,000 a great deal to pay for an airplane he considered "no longer of any great interest to us." Eisenhower also disliked the idea of bribing individuals to defect, feeling it preferable that they do so from ideological conviction. Lieutenant No was therefore persuaded to reject the reward as such, and instead the Committee for Free Asia, a CIA-funded organization, provided him with an equivalent sum in technical education and financial assistance. At this time the United States also withdrew the offer of $50,000 to any subsequent Communist pilot who defected, and even offered to return the Russian-made aircraft to its "rightful owner." Clark later speculated that the reason the Soviets never took up the latter suggestion was because this would have flagrantly disproved their contemporaneous claim that, as a "neutral" power in the Korean conflict, the USSR was entitled to voting representation in this capacity at a forthcoming international conference scheduled to discuss Korean political problems.

Although some observers questioned the actual value of this particular aircraft, given that it was a relatively old model, Clark had no such reservations, claiming it "was the first combat MiG we ever laid hands on long enough to test." This, he argued, later enabled United States pilots to shoot down at least a dozen similar airplanes. Lieutenant No also provided valuable intelligence information on Communist violations of the armistice, particularly on the transfer of MiGs from Manchuria to supposedly nonmilitary bases within North Korea.

—*Priscilla Roberts*

References:

Ambrose, Stephen E. *Eisenhower.* 2 vols. New York: Simon & Schuster, 1983, 1984.

Bailey, Sydney D. *The Korean Armistice.* London: Macmillan, 1992.

Clark, Mark W. *From the Danube to the Yalu.* New York: Harper & Brothers, 1954.

Foot, Rosemary J. *A Substitute for Victory: The Politics of Peacemaking at the Korean Armistice Talks.* Ithaca, NY: Cornell University Press, 1990.

Futrell, Robert F. *The United States Air Force in Korea, 1950–1953.* Rev. ed. Washington, DC: Office of the Chief of Air Force History, 1983.

No, Kum-Sok, with J. Roger Osterholm. *A MiG-15 to Freedom: Memoirs of the Wartime North Korean Defector Who Delivered the Secret Fighter Jet to the Americans in 1953.* Jefferson, NC: McFarland, 1996.

See also: Clark, Mark W.; Eisenhower, Dwight D.; MiG, Operation.

Morrison, Herbert S.
(1888–1965)

British foreign secretary from March to October 1951. Born on 3 January 1888, to a London police constable and his wife, a former domestic servant, Herbert S. Morrison was educated at state schools. He completed his formal schooling at age fourteen and quickly moved into journalism and, from April 1915 onward, into Labour Party politics. In 1922 Morrison became Mayor of Hackney Borough in London, and in 1921 he won a seat on the London County Council, which he soon came to dominate and would continue to do so until 1940. Among his major achievements in London were the creation of the London Passenger Transport Board, slum clearance, the building of Waterloo Bridge, and reform of welfare provisions.

Elected to Parliament in 1923 and 1929, between 1929 and 1931 Morrison served as minister of transport in Ramsay MacDonald's Labour government, losing his seat in the general election of 1931. Returned to Parliament in 1935, in the national wartime coalition government of 1940 Morrison was first minister

of supply and then home secretary and minister of home security. In the latter capacity he used his knowledge of London and its inhabitants to assist its people in enduring the wartime blitz with their sanity and sense of humor intact. In the 1945 Labour government Morrison served successively as lord president of the council, chancellor of the exchequer, and, again, lord president, positions in which he continued to concern himself almost exclusively with domestic affairs.

In 1951 when Ernest Bevin's illness left the post of foreign secretary vacant, Prime Minister Clement Attlee dithered as to whether to appoint Morrison, who it seems gave the appearance, deliberately or not, of coveting the job and so obtained it by default, a prize he may later have regretted. Attlee soon regarded the appointment as an error and he and U.S. Secretary of State Dean Acheson both remarked acidly on Morrison's ignorance of world affairs. Even so, during Morrison's tenure Anglo-American friction over East Asia diminished, partly because of the recall of General Douglas MacArthur, which alleviated fears that Britain might be plugged into a broader war against the People's Republic of China (PRC). Morrison's personal preoccupation with the concurrent Iranian crisis also reduced tensions, inasmuch as the British muted their criticisms of U.S. policies in Asia in the hope of winning U.S. support in the Middle East. In addition, PRC intransigence in spring 1951 in rejecting all moves toward a negotiated settlement and attempting, instead, to keep fighting until it had driven United Nations (UN) forces from Korean territory, radically improved America's image in British eyes. In May 1951 Britain voted for a selective UN embargo on China and accepted Acheson's suggestion of a moratorium on the perennially difficult question of PRC representation in the UN. Morrison also endorsed the principle that the UN commander in Korea be authorized to attack Manchurian military bases should North Korean or Chinese forces launch an unexpected air assault on his troops, although he did insist upon prior American consultation with the British. In addition, in May Morrison made a speech supporting the position of the Second World War Cairo Declaration of 1943 that Taiwan was part of China but opposing its return to the PRC until the Korean crisis had ended.

Morrison did not merely echo U.S. policy, but continued to reveal the same fears of imprudent provocation of China that Attlee demonstrated in 1950. Although Morrison shared Acheson's view that it was unlikely that an armistice would ultimately lead to a settlement of all outstanding political questions in Asia, he refused to preclude the possibility of such a comprehensive scheme. Emphasizing Hong Kong's vulnerability to PRC pressure or takeover and the need to avoid driving China entirely into the Soviet camp,

Morrison was reluctant to broaden the war should armistice negotiations fail. He was also somewhat fearful that domestic political pressures might lead Washington to recklessly expand the war beyond the bounds of prudence. He was therefore only ready to endorse somewhat limited moves, such as bombing Yalu power stations. In December 1950 an irritated Acheson, who already thought Beijing part of the Communist conspiracy, complained of Morrison's—and by extension the British—"familiar exegesis."

Morrison's tenure as foreign secretary ended when the Labour Party lost the October 1951 election. Conservative Anthony Eden replaced him. In opposition Morrison remained a highly effective parliamentarian and party spokesman, contributing frequently to debates, but he lost the leadership contest of 1955 to Hugh Gaitskell. He died on 6 March 1965 at Sidcup.

—*Priscilla Roberts*

References:

Butler, Rohan, and M. E. Pelly, eds. *Documents on British Policy Overseas*. Series II, Vol. 4, *Korea, 1950–1951*. London: Her Majesty's Stationery Office, 1995.

Donoughue, Bernard, and G. W. Jones. *Herbert Morrison: Portrait of a Politician*. London: Weidenfeld & Nicolson, 1973.

MacDonald, Callum A. *Britain and the Korean War*. Oxford: Blackwell, 1990.

Morgan, Kenneth O. *Labour in Power, 1945–1951*. Oxford: Clarendon Press, 1985.

Morrison, Lord of Lambeth. *Herbert Morrison: An Autobiography*. London: Odhams, 1960.

Stueck, William W., Jr. *The Korean War: An International History*. Princeton, NJ: Princeton University Press, 1995.

See also: Acheson, Dean Goodersham; Attlee, Clement R.; Bevin, Ernest; Eden, Anthony; MacArthur, Douglas; Truman's Recall of MacArthur.

Mortars

The need for indirect methods of fire to assist infantry other than air strikes has traditionally been filled by artillery, but the hilly, mountainous terrain of the Korea peninsula often rendered artillery fire impractical. This void was filled by mortars, high-angle-firing weapons designed to fire over heights and enemy fortifications.

In the Korean War the U.S. Army employed three types of mortars: the 60-mm (three per rifle company); the 81-mm (three per infantry battalion); and the 107-mm, more commonly known as the 4.2-inch (six per infantry regiment). British Commonwealth forces used a 3-inch mortar. On the Communist side the Korean People's Army (KPA) and the Chinese People's Volunteer Army (CPVA, Chinese Communist) utilized a 61-mm mortar at company level, an 82-mm mortar at battalion level, and a 120-mm mortar at the regimental level. The slightly larger diameters of the 61-mm and the 120-mm enabled the KPA and the CPVA to take advantage of captured U.S. mortar

ammunition for the American 60-mm and the 107-mm in their own mortars; however, the U.S. troops could not use any captured Communist ammunition because the rounds were too big to fit in the U.S. mortar bores.

Conventional rounds were not the only types of projectiles employed by the United Nations (UN). The 2d Chemical Mortar Battalion, with three 4.2-inch heavy mortar companies, provided direct support of infantry units. It saw heavy action in November and December 1950. During the Chinese spring 1951 offensive in April, elements of the Republic of Korea Army (ROKA, South Korea) collapsed, leaving the 2d Chemical Mortar Battalion trapped, but most of its elements managed to reach UN lines. In October 1952, most probably to dispel Communist propaganda that the United States was employing chemical weapons against noncombatants, the army dissolved the 2d Chemical Mortar Battalion.

Of U.S. mortars used in Korea, the 107-mm (4.2-inch) may have seen the most action. It saw extensive use with the 8th U.S. Cavalry Regiment at Unsan and the 9th U.S. Infantry Regiment at Kunu-ri, which came under heavy Chinese pressure at the end of November 1950.

Mortar fire was also very important in fighting over Heartbreak Ridge between September 1951 and November 1952. Artillery and mortar support fire for the battle during 13–15 September 1951 alone created an army-wide ammunition shortage after the expenditure of nearly 120,000 60-mm, 81-mm, and 107-mm (4.2-inch) mortar rounds.

Mortars were effective in both offensive and defensive operations. On 30 November 1950 U.S. Army troops of "Task Force Faith," named for their commander Lieutenant Colonel Don Faith, were assaulted by the CPVA 80th Division. U.S. commanders believed that the Chinese had orders to take the position at any cost, so the soldiers were ordered to retreat, but in the process they used mortar and artillery fire to inflict heavy casualties on the attackers. U.S. and UN forces also used mortar fire with great effect in March 1951 in Operation RIPPER, when they drove Chinese forces back across the 38th parallel.

Mortars played an important role in the Korean War by providing mobile infantry support fire in all types of terrain and in conditions and locations where standard artillery was impractical. In the "Forgotten War," mortars may be the forgotten weapon, but their supporting fire was responsible for saving entire UN units.

—*William B. Harrington*

References:

Blair, Clay. *The Forgotten War: America in Korea, 1950–1953*. New York: Times Books, 1987.

Summers, Harry G., Jr. *The Korean War Almanac*. New York: Facts on File, 1990.

See also: Chemical Warfare; RIPPER, Operation.

Mu Chŏng (Kim Mu-chŏng)
(1905–1952)

Korean People's Army (KPA, North Korea) general and commander of its II Corps at the start of the Korean War. Mu Chŏng (his family name of Kim has usually been omitted) was born at Kyŏngsŏng, North Hamgyŏng Province. After joining the March First Movement of 1919, he went to China in 1923 and graduated from Henan Military Academy. Mu Chŏng began his military career with the warlord Yen Hsishan and developed an expertise in artillery. An artillery lieutenant during the Northern Expedition, he joined the Chinese Communist Party in 1925. In 1927 he was sentenced to death under the Guomindang court at Wuch'iang but fled to Shanghai. In 1929 he was arrested again but escaped to Hong Kong. Thereafter, Mu Chŏng reportedly became chief of artillery in the People's Liberation Army (PLA, Chinese Communist). He was the only Korean to survive the Long March, cultivating comradeship with Peng Dehuai.

In 1939 and 1940, Mu Chŏng established a Korean unit within the PLA. Early the following year this unit was developed into the North China Korean Youth Federation. Six months later, in combination with new arrivals from the Korean Volunteer Corps, which was receiving Nationalist backing in Nanjing, the federation was reorganized into the North China Korean Independence League, with Kim Tu-bong as its chairman. Under the league the Korean Volunteer Army was established with Mu Chŏng as its commander.

After the liberation, Mu Chŏng was elected in absentia a member of the Central People's Committee at the Committee for the Preparation of Korean Independence organized in Seoul, but in December 1945 he returned to northern Korea. In the initial period he was highly regarded as the "vice-commander" of the Eighth Route Army, or the Chinese Communist choice to assume leadership in Korea, much to the great displeasure of Kim Il Sung. However, Mu Chŏng would hold no official position in the northern leadership until the fall of 1946, when he became deputy chief for artillery in the peace preservation corps, from which the KPA would develop. Evidently, Kim Tu-bong served as the principal spokesman for the Yenan (Chinese exile) faction in northern Korea. In March 1948 Mu Chŏng was elected a member of the Central Committee of the North Korean Workers' Party.

Mu Chŏng was ineffective during the Korean War and was demoted to the less important post of commander of the VII Corps of the KPA. At the third regular meeting of the Central Committee of the Korean Workers' Party held on 4 December 1950, he was removed from the body on charges that he was responsible for the loss of P'yŏngyang in the fall. It is believed that Kim Il Sung purged him because Mu Chŏng's Chinese connection might have heightened his politico-military position following Chinese military intervention in the Korean War. The Chinese leadership helped Mu Chŏng to return to China; however, he was dying of gastroenteritis and returned to P'yŏngyang, where he died in October 1952.

—Hakjoon Kim

References:

Chung'ang Ilbo, ed. *Pirok: Chosŏn Minjujuŭi Inmin Konghwaguk* [The secret records of the Democratic People's Republic of Korea]. Seoul: Chung'ang Ilbo, 1992.

Cumings, Bruce. *The Origins of the Korean War.* 2 vols. Princeton, NJ: Princeton University Press, 1981, 1990.

Suh, Dae-Sook. *Kim Il Sung: The North Korean Leader.* New York: Columbia University Press, 1988.

See also: Korea, Democratic People's Republic of: 1945–1953; Korea, Democratic People's Republic of: 1953 to the Present; March First Movement.

Muccio, John J.
(1900–1989)

First U.S. ambassador to the Republic of Korea (ROK), 1949–1952. Born on 19 March 1900, in Valle Agricola, Italy, John J. Muccio saw service in World War I in the U.S. Army. He then acquired U.S. citizenship and in 1921 graduated from Brown University. Appointed to the U.S. Foreign Service two years later, Muccio held posts in Europe, Asia, and Latin America. In August 1948 he became President Harry S. Truman's special representative to the Republic of Korea (ROK) and then, on 21 March 1949, the first U.S. ambassador.

Muccio presided over the U.S. embassy, Korea Military Advisory Group (KMAG), an Economic Cooperation Administration branch, and the Joint Administrative Services, the mission's supply office. Despite disagreements with ROK president Syngman Rhee, Muccio developed a working relationship with him as well as an admiration for Rhee's intelligence and historical insights. Nevertheless, he recognized Rhee's reverence for General Douglas MacArthur and feared his suspicious nature. Characterizing the ROK leader as an "egomaniac," Muccio feared that Rhee might launch an attack against the Democratic People's Republic of Korea (DPRK, North Korea).

Muccio endorsed Rhee's wish for a permanent U.S. military role in Korea and his government's request for $10 million in additional aid for 1950. A few weeks before the DPRK invaded the ROK, Muccio informed the U.S. Congress of Seoul's military inferiority, an assessment that many did not hold. Muccio worried that the DPRK's military advantage would give it the winning edge in case of an all-out assault of the South. He cited DPRK advantages in artillery, armor, and planes supplied by the USSR.

Ambassador Muccio officially notified Washington of the outbreak of the Korean War. In a dispatch sent almost six and a half hours after the beginning of the invasion, he announced that the DPRK had mounted a full-scale, unprovoked attack. At a meeting of the United Nations Commission on Korea, Muccio expressed confidence in the capability of ROK Army (ROKA) troops, but he also pressed the Department of State to back a KMAG plea to General MacArthur for more ammunition for the ROKA. When Rhee considered a sudden departure from Seoul, Muccio warned that this could demoralize ROKA troops. Muccio's own decision to stay braced Rhee, at least temporarily. Under the pressure of advancing Korean People's Army (KPA, North Korean) forces, Muccio elected to evacuate U.S. civilians from Seoul via Inch'ŏn and Kimpŏ Airfield but delayed this step for a time in hopes of preserving South Korean morale despite the misgivings of some military personnel. Once Rhee left Seoul, the State Department ordered Muccio to follow, and he joined Rhee in Taejŏn.

Muccio conferred with MacArthur on several occasions after the war's outbreak, and he traveled with the general to meet President Truman at Wake Island in October. He and MacArthur were the only participants in the general's party to take prominent roles in the discussions. Muccio later described MacArthur as irritated and uncomfortable and complaining of being "summoned for political reasons" and suggesting the president was "not aware that I am still fighting a war." In his remarks Muccio spoke about Korean political and economic conditions. Both he and MacArthur endorsed a reconstruction aid package and expressed fear of President Rhee's weakened political status. Before their departure, Truman awarded Muccio the Medal of Merit.

In 1952 Muccio pressed Rhee to comply with the pending cease-fire and found the ROK president uncooperative. Despite his reputation of being Rhee's "best and most patient friend in the American community," Muccio urged the State Department to ponder United Nations intervention through the ROKA. On 25 June the State Department directed Muccio and Lieutenant General Mark W. Clark to begin contingency planning in case action was required to stop Rhee's meddling. In November 1952 Muccio was succeeded by Ellis O. Briggs and returned to the United States.

Muccio retired from the Foreign Service in 1961. He died in Washington, D.C., on 19 May 1989.

—*Rodney J. Ross*

References:
Goulden, Joseph C. *Korea: The Untold Story of the War.* New York: Times Books, 1982.
James, D. Clayton. *The Years of MacArthur.* Vol. 3, *Triumph and Disaster, 1945–1964.* Boston: Houghton Mifflin, 1985.
Paige, Glenn D. *The Korean Decision, June 24–30, 1950.* New York: Free Press, 1968.

See also: Briggs, Ellis; Church, John H.; Clark, Mark W.; Korea Military Advisory Group (KMAG); MacArthur, Douglas; Seoul; Syngman Rhee; Truman, Harry S.; Wake Island Conference.

Murphy, Charles S.
(1909–1983)

Special counsel to the president, 1950–1953, speechwriter from 1947 onward, and also a close personal friend to Harry S. Truman. Born on 20 August 1909, in Wallace, North Carolina, Charles Springs Murphy in 1928 joined the civil service as a postal clerk in Wilmington, Delaware; he earned a B.A. and a law degree from Duke University by attending night school. Murphy then moved to Washington to work as assistant counsel in the Office of the Legislative Counsel of the U.S. Senate, scrutinizing the language of draft bills to ensure there were no inaccuracies or errors. In this capacity Murphy, a Democrat, became acquainted with and won the respect of the novice Senator Harry S. Truman of Missouri, who often called upon his expertise and for whom he wrote the bill establishing the wartime committee to investigate the defense industry that Truman chaired.

In 1947 President Truman chose Murphy as a presidential administrative assistant, responsible for steering bills through the numerous congressional pitfalls and hazards they faced. In 1950 he selected Murphy to succeed Clark Clifford as special counsel to the president, his principal responsibility being to ensure the legislative success of programs initiated by the White House. Murphy was known for his meticulous attention to detail and his deep knowledge both of Congress and of legislation in progress. Many viewed the unassuming lawyer as the most able member of Truman's staff.

The plain-spoken Truman also valued Murphy's talent for expressing the president's thoughts in simple and comprehensible words and phrases compatible with his own personality, and the president used him as a major speechwriter. The two men found each other highly congenial, and Murphy regularly attended sessions of Truman's "little cabinet," latenight meetings of a circle of the president's friends and advisers who discussed and decided political and legislative strategies over poker and bourbon. Murphy played an important part in developing the campaign strategy for the presidential election of 1948, in which the supposedly unelectable incumbent won a dramatic upset victory.

Murphy's role in U.S. policy toward the Korean War was relatively limited and essentially supportive. He was present at the 28 November 1950 meeting when Truman told his staff that Chinese intervention in the war had destroyed all hope of a quick and easy victory. He helped to draft several of the president's speeches on the war, including his statement of 27 June 1950, and his 16 December declaration of a national emergency that demanded much higher defense spending, partial mobilization, and restoration of the draft.

Truman discussed with Murphy his April 1952 seizure of the steel plants, a move that the Supreme Court ultimately declared unconstitutional. He was one of the entourage at Truman's October 1950 Wake Island meeting with General Douglas MacArthur, and the following April, when the president finally fired the general, Murphy advised him on public relations tactics.

Overall, Murphy's role was to support and assist the president rather than to initiate policy. This pattern continued into later years, when Murphy assisted his financially straitened former boss in approaching top political figures to win congressional legislation granting all presidents a pension. Even later, he was one of the comparatively few guests invited to attend Truman's funeral and memorial ceremonies.

After Truman left office, Murphy went into private law practice in Washington. He returned to government in 1961 when President John F. Kennedy appointed him undersecretary of agriculture. From 1965 to 1968 he was chairman of the Civil Aeronautics Board, and in 1968 he also became counselor to the embattled President Lyndon B. Johnson. Murphy returned to private law practice when Richard Nixon became president, but behind the scenes the Democratic Party valued his advice and regarded him as a respected elder statesman. He died in Anne Arundel County, Maryland, on 28 July 1983.

—*Priscilla Roberts*

References:

Hamby, Alonzo L. *Man of the People: A Life of Harry S. Truman.* New York: Oxford University Press, 1995.

McCullough, David. *Truman.* New York: Simon & Schuster, 1992.

"Murphy, Charles S(prings)." In *Current Biography, 1950.* New York: H. W. Wilson, 1951.

"Murphy, Charles S(prings)." In *Political Profiles: The Truman Years,* edited by Eleanora W. Schoenebaum. New York: Facts on File, 1978.

See also: MacArthur, Douglas; Truman, Harry S.; Wake Island Conference.

Murphy, Robert D.
(1894–1978)

U.S. ambassador to Japan, 1952–1953. Born in Milwaukee, Wisconsin, on 28 October 1894, to an Irish laborer's family, Robert D. Murphy worked his way through Marquette University and George Washington University Law School, after which he joined the Foreign Service in 1920. Early assignments were followed by ten years in Paris, 1930–1940. During the Second World War Murphy undertook various confidential assignments for President Franklin D. Roosevelt, helping to prepare the ground for the invasion of North Africa, among other missions. From September 1944 until 1949 he was the political adviser in occupied Germany, working closely with Deputy Military Governor Lieutenant General Lucius D. Clay. Both men became early supporters of the economic rehabilitation of the western occupation sectors of Germany, and both generally urged a hard line against Soviet demands. This was particularly the case during the 1948–1949 Berlin Blockade, when Murphy believed administration policy was overly conciliatory.

After eighteen generally uneventful months as U.S. ambassador to Belgium, in 1952 Murphy was appointed ambassador to Japan, the first U.S. diplomat since the war to hold that position. At this time the Truman administration regarded his lack of previous Asian experience as a positive asset, since many of its Far East experts had come under McCarthyite attack for views allegedly overly sympathetic to Asian communism, a charge from which Murphy's well-known hawkish reputation protected him. In this post Murphy worked closely with commander of United Nations (UN) forces in Korea General Lieutenant Mark W. Clark to bring about an armistice. Here again, his uncompromising outlook was much in evidence. Murphy believed that the Soviet Union and the People's Republic of China were using the Democratic People's Republic of Korea (DPRK, North Korea) for their own ends, but that both powers feared extension of the war to China. Murphy therefore maintained that the United States should drive the Chinese People's Volunteer Army (CPVA, Chinese Communist) back into Manchuria, as he believed UN forces were capable of doing, rather than restricting its troops to a limited war. The UN could then force a peace settlement on the Chinese and North Koreans. Murphy also found himself frustrated by what he believed to be intransigent and unreliable maneuvering by Republic of Korea president Syngman Rhee, who stubbornly refused to improve his country's relations with Japan.

When Murphy's old friend and military associate from the Second World War, Dwight D. Eisenhower, assumed the presidency in 1953, he appointed Murphy assistant secretary of state for UN affairs but delayed his transfer until after the armistice had been concluded. Murphy found his role as political adviser during the concluding stages of the armistice negotiations personally difficult; and the contrast with his experiences in Europe at the end of the Second World War, when the United States was dealing from a victorious position, was especially galling. He continued to believe that the United States should have fought the Korean War to a similar victorious end.

In August 1953, after the armistice agreement had been signed, Murphy unenthusiastically took up his UN duties, blaming that organization for having exercised a major "restraining influence" on U.S. prosecution of the war in Korea. Later that year Eisenhower promoted Murphy to deputy undersecretary of state, ranking third in the department. Until Murphy's retirement in 1959, he was a troubleshooter undertaking particularly sensitive missions, with Eisenhower dispatching him to deal with the French during the Suez crisis of 1956 and to Lebanon in 1958 to prepare that nation for the arrival of U.S. troops. Although retired, in 1969 Murphy advised President Richard Nixon on top diplomatic appointments and under Gerald Ford he served on the Foreign Intel-ligence Advisory Committee. Murphy died in New York on 9 January 1978.

—*Priscilla Roberts*

References:

Foot, Rosemary J. *A Substitute for Victory: The Politics of Peacemaking at the Korean Armistice Talks.* Ithaca, NY: Cornell University Press, 1990.

McMahon, Robert J. "Robert D. Murphy." In *Dictionary of American Biography: Supplement Ten, 1976–1980,* edited by Kenneth T. Jackson. New York: Charles Scribner's Sons, 1995.

Murphy, Robert D. *Diplomat among Warriors.* Garden City, NY: Doubleday, 1964.

"Robert D. Murphy." In *Political Profiles: The Eisenhower Years,* edited by Eleanora W. Schoenebaum. New York: Facts on File, 1977.

"Robert D. Murphy." In *Political Profiles: The Truman Years,* edited by Eleanora W. Schoenebaum. New York: Facts on File, 1978.

See also: Clark, Mark W.; Eisenhower, Dwight D.; Syngman Rhee.

N

Najin (Rashin), Bombing of
(August 1950–August 1951)

Port and industrial center in northeast Korea only sixty miles from Vladivostok and less than twenty miles from the Soviet border, which became a controversial bombing target because of its installations and location. Najin (also called Rashin or Racin) in 1950 contained key oil storage tanks and railway yards, as well as docks frequented by Russian ships. It was included in the target lists of major industrial concentrations prepared both by the Strategic Air Command (SAC) and Joint Chiefs of Staff (JCS), but Far East Air Force (FEAF) Bomber Command could not divert adequate resources to strategic bombing until the ground situation had stabilized and additional SAC reinforcements arrived. B-29s attacked the city on 12 August, but cloud cover forced them to deliver their bomb loads by radar, and the results were poor. The inaccurate bombing and news reports that the mission was designed to hinder Soviet submarine operations from the ice-free port heightened U.S. State Department fears that the action might widen the war, and protests were lodged with President Harry S. Truman and Secretary of Defense Louis Johnson. Though Johnson defended the raids, U.S. Air Force Chief of Staff General Hoyt Vandenberg instructed Lieutenant General George Stratemeyer of FEAF to delay further attacks until targets could be reevaluated. General Omar Bradley and Johnson requested permission from the National Security Council to resume the attacks in October, but by then United Nations F-51s had strafed a Chinese airfield and the navy had shot down a Russian aircraft. A worried Truman ordered the State and Defense Departments to study the matter, and the JCS decided on its own to order no further attacks because of the increased tensions.

Najin became an issue again after Chinese intervention in the war. On 15 February 1951 General Douglas MacArthur complained that the Communist side was taking advantage of the port's immunity from air attack to build up reinforcements and supplies. He asked to take advantage of good weather to destroy docks, marshaling yards, and storage facilities by visual bombing. Major General Maxwell Taylor, army assistant chief of staff for operations, recommended at a 16 February meeting that Army Chief of Staff General J. Lawton Collins ask the JCS to lift restrictions, but the JCS expressed concern about the bombers being intercepted or hitting Russian vessels

in the harbor. MacArthur replied that there were no indications that Soviet ships were using the port, while the only source for possible fighters to defend the city were Russian airfields near Vladivostok, "and such an overt act of war is not considered likely." Taylor again recommended that Collins get approval for the air attacks at the next JCS meeting on 19 February, but Secretary of Defense George Marshall, Secretary of State Dean Acheson, and President Truman all agreed that the limitations should not be removed at that time. The JCS informed MacArthur of its decision on 21 February. The prohibition against bombing Najin generated much debate in May during the congressional hearings concerning the relief of MacArthur and the overall situation in the Far East.

MacArthur's successor, Lieutenant General Matthew Ridgway, tried to get the restrictions lifted later that summer. He cabled the JCS that aerial reconnaissance had revealed "extensive stockpiling of matericl and supplies" at the port; and, with its highway and rail complex funneling supplies to all areas in the south, it was "a principal focal point for intensifying the enemy supply build-up in the battle area." In reply to queries about his specific plans, Ridgway assured the JCS that, because of uncertain weather conditions, he would mount only one or two normal visual strikes against the marshaling yard, and he guaranteed that the border would not be violated. The Air Staff supported the request for many reasons. An attack would hamper the Communist supply buildup and might pressure their negotiators out of "dilatory tactics" at the armistice talks. It was in keeping with current JCS directives to conduct no military operations within twelve miles of USSR territory, and it would show the Communists that "all of their sanctuaries are not privileged." Najin was also considered "the last major profitable strategic target in Korea." The Air Staff discounted diplomatic concerns about a secret Democratic People's Republic of Korea (DPRK, North Korea)–USSR treaty giving the Soviets a long-term lease on the port, noting that another port covered in the same agreement had been bombed repeatedly with no Soviet reaction.

The JCS agreed with the Air Staff arguments, and after getting presidential approval, authorized Ridgway to attack Najin. Since the port lay beyond the range of Fifth Air Force fighters, carrier jets provided cover for thirty-five B-29s, which carried out the mission in good weather on 25 August. Bomber Command hit the target area with a reported 97 percent of the more than 300 tons of bombs dropped, and no follow-up raids were necessary.

—*Conrad C. Crane*

References:

Crane, Conrad C. *American Air Power Strategy in Korea, 1950–1953.* Lawrence: University Press of Kansas, 1999.

Futrell, Robert F. *The United States Air Force in Korea, 1950–1953.* Rev. ed. Washington, DC: Office of the Chief of Air Force History, 1983.

Schnabel, James F. *United States Army in the Korean War: Policy and Direction, the First Year.* Washington, DC: Office of the Chief of Military History, Department of the Army, 1972.

Schnabel, James F., and Robert J. Watson. *The History of the Joint Chiefs of Staff: The Joint Chiefs of Staff and National Policy.* Vol. 3, *The Korean War.* Wilmington, DE: Michael Glazier, 1979.

U.S. Senate. *Military Situation in the Far East. Hearings Before the Committee on Armed Services and the Committee on Foreign Relations.* 82d Cong., 1st sess. Washington, DC: U.S. Government Printing Office, 1951.

See also: Acheson, Dean Goodersham; Aircraft (Principal Combat); Bradley, Omar Nelson; Collins, Joseph Lawton; Johnson, Louis A.; Joint Chiefs of Staff (JCS); MacArthur, Douglas; Marshall, George C.; Ridgway, Matthew Bunker; Stratemeyer, George E.; Taylor, Maxwell Davenport; Truman, Harry S.; Vandenberg, Hoyt S.

Naktong Bulge, First Battle of
(5–19 August 1950)

Key battle in August 1950 involving U.S. and Republic of Korea Army (ROKA, South Korean) forces against Korean People's Army (KPA, North Korean) troops along the Naktong River. In early August, Major General John H. Church's 24th Infantry Division numbered 9,882 men (half its authorized strength). An attachment of 486 soldiers and operational control of the 2,000-man ROKA 17th Infantry Regiment brought its aggregate strength to 12,368 men. Rated combat efficiency was 53 percent.

The division manned a thirty-four-mile front; doctrine called for division fronts to be only nine miles. The northern 30,000-yard sector was held by the ROKA 17th Infantry; the next 12,000 yards by the U.S. 21st Infantry with the 14th Engineer Combat Battalion. The Heavy Mortar Company was on line south of the 21st. Next, in the bulge of the Naktong, was the 34th Infantry on a 16,000-yard front. Everywhere the division front was held by isolated squad and platoon enclaves, with huge gaps between. The 3d Battalion, 34th Infantry manned the regimental front with Companies I, L, and K, from north to south. The 1st Battalion, 34th Infantry was regimental reserve, while the 19th Infantry was the division reserve.

At one minute after midnight on 6 August 1950, 800 members of the KPA 4th Division quietly crossed the Naktong and drove deep into the gap between Companies I and L, 34th Infantry. A counterattack by

the 1st Battalion of the 34th Infantry saw its Company A reach the front line, but in effect, the counterattack failed. A subsequent attack by the 19th Infantry and 24th Recon Company relieved some pressure but failed to stay the KPA's advance.

The ROKA 17th Infantry thwarted KPA river crossing attempt on the night of 6–7 August. The next morning the Eighth Army withdrew the 17th. Its place was taken by Task Force Hyzer, named for Lieutenant Colonel Peter C. Hyzer, commanding officer of the 3d Engineer Combat Battalion. It consisted of Hyzer's battalion, a light tank company (less its tanks), and the 24th Recon Company. At the same time Eighth Army commander Lieutenant General Walton H. Walker reduced the 24th Infantry Division's front by 20,000 yards, assigning this to the 1st Cavalry Division on the 24th's right flank.

Counterattacks and fighting on 7–10 August proved fruitless, although the newly arrived 9th Infantry Regiment of the U.S. 2d Division was thrown into the battle. KPA troops now approached the town of Yŏngsan in the 24th Division rear area, and the 2d Battalion, 27th Infantry Regiment of the 25th Division was committed to the southern flank of the 24th Division, attacking successfully northeast toward the town.

On 10 August, Church formed Task Force (TF) Hill, named for Colonel John G. Hill, commander of the 9th Infantry. It included the 9th Infantry (less its 3d Battalion), the 19th and 34th Infantry Regiments, and the 1st Battalion, 21st Infantry. But the force was inadequate.

KPA forces now cut the main supply route east of Yŏngsan. A series of ad hoc defensive positions were formed along this route by headquarters, military police, reconnaissance, and engineer troops, but most soon fell to enemy attack. On 12 August elements of the KPA 10th Division crossed the Naktong and seized a large terrain mass on the division's northern flank (Hill 409) but never moved beyond that point.

On 13 August, the 2d Battalion of the 27th Infantry, joined by the 3d Battalion, attacked again, driving closer to Yŏngsan and making contact with 1st Battalion of the 21st Infantry and the freshly arrived 1st Battalion of the 23d Infantry of the U.S. 2d Division. This meeting opened the supply route.

TF Hill was not strong enough to continue attacking on 14 and 15 August. The KPA attacked the 1st Batallion of the 21st shortly after midnight on the 15th, and then attacked all across the front, penetrating the 2d Batallion of the 9th Regiment, 2d Division's lines. Continuing on 16 August, the KPA pushed the 2d Battalion of the 19th back some 600 yards and forced the 1st Batallion of the 34th Infantry to give ground.

On 17 August TF Hill was disbanded, its components reverting to division control. That day the 1st

Marine Provisional Brigade (5th Marine Regiment, artillery battalion, and tank company) was committed to the fray, attached to the 24th Division.

The Marine 2d Battalion attacked the KPA on Obong-ni Ridge. The army's 9th Infantry, on the Marines' right, was to attack at the same time. The commanders of the 5th Marines and 9th Infantry decided to have the Marines attack first, then support the army attack. This proved to be a mistake, for KPA troops in the army's zone poured deadly fire into the flanks and rear of the attackers. This, coupled with very stubborn resistance, limited the Marines to the seizure of a single knob on the ridge. Then the 9th attacked and eliminated the threat to the Marines from that quarter.

The Marine 1st Battalion continued the assault on Obong-ni, taking two-thirds of the ridge. The Marines defeated a KPA counterattack that night, and the next morning seized the remainder of Obong-ni and a promontory across the valley from it. Army units also continued attacking north of the Marines on 18 August, some its units taking heavy casualties. But KPA troops were dislodged and began fleeing toward and across the Naktong, hastened by heavy, accurate air, artillery, and mortar fire.

By 19 August the United Nations Command had restored the river line, but at the high cost of over 1,800 casualties. The KPA 4th Division, which had numbered about 8,000 men, was reduced to some 3,500 men and lost all of its artillery and heavy equipment.

—*Uzal W. Ent*

References:

Appleman, Roy E. *South to the Naktong, North to the Yalu.* Washington, DC: Office of the Chief of Military History, 1961.

Blair, Clay. *The Forgotten War: America in Korea, 1950–1953.* New York: Times Books, 1987.

Ent, Uzal W. *Fighting on the Brink: Defense of the Pusan Perimeter.* Paducah, KY: Turner, 1996.

Geer, Andrew. *The New Breed: The Story of the U.S. Marines in Korea.* Nashville: Battery Press, 1989.

Montross, Lynn, and Nicholas A. Canzona. *U.S. Marine Operations in Korea, 1950–1953.* Vol. 1, *The Pusan Perimeter.* Washington, DC: U.S. Marine Corps Historical Branch, 1954.

See also: Church, John H.; Naktong Bulge, Second Battle of; Walker, Walton Harris.

Naktong Bulge, Second Battle of
(31 August–9 September 1950)

Second key battle in August–September 1950 involving U.S. and Republic of Korea Army (ROKA) forces against the Korean People's Army (KPA, North Korean) along the Naktong River. On 24 August the U.S. 2d Infantry Division relieved the 24th Infantry Division on the Naktong. An adjustment of the 2d and 1st Cavalry sectors gave the division a front of over

thirty-two miles. Eighth Army commander Lieutenant General Walton H. Walker believed that, with the defeat of the KPA 4th Division earlier in the month, the U.S. 2d Division would be on a relatively quiet front where it could get experience but without serious fighting.

The division had but seven infantry battalions available. The 3d Battalion, 9th Infantry Regiment was defending the airfield at Yŏnil, and the 3d Battalion, 23d Infantry was attached to the 1st Cavalry Division. 2d Division commander Major General Laurence B. "Dutch" Keiser placed his 38th Infantry in the north on a front of almost twelve miles, the 23d Infantry (minus the 3d Battalion) in the center defending somewhat less than ten miles, and the 9th Infantry (minus the 3d Battalion) in the south, including the bulge, with about eleven and a half miles.

The 1st Battalion, 9th Infantry held the southern half of the regimental sector with three companies on line; the 2d Battalion, 19th Infantry held the north with two companies. One company was in reserve.

The 23d placed all three companies of the 1st Battalion on line. The 2d Battalion (minus Company E) was in reserve. Company E was sent to the 9th as an additional reserve unit. The 38th outposted the Naktong with two companies, refusing the regimental flank with two more. Its 3d Battalion was in reserve.

Supported by artillery and mortar fire, elements of the KPA 9th Division crossed the Naktong between 2130 and 2400 on 1 August, striking the 9th Infantry Regiment. The KPA 2d Division attacked the 23d at the same time, overrunning Company C. The attack was so swift and surprising that it also overran the reinforced company-sized Task Force Manchu, which had been assembled in Company B's position in preparation for a raid across the river. Although one or two river-front units still held out, by dawn on 1 September the KPA had already taken Obong-ni Ridge and most of the neighboring Cloverleaf Hill. In one memorable episode, Sergeant Ernest R. Kouma's tank battled the KPA all night, then fought its way through eight miles of KPA-held territory. Kouma was later awarded the Medal of Honor.

The story was the same in the 23d's sector; some troops of the KPA 2d Division attacked frontally, while others exploited gaps to attack CPs, supply points, and mortar and artillery positions and to ambush reinforcements. Companies B and C were all but destroyed.

Part of the KPA 10th Division also attacked the 38th, overrunning Companies E and F. Elements of three KPA divisions (2d, 9th, and 10th) attacked the 2d Division. By daylight on 1 September the KPA had split the 2d Division in two and KPA units had reached Yŏngsan, deep in the division's rear. South of the 2d

KPA soldier captured by Marines on 4 September 1950 during the Second Battle of the Naktong Bulge.
(National Archives)

Division, elements of the KPA 6th and 7th Divisions had penetrated 25th Division's lines, but the division's 27th Infantry was successfully counterattacking.

Remnants of the 9th Infantry, the division engineers, reconnaissance company, part of the division's tank battalion, and some automatic antiaircraft carriers then formed a scratch force to defend Yŏngsan.

General Keiser appointed division artillery commander Brigadier General Loyal Haynes to lead the defense of the division's northern sector and assistant division commander Brigadier General Sladen Bradley to do the same in the south. Meantime, General Walker attached the Marine Brigade to the 2d Division at 1330 on 2 September and alerted the 19th Infantry (24th Division) for possible commitment.

The army-Marine counterattack on 3 September was marked by considerable confusion. The local army commander told the Marines that the line of departure was secured; it was not. The Marines had to seize it before launching the planned attack.

The Marine 2d Battalion attacked from south of Yŏngsan along the MSR (main supply route). Shortly thereafter, it was stopped by stubborn KPA defenders. But the Marine 1st Battalion, attacking on the 2d's left, dislodged this force. The Marines ended the day with the two battalions somewhat scattered but having driven back the KPA. On 4 September the 1st and 3d Battalions continued the attack, forcing KPA units to retreat further. The Marines experienced heavy artillery fire and infantry probes that night.

Early on 5 September a strong KPA counterattack against the 9th Infantry north of the Marines was thwarted by artillery and the Marines' machine gun fire. Then the Marines began their attack, headed for Obong-ni Ridge. Simultaneously elements of the 9th, 23d, and 38th Regiments of the 2d Division also attacked.

Throughout this period the 23d Regiment, aided by 3d Battalion, 38th Infantry, took on the KPA 2d Division and thoroughly defeated it. Fighting in the 23d's sector continued until 16 September, when most of the KPA were eliminated. In the far north of the division sector the KPA 10th Division, after making its initial attacks, retreated onto the massive hill dubbed Hill 409. In the Second Battle of the Naktong River the KPA 2d and 9th Divisions lost between them over 10,000 men. There is evidence that elements of the KPA 4th Division also took part in the battle, but to what extent and with what loss is unknown. KPA forces of varying sizes remained in the 2d Division sector, engaging in some bloody battles, until the 2d broke out of the perimeter later in September.

—*Uzal W. Ent*

References:

Appleman, Roy E. *South to the Naktong, North to the Yalu.* Washington, DC: Office of the Chief of Military History, 1961.

Blair, Clay. *The Forgotten War: America in Korea, 1950–1953.* New York: Times Books, 1987.

Ent, Uzal W. *Fighting on the Brink: Defense of the Pusan Perimeter.* Paducah, KY: Turner, 1996.

Geer, Andrew. *The New Breed: The Story of the U.S. Marines in Korea.* Nashville: Battery Press, 1989.

Montross, Lynn, and Nicholas A. Canzona. *U.S. Marine Operations in Korea, 1950–1953.* Vol. 1, *The Pusan Perimeter.* Washington. DC: U.S. Marine Corps Historical Branch, 1954.

See also: Keiser, Laurence B.; Naktong Bulge, First Battle of; Walker, Walton Harris.

Nam II
(1913–1976)

Democratic People's Republic of Korea (DPRK, North Korea) general and political figure, who was chief delegate at the Korean armistice negotiations. Born on 5 June 1913 at Kyŏngwŏn County, North Hamgyŏng Province, North Korea, the son of a farmer who later fled to Russia to escape the Japanese, Nam Il graduated from a teacher's college in Tashkent. Forsaking a teaching career, he attended the Smolensk Military School in Russia. As a Red Army captain he fought the German army in the Battle of Stalingrad. Later, as chief of staff of a division, he helped the Red Army take Warsaw.

Nam arrived in P'yŏngyang in August 1946, one year after Soviet forces had liberated North Korea from Japanese control. He then became vice minister of education of the North Korean People's Committee under Soviet auspices. In September 1948, on the establishment of the DPRK, Nam was named to the same post. The Ministry of Education was soon a propaganda vehicle for the new regime.

Nam helped the Defense Ministry plan the 25 June 1950 DPRK attack on the Republic of Korea (ROK, South Korea). With the outbreak of the Korean War, he became vice chief of staff of the Korean People's Army. In December 1950 he became chief of staff with the rank of lieutenant general, replacing Kang Kŏn, who had been killed in battle.

Nam was regularly elected to the Central Committee of the Korean Worker's Party. When armistice negotiations began in July 1951, he became head of the DPRK delegation, a position he held for the remainder of the talks. The chain-smoking Nam had considerable nervous energy, although he seldom displayed emotion. He was also known for rudeness, lack of courtesy, and tasteless remarks. U.S. officials soon realized that Nam, despite his title, was subordinate to Chinese representative Xie Fang. He met United Nations proposals with a filibuster, obviously unable to proceed without specific authorization from superiors. After a day or two he would speak firmly on the matter under discussion. Shortly before the signing of the truce agreement, Nam was promoted to full gen-

General Nam Il, senior democratic People's Republic of Korea delegate to the truce talks, leaving the negotiations after they had adjourned for the day, 30 November 1951. (National Archives)

eral so that he would outrank Lieutenant General William K. Harrison, Jr., who signed for the United Nations Command. In August 1953, a month after the agreement, Nam became foreign minister, a post he held until 1959.

Entirely subservient to Kim Il Sung, Nam was one of the few Korean officials of Russian background to survive Kim's purge of Soviet Koreans after the Korean War. In 1954 Nam led the DPRK delegation at the Geneva Conference and proposed the reunification of Korea on the basis of North-South parity, while excluding the United Nations and all external forces. The ROK opposed this plan, and no agreement could be reached.

In 1957 Nam was promoted to DPRK vice-president, a post he held until his death on 7 March 1976 at P'yŏngyang, reportedly in an automobile accident. Nam received a state funeral.

—*Hakjoon Kim*

References:

Goulden, Joseph C. *Korea: The Untold Story of the War.* New York: Times Books, 1982.

Matray, James I., ed. *Historical Dictionary of the Korean War.* Westport, CT: Greenwood Press, 1991.

Nodong Sinmun, 8–10 March 1976.

See also: Geneva Conference of 1954; Harrison, William Kelly, Jr.; Kang Kŏn; Xie Fang (Hsieh Fang).

Namsi, Battle of
(October 1951)

A town in northwest North Korea not far from what was commonly known as MiG Alley. With the Korean War in a stalemate in mid-October 1951, U.S. intelligence discovered three 7,000-foot hard-surfaced airstrips in a twenty-mile radius in northwest Korea—near Saamch'ŏn, T'aech'ŏn, and Namsi. Each had antiaircraft guns, major revetments, and some 1,000 workers for rapid runway repair.

Brigadier General Joe W. Kelly and his B-29s of the Far East Air Force (FEAF) were assigned to destroy the fields. Up to that time most B-29 raids had occurred during daylight with no real MiG opposition. On average the B-29s flew sixteen sorties a day, with three flights of three bombers each attacking rail and road targets or two flights of four bombers attacking bridges.

To destroy the airfields Kelly planned to send three flights of three B-29s using short-range navigation (SHORAN) guidance beacons and receiving direct escort from F-84 Thunderjets and indirect escort from F-86 patrols tying down enemy MiGs. Raids were scheduled from first light to 1000 hours or 1500 hours to last light and conducted along four SHORAN arcs. Flak and the lower altitude limits at which SHORAN beams could be received dictated bombing altitudes.

On 18 October nine B-29s of the 19th Bomb Group (19BG) attacked Saamch'ŏn and nine more from the 98th Bomb Wing (98BW) attacked T'aech'ŏn. The 19BG successfully dropped 306 100-pound bombs on target, but the 98BW failed to rendezvous with its fighter escort and went on to secondary targets. The same thing happened three days later. Thus far no MiGs had defended the airfields.

On 22 October nine B-29s of the 19BG, escorted by twenty-four F-84s, bombed T'aech'ŏn and were attacked by forty MiG-15s. One B-29 crashed in the sea, but its crew was rescued. The next day nine more B-29s of the 307th Bomb Wing, supported by fifty-five F-84s, bombed Namsi. One B-29 aborted at the start. The rest were attacked by fifty MiGs diving through the formations. At the same time one hundred other MiGs struck thirty-four nearby patrolling F-86s, effectively diverting them from the main fight. In the twenty-minute battle each of the three B-29 flights lost at least one bomber. The Communists lost four MiGs (three to the B-29 gunners), while one U.S. F-84 was lost. Only one of the bombers that survived the attacks did not have major damage, as well as dead and wounded men on board.

One air force official called it "one of the most savage and bloody air battles of the Korean War." Still, the campaign continued the next day when eight 98BW B-29s bombed bypass railway bridges at Sunch'ŏn. Supported by sixteen Royal Australian Air Force Meteors and ten F-84s, they were attacked by seventy MiGs with similar results. Another B-29 went down, while seven sustained heavy damage. For two days FEAF commander General Otto P. Weyland halted operations. On 27 October eight B-29s of the 19BG, sixteen Meteors, and thirty-two F-84s were ravaged by ninety-five MiGs.

In many ways, the October raids proved to be the high tide for the Communist air forces in the war. It was also, as Paul Futrell notes, the "swan song of Superfortress daytime operations over Korea."

The *U.S. Air Force Statistical Digest* for fiscal year 1953 officially reported that in one week United Nations (UN) aircraft had engaged 2,166 MiG sorties and shot down thirty-two (twenty-four by F-86s). The FEAF lost fifteen aircraft—seven F-86s, five B-29s, two F-84s, and one RF-80. The B-29 losses were particularly staggering, since before October 1951 only six had been lost in seventeen months; now five had gone down in only one week. In addition, eight B-29s were severely damaged, with fifty-five crewmen dead and twelve wounded.

The results of the campaign of October 1951 were mixed. Kelly decided to fly all future B-29 raids at night. The Communists, for the time being, continued to build up their Korean bases and increase the number and quality of their MiG jets. In December they flew 3,997 sorties. At the same time, U.S. leaders could no longer ignore the need to upgrade FEAF aircraft. In early November Air Force chief of staff General Hoyt Vandenberg began replacing F-80s with an initial deployment of seventy-five new F-86s. In addition, B-29 operations began to use the SHORAN radar system with ever-improving results. By the end of 1951 air force reports determined that the "medium bombers [had] … scored damages" at Namsi, T'aech'ŏn, and Saamch'ŏn faster than Red laborers could effect repairs."

Between January 1952 and April 1953, the Communists made little effort to repair their Korean airfields, opting instead to fly out of Manchurian fields immune from UN attack. As truce talks languished between April and June, laborers rebuilt the airstrips to regain the initiative. Once again UN aircraft destroyed them. The day the final armistice was signed on 27 July, reconnaissance reports stated that all airfields in North Korea were unserviceable for jet aircraft landings. In short, the air battles over Namsi, T'aech'ŏn, and Saamch'ŏn in October 1951, although costly and tactically confining, taught the FEAF important lessons that eventually assured UN air superiority during the Korean War.

—*William Head*

References:

Futrell, Robert F. *The United States Air Force in Korea, 1950–1953*. Rev. ed. Washington, DC: Office of the Chief of Air Force History, 1983.

Mark, Eduard. *Aerial Interdiction: Air Power and the Land Battle in Three Wars*. Washington, DC: Center for Air Force History, 1994.

Thompson, Wayne. "The Air War over Korea." In *Winged Shield, Wing Sword: A History of the United States Air Force*, edited by Bernard C. Nalty. Washington, DC: United States Air Force History and Museum Program, 1997: 3–52.

See also: Aircraft (Principal Combat); United States Air Force (USAF); Vandenberg, Hoyt S.; Weyland, Otto P.

U.S. Air Force napalm attack on suspected Communist positions in a village, 1950. (National Archives)

Napalm

The term *napalm* is derived from the first syllables of two of the fatty acids contained in coconut oil, naphthenate and palmitate, which were added to gasoline to produce an incendiary gel first used in bombing raids over Japan in World War II. In time the term came to designate the gel itself. This early form of napalm was employed in the Korean War as opposed to Napalm-B, composed of gasoline, benzene, and polystyrene, which is a more free-flowing gel developed for use in the Vietnam War. Napalm resembles syrup or jelly, can either be translucent, pale, or brownish, and burns at between 800° and 1200°C in air.

United Nations Command (UNC) forces used napalm-based weaponry and munitions extensively in Korea. On the ground, napalm was projected by flamethrowing tanks, portable flamethrowers worn on the back, specially charged land mines, and 55-gallon drums wired with explosives. One method known as napalm "golden rain" worked much like a primitive fuel-air explosive. It was created by spraying a napalm

mixture into the air above Korean People's Army (KPA, North Korean) troop positions, literally showering them with fire.

U.S. Far East Air Force (FEAF) and U.S. Navy and Marine Corps aircraft employed napalm in close air support missions, for interdiction, and in strategic bombing. In a close air support role, 500-pound bombs filled with thermite and napalm were highly successful against Communist armor. When dropped against the Soviet-built T-34 tank, even a near miss would result in this incendiary mixture igniting the rubber parts of the treads, which would then catch the rest of the tank on fire. Special bunker-busting napalm bombs were also employed against fixed-point targets.

Against troop concentrations, napalm use was mixed. If a direct hit was scored, then it proved to be very effective because of its adhesiveness and high burning temperatures. In such an instance it usually produced two forms of casualties: severe burn cases and carbon monoxide poisoning cases. In a near-miss

A Korean village being bombed. Prisoner interrogation has determined that napalm bombs were the most feared of all weapons used by the U.S. Far East Air Forces in Korea. (National Archives)

scenario, however, Communist troops were usually able to outrun the napalm blast. Still, this exposed them to UN machine gun and artillery fire while they sought new cover.

For interdiction purposes, napalm was employed, along with other aerial munitions, against railroads and roadways. The intent was to slow and disrupt lines of communication so that Communist military forces would not be adequately supplied and reinforced with materiel and soldiers. Napalm was very effective against trains, truck convoys, and the wooden bridges over which they traveled. However, by December 1951, Communist forces had effectively countered these attacks. Men and supplies were moved at night, antiaircraft artillery was increasingly used to protect key bridges and rail lines, and even damages resulting from "maximum-effort" operations were repaired within four to seven days.

Napalm was also used along with other incendiary munitions for strategic bombing purposes—confusingly referred to as close air support or interdiction—from about January 1951 on for policy reasons. During the course of the war the U.S. FEAF Bomber Command devastated the major North Korean cities of P'yŏngyang, capital of the Democratic People's Republic of Korea (North Korea), along with Chinnamp'o, Najin (Rashin), Ch'ŏngjin, and Wŏnsan. One attack upon P'yŏngyang on 11 July 1952 resulted in 1,400 tons of bombs and 23,000 gallons of napalm being delivered by 1,254 aircraft. Such incendiary raids were on a scale with those that took place over Germany and Japan in World War II.

The U.S. FEAF dropped 32,557 tons of napalm ordnance during the course of the Korean War. This was more than twice the total napalm tonnage dropped by the U.S. Army Air Force during World War II. This is in addition to the 10,000–12,000 tons of napalm dropped by U.S. Navy and Marine Corps aircraft. Napalm represented 6.8 percent of the total tonnage of ordnance delivered by the U.S. FEAF. At its height, U.S. monthly production of napalm bombs was estimated to be at about 2,000 compared to 20,500 high-explosive bombs.

—Robert J. Bunker

References:

Björnerstedt, Rolf. *Napalm and Other Incendiary Weapons and All Aspects of Their Possible Use.* Report of the Secretary-General. New York: United Nations, 1973.

Futrell, Robert F. *The United States Air Force in Korea, 1950–1953.* Rev. ed. Washington, DC: Office of the Chief of Air Force History, 1983.

Lumsden, Malvern. *Incendiary Weapons.* Stockholm International Peace Research Institute. Cambridge, MA: MIT Press, 1975.

Swidel, V. W. "Napalm." In *CBW: Chemical and Biological Warfare,* edited by Steven Rose. Boston: Beacon Press, 1969.

See also: Close Air Support.

National Security Act of 1947

Although major reorganizations of the military services had been suggested for decades, it was not until 19 December 1945 that President Harry S. Truman finally set into motion a major revamping of the nation's defense establishment. On that date the president followed up the many studies undertaken by the military services during World War II and sent a message to Congress indicating his support for a consolidation of the armed forces. Numerous congressional hearings followed throughout 1946, and legislation reflecting Truman's ideas, modified to obtain the support of the military, was put forward in 1947. The National Security Act secured passage, and Truman signed it on 26 July 1947. It went into effect on 18 September 1947.

The act established the U.S. Army, U.S. Navy, and U.S. Air Force as separate and equal entities with civilian administrators. Each in turn was supervised by a single, civilian secretary of defense who had cabinet status. The old Navy and War Departments were abolished and replaced by a new organization known as the National Military Establishment. The secretary of defense had authority over all parts of the National Military Establishment and was directed by the president to eliminate duplication of effort between the services in defense procurement, supply, transport, health, research, and storage. He was also to coordinate the national defense budget and its preparation in all parts of the National Military Establishment. The Joint Chiefs of Staff (JCS) held a prominent position in the new organization and continued to formulate strategy, issue military directives, and recommend defense policy to the secretary of defense, the National Security Council, and the president.

The National Security Act of 1947, in addition to dealing with the military services, for the first time brought some rationalization to the nation's intelligence community. The act officially established the Central Intelligence Agency (CIA) from the parts of the World War II–era Office of Strategic Services (OSS) and charged the new agency with coordinating the intelligence-gathering activities of all government departments. The National Security Council (NSC) was another creation of the 1947 law. It was to coordinate the foreign and military policies of the nation and to advise the president on national security matters. Finally, the National Security Resources Board was created to coordinate all military, civilian, and industrial capacities that might be needed for emergency mobilization or future war.

On 10 August 1949, the National Military Establishment was reorganized, with greater authority being granted to the secretary of defense to allow him to enforce cooperation between the services. Thus in 1949 the National Military Establishment was renamed the Department of Defense and was thereafter to consist of the Departments of the Army, Navy, and Air Force, each directed by a civilian secretary, the Joint Chiefs of Staff, the War Council, the Munitions Board, and the Research and Development Board.

By the time of the outbreak of the Korean War in June 1950 the military services of the United States had largely overcome the organizational difficulties caused by the reorganizations put into place by the 1947 act and were able to meet the mobilization and deployment needs presented by the war in a relatively more efficient and timely manner than was possible during earlier twentieth-century military conflicts.

—Clayton D. Laurie

References:

Brune, Lester H. *Chronological History of United States Foreign Relations, 1776 to 20 January 1981.* Vol. 2. New York: Garland, 1985.

Rearden, Stephen L. *History of the Office of the Secretary of Defense: The Formative Years, 1947–1950.* Washington, DC: Office of the Secretary of Defense History Office, 1984.

See also: Central Intelligence Agency (CIA); Joint Chiefs of Staff (JCS); National Security Council (NSC); Truman, Harry S.

National Security Council (NSC)

U.S. agency within the Executive Office of the President, established by the 1947 National Security Act. The close relationship with Great Britain in the Second World War, especially the experience with the Combined Chiefs of Staff, helped U.S. planners recognize the need for a similar U.S. organization. This experience was applied during the war to the development of the organizational structure of the U.S. Joint Chiefs of Staff, as well as to the development of the staff and subcommittee structure of the State-War-Navy Coordinating Committee (SWNCC), established in December 1944 to provide a more regular channel of communication between the State Department and the U.S. military on politicomilitary matters. The "Committee of Three," established during World War II and subsequently abolished, was, in a sense, one of the predecessors of the National Security Council (NSC).

In the immediate postwar period, numerous individuals and groups advocated some kind of high-level coordinating mechanism for national security. One of the more comprehensive of these studies, and the first to suggest the name "National Security Council," was the report prepared by Ferdinand Eberstadt for Secretary of the Navy James Forrestal in September 1945 as a result of the controversy over unification of the armed services. The NSC, established by the enactment of the National Security Act of 1947, flowed from this.

This act, passed by a Republican Congress and approved by a Democratic president, is best known as the legislation that provided for unification of the armed services. However, it was the intent of Congress in passing the act to provide a comprehensive program for the future security of the United States. Title I of the act provides coordinating mechanisms in three other areas of national security activity: national security policy; intelligence; and military, industrial, and civilian mobilization. The National Security Council (NSC), the Central Intelligence Agency (CIA), and the National Security Resources Board (NSRB) were created to coordinate the various activities of the existing executive departments and agencies in these three fields.

The act provided that the function of the NSC should be to "advise the president with respect to the integration of domestic, foreign, and military policies relating to the national security so as to enable the military services and other departments and agencies of the government to cooperate more effectively in matters involving the national security." The CIA was placed under the NSC. The NSC was composed of the president, secretaries of state, defense, army, navy, and air force (service secretaries were excluded in the 1949 amendment to the act), and the chairman of the NSRB The NSRB was formally disbanded in 1953.

—*Youngho Kim*

References:
Central Intelligence Agency. *Organizational History of the National Security Council during the Truman and Eisenhower Administrations*. Washington, DC: U.S. Government Printing Office, 1988.
See also: Central Intelligence Agency (CIA).

NATO (North Atlantic Treaty Organization)

Alliance comprising the United States and eleven western European nations. The North Atlantic Treaty Organization (NATO) came into being on 4 April 1949 and originally was a defensive alliance in response to the growing concern over aggression by the USSR and the spread of communism into Western Europe. The member states declared that an attack against any one of its members would be considered an assault against all.

The European member states hailed NATO as a new U.S. commitment to the defense of Western Europe. The Korean War, however, shifted U.S. foreign policy to the Far East, and the West Europeans believed that increased U.S. military involvement in Korea would damage the flow of military aid to them. These fears soon vanished once the Truman administration's position on the war became clear. Washington believed that a Communist triumph in Asia would pave the way for an attempt to repeat the process in Europe, as did U.S. Far East commander General Douglas MacArthur.

NATO members had to address hard realities laid bare by the war. The military and organizational weakness of NATO in 1950 demanded quick remedies in the face of the crisis. Rearmament in Europe was scarcely under way at the outbreak of war. Also, NATO had only twelve divisions. Efforts to rearm, spurred forward by U.S. Secretary of State Dean G. Acheson, resulted in a substantial increase in defense spending by Britain and France. In fall 1950, the U.S. also pledged to send four additional U.S. divisions to Europe despite the opposition of some in Congress over diverting resources to Europe in time of war in Asia.

These steps proved to be inadequate and raised the explosive issue of allowing military participation by the Federal Republic of Germany (West Germany) in the alliance. Europeans, especially the French, lodged strong protests. The desperate need for manpower, however, produced a proposal by French economic planner Jean Monnet. In October 1950 he introduced the Pleven Plan, named for French Premier René Pleven, that called for a European defense force at the command of NATO that would include German units. Monnet's plan led to the creation of the European Defense Community (EDC) in May 1952. Although the plan ultimately failed (ironically, rejected by the French government), it laid the foundation for West Germany's eventual inclusion in NATO in 1955.

Organizational changes in the command structure of NATO resulted from rearmament and particularly the German question. Command of the military forces of the alliance rested with the Supreme Headquarters Allied Powers Europe (SHAPE), created in January 1951. At that time, General Dwight D. Eisenhower became NATO's first supreme commander. Political restructuring took the form of a council of deputies under the leadership of a secretary-general to carry out the policies of the alliance. These changes, with the exception of continued expansion of the alliance, remain largely unchanged to the present.

—*Eric W. Osborne*

References:

Kaplan, Lawrence S. *NATO and the United States*. New York: Twayne, 1994.

Kauffman, Burton. *The Korean War: Challenges in Crisis, Credibility, and Command*. Philadelphia: Temple University Press, 1986.

MacDonald, Callum. *Korea: The War Before Vietnam*. New York: Free Press, 1986.

See also: Acheson, Dean Goodersham; France; Truman, Harry S.; United Kingdom (UK).

Naval Battles

As in all of the United States' modern wars, in Korea the U.S. Navy and Allied navies had to eliminate their enemy's presence at sea before concentrating on the conflict ashore. Soon after the Democratic People's Republic of Korea (DPRK, North Korean) invasion of the Republic of Korea (ROK, South Korea) on 25 June 1950, the Republic of Korea Navy (ROKN)—composed of submarine chaser *Paektusan* (*PC 701*), one tank landing ship (LST), fifteen minesweepers and minelayers, and 7,000 men—sortied from port in search of the Korean People's Navy (KPN, North Korean navy). It did not take long for *Paektusan*, the crew of which had only recently brought its ship (formerly USS *Whitehead*) to South Korea from the United States, to locate prey. *Paektusan* discovered a KPN 1,000-ton steamer off the east coast in the vicinity of the South Korean port of Pusan. The ROKN combatant sank the KPN ship, perhaps preventing seizure of the one port that would become vital to the United Nations Command (UNC) forces fighting ashore.

In the meantime, UNC help was on the way. With the outbreak of war, Naval Forces Far East commander Vice Admiral C. Turner Joy dispatched his one light cruiser, four destroyers, four amphibious ships, one submarine, ten minesweepers, and an attached frigate of the Royal Australian Navy to Korean waters. Almost simultaneously, U.S. Pacific Fleet commander in chief Admiral Arthur W. Radford transferred his subordinate Seventh Fleet to Admiral Joy's operational control. That fighting fleet, under Vice Admiral Arthur D. Struble, steamed from its home port of Subic Bay, Philippines, on 27 June 1950, made a show of force off the coast of the People's Republic of China, and then headed for Korean waters. Struble's aircraft carrier *Valley Forge*, heavy cruiser *Rochester*, eight destroyers, three submarines, and a number of logistic support ships would be most welcome in the combat theater. The British Commonwealth soon complemented these U.S. naval forces with aircraft carrier

Triumph, two light cruisers, three destroyers, and three frigates. In July the United States strengthened the ROKN with the provision of three decommissioned U.S. submarine chasers, more LSTs, and logistic ships and craft.

In the early hours of 2 July, as the Allied fleets converged on Korea, U.S. cruiser *Juneau*, British cruiser *Jamaica*, and British frigate *Black Swan* discovered four torpedo boats and two motor gunboats of the KPN that had just finished escorting ten craft loaded with ammunition south along the coast in the Sea of Japan. The outgunned KPN torpedo boats turned and gamely pressed home a torpedo attack, but before they could launch their weapons, the Anglo-American flotilla ended the threat; only one torpedo boat survived U.S.-British naval gunfire to flee the scene. After this one-sided battle and for the remainder of the war, North Korean naval leaders decided against contesting control of the sea with the UN navies. Surviving KPN units eventually took refuge in Chinese and Soviet ports.

Freed early from the threat of attack by KPN combatants, major UN warships could concentrate on the ground campaign. At this critical time for UN ground troops—then fighting to hold a precarious lodgment in South Korea—the fleet's carrier-based aircraft, battleships, cruisers, and destroyers poured bombs and shells on North Korean troops, tanks, and vehicles pushing down both coasts of South Korea.

The UN navies still had much to do to deny the KPN use of the sea, however. During July, August, and early September, UN combatants, especially ROKN ships, were needed to disrupt KPN seaborne attempts to resupply the fast-advancing North Korean ground forces. Early in July ROKN minesweeper *YMS 513* sank three Communist supply craft at Chulp'o on the southwestern coast; on the other side of the peninsula, *Juneau* located and destroyed the ammunition vessels that figured in the 2 July sea battle. On 22 July *YMS 513* sank another three supply vessels near Chulp'o. Five days later, submarine chasers *PC 702* and *PC 703*, newly provided by the United States, steamed up the west coast of Korea and, west of Inch'ŏn, sank twelve North Korean sampans loaded with ammunition. During the first week of August, *YMS 302* and other ROKN units destroyed another thirteen Communist logistic craft on the west coast. Between 13 and 20 August the ROKN engaged North Korean supply vessels five times. In one instance, *YMS 503* sank fifteen such vessels and captured thirty.

Combat action was especially heavy on the south coast during the last week of August 1950, when the North Korean command was desperate to reinforce and resupply its troops trying to penetrate the Pusan perimeter. Motor minesweepers *YMS 503*, *YMS 504*,

YMS 512, and *YMS 514*, and *PC 702* sank numerous North Korean craft; many of the embarked troops drowned, while many others were captured.

At the end of the month, the ROKN frustrated a North Korean attempt to seize the port of P'ohang on the Pusan perimeter with troop-laden small boats. Finally, as the UN navies converged on Inch'ŏn for the amphibious assault that would turn the tide in the fall of 1950, *PC 703* sank a KPN minelaying craft and three other vessels in waters off the Yellow Sea port.

Having secured control of the sea off Korea, the UNC could proceed with exploitation of that strategic advantage. With little fear from North Korean counteraction at sea, UN naval forces under Admiral C. Turner Joy deployed U.S. Marine and army troops and South Korean soldiers ashore at Inch'ŏn on 15 September, landed other ground forces at Wŏnsan in northeastern Korea during October, and safely withdrew those forces from Hŏngnam in December when China's entry into the war once again altered the strategic balance. While the fortunes of war on the ground changed a number of times before the 27 July 1953 Armistice, UN forces never lost control of the sea.

—*Edward J. Marolda*

References:

Cagle, Malcolm W., and Frank A. Manson. *The Sea War in Korea.* Annapolis, MD: Naval Institute Press, 1957.

Field, James A., Jr. *History of United States Naval Operations: Korea.* Washington, DC: U.S. Government Printing Office, 1962.

Jane's Fighting Ships. London: S. Low, Marston, 1949–1950, 1951–1952.

See also: Joy, Charles Turner; Korea, Democratic People's Republic of: Navy (Korean People's Navy [KPN]); Korea, Republic of: Navy (ROKN); Radford, Arthur W.; Struble, Arthur D.; United States: Navy.

Naval Forces Far East (NAVFE)

At the beginning of the Korean War, Naval Forces Far East (NAVFE or NavFE), a command existing since 1947, was the principal naval organization directly subordinate to General of the Army Douglas MacArthur's Far East Command (FEC) with its general headquarters in Tokyo. Vice Admiral C. Turner Joy, commander of NAVFE from 26 August 1949, directed an organization broken into four principal components: Amphibious Force Far East (Task Force [TF] 90); Naval Forces, Philippines (Task Force 93); Naval Forces, Marianas (Task Force 94); and Naval Forces, Japan (Task Force 96).

In June 1950 these organizations lacked resources. For warships, Admiral Joy could count only one light cruiser (*Juneau*) and four destroyers at his immediate disposal in TF 96, a unit especially weak in minecraft. His amphibious force (TF 90) totaled five ships, including only one landing craft (*LST-611*).

Moreover, joint training had been woefully inadequate. In June 1949 MacArthur had directed that the three services conduct amphibious exercises, but the first major landing was not scheduled until the fall of 1950.

After the shooting started in Korea, authorities in Washington acted quickly to bolster Joy's forces. On 27 June the Seventh Fleet, based in the Philippines and under the direct control of the commander in chief of the Pacific Fleet, was assigned to NAVFE. Its first warships—one carrier (*Valley Forge*), one heavy cruiser (*Rochester*), and eight destroyers—reached Japanese waters by 28 June and were soon in action. Designated as Task Force 77, this striking force was soon bolstered by other United Nations (UN) warships and supported by a replenishment unit dubbed Task Group (TG) 77.7 (soon redesignated Task Force 79). Henceforth the principal combatant component of the Seventh Fleet—and thus of NAVFE—was TF 77, built around its fast carrier forces.

Over the next three years four vice admirals commanded the Seventh Fleet: Arthur D. Struble (6 May 1950 to 28 March 1951), Harold M. Martin (28 March 1951 to 3 March 1952), Robert P. Briscoe (3 March to 20 May 1952), and J. J. Clark (20 May 1952 through the end of the war). During the war thirteen rear admirals rotated command of TF 77.

In a major reorganization on 12 September 1950, the naval operating commands were recast. Added to the Seventh Fleet organization was Task Force 72, which included the ships involved in the Formosa Patrol. For work closer to the Korea peninsula, the UN Blockading and Escort Force (Task Force 95) was established. Its principal elements included TG 95.1 (west coast group); TG 95.2 (east coast group); TG 95.6 (minesweeping group); and TG 95.7 (Republic of Korea Navy). During the conflict, NAVFE activated additional commands, including two large aviation units: Fleet Air Wing 6 (commissioned 4 August 1950) and Fleet Air Wing 14 (operational on 16 October 1952). Also created was the Logistic Support Force (Task Force 92) (on 3 April 1951).

As units rushed to the theater, NAVFE ballooned. In carriers, the force went from 1 in June to 8 British and U.S. by October 1950. The numbers of battleships, cruisers, and destroyers climbed from 18 to 64. During the same period, the total of warships at the disposal of NAVFE rose from 86 to 274. Such increases in materiel were reflected in personnel. In June 1950, 10,990 U.S. sailors were in the western Pacific; by the end of July 1951 comparable figures totaled 74,335.

In contrast to many of its components, NAVFE enjoyed remarkable command continuity. When Admiral Joy stepped down on 4 June 1952, he was replaced by Vice Admiral R. P. Briscoe, who held his post until the end of the war.

—*Malcolm Muir, Jr.*

References:

Cagle, Malcolm W., and Frank A. Manson. *The Sea War in Korea.* Annapolis, MD: Naval Institute Press, 1957.

Field, James A., Jr. *History of United States Naval Operations: Korea.* Washington, DC: U.S. Government Printing Office, 1962.

See also: Briscoe, Robert Pierce; Joy, Charles Turner; MacArthur, Douglas; Struble, Arthur D.; United States Navy.

Naval Gunfire Support

If, in the thinking of many defense analysts in the late 1940s, the aircraft carrier was obsolete in the nuclear age, the gunship seemed positively antediluvian. Yet during the Korean War the battleship, cruiser, and destroyer once again proved their utility, especially in the support of friendly troops ashore and in the interdiction of Communist forces' communications.

With the great drawdown of the fleet in the five years following V-J Day, the number of battleships on active duty in the U.S. Navy dropped from twenty-three to one and cruisers from ninety to twenty-three. Similar drastic cuts took place in destroyer strength. After all, the Soviet surface fleet was negligible, and the most sensitive targets in the Communist bloc were far removed from coastal areas.

When Korean People's Army (KPA, North Korean) forces crossed the 38th parallel and invaded the Republic of Korea (ROK, South Korea), the U.S. Navy had only one cruiser and four destroyers on duty in Japanese waters. But these were in action at Mukho within four days and, rapidly reinforced by gunships from the Seventh Fleet, they provided support to hard-pressed United Nations Command (UNC) troops retreating toward Pusan. From distant waters came the navy's only active battleship, the *Missouri*, and additional cruisers and destroyers. These U.S. ships were bolstered by gunships from Australia, Canada, Great Britain, New Zealand, and the Netherlands. Over the next three years, the U.S. Navy reactivated the remaining Iowa-class battleships (*Iowa*, *New Jersey*, and *Wisconsin*), five heavy cruisers, and 104 destroyers.

During the conflict naval gunfire provided strong support to important UN operations. For instance, two U.S. and two British cruisers plus six U.S. destroyers assisted the Marines landing at Inch'ŏn on 15 September 1950. At Hŏngnam that December surface warships, including the *Missouri*, covered the withdrawal of ground troops with a large portion of their supplies; in the effort, two heavy cruisers, the *St. Paul* and *Rochester*, expended 3,000 8-inch shells. By the spring of 1951, Secretary of the Navy Francis P. Matthews cited naval gunfire support as one of the key assets of the UN in the conflict.

In fact, shore bombardment had become the primary task of surface warships. Missions included firing in support of fixed positions at the front (in contrast to fluid targets encountered in an amphibious assault); securing both flanks of the UNC battle line; and interdicting rail and road lines running along the northeast coast of Korea. In January 1952 this last effort was formally code-named DERAIL; its greatest success came the next month when shore bombardment halted railroad traffic into Wŏnsan for weeks. But the navy simply did not have enough gunships to maintain this tempo of operations indefinitely.

The overall record is impressive. U.S. warships in one eleven-month period undertook 24,000 fire support missions, during which they expended 414,000 projectiles. Many ships did a great deal of shooting. For instance, one destroyer, the *Swenson*, in four months fired 5,709 rounds of 5-inch ammunition.

The big guns of the battleships turned in the most effective performance. Their 2,700-pound armor-piercing shells proved particularly devastating against hard targets such as railroad tunnels. One Marine Corps report concluded that the 16-inch guns were "pound for pound ... the most efficient rifles in the Korean War." Analysts calculated that a battleship could destroy a bridge in less than one half hour with sixty rounds of 16-inch ammunition. In comparison, at least twelve aircraft sorties were required to achieve a similar result with the attendant risk to aircraft and their crews. During the war the four battleships fired more than 20,000 16-inch projectiles—a much larger number than they had shot in World War II.

Between 25 June 1950 and 31 May 1953, U.S. Navy gunships fired 4,069,626 rounds. In the first two years of the war the warships claimed the destruction of 3,334 buildings, 824 vessels and small craft, 14 locomotives, 214 trucks, 15 tanks, 108 bridges, 93 supply dumps, and 28,566 troops.

These intensive operations revealed certain problems: early in the war, the army and navy possessed neither effective liaison nor a standard doctrine for fire control. Both omissions reflected the prewar sentiment that naval gunfire support was obsolete. Also missing in 1950 were dedicated spotting aircraft: the navy had removed its last float planes from battleships and cruisers two years earlier. Given the exigencies of combat, gunships began experimenting with their helicopters for this work.

With the high pace of operations a variety of problems surfaced, including bore erosion, accidents, and blast damage to ship structures. The cruiser *Helena* did so much shooting that her entire main battery had to be replaced. Her sister ship, *St. Paul*, suffered a serious turret fire in April 1952 that killed thirty men.

The battleship *New Jersey* firing her 16-inch guns near the 38th parallel. (National Archives)

Communist forces also hit back. Surface warships were struck on eighty-five separate occasions, with the damage usually being superficial. However, on 7 May 1952 the destroyer *James C. Owens* took six hits that resulted in ten crew casualties. Even the battleships were not immune; both *New Jersey* and *Wisconsin* were slightly damaged by land-based gunfire. Mines presented a more severe threat to vessels operating close inshore: five destroyers were damaged by these underwater weapons.

Despite such drawbacks, UN soldiers attested to the effectiveness of naval gunfire support. Both army and Marine troops gave it high praise, often comparing it favorably with divisional artillery. Top commanders agreed with these favorable assessments. In December 1950, Douglas MacArthur noted that Communist forces frequently conducted their offensives well inland to avoid the effects of warship bombardment. After the trench stalemate developed, Lieutenant General Matthew Ridgway declared that naval gunfire relieved him of any concern for his flanks. Some analysts noted tellingly that UN front lines near the coast were invariably forward of the battle line inland.

Despite this excellent performance, naval gunfire support suffered cuts during the post–Korean War defense realignment as "New Look" planners of the Eisenhower administration concluded that Korean conditions had been "artificial." Thus, all four battleships, most of the cruisers, and many of the destroyers were consigned to mothballs or the scrap heap. Ironically, the Vietnam War would once again prove the utility of the gunship to hard-pressed troops ashore.

—*Malcolm Muir, Jr.*

References:

Cagle, Malcolm W., and Frank A. Manson. *The Sea War in Korea.* Annapolis, MD: Naval Institute Press, 1957.

Field, James A., Jr. *History of United States Naval Operations: Korea.* Washington, DC: U.S. Government Printing Office, 1962.

Muir, Malcolm, Jr. *Black Shoes and Blue Water: Surface Warfare in the United States Navy, 1945–1975.* Washington, DC: Naval Historical Center, 1996.

———. *The Iowa-Class Battleships:* Iowa, New Jersey, Missouri, *and* Wisconsin. Poole, Dorsett: Blandford Press, 1987.

Reilly, John C., ed. *Operational Experience of Fast Battleships: World War II, Korea, Vietnam.* Washington, DC: Naval Historical Center, 1989.

See also: Helicopter Employment; Helicopter Types and Nomenclature; Hŏngnam Evacuation; Inch'ŏn Landings: Operation CHROMITE; MacArthur, Douglas; Naval Forces Far East (NAVFE); Ridgway, Matthew Bunker; United States Navy.

Nehru, Jawaharlal
(1889–1964)

Prime minister of India. Born on 14 November 1889, at Allahabad in Uttar Pradesh, a northern state of India, Jawaharlal Nehru was born into a prominent upper-caste family. His father was a lawyer and nationalist leader in the Indian Congress Party. Nehru attended school at Harrow and then graduated from Trinity College at Cambridge University in England. He then returned to India, where he became involved in the independence movement against British colonial rule. In the mid-1930s Nehru served as Mahatma Gandhi's chief lieutenant. When independence was secured in 1947, Nehru was selected as the first prime minister of independent India, serving until his death. An ardent nationalist, he perceived foreign policy from a regional perspective of India's relations to Asia rather than globally.

During the Korean War Nehru diplomatically endorsed a policy of nonalignment. A scholar-statesman, Nehru was known for his pacifist philosophy. Uncomfortable with militarism, Nehru strove to minimize potential superpower conflicts; he also was concerned because India shared a border with China. Nehru wanted to resolve the Korean issue peacefully through compromise, appeasement, and accommodation, instead of resorting to warfare. Nehru's diplomacy was compared to a tightrope act in which he criticized aggression but refused to align with the East or West. Neither the United States nor the Soviet Union liked Nehru's nonalignment policy and wanted India to declare allegiance to a side.

When on 25 June 1950, the Democratic People's Republic of Korea (DPRK, North Korea) invaded the Republic of Korea (ROK, South Korea), India's chief delegate to the United Nations (UN) Sir Benegal N. Rau, with Nehru's support, voted for the UN Security Council resolution condemning North Korean aggression. Nehru and Indian leaders instructed Rau not to commit India to any further actions without deliberations. Nehru discussed the situation with U.S. Ambassador Loy W. Henderson, and the Indian government issued a statement in support of the second UN Security Council resolution on 27 June, which

called on member states to offer assistance to the ROK to force the North Koreans to withdraw to the 38th parallel.

Nehru accepted the passing of these resolutions but did not endorse the American idea that the North Korean invasion had been directed by the Soviet Union. He thought that President Harry S. Truman was overreacting to a war of local origins that should be resolved by Koreans. Nehru also resented U.S. interference with his efforts to convince the Soviet Union and China not to intervene in Korea. During the second week of July 1950, he issued the first Indian peace initiative to the United States, Soviet Union, and People's Republic of China (PRC). Nehru asked that the PRC be seated in the UN, for the Soviet Union's UN Security Council boycott to end, for a cease-fire in Korea, and for hope of future reunification. The Soviet Union and China politely acknowledged Nehru's requests but did not commit to fulfilling them. The United States responded angrily about the suggestion of diplomatic recognition of the PRC and said that that demand should not be a condition for ending the war. Despite this discouragement, Nehru continued efforts to achieve Chinese diplomatic recognition and a cease-fire.

Nehru was frustrated by the attitudes of political and military leaders toward him and India. For the most part, the Western powers in Korea did not listen to his ideas, and special delegate to the UN from the PRC General Wu told the UN secretary-general that India's views were unimportant because India had not sent soldiers to Korea. World leaders did not support a thirteen-member Asian-Arab bloc in the General Assembly that Nehru helped to establish to promote a cease-fire and address East Asian concerns. Nehru sank into a depression during 1950. Despite this he continued to speak against war, demand tolerance, and promote international goodwill.

Throughout the Korean War Nehru attempted to keep open lines of communication with Washington, Moscow, and Beijing in hopes of negotiating a settlement. His initiatives, however, were never fully supported by the Communist powers and often made Truman angry. In the fall of 1950 Nehru tried to prevent the war's expansion by sending warnings to Washington and London via Indian ambassador to the PRC K. M. Panikkar. Chinese Foreign Minister Zhou Enlai had told Panikkar that Chinese troops would enter the war if UNC troops moved north of the 38th parallel.

In January 1951 the Commonwealth prime ministers met in London, where Nehru sought to convince the United States not to condemn China and accept its claim to Formosa and membership in the UN. The other Commonwealth leaders refused to support Nehru, and he suggested staging a conference between the United States, the PRC, Great Britain, and the Soviet Union. Nehru believed that the United States had too much influence on policy in Korea, such as approving the bombing of North Korean power plants along the Yalu River. He wrote that he feared that the future of the UN and of world peace "might be decided without proper consultations, and might ultimately depend on the discretion of military commanders who would naturally think more of local military objectives than of large questions affecting the world."

When President Truman dismissed General Douglas MacArthur, Nehru urged the PRC to seek diplomatic resolution to the war. China decided to enter negotiations, however, by submitting demands and concerns through the Soviet Union instead of India. Nehru was isolated from Korean War negotiations until Ambassador Chester Bowles and Eleanor Roosevelt visited India and urged him to convince China to file its complaints of bacteriological warfare independently of truce talks. China withdrew these allegations and tried to have India pressure for the repatriation of prisoners of war (POWs) through Great Britain. The PRC demanded that all POWs be returned.

In late 1952 when the P'anmunjŏm truce talks were stalled, Nehru asked Indian ambassador to the UN V. K. Krishna Menon to initiate a compromise regarding Item 4 about POW repatriation. The Indian proposal called for a cease-fire, repatriation of prisoners wanting to return, and the establishment of a repatriation commission of four neutral powers to monitor the exchange of remaining prisoners, but China and the Soviet Union rejected the idea. However, the Indian peace initiatives and Menon's POW settlement proposal ultimately established the foundation for the July 1953 Armistice Agreement. The United States and China mutually accepted the repatriation commission's final POW agreement, ending the stalemated war. Nehru praised the agreement as an "outbreak of peace."

After the Korean War, Nehru tried to boost India's industrial and economic development. He also focused on encouraging peace within India by creating new states to appease indigenous tribes and religious factions such as the Sikhs. Despite his efforts, violent riots erupted over such issues as Kashmir and government control of private schools.

Seeking to perpetuate his policy of peaceful coexistence and nonalignment with other nations, Nehru refused to join the Soviet or Anglo-American blocs. Active in international diplomacy, he participated in the 1954 Geneva Conference, and he supported disarmament and a ban on nuclear weapons. In 1956 he joined Yugoslavian president Josip Tito and Egyptian president Gamal Abdel Nasser to denounce colonialism and promote a global system of collective security.

In 1961 Nehru ordered Indian troops into Portuguese-controlled areas of the subcontinent. The next year India and China fought along their common border as an unprepared Indian military failed to prevent Chinese troops from gaining Indian territory. Nehru dismissed his defense minister, V. K. Krishna Menon. In January 1964 Nehru became ill during a session of the Indian Congress. He died at New Delhi on 27 May 1964.

—*Elizabeth D. Schafer*

References:

Brecher, Michael. *Nehru: A Political Biography.* New York: Oxford University Press, 1959.

Doody, Agnes G. "Words and Deeds: An Analysis of Jawaharlal Nehru's Non-Alignment Policy in the Cold War, 1947–1953." Doctoral dissertation. Pennsylvania State University, 1961. Unpublished manuscript.

Gopal, Sarvepalli. *Jawaharlal Nehru: A Biography.* 3 vols. Cambridge, MA: Harvard University Press, 1976.

Moraes, Francis Robert. *Jawaharlal Nehru: A Biography.* New York: Macmillan, 1956.

Nehru, Jawaharlal. *Letters to Chief Ministers, 1947–1964,* edited by G. Parthasarathi. 5 vols. Delhi: Oxford University Press, 1985–1989.

Range, Willard. *Jawaharlal Nehru's World View; a Theory of International Relations.* Athens: University of Georgia Press, 1961.

See also: Armistice Agreement; Bowles, Chester; Cease-Fire Negotiations; China, People's Republic of: UN Representation Question; Henderson, Loy; India; Menon, V. K. Krishna; Panikkar, Sardar K. M.; P'anmunjŏm Truce Talks; Rau, Sir Benegal Narsing; Repatriation, Voluntary; Soviet Security Council Boycott; Truce Talks; Truman, Harry S.; Truman's Recall of MacArthur; Union of Soviet Socialist Republics; Zhou Enlai.

Netherlands

As a signatory power of the North Atlantic Treaty Organization (NATO) and the Western European Union defensive alliance of 1948, the Netherlands agreed to provide troops for the United Nations' (UN's) efforts in Korea following the outbreak of war on the divided peninsula. The advance party of the Netherlands force, a battalion, arrived in Korea on 24 October 1950. The entire battalion arrived in Pusan a month later, on 23 November, immediately before the opening of the Chinese offensive. After processing at the United Nations Command (UNC) Reception Center at Taegu, the battalion was attached to the U.S. Eighth Army. As such it represented part of the only reserve available to U.S. commander Lieutenant General Walton Walker. By the next month the Dutch forces were assigned, along with the French Battalion, to the U.S. 2d Division as divisional reserve. The battalion fought in the fierce defensive battles of the first two weeks of January 1951 helping the 2d Division fend off strong Korean People's Army (KPA, North

Korean) V Corps attacks southwest of the town of Wŏnju. In these actions, the Dutch held Hill 247 and assisted in the killing or capturing of some 1,100 KPA troops. This fighting ranged north of Wŏnju to Hoengsŏng and back again by mid-February. On 13 February the battalion fought a gallant rear-guard action in which Dutch commander Lieutenant Colonel M. P. A. den Ouden personally confronted elements of a Chinese breakthrough that had reached the edge of the battalion's command post. Colonel den Ouden and a number of his staff were killed; other staff members were wounded. Excellent covering fire from Dutch troops nevertheless allowed a number of U.S. units to withdraw safely.

In March and April indications arose that the Chinese were about to resume their offensive in the higher ranges of the T'aebaek Mountains southeastward from the Soyang River. Launched on 16 May, that offensive again pushed U.S. and Republic of Korea (ROK) forces back. Included again were the 2d Division and the attached Dutch Battalion. The Dutch drew the assignment to counterattack any Chinese or North Korean breakthrough. This occurred at the juncture of the lines of the U.S. 38th and 23d Infantry regiments, where an ROK Army (ROKA) covering force was collapsed back into the U.S. line by advancing Communist forces. The Dutch only partially fulfilled their mission, confronted as they were by successive waves of thousands of Chinese troops, who literally walked upright through a hail of artillery and small-arms fire directed at the breach. At one point on 17 May the battalion broke under the pressure, though its commander, W. D. H. Eekhout, quickly regained control of his troops. U.S. commanders subsequently pulled the battalion out of the line and sent it two miles to the rear to rest and reorganize at the village of Han'gye. By 28 May, however, Communist forces had been pushed back to about the 38th parallel. In the fighting that followed around Hwach'ŏn Reservoir, Dutch troops and the rest of the 2d Division helped cut off and destroy Communist units attempting to escape the UN counteroffensive. In the words of General Lieutenant Matthew Ridgway, the Dutch Battalion and the 2d Division performed brilliantly and displayed extraordinary heroism in the face of numerically vastly superior Communist forces.

In the spring of 1952 the Dutch Battalion was assigned to the guard units on Koje-do off the southern coast of South Korea. There it assisted in physically suppressing anti-UN demonstrations among Chinese and North Korean prisoners of war.

In the main the Dutch Battalion fit in well among UN forces and conducted itself well in a largely defensive, and occasionally offensive, role between 1950 and 1953. No significant cultural or linguistic difficul-

ties arose between troops from the Netherlands and other contingents as, for example, plagued the Turkish Brigade. Dutch preferences for greater amounts of bread and potatoes in their rations than was given to U.S. forces caused some initial logistical problems. These, however, were fairly quickly overcome and generated no serious frictions in any case. For its service in Korea the battalion earned a U.S. Presidential Unit Citation.

—*D. R. Dorondo*

References:

Hermes, Walter G. *United States Army in the Korean War: Truce Tent and Fighting Front.* Washington, DC: Office of the Chief of Military History, 1966.

Mossman, Billy C. *U.S. Army in the Korean War: Ebb and Flow, November 1950–July 1951.* Washington, DC: U.S. Army Center of Military History, 1990.

Ridgway, Matthew B. "The Second Year: Spring and Summer 1951." In *Pictorial History of the Korean War, 1950–1953: Ridgway and Clark Report.* n.p.: Veterans' Historical Book Service, 1954.

Neutral Nations Repatriation Commission

Commission created by the 27 July 1953 Korean armistice agreement to oversee the final screening of prisoners of war (POWs) from both sides in the Korean War who refused repatriation to their countries of origin. Indian Representative to the United Nations (UN) V. K. Krishna Menon had proposed establishment of a Neutral Nations Repatriation Commission (NNRC) to guarantee each POW freedom of choice. The UN resolution of 3 December 1952 provided the format for the 8 June 1953 POW agreement that set up the NNRC. It consisted of five representatives: two from neutral states friendly to the United States— Sweden and Switzerland—and two from Communist states—Poland and Czechoslovakia. Neutral India was the fifth member, and the Indian representative, Major General Kadenera Subayya Thimayya, served as chairman and executive agent of the NNRC. India also agreed to provide a brigade of troops of about 6,000 men to guard the prisoners while they were being held in compounds within the demilitarized zone (DMZ) near P'anmunjŏm. Major General S. P. P. Thorat had actual command of the troops of the Indian Custodian Force (CFI) supporting the NNRC.

The Republic of Korea (ROK) government of President Syngman Rhee opposed the armistice agreement and insisted that POWs held by the United Nations Command (UNC) refusing repatriation be released in South Korea rather than being transferred to NNRC jurisdiction. Rhee also strongly objected to the selection of India as arbitrator of the POW issue. He regarded India as pro-Communist and therefore not neutral. Because the ROK government refused to permit the Indian custodial troops on South Korean soil, the UNC transported all of them to the DMZ by helicopter. Although Rhee ordered the release of some 27,000 anti-Communist POWs on 18 June 1953, the armistice was concluded with agreement that all remaining nonrepatriated POWs be handed over to NNRC custody. The United States had insisted on a provision that this be completed within sixty days of the conclusion of the armistice. POWs from both sides were then to remain under NNRC jurisdiction for an additional ninety days while representatives of the countries involved endeavored to persuade them to return home. After this, the postwar Korean political conference would hold them an additional thirty days. At the conclusion of this time the NNRC would disband and the remaining POWs would become civilians.

On 22 September 1953 the CFI received from the Communist side 359 UNC nonrepatriated POWs: 23 Americans, 1 British, and 335 South Koreans. Two days later the NNRC took control from the UNC of 7,890 North Korean and 14,702 Chinese POWs. The countries of origin all sent representatives to try to convince the POWs to return home, but the NNRC had difficulty in getting the POWs to attend these sessions, which anti-Communist leaders among the POWs opposed. The Communist side constantly insisted that the NNRC force the POWs to attend, but the NNRC was unable to break the control of the anti-Communist POW organizations over the prisoners and to guarantee conditions for the explanations. If the prisoners would not attend, the explanations could not take place. On several occasions POWs assaulted their guards and attempted to break out of the camps.

UNC representatives were able to meet with only sixty UN POWs. POWs of both sides were under strong and resolute leadership, and only about 3 percent of those who received the briefings decided to accept repatriation. Both sides sought to exploit the repatriation issue for their own propaganda advantage.

The persuasion process was to end on 24 December 1953. The Communists demanded that it continue until all POWs had been briefed, but the UNC refused any extension in the time limit beyond that specified in the armistice terms. India sided with the UNC on this and, in a majority ruling, the Commission advised both sides that the briefings had ended.

During the subsequent thirty days, until 22 January 1954, there was to be a political conference of representatives of the two sides and the NNRC to decide the fate of prisoners not yet briefed. The NNRC was to retain the custody of the POWs within that period. But that conference did not convene because of antagonisms between the UNC and Communist side.

On 20 January 1954 the CFI began the transfer of POWs back to UNC custody. The delivery of 21,805 men to the UNC was completed by 21 January. During this time 104 additional prisoners sought CFI protection and asked for repatriation or asylum. No doubt other prisoners would have chosen repatriation if the opportunity to do so had been available. Only 137 of the Communist nonrepatriates and ten of the UNC nonrepatriates had opted to return home.

Rejecting the position of the NNRC's Polish and Czechoslovakian representatives, on 18 February 1954, the Indian, Swedish, and Swiss members adopted a resolution to dissolve the NNRC three days later. Although the NNRC effort was disappointing to both sides, its activities created precedents and established patterns that were followed in subsequent conflicts.

—*Sunghun Cho*

References:

Neutral Nations Repatriation Commission. *The Final Report of the Neutral Nations Repatriation Commission*, 1954.

Thimayya, Kadenera Subayya. *Experiment in Neutrality*. New Delhi: Vision Books, 1981.

See also: Menon, V. K. Krishna; Syngman Rhee; Thimayya, Kadenera Subayya.

Neutral Nations Supervisory Commission (NNSC)

Commission established to supervise the provisions of the Korean Armistice Agreement dealing with the introduction of military personnel, weapons, and equipment and to investigate armistice violations outside the demilitarized zone (DMZ). The truce negotiations that led to the formation of the Neutral Nations Supervisory Commission (NNSC) dealt with the "concrete arrangements" for the cease-fire and armistice. When negotiations on these arrangements began on 27 November 1951, the two sides had already agreed in principle to the establishment of a Military Armistice Commission (MAC) to supervise the armistice. The United Nations Command (UNC) side now proposed that the MAC include Joint Observer Teams with freedom of movement throughout Korea. They also proposed that, while both sides should be permitted to rotate their personnel and replace equipment, there should be no "reinforcement" (no increase in the numbers of military personnel and other war equipment) while the armistice was in effect. On 3 December 1951 Korean People's Army/Chinese People's Volunteer Army (KPA/CPVA) negotiators proposed a complete ban on the introduction of any new troops and equipment and introduced the idea of supervision of this ban by nations "neutral in the Korean War."

The UNC eventually accepted the idea of neutral nations supervision, so long as both sides were permitted to rotate (but not reinforce) their troops and equipment; that the "neutral" countries be mutually acceptable; and that the NNSC be subordinate to the MAC. Negotiations on this issue stalled for several months when the KPA/CPVA proposed including the Soviet Union; however, the two sides eventually agreed on Czechoslovakia and Poland (nominated by the KPA/CPVA) and Sweden and Switzerland (nominated by the UNC). They also agreed on a rotation figure of 35,000 military personnel per month through five ports of entry for each side. These were Inch'ŏn, Kangnŭng, Kunsan, Pusan, and Taegu in South Korea and Ch'ŏngjin, Hŭngnam, Manp'o, Sinanju, and Sinŭiju in the North.

With the signing of the Armistice Agreement on 27 July 1953, the NNSC went into operation, moving into camps close to the P'anmunjŏm conference site and establishing its operating procedures. It organized twenty Neutral Nations Inspection Teams (NNITs). Ten would operate at the ports of entry and ten mobile teams would be available to investigate violations in other areas outside the DMZ if requested to do so by the MAC or by the senior MAC member of either side.

From the beginning, the inspections were controversial. The North Koreans restricted NNIT access at their official ports of entry and were accused by the UNC of bringing equipment in through other locations. The South Korean government accused the Czech and Polish members of spying and periodically threatened to expel them. Tension also developed within the NNSC between the Poles and Czechs on one side and the Swiss and Swedes on the other. With a four-member, two-faction Commission, deadlocks occurred frequently.

In 1956 the UNC unilaterally suspended NNIT operations in South Korea, citing Communist violations and the obstructive attitude of the Czechs and Poles. The NNSC withdrew its inspection teams but continued to meet weekly at P'anmunjŏm to review reports submitted by the two sides on the rotation of troops and replacement of equipment. As the years went by, both sides found the restrictions against introducing new equipment to be unrealistic and burdensome. In 1957 the UNC, arguing that the KPA persistently violated the armistice prohibitions on introducing new equipment, unilaterally suspended its adherence to that provision.

The NNSC supervisory system was now essentially defunct, but the commission served for many years as an informal channel of communication between the two sides and a moderating influence in the potentially volatile P'anmunjŏm conference area. With the end of the Cold War, however, North Korea became disenchanted with Poland and Czechoslovakia. When Czechoslovakia broke up, the North refused either to recognize the Czech Republic as its NNSC successor or to nominate a replacement, and so in April 1993 the Czech delegation withdrew from the NNSC. In 1995 the Democratic People's Republic of Korea (DPRK)

ejected the Polish delegation from North Korea and severed all contact with the NNSC. The Swiss and Swedish NNSC delegations nonetheless continue to meet weekly, and Poland sends a representative four times a year to sign and validate NNSC documents. Representatives of the three nations also meet periodically in Europe to discuss NNSC business. Thus a small and tenuous NNSC mechanism survives nearly half a century after its establishment.

—*Donald W. Boose, Jr.*

References:

Bailey, Sydney D. *The Korean Armistice.* New York: St Martin's Press, 1992.

Hermes, Walter G. *United States Army in the Korean War: Truce Tent and Fighting Front.* Washington, DC: Office of the Chief of Military History, 1966.

U.S. Department of State, Bureau of Public Affairs. *Foreign Relations of the United States, 1951.* Vol. 7, *China and Korea.* Washington, DC: U.S. Government Printing Office, 1983

———. *Foreign Relations of the United States, 1952–1954.* Vol. 15, *Korea.* Washington, DC: U.S. Government Printing Office, 1984.

See also: Armistice Agreement; Demilitarized Zone (DMZ); Kaesŏng Truce Talks; Military Armistice Commission; Neutral Nations Repatriation Commission; P'anmunjŏm Truce Talks; Truce Talks.

New Zealand

One of the first countries to answer the United Nations call for assistance in Korea. When the war began, U.S. leaders asked that New Zealand deploy a force as a part of the United Nations Command (UNC). New Zealand Prime Minister Sir Sidney George Holland and Chief of the General Staff Major General Sir Keith Lindsay Stewart initially contemplated joining forces with Australia, but the British Commonwealth powers were unable to reach quick agreement on either the type or size of their military commitment, and so on 26 July 1950 the New Zealand government unilaterally decided to send naval and ground forces to Korea.

On 31 December 1950, 1,231 New Zealand officers and men arrived in Korea as part of the 16th Field Regiment, Royal New Zealand Artillery. Commanded by Lieutenant Colonel J. W. Moodie, this unit was the nation's main military commitment, and in January 1951 it was attached to the 27th British Commonwealth Brigade. In April 1951 the artillery unit was followed by part of a divisional signals regiment, a transport platoon, and a light aid detachment.

New Zealand ground forces coordinated well with Australian troops and, because many members of the New Zealand contingent had not been adequately trained in technical matters, Australian artillery officers were attached to supervise their performance. New Zealand soldiers were also incorporated into other Australian units.

In the first week of February 1951 the New Zealanders provided fire support to the U.S. 24th Division, helping its advance to Chuam-ni. The New Zealanders also supported the Republic of Korea Army (ROKA, South Korean) 6th Division in April 1951 above Seoul at the beginning of the Chinese People's Volunteer Army (CPVA, Communist Chinese) spring offensive. Hindered by rugged terrain, the New Zealanders experienced difficulty transporting their equipment and were unable to provide very effective support. The ROKA defense collapsed and the New Zealand troops disengaged, moving south to Kap'yŏng, where the Commonwealth Brigade was in reserve. U.S. IX Corps commander Lieutenant General William M. Hoge ordered the New Zealanders again to move forward, protected by the British Middlesex Battalion; but again the South Koreans retreated, and the New Zealand artillery regiment withdrew to Kap'yŏng. There the U.S. 213th Field Artillery Battalion reinforced the New Zealanders with 155-mm self-propelled howitzers. Here the unit played a vital role by shelling directly in front of Canadian troops and foiling a Chinese advance. CPVA assaults continued until 1 May, when the New Zealanders helped the U.S. 24th Division decisively defeat the CPVA offensive in their sector and advance to Line Kansas. For their role in the fighting ROK president Syngman Rhee awarded the 16th New Zealand Field Artillery Regiment a presidential citation. The New Zealanders later provided artillery support at the Battle of Maryong-san Mountain, where they fired over 50,000 rounds in support of UN forces.

In 1951 the United States urged New Zealand to send additional troops. By this time, however, New Zealanders already constituted about 5 percent of the Commonwealth Division forces, and additional troops were refused. Later the New Zealanders did increase their transportation force from a platoon-size unit to a company.

In July 1951 the United States suggested the formation of a joint Australian–New Zealand force, but New Zealand officials stated their preference to remain with other Commonwealth forces. Thus the New Zealand contingent was merged into the 1st Commonwealth Division when that force was formed that same month. In late 1952 the UNC again requested additional New Zealanders for Korean service, but the appeal was denied. The New Zealand force reached its maximum strength of 1,389 men in 1953, consisting of volunteers who rotated annually on an individual basis.

New Zealand also contributed 1,350 men of its naval forces with the first naval contingent, the frigates HMNZ *Pukaki* and *Tutira*, departing for Korea on 3 July 1950. It was the start of a deployment that lasted for the duration of the war. Within a month these ships had joined the Blockading and Escort Force of the U.S. Naval Command Far East in the Yellow Sea. Other New Zealand naval units patrolled near Wŏnsan, while still others participated in the screening force at Inch'ŏn. The frigates *Taupo*, *Rotoiti*, *Kaniere*, and *Hawea* patrolled the coast. In 1951 and 1952, in a combined endeavor with ROK Marines and the U.S. Navy, these ships shelled Communist guerrillas and insurgents on the islands in the Han River estuary.

A total of 3,794 New Zealanders served in the Korean War, with casualties of 22 killed and 79 wounded in action, 16 dead from other causes, and one missing. One New Zealander was repatriated in Operation BIG SWITCH. While New Zealand's manpower contribution to the war was dwarfed by U.S. and ROK forces, on a per capita basis it was second only to that of the United States.

—*Clayton D. Laurie*

References:

Barclay, C. N. *The First Commonwealth Division: The Story of the British Commonwealth Land Forces in Korea, 1950–1953.* Aldershot, UK: Gale & Polden, 1954.

Carew, Tim. *Korea: The Commonwealth at War.* London: Cassell, 1967.

McGibbon, Ian C. *New Zealand and the Korean War.* 2 vols. Auckland: Oxford University Press, 1996.

Mossman, Billy C. *U.S. Army in the Korean War: Ebb and Flow, November 1950–July 1951.* Washington, DC: U.S. Army Center of Military History, 1990.

Republic of Korea, Ministry of National Defense. *The History of the United Nations Forces in the Korean War.* Vol. 2. Seoul: War History Compilation Commission, 1973.

See also: Hoge, William M.; Kap'yŏng, Battle of; Syngman Rhee.

Nitze, Paul H.
(1907–)

Director of the State Department's Policy Planning Staff (PPS), 1950–1953. Born in Amherst, Massachusetts, on 16 January 1907, to an academic family, Paul H. Nitze in 1928 graduated from Harvard with a B.A. degree in economics, whereupon he entered the New York investment bank Dillon, Read & Company. Among his colleagues was James V. Forrestal, who became undersecretary of the navy in 1940, taking Nitze with him as his assistant. During World War II Nitze held high office in the Board of Economic Warfare and the Foreign Economic Administration, and from 1944 to 1946 he was vice chairman of the U.S. Strategic Bombing Survey. As deputy director of the Office of International Trade Policy in the State Department, 1946–1948, and deputy to the assistant secretary of state for economic affairs, 1948–1949, Nitze helped to formulate and implement the Marshall Plan.

In 1949 Nitze became assistant to George F. Kennan, Soviet expert and formulator of the highly influential containment policy, who then headed the State Department's Policy Planning Staff (PPS). By the end of the year Kennan had resigned his position and Nitze succeeded him. As with fellow Soviet expert Charles E. Bohlen, Kennan depreciated the creation of the North Atlantic Treaty Organization (NATO). He argued forcefully but unsuccessfully that the Soviets did not pose a major military threat to European security and that the ratification of a Western European military alliance with the United States would antagonize the Soviet Union and destroy any prospects for long-term European peace and German unification, yet provide little real protection against potential nuclear attack. Secretary of State Dean Acheson, by contrast, was a strong supporter of the new alliance, as was the temperamentally hawkish Nitze, who had for several years advocated a hard-line position toward the Soviet Union. In his new post he helped to formulate NATO's fundamental structure and to convince Congress to ratify the treaty.

In January 1950, responding to the fall 1949 Soviet detonation of an atomic bomb and the Communist victory in China, Acheson asked Nitze to chair an interdepartmental study group that would conduct a full review of U.S. foreign and defense policy, the first comprehensive survey of its kind. Its report, NSC-68, which was handed to President Truman in April 1950, was largely written by Nitze and argued his (and Acheson's) view that the Soviets were determined on world domination and that by 1954 they would possess nuclear strength sufficient to destroy the United States. To meet this challenge, Nitze recommended that the United States should make itself the leader of the non-Communist world and should rebuild the West until it far surpassed the Soviet Union economically. More significantly, NSC-68 envisaged that the United States would take primary responsibility for the entire non-Communist world's defense and security against outside attack and should possess the ability both to repel a full-scale invasion and to handle limited peripheral wars. To carry out this mission, NSC-68 recommended a massive enhancement of the Free World's military capabilities, and in particular a doubling to quadrupling of U.S. defense spending, the strengthening of NATO's nuclear forces, and the development of more advanced nuclear weapons. NSC-68 estimated that the United States could devote up to 20 percent of its gross national product to defense expenditures without major economic disruptions. Truman, eager to cut government spending and balance the budget, initially rejected these recommendations, preferring a more modest and limited military and foreign policy. The outbreak of the Korean war greatly enhanced the credibility of NSC-68's analysis and prescriptions, and within a few weeks Truman began to implement a per-

manent massive increase of United States defense spending and commitments, including the commitment of substantial U.S. land forces to NATO and the acquisition of additional military bases and allies throughout the world. The U.S. defense budget rose from $13 billion to $52 billion. The broad framework of defense capabilities, commitments, and objectives laid out in NSC-68 would in many respects characterize U.S. strategy for the subsequent forty years.

Nitze agreed enthusiastically with the original U.S. decision to intervene in the Korean conflict. Initially he argued against crossing the 38th parallel, because he feared this might bring Soviet or Communist Chinese forces into the war, but when presentations by Director of the Office of Northeast Asian Affairs John M. Allison and PPS China expert John Paton Davies discounted this possibility, the PPS submitted a memorandum endorsing an attempt to unify all Korea under one Western-oriented non-Communist government. Truman was cautious in accepting these recommendations, authorizing MacArthur to pursue North Korean forces as far as the Yalu River but neither to occupy nor to unify the country. After the November 1950 Chinese military intervention Nitze once again embraced caution, believing that Soviet forces would enter the war only if the overthrow of the Chinese government seemed likely or United Nations forces came too close to the Soviet border.

After Dwight D. Eisenhower became president, Nitze, who was politically unacceptable to the Republican right, left government to head the Foreign Service Educational Foundation. He remained active in Democratic politics, generally advocating the hawkish foreign policies also favored by his friend and patron Acheson. He subsequently held numerous second-rank positions within the national security apparatus, though he never attained the highest-level positions of secretary of state or defense or national security adviser, which were his ultimate ambition. Nitze served under John F. Kennedy as assistant secretary of defense for international security affairs, participating in the deliberations during crises over Berlin and Cuba. From 1963 to 1967 he was secretary of the navy, where he became a proponent of a negotiated Vietnam peace settlement and de-escalation of the ground war. He was one of the "Wise Men," the members of President Lyndon B. Johnson's Ad Hoc Task Force on Vietnam which in March 1968 recommended U.S. withdrawal from the Vietnam conflict. Nitze was deputy secretary of defense, 1967–1969; a member of the U.S. delegation to the Strategic Arms Limitations Talks (SALT) held at Helsinki, 1969–1974; head of the U.S. delegation at the Geneva Arms Control Talks, 1981–1984; and a presidential adviser on arms control, 1984–1989. In the 1970s Nitze was one of the founders of the second

Committee on the Present Danger, which argued that U.S. defenses were dangerously inadequate and attacked SALT II as ineffective; his relatively hard-line views on security won him both respect and office from Ronald Reagan's Republican Party. Interested for decades in the training and education of foreign policy experts, Nitze also founded and endowed the eponymous Washington-based Paul H. Nitze School of Advanced International Studies of Johns Hopkins University, where in his official retirement he kept an office, held a senior research appointment, and remained actively engaged with the intellectual interests that had preoccupied him for almost sixty years.

—*Priscilla Roberts*

References:

Callahan, David. *Dangerous Capabilities: Paul Nitze and the Cold War.* New York: HarperCollins, 1990.

May, Ernest R. *American Cold War Strategy: Interpreting NSC 68.* Boston: Bedford Books, 1993.

Nitze, Paul H., with Ann M. Smith and Steven L. Rearden. *From Hiroshima to Glasnost at the Center of Decision: A Memoir.* New York: Grove Weidenfeld, 1989.

Rearden, Steven L. *The Evolution of American Strategic Doctrine: Paul H. Nitze and the Soviet Challenge.* Boulder, CO: Westview Press, 1984.

———. "Paul H. Nitze: The Last of the Cold Warriors." *Diplomatic History* 17, no. 1 (Winter 1993): 143–146.

Talbott, Strobe. *The Master of the Game: Paul Nitze and the Nuclear Peace.* New York: Alfred A. Knopf, 1988.

See also: Acheson, Dean Goodersham; Allison, John M.; Bohlen, Charles E.; Davies, John Paton; Kennan, George F.; National Security Council (NSC); NATO (North Atlantic Treaty Organization); Truman, Harry S.

Nixon, Richard Milhous
(1913–1994)

Republican congressman from California, who became that state's junior senator in 1951 and his party's vice-presidential candidate in the 1952 campaign. Nixon used Korea as a political weapon with which to attack the Truman administration; as vice-president he handled sensitive negotiations with Syngman Rhee, the president of the Republic of Korea. Born into a grocer's family in Yorba Linda, California, on 9 January 1913, Richard Milhous Nixon graduated from Whittier College, California (1934) and Duke University Law School (1937). He then began the practice of law in Whittier. After wartime stints with the Office of Price Administration in Washington and as an aviation ground officer in the Pacific theater, Nixon served two terms in Congress before winning election to the Senate in the 1950 campaign. Nixon quickly became notorious for red-baiting, a reputation he won through service on the House Un-American Activities Committee, where he aggressively participated in the Alger Hiss espionage

investigation. In his 1950 senate campaign he likewise characterized his opponent, Congresswoman Helen Gahagan Douglas of California, as the "Red Lady," tactics that made him a *bête noire* of the Democratic Party.

Nixon supported the Truman administration's decision to intervene in Korea, but like other Republicans he frequently attacked the specifics of its war policies. He ascribed much responsibility for the outbreak of war to what he characterized as the administration's weak, ineffective, and insufficiently anti-Communist policies, particularly its failure to intervene on Jiang Jieshi's behalf in the Chinese civil war, which he blamed for the subsequent Communist takeover of China. Predictably, he developed close ties to the China lobby, though political opportunism seems to have underpinned his anticommunism. Nixon's rhetoric grew increasingly harsh when United Nations (UN) forces failed to hold North Korean territory after Chinese intervention in late 1950, a tendency further exacerbated by Truman's recall of United Nations Command commander General of the Army Douglas MacArthur the following spring. Nixon went so far as to introduce an unsuccessful Republican Senate resolution demanding MacArthur's reinstatement.

Nixon's selection in 1952 as Dwight D. Eisenhower's running mate in the presidential election was largely due to his anti-Communist credentials and the party's desire to appease the Republican right wing after its favored candidate, Senator Robert A. Taft, failed to win the nomination. Whereas Eisenhower presented a relatively moderate image, Nixon took the low road, launching ferocious assaults on the Truman administration, in which the Korean situation featured prominently, often as a symbol of the failure of Truman's containment policy.

Nixon initially claimed to believe that total victory in Korea was attainable, a position that Eisenhower, who hoped that the P'anmunjŏm armistice talks would deliver a settlement, forced him to modify. Well after he became vice-president, in late 1953 Nixon privately claimed he shared the view of the columnist Joseph W. Alsop, who argued that the July 1953 Korean truce settlement deprived the UN of victory. National Security Council records, however, reveal that he was less than persistent in urging this viewpoint within the Eisenhower administration, behavior that probably reflected his uneasy relationship with the president.

In November 1953 Nixon visited the Republic of Korea on Eisenhower's instructions to extract from President Syngman Rhee a pledge to take no action against the North without informing Eisenhower. Nixon, in whose later foreign policies pragmatism and stated ideology were likewise often at odds, pressed Rhee to exercise even greater circumspection when dealing with the North, and according to his own memoirs succeeding in winning the South Korean president's verbal admission that he recognized that South Korea "could not possibly act alone." Rhee's letter to Eisenhower on the subject, however, merely provided the requested assurance that Rhee would take no unilateral action against the North without notifying the U.S. government. Rhee and Nixon also agreed that Rhee might continue his belligerent public statements, though it remains unclear whether Eisenhower had authorized his deputy to endorse this stance.

After losing the 1960 presidential election to John F. Kennedy and a subsequent trouncing in the 1962 California gubernatorial race, Nixon announced he would leave politics. In 1968, however, he defeated Democratic candidate Hubert H. Humphrey to become the thirty-seventh president of the United States. His victory inaugurated several decades of Republican dominance in the White House, an achievement for which Nixon deserved much of the credit. Foreign policy dominated his presidency: he withdrew U.S. forces from Vietnam, opened relations with the People's Republic of China, inaugurated détente with the Soviet Union, and undertook a major reconceptualization of the U.S. world role in the light of its diminished international weight. One aspect of the latter was U.S. insistence that allies such as Korea bear more of the burden of their own defense. The Watergate scandal, which drove Nixon to resign in August 1974, undercut his foreign and domestic policy successes.

Nixon spent his final two decades in a dogged crusade for rehabilitation, publishing extensively on international affairs and recasting himself as a respected elder statesman and foreign policy expert. He died in New York City on 22 April 1994.

—*Priscilla Roberts*

References:

Ambrose, Stephen E. *Nixon.* 3 vols. New York: Simon & Schuster, 1987–1991.

Caridi, Ronald J. *The Korean War and American Politics: The Republican Party As a Case Study.* Philadelphia: University of Pennsylvania Press, 1968.

Kepley, David R. *The Collapse of the Middle Way: Senate Republicans and the Bipartisan Foreign Policy, 1948–1952.* New York: Greenwood Press, 1982.

Morris, Roger. *Richard Milhous Nixon: The Rise of an American Politician.* New York: Henry Holt, 1990.

Nixon, Richard. *RN: The Memoirs of Richard Nixon.* New York: Grosset & Dunlap, 1978.

Wicker, Tom. *One of Us: Richard Nixon and the American Dream.* New York: Random House, 1991.

See also: China Lobby; Eisenhower, Dwight D.; Jiang Jieshi (Chiang Kai-shek); MacArthur, Douglas; National Security Council (NSC); Syngman Rhee; Taft, Robert Alphonso; Truman's Recall of MacArthur; U.S. Policy toward Korea: 1953 to the Present.

No Name Line, Battle of
(14–18 May 1951)

One of several battle tactical lines established mainly in the spring of 1951 during the several Chinese offensives. Other lines included Lincoln, Utah, Kansas, Missouri, Quantico, and Wyoming. These lines generally constituted both desired defensive and offensive positions. The No Name Line was an eastward extension of Line Lincoln that had its westward terminus in the Seoul area and extended northeastward. No Name also ran in a northeastward direction from a point about midway between the towns of Ch'unch'ŏn and Hongch'ŏn for a distance of about eighteen miles, ending a mile or so southeast of the village of Ŏgumal on the Inje-Han'gye/Hongch'ŏn road (now Korean National Highway 44).

Generally, in the spring and early summer of 1951 the front lines in Korea were below or above the No Name Line, except in May, when the line was manned by four divisions of the X Corps, e.g., the U.S. 1st Marine and 2d Army Divisions, and the Republic of Korea Army (ROKA) 5th and 7th Divisions. These four divisions occupied a northeast diagonally twisting line south of the Soyang River and parallel to the Kansŏng-Hongch'ŏn road.

By 14 May the X Corps G-2 assistant chief of staff for intelligence determined that large numbers of Communist troops—the Chinese People's Volunteer Army (CPVA) and Korean People's Army (KPA)—were in the central sector and that a major attack there was imminent. His conclusions were doubted by Eighth Army headquarters, which continued to believe that Communist forces would aim for Seoul in the west. On 16 May, contrary to the Eighth Army's assessment, the Communists launched their Sixth Spring Offensive and burst upon X Corps with fifteen Chinese and five KPA Divisions, altogether some 175,000 men. The Chinese aimed primarily at the ROKA units on the right, where resistance promptly collapsed. The ROKA troops abandoned most artillery and crew-served weapons and even rifles as they fled to the rear. Two dozen U.S. advisors with the ROKA troops were either killed or captured. Clay Blair wrote, "the ROK bugout, involving about 40,000 men, was the largest and most disgraceful of the Korean War." It left a great gap on the X Corps' right flank and exposed the entire rear of the eastern United Nations Command (UNC) position, directly imperiling the 2d Division, which now faced Chinese troops on three sides. With the departure of the ROKA troops on the right, the Chinese now concentrated on the U.S. 2d Division.

Over the next three days the 2d Division carried out a ferocious defense of its positions and inflicted heavy casualties on the attackers. In the defense the 2d fired awesome amounts of artillery: 17,000 rounds on 16 May and 38,000 rounds on 18 May. The division's position, so far forward of the main line of resistance, was perilously untenable; however, on 18 May it was ordered to withdraw to Han'gye to the rear of the No Name Line. The 2d Division commander assessed Communist casualties in the fighting at more than 20,000 men.

In May the UNC launched a counteroffensive that pushed the Communists back to the No Name Line and beyond. This offensive continued through the summer, and by August and September it had reached well beyond the 38th parallel to the areas to become known as Bloody and Heartbreak Ridges and the Punchbowl. The No Name Line did not thereafter become a location for front-line combat.

—*Sherman W. Pratt*

References:

Blair, Clay. *The Forgotten War: America in Korea, 1950–1953.* New York: Times Books, 1987.

Hastings, Max. *The Korean War.* New York: Simon & Schuster, 1987.

Munroe, Clark C. *The Second United States Infantry Division in Korea, 1950–1951.* Tokyo: Toppan Printing, n.d.

Pratt, Sherman W. *Decisive Battles of the Korean War. An Infantry Company Commander's View of the War's Most Critical Engagements.* New York: Vantage Press, 1992.

See also: Chinese Military Offensives.

Noble, Harold
(1903–1953)

U.S. diplomat. Born in P'yŏngyang on 19 January 1903 to U.S. missionaries living in Korea, Harold Noble graduated from Ohio Wesleyan University in 1924; the next year he completed a master's degree at Ohio State University. He was an instructor at Ewha College in Seoul between 1926 and 1928. In 1929 he obtained a teaching fellowship from the University of California at Berkeley and completed a doctorate in history there in 1931. From that year he was a professor of history at the University of Oregon. During 1939–1940 he taught at Third College in Kyoto, Japan. He was also awarded a Rockefeller fellowship in Chinese and Japanese studies.

During World War II Noble served in the U.S. Marine Corps. He saw service in New Zealand, New Caledonia, and the Solomon Islands as a combat intelligence officer, company commander, and a Japanese language officer.

After the war Noble was a foreign correspondent for the *Saturday Evening Post* in Japan, Korea, China, and Australia. In 1947 he became chief of the publications branch of the Civilian Intelligence Section of the Far East Command. Noble foresaw the forthcoming war in Korea and even predicted its outbreak in an article he wrote.

His many diplomatic positions included that with general headquarters of the Far East Command in Tokyo during 1947–1948; chief of the Political Liaison Office Headquarters in Seoul, Korea, 1948; member of the U.S. delegation to the United Nations General Assembly, 1949–1951; and political attaché and first secretary at the U.S. embassy to the Republic of Korea (ROK).

Noble was an important figure in the Korean War, as he was perhaps the most important U.S. influence on ROK president Syngman Rhee. Rhee had learned to speak English from Noble's father and Noble was a longtime associate of Rhee. Noble wrote several of Rhee's speeches, acted as a conduit during negotiations between Rhee and U.S. Ambassador John Muccio, and was the U.S. diplomat assigned to stay with Rhee when the latter was in Taejŏn after the June 1950 North Korean invasion.

Just before the start of the Korean War, Noble was working to ensure that Rhee would permit free elections in South Korea. He was not in Korea at the time of the North Korean invasion but was immediately recalled by Ambassador Muccio to serve as chief liaison officer to Rhee.

Noble was a staunch opponent of the Democratic People's Republic of Korea (DPRK, North Korea) and a fervent supporter of the ROK. He publicly expressed his desire for forcible reunification of the two Koreas and was subsequently reprimanded for this.

Dissatisfaction with U.S. policies led Noble to resign from the Foreign Service, and in July 1951 he left Korea. He became an executive with the Committee For Free Asia in San Francisco. He was a member of the board of editors of the *Pacific Historical Review*; he was a contributing editor for the *Far Eastern Quarterly*; and he wrote articles and coauthored a book, *What it Takes to Rule Japan* (1946). Noble was in the process of writing another book on Asian affairs when he died of a heart attack on 22 December 1953 on an airplane flight from Honolulu to the continental United States.

—*Monica Spicer*

References:

Findling, John. *Dictionary of American Diplomatic History.* Westport, CT: Greenwood Press, 1980.

Matray, James I., ed. *Historical Dictionary of the Korean War.* Westport, CT: Greenwood Press, 1991.

New York Times, 24 December 1953.

See also: Muccio, John J.; Syngman Rhee.

Nogŭn-ni Railroad Bridge Incident
(July 1950)

Site of alleged massacre of South Korean civilians by U.S. soldiers of H Company of the 2d Battalion, 7th Cavalry Regiment of the 1st Cavalry Division during the Korean War. The railroad bridge at Nogŭn-ni is located near that town a few miles southwest of Hwanggan, North Ch'ungch'ŏng Province, central South Korea. A few days after their deployment to Korea, soldiers of the U.S. 1st Cavalry Division allegedly fired on civilians at the Nogŭn-ni railroad bridge, killing up to 300 people.

In 1997 some 30 Korean survivors of the Nogŭn-ni incident filed for compensation with the Republic of Korea (ROK) government. A low-level ROK commission found that civilians had been killed at Nogŭn-ni but that there was no proof of U.S. involvement. In 1998 a national panel rejected the claim on the basis that the statute of limitations had expired. The incident surfaced again when it received major press coverage in the United States in September 1999, and Secretary of Defense William S. Cohen ordered a new review of the historical evidence with a report to be issued upon its conclusion.

Allegedly, on 26 July U.S. troops instructed some 500 residents of Nogŭn-ni and nearby villages to gather near railroad tracks at Nogŭn-ni. U.S. veterans recall the subsequent events differently, although they are in agreement on a preponderance of women and children among the refugees at the bridge. Reports had circulated among U.S. troops that Korean People's Army (KPA, North Korean) infiltrators might attempt to use refugees to penetrate the battalion's defenses.

On 26 July the civilian refugees were resting near the railroad tracks when they suddenly came under a strafing attack by U.S. aircraft; reportedly upwards of 100 refugees were killed and those who remained sought cover under the railroad bridge. Over the next several days U.S. soldiers kept the refugees pinned down under the bridge and fired on them. Some veterans recall receiving fire from the civilians at the bridge and say that they found disguised KPA soldiers among the dead. Others do not recall being fired upon and say they saw only civilians there. The Korean claimants recall only three days of carnage. On 29 July the 7th Cavalry pulled back and the KPA moved into the area. A North Korean newspaper reported several weeks later that KPA troops had found about 400 bodies in the area.

If proven, this would be the second large-scale massacre of civilians by U.S. troops in a twentieth-century war, the other being the 1968 My Lai Massacre during the Vietnam War. Whatever the outcome of the investigation, the events at Nogŭn-ni must be seen against the background of the initial deployment of U.S. troops from Japan, the vast majority of whom were poorly trained and without combat experience and their injection into the desperate fighting that marked the retreat of United Nations forces to the Pusan perimeter. UN troops had regularly come under fire

from North Korean infiltrators utilizing civilian refugees as human shields. As a consequence, U.S. commanders had indeed issued orders authorizing troops to fire on civilians as a defense against disguised KPA soldiers.

—*Spencer C. Tucker*

See also: Atrocities

Norstad, Lauris
(1907–1988)

U.S. Air Force general, supreme Allied commander of the North Atlantic Treaty Organization (NATO), and early advocate of deploying tactical nuclear weapons to defend Western Europe against Communist attack. Born a minister's son in Minneapolis, Minnesota, on 24 March 1907, Lauris Norstad graduated from the U.S. Military Academy at West Point, in 1930. The following year he received training in the pursuit section of the U.S. Army Air Corps.

When the United States entered World War II, Norstad was serving as assistant chief of staff for intelligence with air force headquarters. In 1943 he began overseas service, first with the Twelfth Army Air Force and later with the Northwest African Air Force. In these positions he helped plan and implement air support for the Allied landings in North Africa, Sicily, and Italy. After his promotion to brigadier general in 1944, Norstad helped plan B-29 raids against Japan, climaxing in the atomic bombings of Hiroshima and Nagasaki in 1945. During the immediate postwar period Norstad served as assistant chief of air staff and played a leading role in the shaping of an independent U.S. Air Force.

When the Korean War began, Norstad was U.S. Air Force deputy chief of staff for operations and acting vice chief of staff. He accompanied W. Averell Harriman on a fact-finding mission to Tokyo in August 1950 and returned with a recommendation that Lieutenant General Matthew B. Ridgway replace Lieutenant General Walton W. Walker as Eighth Army commander if Walker should become a casualty in the fighting in Korea. In October 1950 Norstad was named to command the U.S. Air Force in Europe and assumed additional duty as commander of Allied air forces in Central Europe under Supreme Headquarters, Allied Powers–Europe (SHAPE) in April 1951.

In 1952 Norstad became the youngest American ever to become a full (four-star) general. Between 1953 and 1956 he was air deputy of SHAPE; and, from November 1956 until his retirement in 1963, he served as SHAPE commander. During his time with NATO he worked for increased conventional military preparedness as well as an independent NATO nuclear capability. He favored the expansion of the West

German military and stockpiling of nuclear weapons on German soil. During his tenure in Brussels, Norstad was also an strong advocate for a NATO nuclear force command and was instrumental in increasing from thirty to 100 the number of short-range tactical nuclear missiles in Europe.

During the 1961 Berlin crisis, Norstad advised President John F. Kennedy to publicize the fact that the United States would use nuclear weapons to protect the city, and he was disappointed when the president refused to do so. Norstad also differed with Kennedy on whether land-based or submarine-based nuclear weapons should be deployed to defend Western Europe and whether Britain and France should have veto power concerning their use. These differences led to his resignation in January 1963.

After his retirement, Norstad became president of the international division of the Owens-Corning Fiberglass Corporation, a position he held until 1972. He continued to speak out on defense issues, focusing on the creation of a separate NATO nuclear force and on the need to maintain U.S. troop levels in Europe. Norstad died in Tucson, Arizona, on 12 September 1988.

—Clayton D. Laurie

References:

Lichtenstein, Nelson, and Eleanora W. Schoenebaum, eds. *Political Profiles: The Kennedy Years.* New York: Facts on File, 1978.

Schoenebaum, Eleanora W., ed. *Political Profiles: The Truman Years.* New York: Facts on File, 1978.

See also: Harriman, William Averell; NATO (North Atlantic Treaty Organization); Ridgway, Matthew Bunker; Walker, Walton Harris

North Korea, United Nations Command Occupation of

(October–November 1950)

In October and November 1950 the United Nations Command (UNC) occupied and held effective political control over most of North Korea. The tide of the Korean War had shifted after the 15 September UNC amphibious landing at Inch'ŏn and the Eighth Army's breakout from the Pusan perimeter. UNC forces recaptured Seoul on 27 September, three months after the Korean People's Army (KPA, North Korea) had occupied the city.

There was some question over whether UNC commander General Douglas MacArthur had a mandate to cross the 38th parallel and end the North Korean military threat. The UN objective "to restore international peace and security in the area" was vague and subject to wide interpretation. U.S. policy, laid out in National Security Council document NSC 81/1 and modified as a Joint Chiefs of Staff directive on 27 September, permitted operations into North Korea. It even contained

a long-term provision allowing for the occupation of the country. But as MacArthur led an international force, he was ordered to await UN directives.

On 1 October an impatient Republic of Korea (ROK) president Syngman Rhee ordered the ROK Army (ROKA) into North Korea with the intention of reunifying the peninsula by force. Rhee had presented the UN with a *fait accompli.* This action not only threatened to provoke Soviet and Chinese intervention but further dissuaded India from participating on the UN side.

After extensive General Assembly deliberations, on 7 October the UN passed a resolution authorizing MacArthur to cross the parallel. UNC forces crossed into the Democratic People's Republic of Korea (DPRK) on 9 October, and for the remainder of the month North Korean forces were in retreat.

A UN resolution presented to the Political Committee of the General Assembly on 30 September had recommended that steps be taken to ensure stability throughout Korea. It called for open and free elections to be held in North Korea under UN auspices. The goal was a "unified, independent, and democratic Government in the sovereign state of Korea" but the resolution insisted on UN supervision and never designated any role for the Rhee administration. Subsequently, on 12 October the UN Interim Committee resolved not to recognize any government's claim to control all of Korea. Influential members on the committee doubted that the South Korean government had the right to govern North Korea. A UN General Assembly resolution of 12 December 1948 specified that the ROK had "effective control and jurisdiction" only over South Korea.

Conscientious Interim Committee members also abhorred the oppressive politics of the Rhee regime. South Korean press control laws and the National Security Law of December 1948 violated constitutionally guaranteed rights. These laws prohibited the publication of articles "contrary to the policy of the government" and authorized the imprisonment of anyone who formed a group with the object of "disturbing the peace." Acting under these laws, the South Korean government arrested and detained 89,710 political prisoners between October 1948 and April 1949. Further diminishing Rhee's claim to all Korea was his government's inhumane treatment of prisoners of war during the North Korean occupation of South Korea between June and September 1950. Ultimately, the Interim Committee appointed the UNC as the agency of civil government in North Korea until the arrival of the United Nations Commission on the Unification and Rehabilitation of Korea (UNCURK).

Rhee wrote MacArthur to protest the Interim Committee's resolution, accusing the UN of pandering to the North Korean Communists. Rhee also insisted that the constitution of the Republic of Korea extended over the entire nation and complained that the UNC was not prepared to administer the North. Rhee argued that DPRK propaganda had held that the war was instigated by the United States. If U.S. soldiers moved into the North's cities and villages, this would validate Soviet propaganda and would lead many North Koreans to fight against U.S. "imperialism." Both MacArthur and U.S. Ambassador John Muccio were sympathetic to Rhee's position but forwarded his communication to more skeptical officials in Washington.

Fulfilling earlier pledges to exercise authority over the entire peninsula, Rhee ignored the UN and sent over 32,000 ROK military police, National Police, and civilian administrators into occupied towns in North Korea. Meanwhile, the ROKA continued its move northward to the Yalu River.

The South Korean occupation of large cities such as P'yŏngyang differed from the brutal North Korean occupation of Seoul only in ideological orientation. Right-wing youth groups indoctrinated ambivalent northerners with anti-Communist and counterrevolutionary propaganda. To keep order in P'yŏngyang Rhee appointed Kim Chong-wŏn as head of the military police.

Many Korean Workers' Party members in the North fled in the face of advancing UNC troops. However, thousands destroyed their party identification cards and pledged to cooperate with Rhee's government, only to fall victim to Kim Chong-wŏn's death squads. The DPRK later reported that ROK officials executed hundreds of thousands of North Korean citizens. While this figure is grossly exaggerated, substantiated reports abound of ROKA and attached paramilitary groups pillaging and killing civilians. In October the U.S. 24th Infantry Division complained about the ROKA mistreatment of prisoners and the raping of North Korean women. An Australian UNCURK representative remarked that ROK violence had turned the North Korean people against the UNC. Many North Koreans interviewed by foreign correspondents thought they were better off under the Communists. In late October and early November the *New York Times* and London *Times* published articles detailing ROK atrocities. Despite obvious misgivings, the Truman administration opposed any official condemnation of Rhee because it believed that this would undermine international support for Korean unification.

UN resolutions and U.S. government decisions in late October nonetheless reflected international dissatisfaction with Rhee's conduct. On 23 October 1950, Rhee told a reporter from *U.S. News and World Report* that he was assuming "temporary civil control" over the entire peninsula, despite UN limitations on his authority. British Foreign Secretary Ernest Bevin complained to the U.S. State Department that Rhee's high-handedness might become a source of embarrassment and create an international scandal. Assistant Secretary of State Dean Rusk reassured Bevin by promising that U.S. military personnel would supervise South Korean administration of the North. Meanwhile, atrocities continued. On 28 October more than three weeks after the start of the UN offensive, MacArthur received a civil affairs directive ordering him to occupy and administer the DPRK "in the name and on behalf of the United Nations."

On 24 November MacArthur announced the final UNC offensive. He planned to hand over all administrative responsibilities to UNCURK once his forces occupied all of North Korea. UNCURK representatives finally reached Seoul on 26 November, but Chinese military intervention then rendered them superfluous.

The Chinese military intervention forced a hasty Eighth Army withdrawal that effectively ended UNC occupation of North Korea. Dissatisfied with Communist rule or fearing persecution, approximately 685,000 North Koreans accompanied fleeing ROKA and UNC forces to South Korea in the winter of 1950–1951. As UNC forces withdrew, DPRK authorities imprisoned and executed countless individuals, once again imposing strict Communist rule.

—*Matthew D. Esposito*

References:

Kaufman, Burton I. *The Korean War: Challenges in Crisis, Credibility, and Command.* Philadelphia: Temple University Press, 1986.

MacDonald, Callum. *Korea: The War Before Vietnam.* New York: Free Press, 1986.

Stueck, William W., Jr. *The Korean War: An International History.* Princeton, NJ: Princeton University Press, 1995.

U.S. Department of State, Bureau of Public Affairs. *Foreign Relations of the United States, 1950,* Vol. 7, *Korea.* Washington DC: U.S. Government Printing Office, 1976.

See also: Atrocities; Bevin, Ernest; Inch'ŏn Landings: Operation CHROMITE; Kim Chong-wŏn; MacArthur, Douglas; Muccio, John J.; Rusk, David Dean; South Korea, Occupation by Democratic People's Republic of Korea; Syngman Rhee; 38th Parallel, Decision to Cross; United Nations Commission for the Unification and Rehabilitation of Korea; War Crimes Trials.

Nuclear Warfare

The 25 June 1950 Democratic People's Republic of Korea (DPRK, North Korean) invasion of the Republic of Korea (ROK, South Korea) was viewed by many influential policymakers in the Truman administration as the opening Soviet salvo in World War III. While the Soviets were not a direct military threat in the Korean theater of operations, they had endorsed the attack and trained and equipped the

Korean People's Army (KPA, North Korean) that launched it. The view that the invasion was part of a general Soviet offensive was reinforced by the Soviets' recent detonation of their own atomic bomb in 1949, which broke the U.S. monopoly on nuclear weapons; the USSR fielding of vast conventional military forces on the eastern border of the still-recovering Western European democracies; and the signing of the Sino-Soviet Pact of February 1950 that provided for mutual assistance in case of attack.

U.S. nuclear warfare strategy in regard to the Communist threat dealt with both strategic and operational-level concerns. With regard to strategic policy, the general concept of "preventive" war had formed in the late 1940s and early 1950s. It was based on lessons learned from World War II; namely, that the Allies should have moved more quickly against German and Japanese aggression because such action may have ended the war sooner and would have been the moral thing to do. This perception was strengthened by the view that the bombing of an adversary with nuclear weapons, derived from the experience with Japan, could achieve a quick and decisive U.S. victory.

As early as the Berlin crisis of 1948, the possibility of such a preemptive nuclear strike had been considered. President Harry S. Truman had agreed to put into effect plan BROILER, which would have authorized U.S. forces to drop up to 100 atomic bombs on the Soviet Union, if the Soviets attempted to obstruct the airlift of supplies into Berlin. With the start of the Korean War, high-ranking policymakers in the Truman administration considered the use of nuclear weapons against the Soviet Union. As a result of the North Korean invasion of the South, nonnuclear components of atomic bombs were allowed to leave the continental United States in July 1950 and were stockpiled in the United Kingdom.

Popular support existed in the United States for the use of atomic weapons against the Soviets. In August 1950 Secretary of the Navy Francis Matthews gave a speech advocating such a position to 100,000 cheering supporters at the Boston Naval Yard.

The November 1950 Chinese entrance into the war once again raised the specter of the use of nuclear weapons. While answering a reporter's question in a press conference late that month, President Truman did not rule out the nuclear option and even stated that it might be up to field commanders to make such a decision. This statement was clarified later that day by the White House, which made it clear that only the commander in chief, and not a general such as Douglas MacArthur, could authorize the use of nuclear weapons. During this period the Joint Chiefs of Staff (JCS) never recommended using atomic bombs in the conflict. Its rationale was that they should be used only

in case of forced evacuation from the peninsula or to stave off an impending military disaster. Still, after the Chinese crossed the Yalu River in late 1950, the JCS requested that nonnuclear atomic bomb components be placed aboard the aircraft carrier *Franklin Roosevelt*, which was then stationed in the Mediterranean. Truman endorsed the request.

As the Korean War entered its static phase of opposing trench lines and as armistice talks dragged on, in January 1952 President Truman again considered the use of nuclear weapons. These thoughts were discussed with his aides and written down in his journal but not made known to the public. His idea, which was never carried out, was to issue an ultimatum to the Communist side either to end the war or risk nuclear annihilation.

Shortly after he took office, President Dwight D. Eisenhower had his senior policymakers examine the possibility of using nuclear weapons against the People's Republic of China and the DPRK. In May 1953 the JCS urged the National Security Council to consider their use to resolve the war if armistice negotiations broke down. Administration officials concurred with the JCS recommendation in NSC-147. Because of the 1950 Sino-Soviet Pact, the Soviet Union would be directly drawn into the war. This might lead to implementing war plan SHAKEDOWN, which called for B-36 bombers to drop hundreds of atomic bombs on the Soviet Union. Fortunately for all involved, the signing of the armistice in July 1953 precluded further discussion of this option.

Nuclear operational planning focused on the Korean theater and was based on the needs of U.S. military commanders. It was little more than a sidebar compared to strategic-level issues. With the Chinese entry into the war, General MacArthur requested the right to use nuclear weapons if necessary, and, in late December 1950, he generated a list of targets for atomic destruction. In all, thirty-four atomic bombs would be required. After MacArthur was relieved of his command, in May 1951 his successor, Lieutenant General Matthew B. Ridgway, renewed the earlier request, this time for thirty-eight atomic bombs. Nothing came of these requests, as President Truman retained control of the nuclear arsenal. MacArthur also supported the idea of "a radioactive by-product cordon," as did others.

In the fall of 1951 the U.S. Air Force simulated the use of atomic bombs on the battlefield in Operation HUDSON HARBOR. Individual B-29 bombers flew from Okinawa to North Korea in simulated runs. However, with identifiable concentrations of Communist forces being rare, the exercise was considered operationally unsound. Although U.S. nuclear weapons influenced the strategic conduct of the war and possibly forced the Communists to make concessions leading to the eventual settlement of the war, they had no impact on theater operations.

—*Robert J. Bunker*

References:

Buhite, Russell D., and William Christopher Hamel. "War for Peace: The Question of an American Preventive War against the Soviet Union, 1945–1955." *Diplomatic History* 14 (Summer 1990): 367–384.

Herken, Gregg. *The Winning Weapon: The Atomic Bomb in the Cold War, 1945–1950.* New York: Alfred A. Knopf, 1980.

Hewlett, Richard G., and Francis Duncan. *Atomic Shield, 1947/1952. A History of the United States Atomic Energy Commission.* Vol. 2. Berkeley: University of California Press, 1990.

James, D. Clayton. *The Years of MacArthur.* Vol. 3, *Triumph and Disaster, 1945–1964.* Boston: Houghton Mifflin, 1985.

Snyder, Jack. *Atomic Diplomacy in the Korean War.* Washington, DC: Pew Charitable Trusts, 1993.

Wheeler, Michael O. *Nuclear Weapons and the Korean War.* McLean, VA: Center for National Security Negotiations, 1994.

See also: Eisenhower, Dwight D.; Joint Chiefs of Staff (JCS); MacArthur, Douglas; Ridgway, Matthew Bunker; Truman, Harry S.

O

O'Donnell, Emmett
(1906–1971)

U.S. Air Force general who commanded the Far East Air Force (FEAF) during the period July 1950 to January 1951. Born on 15 September 1906, in Brooklyn, New York, Emmett (Rosie) O'Donnell, Jr., graduated from the U.S. Military Academy, West Point, in 1928 and was commissioned in the infantry. He soon switched to the Army Air Corps and graduated from flying school in 1929. In 1940 he commanded a squadron of the 11th Bombardment Group in Hawaii. He was a major on the outbreak of World War II.

In December 1941 O'Donnell commanded a squadron of the Army Air Corps 19th Bombardment Group in the Philippines. After the Japanese air attack on Clark Field he led a retaliatory U.S. raid against Japanese shipping. Later he commanded Tenth Air Force operations in ferrying supplies over the "hump" into China.

In 1943 O'Donnell returned to the United States to supervise training the 73d Air Wing for bombing operations against Japan. The 73d then relocated to the Marianas, and in November 1944 Brigadier General O'Donnell led the first great air raid on Tokyo.

After overseeing supply runs to U.S. forces in Japan after the war, O'Donnell became information director for the air force from 1946 to 1947. He was then air force deputy director of public relations. In 1948 O'Donnell commanded the Fifteenth Air Force within the air force Strategic Air Command.

On 13 July 1950, O'Donnell was ordered to move both the 22d and the 92d Bombardment Groups to the Far East and engage them in the war as quickly as possible. He accomplished this in only nine days. Soon O'Donnell's bombers were striking North Korean targets.

O'Donnell was highly critical of employing air force bombers in a close air support role; he wanted them used against Communist industrial and command centers. O'Donnell also proposed that his bombers strike Communist staging areas and supply lines in Manchuria. He continued to believe that had bombing attacks been carried out early across the border into China before the People's Republic of China had been able to build up its air defenses and a large number of MiGs, China could have been prevented from sending significant material aid and then large numbers of men to aid the Korean People's Army (KPA, North Koreans).

O'Donnell left Korea in January 1951. At the MacArthur hearings he testified that U.S. bombers should have struck Manchuria in November 1950. With all strategic targets destroyed in North Korea, U.S. bombers were left to "blow up haystacks." He opposed MacArthur's victory plan in Korea, believing it would severely undermine U.S. air capability against the Soviet Union.

After an assignment as deputy chief of air force personnel, O'Donnell was promoted to (four-star) general and commanded the U.S. Pacific Air Forces. He retired from the air force in 1963. After employment as a business consultant, O'Donnell died in McLean, Virginia, on 26 December 1971.

—*Clint Mundinger*

References:

Appleman, Roy E. *South to the Naktong, North to the Yalu.* Washington, DC: Office of the Chief of Military History, 1961.

Futrell, Robert F. *The United States Air Force in Korea, 1950–1953.* Rev. ed. Washington, DC: Office of the Chief of Air Force History, 1983.

New York Times, 27 December 1971.

Who Was Who in America. Vol. 5, *1969–1973.* Chicago: Marquis, 1973.

Who's Who in America, 1950–51. Chicago: Marquis, 1950.

Wolk, Herman S. *The Struggle for Air Force Independence.* Washington, DC: Air Force History and Museums Program, 1997.

See also: Close Air Support; MacArthur Hearings; United States Air Force (USAF).

Office of Defense Mobilization (ODM)

Government agency created by executive order on 16 December 1950 in response to President Harry S. Truman's declaration of a national emergency. After the massive intervention by the People's Republic of China in the Korean War, the Truman administration drastically accelerated the mobilization program. To implement this stepped-up process, Truman created the Office of Defense Mobilization (ODM) and appointed Charles E. Wilson, president of the General Electric Company, to direct its activities. The ODM replaced the older National Security Resources Board, which had been charged to direct Korean mobilization at the beginning of the war.

In creating the ODM, Truman gave to it unprecedented powers to mobilize the whole of America's civilian, industrial, and military resources. The major responsibilities of the ODM were to execute the mandates of the Defense Production Act, to ensure an adequate supply of war materiel to the soldiers in Korea, and to begin the long-term buildup of all of the nation's military forces, specifically those forces prescribed in NSC-68.

Falling under the aegis of the ODM were its various constituent agencies, the most important of which were the National Production Authority (NPA), the Defense Production Administration (DPA), and the Economic Stabilization Agency (ESA). Managerially organized by Charles Wilson, the ODM was designed to function as a policymaking and coordinating agency only. Thus, the NPA, DPA, ESA, and other already existing cabinet-level agencies carried out operational and other day-to-day mobilization activities. Organizationally, the ODM and its constituent parts resembled the typical large, vertically integrated, multidivisional corporation of the day, nearly mirroring the management structure of the General Electric Company. In this sense the ODM was patterned after the War Production Board of World War II.

The ODM made extensive use of industry advisory committees throughout its life span. These advisory committees, comprising nearly all sectors of the industrial economy, worked together with the ODM and other mobilization officials to establish and implement industrial and military production schedules. The use of such committees helped to keep operational functions out of the ODM and also served to ensure that key elements of the private sector worked together on matters of prices, wages, industrial output, and materials allocations.

In general the ODM functioned well. During the Korean War the nation's industrial base, military and civilian production, and weapons development grew at a rapid pace. As examples, by the end of the war aircraft plants churned out nearly 1,000 piston-driven planes per month, four times the number produced in mid-1950, while five times as many jet aircraft were being produced than in mid-1950.

After Charles Wilson resigned as ODM director in April 1952, the agency was headed successively by John R. Steelman and Henry H. Fowler. The ODM continued in existence after the war was over. In 1958, however, President Dwight D. Eisenhower consolidated the ODM and the Federal Civil Defense Agency into one agency under the new banner of the Office of Civil Defense and Mobilization (OCDM). In 1978 that agency was consolidated with several others to form the Federal Emergency Management Agency (FEMA), which remains today as the lineal descendent of the ODM.

—*Paul G. Pierpaoli, Jr.*

References:

Hogan, Michael J. *A Cross of Iron: Harry S. Truman and the Origins of the National Security State, 1945–1954*. Cambridge, UK: Cambridge University Press, 1998.

Pierpaoli, Paul G., Jr. *Truman and Korea: The Political Culture of the Early Cold War*. Columbia: University of Missouri Press, 1999.

Vawter, Roderick W. *Industrial Mobilization: The Relevant History*. Washington, DC: National Defense University Press, 1983.

See also: Defense Production Act; Economic Stabilization Agency (ESA); Eisenhower, Dwight D.; Truman, Harry S.; United States: Home Front; Wilson, Charles Edward.

Office of Price Stabilization (OPS)

U.S. government agency that, under the direction of the Economic Stabilization Agency, administered price controls during the Korean War. Created by executive order on 9 September 1950, the Office of Price Stabilization (OPS) did not become fully operational until January 1951, at which time the Truman administration had decided to freeze prices because of rising inflation. The OPS was responsible for administering the general price freeze of January 1951, as well as setting subsequent price control policies that gradually superseded the general freeze.

The OPS administered price guidelines through thirteen regional and eighty-four district offices maintained by the Department of Commerce throughout the United States. It also acted as an enforcement agency of its price regulations and worked with the Department of Justice to prosecute merchants and individuals suspected of breaking or circumventing pricing regulations. Also, the OPS utilized myriad industry advisory committees and consumer advisory committees to keep key groups in society working collaboratively on mobilization and price stabilization issues. In addition to these unpaid advisors, at its peak of operations, the OPS employed 12,300 workers, the most by far of any Korean-era mobilization agency.

OPS regulations provided set price ceilings for virtually all services and commodities sold in the United States, with the notable exception of food products selling below the Department of Agriculture's price parity program for farmers. The OPS considered requests for price increases above the ceilings or for exemptions from the regulations on a case-by-case basis.

By the spring of 1952, with inflation in retreat, the OPS began lifting or suspending controls on a large number of commodities. President Dwight D. Eisenhower completely liquidated the OPS in the spring of 1953.

—*Paul G. Pierpaoli, Jr.*

References:

Hogan, Michael J. *A Cross of Iron: Harry S. Truman and the Origins of the National Security State, 1945–1954*. Cambridge, UK: Cambridge University Press, 1998.

Pierpaoli, Paul G., Jr. *Truman and Korea: The Political Culture of the Early Cold War*. Columbia: University of Missouri Press, 1999.

Erecting barbed wire on Old Baldy. (National Archives)

Rockoff, Hugh. *Drastic Measures: A History of Wage and Price Controls in the United States.* New York: Cambridge University Press, 1984.
See also: Defense Production Act; Economic Stabilization Agency (ESA); Mobilization; United States: Home Front.

Old Baldy, Battle of
(26 June 1952–26 March 1953)

A hill that was the site of continuous fighting in the Korean War from June 1952 to March 1953. In mid-1952 the front line of the U.S. 45th Division occupied a position south of the Yŏkgok-ch'ŏn River valley. The need for forward defensive positions became apparent because the proximity of Chinese People's Volunteer Army (CPVA, Chinese Communist) forces allowed them easy view of the division's troop movements.

In early June, 45th Division commander Major General David Ruffen established a network of forward outposts to shield troop movements. The opera-

tion, which took place on 6 June, was a success and encountered little resistance except at two hills, one of which was Hill 275, also known as Old Baldy because of the absence of trees on its summit.

Sporadic fighting over Old Baldy escalated on 26 June as CPVA forces attempted to retake the outposts in a series of failed counterattacks that lasted till 29 June. Another CPVA attempt to retake the hill on 3–4 July met with similar results.

This did not deter the Chinese from further attacks. They launched a new offensive that overran Old Baldy on the night of 17–18 July. Retaking the hill proved difficult because of lashing rain that turned the terrain into a quagmire, but the U.S. 23d Infantry Division accomplished the feat on 1 August. Another Chinese assault in September had brief success, but United Nations (UN) forces regained control on 21 September.

Fighting during the ensuing months was not as heavy, but by 20 March 1953 intelligence reports confirmed that a large-scale assault in the area of Old

Soldier of the 5th Marine Regiment scans Communist lines with binoculars, 7 April 1952. Note the trench, resembling World War I warfare. (National Archives)

Baldy was imminent. At the time commander of the U.S. 31st Infantry Regiment and an accompanying Colombian battalion, Colonel William B. Kern had charge of the area encompassing Old Baldy. Kern entrusted its defense to the Colombian battalion, commanded by Lieutenant Colonel Alberto Ruiz-Novoa. On 23 March the Chinese launched a coordinated assault on Old Baldy and neighboring Pork Chop Hill. A massive artillery and mortar barrage on Old Baldy destroyed most of the UN bunkers before a Chinese infantry regiment of about 3,500 men seized the hill. Repeated UN counterattacks on 24–25 March were unsuccessful and produced heavy casualties. Kern finally decided to abandon the effort and withdrew his forces during the night of 25–26 March. The remnants of Ruiz-Novoa's battalion also managed to escape. Eighth Army commander Lieutenant General Maxwell D. Taylor canceled further plans to retake the hill because he did not consider it essential.

The Battle of Old Baldy typified the see-saw hill battles in the static phase of the Korean War. Its loss led to renewed assaults on neighboring Pork Chop Hill. The Chinese occupation of Old Baldy outflanked UN troops on Pork Chop Hill and eventually led to its capture as well.

—*Eric W. Osborne*

References:

Hermes, Walter G. *United States Army in the Korean War: Truce Tent and Fighting Front*. Washington, DC: Office of the Chief of Military History, 1966.

Kaufman, Burton I. *The Korean War: Challenges in Crisis, Credibility, and Command*. Philadelphia: Temple University Press, 1986.

Rees, David. *Korea: The Limited War*. New York: St. Martin's Press, 1964.

See also: Pork Chop Hill, Battle of; Taylor, Maxwell, Davenport.

Oliver, Robert T.
(1907–)

U.S. academician, close friend of Republic of Korea (ROK) president Syngman Rhee, and prominent writer on Korean affairs. Born in Sweet Home, Oregon, in 1907, Robert T. Oliver graduated from Pacific College in Oregon and received his Ph.D. from the University of Wisconsin in speech and communication. He served on the faculty at Bucknell University, at Syracuse University, and later at the Pennsylvania State University. He has written several books on public speaking and has served as the president of the American Speech Association.

In September 1942 Oliver was invited to meet Syngman Rhee in Washington, D.C., by the Reverend Edward Junkin, pastor of the Presbyterian Church in Lewisburg, Pennsylvania, where Oliver was on leave during the war from the faculty of Bucknell University. He became a close friend and associate of Rhee until the latter's death in 1965. Oliver served as an advisor to President Rhee and to the Korean Commission and the Korean delegation to the United Nations. He first began to write and lecture on Korea in 1943 to promote the cause of Korean independence. From 1947 Oliver managed the Washington Bureau of the Korean Pacific Press and was editor of the monthly magazine *Korean Survey*. He registered with the Department of Justice as an agent of the Republic of Korea.

Oliver wrote many newspaper articles on Korea and many of Rhee's speeches. He also frequently exchanged letters with Rhee. When Seoul was captured by North Koreans at the end of June 1950, Rhee's files were seized and were soon quoted by North Korea and the Soviet Union in the course of a propaganda campaign carried on over a radio station and in the United Nations. Portions of letters were made public in garbled and incomplete quotations by the Communist countries in an attempt to blame the ROK and Rhee for the outbreak of the Korean War. In reality, Oliver had objected to any belligerent actions by the ROK. He wrote to Rhee on 30 September 1949, "On the question of attacking northward ... it is very evident to us here that any such attack now, or even talk of such an attack, is to lose American official and public support and will weaken our position among other nations."

From 1944 through 1978 Oliver wrote a half dozen books on Korea. He lives in Chestertown, Maryland.

—Youngho Kim

References:
Oliver, Robert T. *The Case for Korea: A Paradox of United States Diplomacy.* Washington, DC: Korean American Council, 1945.
———. *Korea: Forgotten Nation.* Washington, DC: Public Affairs Press, 1944.
———. *Syngman Rhee and American Involvement in Korea, 1942–1960: A Personal Narrative.* Seoul: Panmun Books, 1978.
———. *Syngman Rhee: The Man Behind the Myth.* New York: Dodd, Mead, 1955.
———. *Why War Came in Korea.* New York: Fordham University Press, 1950.
See also: Syngman Rhee.

OP Harry, Battle for (10–18 June 1953)

U.S. outpost (OP) battle in the last Chinese offensive of the war, won at heavy cost by U.S. forces. The fight for OP Harry was typical of a number of battles along the Eighth Army front just prior to the armistice. Outposts were generally lightly held, platoon- or company-sized positions in front of the main line of resistance (MLR). Outpost Harry was located in the west sector of the Eighth Army front, 2.5 miles southeast of Jackson Heights and eight miles northwest of Kimhwa. The slope of the terrain favored the defenders; OP Harry lay on a table of land slanting toward the U.S. positions that allowed supporting tank fire on three sides. 3d Division commander Major General Eugene Ridings was also determined that OP Harry would be held.

The fight for OP Henry was part of a series of Chinese diversionary attacks against the U.S. IX Corps line to keep the corps fully occupied while their main offensive was in progress. On 10 June 1953, the Chinese began their assault on OP Harry, which was held by elements of the U.S. 3d Division on the left flank of the ROK 9th Division. The Chinese initiated the attack with a company but soon augmented it to two battalions, which succeeded in penetrating the U.S. position. Counterattack followed counterattack, but U.S. forces emerged on top by the morning of the 11th. That night the Chinese resumed their assault, this time with a regiment, and the pattern of the previous night was repeated. The Chinese followed this with a small-scale probe on the 14th and then a two-battalion assault on the 18th. The 3d Division estimated that the Chinese had taken 4,200 casualties in their effort to take OP Harry. The fighting had also been costly for the United Nations Command; a succession of companies of the 3d Division were involved and had paid a heavy price.

—Spencer C. Tucker

References:
Eisenhower, John S. D. *Strictly Personal.* Garden City, NY: Doubleday 1974.
Hermes, Walter G. *United States Army in the Korean War: Truce Tent and Fighting Front.* Washington, DC: Office of the Chief of Military History, 1966.
See also: Chinese Summer Offensives of 1953.

Order of Battle (See Appendix I)

Osan, Battle of
(5 July 1950)

First battle of the Korean War involving U.S. troops, specifically Task Force Smith. Named for its commander, Lieutenant Colonel Charles B. ("Brad") Smith, Task Force Smith comprised 406 officers and enlisted men from the 1st Battalion of the 21st Infantry Regiment and 134 officers and men from the 52d Field Artillery Battery (Battery A plus small contingents from the Headquarters and Service Batteries). It was the first U.S. Army combat unit to enter Korea after the invasion of the South by the Korean People's Army (KPA, North Korean).

Task Force Smith arrived in South Korea by air near Pusan and moved north to Taejŏn by train, arriving there on the morning of 2 July 1950. The men of the task force were confident, believing that as soon as the North Koreans saw their American uniforms they would run away. Smith ordered his men to rest while he and his staff officers drove north to reconnoiter. Some three miles north of Osan, Smith found an ideal blocking position, a line of low rolling hills about 300 feet above the level ground. This position commanded the main railroad line to the east and afforded a clear view to Suwŏn, about eight miles north.

On 4 July the task force was joined at P'yŏngt'aek by part of the 52d Field Artillery Battalion: some of the Headquarters and Service Batteries and all of A Battery with five 105-mm howitzers (one howitzer was left behind at P'yŏngt'aek), seventy-three vehicles, and 134 men under the command of Lieutenant Colonel Miller O. Perry. On the late afternoon of 4 July, Smith, Perry, and others made a reconnaissance of the position Smith had selected. The combined infantry and artillery then moved out of P'yŏngt'aek by truck, arriving at the position about 0300. The U.S. line was about one mile in length and was bisected by the Suwŏn-Osan road.

In cold, rainy weather the men dug foxholes and laid telephone lines to four of the howitzers, placed in a concealed position some 2,000 meters to the south. One 105-mm howitzer was positioned halfway between the battery and the infantry to enfilade the road and serve as an antitank gun. Artillery volunteers formed four .50-caliber machine gun and four 2.36-inch bazooka teams and joined the infantry position to the north. The infantry vehicles were located just to the south of their position, and the artillerymen concealed their trucks just north of Osan. The Americans were vulnerable to enemy flanking attacks, lacked the means to stop tanks, and had no reserves.

At dawn on 5 July, Smith ordered his artillery, mortars, and machine guns to conduct registration fire. Steady rain precluded air support. Shortly after 0700 the Americans detected movement to the north. Within half an hour a column of eight KPA T-34 tanks, part of the 107th Tank Regiment of the 105th Armored Division, approached across the open plain from Suwŏn.

At 0800 the artillery received a request for a fire mission and at 0816 it opened fire against the tanks about 2,000 yards in front of the infantry position. The high-explosive (HE) rounds had no effect on the tanks, which had their hatches closed, but they did kill many KPA infantrymen riding on the tanks. The battery had only six armor-piercing high-explosive antitank (HEAT) rounds available (one-third of the total on hand when the 52d was loading at Sasebo, Japan), all of which were given to the single howitzer forward. Antitank mines would have stopped the enemy advance but there were none in Korea. Smith ordered 75-mm recoilless rifle fire withheld until the column of tanks reached 700 yards range. The recoilless rifle crews then scored direct hits, again without apparent effect. The tanks stopped and opened fire with their 85-mm main guns and 7.62-mm machine guns.

Second Lieutenant Ollie Connor engaged the tanks as they entered the infantry position, firing twenty-two 2.36-inch bazooka rounds at the enemy armor as it passed through and out of the position. All rounds were fired from close range, and a number were fired at the more vulnerable rear ends of the T-34s. The 2.36-inch rounds could not penetrate the T-34 armor, but Conner is credited with disabling two of the tanks. The 3.5-inch bazooka round would have been effective, but there were none in country.

As they approached the lone 105-mm gun forward, the two lead tanks were hit and damaged, probably by HEAT rounds. One caught fire and two of its crew members came out of the turret with their hands up; a third came out with a burp gun and fired it against a U.S. machine gun position beside the road, killing an assistant gunner, possibly the first U.S. ground soldier fatality of the Korean War. The third tank through the pass, however, knocked out the forward 105-mm howitzer with cannon fire. The other tanks then swept on south past the U.S. artillery battery, which fired HE rounds against them. One tank was disabled and ultimately abandoned.

Additional KPA tanks soon swept past the U.S. position, causing some of the battery crewmen to run from their guns. Officers and noncommissioned officers continued to service the guns, and the men returned. One other tank was disabled by a hit in the track. By 1015 the last of thirty-three North Korean tanks had driven through the U.S. position, killing or wounding some twenty Americans by machine-gun and artillery fire. Most of the vehicles parked immediately behind the infantry position were destroyed. The tanks also severed the wire communications link with Battery A.

Fortunately for the Americans, there were no accompanying infantrymen; the tankers were unable to locate the artillery battery firing on them, and the T-34s rumbled on toward Osan. A lull of about an hour followed. The steady rain continued and the defenders used the time to improve their position. At about 1100 three more tanks were sighted advancing from the north. Behind them was a column of trucks, followed by long columns of infantry on foot, the 16th and 18th Regiments of the North Korean 4th Division. The column was apparently not in communication with the tanks that had preceded it.

It took about an hour for the head of the column to reach a point about 1,000 yards from the U.S. position, when Smith ordered fire opened. U.S. mortars and machine guns swept the KPA column but did not stop the three tanks. They advanced to within 300 yards and raked the ridge with shell and machine gun fire. Smith had no communication with the artillery battery, which he believed had been destroyed.

Smith held his position as long as he dared, but casualties among his men rapidly mounted. The Americans were down to fewer than twenty rounds of ammunition apiece and the North Koreans threatened to cut off their position. With KPA tanks to the rear of the American position, Smith consolidated his force in a circular perimeter on the highest ground east of the road. The North Koreans were by now employing mortar and artillery fire. About 1630 Smith ordered a withdrawal, remarking, "This is a decision I'll probably regret the rest of my days." He planned an orderly leapfrogging withdrawal, with one platoon covering another, but under heavy KPA fire many weapons and much equipment was simply abandoned. Many men had not received word of the withdrawal, including three of the eight platoon leaders present. It was at this point that the Americans suffered most of their casualties.

The infantry withdrawal was disorganized from the start. The men came out for the most part in small groups. Some went south toward Osan, but west of the road; others headed west for a short distance, then south to the road leading east from Osan. Most of the infantry passed through or near the battery position.

Shortly after ordering the infantry to withdraw, Smith set out to find Perry. He discovered the artillery still in position east of the road. Smith was surprised to find the battery position intact with only Perry and one other man wounded. The artillerymen disabled their five howitzers by removing sights and breech-blocks. The men then withdrew into Osan, when they discovered KPA tanks near the southern edge of the town. They then turned back and drove east out of Osan. Fortunately there was no KPA pursuit. The infantry element split into many groups, which scattered. Some men headed east, while others went south and around Osan.

At Ch'ŏnan, only 185 men of the task force could be accounted for. Subsequently, C Company commander Captain Richard Dashner came in with 65 more, bringing the total near 250. More men trickled back to U.S. positions during the following week. One survivor even made it from the west coast by sampan to Pusan. In the battle approximately 150 U.S. infantrymen were killed, wounded, or missing. All 5 officers and 10 enlisted men of the forward observer liaison, machine gun, and bazooka group were lost. KPA casualties in the battle before Osan were approximately 42 dead and 85 wounded. The KPA also had four tanks destroyed and two or three damaged but repairable. In the Battle of Osan, Task Force Smith had held up the KPA advance for perhaps seven hours.

The North Koreans continued their offensive south against more and more units of the 24th Division. On 6 July they forced a U.S. withdrawal from the next blocking position at P'yŏngt'aek, held by the 34th Regiment. The 21st Regiment imposed another slight delay on the KPA in front of Choch'iwŏn, but both regiments suffered heavily in these actions. These and other battles during the period until 21 July, did purchase time for the 1st Cavalry and 25th Infantry divisions to arrive from Japan.

—*Spencer C. Tucker*

References:

Appleman, Roy E. *South to the Naktong, North to the Yalu.* Washington, DC: Office of the Chief of Military History, 1961.

Collins, J. Lawton. *War in Peacetime: The History and Lessons of Korea.* Boston: Houghton Mifflin, 1969.

Ent, Uzal W., letter to the author.

Gugeler, Russell A. *Combat Actions in Korea.* Washington, DC: U.S. Army Center of Military History, 1954.

Rees, David. *Korea: The Limited War.* New York: St. Martin's, 1964.

See also: Dean, William Frishe; MacArthur, Douglas; Task Force Smith; Truman, Harry S.; Walker, Walton Harris.

P

Pace, Frank, Jr.
(1912–1988)

U.S. secretary of the army during the Korean War. Born on 5 July 1912 in Little Rock, Arkansas, Frank Pace, Jr., was educated at Princeton and Harvard and became a lawyer specializing in tax law. Service during World War II as a stateside administrator in the Air Transport Command whetted his appetite for public service. After working in the Justice and Post Office Departments in Washington, he became assistant director, then director, of the Bureau of the Budget. His efficient service as director helped him secure the position of secretary of the army in April 1950.

As army secretary Pace was responsible for the training, operations, preparedness, and effectiveness of the U.S. Army. When the Korean War erupted on 25 June 1950, he and other presidential advisers recommended to President Harry S. Truman that the U.S. government do all in its power short of war to assist the Republic of Korea. When General Douglas MacArthur asked to use U.S. troops in combat on 30 June 1950 because of South Korea's near military collapse, Pace concurred and obtained presidential approval. This action marked U.S. entry into the ground war. When MacArthur's forces were approaching the Yalu River in November 1950, Pace contributed to the directive that they should stop at the heights south of the Yalu. On 28 November 1950 Pace helped advise President Truman that, because of massive Chinese intervention in the war, the United States should fully implement NSC-68, which put the United States on a constant war footing during the Cold War. When President Truman decided to relieve MacArthur in April 1950, he wanted Pace, who was in Asia at the time, to deliver the message; but Pace was in Korea and out of contact with Washington. With the press about to break the story, the Truman administration released the news first, and MacArthur learned of his dismissal from his wife. She had been informed by one of MacArthur's aides, who heard it over the radio. Pace did inform Lieutenant General Matthew B. Ridgway that he was MacArthur's replacement.

Under Pace and during the Korean War the army increased in size from 600,000 to 1,500,000 men. New training camps were opened, and National Guard divisions and reservists were called to active duty. Nearly 3 million soldiers served during the war. To share risk among combat troops, Pace instituted a point system whereby troops with sufficient points could rotate out of the combat zone. Racial enlistment quotas and seg-

regated units were abolished, and African-American replacements filled vacancies in white combat units. By the end of Pace's tour in January 1953, the army was almost fully integrated.

The army was also reorganized with the chiefs of infantry, cavalry, and artillery being abolished and the new branches of armor, transportation, and military police established. Pace supported the development of army tactical nuclear weapons, especially the 280-mm atomic cannon.

One of Pace's actions had a long-reaching impact on the army. The Key West Agreement of 1948 had restricted the army to small airplanes and helicopters in roles that would not duplicate air force missions of close air support, transport, or reconnaissance. To meet battlefield needs in Korea, in 1951 and 1952 Pace secured two agreements from Secretary of the Air Force Thomas K. Finletter that expanded the functions of army aviation and the size of the battle zone in which aircraft could operate. These agreements enabled the army to rapidly expand its aviation in the 1950s.

—*John L. Bell*

References:

Bradley, Omar N., and Clay Blair. *A General's Life: An Autobiography.* New York: Simon & Schuster, 1983.

Collins, J. Lawton. *Lightning Joe: An Autobiography.* Baton Rouge: Louisiana State University Press, 1979.

Roosevelt, Kermit. "The Army's Bright Young Boss." *Saturday Evening Post,* 28 October 1950.

Rothe, Anna, ed. *Current Biography.* New York: H. W. Wilson, 1950.

Weigley, Russell F. *History of the United States Army.* Bloomington: Indiana University Press, 1984.

Wolf, Richard I. *The United States Air Force Basic Documents on Roles and Missions.* Washington, DC: Office of Air Force History, 1987.

See also: Finletter, Thomas K.; Ridgway, Matthew Bunker; Truman, Harry S.; Truman's Recall of MacArthur; United States Air Force (USAF).

Pacific Pact

Abortive 1950 attempt to establish an anti-Communist Asian mutual security organization. The Pacific pact scheme, spearheaded by the Philippines, Taiwan, and the Republic of Korea (ROK, South Korea), prefigured the Southeast Asia Treaty Organization (SEATO) and the bilateral Asian-U.S. security pacts concluded later in the 1950s.

The success of Mao Zedong's Communist revolution in China in 1949 altered the course of U.S. foreign policy in Asia. Jiang Jieshi's (Chiang Kai-shek's) Nationalist (Guomindang) forces were driven off the mainland and onto Formosa (Taiwan). U.S. policymakers believed that the "loss" of China to communism rendered defense of the ROK impractical. Previously, the United States had referred to the ROK as a testing ground of U.S. resolve and a battleground between democracy and communism. President Harry S. Truman had gone so far as to suggest that aid to South Korea should be considered equivalent to that for Western Europe.

Even so, from at least 1947 U.S. policy toward Korea was always somewhat ambiguous. Late that year Congress failed to pass a Korean aid bill, and the State, War, and Navy Departments announced their intention of minimizing U.S. financial and military commitments and withdrawing all U.S. troops within two years. In 1949 the official U.S. attitude became still more cautious and ambivalent. The United States canceled $500 million in economic aid, withheld much military support, and withdrew the last of U.S. occupation troops from South Korea. On 1 January 1950, moreover, Secretary of State Dean Acheson excluded the ROK when he detailed the U.S. defense perimeter in the course of a major speech.

ROK president Syngman Rhee responded to the new U.S. policy by requesting an official commitment from the United States comparable to the North Atlantic Treaty Organization (NATO) in Europe. On 16 May 1949, Rhee issued a public statement calling for "a solution to the grave threat against Korea and all Asia by aggressive forces of communism." That solution included the formation of a Pacific pact, a mutual defense treaty between the United States and South Korea comparable to NATO. At the least, Rhee wanted a public declaration of U.S. intent to defend a reunited, independent Korea. Earlier Rhee had made similar requests. On one occasion, he stated that he wanted a "statement by President Truman that the United States would consider an attack against South Korea as an attack against itself."

In requesting a Pacific pact, Rhee found an immediate ally in Nationalist Chinese leader Jiang Jieshi, who had been trying since 1948 to persuade the United States to expand its commitment to non-Communist forces in Asia. He too wanted a pledge equivalent to the one the United States had extended to Europe. Thus on 11 May 1949 Nationalist Chinese Ambassador to the United States V. K. Wellington Koo suggested to Acheson the creation of a Pacific pact. The next day Australian Prime Minister Joseph Benedict ("Ben") Chifley echoed the request, and two days later Rhee followed suit.

Washington turned down this request for a formal alliance. On 18 May 1949, Acheson stated publicly

that a Pacific pact was premature. He also suggested that any such pact would indefinitely commit U.S. troops to the Nationalist Chinese in their fight against the Communists on mainland China. Acheson concluded by saying that the United States favored Indian Prime Minister Jawaharlal Nehru's policy that called on Asian nations to work to end their conflicts before the creation of formal alliances.

Rebuffed by the United States, Jiang and Rhee sought allies in the Pacific. In July 1949 Jiang traveled to the Philippines, where he met with Prime Minister Elpidio Quirino, who endorsed the idea of an anti-Communist Pacific pact. Quirino claimed that such an arrangement did not seek or require U.S. sanction, despite the intent of the members to "do our bit in the American-led crusade against Communism." Jiang next traveled to South Korea, where he and Rhee issued a joint statement proposing an organizational conference of anti-Communist Pacific countries.

This did not alter the U.S. stance. In August 1949 President Truman told Quirino that the United States would "watch sympathetically" as non-Communist Asia worked to bring about mutual security. Quirino also found a less-than-enthusiastic U.S. Congress. A further setback occurred in September, when the North Atlantic Council of Foreign Ministers, meeting in Washington, concurred with the U.S. position that a Communist victory in China was inevitable and further efforts to assist the Nationalists' military would therefore be pointless. Thus the foreign ministers rejected participation in a Pacific pact. In addition, Nehru again characterized the creation of such an alliance as premature.

Nonetheless, Quirino organized a conference. During 26–30 May 1950, representatives of India, Indonesia, the Philippines, Ceylon, Pakistan, and Thailand met in Baguio, the Philippines. Noticeably absent were Syngman Rhee and Jiang Jieshi. Neither attended nor sent representatives because India and Indonesia refused to deviate from their neutral stance even before the conference began. In the end, the Baguio Conference produced little of a concrete nature. No formal Pacific pact emerged, and there was no mutual security declaration. In fact, the official proclamation implied that the representatives opposed Great Power intervention in Asia altogether.

Less than one month later, forces of the Democratic People's Republic of Korea (DPRK, North Korea) crossed the 38th parallel and invaded the ROK, beginning the Korean War. Although early moves for a Pacific pact proved fruitless, the outbreak of the Korean War greatly alarmed many Asian nations and subsequently was a major contributory factor in persuading the United States to establish the 1954

SEATO pact and to negotiate bilateral security treaties with both Taiwan and the ROK.

—Mark A. T. Esposito

References:

Colbert, Evelyn S. *Southeast Asia in International Politics, 1941–1956*. Ithaca, NY: Cornell University Press, 1977.

Hess, Gary R. *The United States' Emergence As a Southeast Asian Power, 1940–1950*. New York: Columbia University Press, 1987.

Oliver, Robert T. *Syngman Rhee: The Man Behind the Myth*. New York: Dodd, Mead, 1955.

Stone, I. F. *The Hidden History of the Korean War*. New York: Monthly Review Press, 1952.

Stueck, William W., Jr. *The Korean War: An International History*. Princeton, NJ: Princeton University Press, 1995.

See also: Acheson, Dean Goodersham; Jiang Jieshi (Chiang Kaishek); Mao Zedong; NATO (North Atlantic Treaty Organization); Nehru, Jawaharlal; Syngman Rhee; Truman, Harry S.

Padilla Nervo, Luis
(1898–1985)

Head of the Mexican Delegation to the United Nations (1945–1952) and president of the Sixth Session of the United Nations (UN) General Assembly (1951–1952). Although Mexico drew closer to the United States economically in the 1940s and 1950s, it always tried to maintain an independent foreign policy both in international affairs in general and at the UN in particular. Luis Padilla Nervo was one of the principal architects of this policy. Born on 19 August 1898 in Zamora, Michoacan, Mexico, Luis Padilla Nervo received his degree in law from the National Autonomous University of Mexico and also attended the University of Buenos Aires, George Washington University, and the University of London. He entered the Mexican diplomatic corps in 1918 and served variously between 1933 and 1945 as Mexico's minister to El Salvador, Panama, Uruguay, Denmark, Cuba, and the United States. Padilla was part of the Mexican delegation to the San Francisco conference of the UN in 1945 and subsequently served as head of the Mexican delegation to the UN from 1945–1952.

As head of the Mexican delegation, Padilla exercised considerable influence among the Latin American nations, which initially composed approximately 40 percent of the membership of the General Assembly. Padilla worked unsuccessfully at the San Francisco meeting of the UN in 1945 to get a permanent "Latin American" seat on the Security Council. Mexico, however, did become the first Latin American nation to be elected to one of the nonpermanent seats on the Security Council in 1946, making Padilla the first Latin American to serve on that powerful body.

With the North Korean attack on South Korea, Padilla supported UN military involvement in Korea as well as UN resolutions calling for a greater role for the General Assembly in cases of international aggres-

sion and branding China as an aggressor after its intervention in Korea. Although supporting a military response, Padilla continued to work for a diplomatic solution to the conflict. He was one of three veteran diplomats assigned to the UN's Good Offices Committee, which had the responsibility of bringing China into negotiations to end the war.

Mexico also had a representative on the UN's Additional Measures Committee (AMC), exploring economic sanctions against China; Mexico was part of the group on the committee trying to delay sanctions for fear that they might provoke a widening of the war. Under growing U.S. pressure, Mexico and the AMC approved a resolution calling for a selective embargo, which was later approved by the General Assembly on 18 May 1951 without a negative vote, although several nations abstained or were absent. While Padilla supported a peaceful resolution in Korea, he opposed an appeal being considered by a bloc of Asian and African countries to halt the fighting along the 38th parallel because it would have bypassed the Good Offices Committee.

As president of the Sixth Session of the General Assembly (1951–1952), Padilla continued his efforts to bring about a negotiated end to the war. He was at the center of an ultimately unused Mexican effort to resolve the problem of dealing with the repatriation of prisoners of war, an issue that had deadlocked the armistice talks. Although he supported the U.S. position on key resolutions relating to the conduct of the war, in other areas such as UN membership, disarmament, UN trusteeships, and economic development, Padilla staked out an independent position for Mexico. In his parting remarks as outgoing president of the assembly in October 1952, Padilla commented on the need for a reconciliation between the United States and the Soviet Union and called for renewed efforts to bring the war to a negotiated conclusion.

After serving as president of the General Assembly, Padilla continued his distinguished diplomatic career. He left the UN to become Mexico's minister of foreign relations, a post he held from 1952 to 1958. After serving as minister of foreign relations, Padilla returned to head the Mexican delegation at the UN from 1958 until 1963, when he was appointed to the International Court of Justice, where he served until 1973. By the end of his career he had received decorations from twenty-four African, Asian, European, and Latin American countries.

Padilla effectively used his position at the UN during the Korean conflict to help maintain Latin American support for UN policy in Asia, without blindly adhering to the positions adopted by the United States on other issues. Padilla Nervo died in 1985.

—Don M. Coerver

References:

Faust, John R., and Charles L. Stansifer. "Mexican Foreign Policy in the United Nations: The Advocacy of Moderation in an Era of Revolution." *Southwestern Social Science Quarterly* 44 (September 1963): 121–129.

Houston, John A. *Latin America in the United Nations*. New York: Carnegie Endowment for International Peace, 1956.

Stueck, William W., Jr. *The Korean War: An International History*. Princeton, NJ: Princeton University Press, 1995.

See also: Latin America; Mexico.

Paek In-yŏp
(1922–)

Republic of Korea Army (ROKA, South Korean) general, later educator. Born in Kangsŏ, North P'yŏngan Province, North Korea, in 1922, Paek In-yŏp is the younger brother of well-known ROKA General Paek Sŏn-yŏp. Paek graduated from the Japanese Military Academy in 1945 and became a second lieutenant in the Japanese army.

After the Second World War, Paek became a colonel in the ROK National Constabulary and was appointed as commander of the 17th Regiment in the Ongjin peninsula. He was a key figure in border fighting with North Korean forces during the period 1948–1949. Paek's regiment was long identified with the "Haeju attack" theory of the beginning of the war—namely, that the war was initiated by ROK forces—which has been proved false. Soon after the outbreak of the war, the 17th Regiment was compelled to withdraw because of resupply problems.

On 7 August 1950, Paek became commander of the Capital Division. He distinguished himself in the later fighting, and in 1953 he studied at the U.S. Army War College. He then became commander of the ROKA VI Corps as a lieutenant general. Paek graduated from the ROK National Defense College in 1953 and retired from the military in 1962. After retirement in 1964, Paek and his elder brother Paek Sŏn-yŏp founded the Sŏnin School in Inch'ŏn City.

—Choo-suk Suh

References:

Paek Sŏn-yŏp. *Kun Kwa Na* [The military and I]. Seoul: Taeryuk Yŏn'gu-so, 1989.

Wŏlgan Chosŏn [Chosŏn monthly], October 1993.

See also: Border Clashes; Paek Sŏn-yŏp.

Paek Sŏng-uk
(1897–1981)

Home minister of the Republic of Korea (ROK), 1950. Born in Seoul in 1897, Paek Sŏng-uk was educated at the Buddhist Central School, which later became Tong'guk University. A supporter of Korean independence, he was exiled to Shanghai, China, after he joined the March First Movement of 1919. It was at this time that he met Syngman Rhee, a generation older and already one of the foremost leaders of the Korean nationalist movement. Paek proceeded to Europe for several years, and lived in France and Germany. In 1925 the University of Würzburg awarded him a doctorate in Buddhism. Paek returned to Korea and spent many years pursuing Buddhist scholarship at a temple on Kŏmgang-san Mountain. When Rhee returned to Korea in 1945 after the country's liberation from the Japanese, Paek resumed contact with him and became one of his strongest supporters. During Rhee's subsequent bitter disputes and conflicts with Lieutenant General John R. Hodge, commander of U.S. occupation forces, Paek remained his staunch ally, publicly stating that Rhee was the only Korean leader capable of uniting the country and heading a future South Korean government.

Paek's one spell of high political office was short and ill-fated. In February 1950 Rhee, who became the first president of the Republic of Korea in 1948, asked Paek's opinion as to the desirability of establishing a parliamentary system, as the opposition in the National Assembly had suggested. Paek expressed strong disapproval of the idea, whereupon Rhee promptly named him home minister, a post in which he exercised direct authority over the local and central bureaucracies and, even more importantly, the police, who were responsible for maintaining internal security, a mandate that ROK leaders tended to define very broadly.

Paek used his position to orchestrate and direct a nationwide propaganda and terror campaign against the creation of a parliamentary system, which was probably partly responsible for the National Assembly's failure to pass a constitutional amendment supporting the switch to such a political system. Simultaneously, Rhee also pressured the National Assembly by threatening to postpone the imminent elections scheduled for the coming May. His tactics, however, proved counterproductive when U.S. officials warned that, if the elections did not take place on time, anticipated U.S. economic and military aid would not be forthcoming, a threat that forced Rhee to accept a compromise and end this particular crisis. After the North Korean invasion of 25 June 1950, Paek (whom Harold J. Noble, at that time first secretary at the U.S. embassy in Seoul, described as a superstitious "fatalist and military pessimist"), was Rhee's only cabinet member to refuse to desert Seoul until the government as a whole left the capital. His courage, however, coexisted with a "gloomy" outlook that so depressed Rhee that on the day the war began, Paek's "defeatism" led the president to demand his resignation.

Paek clung to office only for another month. By mid-July, Noble, Lieutenant General Walton H. Walker, commander of the U.S. Eighth Army in Korea, and U.S. Ambassador John J. Muccio all regarded him as "a serious menace to the successful prosecution of the war so pessimistic that he even infected high police officers with his defeatism." They were determined to replace Paek with the more positive and dynamic Cho Pyŏng-ok, a course of action that they daily recommended to the reluctant Rhee. Although the president preferred the loyal and malleable Paek to Cho or any other contender, ultimately he followed their advice, dismissed Paek, and appointed Cho.

In 1952 Paek ran unsuccessfully for vice-president, his last major excursion into politics. From 1953 to 1961 he served as president of Tong'guk University, his alma mater, and after he retired he continued to lecture privately on Buddhism. Paek died in 1981.

—Priscilla Roberts

References:

Cumings, Bruce. *The Origins of the Korean War.* 2 vols. Princeton, NJ: Princeton University Press, 1981, 1990.

Dobbs, Charles M. *The Unwanted Symbol: American Foreign Policy, the Cold War, and Korea, 1945–1950.* Kent, OH: Kent State University Press, 1981.

Noble, Harold J. *Embassy at War.* Seattle: University of Washington Press, 1975.

"Paek Song-uk." In *Historical Dictionary of the Korean War,* edited by James I. Matray. Westport, CT: Greenwood Press, 1991.

See also: Hodge, John R.; Korea, Republic of: History 1947–1953; Muccio, John J.; Noble, Harold; Syngman Rhee; Walker, Walton Harris.

Paek Sŏn-yŏp
(1920–)

Republic of Korea Army (ROKA, South Korean) officer who rose from division commander with the rank of colonel at the beginning of the Korean War, to corps commander, and then to full general and chief of staff of the army. Born in Kangsŏ, South P'yŏngan Province near P'yŏngyang, on 23 November 1920, Paek Sŏn-yŏp graduated from the Japanese Manchurian Military Academy in 1941. During World War II he was a Japanese army lieutenant. After his return to Korea in 1945, Paek graduated from the U.S. military government's Military English-Language School and joined the Korean constabulary as a company commander.

When the Korean People's Army (KPA, North Korean) began its invasion of South Korea on 25 June 1950, Paek commanded the ROKA 1st Division at Kaesŏng, two miles below the 38th parallel on the Seoul-P'yŏngyang highway. On the day of the invasion his division conducted a surprisingly effective defense and held its positions south of the Imjin River for nearly three days. But his own division was threatened with being cut off by the main KPA attack from the Ŭijŏngbu area when the ROKA 7th Division was forced to give way. Paek then removed his division to the Han River, where he took up positions on 28 June.

Paek established a reputation as an excellent combat leader. In August 1950 he played an important role in the valiant and bloody defense of Taegu, a key point on the axis of the KPA main attack, which was vital in enabling United Nations (UN) forces to hold the Pusan perimeter. Although Paek received proper credit for the defense of Taegu, his success was in part the result of fire support from the neighboring U.S. 1st Cavalry Division, which helped compensate for the lack of his own artillery.

During the Pusan perimeter breakout and subsequent counterattack, Paek and his division came under U.S. I Corps command, the first time Korean army formations were with U.S. Army units at the division level. During the October UN/ROK race to P'yŏngyang, Paek's division, despite being on foot, beat UN motorized units to the Democratic People's Republic of Korea (DPRK, North Korean) capital and took the city on the 19th. During the subsequent advance north of the Ch'ŏngch'ŏn River, on 25 October Paek first encountered Chinese units above Unsan. When he immediately reported this fact to Commanding General of I Corps Frank W. Milburn, it was the first U.S. knowledge of direct Chinese military intervention in the war. Many U.S. generals, including Milburn, 1st Cavalry Division commander Hobart R. Gay, and Eighth Army commander Walton H. Walker, regarded Paek as one of very best ROK generals.

Promoted to major general in April 1951, Paek commanded the ROKA I Corps then positioned on the east coast of Korea north of the 38th parallel. In July when truce talks began, Paek represented the ROK government as one of five UN Command delegates. From November 1951 to April 1952 he commanded Task Force Paek, consisting of the ROK Capital and 8th Divisions. With this force he conducted Operation RATKILLER, which successfully wiped out Communist guerrillas operating in the Chiri-san area in the southern part of Korea. This force killed or captured more than 10,000 guerrillas.

In January 1952 Paek was promoted to lieutenant general and given command of the new ROKA II Corps. Unlike I Corps, the new corps had, in addition to its infantry divisions, an organic artillery battalion and quartermaster and engineer assets.

U.S. Eighth Army commander Lieutenant General James A. Van Fleet was so impressed by Paek's ability that in July 1952 he recommended him to President Syngman Rhee as ROKA chief of staff. Paek served twice in that position: from 1952 to 1954 and from 1957 to 1959. On 31 January 1953 Paek was, at age thirty-two, promoted to four-star general, the first individual in the ROKA to hold that rank.

In May 1953 the U.S. government prepared a contingency plan to remove Rhee from office, as the president was then attempting to sabotage the truce talks. In drawing up their plan, the Americans assumed Paek would side with the United States even though they had not consulted him. The plan was never implemented, as Rhee finally agreed to the U.S. position regarding the truce.

In 1959 Paek became chairman of the ROK Joint Chiefs of Staff, and the next year he retired from the army. Thereafter he served successively as ambassador to Taiwan, France (and concurrently thirteen other nations), and Canada. From 1969 to 1971 he was minister of transportation.

—*To-Woong Chung and Mark R. Franklin*

References:

Appleman, Roy E. *South to the Naktong, North to the Yalu.* Washington, DC: Office of the Chief of Military History, 1961.

Hermes, Walter G. *United States Army in the Korean War: Truce Tent and Fighting Front.* Washington, DC: Office of the Chief of Military History, 1966.

Paek Sŏn-yup. *From Pusan to Panmunjom.* McLean, VA: Brassey's, 1992.

———. *Kun kwa Na* [The army and I: memoirs]. Seoul: Taerkuk Yŏn'gu-so, 1989.

See also: Gay, Hobart Raymond; Kaesŏng Truce Talks; Milburn, Frank William; RATKILLER, Operation; Syngman Rhee; Taegu, Defense of; Van Fleet, James Alward; Walker, Walton Harris.

Paek Tu-jin
(1908–1992)

Republic of Korea (ROK, South Korea) banker, finance minister, and prime minister. Born in Sinch'ŏn, Hwanghae Province, North Korea, on 7 October 1908, Paek Tu-jin grew up in Seoul. He graduated from the College of Commerce of Tokyo Imperial University in 1934. He joined Chosŏn Central Bank in 1934 and served as a trustee there from 1945 to 1950.

A staunch supporter of South Korean president Syngman Rhee, Paek was appointed chief of the foreign aid management agency in 1949. After the outbreak of the Korean War in 1950, he became president of the Korea Industrial Bank. The next year Rhee appointed him both finance minister and the chief of the Planning Agency, thus making him his chief financial advisor.

As chief financial officer of Korea, Paek faced enormous problems, perhaps the most pressing of which was controlling chronic inflation. Paek employed the common-sense approach of paring nonmilitary expenditures as much as possible and collecting taxes, by force if necessary. Paek played a major role in ROK-U.S. economic relations. Both he and Rhee believed that the serious inflation resulted from the advance payments in wŏn, the ROK currency, to the United Nations Command for maintenance costs in Korea. Paek finally secured an economic cooperation agreement with Charles Miller, representing the U.S. government.

In February 1953 Paek implemented a currency reform that replaced the old wŏn with a new hwan at the rate of 100 to 1. When Henry Tasca visited South Korea, Paek worked out a program with him for a long-range reconstruction program. In 1952 Rhee designated Paek acting prime minister, succeeding Chang Ta'ek-sang. Paek became prime minister in April 1953 and served until 1954.

In 1960 Paek was elected to the ROK National Assembly, but he could not serve out his term because of the May 1961 military coup d'état. He became presidential adviser of the ruling Democratic Republican Party in 1967. From 1967 to 1980 he served as an assemblyman. He was again prime minister during 1970–1971, and he was elected speaker (chairman) of the National Assembly in 1971. In 1973 he also chaired the Yujŏng-hoe club, consisting of presidentially designated assemblymen.

Paek was again elected speaker of the National Assembly in 1979, but in the 1980s he held no official position. Paek died in Seoul on 5 September 1992.

—*Choo-suk Suh*

References:

Lyons, Gene M. *Military Policy and Economic Aid: The Korean Case, 1950–1953.* Columbus: Ohio State University Press, 1961.

Matray, James I., ed. *Historical Dictionary of the Korean War.* Westport, CT: Greenwood Press, 1991.

Paek Tu-jin. *Paek Tu-jin Hoegorok* [Memoirs of Paek Tu-jin]. Seoul: Taehan Kongnon-sa, 1975.

See also: Meyer, Clarence E.; Tasca, Henry J.

Pak Hŏn-yŏng
(1900–1955)

Minister of foreign affairs and a vice premier of the Democratic People's Republic of Korea (DPRK, North Korea) during the Korean War and one of the key leaders of the Korean Communist movement. Pak Hŏn-yŏng was born on 1 May 1900 in Yesan, South Ch'ungch'ŏng Province, in southern Korea. He began anti-Japanese activities by joining in the Koryŏ Communist Youth League in Shanghai as early as 1919 and was one of the original members of the Koryŏ Communist Party formed in Shanghai in 1921. In 1925 in Seoul he formed both the Korean Communist Party (KCP) and the Korean Communist Youth League. The Japanese arrested him three times—in 1921, in 1924, and in 1933—in connection with his Communist activities. In 1933 he was imprisoned for six years when he reentered Korea from Shanghai in an effort to reconstruct the KCP. Upon his release in 1939 he achieved some success in uniting existing Korean Communist factions in the K'om Kŭrup (Communist Group). In 1941 he went underground for the duration of the Pacific War, working as a laborer in a South Chŏlla Province brick factory. On 15 August 1945, when the Japanese surrendered, he left for Seoul, saying "I go to begin my future."

After the Korean liberation Pak was the key leader in the short-lived, stormy period of Communist ascendancy in southern Korea. Called in 1945 "the greatest leader of Korean communism," he took the lead in the February 1946 formation of Minjŏn (Democratic National Front), a leftist coalition in southern Korea, and the fall 1946 creation of the Namrodang (South Korean Worker's Party), a merger of the political left in southern Korea. As the leader of the "domestic" faction, Pak was the logical choice to be national leader of post-1945 Korean communism because of his indigenous support, long party experience, and strong intellectual qualifications.

The Americans now intervened, occupying Korea south of the 38th parallel in accordance with World War II agreements with the Soviets. Since their fundamental objectives and the means they used in reaching them differed so radically, U.S. occupation authorities and the Communists in southern Korea were destined to come into conflict. After the 1946 "Autumn Harvest Uprisings," the southern Left saw its strength dissipate and the center of gravity move to P'yŏngyang. Pak and other southern Communist leaders were forced to move north, to be fixed in secondary positions there.

On the September 1948 establishment of the Democratic People's Republic of Korea (DPRK), Pak became a vice premier with Kim Ch'aek and Hong Myŏng-hŭi under Premier Kim Il Sung. Pak also held the important cabinet position of minister of foreign affairs, and he was made vice chairman of the Korean Worker's Party—a fusion of the northern and southern Worker's parties—as well as a member of the all-important seven-member military committee of the party. According to some writers, Pak urged the North Korean invasion of South Korea in an effort to advance his political fortunes against his rival Kim Il Sung. But both men wanted a war against the South to reunify their country under communism. Reportedly, a secret conference was held in March 1950 in P'yŏngyang that was attended by North Korea's top leaders. Kim Il Sung is said to have opened for discussion the possibility of military action against the Republic of Korea. Pak allegedly spoke strongly in favor of such a course, asserting that if the Korean People's Army (KPA) invaded the South, 200,000 underground South Korean Communists would emerge to fight with the northern forces. But in the summer of 1950 the southern population was generally apathetic regarding the North Korean occupation. Few "rose up" to voluntarily greet the KPA armies, which was one of the reasons for the North Korean failure.

After North Korea's military defeats in the fall of 1950, the rivalry between Kim Il Sung and Pak Hŏn-yŏng intensified. Kim Il Sung complained to the Chinese that Pak "has no determination to start a guerrilla struggle in the mountainous area."

Pak Hŏn-yŏng's fate was sealed by the North Korean failure to conquer the South. After the end of the war, Pak and the southern Communists were made scapegoats for the debacle of the war. Kim Il Sung and his allies blamed Pak for failing to produce an uprising in the South that would lead to a Communist victory. Pak, loser in the power struggle with Kim Il Sung, was purged. In December 1955 Kim, who emerged as the "maximum leader," had Pak Hŏn-yŏng executed on a charge of spying for the "U.S. imperialists."

—Jinwung Kim

References:

Cumings, Bruce. *Korea's Place in the Sun: A Modern History.* New York: W. W. Norton, 1997.

Matray, James I., ed. *Historical Dictionary of the Korean War.* Westport, CT: Greenwood Press, 1991.

Scalapino, Robert A., and Lee Chong-Sik. *Communism in Korea.* 2 vols. Berkeley: University of California Press, 1973.

See also: Kim Il Sung.

Pandit, Vijaya Lakshmi
(1900–1990)

Indian ambassador to the United States and chief delegate to the United Nations during the Korean War. Born in 1900, Vijaya Lakshmi Pandit was, like her brother, future Indian Prime Minister Jawaharlal Nehru, active in the Indian movement to secure independence from Britain. She was arrested several times. After India became independent in 1947, Pandit served the new government in a variety of key diplomatic posts, including those of ambassador to the Soviet Union and then to the United States and Great Britain.

As Indian ambassador to the United States during the Korean War, Pandit closely followed her country's nonaligned stance, worked to keep the war from spreading, and sought to bring the war to a peaceful conclusion. She was certainly friendlier toward, and less skeptical of, the West than her brother, and on occasion she sought to soften his criticisms of Truman administration policies. This was a difficult period in U.S.-Indian relations for, although Pandit was well respected by Truman administration officials—Secretary of State Dean G. Acheson found her "a most charming lady"—they also viewed Indian policies as at best naive.

Pandit played little role in V. K. Krishna Menon's prisoner-of-war proposals that helped to end the war, in part because of personal animosity and in part because she did not think that Menon would be able to secure a compromise on the matter.

In 1953 Pandit was elected president of the General Assembly, the first woman to hold that post. In 1970 Pandit moved to Dehra Dun, in north India. Outraged by the proclaimed state of emergency, she campaigned against her niece Prime Minister Indira Gandhi and was a factor in her fall from power. Ailing for some years, she died on 1 December 1990.

—Spencer C. Tucker

References:

New York Times, 2 December 1990.

Pandit, Vijaya Lakshmi. *The Scope of Happiness: A Personal Memoir.* London: 1979.

Reid, Escott. *Envoy to Nehru.* Delhi: Oxford University Press, 1981.

Stueck, William W., Jr. *The Road to Confrontation: American Policy toward China and Korea, 1947–1950.* Chapel Hill: University of North Carolina Press, 1981.

See also: Acheson, Dean Goodersham; India; Menon, V. K. Krishna; Nehru, Jawaharlal.

Panikkar, Sardar K. M.
(1895–1963)

India's ambassador to China from 1947 to 1952 and diplomatic conduit for communications between the People's Republic of China (PRC) and the Western powers. Born on 3 June 1895, at Travancore, India, Sardar K. M. Panikkar was educated at Madras Christian College and Christ Church College, Oxford, where he gained first class honors in modern history. After reading for the bar, Panikkar returned to India and spent short spells as a university professor and editor of the *Hindustan Times.* He then became a public servant, serving in the administrations of several of the Indian princely states. His most senior positions were as foreign minister of Potiala and prime minister of Bikaner State from 1944 to 1947.

Before Indian independence Panikkar was also a member of the Indian delegations at numerous international gatherings and conferences. Throughout his life he wrote extensively on India's history and politics and on international relations, and he became known as a brilliant although far from objective scholar and diplomat, dedicated to the cause of Afro-Asian nationalism. In 1947 he became India's ambassador to China. Panikkar withdrew briefly from China after the Communist Party's final victory in the Chinese civil war and its proclamation of the People's Republic of China on 1 October 1949, but in December of that year Prime Minister Jawaharlal Nehru of India recognized the new regime and, somewhat unconventionally, reassigned Panikkar to Beijing. Panikkar's outspoken support for Asian nationalism, the Chinese revolution, and India's nonaligned Cold War policies, and his scholarly accomplishments were assets that helped him to develop warm and friendly relations with China's new leaders.

During the Korean War Panikkar routinely informed Secretary-General of the Ministry of External Affairs Sir Girja Bajpai of his conversations regarding Korea with PRC Foreign Minister Zhou Enlai and other Chinese leaders. Bajpai, in turn, relayed these messages to the British and U.S. governments, with whose personnel he enjoyed good relations. The British Foreign Office tended to give considerable credence to his reports, whereas U.S. officials were more skeptical, deploring what they considered Panikkar's pro-Communist sympathies and therefore characterizing his observations as unreliable.

Panikkar initially reported that China's leadership seemed relatively uninterested in Korea and that a Chinese military intervention appeared unlikely. In late September, after the success of General Douglas MacArthur's Inch'ŏn counteroffensive raised the possibility that United Nations (UN) forces would cross the 38th parallel dividing the two Korean states, Chinese leaders began to express serious concern over Korea. The most dramatic incidents of Panikkar's involvement with Korea then ensued. On 25 September 1950 acting Chinese Army Chief of Staff General Nieh Yen-jung warned Panikkar that China would intervene militarily should UN forces cross the parallel. In a speech of 30 September, Zhou Enlai publicly made the same threat.

Disregarding these, on 1 October the Republic of Korea Army (ROKA, South Korean) units crossed the 38th parallel. On 3 October earlier Chinese warnings were reinforced when Zhou Enlai summoned Panikkar to a midnight meeting, at which he emphasized that the PRC was prepared to tolerate the presence of South Korean forces in the North, but "American intrusion into North Korea would encounter Chinese resistance." Panikkar immediately cabled this information to Delhi, and it was communicated to both British and American diplomatic representatives. The British were relatively receptive, and although some U.S. State Department officials, notably O. Edmund Chubb and U. Alexis Johnson, argued that the threat of Chinese intervention should not be ignored, top U.S. leaders, including President Harry S. Truman, Secretary of State Dean Acheson, and MacArthur, argued that to hold back at the parallel would be interpreted as evidence of U.S. weakness and irresolution.

On 8 October the UN, at U.S. insistence, passed a resolution authorizing its forces to cross into North Korean territory, and within a few weeks Chinese troops joined the fighting. Panikkar feared that the war would escalate further and that the United States would extend bombing raids to Manchuria, possibly provoking Soviet intervention. He remained in Beijing until 1952, encouraging all moves to bring about a negotiated peace settlement, efforts in which Indian diplomats at the UN were also deeply involved.

After leaving China, Panikkar was successively Indian ambassador to Egypt and to France. In 1961 he returned to the academic world as vice-chancellor of Jammu and Kashmir University in Srinagar. He died at Mysore, India, on 10 December 1963.

—*Priscilla Roberts*

References:

Gopal, Sarvepalli. *Jawaharlal Nehru: A Biography.* London: Jonathan Cape, 1979.

Kux, Dennis. *Estranged Democracies: India and the United States, 1941–1991.* New Delhi: Sage, 1993.

Panikkar, K. M. *In Two Chinas: Memoirs of a Diplomat.* London: Allen & Unwin, 1955.

Stueck, William W., Jr. *The Korean War: An International History.* Princeton, NJ: Princeton University Press, 1995.

Wolpert, Stanley. *Nehru: A Tryst with Destiny.* New York: Oxford University Press, 1996.

See also: Acheson, Dean Goodersham; Bajpai, Girja S.; Clubb, Oliver Edmund; Inch'ŏn Landings: Operation CHROMITE; India; Johnson, U. Alexis; MacArthur, Douglas; Nehru, Jawaharlal; Truman, Harry S.; Zhou Enlai.

P'anmunjŏm Security Agreement

The 22 October 1951 P'anmunjŏm Security Agreement relocated the truce talks from Kaesŏng to P'anmunjŏm and designated the conference site, the base camps of the two sides, and corridors along the roads leading from the base camps to P'anmunjŏm as neutral areas.

Security and access in the conference area had been an issue from the beginning of the truce talks. Kaesŏng was not under the control of either side when the United Nations Command (UNC) agreed on 3 July 1951 to hold the talks there. By the time the negotiations began on 10 July, however, Korean People's Army/Chinese People's Volunteer Army (KPA/CPVA) troops had occupied the town, giving them possession of the negotiation site and control of the conference setting. During the initial negotiations the KPA/CPVA refused to allow journalists to accompany the UNC delegation, citing security considerations. The UNC then proposed a five-mile radius Kaesŏng neutral zone and threatened to change the conference site if the Chinese and North Koreans continued to insist that restrictions on the movements of UNC personnel at Kaesŏng were necessary for their safety. On 15 July the KPA/CPVA agreed to establish the neutral zone.

Despite this agreement, security and access in the conference site continued to be an issue. On 4 August a company of Chinese combat troops marched through the conference area. When the UNC protested, the KPA/CPVA apologized for the incident. They in turn made a series of accusations against the UNC, alleging air attacks and other violations of the neutral zone. On 22 August the KPA/CPVA charged the UNC with bombing and strafing the conference site itself and unilaterally recessed the talks. Apparently the Chinese wanted a pause in the talks while they reassessed their battlefield position and their negotiating strategy.

Although the UNC expressed willingness to resume the talks, it had concluded that the Kaesŏng conference site was disadvantageous. It was also concerned that the Chinese and North Koreans were taking advantage of the large neutral zone to reconstitute their forces in that area, which lay along the main avenue of approach into South Korea.

When the Chinese completed their strategic reassessment in mid-September and decided not to conduct a new major military offensive, the KPA/CPVA side offered to resume negotiations. The UNC, however, declined to resume the negotiations at Kaesŏng. After several weeks of bargaining, the KPA/CPVA side agreed on 24 October to a new conference site at P'anmunjŏm, midway between the two sides, and ratified an agreement reached by the liaison officers on 22 October.

The P'anmunjŏm Security Agreement established a circular area 1,000 yards in radius as the conference site. Armed personnel were excluded from that area except for each side's security detachment of two officers and fifteen men equipped with small arms. The two sides would share in equipping and maintaining the conference facilities. Each side could determine the composition of its own delegation, which would have freedom of movement within the conference site. Three-mile radius areas centered on the two sides' base camps at Kaesŏng and Munsan and a corridor extending 200 meters on either side of the Kaesŏng-P'anmunjŏm-Munsan road were also designated as neutral zones. No hostile acts were to be permitted within or against these areas, nor could aircraft fly over them, except under uncontrollable weather or technical conditions.

When the talks resumed on 25 October 1951, the UNC accepted a KPA/CPVA proposal to establish a joint office of the liaison officers to deal with the administration of the security agreement and to investigate and settle violations. Under a subsequent liaison officer agreement of 24 November 1951, the UNC agreed to allow safe passage between P'yŏngyang and Kaesŏng of two daily KPA/CPVA convoys of up to six trucks and three jeeps each.

The P'anmunjŏm Security Agreement largely removed the issue of equity and security from the truce talks agenda and set the stage for substantive negotiations. However, the long recess, the charges and countercharges, and the difficulty of reaching the agreement did nothing to alleviate an atmosphere of hostility and mistrust that continued to permeate the talks.

—*Donald W. Boose, Jr.*

References:

Chen, Jian. *Mao's China in the Cold War: Inquiries and Reinterpretations.* Chapel Hill: University of North Carolina Press, in press.

Goodman, Allan E., ed. *Negotiating while Fighting: The Diary of Admiral C. Turner Joy at the Korean Armistice Conference.* Stanford, CA: Hoover Institute Press, 1978.

Hermes, Walter G. *United States Army in the Korean War: Truce Tent and Fighting Front.* Washington, DC: Office of the Chief of Military History, 1966.

U.S. Department of State, Bureau of Public Affairs. *Foreign Relations of the United States, 1951.* Vol. 7, *China and Korea.* Washington, DC: U.S. Government Printing Office, 1983.

See also: Kaesŏng Neutral Zone Controversy; Kaesŏng Truce Talks; P'anmunjŏm Truce Talks; Truce Talks.

P'anmunjŏm Truce Talks
(25 October 1951–27 July 1953)

The P'anmunjŏm phase of the Korean truce talks began on 25 October 1951, after the site of the talks had been relocated from Kaesŏng under the terms of the 22 October 1951 P'anmunjŏm Security Agreement. The talks then continued with one long recess until the armistice was signed on 27 July 1953.

When the talks resumed at P'anmunjŏm, the Korean People's Army/Chinese People's Volunteer Army (KPA/CPVA) and the U.S.-led United Nations Command (UNC) negotiators had already agreed on a five-item agenda, the first item of which was agreement on the agenda itself. They had also made considerable progress on the second item, fixing the location of a military demarcation line (MDL) and demilitarized zone (DMZ). After a month of negotiations the two sides agreed on 27 November 1951 to an MDL coinciding with the line of ground contact at that time. The UNC insisted that if the negotiations were not concluded within thirty days of the agreement, the MDL would be the line of contact at the time of the armistice. Although more than a year and a half would pass before the armistice was signed, and ground attacks by both sides would require some adjustments to the final MDL, the line did not change significantly.

The third agenda item, concrete arrangements for implementing the armistice, was a more difficult issue. Both sides agreed that there should be a Military Armistice Commission (MAC) with equal representation from both sides, but the UNC wanted the MAC to have authority to observe and enforce the armistice throughout Korea, while the KPA/CPVA insisted its mandate be limited to the DMZ. The UNC also called for a ban on the repair or construction of airfields to prevent a challenge to UNC air superiority, but the KPA/CPVA rejected this proposal. As the negotiations proceeded on these points, the U.S. government, in consultation with the British, conceived the idea of a "greater sanctions statement," or "joint policy declaration," to be issued by all the UNC nations when the armistice was signed. This declaration would threaten a united and prompt response to renewed aggression and would warn that such response might not be confined

to Korea. As a more effective deterrent than mere legal prohibitions, the declaration would permit the UNC some flexibility on the airfield and inspection issues.

On 3 December 1951 the KPA/CPVA proposed armistice supervision outside the DMZ by nations "neutral in the Korean War." The UNC accepted this approach with some modifications, and by March 1952 the two sides had agreed that the Neutral Nations Supervisory Commission (NNSC) should include representatives from Czechoslovakia, Poland, Sweden, and Switzerland. They also settled on procedures for the rotation of military personnel and replacement of worn-out equipment through five ports of entry for each side. The two sides still disagreed on airfield repair, however, as well as on a new KPA/CPVA demand that the Soviet Union be included in the NNSC. Meanwhile, Agenda Item 5, "Recommendations to the Governments Concerned on Each Side," was quickly resolved. On 19 February 1952, the two sides agreed to recommend that the governments concerned convene a political conference within three months after the armistice to address, "the withdrawal of foreign forces from Korea, the peaceful settlement of the Korean question, etc." The concluding "etc." successfully pushed into the future a number of controversial political topics.

The most difficult matter to resolve, and one that deadlocked the talks for eighteen months, was Item 4, "Arrangements Relating to Prisoners of War." Both sides had initially assumed that all prisoners of war (POWs) would be exchanged at the conclusion of an armistice. However, among the prisoners held by the UNC were many former residents of South Korea who had been inducted into the KPA and subsequently captured. The United States agreed with the Republic of Korea (ROK, South Korean) government that these individuals should be allowed to return to their homes in the South. Many of the Chinese soldiers in the CPVA had originally been in the Nationalist Chinese army, and some of these were likely to prefer to go to Taiwan rather than being forced to return to the People's Republic of China (PRC, Communist China). By the time negotiations began on Item 4, the United States had concluded on both humanitarian and propaganda grounds that no prisoner should be forcibly repatriated against his will. The KPA/CPVA rejected this principle but might have been persuaded to accept some type of voluntary repatriation if most of the Chinese POWs had been willing to return to China. When the UNC screened the prisoners in April 1952, however, only 70,000, including 5,100 Chinese, out of over 170,000 prisoners held by the UNC, indicated a desire for repatriation. The KPA/CPVA flatly refused to negotiate on the basis of this low figure.

On 28 April the UNC presented a "package proposal," suggesting that in return for the UNC dropping the airfield repair ban, the KPA/CPVA concede on the issues of USSR membership in the NNSC and voluntary repatriation. The KPA/CPVA accepted the first two proposals, resolving Item 3, but firmly rejected voluntary repatriation except for former residents of South Korea. Voluntary repatriation was now the only issue standing in the way of an armistice. With the talks deadlocked and no resolution in sight, the UNC declared a unilateral recess on 8 October 1952.

Throughout 1952 each side attempted to influence the other by means of political and military action. The United States sought support in the United Nations and tried to find a formula that the Chinese might accept but that still adhered to the principle of voluntary repatriation. The North Koreans and Chinese carried out a propaganda campaign, accusing the United States of conducting germ warfare and challenging both UNC motives on the POW issue and its management of POW camps. The UNC position was weakened by a series of violent uprisings in those camps. Militarily, the UNC stepped up its air campaign and both sides conducted limited ground offensives to improve their positions and to put pressure on their opponents.

During the fall 1952 United Nations General Assembly session, the Indian delegation proposed a resolution suggesting that prisoners not desiring repatriation be put into the hands of a Neutral Nations Repatriation Commission (NNRC). With the British and other Commonwealth countries strongly supporting this approach, the United States reluctantly joined the majority of the General Assembly in voting for the resolution on 3 December. Although the Chinese and the Soviet Union initially rejected the idea, they reversed their position a few months later.

On 28 March the KPA/CPVA accepted an earlier UNC recommendation for an exchange of sick and wounded prisoners. In a speech two days later, Chinese Premier Zhou Enlai made a proposal, endorsed by the Democratic People's Republic of Korea (DPRK, North Korea) and the USSR, that prisoners not desiring repatriation be transferred to a neutral state. The exchange of sick and wounded prisoners began on 20 April and the truce talks resumed a week later.

Both sides quickly agreed on the principle of voluntary repatriation and the use of an NNRC chaired by India and consisting of representatives of the same countries that constituted the NNSC. Tough bargaining continued, however, until the UNC presented its "final position" on 25 May 1953. The UNC proposal, which contained some concessions, was that all prisoners would be repatriated within sixty days after the armistice. Those refusing repatriation would then be transferred to the NNRC for ninety days, during which representatives of their home countries would have access to them under NNRC supervision. The postwar

political conference would have thirty additional days to deal with any remaining nonrepatriates, who would then either be released or have their fate decided by the United Nations General Assembly.

Washington followed the 25 May proposal with public and private efforts to persuade the Chinese and North Koreans that if they rejected the proposal, the United States was prepared to widen its military effort, possibly including the use of nuclear weapons. Whether they were persuaded by these threats or were simply satisfied that the UNC had met their requirements, the KPA/CPVA accepted the 25 May proposal on 4 June 1953.

ROK president Syngman Rhee, who had opposed an armistice from the beginning, now made a final effort to derail the agreement. He threatened to fight on alone and on 17 June unilaterally released Korean prisoners from the UNC POW camps. This stalled the truce talks, but after Chinese attacks against ROK Army units nearly destroyed two divisions, and with the promise from the United States of a mutual security treaty and a major aid package, Rhee agreed to adhere to the armistice.

The military commanders of the two sides signed the Armistice Agreement on 27 July 1953. Representatives of the sixteen nations that had provided combat forces to the UNC signed the Joint Policy Declaration in New York City the same day. At 2000 hours, after two and a half years of negotiations, the guns finally fell silent in Korea.

—*Donald W. Boose, Jr.*

References:

Chen, Jian. *Mao's China in the Cold War: Inquiries and Reinterpretations*. Chapel Hill: University of North Carolina Press, in press.

Foot, Rosemary J. *A Substitute for Victory: The Politics of Peacemaking at the Korean Armistice Talks*. Ithaca, NY: Cornell University Press, 1990.

Goodman, Allan E., ed. *Negotiating while Fighting: The Diary of Admiral C. Turner Joy at the Korean Armistice Conference*. Stanford, CA: Hoover Institute Press, 1978.

Hermes, Walter G. *United States Army in the Korean War: Truce Tent and Fighting Front*. Washington, DC: Office of the Chief of Military History, 1966.

U.S. Department of State, Bureau of Public Affairs. *Foreign Relations of the United States, 1951*. Vol. 7, *China and Korea*. Washington, DC: U.S. Government Printing Office, 1983.

———. *Foreign Relations of the United States, 1952–1954*. Vol. 15, *Korea*. Washington, DC: U.S. Government Printing Office, 1984.

See also: Armistice Agreement; BIG SWITCH/LITTLE SWITCH, Operations; Civilian Internee Issue; Demilitarized Zone (DMZ); Joy, Charles Turner; Kaesŏng Bombing Proposal; Kaesŏng Truce Talks; Military Armistice Commission; Nam Il; Neutral Nations Repatriation Commission; Neutral Nations Supervisory Commission (NNSC); P'anmunjŏm Security Agreement; Prisoners of War, Rescreening of; Repatriation, Voluntary; SCATTER, Operation.

Partridge, Earle Everard
(1900–1990)

U.S. Air Force general and commander of the Fifth Air Force in Japan and Korea, 1948–1951. During the remainder of the Korean War he headed the Air Force Research and Development Command.

Born in Winchendon, Massachusetts, on 7 July 1900, after service in the U.S. Army in World War I, Partridge studied one year at Norwich University before attending the United States Military Academy at West Point. He graduated from West Point in 1924 and was commissioned in the Army Air Service. Subsequent assignments included flying instructor and service in observation and pursuit squadrons. Partridge also advanced his professional education in the late 1930s with study at the Air Corps Tactical School and the Command and General Staff School. During World War II Partridge rose to be chief of staff of the 12th Bomber Command in North Africa and then of the Fifteenth Air Force in Italy. In June 1944 Partridge commanded the 3d Bombardment Division in Britain and later commanded the Eighth Air Force there.

In 1948 Partridge became commander of the Fifth Air Force in Japan. After the Korean People's Army (KPA, North Korea) invaded South Korea on 25 June 1950, General Douglas MacArthur ordered Partridge, acting commander of the Far East Air Forces, to evacuate Americans from Korea, attack North Korean invasion forces, and to resupply Republic of Korea (ROK) forces. Major General Partridge thus led the air force into the Korean War.

Initially the U.S. Air Force operated under very difficult conditions and Partridge contributed greatly to the September rout of KPA forces. His Fifth Air Force was a tactical unit and executed missions of close air support (CAS), interdiction, air superiority, and reconnaissance. Partridge located his headquarters next to Eighth Army headquarters, and he and Lieutenant General Walton H. Walker established a close working relationship. Partridge served frequently as Walker's liaison pilot in a T-6.

Partridge soon discovered that his F-80 jets based in Japan did not have the range to remain long over targets in Korea, despite the addition of larger wing full tanks. The F-80s could not operate from the primitive fields in Korea, so he converted six squadrons to old propeller-driven F-51s operating from dirt strips. Flying both from Japan and Korea, his squadrons devastated KPA forces and helped prevent the destruction of the Eighth Army. In July his aircraft destroyed many Communist planes, establishing air superiority over all Korea. His planes also destroyed railroad and highway bridges in July and August to interdict resupply to KPA forces along the Pusan perimeter opposite the Eighth Army and to isolate the Inch'ŏn invasion site. Lacking sufficient numbers of forward air controllers for CAS, Partridge developed "Mosquito" flights of T-6s to direct air strikes.

In July and August Partridge tried to coordinate navy and Marine CAS in support of the Eighth Army. The Marines coordinated their CAS attacks with the air force, and the navy tried to, but launchings at sea were dependent on weather. Carriers also launched too many aircraft at once, and the air force lacked the controllers to put them on targets when they arrived over the battlefield. The navy thereupon moved its carriers farther north along the west coast of Korea to launch interdiction strikes. Later they acted independently on the east coast.

After the Inch'ŏn landing, when the Eighth Army invaded North Korea, Partridge's planes blasted a path for it. His provision of CAS was made easier in October when the Eighth Army received sufficient numbers of radios to open a strike-request network. Partridge also supplied forward air controllers to every army unit down to regimental size. North Korean resistance had almost ceased when on 1 November 1950 Partridge received a shock: fast Chinese MiG-15 jets operating from Manchuria attacked his F-51s, and his F-51s and F-80s could not match the MiGs in speed. But in December Partridge received higher performance F-84 and F-86 jets that prevented the MiGs from attacking Eighth Army troops.

As the Eighth Army and X Corps withdrew before the Chinese onslaught, Partridge exerted every effort to provide air support. His most important mission was CAS, dropping proximity-fused bombs and napalm on the Chinese. A new CAS technique utilizing flares enabled B-26s to attack at night. As a result, Chinese troops, who tended to remain concealed during the day and move at night, were caught in the open and mauled.

As United Nations Command forces fell back, Partridge evacuated airfields at P'yŏngyang and elsewhere in the north, falling back on Suwŏn, Taegu, Pusan, and Japan.

In early 1951 Partridge's airmen discovered that the Chinese were improving airfields in northwest North Korea, an area called MiG Alley. The Chinese intended to move fighter-bombers to these fields to support a spring ground offensive, and Partridge ordered the fields repeatedly bombed to prevent their use. This campaign was successful, and the Chinese gave up their effort in July 1951. The Chinese spring offensive thus had no air support, and the attackers on the ground were slaughtered by artillery and Fifth Air Force bombs.

When Partridge departed Japan in the summer of 1951, his command had made substantial contributions to saving South Korea from North Korean domination. In his new assignment as head of the Research and Development Command, Partridge focused on improving weapons used by airmen in Korea. One of his achievements was increasing the speed of the F-86 to make it more competitive with Chinese MiG-15s. During 1954–1955, Partridge returned to Japan as commander of Far East Air Forces. After serving as chief of Continental Air Defense Command from 1955 to 1959, he retired from the air force. In 1960 he became a trustee of Aerospace Corporation. Partridge died on 7 September 1990.

—John L. Bell

References:

Appleman, Roy E. *South to the Naktong, North to the Yalu.* Washington, DC: Office of the Chief of Military History, 1961.

Candee, Marjorie Dent, ed. *Current Biography.* New York: H. W. Wilson, 1955.

Futrell, Robert F. *The United States Air Force in Korea, 1950–1953.* Rev. ed. Washington, DC: Office of the Chief of Air Force History, 1983.

Partridge, Earle E. *Air Interdiction in World War II, Korea, and Vietnam: An Interview with Earle E. Partridge, Jacob E. Smart, and John W. Vogt.* Washington, DC. Office of Air Force History, U.S. Air Force, 1986.

See also: MacArthur, Douglas; United States Air Force (USAF); Walker, Walton Harris.

Pearson, Lester B.
(1897–1972)

Canadian secretary of state for external affairs during the Korean War. Born in Newtonbrook, Ontario on 23 April 1897, Lester B. Pearson began his professional career as a history professor but soon moved into the Canadian diplomatic service. He was appointed first secretary to the Canadian High Commission in London in 1935, then to Canada's legation in Washington, D.C., in 1942. Pearson became Canadian ambassador to the United States in 1945 and, the following year, deputy minister for external affairs in Ottawa. In 1948 he ran for, and won, a seat in the Canadian House of Commons and a place in Prime Minister Louis St. Laurent's cabinet as secretary of state for external affairs. This was the position that he held when the Korean War broke out.

The invasion of the Republic of Korea (ROK, South Korea) by the Democratic People's Republic of Korea (DPRK, North Korea) had surprised Pearson, as had the United States' decision to become militarily involved in the war. However, he soon realized the need for Canadian participation in the United Nations (UN) force to be sent to Korea. Not only was he an ardent believer in collective security, but he also knew that Canada must participate if it was to have any influence in the operation. As the war evolved, Pearson became one of its most active diplomatic forces, especially in the UN, where he often headed the Canadian delegation. He was

particularly important as president of the General Assembly during the crucial last phase of the war in 1952–1953, and he was heavily involved in attempting to influence the United States, which provided the lion's share of the troops of the United Nations Command.

Pearson and the Canadian government doubted the wisdom of having any involvement in Asia, believing that the focus of the Cold War lay in Western Europe and involved the North Atlantic Treaty Organization (NATO). However, if the battle against communism was to be fought in a limited way in Korea, then it would have to be under the UN umbrella. In addition, the Canadians saw the UN as a forum to influence U.S. policies, a view shared by the British and some other nations. Pearson used the UN to present a Canadian perspective of the Korean War, one that was limited and moderate in geographical extent, in strategy, and in ultimate goals. Because of Pearson's activities in brokering UN policies on Korea, Washington sometimes saw him as either a nuisance or a counterproductive agent who seemed to work against the interests of the United States. Yet Pearson repeatedly emphasized his government's basic agreement with U.S. policy and its commitment to contain Communist expansion. More than once he warned the Soviet Union not to assume that there was any breach in fundamental beliefs between the United States and Canada, and he insisted that Canada was still America's closest friend and staunchest ally.

The balancing act that Pearson tried to perform involved molding and restraining U.S. positions informally and discreetly. This was the quiet diplomacy of cajoling and prodding the United States into what Pearson and the Canadian leadership believed were more moderate policies toward the war. If this type of diplomacy failed, then the Canadians had to determine how important a specific issue was and whether it was worth publicly criticizing the Americans for it. On occasion, in a number of speeches to various groups, Pearson did "go public." This was a tactic guaranteed to infuriate the U.S. State Department.

Some of the issues that concerned Pearson during the war dealt with specific military strategy. For instance, the Canadian government did not want a widened war. Of primary concern was the possibility of doing anything that could bring the People's Republic of China into the conflict. Because of that, General Douglas MacArthur's rhetoric and actions were often viewed with suspicion or even outright alarm. Canada agreed with the decision to have UN forces move across the 38th parallel into North Korea, but only with great reluctance. Pearson believed that this act was done more to fulfill U.S. foreign policy goals than to enforce UN resolutions that called only for a restoration of the prewar status quo. Any talk of coming close to the Chinese border or of bombing Chinese bases or pursuing Communist planes into Chinese airspace was not supported by Canada. Pearson was one of a number of Western leaders who was vocal in questioning MacArthur's role and who applauded his eventual dismissal.

Pearson was part of the UN Cease-fire Group that in late December 1950 tried to explore ways to end the fighting. On this issue he tended to agree more with the U.S. position of wanting a cease-fire on the battlefield before any substantive issues could be discussed. He and St. Laurent worked diligently with the Indian government to work out a compromise over the prisoner-of-war (POW) repatriation dispute, in this case breaking with the U.S. State Department and causing a good deal of hard feelings in Washington. Pearson was also associated with the unsuccessful attempt to block a U.S.-sponsored UN condemnation of the Chinese as aggressors. He eventually voted with the U.S. on this resolution but still believed it to be an unwise step in the process of ending the war. In the spring of 1952, Pearson was openly upset over the use of Canadian troops, without prior consultation, to help guard rebellious prisoners on Kŏje-do, an island POW camp where the U.S. administration had failed badly at keeping order.

Pearson continued on at External Affairs after the war and in 1956 helped arrange a solution to the Suez crisis, for which he received the Nobel Peace Prize in 1957. In 1958 he succeeded St. Laurent as leader of the Liberal Party, and in 1963 and 1965 became prime minister in minority governments. In that office he once more was critical of U.S. Asian policy, this time in Vietnam. Pearson retired from public life in 1967 and died in Ottawa on 27 December 1972.

—*Eric Jarvis*

References:

Granatstein, J. L., and Norman Hillmer. *For Better or for Worse, Canada and the United States to the 1990s.* Toronto: Copp Clark Pitman, 1991.

Melady, John. *Korea: Canada's Forgotten War.* Toronto: Macmillan, 1983.

Stairs, Denis. *The Diplomacy of Constraint: Canada, the Korean War, and the United States.* Toronto: University of Toronto Press, 1974.

Stueck, William W., Jr. *The Korean War: An International History.* Princeton, NJ: Princeton University Press, 1995.

See also: Canada; Cease-Fire Negotiations; Kŏje-do Prisoner-of-War Uprising; MacArthur, Douglas; NATO (North Atlantic Treaty Organization); Repatriation, Voluntary; St. Laurent, Louis S.; 38th parallel, Decision to Cross; United Nations Cease-Fire Group; Wrong, Humphrey Hume.

Peng Dehuai (Peng Te-huai)
(1898–1974)

Commander of the Chinese People's Volunteer Army (CPVA) during the Korean War. Born in Wushi

Village, Xiangtan County, Hunan Province, China in 1898, Peng Dehuai secretly joined the Chinese Communist Party (CCP) in early 1928. During the Long March (1935) he became one of Mao Zedong's closest lieutenants, after Lin Biao. Peng was appointed vice-commander of the army under Zhu De in April 1937.

Peng's record as a military commander up until the end of the Civil War was spotty. Of twenty-nine battles he personally directed until 1949, he had fifteen victories and fourteen defeats. He fought best when fighting for survival. He was less successful fighting offensively, but he was an effective tactician and campaigner.

During the Chinese Civil War (1945–1949) Peng did not build a group of loyal supporters. He commanded the Eighth Route Army from 1937 to 1946, but had no troops under his direct command. At the time of the outbreak of the Korean War, Peng was in northwest China (Xinjiang Province) consolidating CCP control. During the war he retained his posts as the deputy commander in chief of the People's Liberation Army (PLA) and commander of the First Field Army.

Peng commanded Chinese forces from October 1950 to 5 September 1954. This information from recently released Chinese records differs with U.S. military assessments during the Korean War that had Peng replacing Lin Biao (commander, Fourth Field Army) as commander in January 1950 or February 1951. Peng arrived in northeast China on 4 September 1950, to lead the intervention forces. He was officially named commander on 8 October 1950, the same day the CPVA was ordered "to march speedily to Korea."

On 10 October 1950, Peng cabled Mao Zedong informing him that, contrary to Peng's original plan to send only two corps and two artillery divisions across the Yalu River, he now intended "to mass all forces south of the Yalu in case bridges are blown." Mao agreed with this plan, and on 13 October 1950, the Central Military Commission formally sanctioned sending Chinese troops into Korea.

Peng's forces began crossing the Yalu River on 19 October, and on the 25th the CPVA had its first exchange of fire with U.S. forces. From October 1950 to June 1951 the Chinese fought five major "counterattacks" under Peng's direction, albeit with detailed guidance from the General Staff (*Nie Rongzhen*), Zhou Enlai, and Mao in Beijing. Zhou provided detailed guidance of all logistics operations and daily operations.

Peng initially attacked along the whole front in a series of three campaigns: 25 October to 1 November 1950; mid-November 1950 to 12 December 1950; and 30 December 1950 to 11 January 1951. During late November or early December 1950, Mao Zedong's only son, Mao Anying, who served as a Russian-language interpreter, died during a U.S. air attack on Peng's headquarters. Peng, who had been entrusted to protect Anying, blamed himself for his death.

During the Fourth Campaign, 25 January to March 1951, the Chinese offensive broke down south and southeast of Seoul, and Li Tianyu was forced to evacuate Seoul on 14 March. On 22 April Peng launched the Fifth Campaign with the aim of retaking Seoul, but U.S. forces under Lieutenant General James A. Van Fleet broke the Chinese offensive north of Seoul. By 21 May 1951, the front line was at a standstill.

In July 1951 armistice negotiations began at Kaesŏng. Between May and July 1953 Peng launched a series of offensives against Old Baldy and Pork Chop Hill. On 11 July 1953, Chinese and North Korean forces launched a massive five-corps offensive against the Republic of Korea Army Corps. The U.S. 3d Division counterattacked, ending major Communist forces' hostilities for the remainder of the war. Peng then concentrated on building elaborate defensive positions for what he later styled an "active defense in positional warfare."

On 27 July 1953, Peng signed the Armistice Agreement worked out at P'anmunjŏm. Kim Il Sung awarded him the National Flag Order of Merit, First Class, and conferred on him the title "Hero of the Korean Democratic People's Republic" on 31 July 1953. Peng left North Korea on 11 August 1953, returning to a hero's welcome in Tiananmen Square in Beijing. He resigned as the CPVA commander on 5 September 1954. Yang Dechi of the North China (Fifth) Field Army assumed command in 1954.

Peng viewed the Korean War more as a strategic than an operational success. In his memoirs he wrote, "signing the armistice, I thought that the war had set a precedent for many years to come—something the people could rejoice in." But Peng continued, "tactically the war revealed to the PLA's leaders just how weak their forces were and just how thin the line that separated success from failure. The victory had been nearly pyrrhic in nature."

The Korean War experience convinced Peng that the PLA needed to modernize its forces for conventional warfare. He placed priority on military training over politics and stressed the importance of modern equipment, professionalism, and new technology to support modern warfare. Following Korea, Peng turned to the Soviet Union to provide a model for modernization and professionalism.

Appointed minister of defense at the First National People's Congress on 28 September 1954, on 1 October Peng initiated a program for modernization of the PLA when he issued Order No. 1, which required the PLA to study the Soviets, grasp modern warfare,

obey orders, and honor discipline. He initiated further reforms (the Four Great Systems) in 1955. On 27 September 1955, Peng was named one of ten marshals of the PLA.

Mao Zedong dismissed Peng from all posts on 17 September 1959, accusing him of leading an "anti-Party clique." At the beginning of the Cultural Revolution (1966–1976) Peng was arrested and brought to Beijing, where he was publicly criticized between January and February 1967. He was imprisoned in April 1967 and later tortured. In 1974, when he fell seriously ill, Mao ordered that Peng receive no medical care. He died on 29 November 1974.

Peng was posthumously rehabilitated as a "a great revolutionary fighter and loyal member of the Party" at the Third Plenum of the Eleventh CCP in 1978.

—*Susan M. Puska*

References:

Domes, Jurgen. *Peng Te-huai, The Man and the Image.* Stanford, CA: Stanford University Press, 1985.

Peng Dehuai. *Memoirs of a Chinese Marshal: The Autobiographical Notes of Peng Dehuai (1989–1974).* Beijing: Foreign Language Press, 1984.

Whitson, William W., with Chen-Hsia Huang. *The Chinese High Command: A History of Communist Military Politics, 1927–71.* New York: Praeger, 1973.

Wilhelm, Alfred D. *The Chinese at the Negotiating Table: Style and Characteristics.* Washington, DC: National Defense University Press, 1994.

See also: China, People's Republic of: Army; Deng Hua (Teng Hua); Gao Gang (Kao Kang); Mao Zedong; Van Fleet, James Alward; Xie Fang (Hsieh Fang); Zhou Enlai.

Peruvian Prisoner-of-War Settlement Proposal

Unimplemented United Nations (UN) resolution aimed at resolving issue of repatriation of prisoners of war (POWs). As armistice negotiations stalled, the main issue increasingly revolved around the question of repatriation of POWs. The United States was pressing for voluntary repatriation of prisoners, while the People's Republic of China (PRC, Communist China) and the Democratic People's Republic of Korea (DPRK, North Korea) insisted on a forced repatriation of all prisoners. The U.S. view had been shaped by the unfortunate results of forced repatriation after World War II as well as the composition and numbers of prisoners held by the UN Command. The PRC and DPRK were alarmed by the propaganda implications of the large numbers of their soldiers that the UN Command claimed did not want to be repatriated.

The continuing impasse over repatriation produced a suspension in armistice talks in October 1952 and led to a number of offers of mediation by different countries, as well as proposals in the UN General Assembly—meeting that same month—to deal with the problem. One of the proposals for settling the

POW controversy came from Peru, which submitted its proposition to the UN General Assembly on 3 November 1952. The centerpiece of the Peruvian plan was voluntary repatriation. The proposal called for the creation of a commission composed of representatives from the principal combatant nations as well as two representatives selected by the General Assembly. One neutral country not a member of the UN would also be invited to have a representative on the commission who would serve as its chair. The commission would preside over the immediate return of all prisoners who "freely expressed" a wish to be repatriated. Prisoners who declined repatriation would be located in a "neutralized zone"—neutral nations or UN Trust Territories—until a final agreement could be reached concerning their disposition. The UN never acted on the proposal, which was publicly rejected by the Soviet Union at the UN on 10 November 1952.

Although the Peruvian proposal was never implemented and had a brief diplomatic life span, it did help push forward a resolution of the repatriation issue. The United States was uneasy over the proposal's vagueness about treatment of those who refused repatriation, but U.S. diplomats frequently referred to the proposal in their discussions concerning an acceptable solution to the problem. U.S. Secretary of State Dean Acheson asked the Peruvian delegation to the UN to defer action on their proposal until the General Assembly considered a proposal from India dealing with repatriation. The Assembly approved the Indian proposal, and the Peruvian proposal, no longer needed, was never submitted to a vote. The Indian delegation admitted that their plan had been influenced by the Peruvian proposal and by another proposal put forward by the Mexican delegation.

The Peruvian POW proposal represented a long-standing interest of Latin American nations in mediating between the superpowers. In the context of the Korean War, it also demonstrated the general diplomatic support on most issues that the United States enjoyed among Latin American nations. On the specific issue of prisoners of war, the proposal incorporated the most important point sought by the United States—no forced repatriation of prisoners.

—*Don M. Coerver*

References:
Houston, John A. *Latin America in the United Nations.* New York: Carnegie Endowment for International Peace, 1956.
Stueck, William W., Jr. *The Korean War: An International History.* Princeton, NJ: Princeton University Press, 1995.
U.S. Department of State, Bureau of Public Affairs. *Foreign Relations of the United States, 1952–1954*, Vol. 15, Part I. Washington, DC: U.S. Government Printing Office, 1984.
See also: Acheson, Dean Goodersham; Armistice Agreement; India; Latin America; Mexico; Padilla Nervo, Luis; P'anmunjŏm Truce Talks; Repatriation, Voluntary.

Philippines

Philippine interest in Korea was marked by various diplomatic initiatives before 1950. Its United Nations (UN) delegation endorsed a resolution passed on 14 November 1947 creating the UN Temporary Commission on Korea (UNTCOK), a body designed to oversee Korean elections. The UN General Assembly agreed, on U.S. recommendation, that Manila should participate in UNTCOK. Filipino president Manuel Roxas assigned Senator Melecio Arranz, and then replaced him with Rufino Luna, as envoy to the commission. Luna supported an Interim Committee resolution of 26 February 1948 for elections in sections of Korea accessible to UNTCOK. According to Luna, an independent and unified Korea were the aims of the pending election. Roxas favored noninvolvement in Korea's domestic matters and a negotiated unity by Koreans themselves.

The Philippines participated in additional UN agencies regarding the peninsula, such as the Commission on Korea (a follow-up to UNTCOK), the Additional Measures Committee, and the Commission on Unification and Rehabilitation of Korea.

Within UNTCOK the Philippine government encouraged U.S. efforts to recognize the Republic of Korea (ROK, South Korea). Manila tendered diplomatic acknowledgment on 22 August 1948, seven days after Syngman Rhee's inauguration, but waited until February 1953 to institute official ties. The next year Rhee considered a pacific security pact, an idea promoted by Philippines president Elpidio Quirino. Despite the fact that the idea originated from Thomas H. Lockett (an officer in the U.S. embassy in Manila) and Philippine interest, as reflected in a meeting between Quirino and the Republic of China's Jiang Jieshi (Chiang Kai-shek), the United States objected and the proposition languished.

Once war began in June 1950, the Philippines, after briefly considering neutrality, endorsed the U.S. decision to stand behind the ROK. Now the recipient of increased U.S. military aid, the Quirino administration weighed the extent of Philippine entanglement. Since the General Military Council and opposition Nationalist party resisted the employment of Filipinos beyond the homeland, Quirino pondered the use of volunteers or American-outfitted units.

At first Quirino limited Manila's contribution to the sending of material goods. But Philippine Foreign Minister Carlos Romulo and Filipino ambassador to the United States Joaquin Elizalde favored a troop commitment and labored to surmount the military and political obstacles. Before committees of the Philippine senate, Romulo argued that a troubled Korea's proximity meant repercussions for the archipelago and reasoned that the national constitution's repudiation of war still permitted military intervention. On 10 August the Philippine house approved a proposal to give "every possible assistance," and President Quirino initially gave a 5,000-man regimental combat team to the UN Command (UNC). Senator Claro Recto, an advocate of an independent policy that shunned loyalty to the United States, scorned the decision.

The leading Philippine contingent reached Korea by 19 September 1950, with four battalions of combat units alternating in and out during the war. Early arrivals were provisioned from mutual security moneys allotted to Manila, with later equipment provided on a repay arrangement through the U.S. Eighth Army. Notwithstanding morale difficulties owing to cold weather and operational conditions, Filipino soldiers performed with merit. Some took part in Operation KILLER, begun on 21 February 1951, in which UNC and South Korean forces regained lost ground and advanced toward the Han River. A general retreat of UNC forces saw many Filipino troops taken prisoner. Despite two years of confinement and brainwashing, none of the Filipino prisoners of war became Communists.

Although Philippine authorities supported the U.S. Korean policy, the Manila press defended General Douglas MacArthur after his dismissal. President Quirino asked him to make a stopover, but Ambassador Elizalde warned about partiality in the controversy. Meanwhile, the Philippines endorsed UN resolutions concerning the means of Korean unification; the establishment of a cease-fire; condemnation of, and sanctions against, the People's Republic of China (PRC, Communist China); and an accounting of enemy atrocities against war prisoners. Manila backed the 1953 truce and participated in an Asian conference on Korea the next year.

—*Rodney J. Ross*

References:

Dobbs, Charles M. *The Unwanted Symbol: American Foreign Policy, the Cold War, and Korea, 1945–1950.* Kent, OH: Kent State University Press, 1981.

Meyer, Milton Walter. *A Diplomatic History of the Philippine Republic.* Honolulu: University of Hawaii Press, 1965.

Stueck, William W., Jr. *The Korean War: An International History.* Princeton, NJ: Princeton University Press, 1995.

See also: Jiang Jieshi (Chiang Kai-shek); KILLER, Operation; Syngman Rhee; United Nations Additional Measures Committee; United Nations Commission for the Unification and Rehabilitation of Korea.

PILEDRIVER, Operation
(1–13 June 1951)

Last United Nations Command (UNC) offensive of the Korean War, before the settling down of lines just north of the 38th parallel. On 27 May 1951 Eighth Army commander Lieutenant General James A. Van Fleet issued Operational Order PILEDRIVER, directing the Eighth Army to attack into the "Iron Triangle," an area (P'yŏnggang in the north, Ch'ŏrwŏn in the west, and Kimhwa in the east) just north of the 38th parallel, roughly in the center of the Korean peninsula that witnessed some of the fiercest fighting of the entire conflict. The purpose of the offensive was to solidify the UNC position along the Kansas-Wyoming Line.

The operation called for I Corps to drive to the areas bounded by Ch'ŏrwŏn and Kimhwa, IX Corps to seize the area from Hwach'ŏn north to Samyang-ni, and X Corps to attack north from the east side of the reservoir and, with the Republic of Korea Army (ROKA) I Corps, to seize the area to Kŏjin-ni on the east coast, cleaning out the Punchbowl north of Sŏhwa, another fortified zone that Communist forces had previously used as a springboard for their offensives.

Van Fleet, believing that Communist forces were severely weakened and that a continuation of the UN attack north could destroy them, expected rapid progress. When the operation commenced on 3 June, however, UN forces immediately hit unexpected stiff resistance, particularly in the I Corps sector. In moving forward, the 1st Cavalry Division encountered three lines of Communist defenses in the Yŏnch'ŏn area. At the same time, the 3d Division, attacking north toward Ch'ŏrwŏn, met heavy resistance and was hit by a vicious Chinese counterattack; one of its battalions was driven back across the Hant'an River. The 25th Division was also held up by tenacious Chinese troops defending the high ground on its objective.

The next day Lieutenant General Edward M. Almond's X Corps on the right flank resumed its attack toward the Punchbowl. For five days the battle raged. So little progress was made that the 7th Marines, on reserve after their rugged battle on the ridge, were sent to the front with the 1st Marines on their right and the ROK Marines on their left. At 0200 on the 11th the ROK Marines took their North Korean foes completely by surprise in a night attack, resulting in wholesale slaughter. This victory allowed them to advance to the Punchbowl.

By 10 June, aided by round-the-clock close air support, the 3d Division, the ROKA 9th Division, and the 10th Philippine Battalion had gained the high ground south of Ch'ŏrwŏn at the western foot of the triangle base, while the 25th Division and the Turkish Brigade fought to within three miles of Kimhwa. The next day the Communists abandoned Ch'ŏrwŏn and Kimhwa, and on 13 June two tank-infantry task forces, one from Ch'ŏrwŏn and the other from Kimhwa, entered the abandoned ruins of P'yŏnggang, the apex of the triangle, and found it, too, deserted. However, UN forces discovered that the Communists were positioned in strength on the high ground north of P'yŏnggang, and I Corps forces subsequently withdrew.

Units of IX Corps also pushed northeast from Kimhwa toward Kŭmsŏng and likewise found the line heavily occupied by Communist troops, who were in the process of establishing a strong defensive line. These UN units also pulled back to Kimhwa.

Because the Iron Triangle was dominated by surrounding heights, neither side attempted thereafter to hold the low ground in strength, though Chinese troops struck back on 17 June and recaptured P'yŏnggang.

The significance of Operation PILEDRIVER was twofold. First, it was the last offensive of the Korean conflict before the settling down of lines just north of the 38th parallel. Second, the Iron Triangle from then on would become a kind of a no-man's-land, belonging to neither side.

—James H. Willbanks

References:

Appleman, Roy E. *Ridgway Duels for Korea.* College Station, TX: Texas A&M Press, 1990.

Blair, Clay. *The Forgotten War: America in Korea, 1950–1953.* New York: Times Books, 1987.

Middleton, Harry J. *The Compact History of the Korean War.* New York: Hawthorn Books, 1965.

Rees, David. *Korea: The Limited War.* New York: St. Martin's Press, 1964.

See also: Almond, Edward Mallory; Iron Triangle; Kansas-Wyoming Line; Milburn, Frank William; Punchbowl; Tenth Corps; Van Fleet, James Alward.

Plimsoll, James
(1917–1987)

Australian representative on the United Nations Commission for the Unification and Rehabilitation of Korea (UNCURK), 1950–1952. Born in Sydney on 25 April 1917, James Plimsoll was educated at Sydney High School and the University of Sydney. He spent four years working in the Economics Department of the Bank of New South Wales before joining the Australian army in 1942. In 1945, still in the military, he became a member of the Australian delegation to the Far Eastern Commission (FEC), a post he held for several years. This impelled him to change his career and become a professional diplomat. While on the FEC he indicated to John M. Allison, then chief of the U.S. State Department's Division of Northeast Asian Affairs, that Australians would find a moderate Japanese peace settlement enabling that country to regain its international position far more tolerable if it were coupled with a security pact between Australia and the United States. This was also the position taken by Sir Percy Spender, who became Australia's minister of external affairs shortly afterward.

On 8 October 1950 the United Nations established UNCURK. This came at a time when UN officials optimistically anticipated victory in Korea in the near future but were by no means delighted by the prospect that Syngman Rhee, the autocratic leader of the Republic of Korea (ROK, South Korea), would simply extend his authority over the entire country. UNCURK was a seven-nation body, the representatives of which were expected to arrive in Korea in mid-November. Meanwhile, they were to form an Interim Committee to "assume provisionally all responsibilities" for governing North Korea until arrangements for unifying the country could be finalized. Plimsoll was appointed Australia's representative on UNCURK, and he immediately set to work attempting to draft an acceptable scheme for nationwide elections that would not necessarily result in a government controlled by Rhee, and for interim arrangements that would ensure that the United Nations Command (UNC), not Rhee, governed UN-occupied North Korean territory.

Plimsoll arrived in Korea in late November, by which time Chinese intervention had eradicated prospects of any imminent UN victory. Even so, UNCURK's personnel remained in Korea, despite the dilution of their authority when the UN subsequently established both the UN Ceasefire Group and the UN Korean Reconstruction Agency. One major reason for this continued presence in Korea was the fact that the fairly youthful and inexperienced Plimsoll swiftly found himself on a personal footing with the elderly and intractable Rhee. This enabled him to exert a certain moderating influence on the authoritarian leader's policies. Plimsoll was heavily involved in UNCURK's efforts to restrain the ROK police and prison authorities. Plimsoll cooperated closely with U.S. Ambassador John J. Muccio in these efforts, a relationship that helped to reinforce the developing Australian-American alliance. U.S. officials, appreciative of Plimsoll's role, strongly resisted his government's attempts to assign him to other duties and insisted that he remain in Korea. They argued that only by staffing UNCURK with representatives of Plimsoll's high caliber could it win respect and acceptance.

The climax of Plimsoll's service on UNCURK came in the South Korean political crisis of mid-1952 after Rhee declared martial law and arrested opposition members of the National Assembly so as to force the passage of a constitutional amendment likely to win him a third term as president. In a personal interview with Rhee, Plimsoll warned him that his behavior had shocked other countries throughout the world and that it would jeopardize continuing UN support for the ROK. Plimsoll subsequently served as an important intermediary in Western negotiations with Rhee, although the stubborn president effectively came through this crisis victorious, obtaining the constitutional amendment he sought and winning a landslide electoral triumph in August.

In late 1952, when an armistice in Korea seemed imminent and the victory of Dwight D. Eisenhower in the U.S. presidential elections was about to remove many of Plimsoll's most fervent American admirers, the Australian government finally recalled him to Canberra to be assistant secretary of the Department of External Affairs. In his later career he would serve with distinction as secretary of the department, as ambassador to Washington, Moscow, and Tokyo, and as high commissioner in London. In 1982 Plimsoll was appointed governor of Tasmania. He died at Government House, Hobart, on 8 May 1987.

—*Priscilla Roberts*

References:

Luard, Evan. *A History of the United Nations.* Vol. 1, *The Years of Western Domination, 1945–1955.* London: Macmillan, 1982.

O'Neill, Robert J. *Australia in the Korean War, 1950–1953.* 2 vols. Canberra: Australian War Memorial/Australian Government Publication Service, 1981, 1985.

Stueck, William W., Jr. *The Korean War: An International History.* Princeton, NJ: Princeton University Press, 1995.

Yoo, Tae-Ho. *The Korean War and the United Nations.* Louvain, Belgium: Librairie Desbarax, 1964.

See also: Eisenhower, Dwight D.; Muccio, John J.; Syngman Rhee; United Nations Commission for the Unification and Rehabilitation of Korea.

Poetry of the Korean War

As is true of the literature in general, the Korean War did not produce a vast outpouring of poetry comparable to the wars that came immediately before and after it. Nevertheless, though small, a powerful body of poetry does exist, almost none of which has received any attention to speak of, undoubtedly for the same complex reasons the Korean War itself has been ignored or shortchanged both historically and in American popular culture. Four poets, in particular, deserve consideration: William Childress, Rolando Hinojosa, William Wantling, and Keith Wilson.

Born in Hugo, Oklahoma, in 1933, William Childress grew up in a family of sharecroppers and migrant cotton pickers. He enlisted in the U.S. Army in 1951, serving in Korea during 1952–1953 as a demolition expert and secret courier. After receiving two college degrees, Childress has had a long and varied career as a teacher, editor, and writer. His Korean War experience is reflected in poems appearing in two collections, *Burning the Years* (1971) and *Lobo* (1972), later consolidated into *Burning the Years & Lobo: Poems 1962–1975* (1986).

Interestingly, the Vietnam War seems to have been a catalyst for Childress (as it was for Wilson). While several of his Korean War poems were written before the U.S. buildup in Vietnam, his poems become more pointed, cynical, and bitter as the Sixties—and the Vietnam War—advance. In one of his finest poems, "Korea Bound, 1952," he compares soldiers on a troop ship—ostensibly free men in a democracy—with Pharaoh's slaves, and in the poem's final irony, they sail past Alcatraz Island, then a federal prison, where the prisoners' "lack of freedom guarantees their lives."

Childress writes movingly about the travails of soldiers and the costs of war in poems such as "The Soldiers" and "Shell Shock," and his empathy for comrades is matched by his contempt for the generals who command them. Both "Combat Iambic" and "Death of a General" are scathingly unrelenting, reminiscent of Siegfried Sassoon at his best. And "The Long March," a poem that begins "North from Pusan," concludes, "…the General/camps with the press corps./Any victory will be his./For us there is only/the long march to Viet Nam."

In "The Long March," Childress makes explicit his rising horror at yet another futile and unwinnable Asian war such as his own. And "For My First Son" is as bitter as bitter gets. After enumerating the "future of steel" toward which his son's "tiny fingers grope"—a flamethrower's blast, trenchfoot, worms, gangrene, shrapnel, empty eyes—Childress concludes, "…these are/the gifts of male birthdays,/the power and glory, and/the lies of leaders send them."

Born in Mercedes, Texas in 1929 of mixed Chicano-Anglo parents, Rolando Hinojosa served two years in the U.S. Army immediately after World War II, then was recalled in 1949, fighting in Korea as a tanker. After the war, he went on to successful simultaneous careers as a university professor and administrator and as a writer. Writing mostly in Spanish, Hinojosa is not well known among English-speaking readers, but in the Spanish-speaking community in the United States, Latin America, and Europe, he has a large following. Many of his characters are Korean War veterans, including his recurring protagonist Rafe Buenrostro, and both *Korean Love Songs*, a 1978 novel-in-verse, and his 1993 novel *The Useless Servants* deal with the war directly.

Korean Love Songs differs from most of Hinojosa's work in two ways: it is in verse and in English. "I had originally tried to write about Korea in Spanish," he explains, "but that experience wasn't lived in Spanish." The narrator of the thirty-eight-poem sequence is Buenrostro, and the action moves from Pusan to North Korea, then south again with the Chinese in pursuit, and finally north once more to the 38th parallel. The sequence forms a narrative whole, with each poem serving as a chapter in the story.

While Anglo-Chicano conflict—a major thread in most of Hinojosa's writing—is present here, the main focus of the book is on the war itself, its ugly reality and terrible cost. "Christ,/What am I doing here?" asks Buenrostro in "Incoming," while in "A Matter of Supplies" he seems to answer himself, "It comes down to this: we're pieces of equipment/To be counted and signed for./On the occasion some of us break down,/And the parts which can't be salvaged/Are replaced with other GI parts, that's all." Hinojosa, who arrived in Korea on 3 July 1950, only eight days after the North Korean attack, makes the turbulent first year of the war come alive.

William Wantling was born in 1933 in what is now East Peoria, Illinois. He volunteered for the marines in 1952 and served in Korea in 1953. In 1958, he ran afoul of the law—probably for narcotics possession, though the record is not clear—and served over five years in San Quentin, where he first began to write poetry. After his release, he earned B.A. and M.A. degrees from Illinois State University but continued to struggle with drugs and alcohol, leading to repeated scrapes with the law and frequent stays in the mental and drug dependency wards of hospitals in Peoria and Normal. He died in 1974 at the age of forty.

The official cause of death was heart failure, but in truth Wantling seems to have burned the candle at both ends until there was nothing left to burn. His poems are frenetic and boisterous, full of restless energy. He wrote only a handful of poems about the Korean War, but they suggest that what he saw and did there when he was still just a teenager changed his life forever, and not for the better.

"Korea 1953" begins with "endless weeks of zero" and a "lurking bunker on a barren hill" where "murder is sanctioned," and ends with men become "as a pack of maddened dogs." In "The Korean," he exposes the cold-blooded savagery of war, but in "Without Laying Claim" he suggests that while war brutalizes, it cannot fully extinguish conscience. The tension between the rough, hard soldier's exterior necessary to survive the ordeal of war and the innate inclination toward a broader range of human emotions is particularly evident in "I Remember," in which a tough lieutenant has to stare straight up into the sun so his men won't notice that he's crying.

Though Wantling survived the war, he could not escape it. Feelings of guilt and remorse dominate "Sure," while rage is the controlling emotion in "The Day the Dam Burst." But instead of turning that rage outward, as he imagines himself doing in the poem, he turned it inward, and eventually it killed him. Wantling's poems are haunting reminders that the costs of war do not end when the guns fall silent.

Born in Clovis, New Mexico in 1927, Keith Wilson aspired to a career as a naval officer. Graduating from the U.S. Naval Academy in Annapolis, Maryland, he served three tours in Korean waters between 1950 and 1953. At first proud to be part of the United Nations' effort, he came to believe that it was in reality only a fig leaf covering far less altruistic U.S. policy aims. Disillusioned, he left the navy and embarked on a career as a university professor and poet.

Wilson's Korean War experiences provide the foundation for perhaps his most important book. First published in 1969 as *Graves Registry & Other Poems*, it contained poems about the war along with poems about his native American Southwest. Says Wilson, "I started writing *Graves Registry* in the winter of 1966 in anger that my government was again fighting an undeclared war in a situation that I, from my experiences in Korea, knew we could never win."

In 1992 Wilson published an updated edition of the book called simply *Graves Registry* and containing the original Korean War poems, additional poems from his 1972 *Midwatch* (including a number that deal explicitly with the Vietnam War), and fifty newer poems. Taken together, they weave the literary and the political into a single tableau that moves skillfully across time and geography.

Wilson's Korean War poems are not about the big battalions and the pitched battles, but rather coastal operations and guerilla raids, shattered villages, and shattered ideals. They are peopled by Americans, but also by Koreans and Japanese, refugees and cripples, and by warriors, but also and more so by the defenseless and the innocent who always become the wreckage of war. "O, do not dream of peace," he scolds in "Commentary," while "such bodies/line the beaches & dead men float/the seas, waving[.]" As in "December 1952," Wilson's poems force us to confront "the cost of lies, tricks/that blind the eyes of the young. *Freedom./ Death. A Life Safe for*. The Dead." They are his explanation of how he began his life expecting to be a career military officer and ended up becoming a teacher instead.

—W. D. Ehrhart

References:

Ehrhart, W. D. "I Remember: Soldier-Poets of the Korean War." *War Literature & the Arts* 9 no. 2 (Fall/Winter 1997): 1–47.

Kaye, Ian E. *Pick & Shovel Poems*. Ilfracomb: Stockwell, 1979. Reprint, Devon, UK: Stockwell, 1979.

———. *Scallywag Poems*. Devon, UK: Stockwell, 1983.

Pyros, John. *William Wantling: A Biography & Selected Works*. Peoria, IL: Spoon River Poetry Press, 1981.

Saldivar, Jose David, ed. *The Rolando Hinojosa Reader*. Houston: Arte Publico Press, 1985.

See also: Film and Literature of the Korean War.

P'ohang, Battle of
(August–September 1950)

Battle that was part of the Communist plan to take the Pusan perimeter at the beginning of the Korean War. By the end of the summer in 1950 the initial Korean People's Army (KPA, North Korean) thrust to crush the Pusan perimeter had failed. Only in the east had the lines of the perimeter defense changed markedly. There Republic of Korea Army (ROKA) defenses had collapsed against a renewed KPA attack on Y'ŏngdŏk, and the 3d ROKA Division had to be evacuated by sea. The ROKA then went back into action against the KPA, which by this time had moved into the east coast port of P'ohang. ROKA troops retook the town, but with the KPA so close, the U.S. Air Force (USAF) evacuated its nearby base at Yŏnil (USAF Field K-3).

By 15 August the only KPA hope for victory was to launch a massive coordinated offensive around the perimeter before the United Nations forces got any stronger. Two new KPA divisions were brought up for this offensive, making an assault force of thirteen infantry divisions, an armored division, and two armored brigades.

The KPA command ordered its 12th Division to attack through the ROKA 8th Division behind the Yŏngdŏk front and capture P'ohang by 26 July 1950. However, ROKA forces fought tenaciously, and it was the end of July before the KPA reached the outskirts of Andong. The battle for this town consumed five days and resulted in heavy casualties in the KPA divisions, as well as in the defending 8th ROKA Division and the Capital Division, which had come up to assist.

Eighth Army commander Lieutenant General Walton Walker called this attack the "last gasp" of an "over-extended enemy." Nevertheless, it was a very forceful move, and the Pusan perimeter almost cracked in several places. In the east, KPA forces retook P'ohang on 6 September, despite an intense U.S. sea and land bombardment. They continued to push to the south to the outskirts of Kyŏngju, and at Yŏngch'ŏn they cut the lateral road running east from Taegu, thereby threatening this key city from the "back door."

Walker moved up everything he could spare to stop the KPA advance: the 21st Infantry Regiment, units of the 9th Regiment, and finally the 24th Division, whose place along the Naktong River had been taken by the 2d Infantry Division. With this assistance and highly effective support from naval vessels firing from offshore, ROKA forces finally rallied sufficiently to retake some of the lost ground. In the end, however, the KPA offensive in the east collapsed as much from its logistical difficulties as from anything else.

—*James H. Willbanks*

Reference:
Appleman, Roy E. *South to the Naktong, North to the Yalu.* Washington, DC: Office of the Chief of Military History, 1961.
See also: Pusan Perimeter and Breakout; Walker, Walton Harris.

Police Action

Term used by President Harry S. Truman to describe the U.S. military response in the Korean War. Article I,

Section 8, of the U.S. Constitution reserves to the Congress the right to declare war. In this the framers of the constitution sought to place the power to wage war with the people through their elected representatives, as opposed to placing this authority with the executive or with the cabinet, as in the British system.

Truman's action was not unique. Earlier U.S. presidents had temporarily committed U.S. military forces without formal declaration of war, the Barbary Wars and Quasi-War with France being but two examples; but in the case of Korea there was not the excuse of a direct attack on U.S. citizens or their property, and none of the other deployments solely on the basis of presidential authority had been as long term or as costly.

On 27 June 1950, citing the threat posed by international communism and in what he called the most difficult decision of his presidency, Truman committed U.S. forces to the Korean fighting without a congressional vote. Only after the fact did he communicate this decision to his cabinet and to congressional leaders of both parties.

Truman's message to the American people amounted to a declaration of war in which he not only committed U.S. fighting forces to Korea but also announced acceleration of military assistance to France in its war in Indo-China. Truman called his response to the fighting in Korea a "police action," in part because it connoted what he sought: a short and limited action. He also said U.S. forces had merely to defeat "a bandit raid." When pressed on the matter he cited as justification the United Nations (UN) Security Council resolution calling on member states to provide military support to the Republic of Korea (ROK, South Korea).

In effect Truman brought the United States into a war by executive decision through the guise of UN resolutions. The president believed that he had to act quickly, but his decision to proceed on his own vastly increased presidential power and set a precedent that surfaced again during the Vietnam War when President Lyndon B. Johnson used the August 1964 Tonkin Gulf Resolution as justification for waging an undeclared war in Indo-China. Of course, Congress can halt any U.S. military venture simply by cutting off funding, but such action is quite difficult once troops have been committed and American blood has been shed.

—*Spencer C. Tucker*

References:
Javits, Jacob K. *Who Makes War: The President versus the Congress.* New York: William Morrow, 1973.
LaFeber, Walter. *The American Age: United States Foreign Policy at Home and Abroad, 1750 to the Present.* New York: W. W. Norton, 1994.
Truman, Harry S. *Memoirs.* Vol. 2, *Years of Trial and Hope.* Garden City, NY: Doubleday, 1956.
See also: Truman, Harry S.

Pongam-do Prisoner-of-War Uprising
(14 December 1952)

Communist prisoner-of-war (POW) uprising that occurred at United Nations Command (UNC) Camp No. 1C on Pongam-do, a small island west of Kŏje-do, near Pusan, South Korea. The UNC garrison consisted of about 100 U.S. administrative personnel and a Republic of Korea Army (ROKA) security battalion. The camp had two separate areas that housed civilian internees (CIs). These CIs had been inmates of the infamous Compound 62 on Kŏje-do, which had erupted with such violence on 18 February 1952. The POWs had been transferred to Pongam-do in July when the large Kŏje-do compounds were broken up.

Between 7 and 13 December, POW camp authorities intercepted several messages indicating imminent coordinated riots. Concerned that the CIs might break out of their enclosures, the commanding general of the Korean Communication Zone Major General Thomas W. Herren alerted the UNC to his possible need for reinforcements from the Korean mainland. On 12 December, however, he informed the commander in chief of the UNC that he believed no immediate danger of a mass breakout existed and that prisoner plans were not of a nature to warrant additional reinforcements. Meanwhile, the camp commander took the precaution of doubling his alert forces to provide for any contingency.

At noon on Sunday, 14 December 1952, CIs in Enclosure 2 began mass demonstrations in their respective compounds. An estimated 3,600 of some 9,200 prisoners in six of the eight compounds of Enclosure 2 were involved in the riot, but Enclosure 1 was quiet. The prisoners probably had the objective of breaking out of the compounds and capturing UNC personnel to bargain with camp authorities and embarrass the UNC. The instigators also sought to influence negotiations at the truce talks then in progress and provoke world opinion.

Pongam-do was a steep, terraced windswept camp. The approach to the buildings housing the POWs was from below, an aid to prisoners throwing stones and other objects down on the guards. It also inhibited the effective use of such mass control weapons as concussion and tear gas grenades. In any case, at the time of the uprising, the wind was blowing across the steep hill and tear gas could not be used effectively. If this had been possible, the riot quite probably would have been quelled with fewer fatalities.

Orders, warning shots, and riot guns had no effect on the demonstrating POWs. Camp authorities were also inhibited by the limited number of security personnel available. This prevented the simultaneous dispatch of significant numbers to each of the six compounds involved. As a result, almost from the start the camp authorities resorted to machine gun and rifle fire to prevent a mass outbreak. The threat of another Kŏje-do situation conditioned events.

Camp authorities soon quelled the riot, and throughout they maintained uncontested control. In the course of suppressing the demonstrations, however, 85 prisoners were killed and another 113 were wounded. The injured were later moved to the field hospital at nearby Kŏje-do. Two U.S. soldiers and two ROKA soldiers were injured by thrown rocks.

At P'anmunjŏm, Communist truce negotiators condemned the actions by the UNC in suppressing the demonstration, questioning why it was necessary to shoot prisoners shouting slogans and demonstrating. They insisted that the UNC take immediate steps to end such "brutalities." The Soviet Union even submitted to the UN General Assembly on 21 December 1952 a protest over the "mass murder of Korean and Chinese POWs" by U.S. armed forces on Pongam-do.

Although the Soviet UN resolution failed to pass, killings of POWs, no matter how justified, caused the UNC considerable embarrassment. The Pongam-do uprising revealed the need for intensive training for security personnel in riot control and the use of special riot-type weapons. Other incidents at Pongam-do later in December, while on a smaller scale, resulted in the deaths of 14 CIs and injuries to an additional 86.

—*Sunghun Cho*

References:

Cho, Sunghun. "Han'guk Chŏnjaeng Chung UN Kun P'oro Chŏngch'aek e Kwanhan Yŏn'gu" [UN Forces POW policies during the Korean War]. Doctoral dissertation, Academy of Korean Studies, Seoul, 1999. Unpublished manuscript.

Headquarters U.S. Army Pacific. "The Handling of Prisoners of War during the Korean War." 1960. Unpublished document.

See also: Kŏje-do Prisoner-of-War Uprising; Prisoner-of-War Administration United Nations Command.

Pork Chop Hill, Battle of
(23 March–11 July 1953)

Name given to a number of small, violent battles fought during the Korean War on and around the western side of the Korea peninsula near the 38th parallel. Hill 234 became known as Pork Chop Hill because of its shape. The hill was originally taken from the Chinese army by United Nations (UN) forces on 6 June 1952 and was made into a defensive outpost, one of many such positions making up the UN Command (UNC) line. These outposts were located on hills or ridges and were built for all-around defense. It was a system created by the stalemated nature of the war by 1952–1953, which emphasized small group combat fought on a seemingly endless number of hills that crossed the center of the peninsula. Victories in these engagements were used, particularly by the Chinese who usually initiated combat, as propaganda in the long-running peace talks being held at P'anmunjŏm.

In November 1952 Chinese troops attacked Pork Chop Hill, which was successfully defended by a battalion from Thailand. The most serious attempts to capture the hill, however, came in the spring and summer of 1953. On 23 March the Chinese launched simultaneous assaults against Pork Chop Hill and the nearby hill known as Old Baldy. Old Baldy was lost by UNC forces, but a U.S. battalion managed to hang on to a portion of Pork Chop Hill; a counterattack retook all of the hill on 24 March. Eighth Army headquarters then decided to give up Old Baldy, but Pork Chop Hill, which now stuck out into the Communist lines, was maintained as a fortified outpost.

Perhaps the best known of the struggles for the hill began after 2200 on 16 April 1953. By moving swiftly and silently, Chinese troops managed to arrive at Pork Chop Hill practically unobserved and get into the UN defenses. They overwhelmed an understrength U.S. force of only seventy-six men, twenty of whom were strung out in listening posts in front of the hill and five more of whom were on patrol at the time. This patrol was the only group that had seen the oncoming Chinese force, but it had been unable to relay a message back to the men on Pork Chop. In conjunction with a small number of survivors who had eluded the Chinese, attempts were then launched to try to retake the hill starting in the early hours of 17 April and lasting into the next day.

The UNC did not at first realize just how complete the Chinese success had been, and as a result many of the units that moved up the rear of the hill were surprised when they came under Communist fire almost immediately. They were routinely thrown back or soon found themselves cut off and surrounded. Confusion was common at this stage, and one U.S. unit even fired into one of their own companies by mistake. There were also shortages of water and ammunition and a lack of communication with headquarters. During the battle both sides poured unusually heavy artillery barrages onto Pork Chop Hill that had the effect of pinning everyone in their dugouts and battered trenches, preventing either side from advancing successfully.

Throughout the battle, Eighth Army command had to decide how many men it was prepared to lose in order to retake and hold Pork Chop Hill. This was a decision that was dependent on how important it was to prevent the Chinese from flaunting a victory at P'anmunjŏm. In the end, it was determined that the hill must be kept, and a final assault led to the recapture of the heights on 18 April. Sporadic fighting for Pork Chop Hill continued into the summer of 1953.

What finally underlined the futility of the Battle of Pork Chop Hill was the decision later made by high command to give Pork Chop Hill back to the Chinese. The evacuation of the hill took place without difficulty on 11 July, two weeks before the armistice. In a way, Pork Chop Hill symbolized the last two years of the Korean War. It was an example of the hopeless, bloody stalemate into which the war had evolved and it pointed toward the type of limited warfare of the future that both the military and civilians found to be so frustrating during the era of the Cold War. Pork Chop Hill ended up within the demilitarized zone created to separate South and North Korea at the war's conclusion.

—*Eric Jarvis*

References:
Hastings, Max. *The Korean War.* New York: Simon & Schuster, 1987.
Hermes, Walter G. *United States Army in the Korean War: Truce Tent and Fighting Front.* Washington, DC: Office of the Chief of Military History, 1966.
Marshall, S. L. A. *Pork Chop Hill: The American Fighting Man in Action, Korea, Spring 1953.* New York: William Morrow, 1956.
See also: Chinese Military Offensives; Eighth United States Army; Film and Literature of the Korean War; Marshall, Samuel Lyman Atwood; Old Baldy, Battle of; P'anmunjŏm Truce Talks.

Potsdam Conference
(17 July–2 August 1945)

Diplomatic conference at the end of World War II that saw the Soviet Union accede to the principles of the Cairo Declaration and that also discussed the future of Korea.

The Allied talks at Potsdam, in which President Harry S. Truman represented the United States, Josef Stalin represented the Soviet Union, and Winston Churchill represented Great Britain (during the conference Churchill was ousted by British election results; Clement Attlee replaced him), focused on plans for the future of Germany and the Soviet entry in the continuing war in the Pacific. Mention of Korea was brief.

This had not been the intention of either U.S. or Soviet policymakers. Having failed to reach a satisfactory arrangement for the postwar status of Korea at the February 1945 Yalta Conference, U.S. diplomats hoped for further consideration of the subject at Potsdam. State Department officials regarded the Korea peninsula as a strategic area that could not be abandoned to the Soviet Union, and they aimed at a four-power trusteeship leading to the independence of a unified Korean state. China, Great Britain, the USSR, and the United States would share administrative responsibility for the territory until the Korean people were "ready" for independence according to the principles proclaimed in the November 1943 Cairo Declaration. President Franklin D. Roosevelt believed that joint involvement in Korea would force the

Soviets to assume equal responsibility for preserving peace and stability in the region. At the end of May 1945 Stalin informally accepted the administrative scheme during talks with presidential envoy Harry Hopkins as the best solution for Korea. U.S. Ambassador to the Soviet Union W. Averell Harriman confirmed in early July that the Soviets had embraced the proposal after talks with the Chinese and that they looked forward to a detailed examination of the arrangements at Potsdam.

This consultation never took place. When Stalin opened discussion of the trusteeship concept in general on 22 July 1945 with the suggestion that Korea be the first issue, British Prime Minister Churchill immediately turned the conversation to the subject of the Italian colonies in Africa. Churchill accused the Soviets of coveting these territories and using the trusteeship concept to get a foot in the door. The talks then dissolved in a sea of acrimony.

Thereafter, new U.S. president Truman largely avoided the topic of Korea at the conference. U.S. military officials did not regard the Korea peninsula as strategic. Their primary focus was the invasion of the Japanese islands, and they left the planning of the invasion of the Japanese-held Korea peninsula to the Soviets. Loss of territory there was considered a *quid pro quo* for the Soviet commitment to enter the war in the Pacific. The sole U.S. contribution to discussion of Korea at Potsdam was the suggestion, quickly accepted by the Soviets, that the 38th parallel be the dividing line for accepting the Japanese surrender in Korea.

No agreement was reached regarding the future of Korea until the December 1945 meeting in Moscow of the foreign ministers of China, Great Britain, the United States, and the Soviet Union. In the interim the Soviet Union had become an indirect partner to the Cairo Declaration through both the Potsdam Declaration and its entry into the war against Japan. The Korea peninsula had been liberated and occupied by Soviet and U.S. troops north and south of the 38th parallel, respectively. Most important, however, was that the U.S. military and political leadership had revised its assessment of the strategic importance of Korea and the reliability of the Soviet Union as a partner. Whereas U.S. policy toward Korea at Potsdam had been rather hazy and unrealistic, the United States now regarded the area as a test of Soviet ambition. Any diplomatic agreement, therefore, would be effective only insofar as the situation on the ground permitted.

The Moscow Agreements of December 1945 essentially confirmed the Cairo Declaration and the original concept of trusteeship for Korea. Based on a Soviet draft, the accord provided for four-power supervision of a provisional Korean government that would lead to a unified national government. The foreign ministers agreed that the trusteeship would last no more than five years. With American and Soviet troops on the spot, Chinese and British interests now clearly took a back seat to the competing world visions of the United States and the Soviet Union. The detailed arrangements for the joint administration of the Korea peninsula contained in the Moscow Agreements thus came too late. American actions in southern Korea undermined the accord almost immediately.

—*Timothy C. Dowling*

References:

Cumings, Bruce. *The Origins of the Korean War.* Vol. 1, *Liberation and the Emergence of Separate Regimes, 1945–1947.* Princeton, NJ: Princeton University Press, 1981.

Lowe, Peter. *The Origins of the Korean War.* New York: Longman, 1997.

Rhee, T. C. "Four Great Powers and Korean Unification: What Can and Cannot Happen?" In *Korean Unification: New Perspectives and Approaches,* edited by Tae-Hwan Kwak, Ghonghan Kim, and Hong Nack Kim. Seoul: Kyungnam University Press, 1984: 225–250.

See also: Attlee, Clement R; Cairo Declaration; Churchill, Sir Winston Spencer; Cold War, Origins to 1950; Harriman, William Averell; Stalin, Josef; 38th Parallel, Division of Korea at; Truman, Harry S.

Prisoner-of-War Administration, Communist

At the outbreak of the Korean War, Democratic People's Republic of Korea (DPRK, North Korean) and Communist Chinese authorities had not anticipated the capture of large numbers of United Nations Command (UNC) prisoners, ultimately some 90,000 people. The stated Communist policy was humane treatment of prisoners of war (POWs). According to this policy the prisoners' lives would be protected and medical care and treatment would be provided for the sick and wounded. But the lack of preparation stymied whatever good intentions the Communist side might have had regarding POWs. There were no policies as to how POW camps should be operated and there were no proper facilities for handling prisoners. Moreover, POWs came to be regarded as pawns in the ideological struggle.

Conditions in North Korean POW camps underwent three distinct phases: from June to November 1950, when Chinese People's Volunteer Army (CPVA, Communist Chinese) forces entered the war; the winter of 1950–1951, when three temporary camps were established; and 1951–1953, when there were permanent camps.

During the first phase the Korean People's Army (KPA, North Korean) had sole charge of UNC prisoners. Republic of Korea Army (ROKA, South Korean) POWs were taken first to Seoul and then to P'yŏngyang, where they remained until early September. Some of them were then moved to the

Graves of American POWs who had been killed by KPA troops, found beside an abandoned train where other unburied bodies of American soldiers were also discovered. (National Archives)

vicinity of Manp'o, where they were held until 31 October 1950. The KPA made use of whatever facilities were available in any given area in which it was desired to establish a POW enclosure. Because in the first months of the war there was no KPA policy for handling POWs, there was no internal camp organization. Housing, food, and medical care were extremely primitive and limited. Despite facts to the contrary, the DPRK claimed that they were treating their prisoners generously and well.

During the second period of the winter of 1950–1951, there was joint administration of UNC POWs by both the KPA and CPVA. But the degree of contribution to be provided by each side was not clearly established, and the majority of POW deaths occurred during this time. The so-called early November 1950 "Death March" transferred the POWs to camps in far northern Korea, again without any sem-

blance of organization and under the control of security police. Upon their capture, unwounded and walking wounded prisoners were herded into groups for marching. Many marches were made in severe cold weather conditions and on foot, over rugged, mountainous terrain. These resulted in the deaths of many POWs. During the marches there was little or no medical attention for the wounded. Malnutrition, lack of medical care, dysentery, pneumonia, and cold weather all took a heavy toll. And in many cases, sick and wounded prisoners were simply taken from the line of march by the guards, and the most seriously wounded were either left behind or killed by small arms fire or by bayonet.

Temporary camps along the route of march were known by different names, such as "Bean Camp," "Mining Camp," and "Death Valley." These temporary camps, first organized in November 1950, were all under KPA jurisdiction, but control passed to the

American soldier, hands tied behind his back, murdered by the Korean People's Army. His boots had been taken, 18 August 1950. (National Archives)

Chinese in the middle of December. The prisoners were housed in huts, but food was inadequate and they died at an exceedingly high rate.

In the third period from the spring of 1951, the Chinese were in sole charge of the POW camps with the exception of those housing South Korean POWs. Conditions began to improve that summer and continued to do so until the end of the war under the so-called lenient policy.

The headquarters for all Communist POW camps was in Pyŏkdong, North P'yŏngan Province. Political officers worked in tandem at all levels with military officers in running the POW network. Decisions regarding POW policy came from the top, and individual camp commanders had little latitude.

Communist authorities announced the existence of camps numbered 1 to 17, but other camps have been identified. Most camps were located in far northern Korea, near the Yalu River. Individual camps were divided into companies, the chief administrative unit. Companies averaged 200 men but ranged in size from 60 to 350 POWs. There were three to seven companies per camp. Each company was further broken down into four or five platoons of about 50 POWs each. Each platoon was further subdivided into five squads with approximately 10 POWs to a squad, which was the basic POW unit.

To facilitate camp control, the Communists first allowed the prisoners to organize themselves along their own military lines, permitting the highest-ranking officer to serve as camp leader and to select his staff in accordance with normal military procedure. This system was abolished in early 1951, replaced by one in which the Communist authorities appointed the leaders.

Camp authorities appointed prisoners to the positions of platoon sergeant, squad leader, and assistant squad leader. Only those POWs who got along with the Communists were selected for these positions. The platoon sergeant called roll and organized platoon details. The squad leader's primary duties consisted of checking the men on details, reporting squad roll call, and reading articles to the squad during indoctrination periods. There were many POW committees, such as mess, sanitation, recreation, and study.

To facilitate further handling of prisoners, the Communists divided prisoners within each camp into companies and platoons along national and ethnic lines; i.e., white Americans, African-Americans, British, Turks, and other UN countries. Further segregation occurred between officers, noncommissioned officers, and enlisted men, as well as between "progressives" and "reactionaries." Progressives were either committed Communists or potential converts. To protect them as a group and take proper retaliatory measures against reactionaries, the Communists segregated the two groups. Progressives received much better treatment, while reactionaries were threatened, put on work details, and beaten.

Prisoners were occasionally shifted between camps, companies, and platoons to prevent them from forming stable prison societies. The Communists also kept firm control over the camps by means of an extensive informant system, augmented by close observation by instructors and guards. These techniques enabled the camp authorities to remain well informed of activities within the compounds.

The complete isolation of compounds from each other and from the outside world prevented organization and planning of concerted resistance. Corporal punishment or solitary confinement in the "hole" were the most commonly used methods to deal with resistance. Indoctrination and utilization of POWs for propaganda purposes were important aspects of Communist POW policy.

From July 1951 the Communists had a developed plan to deal with POWs. Interrogation was developed with a view of gaining tactical and strategic intelligence information. To this was added an effort to secure information of a personal nature to use in indoctrinations. In December 1950 the CPVA established an interrogation center twenty miles from "Death Valley" for detailed interrogation. The KPA used "Pak's Palace," established in April 1951 for POW interrogation.

The primary Communist purpose in indoctrination was not to convert a prisoner to communism as much as to destroy his spirit or to place him under such mental pressure that he could be used for the captors' purposes. Persuasion and coercion were sometimes employed to force prisoners to accept communism. In Camp 5 the authorities transferred sergeants and officers to other camps to prevent their influencing the younger men who remained. Men who consistently made trouble were also moved to other camps, leaving groups of men between the ages of eighteen and twenty-four who, although fairly intelligent, did not have much formal education and were from low-income groups.

The indoctrination program proceeded in stages and included lectures, discussions, and supplementary reading. Subjects included the Korean War, the contradictions between capitalism and socialism, and the advantages of communism. After completion of this formal indoctrination program, prisoners were encouraged to study on their own.

The Communists utilized prisoners to perform various tasks. These ranged from minimal maintenance duties to preserve some semblance of cleanness in the camp to long, hard physical labor. ROKA POWs were not considered prisoners but were referred to as "liberated warriors." As such, they were organized into labor units known as "liberation units" and "liberation construction regiments" and were employed in direct support of the Communist war effort. They worked in mines; dug air-raid shelters and underground bunkers; constructed airfields; planted, cultivated, and harvested crops; and built, repaired, and maintained roads, railway lines, and bridges.

UNC prisoners held by the Communists during the Korean War had to endure horrific conditions. Although the exact number of those who died in captivity will never be known with certainty, it was certainly quite high. One estimate puts the number of dead at about 15,000, including 8,334 Koreans and 6,137 Americans.

—*Sunghun Cho*

References:

Army Security Center, Fort George G. Meade, MD. "U.S. Prisoners of War in the Korean Operation: A Study of Their Treatment and Handling by NK Army and the Chinese Communist Forces," 1954.

Cho, Sunghun. "Han'guk Chŏnjaeng Chung Kongsan'guk ŭl UN Kun P'oro Chŏngch'aek e Taehan Yŏn'gu" [Communist policies regarding UN POWs during the Korean War]. *Han'guk Kŭnhyŏndaesa Yŏn'gu* [Journal of Korean modern and contemporary history] 6 (1997): 217–266.

Kim, Haeng-bok. *Han'guk Chŏnjaeng ŭi P'oro* [POWs in the Korean War]. Seoul: Korean Institute of Military History, 1996.

White, William L. *Captives of Korea.* New York: Charles Scribner's Sons, 1955.

See also: Casualties.

Prisoner-of-War Administration, United Nations Command

The United Nations Command (UNC) initially gave little thought to prisoner-of-war (POW) camps in South Korea. The first camp, at Pusan, held fewer than a thousand prisoners. Numbers of POWs swelled, however, especially after the 15 September 1950 Inch'ŏn landing and Eighth Army breakout from the Pusan perimeter; and by November 1950 the UNC held over 130,000 prisoners.

The Pusan camp was totally inadequate to deal with so many POWs, and the sudden influx of prisoners into the camp revealed how inadequate planning had been. Not only was the camp too small, food and clothing were in extremely short supply, there were not sufficient guards for so many prisoners, and those who were on hand were totally unprepared for their duties. The quality and numbers of guards did not improve and remained a major handicap in UNC camp administration. Prisoners who had been members of the Republic of Korea Army (ROKA) but had been pressed into service in the North Korean army assumed positions of leadership among the prisoners. As they professed to be anti-Communists, the ROKA guards gave them favorable treatment.

With Pusan incapable of handling so many prisoners, the UNC decided for logistical as well as security reasons to move the prisoners to new camps to be built on Kŏje-do, an island twenty miles southwest of the port of Pusan. In January 1951 UNC authorities began the transfer of prisoners to Kŏje-do.

Colonel Hartley F. Dame, the first commander on Kŏje-do, had several formidable obstacles to overcome in establishing the camp. Kŏje-do had no water resources, so the first order of business was to build dams and store rain water to ensure a relatively adequate, independent supply of water sufficient for 118,000 indigenous inhabitants, 100,000 refugees, 150,000 prisoners, and the camp administration. Other major logistical problems included securing food, shelter, and other necessities. The ROK government was responsible for providing the food and transporting it to the camp. Barracks had to be built for the prisoners as well as other housing for the guards and camp administration personnel. Construction began in January 1951, and by the end of the month 50,000 POWs had been transferred to the new camp from the mainland.

The camp, on the north coast of the island, was designed for four enclosures, each of which was to be divided into eight compounds. These compounds were to hold no more than 1,200 men each, but they were soon crammed with up to five times the estimated number of prisoners, a major factor in the events that were to follow. Although Kŏje-do was considered an ideal place to hold POWs, it was also a small island, land was scarce, and there was no opportunity to enlarge the camps. Eventually the areas between the compounds were also used to hold prisoners.

The limited space, along with the limited number of guards and security personnel, and their inadequate training and generally inferior quality, contributed to the inability of the administration to maintain adequate control. This was exacerbated by the belief that the war would not last long and that there was no need for a long-term solution. Thus, corrective actions were not taken.

Part of the problem—in fact a major part of it—was that ROKA troops were used as guards. Antagonism was common between the guards and the prisoners. Control weakened as tension and resentment grew from angry words and threats to physical attacks. The inadequacy of the guard situation was such that to a considerable extent the prisoners themselves ran the compounds, and staunch Communists saw in this an opportunity to embarrass the UNC during cease-fire negotiations. Prisoner provocations reached a peak with the beginning of negotiations at Kaesŏng.

Many of the POWs who had professed strong anti-Communist sentiments feared repatriation to North Korea. During attempts to screen the prisoners they divided into two different groups—anti-Communists and Communists. The Democratic People's Republic of Korea (DPRK, North Korea) and People's Republic of China (PRC) sent agitator agents to be captured so they could organize the prisoners and foment trouble in the camps. These agents formed the nucleus of prisoner resistance to screening.

Bloody clashes soon erupted in the compounds as POW kangaroo courts tried fellow prisoners, death penalties were carried out, and beatings and murders went unpunished. Camp administrators were not allowed to institute judicial actions against the troublemakers, resulting in a further erosion of authority within the camps.

The 2d Logistical Command had charge of all prison camps. The chief of staff of the 2d Logistical Command, Colonel Albert C. Morgan, requested more and better-trained security personnel, but disturbances continued unabated in the camps when Eighth Army commander Lieutenant General James A. Van Fleet inspected the camps. This resulted in a reorganization of the prison security forces.

Another problem was the rapid turnover in commanders on Kŏje-do. In September 1951 Colonel Maurice J. Fitzgerald assumed command. As a result of the disturbances and reorganization, the 8137th Military Police Group was activated that October. In addition to the three assigned battalions, four additional escort guard companies were attached to the group. By November a battalion of the 23d Infantry Regiment was assigned to Kŏje-do, and by December there were more than 9,000 combined U.S. and ROK forces on the island, although this was still far less than the 15,000 originally requested.

Despite an increase in security personnel, violence escalated. On 18 December 1951, a major disturbance between pro- and anti-Communist forces led to more riots and demonstrations that left fourteen dead and twenty-four others injured. As commander of the 2d

Communist POWs at Compound 77, Kŏje-Do in South Korea, 27 May 1952. (National Archives)

Logistical Command Brigadier General Paul F. Yount pointed out, introduction of the screening process had led to the increased violence. Before that, U.S. military personnel had full access to compounds and administered them satisfactorily, although never to the degree desired. By December over 37,000 prisoners had been reclassified as civilian internees. A second screening instituted by commander of the Kŏje-do camp, Colonel Fitzgerald, led to a major upheaval.

The second POW screening was an attempt to correct mistakes made in the first screening and to segregate nonrepatriates from those who wanted to be repatriated to the DPRK or PRC. Communist POWs controlled Compound 62 and refused to admit screening teams. They stated that none of their numbers wanted to remain in South Korea. The ROK screening teams were just as determined to fulfill their assigned duties.

On the morning of 18 February 1952, members of the 3d Battalion of the 27th Infantry Regiment moved in, passing through the gates with bayonets fixed, and divided the camp into four segments. The prisoners grabbed makeshift weapons, including rocks and sticks, and attacked the troops. Totally unprepared for the violent resistance, the troops used concussion grenades in an attempt to stop the attack. When this failed they opened fire, killing 55 prisoners and wounding another 140. The 3d Battalion suffered one killed and 38 wounded.

The UNC blamed the Communist leaders among the POWs, and the Department of the Army directed UNC commander Lieutenant General Matthew B. Ridgway to point out that only 1,500 inmates took part and that only civilian internees, not prisoners of war, were involved. Nonetheless, this event turned out to be a highly useful propaganda weapon for Communist negotiators at the cease-fire talks.

On 20 February General Van Fleet appointed Brigadier General Francis T. Dodd as camp comman-

A North Korean prisoner, Taegu. (Corbis)

dant and ordered him to tighten discipline and gain control of the situation. Unfortunately, the bloody confrontations were not over. Despite Dodd's instructions, on 13 March another confrontation between ROKA troops and Communist inmates resulted in the guards firing on inmates in retaliation for being attacked; 12 prisoners were killed and 26 wounded.

In April a new round of screening was undertaken. Again Communist prisoners sought to obstruct the process; they refused to allow the screening teams into seven of the compounds. The screening went on, nevertheless. This led to the discovery that, of 170,000 prisoners, only 70,000 wished to return home. This brought negotiations at P'anmunjŏm to a standstill as the Communist negotiators renewed their attacks on the screening process.

General Van Fleet then informed General Ridgway that he intended to separate Communist POWs from the anti-Communists and remove the latter to the mainland. Despite the demands that this would mean on personnel and equipment, Van Fleet believed it would lessen the likelihood of violence. Unfortunately, the removal of the non-Communists resulted in a concentration of hard-liners among the Communist prisoners who wished to return home. The POWs would no longer have to worry about fighting among themselves; they could now direct all their efforts against the UNC.

Unrest, tension, lack of moderating influences in the camps, and riots over food and other resources culminated in a riot on 7 May 1952 in which Communist POWs seized General Dodd and then announced that he would not be released until certain demands were met, and that if there were any attempts to use force, he would be killed.

Van Fleet then appointed Brigadier General Charles F. Colson the new camp commander and sent him to Kŏje-do to free Dodd by force, if necessary. Colson received an ultimatum from the prisoners stipulating a number of conditions for Dodd's safe release. Colson then signed a statement conceding that numerous POWs had been killed and wounded by UN guards and guaranteeing "humane treatment" for UNC POWs in accordance with the principles of international law and an end to "forcible" POW screening.

Dodd was released unharmed, but the Communists exploited Colson's statement as proof of UNC atrocities, humiliating the United States and Eighth Army and raising serious questions worldwide over the validity of the voluntary repatriation doctrine. Both Dodd's capture and Colson's statement were major international events and had a devastating impact on the UNC's international image.

Although a subsequent U.S. Army investigating board found both generals blameless, General Van Fleet and UNC commander Lieutenant General Mark W. Clark convened another board of inquiry that reversed the original decision, and both generals were reduced in rank to colonel and retired from the army. General Clark assigned Brigadier General Haydon L. Boatner to command the camp with instructions to clean out the compounds and restore order. On 10 June Boatner sent in paratroopers backed by six M-47 Patton tanks, and after a battle of over an hour in which more than 150 prisoners were killed, brought the situation under control. There was another public outcry, but this was the last major clash in the UNC prison camps.

The UNC also constructed new prison camps on Kŏje-do as well as on the mainland and on Cheju-do. In addition to reduction in the numbers of POWs held in the new compounds, more UNC troops were added as guards—including those from the United Kingdom, Canada, and Greece. Boatner built new enclosures and moved 6,000 civilians away from the vicinity of the camps and to the mainland. On 10 July 1952 General Clark removed POW administration from Eighth Army jurisdiction and placed it under the Korean Communications Zone of the Far East Command.

Another POW camp was established on Pongam-do, where one ROKA battalion and U.S. administrative personnel guarded and maintained 9,000 prisoners. On 24 December 1952, a riot broke out there but was soon suppressed.

Less tumultuous times appeared to be in the offing, but the primary problem of POW repatriation remained. ROK president Syngman Rhee, strongly opposed to an armistice that would leave Korea divided, saw the issue of forced repatriation as a means of breaking up the armistice talks. He ordered the release on the night of 17–18 June of non-Communist UNC prisoners from mainland camps. Some 27,000 militantly anti-Communist POWs broke out of camps at Pusan, Masan, Nonsan, and Sangmudae and disappeared into the general South Korean population. Only 971 were recovered. U.S. troops subsequently replaced the ROK security guards. After that the UNC effectively maintained security and control of the camps.

—*Patricia Wadley*

References:

Blair, Clay. *The Forgotten War: America in Korea, 1950–1953.* New York: Times Books, 1987.

Hermes, Walter G. *United States Army in the Korean War: Truce Tent and Fighting Front.* Washington, DC: Office of the Chief of Military History, 1966.

Vetter, Harold J. *Mutiny on Koje Island.* Rutland, VT: Charles E. Tuttle, 1965.

See also: Boatner, Haydon Lemaire; Clark, Mark W.; Dodd-Colson Prisoner-of-War Incident; P'anmunjŏm Truce Talks; Repatriation, Voluntary; Ridgway, Matthew Bunker; Second Logistical Command; Syngman Rhee's Release of North Korean Prisoners of War; Van Fleet, James Alward.

Prisoner-of-War Code of Conduct

The Military Code of Conduct for Prisoners of War adopted in 1955 [see Documents] was a direct result of the ordeal of U.S. prisoners of war (POWs) of both the North Koreans and Chinese Communists. Before the establishment of the 1955 code, military personnel were merely expected to conduct themselves in a manner that would not bring dishonor upon their country, the military, or themselves. During preliminary and subsequent interrogations they were expected to give only their name, rank, and serial number. They were also expected to try and escape. They were still under military orders, but other than that there were no regulations to guide their conduct. The United States was a signatory of the Geneva Accords concerning the treatment of POWs. A subsequent protocol spelled out how POWs were to be maintained and what was expected of them.

The United States learned in World War II that prisoners were, for the most part, at the whim of their captors. The Germans generally followed the Geneva Accords, as did the Italians. The Japanese did not; brutality was common, prisoners were starved, medical care was virtually nonexistent, and there was no protecting power to guarantee proper treatment of prisoners.

When the Korean War began there was little thought given to the POW issue, let alone how prisoners would conduct themselves. Unfortunately, the People's Republic of China (Communist China) and Democratic People's Republic of Korea (North Korea) considered propaganda a tool of war and a potential weapon against a prisoner's own country. To that end the Communists carried out intense psychological and propaganda campaigns among prisoners. POWs were deprived of food, brutality was common, and medical care was sparse. The Communists also refused to allow visits to their POW camps by the Red Cross or protecting power.

The Communists also instituted a regime to work on POW morale. Enlisted personnel were separated from noncommissioned officers, officers were isolated from their men, and any individual who showed leadership potential was removed. Prisoners were not allowed to consider themselves part of a military organization. The Communists inflicted brutal punishment for the most trivial offenses, and deaths from mistreatment were not uncommon. POWs were also ordered to attend "schooling" and indoctrination classes. All this was done to try to break down POW resistance.

Given these conditions and the length of time many of the men were prisoners, it is not surprising that some "cooperated." More shocking was the fact that twenty-one Americans refused repatriation. As a direct result of the Korean War experience, the U.S. military then decided that not only was intensive ideological indoctrination needed but also a policy of absolute noncompliance with any captor's demands, and that failure to follow this code should result in severe punishment. On 17 August 1955, President Dwight D. Eisenhower signed Executive Order 10631, a code of conduct for members of the U.S. Armed Forces that delineated exactly how members of the military were to conduct themselves as prisoners of war.

—*Patricia Wadley*

References:

Biderman, Albert D. *March to Calumny: The Story of American POWs in the Korean War*. New York: Macmillan, 1963.

Snyder, Don J. *A Soldier's Disgrace*. Dublin, NH: Yankee Books, 1987.

See also: Brainwashing (*Senoe*; *Xinao*); Prisoner-of-War Administration, Communist.

Prisoners of War, Rescreening of

June 1952 action by the United Nations Command (UNC) to determine the status of prisoners of war (POWS) it controlled, specifically those who wished to return home and those who would refuse repatriation. The UNC did not consider rescreening POWs to be desirable. The UNC believed that such a program might lengthen the odds of reaching an armistice agreement. It might also have strengthened Communist allegations that the initial UNC screening was improper.

After the Communist refusal to agree to an exchange of prisoners on the basis of an estimate of only 70,000 POWs desiring repatriation, the UNC cast about for any reasonable means to resolve the deadlock while at the same time remaining firm on the issue of nonforcible repatriation. The UNC side then suggested verification and rescreening after the armistice, to be conducted under the most stringent criteria to determine those who would actually resist repatriation. On 23 April 1952, the UNC proposed that joint Red Cross teams from the two sides, with or without military observers, be allowed to interview the prisoners to verify that those designated as nonrepatriates would forcibly resist being returned to the side from which they came. The UNC also proposed that all POWs of both sides be delivered in groups to the demilitarized zone (DMZ) and there be allowed to express their preferences on repatriation.

The Communists rejected these proposals. They sought to establish the illegality of voluntary repatriation of POWs and halt the screening. Communist agents also sought to instigate riots in the camps, leading to the capture of UNC Kŏje-do POW camp commander U.S. Brigadier General Francis T. Dodd on 7 May 1952. The Communist side said that the Dodd incident proved that voluntary repatriation and screening were only devices for the forceful retention of POWs. Certainly the incident undermined the previous confidence of Allied governments as well as public opinion on the UNC's handling of POWs and the validity of the screening process.

The UN Allies now pressed for some type of rescreening before an armistice that would allow

Communist observation and would contain a commitment by both sides to abide by the results. Worried about an indefinite suspension or even end to the negotiations, the UNC proposed a program for rescreening POWs before the armistice, in which independent observers would be drawn from countries not participating in the war. The UNC also invited the Communists to participate in the rescreening process. But the Communist side insisted that the very act of screening was illegal and unacceptable, and they continued to make a propaganda issue of the screening process.

As a consequence of the Communist refusal to participate, rescreening was carried out unilaterally by the UNC without the participation of neutral or Communist observers. The rescreening was conducted to determine whether a larger proportion of prisoners might want to be repatriated and to screen those prisoners not previously checked.

During the period 23–30 June 1952, previously unscreened POWs were interviewed. Each screening team consisted of one or two officers, six to eight Korean interrogators from the Civil Information and Education Section, four to six fingerprint personnel, and twelve Korean interviewers. In general the procedure paralleled that followed in April. Prisoners were first identified and fingerprinted, then taken to the interview tent. If a prisoner refused to answer the questions or indicated that he would not resist repatriation violently, he was placed on the list to be repatriated and assigned to a repatriate compound.

The rescreening occurred with less chance of violence because hard-core Communist POWs and civilian internees had already been transferred to other camps during Operation BREAKUP. The UNC stressed the objective nature of the screening, in which each POW was given the opportunity to make his own decision and encouraged to return to Communist control. The screening teams screened and identified some 50,000 POWs who had not been screened in April.

Of the 170,000 POWs, approximately 83,000 (76,600 North Korean and 6,400 Chinese) chose to be repatriated, while about 86,000 refused repatriation. The latter represented an increase of 16,000 over the April figure of those refusing repatriation. The UNC recommended to the U.S. Joint Chiefs of Staff that the UNC delegation at P'anmunjŏm be authorized to submit a new final figure to the Communists as soon as possible. But this led to discussion over whether disclosing the revised figure would discredit the initial screening that had produced the figure of 70,000 refusing repatriation.

Finally, on 13 July 1952, the UNC informed Communist negotiators of the revised figure. Korean People's Army (North Korean) Lieutenant General Nam Il, chief North Korean negotiator at the armistice negotiations, rejected the UNC contention that this was an impartial and valid count; he insisted that the final tally should be approximately 110,000 repatriates. The deadlock at P'anmunjŏm over repatriation remained the major issue to be resolved before conclusion of an armistice.

The solution was for some independent and impartial body to reinterview all those POWs not wishing repatriation. The UNC presented new proposals on 28 September 1952, in which all POWs objecting to repatriation would be delivered to the DMZ, where they would be freed from military control of both sides and interviewed by representatives of mutually agreed countries or an international committee. Such a plan was ultimately adopted, but for the time being at least the Communist side remained firmly opposed to the principle of voluntary repatriation, fearing a propaganda defeat in the process.

—Sunghun Cho

References:

Cho, Sunghun. "Han'guk Chŏnjaeng Chung UN Kun ŭi P'oro Chŏngch'aek e Kwanhan Yŏn'gu" [UN Forces POW policies during the Korean War]. Doctoral dissertation, Academy of Korean Studies, Seoul, 1999. Unpublished manuscript.

Hermes, Walter G. *United States Army in the Korean War: Truce Tent and Fighting Front.* Washington, DC: Office of the Chief of Military History, 1966.

Vatcher, William H., Jr. *Panmunjom.* Westport, CT: Greenwood Press, 1973.

See also: Dodd-Colson Prisoner-of-War Incident; P'anmunjŏm Truce Talks; SCATTER, Operation.

Psychological Warfare

Within a day of President Harry S. Truman's announcement that U.S. troops would assist the invaded Republic of Korea (ROK, South Korea) in June 1950, propaganda leaflets were being dropped over the peninsula telling of the decision. Within another day radio broadcasts from Tokyo carried the same message, making psychological warfare the first United Nations weapon used against the Democratic People's Republic of Korea (DPRK, North Korea). Following these early precedents, U.S. forces attached to the United Nations Command (UNC) used psychological warfare to an unprecedented degree relative to the size of the conflict. Although no definitive answer can be made as to its overall impact and effect, psychological warfare did serve as an "enhancer" to UN conventional weapons.

The primary purpose of psychological warfare is to lower enemy morale and to influence populations to resist their leaders, abandon the war effort, or to surrender or resist less intently. Most practitioners recognize that propaganda rarely produces immediate results, but rather has a slow, cumulative effect. Tactically it works best against tired, hungry, cold, and

Whatever the colour, race or creed,
All plain folks are brothers indeed.
Both you and we want life and peace,
If you go home, the war will cease.

Demand Peace!
Stop the War!

Greetings
from
The Chinese People's
Volunteers

KOREA 1951

Chinese People's Volunteer Army propaganda Christmas card dropped on UNC lines in December 1951. (National Archives)

demoralized troops, especially surrounded units, who feel abandoned or betrayed by their officers or leaders, or who feel overwhelmed by enemy numbers, firepower, or material might. During the Korean War most psychological warfare was used on the tactical level rather than at the strategic level.

By 1950 psychological warfare was a well-honed weapon in the U.S. arsenal with an institutional history dating back to World War I. The Korean War experience also drew heavily on the same personnel, doctrine, methods, themes, weapons, and equipment used in both the European and Pacific theaters by U.S. and Allied civilian and military propagandists during World War II. Indeed, many propaganda leaflets and themes, such as the famous "surrender pass" leaflet first used in the earlier conflicts, was also used widely in Korea. The technology for delivering leaflets by aircraft and artillery dated back to World War II, and, in some cases, such as the leaflet artillery shell, to technology developed during World War I. Radio and

loudspeaker broadcasts and equipment used during World War II again provided a significant component of the Korean War arsenal. Even psychological warfare tactical units and headquarters organizations, from the field to Washington, D.C., could trace their origins to similar entities created during the earlier conflicts.

Unlike World Wars I or II, however, the United States was quick to develop psychological warfare in 1950. Soon after the invasion, President Truman developed the Psychological Strategy Board (PSB) to formulate national policy and to coordinate campaigns with the military. The PSB was aided by social scientists of the Operations Research Office at Johns Hopkins University, who were later superseded by analysts and scholars belonging to the army's own Human Resources Research Office.

The U.S. Army, because of persistent pressure applied by Secretary of the Army Frank Pace, Jr., created an unprecedented staff organization in the Pentagon on 15 January 1951: the Office of the Chief of Psychological Warfare, divided into Psychological Operations, Requirements, and Special Operations Divisions. Brigadier General Robert A. McClure, who had commanded Allied psychological warfare efforts in Europe during World War II, was selected to lead the new office. McClure created a staff that drew heavily on the same talent he had used during the prior conflict. Capitalizing on this, he convinced the army to create a psychological warfare center at Fort Bragg, North Carolina, in April 1952 to provide training, equipment, and doctrinal support for all army psychological warfare units, including those in Korea.

U.S. psychological warfare in Korea had other strong supporters in addition to Pace. These included General Douglas MacArthur, Lieutenant General Matthew B. Ridgway, and presidential advisor and assistant for Cold War planning C. D. Jackson, who, after his appointment in the spring of 1953, regularly advised a very interested President Dwight D. Eisenhower on the use of psychological warfare in Korea and in the larger struggle against world communism.

At the tactical level in Korea the situation was initially not as far advanced as at Washington headquarters. Yet as early as 1947 Major General Charles A. Willoughby, MacArthur's assistant chief of staff for intelligence, recreated the World War II Psychological Warfare Section under Colonel J. Woodhall Greene to create contingency plans for the Far East. Although still a small group in June 1950, the Psychological Warfare Section, Far East Command, grew to thirty-five people by December and by 1952 had become the central planning and coordinating agency for all UN psychological warfare activities in Korea.

When the DPRK invaded the ROK in June 1950, however, the only deployable U.S. Army psychological warfare unit was at Fort Riley, Kansas. This unit, the twenty-five-member 1st Loudspeaker and Leaflet Company, was patterned after the five similar self-contained U.S. Army Mobile Radio Broadcast Companies developed during World War II. The 1st Loudspeaker and Leaflet Company arrived in Korea on 8 November 1950 and served as the Eighth Army's tactical propaganda unit during the remainder of the war. In August 1951 this group was joined by the 1st Radio Broadcasting and Leaflet Group. It controlled all strategic psychological warfare operations in Korea including the "Voice of the UN Command" broadcasts that had begun the year before.

As during World War II, the propagandists in the U.S. Army units had backgrounds in journalism, art, advertising, radio, film, or the social sciences. The units employed South Koreans as radio announcers, leaflet writers, and linguists. Printing of leaflets took place in a specially created print shop in Yokohama. Propaganda leaflets drew heavily on themes and formats developed during World War II that were adapted to new audiences in Korea. Colorful art work was a perennial leaflet component, and themes included depictions of the horrors of combat, promises of food and medical treatment in captivity, descriptions of the incompetence of Communist officers and leaders, and exploitation of fears that the soldiers had for their own survival and safety. Other themes emphasized UN firepower and material superiority, the mounting Communist death toll on the battlefield, the backwardness of Communist weapons, tactics, and material, the emptiness of Communist ideology, and the injustice of the Communist cause. Many Communist prisoners of war claimed that the signature of General MacArthur on a surrender pass convinced them that promises of good treatment in captivity would be honored, a similar response to that given by Axis soldiers viewing the same leaflet during World War II.

Once leaflet production facilities were operational, psychological warfare officers (PWOs) attached to Eighth Army headquarters would decide on suitable targets, either on their own initiative or after requests were received from division and corps commanders, many of whom had to first be indoctrinated as to the value of psychological warfare. Once the target was determined, however, the PWO would contact Tokyo, giving the general content for leaflets and where the drop should occur. Tokyo then took the leaflets out of existing stocks or printed them specially for a given situation or even a particular Communist unit. From the printing plant the leaflets were taken to air bases and loaded onto aircraft for drops directly over Communist forces or for transport to the war zone for drops by Korea-based aircraft. Standard smoke artillery shells were also converted to leaflet use and allowed a broad distribution directly over Communist positions during combat operations.

By the spring of 1951 plans were well under way to double the leaflet distribution effort of about 13 million propaganda leaflets per week. In response to these plans, General McClure continued to campaign to improve the air support he claimed he lacked during the first year in Korea.

As during both world wars, the vast majority of propaganda leaflets were delivered by aircraft, initially in loosely wrapped bundles that fell apart as they descended from low-flying planes. Later, air force personnel drew again on their World War II experiences and began using hollow aerial bombs, each with a capacity of 45,000 four-by-five-inch leaflets. Thirty-two bombs constituted an aircraft load. The bombs were released at 15,000 feet or higher, with fuses set to open at 1,000 feet.

By the end of the war about one million individual leaflets could be distributed nightly by a single B-29.

More than 2.5 billion leaflets were dropped over Communist troops and civilians in North Korea by the end of the war, compared with six billion dropped during all of World War II.

In addition to leaflets, the primary medium of tactical psychological warfare, two C-47 aircraft were made available to the Eighth Army to broadcast surrender messages over loudspeakers, a technology fully developed by the U.S. Navy in the Central Pacific and on Okinawa during World War II. These planes had loudspeakers mounted on their bottoms so they could point directly at the ground for better sound projection.

By the spring of 1951 plans were also under way to increase the thirteen hours of daily radio broadcasts made in Korean by adding Chinese-language short-wave radio broadcasts audible to Communist troops throughout Korea and into Manchuria. A shortage of receivers in Communist hands and frequent disruptions of electrical power limited the effectiveness of strategic radio operations during the Korean War.

As in World War II, leaflet and radio propagandists often combined their efforts. In March 1953 the Fifth Air Force, in cooperation with the Eighth Army, began dropping a special leaflet that asked: "Where is the Communist Air Force?"—a direct throwback to the famous 1944 Office of War Information propaganda campaign asking "Where is the Luftwaffe?" These leaflets were dropped on Communist troop concentrations, while Radio Seoul hammered the same theme, hoping to create demoralization, friction between the air forces and ground troops, and foolhardy sorties by Communist pilots undertaken to disprove UNC allegations.

In a twist on the theme described above, on the night of 26 April 1953, two B-29s dropped more than a million leaflets along the Yalu River, offering $50,000 and political asylum to each Russian, Chinese, or North Korean pilot who would deliver his jet to the South. The campaign was named "Project MOOLAH."

By 1953, psychological warfare in all its forms had become a standard UN weapon. Leaflets, radio broadcasts, and loudspeakers were credited as a major factor in the heavy increase in prisoners after July 1951, and interrogations of Communist prisoners of war showed that one in three were influenced to surrender by leaflets. Interrogations of civilians in North and South Korea further revealed that UN radio broadcasts reached a considerable audience and stirred some civilian opposition to the Communist regime. One authority has determined that Chinese enlisted men were found the most amenable to UN psychological warfare messages, while the hard-core North Korean officer corps were least inclined to believe or act on such appeals.

—*Clayton D. Laurie*

References:

Daugherty, William E., and Morris Janowitz, eds. *A Psychological Warfare Casebook*. Baltimore: Johns Hopkins University Press, 1958.

Laurie, Clayton D. *The Propaganda Warriors: The American Crusade against Nazi Germany*. Military Studies Series. Lawrence: University Press of Kansas, 1996.

———. "The U.S. Army and Psychological Warfare Organization and Operations, 1918–1945," U.S. Army Center of Military History, Washington, DC. Unpublished manuscript.

Pease, Stephen E. *Psywar: Psychological Warfare in Korea, 1950–1953*. Harrisburg, PA: Stackpole, 1992.

Sandler, Stanley. "Cease Resistance: It's Good for You. A History of U.S. Army Combat Psychological Operations." Fort Bragg, NC: U.S. Army Special Operations Command, 1995.

See also: Eisenhower, Dwight D.; Jackson, Charles Douglas "C.D."; MacArthur, Douglas; McClure, Robert A.; MOOLAH, Operation; Pace, Frank, Jr.; Ridgway, Matthew Bunker; Truman, Harry S.; Willoughby, Charles A.

Puller, Lewis Burwell
(1898–1971)

U.S. Marine Corps general and icon. Born on 26 June 1898, in West Point, Virginia, Lewis Burwell "Chesty" Puller enrolled in the Virginia Military Institute in 1917 but, impatient to participate in World War I, dropped out to enlist in the Marines in August 1918. Although his formal education was spotty, Puller read widely throughout his life and had a passion for the Civil War, especially the exploits of General Thomas J. "Stonewall" Jackson.

Disappointed not to see World War I service, Puller attended officer candidate school and was commissioned in the Marine reserves in June 1919. Caught in the reduction of the Marine Corps after the war, he was soon on the inactive list. Puller then promptly reenlisted in the Marines as a corporal. From 1919 to 1924 he served in the Haitian gendarmerie as acting first lieutenant. There he demonstrated the rapid marching, aggressive tactics, and leading from the front that became his hallmarks.

In 1924, on his return to the United States, Puller was commissioned a second lieutenant. During the next seven years he was stationed in Philadelphia; Quantico, Virginia; Pensacola, Florida (where he took aviation training but did not earn a pilot's wings); Hawaii; and Nicaragua. He served twice as commander of the Marine detachment on the cruiser *Augusta*, a second time in Nicaragua, and in Beijing (Peking), China, as commander of the Marine detachment at the U.S. legation. Between 1936 and 1939 he was an instructor at the Marine Basic School in Philadelphia, and during 1940–1941 he was with the 4th Marine Regiment in Shanghai, China, where he was promoted to major and battalion commander. Puller was next with the 7th Marines at Camp

Lejeune, North Carolina, where he became a pioneer in jungle warfare training.

In September 1942 the 7th Marines landed on Guadalcanal, and Puller distinguished himself in the 24–25 October defense of Henderson Field. His half-strength battalion held off an entire Japanese regiment, killing more than 1,400 of the attackers. Promoted to lieutenant colonel, he commanded two battalions at Cape Gloucester, New Britain, when their regular commanders were wounded. In February 1944 he commanded the 1st Marine Regiment and landed with it on Peleliu in September. In November he returned to the United States for training duty at Camp Lejeune and was shortly thereafter promoted to colonel.

When the Korean War began, Puller actively sought a combat command. In August 1950 he returned to the 1st Marine Regiment at Camp Pendleton, California. Sent to Korea immediately thereafter, Puller led the 1st in the 15 September Inch'ŏn landing and in the subsequent recapture of Seoul. He won his fifth Navy Cross, the most awarded in Marine Corps history, for inspirational leadership during the withdrawal from the Changjin Reservoir. Promoted to brigadier general in January 1951, Puller was for a short time assistant divisional commander of the 1st Marine Division under Major General Oliver P. Smith.

In May 1951 he returned to the United States to command the 3d Marine Brigade, later redesignated the 3d Marine Division, at Camp Pendleton. Promoted to major general in September 1953, he returned to Camp Lejeune as commander of the 2d Marine Division and later deputy camp commander until his retirement for disability in November 1955 with the rank of lieutenant general.

Although he proved himself a competent staff officer, Puller was first and foremost a warrior. During his long career he won fifty-three decorations, probably the most in Marine Corps history. "Chesty" Puller was also perhaps the most colorful figure in Marine Corps history. Most comfortable when commanding troops in battle, he had only contempt for what he believed were bloated military staffs and their excess creature comforts. One "Pullerism" was "Paperwork will ruin any military force."

Puller died in Hampton, Virginia, on 11 October 1971. A chaplain who served with him in Korea said he was a man who "turned the air around him to heroism and romance and selflessness, who could make men act better than they really were."

—Spencer C. Tucker

References:

Dabney, William H. "The Next Stop Is Saigon." *Marine Corps Gazette.* Vol. 82, No. 6 (June 1998): 30–32.

Davis, Burke. *Marine! The Life of Lewis B. (Chesty) Puller, USMC (Ret.).* Boston: Little, Brown, 1962.

Dictionary of American Biography, edited by Roger J. Spiller. Vol. 2. Westport, CT: Greenwood Press, 1984.

Dictionary of American Biography. Supplement Nine, 1971–1975, edited by Kenneth T. Jackson. New York: Charles Scribner's Sons, 1994.

Hoffman, Jon T. "Lieutenant General Lewis Burwell Puller." *Marine Corps Gazette.* Vol. 82. No. 6 (June 1998): 27–30.

Montross, Lynn, et al. *U.S. Marine Operations in Korea.* 5 vols. Washington, DC: U.S. Marine Corps Historical Branch, 1954–1957.

Schuon, Karl. *U.S. Marine Corps Biographical Dictionary.* New York: Franklin Watts, 1963.

See also: Changjin (Chosin) Reservoir Campaign; Inch'ŏn Landings: Operation CHROMITE; Smith, Oliver Prince; United States Marine Corps.

PUNCH, Operation
(5–9 February 1951)

Operation that cleared the way for the recapture of Seoul in 1951. Operation PUNCH began on 5 February 1951, the same day that X Corps implemented Operation ROUNDUP in the area of Hongch'ŏn, above the town of Hoengsŏng. It was actually an extension of the I and IX Corps push on the Seoul area in late January, code-named Operation THUNDERBOLT, and not part of the X Corps offensive.

Operation PUNCH consisted of a task force built around the U.S. 25th Infantry Division, which was augmented by heavy artillery and armored units and by close air support. The mission of this task force was to destroy all Communist troops in defensive positions in the Hill 440 complex just south of Seoul.

During 5–9 February Operation PUNCH forces pounded Hill 440. By the 9th the Communist Chinese defenders had retreated across the Han River. More than 4,200 Chinese were killed (that number includes the battlefield count and not those carried from the field or wounded). United Nations Command (UNC) forces suffered only 70 casualties. Operation PUNCH cleared the way for I Corps' final assault on Seoul.

—James H. Willbanks

References:

Blair, Clay. *The Forgotten War: America in Korea, 1950–1953.* New York: Times Books, 1987.

Marshall, S. L. A. *Operation Punch and the Capture of Hill 404, Suwon, Korea, February 1951.* Baltimore: Johns Hopkins University Press, 1952.

Middleton, Harry J. *The Compact History of the Korean War.* New York: Hawthorn Books, 1965.

Rees, David. *Korea: The Limited War.* New York: St. Martin's Press, 1964.

See also: Iron Triangle; ROUNDUP, Operation; Seoul; Tenth Corps; THUNDERBOLT, Operation.

Punchbowl

Bowl-shaped valley about 4.4 miles in diameter, surrounded by high hills, about 5 miles north of Line

Kansas, 19 miles north of the 38th parallel, and 6 miles east of Heartbreak Ridge. The Punchbowl was first reached and briefly held by United Nations Command (UNC) forces in April 1951, during the Operation PILEDRIVER offensive. After it was regained in early summer, it thereafter became mainly a "no-mans" zone, vigorously patrolled by both UNC and Communists units, which often set ambushes for each other. The high ground to the north of the Punchbowl was occupied by Communists forces, while that to the south was controlled by UNC forces that from time to time included the U.S. 2d, 3d, 7th, and 40th Army Divisions, the 1st Marine Division, and various Republic of Korea Army (ROKA) divisions.

The high ground to the south and southwest of the Punchbowl was eventually, in summer 1951, mostly controlled by UNC forces. It provided jump-off points for some of the troops supporting or reinforcing 2d Division regiments, or others, in attacks on the Heartbreak Ridge hills in August and September 1951.

At one point in the cease fire talks at P'anmunjŏm, Communist delegates demanded that the Punchbowl, along with Heartbreak Ridge and some other key and hard-won high ground, be returned to them as a condition for agreeing to a cease-fire. The UNC rejected that demand, which was not again brought up by the other side. Today the Punchbowl lies mostly just south of the 4-kilometer-wide (2.5-mile-wide) demilitarized zone (DMZ) with its northern rim at the southern DMZ boundary.

—Sherman W. Pratt

References:

Blair, Clay. *The Forgotten War: America in Korea, 1950–1953.* New York: Times Books, 1987.
Command Reports, 2nd Infantry Division, August–September 1951. National Archives, Suitland, MD.
Pratt, Sherman W. *Decisive Battles of the Korean War. An Infantry Company Commander's View of the War's Most Critical Engagements.* New York: Vantage Press, 1992.
See also: Bloody Ridge, Battle of; Heartbreak Ridge, Battle of; P'anmunjŏm Truce Talks.

Pusan

City in the southeastern corner of the Korea peninsula. Pusan is the second largest city and the largest trading port of the Republic of Korea (ROK, South Korea). When Korea was forced to sign the Kanghwa Treaty with Japan in February 1876, Pusan was opened to foreign trade, along with Chemulp'o (Inch'ŏn) and Wŏnsan. During the Korean War, Pusan was the temporary capital of the ROK after the capture of Taejŏn.

By the beginning of August 1950, Lieutenant General Walton H. Walker's Eighth Army had been pushed below the Naktong River into the so-called Pusan perimeter, where it struggled desperately to maintain a toe-hold on the peninsula. This perimeter was a line encompassing an area some fifty miles wide and a hundred miles deep on the southeastern tip of the peninsula. Walker's forces became stronger as men and munitions poured into Pusan and the North Korean offensive stalled in the face of determined counterattacks.

At midnight on 24 May 1952, ROK president Syngman Rhee declared martial law in Pusan and the surrounding region and jailed numerous members of the National Assembly. These actions became an embarrassment to the United Nations cause. Doubting his prospects to secure another term through the National Assembly, Rhee had sought to amend the constitution to provide for direct popular election of the president. This required action by the National Assembly, which resisted his appeal.

In early 1953 the ROK moved its government from Pusan back to Seoul, a move the United Nations Command vainly sought to postpone for security reasons.

—Jinwung Kim

References:

Blair, Clay. *The Forgotten War: America in Korea, 1950–1953.* New York: Times Books, 1987.
MacDonald, Callum. *Korea: The War Before Vietnam.* New York: Free Press, 1986.
Stueck, William W., Jr. *The Korean War: An International History.* Princeton, NJ: Princeton University Press, 1995.
See also: Pusan Perimeter and Breakout.

Pusan Logistical Command
(see 2d Logistical Command)

Pusan Perimeter and Breakout

The battle for the Pusan perimeter was one of the most skillful mobile defense operations ever conducted by a U.S. commander. Beginning on 5 July 1950 with the Task Force Smith battle near Osan, Lieutenant General Walton H. Walker's U.S. Eighth Army had suffered an unbroken string of defeats. From Ch'ŏnan (6–8 July), to Ch'ŏngju (10 July), to Choch'iwŏn (11–12 July), to the Kŭm River (15–16 July), and finally to Taejŏn (19–20 July), the Korean People's Army (KPA, North Korean) continuously pushed Walker's understrength and poorly trained 24th Infantry Division southward down the peninsula. On 25 July, meanwhile, the 1st Cavalry Division lost Yŏngdong.

Walker's mission became one of trading space for time, delaying and withdrawing until sufficient forces could be built up in Japan for General Douglas MacArthur's Far East Command to effect a deep turning movement by landing forces at Inch'ŏn. By the end of July, however, Walker had run out of space. If his forces withdrew any farther toward the key port of

Eighth Army commander Lieutenant General Walton H. Walker crossing the Naktong River in his jeep with handrail. (National Archives)

Pusan, he would have insufficient depth with which to maneuver the reserves necessary to counter KPA penetrations, and eventually to mass for a counterattack and breakout.

Walker ordered his forces to withdraw behind the line of the Naktong River, and by 1 August the Pusan perimeter (also known as the Naktong perimeter) had been established. Three days earlier, on 29 July, Walker issued his famous "Stand or Die" order. The Eighth Army at that point consisted of the still-understrength 24th and 25th Infantry Divisions and the 1st Cavalry Division. Throughout the course of the campaign, the Eighth Army was reinforced by the 5th Regimental Combat Team (RCT), the 1st Marine Provisional Brigade, regiments of the 2d Infantry Division, and the British 27th Infantry Brigade, all arriving through Pusan.

Walker also had operational control of the five surviving divisions of the Republic of Korea Army (ROKA). The Allied defensive perimeter consisted of a rectangle approximately 100 by 50 miles in the southeast corner of Korea. On the western side the line of defense ran along the Naktong River—except for the southernmost 15 miles where the river turned east, away from the line. The northern boundary was a line through the mountains from Naktong-ni to Yŏngdŏk, on the east coast. The East Sea (Sea of Japan) formed the eastern boundary, and the Tsushima Strait the southern.

Walker had the advantage of operating on interior lines, and he had a robust logistics infrastructure within the perimeter. Pusan was in the southeast corner. With its large natural harbor and location on the Tsushima Strait, Pusan was Korea's chief seaport. Its docking facilities were capable of handling thirty oceangoing vessels simultaneously. The port had a daily discharge capacity of up to 45,000 tons, but shortages of personnel and transportation assets held the daily average to 28,000 tons during the campaign. Walker also had the advantage of an excellent rail loop that connected Pusan with Miryang, Taegu, and P'ohang.

Walker positioned three of his still-understrength U.S. divisions along the Naktong. The 25th Infantry Division was in the south, the 24th Infantry Division in the center, and the 1st Cavalry Division in the north to just above Waegwan. Above the 1st Cavalry Division, the ROKA 1st Division held the north until the defensive line turned to the east. Across the northern flank of the line the ROKA 6th Division held the western portion, the 8th Division and Capital Divisions held the center, and the 3d Division held the eastern end until the line reached the sea near Yŏngdŏk.

As U.S. forces continued to pour in through Pusan they were rushed immediately to the front lines. By mid-August the Allies had over 500 medium tanks in Korea, giving them a greater than five-to-one advantage in armor. On the sea flanks of the perimeter the U.S. Navy was able to provide effective naval gunfire support. The U.S. Fifth Air Force also held air supremacy, which meant that movement within the perimeter could be conducted without regard to cover and concealment. This, of course, enhanced Walker's mobility advantage.

Eleven KPA divisions initially faced the Allies. From south to north along the Naktong were arrayed the 6th, 4th, 3d, 2d, 15th, and 1st Divisions. From west to east along the north flank of the perimeter the North Koreans had the 13th, 8th, 12th, and 5th Divisions. The bulk of the 105th Armored Division was held in reserve. KPA forces also included the 766th Independent Infantry Regiment, in the northeast corner near Yŏngdŏk, and the 83d Motorized Regiment, detached from the 105th Armored Division and in the southwest corner near Kogang-ni. About the middle of August elements of the newly formed 7th Division entered the southern end of the line north of the 6th Division. The 9th Division and elements of the 10th Division also entered the line south and north, respectively, of the 2d Division.

Most of the KPA units, especially the 13th Division, had suffered heavy losses during the fight down the peninsula. The 105th Armored Division had only about forty tanks left. Although intelligence estimates at the time painted a somewhat different picture, the Allies actually held a slight numerical advantage, with some 92,000 troops to 70,000. Many of Walker's soldiers, however, were engaged in securing and operating his extensive logistics infrastructure within the perimeter.

The KPA's primary operational objective was to cut off and isolate the U.S. and South Korean forces on the Korea peninsula, thereby preventing them from reinforcing and building up to the point where they could

go on the offensive. The North Korean geographic objective was the port of Pusan, the main point of entrance for Allied reinforcements and logistics. From the KPA standpoint, the campaign's center of gravity was the forces of the Eighth Army and the ROKA. Once those forces were isolated and neutralized, Pusan would be wide open and vulnerable. Between 5 August and 9 September the KPA attacked the Pusan perimeter along four widely separated concentric axes, all following natural approach corridors.

From 5 to 14 August the KPA tried to envelop the left (southern) flank of the United Nations (UN) line with one division and one armored regiment attacking along the Sunch'ŏn-Chinju-Masan-Pusan axis. Walker responded by reinforcing the 25th Infantry Division with the 5th RCT and the 1st Marine Brigade. Operating as Task Force Kean, the combined army-Marine force launched the first Allied counterattack of the war on 7 August. Striking at the KPA 6th Division at Chinju, the poorly coordinated attack made only limited progress. After five days of back-and-forth fighting, Walker called off the counterattack and shifted his attentions to threats farther to the north.

Between 4 and 19 August the KPA tried to penetrate the UN line in the vicinity of Taegu with five infantry divisions echeloned in depth, supported by elements of the 105th Armored Division. This was a two-pronged attack originating around Sangju. One thrust approached Taegu from Kunwi in the north, the other pointed south of Taegu. From Taegu the axis of attack led straight down the road and rail main lines of communication (LOCs) to Kyŏngsan, Miryang, Samnangjin, and Pusan.

General Walker considered the attack south of Taegu, an area known as the "Naktong bulge," to be the primary threat. Had KPA forces succeeded in this sector, they could have cut the Taegu-Pusan rail loop, threatening the very existence of the entire defensive perimeter. North of Taegu Walker could still afford to trade some space for time. The North Koreans also helped the allies by poorly coordinating the two thrusts. This allowed Walker to continually shift his mobile and armored reserves behind the lines to the points of maximum danger.

Walker moved the 1st Marine Brigade and elements of the 27th Infantry Regiment up from the south and attached them to the 24th Infantry Division. On 17 August the 24th Infantry Division counterattacked the KPA 4th Division and cleared the bulge by the following night. On 24 August Walker moved the 2d Infantry Division into the line and pulled the 24th Infantry Division back into reserve.

North of Taegu, meanwhile, the KPA 13th and 1st Divisions forced their way across the Naktong and by 9 August had collapsed the northwest corner of the

PFC Clarence Whitmore, voice radio operator of the 24th Infantry Regiment, reads the latest news while enjoying chow during a lull in the battle, near Sangju, 9 August 1950. (National Archives)

perimeter, pushing the divisions of ROKA II Corps down on top of the 1st Cavalry Division. To protect his valuable mobile communications system, Walker was forced to evacuate his headquarters from Taegu to Pusan. He also shifted the 27th Infantry Regiment again farther north. The 27th Infantry and the ROKA 1st Division attacked on 18 August and established positions overlooking a long, flat, narrow valley that became known as the Bowling Alley. On 19 August Walker also shifted elements of the 23d Infantry Regiment to reinforce the 27th. During the next six continuous nights the KPA 13th Division unsuccessfully tried to drive the U.S. forces back.

From 9 to 19 August, meanwhile, the KPA 5th Division attempted to infiltrate and envelope the right (north) side of the UN line with three divisions and an independent regiment on the Yŏngdŏk-P'ohang-Kyŏngju-Ulsan-Pusan axis. The North Korean objective was to drive all the way down the east coast to Pusan. The defensive battles along the north flank were an operation primarily under the control of the ROKA I Corps. Walker did send a small task force of artillery and armor, and the South Koreans received massive U.S. air and naval support.

Both geography and hydrography provided perfect conditions for naval gunfire support of the ROKA 3d Division. The straightness of the Korean east coast, the sea depth along the coast, and the high coastal terrain that forced the major roads right to the edge of the coast all meant that the KPA forces were almost constantly within range of the ships' guns. Naval gunfire and tactical air support from the Fifth Air Force helped the ROKA 3d Division overcome its weakness in organic artillery.

Naval and air fires gave the ROKA units a further maneuver advantage by forcing the KPA forces to operate primarily at night and away from the main coastal roads. These fires also allowed the South Koreans to exploit both the advantage of falling back on interior lines and the advantage of UN maritime superiority. The best example of this came during the 16–17 August evacuation of the ROKA 3d Division from Tŏksŏng-ni by sea while the Fifth Air Force maintained a curtain of fire around the beach. By 18 August the 3d Division was moving into battle positions near P'ohang, some twenty-five miles to the south, and still capable of continuing the fight. At that point, however, the Pusan perimeter had been collapsed from the north to about half its original size.

Starting on 27 August the North Koreans launched another round of attacks that fell on the same objectives as the earlier August drives. This time the attacks were well coordinated and hit simultaneously. By 3 September Walker was forced to fight defensive battles in five different locations at the same time.

On the northern flank the ROKA 3d Division was forced out of P'ohang on 6 September and the KPA cut the east-west road to Taegu. In the center by 10 September the North Koreans had pushed the 1st Cavalry Division to within fifteen miles of Taegu. Farther south the 2d Infantry Division was driven back to just short of Yŏngsan in the Naktong bulge. In the far south the KPA broke through the 25th Infantry Division and again threatened Masan.

American casualties during the first two weeks of September 1950 were the heaviest of the war. Yet with the security of Pusan always in the forefront, Walker continued to shift his reserves from danger point to danger point inside his ever-shrinking perimeter. Attaching the 1st Marine Brigade to the 2d Infantry Division, he ordered the clearing of the Naktong bulge for the second time. Walker also centrally positioned one of the 24th Infantry Division's regiments where it could be used to reinforce either the 25th Infantry Division, the 2d Infantry Division, or ROKA units in the north.

By 12 September the North Korean offensive reached its culminating point and stalled. The entire KPA was now overextended, dangerously out of position, and off-balance. All of its effective combat power was arrayed around the Pusan perimeter. Its land and sea LOCs were under constant attack by U.S. naval and air forces. The North Koreans were now a ripe target for a turning movement at operational depth. They still had close to 70,000 troops around the Pusan perimeter. Inside, the Eighth Army now had 84,500 troops and the ROKA some 72,000.

The U.S. X Corps landed at Inch'ŏn on 15 September. The Eighth Army started its breakout the next day. Walker wanted to wait one day after the Inch'ŏn landings to let the reality of being cut off sink in for the North Koreans. On the 16th, however, there was little sign that KPA forces were even aware of the situation to the north, despite a massive bombardment of psychological warfare leaflets and broadcasts.

The Eighth Army plan called for the breakout to be made by the newly activated U.S. I Corps just north of Taegu. I Corps at that point consisted of the 1st Cavalry Division, the 24th Infantry Division, the ROKA 1st Division, the 5th RCT, and the British 27th Infantry Brigade. The 5th RCT and the 1st Cavalry Division were supposed to seize a bridgehead over the Naktong near Waegwan. The 24th Infantry Division would then cross the river and drive along the Kimch'ŏn- Taejŏn-Suwŏn axis to effect a linkup with X Corps. Other units of the Eighth Army would conduct holding attacks along the perimeter to pin the North Koreans in place.

The Eighth Army experienced great difficulty in making the breakout. Walker's units were burned out after almost two months of heavy and continuous combat. They also lacked the proper river crossing equipment, and ammunition was in short supply. Determined KPA troops held on grimly but finally showed signs of breaking on 22 September. The next day the North Koreans began a general withdrawal.

The allies followed in pursuit. The lead U.S. unit was Task Force Lynch, organized around the 1st Cavalry Division's 3d Battalion, 7th Cavalry. At 0826 hours on 27 September just north of Osan, Task Force Lynch linked up with elements of the U.S. 7th Infantry Division's 31st Infantry Regiment.

The battle for the Pusan perimeter was over. At the tactical level the North Korean attacks had mostly been a series of poorly coordinated attempts to penetrate, infiltrate, and/or envelop the Pusan perimeter. At the operational level they added up to one big frontal attack, and a piecemeal one at that. The single biggest flaw in the KPA's operational concept was its inability to achieve the necessary mass at a decisive point. Its only hope had been to achieve overwhelming mass at one point, punch through the thinly held UN lines, and drive straight for Pusan. It failed to do this, although it came the closest at Taegu.

General Walker conducted an effective mobile defense. It was both active and flexible. The perimeter was thinly held, manned by a series of strong points on key terrain that commanded the principal river crossing sites, the major hills, and the road junctions. With his three U.S. divisions and all five Korean divisions on line, Walker carefully husbanded and formed reserves with the units that were coming in through Pusan. Eighth Army had two primary locations for holding reserves, Kyŏngsan and Samnangjin-Miryang, but the reserve forces were committed to wherever a trouble spot erupted. After a given situation was restored, the reserves were withdrawn for commitment elsewhere.

Eighth Army's counterattacks in the south were conducted under the control of the division in the line, after being reinforced by commitment of Eighth Army reserves. For the counterattacks in the north, the counterattacking forces remained under Eighth Army control. At times General Walker had to pull a regiment of a committed division out of the line and shift it elsewhere. For example, after the 25th Infantry Division had stopped the attack toward Masan (5–12 August), the 27th Infantry Regiment was pulled out of the line and sent north to assist the 24th Infantry Division at the Naktong bulge (12–16 August); and then north again (18–25 August) to stop the KPA attack against Taegu on the Kunwi axis.

From the very start General Walker had conducted his defense with the ultimate objective of shifting over to the offensive once the KPA attack reached culmination. Critical to this was maintaining the viability of the internal LOCs, which would be essential to support and sustain any breakout. Walker therefore was able to give up far more ground in the north, where the original line of the perimeter was almost forty miles from the apex of the LOC network at Yŏngch'ŏn. Along the western side of the perimeter the LOCs were much closer, giving the defenders far less flexibility.

By the time I Corps and X Corps linked up on 27 September, the KPA had been all but annihilated. Only 20,000 to 30,000 of its troops besieging Pusan ever returned to North Korea. The defenders paid a high price as well. Between 5 July and 16 September, Eighth Army casualties totaled 4,280 killed in action, 12,377 wounded, 2,107 missing, and 401 confirmed captured.

—*David T. Zabecki*

References:

Appleman, Roy E. *South to the Naktong, North to the Yalu.* Washington, DC: Office of the Chief of Military History, 1961.

Blair, Clay. *The Forgotten War: America in Korea, 1950–1953.* New York: Times Books, 1987.

Ent, Uzal W. *Fighting on the Brink: Defense of the Pusan Perimeter.* Paducah, KY: Turner, 1996.

Hoyt, Edwin P. *The Pusan Perimeter.* New York: Stein & Day, 1984.

Robertson, William G. *Counterattack on the Naktong, 1950.* Fort Leavenworth, KS: Combat Studies Institute, 1985.

See also: Bowling Alley; Inchŏn Landings: Operation CHROMITE; MacArthur, Douglas; Naktong Bulge, First Battle of; Naktong Bulge, Second Battle of; Osan, Battle of; Taegu, Defense of; Task Force Kean; Task Force Smith; Walker, Walton Harris.

Pyŏn Yŏng-t'ae
(1892–1969)

Republic of Korea (ROK) diplomat. Born in Seoul on 15 December 1892, Pyŏn Yŏng-t'ae graduated from Posŏng High School in Seoul in 1909 and from Xinxing School in Manchuria in 1912. He studied at Xiehe University near Beijing (Peking) in 1915 and taught English at Chung'ang High School, Seoul, from 1920 to 1943. To avoid any connection with Japanese colonial authorities during their national mobilization for World War II, in the spring of 1943 Pyŏn moved to a little farm at Pup'yŏng, between Seoul and Inch'ŏn. From 1945 to 1949 he taught English at Korea University, Seoul. Pyŏn's literary works include *My Attitude Toward Ancestor Worship* (1925), *Tales from Korea* (1943), and *Song from Korea* (1948).

In February 1949 ROK president Syngman Rhee sent Pyŏn to the Philippines as his personal envoy, and he was successful in establishing official recognition of the ROK by the Philippines. During this trip Pyŏn had the opportunity to visit with General Douglas MacArthur in Tokyo. Pyŏn exposed Rhee's policy of "unification through military means" as being unrealistic and motivated by domestic politics. Pyŏn did, however, emphasize to MacArthur the need to strengthen ROK military forces.

In February 1951 Pyŏn was a Korean delegate at the United Nations Economic Commission for Asia and the Far East (UNECAFE) held in Lahore, Pakistan. During this conference the Soviet delegate proposed that the ROK's associate membership in UNECAFE be ended because of its government's "non-democratic nature." Pyŏn made a strong impression in his shrewd responses to scathing attacks from the Soviet delegate; he also was able to disarm the Soviet attacks by dispassionately laying out the real situation in Korea. When the Soviet Union obstructed further activities of UNECAFE, its own membership was terminated.

Upon his return to Korea, Pyŏn became minister of foreign affairs. In the late spring of 1951 he went on a speaking tour in the United States in support of U.S. foreign aid around the world. Pyŏn appealed to the American people to protect their own freedom and that of the rest of the Free World by helping to rebuild Korea, thereby forestalling the threat of communism.

Pyŏn led the ROK delegation to the UN General Assembly Seventh Session, from October 1952 to March 1953. There he met with U.S. Secretary of State Dean G. Acheson and stressed the necessity of a mutual defense treaty between the ROK and the United States. During the conference proceedings Pyŏn defended his government, which had been criticized in a report by the UN Commission for the Unification and Rehabilitation of Korea. He also refuted issues regarding prisoners of war raised by the Indian delegation.

Along with General Ch'oe Tŏk-sin and Colonel Yi Su-yŏng, Pyŏn participated at the special UN General Assembly session held in August 1953 in preparation for carrying out Clause 60 of the Military Armistice Agreement on Korea. Pyŏn was successful in blocking Indian participation at the political conference that followed. He was also able to secure representation in its preparatory meeting, which included the ambassadors of the sixteen nations that participated on the UN side in the Korean War. This strengthened the ROK position at the ensuing political conference.

While Pyŏn was in the United States for the Eighth UN General Assembly Session in September 1953, he helped dissuade U.S. politicians and journalists regarding possible "neutralization" of Korea and establishment of a "buffer zone" there. He also informed them about the reality of coercive "persuasion" tactics used by the Communists on anti-Communist prisoners of war.

The 1954 Geneva Conference provided another opportunity for Pyŏn to exhibit his diplomatic skills. He succeeded in frustrating both Nam Il's proposal to institute a Korean Commission with an equal number of members from the two Korean national assemblies and a Philippine proposal to establish a constitutional assembly with representatives from the two Korean states. At that time the Eisenhower administration was considering supporting a policy that would call for general elections in both North and South Korea, establishment of a buffer zone between the People's Republic of China and Korea, and the simultaneous withdrawal of Chinese and United Nations Command (UNC) military forces from Korea. Pyŏn dissuaded the U.S. delegates from supporting such a plan by reminding them of the previous negative experiences following negotiated arrangements with the Communists. Subsequently Pyŏn secured the support of fifteen of the sixteen nations participating in the Korean War on the UN side to endorse the ROK proposal as outlined in a sixteen-nation communiqué, which included the ROK.

After serving as ROK prime minister from June to November 1954, Pyŏn retired from government. He received an honorary doctorate in literature from Korea University in May 1962 and became a professor at Seoul National University and Korea University in 1965. He died in 1969.

—Man-ho Heo

References:
Chŏng In-hŭng, Kim Sŏng-hŭi et al., eds. *Chŏngch'ihak Sajŏn* [Dictionary of political science]. Seoul: Pakyŏng-sa, 1994.
Pyŏn Yŏng-t'ae. *Na ŭi Choguk* [Korea, my country: memoirs]. Seoul: Chayu Ch'ulp'an-sa, 1956.
———. *Oegyo Yŏrok* [The other story of diplomacy]. Seoul: Han'guk Ilbo-sa, 1959.
See also: Acheson, Dean Goodersham; Geneva Conference of 1954; MacArthur, Douglas; Nam Il; Syngman Rhee.

P'yŏngyang

City at the estuary of the Taedong River in North Korea. The oldest city in Korea, reportedly Old Chosŏn was founded there in 2333 B.C. by King Tan'gun, the mythic father of the Korean people. It served as the northern capital during the Koryŏ Dynasty (918–1392). During the Japanese occupation P'yŏngyang was a major industrial and railroad center and, with almost half a million residents, the obvious choice to become the newly proclaimed regime's capital. From the late 1940s, P'yŏngyang has been the capital of the Democratic People's Republic of (DPRK, North Korea), the formation of which was announced on 9 September 1948.

For reasons of both morale and strategy, after September 1950 P'yŏngyang's capture became one of the principal objectives for United Nations Command (UNC) forces, and on 20 October 1950 it was taken by the advancing U.S. Eighth Army. U.S. and South Korean troops alike regarded it as a base for rest and recreation, and some incidents of looting occurred.

Following the late October 1950 Chinese intervention in the war, in mid-November the U.S. State Department proposed a halt to UN offensive operations and a withdrawal to just north of P'yŏngyang and Wŏnsan. UNC commander General Douglas MacArthur rejected this and on 24 November commenced his "final" offensive.

The second and massive Chinese intervention of late November 1950 forced UNC forces to evacuate P'yŏngyang on 3 December 1950, and two days later the city burned to the ground—whether accidentally or as a final vindictive act of retaliation on the part of UNC troops is still unclear. When Communist forces retook P'yŏngyang they circulated vivid pictures around the world of the devastated ruins in a major propaganda coup. From then until the 1953 armistice, the city was a major target for air raids by UN air forces, often using delayed-action bombs that exploded as much as seventy-two hours after they were dropped. Summer 1952 bombing raids also targeted five nearby dams that controlled the water supplies needed for the rice harvest, causing severe flooding in much of the North. P'yŏngyang's population dwindled to 50,000, and these, including Kim Il Sung's government, spent most of the daylight hours in a system of deep bunkers and trenches. One aim of the air raids was the psychological destabilization of P'yŏngyang's population, but, as with similar bombing campaigns in other wars, civilian morale tended to survive relatively intact.

After the 27 July 1953 armistice, P'yŏngyang was rebuilt as a showplace for the DPRK government, although in the later 1990s the ravages of famine began to disturb its immaculate façade. It continues as the DPRK capital and its "special municipality."

—*Priscilla Roberts and Jinwung Kim*

References:

Cumings Bruce, *Korea's Place in the Sun: A Modern History.* New York: W. W. Norton, 1997.

Halliday, Jon, and Bruce Cumings. *Korea: The Unknown War.* New York: Pantheon, 1988.

See also: MacArthur, Douglas; North Korea, United Nations Command Occupation of.

P'yŏngyang: March to and Capture of (October 1950)

The United Nations Command (UNC) invasion of North Korea officially began on 7 October 1950 after the failure of the government of the Democratic People's Republic of Korea (DPRK, North Korea) to respond to UNC commander General Douglas MacArthur's proclamation of the UN resolution demanding its surrender. The invading UNC force consisted of the U.S. I Corps of the Eighth Army in the west and the U.S. X Corps in the east. The U.S. I Corps then driving on the DPRK capital of P'yŏngyang from

the vicinity of Kaesŏng consisted of the 1st Cavalry Division followed by the 24th Infantry Division. In the east along the coast the Republic of Korea Army (ROKA) First Corps had pushed ahead of U.S. X Corps and took the port city of Wŏnsan on 11 October. Two weeks later, on 25 October, X Corps forces landed at Wŏnsan by sea.

The 1st Cavalry Division ran into stubborn Korean People's Army (KPA, North Korean) resistance on its way to Kŭmch'ŏn. A strong KPA roadblock just north of Kaesong temporarily halted two battalions of the 5th Cavalry Regiment, and the 7th and 8th Cavalry Regiments of the division quickly moved forward to aid in taking the town. The 7th Cavalry made a wide sweep to block the main highway north of Kŭmch'ŏn and create a pocket, into which the 5th and 8th Cavalry Regiments slowly pushed the KPA defenders. It took five days of fighting, however, before KPA resistance ceased and Kŭmch'ŏn fell. After this battle, the North Koreans limited their defense to slowing down advancing U.S. troops and ambushing lightly protected service units.

During this time two other divisions moved on line with the 1st Cavalry. On the west the 24th Division moved toward the port of Chinnamp'o. On the right the 1st ROKA Division moved toward P'yŏngyang. In addition, the 27th British Commonwealth Brigade, with its newly attached Australian 3d Battalion, pushed through the 1st Cavalry Division in the center and took over the lead to Sariwŏn.

Attacking UN units were moving so fast that they often overran many KPA units. Confusion over identity of uniforms affected both sides, and members of the 27th Brigade mistook stranded North Korean soldiers as South Korean troops. The North Koreans, on the other hand, thought the Scot Argylls of the 27th Brigade were Russians who had just entered the war to help them.

With the fall of Sariwŏn the race for the capture of P'yŏngyang began. From the south the U.S. I Corps continued to push rapidly north. From the southeast four ROKA divisions carried out a wide envelopment, racing one another to take the city. Capture of the DPRK capital now became a political objective. The North Koreans, however, were not prepared to give up their capital without a fight.

Two divisions led this race for P'yŏngyang: the U.S. 1st Cavalry and the ROKA 1st Division. On 18 October the 1st Cavalry Division was only thirty miles from the city, while the 1st ROKA Division was even closer but was being slowed by strong KPA resistance, the route in front of the ROKA division being heavily mined. As a consequence, on 19 October Company F of the 5th Cavalry Regiment became the first UN unit to reach the DPRK capital; it entered southwest P'yŏngyang at 1100 hours.

Tanks and infantry of the 1st Cavalry Division in pursuit of Korean People's Army forces some 14 miles north of Kaesŏng. (National Archives)

At almost the same time the ROKA 2d Battalion, 12th Regiment arrived at the south edge of the Taedong River. During the afternoon of the 19th the ROKA 11th Regiment secured P'yŏngyang airfield. By nightfall most of the ROKA 1st Division was in the main part of the city north of the Taedong River. After dark the 8th Regiment of the ROKA 7th Division moved into P'yŏngyang from the east.

In spite of the quick capture of much of P'yŏngyang, the KPA continued to resist and planned a last-ditch defense at the administrative center of the city. The next morning, 20 October, however, the ROKA 1st Division took the strongly fortified city administrative center with ease. North Korean defenders were too demoralized by the rapid approach of the Eighth Army to put up any fight and abandoned both guns and entrenchments. By midmorning the ROKA 1st Division reported the city secure. Shortly after-

ward, engineer boats were brought up and the U.S. 5th Cavalry Regiment began crossing the Taedong River. By noon both U.S. and ROKA forces had completely secured the city.

—*Daniel R. Beirne*

References:

Alexander, Bevin. *Korea: The First War We Lost.* New York: Hippocrene Books, 1986.

Appleman, Roy E. *South to the Naktong, North to the Yalu.* Washington, DC: Office of the Chief of Military History, 1961.

Blair, Clay. *The Forgotten War: America in Korea, 1950–1953.* New York: Times Books, 1987.

James, D. Clayton, with Anne Sharp Wells. *Refighting the Last War: Command and Crisis in Korea, 1950–1953.* New York: Free Press, 1993.

Whelan, Richard. *Drawing the Line: The Korean War, 1950–53.* Boston: Little, Brown, 1990.

See also: MacArthur, Douglas; P'yŏngyang; Tenth Corps.

Q

Qin Jiwen (Ch'in Chi-Wen)
(1914–1997)

General and commander of the Chinese People's Volunteer Army (CPVA, Communist Chinese) Fifteenth Army during the Korean War. Born in Huangan, Hubei Province, China, on 16 November 1914, Qin Jiwen in his long military career advanced from soldier to People's Republic of China (PRC) minister of defense. Qin was a capable commander in the Second Field Army against the Japanese when they invaded China and during the Chinese Civil War (1946–1949).

Qin's Fifteenth Army entered Korea in March 1951 in the second wave of reinforcements. After participating in the CPVA's Fifth Offensive, the Fifteenth Army was stationed in the Obong-san Mountain area. Some of its units were deployed on the hilltops of Sanggamnyŏng, a strategically important position for the Chinese defense line that directly threatened Kimhwa on the thirty-eighth parallel. Since the post was exposed to United Nations Command (UNC) attack, five companies from the 45th Division of the Fifteenth Army constructed tunnels to assist in its defense.

Qin directed the Chinese defense at Sanggamnyŏng during a UNC attack during 14 October–25 November 1952. It saw some of the most brutal and fierce fighting of the Korean War. General Qin's troops, deployed on two narrow hilltops of Sanggamnyŏng at the front tip of the Obong-san ranges, absorbed numerous UNC assaults and bombardments. The Fifteenth Army defeated numerous assaults on the surface and used the tunnels with great effectiveness, successfully defending the stronghold for more than one week before a large-scale Chinese counterattack ended the UNC offensive. The Chinese success there helped to strengthen the Communist bargaining position in the armistice negotiations.

After the Korean War, General Qin was promoted to deputy commander of the Yunnan Military District, then deputy commander of the Kunmin Military Region. In 1955 he was promoted to lieutenant general. As a trusted officer under Deng Xiaoping, then political commissar of the Second Field Army, he was promoted to commander of the Chengdu Military Region in 1974, commander of the Beijing Military Region in 1978, and PRC minister of defense in 1988. He served in the latter post until 1993. Qin Jiwen died on 2 February 1997.

—*Richard Weixing Hu*

References:

National Defense University of China. *Zhongguo Jundui Shizhan Shilu* [War cases of the Chinese armed forces]. Vol. 4. Beijing: Guofang Daxue Chubanshe, 1993.

Qin Jiwei. *Qin Jiwei Huiyilu* [Qin Jiwei memoirs]. Beijing: Jiefangjun Chubanshe, 1996.

Wu Rugao et al. *Zhongguo Junshi Renwu Dacidian* [Dictionary of Chinese military figures]. Beijing: Xinhua Chubanshe, 1989.

Zhongguo Junshi Dabaike Quanshu [Chinese military encyclopedia]. Military History, Vol. 3. Beijing: Military Science Press, 1997.

See also: China, People's Republic of: Army.

Quesada, Elwood R.
(1904–1993)

U.S. Air Force general who was instrumental in developing the air-ground coordination techniques for close air support during World War II that were used by the U.S. Air Force in support of ground forces during the Korean War. Born in Washington, D.C., on 13 April 1904, Elwood R. Quesada attended the University of Maryland and Georgetown University. In 1924 he enlisted in the army as a private, becoming a flying cadet in the Army Air Service and receiving his commission upon graduation. In 1929 he won fame by joining fellow aviators and latter-day generals Carl Spaatz, Ira C. Baker, Frank Andrews, and Henry "Hap" Arnold in the record-setting flight of the *Question Mark*, a test plane that the crew kept aloft for 151 hours through air-to-air refueling.

During the 1930s, Quesada had several assignments as personal pilot for a number of prominent government figures such as Secretary of War George H. Dern. Captain Quesada attended the Command and General Staff School at Fort Leavenworth, Kansas, graduating in 1937. Other assignments included service as air attaché in Cuba and Argentina.

In late 1940 Quesada became Arnold's foreign liaison chief and went with him to London in April 1941 to set up lend-lease operations with British air leaders. Three months later in July 1941, Major Quesada assumed command of the 33d Pursuit Group at Mitchell Field, New York. By December 1942 he had risen to the rank of brigadier general and was in command of the 1st Air Defense Wing, making preparations to go to North Africa. Once there, he took command of the XIIth Fighter Command. Quesada led his men in missions over Tunisia, Morocco, Sicily, Corsica, and southern Italy.

In the fall of 1943 Quesada was summoned to England to command the IX Fighter Command (later renamed the IX Tactical Air Command). He led this group in preparations for the Allied invasion of France, and the day after D-Day established his headquarters on French soil. Quesada helped plan the breakout from the Normandy beaches, and he developed the air-ground coordination techniques for close air support that remain part of current U.S. military doctrine. Until the end of the war he directed his command in operations in support of the Allied advance across France and Germany.

After the war, General Quesada went to Washington as assistant chief of staff for the U.S. Air Force. From March 1946 to November 1948 Major General Quesada served as the first commander of the Tactical Air Command. Then he devoted his attention to several projects for the new Joint Chiefs of Staff before assuming command of Joint Task Force Three.

Quesada retired from the air force in 1951. Four years later President Dwight Eisenhower appointed him his special assistant. During the next six years he not only wrote the legislation establishing the Federal Aviation Agency but also served as its first administrator. General Quesada died on 9 February 1993.

—*James H. Willbanks*

References:

Frisbee, John L., ed. *Makers of the United States Air Force.* Washington, DC: Office of Air Force History, 1987.

Futrell, Robert F. *The United States Air Force in Korea, 1950–1953.* Rev. ed. Washington, DC: Office of the Chief of Air Force History, 1983.

Kohn, Richard H., and Joseph P. Harahan, eds. *Air Superiority in World War II and Korea: An Interview with General James Ferguson, General Robert M. Lee, General William W. Momyer, and Lieutenant General Elwood R. Quesada.* Washington, DC: Office of Air Force History, 1983.

Momyer, William W. *Air Power in Three Wars: WWII, Korea, Vietnam.* Washington, DC: Department of the Air Force, 1978.

See also: Close Air Support; Eisenhower, Dwight D.; Forward Air Controllers (FACs).

R

Radford, Arthur W.
(1896–1973)

U.S. admiral, commander in chief, Pacific, and commander in chief, U.S. Pacific Fleet, April 1949 to August 1953, then chairman of the Joint Chiefs of Staff. Born in Chicago, Illinois, on 27 February 1896, Arthur W. Radford graduated from the U.S. Naval Academy in Annapolis in 1916 and saw action aboard the battleship *South Carolina* during World War I. During the interwar period Radford became a naval aviator, spent three years with the U.S. Navy Bureau of Aeronautics, and served with aviation units attached to the *Colorado*, *Pennsylvania*, and *Wright*. He eventually commanded a fighter squadron on the carrier *Saratoga*.

When World War II began in Europe, Radford was commander of the U.S. Naval Air Station, Seattle, Washington. He returned to sea duty in 1940 aboard the aircraft carrier *Yorktown*, then with the U.S. Pacific Fleet, and was aboard it at the time of the 7 December 1941 Japanese attack on Pearl Harbor, Hawaii. Shortly thereafter, Radford was chosen as the director of the navy's aviation training program, which was then undergoing a major expansion. In April 1943 he was promoted to rear admiral and was again assigned to the Pacific Fleet, where he commanded a carrier division that participated in numerous amphibious operations, including the November 1943 landings at Tarawa in the Gilbert Islands. In May 1944 Radford became assistant deputy chief of naval operations for air at the Navy Department in Washington. He was promoted to vice admiral in 1945.

After the war Radford held a number of posts, including vice-chief of naval operations. He was a primary leader in the "Revolt of the Admirals" that erupted in 1949 over the navy's opposition to the Truman administration's emphasis on creating a sizable U.S. Air Force strategic bomber capability, allegedly at the expense of sea power.

Appointed commander in chief, Pacific, and commander in chief of the U.S. Pacific Fleet in April 1949, Radford was a strong anti-Communist and a firm believer that the greatest threat to U.S. national security lay in Asia rather than in Europe. He did not, however, have any direct responsibility for U.S. forces in the Korean War, because after its start one of Radford's subordinate commands, the newly formed U.S. Seventh Fleet, was placed under control of the commander in chief of the United Nations Command (UNC), General Douglas MacArthur. An advocate of an "Asia First" strategy and an admirer of General MacArthur, Radford supported the Inch'ŏn landing plan and approved of the long-range UN goal of a military reunification of the Korea peninsula. He was present at the Wake Island Conference between President Harry S. Truman and MacArthur, later recalling that he had interpreted MacArthur's assurance that UN forces could handle Chinese forces should they intervene to mean that the Communists would not pose a problem so long as U.S. warplanes could strike their bases in Manchuria. As with MacArthur, Radford was frustrated by restrictions placed on UN forces after the intervention of the Chinese People's Volunteer Army (CPVA, Chinese Communist). When in April 1951 Truman relieved MacArthur of his command, Radford gave the returning general a hero's welcome in Hawaii.

In 1952 Radford joined president-elect Dwight D. Eisenhower on his trip to Korea. The admiral, then commander of the Philippine-Formosa area, made a favorable impression on Eisenhower, who the following summer nominated him as chairman of the Joint Chiefs of Staff, a position he accepted and held from 1953 until 1957. As Eisenhower considered alternatives for ending the stalemated Korean War, Radford reportedly recommended threatening the People's Republic of China with attacks on their Manchurian bases and the use of atomic weapons. Radford suggested similarly aggressive measures to the president in the spring of 1954 following French pleas for U.S. military intervention in aid of the beleaguered garrison at Dien Bien Phu in Indo-China.

Retiring from the U.S. Navy in 1957, Radford entered the business world, yet he also served as a military adviser in the presidential campaigns of Republican vice-president Richard M. Nixon in 1960 and Republican senator Barry Goldwater in 1964. He died in Washington, D.C., on 17 August 1973.

—Clayton D. Laurie

References:

Jurika, Stephen, Jr., ed. *From Pearl Harbor to Vietnam: The Memoirs of Admiral Arthur W. Radford.* Stanford, CA: Hoover Institution Press, 1980.

Who's Who in America, 1968–1969. Chicago: Marquis, 1968.

See also: Eisenhower, Dwight D.; Joint Chiefs of Staff (JCS); MacArthur, Douglas; Nixon, Richard Milhous; Truman, Harry S.; Truman's Recall of MacArthur

Radhakrishnan, Sarvepalli
(1888–1975)

Indian Ambassador to the Soviet Union from 1949 to 1952 who contributed to unsuccessful Indian attempts to bring about a negotiated settlement of the Korean War. Born on 5 September 1888, in Tiruttani in the state of Madras, Sarvepalli Radhakrishnan studied at Voorhees College, Vellore, and Madras Christian College. This led to an academic career as a renowned philosopher and scholar. After holding a variety of university positions, Radhakrishnan was appointed to the King George V chair of moral philosophy at the University of Calcutta, where he remained for almost twenty years. As a visitor he also taught and lectured at numerous Western academic institutions, including All Souls College, Oxford; the University of London; and the University of Chicago.

Although not a member of the Congress Party, Radhakrishnan was friendly with both Mohandas K. Gandhi and Jawaharlal Nehru, and he made wide use of the Western contacts available to the Congress Party. He won outstanding nationalist credentials in 1942 when, as vice chancellor of Benares Hindu University, a center for Indian freedom fighters, he resisted the British viceroy's attempts to close down that institution. In 1947 he was elected to the constituent assembly, and in 1949 Nehru appointed him Indian ambassador to the Soviet Union, a post in which he convinced Josef Stalin and other Soviet leaders that India was sincere in adopting a nonaligned posture. The idealistic ambassador believed that India had the potential to provide an ideological bridge between the antagonistic Cold War camps and thereby serve as an important force promoting world peace.

To Radhakrishnan the Korean War initially seemed to offer an outstanding opportunity for India to play just such a conciliatory and mediating role. A few days after the war began, India's Ministry of External Affairs instructed him to explore with both Soviet officials and U.S. diplomats in Moscow the possibility of a negotiated peace settlement. Even before receiving this message, Radhakrishnan had begun to do so, engaging in friendly conversations with Josef Stalin and others. In early July he suggested to Nehru that the United States be asked to support admission of the People's Republic of China (PRC, Communist China) to the United Nations, in exchange for Soviet support in the Security Council for an immediate cease-fire in Korea, the withdrawal of North Korean troops behind the 38th parallel, and the creation of a united and independent Korean state. These proposals became the foundation for Nehru's fruitless July peace initiative, in which he sent messages calling for negotiations to Moscow, Washington, and Beijing. U.S. Secretary of State Dean Acheson turned him down flatly, while Stalin temporized, but with hindsight it seems unlikely that such proposals, an effective abdication of their position in North Korea, could ever have been acceptable to Soviet leaders. As the Korean War pro-

gressed, Radhakrishnan continued to support all peace initiatives but had little influence on policy.

In 1952 Radhakrishnan returned to India and successfully ran for election for the first of what would be two five-year terms as India's vice-president. In 1962 he was elected president, where he exercised a stabilizing influence during India's wars with China and Pakistan and two prime ministerial transitions. Disillusioned with politics, after his retirement in January 1967 Radhakrishnan became a near recluse. He died in Madras on 16 April 1975.

—*Priscilla Roberts*

References:
Copley, Antony R. H. "Radhakrishnan, Sir Sarvepalli." In *Dictionary of National Biography, 1971–1980,* edited by Lord Blake and C. S. Nicholls. Oxford: Oxford University Press, 1986.
Gopal, Sarvepalli. *Jawaharlal Nehru: A Biography.* London: Jonathan Cape, 1979.
Kux, Dennis. *Estranged Democracies: India and the United States, 1941–1991.* New Delhi: Sage, 1993.
Reid, Escott. *Envoy to Nehru.* Delhi: Oxford University Press, 1981.
Stueck, William W., Jr. *The Korean War: An International History.* Princeton, NJ: Princeton University Press, 1995.
Wolpert, Stanley. *Nehru: A Tryst with Destiny.* New York: Oxford University Press, 1996.
See also: Acheson, Dean Goodersham; India; Nehru, Jawaharlal; Stalin, Josef.

Railroads, Korean National

Both United Nations Command (UNC) and Communist forces in Korea relied on railroads as the principal means of meeting their requirements for surface transportation. In June 1950 the Korean railway system, built by the Japanese in the early twentieth century, was in relatively good condition despite some damage during World War II. However, the system was sparse, and the rugged Korean terrain limited railroad capacity and the flexibility of the rail network. Moreover, railway operations in Korea were hampered throughout the war by the destruction of facilities, the lack of indigenous skills, and equipment deficiencies.

In 1950 there were three principal rail lines in Korea. The main line (double-tracked, standard gauge, and well ballasted) extended some 250 miles north from the port of Pusan on the southeastern coast through rugged hills via Taegu, Taejŏn, and Yŏngdŭngp'o to Seoul and then continued north up the western side of peninsula via P'yŏngyang to Sinŭiju on the Manchurian border. A second (single-tracked) line ran up the southeast coast from Pusan via Yŏngch'ŏn and Chech'ŏn to Wŏnju, where it turned eastward and terminated in the east-central mountains. The third principal line ran down the northeast coast from the Korean border with Manchuria and the Soviet Union via Hŭngnam and Wŏnsan to Yangyang just north of the 38th parallel. There was no connection between the two east coast lines, and until the opening of the Seoul-Ch'unch'ŏn line in July 1951 there were no lateral lines across the peninsula south of the 38th parallel, although in the North there were several single-track lateral lines. Feeder lines connected the port of Inch'ŏn and the other important ports and towns of southern and western Korea to the main line.

Capacity throughout the system was limited by steep grades and many curves, bridges, and tunnels, some of which made a 360 degree turn while climbing from one level to another. On the eastern single-track line, for example, there were 96 tunnels and 311 bridges in 310 miles. On 31 July 1951, the capacity of the main line from Taejon to Yŏngdŏngp'o was 18 trains (360 cars and 9,000 tons) per day. The southeast coast route could handle only about nine trains and 3,000 tons per day.

Before World War II the Korean National Railways were run by Japanese management and technical personnel, and Koreans generally performed only menial tasks. In June 1950 the number of experienced Korean personnel was limited, and the levels of training and technical expertise were not high. Consequently, in August 1950 U.S. Army railway operating units were deployed to Korea and used to supervise Korean workers.

When the U.S. 3d Transportation Military Railway Service began operations in August 1950, there were only 270 miles of track, 280 locomotives, 4,300 freight cars, and 450 passenger cars—all in various states of disrepair—available to UN forces. By January 1951 UN forces had the use of 1,080 miles of railroads, 305 locomotives, and 5,225 usable cars, and that month they moved some 340,000 tons of freight. In June 1951, 3,397 trains were dispatched, 769,850 tons were hauled, and 211,486 passengers were transported. In the last year of the war (July 1952 to July 1953), monthly rail movements averaged 1.25 million tons and 300,000 passengers.

—Charles R. Shrader

References:
Appleman, Roy E. *South to the Naktong, North to the Yalu.* Washington, DC: Office of the Chief of Military History, 1961.
Huston, James A. *Guns and Butter, Powder and Rice: U.S. Army Logistics in the Korean War.* Selinsgrove, PA: Susquehanna University Press, 1989.
———. *The Sinews of War: Army Logistics, 1775–1953.* Washington, DC: Office of the Chief of Military History, 1966.
Logistical Problems and Their Solutions. APO 301: Headquarters, Eighth U.S. Army Korea, Historical Section and Eighth Army Historical Service Detachment (Provisional), 1952.
See also: Logistics in the Korean War.

Rashin, Bombing of (see Najin, Bombing of)

RATKILLER, Operation
(2 December 1951–15 March 1952)

Four-phase Republic of Korea Army (ROKA) campaign against Korean People's Army (KPA, North Korean) guerrilla units and independent bandit groups operating behind the main line of resistance within the ROK in late 1951 and early 1952. Because of the seesaw nature of the Korean War in 1950 and 1951, as well as the Inch'ŏn landing in September 1950, large numbers of KPA troops were cut off or purposely left behind in the South to hinder United Nations operations and to harass ROK military and civilian officials as guerrillas. Additional thousands infiltrated through the main line of resistance for the same purposes. During November 1951 there was a significant upsurge in raiding activities as North Korean guerrillas launched well-coordinated attacks on ROK rail lines and installations. Although the raids were not in sufficient strength to inflict serious damage, Eighth Army commander Lieutenant General James Van Fleet decided to eliminate this irritation to the United Nations Command. In mid-November he ordered the ROKA to set up a task force of the Capital and 8th Divisions, minus artillery units. Van Fleet wanted the group organized and ready to stamp out guerrilla activity by the first of December 1951 in a four-phase operation. Since the region around Chiri-san contained the core of guerrilla resistance, Van Fleet directed that the first phase of the task force operations cover this mountainous stretch some twenty miles northwest of the city of Chinju.

On 1 December ROK president Syngman Rhee took the first step in eliminating the guerrilla threat by declaring martial law in southwestern Korea. This restricted the movement of civilians, established a curfew, and severed telephone connections between villages. On the following day Task Force Paek, named after ROKA commander Lieutenant General Paek Sŏn-yŏp, initiated the antiguerrilla campaign named Operation RATKILLER.

Moving in from a 163-mile perimeter, Task Force Paek closed on Chiri-san. The ROKA 8th Division pushed southward toward the crest of the mountains while the Capital Division moved northward to meet it. Blocking forces, composed of National Police, youth regiments, and area security forces, were stationed at strategic points to cut off possible escape routes. As the net was drawn tighter, groups of from 10 to 500 guerrillas each were flushed out, but only light opposition developed. After twelve days, on 14 December 1951, Task Force Paek ended the first phase of Operation RATKILLER with a total of 1,612 guerrillas reported killed and 1,842 captured.

The hunt then shifted north to North Chŏlla Province for phase two of Operation RATKILLER,

Communist guerillas, taken by the ROK Capital Division in the area around Chri-san, being fed at a POW stockade. (National Archives)

with the mountains around Chŏnju the chief objective. From 19 December to 4 January 1952, the ROKA 8th and Capital Divisions ranged the hills to trap both guerrillas and independent bandits hiding in the rough terrain. By the end of December it was estimated that over 4,000 guerrillas or bandits had been killed and some 4,000 captured.

When phase three opened on 6 January 1952, Task Force Paek returned to the Chiri-san region to capture or liquidate guerrillas who had filtered back into the area after phase one. On 19 January the Capital Division carried out the most significant action of the campaign. While the ROKA 26th Regiment took up blocking positions north of the mountains, the ROKA 1st and Cavalry Regiments attacked from the south in two consecutive rings. Although one small guerrilla group broke through the inner ring, it was caught by the outer circle of troops. What was believed to be the core of Communist resistance forces in South Korea perished or were taken prisoner during this final drive. When phase three ended at the close of January 1952, a total of more than 19,000 guerrillas and bandits had been killed or captured in Operation RATKILLER. The last phase, number four, was a mopping-up operation against light and scattered resistance. The ROKA 8th Division returned to the front in early February, while the Capital Division's mobile units sought to catch up with the remnants of the guerrillas. Operation RATKILLER officially terminated on 15 March, when local authorities assumed the remaining tasks of securing the countryside. The overall success of Operation RATKILLER is difficult to assess, as guerrilla activity continued even after the close of the campaign, albeit on a smaller scale.

—*Clayton D. Laurie*

Reference:
Hermes, Walter G. *United States Army in the Korean War: Truce Tent and Fighting Front.* Washington, DC: Office of the Chief of Military History, 1966.
See also: Paek Sŏn-yŏp; Syngman Rhee; Van Fleet, James Alward.

Rau, Sir Benegal Narsing
(1887–1953)

India's permanent representative at the United Nations (UN), 1949–1951, and Indian representative on the Security Council, 1950–1951. Born on 26 February 1887 in Mangalore in the South Kanara District of what was then British India, Benegal Narsing Rau was educated at Madras University, where he won first class honors in three separate subjects, and at Trinity College, Cambridge, where he also took a first-class honors degree in mathematics.

In 1910 Rau joined the Indian Civil Service and earned distinction as a legal specialist, particularly for his work in revising the Indian Statute Book in the

mid-1930s. From 1934 to 1938 he served as India's deputy high commissioner in London. Appointed reforms commissioner in 1938, he served as a judge of the high court of Calcutta from 1939 to 1944; during 1944-1945 he served as prime minister of Jammu and Kashmir. Rau's legal expertise and his diplomatic skills alike were much in demand for difficult and potentially contentious assignments. During the 1940s he twice served as chairman of a committee in charge of codifying Hindu law, and during 1946–1947 he was constitutional adviser to the governments of both India and Burma as they framed new constitutions in preparation for independence.

In 1948 Rau became a member of India's delegation to the UN, and in 1949 he was his country's permanent representative to that body. He was a staunch supporter of Prime Minister Jawaharlal Nehru's nonaligned and independent foreign policy. After India's recognition of the new People's Republic of China (PRC, Communist China) in December 1949, Rau argued his country's case that the UN should also accept Communist China's representatives on the grounds that only by such inclusion would China be forced to accept and respect international obligations and customs.

When North Korean forces invaded South Korea in late June 1950, Rau, India's nonpermanent representative on the UN Security Council, was serving as that body's president. He immediately convened the council in emergency session and, even though he felt some discomfort in doing so in the absence of instructions from his government, voted for the 25 June Security Council resolution calling on North Korean troops to withdraw from the South. Still uncertain as to his government's position, on 27 June he abstained from the subsequent Security Council resolution requesting member states to contribute military forces to the United Nations Command (UNC) to accomplish this objective.

From the beginning of the Korean crisis Rau tried to employ his charm and well-honed diplomatic skills to function as a voice of conciliation and moderation and also to carve out a distinctive role for India as a leading nonaligned nation. In August he was the leader in an abortive effort to set up a subcommittee of the Security Council's nonpermanent members to discuss UN objectives in Korea. As the fortunes of war began to favor the UN forces in September and early October 1950, Rau took the lead in efforts to deter their crossing the 38th parallel. From early November 1950, when Chinese forces intervened, he was a dedicated supporter of a cease-fire. In December 1950 he attempted unsuccessfully to persuade PRC leaders to rein in their troops at the demarcating 38th parallel.

Rau played a central role in drafting and steering through the General Assembly the UN resolution of 14

December 1950, which set up the three-person UN Cease-Fire Group, of which he was a member. In this capacity Rau initially succeeded in concentrating UN energies on the possibilities of a cease-fire, as opposed to the U.S. preference for pushing resolutions condemning the PRC. Soon, however, his efforts proved fruitless, as the Chinese followed in reverse the footsteps of the UNC forces and early in 1951 crossed the 38th parallel. Even so, Rau's maneuvers contributed to delaying passage of such a resolution until 1 February 1951, when the military situation had once more begun to turn in favor of UN forces. He also managed to moderate the resolution's language and recommendations sufficiently to reduce the possibility that the UNC would launch direct military attacks on the Chinese mainland, an abiding worry for Indian diplomats during the Korean conflict.

Although Rau would undoubtedly have welcomed serving on the UN Good Offices Committee established by the 1 February resolution, the Indian government's refusal to participate in its efforts denied him this chance. From then onward, although he personally welcomed all efforts to bring about a cease-fire, his role in the Korean crisis diminished. His name was widely mentioned as a potential successor to the somewhat lackluster UN Secretary-General Trygve Lie, who eventually stood down in 1953; but in late 1951 Rau left the UN to become a member of the International Court of Justice at The Hague. He died suddenly in Zurich, Switzerland, on 29 November 1953.

—*Priscilla Roberts*

References:

Barros, James. *Trygve Lie and the Cold War: The United Nations Secretary-General Pursues Peace, 1946–1953.* DeKalb: Northern Illinois University Press, 1989.

Gopal, S. "Rau, Sir Benegal Narsing." In *Dictionary of National Biography, 1951–1960,* edited by E. T. Williams and Helen M. Palmer. Oxford: Oxford University Press, 1971.

Kux, Dennis. *Estranged Democracies: India and the United States, 1941–1991.* New Delhi: Sage, 1993.

"Rau, Sir Benegal Narsing." In *Current Biography, 1951.* New York: H. W. Wilson, 1951.

Stueck, William W., Jr. *The Korean War: An International History.* Princeton, NJ: Princeton University Press, 1995.

See also: Cease-Fire Negotiations; India; Nehru, Jawaharlal.

Recoilless Rifles

Lightweight artillery developed for infantry use. Recoil—the rearward action of a weapon as it is discharged—is an intrinsic problem of artillery. The laws of physics dictate that the forward-directed energy of an artillery projectile must be counterbalanced by an equal amount of energy directed to the rear. Conventional artillery has long compensated for this often considerable rearward action with various combinations of buffers and springs. Although they are generally effec-

tive, such systems invariably greatly increase the weight of the weapon, hindering mobility. As early as 1910 U.S. Navy experiments indicated that, by redirecting a percentage of the blast rearward, the recoil and thus the weight of a weapon could be greatly reduced.

In the 1930s the German armaments firm Krupp renewed the recoilless weapon experiments in its search for a lightweight gun for airborne and mountain troops. Krupp's efforts resulted in the basic design still in use today. Their technicians mounted a rocket nozzle to the breech of the gun to redirect half the energy of the ignited propellant rearward. They were thus able to virtually eliminate the weapon's recoil and, by eliminating its conventional recoil system, greatly reduce its weight as well.

The Krupp design, however, does incur some liabilities. Although the gun itself is relatively lightweight, the ammunition is considerably heavier than that of conventional artillery. To both propel its shell and counterbalance its recoil, a recoilless weapon charge requires twice the propellant of a normal gun. Moreover, the back-blast and flash generated by the weapon's discharge can reveal its position and is hazardous to personnel directly behind the gun.

The U.S. issued recoilless rifles to its troops in Korea in both 57-mm and 75-mm calibers. The new weapons quickly proved that their relative light weight, accuracy, destructive power, and general versatility far outweighed their liabilities.

The tendency of Communist troops to establish bunkers high along Korea's innumerable hills frustrated the conventional artillery's efforts to neutralize them. These reinforced bunkers, dug beneath the ridge crests, were nearly impervious to indirect artillery fire and air attack. Infantry units, however, found their recoilless rifles mobile enough to manhandle within range of these positions; 75-mm recoilless rifle crews frequently exploited their guns' accuracy and flat trajectory to neutralize such bunkers with a single round at ranges up to 1,200 yards. Although lacking the range and destructive capabilities of the 75-mm gun, the 57-mm gun also had its merits. Many troops preferred it for its lighter weight and effectiveness.

Recoilless rifles also proved their versatility against armor and personnel. At close range the 75-mm guns were credited with the destruction of self-propelled guns as well as tanks. During a 1950 action south of Yudam-ni a single recoilless rifle destroyed numerous Chinese pillboxes and machine gun nests at ranges up to 1,300 yards. Switching to high-explosive ammunition, its crew then routed a company-size attack at a range of within 200 yards. Other recoilless rifle crews found 75-mm white phosphorous rounds particularly effective against night attacks at long range.

—*Jeff Kinard*

A 75-mm recoilless rifle of the 7th Infantry Division in action in Korea. (National Archives)

References:

Chant, Christopher, ed. *How Weapons Work*. London: Marshall Cavendish, 1976.

Marshall, S. L. A. *Commentary on Infantry Operations and Weapons Usage in Korea, Winter of 1950–51*. Chevy Chase, MD: Operations Research Office, 1951.

See also: Artillery; Machine Guns; Small Arms (Pistols, Rifles, Submachine Guns, Automatic Weapons).

Reconnaissance

The seeking out and gathering of information about enemy forces. Reconnaissance may be broken down into two categories: tactical and strategic. Tactical reconnaissance provides information regarding enemy forces that may be of immediate use to field commanders. Strategic reconnaissance yields information gathered for, and distributed to, war planners who interpret it and apply it to operations development. All service branches conduct reconnaissance.

The U.S. Air Force conducted the bulk of United Nations Command (UNC) aerial reconnaissance missions during the Korean War, although it was handicapped at the start of the conflict by having only one specialized reconnaissance squadron in the Far East. Utilizing modified aircraft, given the prefix "R" (for reconnaissance) to their designation, the Far East Air Force flew strategic-level reconnaissance with the RB-17 Flying Fortress and RB-29 Superfortress.

Only in January 1951 was the 67th Tactical Reconnaissance Wing assigned to Fifth Air Force. It flew the RF-51 Mustang, RF-80 Shooting Star, and RB-26 Invader. It also used the RF-86 Sabre jet to photograph the area of MiG Alley, the far north of Korea next to the Chinese border. During the period April 1952 to March 1953, the 67th Reconnaissance Wing carried out an average of 1,792 reconnaissance sorties a month.

The 1st Marine Aircraft Wing's Marine Photographic Squadron (VMJ-1) was later assigned to the Fifth Air Force's command, which broke the tradition of Marine Corps command of its own air assets. The Marines flew the F2H-2P Banshee photo-jet aircraft.

Although overshadowed by the army and air force, UN naval forces accounted for 30 percent of all U.S. reconnaissance operations during the Korean War. Ship patrols scouted out North Korean minelaying activities, and carrier-based missions provided both tactical and strategic intelligence. The UNC also used the Martin PMB-5S Mariner and the British air force's Sunderland, both flying boats (amphibious aircraft), for reconnaissance missions. Naval reconnaissance aircraft patrolled the skies along both the west and east coasts of Korea and along the coast of China.

Ground forces had the greatest need for tactical reconnaissance. In the air the army employed VHF radio–equipped L-17s to direct air force tank-busting aircraft against Communist positions. L-4 and L-5 small aircraft were also utilized to provide UNC forces information on Communist positions to their front. In February 1951 the first Cessna L-19As arrived in Korea. This magnificent aircraft soon replaced the L-4 and L-5 and became the backbone of U.S. Army aviation (reconnaissance, artillery spotting, occasional direction of air strikes, and general liaison) in Korea. The Marines also used this aircraft, designated the OE-1.

Observation helicopters were a new addition to the aviation units in Korea. The Hiller H-23A Raven was used for reconnaissance as well as other missions.

In the early stages of the war, the army neither appreciated the value nor made much use of aerial photography. Largely as a result of this, the UNC failed to detect the large numbers of Chinese People's Volunteer Army (CPVA) troops who moved into North Korea in October and November 1950. Part of this had to do with the delay between the actual photography and the availability of the processed information. There were also few trained photo interpreters available. Aerial photography proved its effectiveness in the 2d Infantry Division's success in crossing the Naktong River. Communist forces did their best to thwart aerial reconnaissance and photography by hiding during the day and moving only at night.

Although there was no military operations specialty for intelligence or reconnaissance when the Korean War began, every U.S. Army regiment had a special reconnaissance platoon and each division had a reconnaissance company with a tank section (usually M-24 Chaffee light tanks). Front-line forces regularly sent out numerous foot patrols to collect information regarding Communist forces. Corporal Gordon M. Craig, 16th Reconnaissance Company, 1st Cavalry Division, and Sergeant First Class Charles W. Turner,

2d Reconnaissance Company, 2d Infantry Division, were both awarded the Medal of Honor for actions behind Communist lines in Korea.

Early in the conflict, specially trained soldiers, known as line crossers, would cross enemy lines mixed in with migrating civilians to collect intelligence. This process was short-lived and disappeared once the front lines became stable and civilians were forced to the rear.

Because the UNC dominated the skies over the Korean peninsula during the war, Communist forces were unable to utilize aerial photography, and their reconnaissance activities were limited largely to ground patrols.

—Jonathan D. Atkins

References:
Field, James A., Jr. *History of United States Naval Operations: Korea.* Washington, DC: U.S. Government Printing Office, 1962.
Futrell, Robert F. *The United States Air Force in Korea, 1950–1953.* Rev. ed. Washington, DC: Office of the Chief of Air Force History, 1983.
Jackson, Robert. *Air War over Korea.* New York: Charles Scribner's Sons, 1973.
Politella, Dario. *Operation Grasshopper.* Wichita, KS: Robert R. Longo; 1958.
Summers, Harry G, Jr. *Korean War Almanac.* New York: Facts on File; 1990.
See also: Aircraft (Principal Combat).

Red Ball Express

Term for supply operation begun in September 1950 to meet the immediate emergency needs of United Nations Command (UNC) forces in Korea. The Red Ball Express was a highly organized and coordinated transportation operation supporting the UNC forces then driving the Korean People's Army (KPA, North Korean) northward. Airlift was extremely limited at this time in the war, and the U.S. Navy was having to clear captured ports of mines before supplies could be moved through them. The term Red Ball Express was taken from a similar operation in the European theater during World War II that used truck convoys to move supplies from the Normandy beaches to the Allied front.

The Red Ball Express cut some twelve hours off the normal sixty hours for shipping from the U.S. supply depot in Yokohama, Japan, to the South Korean port of Pusan. It carried about 300 measurement tons a day, utilizing two express trains from the Yokohama depot to the port of Sasebo.

Once the supplies were in Korea, they moved north by rail and truck. Motor transport was especially critical as UNC forces advanced away from their supply depots at Pusan and Inch'ŏn. During the first months of the Red Ball Express, 76 percent of the Eighth Army's trucks operated around the clock. The U.S. 2d Infantry Division was a primary contributor to the Red

Ball Express, at one point providing 320 trucks to supply I Corps from the Han River.

As the war progressed, South Korea's rail lines were rebuilt and took pressure off of supply by road. Throughout the war, similar rapid transportation of supplies played a vital role in supporting UNC forces. Once the Eighth Army's front stabilized, the supply situation became less critical. The supply lines were shortened and additional aerial resupply became available. The Red Ball Express ended in the summer of 1952.

—*Kevin J. Fromm*

References:

Huston, James A. *Guns and Butter, Powder and Rice: U.S. Army Logistics in the Korean War*. Selinsgrove, PA: Susquehanna University Press, 1989.

Summers, Harry G., Jr. *Korean War Almanac*. New York: Facts on File, 1990.

Westover, John G. *Combat Support in Korea*. Washington, DC: Combat Forces Press, 1955.

See also: Japan Logistical Command; Logistics in the Korean War; Railroads, Korean National; Second Logistical Command.

Red Cross

For over 100 years the International Red Cross and its affiliates have provided aid in disaster and war. In the mid-nineteenth century, Jean Henri Durant of Switzerland and Clara Barton of the United States lobbied for an organization to aid victims of catastrophes. In 1863 representatives of sixteen nations met in Geneva, Switzerland, to discuss the formation of such an organization. The envoys agreed upon two necessities: a need for volunteers to aid victims in natural disasters and war, and universally recognized neutrality for those administering the aid. Members named the organization the International Red Cross (IRC). By March 1882 the U.S. Congress had passed legislation that established the American Red Cross. In July of the same year, President Chester Arthur signed the bill into law.

The IRC and the American Red Cross fulfilled many divergent roles during the Korean War. Soon after the 1950 incursion, the IRC offered to act as an intermediary between the belligerent forces. Also, medical experience during World War II had established the importance of extensive blood supplies. The U.S. Surgeon General immediately launched a drive to collect whole blood, placing the American Red Cross in charge. Soon thereafter, the Red Cross expanded its processing capacity and eventually supplied 75 percent (961,000 units) of all the blood used during the conflict. In addition, organization personnel performed routine medical examinations to decide preliminary treatment. American women, serving as auxiliary personnel or Gray Ladies, supplied aid and comfort to wounded during their recuperation in Tripler Hospital at Hicham Air Force Base, Hawaii.

From the outset of the conflict, the IRC stood ready to provide aid to those involved—regardless of their political affiliation. But the Democratic People's Republic of Korea (DPRK, North Korea) and its allies frequently ignored the beneficent efforts of the IRC and typically used them for political gain. The Communist side repeatedly rejected humanitarian medical shipments and often shuffled United Nations Command (UNC) prisoners to various locations, successfully hampering attempts to confirm conditions and numbers. At one point, People's Republic of China (PRC, Communist Chinese) officials accused UN forces of employing bacteriological warfare and using prisoners of war in atomic bomb experiments. An IRC investigation disproved the reports.

In the spring of 1952, riots erupted at the Kŏje-do prisoner of war camp in the Republic of Korea (ROK, South Korea). Political differences among the Communist prisoners started the unrest, but the problems quickly involved ROK and U.S. guards. In gaining control, sentries opened fire, killing several prisoners. The IRC subsequently evaluated camp conditions and offered suggestions to avoid future incidents. UNC officials adopted several proposals and thus eased tensions.

The American Red Cross arranged emergency leave for men who had serious family problems. This service was a valuable asset to the troops. The agency also maintained "rest centers" behind the lines.

Two Red Cross volunteers, both men, died of wounds sustained during the Korean War. The multiple agencies of the Red Cross continue to provide aid and assistance throughout the world in peace and war.

—*Dean S. Brumley*

References:

Cowdrey, Albert E. *United States Army in the Korean War: The Medic's War*. Washington, DC: U.S. Army Center of Military History, 1987.

Hurd, Charles. *The Compact History of the American Red Cross*. New York: Hawthorne Books, 1959.

U.S. Department of State Bulletin, 9 July 1951; 1 October 1951; 12 March 1952; 12 January 1953.

White, William L. *Captives of Korea: An Unofficial White Paper on the Treatment of War Prisoners, Our Treatment of Theirs; Their Treatment of Ours*. New York: Charles Scribner's Sons, 1955.

See also: Biological Warfare.

Refugees

Civilians displaced by war. Refugees during the Korean War fled their homes in fear of imprisonment, reprisals, or execution by the Communists. This dispersal scattered families, separating spouses, parents, children, and other relatives. As Communist forces pushed south, refugees abandoned their homes and possessions to escape possible dangers and restrictions

Homeless, this brother and sister search empty cans for morsels of food and try to keep warm beside a small fire in the railroad yards in Seoul, Korea, 17 November 1950. (National Archives)

and to seek freedom in the South. Refugees stated that they fled to escape hardships such as forced labor and service in the Korean People's Army (KPA, North Korean). Others wanted to avoid retaliation for anti-Communist activities or those of family members. Refugees were also afraid of Chinese soldiers. Many refugees decided to flee when encouraged by friends or neighbors or when ordered to leave by authorities. Alternatives to fleeing included going underground to fight the Communists, hiding, or cooperating with the Communist occupation forces.

Before the war 3.5 million North Koreans had moved south, while far fewer Communist sympathizers moved into the North. Numerous intellectuals, writers, and political figures were kidnapped from the South to the North. Many who survived fled south after the invasion.

Some civilians used weapons to assist Republic of Korea (South Korean) forces in the defense of cities, such as Taejŏn in July 1950. Most civilians, however, were refugees, carrying their belongings on A-frames and traveling on foot or sometimes by oxcart or railroad car. Following motorized military forces, the refugees were not protected from Communist attacks. Thousands of refugees swarmed in masses on narrow roads and clustered waiting to cross bridges. Crowds of refugees risked death by climbing across the twisted metal of bombed bridges such as the Han River bridge at Seoul or the Taedong River bridge near P'yŏngyang. During winter, refugees suffered the hazards of crossing icy rivers on foot and with handmade rafts. Many left home without being able to tell their families where they were going or were separated en route.

When Chinese forces entered the war in October 1950, the flow of refugees expanded and Allied forces evacuated hundreds of thousands of civilians. Troops stockpiled food and straw at feeding stations, and refugees received inoculations and were dusted with DDT for lice. At the port of Hŭngnam, United Nations

(UN) soldiers filled boats with many times their capacity but were unable to transfer all awaiting refugees, some of whom chose to drown themselves instead of risking their fate with the Communists. Thousands of North Korean refugees were evacuated from other ports. Remaining refugees suffered from the scorched earth policy, which called for the destruction of all supplies from which the Communist enemy could benefit. From December 1950 to January 1951 almost 1 million North Koreans, of a total population of 9,500,000, fled to the South.

Starvation and disease affected refugees. Bitter winter weather caused fingers and toes to be lost to frostbite. Other wounds festered without medical care, and smallpox spread among refugees, who also felt constant fear and anxiety. Air raids and bombings threatened the columns of refugees moving south. Eighth Army commander Lieutenant General Matthew B. Ridgway remarked on 5 January 1951, "The southward exodus of several million refugees before the oncoming communist flood presents perhaps the greatest tragedy to which Asia has ever been subjected."

The UN offered refugees food, shelter, and medical care. The UN Civil Assistance Command, Korea provided clothing, housing, sanitary water supplies, and an education program to rehabilitate refugees. Private relief efforts, such as the International Refugee Organization and CARE, attempted to assist refugees, but many people rejected charity. Chaplains and nuns who opened health clinics also offered humanitarian assistance. Servicemen arranged for shoes and clothing for homeless children and secured toys for orphans at Christmas. "Operation Christmas Kidlift" airlifted war orphans to Cheju-do. By spring 1951, with the stabilization of the fighting front, refugee relief work was more routine than emergency because the number of new refugees significantly decreased.

Efforts then centered on alleviating suffering, improving public health, and assisting in the recovery of the Korean economy. Moving refugees to safety was a priority, but attempts to place refugees in shelters in the Cholla provinces in southwest Korea and other sites were not successful. Many refugees were determined to return to their homes.

Refugees presented danger to the UN Command war effort. Logistically they hindered troop movement along crucial roads. Often KPA soldiers used refugees as shields, driving them ahead of themselves. KPA soldiers also disguised themselves as refugees, wearing traditional white robes over their uniforms, to infiltrate UN lines. These fraudulent refugees served as a military weapon, harassing UN forces, sabotaging equipment, and securing intelligence. Such agents endangered the safety of UN troops, who experienced difficulty in determining who were refugees and who

were not. Legitimate refugees were also at risk of being shot or captured if they were mistakenly considered to be spies. Military police set up checkpoints to screen columns and control refugee traffic from clogging supply routes or impeding military traffic.

After the war, some refugees were fortunate enough to be reunited with family members. However, many refugees never saw their loved ones again nor their homes in the north. Not only was there physical separation but communication was cut as well. Parents mourned missing children, as children searched for their parents and siblings. Many spouses never remarried, hoping to find their wife or husband. In the armistice talks, negotiators discussed the "ten million dispersed families" of North and South Korea. Such separation was devastating in a culture devoted to ancestor worship and rites such as the visiting of graves during the harvest festival (*ch'usŏk*).

Efforts to reunite families were discussed during the armistice negotiations and in subsequent International Committee of the Red Cross meetings. Hoping to locate relatives, individuals published names and photographs of family members in newspapers. Although some contacts were established between families across the North and South, most refugees were not as fortunate.

In 1971 the Red Cross established a telephone line between North and South Korea at P'anmunjŏm for the exchange of information about relatives. Even if families could not visit, they hoped to learn the fate and whereabouts of their relatives. Continued tensions between the two Koreas prevented reunions, and many former refugees have been frustrated in their efforts to locate family members. The theme of family separation has remained popular in Korean television and dramatic plots.

During the summer of 1983 the Korean Broadcasting System televised a "reunion telethon." Individuals held placards with names and photographs, which were then broadcast. On the first day 850 people gave their information and 36 relatives were reunited. The telethon peaked with 238 reunions from 1,256 petitioners. Because of its popularity, the reunion telethon was rebroadcast every Friday for several months, reuniting more than 10,000 relatives. Although Koreans continued to employ posters, newspapers, and computers to search for lost family members, television has proved most useful for the illiterate.

—*Elizabeth D. Schafer*

References:
Kim, Choong Soon. *Faithful Endurance: An Ethnography of Korean Family Dispersal.* Tucson: University of Arizona Press, 1988.
Red Cross Conference in Korea, from Aug. 12, 1971 to Nov. 22, 1972. Seoul: Office of the South-North Red Cross Conference, Republic of Korea National Red Cross, 1972.

Republic of Korea National Red Cross. *The Dispersed Families in Korea.* Seoul: Republic of Korea National Red Cross, 1977.

Riley, John W., Jr., Wilbur Schramm, and Frederick W. Williams. "Flight from Communism: A Report on Korean Refugees." *Public Opinion Quarterly* 15 (Summer 1951): 274–286.

Samuels, Gertrude. "Korea's Refugees—Misery on the March." *New York Times Magazine,* 11 February 1951: 10–11.

Worden, William L. "The Cruelest Weapon in Korea." *Saturday Evening Post* 223, no. 33 (1951): 26–27, 134–136.

See also: Civilian Internee Issue; Hŭngnam Evacuation; Infiltration; Nogŭn-Nl Railroad Bridge Incident; RAT-KILLER, Operation; Ridgway, Matthew Bunker; Scorched Earth Policy; United States Army Military Police.

Repatriation, Voluntary

Policy developed by the United States for humanitarian and propaganda reasons whereby no Communist prisoner of war (POW) would be forced to return home against his will after the war. The Truman administration debated the policy between July 1951 and late February 1952 after the issue was first raised by Brigadier General Robert A. McClure, chief of the U.S. Army's Psychological Warfare Division. McClure had learned that many Chinese POWs had fought under Nationalist leader Jiang Jieshi (Chiang Kai-shek) during the recent civil war in China and had then been impressed into Communist service in Korea. He feared that many would face harsh punishments on their return as had Russian POWs in U.S. custody at the end of World War II. McClure further believed that a policy of voluntary repatriation would enhance the effectiveness of the United Nations' psychological warfare campaigns.

Controversies surrounding voluntary repatriation stalled the truce talks for nearly two years, and little consensus initially existed for the concept among U.S. and United Nations Command (UNC) military and political leaders; President Harry S. Truman was its main proponent. The Communists insisted on the return of all captured nationals, a demand that was strenuously opposed by the United States and the Republic of Korea (South Korea). Other UN members argued that POW issues should not stand in the way of an armistice and that the voluntary repatriation concept seemed to contradict Article 118 of the 1949 Geneva Convention. In addition, it was pointed out that it was very difficult to establish the true wishes of POWs while they were actually in custody.

When the concept was officially announced by UN negotiators at the peace talks on 2 January 1952, the Communists rejected it out of hand. But when UNC negotiators later indicated that as many as 116,000 out of 132,000 Communist POWs and 38,500 civilian internees would probably elect to return home, giving the impression that voluntary repatriation would not discredit Communist ideology, the Chinese agreed on

2 April 1952, to a POW screening to separate potential repatriates from nonrepatriates.

During the week-long Operation SCATTER, which started on 8 April 1952, the UNC produced figures contrary to original expectations, alleging that only 70,000 prisoners (7,200 civilians, 3,800 South Koreans, 52,900 North Koreans, and 5,100 Chinese) of the 170,000 total indicated any interest in returning to their homelands. The Communists were livid on being informed of the outcome of the screening on 19 April, considering it a UNC plot to humiliate them. They walked out of the peace talks on 28 April. As a result, UNC commander in chief (CINCUNC) Lieutenant General Matthew B. Ridgway, who personally opposed the policy, immediately sought permission from Washington to conduct a rescreening under the supervision of a neutral nation or the International Red Cross.

When the truce talks resumed on 7 May 1952, the Communist delegation again refused to accept voluntary repatriation. The UNC was now less enthusiastic about rescreening because of the Kŏje-do POW uprising then under way, and the peace talks remained deadlocked over the issue for the remainder of the summer. Nonetheless, Lieutenant General Mark W. Clark, Ridgway's replacement as CINCUNC, did order rescreening after discovering that Operation SCATTER was marked by irregularities. The UNC then determined that at least an additional 10,000 POWs favored repatriation, bringing the final number to 83,000. The Chinese were assured that this new number of POWs would be returned as part of a new UNC POW offer made on 28 September 1952. When the Communists rejected this approach, U.S. negotiators walked out of the peace talks on 8 October, beginning another stalemate lasting six more months.

The deadlock over voluntary repatriation continued until three events changed the tone of the debate: Dwight D. Eisenhower assumed office as U.S. president in early 1953; Soviet Premier Josef Stalin died in March; and Operation LITTLE SWITCH was carried out successfully in April. Operation LITTLE SWITCH in particular set the stage for the final settlement of the voluntary repatriation issue and resulted in the Communist plan to have all nonrepatriates sent to a neutral state until their fate could be finally determined. This idea was modified by the UNC on 25 May 1953, which proposed that a Neutral Nations Repatriations Commission (NNRC), consisting of representatives from four nations chaired by India would be created to take responsibility for nonrepatriate prisoners within sixty days of the armistice. During a sixty- to ninety-day period after that, the NNRC would maintain order and supervise both Chinese and North Korean prisoners in the POW camps. If nonrepatriates could not be convinced by their comrades to return home, and if their fate could not be resolved by a postwar Korean political conference called for under Agenda Item 4 of the draft armistice agreement, the NNRC would be dissolved and any remaining POWs would be released. Those prisoners willing to return home would be released in an operation designated BIG SWITCH. This proposal was accepted by the Communists on 8 June.

—*Clayton D. Laurie*

References:

Blair, Clay. *The Forgotten War: America in Korea, 1950–1953.* New York: Times Books, 1987.

Fehrenbach, T. R. *This Kind of War: A Study in Unpreparedness.* New York: Macmillan, 1962.

Hermes, Walter G. *United States Army in the Korean War: Truce Tent and Fighting Front.* Washington, DC: Office of the Chief of Military History, 1966.

MacDonald, Callum. *Korea: The War Before Vietnam.* New York: Free Press, 1986.

See also: BIG SWITCH/LITTLE SWITCH, Operations; Clark, Mark W.; Eisenhower, Dwight D.; Jiang Jieshi (Chiang Kaishek); Kŏje-do Prisoner-of-War Uprising; McClure, Robert A.; Neutral Nations Repatriations Commission; Psychological Warfare; Ridgway, Matthew Bunker; Stalin, Josef; Truman, Harry S.

Rest and Recuperation (R&R)

Wartime policy initiated to restore troop morale during the Korean War. Early twentieth-century warfare often had soldiers in combat for the duration of a military conflict. The idea of limited wartime service and rotation of troops was introduced during World War II. In previous wars, soldiers occasionally visited rest areas behind the lines to restore their physical and emotional energy. Studies of World War II troops showed that casualty rates significantly increased when troops were in combat more than 180 days without relief. As a result of these findings and actual events in Korea, on 30 December 1950, the Eighth U.S. Army and the Japan Logistics Command formally established a rest and recuperation (R&R) program called "Operation Relax" for servicemen. R&R was also known as "Little R," while rotation home, which began in Spring 1951, was called "Big R."

Military leaders publicized R&R policies to troops in an effort to offer hope and enhance morale. Servicemen enthusiastically received the news that everyone would take a five-day R&R leave during their combat tour, usually in the sixth or seventh month of service. Priority was given to those who had been in Korea the longest and was not affected by rank or date of rank. Combat effectiveness of units would be retained by selecting individuals—not units—for R&R trips. R&R leaves were scheduled for specific dates so that soldiers could plan their R&R as if it were a holiday. Also, such itineraries ensured that transportation was available and that Special Service hotels and recreational facilities were not overwhelmed. A constant number of soldiers were transported to and from Japan on a daily basis.

The first group of Korean War soldiers to enjoy R&R were members of the 21st Regiment, 24th Division. They left Kimpŏ Airfield on a C-54 transport. Unshaven, dirty, and exhausted, they wore their helmets and fatigues and carried weapons. Upon arrival in Japan, they were processed. At first there were two reception centers: Camp Kokura near Ashiya Air Base on Kyushu and Camp McNeely near Haneda Air Base in the Tokyo-Yokohama area. A third processing center opened in February 1951 at Itami Air Base at Osaka. Railroads and buses were available to take soldiers to other destinations.

At the centers the soldiers were paid in Japanese currency, given clean uniforms, fed steak dinners, and told to "rest and recuperate" as they pleased. They left their uniforms, boots, and weapons at the center to be cleaned and repaired. Instructed as to the location of hotels where they could stay and possible activities, the men were ordered to report back to the center at midnight five days later. During R&R the men sampled entertainment around Japan. Some men arranged for their families and girlfriends to meet them in Japan. Others spent time talking to family in the United States by telephone.

Most soldiers spent R&R dining, dancing, sightseeing, and watching movies. Having saved their money while in service, they indulged in presents and souvenirs for themselves, their families, and members of their units in Korea. Some soldiers used the occasion for debauchery, and R&R was also known as I&I for "intercourse and intoxication," but many men were too tired from combat to do much more than sleep.

R&R helped restore soldiers by removing them from the hazards of combat and the desolation and stagnation of a war zone. Sleeping, eating, and bathing refreshed men, providing them a sense of dignity. Momentarily escaping destruction, danger, and hardship, men savored comforts before returning to the daily risks of being in action. Returning to the reception centers, R&R soldiers received their weapons and equipment. Men were issued winter clothing as needed. A bus then transported them to Ashiya Air Base, where they departed for Seoul and the front.

The Fifth Air Force initially had a more informal R&R program for its forces. When airmen or officers could be spared for three days, they were allowed to go to Japan on available flights without being processed. There were no specific flights scheduled for air force personnel traveling on military orders for R&R, so plans were uncertain compared to army R&R. It was usually easier for air force servicemen to get to Japan than to return; sometimes they waited several days for a flight to Korea. Airmen were allowed three-day leaves every month for awhile until the air force began scheduling R&R like the army. In September 1951 the U.S. Far East Air Force (FEAF) standardized the R&R system by organizing "packets" of forty-six people with an officer or noncommissioned officer in charge who were airlifted to and from Korea as a group.

Celebrations honored specific R&R passengers. For example, in April 1951 Combat Cargo and Japan Logistical Command hosted a welcome ceremony for Sergeant First Class George Quick, the 25,000th army R&R passenger. Governor Yasui gave Quick the keys to the city of Tokyo, and prominent officers attended a cocktail party in Quick's honor. A month later the 75,000th army R&R passenger, First Lieutenant Napoleon L. Donato, was treated to similar events. By August 1951, 91,000 United Nations officers and enlisted men had enjoyed R&R in Japan. Army Corporal Ronald Allnut was the 100,000th passenger, and army Master Sergeant Richard J. Hartnett was the 200,000th R&R honoree. Similar events were staged for certain air force and Combat Cargo passengers to honor the total number of R&R recipients.

By the end of June 1953 the FEAF's 315th Air Division (Combat Cargo) had airlifted approximately 800,000 R&R passengers. At first, R&R soldiers were mostly American, but by the end of the war, members of international forces affiliated with the United Nations Command enjoyed breaks from the front. Medical personnel and Red Cross workers also took R&R vacations from their duties. Because of the variety and number of R&R participants, the Japanese economy thrived from the money invested in luxury goods, hotel rooms, and entertainment.

Soldiers needed this time away from combat duty and stress. Although rotation home was most desired, R&R enabled soldiers to continue their very hazardous yet often monotonous mission in Korea; it was indeed a pleasant interlude amidst the savage war.

—*Elizabeth D. Schafer*

References:

Fehrenbach, T. R. *This Kind of War: A Study in Unpreparedness.* New York: Macmillan, 1962.

Futrell, Robert F. *The United States Air Force in Korea, 1950–1953.* Rev. ed. Washington, DC: Office of the Chief of Air Force History, 1983.

Gray, Bob. "Seoul Liberty." *Leatherneck* 35 (1952): 43–45.

Kellett, Anthony. *Combat Motivation: The Behavior of Soldiers in Battle.* Boston: Kluwer, 1982.

Thompson, Annis G. *The Greatest Airlift: The Story of Combat Cargo.* Tokyo: Dai-Nippon Printing Co., 1954.

See also: Battle Fatigue; Japan Logistical Command; Kimpŏ Airfield; Rotation of Troops System; Strategic and Tactical Airlift in the Korean War; United States Air Force (USAF); United States Army.

Return-to-Seoul Movement

From late 1951 onward Republic of Korea (ROK, South Korean) president Syngman Rhee campaigned strongly to return his government from Pusan to Seoul, Korea's traditional capital ever since the Chosŏn Dynasty began in the late fourteenth century. Rhee accomplished his objective piecemeal in late 1952 and early 1953.

For Rhee the relocation was filled with great symbolic, psychological, and political meaning. It would signify that the Democratic People's Republic of Korea (North Korea) had failed in its effort to conquer the South, and it would confer additional legitimacy upon his domestically somewhat beleaguered government. Two successive United Nations commanders, Lieutenant Generals Matthew B. Ridgway and Mark W. Clark, opposed the transfer, fearing that, should civilians return in large numbers to Seoul, it might prove militarily indefensible against a renewed North Korean offensive.

Seoul was uncomfortably close to the front, and in July 1952 the United Nations Command (UNC) deliberately created the Korean Communications Zone to handle rear-area issues, hoping to confine civilian activities to this sector while reserving the forward area, including the capital, for the military. Both generals feared that returning the government to Seoul would once more entangle the UNC in civilian issues and confrontations with the Rhee government, detracting from their forces' fighting capabilities, which they considered their first priority. Aid workers and foreign governments, moreover, opposed the move because they feared that the cost of rehabilitating Seoul, devastated after two successive "liberations" by Communist and UN forces, would reduce the funds available for more essential relief work.

Such arguments carried no weight with Rhee, whose determination to return remained unwavering. After winning the ROK presidential election of August 1952 he made Seoul his official residence, which forced all leading ROK government officials, UN functionaries, and U.S. and other foreign representatives to travel there to transact business with him. By February 1953 civilians had begun to return to the city, and a piecemeal transfer of government offices was in progress. For military reasons Clark continued to oppose the move, although U.S. Ambassador Ellis O. Briggs recommended his country accept the shift of at least a few ROK officials. On State Department instructions, in March 1953 the two men unsuccessfully attempted to persuade Rhee to return to Pusan. The notoriously stubborn president told them that he would remain there personally, as would most key government officials, though he would for the time being leave their ministries in Pusan, together with the legislature, with which his relations were poor. As armistice talks progressed, the ROK administration shifted inexorably to Seoul, and in May 1953 Briggs himself was obliged to relocate the U.S. embassy to Korea's traditional capital. Once the armistice agreement was signed, all remaining ROK agencies and officials, including the legislature, moved to Seoul.

—*Priscilla Roberts*

References:

Bailey, Sydney D. *The Korean Armistice*. London: Macmillan, 1992.

Clark, Mark W. *From the Danube to the Yalu*. New York: Harper & Row, 1954.

Foot, Rosemary J. *A Substitute for Victory: The Politics of Peacemaking at the Korean Armistice Talks*. Ithaca, NY: Cornell University Press, 1990.

Hermes, Walter G. *United States Army in the Korean War: Truce Tent and Fighting Front*. Washington, DC: Office of the Chief of Military History, 1966.

Oliver, Robert T. *Syngman Rhee and American Involvement in Korea, 1942–1960: A Personal Narrative*. Seoul: Panmun Books, 1978.

Stueck, William W., Jr. *The Korean War: An International History*. Princeton, NJ: Princeton University Press, 1995.

U.S. Department of State, Bureau of Public Affairs. *Foreign Relations of the United States, 1952–1954*. Vol. 15, *Korea*. Washington, DC: U.S. Government Printing Office, 1984.

See also: Briggs, Ellis; Clark, Mark W.; Ridgway, Matthew Bunker; Syngman Rhee.

Ridgway, Matthew Bunker
(1895–1993)

U.S. Army general and, during the Korean War, commander of the Eighth U.S. Army in Korea and later commander in chief of United Nations forces in Korea. Son of a U.S. Army officer, Matthew Bunker Ridgway was born at Fortress Monroe, Virginia, on 3 March 1895. The young Ridgway grew up on various military posts and graduated from the U.S. Military Academy at West Point in 1917.

Unlike most of his classmates, Ridgway was not posted to the First World War in France. Instead, he spent the war on the Mexican border and returned to West Point in 1918 to teach Romance languages. As one of only six officers in the regular army fluent in Spanish, he served in several high-level postings in Latin America during the 1920s. In the 1930s, he was selected to attend the Infantry School, the Command and General Staff School, and the Army War College. He became a protégé of General George C. Marshall, who promoted him to brigadier general at the beginning of World War II.

Ridgway enjoyed regular promotion as a commander of airborne forces (the 82d Airborne Division and then the XVIII Airborne Corps) and had a distinguished record in the war. With the reputation as one of the best corps commanders in the U.S. Army, Ridgway was promoted to Lieutenant General in June 1945. In August 1949 Ridgway became army deputy chief of staff for administration. When U.S. Eighth Army commander Lieutenant General Walton H. Walker was killed in a jeep accident on 23 December 1950, Ridgway was named to replace him. It was a very difficult period for the U.S. forces and the United Nations Command (UNC) in Korea. Chinese forces had pushed UN troops back below the 38th parallel, and morale in the Eighth Army was very low. The Joint Chiefs of Staff (JCS) had ordered a contingency plan for the possible evacuation of UN forces to Japan.

Ridgway immediately employed his legendary motivational talents. He ordered the supply services to provide better and more food, served hot. He secured warmer clothing for the bitter Korean winter. He improved the Mobile Army Surgical Hospitals (MASHs), because he understood that troops would fight better if they knew that they would receive proper medical care if wounded. He removed incompetent or defeatist officers, and he improved reconnaissance and intelligence-gathering capacities. Although Ridgway was forced to withdraw his troops from the South Korean capital of Seoul in early January 1951, he restored their fighting spirit and, in February, launched a massive offensive, Operation KILLER. In that operation, the Eighth Army retook Seoul and drove the Chinese back above the 38th parallel, where the battle lines began to stabilize.

When President Harry S. Truman relieved General Douglas MacArthur of his command on 11 April 1951, General Ridgway was appointed to all of MacArthur's former positions as UNC commanding general, commander in chief of U.S. armed forces in the Far East, and supreme commander of the Allied occupation forces in Japan. Ridgway moved from the field to headquarters in Tokyo, where he oversaw the war for the next thirteen months. Ridgway's accessibility, articulation, and polish made him popular with the press, and he was elevated to national prominence and stature.

Having suffered devastating defeats in several failed offensives, the Chinese and North Koreans in July 1951 offered to begin negotiations at Kaesŏng, on the 38th parallel. Official talks began on 10 July with the Communists proposing an immediate cease-fire. Ridgway and the Joint Chiefs rejected the suspension of military operations until a satisfactory peace was negotiated. Lieutenant General James A. Van Fleet, new commander of the Eighth Army, proposed driving the Communists far back into North Korea. Ridgway and the JCS believed that it would be a mistake to push deep into enemy territory at this point. They wished to concentrate on punishing Communist forces along the

Lieutenant General Matthew Ridgway slogs along a muddy path during his visit to a Marine command post, May 1951. (National Archives)

parallel and employing air power to strike the Communists's long supply lines. Both sides strongly fortified their respective positions, and some of the most bitter fighting of the war occurred over the next two years. The war became one for yards rather than miles.

In late August 1951 the Communists suspended negotiations and did not return to the table until October. Ridgway ordered a new series of attacks east of the Iron Triangle to pressure peace negotiations and to gain territory prior to an armistice agreement. These savage battles during the suspension of peace talks resulted in huge UN casualties, including 2,700 at Bloody Ridge and 3,700 at Heartbreak Ridge. The UNC gained important long-term defensive positions at a cost of 60,000 UNC casualties, 22,000 of whom were Americans. Ridgway emphasized that the UNC would not return to Kaesŏng, which was in Communist territory, and on 25 October the talks

resumed at P'anmunjŏm, five miles east of Kaesŏng. Shortly thereafter, the Communists offered to accept the existing battle lines as the permanent demarcation between North and South Korea if a cease-fire were promulgated immediately. Ridgway rejected the proposal, since he believed that military pressure was necessary to accomplish a favorable peace. And he was not willing to concede Kaesŏng, a former Korean capital, to the Communists. However, the JCS did not consider Kaesŏng to be worth the cost and instructed Ridgway to concede this issue. While the peace talks stalled, Ridgway in November 1951 launched Operation RATKILLER, which eliminated 20,000 Communist guerrillas and bandits in the mountains of South Korea near the border. As 1952 began, repatriation of prisoners of war became the divisive issue that would dominate the rest of the war.

On 12 May 1952 Ridgway replaced General Dwight D. Eisenhower as supreme commander of Allied

Powers in Europe and commander of the North Atlantic Treaty Organization. In October 1953 he became U.S. army chief of staff. After disagreement with the Eisenhower administration over its emphasis on nuclear weapons (the New Look, dubbed "more bang for a buck") at the expense of conventional forces, Ridgway retired from active duty in June 1955. During the 1960s he advocated limiting U.S. involvement in Vietnam, and in 1968 President Lyndon Johnson named him to the Senior Advisory Group, known as the "Wise Men," that recommended U.S. extrication from that conflict. Ridgway died on 26 July 1993, at Fox Chapel, Pennsylvania.

—*Joe P. Dunn*

References:

Appleman, Roy. *Ridgway Duels for Korea*. College Station, TX: Texas A&M Press, 1990.

Blair, Clay. *The Forgotten War: America in Korea, 1950–1953*. New York: Times Books, 1987.

Ridgway, Matthew B. *The Korean War*. Garden City, NY: Doubleday, 1967.

Soffer, Jonathan M. *General Matthew B. Ridgway: From Progressivism to Reaganism, 1895–1993*. Westport, CT: Praeger, 1998.

See also: Bloody Ridge, Battle of; Eisenhower, Dwight D.; Heartbreak Ridge, Battle of; Joint Chiefs of Staff (JCS); Kaesŏng Truce Talks; KILLER, Operation; Marshall, George C.; Mobile Army Surgical Hospital (MASH); P'anmunjŏm Truce Talks; RATKILLER, Operation; Repatriation, Voluntary; Truman, Harry S.; Truman's Recall of MacArthur; Van Fleet, James Alward; Walker, Walton Harris.

RIPPER, Operation
(6–31 March 1951)

March 1951 United Nations Command military operation. In effect, RIPPER was a continuation of Operation KILLER, but on the entire front. Its primary goal was again to inflict maximum casualties on the Communist side and disrupt any new offensive. The secondary objective was to retake the South Korean capital of Seoul. Except for the Republic of Korea Army (ROKA) 1st and U.S. 3d Divisions, on the western front, the operation initially employed (from west to east): the U.S. 25th Infantry Division (I Corps); 24th Infantry and 1st Cavalry Divisions, British 27th Brigade, ROKA 6th and the U. S. 1st Marine Divisions (IX Corps); U.S. 2d Infantry, ROKA 5th and U.S. 7th Infantry Divisions (X Corps); ROKA 7th and 9th Divisions (ROKA III Corps); and ROKA Capital Division (ROKA I Corps).

The offensive was to end on Phase Line Idaho, which ran northeast from the western boundary between the 3d and 25th Divisions to a point about five miles north of Kap'yŏng, thence more or less east-northeast to six or seven miles north of Ch'unch'ŏn. There it trended southeast across the eastern front of

the IX Corps to a point about fifteen miles north of the center of the X Corps front, then slightly north of east to the east coast. Phase Lines Albany, Buffalo, Buster, and Cairo were established to control the attack.

At 0615 on 7 March the 25th Division conducted a model crossing of the Han, preceded by an awesome twenty-minute, 5,000-round bombardment by 148 artillery pieces. Four tanks added 900 main-gun rounds. Overcoming some initial resistance, the division gained Line Albany between 11 and 13 March.

The 24th, 1st Cavalry, ROKA 6th, and 1st Marine Divisions met light to moderate resistance, gradually pinching out the ROKA 6th, and reaching Albany by dark on the 12th.

The Marine advance took them through "Massacre Valley," where a 2d Division force, Support Force 21, had been ambushed and destroyed by Communist forces in mid-February. There a 2d Division team recovered five 155-mm howitzers, six M-5 tractors, four tanks, and a number of trucks. The 2d and ROKA 5th and 7th Divisions (X Corps), overcoming skillful North Korean delaying actions, reached Albany by 14 March.

The ROKA III Corps also had little trouble advancing, and by 13 March the ROKA I Corps was beyond its portion of Line Idaho.

Thinking the Communists might stoutly defend Hongch'ŏn, Eighth Army commander Lieutenant General Matthew B. Ridgway ordered that it be taken in a double envelopment. Accordingly, commanding general of IX Corps Major General William M. Hoge ordered the 1st Cavalry to attack on the 14th from the west while the 1st Marine Division approached from the east. Neither division met much resistance. The same was true of attacks by the 24th and ROKA 6th Divisions, and the 25th Division in I Corps.

By nightfall on 15 March the 25th Division had completely outflanked Seoul, the 24th was on the banks of the Chongpyong Reservoir, the ROKA 6th was on high ground overlooking the Hongch'ŏn River, and the 1st Cavalry was on its banks. The Marines, slowed by strong enemy positions, took the town of Hongch'ŏn and attained the river bank later in the day.

But of more value was the fact that the Communists had abandoned Seoul without a fight. 3d Division patrols crossed on the 12th to find Communist shoreline positions vacant. More patrols crossed east and southeast of the city on the 14th, while five from the ROKA 1st Division entered the city. Aerial reconnaissance revealed that the Communist force had withdrawn to strong positions about five miles north of the city.

Ridgway then ordered I Corps to take Seoul and occupy the first defensible terrain north of it. The ROKA 1st and U.S. 3d Divisions executed the order the next day, sending combat patrols farther north in search of the enemy.

Meantime the 24th, ROKA 6th, 1st Cavalry, and 1st Marine Divisions continued attacking. Only the 1st Cavalry met significant resistance. By nightfall on 19 March the bulk of IX Corps was on or near the Buster-Buffalo Line. The Communists abandoned the area, allowing the IX Corps to attain Line Cairo and seize Ch'unch'ŏn unopposed on 21 March, causing the cancellation of a projected drop just north of the city by the 187th Airborne and two Ranger companies.

In the east, X Corps and the ROKA III Corps reached Line Idaho by 17 March and Ridgway ordered all three corps on the eastern front to patrol well beyond the 38th parallel between the Hwach'ŏn Reservoir and Ch'unch'ŏn on the east coast.

Operation RIPPER gained Seoul without a fight. It also secured substantial territorial gains, but it fell short in inflicting significant casualties on Communist forces. Between 1 and 15 March there had been only 7,151 known Communist dead.

—*Uzal W. Ent*

References:

Appleman, Roy E. *Ridgway Duels for Korea.* College Station, TX: Texas A&M Press, 1990.

Blair, Clay. *The Forgotten War: America in Korea, 1950–1953.* New York: Times Books, 1987.

Mossman, Billy C. *U.S. Army in the Korean War: Ebb and Flow, November 1950–July 1951.* Washington, DC: U.S. Army Center of Military History, 1990.

See also: Hoge, William M.; Ridgway, Matthew Bunker.

Roberts, William L.
(1891–1968)

U.S. Army brigadier general and commander of the Korean Military Advisory Group (KMAG) from its inception until just before the beginning of the Korean War. Born in 1891, William L. Roberts attended the U.S. Military Academy at West Point, graduating in 1913. His military career was undistinguished. During World War I he served in France in the infantry, and in World War II he was with the 10th Armored Division. In 1944 he was a colonel, and at the end of the war he was a brigadier general and assistant divisional commander of the 4th Armored Division.

Having been passed over for promotion to major general, Roberts faced mandatory retirement in June 1950. In 1948 he was assigned to Korea, where on 20 May he became advisor to the director of the Department of Internal Security in the U.S. military government. On the formal establishment of the Republic of Korea (ROK), Roberts commanded the Provisional Korean Military Advisory Group of some 100 men. On 1 July 1949, it expanded into KMAG, an organization of some 500 men. Roberts became chief of KMAG, with his headquarters in Seoul.

As the closest military advisor to U.S. Ambassador John Muccio, Roberts's mission was to train a South Korean army strong enough to deter any attacks from North Korea. Taking up the task with considerable zeal, Roberts was determined to be successful before he had to leave Korea, and he certainly did the best he could with the scant resources available. While he had direct communication with the Department of the Army on military matters, Roberts also regularly informed U.S. Far East Command commander General Douglas MacArthur on the status of the Republic of Korea Army (ROKA).

Roberts directed the establishment of several technical schools, and in August 1949 he ordered that KMAG establish an infantry school to qualify Korean officers as platoon leaders, company commanders, and battalion staff officers. He also sought to prove to Congressmen and other U.S. visitors that military aid to the ROK was an excellent investment; he regularly stage-managed visits by VIPs and journalists to make the case for additional assistance. Publicly, Roberts had only praise for the ROKA; privately he did have doubts, most notably displayed in a long March 1949 letter to Lieutenant General Charles Bolté of the Joint Chiefs of Staff (JCS). In it Roberts warned about ROKA shortcomings, especially in confronting North Korean aircraft, tanks, and heavy artillery. In December Roberts recommended through Ambassador Muccio that the United States sharply increase military aid to the ROK. His proposals included ten T-6 trainers, forty F-51 fighter aircraft, and two C-47 cargo aircraft, signal equipment, 3-inch guns for the Coast Guard, 105-mm howitzers, and more machine guns and mortars (including 4.2-inch).

Roberts professed to be unconcerned about Korean People's Army (North Korean) armor. Given his own long experience with tanks, Roberts should have known better when he stated that Korea was "not good tank country."

Overall, however, reports from Roberts and Ambassador Muccio to Washington were optimistic in their assessment of ROKA capabilities and gave the false impression that it was the best in the Far East and lacked only aircraft and heavy artillery to be invincible. A week before the Korean War began, Roberts left Korea to retire from the army; Colonel W. H. Sterling succeeded him as the chief of KMAG. On his departure, Roberts again expressed confidence in ROKA capabilities. Stopping in Tokyo for a debriefing at MacArthur's headquarters, he told Chairman of the JCS General Omar N. Bradley that the ROKA could "meet any test the North Koreans imposed on it." This assessment led Bradley to write to the JCS after the

KPA invasion: "After my talk with General Roberts, I am of the opinion that South Korea will not fall in the present attack unless the Russians actively participate in the action."

Roberts died in 1968.

—*Monica Spicer and Spencer C. Tucker*

References:

Blair, Clay. *The Forgotten War: America in Korea, 1950–1953.* New York: Times Books, 1987.

Matray, James I., ed. *Historical Dictionary of the Korean War.* Westport, CT: Greenwood Press, 1991.

Sawyer, Robert K. *Military Advisors in Korea: KMAG in Peace and War.* Washington, DC: Office of the Chief of Military History, U.S. Army, 1962.

See also: Bolté, Charles Lawrence; Bradley, Omar Nelson; Korea Military Advisory Group (KMAG); MacArthur, Douglas; Muccio, John J.; Syngman Rhee.

Robertson Mission
(22 June–12 July 1953)

A U.S. diplomatic mission to convince Republic of Korea (ROK, South Korean) president Syngman Rhee to agree to an armistice agreement with the Communists. The mission had been planned months before its start on 22 June 1953, with the general objective to seek Rhee's support for the armistice negotiations. After Rhee's release of 27,000 North Korean prisoners of war (POWs) on 18 June, the mission, headed by Assistant Secretary of State for Far Eastern Affairs Walter Robertson, changed course. Now Robertson, United Nations Command (UNC) commander Lieutenant General Mark Clark, and Ambassadors Ellis Briggs and Robert Murphy recommended to Washington that the United States should go ahead "with full steam" and sign the armistice.

To achieve this goal the UNC had to convince the Communists, who were outraged by Rhee's release of the POWs, that Seoul would abide by the provisions of a future armistice agreement. Legally the UNC did not need the approval of the ROK government to sign the armistice. It was a military agreement between military commanders, and ROK forces had been placed under UNC control by President Rhee himself.

U.S. president Dwight D. Eisenhower sent Robertson to discuss a mutual defense treaty with Rhee to facilitate South Korean approval. Robertson was also allowed to outline U.S.-ROK tactics for a postarmistice political conference with the Communists. He was also authorized to offer U.S. economic assistance to Seoul along the lines recommended by Henry Tasca's recent fact-finding mission.

Robertson's first stop was in Tokyo, where Clark joined him and they flew to Seoul together. Clark had his doubts about the wisdom of sending a special emissary to Rhee. He believed that "those who knew the problem intimately and had had personal contact with him [Rhee] could make better use of a blank-check authority in dealing with him." Still, Clark gave his full support to the mission because he hoped Rhee might appreciate a special envoy straight from Washington.

South Korean crowds, propelled by Rhee's propaganda machine, "welcomed" the emissaries with slogans such as "Go North!" and "Don't Sell Out Korea!" to demonstrate that South Koreans wanted nothing less than the reunification of Korea.

At the beginning of the "Little Truce Talks," Rhee showed willingness to accept Robertson's offers but soon threw in new conditions that seemed unacceptable to Washington. Seoul demanded the immediate withdrawal of Chinese forces from Korean soil and insisted that all POWs in South Korea would be guarded by the ROK armed forces and no Communist indoctrinators would be allowed to approach them. One of Robertson's tasks was to influence Rhee to agree to the transfer of POWs to the demilitarized zone.

Washington instructed Robertson's team to convince Rhee that this was its last and best offer to him. Clark was allowed to put pressure on Rhee by indicating that the UNC was ready to resume negotiations with the Communists. Clark was also permitted to let the ROK president believe that Washington was even willing to withdraw its troops from the peninsula in order to end the war.

On 8 July 1953 the Communists launched a massive offensive that devastated three South Korean divisions; only prompt U.S. military assistance halted the Chinese advance. The offensive was a signal to Seoul that a "march to the North" would not be so easy to accomplish. Now Rhee dropped his demand for immediate Chinese withdrawal in return for a prompt start of negotiations over a U.S.–South Korean mutual defense pact.

During his visit to South Korea, Robertson met with Rhee every day. Although the two never reached a complete agreement, U.S. Secretary of State John Foster Dulles believed that the current stage of negotiations was a good basis for an armistice and that the remaining differences could be solved at a postwar conference. The agreement concluding Robertson's visit pledged the United States to guarantee the creation of a mutual defense pact after an armistice. Washington also agreed to endorse long-term economic aid to the ROK, starting with an initial $260 million. Political talks after the armistice were limited to ninety days, after which the United States and South Korea would withdraw and work out a different way to satisfy Seoul's demands. Robertson also promised that the United States would help expand ROK armed forces to enable them to withstand any future aggression without foreign military aid. In return for all these,

President Rhee agreed to accept the armistice, yet without a promise to sign it.

As a result of the agreement, negotiations in P'anmunjŏm resumed on 10 July and finally led to the Armistice Agreement of 27 July 1953. According to Clark, the significance of the Robertson mission was to prove that South Korea was not a puppet state under U.S. control but a sovereign country.

—*Zsolt Varga*

References:

Berger, Carl. *The Korean Knot: A Military and Political History.* Philadelphia: University of Pennsylvania Press, 1957.

Clark, Mark W. *From the Danube to the Yalu.* New York: Harper & Row, 1954.

Paik, Sun Yup. *From Pusan to Panmunjon.* New York: Brassey's, 1992.

Stueck, William W., Jr. *The Korean War: An International History.* Princeton, NJ: Princeton University Press, 1995.

See also: Briggs, Ellis; Clark, Mark W.; Murphy, Robert D.; P'anmunjŏm Truce Talks; Prisoners of War, Rescreening of; Robertson, Walter Spencer; Syngman Rhee; Syngman Rhee's Release of North Korean Prisoners of War; Tasca, Henry J.

Robertson, Sir Horace C. H.
(1894–1960)

Administrative commander in chief of the British Commonwealth Forces in Korea, 1950–1951. Born on 29 October 1894, in Melbourne, Australia, and educated at the Royal Military College, Duntroon, Horace C. H. Robertson served with distinction at Gallipoli and in Palestine during World War I. He attended the Army Staff College at Camberley and proceeded to hold various staff and instructor positions in the interwar Australian army. During World War II he commanded the 19th Australian Army Brigade in the Libyan campaign, before returning to the Pacific theater to lead Australian troops in the southwest Pacific. In April 1946 he was named commander in chief of the British Commonwealth Occupation Forces in Japan, where he ranked second only to General Douglas MacArthur. Blunt and outspoken, on the third anniversary of the atomic bombing of Hiroshima in August 1948, he told the Japanese people, "This disaster was your own fault," continuing, "The Japanese nation treacherously attacked us without warning."

Although one of the ablest Australian military men of his generation, Robertson was frequently arrogant, tactless, and overbearing, characteristics that could and sometimes did bedevil his relations with peers and subordinates. He remained on good terms with the often difficult and overbearing MacArthur, but his position as the first Dominion officer ever to command a British Commonwealth force that included British troops would in any case have been likely to cause some tensions, and Robertson's personality helped to exacerbate those strains. His time in Japan was marked by sharp disagreements with several of his subordinates and also with British military authorities in London and British officials in Tokyo.

When the Korean War began, Lieutenant General Robertson was appointed administrative commander in chief of British Commonwealth Forces in Korea, with overall responsibility for providing logistical and administrative support to the Commonwealth Division. The core of these forces was those Commonwealth troops still stationed in Japan, which, it had already been decided in May 1950, would shortly be withdrawn, and which were consequently under strength and poorly equipped. Robertson instituted a highly effective reinforcement, equipment, and training program for the one Australian infantry battalion still remaining in Japan, which was sent to Korea in September 1950.

During his time in Korea, serious tensions and disagreements continued to mar Robertson's dealings with British military officials in London and with British subordinates. At the same time, his good relations with the often prickly MacArthur allowed him to serve as an effective communications channel between the United Nations commander in chief and his military and civilian superiors in Australia. Within a few days after the war began, he had won from them the decision to allow MacArthur to use the Royal Australian Air Force's 77 Squadron against North Korean troops. Contrary to MacArthur's original intentions, by Christmas 1950 Robertson had persuaded the commander in chief to impose strict censorship on the reporting of the war, on the grounds that this was necessary to prevent the leakage of restricted information to the Communist Chinese. Robertson, who seems to have found the Americans more congenial than he did the British, was also on good terms with Lieutenant General Matthew B. Ridgway, MacArthur's successor. His efforts contributed to Australia's overall image as a loyal ally of the United States during the Korean War, which in turn played a major part in persuading U.S. officials to sign the 1951 ANZUS (Australia–New Zealand–United States) security pact. In December 1951 Robertson returned to Australia to become director general of recruiting. He retired in 1954 and died in Melbourne on 28 April 1960.

—*Priscilla Roberts*

References:

Farrar-Hockley, Sir Antony. *The British Part in the Korean War.* Vol. 1, *A Distant Obligation.* London: Her Majesty's Stationery Office, 1990.

Grey, Jeffrey. *Australian Brass: The Career of Lieutenant General Sir Horace Robertson.* Cambridge, UK: Cambridge University Press, 1992.

———. *The Commonwealth Armies and the Korean War: An Alliance Study.* Manchester: Manchester University Press, 1988.

O'Neill, Robert J. *Australia in the Korea War, 1950–1953*. 2 vols. Canberra: Australian War Memorial/Australian Government Publishing Service, 1981, 1985.

Wood, James. *The Forgotten Force: The Australian Military Contribution to the Occupation of Japan, 1945–1952*. St. Leonards, NSW, Australia: Allen & Unwin, 1998.

See also: Australia; Far East Command (FEC); MacArthur, Douglas; Ridgway, Matthew Bunker.

Robertson, Walter Spencer
(1893–1970)

U.S. diplomat; assistant secretary of state for Far Eastern affairs, 1953–1959. Born on 7 December 1893, in Nottoway County, Virginia, Walter Spencer Robertson attended the Hoge Military Academy. He then studied at the College of William and Mary and Davidson College but left college in 1912 for a career in banking. During World War II he joined the Army Air Corps and served as a pursuit pilot. After the war he resumed his career with the Richmond banking and brokerage firm of Scott & Stringfellow, becoming a partner in 1925.

Robertson entered government service in 1943 during World War II as Lend-Lease administrator in Australia. The next year U.S. Ambassador to China Patrick J. Hurley invited him to the embassy in Chongqing (Chungking) to be counselor for economic affairs; he later became chargé. He supervised U.S. economic activities in China until mid-1946, when he left government service to resume his business career.

Robertson was a great admirer and friend of Generalissimo Jiang Jieshi (Chiang Kai-shek). He was also one of the chief architects of U.S. pro–Nationalist China policy. Because of his conviction that U.S. policy before 1949 helped Mao Zedong come to power, he urged that the United States not extend diplomatic recognition to the People's Republic of China. He believed that the Nationalists on Taiwan constituted the legitimate Chinese government.

Robertson joined Democrats for Eisenhower during the 1952 election campaign, and in January 1953 president-elect Dwight D. Eisenhower appointed him assistant secretary of state for Far Eastern affairs in the Department of State. In this post, Robertson had a reputation for fervor and stubbornness in his beliefs. He was regarded as even more anti-Communist than Secretary of State John Foster Dulles.

In late June 1953 President Eisenhower sent Robertson to the Republic of Korea (ROK, South Korea) in hopes of persuading President Syngman Rhee to accept the proposed armistice terms. Rhee had proclaimed these terms to be unsatisfactory, insisting that a U.S.-ROK joint defense pact be followed by the reciprocal removal of United Nations Command and Communist military forces from Korea. He also opposed the employment of foreign troops on South Korean soil as guardians of prisoners of war (POWs) and protested any contact between Communist officials and the captives. Rhee threatened a continuation of the war. Then, with Communist military action intensifying, on 17 June 1953 Rhee breached the armistice terms by ordering ROK guards to release Communist POWs who were refusing repatriation.

President Rhee turned down a request by Secretary of State John Foster Dulles to visit Washington for resolution of the impasse. Instead he suggested that Dulles travel to Seoul. The secretary of state, considering such a journey ill-advised before ROK agreement to the armistice, elected to dispatch Robertson instead. Robertson lacked Korean expertise, but his staunch anticommunism led him to identify with Rhee.

Robertson arrived in South Korea amidst popular demonstrations after a tirade by Rhee against the armistice accord. On 26 June Robertson began conversations with Rhee. While Robertson admired Rhee he proved to be skillful in negotiating and was persuasive. He informed the ROK president that the United States was not prepared to continue the war until Korea was reunified. Threatened with a withdrawal of the United Nations Command and given concessions regarding U.S. military assistance for an expanded ROK Army as well as the promise that the U.S. and ROK would resume the war should the armistice fail, Rhee yielded. On 9 July Robertson received a pledge from Rhee that his government would not block the proposed armistice. Robertson departed Korea on 11 July with the crisis at an end.

Three years later President Dwight D. Eisenhower sent Robertson to Taiwan for talks with Jiang Jieshi concerning the defense of Quemoy and Matsu. After his resignation from the State Department in 1959, Robertson returned to Scott & Stringfellow. He died on 19 January 1970, in Richmond, Virginia.

—*Rodney J. Ross*

References:

Alexander, Bevin. *Korea: The First War We Lost*. New York: Hippocrene Books, 1986.

Goulden, Joseph C. *Korea: The Untold Story of the War*. New York: Times Books, 1982.

New York Times, 20 January 1970.

Stueck, William W., Jr. *The Korean War: An International History*. Princeton, NJ: Princeton University Press, 1995.

See also: Dulles, John Foster; Eisenhower, Dwight D.; Jiang Jieshi (Chiang Kai-shek); Marshall, George C.; Robertson Mission; Syngman Rhee.

Rocket Artillery

Both sides in the Korean War used artillery rockets and rocket launchers that had been developed and fielded during World War II. By modern standards these weapons were inaccurate and had very limited

T-66 towed rocket launcher battery in fire support, 27 May 1951. (National Archives)

range. They were, however, capable of delivering short bursts of saturation fire on large areas, which generally produced a greater psychological than a physical effect. The rocket artillery of the period fell into three basic categories: ship to shore, air to ground, and ground to ground.

The U.S. Navy used 5-inch, spin-stabilized shore bombardment rockets with a range of 5,000 yards. They were fired from World War II–era landing craft that had been refitted as rocket ships. These converted craft were designated as Landing Ship, Medium, Rocket (LSMR). At least six of these craft operated in Korean waters, supporting landing operations, such as the one at Inch'ŏn, and evacuations, such as that of Hŭngnam. One LSMR could fire a salvo of 1,020 rockets into an area 500 yards square, with 80 percent of the rockets expected to land in the target area. The first reloading took forty-five minutes, and each subsequent reloading took one-and-a-half to two hours.

Air force and navy jet and propeller fighters carried 5-inch high-velocity aircraft rockets (HVARs) for use against ground targets. These fin-stabilized rockets weighed 140 pounds with a 20-pound high explosive or semi–armor-piercing warhead. They had a range of 1,000 yards. The F-80 Shooting Star carried four HVARs.

The U.S. Army had a small number of multiple rocket launcher batteries in Korea. The standard field artillery rocket was the M-16, a 4.5-inch, spin-stabilized rocket first fielded in 1945. It was an improved version of the 4.5-inch, fin-stabilized M8 rocket introduced in 1943. The M-16 weighed 42.5 pounds and had a range of only 5,250 meters—less than half the range of the 105-mm light howitzer.

The M-16 rocket came with both smoke and high-explosive warheads. It was fired from a variety or towed or truck-mounted launchers. The most commonly used was the T-66 towed rocket launcher. Weighing 1,240

U.S. Marines launch a 4.5 rocket barrage against the Chinese Communist forces, 1951. (National Archives)

pounds, the split-trail T-66 mounted twenty-four launching tubes. A single battery of twelve launchers was capable of delivering a volley of 288 rounds, the equivalent of sixteen battalions of 105-mm howitzers.

Communist forces also had a limited number of Soviet-supplied rockets and rocket launchers. Used by the Korean People's Army (North Korean) for the first time during the Unsan engagement on 1–2 November 1950, the 82-mm RS-82 rockets were fired primarily from a truck-mounted launcher. Introduced in 1941, the RS-82 weighed 17.6 pounds and had a range of 5,500 meters.

After the Korean War, the U.S. Army abandoned multiple rocket launchers in favor of larger, longer-range, single artillery rockets, such as the Little John and Honest John. In the late 1960s and early 1970s, the unguided rockets were replaced with tactical guided missile systems, such as the Lance and Pershing. The Soviets also developed large free-flight rockets, such

as the Frog, and tactical guided missiles, like the Scud, Scaleboard, and SS-21. The Soviets, however, never abandoned multiple rocket launchers.

In the 1980s the U.S. Army and the North Atlantic Treaty Organization resurrected multiple rocket launchers with the introduction of the Multiple Launch Rocket System (MLRS). The MLRS played a major role in the Persian Gulf War. With far greater accuracy, effective ranges now well beyond cannon artillery, and a sophisticated family of warheads, the MLRS only superficially resembles its Korean War ancestors.

—*David T. Zabecki*

References.
Bailey, Jonathan B. A. *Field Artillery and Fire Power*. Oxford: Military Press, 1989.
Bellamy, Chris. *Red God of War*. London: Brassey's, 1986.
Hedekin, Thomas B. "Artillery Rockets." *Field Artillery Journal* (October 1946): 564–573.
See also: Artillery; Unsan, Battle of.

"Rolling with the Punch"

United Nations Command (UNC) battlefield tactic employed generally in the Korean War from early January 1951, after the UNC withdrawal from north of the 38th parallel, to about mid-February, after critical engagements at Chip'yŏng-ni, Wŏnju, and elsewhere.

During this period, Chinese People's Volunteer Army (CPVA, Chinese Communist) and Korean People's Army (KPA, North Korean) forces had been known to hesitate when meeting an American unit with far superior firepower. Rather than continue a frontal assault, the Communists would then halt in place, fan out to the flanks with their superior numbers, and attempt to surround, isolate, and annihilate the UNC units. UNC commanders also noted at this time that Communist forces could not usually maintain the momentum of their assaults for much distance, because after advancing a short distance, they had to wait for weak support and supply forces to catch up. Communist forces in that period had an ability to strike hard initially but to continue only for a short distance. Thus, if UNC forces resisted temporarily when attacked, then recoiled and maintained a short distance from Communist forces, they could remain relatively safe from serious harm.

To counter the enemy's tactics, UNC battalions, especially U.S., would occupy blocking positions in mountain passes or elsewhere, with instructions to inflict as much damage on attacking forces as possible, but when it appeared they might be surrounded and cut off, to withdraw through and under covering fire from a companion unit in position to the rear and go into position behind that unit. The cycle would then be repeated. These actions became known as "rolling with (and just beyond) the punch." The technique was mostly abandoned after the Chip'yŏng-ni battle, where it was established that there was little chance that U.S. units would be encircled.

—*Sherman W. Pratt*

See also: Chinese Military Offensives; Chip'yŏng-ni, Battle of; Kap'yŏng, Battle of; Wŏnju, Battle of.

Rotation of Troops System

U.S. personnel policy during the Korean War. Rotating troops was initially implemented during World War II. Previously, rest areas behind the lines provided soldiers a respite from service, and units were placed in and out of combat together. Since the American Revolution, soldiers enlisted in a unit for a certain length of service time, ranging from a few months to until the war's end. With the rotation system, casualties were replaced by individuals, not units. Soldiers did not remain in action for the duration of the military crisis. Instead, each serviceman was rotated home based on his time in combat.

When the Korean War began, military leaders considered the potential hazards of harsh Korean winters on soldiers' morale and discussed limiting service time. Although some U.S. soldiers in Korea had fought in World War II, many of the reservists and national guardsmen called to service lacked active duty experience and performed poorly in combat. These civilian soldiers wanted to go home, as promised by General Douglas MacArthur in his 1950 "Home by Christmas" speech, and were unenthusiastic about staying in Korea.

In spring 1951, military leaders realized that the war was not going to be resolved quickly; thus, they sought ways to equalize the burden of service. Troops soon heard rumors about a rotation-home policy. Since December 1950 the system of rest and recuperation, known as "R&R" and "Little R," allowed selected soldiers a five-day rest period in Japan away from combat dangers and stress. The "Big R," or rotation to the United States, enabled Korean War soldiers who had served for a certain time in the combat theater to be replaced. Replacements had to arrive before men could return home. On 22 April 1951, the first U.S. soldiers rotated out of Korea.

The rotation of troops system was based on a point system. Each man received four points for every month spent in the combat zone. Three points were given for being located within the area between regimental headquarters and the front line, and two points were given for rear-echelon duties. Service in Japan counted for one point per month, except for soldiers wounded in combat, who received four points until they were reassigned. When a soldier accrued thirty-six points, he was rotated home and discharged, unless he preferred to reenlist. The average infantryman returned home within a year if he survived battle and weather conditions.

The rotation of troops system was controversial in Korea and later in Vietnam. Military efficiency was hindered, as unqualified officers were often promoted because of personnel turnover. "Short-timers" became cautious in combat as the time neared for them to return home. Survival and beating the clock became more important than defeating the enemy. Getting home safely was the primary goal. "There came a chance that I might make it home. I had given up on the idea long before, and the possibility was like a new lease on life," Lieutenant Colonel Anthony B. Herbert recalled. "Like others, I began to fight a little more cautiously, to take fewer chances than before." Soldiers constantly talked about rotation home and sometimes protected high-point men on patrols and missions.

Individual rotation weakened unit cohesion and effectiveness. Experienced soldiers were replaced by reservists, national guardsmen, and draftees unfamiliar with the Korean terrain and mountain combat techniques. Military writer S. L. A. Marshall noted that the Chinese "sit there year after year. The longer they stay the smarter they get. Our youngsters keep moving in and out. They're smart and they've got guts, but they don't stay long enough to learn." Military leaders were acutely aware of the detrimental consequences of the rotation system by mid-1952, when 35,000 men were rotated monthly. Rotation created large demands for personnel and resulted in the drafting of 1.2 million more men, affecting services such as transportation.

—*Elizabeth D. Schafer*

References:

Cohen, Eliot. *Citizens and Soldiers: The Dilemmas of Military Service.* Ithaca, NY: Cornell University Press, 1985.

Fehrenbach, T. R. *This Kind of War: A Study in Unpreparedness.* New York: Macmillan, 1962.

Kellett, Anthony. *Combat Motivation: The Behavior of Soldiers in Battle.* Boston: Kluwer, 1982.

Millett, Allan R., and Peter Maslowski. *For the Common Defense: A Military History of the United States of America.* New York: Free Press, 1984.

See also: Battle Fatigue; Draft; Home-by-Christmas Offensive; MacArthur, Douglas; Marshall, Samuel Lyman Atwood; Rest and Recuperation (R&R); United States Army.

ROUNDUP, Operation
(5–11 February 1951)

Military operation mounted by the United Nations Command (UNC) in February 1951. In early 1951 Eighth Army commander Lieutenant General Matthew B. Ridgway decided to advance the center of the UNC line for an assault on Seoul. He ordered Lieutenant General Edward Almond to launch his X Corps in an offensive to make contact with the Communist forces and ascertain their dispositions and, if possible, their intentions; if the opportunity presented itself, Almond was to disrupt any assemblies for Communist offensive operations. This attack was to be launched simultaneously with the I and IX Corps offensives THUNDERBOLT and EXPLOITATION. It was designed to be a limited offensive that would follow the successful implementation of Operation THUNDERBOLT, which had left the Eighth Army in control of the Han River on its left flank.

The primary objective of Operation ROUNDUP was to advance the central front northward in preparation for a coordinated assault on Seoul, compelling the Communists to evacuate the capital of the Republic of Korea (ROK). Before launching the offensive, Ridgway moved troops from the western sector to reinforce X Corps and the ROK Army (ROKA) III Corps in the center of the peninsula. He instructed X Corps and ROKA III Corps to coordinate an envelopment of Hongch'ŏn, which would bring them abreast and even a little above the two corps on the west.

Beginning on 5 February X Corps, consisting of the ROKA 5th and 8th Divisions, supported by armored and artillery support teams from the 2d and 7th Divisions and the 187th Airborne Regimental Combat Team, advanced northward from Hoengsŏng toward Hongch'ŏn for several days; but resistance grew as UN forces came closer to the main Communist positions. Additionally, the terrain proved much rougher than anticipated. Narrow roads, sharp ridges, and broken ground slowed the attack.

Meanwhile, one Korean People's Army (North Korean) and two Chinese divisions had moved south from Seoul to halt the advance. Intelligence reports warned that a counterattack was possible, but X Corps commander Almond pressed forward. On the night of 11 February the Chinese People's Volunteer Army (Chinese Communist), organized into four armies, counterattacked in force, striking ROKA forces spearheading the X Corps advance and breaking through to establish roadblocks behind UNC lines. X Corps was able to retreat to Wŏnju, but the ROKA 8th Infantry Division was nearly annihilated, losing 7,500 men and all its equipment. U.S. support units, roadbound with their armor and artillery, were cut off and decimated, losing dozens of artillery pieces. The battle soon developed into a frantic defense of Hoengsŏng, but despite heroic efforts on the part of UNC forces, the corps was forced to retreat south of Hoengsŏng at a cost of 11,800 casualties (1,900 of them American).

Ridgway ordered the establishment of defensive positions to halt the retreat, and X Corps was able to reestablish defensive lines north of Wŏnju. While the X Corps was trying to establish its defensive lines, the Communists launched a new attack northwest of Wŏnju at the road junction of Chip'yŏng-ni on X Corps' left flank. For three days three Chinese divisions encircled and assaulted a defense perimeter manned by the 23d Infantry Regiment and the French Battalion. The Chinese wanted Chip'yŏng-ni because it was the key to the entire Eighth Army defense line, and they tried desperately to take it, despite sustaining severe punishment from air attacks as well as the embattled U.S. troops. The 23d held its positions until relief came in the form of an armored task force from the 5th Cavalry Regiment.

In terms of its original objective, Operation ROUNDUP had failed, but the hastily erected defenses and the valiant stand of the 23d Infantry Regiment and the attached French Battalion stopped the Chinese counterattack.

—*James H. Willbanks*

References:

Appleman, Roy E. *Ridgway Duels for Korea.* College Station, TX: Texas A&M Press, 1990.

Blair, Clay. *The Forgotten War: America in Korea, 1950–1953.* New York: Times Books, 1987.

See also: Almond, Edward Mallory; Chip'yŏng-ni, Battle of; Ridgway, Matthew Bunker; Tenth Corps; THUNDERBOLT, Operation.

RUGGED, Operation
(3–6 April 1951)

United Nations Command (UNC) military operation in April 1951. By the end of March 1951, the Eighth Army stood generally just below the 38th parallel, although Republic of Korea (ROK, South Korean) troops on the east coast had moved a few miles above it. With the approval of General Douglas MacArthur, Eighth Army commander Lieutenant General Matthew B. Ridgway elected to continue the advance over the 38th parallel in hopes of achieving maximum destruction of Communist forces, which were assembling in a fortified area known as the Iron Triangle. Communist troops were already in this area in force and appeared to be preparing for their spring offensive. By the first week in April Allied intelligence reported the presence of nine Chinese People's Volunteer Army (CPVA, Communist Chinese) armies (twenty-seven divisions) along with eighteen Korean People's Army (KPA, North Korean) divisions.

Ridgway decided under the circumstances that it would be better for the Eighth Army to move forward than to stand in place. Accordingly, he ordered the commencement of Operation RUGGED, which called for a general advance to a new objective line, KANSAS, which ran along commanding ground just north of the 38th parallel, except along the Imjin River in the west, where UN forces were to remain in position.

On 5 April UN forces moved forward in a general advance from positions across the peninsula. These included the U.S. 3d, 24th, and 25th and the ROK 1st Divisions of the U.S. I Corps in the west; in central Korea it included the U.S. IX Corps, with the U.S. 1st Marine, 1st Cavalry, and ROK 6th Divisions; they were joined by the 4th Ranger Company of the 187th Airborne Regimental Combat Team, then in reserve. In the east the U.S. X Corps, including the U.S. 2d and 7th and the ROK 5th Divisions, also advanced; they were joined along the east coast of Korea by the ROK I and III Corps, comprising four ROK divisions.

These troops rapidly crossed the 38th parallel and by 9 April reached defensive Line KANSAS and began to dig in. With the success of this move, Ridgway decided to add another objective line in the west, which he named UTAH. The purpose of this line, which was essentially a northern bulge of Line KANSAS in the west, was to thrust UN troops to a point just south of Ch'ŏrwŏn, the southwestern anchor of the Iron Triangle.

The result of this advance to KANSAS-UTAH was that UNC forces were in place just in time to defend against the Chinese spring offensive, which began on 21 April 1951.

—*James H. Willbanks*

References:
Blair, Clay. *The Forgotten War: America in Korea, 1950–1953.* New York: Times Books, 1987.
Middleton, Harry J. *The Compact History of the Korean War.* New York: Hawthorn Books, 1965.
Rees, David. *Korea: The Limited War.* New York: St. Martin's Press, 1964.

See also: Almond, Edward Mallory; Eighth United States Army; Iron Triangle; Kansas-Wyoming Line; MacArthur, Douglas; Ridgway, Matthew Bunker; Tenth Corps.

Rusk, David Dean
(1909–1994)

U.S. State Department official, later secretary of state. Born into a modest household in Cherokee County, Georgia, in 1909, David Dean Rusk attended Davidson College in North Carolina and, after graduating in 1931, became a Rhodes scholar at Oxford. He studied and later taught government and international relations at Mills College between 1934 and 1940. Rusk also briefly attended the University of Berlin in 1933. While there, he witnessed Adolf Hitler's rise to power, which had a profound impact on his life and worldview. Later he equated Communist aggression in Europe and Asia with Nazi expansion in Europe. The timid response to Hitler by the Western democracies at the 1938 Munich Conference appalled him. Rusk later advocated meeting Communist expansion with strength.

A strong military heritage and experience in Asian affairs also affected Rusk's outlook. Both his grandfathers had served in the Confederate Army, and Rusk followed the military tradition by joining the Reserve Officers Training Corps in high school and college, where he served as a cadet commander. During World War II Rusk was chief of war plans for General Joseph Stilwell in the China-Burma-India theater. In 1945 he accepted a position with the Pentagon, where, working in the operations division, he and Charles H. Bonesteel III were largely responsible for the U.S. position promoting the 38th parallel as the line dividing Korea between U.S. and USSR occupation forces.

After the war Rusk left the Pentagon and joined the Department of State. He first worked for Secretary of State George C. Marshall, whom Rusk greatly admired. In 1947 Rusk became the State Department's director of special political affairs and then deputy secretary of state in 1949. In 1949 and 1950 the State Department fell under tremendous scrutiny. The "loss" of China and the conviction of Alger Hiss for perjury led conservative critics and Senator Joseph McCarthy to attack the State Department. Rusk had little role in developing President Harry S. Truman's China policy, working instead on United Nations affairs. In 1950, however, he became assistant secretary of state for Far Eastern affairs, volunteering for what was arguably the most difficult job at the State Department.

In May 1949 Rusk worried about U.S. policy in South Korea. He believed that the United States had an "implied commitment" to the South, and he fretted over President Truman's decision to withdraw U.S. troops from South Korea. Rusk also became an advocate of the Republic of Korea (ROK, South Korea), saying in 1950 that although the Syngman Rhee government was not democratic it was progressing in that direction. Moreover, Rusk believed that ROK military forces could repel an "unlikely" attack from the North.

When word came that the Democratic People's Republic of Korea (DPRK, North Korea) had invaded the South, Rusk and Secretary of State Dean Acheson closely monitored the situation for the rest of the night. At 3:00 A.M. on 25 June, Rusk and Acheson formally requested a meeting of the United Nations Security Council. For the rest of the morning Rusk worked with Acheson in forming policy options for President Truman.

During two days of meetings at the Blair House, Rusk was heavily involved in planning the response to the DPRK attack. Drawing on lessons he learned from World War II, Rusk believed that the United States had to act to defend the ROK. He also insisted the matter be taken to the United Nations. With the successful U.S. landing at Inch'ŏn and the liberation of the South, Rusk and the State Department were confronted with the decision of whether to cross the 38th parallel. Some at the State Department worried that not crossing the 38th parallel would leave open the possibility of a future attack from the North. Others believed that the aggressor nation should be punished. Many feared, however, that crossing the 38th parallel and trying to liberate the North would mean a wider war with China and/or the Soviet Union. Beijing had warned that China would fight if U.S. forces invaded the North. Nonetheless, Rusk supported the decision to cross the 38th parallel and advocated the liberation of all Korea. Rusk did not seek a wider war but believed that Chinese military intervention was only a remote possibility.

United Nations commander General Douglas MacArthur also did not believe that China or the Soviet Union would intervene. During a meeting with Truman at Wake Island in October 1950 MacArthur told the president that there was "very little" chance that Soviet or Chinese forces would join the fray. In the midst of MacArthur's assessment, Rusk handed Truman a note in which he urged the president not to risk a wider war with either the Soviet Union or the People's Republic of China. Rusk strongly supported Truman's decision to fire MacArthur over the general's insubordination.

Before leaving government in 1952, Rusk held primary responsibility for shaping the peace treaty with Japan, working closely with future Secretary of State John Foster Dulles. In 1952 Rusk became president of the Rockefeller Foundation. He returned to government in 1961 as secretary of state in the Kennedy administration and remained in that capacity under President Lyndon Johnson. Many of Rusk's views and defense of failed Vietnam policies were based on his Korean War experience. Rusk remained as secretary of state until 1969. He then taught at the University of Georgia between 1970 and 1984. David Dean Rusk died in Athens, Georgia on 20 December 1994.

—Mark A. T. Esposito

References:

Cohen, Warren I. *Dean Rusk.* Totowa, NJ: Cooper Square, 1980.

Rusk, Dean. *As I Saw It,* edited by Daniel S. Papp. New York: W. W. Norton, 1990.

Schoenbaum, Thomas J. *Waging Peace and War: Dean Rusk in the Truman, Kennedy, and Johnson Years.* New York: W. W. Norton, 1988.

See also: Acheson, Dean Goodersham; Dulles, John Foster; Japanese Peace Treaty; Korea: History, 1945–1947; MacArthur, Douglas; Marshall, George C.; McCarthy, Joseph R.; McCarthyism; Syngman Rhee; 38th Parallel; Truman, Harry S.

S

Sanctuaries

Sheltered sites for troops. Sanctuaries were places of refuge where forces were safe from attacks and from which they staged war against nearby opposing forces. In General Douglas MacArthur's 27 September 1950 military order for the invasion of North Korea after the Inch'ŏn landing, he stressed that troops were not to cross the Chinese and Soviet borders even if Chinese troops entered the war. Restrictions also forbade air attacks on Chinese bases in Manchuria in fear of violating Soviet airspace. In turn, the Communists did not attack U.S. bases and communication lines in Japan and the Republic of Korea. President Harry S. Truman and his defense advisors accepted the idea of sanctuaries, preferring to contain any future fight with the Chinese in Korea rather than expanding the war into other territories.

The sanctuary of Manchuria was officially recognized by the United Nations Command (UNC) and the United States in November 1950. Manchuria was a historical route for the invasion of China. In the 1930s Japan used Korean bases to conquer Manchuria and then invade China. The presence of UN forces near the Manchuria-Korea border in fall 1950 alarmed the Chinese. People's Volunteer Army (Chinese Communist) forces used Manchuria to prepare for their entry into the Korean War in late October. Supply depots and airfields were built there to stage air attacks against UNC air and ground forces in North Korea. Siberia and the North Korean port town of Najin (Rashin) also were sanctuaries for Communist forces, who built up industries, arsenals, and rail systems safe from Allied bombs.

The United States wanted to keep Chinese forces out of the Korean War, fearing the Soviet Union would enter the war because of the 1950 Sino-Soviet Treaty of Friendship and Alliance. Granting China a form of neutrality, which it was not legally entitled to because its forces engaged UNC troops, was a sort of "gentlemen's agreement." Political restrictions would protect certain geographic regions from attack. Allied leaders agreed that Chinese army and air forces could consider as sanctuaries the area north of the Yalu River, serving as the North Korean and Chinese boundary, and the territory of Manchuria. Limiting military operations in the Korean War set a precedent for similar sanctuaries during the later Vietnam War.

U.S. military leaders promised not to bomb the Manchurian bases of China's air force. The Chinese pledged not to use aircraft based at sanctuaries against UNC ground troops, Allied bases outside Korea (primarily in Japan), and Allied forces in transit to and from Korea. Chinese aircraft from Manchurian sanctuaries, however, routinely attacked Allied airmen in MiG Alley and shot down planes over North Korea. Allied fighters were forbidden to pursue Communist aircraft because Washington believed that bombing Manchuria would deplete and divert Allied strength from Korean targets and cause too much attrition.

MacArthur criticized the sanctuaries as an "enormous handicap, without precedent in military history." His frustration about prohibitions on bombing sanctuaries and Yalu River bridges and power plants helped bring about his dismissal from command. At the MacArthur hearings in May 1951, he stressed that the Chinese could have been defeated if restrictions on bombing sanctuaries had been removed. "Manchuria and Siberia were sanctuaries of inviolate protection for all enemy forces and for all enemy purposes," MacArthur emphasized, "no matter what depredations or assaults might come from there."

Although military strategists considered bombing airfields and supply lines in the sanctuaries after MacArthur's dismissal, including the possible use of atomic weapons to end the war, the sanctuaries remained safe from Allied attacks despite continued launching of air strikes from Manchuria. The safety of the sanctuaries was ensured by the Allies' fears of retaliation and an expanded war.

—*Elizabeth D. Schafer*

References:

Futrell, Robert F. *The United States Air Force in Korea, 1950–1953.* Rev. ed. Washington, DC: Office of the Chief of Air Force History, 1983.

MacArthur, Douglas. *Reminiscences.* New York: McGraw-Hill, 1964.

Spurr, Russell. *Enter the Dragon: China's Undeclared War against the U.S. in Korea, 1950–1951.* New York: Henry Holt, 1988.

Wilz, J. E. "The MacArthur Hearings of 1951: The Secret Testimony." *Military Affairs* 39 (December 1975): 167–173.

See also: China, People's Republic of: Air Force; China, People's Republic of: Army; Chinese Military Offensives; MacArthur, Douglas; MacArthur Hearings; Manchuria; Manchurian Sanctuary; MiG Alley; Najin (Rashin) Bombing of; Sino-Soviet Treaty of Friendship and Alliance; Soviet Air War in Korea; Truman, Harry S.; Truman's Recall of MacArthur; United States Air Force (USAF); Yalu Bridges Controversy.

Sasebo

Port city on the western coast of the Japanese island of Kyushu. It became the major base for U.S. naval operations during the Korean War. Situated in Nagasaki

Prefecture at the mouth of Omura Bay, Sasebo has a fine natural harbor. In the late nineteenth century it grew from a small village to a naval base, which led to its partial destruction by Allied bombing during World War II. In June 1950 Sasebo, which was the headquarters of the U.S. Army's 34th Infantry Regiment, 24th Infantry Division, served as a secondary naval facility for U.S. Fleet Activities Yokuska.

During the Korean War, Sasebo rapidly eclipsed Yokuska, which was located near Tokyo, 500 miles farther from the theater of war. Sasebo's convenient proximity to the Korean port of Pusan, a mere 156 nautical miles away across the Tsushima and Korean Straits, gave it new importance as the chief wartime anchorage and center for the repair, refitting, and refueling of all U.S. naval forces in the Korean theater. The city also housed a large replacement depot for the U.S. Army. The majority of U.S. military personnel who served in Korea passed through Sasebo at least once during their tour of duty, either when embarking for Korea or when returning home.

—*Priscilla Roberts*

References:

Cagle, Malcolm W., and Frank A. Manson. *The Sea War in Korea.* Annapolis, MD: Naval Institute Press, 1957.

Karig, Walter. *Battle Report: The War in Korea.* New York: Rinehart, 1952.

Kim, Nam G. *From Enemies to Allies: The Impact of the Korean War on U.S.-Japan Relations.* San Francisco: International Scholars Publication, 1997.

See also: Japan; United States Navy.

SATURATE, Operation
(Winter–Spring 1952)

On 27 November 1951, United Nations Command (UNC) commander Lieutenant General Matthew B. Ridgway halted a UN offensive, resulting in a de facto cease-fire. To maintain the gains achieved by the recent offensive during negotiations, he proposed to continue the Fifth Air Force's (5AF's) aerial interdiction campaign. Air force pilots were not happy at this prospect, especially if tactics used in Operation STRANGLE remained unchanged. These missions had always been scheduled at the same morning or afternoon hours against predictable regular targets. Communist flak batteries were concentrated near these targets and took a heavy toll on UN air assets.

In January 1952 planners prepared for a new air campaign—Operation SATURATE—that would vary targets to avoid concentrated Communist defenses. Even as analysts pondered how to improve aerial interdiction, the Far East Air Force (FEAF) began a bomber campaign against specific rail and road "choke points." The most famous of these was the crossroads near Wadong. Between 26 January and 11 March

1952, in this preliminary to Operation SATURATE, 77 B-29s and 125 B-26 sorties dropped 3,928 500-pound bombs on this target. It proved to be a disappointing effort, with only eighteen rail and fifteen road cuts. During the forty-five-day effort, rail traffic was blocked for only seven days and road traffic for just four days.

Planning for Operation SATURATE called for more concentrated around-the-clock raids against shorter rail segments of the four main rail lines in North Korea. Fighter-bombers made daylight attacks, while B-26s struck the same targets at night. FEAF B-29s focused on bridges. The Fifth Air Force picked targets; closely controlled flights; and varied approaches, withdrawals, and altitudes. It also shifted targets based on flak concentrations and weather, and employed photo reconnaissance before, during, and after each raid.

Operation SATURATE officially commenced on 25 February and evolved into a race between U.S. airmen trying to destroy Communist rail lines and repair personnel trying to fix them. One example of this general pattern occurred on 25–26 March in an attack against the Chŏngju-Sinanju line that crossed two small streams. Flak was minimal and weather good for the 307 fighter-bomber sorties that dropped 530 1,000-pound bombs and 84 500-pound bombs on the rail bed and bridges. That night eight B-26s covered the target with 42 500-pound bombs.

The next day, 161 more fighter-bomber sorties dropped 322 1,000-pound bombs. In all, only one F-51 suffered minor flak damage. Aerial reconnaissance indicated that, aided by thawing mountain snows that cause flooding streams, the rail lines became totally impassible.

Even so, by 30 March Communist workers had repaired the road bed, and they had replaced the track by the 31st. The successful cut had lasted five days, but to ensure continued success, the raids needed to be repeated—something dwindling FEAF resources would not allow. Thus raids through May had to be reduced in size.

Despite these problems, Fifth Air Force's focus on cutting shorter lengths of track and its ability to outguess Communist flak placement generally validated the tactics of Operation SATURATE. One U.S. Air Force report noted that the Sinŭiji-Sinanju line was "continually out of operation" throughout April and most of May.

By May, as fighter-bombers were in ever-increasing demand, 243 had been lost and 290 severely damaged since the beginning of aerial interdiction campaigns in June 1951. Concurrently, Fifth Air Force had received only 131 replacements. By late May the 49th and 136th Fighter-Bomber Wings, which were each supposed to have 75 aircraft, had 41 and 39, respectively.

A fully equipped Fifth Air Force could have maintained six major cuts, but the undermanned force simply found North Korea's 600 miles of track too extensive. In mid-May the operation ended. Nearly a year of rail and road interdiction had not had sufficient impact to cause Communist forces to accept UN armistice terms.

During these raids, FEAF aircraft had flown 87,552 sorties, made 19,000 rail cuts; they had also destroyed 34,211 vehicles, 276 locomotives, and 3,820 rail cars. Despite such numbers, Communist forces were able to supply their front-line troops and to build logistical dumps in forward areas. For example, in July 1951, at the height of Operation STRANGLE, the Communists fired 8,000 artillery/mortar rounds. In May 1952, at the end of Operation SATURATE, they fired 102,000 rounds.

Ultimately, air force leaders were reminded that aerial interdiction is a very difficult and costly undertaking. They understood the significant impact of terrain, weather, climate, and Communist defenses on such a campaign. They grasped the need for continuous operations to counter the efforts of massed repair personnel.

The very nature of limited conflict deeply affected aerial operations in both Korea and Southeast Asia. Low-intensity conflict, by definition, seeks to limit the extent and expenditure of the engagement. It is full of political twists and turns, which also limit the employment of military assets. In the case of Korea, and later Vietnam, political restraints of Allied forces, especially air forces, and Communist sanctuaries and resupply proved to be roadblocks that were nearly impossible to overcome. Chinese and Soviet resupply of arms and trucks in Korea was critical, and with Chinese supply areas off-limits to UN attacks, these supplies were all but guaranteed.

The lessons of aerial interdiction during operations such as SATURATE were bought at a high price and should have been deeply ingrained in air power theory and doctrine and U.S. foreign policy when Vietnam unfolded less than a decade later. But to U.S. civilian and military leaders, Korea was the exception to the rules of international politics and military engagement. The strategic confrontation with the Soviet Union in Europe was the Cold War mainstream, not the Third World. Thus in Vietnam most of the same problems arose again during the COMMANDO HUNT aerial interdiction operations of 1968–1972, with the same results.

—*William Head*

References:

Futrell, Robert F. *The United States Air Force in Korea, 1950–1953.* Rev. ed. Washington, DC: Office of the Chief of Air Force History, 1983.

Mark, Eduard. *Aerial Interdiction: Air Power and the Land Battle in Three Wars.* Washington, DC: Center for Air Force History, 1994.

Thompson, Wayne. "The Air War over Korea." In *Winged Shield, Wing Sword: A History of the United States Air Force,* edited by Bernard C. Nalty. Washington, DC: U.S. Air Force History and Museum Program, 1997: 3–52.

See also: Aircraft (Principal Combat); Far East Air Force (FEAF); Logistics in the Korean War; Ridgway, Matthew Bunker; STRANGLE, Operation.

SCATTER, Operation
(29 June 1952)

United Nations Command (UNC) code name for the screening of Communist prisoners of war (POWs) to determine those who wished repatriation. During the armistice talks, Communist negotiators cited the Geneva Convention in demanding the unconditional repatriation of all POWs after the cessation of hostilities. But the issue of POWs during the Korean War was not as simple as in earlier wars. As increasing numbers of Communist military personnel deserted to or were otherwise captured by the UNC, it became evident that a substantial number of POWs believed that they would suffer death or injury if returned to Communist control. Also, with the Communists making a determined effort to organize their POWs, riots and disorders mounted, and murders and atrocities became commonplace in the UNC-administered camps. Such conditions made camp reorganization imperative.

After armistice negotiations deadlocked over the issue of exchange of POWs, in early April 1952 the Communist side requested an estimate of the number of POWs the UNC would repatriate. The UNC pointed out that this figure could only be determined by interviewing individual POWs. At that time the UNC and the Communist side assumed that only a relatively small percentage of prisoners would resist repatriation. Both sides supported screening to determine which POWs and civilian internees (CIs) desired repatriation and which did not.

At the suggestion of the UNC, the Communist side issued an amnesty statement, and the UNC then began screening of POWs in its custody. The plan to screen all internees, known as Operation SCATTER, was conducted by the 2d Logistical Command and was carried out during the period 8–15 April 1952. Operation SCATTER was also designed to separate prisoners who selected repatriation from those who selected nonrepatriation to minimize acts of violence between those opposing groups.

Before screening began, the UNC provided the Communist side's official amnesty statement to all prisoners in UNC custody. POWs were told to carefully consider their individual decisions. POWs were warned of possible reprisals against their families if they refused to return, and they were told that no promises could be made as to their disposition if they refused to return and that they might remain in the camps for many months after repatriates had returned home.

On 8 April 1952, UNC teams began individual polling of the POWs. The interviews were conducted by unarmed UNC personnel including Korean and Chinese linguists. Each prisoner, carrying his personal possessions, was called forward individually and interviewed in private. As soon as the prisoner reached a definite decision, either during or at the conclusion of the interview, he was removed to another camp if he refused repatriation; if not he was kept in a Kŏje-do compound to await return to Communist control. The program proceeded smoothly and with no incidents until UNC personnel attempted to enter the Communist-controlled compounds. Camp authorities feared considerable loss of life if they attempted to do so. Therefore authorities omitted screening of those compounds that had violently opposed the program and merely listed all these POWs for return to Communist control. Many individuals did seek, at risk of their lives, to express their desire not to return to Communist control, and a number of them were murdered by fellow POWs as a result.

Pressed by the Communist side in the armistice talks, early in April the UNC had released a figure of 116,000 likely repatriates. That seemed a reasonable estimate, but based on the screening of the POWs consenting to be interviewed, the UNC discovered to its surprise that only some 70,000 wanted repatriation, as follows: 7,200 CIs, 3,800 POWs of Republic of Korea residence, 53,900 Korean People's Army (North Korean) POWs, and 5,100 Chinese People's Volunteer Army (Chinese Communist) POWs. The vast majority of Chinese POWs had refused repatriation and demanded to be sent to Taiwan. This was a very serious development, because it was clear that Beijing would never accept such an outcome.

The UNC defended the process, reporting that its estimate of 70,000 resulted from a carefully worked-out screening process in an atmosphere that guaranteed each POW freedom of choice. The UNC then affirmed the finality of the 70,000 estimate and indicated that this figure must be accepted in any further negotiations.

The screening necessitated moving those refusing repatriation to other camps to separate them from the Communist prisoners. This operation, known as Operation SPREADOUT, took place from 19 April to 1 May 1952. It relocated some 80,000 nonrepatriate POWs and CIs from Kŏje-do UNC POW Camp One to new camps on the Korean mainland. Anti-Communist Chinese POWs were sent to Cheju-do.

But the screening results were not completely accurate, as many anti-Communist enclosures had taken steps to ensure a majority for nonrepatriation. Some U.S. officials understood that the results would be unacceptable to the Communist side and probably would lead them to charge the UNC with bad faith. Allied governments expressed concern that the number of nonrepatriates was too high in the anti-Communist camps.

When on 19 April 1952, they were informed of the results of the first screening, Communist negotiators were stunned. They insisted on the full repatriation of all POWs and at the same time sought to discredit the UNC screening. They protested that the 70,000 figure was the result of manipulation, and they claimed that the screening had not been impartial and was in violation of the Geneva Convention. The figure resulting from the Kŏje-do screening dealt a fatal blow to prospects of an early armistice.

—*Sunghun Cho*

References:
Cho, Sunghun. "Han'guk Chŏnjaeng Chung UN Kun ŭi P'oro Chŏngch'aek e Kwanhan Yŏn'gu" [UN Forces POW policies during the Korean War]. Doctoral dissertation, Academy of Korean Studies, Seoul, 1999. Unpublished manuscript.
MacDonald, Callum A. *Korea: The War Before Vietnam.* New York: Free Press, 1986.
See also: Civilian Internee Issue; P'anmunjŏm Truce Talks; Prisoners of War, Rescreening of.

Scorched Earth Policy

Term implying the destruction of everything that might be useful to an advancing enemy force. With the massive Chinese military intervention in the war at the end of November 1950, the U.S. Eighth Army was forced to withdraw from North Korea. As United Nations Command (UNC) forces retreated, Eighth Army commander Lieutenant General Walton H. Walker ordered a scorched earth policy. He did so convinced that the advancing Chinese People's Volunteer Army (CPVA, Communist Chinese) forces, with their lengthening supply lines, would have to live off the land, which would be especially difficult in a Korean winter.

Eighth Army engineers fired a large UNC supply dump in the Democratic People's Republic of Korea (DPRK, North Korea) capital of P'yŏngyang and destroyed bridges. Walker ordered that nothing of value be left behind. Eighth Army troops were to burn houses, kill livestock, and destroy food stocks as they retreated. The effects of these efforts on the CPVA forces is difficult to measure, but the policy certainly had catastrophic effects on the North Korean population. The scorched earth policy certainly increased the number of North Koreans who fled south. Perhaps a million people left North Korea for South Korea in the winter of 1950–1951. As X Corps in eastern Korea withdrew, it too practiced a scorched earth policy, destroying everything that might be of use to Communist forces, either by demolition or by naval gunfire.

Walker's successor, Lieutenant General Matthew B. Ridgway, continued this policy. On the morning of 4 January 1951, as the last UNC troops left Seoul, Ridgway ordered the four bridges over the Han River blown. At the same time, demolition charges destroyed the tidal basin at Inch'ŏn and supplies at Kimpŏ Airfield, including 1,600,000 gallons of aviation gasoline, 9,300 tons of engineer material, and twelve railroad cars full of ammunition.

Ridgway then issued an order the same day to end the scorched earth policy. He declared that in the future demolitions would be limited to those that combined "maximum hurt to the enemy with minimum hurt to the civilian population." Water and power plants would be spared and bridges would be destroyed only if this was necessary to delay a Communist advance. There would be no more "destruction for destruction's sake."

—*Spencer C. Tucker*

References:
Blair, Clay. *The Forgotten War: America in Korea, 1950–1953.* New York: Times Books, 1987.
Summers, Harry G., Jr. *Korean War Almanac.* New York: Facts on File, 1990.
See also: Eighth United States Army; Ridgway, Matthew Bunker; Walker, Walton Harris.

Searchlights

During the Korean War both United Nations and Communist forces employed searchlights in nighttime operations. These systems directed high-intensity light at military targets by either manual, radar, or sound-controlled means and were usually mobile. Searchlights having intensity ranging in tens of millions of candlepower existed, and some had beam ranges up to 30,000 feet.

United Nations use of searchlights centered primarily on battlefield illumination. For a short period in late autumn 1951, the U.S. Air Force designated several bombers in each squadron of B-26 Intruders to be outfitted with napalm tank–size 80 million–candlepower searchlights. After limited successes, the fragile searchlights were deemed unsuitable to hold up to the rigors of bombing operations. U.S. Army and Marine units holding defensive positions in October 1952 and March 1953 utilized searchlights in coordination with flares, both hand-launched and dropped from planes, to spot enemy movements. Searchlights were also employed by Allied antiaircraft artillery searchlight batteries to illuminate Communist aircraft and to light

up ground forces by reflecting the beams off low-level clouds.

The Communists used searchlights principally in an air-defense role along the Yalu River, but after February 1952 they used them farther south in support of flak units. Communist forces ultimately employed some 500 searchlights. They were positioned in clusters around key sites and in defensive belts but were constantly moved for defensive purposes.

—*Robert J. Bunker*

References:
Futrell, Robert F. *The United States Air Force in Korea, 1950–1953.* Rev. ed. Washington, DC: Office of the Chief of Air Force History, 1983.
Hermes, Walter G. *United States Army in the Korean War: Truce Tent and Fighting Front.* Washington, DC: Office of the Chief of Military History, 1966.
See also: Antiaircraft Artillery.

Sebald, William J.
(1901–1980)

U.S. State Department political adviser to U.S. Far Eastern commanders Generals Douglas MacArthur and Matthew B. Ridgway, 1946–1952. Born in Baltimore on 5 November 1901, William J. Sebald graduated from the U.S. Naval Academy in Annapolis, Maryland, in 1922. For the next eight years he remained in the navy, spending 1925 to 1928 as a language officer in Japan before resigning in 1930 to earn a law degree. In 1933 Sebald returned to Japan to practice Japanese commercial law, returning to Washington in 1939, where he continued his legal practice until 1941. After wartime service as chief of the U.S. Navy's Pacific division of combat intelligence, he turned to diplomacy, becoming an auxiliary U.S. Foreign Service officer in 1945 and a regular officer two years later.

In 1946 Sebald, one of the relatively few U.S. officials familiar with Japan's language and society, returned to Tokyo to join the U.S. occupation forces as legal assistant to MacArthur's acting political adviser, who died the following year. Sebald then took over three responsibilities: acting political adviser to MacArthur, representing the State Department's interests; chief of the diplomatic section of Far East commander General MacArthur's headquarters; and chairman and American member of the Allied Council for Japan, the largely ineffective international advisory body to the occupation forces. In 1950 he was named political adviser for Japan with the rank of ambassador. Sebald succeeded in developing an excellent relationship with the often difficult MacArthur, and therefore served as a reliable conduit of information to the State Department, which the autocratic general otherwise tended to leave in the dark regarding his policies.

During the Korean War, Sebald continued to perform this function, exercising little influence on major decisions but participating in key meetings, observing, and reporting back to his superiors in Washington. On 14 November 1950, two weeks before Communist Chinese forces intervened en masse, MacArthur described to Sebald his strategy for what he believed would be the war's final stages. This included intimidating the People's Republic of China (Communist China) by bombing bridges crossing the Yalu River into China and, should the Chinese still prove intransigent, bombing "key points" in Manchuria, moves that State Department officials and many of America's allies feared might well bring not only China but also the Soviet Union into the war. Sebald was normally present at MacArthur's meetings with the numerous Washington officials and other functionaries who for one reason or another paid visits to his combat headquarters.

Sebald remained in his post when Lieutenant General Matthew B. Ridgway replaced MacArthur, and he was heavily involved in the preparatory work for the conclusion of the Japanese peace treaty. In July 1951 the Joint Chiefs of Staff declined to allow his participation in the impending Kaesŏng truce talks, fearing that as a nonmilitary figure his presence would draw attention to the negotiations' political nature and implications and perhaps suggest some connection existed between them and the impending Japanese treaty.

Sebald remained in Japan until early 1952, shortly before the U.S. occupation formally ended, and the State Department then replaced him with a regular ambassador. Sebald served as U.S. ambassador to Burma between 1952 and 1954 and as ambassador to Australia from 1957 until 1961, when he retired. For three years (1954–1957), he was assistant secretary of state for Far Eastern affairs. In retirement he wrote his memoirs. Sebald died in Naples, Florida, on 10 August 1980.

—*Priscilla Roberts*

References:

James, D. Clayton. *The Years of MacArthur.* Vol. 3, *Triumph and Disaster, 1945–1964.* Boston: Houghton Mifflin, 1985.

Sebald, William J., with Russell Brines. *With MacArthur in Japan: A Personal History of the Occupation.* London: Cresset Press, 1967.

See also: Japan; MacArthur, Douglas; Ridgway, Matthew Bunker.

2d Logistical Command

The principal logistical base for United Nations (UN) forces throughout the Korean War was the southeastern port of Pusan. A small detachment led by Lieutenant Colonel Lewis A. Hunt arrived in Korea on 30 June 1950 to organize logistical support of U.S. troops, and on 4 July Brigadier General Crump Garvin and his staff arrived in Pusan from Japan and established the Pusan Base Command, which immediately took over port operations and other logistical support for the Eighth U.S. Army in Korea (EUSAK). On 13 July 1950, the Pusan Base Command was reorganized and renamed the Pusan Logistical Command. During the desperate defense of the Pusan perimeter from July to September 1950, personnel of the Pusan Logistical Command performed their critical logistical duties and also assisted in the fortification of the perimeter and prepared to take up defensive positions on the line if needed.

On 19 September 1950, the Pusan Logistical Command was redesignated as the 2d Logistical Command, and Brigadier General Paul F. Yount subsequently assumed command from Brigadier General Garvin. The principal mission of the 2d Logistical Command was to receive, store, and distribute supplies for the EUSAK and to forward EUSAK supply requisitions to the Japan Logistical Command. Headquarters of EUSAK, however, retained direct control of all requisitions for ammunition, petroleum products, and perishable foodstuffs. As of 23 November 1950 the 2d Logistical Command controlled the port, depot, and transportation units at Pusan; the 3d Logistical Command then operated UN logistical facilities on Korea's west coast, the UN Reception Center at Taegu, and a 400-bed Swedish Red Cross field hospital located in Pusan. The 2d Logistical Command was also responsible for management of UN camps for North Korean and Chinese prisoners of war. In November 1950 there were over 130,000 North Korean and Chinese prisoners of war in camps operated by the 2d Logistical Command at Pusan, Inch'ŏn, and P'yŏngyang.

With the evacuation of Inch'ŏn in December 1950, the 2d Logistical Command absorbed most of the units of the 3d Logistical Command, and it eventually controlled some 260 attached and assigned units and was responsible for the administration of all UN logistical and administrative facilities in Korea south of 36° 30′ north latitude. In September 1951 the 2d Logistical Command had five subordinate area commands: the Pusan Area Command (operated by the 3d Logistical Command); the Taegu Military Command; the Inch'ŏn-Seoul Area Command; the Kunsan Area Command; and the Sokch'o-ri Area Command, all of which, except the Pusan Area Command, were operated by provisional units. U.S. military personnel assigned to the 2d Logistical Command generally were used to supervise Korean laborers, who eventually numbered over 100,000. This made the 2d Logistical Command a much larger organization than originally envisioned.

On 16 October 1952, the 2d Logistical Command was transferred to the newly formed Korean Communications Zone (KCOMZ) and subsequently operated the Korean Base Section under KCOMZ. The outstanding performance of the 2d Logistical Command during the Korean War proved the soundness of the logistical command doctrine.

—*Charles R. Shrader*

References:

Appleman, Roy E. *South to the Naktong, North to the Yalu.* Washington, DC: Office of the Chief of Military History, 1961.

Huston, James A. *Guns and Butter, Powder and Rice: U.S. Army Logistics in the Korean War.* Selinsgrove, PA: Susquehanna University Press, 1989.

———. *The Sinews of War: Army Logistics, 1775–1953.* Washington, DC: Office of the Chief of Military History, 1966.

Logistical Problems and Their Solutions. APO 301: Headquarters, Eighth U.S. Army Korea, Historical Section and Eighth Army Historical Service Detachment (Provisional), 1952.

Mossman, Billy C. *U.S. Army in the Korean War: Ebb and Flow, November 1950–July 1951.* Washington, DC: U.S. Army Center of Military History, 1990.

See also: Eighth United States Army; Japan Logistical Command; Korean Communications Zone; Logistics in the Korean War.

Seoul

Capital and largest city of South Korea; site of several major battles during the Korean War. Founded by General Yi Sŏng-gye in 1394, the city of Seoul, which means "capital," was originally called Hansŏng or Hanyang. Situated at the center of the Korea peninsula, the city offered an ideal location. The site was a militarily defensible, natural redoubt adjoining the navigable Han River, which flows into the Yellow Sea. The strategic port of Inch'ŏn, at the mouth of the river, lies nearby and served the capital.

The Chosŏn dynasty ruled the area until 1910, when the Japanese annexed Korea and renamed the city Kyŏngsŏng (Kejo). With the defeat of Japan at the end of World War II and founding of the Republic of Korea, Seoul again became the city's official name.

During the Korean War, Seoul changed hands a number of times. Troops of the Korean People's Army (KPA, North Korean) captured Seoul on 28 June 1950, only three days after they invaded South Korea. After the successful 15 September 1950 Inch'ŏn landing, United Nations Command (UNC) forces recaptured the city on 28 September. UNC forces held the capital until 3 January 1951, when it fell to the Chinese People's Volunteer Army (CPVA, Communist Chinese). UNC forces retook the city on 15 March. Although much of the city was left in ruins by the fighting, Seoul was rebuilt and has developed into a major industrial area. Today it has a population in excess of 10 million people.

—*Mary L. Kelley*

References:

Blair, Clay. *The Forgotten War: America in Korea, 1950–1953.* New York: Times Books, 1987.

Rees, David. *Korea: The Limited War.* New York: St. Martin's Press, 1964.

Riley, John W., Jr., and Wilbur Schramm. *The Reds Take a City: The Communist Occupation of Seoul.* New Brunswick, NJ: Rutgers University Press, 1951.

See also: Inch'ŏn Landings: Operation CHROMITE; Seoul, Recapture of; Seoul, Fall of.

Seoul, Fall of
(25–29 June 1950)

Controlling the Republic of Korea (ROK) capital of Seoul was important to both sides in the Korean War. Indeed, Seoul changed hands four times during the war. The city's location only fifty miles from the border, its industry, and the fact it was the ROK capital and governmental center all contributed to its importance. The Democratic People's Republic of Korea (DPRK, North Korea) made the capture of Seoul a priority for its June 1950 offensive.

The North Korean invasion of South Korea early on 25 June 1950 saw the Korean People's Army (KPA) descend upon an unprepared and unsuspecting South Korea. The prompt capture of Seoul was a primary goal. To cut off ROK Army (ROKA, South Korea) forces north of the Han River and secure the ROK capital, the KPA deployed its 1st and 6th Divisions along the Kaesŏng-Munsan-Seoul corridor, the 4th Division along the Tongduch'ŏn-Ŭijŏngbu-Seoul corridor, and the 3d Division along the P'och'ŏn-Ŭijŏngbu-Seoul corridor. The ROKA 1st and 7th Divisions and elements of the Capital Division were deployed north of Seoul and bore the brunt of the KPA shock troops at the beginning of the war. The ROKA 2d, 3d, and 5th Divisions, deployed in the rear area as a reserve, then moved north of the Han River and on 27 June engaged KPA troops.

By the second day of the invasion, 26 June 1950, Seoul was under siege. In the early hours of that day, Americans began to evacuate the city by ship along the Han River and out of the port of Inch'ŏn. The evacuation also occurred by air. It continued through the night and into the following day, until all 2,000 American dependents and other foreigners had been removed.

On 27 June four U.S. Air Force F-82 Twin Mustang propeller-driven night fighters and several F-80 Shooting Star jet fighters of the Fifth Air Force covering the evacuation shot down three Korean People's Air Force (KPAF, North Korean) Yak-9 attack planes, which had attacked them. Four other Yak-9s were shot down later that same day.

As KPA forces advanced on Seoul, panic set in among the populace. Civilians as well as solders and government officials filled the streets, transporting such valuables as they could. Most fled the city south by one of the four bridges across the Han River, and from there many continued as far south as Pusan.

During the exodus from the city, ROKA Chief of Staff General Ch'ae Pyŏng-dŏk made a costly mistake. There were four bridges spanning the Han River: three for rail traffic and the fourth a three-lane highway crossing. The original plan in event of a DPRK invasion was to destroy these bridges only when KPA tanks entered the city, an event unlikely to occur until 28 June. Despite these plans, during the night of the 27th, as ROK high officials evacuated Seoul, Ch'ae ordered his deputy, General Kim Paek-il, to destroy the bridges that night at 0130. All four bridges were duly blown up, despite the fact that some 4,000 people were on one bridge alone when it was destroyed, killing in the blast or drowning in the Han River some 500–800 people.

The bridges were destroyed several hours before it was necessary, and this action cut off thousands of ROKA solders from their evacuation routes and forced them to abandon their heavy equipment and, in many cases, even their weapons to get across the river. Blame was assigned not to Ch'ae but to the ROKA's chief engineer, who was executed shortly thereafter.

Despite ROKA opposition, the KPA, spearheaded by tanks, continued its relentless drive on Seoul. During the night of 27 June, its 3d Division entered the city.

U.S. Army Major General John Church, who headed a survey team ordered to Korea by U.S. Far East commander General Douglas MacArthur arrived in Seoul on the night of the 27th. Church, amazed at the chaos, took charge, corralling stragglers in an attempt to form a defensive line south of the Han River. The capital itself fell on the 28th. In a radio message to MacArthur, Church advised that only U.S. troops could contain the invasion. After a personal trip to Korea the next day, MacArthur concurred in this assessment. Meanwhile, the North Koreans in Seoul set about rounding up government officials, police officers, and remaining solders for execution.

U.S. tanks move through a roadblock and past marines of the 1st Marine Division in Seoul, 25 September 1950. (National Archives)

The 3d and 4th KPA Divisions suffered 1,500 casualties in the taking of Seoul; the ROKA was shattered. By 28 June the ROK government had fled to Taejŏn and the ROKA command could account for only 22,000 men of the 98,000 men on its rolls only three days earlier.

—Michael D. Mulé

References:

Blair, Clay. *The Forgotten War: America in Korea, 1950–1953.* New York: Times Books, 1987.

Leckie, Robert. *Conflict: The History of the Korean War, 1950–1953.* New York: Putnam, 1962.

Marshall, S. L. A. *Military History of the Korean War.* New York: F. Watts, 1963.

See also: Korea, Democratic People's Republic of, Invasion of the Republic of Korea; MacArthur, Douglas; Seoul; South Korea, Occupation by Democratic People's Republic of Korea; Truman, Harry S.

Seoul, Recapture of
(18–28 September 1950)

After their landing at Inch'ŏn, X Corps of the United Nations Command (UNC) forces pressed eastward with the goal of liberating the Republic of Korea (ROK, South Korean) capital of Seoul. Hard fighting took place before the city was recaptured.

Capturing Seoul was important for several reasons. First, the city was an industrial center and communications hub with north-south rail lines and roads running through it. Retaking Seoul would cut off most Korean People's Army (KPA, North Korean) forces to the south along the Pusan perimeter. Taking the capital would also be a tremendous morale boost for the UNC, especially the Republic of Korea Army.

U.S. forces began their move toward Seoul on 17 September. UNC commander General Douglas

Thousands of South Korean refugees stream south of Seoul on the evacuation of the ROK capital ahead of advancing Communist troops, 5 January 1951. (National Archives)

MacArthur was determined that the capital be retaken by 25 September, three months to the day after the outbreak of the war. The first objective was to capture Kimpŏ airfield. It would provide a place for U.S. aircraft to land, resupply, and provide close ground support to the attackers.

Early on 17 September the 5th Marines ambushed a column of six KPA T-34 tanks and 200 infantry. By the night of the 17th much of Kimpŏ airfield had been taken; it was completely in Marine Corps hands on the 18th. That same day the 7th Infantry Division began landing at Inch'ŏn; and on the 21st the remaining Marine regiment, the 7th, disembarked. By the end of 19 September the 5th Marines had cleared the entire south bank of the Han River on their front; they crossed the river a day later but were then slowed by determined KPA resistance. The 1st Regiment also ran into stiff resistance from a regiment of the KPA 18th Division on the 22nd before it too reached the Han.

X Corps commander Major General Edward M. Almond had made it clear to 1st Marine Division commander Major General Oliver P. Smith that Seoul must fall by 25 June. Fighting was stiff, as the KPA defenders set up barricades and fought street by street and house by house. U.S. air strikes and artillery took their toll of the defenders, leveling sections of the city. The U.S. flag, soon to be replaced by that of the United Nations, was not raised at the Capitol Building by the 5th Marines until the afternoon of 27 September, although Almond announced just before midnight on the 25th that the city had fallen. On 29 September MacArthur presided over an emotional ceremony in the Capitol Building marking the liberation of Seoul and the restoration of the Syngman Rhee government.

On 3 January 1951, in the course of the Third Chinese People's Volunteer Army (Chinese Communist) offensive, the ROK government again abandoned Seoul. The Eighth Army retook the ROK capital for a fourth and final time in the war on 14 March 1951.

—*Michael D. Mulé*

References:

Blair, Clay. *The Forgotten War: America in Korea, 1950–1953.* New York: Times Books, 1987.

Hastings, Max. *The Korean War.* New York: Simon & Schuster, 1987.

Higgins, Marguerite. *War in Korea.* Garden City, NY: Doubleday, 1951.

Marshall, S. L. A. *Military History of the Korean War.* New York: F. Watts, 1963.

See also: Almond, Edward Mallory; Chinese Military Offensives; Inch'ŏn Landings: Operation CHROMITE; Kimpŏ Airfield; MacArthur, Douglas; Seoul, Fall of; Smith, Oliver Prince; Tenth Corps.

Service, John Stewart
(1909–1999)

U.S. Foreign Service officer and one of the "Old China Hands." In the view of many, the Old China Hands were the best-trained and most articulate diplomats in the history of the Foreign Service. Their reward for accurately reporting events in China during the Second World War and the years immediately afterward was to be systematically hounded from their posts and—for a number of them, including Service—public disgrace.

Born in China of missionary parents on 8 August 1909, John Stewart Service grew up in Sichuan Province, attended high school in Shanghai, and then studied art history at Oberlin College in Ohio. He returned to China in 1922 and, after a brief time in banking, joined the Foreign Service. When the Japanese entered Beijing (Peking), he helped escort American refugees to safety. Assigned to the new Nationalist capital at Chongqing (Chungking) as a political officer in 1941, his task was to gather information on all Chinese political parties and factions, including the Communists. Service knew China extraordinarily well and had almost an uncanny instinct regarding events there.

In the Communist witch-hunt hysteria of the early Cold War period, Senator Joseph R. McCarthy attacked Service and other China Hands, including John Carter Vincent, John Paton Davies, and Oliver Edmund Clubb. Accused of being soft on Communism, Service had in fact reported the truth of corruption in the Jiang Jieshi (Chiang Kai-shek) government. As the war progressed, he had predicted a civil war that would lead to a Communist victory if things were unchanged. On 20 March 1944, Service had informed his superiors: "China is a mess ... for the sorry situation as a whole Chiang, and only Chiang, is responsible.... Chiang will cooperate if the U.S., upon which he is dependent, makes up its mind exactly what it wants from him and then gets hard-boiled about it.... This may mean taking an active part in Chinese affairs. But unless we do it, China will not be of much use as an ally. And, in doing it, we may save China."

The China Hands did not—contrary to the charges of their critics—welcome communism. They simply urged that U.S. pressure be brought to bear on Jiang and—failing that—they advocated a policy of U.S. neutrality in what was an inevitable civil war. Had their advice been followed the United States would probably have been able to maintain diplomatic relations with China and the Korean War might have been prevented. Certainly the charge that Service and other Foreign Service officials "lost" China was patently ridiculous. The Chinese themselves accomplished that.

In February 1950 Senator McCarthy specifically charged Service with being "a known associate and collaborator with Communists." Although Service was subsequently cleared by a Senate committee, a Loyalty Review Board named by President Harry S. Truman said there was "reasonable doubt as to his loyalty." Secretary of State Dean G. Acheson dismissed him the same day. Service fought this and in 1956 the Supreme Court ruled 8–0 that the board had no right to review the State Department's findings and that Acheson had no right to dismiss him. Service then rejoined the State Department, retiring from an obscure post in the Liverpool, England, consulate in 1962.

Service then earned a master's degree at the University of California, Berkeley, and became library curator of its Center for Chinese Studies. With the 1970s thaw in relations between the United States and People's Republic of China, Service visited China, even meeting with Chinese Prime Minister Zhou Enlai in 1971. He also published several books on China. John Service died in Oakland, California, on 3 February 1999.

—*Spencer C. Tucker*

References:

Kahn, E. J., Jr. *The China Hands. America's Foreign Service Officers and What Befell Them.* New York: Viking Press, 1975.

Service, John S. *Lost Chance in China. The World War II Dispatches of John S. Service,* edited by Joseph W. Esherick. New York: Random House, 1974.

See also: Acheson, Dean Goodersham; Clubb, Oliver Edmund; Davies, John Paton; Jiang Jieshi (Chiang Kai-shek); McCarthy, Joseph R.; Truman, Harry S.; Zhou Enlai.

Shepherd, Lemuel Cornick, Jr.
(1896–1990)

U.S. Marine Corps general. Born in Norfolk, Virginia, on 10 February 1896, Shepherd graduated from the Virginia Military Institute in 1917. He then accepted a commission in the U.S. Marine Corps. Ordered to France in June 1917 as a second lieutenant, Shepherd was promoted to first lieutenant in August of the same year. He fought with the 5th Marine Regiment (part of the 2d U.S. Army Division) in the battles of Belleau Wood, Aisne-Marne, Saint-Mihiel, and Meuse Argonne. He was wounded three times.

In 1919 Shepherd was promoted to captain and became an aide to Marine Corps Commandant General John Archer Lejeune. After this post he held a variety of assignments, including service on the battleships *Nevada* and *Idaho*, Norfolk Marine Corps Base, and the 4th Marines in China. After graduating from the Field Officers Course at Quantico, Virginia, in 1930 he was deployed to Haiti, where he served for four years. Promoted to major in 1932 and to lieutenant colonel in 1935, he served on the Marine Corps Institute Staff between 1934 and 1936. After graduating from the Naval War College in 1937, Shepherd

commanded a battalion of the 5th Marines. In 1940 he was promoted to colonel after completing a tour on the staff of the Marine Corps Schools.

In March 1942 Shepherd assumed command of the 9th Marine Regiment. After service under General Alexander Vandegrift in the 1st Marine Division on Guadalcanal, Shepherd was promoted to brigadier general in July 1943. Later he commanded units that fought on Cape Gloucester (December 1943) and on Guam (July–August 1944). Promoted to major general, Lejeune commanded the 6th Marine Division in the Okinawa campaign (April–June 1945).

In 1946 Shepherd became assistant commandant of the Marine Corps; from 1948 to 1950 he was commandant of the Marine Corps Schools. In June 1950 he was promoted to lieutenant general and took command of Fleet Marine Forces in the Pacific, with headquarters in Honolulu.

During the Korean War, Shepherd served on General Douglas MacArthur's staff. In the course of a meeting with MacArthur on 10 July, when MacArthur recalled his success with the 1st Marine Division in the Pacific during World War II, Shepherd suggested that he ask the Joint Chiefs of Staff for the division, a request that was granted. Shepherd said the division could be in Korea in six weeks and ready for service by 15 September.

Shepherd participated in planning for the Inch'ŏn landing. He thought the landing a good one but opposed Inch'ŏn as the site, particularly as another location to the south was equally well placed as a base from which to take Seoul. At MacArthur's request, Shepherd accompanied him aboard the flagship *Mount McKinley* to act as his personal adviser on amphibious matters. Shepherd was one of the first Americans to fly into Kimpŏ Airfield after its recapture. In January 1952 he was promoted to (four-star) general and became commandant of the Marine Corps. He retired in January 1956. Recalled later that year to serve as chairman of the Inter-American Defense Board, he again retired in September 1956. Shepherd died in La Jolla, California, on 6 August 1990.

—*Jason B. Berg*

References:

Dupuy, Trevor N., Curt Johnson, and David L. Bongard. *The Harper Encyclopedia of Military Biography.* New York: HarperCollins, 1992.

Heinl, Robert Debs. *Soldiers of the Sea. The United States Marine Corps, 1775–1962.* Baltimore: Nautical and Aviation Publishing Co. of America, 1991.

Langley, Michael. *Inchon Landing. MacArthur's Last Triumph.* New York: Times Books, 1979.

Millett, Allan R. *Semper Fidelis: The History of the United States Marine Corps.* New York: Macmillan, 1990.

See also: Inch'ŏn Landings: Operation CHROMITE; MacArthur, Douglas.

Sherman, Forrest P.
(1896–1951)

U.S. Navy admiral and chief of naval operations between 1949 and 1951. Born on 30 October 1896, at Merrimack, New Hampshire, Forrest P. Sherman attended the Massachusetts Institute of Technology during 1913–1914 and then the U.S. Naval Academy from which he graduated in 1917 because of the wartime accelerations. Sherman served on the *Nashville* in European waters during World War I. In 1922 he completed flight training in Pensacola, Florida. After subsequent assignments in naval aviation, he graduated from the Naval War College in 1927. A variety of other postings both afloat and ashore followed.

When the United States entered World War II, Sherman was serving in the War Plans Division of the Office of the Chief of Naval Operations. He then took command of the carrier *Wasp*, and after its loss in September 1942, he became chief of staff of the commander of the Pacific Fleet Air Force. In November 1943 Sherman was appointed deputy chief of staff to commander of the Pacific Fleet Admiral Chester Nimitz, in which capacity he played a significant role in planning future naval operations.

After World War II, in October 1945 Sherman took command of Carrier Division I. Promoted to vice admiral, he became deputy chief of naval operations that December. In January 1948 he became chief of U.S. naval forces in the Mediterranean. In November 1949 he became chief of naval operations with the rank of admiral. As chief of naval operations, Sherman forcefully defended the navy in a time of shrinking defense budgets. He secured funding for the navy's first nuclear submarine and the modernization of ships, and he was a strong advocate of naval aviation.

Once the Korean War began in 1950, Sherman participated in the series of high-level meetings involving President Harry S. Truman, the service secretaries, presidential advisers, and congressional leaders. He attended the first and second Blair House meetings. Truman endorsed his recommendation for a naval blockade of the Democratic People's Republic of Korea (DPRK, North Korea). Sherman supported MacArthur's call for the use of ground forces, and he oversaw the mobilization of U.S. Navy assets, including expansion of the navy. Later he won congressional approval for construction of a supercarrier.

Sherman and the other chiefs expressed reservations about Operation CHROMITE, General MacArthur's proposed landing behind Korean People's Army (KPA, North Korean) lines at Inch'ŏn. Sherman opposed depriving the Atlantic Fleet Marine Force of the 1st Marine Division, since it might be needed elsewhere, and he disagreed with the site, suggesting a

landing farther south at Kunsan. Yet Sherman did assure Truman that MacArthur would wisely employ units given him.

The Joint Chiefs of Staff (JCS) dispatched Sherman and General J. Lawton Collins to East Asia for more information before granting approval for Operation CHROMITE. MacArthur received them in Tokyo on 21 August. The next day the two visited Korea for talks with Eighth Army commander Lieutenant General Walton H. Walker before flying back to Japan for MacArthur's Inch'ŏn briefing on the 23rd. At that time Sherman and Collins again pressed for the Kunsan site, and, subsequent to conversations with navy and Marine officers, wanted MacArthur to consider P'osŭng-myŏn, nearly fifty miles below Inch'ŏn, as a second alternative. But even before the briefing Sherman had decided to back MacArthur's proposal. When the dangers of moving through Flying Fish Channel, the passageway heading into Inch'ŏn, which could be protected by mines and coastal batteries, were raised, Sherman broke in saying, "I wouldn't hesitate to take a ship up there." MacArthur cried out, "Spoken like a Farragut!" All expected the general's forces to advance beyond the 38th parallel and occupy North Korea once KPA resistance was eliminated. After his last meeting with MacArthur, Sherman declared, "I wish I could share that man's confidence." On 28 August the JCS gave their qualified endorsement to Operation CHROMITE.

As United Nations Command (UNC) troops drove northward, Sherman met Defense and State Department officials on 21 November to consider changing MacArthur's mission out of concern for intervention by the People's Republic of China (PRC, Communist China). Although no alteration of MacArthur's orders ensued, Sherman thought that the general was too scornful of JCS anxiety about offending China's interests.

Later, Sherman urged retaliation if Chinese air forces attacked from Manchuria. He disapproved of a cease-fire. Apparently ready to wage war to defeat the PRC, Sherman emerged as a cautious supporter of MacArthur's proposals to pressure China through a naval blockade, Republic of China military operations, guerrilla activities, and naval as well as air strikes if Chinese assaults against UNC forces carried beyond Korea.

Sherman and the other service chiefs conferred on 5 April after being informed of President Truman's displeasure at MacArthur's public defiance of administration policy. After considering the matter, they recommended that MacArthur be relieved from command. Sherman believed that dismissal was justified, since MacArthur had violated a presidential prohibition on public statements, opposed the idea of limited war, and endangered civilian control of the military. Later Sherman defended the decision at the MacArthur congressional hearings.

Sherman believed in the primacy of Europe in U.S. defense planning. In July he left for Europe on an inspection trip and negotiations regarding U.S. bases in Spain. Sherman died of a heart attack on 22 July 1951, while attending a conference on European defense in Naples, Italy.

—*Rodney J. Ross*

References:

Alexander, Bevin. *Korea: The First War We Lost.* New York: Hippocrene Books, 1986.

Dictionary of American Biography, Supplement Five, 1951–1955, edited by John S. Garraty. New York: Charles Scribner's Sons, 1977.

Goulden, Joseph C. *Korea: The Untold Story of the War.* New York: Times Books, 1982.

James, D. Clayton. *The Years of MacArthur.* Vol. 3, *Triumph and Disaster: 1945–1964.* Boston: Houghton Mifflin, 1985.

New York Times, 23 July 1951.

See also: Blair House Meetings; Collins, Joseph Lawton; Collins-Sherman Visit to Tokyo; Inch'ŏn Landings: Operation CHROMITE; Joint Chiefs of Staff (JCS); MacArthur, Douglas; MacArthur Hearings; Walker, Walton Harris.

Short, Joseph H., Jr.
(1904–1952)

Press secretary to President Harry S. Truman for much of the Korean War, from December 1950 until his death in September 1952. Born in Vicksburg, Mississippi, on 11 February 1904, Joseph H. Short, Jr., initially contemplated a military career. He earned a B.A. degree from the Virginia Military Institute in 1925. Experience on a campus newspaper led him to switch to journalism, and in the later 1920s he held various positions on the *Jackson (Mississippi) Daily News*, the Vicksburg *Post and Herald*, and the *New Orleans Times-Picayune*. He joined the Richmond bureau of the Associated Press (AP) in 1929. Two years later he transferred to the AP's Washington office, where he remained until 1941. A respected newsman, during the Second World War Short moved first to the *Chicago Sun* and then in 1943 to the Washington staff of the *Baltimore Sun*, where he remained until 1950. In the course of covering Harry S. Truman's vice-presidential campaign of 1944, several presidential overseas and domestic trips in 1947, and the long and demanding presidential "whistle-stop" campaign of 1948, Short developed a warm relationship with the president.

When Truman's first press secretary, Charles Ross, died suddenly in December 1950, the president named Short to succeed him, an appointment that gave rise to some comment because it was the first time a professional reporter had held the position. Newspapermen

widely acclaimed the selection of a hardworking and well-liked colleague and former National Press Club chairman, who prided himself on returning every telephone call made to him.

Short attempted to broaden the channels of communication between the White House and reporters and to coordinate the various cabinet departments' information activities and those of the presidency. Short advised Truman on the public relations aspects of the Korean War, attempting to provide diplomatic and tactful public explanations of some of the more controversial issues to which it gave rise, preeminent among which was his announcement of the recall in April 1951 of General Douglas MacArthur.

One of Short's early tasks was to issue a formal presidential statement denouncing the railroad strike as irresponsible and unpatriotic during a national emergency; in April 1952 he likewise depicted the president's ultimately unsuccessful seizure of the nation's steel plants as an essential war measure. Short also functioned as a speechwriter and general adviser to the president on both domestic and international issues, although, as might be expected, his major impact was on the presentation of policy rather than its making. Short's unexpected death from a heart attack on 18 September 1952, was widely blamed on the grueling pressures to which his job subjected him.

—*Priscilla Roberts*

References:

Hamby, Alonzo L. *Man of the People: A Life of Harry S. Truman.* New York: Oxford University Press, 1995.

McCullough, David. *Truman.* New York: Simon & Schuster, 1992.

Nelson, W. Dale. *Who Speaks for the President? The White House Press Secretary from Cleveland to Clinton.* Syracuse, NY: Syracuse University Press, 1998.

"Short, Joseph (Hudson Jr.)." In *Current Biography, 1951.* New York: H. W. Wilson, 1952.

Stein, Meyer L. *When Presidents Meet the Press.* New York: Messner, 1969.

Swain, Martha H. "Joseph Hudson Short, Jr." In *Dictionary of American Biography, Supplement Five, 1951–1955,* edited by John A. Garraty. New York: Charles Scribner's Sons, 1977.

See also: Steel Plants, Truman's Seizure of; Truman, Harry S.; Truman's Recall of MacArthur.

SHOWDOWN, Operation
(13 October–8 November 1952)

Limited offensive operation by United Nations Command (UNC) forces to take hills in the Iron Triangle. With peace talks at P'anmunjŏm recessed, the Communists launched their largest offensive of the year on 6 October 1952. With substantial artillery fire and massive infantry attacks, the Communist forces drove back the Eighth Army west of the Iron Triangle to split I and IX Corps. Hoping to influence U.S. public opinion in the few weeks before the U.S. presiden-

Troops of the 17th Regiment, U.S. 7th Infantry Division, taking a break along a very muddy road. (National Archives)

tial election, the Chinese pressed the attack for ten days until resistance from the Republic of Korea Army (ROKA, South Korean) 9th Division artillery and close air support forced them to withdraw.

To counter the Communist offensive and strengthen the battered IX Corps position on the extreme southeast apex of the Iron Triangle near Kimhwa, the UNC planned an immediate limited offensive to seize Communist positions in the Iron Triangle complex. This offensive, Operation SHOWDOWN, was intended to convince the Communists that failure to reach an agreement would prove costly to them militarily.

The attack was launched on 14 October by four battalions: two from the U.S. 7th Infantry Division and two from the ROKA 2d Infantry Division, with one battalion from each executing a diversionary attack. The four other battalions assaulted the northeast corner of the hill at Kimhwa, where Chinese observation teams overlooked a UN supply route through the valley.

In spite of heavy artillery and air support, the operation did not go according to the UNC plan. The Chinese put up fierce resistance, stalling the UN attacks. Both sides then brought up more manpower. The UNC did not accurately assess Chinese resistance in its prebattle estimations; it had planned on an assault of no more than five days' duration with an estimated total cost of only 200 casualties to seize the entire ridge line. What was expected to be a speedy operation dragged on for three weeks and was the heaviest fighting since late 1951. The Chinese infantry were too well dug in to be dislodged by the piecemeal UN attacks.

By 8 November 1952, the UNC broke off its assaults. The Chinese still held most of the hills in the Triangle, with the exception of one corner of Triangle Hill, half of Sniper's Ridge, and most of Jane Russell Hill. The minor gains in territory achieved were insufficient compensation for the enormous loss of life.

What was originally planned to be a limited offensive operation had resulted in bloody stalemate in which U.S. and ROKA forces sustained an appalling 9,000 casualties in twenty-five days of heavy fighting, nearly twenty times the original UNC estimate.

The Chinese forces lost twice as many men—19,000—but they proved that they were willing to trade men for real estate. This "limited battle in a limited war" had its effects politically in the United States. President Harry S. Truman's public approval rating plummeted below 25 percent at the conclusion of this operation. Eighth Army commander Lieutenant General Mark Clark characterized the offensive as "unsuccessful," and it caused him to resume emphasis on air pressure tactics to break the armistice deadlock.

—*Bradford A. Wineman*

References:

Blair, Clay. *The Forgotten War: America in Korea, 1950–1953.* New York: Times Books, 1987.

Fehrenbach, T. R. *This Kind of War: A Study in Unpreparedness.* New York: Macmillan, 1962.

Hastings, Max. *The Korean War.* New York: Simon & Schuster, 1987.

Hermes, Walter G. *United States Army in the Korean War: Truce Tent and Fighting Front.* Washington, DC: Office of the Chief of Military History, 1966.

Rees, David. *Korea: The Limited War.* New York: St. Martin's Press, 1990.

See also: Clark, Mark W.; Truman, Harry S

Shtykov, Terentii Fomich
(1907–1964)

Soviet ambassador to the Democratic People's Republic of Korea (DPRK, North Korea) between 1948 and 1951, who supported Kim Il Sung's policy of invading the Republic of Korea (ROK, South Korea). Born in the Russian province of Vitebsk in 1907, Terentii F. Shtykov joined the Bolshevik Party in 1920. He served as secretary for the regional party organization in Vy'borg in 1937 before advancing to second secretary of the Leningrad Oblast just before the Second World War. A client of Leningrad party boss Andrei Zhdanov, Shtykov served on several fronts around Leningrad during the Second World War before being transferred to the Far Eastern front in 1945. He rose to the rank of colonel-general. Highly decorated, Shtykov received three Orders of Lenin, three Orders of Kutuzov (first class) and the Order of Suvarov, yet he was essentially a political officer.

As a member of the Military Council and deputy commander of the Maritime Military District of the Soviet Union, Shtykov played a pivotal role in the construction of the DPRK. Along with commander of the Soviet First Far Eastern Front (Army Group) Marshal Kiril A. Meretskov, he led the delegation that accepted the Japanese surrender in northern Korea on 19 August 1945. Shtykov then supervised the selection of personnel for the Soviet Civil Administration in Korea, headed the Soviet delegation to the Joint Soviet-American Commission on Korea (20 March 1946 to 18 October 1948), and guided the drafting of the new DPRK Constitution, as well as the law on land reform and the Communist Party statutes in 1946.

As a negotiator, Shtykov was stubborn and followed the Stalinist line to the letter. His American counterparts noted Shtykov as a hot-tempered authoritarian, who was neither politically profound nor intellectual.

Shtykov's influence on Korean politics was nonetheless immense. Through his position on the Military Council and his links to Zhdanov, Shtykov became the most authoritative voice on Soviet policy in Korea until the war turned against the DPRK in late 1950. His support for Kim Il Sung over Pak Hŏn-yŏng may have been the decisive factor in Stalin's choice of the former to be premier of the new North Korean administration in February 1946. Shtykov supported Kim and his policies unflinchingly while serving as ambassador to P'yŏngyang. It is likely that it was Shtykov who first convinced Stalin to approve an attack on the ROK. It is almost certain that he used the wide latitude afforded him as ambassador to support the invasion plans in early 1950.

Shtykov was deprived of rank and reassigned to the Russian provinces in 1951. After several years as First Secretary of the Novgorod Oblast and Maritime Krai Party organization, he surfaced in 1959 as ambassador to Hungary. Recalled in 1960, he served as chairman of the State Control Commission for the Council of Ministers of the Russian Soviet Federal Republic in Moscow until his death there on 25 October 1964.

—*Timothy C. Dowling*

References:

Goncharov, Sergei N., John W. Lewis, and Xue Litai. *Uncertain Partners: Stalin, Mao, and the Korean War.* Stanford, CA: Stanford University Press, 1993.

Ree, Erik van. *Socialism in One Zone: Stalin's Policy in Korea, 1945–1947.* Oxford: Berg, 1989.

Simmons, Robert R. *The Strained Alliance: Peking, Pyongyang, Moscow, and the Politics of the Korean Civil War.* New York: Free Press, 1975.

See also: Korea, Democratic People's Republic of: 1945–1953; Korea: History, 1945–1947.

Sin Ik-hŭi
(1894–1956)

Speaker of the Republic of Korea (ROK, South Korea) National Assembly during the Korean War. Born at Kwangju, near Seoul, on 11 July 1894, Sin Ik-hŭi was an enthusiastic independence activist. In 1908 he went to study at Waseda University in Japan, and during this time he organized a Korean student union. Returning to Korea in 1913, he took up teaching and became deeply involved in the independence movement.

In 1918 Sin began working with overseas agitators for the independence movement in Manchuria, Beijing (Peking), and Shanghai, and he also played an important role domestically in the March First Movement by discussing with other nationalists the means by which independence might be achieved. In March 1919, because of his role in the March First Movement, Sin went into enforced exile in Shanghai for twenty-six years, until independence. During his period of exile he drafted much of the constitution for the Korean Provisional Government (KPG) and held various key posts in its government-in-exile, including minister of home affairs, minister of justice, and minister of foreign affairs.

At the conclusion of World War II, Sin returned to Korea in December 1945 as a key figure in the KPG, but his political ideas differed from those of Kim Ku. When Syngman Rhee argued in 1946 that South Korea should form a separate government from North Korea, most of the KPG groups objected. They refused to change their policy, insisting on a unified Korean government. Nonetheless, a separate ROK was established in 1948. Sin was the most prominent KPG political leader who accepted Rhee's policy and became active in the establishment of the ROK.

Sin's strong anti-Communist stance should have led him closer to Rhee. In fact, as soon as Sin returned to Korea, he had created the Chung'ang activist group, which operated under the KPG banner. This group made an attempt on Kim Il Sung's life, but it was soon dissolved as a result of dissension within the KPG. In 1946 Sin seceded from Kim Ku's KPG group by becoming vice-president of a right-wing organization that enthusiastically followed Rhee's leadership. Furthermore, Sin took the lead in forming the Taehan Anti-communism Association, and he made a speaking tour of the country to spread his anti-Communist message. At the same time Sin founded a college and also published a newspaper.

Anti-Communism, antitrusteeship, and independence from the U.S. military government were Sin's political guideposts during the first few years after independence. Shortly after the establishment of the ROK, Sin suggested that Rhee's first cabinet should include the KPG group that had opposed establishment of a separate ROK government, but Rhee rejected the idea. Because of this, Sin gradually distanced himself from Rhee. Finally, in 1947 Sin merged his group and another right-wing nationalist organization to form a new political party, and he became its leader. In February 1949 this party joined with the Korean Democratic Party to form the Democratic Nationalist Party in opposition to Rhee.

Chosen as speaker of the National Assembly following Rhee's inauguration as president in August 1949, Sin was in that post when the Korean War began and was still serving during the 1952 political crisis when Rhee pushed the National Assembly to revise the constitution for his second seizure of power. Sin not only kept the position of speaker for three terms, but he was able to increase his political power during that time.

In 1955 the Democratic Nationalist Party was expanded to form the Democratic Party, and Sin led this new opposition party. He ran against Rhee in the 1956 presidential election on the Democratic Party ticket, and a campaign speech delivered alongside the Han River brought him enormous popularity. However, Sin died suddenly of apoplexy on 5 May 1956, while traveling by train to campaign in the Honam region. His running mate for vice-president, John Myŏn Chang, was victorious in the election. Many in Korea still remember Sin as a capable political leader who resisted Rhee's dictatorship. Although Sin opposed Rhee politically, he still supported Rhee's anti-Communist and anti-Japanese platforms.

—*Insook Park*

References:

Kim, Hakjoon. *Haebang Kong'gan ŭi Chuyŏkdŭl* [The principal actors of the liberation period]. Seoul: Tonga Ilbo-sa, 1996.

Matray, James I., ed. *Historical Dictionary of the Korean War.* Westport, CT: Greenwood Press, 1991.

Park, Myung-Lim. *Han'guk Chŏnjaeng ŭi Palbal kwa Kiwŏn* [The outbreak and origins of the Korean War]. Vols. 1, 2. Seoul: Nanam, 1996.

See also: Syngman Rhee.

Sin Sŏng-mo
(1891–1960)

Defense minister and concurrently acting prime minister of the Republic of Korea (ROK, South Korea) at the outbreak of the Korean War. Born at Ŭiryŏng, South Kyongsang Province, on 26 May 1891, Sin Sŏng-mo graduated from Posong Law School in Seoul in 1910. That same year he fled to Vladivostok after the Japanese annexation of Korea and started his life in exile under the tutelage of Sin Ch'ae-ho, one of the best-known leaders of the Korean independence movement. Graduating from a maritime school in Shanghai in 1913, Sin served as an ensign at Chinese navy headquarters. In 1919 he joined the Korean Provisional Government, and in 1923 he was arrested in China by the Japanese police and returned to Korea and imprisoned. Upon his release in 1925, he went to Britain, where he graduated from the London School of Navigation and secured a master's license. Between 1930 and 1945 Sin worked as a captain for British and Indian commercial ship companies.

On his return to Korea in November 1948, Sin received a cordial welcome from President Syngman Rhee. The next month he was appointed minister of the interior. In March 1949 he left that post to become minister of defense, a post in which he served until May 1951. Between April and October 1950 Sin also served concurrently as the acting prime minister.

Immediately preceding the outbreak of the war, Sin, on several occasions, publicly warned about the possibility of a North Korean attack. On 10 May he held a press conference in which he stated that Korean People's Army (KPA, North Korean) troops were moving toward the 38th parallel and there was an imminent danger of invasion from the North. On 8 June he stated that the ROK government was considering issuing a national mobilization order, and he actually ordered ROK armed forces onto emergency alert. At the same time, in his public pronouncements Sin was confident. In the course of the 10 May press conference he said that following a KPA invasion, the ROK Army (ROKA) would counterattack across the 38th parallel. Such boasting was largely public posturing about the ability of the government to handle any possible crisis. Sin had previously said in the National Assembly that the ROKA would take breakfast at Kaesong, lunch in P'yŏngyang, and supper at Sinŭiji. The Democratic People's Republic of Korea (North Korean) government used Sin's boastful words after the war as evidence for their claim that the war began with an ROKA invasion of the North.

Sin did not have a good sense of reality when the war broke out. Without undertaking any military measures, he simply urged that Rhee remove the government from Seoul. Even the emergency cabinet meeting on June 27 was not initiated by him, but rather by former Prime Minister Yi Pŏm-sŏk. Rhee, Sin, and chief of staff of the ROK armed forces Ch'ae Pyŏng-dŏk lacked military knowledge and experience. Blame for the poor military situation in which the ROK found itself at the beginning of the war rests in large part with those three men. Sin was remarkable in carrying out what Rhee ordered, but not in counseling what the president needed. Largely because of this he had a long tenure in the cabinet.

Sin's departure from the cabinet was brought about by two incidents early in 1951. One was the scandal related to the ROK National Guard, when leaders misappropriated public funds for themselves, and as a result more than 1,000 enlisted guardsmen died of starvation and illness. The other was when ROKA troops, while searching for Communists, massacred innocent civilians at Kŏch'ang in South Kyŏngsang Province. As defense minister, Sin was blamed for both scandals. The Assembly then voted to remove

him from the cabinet. Subsequently, Rhee appointed Sin chief of the ROK mission to Japan with the equivalent rank of ambassador. Sin died on 29 May 1960.

—To-Woong Chung

References:

Noble, H. J. *Embassy at War*. Seattle: University of Washington Press, 1975.

Park, Myung Lim. *Han'guk Chŏnjaeng ŭi Palbal kwa Kiwŏn* [The outbreak and origins of the Korean War]. Vol. 2. Seoul: Nanam, 1996.

War History Compilation Committee, Ministry of National Defense. *Han'guk Chŏnjaeng-sa* [History of the Korean War]. Vol. 1. Seoul: Ministry of National Defense, 1967.

See also: Ch'ae Pyŏng-dŏk; Korea, Republic of: National Guard Scandal; Syngman Rhee; Yi Pŏm-sŏk (Lee Bum Suk).

Sin T'ae-yŏng
(1891–1959)

Republic of Korea Army (ROKA, South Korea) general and minister of defense for the ROK toward the end of the Korean War. Born in Seoul in 1891, Sin T'ae-yŏng was educated in the same city at the Royal Boy's Military School and Royal Military School in the late Chosŏn Dynasty (1392–1910). In 1914 he graduated from the Japanese Military Academy and began his military career for Japan, attaining the rank of lieutenant colonel at the time of the Japanese surrender in 1945.

Sin spent three years in self-imposed exile, rejecting an offer to supervise the formation of the ROKA. He resumed his military career with the rank of colonel in the fall of 1948 when antigovernment and leftist elements in the military in South Korea staged the Yŏsu-Sunch'ŏn Rebellion. Promoted in May 1949 to brigadier general and five months later to major general, he then became the chief of staff of the ROKA. In April 1950 he resigned from the post because of differences with the U.S. Korea Military Advisory Group (KMAG). It was said that he predicted the imminent North Korean invasion of the South and stressed the importance of ROK military preparedness. Two months later the Korean War began, and he was appointed commander of the defense of North Chŏlla Province but was removed in July 1950 because of conflicts with Defense Minister Sin Sŏng-mo. In January 1952 he was reinstated, and two months later he was promoted to lieutenant general. Soon Sin was appointed minister of defense, a post he retained until June 1952, when Son Wŏn-il replaced him. From 1954 to 1956 he was commander of the national militia.

Sin died in Seoul in 1959. His son, Ŭng-kyun, an ROKA lieutenant general and ambassador to the Federal Republic of Germany, died in 1996.

—Hakjoon Kim

Reference:
Republic of Korea, Ministry of Defense records.
See also: Korea, Republic of: History, 1947–1953; Korea, Republic of: History, 1953 to the Present; Yŏsu-Sunch'ŏn Rebellion.

Sino-Soviet Treaty of Friendship and Alliance (14 February 1950)

Despite its name, the negotiations leading up to the Sino-Soviet Treaty of Friendship and Alliance actually exacerbated the growing tensions between the two colossal Communist powers and consequently may have emboldened U.S. war hawks in responding to the outbreak of hostilities in Korea. Mao Zedong himself headed the Chinese delegation to Moscow in December 1949, where he also paid homage to Josef Stalin on the occasion of his seventieth birthday (21 December). Stalin expected obedience from the Chinese leader, while Mao sought respect and generosity from his senior Communist comrade. Both were disappointed. After two months of difficult negotiations over border disputes, economic assistance, and a military alliance, a treaty was finally signed on 14 February 1950.

While the relationship between the two leaders was no warmer than before, the treaty did provide some benefits for both sides. Its centerpiece was a thirty-year military alliance in which each signatory agreed to "render military and other assistance with all the means at its disposal" in the event of attack "by Japan or States allied with it" (an oblique reference to the United States). The use of Japan as the focal point meant that the USSR would not be obligated to provide assistance if the United States attacked China with another ally (such as Taiwan or South Korea). The USSR also agreed to give up the strategic naval base of Port Arthur, but Soviet military forces would remain there until the end of 1952 as a deterrent to possible Japanese or American imperialistic plans. Finally, the Soviet air force was to provide temporary assistance against air raids on coastal targets by the Nationalist forces in Taiwan. Reportedly, an offer by Stalin to provide military advisors (spies) was politely declined. The tepid nature of the Soviet military commitment to China may have led U.S. policymakers to assume incorrectly that China would hesitate to intervene militarily in Korea without a stronger guarantee of Soviet support.

The territorial and economic sections of the treaty were mostly decided in favor of China, but Stalin extracted numerous significant concessions. Most of the disputed territory occupied by Soviet forces during the war was returned to China, including Port Dalny, Port Arthur, the Manchurian railroads, and parts of Sinjiang. In this last area, however, the Soviets were given the right to exploit the raw materials. Mao's biggest capitulation to Soviet wishes was in agreeing that Outer Mongolia, claimed by China, would retain its nominal independence and its very real subservience to Moscow. In terms of economic assistance, Mao asked for and received a relatively paltry $300 million loan, paid out over five years, with a one percent annual interest rate. The ten-year repayment plan for the loan stipulated that payments would come in the form of "raw materials, tea, gold, [and] American dollars." The fact that more substantial economic aid was not offered by the more industrialized Soviet state to its almost entirely agrarian Communist neighbor is an unmistakable indication that Stalin did not relish the idea of an industrialized China on his border. And yet, if China was to follow the USSR's lead in "building communism," it would mean first and foremost constructing a strong industrial base. This economic abandonment of a Communist brother was typical, insofar as Stalin invariably placed Soviet national interests ahead of ideological considerations. His treatment of other allies (or satellites) was usually far more exploitative.

Stalin's arrogant and miserly treatment of Mao in the negotiations leading up to the Sino-Soviet Treaty of Friendship and Alliance had unintended consequences. Mao and the other leaders of the Chinese Communist Party (CCP) had to realize that they could expect only parsimonious assistance from the USSR and that their foreign policy objectives would not always coincide. Stalin tried to isolate China and make it more dependent on the USSR, but instead he pushed the CCP toward greater and greater independence. When word reached Washington of the growing divisions within the Communist world, U.S. policymakers apparently accepted the false assumption that cracks in Communist solidarity would make both China and the Soviet Union less likely to intervene in Korea. This miscalculation certainly contributed to the catastrophic decision to send General Douglas MacArthur's forces across the 38th parallel, which triggered Chinese intervention.

—*Edward Sharp*

References:
Beloff, Max. *Soviet Policy in the Far East, 1944–1951.* London: Oxford University Press, 1953.
Simmons, Robert R. *The Strained Alliance: Peking, Pyongyang, Moscow, and the Politics of the Korean Civil War.* New York: Free Press, 1975.
Stueck, William W., Jr. *The Korean War: An International History.* Princeton, NJ: Princeton University Press, 1995.
See also: China, People's Republic of; Japan; Korea, Democratic People's Republic of, Invasion of the Republic of Korea; Mao Zedong; Soviet Security Council Boycott; Stalin, Josef; Union of Soviet Socialist Republics; Vyshinskii, Andrei Ianuarovich; Zhou Enlai.

SMACK, Operation
(25 January 1953)

Bungled military offensive by the U.S. 7th Infantry Division. Designed as a showpiece of air-tank-artillery coordination, its purpose was partly to impress the recently sworn-in president, Dwight D. Eisenhower, with the military's resolve and capacity to win. Operation SMACK's failure had decidedly unfavorable repercussions for the United Nations Command (UNC) and in particular for Lieutenant General Mark W. Clark, its bellicose commander in chief, who was eager to fight until a complete victory was won and Korea's reunification accomplished.

Operation SMACK's objective was to capture the Communist-held redoubt of Spud Hill in the west-central portion of the UNC lines. The UNC also hoped to take Communist prisoners who might provide useful intelligence information. Numerous high-ranking U.S. Army and Air Force officers and a dozen press representatives were invited to observe the offensive. So stage-managed was the occasion that the division had produced a six-page, three-color brochure for their guests' information and convenience; the title page set out the day's "scenario."

Such blatant hubris received what might be considered its just reward. Despite careful advance preparations, including a week's prior air and artillery bombardment, SMACK quickly went astray. Far East Air Force and Marine Corps aircraft mostly missed their preselected targets, flamethrowers and automatic weapons jammed or misfired, smoke screens were incorrectly located, and the initial infantry troop assault was blocked and the men caught in a defile. All three infantry platoon leaders were wounded, and within a few hours U.S. troops were withdrawn from Spud Hill.

Seventy-seven United States casualties, several hundred thousand pounds of bombs, tens of thousands of rounds of heavy- and light-caliber ammunition, 2,000 tank rounds, and 650 grenades brought a return of sixty-five Communist casualties and none of the anticipated prisoners. Moreover, Communist forces had been far less enthusiastic in their use of artillery and had employed no air power whatever. Even making all allowances for the traditional U.S. strategy of making lavish use of technology to minimize casualties, the balance sheet was disproportionately unfavorable to the Americans, who had failed to gain their objective.

Operation SMACK mushroomed into a well-publicized embarrassment when an enterprising newspaper correspondent, recently arrived in Korea and present neither at the detailed prebriefing nor the actual event, wrote a piece in which he charged that American soldiers had died needlessly in a poorly planned "demonstration" show mounted as a publicity event for the military's top brass. His story featured prominently the use of the ill-chosen word "scenario," the egregious brochure, and the presence of high-ranking spectators. Friendly reporters hastened to defend the military, and Eighth Army commander Lieutenant General James Van Fleet issued a public statement, but the damage was done.

U.S. Army Chief of Staff General J. Lawton Collins was obliged to testify before the congressional armed services committees, where he characterized the operation as a test of coordinated assault methods rather than a needless publicity exhibition. Congress accepted his explanation, and the incident was considered closed. Even so, the failure to achieve such a small, limited, and long-prepared objective cast serious doubt on the military's competence and severely weakened Clark's credibility in dissenting from Eisenhower's policy of seeking a negotiated peace.

—*Priscilla Roberts*

References:
Clark, Mark W. *From the Danube to the Yalu.* New York: Harper & Row, 1954.
Fehrenbach, T. R. *This Kind of War: A Study in Unpreparedness.* New York: Macmillan, 1962.
Hermes, Walter G. *United States Army in the Korean War: Truce Tent and Fighting Front.* Washington, DC: Office of the Chief of Military History, 1966.
See also: Clark, Mark W.; Collins, Joseph Lawton; Eisenhower, Dwight D.; Van Fleet, James Alward.

Small Arms (Pistols, Rifles, Submachine Guns, Automatic Weapons)

Personal infantry weapons. The typical combatant during the Korean War, regardless of nationality, entered action armed with World War II or earlier weaponry. It fell to the nations with the largest stocks of existing small arms—the United States and the Soviet Union—to act as the primary sources of arms to the opposing forces.

The United States provided Republic of Korea (South Korean) forces with U.S.-made weapons and supplemented the small arms issues of its United Nations (UN) allies. Rifles and carbines were the standard infantry arms, while officers and specialized personnel generally carried pistols. Light automatic weapons also reinforced the firepower of ground forces.

The U.S. .30-caliber M1 (Garand) rifle was the standard rifle for U.S. forces as well as many of their UN allies. The gas-operated, semiautomatic Garand is chambered for the .30-06 cartridge and is fed by eight-round stripper clips. Two telescopically equipped sniper versions, the M1C and the M1D, were also issued.

The U.S. .30-caliber M1 carbine was intended as a lightweight, semiautomatic weapon for company-grade officers and special troops. The M1 carbine weighs 5.5 pounds and measures a compact 35.6 inches in length. Later modifications include the M1A1, a folding-stock version intended for paratroops, and the selective-fire M2.

The U.S. .45-caliber Model 1911A1 pistol was the standard sidearm of U.S. forces in Korea. Adopted in 1911, the Model 1911 is a recoil-operated semiautomatic pistol that is fed by a seven-round magazine. The U.S. government also purchased commercially available sidearms, including the Colt .32- and .380-caliber automatic pistols, the Colt Detective Special Revolver, Colt Police Positive Revolver, Colt Special Official Police Revolver, and the Smith & Wesson Military and Police Revolver. All are chambered for the .38-caliber Special cartridge.

The .45-caliber Thompson Model 1928A1 submachine gun as issued to troops in Korea is an open-bolt, blowback, selective-fire weapon. Chambering the same cartridge as the Colt Model 1911, the Thompson accepts a twenty-round, detachable box magazine. Although reliable, Thompsons weigh a heavy 10.45 pounds and were expensive to manufacture. During World War II these shortcomings led the government to explore alternative submachine gun designs that saw service in Korea. These included the Harrington & Richardson .45-caliber Reising Models 50 and 55 submachine guns and the .45-caliber M3 and M3A1 submachine guns. In contrast to the Thompson's wooden stocks and milled steel construction, the M3 and M3A1 were equipped with retractable wire stocks and were manufactured using simplified stamped steel techniques. Although relatively reliable, their rather crude appearance earned them the nickname of "grease gun."

The M1918A2 Browning Automatic Rifle (BAR) provided squad-level automatic firepower for U.S. troops in World War I, World War II, and the Korean War. The gas-operated BAR fires the standard .30-06 U.S. rifle cartridge and is fed by a twenty-round detachable magazine. It is a full-automatic–only weapon with two settings: slow, with a cyclic rate of 300 to 450 rounds per minute (rpm); and fast, with a rate of 500 to 650 rpm.

Other UN contingents, notably Belgium, France, and the United Kingdom, issued their own small arms. Fabrique Nationale d'Armes de Guerre (FN) of Herstal lez Liège, Belgium, had long manufactured American John Browning's designs, including the BAR. The Belgian army adopted the FN Self-Loading Rifle M1949 in U.S. caliber 30-06. It is a gas-operated semiautomatic weapon with a ten-round magazine capacity.

Another Browning design, the highly successful 9-mm FN Browning High Power Pistol, served as the standard military sidearm of Belgium as well as Denmark, the Netherlands, The Republic of China (Nationalist China), the United Kingdom, and Canada. In appearance and mechanism, the High Power resembles Browning's earlier design, the Colt Model 1911A1. Significant changes include the caliber—9-mm—and the thirteen-round magazine capacity.

Belgian troops also utilized the Vigneron M2 Submachine Gun. It chambers the 9-mm parabellum cartridge, fed by a thirty-two–round magazine. The Vigneron is a selective-fire weapon, similar in operation to the British Sten, and is primarily constructed of steel stampings.

As produced by FN, the Belgian BAR, although chambered for the standard U.S. .30-06 caliber, boasts a number of improvements over its American cousin. The Belgian BAR Type D features a quick-change barrel and an adjustable cyclic rate. It is also fitted with a pistol grip and carrying handle, and it accepts either a tripod or a bipod with a butt rest.

France issued domestic, U.S., British, and captured World War II German small arms. Many French soldiers carried the 7.5-mm MAS1936 rifle—a conventional bolt-action, pre–World War II design. Later models include the MAS1936 M51 (equipped with an integral grenade launcher) and the folding-stock 1936 CR39 rifle. The standard French service rifle—the semiautomatic 7.5-mm M1949 (MAS)—is simple to operate and maintain and is fed by a ten-round detachable magazine. Although it does not accept a bayonet, it is equipped with an integral grenade launcher and sights.

There was also little standardization in French sidearm issues. Post–World War II armorers faced a logistical nightmare of captured German 9-mm P08 Lugers and P-38s, U.S. .45-caliber 1911s and 1911A1s, prewar French 7.65-mm M1935s, and the new French 9-mm M1950. The M1950 is a nine-round hybrid of the M1935 series and Colt 1911 series designs chambered for the 9-mm cartridge. It resembles its forebears in both appearance and function.

The French 9-mm submachine gun M1949 (MAT49) is predominantly of stamped steel construction and is an excellent weapon in all respects. It is blowback-operated, capable of automatic fire only, and accepts a thirty-two–round box magazine. The M1949 is equipped with a grip safety and was very popular among French troops for its compactness afforded by a retracting wire stock and folding magazine.

The standard French squad automatic weapon was the 7.5-mm Model 1924 M29 light machine gun. It is a gas-operated selective-fire weapon very similar in function to the BAR. The M29 differs from the BAR in that it is fed by a top-mounted box magazine and is equipped with a front trigger for semi-automatic fire and a rear trigger for its fully automatic mode.

Great Britain and Canada issued the battle-proven yet relatively obsolescent .303-caliber Enfield Rifle No. 4 Mark 1 (SMLE). Australia continued to use the earlier SMLE No. 1 Mark 3*. The Enfield is a robust bolt-action weapon fed by a detachable ten-round magazine. A sniper version, the Rifle No. 4 Mark I (T), was issued equipped with the No. 32 telescope.

The .38-caliber Enfield "Pistol" No. 2 Mark I was the standard sidearm of British Commonwealth troops. The Enfield is a six-chambered, top-break, double-action revolver. Its cousin, the No. 2 Mark I*, was introduced during World War II and is a double-action–only weapon. Commonwealth troops also carried the Canadian Inglis-manufactured 9-mm Browning High Power as well as numbers of U.S. Colt 1911s, 1911A1s, and obsolescent British .455-caliber Webley revolvers.

The 9-mm selective-fire Sten Mark V submachine gun saw extensive use in Korea. Australia also issued two native-designed submachine guns—the 9-mm Austen Mark I and Mark II and the 9-mm Owen Mark I. These weapons are somewhat similar to the Sten. The Bren Light Machine Gun is a gas-operated, selective-fire squad weapon fitted with a top-mounted thirty-round magazine. The Bren, in Marks 1 through 4, was manufactured in the standard British .303 rifle caliber in England, Canada, and Australia.

Communist China initially armed its own as well as North Korean infantry with captured World War II Japanese, Chinese, and U.S. weapons abandoned by the Nationalists after China's civil war. As the war progressed, the Soviet Union replaced weapons lost to attrition with Soviet and captured World War II German armaments. The Chinese, in turn, eventually retooled their arsenals to copy the Soviet models.

A pre–World War I Russo-Belgian design, the bolt-action, 7.62-mm Mosin-Nagant series, was the most widely used Communist rifle. The Model 1891 rifle, the Model 1891/30 rifle, and the Model 1944 carbine are all fed by five-round magazines and share identical bolt actions. A sniper model of the M1891/30, equipped with either the PU or more powerful PE telescope, was also issued.

The most common sidearms in Communist service were the Mauser Models 1896 and 1912 "Broomhandles," and the Tokarev Models 1895 and 1933. The Tokarev Model 1933 is a modified Browning design. Communist China also manufactured the Model 1933, designating it as Type 51. The Model 1933 is a recoil-operated semiautomatic pistol that is fed by an eight-round magazine. The Soviets also furnished numbers of their obsolescent 7.62-mm Model 1895 double-action revolvers. The Mauser Model 1912 "Broomhandle" semiautomatic pistol was a particular favorite among Chinese troops. It is chambered for either the 7.63-mm Mauser cartridge or the 9-mm parabellum cartridge. China also produced a number of copies in U.S. caliber .45. The Mauser accepts a wooden shoulder stock/holster and is fed by a ten-round integral magazine.

The Soviet Union also supplied China and North Korea with thousands of submachine guns. The various models are essentially similar in appearance and operation. The most common models were the PPD Model 1934/38, PPD Model 1940, PPSH Model 1941, and the PPS Model 1943. All are chambered for the 7.62-mm pistol cartridge. Later marks differed from earlier models in their more simplified construction and feed systems. All models except the fully automatic only PPS M1943 are selective-fire weapons.

The most common Communist-produced squad-level automatic weapons were the 7.62-mm DP and DPM. They are conventional gas-operated, air-cooled light machine guns. Both weapons are fed by forty-seven–round drum magazines.

—*Jeff Kinard*

References:

Hobart, F. W. A. *Pictorial History of the Machine Gun.* London: Allan, 1971.

Hogg, Ian, and John Weeks. *Military Small Arms of the Twentieth Century.* Chicago: Follett, 1973.

Smith, W. H. B. *Small Arms of the World,* 9th ed. Harrisburg, PA: Stackpole, 1969.

See also: Machine Guns.

Smith, Oliver Prince
(1893–1977)

U.S. Marine Corps general and commander of the 1st Marine Division during the Korean War. Born in Menard, Texas, on 26 October 1893, Oliver Prince Smith worked his way through the University of California, Berkeley, where he was a member of the Reserve Officers Training Corps and graduated in 1916. Smith was a Christian Scientist all his life and remained a deeply religious person who neither drank nor swore. After graduating from the University of California, he worked for Standard Oil Company. When the United States entered the World War I, Smith applied for a Marine Corps reserve commission, which was granted in May 1917. He was then sent to Guam, where he received a regular commission.

In 1919 Smith was assigned to Mare Island Marine Barracks, San Francisco. He commanded the Marine detachment on board the battleship *Texas* from 1921 to 1924. Between 1924 and 1928 he was in the personnel section of Marine Corps headquarters in Washington. After spending three years in Haiti working with the gendarmerie, Smith attended the Army Infantry school in Fort Benning, Georgia, graduating in 1932; he was then an instructor in the Marine Corps Schools at Quantico, Virginia. He served on the staff of the naval attaché at the Paris embassy from 1934 to 1936 and then returned to Quantico, where he was again an instructor between 1936 and 1939. After a year with the Fleet Marine Force, Pacific, in 1940 he commanded a battalion of the 6th Marine Regiment, and from May 1941 until March 1942 he was with that battalion in Iceland. After two years with headquarters staff, in January 1944 he received command of the 5th Marine Regiment of the 1st Marine Division and led it through the New Britain campaign. Promoted to brigadier general, in April he became assistant commander of the 1st Division. He saw action on Peleliu in September and October, and in November he was made deputy chief of staff to General Simon B. Buckner's Tenth Army. After combat on Okinawa during April and June 1945, Smith was named commandant of the Marine Corps Schools at Quantico.

In April 1948 Smith became assistant commandant and chief of staff of the Marine Corps under General Clifton B. Cates. Promoted to major general, in June 1950 Smith took command of the 1st Marine Division at Camp Pendleton, California. He had only twenty days to prepare the division for Korea; and on 15 September 1950, Smith led the division—which made up about half of Major General Edward M. Almond's X Corps—in the Inch'ŏn landing. Smith and Almond did not get along, primarily because Almond insisted on depreciating him and failed to understand the requirements of the Marines.

Smith was present in Seoul for the ceremony staged by United Nations Command commander General Douglas MacArthur turning the city back to the South Koreans. The 1st Marine Division then relocated to Inch'ŏn and was shifted by sea to the port of Wŏnsan on the east coast of Korea. At the end of October the division began an advance to the Yalu River.

Smith had serious misgivings about General Douglas MacArthur's troop dispositions for the final push to the Yalu, enough so that he communicated to Marine Commandant General Clifton B. Cates in Washington his doubts about the wisdom of a campaign in the bitter cold of a Korean winter with his division scattered along one road from Hŭngnam to the Yalu. Smith also expressed concern about the gap between his division and the Eighth Army on his left. For a Marine general in the field to counsel caution in carrying out the orders of a commander took some courage. But Smith slowed the Marine advance to about a mile a day, took care not to string out his units any more than was absolutely necessary, and hurried the establishment of a base at Hagaru-ri. In all probability this saved his division from annihilation in the next few weeks.

When the Chinese People's Volunteer Army (CPVA,Communist Chinese) resumed its offensive at the end of November, Smith's division was trapped with its main elements seventy-eight miles north of the port of Hŭngnam at the Changjin (Chosin) Reservoir. On the night of 27–28 November, the Chinese attacked the Marines in zero-degree weather. Ultimately, the Chinese fed twelve divisions (three armies) into the battle. The Marines then began an epic thirteen-day retreat, in which they brought out their wounded and their equipment with them. The first stage was from Yudam-ni to the base at Hagaru-ri, which they reached on 3 December in one of the most masterful withdrawal operations in the history of war, fought against heavy odds. When General Smith met U.S. correspondents at Hagaru-ri, they questioned him about the retreat and he replied, "Gentlemen, we are not retreating. We are just attacking in another direction."

The next stage of the withdrawal, to Kot'o-ri, began on 6 December. It took thirty-eight hours to cover eleven miles through snow under incessant Chinese attack. Smith again regrouped his forces for a retreat ten more miles to Chinhŭng-ni. On 8 December the first troops in the force began to fight their way toward the sea and safety. By 11 December what remained of the command reached the Hamhŭng-Hŭngnam area. Marines remembered the withdrawal with pride; Chinese survivors recalled the devastating effects of air strikes and artillery.

After the evacuation from Hŭngnam at the end of December, the divided command was ended, and Smith's 1st Marine Division was incorporated into the Eighth Army as part of IX Corps. During the February 1951 counteroffensive when army Major General Bryant E. Moore suddenly died, Eighth Army commander Lieutenant General Matthew B. Ridgway named Smith to command IX Corps, one of the rare instances in which a Marine general has commanded army troops at the division or corps level. He continued in that capacity until March.

In April 1951 Smith returned to the United States as commander of Camp Pendleton, California. Promoted to lieutenant general in 1953, he commanded the Fleet Marine Force, Atlantic, from July 1953 until September 1955. Smith retired on 1 September 1955, when he was promoted to general. Smith died in Los Altos, California, on 25 December 1977.

—*Spencer C. Tucker*

References:

Blair, Clay. *The Forgotten War: America in Korea, 1950–1953.* New York: Times Books, 1987.

Dictionary of American Military Biography, edited by Roger J. Spiller. Vol. 3. Westport, CT: Greenwood Press, 1984.

Heinl, Robert D. *Victory at High Tide: The Inchon-Seoul Campaign.* Philadelphia: J. B. Lippincott, 1968.

Montross, Lynn, et al. *U.S. Marine Operations in Korea, 1950–1953.* 5 vols. Washington, DC: U.S. Marine Corps Historical Branch, 1954–1972.

New York Times, 26 December 1977.

See also: Almond, Edward Mallory; Cates, Clifton B.; Changjin (Chosin) Reservoir Campaign; Hŭngnam Evacuation; Inch'ŏn Landings: Operation CHROMITE; MacArthur, Douglas; Ridgway, Matthew Bunker; Wŏnsan Landing.

Smith, Walter Bedell
(1895–1961)

Director of the Central Intelligence Agency, September 1950 to February 1953, then undersecretary of state until 1954. Born in Indianapolis, Indiana, on 5 October 1895, Walter Bedell Smith briefly attended Butler University. Early on, he decided to pursue a military career, and in 1910 he enlisted as a private in the Indiana National Guard. After the United States entered World War I, he was called up for active duty. He attended officer training school, and in 1918, as a second lieutenant in the 39th Infantry, he saw active service in France at Chateau-Thierry and the Second Battle of the Marne.

In the years following the war, Smith—who had risen to the rank of major by the end of the 1930s—acquired the organizational, administrative, and planning skills essential to managing modern warfare. He served with the Bureau of Military Intelligence, the Bureau of the Budget, and the Federal Liquidation Board, and he had several assignments either studying or instructing at the Infantry School at Fort Benning, Georgia, the Command and General Staff School at Fort Leavenworth, Kansas, and the Army War College. General George C. Marshall, Chief of Staff of the U.S. Army from 1939, noted Smith's abilities, and that October summoned him to Washington to assist in the rapid buildup of the U.S. military.

Smith served successively as assistant secretary and secretary to the General Staff, and in 1942 he became secretary to both the newly created Joint Chiefs of Staff (JCS) and the Anglo-American Combined Chiefs of Staff. In September 1942 Smith was assigned as chief of staff to General Dwight D. Eisenhower, a position he held until the end of 1945. Smith won a stellar reputation as one of the finest chiefs of staff in any army. He also assisted Eisenhower in his complicated wartime dealings with the French and diplomatic negotiations leading up to the surrender of Italy.

Smith returned to Washington in January 1946 as chief of the Operations and Planning Division of the JCS, but two months later President Harry S. Truman appointed him ambassador to the Soviet Union, where he remained until 1949. Smith's experiences in this post, as the Cold War steadily and rapidly intensified, convinced him that the United States must take a firm line to contain Soviet expansion, but he also believed that the Soviets did not deliberately seek war and would back down when confronted by U.S. strength.

Smith frequently offered suggestions, all ultimately fruitless, as to possible means of breaking the Soviet-American deadlock over the future of Korea.

In September 1950 Truman named Lieutenant General Smith, then commanding the First Army, as director of the Central Intelligence Agency (CIA); Smith was promoted to general in July 1951. The president hoped he would improve leadership and organization within the agency, then attracting heavy criticism for its failure to predict the North Korean invasion of South Korea. Smith's reputation as both an outstanding bureaucrat and a staunch anti-Communist helped to deflect further criticism from the CIA, which he centralized and coordinated, persuading General Douglas MacArthur not only to allow the agency to operate in Korea but to also utilize its intelligence. Under Smith the CIA nonetheless wrongly predicted that China would not intervene in the Korean conflict, and it also failed to anticipate assorted coups in Latin America.

Smith tightened the flow of intelligence, restricting the overall picture to a few high-ranking officers, and instituted a training program to develop a group of career intelligence officers. On occasion, notably during the 1952 presidential campaign, his uncompromising anti-communism led him to allege that Communist agents had long since infiltrated both the State Department and the CIA, suggestions that provided ammunition for McCarthyite attacks on the Truman administration.

Smith took a hawkish line toward the Korean War, viewing the Democratic People's Republic of Korea (North Korea) and the People's Republic of China (PRC, Communist China) as mere Soviet pawns who were being used to implement a global Soviet strategy. He believed that the Soviets, though unwilling to go to war directly with Western countries in Europe, were prepared to sanction a Sino-American war in Asia, with the objective of weakening America's commitment to Europe and impeding European rearmament. He therefore strongly supported the enhancement of U.S. budgetary and personnel commitments to the North Atlantic Treaty Organization. A hard-liner, Smith advocated that the United States should put as much pressure on the PRC as was necessary to bring about a satisfactory settlement of the conflict. He was even ready to sanction the use of Guomindang Republic of China troops in the war. On the whole, the Truman administration and its United Nations allies followed a course somewhat milder than that recommended by Smith.

As one of the few Truman appointees to survive the transition to the Eisenhower administration, Smith provided a degree of continuity. As undersecretary of state in the Eisenhower administration, he helped new Secretary of State John Foster Dulles to devise policy toward Korea. Smith was particularly active in formulating a complicated compromise proposal designed to resolve the vexing question of repatriation of prisoners of war, one of the major sticking points in the peace negotiations, which cleared the way to the eventual 1953 P'anmunjŏm armistice agreement. Smith's last major assignment in the State Department, before he retired in 1954, was to represent the United States at the Geneva Conference that year, a meeting whose decidedly overoptimistic objectives included facilitating Korea's potential reunification and resolving the growing difficulties in Indo-China.

After his retirement, an embittered Smith, who never received either the fifth star or the promotion to chief of staff of the army he believed his services merited, turned to business, amassing a considerable estate. Smith took advantage of his Pentagon, CIA, and State Department connections when he actively sought assorted high positions with various corporations, including United Fruit, AMF Atomics Incorporated, the Associated Missile Products Company, the American Machine and Foundry Company, RCA, and the Corning Glass Company, at least some of which—notably United Fruit—had benefited by actions Smith took as undersecretary of state. In 1958 Dulles appointed Smith, a staunch and vocal supporter of nuclear expansion, his special advisor on disarmament. Smith died on 9 August 1961 in Washington, D.C.

—Priscilla Roberts

References:

Ambrose, Stephen E. *Ike's Spies: Eisenhower and the Espionage Establishment.* Garden City, NY: Doubleday, 1981.

Brands, H. W., Jr. *Cold Warriors: Eisenhower's Generation and American Foreign Policy.* New York: Columbia University Press, 1988.

Breuer, William B. *Shadow Warriors: The Covert War in Korea.* New York: Wiley, 1996.

Crosswell, D. K. R. *The Chief of Staff: The Military Career of General Walter Bedell Smith.* New York: Greenwood Press, 1991.

Dictionary of American Biography, Supplement Seven, 1961–1965, edited by John A. Garraty. New York: Charles Scribner's Sons, 1981.

Mayers, David. *The Ambassadors and America's Soviet Policy.* New York: Oxford University Press, 1995.

Montague, Ludwell Lee. *General Walter Bedell Smith As Director of Central Intelligence, October 1950–February 1953.* University Park: Pennsylvania State University Press, 1992.

Ranelagh, John. *The Agency: The Rise and Decline of the CIA.* New York: Simon & Schuster, 1986.

Smith, Walter Bedell. *My Three Years in Moscow.* Philadelphia: J. B. Lippincott, 1949.

Snyder, William P. "Walter Bedell Smith: Eisenhower's Chief of Staff." *Military Affairs* 48, no. 1 (January 1984): 6–14.

See also: Central Intelligence Agency (CIA); Eisenhower, Dwight D.; Joint Chiefs of Staff (JCS); MacArthur, Douglas; Truman, Harry S.

Son Wŏn-il
(1909–1980)

Republic of Korea (ROK, South Korean) Navy admiral and chief of staff at the outbreak of the Korean War in 1950, later defense minister. Born in Kangsŏ, South P'yŏngan Province, Korea, on 5 May 1909, Son Wŏn-il went to China and Germany during the period of the Japanese colonial administration to study navigation. He secured a master's license in Germany in 1933 and then gained maritime experience at sea in European waters. Immediately after the end of Japanese rule in 1945 and anticipating imminent Korean independence, he moved to organize the nucleus of a future navy. Son was a dominant figure in naval circles during the period from 1945 to 1950.

In November 1945 officials in the U.S. military government in Korea suggested to Son that he help establish a coast guard to maintain coastal security and stop smuggling. Believing that this would evolve into a navy, Son agreed, and the next year he became the commandant of the Coast Guard. In August 1948, with the establishment of the ROK, the Coast Guard was indeed transformed into a regular navy. Son became its chief of staff with the rank of commodore. When the Korean War began in June 1950, Son was in the middle of the Pacific Ocean overseeing the passage to Korea of three patrol ships secured from the United States. He did not return to Korea until 14 July.

In June 1950 the ROK Navy (ROKN) consisted of 6,900 men and seventy-one ships, largely ex-U.S. and ex-Japanese minesweepers and picket boats. It had bases at seven major ports—Inch'ŏn, Kunsan, Mokp'o, Yŏsu, Pusan, P'ohang, and Mukho—and its service installations were at Chinhae. The surprise naval invasion by the Democratic People's Republic of Korea (DPRK, North Korea) of 25 June consisted of a number of small landings along the east coast of South Korea. Although no ROKN ships were immediately available in the area to oppose these landings, units did quickly put to sea from the south. In the first critical hours of the invasion the ROKN fought well, sinking a North Korean armed steamer northeast of Pusan with 600 men. Soon U.S. Navy units began to arrive, and any DPRK naval threat was largely removed.

In September 1950 Son participated in the Inch'ŏn landing as commander of ROK units, including the ROK Marine Corps of 2,800 men and the 17th Infantry Regiment. Son personally led Marines in street fighting in Inch'ŏn, Pup'yŏng, Kimp'o, and Seoul, and he pushed them to be first to take over the Capitol Building in Seoul early in the morning of 27 September.

In June 1953 Son retired from the navy to become defense minister, a post he retained until 1956. The next year he became the first ROK ambassador to the

Federal Republic of Germany. He died in Seoul on 15 February 1980.

—*To-Woong Chung*

References:

Han'guk Ilbo, 30 September–21 December 1976.

Hong, Ŭn-hye, ed. *Uridŭl ŭn Ibada Wihae* [We are for this sea: memoirs]. Seoul: Kain k'hoek, 1990.

Republic of Korea, War History Compilation Committee. *Han'guk Chŏnjaeng-sa* [History of the Korean War]. Vol. 1. Seoul: Ministry of National Defense, 1967.

See also: Inch'ŏn Landings: Operation CHROMITE; Korea, Republic of: Navy (ROKN).

Song Shilun
(1907–1991)

Deputy commander of the Chinese People's Volunteer Army (CPVA, Chinese Communist) and commander of the Ninth Army Group during the Korean War. Born in Liling, Hunan Province, on 10 September 1907, Song started his long military career when he entered the well-known Whampoa Military School in 1926. He was chief of staff of the Red Army's Thirty-fifth Army in 1930, and later commander of the Red Army Thirtieth and Twenty-eighth Armies. In 1938 Song was promoted commander of the Fourth Army in the Eighth Route Army. He and General Deng Hua (later the deputy commander of the CPVA) directed numerous operations in Eastern Hebei Province during the War of Resistance against the Japanese. When the Civil War began, he was the Chinese Communist Party's director of military liaison affairs stationed in Beijing. He became commander of the Tenth Army, East China Field Army, in 1946. He was promoted to commander of the Ninth Army Group in 1948, directing the cross–Yangtze River campaign and the Shanghai campaign in 1949.

When the Korean War began, Song led three armies of the People's Liberation Army (PLA, Chinese Communist) Ninth Army Group to enter the war in late 1950. During the second Chinese offensive, he commanded the Eastern Front. His army group later participated in the fifth offensive campaign and the Sanggamnyŏng campaign. He returned from Korea in 1952 and was appointed director of the PLA Advanced Infantry School in Shijiazhuang. He was promoted to general in 1955. In 1957 Song was named vice-president of the PLA Academy of Military Sciences, and in 1972 he became its president. He died in Shanghai on 17 September 1991.

—*Richard Weixing Hu*

References:

Guo Huaruo et al. *Jiefangjun Junshi Dacidian* [Dictionary of CPLA military history]. Changchun: Jilin People's Press, 1993.

Wu Rugao et al. *Zhongguo Junshi Renwu Dacidian* [Dictionary of Chinese military figures]. Beijing: Xinhua Chubanshe, 1989.

Zhongguo Junshi Dabaike Quanshu [The Chinese military encyclopedia]. Military History, Vol. 3. Beijing: Military Science Press, 1997.

Zhongguo Renmin Jiefangjun Jiangshui Minlu [Brief biographies of CPLA marshals and generals]. Vols. 1–3. Beijing: PLA Press, 1986, 1987.

See also: China, People's Republic of Army; Chinese Military Offensives.

South Africa, Union of

The South African government announced on 4 August 1950 that a fighter squadron had been offered for service with United Nations Command (UNC) forces in Korea. This offer was accepted two weeks later. The South African Air Force (SAAF) designated 2d Squadron as the unit. In response to a request for approximately 200 officers and men, some 332 officers and 1,094 other ranks volunteered. Of this group, 50 officers and 157 men were selected to serve in the squadron, the origins of which lay in 1940 in East Africa, the Middle East, and Italy as the "Flying Cheetahs." The 2d Squadron's first commander in Korea was Commandant S. van Breda Theron.

After a long sea voyage to the Far East, the 2d Squadron disembarked in Japan on 4 November 1950. There it began familiarization with U.S. Air Force (USAF) procedures, as it would fly in conjunction with U.S. forces. It also received its first aircraft, veteran USAF North American F-51 Mustang fighter-bombers. These aircraft were subsequently painted with SAAF markings: dark blue rounders with white centers emblazoned with a red, leaping springbok; tricolor vertical tail-fin flashes; and, on occasion, red propeller spinners. The unit's first flights staged to Airfield K-9 (Pusan East) on 16 November 1950, but immediately it began preparations for moving forward to a front-line base at K-24 (P'yŏngyang East), where it was in place by 22 November.

During the period January to November 1951, the 2d Squadron (attached to the USAF's 18th Fighter-Bomber Wing) flew some of its most intense and frequent missions of the entire war. Missions primarily included close air support of ground forces and interdiction of Communist supply lines. Fifty-nine percent of all aircraft lost by the squadron to enemy action or accidents were destroyed between January and November 1951.

By October 1951 the nature of the ground war had changed essentially to maintaining the front lines while truce talks progressed. Aerial attacks consequently became a principal means by which the UNC exerted pressure on Communist forces. South African pilots flew numerous close support and rail interdiction missions during this period, with special emphasis on flak suppression for bomber sorties.

At the end of 1952, the 2d Squadron converted from the venerable but war-weary Mustangs to Republic F-86F Sabre fighter-bombers. Production schedules and demands by USAF units delayed delivery of the jets, but on 25 February 1953 the South Africans flew their first operational sorties. In addition to their traditional close support and interdiction roles, the Cheetahs also flew air-to-air combat missions in light of the Sabre's superior performance. Patrols ranged along the Yalu and Ch'ŏngch'ŏn rivers as well as UNC front lines and Communist supply corridors.

After the armistice, the 2d Squadron remained operational for training and supervision of Communist adherence to the cease-fire. The squadron was based at Airfield K-55 at Osan-ni, south of Seoul. On 28 October 1953 the 18th Fighter-Bomber Wing staged a formal Retreat for the Flying Cheetahs preceding the departure for South Africa of the squadron's remaining personnel. During the squadron's three years of service, thirty-four SAAF members were killed in action or declared missing and presumed dead; eight served time as prisoners of war. The squadron received presidential unit citations from both the United States and the Republic of Korea.

—*David R. Dorondo*

References:

Futrell, Robert F. *The United States Air Force in Korea, 1950–1953*. Rev. ed. Washington, DC: Office of the Chief of Air Force History, 1983.

Moore, Dermot, and Peter Bagshawe. *South Africa's Flying Cheetahs in Korea*. Johannesburg: Ashanti, 1991.

Schafer, Elizabeth. "South African Forces." In *The Korean War: An Encyclopedia*, edited by Stanley Sandler. New York: Garland, 1995.

South Korea, Occupation by Democratic People's Republic of Korea
(July–September 1950)

In the three months after its 25 June 1950 invasion of the Republic of Korea (ROK, South Korea), the Democratic People's Republic of Korea (DPRK, North Korea) came to control 90 percent of the peninsula. Within days the Korean People's Army (KPA) had largely defeated an outclassed Republic of Korea Army (ROKA). As the KPA overran Ongjin, Seoul, and Ch'unch'ŏn, DPRK leader Kim Il Sung ordered thousands of Communist Party members to take administrative control of the occupied territory. His three principal objectives in early July were to unify the divided country by military force, establish a Communist government in Seoul, and reinstate the People's Committees founded by the South Korean Worker's Party and forced to disband in 1948.

Although many did so, not all South Koreans fled from advancing KPA forces or hid in fear of their lives. Indeed, initially the DPRK and KPA enjoyed considerable popular support among Southerners. Thousands of South Korean Communists and nationalist sympathizers welcomed the North Koreans as "liberators" and declared themselves supporters of Kim Il Sung's cause. Many civilians in Seoul donned red arm bands to show their allegiance to the invading army. Some fifty deputies from the ROK National Assembly declared their loyalty to the DPRK, and the U.S. Central Intelligence Agency (CIA) reported that more than 50 percent of Seoul's student population actively collaborated with the North Koreans. In Inch'ŏn, a Communist stronghold, locals welcomed the KPA with a grand celebration. Many South Korean workers enlisted in the northern army or offered their services in Communist-controlled factories. Among South Koreans rallying to the DPRK were nationalists who wanted to see the peninsula reunited under one Korean government. Others were disillusioned with the corruption and economic injustice prevalent in Syngman Rhee's ROK.

Just as KPA officers had prepared meticulously for the military invasion of the South, so too did the Communist leadership follow a detailed blueprint to transform the political, economic, and social structures of South Korea. Communist Party officials took over public buildings, formed People's Committees in every major city, and selected puppet mayors for every occupied town and village. Former Korean Workers' Party leader and Minister of Justice Yi Sŭng-yŏp became the leading political figure in the South in his capacity as secretary of the Central Committee.

Radio addresses and other media bombarded the southern population with DPRK propaganda. In broadcasts Kim Il Sung emphasized the popular and democratic nature of his movement. Such themes struck a chord with a people who tired of what they were told was neocolonial rule, monopoly capitalism, and the authoritarian Syngman Rhee regime. Communist propaganda referred to Rhee as the "running dog of American imperialism" and the "puppet of the warmongers of Wall Street." The early ROKA military failures and its execution of political prisoners helped this effort.

Anti-American rhetoric often bordered on the ridiculous, however. One Communist placard in occupied Seoul read: "The American imperialists would have made you, our compatriots, migrate to South America." Such propaganda was disseminated by radio, loudspeaker, and printed leaflets. Public buildings were adorned with enormous posters of Josef Stalin and Kim Il Sung.

In rural areas Communist orators branded South Korea's landed class as enemies of the people. Ideologues promised to eliminate the "brutal totalitari-

Koreans from Hamhung identify the bodies of some 300 political prisoners who were killed by the North Korean Army by being forced into caves, which were subsequently sealed off so that they died of suffocation, 19 October 1950. (National Archives)

an dictatorship," destroy social hierarchies, nationalize industry, and introduce sweeping land reform. They also promised the "oppressed masses" an end to unemployment, an eight-hour workday, a welfare program, improved medical care, equality for women, better education, lower food prices, and a higher standard of living. Peasants, afraid at first, soon flocked to the cause.

On 15 August the occupiers held elections, featuring only Communist candidates, throughout the South. Meanwhile police implemented a modified version of the DPRK legal system in Seoul. North Koreans predominated in the new government; they controlled all means of communication, nationalized radio stations, expelled foreign correspondents, suppressed opposition newspapers, and even confiscated radios to silence United Nations (UN) broadcasts.

The new government also took complete control of the South Korean economy. Within a month Communist officials had confiscated property that belonged to the ROK government, members of the Rhee administration, Japanese nationals, some international corporations, and the landed elite.

On a social level the KPA sold itself as an army of liberation. Soldiers distributed rice and other foodstuffs to the poor. The occupiers also announced a series of measures that would have radically redistributed land and resources to a greater number of people. They also emptied jails of all political prisoners. KPA soldiers and personnel shook the hands of Korean women to symbolize the equality of the sexes. The new roles of women and young adults were redefined through active participation in two formative but short-lived social organizations, the Women's Alliance and the Youth Alliance.

Although they adopted no systematic policy of terror, North Korean officials in the South were as guilty as Rhee's government in persecution of political opponents; they also committed widespread atrocities during the three months of their rule in the South. The occupation government also engaged in forced migration on a limited scale as soldiers rounded up inhabitants of certain sectors of Seoul for relocation in North Korea. The DPRK claimed to be saving the lives of these South Korean migrants from potential U.S. air raids and promised them new homes and jobs in North Korea. Those forced to leave for the North arrived in P'yŏngyang, only to be told by a DPRK official that nothing had been prepared for them. When they returned to Seoul they found their former homes occupied by complete strangers and their possessions gone. South Koreans who wrote memoirs about this experience claimed that this was the punishment for noncooperation.

In Seoul and elsewhere Communist officials rounded up prisoners of war (POWs), ROK policemen, public officials, and property owners. Many were summarily executed. Others, bound at the wrists, were forced to stand in lines for hours, awaiting interrogation by People's Courts. Often the judges in these improvised trials were newly released political prisoners of the Rhee administration seeking retribution against their former oppressors. "Reactionaries" were quickly liquidated after summary trials.

Mass murders of South Korean civilians and POWs were too common to escape international attention. The KPA routinely executed South Korean POWs, and the UN Command later estimated that between June and September 1950 some 20,000 to 22,000 South Korean civilians were executed by the North Korean authorities. The majority of the killings occurred during the latter month as the regime collapsed following the mid-September UN invasion at Inch'ŏn.

The DPRK occupation of the South effectively ended with the 27 September UN liberation of Seoul. The three-month–long DPRK occupation of the South, however, served to solidify Rhee's subsequent control there. The experience chastened most Southerners; they now came to believe that Rhee's government was preferable to one headed by Kim Il Sung.

—Matthew D. Esposito

References:

Hastings, Max. *The Korean War*. New York: Simon & Schuster, 1987.

MacDonald, Callum. *Korea: The War Before Vietnam*. New York: Free Press, 1986.

Nam, Koon Woo. *The North Korean Communist Leadership, 1945–1965: A Study in Factionalism and Political Consolidation*. Tuscaloosa: University of Alabama Press, 1974.

Riley, John W., and W. Schram. *The Reds Take a City: The Communist Occupation of Seoul, with Eyewitness Accounts*. New Brunswick, NJ: Rutgers University Press, 1951.

See also: Kim Il Sung, Korea: Democratic People's Republic of: 1945–1953; Stalin, Josef; Syngman Rhee; Yi Sŭng-yŏp.

South Korean Demonstrations for Unification

Demonstrations and protests began in July 1951 as a result of the start of the Kaesŏng truce talks and continued throughout the remainder of the war. What had been intended at the end of World War II to be two temporary occupation zones for the surrender of Japanese forces now seemed as a consequence of the Cold War to be a permanent partition. Seeing the 38th parallel develop as a permanent boundary dividing two Korean states alarmed many Koreans, and the Korean War was in large part a manifestation of Korean nationalism. Throughout the war the objective of both the Democratic People's Republic of Korea (DPRK, North Korea) and the Republic of Korea (ROK, South Korea) was to reunify the peninsula, but under their own government and ideals.

The ROK government supported, and abetted, the South Korean demonstrations for unification, but they did represent the genuine sentiment and aspirations of every segment of the population, from student and youth groups to veterans.

The possibility of a truce or cease-fire with the DPRK was unacceptable to South Koreans. Many Koreans believed that anything short of complete victory over the DPRK and reunification of Korea would be a betrayal by the big powers and the United Nations (UN). They were dissatisfied and angry over the course of the armistice negotiations; South Koreans did not want their suffering or sacrifices to have been in vain. ROK president Syngman Rhee had always been a staunch nationalist, so much so that before June 1950 the Truman administration had been worried that he might embroil the United States in a war with the DPRK.

The demonstrations arose as a response to deadlocks in the armistice negotiations regarding exchanges of prisoners of war. Rhee hoped that the demonstrations might bring a resumption of the war, with a renewed UN Command (UNC) offensive into North Korea that would bring reunification of the peninsula under his rule.

On 2 April 1953, the ROK National Assembly unanimously passed a resolution opposing any agreements or armistice that did not bring reunification. Rhee carefully orchestrated all this behind the scenes, inflaming public opinion where he could. This also brought tensions among the population against UNC troops. Walkouts of mess boys and strikes by dock workers were intended to demonstrate to the world that South Koreans would not let foreign powers determine the fate of their country. Such demonstrations, which began in Seoul, Pusan, and Inch'ŏn and then spread to other locations, continued throughout the war.

Both the Truman and Eisenhower administrations and major U.S. allies were eager to reach a cease-fire agreement and were not swayed by Rhee's hopes for renewed UNC offensive operations. Finally, in return for extensive U.S. military support to the ROK, Rhee agreed not to undermine the armistice agreement.

—*Kevin J. Fromm*

References:

James, D. Clayton, with Anne Sharp Wells. *Refighting the Last War: Command and Crisis in Korea, 1950–1953*. New York: Free Press, 1993.

Matray, James I., ed. *Historical Dictionary of The Korean War*. Westport, CT: Greenwood Press, 1991.

Stueck, William W., Jr. *The Korean War: An International History*. Princeton, NJ: Princeton University Press, 1995.

See also: Armistice Agreement; Cease-Fire Negotiations; Kaesŏng Truce Talks; P'anmunjŏm Truce Talks; Syngman Rhee; Syngman Rhee's Release of North Korean Prisoners of War; Truce Talks.

Soviet Air War in Korea
(1950–1953)

Early on the afternoon of 1 November 1950, the first MiG-15s flew into action against U.S. Air Force (USAF) units bombing targets near the Yalu River. This action marked the beginning of the air war in MiG Alley and a dramatic change in the prosecution of the war in general. The fact that the MiG-15 pilots were Soviet and that at least two Fighter Air Divisions (FADs) from the Soviet Air Force or Soviet Air Defense Force fought in MiG Alley had been a Soviet state secret until the end of the Cold War. Many United Nations (UN) pilots reported sighting Russian pilots or hearing Russian spoken over the radio, but the USSR and the United States never officially acknowledged the active involvement of Soviet pilots and antiaircraft troops in the Korean air war.

For the United States and UN, the clashes between F-86s and MiG-15s for aerial superiority over the northwest corner of Korea quickly became the most highly publicized element of the war, eclipsing the bloody war of attrition on the ground. Russian pilots were not engaged in trying to gain aerial superiority but were trying instead to ensure that Mao Zedong's field armies were committed into action and, once in action, stayed supplied. The Soviet-piloted MiG-15s were ordered to Dandong (Antung) airfield to defend the railroad bridge across the Yalu River between Dandong and Sinŭiju and the hydroelectric facilities at the Sup'ung Reservoir.

Soviet Premier Josef Stalin and Mao had cemented their official relationship by signing the Sino-Soviet Treaty of Friendship, Alliance, and Mutual Assistance on 14 February 1950. Soviet pilots began flying air defense missions over Chinese cities in the early spring of 1950 with the first MiG-15 aerial victories coming against Chinese Nationalist bombers in southern China. When Stalin, finally convinced that the United States would not or could not intervene, and eager to make up for recent setbacks in Eastern Europe, relented and allowed Kim Il Sung to invade South Korea, he committed a foreign policy blunder that would require help to counteract.

Stalin did not want to use Soviet ground troops to shore up the defeated Korean People's Army after the 15 September UN Command Inch'ŏn landing, and Mao did not want to send his forces into action without air support. The game of brinkmanship played by the two Communist leaders during the first two weeks of October 1950 accelerated the feelings of mutual distrust that helped lead to the Sino-Soviet split later in the decade. Mao wanted the active participation of Soviet air units over the battlefield, and Stalin tried to limit his involvement to defending Chinese airspace in accordance with the February treaty. By 14 October Chinese troops began crossing the Yalu in force. When reports reached Stalin that U.S. aircraft were bombing targets in Manchuria, he ordered Ivan Belov's 151st FAD (along with regiments from the 28th and 50th FADs), that had been training Chinese pilots to fly the MiG-15, into action.

Belov's units became the initial core of the Soviet Sixty-fourth Fighter Air Corps (FAC), headquartered in Shenyang and responsible for the defense of Manchuria. The Sixty-fourth FAC included the antiaircraft divisions, ground control radars, and radar-controlled searchlight units deployed in North Korea. These units, along with their Chinese and North Korean comrades, were responsible for shooting down more U.S. pilots than were the more glamorous MiG-15s. As many as 70,000 Soviet officers and men manned the Sixty-fourth, but, even so, it was smaller than the Sixty-seventh FAC, headquartered in Beijing, that controlled Soviet air units deployed in the rest of eastern and southeastern China. These other Soviet units included bomber and Shturmovik (assault) divisions equipped with Tu-2 and Il-10 aircraft. Together the 64th and Sixty-67th FACs were responsible for creating a modern Chinese air force that quickly became the third largest in the world.

In addition to Belov's original FADs, other Soviet MiG-15 units that fought in Korea included the 303d, 324th (commanded by the leading Allied World War II ace, Ivan Kozhedub), 97th, 216th, 32d, and 190th FADs. Georgii Lobov commanded the 303d; he succeeded Belov as the second commander of the 64th FAC and was paired with the 324th from April 1951 until early 1952. These two units inflicted some of the bloodiest assaults suffered by the USAF's Bomber Command during its campaign against the Yalu bridges. The air battles in early April and on 23 October 1951, known to the USAF as "Black Tuesday," resulted in such heavy losses for U.S. B-29s that they were banned from daylight combat in MiG Alley.

While the railroad bridge between Dandong and Sinŭiju was never dropped, the hydroelectric facilities at Sup'ung did not escape the war unscathed. The USAF and U.S. Navy combined their forces in the summer of 1952 to inflict serious damage on the Yalu dams. The success of U.S. F-84s and A-1 Skyraiders revealed the weakness of the Soviet air defense system. The P-3a radar could not detect low-flying aircraft, and the MiG-15 was designed to fly high and blow up large bombers; it could not dogfight well at low altitudes, particularly without its accustomed ground control direction.

As the war progressed, more Chinese and North Korean pilots flew in MiG Alley and fell victim to the increasing numbers of improved F-86s. Soviet pilots continued to bear the brunt of the aerial combat. The F-86 pilots also began patrolling across the Yalu into Manchuria looking to gain an advantage over the speedy MiG-15. While the F-86 (particularly the E and F models) was a superior dogfight aircraft, particularly in the hands of highly trained U.S. pilots, and gained an impressive kill ratio, the Soviet piloted MiG-15s kept the major supply artery open to the Chinese and North Korean field armies. The result was a stalemate in the air that paralleled the one on the ground, leaving both sides in a state of armed confrontation.

—*Mark A. O'Neill*

References:

Gagin, V. V. *"Vozdushnaia voina v koree (1950–1953 g.g.)"* [Air war in Korea, 1950–1953]. Voronezh: Izdatel'stvo "Poligraf," 1997.

Gordon, Yefim, and Vladimir Rigmant. *MiG-15: Design, Development, and Korean War Combat History*. Osceola, WI: Motorbooks International, 1993.

No, Kum-Sok, with J. Roger Osterholm. *A MiG-15 to Freedom: Memoirs of the Wartime North Korean Defector Who Delivered the Secret Fighter Jet to the Americans in 1953*. Jefferson, NC: McFarland, 1996.

O'Neill, Mark A. "The Other Side of the Yalu: Soviet Pilots in Korea." Doctoral dissertation, Florida State University, 1996.

See also: Air Power in the War; Aircraft (Principal Combat); Kim Il Sung; Mao Zedong; Soviet Airfield Incident; Stalin, Josef.

Soviet Airfield Incident
(8 October 1950)

Incident that threatened war with the Soviet Union and strained the deteriorating relationship between President Harry S. Truman and General Douglas MacArthur. Following the Inch'ŏn landing on 15 September 1950, United Nations Command (UNC) forces under MacArthur's command drove Korean People's Army (KPA, North Korean) forces back into North Korea to an area in proximity to the Yalu River, the border between Korea and China.

On 27 September the Truman administration instructed MacArthur to use only Republic of Korea (South Korean) military units in provinces neighboring China and under no circumstances to attack targets in Manchuria. Washington feared any incident outside of Korea that might have been interpreted as a direct attack rather than a military mistake. Any such attack would herald the possibility of a widened war with China or the Soviet Union and even the possibility of world war and had to be avoided at all costs.

The administration's fears were realized on 8 October 1950. Despite the order to MacArthur, two F-80 Shooting Star fighters of the 49th Air Group repeatedly strafed a Soviet airfield sixty-two miles north of the Korean border and eighteen miles southwest of Vladivostok. The two pilots, both young and inexperienced, made a navigational error while flying in marginal weather and mistook the airfield for a Democratic People's Republic of Korea (North Korean) installation.

The following day the Soviet government vehemently protested what it saw as a gross violation of its territory. Initially the State Department refused to accept responsibility for the attack and claimed that the fighter planes were under the UN rather than U.S. command. The incident, however, may have been one of the reasons behind a conference that took place between President Truman and General MacArthur on 15 October 1950 at Wake Island in the Pacific. Four days later, on 19 October, the State Department issued an apology to the Soviet government. The U.S. government promised to pay for all damages incurred in the attack.

At the same time the UN received a report from MacArthur that declared the attack had resulted from navigational error and poor judgment, as the target was not properly identified before the strike. The report also stated that the commander of the 49th Air Group had been relieved and the two pilots punished. In actuality, neither punishment was severe nor permanently damaging. The air group commander received a new command as director of combat operations for the Fifth U.S. Air Force, while the two pilots escaped punishment once a court-martial refused to convict them.

—*Eric W. Osborne*

References:

Futrell, Robert F. *The United States Air Force in Korea, 1950–1953*. New York: Van Rees Press, 1961.

Hoyt, Edwin P. *On to the Yalu*. New York: Stein & Day, 1984.

Spanier, John W. *The Truman-MacArthur Controversy and the Korean War*. Cambridge, MA: Belknap Press, 1959.

See also: MacArthur, Douglas; Truman, Harry S.; United States: Air Force (USAF); Wake Island Conference.

Soviet Security Council Boycott
(13 January–1 August 1950)

The USSR boycott of the United Nations (UN) Security Council was ostensibly a protest against the refusal by the United States and its allies to seat the UN ambassador from the People's Republic of China (PRC). An unintended consequence of this boycott was that the United States was able to dominate the Security Council without the Soviet ambassador exercising his veto power. Specifically, Soviet ambassador Jacob Malik was not able to veto the U.S. proposal of 27 June 1950 to authorize the use of military force in defense of South Korea. Malik returned to his seat on 1 August 1950, in time to assume the rotating chairmanship of the Security Council. The end of the boycott was a tacit admission that the tactic had backfired. Malik could not undo the June resolutions on Korea, although he vigorously attacked them for propaganda purposes, but he could end U.S. domination of the Security Council, argue for a negotiated settlement of the war, and build support for UN recognition of the PRC.

The UN Security Council was made up of five permanent members (the United States, the USSR, France, the United Kingdom, and China), each of whom had veto power over the council's resolutions, and six temporary members. Dr. Tsiang Ting-fu, the delegate from the Republic of China (Taiwan), held the Chinese seat, even after Mao Zedong's forces had emerged victorious in the Chinese civil war. Presumably, Soviet leader Josef Stalin was distressed that his Communist ally was not given a seat in the UN, although it is possible that he provoked the controversy to keep China isolated and dependent on the USSR (a theory originally attributed to French UN delegate Jean Chauvel). Stalin withdrew his UN ambassador in January, causing a predictable polarization among members, most of whom had been ready to seat the PRC delegate before the boycott. Several months later, when the Korean People's Army (North Korean) invaded the Republic of Korea (South Korea), the Soviets found themselves without their Security Council veto. On the first day of the invasion, 25 June 1950, the United States convened a session of the UN Security Council and pushed through a resolution condemning the attack and demanding an "immediate cessation of hostilities." Two days later, another resolution was passed allowing member nations to provide "such assistance to the Republic of Korea as may be necessary to repel the armed attack." These resolutions gave the United States a mandate to intervene militarily in the name of the UN.

The coincidence of the Security Council boycott with the commencement of hostilities in Korea might be taken as circumstantial evidence that the Soviets did not plan the latter event. While such a conclusion may have some validity, it is more plausible that Stalin simply made a costly blunder in allowing Kim Il Sung to proceed with his invasion of the South during that time. In any case, the Soviet boycott of the UN Security Council gave the Truman administration the unexpected advantage of being able to intervene in Korea under the guise of the UN.

—*Edward Sharp*

References:

Brook, David. *The United Nations and the China Dilemma*. New York: Vintage Press, 1956.

Simmons, Robert R. *The Strained Alliance: Peking, Pyongyang, Moscow, and the Politics of the Korean Civil War*. New York: Free Press, 1975.

Stueck, William, W., Jr. *The Korean War: An International History*. Princeton, NJ: Princeton University Press, 1995.

See also: China, People's Republic of; China, People's Republic of: UN Representation Question; China, Republic of; Cold War, Origins to 1950; Kim Il Sung; Korea, Democratic People's Republic of, Invasion of the Republic of Korea; Lie, Trygve; Malik, Jacob (Iakov) Alexandrovich; Mao Zedong; Sino-Soviet Treaty of Friendship and Alliance; Stalin, Josef; Union of Soviet Socialist Republics; Vyshinskii, Andrei Ianuarovich.

Special Operations

Unconventional warfare is a topic little discussed in connection with the Korean War, but both sides practiced it. Special operations include behind-the-lines reconnaissance, demoralization, propaganda, sabotage, and guerrilla warfare.

The United Nations Command (UNC) supported guerrilla bands in North Korea, providing both training and supplies. Conversely, the Democratic People's Republic of Korea (North Korea) had units operating in the Republic of Korea (ROK, South Korea), as well as special units attached to regular infantry line units.

The UNC, and primarily the U.S. Army, supported partisan activities in the North. Along with equipment, the army provided the partisans with military advisors to train unconventional units in guerrilla warfare, cutting communication lines, and other sabotage. The U.S. Eighth Army's G-3 (training) section first organized these units under the command of Colonel John McGee, the former U.S. Army guerrilla leader in the Philippines in World War II. This special operations unit was later designated Army Unit 8086. Along with training, food, and ammunition, the U.S. Army also sent personnel along with the partisans to act as advisors, actually fighting alongside them. The program was very successful, and by July 1951 this force of some 7,000 partisans claimed to have killed 2,112 Chinese and North Korean soldiers and captured another 169.

In the summer of 1951 Lieutenant Colonel Jay Vanderpool, who also had seen action as a guerrilla in the Philippines during World War II, replaced Colonel McGee. Vanderpool modernized a fleet of junks used by the partisans for hit-and-run operations. He also enhanced their armament to include 106-mm recoilless rifles. In March and June 1951 Vanderpool, assisted by a British officer who had served with the Special Air Service, expanded his partisan operations to include parachute infiltration. Partisan activities continued to grow. One estimate is that UNC partisans during the war killed 9,095 Communist soldiers and captured another 385.

In December 1952 these special operations units were reassigned from the U.S. Eighth Army to the Army Forces Far East, which was given sole charge of covert operations. At peak strength, special operations units consisted of seven regiments and a total of over 22,227 personnel. After the armistice was signed in July 1953, the unit, then commanded by Colonel Glenn Muggleburg, pulled out of North Korea and was assimilated into the Republic of Korea Army (ROKA).

The North Koreans also conducted special operations. At the beginning of the war there were only a few guerrilla activities by the Korean People's Army (KPA). Guerrilla warfare in the South eventually intensified, and a force of some 5,000 partisans operated below the 38th parallel, led by 1,700 Communist advisors. At the time there were two main groups of guerrilla units opposed to the ROK. The first of these was actually a part of the KPA and was sanctioned by the government; the other was little more than bandits with only slight or no affiliation to one government or the other. In October 1950 the Chinese People's Volunteer Army (Chinese Communist) brought in its own guerrilla units. At Dandong during 7–22 January 1951, UN forces encountered the heaviest guerrilla fighting in its rear areas of the entire war. Partisans cut lines of communication and created considerable confusion.

KPA Chief of Staff Nam Il issued a document outlining specific missions for the Korean Worker's Party guerrilla forces. These included forward reconnaissance of UNC positions, spreading propaganda, harassing UNC forces, reinstituting the Communist way of life in southern villages, leading the people against UNC forces, cooperating with other guerrilla groups in sabotage operations, and acting as home guards. Among actual KPA units, the most important were the 766th Independent Unit, the 560th Army Unit, and the 945th and 956th Independent Naval

Infantry units. These served effectively throughout the war, conducting various covert raids on a multitude of UNC targets. These were conducted by rapid naval insertion at targets along the eastern coast of South Korea, such as at Chumunjin, Kangnŭng, Nakp'ungni, Samch'ŏk, and Imwŏnjin. These special operation units were often attached to regular KPA units and would change into civilian clothes or ROKA uniforms and carry out reconnaissance on UNC positions. Another technique was to blend in with the refugees prior to a large-scale Communist attack, then draw out hidden weapons and strike UNC forces from behind.

Eventually the UNC recognized these guerrilla operations as a major threat to security in South Korea and the war effort. The UNC sought to counter these widespread partisan attacks by building up the National Police force. The UNC also conducted whole operations, such as Operation RATKILLER, between December 1951 and June 1952. The sole purpose of this operation was to end Communist guerrilla activity in South Korea. The results were more than satisfying to the UNC. Some 8,000 guerrillas were killed and many sympathizers were arrested. By the July 1953 armistice, Communist guerrilla activity had diminished drastically, to the point where Communist guerrillas were merely fighting for survival.

—*Alec McMorris*

References:

Bermudez, Joseph S., Jr. *North Korean Special Forces.* Annapolis, MD: Naval Institute Press, 1998.

Breuer, William B. *Shadow Warriors: The Covert War in Korea.* New York: Wiley, 1996.

Evanhoe, Ed. *Dark Moon; 8th Army Special Operations in the Korean War.* Royal Leamington Spa, UK: Korvel, 1995.

Malcom, Ben S. *White Tigers: My Secret War in North Korea.* Washington, DC: Brassey's, 1996.

Matray, James I., ed. *Historical Dictionary of the Korean War.* Westport, CT: Greenwood Press, 1991.

See also: Nam Il; RATKILLER, Operation; United States: Rangers.

Spender, Sir Percy C.
(1897–1985)

Australian minister for external affairs from 1949 to 1951, and ambassador to the United States from 1951 to 1958. Born in Sydney on 5 October 1897, Percy C. Spender was educated at the University of Sydney. Admitted to the New South Wales bar in 1923, Spender enjoyed a successful career as a barrister before running successfully for the House of Representatives as a Conservative member of parliament in 1937.

When the Conservatives regained power in 1949, Prime Minister Robert G. Menzies appointed Spender as minister of external affairs. Unlike the premier, who thought such an alliance both unlikely and unnecessary,

Spender firmly believed that Australia's security depended on entering into a regional defense pact with the United States similar to the North Atlantic Treaty Organization (NATO) alliance established by the West European countries in 1949. As with many Australians, he had bitter memories of World War II, when in his opinion Britain virtually abandoned Australia to face Japan alone, and such help as his country received came primarily from the United States.

The Korean War provided Spender with the opportunity to make these hopes reality. By early July, Australia had provided naval support and a fighter squadron to the United Nations Command in Korea, but under the anglophile Menzies it followed the British lead and was initially reluctant to commit ground forces. On 26 July, when Menzies was incommunicado on the Atlantic, making a sea crossing from Britain to the United States, Spender learned that the British government had finally decided to send troops to Korea. He quickly persuaded Acting Prime Minister A. W. Fadden to follow suit; this trumped the British, as the announcement that Australia would commit one battalion (later increased to two) was made one hour before that of the British.

Despite Menzies's benevolent skepticism, the energetic Spender exploited the prestige that Australia had gained by sending ground forces to Korea to win the backing of the Truman administration and U.S. Congress for the ANZUS treaty, the regional mutual security pact between Australia, New Zealand, and the United States that was his most cherished objective. This was negotiated and concluded in 1951, and it was fitting that Spender, its foremost architect (who resigned as minister of external affairs in May 1951 to become Australia's ambassador to the United States), should have signed his greatest triumph on his country's behalf in September 1951. The ANZUS treaty and the close alliance and cooperation with the United States and opposition to the spread of communism in Asia that it implied would be the fundamental principles of Australian foreign policy for at least the next two or three decades.

Within this framework of loyal support of the powerful U.S. ally, Spender, as with other Australian diplomats, believed himself free to express some reservations on U.S. policies toward Korea. As minister of external affairs and ambassador, he was one of the more forceful and energetic participants in the Korean War briefing meetings. These somewhat sporadically scheduled Washington gatherings of representatives from the principal countries contributing to the United Nations forces in Korea were intended to promote Allied unity and ensure that all the nations involved were receiving accurate information on the course of the fighting and of negotiations.

Spender also used his frequent meetings with U.S. officials to express his views. In late 1950 he made known Australia's concern that the United States might launch direct attacks on mainland Chinese territory to retaliate for Chinese intervention in Korea, thereby possibly expanding the war. In December 1950 he indicated that Australia shared British Prime Minister Clement Attlee's alarm over the possibility that the United States might employ atomic weapons in the war.

Although Australia followed the U.S. line on non-recognition of the People's Republic of China (PRC), early in 1951 Spender suggested that the United States consider withdrawing its support and recognition from Jiang Jieshi's Nationalist regime on Taiwan as part of the price of a peace settlement with the PRC, a proposal U.S. officials refused to consider. On several other occasions he urged that the United States adopt a relatively moderate and conciliatory stance toward its Communist antagonists, be circumspect in its condemnation of the Chinese, refrain from escalating the war, and make every effort to reach an acceptable negotiated peace settlement. As befitted the increasingly special Australian-American relationship, Spender's advocacy of restraint was generally undertaken in private, and, when U.S. officials felt sufficiently strongly on an issue, they could normally count on public Australian support, however reluctantly given.

Spender remained ambassador to the United States until 1958, when he became a member of the International Court of Justice at The Hague, of which he served as president from 1964 to 1967. He died in Sydney on 3 May 1985.

—*Priscilla Roberts*

References:

Barclay, John St. J. *Friends in High Places: Australian-American Diplomatic Relations.* Melbourne: Oxford University Press, 1985.

Bridge, Carl, ed. *Munich to Vietnam: Australia's Relations with Britain and the United States Since the 1930s.* Melbourne: Melbourne University Press, 1991.

Harper, Norman. *A Great and Powerful Friend: A Study of Australian American Relations between 1900 and 1975.* St. Lucia: Queensland University Press, 1987.

McIntyre, W. David. *Background to the ANZUS Pact: Policy-Making, Strategy, and Diplomacy, 1945–55.* New York: St. Martin's Press, 1995.

O'Neill, Robert J. *Australia in the Korean War, 1950–1953.* 2 vols. Canberra: Australian War Memorial/Australian Government Publishing Service, 1981, 1985.

Spender, Sir Percy. *Exercises in Diplomacy: The ANZUS Treaty and the Colombo Plan.* New York: New York University Press, 1969.

———. *Politics and a Man.* Sydney: Collins, 1972.

See also: ANZUS (Australia–New Zealand–U.S.) Treaty; Attlee, Clement R.; Australia; Jiang Jieshi (Chiang Kai-shek); Menzies, Robert G.

St. Laurent, Louis S.
(1882–1973)

Prime minister of Canada during the Korean War. Born in Compton, Quebec, on 1 February 1882, Louis St. Laurent began his career as a lawyer. He moved into political life when chosen to be in the cabinet of Prime Minister William Lyon Mackenzie King, first as justice minister, then as secretary of state for external affairs from 1946 to 1948. After King's retirement, St. Laurent became prime minister in 1948. He thus came into the prime ministership with a knowledge of international diplomacy and with some background in the problems of post–World War II Korea.

St. Laurent was initially unconcerned about the news of North Korea's invasion of the South. He and his cabinet believed that Canada had little or no interests in Asia and that the United States would not respond to the invasion militarily. Thus, at first, there was no crisis atmosphere in Ottawa over the Korean problem. However, once the United Nations (UN) and the government of the United States decided to react forcefully, it then fell on Canada to follow suit.

St. Laurent's government decided to send three Royal Canadian Navy destroyers to Korean waters and to provide transport planes to ferry supplies from North America to U.S. bases in Japan. Public opinion in Canada, however, found this contribution too timid, and the U.S. government claimed that it was simply a "token" commitment.

Despite this, St. Laurent was not prepared to send ground troops at this point because Canada's already overstretched military could not easily be extended to include a significant role in Asia. It is important to note in this regard that St. Laurent was a bilingual French Canadian from Quebec, a province that traditionally distrusted Canadian involvement in foreign wars and that had opposed the use of conscription for overseas service during both world wars. Consequently, any possible force that might in the future be sent to Korea would have to be made up of volunteers, not draftees.

During much of the war, St. Laurent seemed to be overshadowed by his energetic secretary of state for external affairs, Lester Pearson. But St. Laurent and Pearson were in agreement about the difficulties that Canada faced over Korea. Both saw the "police action" as an extension of the duties of being a member of the UN and not as being part of an U.S. anti-Communist crusade. Because of this, they wanted the UN to control the strategy and goals of the intervention and to limit as much as possible the enormous U.S. influence over both. The Canadian government was particularly uneasy about the possibility of the conflict spreading to other parts of Asia, or of doing anything that might provoke the People's Republic of China or the Soviet Union. As a result, St. Laurent was deter-

mined that any Canadian contribution would be made solely in response to UN decisions, and while UN forces would, and should, be led by the United States, they had to remain a model of collective security.

Finally, after growing domestic and foreign pressure, the Canadian government decided on 17 July 1950 to send ground troops to Korea. This decision was not announced until 7 August, when St. Laurent went on national radio to explain his government's action. He claimed that while Canada's primary interest was in the defense of Western Europe through the North Atlantic Treaty Organization (NATO) alliance, there was a need for cooperation with the UN in Korea.

Because of the difficulty faced by the Canadian military in dealing with both regions, a special infantry brigade would be recruited for Korea. St. Laurent called for volunteers, especially World War II veterans, to join the unit. The resulting response at recruiting stations across Canada, including Quebec, was overwhelmingly positive. Because of this, a troop commitment to Korea was made without lessening Canada's role in NATO or resorting to conscription.

The determination to send troops to Korea and the public announcement of that decision proved to be St. Laurent's most important achievements in the war. He was also involved, with Pearson, in negotiating resolutions and brokering compromises in the UN. In 1951, in particular, he worked behind the scenes in attempting to arrive at a cease-fire agreement with Indian Prime Minister Nehru, an action that U.S. officials saw as objectionable both in method and outcome.

St. Laurent and his Liberal government were reelected in 1953 but defeated in 1957. He left public life at that point and returned to practicing law. He died in Quebec City on 25 July 1973.

—*Eric Jarvis*

References:

Granatstein, J. L., and Norman Hiller. *For Better or for Worse, Canada and the United States to the 1990s.* Toronto: Copp Clark Pitman, 1991.

Melady, John. *Korea: Canada's Forgotten War.* Toronto: Macmillan, 1983.

Stairs, Denis. *The Diplomacy of Constraint: Canada, the Korean War, and the United States.* Toronto: University of Toronto Press, 1974.

Stueck, William W., Jr. *The Korean War: An International History.* Princeton, NJ: Princeton University Press, 1995.

See also: Canada; Cease-Fire Negotiations; Nehru, Jawaharlal; Pearson, Lester B.; Wrong, Humphrey Hume.

Stalin, Josef
(1879–1953)

Ruler of the Soviet Union from the late 1920s until 1953. Born Iosif Vissarionovich Dzhugashvili in Gori, Georgia, on 21 December 1879, on his mother's insistence he entered a seminary in Tiflis in 1894 but was expelled in 1899, already on the road to becoming a revolutionary. In 1901 he joined the Social Democratic Party in Tiflis. Arrested by the Tsarist police the next year, he was exiled to eastern Siberia. He escaped and returned to Tiflis in 1904, where he became a Bolshevik and took the alias Koba. Stalin raised money for the party by organizing bank robberies in Georgia. He spent a few years with the Baku Bolshevik committee and then went to St. Petersburg, where he adopted the name Stalin ("man of steel"). In 1913 he was arrested for a fourth time and exiled to western Siberia. There he remained until the Russian Revolution of March 1917, when he returned to St. Petersburg and became a leading figure in the Bolshevik coup d'état of November 1917.

As a key figure in the government, Commissar for Nationalities, Stalin took an active role in the Civil War, clashing on occasion with political rival Commissar for War Leon Trotsky. Stalin served as general secretary of the Communist Party between 1922 and 1953 and as Soviet premier from 1941 to 1953.

After the 1924 death of Lenin, Trotsky and Stalin vied for power. Victorious over Trotsky at the end of the 1920s, Stalin carried out massive industrialization efforts, the collectivization of agriculture, and extensive purges of the party and military. His policies directly resulted in the deaths of millions of Soviet citizens. Stalin anticipated a war with Nazi Germany at some point but sought to buy time by signing the 23 August 1939 nonaggression pact, which, in its secret provisions, divided up Eastern Europe between the USSR and Germany and provided substantial economic advantages to Germany.

Caught off guard by the June 1941 German invasion of the Soviet Union, Stalin literally had to be forced back to the leadership, but he learned to be a competent war leader and directed his country to victory in the Great Patriotic War in 1945.

At the 1943 Teheran Conference, Stalin agreed with the principle adopted at the earlier Cairo Conference, which he had not attended, that an appropriate course for Korea would be independence following a period of apprenticeship. According to U.S. president Harry Truman, in private talks at the 1945 Yalta Conference, Stalin not only agreed with President Franklin Roosevelt's plan that the Soviet Union, the United States, and China form a three-power trusteeship over Korea, but he even suggested adding Great Britain. This plan was never carried out. With Japan's military collapse imminent, the United States suggested the 38th parallel as a practical demarcation line for the surrender of Japanese forces, and Stalin readily agreed. President Harry S. Truman never intended this as a permanent line of division.

An early portrait of Russian leader Josef Stalin. (Library of Congress)

By 1948 the Soviets insured the creation of a Communist state in North Korea under the leadership of Kim Il Sung, who was reported to have fought in the Red Army at Stalingrad. The resultant Democratic People's Republic of Korea (DPRK, North Korea) was armed and advised by the Soviet military, even after the Soviet military withdrawal in December 1948. A year later, thanks in part to Soviet assistance, Mao Zedong's Communists won control of China. According to Nikita Khrushchev's memoirs, in late 1949 Stalin approved Kim's plan to reunite Korea by force. A report prepared for Soviet leader Leonid Brezhnev in 1966 indicated that final approval came in March and April 1950 when Kim traveled to Moscow with a detailed plan. Stalin was doubtless reassured by Washington's apparent exclusion of Korea from its defensive perimeter, but less so by Kim's claim that the conquest would be easy. Stalin nonetheless ordered that North Korean weapons and equipment needs be met, and Soviet military advisers assisted in the drafting of war plans. At Stalin's behest, Kim subsequently won approval from Mao in China for his war plans. Talks between Beijing and P'yŏngyang led to the release of thousands of Korean troops then serving in the People's Republic of China (PRC) army. They were sent to the DPRK and became the backbone of new divisions in the Korean

People's Army (KPA, North Korean) formed for the invasion of the South.

Despite Kim's optimism that the war would be won before the United States would be able to rescue the Republic of Korea (South Korea), Stalin ordered all Soviet military advisors serving with the KPA to withdraw. After the Inch'ŏn landing completely reversed the early KPA successes, on 1 October Stalin, in response to a plea from Kim Il Sung, pressured Mao to enter the war and rescue the DPRK. In a 5 October telegram to Mao, Stalin stated that the United States should not be feared because together the Soviet Union and the PRC were stronger than the United States and Great Britain. He wrote, "If war is inevitable, let it be waged now, and not in a few years when Japanese imperialism will be restored as a U.S. ally and when the U.S. and Japan will have a ready-made bridgehead on the continent in the form of all Korea run by Syngman Rhee." This telegram, prompted by the news that Mao had decided not to enter the war at this time, had the desired effect.

PRC Foreign Minister Zhou Enlai (Chou En-Lai) had already flown to meet with Stalin on 11 October at the Black Sea resort of Sochi, where he secured Soviet agreement to supply sufficient tanks and artillery to equip ten Chinese divisions. But a few hours after the initial decision, Stalin must have had second thoughts, because Zhou was then informed that the Soviet Union would loan the promised munitions and supplies and that it would be two and a half months before the Soviet Air Force could assist the Chinese. The Kremlin also opposed a large-scale Chinese intervention because Soviet leaders feared it might provoke a general war, for which the USSR was unprepared. This caused Mao to put Chinese entry into the war on hold until he could secure unanimous support from the Chinese politburo. This decision, made without assurances of Soviet air cover, impressed Stalin, who then promised a loan of 5.6 billion rubles to cover equipping 100 Chinese divisions. Stalin also approved turning over aircraft from two Soviet air divisions stationed in Shenyang and Shanghai to the Chinese and sent thirteen air divisions to protect China, including nine fighter divisions, three attack aircraft divisions, and a bomber division. This was with the proviso that they would assist in China's air defense and not be used over Korea.

The Korean War gave Stalin a confidence in Mao that he had not previously held, thus placing Sino-Soviet relations on a more solid footing, although this does not mean that the Communist allies were always in agreement. After the Chinese military offensive in Korea had been halted and a United Nations counteroffensive had retaken Seoul, Stalin offered a proposal for a cease-fire and mutual withdrawal from the 38th parallel.

Although Mao urged Soviet involvement in the cease-fire negotiations, Stalin insisted that the Chinese handle this. Recently released Soviet documents indicate that, despite the start of negotiations, Stalin saw advantages in prolonging the war and urged Mao to take a hard line. Soviet propaganda continued to charge the United States as an aggressor looking for a future war. U.S. ambassador to Moscow Admiral Alan G. Kirk failed over a two-year period to secure a meeting with Stalin, although he did manage to meet with Deputy Foreign Minister Andrei Gromyko, who claimed ignorance of PRC attitudes toward cease-fire talks. Before his departure from the Soviet Union, Kirk met with Foreign Minister Viacheslav Molotov, who indicated that the Soviets would not pressure Communist negotiators to change their stance at the talks. Stalin was then in poor health, and no compromise was found until after his death. Stalin, easily one of the most horrific and fascinating individuals in world history, died in Moscow on 5 March 1953.

—*Claude R. Sasso*

References:

Goncharov, Sergei N., John W. Lewis, and Xue Litai. *Uncertain Partners: Stalin, Mao, and the Korean War*. Stanford, CA: Stanford University Press, 1993.

Khrushchev, Nikita. *Khrushchev Remembers, with an Introduction, Commentary and Notes by Edward Crankshaw*. Boston: Little, Brown, 1970.

Volkogonov, Dmitri. *Stalin: Triumph and Tragedy*. New York: Grove Weidenfeld, 1988.

Woodrow Wilson International Center for Scholars. "Cold War International History Project (CWIHP)." <http://cwihp.si.edu/default.htm>.

See also: Gromyko, Andrei Andreyevich; Kim Il Sung; Kirk, Alan Goodrich; Malik, Jacob (Iakov) Alexandrovich; Mao Zedong; Molotov, Viacheslav Mikhailovich; Soviet Air War in Korea; Syngman Rhee; Truman, Harry S.; Zhou Enlai.

Steel Plants, Truman's Seizure of
(8 April 1952)

Controversial action taken by President Harry S. Truman during the national emergency created by the Korean War. In November 1951 a labor union representing steelworkers called for a pay increase for its members. The workers had received no increase since 1950, despite record steel production caused by the war, which greatly increased the profits of the companies. The union declared that, barring a wage agreement, its members would strike on 31 December. Truman realized the impact a strike would have on the war effort and tried to avert a production stoppage. He referred the question to his Wage Stabilization Board (WSB), and union workers decided to stay on the job until 8 April, pending an agreement.

Negotiations failed when the steel companies refused the WSB's proposed pay increase unless they were allowed to raise the price of steel. Their refusal confronted Truman with a difficult problem. He viewed the demands of the companies as simple profiteering and refused to allow an increase in the cost of the war. Truman believed this decision left only one course of action in order to safeguard the flow of supplies to Korea and sustain the rearmament of Western Europe. On 8 April 1952 the president issued Executive Order 10340, which authorized the secretary of commerce to take control of eighty-seven major steel factories affected by the strike.

This action did not go unchallenged by members of Congress or the public. The Justice Department was the first to act, arguing in court that Truman had no statutory support for his action. This stance baffled Truman, because he believed he had acted well within his authority, following his declaration of a national emergency and the commitment of U.S. troops to Korea. Steel was indispensable to the war effort. Truman also based his order on his authority as president and commander in chief of the U.S. armed forces, enabling war powers enumerated in the Defense Production Act of 1950, and the laws and authority of the Constitution. He saw the seizure of the mills as a last resort, forced on him by the refusal of the companies to negotiate.

The steel companies then decided to sue the federal government for the return of their property. Their suit was filed in the federal district court of Judge David A. Pine. There Truman administration officials sought in vain to defend their position. Assistant Attorney General Homer Baldridge asserted to Judge Pine that courts could not restrict presidential power in the event of a national emergency. Not only was the administration's case weak, but the public also reacted negatively to the seizure of the steel mills. In a news conference on 17 April, reporters challenged Truman's authority on the basis that a president's power cannot be absolute even in time of crisis.

Truman certainly recognized the unpopularity of his decision and, after the news conference, he did his best to defuse the situation. A few days later the president sent a letter to the Senate in which he allowed Congress to reverse his action.

This letter and repeated public attempts to defend the seizures could not stop the suit in district court. On 29 April Judge Pine wrote a scathing opinion of the president's actions. He rejected the administration's assertion of presidential power on grounds that a strike, although it might harm the United States, was less damaging than unrestricted executive power.

The final blow to Truman's action came in a Supreme Court decision of 2 June 1952, when in a vote of 6–3 the high court found Truman's action unconstitutional. This was a major defeat for Truman, but more important was the effect of the vote on the country's war effort. After the Supreme Court verdict the steel strike went forward; it lasted seven weeks, saw the loss of 20 million tons of steel production, and cut projected civilian as well as military output substantially.

—Eric W. Osborne

References:

Fisher, Louis. *Presidential War Power.* Lawrence: University Press of Kansas, 1995.

Marcus, Maeva. *Truman and the Steel Seizure Case: The Limits of Presidential Power.* New York: Columbia University Press, 1977.

McCullough, David. *Truman.* New York: Simon & Schuster, 1992.

See also: Mobilization; Truman, Harry S.; Truman's Domestic Agenda and the Korean War; Wage Stabilization Board (WSB).

Stevenson, Adlai E.
(1900–1965)

U.S. Democratic presidential candidate in 1952. Born in Los Angeles, California, on 5 February 1900, Adlai Ewing Stevenson came from a prominent Illinois political family. After attending local Illinois schools and the elite Choate School, he spent four years at Princeton University, after which he earned a law degree, first attending Harvard Law School and then graduating from Northwestern University Law School. Entering the leading Chicago law firm, Cutting, Moore and Sidley, Stevenson rapidly won social prominence and a wide circle of intellectual friends, serving in many public service organizations. The most notable of the latter was the Chicago Council on Foreign Relations, of which he was elected president in 1935 and to which he devoted much of his energy, winning a reputation as a stellar public speaker.

A firm supporter of U.S. intervention in the Second World War, in 1940 Stevenson headed the Chicago chapter of the Committee to Defend America by Aiding the Allies. In 1941 Stevenson joined Frank Knox, a Chicago newspaper publisher and the new secretary of the navy, as his administrative assistant and speechwriter. Stevenson remained in the Navy Department until Knox's death in 1944. Shortly afterward he joined the State Department as a special assistant to the secretary of state. He remained there until 1947, serving on the U.S. team at the 1945 San Francisco Conference that created the United Nations (UN) and on several U.S. delegations at successive UN General Assemblies.

Returning to Illinois, in 1948 Stevenson was elected governor on the Democratic ticket, launching an activist and progressive social reform program and attempting to eradicate corruption. An outspoken opponent of the rising force of McCarthyism,

Stevenson quickly won national recognition as a rising political star of remarkable eloquence. The Democratic National Convention in 1952 saw an open contest, as incumbent president Harry S. Truman, damaged by McCarthyism and the Korean war, had chosen not to run again. Drafted on the third ballot, Stevenson faced an uphill battle against Dwight D. Eisenhower, the popular Republican candidate.

Little divided the two presidential candidates on foreign policy; both were staunch Cold War warriors who implicitly endorsed the Truman administration's containment stance. Even so, Eisenhower acquiesced in the bitter attacks of his running mate, Richard M. Nixon, and Senator Joseph R. McCarthy on Stevenson and the Democrats, accusations that followed the K1C2 strategy of focusing on the issues of Korea, communism, and corruption in government.

Stevenson, who had supported the commitment in Korea, attempted to distance himself from the Truman administration and especially from its successive petty corruption scandals, establishing his campaign headquarters in Springfield, Illinois, and rarely asking the president to appear on his behalf. Stevenson delicately suggested that, although he supported the war, had he been president he would have avoided some of Truman's mistakes, trying to tread the fine line between disloyalty on the one hand and implication in the administration's problems on the other. He suggested that the United States should have given stronger guarantees of support to the Republic of Korea and should have been more cautious in crossing the 38th parallel. In practice, Stevenson's position on Korea differed little from that of Eisenhower, and he offered no new initiatives, but rather an indefinite continuation of the existing stalemate. He reversed Eisenhower's tactic of blaming the war's outbreak on Democratic incompetence, suggesting instead that responsibility lay with the Republicans for their failure to give sufficient support to the Truman administration's foreign policies. In October 1950, however, Eisenhower seized the initiative from Stevenson by promising to visit Korea in person if elected. Stevenson mocked but could not match this pledge, particularly since he himself had already privately decided to do likewise were he victorious.

Defeated in the November 1952 elections, Stevenson embarked in 1953 on a world tour of several months, during which he visited Korea and heard the U.S. military's view that full victory would be impossible without major additional U.S. troop and budgetary commitments. In articles for *Life* magazine, he expressed admiration for many of the Taiwan Nationalist government's social policies but admitted its police-state methods were unpopular and the army far weaker than it was portrayed; in Indo-China he

enunciated one of the earliest versions of the domino theory. Until his death Stevenson never doubted that the U.S. commitment to Korea, however expensive and frustrating, was justified as part of his country's overall Cold War policy.

In 1956 Stevenson again ran unsuccessfully for the presidency. Appointed U.S. ambassador to the UN in 1961 by John F. Kennedy as a consolation prize—he had wanted to become secretary of state—Stevenson spent the remainder of his life in that position. On 14 July 1965, he died in London of a sudden heart attack.

—*Priscilla Roberts*

References:

Broadwater, Jeff. *Adlai Stevenson and American Politics: The Odyssey of a Cold War Liberal.* New York: Twayne, 1994.

Johnson, Walter, ed. *The Papers of Adlai E. Stevenson.* 8 vols. Boston: Little, Brown, 1972–1979.

Martin, John Bartlow. *Adlai Stevenson of Illinois: The Life of Adlai E. Stevenson.* Garden City, NY: Doubleday, 1976.

———. *Adlai Stevenson and the World: The Life of Adlai E. Stevenson.* Garden City, NY: Doubleday, 1977.

McKeever, Porter. *Adlai Stevenson: His Life and Legacy.* New York: William Morrow, 1989.

See also: Eisenhower, Dwight D.; K1C2 (Korea, Communism, Corruption); McCarthy, Joseph R.; McCarthyism; Nixon, Richard Milhous; Truman, Harry S.

STRANGLE, Operation
(May–December 1951)

United Nations Command (UNC) bombing campaign. In late May 1951, as UNC forces pushed Communists troops toward the 38th parallel, the Fifth Air Force was given responsibility for the aerial interdiction of the Communists' seven main transport and communication highways leading to the front. Named for an Allied aerial interdiction campaign conducted in Italy in 1944 during World War II, Operation STRANGLE unfolded as a joint campaign in which northern South Korea was divided into three target areas to be attacked by air force fighter-bombers, Task Force 77 navy fighters, and 1st Marine Wing aircraft. Targets were mostly vehicular roads along with bridges, tunnels, and some rail lines.

Operations began on 31 May when F-51s "postholed" main roads with 500-pound bombs where repairs and bypasses were most difficult to effect. B-26s then dropped inert M-83 cluster bombs, which were detonated by Communist traffic. B-29s attacked bridges.

As June unfolded and Communist forces retreated, Allied air raids turned toward airfields, rail marshaling yards, and logistics supply centers. At first, Operation STRANGLE was very successful, but as UNC forces slowed their offensive in mid-June, Communist forces were able to resupply and regroup their front-line troops more easily, and Operation STRANGLE bore diminishing results.

Much as was the case twenty years later during COMMANDO HUNT operations in Vietnam, a key to the Communists' ability to thwart STRANGLE was the enormous number of labor troops deployed to quickly repair or bypass bomb damage. Repair materials such as rocks, timber, and churned-up soil were always in ready supply.

Also, as would be repeated in Vietnam, the difficulty in destroying trucks, the ease of repairing vehicles, and the vast number of new trucks supplied to the North Koreans by the Soviet Union made interdiction almost impossible. UNC air forces, with limited resources because of Cold War commitments in Europe and elsewhere, could not long afford to maintain the initial pace of the campaign.

By July, Far East Air Force (FEAF) officials reported that Operation STRANGLE was unsuccessful. Despite this report, the campaign continued, turning to new targets such as North Korean small-arms factories and Soviet and Chinese arms supplies moving by rail.

Rail traffic and tracks seemed an inviting target, but both proved to be difficult to destroy. Even when stretches of track or rail bridges were destroyed, Communist forces would simply transfer supplies from one train on one side to another on the other side. Here again, large labor crews usually repaired the damage very quickly. Worst of all, the Communists placed very effective antiaircraft artillery (AAA) batteries or MiG interceptor fields around regularly attacked targets, dramatically elevating the price for destroying the target.

By the end of July, U.S. Air Force planners estimated that it would take six to eight months of a concentrated air campaign to interdict enemy rail or road supply efforts. Air force leaders believed their resources allowed for no more than ninety days.

Plans for a new operation culminated on 18 August when a six-month operation, also named STRANGLE, began. To this day, there is controversy over whether this was STRANGLE II or STRANGLE I Phase II. According to FEAF officials, STRANGLE II, which lasted until 23 December, was designed to "cripple the Communist logistics system to the extent that rapid redeployment of their forces and supplies in support of a sustained offensive is impossible."

The original operation focused on truck traffic, while the second concentrated on destroying fifteen- to thirty-mile sections of rail track and/or rail bridges. STRANGLE II employed "group gaggles" of up to sixty-four fighter-bombers carrying 500-pound and 1,000-pound bombs to drop on the 56-inch–wide tracks. These raids were supported by B-29 missions against rail bridges and airfields. Only a direct hit did any real damage, and only 25 percent of bombs hit their targets. Considering that similar attacks in World War II had only a 12.9 percent success rate, the FEAF did well.

By November, rail lines were being destroyed faster than the Communists could repair them. As one official declared, "the United Nations' victory in the air battle against North Korea's railroads seemed imminent." An increase in MiG attacks and the effectiveness of new AAA batteries raised the price of the campaign to alarming levels. Most missions had to be reduced and replanned. They did not reach initial levels again until late November 1951. By then, massive Communist repair efforts had reversed the tide of battle.

In December, Fifth Air Force reports concluded that "Red railway repairmen and bridge builders 'have broken our railroad blockade … and won the use of all key rail arteries.'" As with most Korean air campaigns, STRANGLE I and II had both positive and negative results. On a positive note, senior North Korean prisoners captured later confirmed that their leaders had called off a major August offensive because of the destruction of 40,000 trucks. However, never in six months did the FEAF ever effectively stop Communist resupply of their combat forces nor "isolate the battlefield."

As was the case with aerial interdiction efforts in Vietnam, in Korea air power hobbled the Communists but did not destroy their capacity to wage war, and to do even that required efforts by both air and ground forces.

—*William Head*

References:
Futrell, Robert F. *The United States Air Force in Korea, 1950–1953.* Rev. ed. Washington, DC: Office of the Chief of Air Force History, 1983.
Mark, Eduard. *Aerial Interdiction: Air Power and the Land Battle in Three Wars.* Washington, DC: Center for Air Force History, 1994.
Thompson, Wayne. "The Air War over Korea." In *Winged Shield, Wing Sword: A History of the United States Air Force,* edited by Bernard C. Nalty. Washington, DC: United States Air Force History and Museum Program, 1997: 3–52.
See also: Antiaircraft Artillery; Logistics in the Korean War.

Strategic and Tactical Airlift in the Korean War

Air transport, including the use of helicopters for the movement of personnel and supplies, came into its own during the Korean War. The use of modern transport aircraft gave United Nations forces in Korea an important advantage over their North Korean and Chinese Communist opponents, who did not enjoy the speed and flexibility in logistical movements that air transport afforded. The distance from the United States to the Far East and the rugged terrain of Korea itself made the use of transport aircraft and helicopters for troop movements and the delivery of high-priority cargo extremely important, although ocean transport continued to be the principal means of transoceanic troop and cargo movements. About 1 percent of all cargo moved from the United States to Korea during the Korean War was moved by air, as was about 5 percent of all cargo moved from Japan to Korea. Most air shipments were restricted to critical items such as whole blood, blood plasma, rockets, radio batteries, and replacement parts.

Strategic Airlift

Strategic (intercontinental) airlift was the responsibility of the U.S. Air Force's Military Air Transport Service (MATS). Established in 1947, MATS was organized in three main divisions: Continental, Atlantic, and Pacific. In June 1950, the MATS Pacific Division was assigned fewer than 60 transport aircraft. On the outbreak of the war the Pacific Division was immediately reinforced with 40 aircraft from the Atlantic and Continental Divisions and two troop carrier groups with 75 C-54 Skymasters, the workhorse transport of the Korean War era. Canada also contributed Royal Canadian Air Force No. 426 Transport Squadron with 6 North Star aircraft, and Belgium added 2 C-54s.

By mid-August 1950 the MATS Pacific Division had over 250 aircraft flying on the three regular trans-Pacific routes, and deliveries to the Far East Command averaged 106 tons per day. The Great Circle route from McChord Air Force Base (AFB), Washington, to Tokyo via Alaska was 5,688 miles long and took thirty hours. The mid-Pacific route from Fairfield-Suisun (Travis) AFB, California, to Tokyo via Hawaii was 6,718 miles long and took 34 hours. The other Pacific route from Travis AFB to Japan via Hawaii, Johnson Island, Kwajalein, and Guam was over 8,000 miles long and took forty hours.

On the long Pacific flights, the C-54 could carry about five tons. At the peak there were 200 such aircraft available, each of which could make three round trips per month from the West Coast to Japan. One trans-Pacific round trip by a C-54 cost about $25,000, or $5,000 per ton (or a mere $2,500 per ton if the aircraft were loaded both ways). For every ton moved by MATS over the trans-Pacific routes, the U.S. Navy moved 270 tons by sea at a cost of only about $38 per ton. Commercial charter flights were also used.

In May 1950 Japan received only 70 tons of cargo by air per month; by the end of August 1950 it was receiving over 100 tons per day. In 1951 some 23,000 tons of cargo and 68,000 passengers were flown to the Far East. In 1952 the trans-Pacific airlift increased to 30,000 tons and 175,000 passengers plus about 54,000 medical evacuation patients. Aeromedical evacuation was an important innovation that significantly improved the survival rate and decreased the time

casualties had to wait before reaching definitive treatment. In all, 443,196 casualties were evacuated by air from Korea to the United States during the Korean War.

Tactical Airlift

Tactical (intratheater) airlift was the responsibility of the air force component of the U.S. Far East Command, Far East Air Force (FEAF), and it included flights from Japan to Korea as well as within Korea itself. When the war began, FEAF lacked sufficient intratheater airlift to meet the quickly expanding requirements. On 10 September 1950 all FEAF transport assets were consolidated under the Combat Cargo Command (Provisional). Commanded by Major General William H. Tunner, who had directed the airlift "over the Hump" in the China-Burma-India theater in World War II, as well as the Berlin airlift in 1948–1949, the Combat Cargo Command quickly expanded and by mid-December 1950 it had some 260 aircraft available. On 25 January 1951 the provisional Combat Cargo Command was disestablished and replaced by the 315th Air Division (Combat Cargo). Brigadier General John P. Henebry replaced General Tunner as commander of the 315th Air Division on 8 February 1951.

Units assigned to the Combat Cargo Command/ 315th Air Division included the 374th Troop Carrier Wing (two squadrons of C-54s, later C-124 Globemasters); the 21st Troop Carrier Squadron with C-47 Skytrains (also known as the "Dakota," or more popularly, as the "Gooneybird") augmented by the six C-47s of the Royal Hellenic Air Force's Flight 13 in November 1950 and by troop carriers of the Royal Thai Air Force; the 61st Troop Carrier Group with three C-54 squadrons; and the 314th Troop Carrier Group with four C-119 Flying Boxcar ("Packet") squadrons. The 483d Troop Carrier Wing, an Air Force Reserve unit from Portland, Oregon, equipped with C-119s, joined in spring 1952. The 315th Air Division (Combat Cargo) was also augmented by a Marine Corps squadron of R5Ds (C-54s). Since the runways and ground facilities of Korean airfields were generally limited, all of the 315th Air Division's transports were based in Japan, principally at Tachikawa Air Base outside Tokyo. In Korea the principal cargo fields were K-9 at Pusan (East), K-2 at Taegu (No. 1), K-14 at Kimpŏ near Seoul, K-46 at Hoengsŏng, and K-47 at Ch'unch'ŏn.

Air shipments from Japan to Korea began on 28 June 1950 when an aerial port of embarkation was established at Tachikawa. Air cargo movements from Tachikawa to Korea averaged 50 tons per day, and in October 1950 over 12,500 tons were delivered. Air shipments from Japan to Korea between 1 January and

30 June 1951 totaled some 85,799 short tons. During the course of the Korean War, the 315th Air Division, averaging 140 combat-ready aircraft, flew 15,836,400 ton miles and 128,336,700 passenger miles in 210,343 sorties. A total of 391,773 tons of freight, 2,605,591 passengers, and 307,804 medical evacuation patients were handled. In general, the amount of cargo moved by air within the Far East Command exceeded that moved over the trans-Pacific routes. Between 1 September 1950 and 1 March 1951, a total of 2,123,925 measurement tons of cargo were delivered by air to Korea, 1,612,148 measurement tons (75.9 percent) from Japan and 511,777 measurement tons (24.1 percent) directly from the United States. During the same six-month period, aircraft delivered an average of 28.49 pounds per person per day to Korea.

The FEAF air transport units participated in a number of special air operations during the Korean War. In October–November 1950, the bulk of the I and IX U.S. Corps north of P'yŏngyang were supported by air at a rate of 1,000 tons per day. During the December 1950 evacuation of Hŭngnam, the Combat Cargo Command transported 1,300 tons of cargo, 196 vehicles, 3,600 troops, and several hundred refugees. The 21st Troop Carrier Squadron and the 61st Troop Carrier Group received the Presidential Unit Citation for gallantry in support of operations around the Changjin (Chosin) Reservoir in December 1950, and in one of the more unusual operations, FEAF C-119s dropped eight treadway bridge sections to army engineers at Kot'o-ri, permitting Marine Corps and army units withdrawing from the Chosin Reservoir to bridge a gap in the roadway in the Funchilin Pass. FEAF troop carrier aircraft also supported parachute assaults by the 187th Airborne Regimental Combat Team at Sukch'ŏn-Sunch'ŏn north of P'yŏngyang on 20 October 1950 and at Munsan-ni on 23 March 1951.

Use of Helicopters

Helicopters had seen limited use for medical evacuation and liaison purposes during World War II, but in Korea the use of helicopters became a standard practice on the modern battlefield. The familiar Bell H-13 with two external litters was used extensively for aeromedical evacuation from the front lines to field hospitals, and in Korea helicopters were used for the first time to move combat troops and deliver supplies to forward units. U.S. Air Force and Marine Corps helicopter units led the way. The first helicopter medical evacuations in Korea were accomplished in late July 1950 by a detachment of the air force's 3d Air Rescue Squadron under the command of Captain Oscar N. Tibbetts. Marine Corps helicopter squadron VMO-6 accomplished its first medical evacuation by helicopter on 4 August 1950. On 11 November 1951, Marine Helicopter

Transport Squadron 161 lifted 950 troops to the front and returned an equal number to the rear. Another Marine battalion was relieved by helicopter the following month, and the success of the Marine Corps use of helicopters for troop movements prompted Eighth Army commander in Korea Lieutenant General Matthew B. Ridgway to request that four army helicopter battalions be made available. By the end of the war, aeromedical evacuation, troop movements, and supply deliveries by helicopter were almost routine procedures. U.S. Army aviators flew Mobile Army Surgical Hospital (MASH) H-13s, which were attached to each infantry division.

—*Charles R. Shrader*

References:

Cowdrey, Albert E. *United States Army in the Korean War: The Medic's War.* Washington, DC: U. S. Army Center of Military History, 1987.

Futrell, Robert F. *The United States Air Force in Korea, 1950–1953.* Rev. ed. Washington, DC: Office of the Chief of Air Force History, 1983.

Hermes, Walter G. *United States Army in the Korean War: Truce Tent and Fighting Front.* Washington, DC: Office of the Chief of Military History, 1966.

Huston, James A. *Guns and Butter, Powder and Rice: U. S. Army Logistics in the Korean War.* Selinsgrove, PA: Susquehanna University Press, 1989.

See also: Aircraft (Principal Combat); Helicopter Employment; Helicopter Types and Nomenclature; Logistics in the Korean War; Military Air Transport Service (MATS); Military Sea Transport Service (MSTS); United States Air Force (USAF); United States Navy.

Stratemeyer, George E.
(1890–1969)

U.S. Air Force general and commander of the Far East Air Force (FEAF) during the Korean War. Born on 24 November 1890, in Cincinnati, Ohio, George Edward Stratemeyer grew up in Peru, Indiana. He attended the U.S. Military Academy at West Point with Dwight D. Eisenhower and Omar N. Bradley, graduating in 1915. He then served in the infantry on the Texas border.

Stratemeyer completed flight training in 1917 at Rockwell Field in San Diego, California, and was commander at the School of Military Aeronautics at Ohio State University during World War I. He was chief test pilot at Kelly Air Force Base, Texas, and Chanute Field, Illinois, and transferred to the Army Air Corps in 1920. Stratemeyer then spent three years in Hawaii and taught tactics at West Point between 1924 and 1929. He graduated from the Air Corps Tactical School at Langley Field, Virginia, in 1930, and the Command and General Staff School at Fort Leavenworth, Kansas, in 1932. After teaching at the latter for several years, Stratemeyer was promoted to lieutenant colonel and commanded the 7th Bombardment Group at Hamilton

Field, California, from 1936 to 1938. In the following years he graduated from the Army War College, was appointed commander of the Southeast Air Corps Training Center at Maxwell Field, Alabama, and served as chief of the Air Corps in Washington, D.C. He became a major general in 1942.

During World War II Stratemeyer directed air operations in the China-Burma-India theater, where his troops performed major air supply work. In September 1943 Stratemeyer proposed a plan whereby B-29s would bomb Japan from a base in India and small bases in China, and President Franklin D. Roosevelt approved Stratemeyer's plan, code-named MATTER-HORN. By April 1944 Stratemeyer was commander of the Army Air Force in the China theater with his headquarters at Chongqing (Chungking) through March 1946. Stratemeyer was widely praised for his efforts in the Chongqing airlift, in which 200,000 Chinese troops and 5,000 horses were relocated from western to eastern China. He was promoted to lieutenant general in 1945.

In February 1946 Stratemeyer returned to the United States to supervise the new Air Defense Command. He promoted air force autonomy and a large Air National Guard in the 1948 reorganization in which the Air Defense Command was renamed the Continental Air Command. Known for convincing subordinates to do what he wanted, Stratemeyer was considered a skilled military air tactician. He was certainly a forceful champion of a strengthened air force.

In April 1949 Stratemeyer moved to Tokyo as commanding general of the Far East Air Force (FEAF). This consisted of the Fifth Air Force in Japan, Thirteenth Air Force in the Philippines, Twentieth Air Force in Okinawa, eighteen groups of fighters and fighter-bombers, and one wing of B-26 and B-29 bombers. He was flying between San Francisco and Hawaii en route to Tokyo when the Korean War began. When he landed in Seoul, Republic of Korea Army (ROKA, South Korean) troops were in retreat and Americans were evacuating.

President Harry S. Truman ordered U.S. forces into action south of the 38th parallel but believed that air power was the best way to stop the invasion. Stratemeyer agreed and helped organize direct air support during the crucial early days of the war. He ordered air attacks on advancing Korean People's Army (KPA, North Korean) forces and air cover for the evacuation of U.S. civilians from Seoul; and he flew reconnaissance missions and planned how to use available combat aircraft to defend South Korea. Stratemeyer proudly noted that three-fourths of the men under his command during the Korean War were from the air force reserve training program he had established in peacetime.

When General Douglas MacArthur visited Korea on 29 June Stratemeyer asked that he approve air operations to gain control of the air and to identify targets for future air attacks in North Korea. President Truman supported MacArthur's order for bombing North Korea, and Stratemeyer cabled Fifth Air Force commander Major General Earle E. Partridge: "Take out North Korean airfields. No publicity. MacArthur approves." The goal was to "isolate the battlefield" and to attack communication lines, factories, and industries vital to the North Koreans.

The United States quickly gained air superiority over the small Korean People's Air Force (KPAF, North Korean) and proceeded to bomb supply lines and provide tactical support to ground forces. Some 100 heavy bombers in Stratemeyer's command struck a twenty-seven–mile area along the upper Naktong River in August. A thousand tons of bombs were dropped within twenty-six minutes to rout KPA troops. This was one of the most massive U.S. bombings since Normandy. It was, however, unsuccessful. Stratemeyer instructed that no similar bombings would be ordered unless conditions were desperate.

After the massive intervention by the Chinese People's Volunteer Army (CPVA, Chinese Communist) at the end of November, Chinese and Soviet jet aircraft posed a threat to United Nations operations in far North Korea along and south of the Yalu River, an area known as MiG Alley. With United Nations Command (UNC) aircraft too far away to escort bombing missions to the North, Stratemeyer devised new tactics to meet this situation. Allied air power, however, was unable to prevent Chinese resupply overland. It never could "isolate the battlefield."

Stratemeyer opposed MacArthur's flouting of directives, such as ordering the bombing of bridges across the Yalu in early November 1950. He told Air Force Chief of Staff General Hoyt S. Vandenberg and President Truman that such raids should be limited to south of the river, restrictions that MacArthur later blamed for the failure of his Home-by-Christmas offensive. Stratemeyer did upset Secretary of Defense George C. Marshall when he suggested that the air force should be allowed to pursue unlimited military operations against China. When UNC troops halted the Chinese offensive, Stratemeyer encouraged strategic bombing of industries and supply centers in the North instead of supporting Allied ground forces. This heightened the army–air force close support controversy.

Although loyal to MacArthur, Stratemeyer did not question the presidential authority to remove him from command. In a March 1951 press release, Stratemeyer stressed, "A decision to extend [our operations] beyond the confines of Korea is not one that should be made by the field commander."

Stratemeyer suffered a heart attack in May 1951, and General Otto P. Weyland took over his command. Retiring from active duty on 31 January 1952, Stratemeyer focused his attention on anti-Communist activities. He attempted to convince the Senate not to censure Senator Joseph R. McCarthy, and in 1954 he chaired Ten Million Americans Mobilizing for Justice, collecting signatures opposing such censure. Angry about restrictions placed on the U.S. military during the Korean War, Stratemeyer testified to the Senate Subcommittee on Internal Security in 1954: "We were required to lose the war. We weren't allowed to win it.... I wasn't permitted to do a job, and certainly General MacArthur was handcuffed." Stratemeyer died in Orlando, Florida, on 9 August 1969.

—*Elizabeth D. Schafer*

References:

Appleman, Roy E. *South to the Naktong, North to the Yalu.* Washington, DC: Office of the Chief of Military History, 1961.

Blair, Clay. *The Forgotten War: America in Korea, 1950–1953.* New York: Times Books, 1987.

Current Biography, 1951. New York: H. W. Wilson, 1952.

Futrell, Robert F. *The United States Air Force in Korea, 1950–1953.* Rev. ed. Washington, DC: Office of the Chief of Air Force History, 1983.

New York Times, 11 August 1969.

See also: Aerial Combat; Air Power in the War; Airborne Operations; Aircraft (Principal Combat); Bradley, Omar Nelson; China, People's Republic of: Air Force; Close Air Support; Eisenhower, Dwight D.; Far East Air Force (FEAF); Home-by-Christmas Offensive; MacArthur, Douglas; Marshall, George C.; McCarthy, Joseph R.; MiG Alley; Partridge, Earle Everard; Truman, Harry S.; United Nations Command Air Forces; United States Air Force (USAF); Vandenberg, Hoyt S.; Weyland, Otto P.

Struble, Arthur D.
(1894–1983)

U.S. Navy officer, commander of the Seventh Fleet at the outset of the Korean War. Born in Portland, Oregon, on 28 June 1894, Arthur D. Struble won an appointment to the U.S. Naval Academy in Annapolis, Maryland, graduating in 1915.

Commissioned in the U.S. Navy, Struble spent World War I on board the battleship *South Dakota*, the cruiser *St. Louis*, the store ship *Glacier*, and the destroyer *Stevens*. In 1919 and 1920 Struble served as executive officer and then commanding officer of the destroyer *Shubrick*, which was involved in the Haiti crisis of that period. For the next two decades his assignments alternated between service at sea on battle staffs and warships and ashore at the U.S. Naval Academy, navy headquarters in Washington, and the naval district headquarters in San Francisco, California. The 7 December 1941 Japanese attack on Pearl Harbor found him in command of the light

cruiser *Trenton*, then operating near the Panama Canal.

After a tour in the office of the chief of naval operations early in the war, Struble served as chief of staff of the Western Naval Task Force, the U.S. Navy's major command for the June 1944 Normandy invasion. Convinced of his special talents in amphibious warfare, in August 1944 the navy gave him command of an amphibious group that led the assaults on Leyte, Mindoro, and Luzon in the Philippines. His outstanding performance in these operations earned him the Distinguished Service Medal.

From September 1945 to April 1948, Struble directed the Pacific Fleet's mine clearance and amphibious forces, gaining valuable insight on coastal and inshore operations in the Far East. Rear Admiral Struble complemented this experience with service in Washington as deputy chief of naval operations (Operations) and as naval deputy on the Joint Chiefs of Staff.

In May 1950 Struble was promoted to vice admiral and selected as commander of the Seventh Fleet. In Washington when the Korean People's Army (KPA, North Korean) invaded the Republic of Korea (South Korea), Struble flew to the Far East in time to direct the first carrier strikes on P'yŏngyang. At the same time he oversaw execution of President Harry S. Truman's order on 26 June that the Seventh Fleet "neutralize" the Strait of Taiwan by placing naval forces between mainland China and Taiwan. Surface ships, carrier-based and shore-based aircraft, and submarines of his command promptly established patrols in the disputed waters off China. Units of the navy's Taiwan Patrol Force would carry out this mission for the next two decades.

The right man in the right place, Struble developed the operational plan and led the forces that executed the September 1950 masterful amphibious assault at Inch'ŏn (Operation CHROMITE). Under his control, as commander of Task Force Seven, for Operation CHROMITE were 230 U.S. and Allied aircraft carriers, the battleship *Missouri*, cruisers, destroyers, minesweepers, and amphibious vessels and the U.S. X Corps, composed of the 1st Marine Division and the army's 7th Infantry Division. Careful staff planning, accurate intelligence, successful deception operations, and effective logistic support measures helped ensure the success of Operation CHROMITE. The Inch'ŏn assault was a classic demonstration of amphibious warfare. General Douglas MacArthur's bold plan, executed by Vice Admiral Struble and the Marines, soldiers, sailors, and airmen of the United Nations coalition under his command, soon freed South Korea from the invading KPA.

In addition to the landings at Inch'ŏn and Wŏnsan, the latter in northeast Korea, and the successful evacuation of the X Corps from Hŭngnam in December, Struble directed the fleet's air interdiction and close air support strikes, naval gunfire support, and other combat operations during the critical first phase of the Korean War. Naval forces under his command helped stop KPA ground offensives and protect the Allied reinforcements pouring into the port of Pusan, and brought naval power to bear on KPA forces ashore.

Detached as commander of the Seventh Fleet on 28 March 1951, Vice Admiral Struble returned to the United States to lead the First Fleet on the West Coast and then to serve with the Joint Chiefs of Staff in Washington. From May 1952 to May 1955 he worked on the Military Staff Committee of the United Nations. Before retirement from the navy on 1 July 1956, Struble commanded the Eastern Sea Frontier and the Atlantic Reserve Fleet. Vice Admiral Struble died in Chevy Chase, Maryland, on 1 May 1983.

—*Edward J. Marolda*

References:

Cagle, Malcolm W., and Frank A. Manson. *The Sea War in Korea.* Annapolis, MD: Naval Institute Press, 1957.

Field, James A., Jr. *History of United States Naval Operations: Korea.* Washington, DC: U.S. Government Printing Office, 1962.

U.S. Navy Biographical Files, Operational Archives, Naval Historical Center, Washington, D.C.

Utz, Curtis A. *Assault from the Sea: The Amphibious Landing at Inchon.* Washington, DC: Naval Historical Center, 1994.

See also: Inch'ŏn Landings: Operation CHROMITE; MacArthur, Douglas; Truman, Harry S.; United States Navy.

Student Volunteer Troops (Republic of Korea)

In July 1950, in a gesture that had little concrete impact on the war, student volunteer troops were sent to augment Republic of Korea (ROK, South Korean) armed forces. In March 1949 the ROK government established the Student National Defense Corps, an organization whose objectives included not merely strengthening the country's security through compulsory military training but also inculcating civic values in the nation's youth. All university students were expected to devote a certain number of hours to military training.

The Republic of Korea Army (ROKA) was only established in 1948, and at the outbreak of war it was still small, consisting of 67,559 officers and men, who were poorly trained and underequipped. At the start of the war, the ROKA was virtually overwhelmed by Northern forces, and for the most part retreated in disarray. Calling on every available reservoir of personnel, the ROK government quickly organized student volunteer units, which were sent to the battlefront from July 1950 onward to fight with the regular army. By no means were all these volunteers particularly eager to experience active service, and few if any had adequate

military training. Those unable to learn quickly soon died in combat, and student casualties were high. In the war's early stages the ROKA—disorganized, ill-equipped, and ill-paid—was badly led and fought poorly, leading to high desertion rates. These characteristics were even more pronounced among the untried student volunteers.

In spring 1951 the U.S. military, determined to improve the disappointing performance of its South Korean allies, instituted a concentrated training program for all ROK armed forces. This included student volunteers, who were treated as regular troops for the conflict's duration. Early in the war almost all ROKA divisions at the front were attached to U.S. Army units. This modernized training program cut casualties and losses of equipment by fifty percent and made the ROKA into an effective fighting force. It also professionalized the surviving student volunteer troops and, at least for the period of the war, virtually eliminated the difference between them and other conscripts.

After the war, military training was still a compulsory part of the program of study for South Korean college students. The Student National Defense Corps remained in existence until 1988, when it was abolished.

—*Priscilla Roberts*

References:

Paik, Sun Yup. *From Pusan to Panmunjom.* New York: Brassey's, 1992.

Sawyer, Robert K. *Military Advisors in Korea: KMAG in Peace and War.* Washington, DC: Office of the Chief of Military History, U.S. Army, 1962.

See also: Korea, Republic of: Army (ROKA); Korean Augmentation to the United States Army (KATUSA).

Sukch'ŏn and Sunch'ŏn Airborne Operation (20–23 October 1950)

One of two United Nations command (UNC) airborne operations during the Korean War. It involved the 187th Airborne Regimental Combat Team at Sukch'ŏn and Sunch'ŏn north of the Democratic People's Republic (DPRK, North Korean) capital of P'yŏngyang.

UNC commander General Douglas MacArthur had hoped to use airborne forces in conjunction with his amphibious landing at Inch'ŏn, but none were then available in the theater of operations. The 4,000-man 187th, commanded by Colonel Frank S. Bowen, Jr., arrived in Japan only on 20 September 1950. Its operational readiness date was 21 October; pending this MacArthur held the 187th under his control in GHQ (general headquarters) reserve at Kimpŏ Airfield near Seoul.

With the UN advance north of the 38th parallel, MacArthur planned to employ the 187th in air drops some twenty-five miles north of P'yŏngyang to cut off the escape north of Korean People's Army (KPA, North Korean) units and DPRK officials and to rescue UN prisoners of war. This would be a formidable task for a regimental combat team, especially one that had never made a combat jump and was light on equipment and firepower support.

The operation was planned to coincide with the projected 187th combat readiness date but, when he learned that the DPRK government had fled P'yŏngyang along with much of the KPA, MacArthur moved it up to 20 October. The plan called for the paratroopers to cut two highways and a rail line running north from P'yŏngyang.

On 20 October the troopers loaded aboard 113 C-119 Flying Boxcars and C-47 Skytrains of the 324th and 21st Troop Carrier Squadrons. The congestion of so many aircraft at Kimpŏ Airfield for this operation put a crimp in other activities there, including an emergency supply lift to Eighth Army. At noon the weather cleared over the drop zones and the planes took off, escorted by fighters of the Far East Air Force (FEAF). This was the first time C-119s were employed in a combat jump.

Before the drop, FEAF fighters and fighter-bombers strafed and bombed the drop zones. The air armada included MacArthur's own airplane from Tokyo with the general and reporters aboard. MacArthur wanted to see the jump and have his presence noted.

The drops, led by Bowen himself, began about 1400. The troopers encountered no antiaircraft fire and only sporadic ground fire. Only one trooper of some 2,800 was killed in the drop. Forty-seven were injured. For the first time in a combat operation, heavy equipment was also parachuted. This included vehicles, twelve 105-mm howitzers of the 674th Field Artillery Battalion on wooden pallets (nine of which were recovered in serviceable condition), and tons of ammunition and other equipment. The drop was highly successful.

Once on the ground the 1st Battalion secured hills east and north of Sukch'ŏn and blocked the road. The 3d Battalion also quickly secured its objective of several low hills south of Sukch'ŏn. There was little KPA opposition.

At Sunch'ŏn the 2d Battalion also encountered little KPA resistance. Two of its companies set up positions south and west of Sunch'ŏn, while the third advanced on Sunch'ŏn. It was soon involved in a firefight with what turned out to be elements of the Republic of Korea Army (ROKA, South Korean) 6th Infantry Division advancing toward the North Korean border with China. No one had informed the paratroopers that the 6th Division would be there that day, but fortunately there were few casualties before fire was halted.

That afternoon MacArthur landed in P'yŏngyang and described the paratroop operation as a brilliant stroke that would bring about the final destruction of the KPA. He estimated some 30,000 KPA were trapped between the 187th and the UN forces now moving north of P'yŏngyang. He did not mention the ROKA 6th Division.

On 21 October the 3d Battalion moved south from Sukch'ŏn to meet the advancing 27th British Commonwealth Brigade of the U.S. I Corps. North of Yongyu the 3d Battalion ran into the rear-guard KPA 239th Regiment. During the night of 21–22 October the 239th attempted to break through the paratroopers but was unsuccessful. The KPA regiment of some 2,500 men was all but destroyed. The 3d Battalion reported it killed about 800 and captured another 680.

On 23 October the 187th returned to P'yŏngyang. In the entire operation it had suffered 111 casualties, but more than a third of these were jump-related. While the 187th had captured 3,818 KPA prisoners, the operation was too late; none of these were high-ranking officers or DPRK officials, and the operation had failed to cut off the bulk of the KPA forces, which had already withdrawn north of Sukch'ŏn and Sunch'ŏn when the operation began. Most UN prisoners of war had also been withdrawn to the north or massacred.

—*Spencer C. Tucker*

References:

Appleman, Roy E. *South to the Naktong, North to the Yalu.* Washington, DC: Office of the Chief of Military History, 1961.

Blair, Clay. *The Forgotten War: America in Korea, 1950–1953.* New York: Times Books, 1987.

James, D. Clayton. *The Years of MacArthur.* Vol. 3, *Triumph and Disaster, 1945–1964.* Boston: Houghton Mifflin, 1985.

See also: Airborne Operations; Inch'ŏn Landings: Operation CHROMITE; MacArthur, Douglas.

Sup'ung (Suiho) and the Korean Electric Power Plant Campaign
(23–26 June 1952)

In the summer of 1952, with armistice negotiations at a year-long impasse, Far East Air Force (FEAF) officials proposed a new campaign against North Korean hydroelectric plants. This, they believed, would force the Communists to accept United Nations Command (UNC) truce terms.

On 17 June 1952, Lieutenant General Mark W. Clark, who had replaced Lieutenant General Matthew B. Ridgway as UN commander on 28 April, approved the strikes. Two days later, the Joint Chiefs of Staff and President Harry S. Truman confirmed the action, which lasted from 23 to 27 June.

The targets were the Sup'ung, Changjin, Pujŏn, and Hŏch'ŏn power plants. The Japanese had built this large hydroelectric power complex on the Yalu River.

At the time it was the fourth largest hydroelectric complex in the world. Centered around Sup'ung, the complex employed impounding dams with adjacent powerhouses to exploit the large volume of water. By 1948, it produced 300,000 kilowatts of power, with half of this going to Manchuria as surplus.

Plans called for Fifth Air Force fighter-bombers, FEAF bombers, and navy fighters/fighter-bombers to strike Sup'ung first on 23 June. Once the attack was under way, the other dams would be hit. In conjunction, B-29s were to make night raids against Changjin. The attacks, scheduled to begin at 0930, were delayed by bad weather until 1600. While 84 F-86s patrolled overhead, 35 navy Skyraiders from the carriers *Boxer*, *Princeton*, and *Philippine Sea* dive-bombed Sup'ung. Simultaneously, 35 F9F jets flew flak suppression. This was followed by attacks from 79 F-84s and 45 F-80s, which dropped 145 tons of bombs.

The attack was a complete success. Ground fire was completely neutralized. Even though 250 MiG-15s were stationed thirty-eight miles away at Dandong (Antung), none confronted the F-86s. In fact, 160 fled to Manchuria. Only two U.S. planes suffered minor damage. The raid was so successful that planned night bomber raids were diverted elsewhere.

Reconnaissance reported that 90 percent of North Korean power had been knocked out: eleven of the thirteen power plants were "unserviceable" and the other two "doubtful." In addition, thirty of fifty-one major Chinese factories in Manchuria were without power. Sup'ung alone was 120,000 kilowatts short for the last half of 1952, and the Chinese could never compensate for this loss.

Smaller attacks continued through the night of 27 June. Altogether, the four-day effort had seen 730 5AF fighter-bomber sorties and 238 air superiority sorties without a single loss. The Seventh Fleet had flown 546 sorties, losing two planes to ground fire, and both pilots were rescued. FEAF commander General Otto P. Weyland later declared that the hydroelectric attacks were one of two strikes that were "spectacular on their own merit."

Throughout the remainder of the year, as Communist engineers and repair personnel attempted to repair the dam complex, FEAF Bomber Command sent in B-26s and B-29s on night raids against the dams. On 12–13 September, six B-29s, carrying 2,000-pound armor-piercing bombs, attacked Sup'ung, supported by six B-26s, which knocked out eight of thirty large searchlights and suppressed flak, and by six other radar-jamming B-29s. While one B-29 was lost and three severely damaged, they scored five direct hits, totally neutralizing Sup'ung again.

By February 1953, Fifth Air Force intelligence discovered that two generators at Sup'ung were again

operating. Expecting more B-29 raids, the Communists had positioned 141 heavy guns near the complex. Instead, on 15 February, 22 F-84s of the 474th Fighter Bomber Wing, supported by 82 F-86s, made a low-level raid. It was a total success, and the Sabre jets downed three MiGs, without loss.

In May General Clark gave FEAF approval to strike Sup'ung as needed. To this end the 5AF kept Sup'ung shut down with raids on 10–11 and 30 May. Another raid was in the works but never run because the final truce was signed.

There has been disagreement over the effectiveness of the Sup'ung raids. Some have argued that they had little if any effect on Communist negotiators. They argue that massive protests in Great Britain over the raids actually hardened the Communist position. They also questioned whether the raids had any major impact on the North Korean economy or its ability to wage war.

It is clear that many in Korea and Manchuria suffered, since almost all of the electric power from these plants was shut off for almost all of the last thirteen months of the war. Moreover, the simultaneous destruction of irrigation dams and dikes flooded fields, destroyed crops, and interrupted food production and supply. This and the threat of further attacks had to have had some influence on Communist leaders.

As was the case in Vietnam, the misery of the common citizen mattered little to Chinese or North Korean leaders. Even so, it seems likely that, at least to some extent, the Sup'ung raids, especially the June campaign, forced Communist negotiators to accept UN terms before the effects of the raids became too severe. To this end, the Sup'ung campaign did have an impact on the outcome of the Korean War.

—*William Head*

References:

Clodfelter, Mark. *The Limits of Air Power: The American Bombing of North Vietnam.* New York: Free Press, 1989.

Futrell, Robert F. *The United States Air Force in Korea, 1950–1953.* Rev. ed. Washington, DC: Office of the Chief of Air Force History, 1983.

Momyer, William W. *Air Power in Three Wars: WWII, Korea, Vietnam.* Washington, DC: Department of the Air Force, 1978.

Thompson, Wayne. "The Air War over Korea." In *Winged Shield, Wing Sword: A History of the United States Air Force,* edited by Bernard C. Nalty. Washington, DC: U.S. Air Force History and Museum Program, 1997: 3–52.

See also: Clark, Mark W; Far East Air Force (FEAF); Joint Chiefs of Staff (JCS); Ridgway, Matthew Bunker; Truman, Harry S.; Weyland, Otto P.

Syngman Rhee
(1875–1965)

First president of the Republic of Korea, from 1948 to 1960. Born in Hwanghae Province, Korea on 26 April

1875, to an aristocratic though impoverished Korean family, Syngman Rhee received an education that encompassed both Asian and Western traditions. After classical Confucian training he studied at an American Methodist missionary school, where he learned English. By his late teens Rhee was a dedicated Korean nationalist, determined to end his country's domination by Japan. In 1896 he and like-minded associates formed the Independence Club, which the Japanese destroyed two years later. Rhee was arrested and tortured and remained in prison until 1904, during which time he converted to Christianity.

Upon his release he went to study in the United States and, after some time at Harvard and George Washington Universities, in 1910 was awarded a Ph.D. from Princeton University, the first Korean to gain a doctorate there. His return to Korea that year coincided with the complete Japanese takeover of the country.

For the subsequent thirty-five years Rhee remained in exile in the United States, advocating Korean independence and supported by donations from the Korean community and American sympathizers. In 1919 he was elected president of the Korean Provisional Government based in Washington, although some years later he lost this position because of internal factionalism within the Korean exile movement. During the Second World War Rhee became Korea's best-known political figure overseas, campaigning ardently for Korea's independence and, after the Japanese surrender, its unification.

On 16 October 1945 a U.S. military aircraft returned the seventy-year-old Rhee to Korea, which was then divided at the 38th parallel into Soviet and U.S. zones of occupation. Each of the occupying powers swiftly moved to press its claims to political leadership and power of its preferred Korean candidate. On 20 October Rhee delivered an address at the welcoming ceremonies for the U.S. forces, attended by commander of U.S. forces in Korea Lieutenant General John W. Hodge, while the Soviets elevated young Communist anti-Japanese guerrilla leader Kim Il Sung as their chosen protégé. From then until his fall from power in 1960, Rhee's often stormy dealings with his U.S. sponsors would illustrate the numerous difficulties and pitfalls of the client-patron international relationships on which the United States embarked in Asia after the Second World War, problems equally characteristic of its relations with the Chinese Guomindang's Jiang Jieshi (Chiang Kai-shek) and successive leaders of the Republic of Vietnam.

By October 1945 two rival provisional governments, the leftist Korean People's Republic (KPR), with a strong Communist emphasis, and the conservative Korean Democratic Party (KDP) had emerged.

Neither party was recognized by the occupying powers, which had committed themselves to setting up a United Nations (UN) trusteeship to administer Korea for the indefinite future. Both political groupings nominated Rhee as one of their leaders and both united in opposing the trusteeship plan, but otherwise they had little in common.

Rhee himself quickly alienated his American protectors by using fiercely anti-Soviet rhetoric and attacking the trusteeship scheme, tactics that dug a deep rift between him and Hodge. Initially Rhee used his prestige as a patriotic scholar-statesman and long-time advocate of Korean independence to persuade leaders of both the KPR and KDP to join together and oppose Korean trusteeship in a Council for the Rapid Realization of Korean Independence, the one cause on which all could unite. Before long, hostility between elements of the left and right, together with Rhee's own undisguised antipathy for its Communist members, led to its fragmentation. Rhee allied himself with officials of the KDP and with leaders from yet another exile group, the Chongqing-based Korean Provisional Government (KPG), closely tied to China's Guomindang, whose members also began to return that fall.

In December 1945 U.S. occupation authorities banned the left-wing KPG, using as a pretext its continuing claims to be the government of Korea. Although Hodge did not publicly endorse the more conservative KDP, he increasingly leaned in its favor. Even so, Rhee's obstinacy and outspokenness in dealing with the U.S. commander and other representatives quickly became and remained legendary.

By January 1946 each occupying power had established control in its own zone. During the next two years, successive attempts to reach agreement on the establishment of a UN trusteeship overseeing a unified provisional government of all Korea—the strategy that the United States and the Soviet Union endorsed at the Moscow Conference of December 1945—ran aground because of the reluctance of both occupying powers to contemplate a settlement that their rival might be able to exploit to win a preponderant position on the Korea peninsula. Talks finally collapsed in August 1947. Meanwhile, two separate and fundamentally different regimes began to emerge. In the North the Korean Communist Party under Kim Il Sung strengthened its hold, and opposition to its rule was forcibly eliminated. In early 1947, elections in the North brought about the formation of the People's Assembly and People's Committee, headed by Kim Il Sung, as North Korea's governing bodies. In the South, assassinations of politicians of every orientation became common, complicating the U.S. military government's unsuccessful attempts to organize a coalition of moderates that would exclude both rightist extremists such as Rhee and his counterparts on the left.

Rhee campaigned throughout the South, his emotional demands for Korean independence reinforcing his patriotic credentials, and created solid bases of support inside the police and the bureaucracy. His followers established youth groups and unions opposed to those backed by the Communists, and, despite his poor relations with the Americans, by late 1947 Rhee's skill and acumen had positioned him to become the U.S. zone's indisputable leading political figure. In May 1948 elections in the South, held under UN authorization, conservative forces won a majority. Shortly thereafter, in a 180–16 vote, the new National Assembly elected Rhee as first president of the newly established Republic of Korea (ROK), which took over the responsibilities of the U.S. military government and quickly won American diplomatic recognition.

Rhee almost immediately faced challenges from the National Assembly to his presidential authority over cabinet appointments and the establishment of a parliamentary system, which he beat back only by expending substantial political capital. By introducing land reform, however, he enhanced his standing with farmers, while compensating landowners with formerly Japanese industrial plants. He also instituted policies that successfully combated illiteracy.

Rhee's outlook was always that of a Confucian, authoritarian ruler governing for what he perceived as the good of the country, and he had little affinity for liberal democracy. He successfully and bloodily suppressed armed Communist guerrilla uprisings in the South, backed by the North, and he purged suspected Communists in the bureaucracy. Subsequently, Rhee and other politicians declared that the ROK's military forces should march north and unify the country on their terms, and in 1949 and 1950 there were frequent border clashes along the 38th parallel, incidents in which neither side was guiltless.

These episodes and Rhee's rhetoric alarmed U.S. officials, who decided in 1948 to withdraw their forces entirely from the peninsula, a process that was completed in June 1949. Washington was unresponsive to Rhee's demands for further military aid, and U.S. representatives were also concerned by Rhee's reluctance to raise taxes to fight inflation and his readiness to postpone scheduled National Assembly elections. Even so, U.S. support assured the ROK substantial assistance from the UN as well as from the Economic Cooperation Administration, and the establishment of a training program for the South Korean armed forces, to which the 500-strong U.S. Korea Military Advisory Group (KMAG) remained attached. Even so, by May 1950 Rhee's domestic political dominance was deteri-

orating; in a general election in which 85 percent of the population voted, his party won 56 seats in the General Assembly, as opposed to 26 for the Democratic Nationalist Party and other opposition groups and 128 independents.

Both sides bore responsibility for the sporadic border clashes. But on 25 June 1950 the Democratic People's Republic of Korea (North Korea) launched a well-planned, full-scale invasion of the ROK. Recent findings from newly opened Soviet and East European archives have disproved earlier allegations by such historians and journalists as Bruce Cumings and I. F. Stone that Rhee, in collaboration with the United States, deliberately provoked the war.

Rhee initially ignored the U.S. ambassador's advice to leave Seoul and relocate his government at Pusan, stating that he preferred death at enemy hands to doing so, but the imminent prospect that this fate would materialize persuaded him to follow the counsel he had earlier rejected. Once UN troops reversed the tide of war and achieved military success in fall 1950, crossing the 38th parallel, Rhee claimed the right to appoint provisional governors in liberated areas of the North. The UN refused; it claimed authority not only to govern such areas but also to institute Korea-wide elections once the war had ended.

Throughout the war Rhee demanded the unification of all Korea under his leadership and attempted to sabotage all measures that might undercut this goal. His aim of a united Korea was increasingly at odds with the U.S. and West European readiness to negotiate a settlement that would effectively restore the antebellum status quo. In late 1950 Rhee told President Harry S. Truman that the Korean people demanded their country's unification and he would refuse to recognize any settlement reached by the United States or other powers that did not accomplish this objective. This ultimatum further soured the always poor relations between the two leaders, which remained frosty until Truman left office in 1953. Rhee was, however, sufficiently astute to realize that public or private criticism of UN Command (UNC) forces and tactics, even those with which he disagreed, such as the UNC policy of keeping South Korean troops under strict control and discipline, would be counterproductive. He enthusiastically endorsed General Douglas MacArthur's aim of expanding the war to Chinese territory and continuing it to complete victory, and he was shocked when in April 1951 Truman removed the insubordinate general from his UNC command.

Other issues generated tension between the United States and Rhee. The war experience revealed the level of official corruption and maladministration in the National Guard, whose survivors struggled back to Seoul in rags complaining of nonexistent supplies because of financial misappropriation. Atrocities by ROK Army (ROKA) troops, most notably the February 1951 Kŏch'ang massacre, in which 719 villagers died (and the official investigation of which Rhee quickly ended), tarnished the image of the ROK armed forces and led their American allies to regard them with disgust. Increasingly, Western officials criticized Rhee's administration, but they did little to prevent his subverting of the constitution so as to remain president in the elections of 1952; even President Truman merely expressed concern over the situation.

Rhee and newly appointed minister of the interior and political ally Yi Pŏm-sŏk (Lee Bum Suk) organized a campaign of intimidation against his opponents and worked with the National Assembly, which was empowered to elect the president, to impose martial law on the temporary capital of Pusan in May 1952. Rhee threatened to disband the assembly if it failed to allow popular elections for the presidency.

In early July, after an assassination attempt on Rhee that may well have been staged and that served as a pretext to arrest many of his opponents, the National Assembly bowed to pressure, acceded to Rhee's demands, and amended the constitution to create an upper house and a popularly elected president. Predictably, in subsequent elections in August 1952, Rhee obtained 5 million votes and his closest opponent a mere 800,000. Rhee's repression of his political opponents and his intransigence led both the Truman and Eisenhower administrations to contemplate implementing Operation EVERREADY, a plan to remove him from power.

For the remainder of the war, Rhee's greatest preoccupation was his ultimately unsuccessful effort to sabotage ongoing armistice negotiations and ensure that hostilities continued until all Korea was unified under his rule. By April 1953 both Communist and UNC forces had wearied of war and were prepared to reach a compromise on the thorny issue of the repatriation of prisoners of war, which for almost two years had stalemated progress toward a settlement. Rhee promptly threatened to withdraw all ROK troops from the UNC should the settlement permit any Chinese People's Volunteer Army (Chinese Communist) troops to remain on Korean soil, even in the North, and he rejected a U.S. offer of massive military assistance and economic aid for South Korean rehabilitation. On 4 June, after the peace negotiations at P'anmunjŏm had finally agreed on all aspects of the repatriation of prisoners of war, Rhee publicly stated the conditions on which he would endorse a settlement, mandating the simultaneous withdrawal of all UN and Chinese troops from Korean territory. He would accept only this, he said, on condition that the ROK should conclude a mutual security pact with the United States and receive massive economic aid and the commitment of substantial U.S. military and naval forces to South Korea.

Rhee made these demands secure in the knowledge that the Communist side would find them unacceptable and continue to fight. After threatening to withdraw his troops—which by then constituted two-thirds of those manning the front line—from UNC command, Rhee hinted that even after an armistice they might refuse to lay down their arms. On 18 June 1953 he ordered the release of some 25,000 prisoners of war not scheduled for repatriation. Many were formed into labor battalions and enlisted in the ROKA; others vanished into the countryside. Rhee hoped this incident, which enraged Communist delegates to the armistice talks, would generate recriminations so bitter as to sabotage the negotiations completely; but if anything it made the exasperated participants on both sides even more determined to reach an agreement in which Rhee would be forced to acquiesce. UN and Communist representatives united in denouncing Rhee's unilateral action and agreed to resume their truce talks on 12 July 1953. The same day, the United States dispatched Assistant Secretary of State Walter Robertson to Seoul to persuade Rhee not to obstruct any settlement. After two weeks, Robertson finally extracted Rhee's pledge to accept a cease-fire, which was then signed immediately, on 27 July 1953. In return Rhee secured a U.S.-ROK mutual security treaty, which was concluded almost immediately, on 8 August 1953; $200 million in immediate economic aid, only the first installment of a long-term aid program; and U.S. assistance in expanding the ROKA to twenty divisions.

While Rhee had driven a hard bargain, he found other consequences of the Korean War less attractive. Much as he hated the Communists, he reserved his greatest antipathy for the Japanese, Korea's long-term enemies and oppressors, and often stated that, given the choice, he would join forces with Communists to fight Japan. From the late 1940s he greatly resented the United States' Cold War–fueled policy of giving a higher priority to the revival of the Japanese economy than to that of Korea, and he was even more alarmed by the 1950 Japanese peace treaty with the United States, under which the two nations became de facto military allies.

Age seventy-eight when the Korean War ended, Rhee remained ROK president until 1960, but he failed to meet popular expectations of modernization and political and economic development. His rule became increasingly personalized and authoritarian, and in April 1960 mass demonstrations against him led Rhee, under some U.S. pressure, to resign the presidency and return to private life. The following month he left Korea for exile in Hawaii, and five years later, on 19 July 1965, he died in Honolulu at age ninety.

—*Priscilla Roberts*

References:

Allen, Richard C. *Korea's Syngman Rhee: An Unauthorized Portrait.* Rutland, VT: Charles E. Tuttle, 1960.

Cumings, Bruce. *Child of Conflict: The Korean-American Relationship, 1943–1953.* Seattle: University of Washington Press, 1983.

———. *Korea's Place in the Sun: A Modern History.* New York: W. W. Norton, 1997.

Oliver, Robert T. *Syngman Rhee and American Involvement in Korea, 1942–1960: A Personal Narrative.* Seoul: Panmun Books, 1978.

Stueck, William W., Jr. *The Korean War: An International History.* Princeton, NJ: Princeton University Press, 1995.

See also: EVERREADY, Operation; Hodge, John R.; Jiang Jieshi (Chiang Kai-shek); Kim Il Sung; Korea, Republic of: History, 1947–1953; Korea, Republic of: History, 1953 to the Present; MacArthur, Douglas; Robertson Mission; Robertson, Walter Spencer; Syngman Rhee's Release of North Korean Prisoners of War; Truman, Harry S.; Yi Pŏm-sŏk (Lee Bum Suk).

Syngman Rhee, Assassination Attempt on
(25 June 1952)

Purported attempt to assassinate Republic of Korea (South Korean) president Syngman Rhee on 25 June 1952 during a ceremony in Pusan. This marked the second anniversary of the beginning of the Korean War and was attended by 50,000 people, including the U.S. ambassador. A lone gunman confronted Rhee and pulled the trigger of his pistol twice, but it misfired each time. The police then overpowered the suspect, sixty-two-year-old Yu Si-t'ae. Under interrogation he was said to have admitted his membership in the ultranationalist Blood and Justice Association.

The police claimed that this episode was only part of a larger plot involving the opposition Democratic Nationalist Party. Even today it is still not altogether clear whether this attempt was a political ploy, stage-managed by Rhee, as the president's opponents alleged and as U.S. officials, including U.S. Chairman of the Joint Chiefs of Staff General Omar N. Bradley and State Department official H. Freeman Matthews were inclined to suspect.

In Rhee's defense, one might note that the assassination of political opponents was and would remain for some decades a reasonably common tactic in both North and South Korea's violent and somewhat ungentlemanly political scene, and no party was innocent of its use. Yet the timing and setting of this botched attempt proved so remarkably convenient for Rhee that it is difficult to believe that it was purely coincidental.

Whatever its genesis, Rhee used the incident to his own political advantage. At this time a political crisis had resulted from his attempts to change the constitution so as to win a third two-year term as president. To do so Rhee and the newly appointed home minis-

ter and political ally Yi Pŏm-sŏk organized a campaign of intimidation against his opponents and the National Assembly, which was empowered to elect the president, by imposing martial law on the temporary capital of Pusan in May 1952 and threatening to disband the assembly if it failed to allow popular elections for the presidency. The Democratic Nationalist Party (DNP) was in the forefront of the opposition to these plans.

Rhee used the assassination attempt to justify the arrest of two DNP members and a campaign of political terror against his opponents, who ultimately acquiesced in his plans to change the constitution to allow the popular election of the president. Rhee promptly won this contest in August 1952 in a lopsided vote of 5 million to 800,000.

—*Priscilla Roberts*

References:

Allen, Richard C. *Korea's Syngman Rhee: An Unauthorized Portrait.* Rutland, VT: Charles E. Tuttle, 1960.

Cumings, Bruce. *Child of Conflict: The Korean-American Relationship, 1943–1953.* Seattle: University of Washington Press, 1983.

Oliver, Robert T. *Syngman Rhee and American Involvement in Korea, 1942–1960: A Personal Narrative.* Seoul: Panmun Books, 1978.

Ra, Jong Yil. "Political Crisis in Korea, 1952: The Administration, Legislature, Military and Foreign Powers." *Journal of Contemporary History* 27, no. 2 (April 1992): 301–318.

Stueck, William W., Jr. *The Korean War: An International History.* Princeton, NJ: Princeton University Press, 1995.

See also: Bradley, Omar Nelson; Matthews, H. Freeman; Syngman Rhee; Yi Pŏm-sŏk (Lee Bum Suk).

Syngman Rhee's Release of North Korean Prisoners of War
(18 June 1953)

Release of prisoners that threatened to end Korean War armistice talks. Although peace talks had begun in July 1951, discord over repatriation of prisoners of war (POWs) had prevented any agreement during 1951 or 1952. The Communist side, however, returned to the peace table in April 1953 and showed signs of seeking a settlement. Yet Republic of Korea (ROK, South Korean) president Syngman Rhee remained adamant that the war should not end until Korea was unified under ROK rule and the POW issue was settled. Throughout April and May 1953, he pressed the United States for permission to release Korean People's Army (North Korean) POWs because he feared that Communist officials would take advantage of the Neutral Nations Repatriation Commission and coerce nonrepatriates to return home.

First dismissing Rhee's opposition to the peace settlement as bluff, President Dwight D. Eisenhower's administration soon began to take his threats of unilateral action more seriously. Yet President Eisenhower's advisors convinced him that releasing North Korean POWs unilaterally or reopening negotiations on Item 4 might jeopardize the entire settlement. Eisenhower agreed, yet fears remained that Rhee would do something to sabotage the talks or would refuse to abide by any settlement.

By 18 June 1953 the armistice agreement was all but complete. At this time, however, Rhee unilaterally ordered the release of 25,000 anti-Communist North Korean POWs in protest of the proposed settlement. A United Nations Command (UNC) announcement of that date stated:

> Between midnight and dawn today, approximately 25,000 [of 35,400] military anti-communist North Korean prisoners of war broke out of UNC POW camps at Pusan, Masan, Nonsan, and Sang Mu Dai, Korea. Statements attributed to high officials of the Republic of Korea now make it clear that the action had been secretly planned and carefully coordinated at top levels in the Korean Government and that outside assistance was furnished the POWs in their mass breakout. ROKA [ROK Army] security units assigned as guards at the POW camps did little to prevent the breakouts and there is every evidence of actual collusion between the ROK guards and the prisoners.... U.S. personnel at these non-repatriate camps, limited in each case to the camp commander and a few administrative personnel, exerted every effort to prevent today's mass breakouts, but in the face of the collusion between the ROKA guards and the prisoners, their efforts were largely unsuccessful. The large quantities of non-toxic irritants employed proved ineffective because of the great numbers of prisoners involved in the nighttime breakouts. Nine prisoners were killed and sixteen injured by rifle fire. There were no casualties among U.S. personnel. As of 1 o'clock this afternoon 971 escaped POWs have been recovered. The ROKA security units which have left their posts at non-repatriate camps are being replaced by U.S. troops.

Although UN officials denied any knowledge of, or responsibility for, Rhee's actions and issued a formal written apology at P'anmunjŏm on 20 June, the Communist side denounced the release as a breach of faith.

The POW release prompted an immediate meeting of the U.S. National Security Council. President Eisenhower was convinced that Rhee's move would cause the armistice to collapse, but Secretary of State John Foster Dulles and other administration officials believed that the Communists would overlook the incident, as they too wanted an armistice. After further cabinet and congressional meetings, Eisenhower decided to send Assistant Secretary of State for Far Eastern Affairs Walter S. Robinson to meet with commander in chief of United Nations Command General Mark W. Clark and Rhee in what became known as the "Little Truce Talks." These lasted twelve days. Robinson, who arrived in Korea on 25 June 1953, had been instructed to offer Rhee long-term U.S. military and economic aid if he would cooperate, allaying any fears that the United States would abandon the ROK. If Rhee did not cooperate, he was to be told that the United States would sign the armistice and withdraw its forces, leaving the ROK to fight on alone. If this failed, Robinson and Clark had a plan to launch a coup d'état (Operation EVERREADY) to replace Rhee with Prime Minister Chang T'aek-sang.

The talks, which occurred in the midst of a new Communist offensive, were successful. On 9 July Rhee agreed to end his efforts to scuttle the settlement.

The unilateral POW release and Washington's surprised reaction to it indicated to the Communists that Rhee had acted on his own. Although this event did no more than delay the armistice, it forced the Eisenhower administration to deal with Rhee's fears. It also proved that the real POW issue all along had been the fate of Chinese, rather than North Korean, POWs.

—*Clayton D. Laurie*

References:

Blair, Clay. *The Forgotten War: America in Korea, 1950–1953.* New York: Times Books, 1987.

Hastings, Max. *The Korean War.* New York: Simon & Schuster, 1987.

Hermes, Walter G. *United States Army in the Korean War: Truce Tent and Fighting Front.* Washington, DC: Office of the Chief of Military History, 1966.

See also: Chang T'aek-sang; Clark, Mark W.; Dulles, John Foster; Eisenhower, Dwight D.; EVERREADY, Operation; National Security Council (NSC); Neutral Nations Supervisory Commission (NNSC); Syngman Rhee.

T

Taegu, Defense of
(August–September 1950)

During the periods 4–24 August and 2–15 September 1950, Korean People's Army (KPA, North Korean) forces made two major efforts to capture Taegu, a major South Korean road and railway hub as well as the site of the U.S. Eighth Army headquarters. Its capture would sever the only east-west highway and rail line serving the northern flank of the Pusan perimeter.

Defending Taegu in August were the U.S. 1st Cavalry Division, on a thirty-five–mile front along the Naktong River; the Republic of Korea Army (ROKA, South Korean) 1st Infantry Division, to the north of the 1st Cavalry, along the river for twenty-five miles to near Naktong-ni, then facing north for six more miles; and the ROKA 6th Infantry Division, to the right of the 1st, on a front of eight miles. The KPA 10th Division and part of the 3d Division faced the U.S. 1st Cavalry.

Between 5 and 8 August 1950, the KPA 13th Division crossed the Naktong into the ROKA 1st Division's northern sector. Some of them utilized "underwater bridges," sandbags and oil drums making a ford a few feet below the river's surface. Air strikes, artillery, and mortar fire failed to stop the crossing. On 7 August elements of the KPA 15th Division attacked the ROKA 1st Division's southern sector, broke through, and headed east toward Tabu-dong, six miles away.

The ROKA 1st Division's 12th Regiment withdrew from its positions to occupy the high ridges north of Tabu-dong, including the towering Yuhak-san, but found them occupied by elements of the KPA 13th Division. A bloody fight ensued.

By 15 August the ROKA 1st Division, bloodily engaged with the KPA 13th and 15th Divisions, asked the Eighth Army for help. Two regiments were sent: the U.S. 27th Infantry (24th Division) and ROKA 10th Infantry (8th Division). While the ROKA 1st was thus engaged, the KPA 1st Division attacked the ROKA 6th, which executed a fighting withdrawal. Finally, the ROKA 6th dug in along the high ground northeast of Tabu-dong, on the ROKA 1st Division's right flank.

On 9 August the KPA's 3d Division's 7th Infantry Regiment crossed the Naktong against the 5th Cavalry, seizing Hill 268 (Triangulation Hill). A counterattack by the 1st Battalion of the 7th Cavalry Regiment forced the KPA from the hill and back across the river.

On the night of 11–12 August, elements of the KPA 10th Division crossed the Naktong into positions of the 2d Battalion, 7th Cavalry, and continued attacking for the next two days. About 1800 on 12 August the 1st Battalion of the 7th Cavalry Regiment arrived on the 2d Battalion's left but was forced back by the KPA, refusing the Cavalry Division's left flank. The 7th counterattacked on 14 August and drove the KPA back across the river with heavy losses.

That day elements of the KPA 3d Division, supported by tanks of the KPA 105th Division, crossed the river into the sector of the 13th Regiment, ROKA 1st Division, just north of the town of Waegwan, then turned south and into the flank and rear of the U.S. 5th Cavalry Regiment of the 1st Cavalry Division. On the 15th a KPA force, mistaken by a U.S. officer as expected reinforcing South Koreans, captured the officer and some forty to forty-five other Americans. On the 17th, as counterattacking Americans began forcing the North Koreans from the hill, KPA soldiers herded their U.S. captives into a gully and murdered them. Six of the prisoners survived the massacre, but one died the following day. Some of the murderers were later captured by U.S. troops, but it is unclear what happened to them.

On 18 August the ROKA 1st Division, reinforced by the U.S. 27th Infantry, began counterattacking the KPA 13th Division. The 27th advanced up a deep valley north of Tabu-dong, while the ROK forces attacked along high, steep mountains on each flank. The attack was halted about 2000. Shortly thereafter, a KPA tank-infantry force attacked the 27th, but infantry rocket launchers and U.S. tank fire halted the KPA attackers, destroying at least two tanks, a self-propelled (SP) gun, and a few trucks. After the KPA force was repelled, the 27th organized a two-battalion defensive position across the valley. From the 18th through the 25th the KPA attacked the 27th almost every night, in what became known as the Bowling Alley (because the artillery and tank fire in the valley sounded like the noise of a bowling alley), losing thirteen tanks and five SP guns. The ROKA 1st Division flanking the 27th also held fast.

Some KPA troops infiltrated the high, steep ridges on the right of the ROKA 1st Division and attacked artillery positions and vehicles in rear areas. On 21 August the 2d Battalion, 23d Infantry was deployed to protect the artillery. The KPA attacked the battalion on 22 August, but it was repulsed. Counterattacking between 23 and 25 August, the 2d Battalion of the 23d, joined by the 3d Battalion, killed at least 523 members of the KPA 1st Regiment, ending the threat to the rear area and artillery. Elements of the ROKA 1st Division,

Refugees fleeing from the combat area near Taegu, 20 August 1950. (National Archives)

meantime, drove KPA troops from Kasan, a high mountain overlooking the valley to Taegu.

The KPA tried again to seize Taegu in early September. This time the U.S. 1st Cavalry Division was deployed west and north of the city, with the newly arrived British 27th Brigade on the left, the 1st Cavalry Division's 5th Cavalry Regiment to its north in the Waegwan area, the 7th Cavalry Regiment in the center, and the 8th Cavalry Regiment in the old Bowling Alley area, facing north. The division front was thirty-five miles long. The ROKA 1st Division was on the cavalry's right. From east to west opposing the cavalry were the KPA 1st, 13th, and 3d Divisions.

On 2 September the 1st Cavalry Division launched attacks ordered by U.S. Eighth Army commander Lieutenant General Walton H. Walker to try to relieve KPA pressure on the U.S. 2d and 25th Divisions to the south. Most failed, but a 5th Cavalry attack on 4

September drove the KPA from Hill 303, where the massacre had occurred the previous month.

KPA pressure increased, and it retook towering Kasan. Two companies were sent to take it back, but, battling superior KPA forces on 4 and 5 September, they were driven off. Also on 2 September elements of the KPA 13th Division attacked the 8th Cavalry and slowly drove it back. By 5 September the situation was worsening; KPA forces heavily infiltrated rear areas, established blocks on the main supply route, captured Tabu-dong, and infiltrated the center south of Hill 518, which the 7th Cavalry had been fighting to take. Waegwan, on the 1st Cavalry Division's left, was in no-man's land. It was thus imperative that the 8th Cavalry shorten its lines and reorganize and consolidate. On 6 September it carried out withdrawals of approximately two to five miles. On the 7th elements of the division began attacking their advancing enemy.

Bloody fights for a number of hills ensued, including Hills 174, 203, and 314 in the 5th and 7th Cavalry's area and Hill 570 in the area of the 8th Cavalry. These battles continued until 15 September. One of the bloodiest of these was over Hill 174. Won and lost several times, it was taken for the last time by Company I, 5th Cavalry, on 16 September, only to find that the KPA had withdrawn.

On its new positions the 1st Cavalry Division stopped the KPA advance but at a heavy price. The companies of the 3d Battalion, 8th Cavalry Regiment were at or below 50 percent strength; the 5th Cavalry's strength was so low that it was virtually not combat effective; and one company of the 1st Battalion of the 7th Cavalry Regiment was down to only fifty men.

—*Uzal W. Ent*

References:

Appleman, Roy E. *South to the Naktong, North to the Yalu.* Washington, DC: Office of the Chief of Military History, 1961.

Blair, Clay. *The Forgotten War: America in Korea, 1950–1953.* New York: Times Books, 1987.

Ent, Uzal W. *Fighting on the Brink: Defense of the Pusan Perimeter.* Paducah, KY: Turner, 1996.

See also: Haman, Breakthrough; Inch'ŏn Landings: Operation CHROMITE; Naktong Bulge, First Battle of; Naktong Bulge, Second Battle of; P'ohang, Battle of; Walker, Walton Harris.

Taejŏn Agreement
(12 July 1950)

Bilateral pact between the Republic of Korea (ROK, South Korea) and the United States that set the status and rights of U.S. armed forces stationed in Korea. It was concluded with an exchange of notes between the ROK Ministry of Foreign Affairs and the U.S. embassy at Taejŏn, then the interim capital city of the ROK, on 12 July 1950, during the early period of the Korean War.

The formal title of the agreement was "The Agreement Relating to Jurisdiction over Criminal Offenses Committed by the United States Forces in Korea between the Republic of Korea and The United States of America." Thus it was not an agreement that transferred authority over ROK military forces to the United Nations Command (UNC), as is often mentioned in South Korea.

Its origin dated back to the summer of 1948. On 24 August 1948, immediately after the creation of the ROK under U.S. auspices, South Korean President Syngman Rhee and commanding general of U.S. forces in Korea Lieutenant General John R. Hodge signed a pact titled "The Executive Agreement between the President of the Republic of Korea and the Commanding General, United States Army Forces in Korea, concerning Interim Military and Security Matters during the Transitional Period."

Under this agreement the ROK government granted U.S. military authorities the right to use necessary facilities and areas as well as exclusive control over members of the U.S. armed forces, the civilian component, and their dependents until the complete withdrawal of U.S. troops. With the outbreak of the Korean War in June 1950, U.S. forces returned to Korea, and the Taejŏn Agreement was completed on 12 July 1950. It went into effect the same day it was signed.

The Taejŏn Agreement regarded U.S. armed forces as a rescue force that came to Korea's assistance in a life-or-death situation. As such, it allowed U.S. military authorities to exercise full criminal jurisdiction over U.S. forces. Regardless of the kinds and location of crimes committed by American personnel, U.S. courts-martial could exercise exclusive jurisdiction over all U.S. troops stationed in Korea.

Also by this pact the ROK government and Ministry of Foreign Affairs conceded that because they were faced with stemming the North Korean military invasion, U.S. armed forces in Korea would not be subject to the authority of any institutions other than the U.S. military authorities.

Similar to this very unequal and so-called "backward nation" status-of-forces agreement was the "Agreement on Economic Coordination between the Republic of Korea and the United States," signed in Pusan on 24 May 1952, whereby South Korea promised to offer privileges and concessions to "on-duty" U.S. servicemen and military organizations. Because the American signatory was Clarence E. Meyer, this was referred to as the Meyer Agreement.

ROK president Syngman Rhee transferred authority over the ROK's armed forces to the UNC by an arrangement separate from the Taejŏn Agreement. On 15 July 1950 he sent a letter to UNC commanding general Douglas MacArthur, stating that for "the joint military effort of the United Nations on behalf of the Republic of Korea, I am happy to assign to you command authority over all land, sea, and air forces of the Republic of Korea during the period of the continuation of the present state of hostilities" and "the Korean Army will be proud to serve under your command." Three days later MacArthur welcomed the transfer of the operational authority by replying, "I am proud indeed to have the gallant Republic of Korea forces under my command."

Because the Taejŏn Agreement was so unequal, the ROK and the U.S. governments agreed on negotiations to complete a status of forces agreement for U.S. troops stationed in Korea. These began immediately after the signing of the U.S.-ROK Mutual Security Treaty, which went into effect with a communiqué between Syngman Rhee and U.S. Secretary of State

John Foster Dulles on 7 August 1953. But for a long time negotiations fell short of the Koreans' expectations. Finally, on 9 July 1966, the ROK and the United States concluded "Agreement under Article IV of the Mutual Defense Treaty between the United States of America and the Republic of Korea, Regarding Facilities and Areas and the Status of United States Armed Forces in the Republic of Korea," also known as the Status of Forces Agreement (SOFA).

Under Article 22 of this pact, the Taejŏn Agreement became null and void, with the ROK having "exclusive jurisdiction" over U.S. forces with respect to criminal offenses "except during hostilities and martial law."

—*Jinwung Kim*

References:

Headquarters, United States Forces, Korea. *The United States of America and the Republic of Korea Status of Forces Agreement with Related Documents.* Seoul: Headquarters, U.S. FIK, 1967.

Matray, James I., ed. *Historical Dictionary of the Korean War.* Westport, CT: Greenwood Press, 1991.

Yi, Sŏk-u. *Hanmi Haengjŏng Hyŏpjŏng Yŏn'gu* [A study of the ROK-U.S. Status of Forces Agreement]. Seoul: Min, 1995.

See also: Coulter, John Breitling; Dulles, John Foster; MacArthur, Douglas; Meyer, Clarence E.; Syngman Rhee; United States–Republic of Korea Mutual Defense Treaty.

Taejŏn, Defense of
(19–20 July 1950)

Battle in which U.S. and Republic of Korea Army (ROKA, South Korean) forces tried to stave off the Korean People's Army (KPA, North Korean) advance. By 19 July 1950 Major General William F. Dean's 24th Division was forced into the environs of Taejŏn city. Dean placed Colonel Charles E. Beauchamp, commander of the 34th Infantry Regiment, in charge of its defense. Beauchamp also had the remnants of the 19th and 34th Regiments, the 24th Reconnaissance Company, and what was left of the division's artillery. A number of headquarters and service support units were in the city itself. Dean and one or two members of his staff were also in Taejŏn.

Beauchamp placed the 1st Battalion, 34th Infantry, with the 2d Battalion, 19th Infantry to its left, along the Kapch'ŏn River, defending the Kongju and Nonsan roads, respectively. Surviving artillery was moved from near the Taejŏn airstrip to the southern outskirts of the city. The 3d Battalion, 34th Infantry was placed west and north of the city. Elements of the 21st Infantry, not under Beauchamp's command, with an attached tank company, were deployed across four miles of hills some three to four miles east of Taejŏn and a mile beyond where a railroad and a highway tunnel were located. Their mission was to patrol the road and keep it open east of town.

During a visit on the morning of 18 July, Eighth Army commander Lieutenant General Walton H. Walker told Dean that he needed two days to bring the newly arrived 1st Cavalry Division into position some miles to the rear of Taejŏn.

Beauchamp later wrote that Walker visited him and ordered him to hold the Taejŏn road network for three days. This turned out to be one day too long. Beauchamp recalled that General Dean was not present during this visit and that no one told him about the 1st Cavalry, although on the 20th Dean told him that a battalion of the 21st was coming to support the withdrawal.

The KPA's 5th Regiment attacked the 1st Battalion of the 34th before dawn on 20 July, forcing it out of position, uncovering the 2d Battalion of the 19th's right flank. This forced the 2d Battalion to withdraw as well. By 1000 the road to Taejŏn was open. A feeble counterattack by the 3d Battalion of the 34th failed. Just before this attack, the acting 3d Battalion commander mysteriously disappeared, thrusting command onto a staff captain.

In the battle for Taejŏn, eight KPA tanks were destroyed by the newly issued 3.5-inch rocket launcher. One tank was destroyed by a team led by General Dean. Beauchamp, his executive officer, and Dean were all absent from the command post at critical times during the battle. This produced additional confusion and delay in decision making and the execution of orders.

In fighting its way out of Taejŏn and running a gauntlet of ambushing fire on the road toward 21st Infantry lines, Beauchamp's command suffered terrible casualties. Beauchamp himself escaped late in the day with a small force. A belated and feeble counterattack at the tunnel area—the ambush's choke point—failed. Small groups of GIs made their way out cross-country, although many were killed or captured. Dean became separated and was later captured.

Of 3,933 men engaged in and around Taejŏn, 1,150 were casualties. But the battles on the Kŭm River and at Taejŏn delayed the KPA for six days, enabling the 25th Infantry and 1st Cavalry Divisions to position themselves further to slow the KPA advance.

—*Uzal W. Ent*

References:

Appleman, Roy E. *South to the Naktong, North to the Yalu.* Washington, DC: Office of the Chief of Military History, 1961.

Blair, Clay. *The Forgotten War: America in Korea, 1950–1953.* New York: Times Books, 1987.

Ent, Uzal W. *Fighting on the Brink: Defense of the Pusan Perimeter.* Paducah, KY: Turner, 1996.

Toland, John. *In Mortal Combat: Korea, 1950–1953.* New York: William Morrow, 1991.

See also: Dean, William Frishe; Walker, Walton Harris.

Taft, Robert Alphonso
(1889–1953)

Republican leader of the U.S. Senate during the Korean War and fierce critic of Truman administration policies toward Korea. Born in Cincinnati, Ohio, on 8 September 1889, Robert Alphonso Taft was the eldest son of Republican president William Howard Taft. The scion of a family that had been politically prominent for several previous generations, Taft was subjected to strong expectations and ambitions that he should continue this tradition, resulting in a personality both driven and self-contained. He was educated at the Taft School for Boys in Watertown, Connecticut, Yale University (graduating in 1910), and Harvard Law School (graduating in 1913), where he headed his class.

In 1914 Taft joined the law firm of Maxwell and Ramsey in Cincinnati. In 1917, after U.S. intervention in World War I, he became assistant counsel to the newly formed U.S. Food Administration, headed by Herbert Hoover, and at the end of the war Taft followed his boss to Europe as a legal adviser to the American Relief Administration. For the rest of his life, Taft's views on both domestic and international affairs would reveal the influence of Hoover, who firmly believed that big government was inevitably counterproductive, inefficient, costly, and injurious to individual rights; that statist planning distorted the workings of the market; and that, while the United States should play a humanitarian international role, it should give the protection of its own interests a far higher priority than defending those of other countries.

In 1920 Taft supported Hoover's unsuccessful bid for the presidency. Setting up his own law practice, Taft, Stettinius, and Hollister, which quickly became one of Cincinnati's top legal firms, he also became deeply involved in local and state politics, winning election to a variety of offices despite his dry, humorless, didactic, and professorial style. Hostile to most New Deal measures of the 1930s, including welfare and relief payments, progressive taxes, deficit spending, and government economic intervention, by the time Taft won election to the Senate for Ohio in 1938, he was firmly identified with his party's conservative wing.

Taft was equally critical of President Franklin D. Roosevelt's foreign policies. When the Second World War began, he opposed U.S. aid to the Allies, supporting the "America first" policies enunciated by Hoover and others, insisting that war would destroy American civil liberties and that Germany posed no danger to the western hemisphere. After U.S. intervention, Taft constantly assailed what he viewed as the excesses of domestic controls and propaganda, while opposing the creation of the World Bank or any other international organization apart from the United Nations. Although

Taft became somewhat more liberal domestically, favoring federal aid to education, public housing, and a minimum income for all, he still believed firmly in limited government, fiscal conservatism, and checks on the power of organized labor.

In 1946 Taft became the floor leader of the Republican Party, a ratification of his existing standing as a major figure within the bipartisan conservative coalition that effectively dominated Congress. Immune to appeals for bipartisanship, as the Cold War developed he opposed heavy defense expenditures, voted in 1946 against the large American loan to Britain, complained that U.S. military and economic support for Greece and Turkey and the Marshall Plan were all too expensive, and opposed the creation of the North Atlantic Treaty Organization (NATO) as being likely to provoke the Soviet Union into escalating the Cold War. Taft believed that U.S. nuclear air power could safeguard the United States from any foreign attack, and that his country should not commit troops outside the western hemisphere.

By the time the Korean War began, Taft, although one of the most prominent Republican senators, who had earned the nickname "Mr. Republican," had lost two potential presidential nominations, those of 1940 and 1948, to more attractive candidates, and Harry S. Truman's unexpected presidential victory in 1948 shocked Taft and the Republican Party. As Republican majority leader, Taft therefore moved to take advantage of the Korean War to shore up both his party's and his own political fortunes in the forthcoming 1952 presidential campaign. Three days after the North Korean invasion, Taft decried the administration's failure to seek either a formal declaration of war or a congressional resolution authorizing the use of force in Korea. He also laid much of the responsibility for the war upon the administration's "bungling and inconsistent foreign policy," by which he referred among other matters to Secretary of State Dean Acheson's National Press Club speech of January 1950. He even suggested that the United States might do well to pull out of Korea and base its defenses on a line running through the island positions of Taiwan and Japan. Although he reluctantly supported Truman's initial decision to commit forces to Korea, after Communist China's intervention in late 1950, Taft began to accuse the president of mishandling the war.

After Truman's recall of commander in chief Douglas MacArthur in spring 1951, Taft defended the general, abandoning his own customary restraint and publicly advocating MacArthur's preferred and highly provocative measures of bombing Chinese supply lines in Manchuria and including Guomindang troops from the Republic of China on Taiwan in United Nations forces. He tolerated the extremist tactics of

Senator Joseph R. McCarthy, even though he found them personally distasteful, in the belief that they were likely to enhance the Republican Party's chances of victory.

Campaigning for the 1952 Republican nomination (which he lost to the internationalist war hero Dwight D. Eisenhower), Taft harped constantly on the refrain that the Democratic administration had blundered unnecessarily into an expensive war that it could neither win nor end with honor. Eisenhower and other Republican candidates continued to stress this theme in the successful fall election campaign. Selected as Republican majority leader after the election, a more demure Taft then unsuccessfully attempted to rein in the excesses of McCarthyism. Taft died of cancer on 31 July 1953, in a New York City hospital.

—Priscilla Roberts

References:

Caridi, Ronald J. *The Korean War and American Politics: The Republican Party As a Case Study.* Philadelphia: University of Pennsylvania Press, 1968.

DeJohn, Samuel, Jr. "Robert A. Taft, Economic Conservatism, and Opposition to United States Foreign Policy, 1944–1951." Doctoral dissertation, University of Southern California, Los Angeles, 1976. Unpublished manuscript.

Kepley, David R. *The Collapse of the Middle Way: Senate Republicans and the Bipartisan Foreign Policy, 1948–1952.* New York: Greenwood Press, 1982.

Matthews, Geoffrey. "Robert A. Taft, the Constitution and American Foreign Policy, 1939–53." *Journal of Contemporary History* 17, no. 3 (July 1982): 507–522.

Patterson, James T. *Mr. Republican: A Biography of Robert A. Taft.* Boston: Houghton Mifflin, 1972.

Ricks, John Addison. "'Mr. Integrity' and McCarthyism: Senator Robert A. Taft and Senator Joseph R. McCarthy." Doctoral dissertation, University of North Carolina, 1974. Unpublished manuscript.

Sylvester, John A. "Taft, Dulles and Ike: New Faces for 1952." *Mid-America* 76, no. 2 (April 1994): 157–179.

Taft, Robert A. *A Foreign Policy for Americans.* Garden City, NY: Doubleday, 1951.

See also: Acheson, Dean Goodersham; MacArthur, Douglas; McCarthy, Joseph R.; McCarthyism; Truman, Harry S.; Truman's Recall of MacArthur.

TAILBOARD, Operation (see Wŏnsan Landing)

Taiwan, Neutralization of
(27 June 1950)

U.S. plan to halt possible hostilities between the People's Republic of China (PRC, Communist China) and the Republic of China (Taiwan). At the end of the Second World War, the Chinese Civil War resumed between the Nationalists led by Jiang Jieshi (Chiang Kai-shek) and the Communists led by Mao Zedong. Although Mao had asked the United States to remain neutral, Washington actively supported Jiang and the Nationalists. In 1949 the Communists won the war and pushed the Nationalist forces off the mainland onto the island of Taiwan. Here, Jiang and his followers established the Republic of China (ROC).

By 1950, both the Communists and Nationalists postured for diplomatic advantage. Jiang vowed to retake the mainland and restore his regime to power, while Mao pledged to reunite Taiwan with the mainland. In the United Nations (UN), despite opposition from some of its allies, the United States backed Jiang and the Nationalists as the legitimate government of China.

The Truman administration realized that Korea could have ramifications on the China front, and Washington sought to forestall any renewal of conflict between the two rival Chinese governments. Concurrent with the opening of hostilities in Korea, the Truman administration worked hard to prevent the two Chinas from capitalizing on the situation to attack one another. Shortly after the start of the Korean War, on 27 June 1950, President Harry S. Truman ordered the U.S. Seventh Fleet to the Taiwan Strait.

U.S. leaders saw communism as monolithic; and Truman, in any case, believed that the PRC might seek to take advantage of fighting in Korea to take Taiwan. Such a move would have materially strengthened the Communist bloc and thus compromised U.S. national security interests in Asia. In addition, Truman sought to quiet domestic political opponents who would demand to know why U.S. forces were not being used to protect Taiwan when they were being employed in Korea.

Truman's action was meant to achieve three results: to forestall PRC leaders from using the fighting in Korea to launch an invasion of Taiwan; to prevent Jiang from initiating his promised assault to retake the mainland; and to keep UN attention focused on Korea. Either of the first two could have precipitated a wider war.

The PRC immediately denounced the U.S. action. It claimed that Taiwan was a part of China and not an independent nation. The PRC asserted that the U.S. action interfered with its sovereign rights and constituted armed aggression against it. The PRC did not, however, initiate military action involving the Seventh Fleet.

The U.S. naval presence between Taiwan and the mainland prevented conflict there. Overall, this neutralization of Taiwan worked to the advantage of the United States, which did not have to worry about a renewal of the Chinese Civil War as it helped the Republic of Korea (South Korea) in its war against the Democratic People's Republic of Korea (North Korea).

When the fighting ended in Korea, the United States could no longer justify its involvement in the dispute between Taiwan and the PRC as the result of wanting to avoid a wider regional conflict. The next year, 1954, the United States signed a defensive treaty with Taiwan that considered any armed attack on Taiwan as a breach of U.S. national security interests and committed the United States to act "to meet the common danger in accordance with its constitutional processes."

Washington pursued a one-China policy until 1978, when the United States officially recognized the PRC. Through the 1990s, however, the ROC has remained an ally of the United States and has maintained its independence.

—*David R. Buck*

References:

Accinelli, Robert. *Crisis and Commitment: United States Policy toward Taiwan, 1950–1955*. Chapel Hill: University of North Carolina Press, 1998.

Stueck, William W., Jr. *The Road to Confrontation: American Policy toward China and Korea, 1947–1950*. Chapel Hill: University of North Carolina Press, 1981.

See also: China, People's Republic of; China, Republic of; Jiang Jieshi (Chiang Kai-shek); Mao Zedong; Truman, Harry S.

Tasca, Henry J.
(1912–1979)

U.S. diplomat. Born in Providence, Rhode Island, on 23 August 1912, Henry J. Tasca graduated with a B.S. degree from Temple University in 1933. He completed his M.B.A. at the University of Pennsylvania in 1934, and three years later he earned his Ph.D. there. He also attended the London School of Economics for one year as a Penfield scholar.

Tasca then joined the U.S. Foreign Service as an economic analyst, working in the Department of Trade Agreements. He became assistant director of the Trade Regulation and Commercial Policy Project in 1938 and was an economic advisor specializing in trade for the National Defense Commission.

During World War II Tasca joined the navy and served as a lieutenant commander. Immediately after the war he went to work at the Rome embassy as a representative of the Treasury Department. Additionally he was a special assistant to the secretary of the treasury and an alternate executive director with the International Monetary Fund during 1948 and 1949.

In 1950 Tasca was with the Department of Economic Affairs for the Marshall Plan as staff director of plans and policy. Soon afterward he served as an economic advisor to W. Averell Harriman, President Truman's special assistant for national security affairs. After that, he served overseas as a U.S. deputy special representative.

In 1953, President Dwight D. Eisenhower wanted a firsthand report on the economic situation in the Republic of Korea (ROK, South Korea), and on 9 April he named Tasca as his special representative to conduct a thorough investigation of the situation to make recommendations to the president and the National Security Council (NSC) concerning U.S. assistance to the ROK economy.

The Tasca Mission actually followed the Meyer Mission, headed by Clarence E. Meyer. Meyer's mission had been geared more toward the financial relationship during the war between the ROK and the United Nations, while Tasca surveyed the ROK economy and the effects of the war on it.

On 17 April 1953 Tasca arrived at Pusan, and for the next seven weeks he examined the situation in South Korea, meeting with various members of the United Nations Reconstruction Agency, the ROK National Assembly, the Korean Chamber of Commerce, and officials in the ROK government. Tasca returned to the United States on 15 June and submitted an extensive and comprehensive report.

Tasca's report revealed the devastating effects of the war on the ROK, including 2.5 million refugees and some 60,000 demolished homes. U.S. charities provided half of the subsistence for the population. Inflation had skyrocketed and per capita income had plummeted, leaving the population unable to achieve even its former standard of living without extensive economic assistance. Tasca's initial recommendations called for a $1 billion payout over a three-year period, although he wanted a thorough reorganization of agencies that would disperse these funds. Tasca also urged the rebuilding and expansion of the ROK armed forces as an important step of reconstruction.

Tasca's report was reviewed by the NSC and approved by President Eisenhower on 23 June 1953. It provided concrete evidence that the Eisenhower administration was committed to a long-term involvement in restoring the ROK's economy and morale. Congress ultimately provided over $600 million to rebuild South Korea.

Tasca next became director of the Foreign Operations Administration in Rome. In 1956 he moved to Bonn, where he served four years. Between 1960 and 1965 he was deputy assistant secretary for African affairs, and from 1965 to 1974 he served as ambassador to Morocco and then to Greece.

Tasca retired in Rome and wrote two books concerning U.S. trade policy. He died in an automobile accident in Lausanne, Switzerland, on 22 August 1979.

—*Monica Spicer*

References:

Hermes, Walter G. *United States Army in the Korean War: Truce Tent and Fighting Front*. Washington, DC: Office of the Chief of Military History, 1966.

Matray, James I., ed. *Historical Dictionary of the Korean War*. Westport, CT: Greenwood Press, 1991.

New York Times, 25 August 1979.

See also: Eisenhower, Dwight D.; Harriman, William Averell; Meyer, Clarence E.; Refugees; Truman, Harry S.

Task Force Kean
(9–12 August 1950)

In early August 1950 Eighth Army commander Lieutenant General Walton H. Walker decided to begin the first big United Nations Command offensive of the war to build up the confidence of his soldiers. Named Task Force Kean after 25th Division commander Major General William B. Kean, this force consisted of the 25th Division plus the just-arrived 5th Regimental Combat Team (RCT), and the 1st Marine Brigade.

The mission was assigned to four regiments. The 35th Infantry Regiment of the 25th Division would attack west along the north Mason Road to Much'on-ni. The 5th RCT would attack from the south road at Chindong-ni and link up with the 25th at Much'on-ni. The 5th Marine Regiment was to attack along the coast road from Chindong-ni to Kosŏng and Sach'ŏn. The 24th Regiment was to secure the area behind the attacking forces. In the last phase of the attack, the 5th Marines from Sach'ŏn were to link up in Chinju with the 5th RCT and 35th Infantry attacking west from Much'on-ni.

The Eighth Army, however, was unaware of the movement of the Korean People's Army (KPA, North Korean) 6th Division, attacking rapidly from the west toward Pusan, which would run head-on into Task Force Kean. As early as 2 August several thousand North Koreans had infiltrated the great hill mass of Sŏbuk-san between the north and south routes to Pusan. This hill mass was very steep and honeycombed with old mines. Most roads leading into these hills approached from the west, with few from the east.

The operation, which began on 7 August, initially moved slowly because KPA forces at Sŏbuk-san were able to impede U.S. units massing along the coast road at Chindong-ni. For four days, constant fighting ensued between these forces. Not until 9 August did Kean believe that lines of communication had been cleared sufficiently for the 5th RCT and 5th Marines to begin their attack.

On 9 August the 5th Marines moved rapidly into the attack. By the 11th they reached the town of Kosŏng. This attack was supported by Marine Corps F4U Corsairs and U.S. Air Force F-51 Mustang aircraft. KPA resistance was so weakened by this air support that fresh Marine units continued to push on unopposed until they were a few miles from Sach'ŏn. Here on 12 August the KPA tried to ambush the Marines and counterattack. This was only a partial success, because alert Marines, supported by Corsairs, were able to control the surrounding hills and retain their positions. Subsequently, the Marines received orders to return to Chindong-ni to help extricate the 5th RCT, which had been cut off by KPA units and needed assistance.

The central force of Task Force Kean encountered the heaviest fighting and experienced the most casualties. On 10 August the 1st and 2d Battalions of the 5th RCT had jumped off in the attack to link up with the 35th Infantry at Much'on-ni. In spite of light KPA resistance in the Sŏbuk-san hill mass, the regiment pushed on to the narrow pass beyond Pongam-ni. The 3d Battalion of the 5th RCT passed through the other two battalions and dashed over the pass to Sŏngdong to link up with the 35th Infantry. Here the battalion followed the railroad tracks up Chinju pass to high ground overlooking Chinju. The battalion then dug in defense positions for the night while the rest of the regiment remained near Pongam-ni. On the morning of the 12th a company of North Koreans, their helmets camouflaged with tree branches, attacked Company I but were driven off.

While the 3d Battalion of the 5th RCT was locked in fighting close to the Chinju objective, more activity was taking place in the regiment's rear. On the night of 10 August, KPA units attacked the 1st Battalion and artillery units in Pongam-ni. KPA mortar and artillery fire landed all around, and many injuries resulted from rock fragments thrown up by detonations. At the height of the conflict the commanders of both the 1st Battalion and 555th Field Artillery Battalion (FAB) were wounded. When daylight came, U.S. air strikes drove the KPA units back into the hills.

Eighth Army headquarters now pressured General Kean to speed up his attack. The Marines were having great success on their route, while the 5th RCT was moving too slowly. In response, the 2d Battalion and the 555th FAB of the 5th RCT were sent through the pass northwest of Pongam-ni to join the 3d Battalion outside Chinju. The rest of the regiment at Pongam-ni lined up in column and prepared to traverse the pass at daybreak. Before dawn the KPA attacked the unprotected artillery and regimental supply train from all sides. The resulting attack, known as "Bloody Gulch," was almost a massacre. KPA tanks approached unopposed and fired at point-blank range directly into the emplacements of the 555th FAB and of the newly arrived 19th FAB. Together these two units lost about 190 men killed and 140 wounded in the engagement.

On 12 August Task Force Kean received orders to return to its original lines. With the help of close air support from U.S. Air Force F-51s and Marine Corps F4Us, the task force withdrew. Most of the 5th RCT withdrew through the 35th Infantry. In spite of high losses, Task Force Kean was the first major offensive of the Eighth Army that stopped the KPA thrust from the southwest toward its goal of the port of Pusan.

—*Daniel R. Beirne*

References:

Appleman, Roy E. *South to the Naktong, North to the Yalu.* Washington, DC: Office of the Chief of Military History, 1961.

Blair, Clay. *The Forgotten War: America in Korea, 1950–1953.* New York: Times Books, 1987.

Ent, Uzal W. *Fighting on the Brink: Defense of the Pusan Perimeter.* Paducah, KY: Turner, 1996.

Hoyt, Edwin P. *The Pusan Perimeter.* New York: Stein & Day, 1984.

Toland, John. *In Mortal Combat: Korea, 1950–1953.* New York: William Morrow, 1991.

See also: Eighth United States Army; Kean, William Benjamin; Walker, Walton Harris.

Task Force Seventy-seven (see Naval Forces Far East [NAVFE])

Task Force Smith

First U.S. Army unit to enter combat in Korea. On 30 June 1950, President Harry S. Truman authorized General Douglas MacArthur to commit ground forces under his command to Korea, and he in turn instructed General Walton H. Walker, commander of the Eighth Army, to order the 24th Division there. Early on 1 July, the Eighth Army provided that a makeshift infantry battalion of the 24th Division be flown to Korea in the six C-54 transport aircraft that were available. The remainder of the division would follow by ship. The initial force was to make contact with the Korean People's Army (KPA, North Korean) and fight a delaying action. MacArthur called Task Force Smith an "arrogant display of strength" and hoped it would fool the North Koreans into believing a larger force was at hand. Some officers assumed that even this small U.S. force would give the North Koreans pause once they realized whom they were fighting.

Task Force Smith was named for Lieutenant Colonel Charles B. ("Brad") Smith, commanding officer, 1st Battalion, 21st Regiment, 24th Infantry Division. Task Force Smith consisted of half of the battalion headquarters company; half of the communications platoon; understrength rifle companies B and C; two 75-mm recoilless rifles each and crews from Companies D and M (the heavy weapons companies of the 1st and 3d Battalions, respectively); a medical platoon from the 21st Regimental Medical Company; two 4.2-inch mortars from the 21st Infantry's heavy mortar company, each manned by a private from that company as well as a noncommissioned officer and four or five men from Company B. In addition to their rifles the infantrymen had six 2.36-inch bazooka rocket launchers, and four 60-mm mortars. Each man was issued 120 rounds of ammunition and two days' C

rations. Most of the men were twenty years old or less; only a sixth had seen combat. As finally dug in, Task Force Smith consisted of 17 officers and 389 enlisted men in its infantry element. The artillery element of 134 officers and enlisted men, which joined the task force on 4 July, came from the 52d Field Artillery Battalion. It consisted of a small contingent from the headquarters and service batteries, and all of Battery A, with five 105-mm howitzers (one howitzer was left behind at P'yŏngt'aek) and seventy-three vehicles. Lieutenant Colonel Miller O. Perry commanded the artillery element, which had 9 officers and 125 enlisted men.

From Smith on down the men of the task force were enthusiastic about the assignment and believed the operation in Korea would be a "piece of cake," with the North Koreans running away when they saw the American uniforms. The task force left Japan by air on the morning of 1 July and received an enthusiastic welcome by South Koreans on their arrival, which provided a deceiving boost to morale. 24th Division commander General William Dean then ordered Smith to block the main road to Pusan as far north as possible. This decision resulted in the 5 July 1950 Battle of Osan.

—*Spencer C. Tucker*

References:

Appleman, Roy E. *South to the Naktong, North to the Yalu.* Washington, DC: Office of the Chief of Military History, 1961.

Collins, J. Lawton. *War in Peacetime. The History and Lessons of Korea.* Boston: Houghton Mifflin, 1969.

Gugeler, Russell A. *Combat Actions in Korea.* Washington, DC: U.S. Army Center of Military History, 1954.

Rees, David. *Korea: The Limited War.* New York: St. Martin's Press, 1964.

See also: Dean, William Frishe; MacArthur, Douglas; Osan, Battle of; Truman, Harry S.; Walker, Walton Harris.

Taylor, Maxwell Davenport
(1901–1987)

U.S. Army general and diplomat, commander of the Eighth Army during the Korean War and later chairman of the Joint Chiefs of Staff (JCS). Born in Keytesville, Missouri, on 26 August 1901, Maxwell D. Taylor graduated in 1922 from the U.S. Military Academy at West Point as first captain and fourth in his class. Commissioned in the engineers, he transferred to the field artillery in 1926. Sent to Paris to study French, he returned to teach French and Spanish at West Point (1928–1932). After graduation from the Command and General Staff College in 1935, Taylor studied Japanese in Tokyo. He was briefly assistant military attaché in Beijing, and in 1940 he graduated from the Army War College and was then assigned to Latin America to study defense needs. He then commanded the 12th Artillery Battalion at San Antonio,

Lieutenant General Maxwell D. Taylor and Brigadier General Ralph M. Osborne are shown in conference as they arrive for an inspection tour of Freedom Village, Korea. (National Archives)

Texas. In July 1941 Taylor was assigned as secretary to the army chief of staff.

In the spring of 1942 Taylor became the chief of staff of Major General Matthew B. Ridgway's 82d Infantry Division and remained with it when it became the 82d Airborne Division. Promoted to brigadier general that December, he participated in combat in Sicily and Italy in 1943, and in September he made a dramatic trip behind German lines to Rome to investigate the feasibility of a paratroop drop to secure the city. In March 1944 he took command of the 101st Airborne Division and dropped with it into Normandy on the night of 5–6 June 1944. He commanded the division in its September drop around Eindhoven, Operation MARKET-GARDEN, when he was wounded.

After the war Taylor served as superintendent of the U.S. Military Academy (1945–1949), where he helped to modernize its curriculum. In 1949 he commanded U.S. forces in Berlin, and in August 1951 he became

deputy chief of staff of the army for operations (G-3), a position in which he favored desegregation of the army.

On 11 February 1953 Lieutenant General Taylor succeeded Lieutenant General James A. Van Fleet as commander of the Eighth Army in Korea. Van Fleet had grown increasingly frustrated with Washington's conduct of the last two years of the war. Taylor inherited this situation. He was acutely aware of president-elect Dwight D. Eisenhower's desire to minimize United Nations Command (UNC) casualties and bring about an early and honorable end to the war. He also had to deal with Republic of Korea president Syngman Rhee's opposition to an armistice arrangement that would leave Korea divided at the 38th parallel. Taylor chose to regard recent Chinese attacks as mere face-saving measures and refused to allow the UNC to retake Old Baldy and Pork Chop Hill. Taylor directed military operations in Korea until the armistice in July 1953.

In November 1954 Taylor was promoted to general and was made commander in chief of the Far East Command. In June 1955 Taylor succeeded General Matthew B. Ridgway as army chief of staff, a post he held until July 1959. He took issue with the doctrine of massive nuclear retaliation advocated by the Eisenhower administration and Chairman of the JCS Admiral Arthur W. Radford; Taylor favored a larger military capable of flexible response. When Radford's view prevailed, in July 1959 Taylor resigned.

Taylor then wrote *The Uncertain Trumpet* (1960), in which he urged a reappraisal of U.S. military policy and a buildup of conventional forces and the doctrine of flexible response. Taylor believed that brush-fire wars, not nuclear conflicts, presented the greatest military challenge to the United States.

In 1961 President John F. Kennedy, a firm proponent of flexible response, made Taylor his military adviser. After a trip to Vietnam in October 1961, Taylor urged that Kennedy send additional military aid and advisors there as well as 8,000 ground combat troops. In October 1962, in an unprecedented move, Kennedy recalled Taylor from retirement to serve as chairman of the JCS. In this post Taylor urged a forceful commitment to the Republic of Vietnam and the bombing of North Vietnam.

Taylor undertook his most controversial role in July 1964, when he became U.S. ambassador to the Republic of Vietnam. Disillusioned by early 1965, Taylor urged that U.S. ground troops be used only in an enclave approach to protect major population centers. He believed that the South Vietnamese lacked motivation rather than personnel and that U.S. troops would encourage them to do less of the fighting. He lost this battle to General William Westmoreland's search-and-destroy approach of seeking out and doing battle with major Communist units.

Returning to Washington in July 1965, Taylor joined the group of President Lyndon Johnson's senior policy consultants known as the "Wise Men." In retirement he wrote his memoirs, published as *Swords and Plowshares* (1972). A daring and resourceful combat leader and important military thinker, Maxwell Taylor died in Washington, D.C., on 19 April 1987.

—*Spencer C. Tucker*

References:

Blair, Clay. *The Forgotten War: America in Korea, 1950–1953.* New York: Times Books, 1987.

Taylor, John M. *General Maxwell Taylor: The Sword and the Pen.* New York: Doubleday, 1989.

Taylor, Maxwell D. *Swords and Plowshares.* New York: W. W. Norton, 1972.

See also: Eisenhower, Dwight D.; Joint Chiefs of Staff (JCS); Ridgway, Matthew Bunker; Syngman Rhee; Van Fleet, James Alward.

X Corps

Separate United Nations command activated on 26 August 1950, specifically for the Inch'ŏn invasion. General Douglas MacArthur authorized Major General Edward M. Almond to establish a planning group for Operation CHROMITE, code name for the Inch'ŏn landing. This group, known as Force X, initially experienced difficulties in requisitioning supplies because it was not listed as an official organization. Almond then requested that MacArthur upgrade it to a corps. MacArthur agreed, and Almond kept the numerical designation of X, MacArthur noting that the World War II X Corps had been associated with the U.S. Eighth Army since 1944 and had provided occupation troops in Japan until the corps was deactivated in January 1946.

X Corps came directly under MacArthur's Far East Command (FEC) as a self-sustaining "miniature army" of two reinforced divisions, a tactical air command, a complete artillery group, and engineer and signal units. It also had additional support units for ordnance, maintenance, medical services, transportation services, and the like. X Corps was not dependent on the Eighth U.S. Army in Korea (EUSAK) for supplies. MacArthur designated Almond, his loyal chief of staff, to command X Corps, a decision made in consultation with the Joint Chiefs of Staff (JCS).

Already concerned with the end of command unity brought by the separation of X Corps from EUSAK, the JCS believed that MacArthur was trying to avoid having to place Almond under EUSAK commander Lieutenant General Walton H. Walker, with whom he had quarreled. The JCS also pointed out that Almond was only a major general, not a lieutenant general as was usual for a corps commander, and that he had no experience with amphibious warfare. They suspected that MacArthur had selected Almond for the command because of his unquestioning loyalty and that MacArthur had planned to reward him by securing his promotion to lieutenant general later. At the same time, Almond retained his position as MacArthur's chief of staff because MacArthur professed to believe that after the Inch'ŏn landing, the war would soon be over.

On 31 August FEC General Order 24 officially gathered X Corps units to prepare for the Inch'ŏn landing. U.S. and Republic of Korea (ROK) troops collected at embarkation camps in Japan. The 1st Marine Division was the foundation of X Corps; it was supplemented with the U.S. 7th Infantry Division and other U.S. Army and Korean marine units.

X Corps soon grew to 70,457 men. Pre-invasion difficulties to be surmounted included communication problems between U.S. and ROK soldiers and insufficient supplies. Only the highest-ranking X Corps officers knew what was in the offing, and often requisitions were not expeditiously filled because supply sources did not recognize the urgency for the delivery of goods. Some, including General Walker, also expressed concern about an army officer commanding Marines in an amphibious operation.

Despite these problems, the 15 September landing at Inch'ŏn went well. As soon as the 7th Marine Regiment was ashore and had secured the beachhead, Almond took over operational command from amphibious commander Rear Admiral James H. Doyle.

Aggressive, tactless, and egotistical, Almond soon sparred with other commanders once ashore. Anxious to recapture Seoul quickly on MacArthur's urging, Almond accused his subordinates of moving too slowly. Tensions soon developed between him and Major General Oliver P. Smith, commander of the 1st Marine Division. Almond also resisted efforts by EUSAK to join forces in pursuit of North Korean troops retreating north to P'yŏngyang. Almond's chief of staff, Major General Clark L. Ruffner, remarked that Almond "could precipitate a crisis on a desert island with nobody else around." Friction between Almond and his subordinates clearly impeded the effectiveness of X Corps.

Despite pleas from EUSAK after the recapture of Seoul that MacArthur restore unity of command, he refused, and decided to reembark X Corps from Inch'ŏn and send it by sea around the tip of the peninsula for an amphibious landing at Wŏnsan. X Corps's mission was to move west from Wŏnsan to assist EUSAK in capturing the Democratic People's Republic of Korea (North Korean) capital of P'yŏngyang.

ROK troops had already secured the harbor at Wŏnsan while X Corps was en route. The Marines spent almost two weeks at sea, which time they dubbed "Operation Yo-Yo," waiting for Wŏnsan harbor to be cleared of mines. Finally landing on 25 October, the 1st Marine Division began moving north to Hŭngnam and the Changjin Reservoir because P'yŏngyang had fallen to ROK forces on the 19th. MacArthur and Almond planned for X Corps to be the first troops to reach the Yalu River. By November 1950 X Corps consisted of 84,785 troops.

On 11 November Almond issued Operation Order 6 for X Corps to advance immediately to the Yalu River. Because of limited North Korean resistance he and MacArthur hoped to end the war by Christmas. Determined to reach the China border, Almond did not consider EUSAK requests for assistance. X Corps and EUSAK were now separated by the T'aebaek Mountain range. Isolated from United Nations Command forces to the west, X Corps received its supplies from Japan.

Because Almond simply followed MacArthur's directives, his command decisions were not always the best. MacArthur discounted the threat of Chinese intervention, and Almond blindly followed his orders, rushing troops forward without considering the risk posed by Communist soldiers. Determined to win the race to the Yalu, Almond scattered X Corps forces across the front in an uncoordinated fashion. He also sharply criticized more conservative commanders, such as General Smith, who were much more careful in their troop dispositions. Almond diverted units, and conflicting orders created confusion that only intensified when the Chinese struck in force on 25 November.

Overwhelming Chinese strength forced X Corps back on Hŭngnam, resulting in one of the largest amphibious evacuations in history. In February 1951 Almond received his third star for the Hŭngnam evacuation during early December 1950. This was in recognition of the very few casualties and equipment losses suffered by X Corps as it withdrew to Pusan.

The debacle in North Korea at the hands of the Chinese stemmed in part from the divided command. The JCS directed MacArthur to end this and to place X Corps under EUSAK control. On 9 December MacArthur directed Almond to report to new EUSAK commander Lieutenant General Matthew B. Ridgway.

For the remainder of the war, X Corps served as the third corps of EUSAK, participating in combat actions through the July 1953 armistice. In July 1951 Almond was reassigned as commander of the Army War College, Carlisle Barracks, Pennsylvania. Major General Clovis E. Byers replaced Almond as commander of X Corps. Lieutenant General Isaac D. White was commander of X Corps when the armistice was signed.

X Corps received two ROK Presidential Unit Citations for its actions at Inch'ŏn and Hŭngnam and its overall combat performance. Although MacArthur had envisioned X Corps serving as the postwar U.S. military headquarters for South Korea, it was deactivated on 27 April 1955, and its flag was retired to Fort Riley, Kansas.

—*Elizabeth D. Schafer*

References:

Appleman, Roy E. *East of Chosin: Entrapment and Breakout in Korea.* College Station, TX: Texas A&M Press, 1987.

———. *Escaping the Trap: The US Army X Corps in Northeast Korea, 1950.* College Station, TX: Texas A&M Press, 1990.

———. *South to the Naktong, North to the Yalu.* Washington, DC: Office of the Chief of Military History, 1961.

Blair, Clay. *The Forgotten War: America in Korea, 1950–1953.* New York: Times Books, 1987.

Cowart, Glenn C. *Miracle in Korea: The Evacuation of X Corps from the Hungnam Beachhead.* Columbia: University of South Carolina Press, 1992.

Heinl, Robert D. *Victory at High Tide: The Inchon-Seoul Campaign.* Philadelphia: J. B. Lippincott, 1968.

Mossman, Billy C. *U.S. Army in the Korean War: Ebb and Flow, November 1950–July 1951*. Washington, DC: U.S. Army Center of Military History, 1990.

Schnabel, James F. *United States Army in the Korean War: Policy and Direction, the First Year*. Washington, DC: Office of the Chief of Military History, Department of the Army, 1972.

Stanton, Shelby. *America's Tenth Legion: X Corps in Korea*. Novato, CA: Presidio Press, 1989.

Stewart, Richard W. *Staff Operations: The X Corps in Korea, December 1950*. Fort Leavenworth, KS: U.S. Army Command and General Staff College, 1991.

See also: Almond, Edward Mallory; Amphibious Force Far East (Task Force Ninety); Changjin (Chosin) Reservoir Campaign; Collins, Joseph Lawton; Doyle, James H.; Eighth United States Army; Far East Command (FEC); Hŭngnam Evacuation; Inch'ŏn Landings: Operation CHROMITE; Joint Chiefs of Staff (JCS); MacArthur, Douglas; Ridgway, Matthew Bunker; Smith, Oliver Prince; Walker, Walton Harris; Wŏnsan Landing.

Thailand

The first Asian country to offer military personnel to the United Nations Command (UNC), Thailand provided air, naval, and ground troops. Traditionally, Thailand had practiced a neutral foreign policy, remaining friendly with major Asian powers without sacrificing its independence. After World War II, however, Thailand sought an alliance with the United States to secure weapons and financial assistance. U.S. diplomats realized the importance of a stable Thailand in the midst of the Indo-Chinese War. The United States gave Thailand aid and promised to protect it from Communist guerrillas. In 1947 Phibun Songgram seized power in a coup d'état, and the Thai military controlled the country through the 1950s.

After the 25 June 1950 invasion of the Republic of Korea (ROK, South Korea) by the Democratic People's Republic of Korea (DPRK, North Korea), Phibun offered rice for refugee relief and said he would send troops if asked. Phibun hoped that by sending only a small number of troops, Thailand would secure sophisticated military aircraft and equipment for use in Korea that could be kept after the war.

Although much of the Thai press and many civilian members of the government were opposed to sending troops to Korea, Phibun addressed Parliament, emphasizing the possible economic benefits of Thai participation in the war on the U.S. side. The Thai National Defense Council and cabinet unanimously agreed to send troops, and this united military support convinced reluctant civilian legislators to cooperate. Thailand sent 4,000 ground troops as well as 40,000 metric tons of rice valued at $4,368,000. The United States welcomed Thailand's contribution as proof of regional support for the ROK and as a counter to Communist propaganda that claimed the military action was supported solely by Western "imperialists."

Attached to the U.S. 2d Infantry Division, the Thai Infantry Battalion was perhaps best known for its defense of Pork Chop Hill in November 1952 against vicious Chinese attacks. Thailand also provided two frigates, the HMRTN *Bangpakon* and *Prasae*. A detachment of Royal Thai Air Force was attached to the U.S. Air Force 21st Troop Carrier Squadron, flying C-47 Skytrains. Thai forces suffered 136 dead from all causes and 469 wounded.

Thailand also supported U.S.-sponsored resolutions in the United Nations against the People's Republic of China (PRC) and DPRK, including the February 1951 UN censure vote of the PRC for entering the war and the May 1951 embargo decision.

In return, Thailand received millions of dollars in U.S. aid for a variety of public improvement projects, and the World Bank approved a $25,400,000 loan to rehabilitate Thailand's transportation and irrigation systems, the first such loan to a Southeast Asian nation.

The 17 October 1950 Mutual Defense Assistance Agreement between the United States and Thailand confirmed that each nation would provide military equipment and services if requested and that Thailand could keep military equipment given by the United States. During the Korean War the United States sent sufficient arms to Thailand to equip ten army battalions, as well as fighter planes and naval vessels. The United States also established a military assistance advisory group to train Thai soldiers. U.S. military assistance to Thailand totaled $4.5 million in 1951, $12 million in 1952, and $56 million in 1953. Thailand participated in the 1954 Geneva Conference and was a founding member of the Southeast Asia Treaty Organization (SEATO), with Bangkok being selected as SEATO's headquarters. Thailand remained a critical ally for the United States during the Vietnam War.

—*Elizabeth D. Schafer*

References:

Darling, Frank C. *Thailand and the United States*. Washington, DC: Public Affairs Press, 1965.

Fineman, Daniel. *A Special Relationship: The United States and Military Government in Thailand, 1947–1958*. Honolulu: University of Hawaii Press, 1997.

Hayes, Samuel P., ed. *The Beginning of American Aid to Southeast Asia: The Griffin Mission of 1950*. Lexington, MA: Heath Lexington Books, 1971.

Randolph, R. Sean. *The United States and Thailand: Alliance Dynamics, 1950–1985*. Berkeley: Institute of East Asian Studies, University of California, 1986.

Republic of Korea. *The History of the United Nations Forces in the Korean War*. 6 vols. Seoul: Ministry of National Defense, 1972–1977.

Stueck, William W., Jr. *The Korean War: An International History*. Princeton, NJ: Princeton University Press, 1995.

See also: China, Republic of; Geneva Conference of 1954; Pork Chop Hill, Battle of; United Nations Command Air Forces; United Nations Command Ground Forces, Contributions to.

Thimayya, Kadenera Subayya
(1906–1965)

Indian army general and chairman of the Neutral Nations Repatriation Commission (NNRC) in the Korean War. Born in Coorg, southern India, on 31 March 1906, Kadenera Subayya Thimayya was opposed to British rule. His socially prominent family owned a coffee plantation, and at age 16 Thimayya was selected to attend the new Prince of Wales Royal Indian Military College at Dehra Dun. An excellent student and superb athlete, Thimayya in 1924 was one of the six Indian cadets selected for further training at the Royal Military Academy at Sandhurst. In Britain for the first time, he became aware of social and racial discrimination, and this helped fuel his own sense of Indian nationalism.

Commissioned in 1926, Thimayya returned to India and served in the Highland Light Infantry Regiment, one of the most exclusive units in the British army. During World War II he fought against the Japanese in Burma.

As an officer in the British Indian army, Thimayya had little opportunity to take part in the Indian struggle for independence. He did, however, actively protest against the army's policy of denying promotion to qualified Indian officers. He simply refused to accept the tradition that relegated Indian officers to an inferior position.

In 1947, when India received its independence, Brigadier General Thimayya caught the attention of Prime Minister Jawaharlal Nehru. His 4th Division helped restore order in the East Punjab, along the new India-Pakistan border. Thimayya emerged from this fighting as something of a national hero. He served with distinction in the 1947 war with Pakistan over Kashmir.

In 1953 during the Korean War, India was asked to provide the chairman for the NNRC and some 6,000 troops to maintain order in the prisoner-of-war (POW) camps. They would oversee the screening of Communist and United Nations Command (UNC) POWs at P'anmunjŏm who had refused repatriation. Nehru appointed Thimayya to the post.

Thimayya proved ideally suited for this very difficult assignment. Diplomatic yet firm, he won the respect of the prisoners and of Communist and UNC representatives. Although he allowed the Communists to broadcast daily ten-minute loudspeaker appeals to their countrymen to return home, he correctly predicted to UNC officials that this would have the opposite effect. Thimayya also proved adept in dealing with Republic of Korea (ROK) president Syngman Rhee. When Rhee threatened to liberate the prisoners unilaterally, Thimayya arranged to replace the ROK Marines with U.S. Marines. He also made sure that the

proceedings were concluded within the agreed upon eight-week schedule.

On his return from Korea, Thimayya immediately took over the Western Command, one of the India's three major military commands. However, the Korean experiences were a troubling memory and, with the help of Humphrey Evans, in late 1954 he wrote his memoirs. But because the Indian government did not believe the time was appropriate for its publication, the manuscript was stored away for nearly twenty years. Only well after Thimayya's death, in 1981, did his widow Nina Thimayya publish his memoirs, *Experiment in Neutrality*. The book treats his activities as head of the NNRC and was translated into Korean in 1993.

Between 1957 and 1961 Thimayya served as Indian army chief of staff. He retired from the army on 10 April 1961. He then commanded UN peacekeeping troops on the troubled island of Cyprus. He died in Nicosia on 12 December 1965.

—*Sunghun Cho*

References:

Evans, Humphrey. *Thimayya of India*. New York: Harcourt Brace, 1960.

Gopal, Sarvepalli. *Jawaharlal Nehru: A Biography*. 3 vols. Cambridge, MA: Harvard University Press, 1976.

Thimayya, Kadenera Subayya. *Experiment in Neutrality*. New Delhi, India: Vision Books, 1981.

Times of India, 20 December 1997.

See also: India; Nehru, Jawaharlal; Neutral Nations Reparation Commission; Syngman Rhee.

3d Logistical Command

The U.S. Army's 3d Logistical Command was established on 19 September 1950 to provide support for the newly formed U.S. X Corps scheduled for Operation CHROMITE, the amphibious assault at Inchŏn on Korea's west coast. On 6 October 1950 the 3d Logistical Command, commanded by Brigadier General George C. Stewart, assumed responsibility for the operation of the port of Inchŏn. The 3d Logistical Command subsequently supported United Nations (UN) forces during the drive to the North Korean capital of P'yŏngyang and on toward the Yalu River and the subsequent withdrawal southward following the Chinese intervention in November and December 1950. In December 1950 Colonel John G. Hill replaced Brigadier General Stewart as commander of the 3d Logistical Command, and he supervised the forced evacuation of the port of Inchŏn and other UN logistical facilities in the Inchŏn-Seoul area. The evacuation was conducted successfully, but some 1.6 million gallons of petroleum products, 9,300 tons of engineer supplies, and twelve railcars of ammunition had to be abandoned or destroyed. The port of Inchŏn was also demolished, a senseless move, since UN forces controlled the seaward approaches and the Communists would have been unable to utilize the port in any event. After the withdrawal from Inch'ŏn, on 1 January 1951 the Eighth Army in Korea attached the 3d Logistical Command to the 2d Logistical Command. Subsequently the 3d Logistical Command operated the port of Pusan and logistical facilities in the Pusan area.

—*Charles R. Shrader*

References:

Appleman, Roy E. *South to the Naktong, North to the Yalu.* Washington, DC: Office of the Chief of Military History, 1961.

Mossman, Billy C. *U.S. Army in the Korean War: Ebb and Flow, November 1950–July 1951.* Washington, DC: U.S. Army Center of Military History, 1990.

See also: Inchŏn Landings: Operation CHROMITE; Logistics in the Korean War; Tenth Corps.

38th Parallel, Decision to Cross

Two weeks after the successful Inch'ŏn landing of 15 September 1950, United Nations Command (UNC) forces launched an offensive north across the 38th parallel. The decision to do so had been under consideration from the opening days of the war. Initial UNC objectives established by the UN Security Council resolution of 27 June 1950 were to "repel the armed attack and to restore international peace and security in the area." This clearly required driving the attacking forces back to the 38th parallel, but both U.S. policy and earlier UN General Assembly resolutions identified the long-range goal of a free, united, and independent Korea. Republic of Korea (ROK, South Korean) president Syngman Rhee and some of President Harry S. Truman's advisors saw the war as an opportunity to achieve that goal.

On 13 July 1950, Syngman Rhee publicly declared that the North Korean attack had "obliterated" the 38th parallel as a boundary. On the same day General Douglas MacArthur, meeting in Tokyo with members of the U.S. Joint Chiefs of Staff (JCS), advised that he intended to destroy the North Korean forces, not just drive them back, and that he might have to occupy all of Korea to do so. Chinese intervention, he argued, could be dealt with by atomic bombs. On 17 July President Truman ordered a formal study to determine if the UNC should conduct operations north of the 38th parallel. The issue was secretly debated over the next few weeks in a series of policy papers and meetings.

Those who favored the move argued that peace and security could not be restored while the North Korean threat existed. They saw a moral obligation to take advantage of the opportunity to reunify Korea and believed that the aggressor should be punished by more than a mere return to the status quo. Some argued that unification of Korea under a non-Communist government would provide important strategic advantages. The arguments against moving north were based on fears of provoking Soviet or Chinese intervention with consequent risk of general war.

U.S. officials also sounded out the UN allies. Members of the UN Commission on Korea agreed on 5 August that the goal of the UN effort should be a unified, independent, democratic Korea. U.S. Ambassador Warren R. Austin endorsed that goal in UN speeches on 10 and 17 August 1950. U.S., British, and French officials agreed on 1 September that, while UN forces should not proceed north without prior UN direction, a resolution should be put before the UN General Assembly reiterating the goal of Korean independence and unification.

Clearly, the Truman administration saw the decision to cross the 38th parallel as a weapon with which to fight its domestic critics. Under enormous pressure and vituperative attacks from conservatives—mostly Republicans—the Truman administration attempted to wrest the initiative by rolling back—not simply containing—communism. Crossing the 38th parallel would do just that and, it was hoped, would neutralize McCarthyite attacks, which had been fully unleashed by the sudden outbreak of war in June 1950.

On 11 September President Truman approved the final version of the formal study, NSC 81, which recommended postponing a decision, but anticipated that the UN commander would receive approval to conduct operations north of the parallel unless the Soviets or Chinese intervened first. NSC 81 recommended that MacArthur be ordered to prepare plans to occupy North Korea but not to execute those plans without explicit presidential approval. The JCS informed General MacArthur of the gist of NSC 81 on 15 September, the same day of the Inch'ŏn landing.

UNC military success emboldened President Truman and his advisors to approve the offensive north. Secretary of Defense Louis Johnson's resignation and his replacement by George C. Marshall on 21 September delayed that decision until 27 September. On that date the JCS, with President Truman's approval, informed MacArthur that his objective was now the destruction of the Korean People's Army (North Korean); authorized him to conduct operations north of the 38th parallel provided the Soviets or Chinese had not intervened or threatened to intervene; and directed him to submit plans for invading and occupying North Korea.

On 28 September MacArthur submitted his plan, advising the JCS that he would issue a surrender proclamation on 1 October and, if he received no response, would then enter North Korea to accomplish his objectives. The president approved, and on 29

United Nations forces in the withdrawal from P'yŏngyang, recrossing the 38th Parallel. (National Archives)

September the JCS ordered MacArthur to carry out his plan on schedule. Later the same day Marshall sent a personal message to MacArthur, telling him not to announce in advance his intention to cross the parallel (presumably to avoid public debate that might jeopardize ongoing UN deliberations on the General Assembly resolution). Marshall told MacArthur to "feel unhampered tactically and strategically to proceed north of the 38th parallel."

On 1 October MacArthur broadcast his surrender message, and lead elements of the ROK Army (ROKA) 3d Division crossed the parallel on the east coast of Korea. UNC Operations Order No. 2, issued on 2 October, directed the Eighth Army to attack north toward P'yŏngyang. X Corps was to conduct an amphibious landing at Wŏnsan with a subsequent attack to link up with the Eighth Army. Resupply and the redeployment of X Corps caused a delay in executing the order.

On 3 October Chinese Premier Zhou Enlai warned Indian Ambassador Sardar H. M. Panikkar that if U.S. troops crossed the parallel, China would intervene. The U.S. leadership dismissed Zhou Enlai's threat as a ploy in support of Soviet negotiations in the UN. Although the Chinese had begun mobilizing in Manchuria in the summer of 1950, U.S. intelligence could provide no clear-cut military indication of Chinese preparations for intervention. Both the United States and the UN were inclined to accept MacArthur's assessment that Chinese intervention was unlikely and that his forces could deal with the Chinese if they did intervene.

On 7 October, after a week of debate, the UN General Assembly passed a resolution recommending steps to ensure "conditions of stability throughout Korea" and actions "for the establishment of a unified, independent and democratic Government in the sovereign state of Korea." On the same day, MacArthur gave the go-ahead and 1st Cavalry Division patrols began to cross the parallel.

On 9 October MacArthur transmitted a second surrender message and Lieutenant General Walton H. Walker gave orders to the Eighth Army "to strike out for P'yŏngyang without delay." Later on the 9th the 1st Cavalry Division, the British 27th Brigade, the ROKA 1st Division, and elements of the U.S. 24th Division crossed the 38th parallel in the west in force. The offensive north had begun.

—Donald W. Boose, Jr.

References:

Condit, Doris M. *History of the Office of the Secretary of Defense.* Vol. 2, *The Test of War, 1950–1953.* Washington, DC: Office of the Secretary of Defense, 1988.

Kaufman, Burton I. *The Korean War: Challenges in Crisis, Credibility, and Command.* Philadelphia: Temple University Press, 1986.

Matray, James I. "Truman's Plan for Victory: National Self-determination and the 38th parallel Decision in Korea." *Journal of American History* 66 (September 1979): 313–314.

Schnabel, James F. *United States Army in the Korean War: Policy and Direction, the First Year.* Washington, DC: Office of the Chief of Military History, Department of the Army, 1972.

Schnabel, James F., and Robert J. Watson. *The History of the Joint Chiefs of Staff: The Joint Chiefs of Staff and National Policy.* Vol. 3, *The Korean War, Part 1.* Washington, DC: Historical Division, Joint Secretariat, Joint Chiefs of Staff, 1978.

Stueck, William W., Jr. *The Korean War: An International History.* Princeton, NJ: Princeton University Press, 1995.

See also: Austin, Warren; Collins-Vandenberg Visit to Tokyo; Johnson, Louis A.; Joint Chiefs of Staff (JCS); MacArthur, Douglas; Marshall, George C.; North Korea, United Nations Command Occupation of; Panikkar, Sardar K. M.; Truman, Harry S.; Zhou Enlai.

38th Parallel, Division of Korea at

Despite Korea's strategic location in Northeast Asia, the United States exhibited little interest in the peninsula until World War II in the Pacific dramatically changed the strategic balance and altered American perceptions of U.S. interests in the region. During the conflict President Franklin D. Roosevelt viewed Soviet cooperation as essential to the war effort and to postwar peace and stability. Until the end of the war in East Asia, U.S. military and political leaders desired Soviet intervention against Japanese forces on the Asian continent, although they realized Soviet occupation of Korea, Manchuria, and perhaps even part of Japan might jeopardize U.S. interests in the region. It was a price Washington was willing to pay to lessen American casualties and end the war sooner than might otherwise have been possible. Moreover, the United States had no ground forces anywhere near Northeast Asia to counterbalance potential Soviet influence.

Wishing to limit the Soviet Union's postwar influence in East Asia but to avoid provoking a Russian preemptive action, Roosevelt and his advisors proposed a vaguely defined postwar international trusteeship for Korea under the United States, Great Britain, China, and the Soviet Union. Although the Allied leaders discussed the concept from time to time during the war, they failed to agree on the details of the trusteeship.

In Cairo on 1 December 1943, U.S., British, and Chinese leaders declared that Korea should become free and independent "in due course," implying some temporary period of external supervision. Later, at Teheran, Soviet leader Josef Stalin endorsed the declaration. At the February 1945 Yalta Conference the Soviet leader confirmed an earlier promise to enter the Pacific War two or three months after the defeat of Germany, and the U.S. and British leaders consented to Soviet concessions in Sakhalin, the Kurile Islands, and northern China. The Allies also agreed to a four-power Korean trusteeship but, again, details were left ill-defined.

After Roosevelt's death in April 1945, U.S.-Soviet relations deteriorated. President Harry S. Truman's advisors favored a tougher line toward Russia, and conflicting U.S. and Soviet views on lend-lease, combined operations, and the postwar treatment of Germany and Eastern Europe also soured relations. In May, acting Secretary of State Joseph C. Grew argued that the United States should seek firm Soviet commitment to the Korean trusteeship before implementing the Yalta Agreement. The service secretaries agreed that such a commitment was desirable but noted that the United States had little political leverage. The Soviets would enter the Pacific war at a time of their choosing and could occupy mainland Northeast Asia before U.S. forces could reach these areas.

At the July 1945 Potsdam Conference, the Allied Chiefs of Staff discussed U.S.-Soviet military operations when Russia entered the war, including the coordination of air and naval boundaries near Korea. But except for a brief and inconsequential exchange on 22 July, the political leaders never discussed Korea.

While the Potsdam talks were under way, U.S. officials decided to prepare to occupy Korea as well as Japan if the Japanese surrendered unexpectedly. This decision appears to have been driven by concerns about Soviet actions and intentions and by a new confidence based on the successful atomic bomb test during the Potsdam Conference. They considered that use of the bomb might cause Japan to surrender without an invasion, allowing the United States to establish a presence in Korea without expending American lives in the process.

On 23 July Secretary of War Henry L. Stimson advised President Truman that, "now with our new weapon we would not need the assistance of the

Russians to conquer Japan." But Army Chief of Staff George C. Marshall cautioned that, with troops massed on the Manchurian border, the Soviets could attack anyway, getting "virtually what they wanted in the surrender terms."

Just before Potsdam, the Joint Chiefs of Staff directed the Pacific commanders to include Korea in their plans for the occupation of Japan. On 25 July, after discussions at Potsdam with his Soviet counterpart, Marshall ordered the U.S. Army to prepare to move troops into Korea and alerted General Douglas MacArthur that decisions on the occupation of Japan were imminent.

MacArthur's plans for the occupation were still under development, however, when the first atomic bomb was dropped on Hiroshima on 6 August 1945. Two days later the Soviet Union declared war on Japan. On 9 August the United States dropped the second atomic bomb at Nagasaki and Soviet troops crossed the Manchurian border. On 10 August the Japanese asked for an armistice, sparking intense activity by U.S. planners to develop the necessary instruments of surrender. Two staff officers, Colonels Charles H. Bonesteel III and Dean Rusk, were tasked with drafting General Order 1, designating in detail the particular Allied authority to whom the Japanese forces in each area of the Far East were to surrender. Their guidance was to place the line in Korea as far north as possible considering that Soviet troops were advancing rapidly while the closest U.S. forces were on Okinawa, 600 miles away. Bonesteel and Rusk recommended the 38th parallel, dividing the country roughly in half, with the capital of Seoul in the American zone. On 15 August President Truman approved General Order 1, sending copies to Moscow and London. Stalin made no objection.

On 15 August the Japanese accepted the terms of surrender, and the U.S. occupation force, Lieutenant General John R. Hodge's XXIV Corps, began preparations for the imminent move to Korea. Few of the preliminary actions necessary to implement the occupation plan had been carried out and, although the corps headquarters and one division were on Okinawa, the other units and the shipping to transport them were scattered throughout the western Pacific. Shipping was at a premium and movement of troops to Japan had first priority.

At the time of the Japanese surrender, no civil affairs units had been designated or trained for Korea. The XXIV Corps military government expertise consisted of twenty civil affairs officers (none with any knowledge of Korea) and six paroled Japanese-speaking Korean prisoners of war attached to the corps as translators. Even more serious was a lack of policy guidance. General MacArthur, still under the impres-

sion that the occupation was to be on a quadripartite basis, requested clarification from Washington. He was told that no other countries had "declared intentions," so the initial occupation of Korea would be by U.S. and Soviet forces only. International arrangements for Korea were under "urgent consideration" by the State Department. Neither MacArthur nor Hodge had received any instructions on such key questions as Korean independence, the severing of Korea from Japanese influence, and domestic Korean politics. The initial directive on civil affairs administration did not arrive until 17 October, more than a month after Hodge's occupation force had arrived in Korea.

An advance party from Hodge's headquarters flew to Korea on 4 September. There they made contact with the Russian consulate, which had continued to operate in Seoul after the USSR's declaration of war against Japan, and learned that Soviet occupation forces had stopped at the 38th parallel. On 5 September, after a week-long delay due to devastating typhoons, the lead elements of the occupation force finally embarked for Korea, landing at Inch'ŏn on the afternoon of 8 September.

The occupation force entered a peninsula seething with repressed nationalism, fervor for independence, and hostility among factions of left and right. Returning exile groups, each with its own claim, added to the political ferment. Overlaying the domestic tensions was a growing U.S.-Soviet animosity. In December 1945 the foreign ministers of the victorious powers agreed to implement the four-power trusteeship and established a U.S.-Soviet joint commission to work out the details and begin the process toward Korean independence.

U.S.-Soviet antagonism and domestic Korean pressures soon crippled the joint commission, however, and in 1947 the United States put the Korean question before the United Nations (UN). The General Assembly established the UN Temporary Commission on Korea (UNTCOK) to supervise elections with the goal of a free and independent Korea. The Soviets denied the legitimacy of the UN action and refused UNTCOK entry into the North. UNTCOK duly observed elections in the South, leading to the formation of the Republic of Korea under Syngman Rhee. Soon thereafter, the Democratic People's Republic of Korea was established in the North under Soviet auspices. By 1949 two rival regimes, each with a great power sponsor, faced each other across the 38th parallel, and the division of Korea was complete.

—Donald W. Boose, Jr.

References:

Cumings, Bruce. *The Origins of the Korean War: Liberation and the Emergence of Separate Regimes, 1945–1947.* Princeton, NJ: Princeton University Press, 1981.

Matray, James I., ed. *The Reluctant Crusade: American Foreign Policy in Korea, 1941–1950.* Honolulu: University of Hawaii Press, 1985.

Sandusky, Michael. *America's Parallel.* Alexandria, VA: Old Dominion Press, 1983.

See also: Cairo Declaration; Hodge, John R.; Korea: History, 1945–1947; MacArthur, Douglas; Marshall, George C.; Potsdam Conference; Rusk, David Dean; Stalin, Josef; Syngman Rhee; Truman, Harry S.; U.S. Policy toward Korea before 1950.

THUNDERBOLT, Operation
(25 January–10 February 1951)

A reconnaissance in force launched by the U.S. I and IX Corps in late January 1951 intended to provide the commander of the U.S. Eighth Army in Korea, Lieutenant General Matthew B. Ridgway, with accurate intelligence before the United Nations Command's (UNC's) drive back to the 38th parallel.

Based on the success of Operation WOLFHOUND and Task Force Johnson, which demonstrated that few Communist forces stood between the UNC and the 38th parallel and showed the feasibility of limited offensive operations, Ridgway sought to determine the capabilities of his forces and the disposition of Communist forces in South Korea. Operation THUNDERBOLT called for a controlled advance by elements of the U.S. I and IX Corps with the intent of pressing to the Han River near Seoul, while determining the Communist military situation and inflicting the maximum possible punishment. The corps would advance by phase lines under the I Corps commander's direction and the U.S. X Corps would protect the UNC's right flank. The navy planned two diversionary operations to give the appearance of amphibious invasion and draw attention away from the main effort.

The operation commenced on 25 January with the U.S. 25th Infantry Division leading I Corps and the U.S. 1st Cavalry Division leading IX Corps. Employing Ridgway's "meat grinder" technique for the first time, the offensive advanced slowly from phase line to phase line, more a result of Ridgway's requirements for close coordination and thorough ground searches than of Communist opposition. Ridgway expanded the operation by adding the U.S. 3d Infantry Division to I Corps' advance on 27 January and the U.S. 24th Infantry Division to IX Corps' advance on 28 January. As the situation became clearer and Communist resistance significantly increased, units measured progress in yards instead of miles.

Owing to the dramatic increase in UNC participation and Communist resistance, on 30 January Ridgway converted the reconnaissance in force to a deliberate attack, and he increased the use of air assets to aid the advance. He also began planning Operation ROUNDUP, which would send his remaining forces forward in a manner similar to that of THUNDERBOLT. Operation ROUNDUP began on 5 February 1951, thus beginning an army-wide advance to the north. Continuing its methodical advance, UNC forces reached the south bank of the Han River by 10 February 1951, stopping just short of Seoul.

Conceived as a reconnaissance in force, Operation THUNDERBOLT showed that few Communist forces opposed the UNC in South Korea, and it demonstrated the success of the "meat grinder" technique. Operation THUNDERBOLT and the follow-on offensives placed the UN forces in a favorable position to begin subsequent operations that would allow the UNC to recapture Seoul, recross the 38th parallel, and begin peace negotiations by mid-1951.

—*Timothy A. Sikes*

References:

Blair, Clay. *The Forgotten War: America in Korea, 1950–1953.* New York: Times Books, 1987.

James, D. Clayton, with Anne Sharp Wells. *Refighting the Last War: Command and Crises in Korea, 1950–1953.* New York: Free Press, 1993.

Stokesbury, James L. *A Short History of the Korean War.* New York: William Morrow, 1988.

U.S. Army, 1st Cavalry Division. *The First Cavalry Division in Korea.* Atlanta: Albert Love Enterprises, n.d.

See also: "Meat Grinder" Strategy; ROUNDUP, Operation; WOLFHOUND, Operation.

Tomlinson, Frank S.
(1912   )

British career diplomat and counselor in the British embassy in Washington, D.C., between 1951 and 1953. Born in Sydney, Australia, on 21 March 1912, and educated at University College, Nottingham, Frank Stanley Tomlinson entered the British Consular Service in 1935. He held various junior positions in Japan, South Vietnam, the United States, and the Philippines before returning to Britain in 1947 to serve in the Foreign Office.

In 1951 Tomlinson was posted to the British embassy in Washington, where he attended and was one of the more active contributors to the Korean War briefing meetings. These somewhat sporadically scheduled Washington gatherings of representatives from the principal countries contributing to the United Nations forces in Korea were intended to promote Allied unity and ensure that all the nations involved were receiving accurate information on the course of the fighting and of negotiations. Tomlinson served as a highly dependable conduit for the passage of information between U.S. and British officials. He accurately presented and explained to U.S. government representatives London's views on issues relating to the Korean War.

Tomlinson received instructions from London, which he followed faithfully, to work for an early cease-fire and avoid any broadening of the war, concerns that were constant preoccupations of British diplomacy during the Korean War. Tomlinson was particularly active on policies and issues related to the People's Republic of China (PRC, Communist China), ably setting forth the relatively conciliatory attitude the British advocated on such matters as Taiwan and United Nations seating as an alternative to the far more uncompromising U.S. position. After leaving Washington, Tomlinson held several more second-rank Foreign Office appointments, including head of its Southeast Asia Department, British Consul General in New York, and British High Commissioner in Colombo, ending his career as deputy undersecretary of state at the Foreign and Commonwealth Office. On his retirement in 1972 he moved to Wiltshire.

—*Priscilla Roberts*

References:

Butler, Rohan, and M. E. Pelly, eds. *Documents on British Policy Overseas. Series II,* Vol. 4, *Korea, 1950–1951.* London: Her Majesty's Stationery Office, 1995.

Danchev, Alex. *Oliver Franks: Founding Father.* New York: Oxford University Press, 1993.

Lowe, Peter. *Containing the Cold War in East Asia: British Policies toward Japan, China and Korea, 1948–1953.* Manchester: Manchester University Press, 1997.

MacDonald, Callum A. *Britain and the Korean War.* Oxford: Blackwell, 1990.

Stueck, William W., Jr. *The Korean War: An International History.* Princeton, NJ: Princeton University Press, 1995.

See also: Churchill, Sir Winston Spencer; Eden, Anthony; Franks, Oliver; United Kingdom (UK).

Triangle Hill, Battle of
(14 October–5 November 1952)

Battle involving United Nations and Chinese forces following the Battle of White Horse Hill. At the time of the Battle of Triangle Hill, United Nations Command (UNC) forces were in a holding pattern defending key hilltops along the front. Eighth Army commander General James A. Van Fleet sought to seize the initiative, and he targeted an area about three miles north of Kimhwa where only 200 yards separated the two sides. This area comprised Hill 598 (Triangle Hill) and Sniper Ridge, where UNC casualties had been high. If the Chinese could be pushed off Triangle Hill, they would have to retreat some 1,250 yards to the next defensive position. Operation SHOWDOWN, launched on 13 October, encompassed what became known as the Triangle Hill Complex: Triangle Hill, Sandy Ridge, Pike's Peak, Jane Russell Hill, and Sniper Ridge.

The assault on Triangle Hill was Van Fleet's response to the ongoing Chinese attack on White Horse Hill. Triangle Hill was not expected to be a difficult assault and was projected to last five days with approximately 200 UNC casualties. The attackers planned to support their infantry assault with sixteen artillery battalions, consisting of 288 artillery pieces, and more than 200 fighter-bomber sorties. From the beginning the operation was plagued with problems, when the number of days of preparatory air strikes was cut from five to only two, to support operations at White Horse Hill.

A battalion of the 135th Regiment, 45th Division, Fifteenth Chinese People's Volunteer Army (CPVA, Chinese Communist) defended Triangle Hill. This was an elite formation, well dug in and with adequate ammunition. U.S. 7th Division commander Major General Wayne Smith assigned the task of taking Triangle Hill to Colonel Lloyd Moses's 31st Infantry Regiment. Although the original plan called for only one assaulting battalion, Moses determined he would need two.

The contest for Triangle Hill, which began on 14 October, was fierce. The Chinese proved tenacious in defense. At one point U.S. troops believed that the Chinese had to have been on drugs when one Chinese battalion moved through its own artillery and mortar fire. At the end of the first day's fighting, despite taking heavy casualties, the Chinese had repelled the two attacking U.S. battalions. On 15 October the attackers did capture Hill 598 but then encountered stiff resistance at the base of Pike's Peak.

Casualties multiplied as both sides fed additional forces into what had become a matter of face for each. Eventually 7th Division battalions were expended at the rate of one a day. General Smith frequently rotated his troops to keep them fresh.

By 16 October the UNC had three battalions on Triangle Hill. The Chinese then committed the 134th Regiment of the 45th Division and managed to hold Pike's Peak. On 25 October, when the Republic of Korea Army (ROKA, South Korean) 2d Division relieved the 7th Division, the Chinese again controlled Pike's Peak. In twelve days of battle, the 7th Division sustained more than 2,000 casualties. Eight of its nine infantry battalions fought in the battle. The ROKA 2d Division was forced from Triangle Hill on 30 October.

Because of the high number of casualties, on 5 November General Jenkins ended further attacks on Triangle Hill, conceding its possession to the Chinese. In this battle UNC forces had suffered some 9,000 casualties, while the Communist side had lost more than 19,000. This UNC failure and resulting high number of casualties was a test of the formidable strength and depth of the Communist lines and led UNC commander General Lieutenant Mark W. Clark thereafter to keep his forces on the defensive.

Lessons from other hill battles were again illustrated here. These included the need for attacking troops to close quickly with defenders, to keep the attack moving, not to allow troops to become pinned down, and to dig in quickly and provide defensive cover.

During this battle Van Fleet tested out a new strategy of concentrating heavy firepower against Communist artillery by reorganizing the ratio of 8-inch howitzers and 155-mm guns to allow maximum effect from the firepower. On 3 November Van Fleet implemented his counterbattery program, concentrating heavy firepower against Communist artillery on Triangle Hill with three 8-inch howitzers and three 155-mm gun battalions. But because of caves, tunnels, and heavy overhead protection, it took more than fifty rounds of accurate fire to destroy each Communist artillery piece. Thus the counterbattery program was of limited use and could only be used within the normal ammunition allotment, at least until the overall supply of heavy artillery shells increased.

The Chinese defense of Triangle Hill and subsequent repulse of UNC forces counterbalanced the Chinese loss at White Horse Hill. The Chinese showed their willingness to absorb large losses to defend their positions.

—*Carol I. Yee*

References:

Hermes, Walter G. *United States Army in the Korean War: Truce Tent and Fighting Front.* Washington, DC: Office of the Chief of Military History, 1966.

MacDonald, Callum. *Korea: The War Before Vietnam.* New York: Free Press, 1986.

See also: SHOWDOWN, Operation; Van Fleet, James Alward; White Horse Hill, Battle of.

Tripartite Meetings
(November 1951)

Meetings that dealt in part with the Korean War. The Tripartite Meetings of British, French, and U.S. foreign ministers were held during the entire month of November 1951, in conjunction with two other contemporaneous broader international gatherings: the Sixth Session of the United Nations General Assembly that met in Paris and the Eighth Session of the North Atlantic Treaty Organization (NATO) Council held in Rome. In bilateral and tripartite discussions, U.S. Secretary of State Dean Acheson, British Foreign Secretary Anthony Eden, and French Minister of Foreign Affairs Robert Schuman covered a wide range of issues. These included Iran, NATO, Australia, Egypt, the European Defense Community, Germany, and Korea.

The major issue involving Korea was the possibility of cease-fire arrangements, discussions as to which were then in progress at P'anmunjŏm between the combatants. On 28 November 1951, Acheson and Eden discussed Item 3 on the agenda, namely, the establishment of an inspection organization that could supervise and enforce a cease-fire and take action on any breaches. They considered five different forms of inspection, which were, in decreasing order of severity: complete inspection anywhere behind the lines on both sides; inspection only at specified key points; air inspection; inspection limited to a zone stretching twenty-five miles behind the lines; and inspection limited to the demilitarized zone. Acheson faced the dilemma that, although he and top U.S. military officers believed that only a strong system of inspection would enable the United States to anticipate a future North Korean offensive, he feared that demands for this would compromise and perhaps deadlock the ongoing truce talks. He wished to obtain British endorsement of a strong joint policy (greater sanctions) statement designed to emphasize that any future violation of the cease-fire would bring immediate and heavy consequences to the violators, thereby compensating for any potential shortcomings in the inspection provisions per se.

Acheson and Eden held lengthy discussions on the subject, in which, as so often was the case during the war, the British were caught between their desire to please the United States and their fear of provoking China and thereby compromising their position in Hong Kong and other Asian locales. Eden promised to consult with Prime Minister Winston Churchill as to whether Britain would join in a declaration by all the powers who had contributed to the United Nations forces, warning of the potentially serious consequences of any future cease-fire violation, and specifically suggesting that these might include bombing Chinese airfields in Manchuria or the imposition of an Anglo-American naval blockade of the Chinese coast. It was agreed, however, that this public statement would not be issued unless and until the cease-fire had been signed without reaching agreement on a system of inspections satisfactory to the Western powers. After Eden's return to London the matter was discussed by Churchill, other government ministers, and the British chiefs of staff and within the Foreign Office.

By late December 1951 the British had watered down the proposed statement so that it bore less of the character of an ultimatum and refrained from mentioning concrete retaliatory measures, stating instead that a "breach of the armistice would be so grave that, in all probability, it would not be possible to confine hostilities within the frontiers of Korea." The British agreed that United Nations commander in chief Lieutenant General Matthew Ridgway should be authorized to conclude an armistice agreement even if supervision and inspection arrangements were considered less than satisfactory, and that they would accept limited bombing raids as suitable retaliation for any breach of its terms.

Discussions continued, and in late February 1952 all sixteen nations with troops in Korea agreed to endorse the much-revised and modified joint statement.

—Priscilla Roberts

References:

Acheson, Dean. *Present at the Creation: My Years at the State Department.* New York: W. W. Norton, 1969.

Butler, Rohan, and M. E. Pelly, eds. *Documents on British Policy Overseas. Series II,* Vol. 4, *Korea, 1950–1951.* London: Her Majesty's Stationery Office, 1995.

Dockrill, Michael. "The Foreign Office, Anglo-American Relations and the Korean Truce Negotiations, July 1951–July 1953." In *The Korean War in History,* edited by James Cotton and Ian Neary. Manchester: Manchester University Press, 1989: 100–119.

Eden, Anthony. *Full Circle.* Boston: Houghton Mifflin, 1960.

Foot, Rosemary J. *A Substitute for Victory: The Politics of Peacemaking at the Korean Armistice Talks.* Ithaca, NY: Cornell University Press, 1990.

Lowe, Peter. *Containing the Cold War in East Asia: British Policies toward Japan, China and Korea, 1948–1953.* Manchester: Manchester University Press, 1997.

MacDonald, Callum A. *Britain and the Korean War.* Oxford: Blackwell, 1990.

Poidevin, Raymond. *Robert Schuman: Homme d'État, 1886–1963.* Paris: Imprimérie Nationale, 1986.

Stueck, William W., Jr. *The Korean War: An International History.* Princeton, NJ: Princeton University Press, 1995.

See also: Acheson, Dean Goodersham; Eden, Anthony; France; Ridgway, Matthew Bunker; United Kingdom (UK).

Troop Ships

A vital component of the U.S. war effort in Korea. The invasion of the Republic of Korea (ROK, South Korea) on 25 June 1950 presented the United States with a difficult situation. The ROK Army (ROKA) was unable to stop the attack by the Democratic People's Republic of Korea (DPRK, North Korea). President Harry S. Truman then committed U.S. forces to Korea. But the United States had few troops in Asia at the outbreak of the conflict. Obviously, large numbers of men would have to be transported to Korea.

The distance between the United States and Korea made this task appear daunting. Almost 5,000 nautical miles separated San Francisco, one of the major embarkation points for troops on the west coast, and Korea. The distance between Korea and embarkation points on the east coast via the Panama Canal was almost 8,100 nautical miles. As transcontinental air transport was not a feasible option in 1950, troop ships carried the bulk of U.S. forces to Korea.

The task of coordinating and overseeing the use of troop ships lay with the U.S. Navy's Military Sea Transport Service (MSTS). The MSTS used commercially chartered vessels and U.S. Navy transport ships operated by navy personnel and those of the navy's civil service branch. Because of a decline in shipbuilding after World War II, many of these ships were World War II transports of the Liberty and Victory classes. These vessels had been mass produced during the war and, although originally designed as freighters, many were rebuilt as troop transports. MSTS's logistical efforts also benefited organizationally from the World War II experience of deploying ships with men and supplies from U.S. embarkation points across the Pacific.

Sea transport was vital in the early going. The number of transport ships rose from 25 in July 1950 to 263 by that November. The steady increase in their numbers during these months allowed the United States to transport nearly 100,000 men to Korea during the first three months of the war. Six of every seven people who went to Korea traveled by sea. During the war, MSTS transports carried 4,918,919 passengers to and from the United States as well as within the Asian theater of operations.

Troop ships also contributed greatly to combat operations. Captain Virginius Roane commanded the U.S. Navy's Transport Force in the Asian theater and he used his ships there to good effect, particularly in the 15 September 1950 Inch'ŏn landing, when his force landed 60,000 U.S. and 6,000 ROKA troops. Roane's force also proved its worth in the later evacuation of United Nations forces from Hŭngnam in North Korea.

It is difficult to overemphasize the logistic importance of troop ships. The United States could not have projected its military might across the Pacific without them.

—Eric W. Osborne

References:

Field, James A., Jr. *History of United States Naval Operations: Korea.* Washington, DC: U.S. Government Printing Office, 1962.

Huston, James A. *The Sinews of War: Army Logistics, 1775–1953.* Washington, DC: Office of the Chief of Military History, United States Army, 1966.

Love, Robert W., Jr. *History of the U.S. Navy.* Vol. 2, *1942–1991.* Harrisburg, PA: Stackpole, 1992.

See also: Military Sea Transport Service (MSTS).

Truce Talks
(July 1951–July 1953)

Korean War truce talks began at Kaesŏng on 10 July 1951 and continued with two long recesses and one relocation of the conference site until the armistice was signed on 27 July 1953. The talks took place after the 1951 Chinese spring offensive stalled and a subsequent counteroffensive by the U.S.-led United Nations Command (UNC) met increasing Chinese and North Korean resistance north of the 38th parallel. The People's Republic of China (PRC, Communist China) and the United States, having concluded that military victory was unobtainable at an acceptable cost, then sought a negotiated settlement. Being unable to fight on alone, the Democratic People's Republic of Korea (DPRK, North Korea) and Republic of Korea (ROK, South Korea) could only acquiesce.

On 23 June 1951, after preliminary U.S.-Soviet contacts, Soviet deputy foreign minister Jacob Malik suggested in a radio speech that the two sides should seek a cease-fire. On 30 June Lieutenant General Matthew B. Ridgway, commander in chief of the UNC (CINCUNC), proposed that the talks begin aboard a Danish hospital ship moored in Wŏnsan harbor. In their response, Kim Il Sung, supreme commander of the Korean People's Army (KPA, North Korean) and Peng Dehuai, commander of the Chinese People's Volunteer Army (CPVA, Chinese Communist), proposed Kaesŏng, a town in western Korea near the 38th parallel. The UNC accepted. Kaesŏng, the old Korean capital, lay between the lines and was then unoccupied by either side. By the time liaison officers met there on 8 July to make preliminary arrangements for the talks, however, KPA and CPVA forces had moved into Kaesŏng, giving them control of the conference site.

Each side was represented at the truce talks by a negotiating team of five generals or admirals. These principals were assisted by liaison or staff officers who worked out the details of agreements and maintained contact during the long recesses. Much of the most productive negotiating was done by subdelegations consisting of two principals from each side aided by staff assistants. KPA/CPVA negotiators operated from a location near Kaesŏng. UNC negotiators maintained a base camp at Munsan, some fifteen miles southeast of Kaesŏng.

Key KPA/CPVA policy decisions were coordinated among the Chinese, North Korean, and Soviet leaders, with China providing direction and guidance to the KPA/CPVA delegation. Instructions were transmitted through a team headed by Chinese vice foreign minister and deputy chief of staff of the Chinese army Li Kenong, who directed negotiations from behind the scenes. The chief KPA/CPVA delegate at the table was Lieutenant General Nam Il, KPA chief of staff and North Korean vice foreign minister. He was assisted by two North Korean and two Chinese generals or admirals.

On the UNC side, the Republic of Korea (ROK, South Korea) and the major UN allies could occasionally influence policy, but the U.S. government took sole responsibility for directing the UNC negotiators, transmitting instructions through the U.S. Joint Chiefs of Staff to CINCUNC. Vice Admiral C. Turner Joy, commander of U.S. Naval Forces Far East, served as UNC chief negotiator until May 1952, when he was replaced by Lieutenant General William K. Harrison, who served as UNC chief delegate until the armistice was signed. The UNC principals also included three other U.S. generals or admirals and one ROK Army general.

While both sides sought an armistice, each had its own objectives. Neither side trusted the intentions of the other and both believed that any concession would be taken as a sign of weakness, and each side was convinced that military pressure was essential to force the other side to compromise. Ideological differences and the bitter nature of the war intensified the mutual suspicion and hostility that marked the talks. During the first meeting both sides acted in a businesslike manner, but the underlying antagonisms were evident. UNC delegates refused food and other amenities offered by the KPA/CPVA, while the Chinese and North Koreans took advantage of their control of the setting to portray themselves as victorious hosts. They also restricted access to the conference site, denying entry to journalists accompanying the UNC negotiators. After several days of sparring on this issue, the KPA/CPVA agreed, on 15 July 1951, to establish a Kaesŏng Neutral Zone to which both sides would have equal access.

During the next two weeks the negotiators worked out a five-point agenda, Item 1 of which was adoption of the agenda, while Items 2 through 5 provided the format for the eventual Armistice Agreement. Item 2, fixing a military demarcation line (MDL) and establishing a demilitarized zone (DMZ), became Armistice Article I. Item 3, concrete arrangements for a cease-fire, an armistice, and a supervising organization, became Article II. Item 4, arrangements relating to prisoners of war, became Article III. And Item 5, recommendations to the governments of the countries concerned, became Article IV.

The first substantive issue was the location and nature of the MDL and DMZ. The KPA/CPVA side insisted on an MDL along the 38th parallel. The UNC, whose forces had pushed north of the parallel except for an area near Kaesŏng, sought a line well north of the existing line of ground contact. By 22 August the two sides had narrowed their differences and were close to agreement on an MDL based on the ground contact line. The KPA/CPVA then declared a unilateral recess, ostensibly in protest against UNC air attacks against the conference site, but probably to pause negotiations while they reassessed their strategy and prepared for a possible new military offensive.

During the long recess, the UNC, which had been dissatisfied with the Kaesŏng site from the beginning, sought to relocate the talks to a more neutral location. The KPA/CPVA eventually concurred, and under the terms of the 22 October P'anmunjŏm Security Agreement the talks were relocated to a new site several miles to the east.

When negotiations resumed at P'anmunjŏm on 25 October 1951, the remaining Item 2 issues were the precise location of the MDL and when it would come into effect. Ridgway believed that recent UNC ground offensives had brought the Communists back to the table and feared that immediate agreement on the truce line would make further offensives impossible. He thus insisted that the truce line be the line of ground contact when the armistice was signed. The UNC also proposed adjusting the current line of contact, giving up ground near the east coast of Korea in return for placing Kaesŏng in the UNC zone. The KPA/CPVA insisted on immediate agreement on the location of the MDL and refused to give up Kaesŏng. Ridgway's efforts to regain Kaesŏng were prompted by recognition of the military importance of the area as the main avenue of approach into the south and by strong pressure from Syngman Rhee, to whom the old Korean capital had important symbolic significance. Neither of these arguments was persuasive to U.S. leaders in Washington, who believed the armistice would soon go into effect and did not want to delay agreement over what they saw as trivial issues. They thus ordered the UNC to concede these points with the proviso that if the armistice was not concluded within thirty days, the MDL would be the line of contact at the time the armistice was signed. On this basis Item 2 was resolved on 27 November 1951. Although the truce talks went on long after the thirty-day time limit and subsequent fighting required some adjustments, the line changed little by the time of the armistice.

The two sides then addressed Item 3. They quickly agreed on the establishment of a military armistice commission (MAC) with equal representation from both sides, but they differed as to the nature and scope of its activities. The UNC wanted a supervisory mechanism with the power of inspection throughout Korea and, fearing a challenge to UNC air superiority, also called for a ban on the repair or construction of airfields. The KPA/CPVA side accepted MAC supervision inside the DMZ but rejected the airfield repair ban and inspections outside the DMZ.

On 3 December 1951, the KPA/CPVA suggested supervision of the armistice outside the DMZ by nations "neutral in the Korean War," and the UNC eventually accepted this concept. By March 1952 the two sides had agreed to Czechoslovakia, Poland, Sweden, and Switzerland as members of the Neutral Nations Supervisory Commission (NNSC) as well as on procedures for the rotation of military personnel through five ports of entry for each side. Thus Item 3 had been resolved except for airfield repair and a new KPA/CPVA demand that the Soviet Union be included in the NNSC. Resolution of these matters soon became embroiled in the far more difficult issue of repatriation of prisoners of war (POWs).

Both sides had initially assumed that all POWs would be exchanged at the conclusion of an armistice. By the time negotiations began on Item 4, however, the UNC had determined that former residents of South Korea impressed into the KPA should be permitted to stay in the South. U.S. president Harry S. Truman had also concluded that Chinese and North Korean prisoners should not be repatriated against their will. He was heavily influenced in this by memories of the tragic post–World War II fate of millions of Soviet POWs who had been forcibly repatriated, many suffering long imprisonment or death. Truman's rationale for voluntary repatriation was humanitarian, but other U.S. officials foresaw a moral and propaganda victory if large numbers of Chinese and North Korean soldiers rejected communism. They also believed that fear of such military defectors would deter future Communist aggression. General Ridgway and others argued against this policy, concerned that it would delay an armistice and jeopardize UNC prisoners held by the KPA/CPVA. There were also well-justified concerns that pro–Nationalist Chinese prisoners, South Koreans, and Nationalist Chinese with access to the camps would pressure POWs into rejecting repatriation. But President Truman remained adamant.

When discussion of Item 4 began on 11 December 1951, the KPA/CPVA proposed that all POWs simply be exchanged. The UNC, with voluntary repatriation still under debate in Washington, proposed an initial exchange of information on POWs and called for Red Cross inspections of POW camps. The KPA/CPVA rejected Red Cross visits, an issue that the UNC subsequently dropped, but the Communist side agreed to exchange POW data.

When POW lists were exchanged on 22 December, the UNC was shocked to discover that the KPA/CPVA lists contained only 11,559 names out of 99,500 ROK and UNC soldiers listed as missing in action. The KPA/CPVA claimed that the discrepancy arose because they had released many prisoners at the front and because U.S. bombing had killed some UNC POWs. They in turn complained that the UNC list was more than 44,000 less than an earlier list the UNC had passed to the Red Cross. The UNC side acknowledged some faulty initial counting and advised that it had reclassified some 37,000 former ROK residents as civilian internees and removed them from the POW rolls.

On 2 January 1952, the UNC proposed a method for dealing with POWs that involved voluntary repatriation. The KPA/CPVA rejected the principle and, although all the other POW-related issues were resolved by early February, voluntary repatriation was an insurmountable obstacle.

While negotiations on Items 3 and 4 stalled, Item 5, recommendations to the governments concerned, proved easy to resolve. On 6 February 1952, General Nam Il proposed a postwar political conference within three months of the signing of the armistice to discuss withdrawal of foreign forces from Korea, specific recommendations for peaceful settlement of the Korean question, and other problems relating to peace in Korea. The UNC accepted the proposal, with the replacement of "other problems relating to peace in Korea" with the nonspecific term "etc." and a few other changes. Item 5 was resolved on 19 February 1952.

In March 1952 the KPA/CPVA side began to show some flexibility on Item 4, at least regarding prisoners who had been residents of South Korea. On 1 April a UNC staff officer suggested that as many as 116,000 Communist POWs might choose repatriation, but that estimate proved to be woefully optimistic. On 19 April, after screening the prisoners to determine their repatriation desires, the UNC informed the KPA/CPVA that only 70,000 out of over 170,000 prisoners held by the UNC desired repatriation. The KPA/CPVA negotiators stated flatly that such a low figure could not possibly be the "basis for further discussion." On 28 April the UNC presented what it referred to as a package proposal. It dropped the ban on airfield repair and, in return, asked the KPA/CPVA to concede on Soviet participation in the NNSC and voluntary repatriation. The KPA/CPVA accepted the first two proposals, effectively resolving Item 3, but it firmly rejected voluntary repatriation except for former residents of South Korea.

With the talks now deadlocked, the tone at P'anmunjŏm became increasingly hostile. The Chinese and North Koreans began an intense propaganda offensive, accusing the United States of conducting germ warfare. Bloody uprisings in the UNC-controlled POW camps provided fuel for the campaign, embarrassed the UNC, and cast doubt on its administration of the camps and the legitimacy of the screening. On 8 October, with no progress in sight, the UNC declared a unilateral recess.

Neither side was prepared to initiate a major offensive, but both now increased their military activity to put pressure on their opponents. Lieutenant General Mark W. Clark, who had replaced Ridgway as CINCUNC in May, gained approval to conduct the largest air attacks of the war against the North Korean capital of P'yŏngyang and to destroy hydroelectric dams on the Yalu River. Both sides carried out ground attacks. The Chinese stepped up their propaganda campaign and conducted a major reinforcement of their forces in Korea.

With no progress at P'anmunjŏm, the truce talks became an issue at the UN, with several countries putting forth proposals. The one that garnered the most support was that of the Indian delegation, strongly supported by the British and other Commonwealth countries. It called for a neutral nations repatriation commission (NNRC) to deal with the prisoner issue. The United States preferred a resolution that would simply endorse the UNC position but, under pressure from its allies, agreed to support the Indian resolution with some amendments. The General Assembly passed the resolution on 3 December.

The Indian resolution would eventually provide the basis for resolution of the POW repatriation issue, and, as 1953 began, other events that would eventually lead to an armistice were under way. The new Eisenhower administration took office in the United States and was committed to ending the war. North Korea, with its economy devastated, and China, strained by its war effort and eager to begin economic reconstruction, were apparently prepared to return to the truce talks, although they preferred that the United States make the first move. That came on 22 February when Clark, following up a Red Cross proposal, called for an exchange of sick and wounded prisoners.

On 5 March Soviet leader Josef Stalin died. His successors were clearly predisposed to a settlement in Korea and encouraged the Chinese and North Koreans to conclude an armistice. On 28 March the KPA/CPVA accepted Clark's proposal. Two days later Chinese Premier Zhou Enlai made a speech in which he proposed that prisoners not desiring repatriation be transferred to a neutral state. Kim Il Sung publicly endorsed this policy the next day, as did the Soviet foreign minister on 1 April. The Communists had now accepted the principle of voluntary repatriation, and events began to move quickly. The exchange of sick and wounded prisoners, Operation LITTLE SWITCH, began on 20 April, and the truce talks resumed on 26 April. The KPA/CPVA put the NNRC concept on the table, suggesting the NNRC be composed of the same members as the NNSC plus India.

The two sides were now close to agreement, but UNC negotiators still found some aspects of the KPA/CPVA proposal unacceptable. They also introduced two new demands: that the NNRC work on the basis of consensus, rather than majority vote; and that South Korean nonrepatriates not be turned over to the NNRC. Both positions were contrary to the Indian UN resolution, which the U.S. government had previously supported, and the Eisenhower administration ultimately decided not to jeopardize the armistice over these issues. On 25 May the UNC presented what it called its final position. Dropping both of the new conditions, it called for the repatriation of all prisoners within sixty days after the signing of the armistice. Those refusing repatriation were to be transferred to the NNRC for a ninety-day period, during which representatives of their home country would have access to them under NNRC supervision. After ninety days the postwar political conference would deal with any remaining nonrepatriates, with the proviso that after an additional thirty days the nonrepatriates would either be released or their fate decided by the UN General Assembly.

The Chinese and North Koreans were under some pressure to accept. Earlier in May the UNC had attacked irrigation dams near P'yŏngyang to disrupt rail and road lines. Although the North Koreans were eventually able to neutralize the effects by draining the reservoirs, these attacks further strained the North Korean infrastructure and demonstrated a UNC willingness to step up its military action. On 20 May President Dwight D. Eisenhower and his advisors had concluded that if the KPA/CPVA rejected the final offer, the UNC would initiate a military offensive that might include attacks on China and use of nuclear weapons. To signal this resolve, CINCUNC publicly warned that if the KPA/CPVA did not accept the 25 May proposal, the UNC would widen its war effort. U.S. officials attempted to transmit veiled nuclear threats to the Chinese through India and other countries. On 4 June General Nam Il responded to the UNC by declaring, "We basically agree to the new proposal which your side put forward on 25 May." On 8 June the two sides concluded an agreement on voluntary repatriation, and staff officers began a final review of the armistice language.

Feeling betrayed by the 25 May UNC concessions, ROK president Syngman Rhee now made a final effort to derail the armistice. He made strong overtures to President Eisenhower, ordered public demonstrations, threatened to remove the ROK Army from the UNC, said he would attack any Indian troops that set foot on ROK soil, and on 17 June unilaterally released Korean prisoners from the UNC POW camps. Eisenhower sent a mission headed by Walter S. Robertson to negotiate with Rhee. With the promise of future U.S. support, a ROK-U.S. mutual security treaty, and a major aid package—and after the Chinese initiated a series of heavy attacks aimed at ROK units, nearly destroying two ROK Army divisions—Rhee agreed to abide by the armistice. On 27 July 1953 General Clark, Marshal Kim Il Sung, and General Peng Dehuai signed the Armistice Agreement in separate ceremonies, Kim and Peng near P'anmunjŏm and Clark at Munsan. At 1100 the next morning, the Military Armistice Commission began its first meeting at P'anmunjŏm.

—Donald W. Boose, Jr.

References:

Chen, Jian, ed. "China's Strategy to End the Korean War." In *Mao's China in the Cold War: Inquiries and Reinterpretations.* Chapel Hill: University of North Carolina Press, in press.

Foot, Rosemary J. *A Substitute for Victory: The Politics of Peacemaking at the Korean Armistice Talks.* Ithaca, NY: Cornell University Press, 1990.

Goodman, Allan E., ed. *Negotiating while Fighting: The Diary of Admiral C. Turner Joy at the Korean Armistice Conference.* Stanford, CA: Hoover Institute Press, 1978.

Hermes, Walter G. *United States Army in the Korean War: Truce Tent and Fighting Front.* Washington, DC: Office of the Chief of Military History, 1966.

Stueck, William W., Jr. *The Korean War: An International History.* Princeton, NJ: Princeton University Press, 1995.

U.S. Department of State, Bureau of Public Affairs. *Foreign Relations of the United States, 1951.* Vol. 7, *China and Korea.* Washington, DC: U.S. Government Printing Office, 1983.

———. *Foreign Relations of the United States, 1952–1954.* Vol. 15, *Korea.* Washington, DC: U.S. Government Printing Office, 1984.

See also: Agenda Controversy; Armistice Agreement; BIG SWITCH/LITTLE SWITCH, Operations; Cease-Fire Negotiations; Chinese Military Offensives; Civilian Internee Issue; Clark, Mark W.; Dam Raids of 1953; Demilitarized Zone (DMZ); Eisenhower, Dwight D.; Harrison, William Kelly, Jr.; Joy, Charles Turner; Kaesŏng Bombing Proposal; Kaesŏng Truce Talks; Li Kenong (Li K'e-nung); Malik, Jacob (Iakov) Alexandrovich; Menon, V. K. Krishna; Military Armistice Commission; Nam Il; Neutral Nations Repatriation Commission; Neutral Nations Supervisory Commission (NNSC); P'anmunjŏm Security Agreement; P'anmunjŏm Truce Talks; Prisoners of War, Rescreening of; Repatriation, Voluntary; Ridgway, Matthew Bunker; Robertson Mission; SCATTER, Operation; Stalin, Josef; Sup'ung (Suiho) and the Korean Electric Power Plant Campaign; Syngman Rhee; Truman, Harry S; Zhou Enlai.

Truman, Harry S.
(1884–1972)

President of the United States from 1945 to 1953. Born in Lamar, Missouri, on 8 May 1884, Harry S. Truman moved several times as a youth. He spent most of his formative years in Jackson County, Missouri, on his family's 600-acre farm near Grandview. He hoped for a college education and tried to secure appointments to the U.S. Military Academy, West Point, and to the U.S. Naval Academy, Annapolis, but was turned down because of bad eyesight. In World War I he served as an officer with Battery D of the 129th Field Artillery and rose to the rank of captain.

After World War I Truman studied law at night at Kansas City School of Law and won election, with the aid of "Boss" Tom Pendergast, to a judgeship on the Jackson County court. He served in that position between 1926 and 1934. In 1934 he was elected to the U.S. Senate and was reelected in 1940, achieving prominence as the chair of the Senate committee to investigate the national defense program.

President Franklin D. Roosevelt included Truman on the 1944 Democratic Party ticket as a compromise vice-presidential candidate replacing Henry Wallace, who was regarded as being too liberal. When Roosevelt died of a cerebral hemorrhage on 12 April 1945, Truman became the thirty-third president of the United States. Although he had little experience in foreign policy and had not been included in many major policy decisions, Truman guided the United States through the conclusion of World War II. He did not shrink from difficult decisions, especially that of employing the atomic bomb against Japan.

Less willing than Roosevelt to work with Soviet leader Josef Stalin, Truman provided firm leadership in the Cold War. He implemented the policy of containing Communist expansion, known as the Truman Doctrine, by coming to the aid of Greece and Turkey in 1947. His administration also undertook to strengthen Europe against Communist subversion with the Marshall Plan that same year.

Truman was reelected president in 1948 in the midst of the first major confrontation of the Cold War, the Berlin airlift. However, the 1949 Communist victory in China and the Soviet Union's successful test of an atomic bomb intensified attitudes in the United States toward the Cold War.

In his memoirs Truman pointed out the uncompromising nature of the Soviet position after World War II regarding Korea and his appeal to the United Nations to resolve the issue there. Although the U.S. military government ended with elections and the proclamation of the Republic of Korea (ROK) in the South on 15 August 1948, the U.S. National Security Council recommended extensive military and economic aid for South Korea, and a defense agreement was signed with that country on 26 January 1950. Unfortunately, in a speech two weeks earlier, Secretary of State Dean Acheson had excluded the ROK from the U.S. defense perimeter. Fearful that ROK president Syngman Rhee might use them for offensive purposes, the Truman administration had opposed providing tanks or medium or heavy artillery to the ROK.

Despite the failure of his administration to anticipate an invasion of the ROK by the Democratic People's Republic of Korea (DPRK, North Korea), President Truman reacted decisively to the 25 June 1950 invasion. Truman later compared the attack to Nazi Germany's aggression in the late 1930s when he wrote, "If the Communists were permitted to force their way into the Republic of Korea without opposition from the free world, no small nation would have the courage to resist threats and aggression by stronger Communist neighbors." Truman saw Moscow's hand in the invasion and believed that the Soviet Union was trying to secure South Korea "by default" on the

President Harry S. Truman signs the National Emergency Proclamation at the White House, 16 December 1950. (National Archives)

assumption that the United States would be too fearful of another world war to intervene.

Truman adroitly handled the Korean issue in the United Nations. In this he benefited from the Soviet boycott of the Security Council—conducted in protest over the exclusion from the United Nations of the People's Republic of China (PRC, Communist China)—and the failure of the DPRK to pull back across the 38th parallel. Truman also sent the Seventh Fleet to protect Formosa (Taiwan), strengthened U.S. forces in the Philippines, and increased aid to French forces fighting in Indo-China.

Truman rejected an offer from the Chinese Nationalists to fight in Korea, believing that this might provoke the PRC to enter the conflict. Fear of Soviet designs against Western Europe was also a major preoccupation. Truman wanted to avoid a third world war and would not approve reconnaissance flights over Darien, Port Arthur, and Vladivostok, which might have provoked a Soviet response.

Truman appointed General Douglas MacArthur as commander of United Nations (UN) forces in Korea and supported his requests for more troops. The conflict led to the calling up of four National Guard divisions to active duty, an increase in the size of the regular army, and an emergency appropriation of $10 billion for defense purposes. The United States was unprepared militarily for the war and, by summer's end, Truman announced plans to significantly strengthen U.S. military forces and to double the armed forces to 3 million men, warning that the nation's defense burden would become greater still.

Four days before MacArthur's 15 September 1950 landing at Inch'ŏn that would dramatically change the war, Truman asked for Defense Secretary Louis A. Johnson's resignation. General of the Army George C. Marshall replaced Johnson, whose abrasive personality and ego had offended many. Truman was not fond of MacArthur but approved his Inch'ŏn plan, despite reasonable concerns raised by chairman of the Joint Chiefs of Staff (JCS) General Omar N. Bradley and others. He also approved MacArthur's request, with JCS concurrence, to pursue the North Koreans across the 38th parallel with the proviso that he not carry the war into Chinese or Soviet territory.

Truman sought a personal meeting with MacArthur, which took place on Wake Island on 15 October 1950. There they discussed the possibility of Chinese or Soviet intervention almost as an afterthought. MacArthur dismissed the possibility of Chinese intervention and maintained that, should the Chinese intervene, they would be able to get no more than 60,000 men across the Yalu River into North Korea in the face of U.S. bombing. MacArthur was proved wrong in both assessments when the PRC made good on its threat to enter the conflict. Truman reluctantly approved MacArthur's plea to bomb bridges over the Yalu, with the proviso that it was vital "to avoid violation of Manchurian territory and airspace."

As UN forces reeled from the massive PRC military intervention, on 30 November 1950, Truman was asked about the possibility of using the atomic bomb in the war. He responded, "There has always been active consideration of its use." America's Western European allies reacted with alarm to this statement, but at this time the Truman administration was more concerned by the fact that the USSR had just completed military maneuvers involving half a million men and had consolidated their Siberian commands under one commander. While Truman declared a national emergency, he and his principal military advisers believed that Korea was "not the place to fight a major war."

Concerned with the direction of U.S. policy, British Prime Minister Clement R. Attlee visited Washington in December 1950. In a victory for Truman, the joint statement at the end of five days of talks indicated that while the two governments would seek a negotiated settlement to end the war, there would be no "thought of appeasement or rewarding aggression." However, Attlee received assurances that Chinese industrial targets would not be bombed, that tentative plans for an economic blockade and efforts to foment internal unrest in China would be abandoned, and the atomic bomb would not be employed there without prior consultation with London.

Although relieving General MacArthur from his command had already been suggested, Truman preferred standing by his commander in the field. Nonetheless, Truman was angered by an interview with MacArthur published in *U.S. News and World Report* wherein MacArthur sought to lay the blame for the UN retreat before the Chinese forces on the administration's limited war restrictions. To curb MacArthur, the administration issued a series of extraordinary directives that required prior State Department or White House clearance before the release of any statements of a political nature. This did not keep MacArthur from announcing his own ultimatum to the Chinese, demanding their surrender and scuttling any possibility of an early cease-fire. Frustrated by MacArthur's repeated challenges to his administration's policy in Korea, Truman now began to consult his advisors about the possibility of removing the general from command. Truman was, however, concerned over the political impact of removing his field commander on Republicans in Congress and wanted the unanimous concurrence of the JCS before taking such a momentous step.

Then, on 5 April 1951, Republican House Minority Leader Joseph Martin released a letter written by MacArthur, which revealed the general's disagreements with the administration on war policy and argued that there was "no substitute for victory." After midnight on the 11th, the president called a hasty news conference to announce that he was relieving MacArthur from his commands. The timing was dictated by fears that press reports of the planned action might get to MacArthur first and allow him to resign before Truman's relief order arrived. MacArthur had forced this decision, which did, however, serve to preserve the vital principle of civilian control of the military and to preserve the president's policy of fighting a limited war in Korea.

Lieutenant General Matthew Ridgway, MacArthur's successor, carried out the Truman administration policy of doing nothing to broaden the conflict. Truman approved a National Security Council policy statement of 17 May 1951 that sought stabilization of the fighting and an armistice, but on 10 June the JCS secured approval for Ridgway to operate north of the 38th parallel to enhance the chances for armistice talks by maximizing Chinese casualties. Although talks did get under way in July, they achieved little.

Truman chose not to stand for re-election in 1952. After the presidential elections, on 18 November Truman met with president-elect Dwight D. Eisenhower, but he was unable to obtain Eisenhower's signature on a joint communiqué to oppose an Indian plan that required the forcible repatriation of prisoners of war. The Communist side used the Truman administration's insistence on voluntary repatriation to stall the truce talks. Despite this, Eisenhower authorized Republican Senator Alexander Wiley to announce the next day that the president-elect favored "non-forcible repatriation." This, coupled with a Soviet attack on the Indian plan, helped the Truman administration reach a compromise on the issue that was closer to its position. Subsequently, when Stalin's death and the Eisenhower administration's threat of the use of tactical nuclear weapons brought an armistice agreement, Truman made no public comment, but he did harbor some resentment that his own efforts to end the war might not be fully appreciated.

After leaving office Truman wrote his memoirs and arranged his papers to be placed in his presidential library in Independence, Missouri. Former Secretary of State Acheson contributed his papers, as did many other administration officials. With the help of Speaker of the House of Representatives Sam Rayburn and Senate majority leader Lyndon Johnson, Truman urged passage of a law allowing former presidents financial support for staff and offices and free mailing privileges. Such a law was subsequently approved.

Truman was present when President Johnson came to the Truman Library on 30 July 1965 to sign the Medicare bill, which was similar to legislation Truman had proposed nearly twenty years before. Harry S. Truman died in Kansas City, Missouri, on 26 December 1972.

—*Claude R. Sasso*

References:

Kaufman, Burton I. *The Korean War: Challenges in Crisis, Credibility, and Command,* 2nd ed. New York: McGraw-Hill, 1997.

McCullough, David. *Truman.* New York: Simon & Schuster, 1992.

Pemberton, William E. *Harry S. Truman: Fair Dealer and Cold Warrior.* Boston: Twayne, 1989.

Truman, Harry, S. *Memoirs.* Vol. 2, *Years of Trial and Hope.* Garden City, NY: Doubleday, 1956.

See also: Acheson, Dean Goodersham; Attlee, Clement R.; Bradley, Omar Nelson; Harriman, William Averell; Johnson, Louis A.; Joint Chiefs of Staff (JCS); MacArthur, Douglas; Marshall, George C.; Martin, Joseph W.; NATO (North Atlantic Treaty Organization); Ridgway, Matthew Bunker; Syngman Rhee; Truman-Eisenhower Transition Meeting; Truman's Cease-Fire Initiative; Truman's Domestic Agenda and the Korean War; Truman's Recall of MacArthur; Wake Island Conference.

Truman-Eisenhower Transition Meeting
(18 November 1952)

Meeting between President Harry S. Truman and president-elect Dwight D. Eisenhower, held at the White House shortly after Eisenhower's election victory but two months before his inauguration. This was the only personal encounter between the two during the interregnum and was largely devoted to issues arising from the Korean War, particularly the vexing question of the forced repatriation of prisoners of war. In their respective memoirs the two presidents gave somewhat different accounts of this occasion: Truman claimed that Eisenhower was "overwhelmed" by the information he acquired, while Eisenhower recalled that the briefing "added little to my knowledge."

After a private meeting between the two in which Truman offered to provide Eisenhower with any information he required during the transition, the principals and their advisers moved to the cabinet briefing room, where Secretary of State Dean Acheson surveyed a variety of international issues and problems, focusing particularly on the Korean situation. At this time Acheson and Truman were particularly concerned by the prisoner-of-war proposal unveiled at the United Nations the day before by Indian representative V. K. Krishna Menon, with backing from Great Britain and Canada. They feared its vague wording might circumvent the Truman administration's demand for exclusively voluntary repatriation. Acheson suggested that Eisenhower sign a public communiqué stating that he supported the administration's position that no prisoner of war could be "forcibly repatriated." Eisenhower, wary of committing himself at this point to any definite stance, agreed only to a vague statement that he was cooperating with Truman during the transition but that, as the United States Constitution decreed, Truman would be fully in control of the executive branch until the inauguration took place.

Upon further reflection, Eisenhower essentially acceded to Truman's request. The following day, 19 November, he authorized Republican member of the Senate Foreign Relations Committee Alexander Wiley, a delegate to the United Nations, to state publicly that the president-elect endorsed the principle of "non-forcible repatriation." Eisenhower's open support for the Truman administration's position, together with a Soviet attack on the Menon plan, enabled Acheson to obtain modifications in the original proposal that made it acceptable to him and Truman, alterations that were enshrined in the United Nations resolution of 3 December 1952.

—*Priscilla Roberts*

References:

Ambrose, Stephen E. *Eisenhower.* 2 vols. New York: Simon & Schuster, 1983–1984.

Brauer, Carl M. *Presidential Transitions: Eisenhower through Reagan.* New York: Oxford University Press, 1986.

Hamby, Alonzo L. *Man of the People: A Life of Harry S. Truman.* New York: Oxford University Press, 1995.

Mosher, Frederick C., W. David Clinton, and Daniel G. Lang. *Presidential Transitions and Foreign Affairs.* Baton Rouge: Louisiana State University Press, 1987.

See also: Acheson, Dean Goodersham; Eisenhower, Dwight D.; Menon, V. K. Krishna; Truman, Harry S.

Truman's Cease-Fire Initiative
(20 March 1951)

Early in 1951 President Harry S. Truman contemplated making a public appeal for a truce in the Korean War, a decision sabotaged by commander of United Nations (UN) forces General Douglas MacArthur, who publicly demanded that his opponents surrender. MacArthur's unregenerately insubordinate behavior on this and several other occasions precipitated Truman's April 1951 decision to relieve him of his command.

By late March 1951 the military situation of UN forces in Korea was clearly improving, as they recovered from the initial shock of the November 1950 Chinese intervention and began to retake lost ground. Lieutenant General Matthew Ridgway's Eighth Army was close to regaining the 38th parallel, the prewar boundary between the north and south. Encouraged by these successes, Truman's advisers began to suggest that he issue a public statement, cleared in advance with the other governments represented in the UN forces, requesting the Communist side reach first a cease-fire and then a negotiated settlement of the war. The president also intended his message to state that, should their opponents ignore these overtures, UN forces would have no alternative but to continue fighting.

On 20 March 1951, the U.S. Joint Chiefs of Staff informed MacArthur that this statement was in the final stages of preparation. MacArthur promptly issued his own cease-fire appeal, which demanded that the Communist side surrender, denigrated Chinese Communist military capabilities, and restated the general's well-known opinion that "the fundamental questions continue to be political in nature and must find their answer in the diplomatic sphere." Truman interpreted MacArthur's statement as an example of gross insubordination, an implicit attempt to ignore his presidential prerogatives, and one that undercut his own planned declaration and tacitly criticized national policy. In his memoirs Truman wrote that MacArthur's statement effectively presented the Communist side with an ultimatum and implied that if the Chinese did not surrender, the United States and its allies might launch a full-scale attack on Chinese territory. According to Secretary of Defense George C. Marshall, MacArthur's statement was the final episode

persuading Truman that he could no longer tolerate the challenges and defiance the general continually presented to his presidential authority and should therefore recall him. In April 1951 Truman did just that.

—*Priscilla Roberts*

References:

Foot, Rosemary J. *A Substitute for Victory: The Politics of Peacemaking at the Korean Armistice Talks.* Ithaca, NY: Cornell University Press, 1990.

Hamby, Alonzo L. *Man of the People: A Life of Harry S. Truman.* New York: Oxford University Press, 1995.

James, D. Clayton, with Anne Sharp Wells. *Refighting the Last War: Command and Crisis in Korea, 1950–1953.* New York: Free Press, 1993.

Schaller, Michael. *Douglas MacArthur: The Far Eastern General.* New York: Oxford University Press, 1989.

Schnabel, James F. *United States Army in the Korean War: Policy and Direction, the First Year.* Washington, DC: Office of the Chief of Military History, Department of the Army, 1972.

See also: MacArthur, Douglas; Marshall, George C.; Ridgway, Matthew Bunker; Truman, Harry S.; Truman's Recall of MacArthur.

Truman's Domestic Agenda and the Korean War

In a January 1949 State of the Union Address, President Harry S. Truman formally enunciated his Fair Deal program, an ambitious domestic reform agenda that traced its origins back to 1945. Over the interceding years Truman had slowly added to his vision so that by the start of 1949 the Fair Deal encompassed issues ranging from public housing to health care to civil rights. By the end of 1949, however, the Fair Deal was already beginning to founder amidst a barrage of foreign policy and national security crises. The final blows came in 1950, and it is no exaggeration to say that the Korean War dealt the coup de grace to the Fair Deal—indeed to most of Truman's domestic agenda.

The Truman administration's hopes of fulfilling the Fair Deal began to wither in early 1949. Ominous signs of a deteriorating international situation combined with mounting tensions between Washington and Moscow began to divert attention away from the Fair Deal. The Russians' detonation of their first atomic weapon in September 1949 shocked Washington and the world. It also marked a new and dangerous turn in the Cold War, as the United States could no longer rely on its atomic monopoly. One month later, Communist forces triumphed in the Chinese civil war. The world's most populous nation had now joined the Communist bloc. At the same time the Soviet Union formally established the German Democratic Republic, ensuring a divided Germany.

The year 1950 brought more crises. The Soviets boycotted the United Nations Security Council and signed a mutual assistance and defense pact with China. Alger Hiss, originally accused of espionage, was convicted of perjury, but only because the espionage charge had exceeded the statute of limitations. The British government uncovered a spy ring that seemed to prove that the Soviets had received secret atomic information through their infiltration of the Manhattan Project and other U.S. atomic weapons programs. Then came the relentless attacks of Senator Joseph McCarthy, who began a four-year-long anti-Communist witch hunt, much of which was aimed at the Truman administration and the Democratic Party. Amidst this atmosphere of crisis and anti-Communist hysteria, it is little wonder that the Truman administration felt obliged to further deemphasize domestic policies in the name of defense and national security.

In January 1950 Truman administration officials decided to counter the Soviets' newly acquired atomic capability by launching an all-out effort to develop, test detonate, and deploy a hydrogen, or thermonuclear, bomb. The United States accomplished this feat by 1952. Also in January 1950, Truman gave the Departments of State and Defense authority to systematically appraise the nation's military and industrial capabilities and to draw plans to augment those capabilities in light of the deepening Cold War. This planning resulted in the drafting of the seminal Cold War document NSC-68. After the outbreak of war in Korea in June 1950, NSC-68 quickly became the national blueprint for waging the Cold War on a global scale. NSC-68 would serve as the U.S. defense and military guidepost for nearly a generation.

Selling NSC-68 to Harry Truman was no small task. He was a fiscal conservative who had staked his second administration on continued domestic reform, small defense outlays, and balanced budgets. The massive defense spending envisioned in NSC-68 was therefore anathema to Truman. The president also greatly feared ceding too much authority to the military and national security establishments. Thus, the fate of NSC-68 hung in the balance until war erupted in Korea. Only after that did Truman agree, albeit reluctantly, to implement NSC-68.

The economic philosophy that underwrote the prescriptions in NSC-68 were based on the ideas of Leon Keyserling, chairman of the Council of Economic Advisors. His economic philosophy would later become the administration's de facto wartime domestic economic policy. Keyserling, a proponent of Keynesian economics, believed that sustained economic growth powered by close public-private cooperation and government supervision would enable the United States to spend considerably more for defense without harming the economy in the long term. In the short term, however, budget deficits and debt, the bane

of Congress and the White House, were the most likely results. For this and other reasons enumerated above, Truman delayed taking action on NSC-68 until June, when war erupted in Korea.

After Truman decided to intervene in the war, he asked Congress to grant him specific wartime powers to place the nation on heightened alert. Congress complied and the result was the Defense Production Act, which Truman signed into law in September. He also requested an emergency $6 billion appropriation with which to augment U.S. military capacity in Korea and Western Europe. Once more, Congress complied. Thus, by July the United States had begun to mobilize, but the effort was half-hearted and disorganized.

Mobilization proceeded slowly for several reasons. First, Truman sought to keep the Korean War limited and to establish the antebellum status quo on the Korean peninsula, making an expansive mobilization program unnecessary. Second, Truman administration officials still clung to the hope of fulfilling the Fair Deal, which made them reluctant to spend large amounts of money on defense. However, the nation's attention and resources continued to be focused on the war, which was going badly, and on Senator McCarthy, who grew more vitriolic by the day. Truman's hopes notwithstanding, the Fair Deal seemed all but dead.

After the successful United Nations Command landing at Inch'ŏn in September, Truman changed course and decided to go for broke. Circumventing the original United Nations resolutions, he ordered General MacArthur to move his forces north toward the Yalu River, thereby reuniting Korea. With these orders also came the decision by Truman to begin implementing fully—albeit gradually—the dictates of NSC-68. This decision marked a radical shift in U.S. defense and mobilization policy. Once NSC-68 was approved, the Korean-era mobilization program became a dual effort: the U.S. continued to mobilize for the short-term Korean period and for the long haul of the Cold War. Implicit in this process was the decision to construct a permanent military and industrial mobilization base so that the nation would not again have to mobilize from scratch. Never before had the United States committed itself to such readiness in the absence of a major or total war. Until the disastrous Chinese intervention in late November, the Truman administration continued to move rather slowly in its mobilization effort. No new mobilization agencies were created, and mandatory economic and material controls were eschewed in favor of voluntary efforts.

After the Chinese intervention, the Korean War and the attendant mobilization program entered a completely new phase. Fearing a wider Asian war and perhaps even a third world war, Truman decided to revert to the original goal of merely preserving the prewar integrity of South Korea. Total victory and Korean unification were abandoned. At the same time, Truman decided to substantially accelerate the United States' mobilization program. On 16 December 1950, he declared a national emergency and began to establish a panoply of powerful civilian mobilization agencies. In doing so, Truman ensured the rapid and complete military, industrial, and economic buildup proposed in NSC-68. By 1951 the defense budget had nearly tripled from the pre–Korean War level of $13.9 billion to $42.9 billion. Mobilization agencies such as the Office of Defense Mobilization, Defense Production Administration, Office of Price Stabilization, Economic Stabilization Agency, and the Wage Stabilization Board began to exert control over vast portions of the U.S. economy. From December 1950 through the remainder of his term, Truman's domestic policy revolved around the massive mobilization program and his efforts to defend against McCarthyite attacks.

From January 1951 through April 1953, the U.S. government controlled nearly all prices and wages. In July 1951 the Truman administration implemented the Controlled Materials Plan (CMP) in response to critical shortages of industrial raw materials and bottlenecks in military production. The CMP controlled both the allocation of materials and the prioritization of industrial production. Although Korean War controls were not as sweeping as those of World War II and did not include product rationing, they were still an unprecedented foray into government planning during a period in which no war had been officially declared.

It was not surprising that the vast array of wartime controls became quickly unpopular, as did the war effort itself. Conservative Democrats and Republicans in particular came to be the most vocal opponents of Truman's wartime domestic policies. They objected to the president's military and foreign policies and they abhorred his domestic policies that to them seemed to smack of government regimentation, if not socialism. To make matters worse, Truman's firing of the vainglorious General MacArthur in April 1951 further fanned the flames of resentment and partisanship among his adversaries.

As President Truman's popularity continued to plummet, so too did his relations with Congress. In the summer of 1951 and again in the summer of 1952, Congress registered its disapproval by trimming wartime controls legislation found in the Defense Production Act. By 1952 Truman had all but lost the support of Congress, which now included a significant loss of support from within the Democratic party itself. As a result, Truman chose not to seek another term in office.

Congressional efforts to undermine wartime controls legislation had only a negligible effect on the U.S. economy. Spectacular growth combined with Truman's decision to slow down and stretch out the long-term military buildup ensured that inflation and shortages remained largely at bay. However, congressional reluctance to raise taxes high enough to keep the mobilization on a pay-as-you-go basis did result in budget deficits and a mounting national debt. For this Truman took most of the blame, even though he continued to preach about the evils of deficits and had repeatedly asked Congress to keep appropriations apace with spending. Congress demurred, and Truman was forced to take the heat for perceived military failures as well as for mounting budget deficits. By early 1952 the Korean War, in the minds of many Americans, had become "Truman's War."

As the battlefield operations stabilized while the peace talks stalled, the mobilization program continued to grind on. By 1952 the United States was quantifiably stronger and safer than it had been just eighteen months before. This did not mean, however, that Truman would enjoy an unremarkable last year in office. One of the last challenges that Truman and his mobilization program faced was the Steel Crisis of 1952. Confronted with a potentially paralyzing strike in the steel industry, and arguing that America's soldiers and national defense would be imperiled by steel shortages, Truman ordered a government seizure of the nation's steel mills. The constitutionality of the order was challenged, and in June 1952 the U.S. Supreme Court handed the president a stinging defeat by overturning his order. The crisis was ended, and with it went the last vestiges of Truman's clout and popularity.

Despite the vexing economic, political, and military problems that faced the Truman administration, when viewed in its entirety Truman's wartime domestic policy can only be considered a success. His administration kept inflation in check, shortages to a minimum, and economic growth astoundingly high. What is more, U.S. industrial output soared and unemployment fell to record-low levels. There were no major or enduring dislocations to the nation's economy. To the contrary, the Dow Jones industrial average enjoyed double-digit gains from 1950 to 1952 and the nation's gross national product surged by nearly 5 percent between 1951 and 1952. As successful as his Korean War policies may have been, however, Truman remained profoundly disappointed that partisan politics and wartime exigencies had completely derailed his Fair Deal.

The singular achievement of Truman's Korean War policies may be found in the stunning successes of the military mobilization effort. In less than three years, the size of the U.S. armed forces more than doubled and production of military hard goods increased sevenfold. The number of naval vessels also doubled and the strength of the air force increased from 48 to 100 wings during the same period. The Truman administration accomplished these feats by fostering and relying on administrative decentralization, increased volunteerism, equity of sacrifice, and close public-private cooperation.

—*Paul G. Pierpaoli, Jr.*

References:

Hamby, Alonzo L. *Beyond the New Deal: Harry S. Truman and American Liberalism.* New York: Columbia University Press, 1973.

Hogan, Michael J. *A Cross of Iron: Harry S. Truman and the Origins of the National Security State, 1945–1954.* Cambridge, UK: Cambridge University Press, 1998.

Kaufman, Burton I. *The Korean War: Challenges in Crisis, Credibility, and Command.* Philadelphia: Temple University Press, 1986.

Pemberton, William E. *Harry S. Truman: Fair Dealer and Cold Warrior.* Boston: Twayne, 1989.

Pierpaoli, Paul G., Jr. *Truman and Korea: The Political Culture of the Early Cold War.* Columbia: University of Missouri Press, 1999.

See also: Cold War, Origins to 1950; Controlled Materials Plan (CMP); Defense Production Act; Economic Stabilization Agency (ESA); MacArthur, Douglas; McCarthy, Joseph R.; McCarthyism; Mobilization; Nitze, Paul H.; Office of Defense Mobilization (ODM); Office of Price Stabilization (OPS); Steel Plants, Truman's Seizure of; Truman, Harry S.; Truman's Recall of MacArthur; United States: Home Front; Wage Stabilization Board (WSB); Wilson, Charles Edward.

Truman's Recall of MacArthur

President Harry S. Truman's recall of United Nations (UN) commander in Korea General Douglas MacArthur occurred against a backdrop of events that shocked Western policymakers. Entry of the People's Republic of China (PRC, Communist China) into the war in late 1950 increased fears about possible intervention by the USSR, a prospect that increased once U.S. forces advanced north of the 38th parallel. With Washington and its allies unprepared for a global conflict, the Truman administration soon embraced the UN's measures to stop the fighting.

General MacArthur, reluctant to restrict the conflict to Korea, favored a policy to offset the military capability and perceived aggressive tendencies of the PRC. Apprehensive about a deadlock along the 38th parallel, he urged the U.S. Joint Chiefs of Staff (JCS) in February 1951 to authorize attacks on Najin (Rashin), a harbor close to Soviet territory, and electric installations on the Yalu River. The general opposed a strategy of static warfare, lamenting to newspapermen on 7 March about the "savage slaughter" of Americans that

was sure to result from attritional combat. Openly censuring those supporting a pause at the parallel, MacArthur asked the JCS for atomic bombs to defend Japan. Despite knowledge of Truman's readiness to negotiate, he advised against military restraints, and on 24 March he made known his own scheme to end hostilities.

The UN commander's challenge not only undercut a presidential peace bid; it defied civilian policymaking and alarmed Allied governments. After a conference with Secretary of State Dean G. Acheson, Deputy Secretary of Defense Robert A. Lovett, and Assistant Secretary of State Dean Rusk, Truman sent MacArthur a subtle rebuke, reminding him of a directive dated 6 December 1950 obligating commanders to refrain from public statements respecting delicate military and diplomatic subjects.

MacArthur's insubordination climaxed on 5 April. Representative Joseph W. Martin, Republican minority leader, made public a letter in which the general applauded the congressman's support of MacArthur's disapproval of America's European allies and strategic limitations. The general endorsed Martin's proposed aid for Jiang Jieshi's (Chiang Kai-shek's) attack on the Chinese mainland, labeling the Far East the principal cold war theater, where "no substitute for victory" should be tolerated. London's *Daily Telegraph* reported an interview with MacArthur in which he grumbled about restrictions on his military options; and *The Freeman*, a conservative American journal, printed a remark credited to MacArthur saying political judgments prevented enlargement of the Republic of Korea Army (South Korean).

Truman met with Acheson, Secretary of Defense George C. Marshall, JCS chairman General of the Army Omar N. Bradley, and Ambassador W. Averell Harriman—"the Big Four"—on 6 April to determine what action to take. Conferring again in Marshall's office that day, the Big Four still failed to reach a decision.

Later Marshall, at the insistence of Truman, examined the recent communication between the JCS and MacArthur. When the Big Four gathered with the president the next day, they found him incensed over the *Freeman* article. They then recommended the general's dismissal, a determination that Truman waited to disclose until 9 April, once he learned that the JCS all concurred from "a military point of view only."

Truman signed the recall orders on 10 April. He hoped to have Secretary of the Army Frank Pace, who was in Korea, go to Tokyo and convey the dismissal to MacArthur in person, with the White House announcement coming thereafter. But the message failed to reach Pace, and, when Truman learned that the Chicago *Tribune* planned to break the news of the general's removal, his press secretary reported the decision on 11 April. Before the order could be delivered to him, MacArthur learned of his relief while at his residence, where he was entertaining guests at lunch. The orders informed the general of his dismissal as UN commander, U.S. commander in chief, supreme commander for the Allied Powers in Japan, and commanding general of U.S. Army, Far East.

The U.S. public's reaction to MacArthur's firing was extraordinarily emotional. Most letters pouring into the White House supported the general. City governments prepared cordial receptions, and Congress invited him to speak on 19 April. A California community hanged Truman in effigy, while state lawmakers debated the controversy and asked MacArthur to address them. MacArthur's legislative backers inserted in the *Congressional Record* many angry messages from constituents critical of the president. While the Hearst, McCormick, and Scripps-Howard news chains portrayed the general as a victim and Truman as a scoundrel, a number of newspapers—such as the *New York Times*, the *Washington Post*, and the *Atlanta Journal*—defended the president. A Gallup poll of mid-April found most respondents opposed to MacArthur's relief, yet the bulk of American reporters assigned to Washington, D.C., East Asia, and the UN sided with Truman. While Eighth Army enlisted men in Korea took their commander's dismissal in stride, Republican conservatives damned the president, and Senator William E. Jenner of Indiana called for his impeachment.

—Rodney J. Ross

References:

Donovan, Robert J. *Tumultuous Years: The Presidency of Harry S. Truman.* New York: W. W. Norton, 1982.

James, D. Clayton. *The Years of MacArthur.* Vol. 3, *Triumph and Disaster, 1945–1964.* Boston: Houghton Mifflin, 1985.

MacArthur, Douglas. *Reminiscences.* New York: McGraw-Hill, 1964.

Spanier, John W. *The Truman-MacArthur Controversy and the Korean War.* Cambridge, MA: Belknap Press, 1959.

Truman, Harry S. *Memoirs.* Vol. 2, *Years of Trial and Hope.* Garden City, NY: Doubleday, 1956.

See also: Acheson, Dean Goodersham; Bradley, Omar Nelson; Harriman, William Averell; Jiang Jieshi (Chiang Kai-shek); Joint Chiefs of Staff (JCS); MacArthur, Douglas; Marshall, George C.; Martin, Joseph W.; Pace, Frank, Jr.; Truman, Harry S.

Tsarapkin, Semion Konstantinovich
(1906–1984)

Soviet minister to Korea between 1946 and 1948 and delegate to the United Nations from 1949 to 1954. Born in the Ukraine in 1906, Semion Tsarapkin went to work in a smelting plant before entering advanced political training. He graduated from the Institute of Oriental Studies in Moscow and entered the Soviet Foreign Service in 1937. After assisting in the negotiations for the August 1941 German-Soviet Non-Aggression Pact, Tsarapkin became chief of the Second Far East Department of the Commissariat of Foreign Affairs. In 1944 he transferred to the American Department and attended the conferences at Dumbarton Oaks, San Francisco, and Potsdam. Tsarapkin was also present at the Conference of Foreign Ministers, held 16–26 December 1945, in Moscow at which the postwar fate of the Korea peninsula was discussed. Two weeks later, Tsarapkin accompanied the Soviet delegation to Seoul, headed by Terentii Shtykov, as minister extraordinaire and plenipotentiary. Tsarapkin continued as the principal representative of the USSR People's Commissariat of Foreign Affairs in Korea from 1946 to 1948.

Known for his intelligence and aloofness, Tsarapkin allowed Shtykov to play the lead in negotiations and was only an occasional contributor to Soviet policy in Korea. At times, however, it appeared that Tsarapkin was the true authority within the Soviet delegation. As was Shtykov, he was a tough negotiator who adhered faithfully to the Stalinist line, but Tsarapkin was more sophisticated and controlled than his nominal chief.

His most visible role was as one of the five commissioners in the Soviet delegation to the Joint Soviet-American Commission of 1946. Tsarapkin headed the Soviet representation to the first subcommission, charged with determining the conditions for and order of consultation with Korean parties and organizations in the process of creating an all-Korean government. He staunchly defended the Soviet position that any groups or individuals who had, at any time, opposed the Moscow Decision of December 1945 were to be disbarred from participation, until Moscow ordered him to compromise. Even then Tsarapkin gave only minimal ground and on at least one occasion overruled Shtykov when it appeared the latter was ready to accede to U.S. proposals.

Upon leaving Korea, Tsarapkin joined the Soviet delegation to the United Nations (UN) in 1949 as a deputy to the Security Council. He often served as the Soviet spokesman when Jakob Malik was ill, and he participated in the Soviet boycott of the UN in 1950. He became the Soviets' deputy permanent representative to the UN in March 1951 and served in that capacity until he was recalled to the Soviet Union in 1954 to become head of the foreign ministry's division of internal organizations.

Tsarapkin is credited with opening the discussions that led to the armistice talks at Kaesŏng in 1951. As the newly arrived deputy permanent representative of the Soviet delegation to the UN, in late May, Tsarapkin casually mentioned at the end of a conversation with Thomas J. Cory, an advisor to the U.S. delegation, that the USSR would support armistice talks. After tentative conversations with George F. Kennan of the U.S. State Department regarding the Soviet position and a trip to Moscow, Malik officially proposed talks in a radio broadcast on 23 June 1951. Tsarapkin participated in the Kennan-Malik talks, but the full extent of his role became clear only later. The incident is typical of Tsarapkin's style and career.

Later Tsarapkin also advised the foreign ministry on technical standards for nuclear testing control systems and served as the USSR's chief delegate at the Geneva Conference of 1958 to discuss a nuclear test ban. He was posted to the Federal Republic of Germany from 1958 to 1961 and subsequently served as a roving ambassador until his death in 1984.

—*Timothy C. Dowling*

References:

Goodman, Allan E. *Negotiating while Fighting: The Diary of Admiral C. Turner Joy at the Korean Armistice Conference.* Stanford, CA: Stanford University Press, 1978

Van Ree, Erik. *Socialism in One Zone: Stalin's Policy in Korea, 1945–1947.* Oxford: Oxford University Press, 1988.

See also: Cory, Thomas J.; Geneva Conference of 1954; Kaesŏng Truce Talks; Kennan, George F.; Kennan-Malik Conversations; Korea, Democratic People's Republic of: 1945–1953; Malik, Jakob (Iakov) Alexandrovich; Potsdam Conference; Shtykov, Terenti Fomich; Soviet Security Council Boycott; Union of Soviet Socialist Republics.

Tsiang Ting-fu Fuller (Jiang-Tingfu or Chiang T'ing Fu)
(1895–1965)

Republic of China (ROC, Nationalist China) diplomat and scholar. Born on 7 December 1895 in Shaoyang, Hunan Province, Tsiang Ting-fu began a classical education; in 1906 he continued studies under American Presbyterian missionaries in Xiangtan (Hsiang-t'an). Tsiang then went to the United States and attended Park and Oberlin Colleges, graduating in 1914 and 1918, respectively. Tsiang then moved to France as a YMCA secretary attached to the Chinese labor battalion with the French army during World War I. After the war, Tsiang returned to the United States and earned his doctorate in modern history at Columbia University in 1923.

In 1923 Tsiang returned to China to teach at Nankai University in Tianjin (Tientsin). There he pioneered study of China's diplomatic history from a Chinese perspective. In 1929 he moved to Xinghua (Tsinghua) University in Beijing where, as chairman of the history department, he assembled a comprehensive library collection and a renowned faculty, advancing Modern China Studies.

After Japan's invasion of China, Tsiang argued that China should avoid war until it had fully prepared and gained allies. This gained the attention of Generalissimo Jiang Jieshi (Chiang Kai-shek), who in 1934 summoned Tsiang to discuss his views. Subsequently Tsiang visited Moscow to garner support against the Japanese. About this time Tsiang altered his family name to Tsiang to avoid confusion with the generalissimo's family name. Tsiang began official government service in 1935 as political director of the national executive committee.

In 1936 Tsiang became China's ambassador to the Soviet Union. In 1937 he secured a Sino-Soviet nonaggression pact. Despite this apparent diplomatic success, he correctly predicted that the Soviets would be unenthusiastic in their support of Nationalist China. This view was contrary to that of other Chinese leaders, and Tsiang was recalled in 1938.

From 1938 to 1940 Tsiang supervised the removal of government offices and hospitals to Chongqing (Chungking) to escape the Japanese offensive. He also coordinated the national budget. From 1942 through 1946 Tsiang worked in postwar relief planning. He resigned in 1946 due to a policy disagreement with T. V. Soong, Jiang's brother-in-law and financial advisor. Accepting a professorship at the University of California, he prepared to resume academic life. Pressed by friends, however, he accepted a temporary assignment as China's representative to the United Nations (UN) Economic Commission for Asia and the Far East. Shortly afterward, Tsiang became China's representative to the UN Security Council. In the UN Tsiang attempted to use Chinese influence to encourage peaceful resolution of postwar boundary settlements.

With the establishment of the People's Republic of China (PRC, Communist China) in 1949 the position of the ROC in the UN came under increasing challenge. In protest of Tsiang's presence, the Soviet Union boycotted the Security Council for much of 1950, a move that proved critical in allowing UN support for actions in Korea. Subsequently, as the debate on the ROC presence in the UN intensified, Tsiang reminded members that his state was the legitimate government, based on a constitution approved by duly elected representatives of the Chinese people. Although Tsiang failed to convert many to his cause, he did gain wide respect.

In 1961 Tsiang concurrently served as ambassador to the United States and the UN, although the next year he was replaced in the UN. Tsiang remained ambassador to the United States until April 1965, when he retired to again pursue the study of Chinese diplomatic history. Diagnosed with cancer, Tsiang returned to New York for treatment, where he died on 9 October 1965.

—*K. W. T. Madden*

References:

Boorman, Howard L., ed. *Biographical Dictionary of Republican China.* New York: Columbia University Press, 1967.

Current Biography, 1948. New York: H. W. Wilson, 1949.
New York Times, 28 April and 11 October 1965.
See also: Jiang Jieshi (Chiang Kai-shek).

Turkey

As had often happened in Turkey's modern history, the nation emerged from World War II caught between rival military and political blocks. The Soviet Union applied heavy pressure on Turkey after the war to secure control of the straits between the Black Sea and the Mediterranean. Soviet pressure on both Turkey and Greece in fact led to the Truman Doctrine and was a major factor in galvanizing opinion in the United States regarding the Cold War. Ankara also feared outright Soviet aggression. With North Korea's invasion of South Korea in June 1950, this fear became acute, and Ankara agreed to contribute troops to a United Nations (UN) force on the Korea peninsula.

Turkey's motives were not wholly altruistic. It hoped in return to gain reciprocal U.S. commitments to its defense in the Eastern Mediterranean region. More specifically, the Turkish government hoped to fulfill its insistent desire for admission to the North Atlantic Treaty Organization (NATO); NATO had celebrated its first anniversary just two months before the outbreak of the war in the Far East. In fact, Turkey would eventually be invited to join NATO on 22 October 1951 in partial recognition for its service in Korea. With these diplomatic considerations in mind, Turkey agreed on 25 July 1950 to raise and deploy a brigade to the UN effort in Korea.

The Turkish troops arrived at Pusan in the second week of October 1950 with a nominal strength of 5,190 men. They were commanded by General Tashin Yazici, who had fought against British Empire forces at Gallipoli in World War I.

While the employment of the Turkish Brigade partially reflected both the U.S. and the UN desires to show the world a broad anti-Communist coalition in Korea, the Turks' actual effectiveness in combat became a subject of Allied dispute. The brigade's first major action came in the intense fighting in and around the North Korean road junction of Kunu-ri in the last week of November 1950. At that time the brigade was positioned on the right flank of the U.S. Eighth Army's 2d Infantry Division.

Chinese People's Volunteer Army (CPVA, Chinese Communist) and Korean People's Army (KPA, North Korean) forces had broken the front of the Republic of Korea Army (ROKA) II Corps. That unit's defeat and retreat threatened to expose the Eighth Army's right flank. The Turkish Brigade was ordered to help stem the Communist advance.

Turkish participation began inauspiciously. Overwhelmed by the initial confusion of the UN retreat, the Turks fought their first major battle and in the process mistook retreating ROKA troops for those from the KPA. In ensuing after-action reports, and more particularly in press accounts of the fighting, the Turks were praised for having won a significant victory. It would be some time before the public learned the error. Accusations by the Turks of poor liaison on the part of the Eighth Army's contact officers heralded the beginning of a series of such charges and countercharges, all made worse by enduring linguistic difficulties. The press also noted that individual Turkish and Greek soldiers of the UN command had to be kept separated, for they were known to fight each other as fiercely as either fought the Chinese or North Koreans. Indeed, the Turks banned wearing of the UN colors of blue and white by their troops; these are also the colors of Greece and therefore anathema to a Turk.

Despite initial—and, in retrospect, probably inevitable—setbacks, the Turks recovered. By all accounts they thereafter fought fiercely against Communist troops, even while suffering heavy losses in an ambush of two of the brigade's supply columns south of Kunu-ri on 29 November. After a northerly advance of about seven miles from the village of Sunch'ŏn toward the brigade's rear area, Turkish motorized supply columns ran into advancing Communist forces and were ground down in the heavy fighting that followed.

In these first battles the Turks demonstrated behavior that subsequently came to characterize other UN soldiers' descriptions of the brigade. Stories of Turk bravura assumed the stuff of legend: officers throwing down their hats, refusing orders to retreat further, and "dying on their fur;" repeated bayonet charges by Turkish infantry in both offensive and defensive situations; small units being wiped out rather than surrendering when isolated by Chinese forces; Chinese infantry being silently beheaded in their sleep by stealthy Turkish patrols. While such stories could not always be confirmed, many Allied soldiers reported them. True or not, reports of Turks' fury with the bayonet at least raised morale among the UN forces in the face of Chinese successes in the dark days of fall, winter, and early spring of 1950–1951. U.S.Lieutenant General Matthew Ridgway took note of this and decided to have all infantry units fix bayonets to their rifles. Such apparent bravery on the part of the Turks and attendant casualties also flew in the face of General Douglas MacArthur's statement before the U.S. Senate that the non-U.S. and non-Korean units "had no impact on the tactical situation." This sentiment particularly galled some observers, given the fact that the Turks had deployed to Korea at a time of significant tensions in their own part of the world; and when the U.S. government quietly excused itself for the heavy losses suffered by the brigade at Kunu-ri, Ankara reportedly could not understand what the fuss was about. It was, after all, the duty of Turkish soldiers to die if necessary.

As UN forces attempted to regain the initiative after the turn of the year, the Turks once again found themselves in action. Refitted and reorganized to replace the losses at Kunu-ri, the Turks subsequently fought in the recapture of Seoul in January 1951 and were later assigned to protect Kimpŏ Airfield. In the spring, the brigade was assigned to the U.S. 25th Infantry Division's sector.

The front had begun to stabilize in anticipation of a successful outcome to truce talks. As both sides entered the long period of strategic stalemate and attempted to adjust the front to their respective advantage, Communist forces planned a major assault. The main effort of the Chinese offensive between 22 and 30 April 1951 drove the brigade and other UN forces back to the Han River, on the southern bank of which the Turks took up positions on 30 April. After recovering this lost ground by June 1951, the brigade fought small actions as the main line of resistance wavered back and forth across the middle of the peninsula. In spring 1953, during the last of the Chinese offensives along the putative truce line, Turkish forces commanded by Brigadier General Sirri Acar fought a series of intense, sometimes hand-to-hand, battles with Chinese troops. At the time the Turks were assigned positions in the complex of outposts and bunkers called NEVADA, the retention of which the UN command deemed critical. The Turks were ordered to hold at all costs. In the course of this fighting northeast of P'anmunjŏm, the Turks suffered approximately 395 killed and wounded but inflicted some 3,000 casualties upon the Communists. Having delayed and frustrated Chinese efforts to modify the lines, on 29 May the Turkish troops were eventually withdrawn from the line.

Although the Turkish Brigade was sometimes faulted for being badly led, the Turks replied that insufficient liaison was provided by the UN command, particularly regarding language barriers. The Turkish troops' Islamic faith also occasionally created frictions and/or misunderstandings. For example, the Turks would not allow pork in their rations. This, however, was hardly a Turkish monopoly, as other units such as Indian Hindus would eat no beef. Fortunately, more serious frictions, such as the feared hostility between Turks and British Commonwealth soldiers as a result of the memories of World War I, never materialized. In any event, the Turks' resolution in combat and ability to endure the harsh conditions of Korea were noted by other units. No Turkish troops, for example, died in captivity or went over to the Communist side.

—*David R. Dorondo*

References:
Appleman, Roy E. *South to the Naktong, North to the Yalu.* Washington, DC: Office of the Chief of Military History, 1961.
Fehrenbach, T. R. *This Kind of War: A Study in Unpreparedness.* New York: Macmillan, 1963.
Hermes, Walter G. *United States Army in the Korean War: Truce Tent and Fighting Front.* Washington, DC: Office of the Chief of Military History, 1966.
Mossman, Billy C. *U.S. Army in the Korean War: Ebb and Flow, November 1950–July 1951.* Washington, DC: U.S. Army Center of Military History, 1990.
See also: Kunu-ri, Battle of; MacArthur, Douglas; Ridgway, Matthew Bunker.

Twining, Nathan Farragut
(1897–1982)

U.S. Air Force general and director of personnel and deputy chief of staff during the Korean War. Born on 11 October 1897, in Monroe, Wisconsin, Nathan Farragut Twining graduated from the U.S. Military Academy, West Point, during World War I. He volunteered for the Army Air Corps in the 1920s and received most of his training before 1941 in tactical aviation.

During World War II Twining rendered his greatest service in strategic bombing. Successively he commanded the Thirteenth Air Force in the Pacific in 1943, the Fifteenth Air Force in Italy from 1944 to 1945, and the Twentieth Air Force in the Pacific in 1945. It was Twining's B-29s that dropped the two atomic bombs on Japan. After commanding the Air Technical Services in Ohio between 1945 and 1947, he was commander in chief of the Alaska Command until he was ordered to Washington in 1950 to be director of air force personnel. In this position Twining was responsible for securing the airmen needed to enlarge the air force early in the Korean War. His major contribution in this position was weeding out incompetent National Guard and reserve officers who reported for active duty.

In October 1950 Air Force Chief of Staff Hoyt S. Vandenberg appointed Twining his deputy to supervise day-to-day air force operations. Because Vandenberg was frequently ill, Twining sometimes fulfilled his duties as well. A major problem in late 1950 was an army staff complaint that tactical aviation in Korea was inadequate. Twining sent investigators to Korea to recommend improvements and help him prepare for congressional testimony. The investigators interviewed Eighth Army commander Lieutenant General Walton H. Walker, who testified that the army could not have survived in 1950 without tactical air support. Such statements and evidence that tactical air support had enabled the army to make an orderly withdrawal under Chinese pressure in 1950 and 1951 prevented a congressional inquiry. In 1952 Twining modernized aviation units in Korea to ensure air superiority and bring increased pressure on the Communist side during armistice talks.

Much of Twining's time in 1951 and 1952 was spent on air force reorganization. Research and development and aircraft procurement and maintenance were under one command. Twining supervised their separation into two commands for greater efficiency in the expected expansion of the air force. He also instituted a postgraduate course at Air University so that thousands of new officers could learn air force doctrine.

Twining also devoted much time to the politics of air force expansion. When Robert A. Lovett became secretary of defense in 1951, he asked the Joint Chiefs of Staff (JCS) to recommend a force structure adequate to halt possible Communist aggression, as called for in NSC-68. The JCS recommended 143 wings for the air force, a victory for the politicking of Vandenberg and Twining and an increase over the 95 wings previously authorized. President Harry S. Truman accepted the plan and asked for its implementation by 1955. Still, the air force staff had to decide on the allocation of resources among the tactical and strategic bombing wings. Vandenberg and Twining favored an increase in tactical wings, but Secretary of the Air Force Thomas K. Finletter wanted more strategic bombing wings. From May to September 1952 Twining became acting chief of staff during Vandenberg's illness. Twining came to agree with Finletter's position and testified before Congress that B-52s and hydrogen bombs could hold the Communist powers in check.

When new president Dwight D. Eisenhower began budget discussions in 1953, he proposed a severe cut in the air force budget and a decrease in the number of wings from 143 to 120. Vandenberg and General Curtis E. LeMay attacked the budget as endangering security, but Twining was willing to accept it. Vandenberg thereupon resigned in May 1953, and Twining was appointed chief of staff. Given Eisenhower's dependence on massive retaliation by strategic bombing, Twining was forced to let the budget ax fall on tactical units. By this time, however, an armistice had been concluded in Korea and the fighting there was over.

Twining was chief of staff from 1953 to 1957 and was chairman of the JCS between 1957 and 1960. He retired from the air force in 1960.

In 1966 Twining published a critique of defense policy entitled *Neither Liberty nor Safety*. This book revealed Twining's disagreement with the Truman administration's decision to keep the Korean War limited in scope. Twining wrote that he was appalled that the Truman administration publicly announced that it would not use the atomic bomb and would not attack bases in China. Twining believed that such announcements had sapped the power of the air force and made the United States a "paper tiger."

After retirement from the air force, Twining continued an active life. He served as vice chairman of textbook publisher Holt, Rinehart and Winston and as a director of United Technologies. Still interested in defense issues, Twining lobbied for an anti-ballistic missile program and was critical of U.S. policy during the Vietnam War. He died at Lackland Air Force Base, Texas, on 29 March 1982.

—John L. Bell

References:

Frisbee, John L. *Makers of the United States Air Force.* Washington, DC: Air Force History and Museums Program, 1996.

McCarley, J. Britt. "General Nathan Farragut Twining: The Making of a Disciple of American Strategic Air Power, 1897–1953." Doctoral dissertation, Temple University, 1989. Unpublished manuscript.

Twining, Nathan F. *Neither Liberty nor Safety: A Hard Look at U.S. Military Policy and Strategy.* New York: Holt, Rinehart and Winston, 1966.

See also: Dean, William Frishe; Eisenhower, Dwight D.; Finletter, Thomas K.; Joint Chiefs of Staff (JCS); Lovett, Robert A.; Truman, Harry S.; Vandenberg, Hoyt S; Walker, Walton Harris.

U

Union of Soviet Socialist Republics

In 1950 the Union of Soviet Socialist Republics (USSR) was the acknowledged leader of the Communist world. The Soviet Foreign Ministry played an integral role in all aspects of the diplomacy behind the Korean War, even though that role was often indirect. As the sole designer of Soviet foreign policy, Josef Stalin attempted to be something of a puppet master in his relations with other Communist states, with varying degrees of success. The Soviet Union, born out of the 1917 Bolshevik Revolution and the ensuing civil war, was the world's first Communist regime. As a result of its longevity, substantial economic power, and formidable military strength, the many new socialist and Communist governments created since 1945 were obliged to submit to a certain level of guidance from the USSR.

The Soviet Union, by far the largest country in the world, covered more than 8.6 million square miles, eleven time zones, and two continents. Straddling the Ural Mountains (the traditional dividing line between Europe and Asia) gave the USSR a decidedly split personality, with crucial national interests in both areas. Fifteen supposedly sovereign republics constituted the union, but most political authority was concentrated in Moscow, the Soviet capital and the country's largest city. Russia (the Russian Soviet Federated Socialist Republic) accounted for about three-quarters of the territory of the USSR and just over half of the population, which was close to 200 million in 1950. The other fourteen republics, named for their respective ethnic majorities, were on the outside edge of the country in the west and south. Of the roughly 180 distinct nationalities, who spoke 125 languages and dialects, the most numerous were Russians (55 percent), Ukrainians (18 percent), Uzbeks (5 percent), and Belorussians (4 percent). The many Soviet peoples, divided by language, culture, religion, and historical animosities, were united by the use of Russian as the country's lingua franca and by the experience of Soviet rule.

The ruling house of the Russian Empire, the Romanov Dynasty, came to an abrupt end after more than 300 years during the spontaneous 1917 February (March by the Western calendar) Revolution in Petrograd, the tsarist capital. Brutal and inept, Tsar Nicholas II was unable to keep his exhausted subjects united in the vast war effort during World War I. Another eight months of misery, hunger, and defeat left Russia ripe for another upheaval. Vladimir Il'ich Lenin—who incessantly promised "Peace, Bread, and Land" for the soldiers, workers, and peasants—had gained great popularity among those groups by autumn 1917. Pushing his fellow Bolshevik leaders relentlessly toward armed uprising, Lenin eventually succeeded in provoking the famous October Revolution (November by the Western calendar), which began 74 years of Communist Party rule in Russia. Lenin pulled Russia out of the war, despite protests from Britain and France, and endorsed peasant seizures of noble lands. The Bolsheviks emerged victorious from a bloody civil war that left them in control of most of the former Russian empire. After the hostilities of the civil war had ended and British, French, Japanese, and U.S. interventions had been repulsed, Lenin abandoned the crude economic despotism of War Communism in favor of the New Economic Policy (NEP). The extreme excitement of revolution and civil war gave way to the more mundane tasks of state building and revival of the economy through a limited return to market forces, especially in the agricultural and light manufacturing sectors. The NEP was initially successful, but it gave life to the regime's class enemies (bourgeois capitalists) and it eventually stalled. This was the situation that confronted Lenin's successors after his death in 1924.

Josef Stalin's response to the NEP's temporary stagnation, once he had eliminated his main rivals, was to instigate a new revolution. By 1928 he was secure enough at the top to embark on dual policies of forced collectivization of agricultural lands and a break-neck five-year plan for rapid industrialization. Organizing peasants into collective farms gave the state control over agricultural production, but the peasants resisted and consequently several million of them died and millions more were forced to leave their villages. The First Five-Year Plan, although chaotic and based on unachievable goals, created revolutionary excitement among Communists that had been missing since 1921. More importantly, it produced astonishing economic growth, particularly in heavy industry (coal, oil, iron, steel, and machinery). The impressive industrial achievements of the First and Second Five-Year Plans made Stalin a legend in Communist circles around the world and allowed the Soviet Union to defeat the German invaders during World War II.

The brutality of Stalin's reign extended far beyond his drastic economic policies. His infamous "purges" of the Communist Party, government, and Red Army led to the arrest, conviction, and sentencing of millions of innocent people. Some were executed, others were sent to "gulag" prison camps in Siberia to perform hard labor under unimaginably harsh conditions, and a lucky few were merely expelled from the Communist Party. The purges are a testament to Stalin's extreme paranoia and ruthlessness, traits that would become more pronounced as he aged. Stalin's credibility outside the USSR and the fighting effectiveness of the Red Army were severely compromised by the show trials of prominent old Bolsheviks and by the decimation of the officer corps.

Although the Soviet experience in the Second World War began with a long series of catastrophic defeats at the hands of Germany and its allies, it ended in triumph. At a cost of well over twenty million dead, the USSR emerged as the master of Eastern Europe and one of the world's two great military superpowers. Unfortunately, the Soviet Union's wartime alliance with the other superpower, the United States, rapidly deteriorated into a relationship characterized by mutual suspicion, open hostility, and venomous rhetoric. By 1947 this conflict had become the infamous Cold War, which would last for more than forty years. After the end of World War II, Korea became an early and bloody battlefield of the Cold War.

World War II discussions between China, Britain, and the United States on the future of Japanese imperial possessions lead to the Cairo Declaration of 30 November 1943. The agreement, informally accepted by Stalin in May 1945, stipulated that Korea should become an independent country "in due course." At the Potsdam Conference in July, Stalin agreed that Korea would be put under an international trusteeship, jointly administered by the United States, USSR, China, and Great Britain. On 9 August 1945, a few days before the Japanese surrender, the Red Army occupied the Korean peninsula north of the 38th parallel, ostensibly liberating it from thirty-five years of Japanese rule. A month later, U.S. troops occupied the southern half of the peninsula. The dividing line of the 38th parallel was intended merely as a directive for Japanese forces in Korea. Those north of the line would surrender to Soviet officers and the rest would surrender to U.S. officers. Foreign ministers of the two occupying powers agreed on 27 December 1945 in Moscow that a united Korea would become free and independent after a five-year trusteeship, but Cold War politics doomed this plan to failure.

Within North Korea the USSR supported veteran Communist Kim Il Sung, who had received training and military experience in the Soviet Union. The Communists won a series of rigged local and regional elections in November 1946 and formed a provisional government. On 1 May 1948, a new Soviet-inspired constitution was announced and a permanent government set up soon thereafter. Kim Il Sung, who ended

up ruling the Democratic People's Republic of Korea (DPRK, North Korea) for its first forty-six years, maintained cordial relations with the Soviet Union until it dissolved in 1991, but he showed greater independence each year that he remained in power.

In contrast to North Korea, Soviet relations with the People's Republic of China (PRC, Communist China) were defined partly by the fact that Mao Zedong's 1949 victory in the decades-long civil war was his own. He owed very little to Moscow, whose intermittent assistance occasionally proved to be more harmful than helpful. Nonetheless, Mao was willing to play the role of respectful junior partner to Stalin in the affairs of international communism. In February 1950 Mao and Stalin signed the Sino-Soviet Treaty of Friendship and Alliance, which solidified their relationship on the surface but also showed some underlying tensions. The two Communist giants resolved their border disputes, worked out a modest economic aid package for China, and agreed to a limited military alliance. Stalin was hoping for more obedience from China, while Mao wanted greater assistance from the USSR with the PRC's industrial development and national security. The result was that China followed a more independent path after the death of Stalin, who commanded great respect in Beijing despite his high-handed tactics.

The Soviet role in the start of the Korean War is murky because Stalin wanted to perpetuate the fiction that he was not involved at all. Kim Il Sung's attempt to unify North and South Korea by military force in 1950 was undoubtedly his own idea, but the general plan (if not the exact timing) was certainly approved by both Stalin and Mao. There can be no doubt that Stalin and perhaps even Mao could have prevented the initial invasion by expressing strong opposition to Kim's plan. For Stalin, the risks were small and the potential gains were substantial. If his client state in the North swallowed the U.S. protectorate in the South, then Stalin would share the glory without expending any resources. On the other hand, if the Americans intervened, the crisis would make China, the DPRK, and Stalin's satellites in Eastern Europe more dependent on Soviet diplomatic leadership.

And yet, when the war started, Stalin ended up making a major diplomatic blunder. Because the USSR was then staging a boycott of the United Nations (UN), the Soviet delegate was not present in the Security Council to veto the U.S.-sponsored resolutions authorizing UN members to use force against North Korea. Later, when U.S. forces were driving toward the 38th parallel, the Soviets led the diplomatic effort to prevent them from crossing that line. Stalin was determined not to commit Soviet forces, but he did sanction Chinese intervention and supply arms to both of his allies in the conflict. While the Soviets were not an official party to the armistice negotiations, they played a crucial behind-the-scenes role. Their initial intransigence on the issue of prisoner-of-war repatriation may have helped stall the negotiations, but after Stalin's death in March 1953, their position softened slightly and Soviet leaders pushed to move the talks forward again.

As the leader of the Communist world, Josef Stalin sought to manipulate the course of international affairs to consolidate his standing. By supporting Kim Il Sung's invasion of South Korea, Stalin had the opportunity to expand his influence in Asia, enhance his reputation, and maintain a diplomatic wedge between the United States and China. The war did not work out as planned, but the costs for Stalin were seemingly minimal. He miscalculated, however, the war's impact on Sino-Soviet relations. Mao learned two valuable lessons: Soviet aid for its Communist brethren would be miserly and China was strong enough on its own to fight the United States to a standstill. The resulting boost to Mao's confidence allowed him to chart an increasingly independent course after 1953. Although the DPRK remained on good terms with the USSR, Kim Il Sung placed great value on self reliance for the DPRK after the war.

—Edward Sharp

References:

Beloff, Max. *Soviet Policy in the Far East, 1944–1951.* London: Oxford University Press, 1953.

MacKenzie, David, and Michael W. Curran. *A History of Russia, the Soviet Union, and Beyond,* 5th ed. Belmont, CA: Wadsworth, 1998.

Medish, Vadim. *The Soviet Union,* 4th ed. Englewood Cliffs, NJ: Prentice-Hall, 1991.

Ulam, Adam. *Expansion and Coexistence,* 2nd ed. New York: Holt, Rinehart and Winston, 1974.

See also: China, People's Republic of; Cold War, Origins to 1950; Japan; Kim Il Sung; Korea, Democratic People's Republic of; Invasion of the Republic of Korea; Korea: History, 1945–1947; Mao Zedong; P'anmunjŏm Truce Talks; Sino-Soviet Treaty of Friendship and Alliance; Soviet Security Council Boycott; Stalin, Josef; Vyshinskii, Andrei Ianuarovich.

United Kingdom (UK)

The United Kingdom (UK) was the chief Western ally of the United States during the Korean War. At the outbreak of the conflict, the attention of the British people was focused on rising Cold War tensions and domestic conditions. In 1950 Prime Minister Clement Attlee's Labour government faced an uncertain future. The Labour Party's attempts to improve Britain's war-damaged economy after the war resulted in continuing public hardships. The British people had grown increasingly tired of the austerity ushered in by the Labour government in the name of societal improvement through socialism. They held much less faith in the Labour government in 1950 than they had in 1945 when it assumed power.

The 25 June 1950 invasion of the Republic of Korea (ROK, South Korea) by the Democratic People's Republic of Korea (DPRK, North Korea) dashed hopes for British economic recovery. Atlee and his senior officials were aware of the U.S. stance that a failure of the West to react in Korea would encourage Communist expansion in other areas. The British concurred with this view and were particularly concerned about the threat of Communist aggression in Western Europe. Atlee recognized that the UK had to support the United States, not only to meet Communist expansion in Asia but also to strengthen those in the United States who advocated an American commitment to the defense of Europe. Many British officials feared a lack of support for the United States would strengthen those who believed in a Fortress America foreign policy and possibly threaten the rearmament of Europe embodied in the North Atlantic Treaty Organization (NATO).

On 28 June 1950, three days after the United Nations (UN) resolution condemning the DPRK's invasion of the ROK, Atlee spoke in the House of Commons. He told the members of Parliament that Britain would fulfill its pledge to the UN and provide military assistance to the ROK.

By the end of June, the British and Australian governments had offered their air and naval units stationed at Japan to the UN Command. The issue of providing troops, however, presented two problems for Atlee's government. Any contribution of ground forces required steps toward rearmament that the Labour government had previously tried to avoid in favor of focusing resources on the domestic front. Also, British armed forces were already committed to Malaya, where Communist insurgents threatened colonial rule, and to Hong Kong after the Communist victory in China in 1949. Britain's low defense budget and overseas requirements resulted in the initial commitment to Korea of only one infantry brigade in June and an additional two infantry battalions in August. The need for a greater role necessitated greater defense spending. In January 1951 the British government projected a military spending program of £4.7 billion over the next three years. This doubled the defense estimates put forward at the beginning of 1950 and placed a considerable strain on the economy.

Increasing U.S. pressure and the need for influence in U.S. foreign policy decisions in Korea required the new defense estimate, but so too did the rearmament of Europe. The drain on U.S. resources resulting from the Korean War required increased defense spending in Europe to continue western rearmament. The inadequacy of the new defense estimate presented Atlee's government with the explosive issue of the rearmament of the Federal Republic of Germany (West Germany). Unlike the problem of defense spending, this issue proved difficult but not impossible to solve. Although the problem dogged Atlee's administration until its fall from power, the creation of the European Defense Community in May 1952 defused the issue, as it incorporated German forces into a multinational army under the control of NATO.

Atlee's foreign policy was similar to that of the Truman administration, but it had to address British interests in Asia as well. Atlee's government supported the war effort, but after the rout of the North Koreans, it maintained that all military operations in the DPRK should be conducted well south of the Chinese and Russian borders. From the outset the British demanded that the conflict not extend outside Korea without prior consultation. Although the Truman administration agreed that a widened war would be disastrous, many top U.S. officials, such as Secretary of State Dean Acheson, believed British self-interest clouded their judgment on foreign policy matters.

The November 1950 intervention in the fighting by the People's Republic of China (PRC, Chinese Communist) brought about the situation that Britain had sought to avoid and strained relations with the United States. Atlee's government was profoundly opposed to direct confrontation with China because of the potential damage to Britain's Asian trade interests and the threat the PRC posed to their Far East colonies of Malaya, Hong Kong, and Singapore. The Chinese intervention clearly showed the differing attitudes between the UK and the United States over China. Atlee believed that negotiations must immediately take place over Korea. The United States, however, held that negotiations were impossible until the military situation had been stabilized. London also disagreed with Washington's position that the Chinese invasion had occurred with the approval of the Soviet Union. Truman administration officials believed that communism was monolithic and had to be contained. The British tried to argue that the Chinese were not pawns of the Soviets and that U.S. foreign policy must detach the two. Although this did not fall on completely deaf ears in Washington, the Truman administration refused to concede defeat in Korea, something that Atlee was willing to do in hopes of a cease-fire.

London's fear of a wider war seemed to have been realized when Truman hinted of the possibility of a nuclear attack against the Chinese. This prompted Atlee to fly to Washington in December 1950 to seek U.S. assurance that it would not exercise that option.

The British position at this point was precarious. Atlee did not want to betray the United States in Korea. This would cause a political and strategic crisis by destroying the "special relationship" between the two powers and would threaten future U.S. commitment to the defense of Europe. The British consequently pursued a path of supporting the United States but also trying to influence U.S. foreign policy.

Atlee's government saw the opportunity to influence U.S. policy when the war ground to a stalemate in mid-1951. The Labour government, however, had little time to act, as it lost the general election of October 1951. The Korean War had contributed directly to Labour's defeat, as the issue of rearmament burdened the economy and split the party. It was so contentious that many, including Minister of Health Aneurin Bevan, resigned in the belief that rearmament was a threat to socialism and the welfare state in Britain.

Winston Churchill, leader of the Conservative Party, now became prime minister and named Anthony Eden as his foreign secretary. Churchill took office during the P'anmunjŏm truce talks and fully recognized Britain's subordinate role because the country's military contribution was negligible. The British troop contribution, the Commonwealth Division, consisted of two British brigades, one Canadian brigade, two Australian battalions, and a New Zealand artillery regiment by the time he became prime minister. Britain had a large naval presence but did not have a fighter aircraft to match the Soviet MiG-15 fighter flown by the Communists, which consequently handicapped naval effectiveness. Britain could barely claim the right of consultation on major issues, much less a place at the negotiating table.

Churchill's foreign policy resembled that of Atlee, with some exceptions. The prime minister wanted a speedy end to the war, but not at the price of major concessions to the Communists. He believed that long-lasting peace required negotiation from a position of strength in both Asia with the Chinese and North Koreans and in Europe with the Soviets. Churchill believed such a peace would pave the way for his goal of a wide-ranging summit with the Communists over global affairs.

Attaining these goals met frequent obstacles posed by the war and particularly negotiations for peace. The two stumbling blocks were safeguards for Communist compliance of an armistice and the prisoner of war (POW) repatriation issue. Differing opinions in Washington and London over these problems severely strained the special relationship. The United States considered issuing a warning of the possibility of sanctions, such as an economic blockade of the Chinese coast and further military action against the PRC should the Communists violate the armistice. Churchill and Eden both opposed this because of the possibility of provoking a world war. The British believed that the Communists would abide by the armistice and they

Troops of the 29th British Brigade taking a break during the withdrawal to new defensive positions, April 1951. (National Archives)

wanted any warning to be in the most general terms. Truman and Acheson clearly expressed their irritation with London's stance on the issue.

A more divisive issue was that of voluntary repatriation of prisoners of war. Truman insisted on voluntary repatriation with no concessions, which China vehemently opposed. The British supported the U.S. position but objected to another American suggestion that military pressure be applied to force China to agree to voluntary repatriation. The British objected on the same grounds as in the past and began searching for an alternate solution.

The answer was to employ the help of India, which had strong diplomatic channels to Beijing. Churchill saw Indian support as vital to resolving the POW issue. The Truman administration rejected this view out of distrust for the Indians because of their ties to the Communist bloc. The Americans also believed that the Indian proposal to the UN on POWs did not properly address the issue of defectors. The British again found themselves trying to avoid a serious clash with the United States while pursuing the course that they believed could most quickly end the war. A solution presented itself in late 1952 when the Chinese endorsed a Soviet suggestion that a cease-fire take place first before resolution of the POW issue.

The election of Dwight D. Eisenhower as president of the United States relieved the tension between Britain and the United States over foreign policy. Eisenhower was also against forcible repatriation of POWs, but he wanted a solution as soon as possible and was sympathetic to India's efforts.

Eisenhower's election, however, did not resolve basic differences of opinion between Washington and

Commandos of the 41st Royal British Marines plant demolition charges along railroad tracks of a Communist force supply line eight miles south of Songjin, 10 April 1951. (National Archives)

London over foreign policy in Asia. New U.S. secretary of state John Foster Dulles again considered methods of applying pressure on the PRC to break the truce talks deadlock. And Eisenhower hinted at the possibility of using nuclear weapons. Although the British did not believe that the U.S. president would authorize a nuclear strike, they did object again to increased pressure on the Chinese. In spring 1953 Churchill looked to Russian assistance to solve the crisis, especially after Stalin's death in March 1953, after which the Soviets seemed more receptive to the West. Churchill tried to improve relations with Moscow and talked with Foreign Minister V. M. Molotov on the POW issue. Washington hotly contested the British action, and relations again suffered.

British policy ultimately succeeded despite the past disagreements with Washington. The Indian resolution finally gained acceptance with the Communists, who

agreed to a revised form of the plan on 4 June 1953. After some objection to the peace, particularly from ROK president Syngman Rhee, the armistice was signed on 27 July 1953.

Britain made a significant military commitment to UN Command forces. The Royal Navy provided the aircraft carriers HMS *Triumph*, *Glory*, *Ocean*, and *Theseus*; cruisers *Belfast*, *Jamaica*, *Birmingham*, *Kenya*, and *New Castle*; destroyers *Cossack*, *Consort*, *Cockade*, *Comus*, and *Charity*; frigates *Black Swan*, *Alacrity*, *Heart*, *Morecome Bay*, *Mounts Bay*, and *Whitesand Bay*; hospital ship *Maine*; and other vessels. On 29 August 1950 the first of the British land contingents arrived: the 27th Infantry Brigade from Hong Kong. It was followed by tank units and then the 29th Infantry Brigade. Later, the 27th and 29th Brigades were joined into the 1st British Commonwealth Division. With this division were spotter aircraft from the Royal Air Force and also three squadrons of Sunderland flying boats, and the Royal Navy flew Sea Fury, Firefly, and Seafire aircraft from its carriers to provide ground support and interdiction missions. Britain also provided artillery, antiaircraft artillery, and engineer units. At peak strength, British ground forces totaled 14,198 soldiers.

The British contribution to the Korean War was significant in other ways as well. Churchill's government greatly contributed to the end of the conflict through its support of the Indian initiative on POWs and conciliation with all parties concerned in the war, including the Soviets. At war's end the UK had lost 1,078 men, including missing in action. The price was a high one for the strained resources of the UK, but participation in the war protected and furthered its interests throughout the world.

—Eric W. Osborne

References:

Bartlett, Christopher J. *A History of Postwar Britain, 1945–1974.* London: Longman, 1977.

Grey, Jeffrey. *The Commonwealth Armies and the Korean War: An Alliance Study.* Manchester: Manchester University Press, 1988.

Lowe, Peter. *Containing the Cold War in East Asia: British Policies towards Japan, China, and Korea, 1948–1953.* Manchester: Manchester University Press, 1997.

Summers, Harry G., Jr. *Korean War Almanac.* New York: Facts on File, 1990.

Young, John W., ed. *The Foreign Policy of Churchill's Peacetime Administration, 1951–1955.* Worcester, UK: Leicester University Press, 1988.

See also: Acheson, Dean Goodersham; Alexander-Lloyd Mission; Australia; Bevan, Aneurin; Bevin, Ernest; Canada; Cassels, Sir Archibald James H.; Churchill, Sir Winston Spencer; Defectors; Dulles, John Foster; Eden, Anthony; Eisenhower, Dwight D.; India; Lloyd, John Selwyn; Menon, V. K. Krishna; Molotov, Viacheslav Mikhailovich; Nehru, Jawaharlal; New Zealand; Order of Battle: United Nations, North Korea, and People's Republic of China; Panikkar, Sardar K. M.; P'anmunjŏm Truce Talks; Repatriation, Voluntary; Truman, Harry S.; Union of Soviet Socialist Republics; U.S. Policy toward Korea before 1950; U.S. Policy toward Korea: 1950–1953; West, Sir Michael M. A. R.

United Nations Additional Measures Committee

The Additional Measures Committee was established by United Nations (UN) General Assembly Resolution 498(V) of 1 February 1951, with a mandate to explore sanctions against the People's Republic of China (PRC, Communist China) and the Democratic People's Republic of Korea (North Korea). The United States had sought political and economic, as well as military, countermeasures since the PRC had entered the Korean War in late autumn 1950. Among the measures considered were a trade embargo and the freezing of Chinese assets in the United States. The State Department, concerned about any action that

might jeopardize support for the war by a majority of UN states, recommended against a unilateral embargo and sought UN support for collective action. U.S. efforts in the UN were complicated by an Indian-led group of Asian and Middle Eastern nations who sought to broker a cease-fire and by British reluctance to take measures against China so long as there was hope that cease-fire overtures might bear fruit. Chinese rejection of overtures by the UN Cease-Fire Group in January 1951 gave the United States added leverage and led to passage of the 1 February resolution.

This resolution, the first passed under the Uniting for Peace procedure, condemned Chinese intervention as aggression and established the Additional Measures Committee to consider and report on measures "to meet this aggression." The resolution also established a Good Offices Committee to seek a cessation of hostilities. The Additional Measures Committee was authorized to delay its report if the Good Offices Committee made satisfactory progress.

The Additional Measures Committee was to be composed of the same members as the Collective Measures Committee established by the 7 November 1950 Uniting for Peace resolution. However, at the first meeting on 16 February 1950, the Collective Measures Committee representatives from Burma and Yugoslavia declined to participate. The membership thus consisted of representatives from Australia, Belgium, Brazil, Canada, Egypt, France, Mexico, the Philippines, Turkey, the United Kingdom, the United States, and Venezuela.

The U.S. member sought the imposition of both political measures (nonrecognition and exclusion from the UN) and economic sanctions as soon as possible. The British, fearing widening of the war and Chinese action against Hong Kong, opposed political sanctions. Other members of the committee were inclined to wait to see if the Good Offices Committee made progress before imposing any sanctions. On 8 March 1951, the members of the Additional Measures Committee established a subcommittee consisting of Australia, France, the United Kingdom, and the United States. After a month of deliberations, the subcommittee agreed to focus on economic sanctions.

The PRC's refusal to recognize the legitimacy of the Good Offices Committee and the initiation of the Chinese fifth phase (spring) offensive in April 1951 strengthened U.S. arguments for the imposition of sanctions. On 3 May 1951, the subcommittee recommended, and the committee accepted, a U.S. proposal for economic, but not political, sanctions. On 14 May, the full committee delivered its report, noting that a number of countries had already imposed economic measures and recommending an embargo on the export of weapons, munitions, and strategic materials to North Korea and China. This recommendation was incorporated into UN General Assembly Resolution 500(V) of 18 May, which also called upon the Additional Measures Committee to report on the effectiveness of the embargo and the desirability of relaxing or continuing it. This report could be deferred if the Good Offices Committee reported satisfactory progress. The initiation of truce talks in July 1951 brought the efforts of the Additional Measures Committee to an end.

—Donald W. Boose, Jr.

References:

Goodrich, Leland Matthew. *Korea: A Study of U.S. Policy in the United Nations.* New York: Council on Foreign Relations, 1956.

Seyersted, Finn. *United Nations Forces in the Law of Peace and War.* Leyden: A. W. Sijthoff, 1966.

Yearbook of the United Nations, 1951. New York: Columbia University Press, 1952.

See also: United Nations Cease-Fire Group; United Nations Collective Measures Committee; United Nations Good Offices Committee.

United Nations Cease-Fire Group

Also known as the Group of Three, the United Nations (UN) Cease-Fire Group was formed in response to UN General Assembly Resolution 384(V) of 14 December 1950. This resolution requested the president of the General Assembly to establish a group of three individuals, including himself, to determine the basis on which a satisfactory cease-fire in Korea could be arranged and to make recommendations to the General Assembly as soon as possible.

Resolution 384(V) had its genesis in lengthy UN negotiations that began after the entrance of the People's Republic of China (PRC, Communist China) into the war. On 10 November 1950, following the initial clashes between United Nations Command (UNC) and Chinese People's Volunteer Army forces, the United States proposed a Security Council resolution calling on China to withdraw its troops from Korea. When the Soviet Union vetoed this resolution, the U.S. delegation, making use of the Uniting for Peace procedure, introduced a similar resolution in the General Assembly on 7 December. The earlier resolution had almost unanimous support, but by the time the General Assembly took up the proposal the situation had changed. UN members, concerned about Chinese military success and shaken by U.S. president Harry S. Truman's 30 November 1950 public statement that he would consider using atomic bombs in Korea, were inclined to seek a negotiated settlement. Behind the scenes the British urged the United States to exercise restraint, privately suggesting that U.S. recognition of China and withdrawal of U.S. forces from the vicinity of Taiwan might bring an end to the Korean fighting

and drive a wedge between the Chinese and the Soviets. U.S. leaders rejected these proposals but recognized that they would have to compromise to maintain Allied support. Thus the United States voted in favor of an Indian proposal put forth on 12 December by thirteen Asian and Middle Eastern states for the formation of a group consisting of the General Assembly president and two other persons to investigate the possibility of a cease-fire. This proposal was incorporated in the 14 December 1950 resolution that established the Cease-Fire Group.

General Assembly President Nasrollah Entezam of Iran chose Lester B. Pearson of Canada and Sir Benegal N. Rau of India to join him in the group, which immediately set about its work by asking the United States, representing the UNC, what conditions it would accept for a cease-fire. The U.S. government had already deliberated on its cease-fire conditions and was able to respond immediately. Washington wanted a twenty-mile demilitarized zone with its southern boundary generally along the 38th parallel, UN supervision of the cease-fire, cessation of reinforcement or replacement of armed forces and military equipment in Korea, a one-for-one exchange of prisoners of war, and General Assembly confirmation of the cease-fire.

On 16 December the Cease-Fire Group sent messages to the PRC Ministry of Foreign Affairs and to a Chinese delegation that was in New York attending UN discussions on the Taiwan issue. Receiving no replies, it sent a second message to the Chinese Foreign Ministry on 19 December. China, the forces of which were already advancing south of the 38th parallel, was unlikely to accept a cease-fire zone north of that line and denied the legitimacy of the Cease-Fire Group. On 21 December the Chinese notified the UN that it considered the 14 December resolution null and void, since it had been passed without PRC participation. Two days later they transmitted a message from Foreign Minister Zhou Enlai to Entezam as General Assembly president, ignoring his membership in the Cease-Fire Group. Zhou identified Chinese conditions for a cease-fire as withdrawal of all foreign troops, settlement of the Korean question by the Korean people themselves, U.S. withdrawal from Taiwan, and PRC representation in the UN.

On 2 January 1951 the Cease-Fire Group reported to the First Committee that it had not been able to meet with a Chinese representative and were unable to make a recommendation. The Cease-Fire Group then privately circulated a list of "five principles" offering a step-by-step approach to a Korean settlement. On 11 January the Group made a supplementary report setting forth these principles: (1) a cease-fire, including safeguards to prevent secret offensive preparations, (2) follow-up discussions on restoring peace, (3) withdrawal of all foreign forces followed by elections throughout Korea, (4) a temporary UN administration of Korea pending election arrangements, and (5) establishment of a four-party body composed of the United States, China, the Soviet Union, and the United Kingdom to settle all "Far Eastern problems." The fifth principle opened the door to discussion of Taiwan and China's UN seat and was domestically unpopular in the United States, but refusal to support the principles would leave the United States open to charges of obstructing the search for peace. Hoping that China and the Soviet Union would reject the five principles, President Harry S. Truman reluctantly directed U.S. ambassador to the UN Warren Austin to endorse them. The First Committee transmitted a statement of the principles to the Chinese on 13 January. The Chinese replied on 17 January, rejecting the principles and counterproposing withdrawal of all foreign troops followed by a four-party conference to be held in China to discuss Korea, the U.S. withdrawal from Taiwan, and other Far Eastern problems.

The United States saw the Chinese reply as an outright rejection of the five principles and pushed for immediate condemnation of China as an aggressor and imposition of sanctions. Others saw the reply as the potential basis for negotiations. The result of the subsequent debate was a UN resolution on 1 February 1951 accusing China of aggression, establishing an Additional Measures Committee to identify potential sanctions, and establishing a Good Offices Committee to carry on the search for a peaceful settlement. With the establishment of the Good Offices Committee, the role of the Cease-Fire Group ended.

—*Donald W. Boose, Jr.*

References:

Finley, Blanche. *The Structure of the United Nations General Assembly: Its Committees, Commissions and Other Organisms, 1946–1973.* Vol. 1. Dobbs Ferry, NY: Oceana, 1977.

Goodrich, Leland Matthew. *Korea: A Study of U.S. Policy in the United Nations.* New York: Council on Foreign Relations, 1956.

Luard, Evan. *A History of the United Nations.* Vol. 1, *The Years of Western Domination, 1945–1955.* New York: St. Martin's Press, 1982.

Yearbook of the United Nations, 1950. New York: Columbia University Press, 1951.

Yearbook of the United Nations, 1951. New York: Columbia University Press, 1952.

See also: Austin, Warren; Entezam, Nasrollah; Pearson, Lester B.; Rau, Sir Benegal Narsing; Truman, Harry S.; United Nations Good Offices Committee, Uniting for Peace Resolution; Zhou Enlai.

United Nations Civil Assistance Command in Korea (UNCACK)

Organization responsible for short-term assistance to Korean civilians using U.S. Army funds appropriated by Congress under the Civilian Relief in Korea program.

Before the war, U.S. aid to Korea had been funneled through the Economic Cooperation Administration, which continued to operate until April 1951. When hostilities began, the U.S.-led United Nations Command (UNC) began to provide assistance to Korean civilians caught in the combat zone. UN Security Council Resolution S/1657 of 31 July 1950 requested that the Unified Command (the U.S. government acting as UN executive agent in Korea) take responsibility for determining requirements and establishing procedures for the relief and support of Korean civilians. A 29 September 1950 U.S. presidential directive gave the Economic Cooperation Administration responsibility for planning the postwar rehabilitation of Korea, while the commander in chief of the UNC (CINCUNC) was responsible for short-term civil assistance. The CINCUNC gave this task to the Eighth U.S. Army Civil Assistance Headquarters, renamed UN Civil Assistance Command in Korea (UNCACK) on 11 January 1951.

UNCACK's initial task was to safeguard the rear areas by preventing disease and unrest through provision of food, medicine, clothing, and other goods to meet immediate civilian requirements. But it eventually took on a range of responsibilities, including providing food to prisoners of war, resettling civilian internees, assisting veterans, conducting financial and economic coordination, and carrying out short-term rehabilitation and reconstruction projects.

On 1 December 1950 the General Assembly established the UN Korea Reconstruction Agency (UNKRA) to take over the task of long-term relief and rehabilitation. However, the United States was reluctant to allow an independent agency to operate in Korea while military operations were still taking place. Thus, under a 21 December 1951 memorandum of understanding, CINCUNC retained control over economic assistance and relief efforts, with UNCACK as his oversight agency. All persons from the UN or its specialized agencies serving in Korea (except for members of the UN Commission for the Unification and Rehabilitation of Korea) came under contract to UNKRA and, with the exception of a small UNKRA planning staff, all were seconded to UNCACK.

On 10 July 1952 UNCACK was transferred to a newly organized Korean Communications Zone, which assumed responsibility for all logistic support, civil affairs, and prisoner-of-war control south of the combat zone in Korea. On 1 July 1953, UNCACK was redesignated Korean Civil Assistance Command (KCAC) and was placed directly under the authority of CINCUNC. KCAC retained all UNCACK responsibilities and also supervised a new Armed Forces Assistance to Korea program under which U.S. military supplies and equipment could be diverted to civilian reconstruction projects.

On 7 August 1953 the United States put in place a new postwar civil assistance structure. CINCUNC retained overall responsibility for civil assistance but was assigned an economic advisor with the title of economic coordinator. The Office of the Economic Coordinator administered U.S. bilateral assistance and coordinated the military (KCAC) and international (UNKRA) civil assistance programs. KCAC finally ceased operations in November 1955, when all its duties were assumed by the Office of the Economic Coordinator.

—*Donald W. Boose, Jr.*

References:

Hermes, Walter G. *United States Army in the Korean War: Truce Tent and Fighting Front.* Washington, DC: Office of the Chief of Military History, 1966.

Lyons, Gene M. *Military Policy and Economic Aid: The Korean Case, 1950–1953.* Columbus: Ohio State University Press, 1961.

United Nations. *Report of the United Nations Commission for the Unification and Rehabilitation of Korea.* New York: United Nations, 1951, 1952, 1953, 1954, 1955.

United Nations Command. *Civil Assistance and Economic Affairs: Korea, 1 October 1951–30 June 1952, 1 July 1952–30 June 1953, 1 July 1953–30 June 1954,* and *1 July 1954–30 June 1955.* Tokyo: United Nations Command, 1952, 1953, 1954, 1955.

———. *Civilian Relief and Economic Aid: Korea, 7 July 1950–30 September 1951.* Tokyo: United Nations Command, 1951

See also: Civilian Internee Issue; Korean Communications Zone; Tasca, Henry J.; United Nations Command (UNC); United Nations Commission for the Unification and Reconstruction of Korea; United Nations Korean Reconstruction Agency (UNKRA).

United Nations Collective Measures Committee

The Collective Measures Committee was established on 3 November 1950, by United Nations (UN) General Assembly Resolution 377D(V), the Uniting for Peace Resolution. This resolution also established a Peace Observation Commission, recommended that each member state maintain forces for service as UN units, and requested that the secretary-general appoint a panel of military experts to advise member states on organizing, training, and equipping those forces. The Collective Measures Committee was to consult with the secretary-general and other member states to identify ways, including the use of armed force, to "maintain and strengthen international peace and security." The Committee was also to approve the panel of military experts and receive reports from member states on the forces that they had earmarked for UN service.

João Carlos Muniz of Brazil served as chairman for most of the active life of the committee, which was originally composed of representatives from Australia, Belgium, Brazil, Burma, Canada, Egypt, France,

Mexico, the Philippines, Turkey, the United Kingdom, the United States, Venezuela, and Yugoslavia. On 1 February 1951 the General Assembly passed Resolution 498(V) forming the Additional Measures Committee to identify nonmilitary punitive measures against the People's Republic of China (Communist China) and the Democratic People's Republic of Korea (North Korea). By the terms of the resolution, the Additional Measures Committee was to have the same membership as the Collective Measures Committee, but representatives of Burma and Yugoslavia refused to serve in the new organization.

The Collective Measures Committee met twenty times from 5 March 1951 to 27 August 1954 and made three reports to the General Assembly. In its first report of October 1951, it discussed a number of political, economic, financial, and military measures that could be instituted to coordinate the efforts of states responding to aggression. Setting forth a set of "guiding principles," the committee recommended military collective action, an approach similar to that used for the UN Command in Korea: one nation to provide the leadership as "executive military authority." Other states would provide national contingents under the operational control of the lead nation. The committee's report on national contributions to a UN force revealed that few of the member states that had supported the Uniting for Peace Resolution were actually willing to earmark forces, and none requested advice from the panel of experts, which never became more than a nominal list.

In its second report a year later, the committee made some preliminary observations on the concept of a UN Volunteer Reserve. The General Assembly noted but did not act on the committee's proposals. On 30 August 1954 the Committee made its third report, recommending that it should remain available for further study of the issue of actions in support of collective security.

General Assembly Resolution 809(IX) of 4 November 1954 directed the Collective Measures Committee to "remain in a position to pursue further studies … to strengthen the capability of the United Nations to maintain peace" and to report as appropriate. In fact the Committee made no more reports after 1954 and ceased to exist in 1992.

—*Donald W. Boose, Jr.*

References:

Finley, Blanche. *The Structure of the United Nations General Assembly: Its Committees, Commissions and Other Organisms, 1946–1973.* Vol. 1. Dobbs Ferry, NY: Oceana, 1977.

Russell, Ruth B. *The United Nations and United States Security Policy.* Washington, DC: Brookings Institution, 1968.

Seyersted, Finn. *United Nations Forces in the Law of Peace and War.* Leyden: A. W. Sijthoff, 1966.

United Nations. *Yearbook of the United Nations. 1950, 1951, 1952, 1953, 1954.* New York: Columbia University Press, 1951, 1952, 1953, 1954, 1955.

See also: United Nations Additional Measures Committee; United Nations Command (UNC); Uniting for Peace Resolution.

United Nations Command (UNC)

The United Nations Command (UNC), a U.S.-led multinational force, was established in response to UN Security Council resolutions of 25 and 27 June and 7 July 1950. The first two resolutions condemned the Korean People's Army (North Korean) invasion of South Korea as a "breach of the peace" and recommended UN member states assist the Republic of Korea (ROK, South Korea) in repelling the armed attack and in restoring "international peace and security in the area." While not citing specific provisions of the UN charter, the resolution reflected the language of Chapter VII, which deals with breaches of the peace and, in Article 39, gives the Security Council the power to make recommendations. By 30 June U.S. president Harry S. Truman had authorized General Douglas MacArthur, Commander in Chief of the U.S. Far East Command (FEC), to use U.S. forces to assist the ROK, including air and naval strikes in North Korea, and had ordered a naval blockade of the Korean coast. The United Kingdom, Australia, Canada, New Zealand, and the Netherlands had also dispatched forces.

The United States, already engaged in Korea and providing substantial forces, was the logical choice to lead the military effort. Accordingly, the 7 July resolution recommended that UN states place their forces under a "unified command under the United States," requested the United States designate the commander, authorized the command to fly the UN flag, and asked the United States to provide reports "as appropriate."

On 8 July President Truman designated General MacArthur commander in chief of UN forces in Korea. On 14 July U.S. Army Chief of Staff General J. Lawton Collins presented General MacArthur a flag provided by the Security Council that had flown over the UN mission in Palestine. That same day President Syngman Rhee assigned "command authority" over all ROK forces to General MacArthur. On 24 July MacArthur formally established the UNC, issuing UNC General Order No. 1 and raising the UN flag over his Tokyo headquarters. In the course of the war, fifteen nations, in addition to the United States and the ROK, contributed military forces to the UNC. These additional nations constituted about 10 percent of the ground, 7 percent of the naval, and 1 percent of the air forces in the UNC. Five other nations contributed medical units. During the war, the position of UNC commander in chief (CINCUNC) was held successively by General MacArthur (from 8 July 1950 to 11

April 1951), Lieutenant General Matthew B. Ridgway (from 11 April 1951 to 12 May 1952), and Lieutenant General Mark W. Clark (from 12 May 1952 to 7 October 1953).

The UNC was, for all practical purposes, a U.S. military command. The U.S. government sought UN approval for major political decisions, such as the determination of war aims, response to the Chinese intervention, civilian relief measures, and the armistice, but it maintained a free hand on operational matters. The chain of command ran from the U.S. president through the U.S. Joint Chiefs of Staff (JCS) to CINCUNC. All communications were transmitted through the army chief of staff, the designated executive agent for Far East Command and UNC matters. CINCUNC sent his reports through the JCS to the Defense Department. After interagency coordination, the State Department drafted the final version and presented it to the UN. The FEC headquarters, with the addition of a British deputy chief of staff in July 1952, served as the UNC headquarters. The United States rejected a proposal for a UN committee to assist CINCUNC but accepted the attachment of a representative of the secretary-general to the UNC headquarters. Senior military representatives of the participating states had direct access to CINCUNC on "major policy" matters affecting their forces. Otherwise they were to carry out CINCUNC's orders, with the right to subsequently protest in case of disagreement. The Committee of Sixteen, consisting of UN diplomatic representatives of the states providing military forces, met weekly in New York to keep the participating states informed of military operations, but it was not a mechanism for advance coordination of those operations.

UNC military operations were not charged to the UN budget. Participating states either paid for their own forces or entered into bilateral agreements with the United States for logistical support. Offers of assistance were communicated to the United States or the UN secretary-general. The United States then negotiated bilateral agreements with each government concerned.

While all operationally effective ships and air units were welcome, the minimum size for ground units was set at battalions of approximately 1,000 soldiers each (Luxembourg's small contingent served as part of the Belgian Battalion). With the exception of British Commonwealth forces, which eventually formed an entire division, incoming UN units were trained and equipped at a reception center in Taegu. These national contingents were fully integrated into the FEC component commands: U.S. Eighth Army, Far East Air Force, and Naval Forces Far East, which were designated as UNC component commands while retaining their identity as FEC subordinates.

In the course of the war, the UNC assumed extensive powers and responsibilities for civil relief and control of resources to, in the words of one agreement, "facilitate the conduct of military operations, relieve hardship and contribute to the stabilization of the Korean economy." The UNC never entered into a status-of-forces agreement (SOFA) with the ROK, but it concluded separate agreements on such matters as economic coordination, currency control, and claims settlement as well as various ad hoc arrangements.

When Japan regained sovereignty in 1952, the United States and Japan exchanged notes governing Japanese support of UN actions. This was formalized on 19 February 1954 when Japan, the United States "acting as the Unified Command," and eight of the participating states signed a UNC-Japan SOFA providing for access, transit, and basing rights. Eventually, seven U.S. bases in Japan were designated as UNC bases.

CINCUNC signed the July 1953 Armistice Agreement on behalf of all UNC military forces. The sixteen participating nations signed a joint policy statement supporting the armistice and pledging united resistance should there be a renewal of the conflict in Korea. In 1957 the UNC headquarters moved from Tokyo to Korea, leaving a small UNC (Rear) headquarters to coordinate with the Japanese government.

Security Council resolutions pertaining to the UNC contain no termination date. Pending a permanent political settlement restoring "international peace and security," the United Nations Command remains in Korea. The UNC staff is colocated with that of the ROK/U.S. Combined Forces Command (CFC) in Seoul and is commanded by the same U.S. four-star general who serves concurrently as commander in chief of CFC and commander of U.S. Forces in Korea. The UNC remains responsible for the southern half of the Korean demilitarized zone. Special units assigned to the command include a UNC security force in P'anmunjŏm, a UNC honor guard company in Seoul, the UNC component of the Military Armistice Commission, and liaison detachments from the majority of the original UN participating nations.

—*Donald W. Boose, Jr.*

References:

Bowett, D. W. *United Nations Forces: A Legal Study.* New York: Praeger, 1964.

Hermes, Walter G. *United States Army in the Korean War: Truce Tent and Fighting Front.* Washington, DC: Office of the Chief of Military History, 1966.

Higgins, Rosalyn. *United Nations Peacekeeping, 1946–1967: Documents and Commentary.* Vol. 2, *Asia.* London: Oxford University Press, 1970.

Schnabel, James F., and Robert J. Watson. *The History of the Joint Chiefs of Staff: The Joint Chiefs of Staff and National Policy.* Vol. 3, *The Korean War, Part 1.* Washington, DC: Historical Division, Joint Secretariat, Joint Chiefs of Staff, 1978.

Seyersted, Finn. *United Nations Forces in the Law of Peace and War.* Leyden: A. W. Sijthoff, 1966.

See also: Clark, Mark W.; Collins, Joseph Lawton; Far East Command (FEC); MacArthur, Douglas; Ridgway, Matthew Bunker; Syngman Rhee; Taejŏn Agreement; Truman, Harry S.; United Nations Command Ground Forces, Contributions to.

United Nations Command Air Forces

The United States provided the vast majority of the air arsenal deployed by the United Nations Command (UNC). Other nations made significant contributions, however. At the start of the Korean War, the Republic of Korea Air Force (ROKAF) deployed only twenty-two liaison and trainer aircraft: L4s, L5s, and T-6s. Most of these were destroyed in the early fighting. On 2 July 1950 the United States provided ten F-51 Mustangs, and in short order ROKAF pilots were flying them in combat and carrying out interdiction and ground support roles.

British Commonwealth nations provided the remainder of other UNC air units. When the war began on 25 June 1950, the 77th Mustang Fighter Squadron of the Royal Australian Air Force was stationed in Japan. By 29 June the squadron and its F-51s were fully operational; they were among the first UNC armed forces to fight in Korea. Australian pilots flew interdiction and ground support missions for the duration of the war, occasionally escorting bombers; and later, in jets, they challenged Chinese MiG-15s. In October 1951 Australia sent to Korea its only aircraft carrier, the HMAS *Sydney*, along with the 20th Carrier Air Group: two squadrons of Sea Furies and one of Fireflies. It remained in Korean Waters until February 1952.

Great Britain sent the carriers HMS *Triumph*, *Ocean*, *Glory*, and *Theseus*. From these British pilots flew Sea Fury, Firefly, and Seafire aircraft. British pilots also flew spotter aircraft in support of their ground units, and there were three squadrons of Sunderland flying boats for reconnaissance.

South Africa sent its South African Air Force Second Squadron, the "Flying Cheetahs." It flew U.S. F-51s and later F-86 jets.

In addition, other nations provided assistance to the UNC in the form of transport aircraft. Belgium provided several DC-4 transport aircraft; Greece supplied Flight 13 of the Royal Hellenic Air Force with eight C-47s; Canada and Thailand also provided transport aircraft during the war.

UNC land-based aircraft other than those of the United States flew a total of 44,874 sorties, including 15,359 interdiction and 6,063 close air support missions. They also flew 3,025 counter-air sorties, during which they shot down three Communist aircraft. UNC air forces also flew 6,578 cargo missions, and 13,848 other flights. A total of 152 aircraft were lost.

—*Frank D. Skidmore and Spencer C. Tucker*

References:

Field, James A., Jr. *History of United States Naval Operations: Korea*. Washington, DC: U.S. Government Printing Office, 1962.

Futrell, Robert F. *The United States Air Force in Korea, 1950–1953*. Rev. ed. Washington, DC: Office of the Chief of Air Force History, 1983.

Hallion, Richard P. *The Naval Air War in Korea*. Baltimore: Nautical and Aviation Publishing Co. of America, 1986.

Summers, Harry G. Jr. *Korean War Almanac*. New York: Facts on File, 1990.

See also: Aircraft (Principal Combat); Australia; Korea, Republic of: Air Force (ROKAF); South Africa, Union of; United Kingdom (UK); United States Air Force (USAF); United States Army; United States Marine Corps; United States Navy.

United Nations Command Ground Forces, Contributions to

Twenty-one nations sent personnel to United Nations Command (UNC) forces in Korea; sixteen sent military detachments and five sent medical detachments. During the course of the war the United States provided some 50 percent of the total ground forces; the Republic of Korea, 40 percent; and the remaining UN states, 10 percent.

On 31 July 1953, UNC ground forces strength was 932,539 personnel: 590,911 from the Republic of Korea (South Korea) in both army and Marines; 302,483 in the U.S. Army and Marine Corps; and 39,145 from other UN countries.

U.S. strength was in seven army divisions, one marine division, army and corps headquarters, and logistical and support forces. The United Kingdom (UK) was the second largest contributor with two brigades of five infantry battalions, two field artillery regiments, and one armored regiment; the UK also sent a Royal Marine detachment. In July 1953 the UK had a total of 14,198 personnel in UNC ground forces in Korea.

Canada supplied one brigade of three infantry battalions, one artillery regiment, and supporting armored, antitank, and service forces, for a total of 6,146 personnel in July 1953.

Turkey sent a brigade (5,455 men). Australia contributed two infantry battalions (2,282 men), and New Zealand sent an artillery regiment and other supporting troops (1,389). France, then fighting its own war in Indo-China, nonetheless supplied an infantry battalion, as did Belgium, Colombia, Ethiopia, Greece, the Netherlands, the Philippines, and Thailand (each about 1,000 men). Tiny Luxembourg sent a small force that served with the Belgian battalion (a platoon of 44 men in July 1953). India provided a medical detachment (in July 1953, 70 men, down from a high of 333), as did Denmark, Italy (77), Norway (105), and Sweden (154).

—Spencer C. Tucker

References:

Stueck, William W., Jr. *The Korean War: An International History*. Princeton, NJ: Princeton University Press, 1995.

Summers, Harry G., Jr. *Korean War Almanac*. New York: Facts on File, 1990.

"United Nations Allies in the Korean War." *Army Information Digest* 8, no. 9 (1953): 57.

See also: Australia; Belgium; Canada; Casualties; Colombia; Ethiopia; France; Greece; India; Korea, Republic of: Army (ROKA); Korea, Republic of: Marines; Luxembourg, Grand Duchy of; Netherlands; New Zealand; Order of Battle: United Nations, North Korea, and People's Republic of China; Philippines; Thailand; United Kingdom (UK); United States Army; United States Marine Corps.

United Nations Commission for the Unification and Rehabilitation of Korea

Organization created in accordance with United Nations (UN) General Assembly Resolution 376(V) of 7 October 1950, the same resolution that authorized the U.S.-led United Nations Command (UNC) to conduct operations north of the 38th parallel. At the time, the UNC was on the counteroffensive and the U.S. and its allies in the UN believed that military victory and the reunification of Korea were in sight. The U.S. government, believing that the existing UN Commission on Korea (UNCOK) was inadequate to the task, had pressed the UN to create a new organization to supervise the unification, long-term reconstruction, and security of Korea.

The United Nations Commission for the Unification and Rehabilitation of Korea (UNCURK) was composed of representatives from Australia, Chile, the Netherlands, Pakistan, the Philippines, Thailand, and Turkey, with the chairmanship rotating monthly. UNCURK assumed UNCOK's functions of encouraging reunification and being available for observation and consultation. It was also charged with representing the UN in bringing about a "unified, independent and democratic government of all Korea" and was to exercise responsibilities regarding relief and rehabilitation as the General Assembly might direct.

Pending the commission's arrival in Korea, an interim committee composed of the same members as UNCURK met at UN headquarters "to consult with and advise the Unified Command" (the U.S. government acting for the UN in Korea). At the committee's first meeting on 10 October 1950, the Australian representative, James Plimsoll, who had been given broad powers by his government, immediately began to exercise a strong influence on the proceedings. UNC forces were already moving into North Korea, and Plimsoll was concerned that commander in chief of the UNC (CINCUNC) General Douglas MacArthur might turn the occupied territory over to the Rhee government, ending any possibility of UNCURK-supervised elections. To forestall such an act, Plimsoll recommended, and the Interim Committee adopted on 12 October, a resolution advising CINCUNC to administer the occupied territory pending future UNCURK action. Republic of Korea (ROK) president Syngman Rhee reacted strongly, calling the committee's resolution unacceptable and announcing that he was dispatching previously appointed governors to take control of the northern provinces. The United States ultimately sided with the committee, and on 30 October Rhee was persuaded to issue a statement pledging full cooperation with UNCURK. Nonetheless, the relationship had started badly, and UNCURK's view of the Rhee government was further jaundiced by press reports of torture and summary executions by ROK officials accompanying the UNC into North Korea.

The commission then found itself divided on the key issue of elections in a reunified Korea. Rhee insisted that his appointed governors take over. Some members of the commission favored a British proposal for nationwide elections, while others accepted U.S. arguments that elections should be held only in the North. Plimsoll sought a compromise whereby elections would be held initially in the North to select an interim legislature. That body would then negotiate with the existing ROK National Assembly to write a constitution under which nationwide elections would take place.

This issue was still unresolved on 20 November, when the commission held its first meeting in Tokyo. The next day General MacArthur welcomed the UNCURK members, encouraged them to establish a good working relationship with the Rhee government, and argued in favor of elections in the North only. He was optimistic that military operations would be concluded within a month, but immediately after UNCURK initiated its Korea-based operation, on 26 November the Chinese intervention ended all hope of early reunification and the election issue became moot.

Although most members of UNCURK believed that the Chinese attack ended their mission, their home governments directed them to stay in Korea. UNCURK left Seoul on 3 January, one day ahead of advancing Communist forces, and relocated its operation to Pusan, where it would remain until 18 June 1954.

With its primary mandate of supervising reunification foreclosed, UNCURK turned to its other functions. It formed a committee to study relief and economic issues, a second committee to study the situation in North Korea, and an observation group. The observation group's first report, issued on 7 December 1950, made use of prisoner-of-war interrogations, information supplied by the UNC, and field visits to describe the Chinese intervention. Later that month UNCURK established an ad hoc group to study the refugee issue. Over the years UNCURK observed

and reported on the development of representative government in South Korea, UNC administration of areas north of the 38th parallel, the ROK government's attitude and actions toward the armistice, and economic and social matters.

While UNCURK continued to observe and report, its influence and impact were limited by declining interest on the part of many of the participating nations, an increasingly strained relationship with the Rhee government, and lack of support from the UN secretary-general and the United States. After the Chinese attack, UNCURK attempted to play a role in bringing about an end to hostilities, but its efforts were generally ignored. Instead, the General Assembly established a three-person cease-fire group and, later, a good offices committee to attempt cease-fire negotiations. The existence of these groups undermined UNCURK's authority, as did establishment of the UN Korea Reconstruction Agency (UNKRA) to conduct long-term relief and rehabilitation in Korea. While UNCURK remained the principal UN representative in Korea, its authority over UNKRA was limited.

After the truce talks began in July 1951 with no role for UNCURK, members of the commission began to question its value. UN secretary-general Trygve Lie argued for the abolition of UNCURK and its replacement by a single mediator. U.S. officials considered the commission ineffective and found it inconvenient to have an independent body with no U.S. representation operating in Korea. Preparing for the fall 1951 session of the UN General Assembly, the State Department planned to recommend that UNCURK be replaced with either a single UN political representative (preferably an American) or a smaller body on which the United States would be represented. In either case, the new UN organization would be based in New York rather than Korea and would have a much narrower mandate than UNCURK. In the end, however, the U.S. delegation simply recommended, and the General Assembly agreed, that discussion of Korean political issues, including the future of UNCURK, be postponed pending the outcome of the truce talks.

UNCURK played its most prominent, and perhaps most useful, role during the ROK political crisis of 1952. On 24 May President Rhee declared martial law in Pusan (seat of the ROK government) and jailed several opposition legislators, claiming the existence of a Communist conspiracy. His real motivation was to ensure victory in upcoming elections by forcing the National Assembly to pass a constitutional amendment providing for direct presidential election. UNCURK, led by James Plimsoll and acting in close consultation with the U.S. Embassy and the UNC, called on Rhee to end martial law and release the jailed politicians. When

Rhee refused, the commission made its overtures public. The crisis eventually ended in early July when Rhee released most of the prisoners and the ROK legislators, having been rounded up by Rhee's police and confined in the National Assembly building, and passed a compromise constitutional amendment.

During the crisis the U.S. State Department found UNCURK to be a valuable asset. When, at one point, the United States contemplated using UNC forces to take Rhee into custody, they sought UNCURK's views. If carried out, the action would have been triggered by an UNCURK request. Although the U.S. military was never reconciled to UNCURK's presence as the only UN agency in Korea not under CINCUNC control, the U.S. government saw UNCURK as a useful link between the UN and the UNC and a symbol of international interest in Korea.

After the signing of the armistice and after the 1954 Geneva Conference on Korea, the issue of UNCURK's future rose once again. With no access to North Korea and little influence on the South Korean government, UNCURK's ability to carry out its mandate was essentially gone. UN secretary-general Dag Hammarskjöld argued for its dissolution, but the United States continued to view the Commission as a valuable manifestation of UN involvement in Korea. UNCURK survived, making periodic reports to the General Assembly, until 1973. In that year, following the initiation of dialogue between North and South Korea, UNCURK members concluded that their presence was no longer required and recommended that the commission be dissolved. On 28 November 1973, the General Assembly, expressing the hope that the inter-Korean dialogue would continue "so as to expedite the independent peaceful reunification of the country," dissolved the commission.

—*Donald W. Boose, Jr.*

References:

O'Neill, Robert. *Australia in the Korean War, 1950–1953.* Vol. 1, *Strategy and Diplomacy.* Canberra: Australian War Memorial/Australian Government Publishing Service, 1981.

United Nations. *Report of the United Nations Commission for the Unification and Rehabilitation of Korea.* New York: United Nations, 1951, 1952, 1953, 1954, 1955.

———. *Yearbook of the United Nations. 1950, 1951, 1952, 1953.* New York: Columbia University Press, 1951, 1952, 1953, 1954.

U.S. Department of State, Bureau of Public Affairs. *Foreign Relations of the United States, 1950.* Vol. 7, *Korea.* Washington, DC: U.S. Government Printing Office, 1976.

———. *Foreign Relations of the United States, 1951.* Vol. 7, *China and Korea.* Washington, DC: U.S. Government Printing Office, 1983.

———. *Foreign Relations of the United States, 1952–1954.* Vol. 15, *Korea.* Washington, DC: U.S. Government Printing Office, 1984.

See also: Cease-Fire Negotiations; Hammarskjöld, Dag; Lie, Trygve; MacArthur, Douglas; North Korea, United Nations Command Occupation of; Plimsoll, James; Syngman Rhee; United Nations Cease-Fire Group; United Nations Good Offices Committee; United Nations Korean Reconstruction Agency (UNKRA).

United Nations Good Offices Committee

The Good Offices Committee was established in response to United Nations (UN) General Assembly resolution 498(V) of 1 February 1951, which also established the Additional Measures Committee. Both committees represented attempts to deal with intervention in the Korean War by the People's Republic of China (PRC, Communist China). While the United States pressed for a UN resolution that would brand the PRC an aggressor and impose sanctions, the British Commonwealth nations and a group of Asian and Middle Eastern states opposed actions that might widen the war, and they sought ways to bring hostilities to an end. The 1 February resolution reflected something of a compromise: it identified the PRC as an aggressor and established the Additional Measures Committee to explore sanctions. But it also called upon General Assembly president Nasrollah Entezam of Iran to designate two persons to meet with him to use their "good offices" to "bring about a cessation of hostilities in Korea and the achievement of United Nations objectives in Korea by peaceful means." The Additional Measures Committee was authorized to delay its report on recommended sanctions so long as the Good Offices Committee reported satisfactory progress.

Many UN delegates anticipated that the new committee would have the same membership as the UN Cease-Fire Group established on 14 December 1950, consisting of Entezam, Lester B. Pearson of Canada, and Sir Benegal N. Rau of India. But Rau's government had voted against the 1 February resolution and Pearson believed that his ability to communicate with the Chinese had been undermined by his support for the resolution calling China an aggressor. Both declined to serve, and Sven Grafström of Sweden and Dr. Luis Padilla Nervo of Mexico agreed to take their places. Since Mexico was already represented on the Additional Measures Committee, Dr. Padilla Nervo provided a connection between the two groups.

Although the Chinese immediately condemned the 1 February resolution as null and void, the members of the Good Offices Committee attempted to carry out their mandate. On 14 February Grafström tried to persuade the Chinese to establish contact with General Assembly president Entezam, but the Chinese refused to reply to his overture. The Chinese indicated through various channels that they might be interested in some other approaches, such as a multinational conference, but they would not deal with the Good Offices Committee. The Chinese spring offensive of 1951 led to increased U.S. pressure for the imposition of sanctions. On 14 May 1951, in the absence of progress by the Good Offices Committee, the Additional Measures Committee proposed economic sanctions against the PRC and the Democratic People's Republic of Korea (North Korea).

In June 1951 the members of the Good Offices Committee made a final effort to contact the Communist powers but were rebuffed by both the Soviet Union and China. With the beginning of truce talks in July 1951, the committee ended its efforts.

—*Donald W. Boose, Jr.*

References:

Finley, Blanche. *The Structure of the United Nations General Assembly: Its Committees, Commissions and Other Organisms, 1946–1973.* Vol. 1. Dobbs Ferry, NY: Oceana, 1977.

Goodrich, Leland Matthew. *Korea: A Study of U.S. Policy in the United Nations.* New York: Council on Foreign Relations, 1956.

Stueck, William W., Jr. *The Korean War: An International History.* Princeton, NJ: Princeton University Press, 1995.

Yearbook of the United Nations, 1951. New York: Columbia University Press, 1952.

See also: Cease-Fire Negotiations; Entezam, Nasrollah; Grafström, Sven; United Nations Additional Measures Committee; United Nations Cease-Fire Group.

United Nations Korean Reconstruction Agency (UNKRA)

Agency established by United Nations (UN) General Assembly Resolution 410(V) of 1 December 1950, which also provided for a negotiating committee to arrange for financial and materiel contributions. The General Assembly had already established the UN Commission for the Reunification and Rehabilitation of Korea (UNCURK), the rehabilitation functions of which were to be based on recommendations from the Economic and Social Council (ECOSOC). ECOSOC recommended a $250 million program administered by an agency separate from UNCURK and headed by an agent-general with broad operational responsibilities who would report to an advisory committee. UNCURK's role was limited to advice on matters relating to Korean political unification, the designation of authorities with which the UN Korea Reconstruction Agency (UNKRA) would deal, and on the timing and location of UNKRA programs. The United States agreed to provide 65 percent of UNKRA funding, while the other UN members contributed 35 percent.

On 7 February 1951, UN secretary-general Trygve Lie appointed an American, J. Donald Kingsley, as UNKRA's first agent-general. Later that month, Kingsley met with commander in chief of the United Nations Command (CINCUNC) General Douglas MacArthur in Tokyo, then flew to Pusan to meet with the members of UNCURK. It soon became clear that issues of control and funding would affect UNKRA's activities. The U.S. military was adamant that UNKRA projects not interfere with military operations and that CINCUNC have final authority. UNCURK, however, pushed for an independent program under UN direction. Kingsley accepted UNC primacy but believed UNKRA could provide technical assistance and begin planning without affecting military operations and that such activities did not require military supervision.

Issues of control also affected UNKRA funding. The U.S. Congress insisted that CINCUNC have the final say in the use of UNKRA funds, most of which came from U.S. taxpayers. But other UN nations were reluctant to contribute to a program controlled by the U.S. military.

Funding never reached adequate levels, but the control issue was finally resolved in CINCUNC's favor by a 21 December 1951 UNC-UNKRA memorandum of understanding. UNKRA was allowed to begin work, with CINCUNC retaining actual control over economic assistance and relief efforts as long as the war continued. A small number of long-range planners operated directly under the agent-general, but all other UNKRA personnel came under the UNC military relief organization: the UN Civil Assistance Command in Korea. In October 1952 UNC, UNKRA, and Republic of Korea rehabilitation efforts were brought together under a single coordinating committee. Just before the signing of the Armistice Agreement, UNKRA, now under John B. Coulter, former Eighth Army deputy commander for civil affairs, was absorbed into the U.S.-controlled Korea foreign aid program.

When UNKRA was dissolved on 31 August 1960, its projects had been financed by international donations of just over $142 million, of which $92.9 million were provided by the United States. While the agency never developed the kind of program envisioned by its sponsors, UNKRA nonetheless made valuable contributions to the rebuilding of Korean industry, agriculture, fisheries, and community infrastructure as well as the rehabilitation of education, public health, and financial administration.

—*Donald W. Boose, Jr.*

References:

Lyons, Gene M. *Military Policy and Economic Aid: The Korean Case, 1950–1953.* Columbus: Ohio State University Press, 1961.

United Nations. *Yearbook of the United Nations, 1950, 1951, 1952, 1953.* New York: Columbia University Press, 1951, 1952, 1953, 1954.

U.S. House of Representatives Committee on Government Operations, Subcommittee on International Operations. *Hearings on Relief and Rehabilitation in Korea.* 83d Cong., 2d sess., 13, 14, and 16 October 1953. Washington, DC: U.S. Government Printing Office.

———. *Relief and Rehabilitation in Korea.* 83d Cong., 2d sess., 29 July 1954. H. Rept. 2574. Washington, DC: U.S. Government Printing Office.

See also: Coulter, John Breitling; Kingsley, J. Donald; Lie, Trygve; MacArthur, Douglas; United Nations Civil Assistance Command in Korea (UNCACK); United Nations Commission for the Unification and Rehabilitation of Korea.

United Nations Peace Observation Commission

The Peace Observation Commission was established under the provisions of the Uniting for Peace Resolution: United Nations (UN) General Assembly Resolution 337A(V) of 3 November 1950. The framers of the resolution believed that both the UN Commission on Korea and the UN Special Committee on the Balkans had performed useful work in determining the facts surrounding aggression and threats to peace in Korea and Greece. Accordingly, they included a provision for the establishment of the fourteen-member Peace Observation Commission to "observe and report on the situation in any area where there exists international tension the continuance of which is likely to endanger the maintenance of international peace and security." The commission could be dispatched by the Security Council, the General Assembly if the Security Council was not exercising its function, or the Interim Committee when the General Assembly was not in session, but could only be sent into the territory of states that invited or consented to the intrusion. Membership of the commission included representatives of the five permanent members of the Security Council (the Republic of China, France, the Soviet Union, the United Kingdom, and the United States) plus nine others. From 1951 to 1955 these were Colombia, Czechoslovakia, India, Iraq, Israel, New Zealand, Pakistan, and Sweden.

The Peace Observation Commission played no role in the Korean War. On 7 December 1951 the General Assembly passed Resolution 508 B (VI) that requested the Peace Observation Commission establish a Balkan subcommission to replace the UN Special Committee on the Balkans. The subcommission was to consist of three to five persons and would have authority to dispatch observers into any area of international tension in the Balkans, so long as the affected states consented. In January 1952 Greece requested an observer mission be sent to its frontier areas. On 23 January 1952, the Peace Observation Commission accordingly formed a subcommission, which subsequently agreed to send observers. Colombia, France, Pakistan, Sweden, and the United States contributed observers, while the United Kingdom provided the principal observer. The observers submitted reports until 1954, when the mission was withdrawn at the request of the Greek government. That same year the Thai government requested the commission send observers to ensure that the fighting in Indo-China did not spread to Thailand. The USSR vetoed the proposal, and no action was taken.

In the early 1960s the United States and the Soviet Union engaged in disarmament talks, including discussion of a UN peace force. The U.S. proposals included a role for the Peace Observation Commission, but the discussions never bore fruit. The Peace Observation Commission never met again after 1963, but it remained in existence with occasional minor changes in membership until it was abolished by a General Assembly decision on 23 September 1983.

—*Donald W. Boose, Jr.*

References:

Bowett, D. W. *United Nations Forces: A Legal Study.* New York: Praeger, 1964.

Russell, Ruth B. *The United Nations and United States Security Policy.* Washington, DC: Brookings Institution, 1968.

United Nations. *Yearbook of the United Nations, 1950, 1951, 1952, 1953.* New York: Columbia University Press, 1951, 1952, 1953, 1954.

———. *Yearbook of the United Nations.* Vol 37, *1983.* New York: United Nations, Department of Public Information, 1987.

See also: United Nations Collective Measures Committee; Uniting for Peace Resolution.

United States Air Force (USAF)

The U.S. Air Force (USAF) that entered the Korean War was not the robust high-tech service we know today. Led by Secretary of the Air Force Thomas Finletter (from April 1950 until January 1953) and Chief of Staff of the Air Force General Hoyt S. Vandenberg (from April 1948 until July 1953), the newest U.S. military service was not yet three years old when the Democratic People's Republic of Korea (DPRK, North Korea) launched its invasion of the Republic of Korea (South Korea) on 25 June 1950. The structure and policies of the mid-1950 USAF were deeply influenced by the experiences of—and the doctrine developed before and during—World War II, as well as the severe military budget cuts of the late 1940s.

The basis for U.S. air strategy in World War II was the Air War Plans Division's AWPD-1 report of August 1941, which became part of the Joint Board of the Army and Navy's war plan presented to President Franklin D. Roosevelt on 11 September 1941. It was written by Colonel Harold L. George, Lieutenant Colonel Kenneth Walker, and Majors Laurence S. Kutter and Haywood S. Hansell, all former instructors at the Air Corps Tactical School. The first real U.S. airpower doctrine, AWPD-1 was offensive in nature and called for major increases in pilots and planes. Based on the principles and theories of airpower prophets such as American Billy Mitchell and Italian Giulio Douhet, it became the basis for AWPD-42 and the 1942–1945 "Combined Bomber Offensive."

The authors of AWPD-1 believed that big four-engine bombers—which were, at first, faster than Communist fighters—would always get through to carry the war beyond the battle front and destroy an enemy's ability to make war as well as the will of its people. In late 1942 this doctrine became the basis of daylight precision bombing raids over Europe. There were, however, oversights in the theory. The introduction of high-speed fighters and radar, directed antiaircraft artillery, and the resolve of civilian populations initially reduced predicted results.

In 1943, doctrine (Army Field Manual 100-20) and policy revisions introduced fighter escort to the equation and made airpower a decisive factor in the Allied victory, or so reported the U.S. Strategic Bombing Survey conducted from 1944 to 1945. The survey team seemed to confirm what most airmen already believed when it concluded in its official report that even though some mistakes had been made, "Allied airpower was decisive in Western Europe." The U.S. Army Air Forces' (USAAF's) success also led to the creation of the USAF in September 1947.

At the end of World War II the USAAF had 79,000 planes and 2.3 million people. This quickly shrank during the economizing of the late 1940s, led by congressional pressures to balance the budget. To many civilian leaders, the lesson of World War II was that strategic air assets had delivered the nuclear knockout blow against Japan. As the Cold War evolved, they reasoned that future U.S. defense, based on strategic nuclear bombers and missile forces, would be more effective against the Soviet Union and other potential enemies and cheaper than maintaining "expensive" conventional military forces.

This was a policy with which USAF leadership disagreed. It caused the USAF's first secretary, W. Stuart Symington, to retire in April 1950 and General Vandenberg to describe his charges as a "shoestring air force."

Faced with shrinking funds, one of most contentious internal U.S. military controversies erupted over whether to build costly supercarriers or a fleet of B-36 intercontinental bombers. Even though Secretary of Defense Louis A. Johnson supported the B-36 program and canceled the carrier program, the subsequent "revolt of the admirals" and heated Congressional hearings significantly delayed the B-36's development. While the USAF eventually survived the controversy, the delay meant that it would have to fight the Korean War with the B-29 (by now designated a medium bomber) as its primary bomber asset. The Korean

War made funds plentiful and the carrier program was restored, thus temporarily ending the controversy.

The B-29 was not the only aged aircraft USAF forces used in the early days of the Korean conflict. In spite of Vandenberg's earlier pleas for modern tactical jet aircraft, the USAF flew its earliest missions with World War II propeller-driven F-51s and B-26s. In the first aerial engagements, F-82 Twin Mustangs shot down the first three Communist fighters of the war. Even the primary U.S. jet fighters of the time, the F-80 and the F-84, were not equal to the MiG-15, which the Soviet Union soon began supplying in large quantities to its Communist allies. Only the subsequent introduction of, and later upgrades to, the F-86 allowed the USAF to maintain air superiority during the war.

USAF forces fighting in Korea were designated the Far East Air Force (FEAF). Its personnel and aircraft helped secure the Pusan perimeter. So effective was the early B-29 bombing campaign that FEAF leaders halted the raids in September because the DPRK nonindustrial state simply provided no more targets.

Early on, USAF assets also obliterated North Korean air forces despite restrictions against flying outside of South Korea. Once pilots could fly over the entire peninsula, they found the long columns of Communist troops and supplies to be ideal targets.

During the Inch'ŏn landings and the push north, the USAF provided close air support. When the Chinese invaded in November, the USAF helped protect the Allied withdrawal. During the stalemate in negotiations between June 1951 and July 1953, the ground war became a holding action while the USAF focused on aerial interdiction, hydroelectric raids, nighttime bombing raids, and air-to-air combat over a sector of northern Korea near the Yalu River known as MiG Alley. Most of the famous air battles and pilots of the war came from the dogfights over this area.

During the war, U.S. air forces maintained air superiority in spite of being markedly outnumbered. Thus, United Nations ground forces seldom suffered Communist air raids. Aerial interdiction was only partially successful. A lack of air assets prevented constant pressure on Communist supply and communications lines. Limited ground attacks also allowed Communist forces to preserve their resources, thus the basic principle of interdiction—forcing the enemy to use up its supplies faster than they can be replenished—was missing from the aerial interdiction equation in Korea.

As the two sides came closer to a cease-fire in 1953, the Communists held things up with a demand that all their prisoners of war be forcibly repatriated. President Dwight D. Eisenhower then ordered USAF attacks on northern irrigation dams and dikes. This and the implied threat of air attacks—including nuclear strikes—against targets in Manchuria led the Communists to end the conflict.

During the war the USAF budget and force strength, as well as those of the other services, rose dramatically. The original fiscal year (FY) 1950 USAF authorizations called for 416,000 officers and airmen and $11 billion. In July the Army and Air Force Authorization Act and the first funding supplement raised these to nearly 550,000 men and $16 billion (24,000 aircraft). By the end of the war, USAF forces had grown to 977,593 and its funding to $22.3 billion in FY1952 and $20.7 billion in FY1953.

During most of the war, General Vandenberg, one of the air force's most dedicated and persuasive leaders, served as chief of staff of the air force. In addition, Robert A. Lovett, formerly assistant secretary of war for air from 1941 to 1945, was first Secretary of Defense George C. Marshall's deputy secretary (between 21 September 1950 and 12 September 1951) and then secretary of defense in his own right until 20 January 1953. A long-time proponent of airpower, he and Vandenberg both pushed for a more flexible and multifaceted USAF, one focused on its primary strategic mission of delivering a nuclear strike against the Soviet Union, but one also able to perform numerous conventional strategic, tactical, and airlift missions.

It was mainly because of their efforts that more and better F-86s reached Korea. Even so, during the last two years of the war, only the 4th Fighter Wing and the 51st Fighter Wing with 100 to 125 F-86s were stationed in East Asia to confront 500 to 600 MiG-15s over northern Korea. Add to this a 45 percent mission incapable rate for F-86s, and the Korean aerial combat numbers are nothing short of remarkable. USAF pilots downed 792 MiGs and lost only 78 aircraft—a 10-to-1 ratio. The numbers were the result of superior U.S. pilots, many veterans of World War II, and such innovations as additional engine power and the A-1 radar-computed gunsight in the F-86F.

Given its track record in Korea, the USAF should have fared well after the war. In relative terms it did. But under President Eisenhower and his secretary of defense Charles E. Wilson (from 1953 to 1957), and Secretary of the Air Force Harold L. Talbott (from 1953 to 1955), the postwar era saw a return to military budget cuts for all services and a focus on the strategic nuclear role of the USAF, which many civilian leaders believed provided the United States with "more bang for the buck."

Indeed, it was the budget battle between Wilson and the normally congenial Vandenberg that caused the latter to retire in July 1953, to be replaced by General Nathan F. Twining (from 1953 to 1957), later first USAF chair of the Joint Chiefs of Staff. During the remainder of the 1950s, the air force experience was dominated not by the lessons of limited war taught in Korea but by the apparent lessons of Hiroshima and Nagasaki. General Curtis LeMay's Strategic Air Command and efforts by all the services to control the development and deployment of intercontinental ballistic missiles dominated military policy and thinking throughout the Eisenhower years.

These policies, while successful in deterring Soviet expansion in Europe and Chinese designs in Asia, lost sight of the need for a world power such as the United States to project its will into less-developed corners of the world and to fight what Ed Rice has dubbed "Wars of the Third Kind." Thus, many of the important skills developed in and lessons learned during Korea were forgotten by the time the United States entered the war in Southeast Asia. Lost during the Vietnam War were air-to-air combat skills, with the result that until late in the war, aerial combat ratios were 1 to 1. There was a lack of adaptable tactical weapons systems and conventional bombers, as well as a repeat of aerial interdiction mistakes during COMMANDO HUNT. Even so, during the Korea conflict, superior leadership and dedicated and selfless airmen, overcoming numerous hardships and restrictions, proved decisive in the U.S. effort to preserve the sovereignty of the Republic of Korea.

—William Head

References:

Condit, Doris M. *History of the Office of the Secretary of Defense.* Vol. 2, *The Test of War, 1950–1953.* Washington, DC: Office of the Secretary of Defense, 1988.

Futrell, Robert F. *The United States Air Force in Korea, 1950–1953.* Rev. ed. Washington, DC: Office of the Chief of Air Force History, 1983.

Thompson, Wayne. "The Air War over Korea." In *Winged Shield, Wing Sword: A History of the United States Air Force,* edited by Bernard C. Nalty. Washington, DC: U.S. Air Force History and Museum Program, 1997: 3–52.

See also: Aircraft (Principal Combat); Eisenhower, Dwight D.; Finletter, Thomas K.; Johnson, Louis A.; Lovett, Robert A.; Marshall, George C.; Twining, Nathan Farragut; Vandenberg, Hoyt S.; Wilson, Charles Edward.

United States Army

As in all of the United States' wars, the vast majority of the troops who fought in Korea were U.S. Army soldiers. The U.S. Army's direct involvement in Korea started immediately after the end of World War II. On 3 September 1945, U.S. Army and Army Air Force occupation units started moving into Korea to secure the surrender of Japanese forces south of the 38th parallel and to preserve law and order in the country. At its peak, U.S. Army forces in Korea reached a strength of almost 45,000 men. The last occupation troops left on 29 June 1949, but 482 military advisors remained in the form of the Korea Military Advisory Group (KMAG) to the Republic of Korea.

Officially established on 1 July 1949, KMAG assumed the functions of the provisional military advisory teams that had been operating as part of the occupation force since January 1946. Its mission was "to advise the government of the Republic of Korea in the continued development of the Security Forces of that government." As a part of the U.S. Mission in Korea, KMAG was under the control of U.S. ambassador John J. Muccio. In purely military matters, KMAG coordinated directly with the Department of the Army. After the start of the war, KMAG became a subordinate command of the U.S. Eighth Army. KMAG's wartime strength rose to 1,308 men.

The principal U.S. military headquarters responsible for Korea was the Far East Command (FEC), headquartered in Tokyo. The FEC was established on 1 January 1947, as one of the worldwide geographical commands created by the National Security Act of 1947. The original intent was for the FEC to be a unified command, consisting of three coequal service component commands and a joint staff drawn from officers of all the services. In its early years, however, the FEC was little more than a continuation of its World War II predecessor, the Southwest Pacific Command. Still commanded by General of the Army Douglas MacArthur, the FEC at the outbreak of the Korean War was essentially managed by an army staff under an army commander.

In addition to being the FEC commander in chief, MacArthur was also supposed to be the commander of the army component, U.S. Army Forces Far East. (This "dual hatting" remains a common command arrangement in unified commands to this day.) That organization, however, existed only on paper. On 24 July 1951, the FEC also became the United Nations Command (UNC). The other service component commands under the FEC were Naval Forces Far East, commanded by Vice Admiral C. Turner Joy, and the Far East Air Force, commanded by Lieutenant General George E. Stratemeyer. The FEC finally evolved into a true unified command under its last wartime commander, when Lieutenant General Mark W. Clark finally activated U.S. Army Forces Far East on 1 October 1952.

The U.S. Eighth Army was the primary command and control headquarters for army and all ground combat operations during the Korean War. At the start of the war its headquarters were in Yokohama, Japan. On 13 July 1950, Eighth Army established its forward headquarters in Taegu, Korea, and Lieutenant General Walton H. Walker assumed command over all army forces on the peninsula. On 14 July 1951, South Korean president Syngman Rhee placed all the ground forces of the Republic of Korea Army under the command of

FEC/UNC. Three days later the Eighth Army assumed operational control of those forces. The Eighth Army also exercised command over U.S. Marine Corps ground units committed on the peninsula.

When the Eighth Army transferred its headquarters to Korea, the lack of an army component headquarters in Japan caused problems in the management of army logistical support. This led to the activation on 24 August 1950 of the Japan Logistics Command, headquartered in Yokohama. In October 1952 the Japan Logistics Command was inactivated and its functions absorbed by U.S. Army Forces Far East.

Meanwhile, on 4 July 1950, the Eighth Army established the Pusan Base Command to manage logistics and support operations in Korea. That organization later was designated the Pusan Logistical Command, and then the 2d Logistical Command. In July 1952 the Korean Communications Zone (KCOMZ) was established for logistics and territorial operations behind the Eighth Army's rear boundary, which was set at roughly the 38th parallel. A subordinate command of U.S. Army Forces Far East, KCOMZ absorbed the 2d Logistical Command in October.

Below the level of the Eighth Army, ground combat operations in Korea were controlled by corps. Usually commanded by a lieutenant general, a corps is a flexible organization, to which divisions and other units can be assigned as needed for specific operations. Throughout the course of the war, divisions operating in Korea were assigned to different corps at different times. I Corps was established in Korea on 13 September 1950, just before the Eighth Army's breakout from the Pusan perimeter. IX Corps was established on 23 September, just after the breakout.

On 26 August X Corps was organized in Japan to command the forces for the Inch'ŏn landings. Initially directly subordinate to the FEC, X Corps remained independent of the Eighth Army for several months after the landing. Many historians have been very critical of this unusual command arrangement. X Corps finally came under the Eighth Army on 24 December 1950. A XVI Corps headquarters was established in Japan in 1951, but that organization never operated in Korea.

The division, commanded by a major general, is normally the largest tactical unit in the U.S. Army. The two basic types of divisions in 1950 were infantry and armored. No armored divisions served in Korea, and the 1st Cavalry Division was an infantry division in all but name. The other army divisions serving in Korea included the regular 2d, 3d, 7th, 24th, and 25th Infantry Divisions, and the 40th and 45th Infantry Divisions mobilized from the California and Oklahoma National Guards, respectively.

The organization of the U.S. divisions was essentially the same as the "triangular" structure of World War II, with some modifications having been made in November 1946. A Korea-era infantry division was a fixed unit, normally consisting of nine infantry battalions, four artillery battalions, a heavy tank battalion, an engineer battalion, an air defense battalion, a medical battalion, a reconnaissance squadron, and various support companies. Its authorized wartime strength was 17,700 soldiers, 141 tanks, and 72 light and medium howitzers.

Between the division headquarters and the battalions, each division had three regiments, intermediate-level headquarters commanded by a colonel. A regiment controlled three infantry battalions, a tank company, a 4.2-inch mortar company, and a medical company. The U.S. Army today no longer uses regiments, which were fixed organizations with unique numerical designations. The command level between the divisions and the battalions is now the brigade, which is only identified by its own number within the division. The brigade has a more flexible structure but is roughly the same size as the Korea-era regiment and is commanded by a colonel.

The divisional artillery, in many divisions in Korea commanded by a brigadier general, was a regimental-size organization that controlled the division's four artillery battalions. The three 105-mm howitzer battalions had the mission of providing direct support to each of the three infantry regiments, and the 155-mm howitzer battalion provided general support fires to the division as a whole. The divisional artillery also controlled the antiaircraft artillery automatic weapons battalion, which often was used in a ground support role.

The battalion, commanded by a lieutenant colonel, has always been the basic tactical unit in the U.S. Army. An infantry battalion of the period had a headquarters company, three rifle companies, and a weapons company. The headquarters company provided the battalion administration, maintenance, and supply functions. The weapons company consisted of an 81-mm mortar platoon, a 75-mm recoilless rifle platoon, and a machine gun platoon with both light and heavy machine guns. An artillery battalion had a headquarters and service battery and three firing batteries. A tank battalion had a headquarters company and three tank companies. The standard infantry battalion strength was 40 officers and 935 enlisted soldiers. An artillery battalion was somewhat smaller, with about 500 soldiers. In cavalry (reconnaissance) units the battalion-level organization is called a squadron. The battalions within a given regiment were numbered sequentially.

Wartime Authorization of a Typical Infantry Division

Divisional headquarters company	1
Engineer battalion	1
Heavy tank battalion	1
Medical battalion	1
Reconnaissance troop	1
Military Police company	1
Signal company	1
Maintenance company	1
Supply company	1
Replacement company	1
Regimental headquarters companies*	3
Infantry battalions*	9
Medium tank companies	3
4.2-inch mortar companies	3
Medical companies	3
Divisional artillery headquarters battery†	1
105-mm artillery battalions (DS)	3
155-mm artillery battalion (GS)	1
Antiaircraft automatic weapons battalion	1
Soldiers	17,700
Tanks	141
Howitzers	72

Notes:
* The regiments of the 1st Cavalry Division were designated cavalry regiments. They were, however, standard infantry regiments in all but name only. Their subordinate units were designated cavalry battalions and rifle companies.
† The divisional artillery headquarters controlled the division's three direct support (DS) battalions, one general support (GS) battalion, one antiaircraft artillery automatic weapons battalion, and any other nondivisional battalions designated to reinforce the division for a specific operation.

The company (battery in the artillery and troop in the cavalry) is the lowest level of command in the U.S. Army. Commanded by a captain, an infantry rifle company in Korea consisted of a company headquarters, three rifle platoons, and a weapons platoon with a 60-mm mortar section and a 57-mm recoilless rifle section. A rifle company had six officers and 195 enlisted soldiers. Artillery batteries and tank companies had only about half as many soldiers. A medium tank company had seventeen tanks. At the start of the war, an artillery battery consisted of a headquarters section and four howitzer sections. During the course of the war that increased to six howitzer sections per battery, effectively increasing the divisional artillery strength by 50 percent.

The U.S. Army designates companies, batteries, and troops alphabetically. Under the Korea-era regimental system all the infantry companies in a regiment were lettered in sequence. The three rifle companies in the 1st Battalion were designated A, B, and C, with Company D being the weapons company. The rifle companies in the 2d Battalion were E, F, and G, with company H being that weapons company. The headquarters company of each battalion was simply designated HQ Company, 1st Battalion, etc. The rifle platoon, led by a lieutenant, had three rifle squads and a weapons squad. The nine-man rifle squad was led by a sergeant first class squad leader and a sergeant assistant squad leader. The squad's basic firepower consisted of a corporal armed with a Browning Automatic Rifle, and six riflemen armed with M-1 rifles. The weapons squad had a light machine gun section and a 2.36-inch rocket launcher (later 3.5-inch rocket launcher) section.

The army also had various separate units and organizations that operated either independently or attached to a division for specific operations. The regimental combat team (RCT) was essentially a reinforced regiment, organized to operate independently of a division. An RCT was formed around an infantry regiment with an attached artillery battalion, and in some cases additional armor and engineer elements. Often commanded by a brigadier general, most RCTs were ad hoc organizations put together for a specific operation.

The Fifth RCT operated at times as part of the Twenty-fourth and Fortieth Infantry Divisions, and at other times under the direct control of Ninth or Tenth Corps. Only two battalions of the Twenty-ninth RCT went to Korea, and both were later integrated into the Twenty-fifth Infantry Division. The 187th Airborne RCT was officially part of the Eleventh Airborne Division. As the only airborne unit in Korea, however, it operated most often under the direct control of the Eighth Army. The 187th RCT made the only two airborne assaults of the war. One of the unit's commanders in Korea was then–Brigadier General William C. Westmoreland, who later commanded U.S. forces in Vietnam.

Seven ranger companies also served in Korea. Organized in Korea on 14 October 1950, the Eighth Army Ranger Company was later attached to the 25th Infantry Division. Six other ranger companies, meanwhile, were organized at the Army Infantry School at Fort Benning, Georgia, and trained for Korea. The 1st Ranger Company was assigned to the 2d Infantry Division; the 2d Ranger Company was assigned to the 7th Infantry Division; the 3d Ranger Company was assigned to the 3d Infantry Division; and the 4th Ranger Company was assigned to the 1st Cavalry Division. When the 5th Ranger Company arrived in Korea, it was assigned to the 25th Infantry Division and the Eighth Army Ranger Company was inactivated. The last of these units to arrive in Korea was the 8th Ranger Company, which was assigned to the 24th Infantry Division.

Trained in both airborne and special operations, the 117-man ranger companies were the direct successors of the ranger battalions of World War II. They were used primarily as scout and long-range penetration units. All six companies were inactivated by 1 August 1951, and most of their soldiers were reassigned to the 187th Airborne RCT. One of the commanders of the original Eighth Army Ranger Company was Captain John Paul Vann, and one of his sergeants was David Hackworth. Both would become prominent figures in the Vietnam War.

An Army unit's authorized strength and its actual strength in the field are always two different things. This was especially true in the first half of 1950, just before the start of the war. Following the post–World War II demobilizations, the Army's goal had been a combined air and ground strength of 1.5 million troops, backed up by a reserve force capable of mobilizing 4 million within a year. By early 1950, however, the Army had shrunk to only 591,487 officers and men organized into ten divisions, five separate regimental combat teams, and the Constabulary force in Germany.

Considering the U.S. nuclear monopoly in the late 1940s, few people in the national leadership saw any requirement for maintaining strong, combat-ready conventional forces. Many believed the Army to be obsolete.

With the exception of one division stationed in Germany, all of the Army's divisions in early 1950 were manned and equipped to no more than two-thirds of their authorized strength. Almost all of the weapons and equipment were of World War II vintage. All four of the divisions (1st Cavalry Division; 7th, 24th, and 25th Infantry Divisions) occupying Japan had only two battalions per infantry regiment and two firing batteries per artillery battalion. The divisional antiaircraft artillery battalion had only one battery, and the heavy tank battalion had only one company. Rather than having heavy tanks, this tank company actually was armed with the M-24 Chaffee light tank, which soon proved worthless against the Soviet-made T-34s. The U.S. Army of 1950 was a "hollow force" in every sense of the term.

With the start of the Korean War, the Army went through its third crash expansion within the last 40 years. At its peak strength in 1952 the Army had 1,596,419 soldiers in the active force, which included mobilized reservists and National Guardsmen. The number of active divisions rose to twenty. Eight of those divisions served in Korea but never more than six at any given time. A total of 80 infantry battalions, 54 field artillery battalions, and eight tank battalions served in Korea at various times during the war. The Army's maximum strength in Korea was never more than 275,000.

The crash expansion program could do little to help the Eighth Army's understrength divisions in the desperate months of August and September 1950. Heavy fighting in those months reduced some American units to half of their authorized strength. The Korean Augmentation to the U.S. Army (KATUSA) program was a stopgap measure designed to keep the U.S. units in action. In theory, KATUSAs were members of the ROKA and were paid by the ROK government, but they were trained and equipped by the U.S. Army and assigned to American units. In practice, however, many KATUSAs were little more than schoolboys, drafted off the streets.

Many KATUSAs could not speak even a few words of English. Each KATUSA was supposed to be paired with an American soldier in a "buddy system." Some divisions, however, grouped their KATUSA soldiers into all-Korean squads. Despite their uneven record of effectiveness from unit to unit, the KATUSAs constituted a significant percentage of many U.S. divisions. At the end of September 1950, the 1st Cavalry Division had 2,961 KATUSAs and only 13,859 American troops; and KATUSAs accounted for one-third of the 7th Infantry Division. By late 1952 there were 27,000 Korean augmentation soldiers serving in U.S. Army units. The program was actually retained after the war, and in the mid-1990s there were still some 7,000 KATUSA troops in American units in Korea.

As in every major American war, with the conspicuous exception of Vietnam, a very large percentage—often the majority—of the soldiers who served were reservists or National Guardsmen. In the case of Korea, the United States clearly could not have been successful without them. On 27 July 1950, the U.S. Congress authorized President Harry S. Truman to extend involuntarily for one year all active force enlistments due to terminate prior to 9 July 1952. That, however, was little more than another stopgap measure.

Simultaneously, on 30 June 1950, Congress passed the Selective Service Extension Act of 1950, which authorized the Selective Service System to induct 50,000 men in September. It would be months, however, before those new soldiers could be trained adequately and transported to the war zone.

The Army clearly needed an immediate influx of manpower. The Selective Service Extension Act also authorized the President to mobilize, for a period of 21 months, units of the National Guard and units and individual soldiers and officers of the Organized Reserve Corps (ORC).

In 1950 the Army's pool of trained reservists consisted of 324,761 soldiers in the Army National Guard (ARNG), and 184,015 in the Organized Reserve Corps (ORC). Both groups were categorized as "drilling reservists," citizen-soldiers who—either individually or in units—received pay for participating in regularly scheduled training. The Army also had two additional reserve manpower pools, neither of which received training nor pay. Both the 324,602-man Volunteer Reserve and the 91,800-man Inactive Reserve consisted largely of World War II veterans who had not even worn a uniform since their demobilization in 1945 or 1946.

Starting on 14 August 1950, 138,600 National Guard troops were called into federal service with their units. The activated units included eight of the National Guard's 27 divisions. The 40th and 45th Infantry Divisions ultimately served in Korea; the 28th and 43d Infantry Divisions were sent to Europe to reinforce NATO; and the 31st, 37th, 44th, and 47th Infantry Divisions remained in the United States as training divisions and manpower pools of individual replacements.

The Army Reserve provided a total of 244,300 officers and soldiers during the war. More than 80 percent on the initial 1950 call-up of 197,727 was sent to active Army units as individual replacements. Since the most pressing and immediate need was for fillers to flesh out the skeletonized active Army units, the majority of those called up from the Army Reserve came from the Volunteer Reserve and Inactive Reserve, rather than from the better trained units of the Active Reserve. Many of those units were left untouched against the contingency that they would have to be mobilized later to counter any Soviet threats in Europe. In the end, this was the most controversial aspect of the mobilization of the Army Reserve.

The Korean War arguably was the driving force that led to the desegregation of the U.S. Army. Although in 1948 President Truman had issued Executive Order 9981 to integrate the armed forces, the actual execution of that order was being carried out at a glacial pace. At the start of the war, the majority of black soldiers were still assigned to segregated units, in which almost all the senior officers were white. The first major all-black unit in Korea was the 25th Infantry Division's 24th Infantry Regiment. That unit was followed by the 2d Infantry Division's 3d Battalion, 9th Infantry Regiment, the 3d Infantry Division's 3d Battalion, 15th Infantry Regiment, and the 64th Tank Battalion.

With combat units in Korea desperately short of men, and the pool of qualified black soldiers growing in Japan, the Army soon had no alternative but to start assigning them to previously all-white units. This started happening in early 1951 as an expediency measure. Later that year, FEC commander-in-chief General Matthew B. Ridgway finally ordered the immediate integration of all combat units in Korea.

The 24th Infantry Regiment was inactivated on 1 October, and its soldiers were reassigned among other Eighth Army units. That started a ripple effect throughout the Army, and by July 1953 about 90 percent of the Army's black soldiers were in integrated units. Strength levels of black soldiers and officers in Army Forces, Far East (including Japan and other areas outside of Korea) reached 51,700.

While Korea was a watershed for the integration of blacks, the integration of women into the Army remained many years in the future. In 1950, all women in the Army were assigned to either the Army Nurse Corps (ANC) or to the Women's Army Corps (WAC). For most of the war, WACs were not permitted to serve in Korea itself. They served at FEC headquarters in Japan, and in late 1952 about ten female officers and soldiers did serve in Korea in administrative positions. By 1952 WAC strength armywide was about 10,000.

Army nurses did serve in Korea. A contingent of fifty-seven Army nurses landed at Pusan as early as 5 July 1950, and many served in Mobile Army Surgical Hospitals (MASHs) directly behind the front lines. By the end of the war, more than 540 Army nurses had served in Korea.

Between 25 June 1950 and 27 July 1953, 2,834,000 U.S. Army soldiers served in Korea. A total of 27,704 died as the result of hostile action; 9,429 died from other causes; and 77,596 were wounded in action. The majority of the 8,177 Americans listed as missing in action were U.S. Army soldiers.

—*David T. Zabecki*

References:

Appleman, Roy E. *South to the Nakonq, North to the Yalu.* Washington, DC: Office of the Chief of Military History, 1961.

Collins, J. Lawton. *War in Peacetime: The History and Lessons of Korea.* Boston: Houghton Mifflin, 1969.

Hackworth, David and Julie Sherman. *About Face. The Odyssey of an American Warrior.* New York: Simon and Schuster, 1989.

House, Jonathan M. *Toward Combined Arms Warfare: A Survey of 20th-Century Tactics, Doctrine, and Organization.* Fort Leavenworth, KS: U.S. Army Command and General Staff College, 1984.

Schnabel, James F. *United States Army in the Korean War: Policy and Direction, the First Year.* Washington, DC: Office of the Chief of Military History, Department of the Army, 1972.

Stuckey, John D., and Joseph H. Pistorious. *Mobilization of the Army National Guard and Army Reserve: Historical Perspective and the Vietnam War.* Carlisle Barracks, PA: U.S. Army War College, 1984.

Summers, Harry G., Jr. *Korean War Almanac.* New York: Facts on File, 1990.

See also: African-Americans and the Korean War; Clark, Mark W.; Eighth United States Army; Far East Command (FEC); Japan Logistical Command; Joy, Charles Turner; Korea Military Advisory Group (KMAG); Korean Augmentation to the United States Army (KATUSA); MacArthur, Douglas; Mobile Army Surgical Hospital (MASH); Muccio, John J.; National Security Act of 1947; Ridgway, Matthew Bunker; Second Logistical Command; Stratemeyer, George E.; Syngman Rhee; Tenth Corps; Truman, Harry S.; Walker, Walton Harris; Women in the Military.

United States Army Engineers

Combat soldiers who perform military engineering tasks. The U.S. Army engineers carried out normal military engineering roles in the Korean War, and they also fought in battles. Army engineers underwent a fourteen-week course at Fort Belvoir, Virginia. Engineers spent six weeks in basic infantry training and then eight weeks learning specific military engineering skills such as mine laying, bridge building, obstacle construction and demolition, and assault river crossings.

Army engineers were crucial to the United Nations Command (UNC) effort in the Korean War. They were involved in a cycle of building, fighting, destroying, and rebuilding. Engineers ensured the continuation of supply deliveries and communications. They also inhibited Communist military movements and provided critical combat support.

When the Korean People's Army (KPA, North Korea) invaded the Republic of Korea (South Korea), U.S. officers from the Far East Command headquarters traveled to Korea to evaluate the need for engineers. Noting the mountainous terrain and primitive nature of existing roads, ports, airfields, and railroads, they recognized the urgent need for army engineers to establish UNC supply routes as well as to create roadblocks and minefields to stop the KPA advance. Engineers soon were playing a key role in the UNC military effort.

Army engineers were assigned to infantry battalions and regiments or formed combat engineer battalions as part of infantry divisions. Special engineer units included topographical and petroleum engineers. The 3d Engineer (Combat) Battalion of the 24th Infantry Division was the first group of engineers in the war zone, arriving at Pusan on 5 July

1950. It faced a staggering number of tasks, including normal engineer duties, assisting Allied troop movement, and impeding Communist forces. When needed, engineers halted their construction or demolition duties to fight. Conducting reconnaissance as well as fixing roads and bridges, engineers were the last soldiers across the Kŭm River during the UNC retreat.

During the summer of 1950, engineers defended strategic cities and sites to ensure the flow of UNC supplies. During the Inch'ŏn landing, engineers moved cargo, and, as Allied troops moved north from the Pusan perimeter, engineers helped them cross the Naktong River. Engineers used assault boats to transport troops and equipment, including tanks, while under KPA fire. With the help of Korean civilians, army engineers also helped bridge the Kŭm River.

When, at the end of November, UNC forces retreated south, engineers helped defend the Allied perimeter. They kept routes open for retreating forces and demolished the bridges they had built earlier as well as destroying military supplies that might fall into Communist hands. They also erected obstacles across roads to slow Communist troops.

In December 1950 engineers helped evacuate troops and refugees from the North Korean port of Hŭngnam. When the Chinese opened an offensive on New Year's Day 1951, engineers quickly built bridges for the UNC infantry to advance. Creating roads across mountains and rice paddies, engineers had to deal with frozen ground and had to clear snowfall to keep roads open. Then the spring thaw produced muddy roads and flooded streams that hindered supply deliveries. The army flood prediction service warned about the effects of torrential rains in the mountains, and engineers attempted to prevent flood debris from destroying bridges.

During the UNC spring offensive, engineers rebuilt bridges and roads that they had destroyed in the previous winter's retreat. They also cleared new paths through mountainous areas. This led the 3d Engineers to embrace the slogan, "Where danger goes dynamite makes the way." Knowing the UNC advance depended on a reliable road network, engineers often worked under Communist fire. Engineers improvised both materials and technology, such as using trams to move tons of supplies up steep grades.

In February 1951 the U.S. Army established the Engineer School, Korean Army. There U.S. soldiers taught combat engineering skills to the South Koreans. Some army engineers were also assigned to air force aviation engineer units because of a shortage of qualified aviation engineers. Known as Special Category

Army With Air Force, they helped repair and improve airfields. During the war, three army engineers earned the Medal of Honor.

After the July 1953 truce, army engineers helped with Operation GLORY, building shelters and buildings for the exchange of war dead.

—*Elizabeth D. Schafer*

References:

Armstrong, Frank H., ed. *The 1st Cavalry Division and their 8th Engineers in Korea.* South Burlington, VT: Bull Run, 1997.

Farquhar, William R., and Henry A. Jeffers. *Bridging the Imjin.* Fort Belvoir, VA: U.S. Army Corps of Engineers, 1989.

Huston, James A. *Guns and Butter, Powder and Rice: U.S. Army Logistics in the Korean War.* Selinsgrove, PA: Susquehanna University Press, 1989.

Hyzer, Peter C. "Third Engineers in Korea, July–October 1950." *Military Engineer* 43, no. 292 (1951): 101–107.

———. "Third Engineers in Korea, Part II, November 1950–February 1951." *Military Engineer* 44, no. 300 (1952): 252–259.

———. "Third Engineers in Korea, Part III, March–April 1951." *Military Engineer* 44, no. 301 (1952): 356–361.

Mapp, Thomas H. "Engineer Training for Koreans." *Army Information Digest* 7 (1952): 9–16.

Strong, Paschal N. "Army Engineers in Korea." *Military Engineer* 44 (1952). 405–410.

Westover, John G. *Combat Support in Korea.* Washington, DC: Combat Forces Press, 1955.

See also: Graves Registration; Hŭngnam Evacuation; Inch'ŏn Landings: Operation CHROMITE; Appendix: Medal of Honor Winners; Pusan Perimeter and Breakout; Scorched Earth Policy; United States Army.

United States Army Military Police

Military police (MPs) provide security, riot control, and law enforcement in both peace and war. In September 1941 the Corps of Military Police became a separate branch of the army, and during World War II 209,250 officers and men served as military police, the largest police force in modern history.

Most military police units were demobilized after World War II, although some MPs were stationed overseas with U.S. troops. In 1947 the MP Corps numbered 2,078 officers and 19,630 enlisted men. On 2 July 1950, the 24th MP Company moved to Korea from Japan and over the next weeks other MP companies followed, including the African-American 512th, which was responsible for port security in Pusan and helped keep the main United Nations Command (UNC) supply route north open.

In Korea MPs pursued four primary missions: controlling and screening refugees, monitoring traffic, guarding prisoners of war (POWs), and providing security, especially behind friendly lines. Keeping roads open for UNC supplies and troop movements was a major job. MPs apprehended and escorted stragglers to their units; they also provided railroad security, supervised the Korean Security Guard Company that patrolled a vital gasoline pipeline, and used trained military dogs for contraband searches. MPs monitored traffic through crucial mountain passes, road junctions, and security checkpoints, detaining suspicious individuals for questioning. They patrolled with motor vehicles, created road maps, and reported on current conditions. They investigated abandoned dwellings looking for infiltrators.

MPs also participated in combat. An MP company was assigned to every army division, and these often provided headquarters security against attack. MPs also routinely fought Communist guerrillas operating behind UNC lines. Because they were frequently in isolated locations, MPs often found themselves targets for Communist attacks. Often the last to leave areas after UNC troops withdrew, military policemen occasionally fought advancing Communist forces as infantry.

In October 1951, the 8137th MP Group was established on Kŏje-do, consisting of three MP battalions and four companies, to guard approximately 160,000 Communist POWs and civilian internees. Despite being reinforced by another MP battalion, this MP Group endured a POW riot in May 1952, during which the commandant, Brigadier General Francis T. Dodd, was captured.

Military policemen provided security during the peace talks and have helped monitor the demilitarized zone since the war's end. A total of 42,000 men served in the MPs at the peak of the Korean War, and 54 military policemen were killed and 151 wounded in the conflict. Today the U.S. Army Military Police School at Fort McClellan, Alabama, instructs more than 14,000 army, air force, navy, marine, and civilian personnel annually.

—*Elizabeth D. Schafer*

References:

Berryman, Eric J., and William C. Truckey, compilers and eds. *Soldiers of the Gauntlet: Memories of the 720th Military Police Battalion, United States Army, 1942–1992.* Largo, FL: 720th Military Police Association, 1995.

History of the Military Police Corps. Fort McClellan, AL: U.S. Army Military Police School, 1987.

History of the Provost Marshal Section Far East Command, 1 Jan 1950 through 31 Oct 1950. U.S. Army Military Police Board Report. Fort McClellan, AL: n.p., 1951.

Westover, John G. *Combat Support in Korea.* Washington, DC: Combat Forces Press, 1955.

Wright, Robert K., Jr., compiler. *Military Police.* Washington, DC: U.S. Army Center of Military History, 1992.

See also: African-Americans and the Korean War; Dodd-Colson Prisoner-of-War Incident; Kŏje-do Prisoner-of-War Uprising; Prisoner-of-War Administration, United Nations Command; Refugees; Special Operations; United States Army.

United States Army Signal Corps

Military communications organization. Authorized by Congress in 1863, The U.S. Army Signal Corps played a vital role in Korea. In June 1950 the Army Reorganization Act stripped the Signal Corps of its combat status gained in 1920 and made it an army service branch. Major General Spencer B. Akin, the army's chief signal officer, had served on General Douglas MacArthur's staff during World War II. He retired in May 1951 and was succeeded by Major General George I. Back, who served through the remainder of the war.

When the Korean War began there were 48,500 personnel in the Signal Corps. Reserve officers and units were called to service, and the first signal personnel arrived in Korea in August and September 1950. A shortage of skilled cryptographers, however, delayed the receipt and interpretation of messages.

Because of post–World War II budget cuts, communications were limited by obsolete equipment and untrained personnel. This affected combat performance and troop movement early in the war. Signal Corps personnel attempted to maintain communications during offensives and withdrawals, advancing or evacuating equipment as required.

Korean War signal soldiers benefited from such technological advances as radar and FM (frequency-modulated) radios. Signalmen soon realized, however, that World War II methods and equipment were not entirely suited to Korea. Extremes of climate and temperatures and rugged, mountainous terrain challenged signal operators and their equipment. Working in open, unprotected areas, members of the Signal Corps often fought Communist forces to save their lives as well as protect their communication equipment. Shortages of polyethylene insulation and nylon to cover wires, synthetic manganese dioxide for batteries, and quartz crystals for radios led to creative solutions for unique situations. During the Korean War, the Signal Corps employed such new equipment as the easier-to-transport tactical radioteletype AN/GRC-26. Lighter field wire with improved audio transmission capabilities was also introduced, as was an improved ground radar to locate mortars. Transistorized equipment replaced vacuum-tube equipment. Signal Corps engineering laboratories at Fort Monmouth, New Jersey, produced a variety of more compact, efficient, faster, and powerful communications equipment.

The Mukden cable, buried a meter under the main highway that ran the length of the peninsula, was the primary system for telephone and telegraph communications in Korea. Signalmen repaired the cable when it was struck by bombs; they also strung wire through rice paddies and across hills; and they repaired breaks in wire caused by vehicles or by civilians who cut the wire and used it to tie bundles. Signalmen often found it difficult to transport equipment for repeater stations, which weighed as much as two tons. These elevated and isolated sites were often targeted by the Communists. Mobile repeater stations followed infantry units when roads allowed.

Weather conditions wreaked havoc on wire communications. In winter, batteries froze and soldiers experienced difficulties laying wire while wearing thick gloves. In summer, heat and humidity damaged equipment. As a result, wire communications were often unreliable.

Critical for quick tactical communications over long distances, VHF (very high frequency) radio companies were the backbone of the Korean War Signal Corps. Signalmen learned to bounce radio signals off steep hills, a technique not in the Signal Corps manual. Personnel could operate on slopes instead of summits, and this kept them out of chilling winds so harmful to humans and electronics.

Signal Corps responsibilities included taking motion pictures and photographs. These could reveal potential routes of advance and Communist foxholes, but they were also used as publicity for hometown newspapers.

The aviation section of the Signal Corps, the 304th Signal Operation Battalion, transported as much as 34,000 pounds of messages monthly between corps headquarters and the front. Delivering documents within hours instead of the days required by jeep, the cargo included maps and charts not easily transmitted by radio or telegraph. Carrier pigeons were also used to send messages.

During the war the Signal Corps suffered 334 casualties. After the conflict, Army Signal Corps units remained in Korea to provide communications for the Eighth Army. The Signal Corps also benefited from increased defense spending and new sophisticated satellite communication equipment.

—*Elizabeth D. Schafer*

References:

Huston, James A. *Guns and Butter, Powder and Rice: U.S. Army Logistics in the Korean War.* Selinsgrove, PA: Susquehanna University Press, 1989.

Purkiser, Herman L. "What's New in Signals?" *Military Review* 31 (January 1952): 3–13.

Raines, Rebecca Robbins. *Getting the Message Through: A Branch History of the U.S. Army Signal Corps.* Washington, DC: U.S. Army Center of Military History, 1996.

Westover, John G. *Combat Support in Korea.* Washington, DC: Combat Forces Press, 1955.

Zahl, Harold A. "Toward Lighter Signal Equipment." *Army Information Digest* 8 (June 1953): 31–35.

See also: MacArthur, Douglas; United States Army.

United States Coast Guard

During the Korean War the U.S. Coast Guard assumed a number of noncombat missions. These included search and rescue, loran, and port security. Although the Coast Guard was not transferred to U.S. Navy control as occurred in the Second World War, the navy requested that the Coast Guard deploy additional search-and-rescue units in the Pacific because of the augmentation of flights from the United States to the Far East. These outfits each contained an aviation detachment, one or more cutters, and a command post with the requisite communication capability. Such units were indeed stationed at Sangley Point in the Philippines and at Guam, Wake, Midway, and Adak Islands.

Loran, or electronic navigational aid systems, capabilities also emerged as a role for the Coast Guard. With the other armed services dispatching supplemental forces to South Korea, safety demands on and above the Western Pacific rose considerably. The Coast Guard swiftly established makeshift loran sites that provided coverage for heavy air and sea traffic areas between Korea and the Philippines.

With the Cold War turning hot, the Coast Guard also implemented stricter port security measures, mirroring action taken during the Second World War. Focusing on the conflict in Korea, the Coast Guard placed special emphasis on the prevention of sabotage of ships carrying military cargoes to the Far East. But the USSR's detonation of an atomic bomb, combined with the war in Korea, forced the Coast Guard to implement additional deterrents to prevent the importation of Soviet nuclear devices into American harbors.

To accomplish its increased duties, especially port security, the Coast Guard required more personnel. These were obtained through extension of enlistments, securing new recruits, and expansion of the officer corps. Selected because they required minimal training for port security, petty officers serving at stations and on ships were transferred to port duty. To provide sufficient replacements, classes at petty officer schools were expanded to maximum-size enrollments, and larger numbers of Coast Guard personnel were sent to navy schools. In an effort to prevent disenchantment and to retain manpower, the Coast Guard permitted individuals whose enlistments were up to join the reserve instead of staying on active duty. New recruits also began to bolster the enlisted ranks of the Coast Guard, while enlargement of the officer corps emerged by commissioning recent graduates of universities and merchant marine academies and by temporary appointments. By June 1953 the Coast Guard numbered more than 34,000 officers and enlisted personnel. With the conclusion of hostilities in Korea, the

Coast Guard once again shifted to its traditional peace-time activities.

—*R. Blake Dunnavent*

References:

Capron, Walter C. *The U.S. Coast Guard.* New York: Franklin Watts, 1965.

Johnson, Robert Erwin. *Guardians of the Sea: History of the United States Coast Guard, 1915 to the Present.* Annapolis, MD: Naval Institute Press, 1987.

Waters, John M., Jr. *Rescue at Sea.* Princeton, NJ: Van Nostrand, 1966.

See also: United States: Home Front; United States Navy.

United States: Home Front

In the late 1940s and early 1950s hysteria over communism gripped the United States. The world was plunged into the Cold War and communism seemed to be on the march across the globe. In 1948 the Soviet Union blockaded Berlin, and the West responded with the Berlin Airlift. In 1949 the United States took the lead in the formation of the North Atlantic Treaty Organization to prevent, or at least impede, a Russian invasion of Western Europe. In February 1948, in a Soviet-supported coup, the Communists took power in Czechoslovakia; the USSR now completely dominated Eastern Europe. The next year the Communists came to power in China, the most populous nation on earth. Most troubling of all to Americans, in 1949 the U.S. nuclear monopoly ended when the Soviets successfully exploded an atomic bomb.

At home, Congress sought scapegoats to account for the distressing turn of events overseas. Congressman Richard M. Nixon made a name for himself as a member of the House Un-American Activities Committee (HUAC), which endeavored to root out suspected Communists in government. Former State Department official Alger Hiss was found guilty of perjury, following the most sensational of HUAC investigations. But the person who came to symbolize the "Red Scare" more than anyone else was Senator Joseph McCarthy. During four years of prominence (1950–1954), McCarthy brazenly leveled unprovable charges of treason against leading figures in government, the military, academia, and entertainment. Many Americans were receptive to such a demagogue, particularly with the advent of the Korean War in June 1950.

Americans overwhelmingly supported President Harry S. Truman's decision to intervene in Korea. The American people and their leaders in Washington believed that this latest Communist aggression, which they saw as Moscow-inspired, had to be met with force.

But as the summer drew on and United Nations forces continued to retreat and suffer heavy casualties, public support began to erode. It had been only five years since the end of World War II, and Americans were not enthusiastic about the prospects of another protracted war. Truman understood this sentiment and declared in his first press conference after the North Korean invasion of the South, "We are not at war." He preferred to refer to the conflict as a United Nations "police action." This term repeatedly returned to haunt Truman as U.S. casualties mounted and the stalemate deepened.

American spirits revived briefly as, with General Douglas MacArthur's victory at Inch'ŏn and the Eighth Army's breakout from the Pusan perimeter, the tide turned in favor of the United Nations Command. To relieved Americans it now seemed that the war would indeed be over by Christmas. However, massive Chinese intervention in November 1950 on behalf of the Democratic People's Republic of Korea (DPRK, North Korea) dashed hopes for a quick, decisive victory.

Americans were now faced with the stark choices of bloody stalemate or escalation at the risk of sparking World War III. Public opinion polls showed that over 50 percent of Americans believed that World War III had already begun. In December 1950 President Truman sent shock waves through the nation and the world when he announced that the use of atomic weapons was under "active consideration."

Americans, frustrated by the failure to secure victory in Korea, vented their anger against the Truman administration. Public frustration reached a fever pitch when in April 1951 Truman fired the very popular General MacArthur. Though many knowledgeable critics applauded the president's decision, Truman's public approval ratings sank dramatically. On his return to the United States, MacArthur received a tumultuous welcome in cities across the country as the public displayed its disdain for Truman and his handling of the war.

The vitriolic firestorm that followed the firing briefly rekindled the "Great Debate" over U.S. foreign policy. In hearings over the firing of the general, Congress debated the choices of escalation or limited war. However, it soon became clear to the press and public that the escalation favored by General MacArthur would probably lead to a wider, bloodier war. Americans thus found themselves stuck in a limited war for limited gains. As the war dragged on month after month in stalemate along the 38th parallel, the public slowly lost interest and focused instead on living the "American Dream" at home. Public attention also concentrated on continuing wage and price controls, which had become increasingly unpopular.

The 1950s were a time of great prosperity in the United States. A growing middle class with money to spend brought to maturation today's consumer society. Suburbs, copying the "Levittown" pattern of identical

Catching up on his letters home during a break in action against the Chinese Communist forces along the front, is PFC Dwight Exe of the 5th Cavalry Regiment, 15 November 1951. (National Archives)

houses one after another, sprang up across the United States as affluent whites moved out of urban areas in droves. The GI Bill of Rights, passed during the late stages of World War II, provided a college education and low-cost housing loans to millions of veterans. Television surpassed radio as the most popular medium for entertainment and news. In San Bernardino, California a small drive-in hamburger stand named McDonald's catered to the needs of an increasingly mobile public. Car ownership increased dramatically throughout the fifties.

Life was not ideal for all, however, as "Jim Crow" racial segregation in the South, and more subtle bigotry elsewhere, conspired to maintain the status of American blacks as second-class citizens. In Greenwich Village and San Francisco, the "Beat" counterculture began. Led by such poets and authors as Allen Ginsberg and Jack Kerouac, the Beats decried the conformity and crass commercialism of U.S. society.

In 1952 Americans rejected the Truman administration and its policies by electing Republican Dwight D. Eisenhower over Democratic opponent Adlai Stevenson. During the presidential campaign, "Ike" had promised: "I shall go to Korea." Though he enunciated no clear plan of bringing the war to a close, Eisenhower struck a responsive chord in Americans with his promise to personally attend to ending the conflict.

Finally, on 27 July 1953, a truce was signed that effectively ended the war. However, there was little celebrating in the United States. Lieutenant General Mark Clark reflected the sentiments of many Americans when he said, "I cannot find it in me to exult in this hour." Korea quickly became the "forgotten war" for an American public eager to get on with other things and forget the bitter stalemate that had cost 36,914 U.S. war-related deaths. Sandwiched as it was between the more spectacular World War II and the more divisive Vietnam conflict, Korea would long remain the forgotten war on the American home front.

—*Duane L. Wesolick*

References:

Blair, Clay. *The Forgotten War: America in Korea, 1950–1953*. New York: Times Books, 1987.

Halberstam, David. *The Fifties*. New York: Fawcett Columbine, 1993.

McCullough, David. *Truman*. New York: Simon & Schuster, 1992.

Pierpaoli, Paul G., Jr. *Truman and Korea: The Political Culture of the Early Cold War*. Columbia: University of Missouri Press, 1999.

Rovere, Richard. *Senator Joe McCarthy*. London: Purnell & Sons, 1960.

See also: Antiwar Sentiment in the United States; Clark, Mark W.; Cold War, Origins to 1950; Eisenhower, Dwight D.; Eisenhower's Trip to Korea; MacArthur, Douglas; MacArthur Hearings; McCarthy, Joseph R.; Nixon, Richard Milhous; Police Action; Truman, Harry S.; Truman's Domestic Agenda and the Korean War; Truman's Recall of MacArthur.

United States Marine Corps

The U.S. Marine Corps played a major role in the Korean War. In June 1950 the corps had fallen from an all-time high total of 485,833 personnel at the end of the Second World War to just 74,279 personnel worldwide. This did not keep Marine Corps Commandant General Clifton B. Cates from proposing that marines be sent to fight in Korea immediately after the 25 June 1950 invasion of the Republic of Korea (ROK, South Korea) by the Democratic People's Republic of Korea (North Korea). Chief of Naval Operations Admiral Forrest P. Sherman delayed volunteering the Marines immediately and waited until 1 July, the day after President Harry S. Truman decided to commit ground troops. Far East Command commanding general Douglas MacArthur was delighted with the news, as he was already planning an amphibious operation behind the lines of the Korean People's Army (KPA, North Korean). On 2 July MacArthur requested the dispatch of a Marine regimental combat team; the Joint Chiefs of Staff and Truman concurred on 3 July. On 10 July, on the urging of Fleet Marine Forces in the Pacific commander Lieutenant General Lemuel C. Shepherd, MacArthur revised his request to a full division with supporting aircraft.

Meanwhile, in less than two weeks, on 12 July, the Marines activated the 1st Brigade at Camp Pendleton, California. It consisted of the 5th Marine Regiment and Marine Aircraft Group 33, 6,600 men in all. The 1st Brigade sailed for the Far East on 15 July and debarked at Pusan beginning on 2 August.

Having stripped the 1st Marine Division of much of its resources, Marine headquarters had to rely on the 2d Marine Division (then at one-third wartime strength) and reserves. On 29 July 1950, the Organized Marine Corps Reserve was activated; then on 15 August 1950, the Marine Corps Reserve was called up. By September the Marines had activated 33,258 officers and men. By the end of March 1951, the 90,044-man Marine Volunteer Reserve had activated 51,942 officers and men. Many Marines were dispersed among active Marine Corps units as replacements.

Many of the first Marine reservists recalled to active duty were incorporated into the 1st Marine Division, which made the amphibious landing at Inch'ŏn on 15 September 1950. A total of 1,809 of the 3,836 men of the 3d Infantry Regiment of the 1st Marine Division were reservists, as were nearly a fifth of the Marines who participated in the Inch'ŏn landing. Members of Marine aviation units were also recalled to active duty. Eventually twenty of thirty fighter squadrons and all ten ground-control squadrons in the reserve were called up and integrated into regular Marine aircraft wings. A year after the Korean War began the Marine Corps had grown to nearly 200,000 personnel, and the

Puppies adopted by members of the 7th Marine Regiment. (National Archives)

military expansion following the start of the war envisioned a corps of 400,000 men.

The Marines established an enviable fighting record during the Korean War, particularly as far as U.S. public opinion and Congress were concerned. This included operations in the August–September 1950 defense of the Pusan perimeter, the 15 September 1950 Inch'ŏn landing, and the October–December 1950 Changjin Reservoir campaign (and especially the 1st Marine Division's epic fighting withdrawal).

From January 1951 to March 1952 the Marines held the eastern portion of Eighth Army's defensive positions in the Hwach'ŏn Reservoir Punchbowl area. Then until the end of the war in July 1953, they manned the western sector and approaches to the ROK capital of Seoul.

The 1st Marine Air Wing provided valuable service to the United Nations Command during the conflict. Marine F4U Corsairs and the new F9F Panther jets provided valuable close air support to Marine and army ground operations, the quality of this support being much envied by the army. The 1st Marine Division headquarters was unhappy over the diversion of its air assets to support other ground troops, especially as the Marines believed that the army did not adequately direct close air support strikes. Marine aircraft also escorted bombers and provided battlefield reconnaissance, and the Marines pioneered using helicopters in medical evacuation, transport of troops (a first in warfare), and resupply.

A total of 424,00 Marines served in Korea, suffering 4,267 killed in action, 339 deaths from other causes, and 23,744 wounded in action. Statistically, Marines proved less susceptible to Communist "brainwashing" than did U.S. Army prisoners of war (POWs). A higher percentage of Marines also survived captivity than their army counterparts, and five were decorated

U.S. Marines fighting in the streets of Seoul, 20 September 1950. (National Archives)

for meritorious service while POWs. No Marine was among the 192 convicted of misconduct, nor were there any Marines among the 21 Americans who refused repatriation at the end of the war.

Despite the exemplary record in Korea, there were concerns over the drafting of 72,000 men into the corps during the war, which many veterans believed had reduced overall effectiveness. Marine officers also worried about using Marines as conventional ground troops, and the corps certainly had much to learn about fighting in cold-weather conditions. But the Marines had learned a great deal, including the potential of the helicopter in vertical envelopment. Overall, the Marine Corps emerged from the war three times larger in personnel strength than when the conflict had begun, its place in the minds and hearts of the American public secure thanks to the performance of its 1st Division.

—*Spencer C. Tucker*

References:

Cameron, Craig M. *American Samurai: Myth, Imagination, and the Conduct of Battle in the First Marine Division, 1941–1951.* New York: Cambridge University Press, 1994.

Giusti, Ernest H. *The Mobilization of the Marine Corps Reserve in the Korean Conflict.* Washington, DC: Historical Branch, G-3 Division Headquarters, U.S. Marine Corps, 1967.

Meid, Pat, and James M. Yingling. *U.S. Marine Operations in Korea, 1950–1953.* Vol. 5, *Operations in West Korea.* Washington, DC: U.S. Marine Corps Historical Branch, 1972.

Millet, Allan R. *Semper Fidelis. The History of the United States Marine Corps.* New York: Free Press, 1980.

Montross, Lynn. *Cavalry of the Sky: The Story of U.S. Marine Combat Helicopters.* New York: Harper & Brothers, 1954.

Montross, Lynn, et al. *U.S. Marine Operations in Korea.* 5 vols. Washington, DC: U.S. Marine Corps Historical Branch, 1954–1957.

See also: Brainwashing (Senoe; Xinao); Casualties; Cates, Clifton B.; Changjin (Chosin) Reservoir Campaign; Inch'ŏn Landings: Operation CHROMITE; Joint Chiefs of Staff (JCS); MacArthur, Douglas; Sherman, Forrest P.; Truman, Harry S.; United States: Reserve Forces.

United States: National Guard

National Guard forces were to augment regular forces in times of need. Certainly they played a key role in the Korean War; 84 percent of the Air National Guard (45,000 men) and 34 percent of the Army Guard (138,600 personnel) were mobilized during the conflict.

At the outset of the Korean War, the Joint Chiefs of Staff (JCS) knew that Army and Air National Guard units were available for call to active duty, but they seemed to believe that the recall of individual reservists (not National Guardsmen) and activation of logistical units from the Organized Reserve would be sufficient. On 25 July 1950 Army Chief of Staff General J. Lawton Collins recommended against calling up full Army Guard divisions. He based this partially on his belief that they would have little effect on the war in Korea, since it would take months to bring the divisions to a combat-ready status. However, the rapid advance of North Korean forces soon changed his mind; on 31 July he recommended that four National Guard divisions and two National Guard regimental combat teams be activated.

Army National Guard

During the Korean war, a total of eight National Guard divisions, three regimental combat teams (RCTs) and 714 company-sized units were called to active duty.

President Harry Truman did not wait for General Collins. On 22 July 1950 he alerted the first two of what would become a total of nineteen increments of National Guard units for active duty. These two increments included 24 battalion-sized units. Twenty of these were 90- and 120-mm anti-aircraft battalions, situated near major cities and military installations on both coasts of the United States. Antiaircraft commands were activated because the United States believed that the Soviet Union was behind the North Korean invasion of the South, part of a greater international Communist plan, which might include an attack on Western Europe or the United States itself. By 29 July three increments of Guard units had been alerted for activation in August, totalling 106 battalion and smaller commands.

As North Korean troops forced U.S. and South Korean defenders into what became known as the Pusan Perimeter, more Army Guardsmen were activated. The fourth increment, consisting of the 28th Infantry Division (Pennsylvania), 40th Infantry Division (California), 43d Infantry Division (Rhode Island-Connecticut-Vermont), 45th Infantry Division (Oklahoma), and the 196th (South Dakota) and 278th (Tennessee) Regimental Combat Teams

were alerted on 31 July and activated on 1 September 1950.

These four increments provided the bulk of Army Guard units that served in Korea. The final fifteen increments supplied only five battalions and two smaller units for Korean service (although many other commands were called to active duty elsewhere during the war, including the 31st Infantry Division (Alabama and Mississippi); 44th Infantry Division (Illinois); 37th Infantry Division (Ohio); and 47th Infantry Division (Minnesota and North Dakota).

The Army took thousands of guardsmen from the activated divisions as individual replacements, many of them for Korea. This considerably extended the time required for these divisions to become combat ready. For example, the 28th Infantry Division was activated on 5 September 1950, with a strength of 10,416 personnel. Draftees filled the division to full strength by November. On the 6th of that month, the 28th embarked on a 28-week training program designed to make the command combat-ready. However, on 2 February 1951, and again in March, the Army levied the 28th for a total of 6,000 trained fillers, destroying the division's training timetable. As a result, the 28th was not ready for deployment until mid-November 1951, when it was sent to Germany. The 43d Infantry Division also went to Germany about the same time.

General Douglas MacArthur asked for four of the National Guard divisions for his command. Only the 40th and 45th—both but partially trained—were sent to Japan in April 1951 to finish training and to provide security for Japan. Both divisions formed special commands back in the United States to train fillers who had insufficient training for deployment. When it deployed to Japan, the 45th Division was rated 43 percent combat effective. The 40th Division, was in a similar situation, being 3,000 men short of operational strength.

Originally, the Joint Chiefs of Staff prohibited these divisions from being employed in Korea. However, this order was later changed. The 45th deployed to Korea between 5 and 29 December 1951, replacing the 1st Cavalry Division, which went to Japan. Between early January and early February 1952 the 40th Division deployed to Korea, replacing the 24th Infantry Division, which also returned to Japan. Thus, Japan remained defended by two U.S. Army divisions.

The four Guard divisions remaining in the U.S.— the 31st, 37th, 44th and 47th—continued to supply trained fillers for other Army commands throughout their active duty during the war.

Listed below are the Army National Guard commands that served in Korea during the war:

Organization	State	Mobilization increment	Korean Service from
40th Inf Div	CA	4	11 Jan 52
45th Inf Div	OK	4	5 Dec 51
145th Field Artillery Battalion (FAB)	UT	5	5 Dec 51
176th Armored FAB	PA	3	17 Feb 51
196th FAB	TN	3	9 Feb 51
204th FAB	UT	3	2 Feb 51
213th Armored FAB	UT	3	16 Feb 51
300th Armored FAB	WY	3	16 Feb 51
623d FAB	KY	4	23 Dec 51
936th FAB	AR	3	10 Feb 51
937th FAB	AR	3	10 Feb 51
955th FAB	NY	3	2 Feb 51
987th Armored FAB	OH	1	16 Feb 51
213th AAA Gun Bn	PA	2	11 Nov 51
773d AAA Gun Bn	NY	16	18 Oct 52
227th AAA Group Hq & Hq Battery	FL	17	21 Mar 52
235th FA Observation Bn	PA	7	10 Dec 52
116th Engineer Combat Bn (ECB)	ID	5	28 Feb 51
151st ECB	AL	2	9 Feb 51
194th ECB	TN	3	16 Feb 51
378th ECB	NC	1	24 Feb 51
1092d ECB	WV	3	3 Mar 51
1343d ECB	AL	2	9 Feb 51
138th Engineer Pontoon Bridge Co.	MS	1	16 Feb 51
1169th Engineer Group Hq & Hq Co.	AL	1	28 Feb 51
437th Engineer Treadway Bridge Co.	MI	1	2 Mar 51
2998th Engineer Treadway Bridge Co.	TN	3	27 Feb 51
101st Signal Battalion	NY	3	7 Apr 51
30th Ordnance Battalion Hq & Hq Det.	NJ	1	21 Mar 51
32d Ordnance Battalion Hq & Hq Det.	IL	3	10 Jul 51
106th Ordnance Heavy (H) Maintenance Co.	MO	3	26 Mar 51
107th Ordnance (H) Maintenance Co.	AL	3	8 Jan 51
568th Ordnance (H) Maintenance Co.	TN	1	19 Mar 51
107th Transportation Truck Co.	AL	3	8 Jan 51
121st Transportation Truck Co.	PA	3	4 Jan 51
131st Transportation Truck Co.	PA	3	1 Jan 51
167th Trans. Truck Bn Hq & Hq Det.	PA	3	1 Jan 51
231st Trans. Truck Bn Hq & Hq Det.	MD	3	1 Jan 51
252d Transportation Truck Co.	AL	3	1 Jan 51
715th Transportation Truck Co.	DC	1	5 Jan 51
726th Transportation Truck Co.	MD	3	31 Dec 50
32d Quartermaster Group Hq & Hq Det.	PA	7	17 Feb 52
217th Medical Collecting Co.	AR	3	4 May 51

Air National Guard

Sorting out the order of battle for Air National Guard commands called to active duty in the war is difficult. Three sources supposedly giving complete information are at times contradictory. Some commands carried the designation of groups when mobilized but were redesignated as wings following activation. The 116th and 136th Fighter Bomber Wings, each with squadrons listed here, served in Japan and Korea. In addition to redesignated groups as wings, the Air Force also reorganized or redesignated other Air Guard units once they were mobilized.

At the outset of the Korean War the Air Force first asked for reserve volunteers to serve on active duty. In July 1950 it started to recall reservists and the following month it began to mobilize Air Force Reserve flying units. On 10 October 1950, the Air Force began mobilizing Air Guard wings and their fighter squadrons and support units. The first of these were:

116th Fighter Bomber Wing (Georgia),
136th Fighter Bomber Wing (Texas),
137th Fighter Bomber Wing (Oklahoma),
111th Fighter Bomber Squadron (Texas),
125th Fighter Squadron (Oklahoma),
127th Fighter Bomber Squadron (Kansas),
128th Fighter Bomber Squadron (Georgia),
154th Fighter Squadron (Arizona),
156th Fighter Bomber Squadron (North Carolina),
157th Fighter Bomber Squadron (South Carolina),
158th fighter Bomber Squadron (Georgia),
159th Fighter Bomber Squadron (Florida),
160th Fighter Squadron (Alabama),
165th Fighter Squadron (Kentucky),
167th Fighter Bomber Squadron (West Virginia),
182d Fighter Bomber Squadron (Texas),
196th Fighter Bomber Squadron (California).

Before the Korean War, Air National Guard units did not have specific wartime missions. Much of their equipment, especially aircraft, was obsolete, training was often poor, and the units were generally unprepared for combat. Guard units were almost randomly assigned to major air commands, regardless of their previous training and equipment. As with the Army Guard, Air Guard units were stripped of many key personnel for employment in other commands as fillers. As a result most units took from three to six months to become combat ready.

Despite this, Air Guard units assigned to Japan and Korea compiled excellent combat records. They flew 39,530 combat sorties and destroyed 39 Communist aircraft. Four pilots became aces, shooting down a combined 29 Communist aircraft.

Air National Guard units serving in Japan and Korea during the war are listed below (official abbreviations

are as follows: AC&W, aircraft control & warning; BS, bomber squadron; FBS, fighter bomber squadron; FBW, fighter bomber wing; FG, fighter group; FIG, fighter interceptor group; FIS, fighter interceptor squadron; FIW, fighter interceptor wing; FS, fighter squadron; FW, fighter wing; TRW, tactical fighter wing; TRS, tactical reconnaissance squadron; TRW, tactical reconnaissance wing.

Organization	State	Location	Aircraft	Activated
116th FBW	GA	France/Japan		10 Nov 50
158th FBS*	GA	Japan	F-80, F-84	10 Oct 50
159th FBS*	FL	Japan	F-84	10 Oct 50
196th FBS*	CA	Japan	F-80C	10 Oct 50
136th FBW	TX	Japan/Korea		10 Oct 50
111th FBS**	TX	Korea	F-51D	10 Oct 50
154th FS**	AR	Japan/Korea	F-51D,F-84e	10 Oct 50
182d FBS**	TX	Japan/Korea	F-51 & F-84	10 Oct 50

*Part of 116th FBW
**Part of 136th FBW

These commands served in the U.S. (date is that of activation):

101st FIW (ME), 1 Feb 1951; 102d BS (NY), 1 Mar 1951*; 103d FBS (PA), 1 Apr 1951; 108th FBW (NJ), 1 Mar 1951; 105th FS (TN), 1 Mar 1951; 106th TRS (AL), 2 Apr 1951; 107th FBS (MI), 1 Feb 1951; 108th BS (IL), 1 Apr 1951; 109th FIS (MN), 1 Mar 1951; 110th FS (MO), 1 Mar 1951; 111th FG (PA), 1 Apr 1951; 113th FBW (DC), 1 Feb 1951; 113th FS (IN), 1 Feb 1951; 114th BS (NY), 1 Mar 1951*; 115th FBS (CA), 1 Apr 1951; 117th FBS (PA), 1 Apr 1951; 118th TRW (TN), 1 Apr 1951; 118th FS (CT), 1 Feb 1951; 120th FS (CO), 1 Apr 1951; 121st FIS (DC), 1 Feb 1951; 122d FW (IN), 1 Feb 1951; 123d FIS (OR), 1 Feb 1951; 124th FS (IA), 1 Feb 1951; 124th AC&W (OK), 1 Nov 1951; 125th AC&W (MO), 1 Nov 1951; 126th FIS (WI), 1 Feb 1951; 127th FW (MI), 1 Feb 1951; 128th FG (WI), 1 Feb 1951; 132d FW (IA), 1 Apr 1951; 132d AC&W (MN), 1 Oct 1951; 132d FIS (ME), 1 Feb 1951; 133d FS (NH), 1 Apr 1951; 133d FIW (MN), 1 Mar 1951; 134th FS (VT), 1 Feb 1951; 135th AC&W (LA), 1 Oct 1951; 136th FIS (NY), 1 Mar 1951; 140th FBW (CO), 1 Apr 1951; 141st FBS (NJ), 1 Mar 1951; 142d FBS (DE), 1 Feb 1951; 142d FIG (OR), 1 Mar 1951; 146th FW (CA), 1 Apr 1951; 148th FBS (PA), 1 Feb 1951; 148th AC&W (OR), 1 May 1951; 149th FS (VA), 1 Mar 1951; 153d FS (MS), 1 Mar 1951; 155th TRS (TN), 1 Apr 1951; 157th AC&W (MO), 1 Nov 1951; 163d FS (IN), 1 Feb 1951;

166th FS (OH), 1 Feb 1951; 171st FS (MI), 1 Feb 1951; 172d FS (MI), 1 Feb 1951; 173d FS (NE), 1 Apr 1951; 174th FS (IA), 1 Apr 1951; 175th FS (SD), 1 Mar 1951; 176th FIS (WI), 1 Feb 1951; 178th FIS (ND), 1 Apr 1951; 179th FIS (MN), 1 Mar 1951; 185th TRS (OK), 1 Apr 1951; 186th FS (MT), 1 Apr 1951; 187th FBS (WY), 1 Apr 1951; 188th FS (NM), 1 Feb 1951; 190th FS (ID), 1 Apr 1951; 191st FBS (UT), 1 Apr 1951; 192d FBS (NV), 1 Mar 1951; 196th FS (CA), 1 Mar 1951; 197th FS (AZ), 1 Feb 1951.

*102nd and 1114th Bomber Squadrons became medium bomber squadrons on active duty, equipped with B-29s.

The following commands served in France: 112th FBS (OH), 10 Oct 1950; 117th TRW (AL), 20 Dec 1950; 125th FS (OK), 10 Oct 1950; 127th FBS (KS), 10 Oct 1950; 128th FBS (GA), 10 Oct 1950; 137th FBW (NY), 10 Oct 1950; 157th TRS (SC), 10 Oct 1950; 160th TRS (AL), 10 Oct 1950.

These commands served in England: 116th FIS (WA), 1 Feb 1951; 123d FBW (KY), 18 Sep 1951; 156th FBS (NC), 10 Oct 1951; 165th FBS (KY), 10 Oct 1951; 167th FBS (WV), 10 Oct 1950.

The 170th FS (IL), 1 Mar 1951 served in Iceland.

The twenty-two Air national Guard wings represented a significant increase in the Air Force's structure and efficiency during the Korean War.

—*Uzal W. Ent*

References:

Berebitsky, William. *A Very Long Weekend.* Shippensburg, PA: White Mane Publishing Co., 1996.

Ent, Uzal W., Robert Grant Crist, Editor. *The First Century. A History of the 28th Infantry Division.* Harrisburg, PA: Stackpole Books, 1979.

Francillon, René J. *The United States Air National Guard.* London: Aerospace Publishing, 1993.

Futrell, Robert F. *The United States Air Force in Korea, 1950-1953.* Washington, D.C.: Office of Air Force History, United States Air Force, 1983.

———. *The Air National Guard and the American Military Tradition.* Washington, D.C.: Historical Services Division, National Guard Bureau, 1995.

Gross, Charles G. *Prelude to the Total Force: The Air National Guard 1943-1969.* Washington, D.C.: Office of Air Force History, United States Air Force, 1985.

Hermes, Walter G. *Truce Tent and Fighting Front.* Washington, DC: Office of the Chief of Military History, United States Army, 1966.

Hill, Jim Dan. *The Minute Man in Peace and War.* Harrisburg, PA: The Stackpole Co. 1964.

Schnabel, James F. *United States Army in the Korean War: Policy and Direction, the First Year.* Washington, DC: Office of the Chief of Military History, Department of the Army, 1972.

See also: Collins, J. Lawton; Joint Chiefs of Staff (JCS); Order of Battle; United States: Air Force, Army, Engineers, Reserve Forces, Signal Corps.

United States Naval Construction Battalions (Seabees)

Since their creation during World War II, naval construction battalions, known as Seabees, have lived by their motto of "We build, we fight." Seabees have participated in every major conflict involving the United States since their creation. They have built entire bases, bulldozed and paved thousands of miles of roadway and airstrips, and been responsible for countless other construction projects.

During the Korean War the Seabees were part of Task Force 90. In the course of the conflict they grew in strength from 3,300 to 14,000 men, including reservists and active-duty personnel. Seabees first saw action during the Inch'ŏn landing. Contending with thirty-foot tides and swift currents, they put pontoon causeways into position just before the first assault, all the while under constant fire from the Korean People's Army (KPA, North Korean).

Seabees participated in the war's other amphibious landings. At Wŏnsan, they not only were tasked with setting up pontoon structures but carried out ship repair, inspected abandoned North Korean ships, and cleared mined tunnels.

When the People's Republic of China (PRC, Communist China) entered the war, Seabees were called upon to do their work in reserve and help evacuate troops from the same harbors they were so instrumental in invading. Their pontoon causeways were now used to load troops and equipment onto ships instead of putting them ashore.

Seabees were not used strictly for amphibious landings. They also built airfields for Marine air groups. This was a difficult task, as many of the airstrips were under constant Communist fire but had to remain open. One of the most amazing stories of Seabees in the war occurred on Yo-do, a small island in Wŏnsan harbor, in 1952. U.S. Navy aircraft often had to ditch without making it back to their carriers, and the Seabees were given thirty-five days to create an emergency airstrip on Yo-do for emergency recovery of aircraft. Although under constant KPA fire, they constructed the 2,400-foot runway in only sixteen days. In July alone, eight F4U Corsairs landed safely on the island.

After the Korean War the Seabees reorganized. From 1949 to 1953, thirteen battalions of two distinct types were established. The first were known as amphibious construction battalions, the landing and docking units. Their mission was to place causeways and ship-to-shore fuel lines, construct pontoon docks, and perform other functions for the rapid landing of men, equipment, and supplies. The second type, naval mobile construction battalions, were land-based crews. They were responsible for various land construction tasks, including camps, roads, tank farms, airstrips, permanent waterfront structures, and many other facilities.

—*Matthew S. Carman*

References:

Cagle, Malcolm W., and Frank A. Manson. *The Sea War in Korea.* Annapolis, MD: Naval Institute Press, 1957.

Field, James A., Jr. *History of United States Naval Operations: Korea.* Washington, DC: U.S. Government Printing Office, 1962.

"Seabees." U.S. Navy Facts File: <http://www.chinfo.navy.mil/navpalib/factfile/personnel/seabe es/seabee1.html>.

Summers, Harry G., Jr. *Korean War Almanac.* New York: Facts on File, 1990.

Transano, Vincent A. "History of the Seabees." Naval Historical Center: <http://www.history.navy.mil/faqs/faq67-1.htm>.

See also: Amphibious Force Far East (Task Force Ninety); United States Navy.

United States Navy

Sea control was utterly necessary for the successful prosecution of the United Nations (UN) war effort in Korea. Reinforced by warships from Allied nations, the U.S. Navy was able to maintain the logistical umbilical cord, to blockade the North Korean coast, to back troops ashore with gunfire and close air support, and to assist in campaigns against Communist communications and strategic targets. In carrying out these tasks, the U.S. Navy reaffirmed its place as a key element in the U.S. defense establishment and won the political support necessary to modernize and expand its operating forces.

These capabilities and trends ran counter to the prewar expectations of many defense analysts who saw strategic air power wielded by the air force as paramount; some planners reserved for the navy only the missions of convoy and patrol, fundamentally defensive tasks. Strapped by increasingly severe budget cuts, the once-mighty U.S. Navy presented itself at the beginning of the Korean War as a sorry spectacle: the number of combatants had been sliced from a high of 1,200 warships and 41,000 aircraft in 1945 to 237 warships and 4,300 airplanes by June 1950. Personnel had plummeted from 3,400,000 in 1945 to 382,000 by late spring 1950. Ships still flying commissioning pennants were frequently manned by only two-thirds of their authorized wartime complements. The Marine Corps dropped from six large divisions and 669,000 men to two skeletal divisions and a total strength of 74,000 men.

Caught in this downward spiral, the navy's leadership had bloodied itself in a vicious fight against the air force in 1949; the so-called revolt of the admirals ended with both the secretary of the navy and the chief of naval operations resigning in protest. By 1950 the navy, dispirited and shorn of warships, had lost the confidence of much of the American public.

Yet when the Democratic People's Republic of Korea (DPRK, North Korea) invaded the Republic of Korea (ROK, South Korea) across the 38th parallel, U.S. command authorities immediately turned to the navy, initially to withdraw American noncombatants and then to resupply ROK forces. On 25 June President Harry S. Truman ordered the Seventh Fleet to patrol waters off Formosa and Korea. The next day the president authorized combat operations by U.S. air and naval forces in backing the ROK.

U.S. warships, with reinforcements from the British Commonwealth, quickly found themselves in action. Cruisers and destroyers conducted their first shore bombardment at Mukho on 29 June. On 2–3 July 1950, U.S. surface warships won the only sizable naval engagement of the war by virtually annihilating a North Korean flotilla of torpedo boats and trawlers near Chumunjin. In the Yellow Sea, carriers launched their first strikes on 3 July when aircraft from the *Valley Forge* and HMS *Triumph* struck airfields at Haeju and P'yŏngyang.

As warships and support vessels again proved their utility, Congress voted a $2.7 billion supplement to the navy's budget. Part of the windfall went to recommissioning 48 major combatants and 430 minor warships and auxiliaries. Other portions of the funding went to bring 1,000 aircraft back into service. This materiel buildup, which continued for the remainder of the conflict, was necessarily matched by a corresponding increase in personnel. The navy's authorized personnel strength almost doubled by June 1951 from 382,000 to 688,971. Three key sources of manpower made this expansion possible: the involuntary retention of personnel, the draft, and the recall of reservists. By the middle of the war, over 25 percent of those in navy uniform were reservists.

This investment in materiel and manpower ultimately paid great dividends. In the interim the navy put the 1st Cavalry Division ashore on 18 July 1950 at P'ohang. This force was critical to the holding of the Pusan perimeter. Then in September, the navy helped make possible General Douglas MacArthur's great strategic counterstroke at Inch'ŏn. Charged with supporting the marine landing force, commander of Naval Forces Far East Vice Admiral C. Turner Joy assembled six aircraft carriers, the greatest concentration of naval air power since World War II. Directly backing the invasion force of 230 ships were 2 American and 2 British cruisers, 6 destroyers, and 3 rocket landing craft, which beat down the North Korean coastal defenses at Flying Fish Channel and Wŏlmi-do.

Far less successful was the subsequent landing at Wŏnsan. Unnecessarily complicated, the operation

A snowstorm slows Task Force 77 air operations from the U.S. aircraft carrier *Essex* (CV-9). The planes wait for a lull in the storm to resume operations, 18 January 1952. (National Archives)

saw the navy transport 30,000 troops of two divisions from Inch'ŏn and Pusan to the North Korean port. There the navy confronted a complex minefield laid with Soviet assistance. Short of minesweepers, the navy was slow to clear paths through the 2,000 mines; thus, the first waves crossed the beach sixteen days after ROK Army (ROKA) troops initially entered the city from the south.

Nonetheless, the demonstrated amphibious capability of the U.S. Navy and Marine Corps enabled the United Nations Command (UNC) later in the war to pose credible threats to North Korean rear areas on several occasions. For instance, in January 1951, navy diversionary movements in support of Operation THUNDERBOLT threatened Kansŏng, Kosŏng, and Inch'ŏn. The deception at Inch'ŏn compelled Communist forces to divert at least one division to guard that key port. The next month the navy assisted Operation RIPPER by a feint at Chinnamp'o.

Several times the U.S. Navy also offered hard-pressed ground units a respite at the water's edge. The most noted such episode occurred in December 1950 when the navy evacuated UN troops cut off in northeastern Korea by the Chinese entry into the war. At Hŭngnam, navy vessels lifted off 105,000 troops, including almost the entire ROKA I Corps; 91,000 Korean refugees; 17,500 vehicles; and 350,000 tons of supplies. One tank landing ship (LST) left Hŭngnam jammed with 8,400 Korean civilians.

The navy fulfilled other combat missions. Aside from striking at strategic targets, naval aircraft played a major role in the perennial UNC attempt to deprive Communist front-line forces of essential supplies. Named in 1951 Operation STRANGLE and then Operation SATURATE, the air effort was supplemented by gunfire from warships offshore and by commando raids launched from the sea.

Less heralded but more effective was the navy's blockade of North Korea. The sea barrier closed off three main avenues for the Communists to reinforce and resupply their ground units: deep-water shipping along the east coast; shallow-water coastal shipping on the Yellow Sea; and deep-water shipping routes to the Asiatic seaports in China and Manchuria. Normally swarming with commercial vessels, the waters around North Korea were swept almost completely clean by UN blockaders.

For much of the struggle, the navy paid especially close attention to the three principal North Korean ports of Hŭngnam, Sŏngjin, and Wŏnsan. The siege of the latter was especially prolonged. U.S. warships patrolled in the harbor for 861 straight days with the exception of a short period during Typhoon Karen in August 1952. So protracted did the siege become that the relieving officer, upon taking tactical command, inherited from his predecessor a golden key to the city and the honorific title of Mayor of Wŏnsan. Farther afield, the Seventh Fleet, beginning on 26 June 1950, patrolled in the Formosa Strait in response to an order from President Truman to prevent a Communist attack on Taiwan, or a Nationalist invasion of the mainland, thereby keeping the war limited.

Early in the conflict, navy leaders were concerned about possible Soviet submarine activity. Destroyers and naval aircraft maintained antisubmarine patrols against submarines based at Vladivostok that might interfere with UNC naval assets. Although this concern lessened as the conflict progressed, it could never be ignored. Numerous underwater contacts were reported and some were attacked, but without identifiable result. Although the U.S. Navy maintained submarines as part of the Seventh Fleet, their activities are not mentioned in official histories. However, several British commando operations were launched from U.S. Navy submarines.

Utterly essential to UN prosecution of the war was the logistic support provided to Allied forces by the navy's Military Sea Transport Service (MSTS), a unified organization set up to furnish sea transportation for Defense Department personnel and cargo. The MSTS carried the bulk of resources necessary for the conduct of the war: 4,918,919 passengers; 52,111,299 tons of cargo; and 21,828,879 tons of petroleum. For every ton of supplies airlifted to Korea, 270 tons went by sea (and every ton sent by air required 4 tons of aviation fuel to be shipped by sea). For every individual who flew to Korea, 6 traveled by sea. Overall monthly cargo requirements approximated those of World War II in the Pacific; to transport these vast quantities, approximately 360 ships were needed "in the pipeline" on a constant basis.

With continuous air and gunship operations, at-sea replenishment gave naval operating forces a key advantage. In July 1950 four oilers moved quickly to the theater. Improvements in technique were made, with night replenishment operations becoming standard in 1952, and by the end of that year an entire carrier task force could be topped off with fuel, ammunition, and other necessities within a nine-hour period.

Among support vessels that once more proved invaluable was the LST, with its ability to land or evacuate forces from almost any beach without winches or stevedores. Virtually all of these amphibious ships were World War II vessels hastily returned to service, some under the auspices of the Shipping Control Administration Japan. These proved especially important early in the war, when thirty-eight of the "Scapjap" ships brought in the supplies necessary for the maintenance of the Pusan perimeter. Vice Admiral Joy contended that "the LST has possibly made the greatest single contribution to the success of the UN forces in Korea."

On the other hand, submarines saw little action. Early in the conflict, U.S. submarines conducted patrols off the China coast and in La Pérouse Strait. At the same time, the navy guarded against intervention by Soviet submarines. Numerous contacts were attacked early in the war, and the carriers of Task Force 77 frequently shifted station as a precautionary measure.

In one notable sphere, mine warfare, the navy revealed an important weakness. Landings at Wŏnsan and Chinnamp'o were held up by lack of minesweeping capability. Mines also caused the navy's greatest losses during the war. Five small craft (4 minecraft—*Magpie, Partridge, Pirate,* and *Pledge*—and 1 fleet tug, *Sarsi*) were fatally damaged while conducting their dangerous work. Five destroyers (*Barton, Brush, Ernest G. Small, Mansfield,* and *Walke*) struck mines, although none sank. Fortunately for the U.S. Navy, the Communists usually employed simple contact mines rather than more sophisticated types. Eventually the navy extemporized effective countermeasures, in part by turning to Japan for personnel and minesweepers. By the end of the war the navy calculated that it had destroyed 1,535 mines.

Aside from operational losses and mines, the other principal source of danger for naval personnel was gunfire from shore batteries. During the war, Communist artillery fire hit 85 U.S. warships. Damage was usually minor, although the destroyer *John R. Pierce* was struck seven times off Tanch'ŏn on 6 August 1952 and suffered ten casualties. One hit on the heavy cruiser *Los Angeles* off Wŏnsan on 2 April 1953 cost the ship thirteen wounded.

Given the length of the war and the navy's prominent role in it, personnel casualties were surprisingly light: 493 killed in action, died of wounds, or missing in action; 1,576 wounded; 209 prisoners; and 4,043 nonbattle deaths. Marine casualties were much higher: 4,267 fatalities to hostile action; 339 other deaths; 23,744 wounded; 616 prisoners; and 1,261 nonbattle deaths.

By the end of the war the navy had resumed its rightful place in defense affairs. As General James Van Fleet noted, "We could not have existed in Korea without the navy." Navy funding rose from $4.1 billion in 1950 to $10 billion in 1952. Because carrier aviation had proved so useful, appropriations for naval aviation remained at a markedly higher level after the war. For virtually every year during the remainder of the decade, Congress authorized construction of a new supercarrier able to operate supersonic jet aircraft. Guided missile development, especially for antiaircraft work, was accelerated. The navy also began construction of special minesweepers to counter magnetic mines and of improved large amphibious craft (dock landing ships and LSTs). Planning started on a helicopter assault ship capable of putting a marine battalion ashore and on large "one-stop" replenishment vessels. Oddly, surface warships fared poorly in the postwar era, as all of the navy's battleships and most of its cruisers went into mothballs. Nonetheless, the U.S. Navy was a far stronger force in 1955 than it had been in 1950.

—Malcolm Muir, Jr.

References:

Cagle, Malcolm W., and Frank A. Manson. *The Sea War in Korea.* Annapolis, MD: Naval Institute Press, 1957.

Field, James A., Jr. *History of United States Naval Operations: Korea.* Washington, DC: U.S. Government Printing Office, 1962.

Hallion, Richard P. *The Naval Air War in Korea.* Baltimore: Nautical and Aviation Publishing Co. of America, 1986.

Love, Robert W., Jr., ed. *The Chiefs of Naval Operations.* Annapolis, MD: Naval Institute Press, 1980.

Melia, Tamara Moser. *"Damn the Torpedoes": A Short History of U.S. Naval Mine Countermeasures, 1777–1991.* Washington, DC: Naval Historical Center, 1991.

Riley, John C., Jr., ed. *Operational Experiences of Fast Battleships: World War II, Korea, Vietnam.* Washington, DC: Naval Historical Center, 1989.

See also: Aircraft Carriers; Inch'ŏn Landings: Operation CHROMITE; Joy, Charles Turner; MacArthur, Douglas; Military Sea Transport Service (MSTS); Mine Warfare; Naval Battles; Naval Forces Far East (NAVFE); Naval Gunfire Support; RIPPER, Operation; SATURATE, Operation; STRANGLE, Operation; THUNDERBOLT, Operation; Troop Ships; Truman, Harry S.; U.S. Naval Air Operations; Van Fleet, James Alward; Wŏnsan Landing.

United States: Rangers

The term *rangers* connotes small, highly trained elite units executing raids, patrols, or other operations behind enemy lines. The term also elicits images of intense esprit de corps and proficiency in unconventional warfare; it originated in the colonial period of U.S. history when special troops "ranged" between frontier posts. During the Korean War, senior commanders often misunderstood ranger capabilities and limitations, which resulted in misuse of ranger units.

When the Korean People's Army (KPA, North Korean) crossed the 38th parallel in June 1950 it employed several irregular units to infiltrate Republic of Korea (South Korean) lines to seize specific objectives. U.S. commanders soon realized that Korea's rugged, mountainous terrain offered the perfect conditions for infiltrating small-unit raiders. U.S. Army Chief of Staff General J. Lawton Collins recommended forming a special company to be attached to each division for reconnaissance and limited attacks behind Communist lines. He proposed that each company consist of a small headquarters section and three rifle platoons of three squads each. On 29 September 1950, Colonel John G. Van Houton activated the Ranger Training Center (Airborne) at Fort Benning, Georgia. Calls for volunteers went to the 101st and 82d Airborne Divisions, as regulations required volunteers to be airborne qualified.

On 2 October the first six-week training cycle began, concentrating on methods of small-unit raids, forced marches, land navigation, demolitions, and directing artillery and tactical air support. The 1st through 4th Ranger Infantry Companies (Airborne) graduated on 13 November, with the 1st, 2d, and 4th receiving orders for immediate movement to Korea. The 3d remained at Fort Benning to assist with the second training cycle, which increased to eight weeks, followed by four weeks of cold-weather and mountain-warfare training at Camp Carson, Colorado. The 2d Company, initially designated the 4th, was an all-black unit. As the first six ranger companies arrived in Korea, the U.S. Eighth Army did not assign all companies to specific divisions. For example, the 4th Ranger Company remained a "floater" and served with the 187th Regimental Combat Team (Airborne), the 1st Marine Division, and U.S. IX Corps.

A single U.S. ranger company from Japan engaged in several combat actions before the arrival of the Fort Benning companies. The 8213th Ranger Company, activated at Camp Drake, Japan, on 25 August 1950, consisted of airborne-qualified volunteers from several combat units stationed in Japan. The 8213th served with IX Corps, the Turkish Brigade, and the 25th Infantry Division until its deactivation in March 1951. The 8213th, as part of Task Force Dolvin (commanded by Lieutenant Colonel Welborn G. Dolvin), spearheaded the 25th Infantry Division's drive toward the Yalu River in November 1950. As the northernmost unit of the division, the rangers met the brunt of the Chinese attacks in bloody hand-to-hand combat. Of the eighty-five rangers who occupied defensive positions on the night of 25–26 November, only twenty-one survived. After reorganizing with new personnel, the company joined in the recapture of Seoul in February 1951.

Periodically remaining in reserve to lead counterattacks, ranger companies generally fought as regular infantry. Company commanders with the rank of only captain sometimes faced insurmountable problems coordinating operational support with divisional staffs. Often misused by parent divisions and lacking adequate logistical support, some ranger units suffered casualty rates of 90 percent. Replacements were usually available, however, both from the United States and from volunteers from their parent units in Korea.

Occasionally the Eighth Army appropriately employed the distinctive combat capabilities of the Rangers. On 23 March 1951, the 2d and 4th Ranger Companies were attached to the 187th Regimental Combat Team (RCT) and executed a parachute assault near Munsan-ni. As part of the 187th's mission to cut off retreating Chinese troops, the rangers struck southwest of the drop zones and, with minimal casualties, captured the town of Munsan-ni.

On 7 April the 4th Ranger Company was released from the 187th RCT; IX Corps commander Lieutenant General William M. Hoge planned to use the company to capture the Hwach'ŏn Reservoir to prevent Chinese People's Volunteer Army (CPVA, Communist Chinese) forces from flooding Pukhan River Valley to impede the 1st Cavalry Division's advance north along Route 17. Hoge believed the specially trained rangers were ideal to seize the dam in a small raid and put the floodgates out of commission. Hoge attached the 4th Ranger Company to the 1st Cavalry Division, but the division commander was not aware of the raid concept and assigned the 7th Cavalry Regiment to disable the floodgates. On 8 April he attached the rangers to the 2d Battalion, 7th Cavalry, tasked to attack the dam.

Early in the afternoon of 9 April the 7th Cavalry launched its attack, but rugged terrain and heavy enemy resistance stalled the advance. Steep hills and ridgelines placed the objective outside the range of divisional artillery. Finally, a single 155-mm howitzer moved into range of the dam but provided very little support from its maximum range. Heavy Chinese mortar and interlocking machine-gun fires completely halted the attack.

On 10 April CPVA forces repulsed a second attack; Hoge then ordered a determined assault by the entire 7th Cavalry Regiment. The next day the rangers and the 2d Battalion, augmented by heavy weapons and supported by other regimental units, moved forward to attack the dam. Divisional artillery batteries displaced

forward to support the offensive. Rain, sleet, and snow added to the misery of the advancing U.S. troops.

As the day wore on, the 7th Regiment commander made an attempt to utilize the rangers as Hoge envisioned. Combat engineers brought forward nine assault boats, and two platoons of rangers embarked to cross the reservoir to disable the floodgates. Under cover of darkness and poor weather conditions, both boats crossed undetected, but intense small arms fire halted the rangers on the banks of the reservoir.

After daylight, part of the assault force turned back to the south shore. The remaining rangers were unable to advance and expended most of their ammunition beating off Chinese counterattacks. An infantry company crossed in additional boats to reinforce the rangers, but by midafternoon only one platoon managed to reach them. The Chinese continued to move in more troops and halted the 7th Cavalry advance. All the rangers withdrew from the high ground they occupied to join the supporting company along the beach of the reservoir. After dark both companies returned to the south shore, and the Chinese made no strong attempt to stop the evacuation.

Lack of planning, poor coordination, lack of boats and motors, and insufficient fire support doomed any chance of success for the dam attacks. Ironically, flooding did not become a problem because of the low water level in the reservoir.

In July 1951 the U.S. Army directed the deactivation of all ranger companies in Korea. The companies continued to depend on erratic support from their parent divisions and were constantly misused. Additionally, the war had become static, preventing non-Asians from operating undetected behind Communist lines.

Most airborne-qualified rangers joined the 187th RCT, while the others transferred to infantry companies. The Joint Advisory Commission, Korea, a cover name for the Central Intelligence Agency, recruited a few airborne-qualified rangers into the 8227th Army Unit (Special Activities Group), where the men participated in clandestine operations along the North Korean coast. By October all ranger companies in Korea had disbanded.

After the ranger companies disbanded, army planners realized the need for troops capable of mounting ranger operations. On 2 October 1951, the Ranger Department replaced the Ranger Training Command at Fort Benning, with the mission of training junior officers and noncommissioned officers who would return to their regular infantry units. These specially trained personnel were then expected to pass on their ranger skills to other soldiers, instilling élan and determination to all infantry units.

—Stanley S. McGowen

References:

Appleman, Roy E. *Disaster in Korea: The Chinese Confront MacArthur.* College Station, TX: Texas A&M Press, 1989.

Blair, Clay. *The Forgotten War: America in Korea, 1950–1953.* New York: Times Books, 1987.

Mossman, Billy C. *U.S. Army in the Korean War: Ebb and Flow, November 1950–July 1951.* Washington, DC: U.S. Army Center of Military History, 1990.

Rottman, Gordon L. *US Army Rangers & LRRP Units 1942–87.* London: Osprey, 1987. Reprint, 1997.

See also: Collins, Joseph Lawton; Hoge, William M.; Special Operations.

United States: Reserve Forces

During the Korean War the U.S. government relied heavily on reserve-component forces to assist active-duty units in fighting the war. These components included the Army National Guard, the Air National Guard, the Army Reserve, the Air Force Reserve, the Navy Reserve, and the Marine Corps Reserve. All played important roles in the war.

In 1950 reserve units reflected the active forces in that they too were not well trained or prepared to fight a war. As with every major conflict in its history, the United States had drastically reduced the size of its military after World War II, and in June 1950 active and reserve-component units were undermanned. They suffered from insufficient training as well as inadequate equipment to fight an all-out war.

Reserve commands trained in the United States before they were sent to Korea, Europe, or elsewhere in the world. Reserve units that remained in the United States during the war saw much of their equipment sent to Korea. For instance, the Army National Guard provided tanks and motor vehicles and the Air National Guard sent jet aircraft as well as spare parts and other items. Stateside units found themselves stripped down to only about a third of their authorized equipment inventory.

At the start of the Korean War the army had 591,487 men and women on active duty. The Army National Guard had 324,761 personnel in 4,883 units; the Army Active Reserve had 184,015 in 934 units. In addition there was an inactive 324,602-person Volunteer Reserve and a 91,800-person Inactive Reserve.

During the entire course of the war 244,300 officers and soldiers of the Army Reserve were called to active duty, not including 43,000 reserve officers on active duty at the beginning of the war. Many of those called to active duty were used as fillers and for replacement.

The Air National Guard played an important role during the war. Newly formed after World War II, in June 1950 it had only 373 jet fighters and a total of 2,655 aircraft. Its pilots were poorly trained, the consequence of a restriction of 110 hours of flying time per year imposed for reasons of economy; there had also been little money for aviation fuel. During the war ten Air Force Reserve wings were activated, along with more than 100,000 individual reservists. The Air Force Reserve and the Air National Guard suffered from lack of equipment as well as insufficient training. As with the Army Reserve and the National Guard, active-duty units requisitioned much of the equipment belonging to the air units, and when they were called up many reserve units had only about a third of their authorized equipment.

Navy Reserves made a significant contribution to the U.S. war effort. Reserve ships and crews made up a quarter of the U.S. naval presence in Korean waters during the war. On 25 July 1950 the navy activated the carrier *Princeton.* It was recommissioned on 28 August 1950, with a largely reservist crew. Carriers *Bon Homme Richard, Essex,* and *Antietam* followed in 1951. A total of twenty-two Naval Reserve squadrons of some 6,000 officers and 15,000 enlisted personnel were deployed with the Seventh Fleet.

The Marine Corps had to rely heavily on reserves. In June 1950 the Marine Corps had 74,279 personnel serving worldwide, down from a total of 485,833 at the end of the Second World War. Marine Corps reserves numbered twice the amount of active-duty personnel. On 29 July 1950 the Organized Marine Corps Reserve was called to active duty; on 15 August 1950 the Marine Corps Reserve was activated. By September 1950 the Marines had called up 33,528 officers and soldiers. By the end of March 1951 the 90,044-man Marine Volunteer Reserve had activated 51,942 officers and soldiers. A large number of the first reservists recalled to active duty were immediately incorporated into the 1st Marine Division, which made the amphibious landing at Inch'ŏn on 15 September 1950. Nearly a fifth of the Marines who participated in the landing were reservists. Many Marine reservists called up were later dispersed among active units as replacements. Members of Marine aviation units were also recalled to active duty. Eventually, twenty of thirty fighter squadrons and all ten ground-control squadrons in the reserve were called up and integrated into regular Marine aircraft wings.

Reserve units and personnel played an important role in the Korean War in terms of both personnel and equipment. Equipment shortages were overcome, as was, in time, their lack of training. One-quarter of the top combat decorations won in the first year of the war went to reservists.

It is noteworthy that most of the reservists called up came from the unpaid and untrained inactive and volunteer reserves, and most of them were World War II veterans. The reserve formations that were kept in the United States or sent to Europe were important in that they freed regular formations to fight in Korea.

—Robert J. Arvin, III

References:

Collins, J. Lawton. *War in Peacetime: The History and Lessons of Korea*. Boston: Houghton Mifflin, 1969.

Field, James A., Jr. *History of United States Naval Operations: Korea*. Washington, DC: U.S. Government Printing Office, 1962.

Futrell, Robert F. *The United States Air Force in Korea, 1950–1953*. Rev. ed. Washington, DC: Office of the Chief of Air Force History, 1983.

Gugeler, Russell. *Combat Actions in Korea: Infantry, Artillery, Armor*. Washington, DC: Combat Forces Press, 1954.

Montross, Lynn, and Nicholas A. Canzona. *U.S. Marine Operations in Korea, 1950–1953: The Inchon-Seoul Operations*. Washington, DC: U.S. Marine Corps Historical Branch, 1955.

Sandler, Stanley, ed. *The Korean War: An Encyclopedia*. New York: Garland, 1995.

Schnabel, James F. *United States Army in the Korean War: Policy and Direction, the First Year*. Washington, DC: Office of the Chief of Military History, Department of the Army, 1972.

Stuckey, John D., and Joseph H. Pistorious. *Mobilization of the Army National Guard and Army Reserve: Historical Perspective and the Vietnam War*. Carlisle Barracks, PA: U.S. Army War College, 1984.

Summers, Harry G., Jr. *Korean War Almanac*. New York: Facts on File, 1990.

See also: United States Air Force (USAF); United States Army; United States Marine Corps; United States; National Guard; United States Navy.

United States–Republic of Korea Mutual Defense Treaty
(26 January 1954)

Bilateral agreement in which the United States essentially guaranteed the security of the Republic of Korea (ROK, South Korea) against future aggression by the Democratic People's Republic of Korea (DPRK, North Korea). In the spring of 1953, recently elected U.S. president Dwight D. Eisenhower and his advisors were cautiously optimistic about the resumption of stalled armistice talks, but they recognized the need to restrain and placate ROK president Syngman Rhee, who rejected any compromise with the Communists. Rhee's continual insistence on "no armistice without unification" and his threats not to honor any truce that did not expel the Chinese People's Volunteer Army (Chinese Communist) from Korea and to continue the war alone created doubts about ROK adherence to any negotiated settlement. To Rhee, any agreement that left Chinese Communists in Korea meant the acceptance of a "death sentence" by the ROK. Early in June 1953 President Eisenhower responded to such threats and concerns by assuring Rhee that the United States would continue to seek unification of the two Koreas by "all peaceful means" and by offering to negotiate a mutual security pact and to extend economic aid promptly after the acceptance of an armistice. But Rhee wanted an immediate defense agreement.

The release of 25,000 North Korean prisoners of war on 18 June 1953 complicated the situation and gave Washington a renewed sense of urgency to bring Rhee into line. The subsequent mission by Assistant Secretary of State Walter Robertson (from 22 June to 12 July 1953) resulted in the promise of a mutual security pact, among other pledges from the United States, in exchange for a guarantee that the ROK leader would not obstruct implementation of the terms of an armistice.

Within two weeks of the armistice signing on 27 July 1953, Secretary of State John Foster Dulles initialed the promised bilateral security pact in Seoul on 8 August 1953. Consisting of six articles, the U.S.-ROK Mutual Defense Treaty paralleled existing U.S. agreements with the Philippines and Australia/New Zealand. In the document, the United States pledged to come to the aid of the ROK in the event of an armed external attack on territory recognized by the U.S. as being lawfully brought under the administrative control of the ROK. Subsequent hearings before the Senate Foreign Relations Committee in January 1954 clarified that the United States held no treaty obligations in the event of any unilateral aggressive action by the ROK toward the DPRK or in the event of an internal insurrection against the ROK government; on 26 January 1954, the U.S. Senate ratified the pact by a vote of 81–6. The treaty entered into force with the exchange of ratification documents in Washington on 17 November 1954.

Despite initial efforts to limit its commitment, the United States, by agreeing to this mutual defense pact, recognized its unilateral responsibility for the security of the ROK. As a result, U.S. forces remain in Korea nearly half a century later.

—*Mark W. Beasley*

References:

Ambrose, Stephen E. *Eisenhower: The President*. New York: Simon & Schuster, 1984.

Collins, J. Lawton. *War in Peacetime. The History and Lessons of Korea*. Boston: Houghton Mifflin, 1969.

Stueck, William W., Jr. *The Korean War: An International History*. Princeton, NJ: Princeton University Press, 1995.

U.S. Department of State. *United States Treaties and Other International Agreements*. Vol. 5, Part. 3, *1954*. Washington, DC: U.S. Government Printing Office, 1956: 2368–2376.

U.S. Senate Committee on Foreign Relations. *Mutual Defense Treaty with Korea: Hearings Before the Committee on Foreign Relations*. 83d Cong., 2d sess., 13–14 January 1954. Washington, DC: U.S. Government Printing Office.

See also: Dulles, John Foster; Eisenhower, Dwight D.; Robertson Mission; Robertson, Walter Spencer; Syngman Rhee; Truce Talks.

Uniting for Peace Resolution

United Nations (UN) General Assembly Resolution 377(V) of 3 November 1950, the Uniting for Peace resolution, was a means whereby the United States and its UN allies, then in a majority, could bypass the UN Security Council. The UN Charter confers on the Security Council primary responsibility for the maintenance of international peace and security. Because each of the five permanent members has veto power, the council can take no action without consensus among those nations. The post–World War II U.S.-Soviet confrontation frequently resulted in Security Council deadlock. Security Council resolutions that established the UN effort to assist the Republic of Korea were possible only because the Soviet Union was boycotting the council at the time. When the Soviet delegate resumed his UN seat in August 1950, further Security Council action on Korea became impossible. This gave impetus to long-standing efforts by the United States and its supporters to use their General Assembly majority to sidestep the Soviet veto.

These efforts came to fruition with the 3 November 1950 Uniting for Peace Resolution. The essence of the resolution was the assertion that the General Assembly could *recommend* that member states take action to maintain international peace and security when deadlock among the five permanent members prevented the Security Council from *directing* action. The resolution also provided for emergency sessions of the Assembly within twenty-four hours of a request from seven (later nine) Security Council members or a majority of UN members. In addition, Resolution 377(V) established the Peace Observation Commission and the Collective Measures Committee and called on the member states to earmark and prepare military forces and other resources for use in UN-sponsored collective actions.

U.S. allies in the UN were somewhat reluctant to support the Uniting for Peace Resolution, seeing a potential danger to their own policies in General Assembly majority action and the bypassing of the great-power veto. This was not a problem for the duration of the Korean War, as the Western bloc continued to hold a commanding majority in the General Assembly. Eventually, however, the increasing number of nonaligned nations in the UN shifted the balance.

The first use of the Uniting for Peace procedure came with passage on 1 February 1951 of a General Assembly resolution identifying the People's Republic of China (PRC, Communist China) as an aggressor in Korea and initiating the consideration of sanctions against China and North Korea. In November 1956 the General Assembly met in accordance with the Uniting for Peace procedures to address both the Suez crisis and the Soviet invasion of Hungary after Franco-British and Soviet Security Council vetoes.

The Peace Observation Commission and Collective Measures Committee did no substantive work after 1954 and have since been abolished. Nothing came of the plan to have member states earmark forces for UN collective action. But the Uniting for Peace process has become a permanent part of UN procedure. Nine of the ten emergency General Assembly sessions to date have been called in accordance with that policy, and the procedure provided a foundation for subsequent UN peacekeeping operations.

—*Donald W. Boose, Jr.*

References:

Acheson, Dean. *Present at the Creation: My Years in the State Department.* New York: W. W. Norton, 1969.

Bowett, D. W. *United Nations Forces: A Legal Study.* New York: Praeger, 1964.

Luard, Evan. *A History of the United Nations.* Vol. 1, *The Years of Western Domination, 1945–1955.* New York: St. Martin's Press, 1982.

Russell, Ruth B. *The United Nations and United States Security Policy.* Washington, DC: Brookings Institution, 1968.

United Nations. *Yearbook of the United Nations, 1950.* New York: Columbia University Press, 1951.

See also: Cease-Fire Negotiations; Soviet Security Council Boycott; 38th parallel, Decision to Cross; United Nations Collective Measures Committee; United Nations Peace Observation Commission.

Unsan, Battle of
(1–2 November 1950)

First major battle between Chinese People's Volunteer Army (CPVA, Communist Chinese) and U.S. forces in the Korean War. Reacting to the evidence of the sudden Chinese entrance, U.S. Eighth Army Commander Lieutenant General Walton H. Walker ordered the 1st Cavalry Division, which had been at P'yŏngyang, to block the Chinese force that had overrun Republic of Korea Army (ROKA, South Korean) forces and was attacking toward Unsan. On 1 November the U.S. 8th Cavalry Regiment was rushed to Unsan to replace the badly mauled ROKA units. Hardly had the 1st and 2d Battalions of the 8th taken their defensive positions north and west of Unsan when they were assaulted by the 115th and 116th Divisions of the Chinese Thirty-ninth Army. Waves of Chinese infantry attacked on the evening of 1 November, supported only by mortars. These attackers used bugles and signal flares as a means of control. Swarms of Chinese infantry engulfed the U.S. positions and drove a wedge between the two U.S. battalions.

These two 8th Cavalry battalions fell apart and were driven back into Unsan. The 3d Battalion of the 8th Cavalry, three miles south of Unsan, was then ordered to help the remnants of the 1st and 2d Battalions in their withdrawal from Unsan. The Chinese attack was too rapid, however; by early morning of 2 November the attackers overran the 3d Battalion before it could begin its mission. Hand-to-hand fighting ensued, and by midmorning of 2 November little was left of the 8th

Cavalry Regiment. Small groups of survivors retreated on foot around Chinese roadblocks in the regiment's rear. A counterattack by the 5th Cavalry Regiment to break through these roadblocks was unsuccessful and resulted in over 350 additional U.S. casualties. With more than 600 men killed or captured, the 8th Cavalry Regiment was almost destroyed.

In this first engagement with the Chinese army in the Korean War, an interesting act of humanitarianism occurred. Many American walking wounded from the 5th and 8th Cavalry Regiments captured by the Chinese were placed along a road for U.S. medics to pick up. By dark a number of truckloads of U.S. wounded had been returned to American lines.

The sudden attack by the CPVA created a period of confusion throughout the Eighth Army's chain of command. Steps were immediately taken to withdraw I Corps below the Ch'ŏngch'ŏn River.

—Daniel R. Beirne

References:

Blair, Clay. *The Forgotten War: America in Korea, 1950–1953.* New York: Times Books, 1987.

Hoyt, Edwin P. *The Day the Chinese Attacked: Korea 1950.* New York: Paragon House, 1993.

Spurr, Russell. *Enter the Dragon. China's Undeclared War against the U.S. in Korea, 1950–1951.* New York: Henry Holt, 1988.

Summers, Harry G., Jr. *Korean War Almanac.* New York: Facts on File, 1990.

See also: Chinese Military Offensives.

U.S. Naval Air Operations

During the Korean War U.S. naval aircraft flying from carriers and shore bases made a major contribution to the United Nations Command (UNC) aerial campaign against Communist forces. Naval aviation assisted the air force in several important missions, including attacking strategic targets well behind Communist lines. The first such effort came on 18 July 1950, when the carrier *Valley Forge* launched strikes against the oil refineries at Wŏnsan, North Korea. In spring 1952, the navy cooperated with the air force in striking at the North Korean electrical power grid and scored substantial successes against the Sup'ung hydroelectric facility. On 1 September 1952, 142 aircraft from three carriers carried out the largest navy attack of the war, wrecking the Aoji oil refinery just eight miles from Soviet territory. So complete was the damage wrought by the strategic campaign that a shortage of targets plagued pilots toward the end of the war; at one point, jets from the *Boxer* were reduced to attacking a coal dump and bombing sheep.

Naval aircraft also took part in—and suffered the frustrations inherent in—the UNC interdiction effort, conducted principally in 1951 and optimistically dubbed Operation STRANGLE. Assigned the task of cutting Communist supply lines in northeastern Korea, naval aviators quickly focused on a key railroad bridge near Kilju. Damaged first on 3 March by airmen commanded by Lieutenant Commander Harold G. Carlson from the *Princeton,* the bridge was quickly repaired and again attacked. In what rapidly evolved into a campaign dubbed "the Battle of Carlson's Canyon," the contest served as a model for James Michener's *The Bridges at Toko-ri.* In a struggle that typified the entire STRANGLE campaign, after extraordinary efforts the aviators knocked out the bridge, but Communist workers then built a bypass around the ruins and continued their traffic.

In October 1951 naval aviators abandoned their concentration on bridges in preference to rail cuts and again piled up impressive records, at one point slicing Communist rail lines with 211 cuts in one day. Night operations from carriers began early the next year, although the lack of a specialized night carrier hurt the effort. Ultimately naval analysts concluded that interdiction was so costly (the price of one rail cut totaled $18,000; the cost of the explosives to displace 30 cubic yards of dirt came to $100 per cubic yard) that the campaign hurt the UN war effort more than it did the Communists.

Certainly one of the most unusual attack missions flown by naval aircraft during the conflict was the 1 May 1951 attack on the Hwach'ŏn Dam. AD-1s flying from the *Princeton* breached the floodgates with six torpedoes; the cascading Pukhan River slowed the Communist ground offensive. This strike was the last in warfare by planes dropping torpedoes.

Nearer the navy's taste was close air support (CAS). Early in the war, carrier aircraft proved particularly valuable in this role because they could loiter longer over the front than air force jets based in Japan. Despite initial problems in air-ground communications, soldiers and marines frequently commented on the effectiveness of naval CAS. Nowhere was this more apparent than in the withdrawal from Chosin and the evacuation of Hŭngnam in December 1950. Outside the latter port, 400 navy and Marine aircraft blasted Communist ground forces. When the navy found itself committed to the interdiction mission in 1951, Marine aircraft and planes from two escort carriers (*Badoeng Strait* and *Sicily*) helped fill the gap in CAS until it became a top priority again in April 1952.

Much less publicized than CAS, but quite essential, was the work of the patrol squadrons. Land-based P2V Neptunes or Martin PBM-5 flying boats maintained a constant watch over the Formosa Strait, thereby freeing Seventh Fleet warships for operations off Korea. Patrol aircraft also hunted mines, enforced the naval blockade of North Korea, and made weather flights.

Several notable figures piloted naval aircraft during the conflict. Ted Williams, the Red Sox baseball player, flew Panthers; in early 1953 his plane was set afire by antiaircraft fire, although he managed a safe emergency landing. Two future astronauts, John Glenn and Neil Armstrong, flew combat missions in Marine and navy fighters.

Fine pilots like these managed to compensate for inadequacies in their naval aircraft. The Communist MiG-15 proved an unpleasant surprise, possessing distinct advantages over the front-line navy fighters (the F2H Banshee and the F9F Panther) in terms of speed and altitude capabilities. Despite these handicaps, navy pilots outscored the Communists early. Other triumphs followed: in November 1952, *Oriskany* Panthers downed all but one or two Soviet MiGs that sortied from Vladivostok. That same month, a navy F3D Skyknight won the first night combat between jets by destroying a Yak-15. By the end of the war the navy had claimed twenty-three aerial victories and produced one ace in the conflict, Lieutenant Guy P. Bordelon, who shot down five nightfliers. Nonetheless, the Communist edge in materiel was sufficiently sobering that the Bureau of Aeronautics gave high priority to air superiority fighters, leading shortly after the end of the war to the F9F Cougar and ultimately to the supersonic F8U Crusader.

The navy was more fortunate in finding in its inventory some fine attack aircraft. Although the F4U Corsair proved vulnerable to ground fire, the AD Skyraider could carry large stores of ordnance and possessed a superior loiter time. The F2H Banshee fighter, sturdy and easy to maintain, did double duty in the rail interdiction role.

By the end of the war, navy and Marine aircraft had conducted 275,912 sorties, fully 41 percent of all combat missions flown during the conflict. These planes fired 274,189 rockets and dropped 178,399 tons of bombs—figures significantly higher than their totals for World War II. Evaluators credited the aircraft with killing 86,265 troops and destroying 44,828 buildings, 391 locomotives, 5,896 railroad cars, 7,437 vehicles, 249 tanks, and 2,005 bridges. On the debit side, the navy and Marines lost 5 planes to Communist fighters, 559 to antiaircraft fire, and 684 to operational causes. Some veterans argued that the Korean War, with its longer flying hours and tours, its worse weather, and its tougher antiaircraft defenses, was more demanding of aviators than World War II in the Pacific.

—*Malcolm Muir, Jr.*

References:

Cagle, Malcolm W., and Frank A. Manson. *The Sea War in Korea.* Annapolis, MD: Naval Institute Press, 1957.

Clark, Joseph J., with Clark G. Reynolds. *Carrier Admiral.* New York: David McKay, 1967.

Field, James A., Jr. *History of United States Naval Operations: Korea.* Washington, DC: U.S. Government Printing Office, 1962.

Hallion, Richard P. *The Naval Air War in Korea.* Baltimore: Nautical and Aviation Publishing Co. of America, 1986.

See also: Aerial Combat; Air Power in the War; Aircraft (Principal Combat); Aircraft Carriers; Close Air Support; Hŭngnam Evacuation; SATURATE, Operation; STRANGLE, Operation; Sup'ung (Suiho) and the Korean Electric Power Plant Campaign.

U.S. Policy toward Korea before 1950

The first direct contact between the United States and Korea occurred in August 1866. W. B. Preston, an American merchant and owner of the ship *General Sherman,* attempted to persuade Korea to open trade relations with the United States. After arriving off Korea, Preston ordered the *General Sherman* up the Taedong River toward P'yŏngyang. Local officials warned the foreigners several times not to continue, but Preston and ship captain Page ignored these warnings. The Koreans then attempted to destroy the *General Sherman* with cannon fire from the river banks and with fire rafts set to drift toward the American schooner. But the Americans maneuvered the vessel out of harm's way. When the Koreans tried to attack the ship with their own vessels, the schooner's superior weapons promptly repelled them. Later, Preston and Page took a local official hostage in an attempt to improve their bargaining position. This only increased Korean outrage. When the *General Sherman* ran aground on a sandbar, the Koreans had their first opportunity to seek revenge. Again they employed fire rafts, this time with success against an immobile target. Furious at what they considered the arrogance and barbaric behavior of the Americans, the Koreans showed no mercy toward the surviving crew. When they reached the shore, all crew members were beaten to death by angry mobs or later executed.

News of the fate of the *General Sherman* and its crew reached Washington almost a year later by way of the U.S. embassy in China. Rumors circulated that there were American survivors being held prisoner in Korea. In response to these rumors, Washington dispatched Commander John C. Febiger in the *Shenandoah* to investigate. He sailed from Chefoo, China, in March 1868. Febiger found no evidence of survivors, but he did obtain an official Korean account of the events. The Korean government's position was that the destruction of the *General Sherman* and the execution of its crew resulted from the aggressive and irresponsible actions of the ship's crew. The Korean government also made it very clear that it had no interest in opening its doors to the West.

In April 1870, U.S. Secretary of State Hamilton Fish authorized Minister to China Frederick F. Low to open negotiations with Korea and secure a treaty for the protection of shipwrecked seamen. After conferring with the Navy Department, the State Department directed Asiatic Squadron Commander Admiral John Rodgers to escort Low on his mission. The Low-Rodgers expedition, an armada of five navy ships with more than 1,200 sailors and marines, arrived off the shores of Kanghwa Island, Korea, at the end of May 1871.

On 1 June a surveying party from the expedition came under fire from one of many Korean shore fortifications. The survey party then returned fire. The exchange lasted no longer than ten minutes, but the Americans, while suffering no serious casualties, inflicted extensive damage to the Korean fort. Admiral Rodgers believed that it was essential to demonstrate U.S. strength and capability to the Koreans, and he developed a plan to punish the attack.

The U.S. response began on 10 June 1871, and it ended the next day. It included a massive naval bombardment of Korean shore fortifications, an amphibious assault by U.S. Marines, and the capture of several Korean forts. This experiment at "gunboat diplomacy" was a failure. The Low-Rodgers mission departed Korea without the desired treaty.

In the latter part of the nineteenth century, Americans obtained what little they knew of Korea from the press, which was for the most part, negative. An example of this negative reporting appeared in a *New York Times* editorial on 21 June 1880: "It does not appear that the Coreans [sic] are any better or any worse for their seclusion from the world … and they have none of the vices of barbarism, unless we should find that their uncomfortable habit of massacring all shipwrecked foreigners who fall upon the coast as barbaric." Despite this negative impression, the United States persisted in trying to establish relations with Korea.

During the same period, Chinese officials were increasingly concerned with growing Japanese militarism and expansionism. China supported a U.S.-Korean treaty, which it hoped could prevent Japan from securing hegemony over Korea. In May 1882 Chinese intermediary Viceroy Li Hung-Chang persuaded Korea's King Kojong to sign the Treaty of Peace, Amity, Commerce, and Navigation with the United States. Central to this treaty, from King Kojong's perspective, was Article 1, which stated, "If other Powers deal unjustly or oppressively with either Government, the other will exert their good offices, on being informed of the case, to bring about an amicable arrangement, thus showing their friendly feelings."

In spite of this treaty, U.S. government officials saw little strategic or commercial value in Korea. The U.S. government saw the treaty primarily as a means to improve the treatment of U.S. sailors shipwrecked on the peninsula.

The U.S. State Department's policy toward Korea in the last decade of the nineteenth century demonstrates U.S. indifference toward that country. From the beginning, the State Department had no interest in Korean domestic affairs and little in Korea's foreign affairs. The State Department continuously warned its diplomats in Seoul to remain neutral and disapproved of any U.S. involvement in Korean domestic or foreign affairs. In a diplomatic dispatch, Secretary of State Frederick T. Frelinghuysen informed U.S. Minister in Seoul George C. Foulk: "Seoul is the center of conflicting and almost hostile intrigues involving the interests of China, Japan, Russia, and England, and … it is clearly the interest of the United States to hold aloof from all this and do nothing nor be drawn into anything which would look like taking sides."

Despite Washington's policy line, U.S. diplomats in Seoul continued to give King Kojong the impression that the United States would assist in maintaining Korea's independence. One of those diplomats, Minister Horace N. Allen, informed the State Department that King Kojong was confident the United States would ensure Korea's independence after the Russo-Japanese War.

President Theodore Roosevelt did not intend to interfere in Korea against the Japanese; however, he believed Korea to be incapable of defending itself. He also knew there was little he could do to prevent a Japanese takeover of the peninsula and believed that Japan might play a crucial role in halting the expansion of the Russian Empire. Rather than coming to the aid of Korea, as King Kojong expected, Roosevelt supported the 27 July 1905 Taft-Katsura Memorandum, in which the United States sanctioned the Japanese takeover of Korea and, in return, the Japanese promised not to take any aggressive action against the Philippines.

In October 1905 King Kojong wrote to President Roosevelt requesting that the United States offer its "good offices" as stated in the 1882 treaty and intervene on behalf of Korea to prevent Japanese encroachment. Washington ignored the request and withdrew its legation from Seoul on 24 November 1905. Six days later, Korea became a protectorate of Japan.

In 1907 King Kojong again appealed for assistance when he sent his emissary, Yi Chun, to the Second International Peace Conference at the Hague. Yi claimed that the protectorate convention with Japan was signed under coercion and therefore was null and void. The Japanese argued that Korea had forfeited its diplomatic rights under the protectorate convention and therefore should not be allowed a separate delegation at the conference. The Japanese prevailed and, having grown impatient with the Korean monarch's persistence, forced him to abdicate his throne. Japan formally annexed Korea in August 1910.

Koreans at home and abroad continued to believe that the United States would facilitate their independence. On 8 January 1918, during World War I, President Woodrow Wilson announced his Fourteen Points for peace and espoused the principle of self-determination. Koreans became aware of what was happening in Europe, where smaller nations were about to gain their independence. Having suffered more than a decade of an oppressive Japanese government, they sought ways to capitalize on Wilson's principle of self-determination and bring about Korea's independence.

Syngman Rhee, leader of the Washington-based Korean Commission, was one of those inspired and motivated by Wilson's Fourteen Points. Rhee attempted to attend the Paris Peace Conference with the intent of drawing attention to Korea's situation and persuading President Wilson to recognize Korean independence; but the State Department refused to issue passports to Rhee and his associates, claiming that as subjects of Japan they would have to obtain their passports from Japanese officials.

During the period between the signing of the Taft-Katsura agreement and the end of World War I, the relationship between the United States and Japan changed considerably. Both had emerged as world powers with impressive naval forces, and both were equally suspicious of the other's capabilities and intentions. A naval arms race ensued that led many to believe that war between the two nations was inevitable. In an effort to ease tensions, avoid a new arms race, and reconcile differences, the United States invited Japan to participate in the Washington Conference on the Limitation of Armaments beginning in November 1921.

The Korean Commission saw the conference as another opportunity to publicize Korea's struggle for independence. Changing its name to the Conference on Limitations of Armaments, the commission drafted an appeal, which it submitted to the U.S. delegation on 1 October 1921. The commission argued that several Western powers had negotiated a treaty with Korea before the Japanese annexation, and therefore "must still regard Korea as a separate entity and the treaties in force." U.S. Secretary of State Charles E. Hughes did promise to warn the Japanese regarding their treatment of the Korean people, but the Korean Commission failed to obtain recognition of Korea's right to independence.

Not until World War II did the United States take a real interest in Korea. President Franklin D. Roosevelt favored a trusteeship in Korea, whereby the United States, Great Britain, China, and the Soviet Union would temporarily govern the country until Korea could govern itself. Roosevelt wanted to establish a lasting peace after winning the war and believed that the key to such an endeavor was strengthening U.S.-Soviet relations. He also believed that a U.S.-Soviet trusteeship in Korea would not only provide Russia with the incentive for entering the war in the Pacific but would also form the beginnings of U.S.-Soviet cooperation.

When President Roosevelt died in April 1945, the tone of U.S. policy toward Russia changed, as did U.S. policy toward Korea. Korea became a pawn in a power struggle between the United States and the Soviet Union. Both countries agreed to the 38th parallel as a rough demarcation line for the surrender of Japanese forces; the Soviets would take the Japanese surrender in Korea north of that line and the United States would do the same south of it.

Efforts to reunify the two halves of Korea foundered in the Cold War, and when the Communist northern government refused to allow a United Nations commission into its territory, in May 1948 the commission held elections in the southern half of Korea, and Syngman Rhee was elected president of the Republic of Korea (ROK). The North responded by inaugurating the Democratic People's Republic of Korea (DPRK) with Kim Il Sung as its premier.

By June 1949 the United States had withdrawn its remaining forces from South Korea and left behind the 500-man Korea Military Advisory Group (KMAG) to train ROK forces. On 12 January 1950 Secretary of State Dean Acheson defined the U.S. strategic defense perimeter in Asia as excluding the Korean peninsula. This situation encouraged the DPRK, which had built up its military forces with substantial Soviet aid. On 25 June 1950, the DPRK launched a well-executed surprise invasion of the South. This act initiated the Korean War and dramatically changed U.S. policy toward Korea and all of East Asia.

—*Mark R. Franklin*

References:

Burnette, Scott S., ed. *Korean-American Relations: Documents Pertaining to the Far Eastern Diplomacy of the United States.* Vol. 3, *The Period of Diminishing Influence, 1896–1905.* Honolulu: University of Hawaii Press, 1989.

Cumings, Bruce. *The Origins of the Korean War.* Princeton, NJ: Princeton University Press, 1981, 1990.

George, Douglas Edward. "The Low-Rodgers Expedition: A Study in the Foundations of U.S. Policy in Korea." Thesis. Monterey, CA, Naval Post Graduate School, 1988. Unpublished manuscript.

Koo, Youngnok, and Dae Sook Suh, eds. *Korea and the United States: A Century of Cooperation.* Honolulu: University of Hawaii Press, 1984.

Ky, Dae Yeol. *Korea under Colonialism: The March First Movement and Anglo-Japanese Relations.* Seoul: Seoul Computer Press, 1985.

Lee, Yur Bok, and Wayne Patterson, eds. *One Hundred Years of Korea-American Relations, 1882–1982*. University of Alabama Press, 1986.

McCune, George M., and John A. Harrison, eds. *Korean-American Relations: Documents Pertaining to the Far Eastern Diplomacy of the United States*. Vol. 1, *The Initial Period, 1883–1886*. Berkeley: University of California Press, 1951.

Palmer, Spencer J., ed. *Korean-American Relations: Documents Pertaining to the Far Eastern Diplomacy of the United States*. Vol. 2, *The Period of Growing Influence, 1887–1895*. Berkeley: University of California Press, 1963.

See also: Acheson, Dean Goodersham; China, Republic of; Geneva Convention of 1949; Japan; Korea: Democratic People's Republic of, 1945–1953; Korea: Geography and History to 1945; Korea: History, 1945–1947; Korea, Republic of: History, 1947–1953; Potsdam Conference; Syngman Rhee.

U.S. Policy toward Korea: 1950–1953

When President Harry S. Truman began his second term of office on 20 January 1949, U.S. policy toward East Asia was in crisis. The central issue in the region, which was emerging as the Cold War's second front, was what to do about China. This had profound security ramifications both for U.S.-occupied Japan and for the situation on the Korean peninsula. In China, Mao Zedong (Mao Tse-tung) and the Communists continued to gain in their civil war against Jiang Jieshi (Chiang Kai-shek) and the Nationalists. Mao also appeared to be taking a more anti-American stance and was moving closer the Soviet Union. On the Korean peninsula, veteran Communist Kim Il Sung, who had ties to both China and the USSR, ruled the North as head of the Democratic People's Republic of Korea (DPRK). The situation in Korea between the DPRK and the Republic of Korea (ROK), led by U.S.-educated Syngman Rhee, was uncertain, as both sides sought reunification of the artificially divided peninsula.

Against the backdrop of an evolving U.S. policy of containing the USSR in Europe, the situation in Asia caused Truman and Secretary of State Dean G. Acheson to seek a more realistic and pragmatic policy with both China and Korea. With the Communists controlling most of the mainland, in October 1949 Mao proclaimed in Beijing (Peking) the People's Republic of China (PRC). During the final months of 1949 Jiang was forced to relocate the Nationalist government and major elements of its military to Taiwan (Formosa). Despite significant political support in the U.S. Congress for maintaining military and economic assistance to the Nationalists and formulating a strategy to oppose Communism in Asia, the Truman administration's focus was on Europe, and it continued to distance the United States from events in both China and Korea.

Truman's cautious policy was in accordance with his administration's assessment that without massive U.S. military aid and assistance and direct involve-ment of U.S. military forces, that the Nationalists on Taiwan would soon fall. Despite pressure from the Republican opposition, at a press conference in January 1950 Truman announced that the United States would not seek bases on Taiwan, become involved in the continuing civil war, or provide further military aid or advice to the Nationalists. U.S. domestic policy toward China was further complicated when the United States' major European ally, Great Britain, announced in early January its recognition of the PRC. It was becoming obvious that United States would have to go it alone if it adopted a pro-Jiang China policy.

The controversial and ambiguous nature of U.S. East Asia policy was further highlighted in January when Congress initially failed to pass an appropriations bill for continuing economic assistance to the ROK. This heightened the perception of an American retreat from Korea following the withdrawal of U.S. combat forces. U.S. forces had initially occupied Korea south of the 38th parallel in September 1945. In early 1948, Washington began to redeploy U.S. combat units, and by early 1950, only the 500-man Korea Military Advisory Group (KMAG) remained to train and support the ROK armed forces. Soviet military units had also been withdrawn from the North, but they too had left behind administrative and training cadres.

This minimal U.S. military presence, coupled with the end of economic aid, signaled the reduced strategic importance of, and the diminished American commitment to, the ROK. Although the economic aid legislation was later passed, as Secretary of State Acheson later asserted, "the damage had been done. Without question, the government and the people of the United States wished to end their responsibility for the government and the future of Korea." In a speech on 12 January 1950, Acheson himself did further damage when he implied that Korea and Taiwan were outside the U.S. defensive perimeter in East Asia. Japan was the key regional state for U.S. Far East security.

In February 1950 the Chinese and the Soviets signed a treaty that called on the USSR to provide significant economic aid to China and established a formal military alliance between the two states. The implicit withdrawal of U.S. protection from the Chinese Nationalists and from the regime in South Korea left the door wide open for Mao's planned invasion of Taiwan. With the U.S. pullback from Korea and the Sino-Soviet alliance, the way also seemed clear for the reunification by force of the Korean peninsula by the Kim Il Sung regime. In addition to the apparent diplomatic withdrawal, U.S. military order of battle in the region had been reduced significantly. General Douglas MacArthur's Far East Command consisted of only four infantry divisions and one regimental combat team. This occupation force in Japan and Okinawa was not at full strength and was not properly equipped and trained. The air and naval elements in the theater, while significant, also suffered from shortages and training deficiencies. Muddled diplomacy and military unpreparedness combined to expose U.S. weakness in East Asia.

The United States' politically contentious and ambiguous policies toward both Jiang and the Nationalists on Taiwan and the regime of President Syngman Rhee in South Korea were severely tested by the attack by North Korea early on 25 June 1950. After a series of meetings with his senior foreign policy and military advisors, President Truman decided to provide military equipment to the ROK, but initially he authorized only a limited commitment of U.S. air and naval units. The president did order the Seventh Fleet into the Taiwan Strait to deter a concurrent escalation of fighting between the two Chinas. The Truman administration was concerned over possible future actions by the Soviet Union and China, along with the rapidly deteriorating situation of the ROK forces fighting to stop the offensive by the Korean People's Army (KPA, North Korean).

In addition to its own unilateral actions, the United States forwarded the matter to the United Nations (UN), which condemned the North Korean invasion. The United States also requested that member states provide military support to assist the ROK defenders. Since the USSR was boycotting the Security Council, the UN resolution condemning the North passed unanimously. (At that time the Nationalist government represented China in the UN, which was the reason for the Soviet boycott of the Security Council.) Washington then began the process of gaining UN agreement for direct military action by member states under U.S. command.

General MacArthur, who conducted a personal reconnaissance to Korea on 29–30 June, passed his appraisal of the situation and of the military performance of the Republic of Korea Army (ROKA) to Washington. He recommended direct U.S. military action to stem the invasion. Truman then authorized MacArthur to commit U.S. ground combat forces to the defense of South Korea. After five days of fact-finding and debate, the United States was at war with the DPRK, but on a limited scale and with no authorization to strike Soviet or Chinese targets.

The initial U.S. policy was to stop the invasion and restore the territorial integrity of South Korea. On 7 July the UN passed a resolution that called for a multinational effort under the direction of General MacArthur. Even as defenses were being organized, MacArthur began planning a bold counterstroke.

In September MacArthur's Inch'ŏn campaign (Operation CHROMITE) collapsed the KPA assault and put UN forces on the offensive. After two months of tough fighting just to hang on in Korea, the Truman administration was now confronted with the policy issue of whether or not to allow MacArthur to cross the 38th parallel with ground forces. This action had the potential to trigger the direct intervention by either China or Russia or both.

The policy that emerged left MacArthur significant room for interpretation and provided wide latitude for him to react to the exigencies of the developing situation. Except for tactical actions necessary to carry out the primary military objective of the destruction of the KPA, U.S. ground forces would stay south of the 38th parallel; ROKA forces could conduct limited operations north of that line. Under no circumstances were U.S. naval or air forces authorized to engage targets in China or Russia without prior approval by Washington. Furthermore, if either the Chinese or the Russian forces entered the war, MacArthur's forces were to assume the defensive.

The KPA, clearly defeated in the South, now retreated into North Korea but refused to surrender. On 1 October ROKA forces entered North Korea against minimal resistance. MacArthur reorganized the UN forces and prepared for further military action to destroy the KPA. In early October—avoiding the UN Security Council, as the Soviet Union had ended its boycott of that body—the United States pressed the General Assembly for a resolution to guide follow-on actions. The resultant 7 October UN General Assembly resolution called for "all appropriate steps to ensure stability throughout Korea" and for UN oversight of elections and the formation of a unified democratic Korean government. With this new "guidance," and despite specific warnings from Beijing and growing intelligence evidence of a Chinese build-up in Manchuria, U.S. forces entered North Korea on 9 October. Planning began in earnest for the occupation of North Korea and a phased program under UN auspices leading to a reunified and democratic Korea.

A United Nations Command (UNC) military victory appeared to be within reach when the PRC intervened militarily. Chinese forces began to deploy into North Korea in October. MacArthur, who had previously discounted Chinese intervention, now called for air strikes against Chinese targets. While Washington finally agreed to air strikes to destroy the bridges over the Yalu River, President Truman and key military leaders in Washington were forced to reassess the situation. Truman was determined not to widen the war if at all possible, while MacArthur argued the military necessity of hitting targets in Manchuria that supported the Chinese deployment.

The size and initial success of the massive, late-November Chinese intervention changed the entire complexion of the conflict. UNC forces, after losing Seoul for a second time, finally stopped the Chinese, mounted a major offensive, and were able to restore a defensive line just north of the 38th parallel. The military stalemate on the ground and a sober appraisal of the strategic costs of all out-war with China and possibly also the Soviet Union, precipitated a major policy change in Washington. The growing feud between Truman and MacArthur over how to deal with China culminated with the general's removal from command in April 1951. The core issues of this politically contentious action were the definition of military victory, civilian control over the military, and a fundamental disagreement over the Truman administration's decision to limit the war and to seek a diplomatic settlement.

By May 1951 the war had settled into a costly stalemate with neither side willing to expend the personnel and resources for decisive offensive operations to break the deadlock on the ground. The unification by force of the Korean peninsula was no longer possible without expanding the conflict. The Truman administration now was willing to settle for a diplomatic solution and a return to the antebellum status quo, and the Soviets and the Chinese were also ready to negotiate.

Meetings over a settlement began on 10 July 1951. However, from the very beginning the negotiations bogged down over both major and minor issues. Off and on over the next eighteen months the talks dragged on as disagreements over venues, meeting agendas, cease-fire agreements, the exchange of prisoners, withdrawal of foreign forces, the demarcation line, and the widening of the talks to include the Taiwan situation prolonged the complicated negotiations. In the meantime, both sides attempted to display and confirm their resolve by continuing limited military actions with significant additional casualties.

In December 1952 president-elect Dwight D. Eisenhower visited Korea to make his own personal appraisal. Despite additional pressures exerted by the new administration, there was more than six months of bitter fighting, including a major Communist assault in June, before the difficult negotiations succeeded and the armistice was signed on 27 July 1953. Critical to the negotiations was ROK president Syngman Rhee. He strongly opposed a settlement that would leave Korea divided and Chinese troops in North Korea. To secure his support, the Eisenhower administration had to promise substantial additional aid and a postconflict security pact. Rhee was placated, but the armistice that ended the fighting left Korea politically and geographically divided.

—*J. G. D. Babb*

References:

Acheson, Dean. *The Korean War.* New York: W. W. Norton, 1971.

Alexander, Bevin. *Korea: The First War We Lost.* New York: Hippocrene Books, 1986.

Appleman, Roy E. *South to the Naktong, North to the Yalu.* Washington, DC: Office of the Chief of Military History, 1961.

Donovan, Robert J. *Tumultuous Years: The Presidency of Harry S. Truman.* New York: W. W. Norton, 1982.

Foot, Rosemary J. *The Wrong War: American Policy and the Dimensions of the Korean Conflict, 1950–53.* Ithaca, NY: Cornell University Press, 1985.

Hermes, Walter G. *United States Army in the Korean War: Truce Tent and Fighting Front.* Washington, DC: Office of the Chief of Military History, 1966.

Oberdorfer, Don. *The Two Koreas: A Contemporary History.* Reading, MA: Addison-Wesley, 1997.

Schnabel, James F. *United States Army in the Korean War: Policy and Direction, the First Year.* Washington, DC: Office of the Chief of Military History, Department of the Army, 1972.

See also: Acheson, Dean Goodersham; Eisenhower, Dwight D.; Inch'ŏn Landings: Operation CHROMITE; Jiang Jieshi (Chiang Kai-shek); Kaesŏng Truce Talks; Kim Il Sung; MacArthur, Douglas; Mao Zedong; P'anmunjŏm Truce Talks; Syngman Rhee; Truce Talks; Truman, Harry S.; United States–Republic of Korea Mutual Defense Treaty; U.S. Policy toward Korea: 1953 to the Present.

U.S. Policy toward Korea: 1953 to the Present

U.S. policy toward Korea since 1953 is a legacy of a conflict for which no final peace treaty has been signed. Today, fifty years after the outbreak of the Korean War, the United States maintains nearly 100,000 military personnel in the Asia-Pacific Theater, of which some 37,000 are stationed in the Republic of Korea (ROK), including the 2d Infantry Division, which deployed to the Korean peninsula in 1950. The United States remains committed to the defense of the ROK under the terms of a mutual security treaty promulgated in August 1953.

President Dwight D. Eisenhower took office in January 1953. Following the Truman administration's lead, he was determined to end the costly war and stalemate as soon as possible. Eisenhower saw a negotiated settlement as the only solution. However his ROK counterpart Syngman Rhee continued to push for the reunification of Korea by military force. This was impossible without massive U.S. assistance, and Rhee grudgingly stepped back from his position on reunification and agreed to the terms of the settlement. As a quid pro quo he demanded assurances that the United States would not abandon the ROK and would remain fully committed to the defense of South Korea.

Within a month of the signing of the armistice, the Eisenhower administration concluded a defense treaty with the ROK. The United States also promised significant military assistance to build up the ROK armed forces. However, the United States also began planning for a significant drawdown of its forces. A senior U.S. officer continued to command all Allied forces, including ROK units, in South Korea since July 1950.

After further negotiations with the ROK and direct warnings to Beijing of the consequences of a renewed offensive, two of eight U.S. infantry divisions and several air force units on the peninsula were withdrawn in 1954. In addition, negotiations with the People's Republic of China (PRC, Communist China) continued on the withdrawal of its troops from North Korea. The PRC agreed to reduce its forces, and in August 1954 Washington announced the withdrawal of four additional U.S. divisions. Despite opposition by the ROK and some U.S. members of Congress, this redeployment was completed in 1955.

A tense truce continued in Korea through the 1950s with both the ROK and the Democratic People's Republic of Korea (DPRK, North Korea) continuing to expand their military capabilities, with equipment and training provided by their Cold War sponsors. In the North the Kim Il Sung regime received economic support from both the PRC and the Soviet Union and was able to build its economy and consolidate its power. In the South the increasingly autocratic, corrupt, and harsh Rhee administration was rapidly losing popular support as the economy struggled. In 1960, following a series of student demonstrations and increasing political opposition, Rhee was finally forced from office. After a brief attempt by more moderate and democratic elements to institute economic and governmental reforms failed, Major General Park Chung Hee led a successful coup and seized power in May 1961. U.S. forces and the majority of ROK units did not interfere with the military takeover, and there was no attempt to exploit the situation by the DPRK and their Communist patrons.

By 1963 Park had successfully consolidated his power and gained a measure of political legitimacy when he was popularly elected as the nation's president. This period of political turbulence in South Korea coincided with a series of Cold War–related crises for the Kennedy administration. The Bay of Pigs fiasco, the deteriorating situation in South Vietnam, tensions with the Soviet Union in Europe, and the momentous Cuban missile crisis pushed the security and domestic political situation in the ROK into the background. When the Johnson administration took office in 1963, its primary focus in Asia was the expanding war in Vietnam. The United States began a gradual buildup of forces in South Vietnam that offered economic opportunities for the ROK but also had the potential to draw off U.S. military units and equipment critical to the defense of South Korea.

To show solidarity with its ally and in an effort to ensure that U.S. forces in South Korea would not be shifted to Southeast Asia, the Park government sent 45,000 ROK Army (ROKA) troops to Vietnam. In 1966, President Johnson and other senior members of his administration visited Korea and pledged that no U.S. troops would be withdrawn and that American support for the defense of the ROK was a key element of U.S. Asian policy. However, two incidents in 1968 and another in 1969 tested the relationship and identified limitations in the U.S. commitment.

In January 1968, North Korean forces attacked and captured the USS *Pueblo*, a spy ship gathering electronic intelligence off the DPRK coast. The muted U.S. reaction to this provocation was a regional show of force by aircraft carrier battle groups. This was followed by eleven months of North Korean intransigence and sporadic negotiations before the *Pueblo*'s crew was released. Then in February 1968, North Korean commando forces attempted to assassinate President Park at the Blue House in Seoul. Again, despite a clear military provocation, Washington called for enhancing the defensive posture of ROK and U.S. forces and a diplomatic response. At the height of American commitment to the war in Vietnam, the Johnson administration would not support a retaliatory military strike by the ROK against North Korea that could possibly escalate into wider conflict.

In April 1969, shortly after President Richard M. Nixon took office, North Korean forces shot down a U.S. EC-121 intelligence collection aircraft with the loss of its thirty-one–man crew. Again the United States conducted a naval show of force and deployed additional aircraft to South Korea, but it carried out no punitive response. This lack of military response to North Korean aggression cast doubt on the strength of the U.S. commitment to the ROK in any situation short of a full invasion. In June 1969 the situation was further complicated for the ROK when President Nixon announced a new security doctrine.

The Nixon Doctrine was a major policy change, and the Park regime perceived it as having a direct and negative impact on the U.S.-ROK mutual defense relationship. Nixon attempted to assure the United States' allies that the United States would live up to its treaty commitments and continue to provide nuclear protection. What concerned the ROK was Washington's demand that Allied and friendly nations supply the troops and bear a greater share of the costs of conventional weapons for their own defense.

In early 1971 Nixon ordered the withdrawal of one of the two remaining U.S. Army divisions from Korea. More significantly, Nixon's national security advisor Henry Kissinger began secret negotiations with Beijing that led to the 1972 visit by President Nixon to the PRC. As the United States pulled out of Vietnam, the stage had been set for the eventual full diplomatic recognition and the normalization of relations with the PRC at the expense of the Republic of China. This event shook the Park regime's confidence in U.S. security commitments. Even without significant Soviet or Chinese support, the DPRK's military was superior to that of the South, and the ROK's ability to defend itself was problematic. The confidence of the ROK was further eroded when the PRC reacted to North Korea's concerns over Sino-U.S. rapprochement by extending it a new military and economic aid package—this while promises of more modern U.S. equipment were being delayed and combat forces withdrawn. The Park regime began to seek direct talks with the DPRK, and a short period of détente supported by the United States followed.

By the mid-1970s, as President Nixon became embroiled in the Watergate controversy, the Park regime was losing popular support. It became increasingly dictatorial in an attempt to retain power. Concurrently, after a period of popular and promising negotiations, relations with the North again began to deteriorate. Shortly after Nixon resigned, new president Gerald Ford was confronted by a new crisis on the Korean peninsula.

In August 1976, two U.S. Army officers were brutally murdered in the demilitarized zone (DMZ) while supervising the trimming of a tree in the Joint Security Area (JSA). Ford immediately ordered the deployment of additional air and naval forces to Korea. Under the cover of B-52 bombers and other supporting aircraft, the tree was removed, but the United States took no further action. This incident did result in a change in the deployment of troops within the JSA. Once again the United States was less than decisive or resolute in its response to North Korean aggression. President-elect Carter campaigned for further withdrawals of U.S. forces from Korea, and Seoul again feared abandonment by its ally. The U.S. intelligence community, however, conducted an extensive reexamination of the military balance on the peninsula. This concluded that the North was stronger militarily than was previously estimated. Caught up in a contentious domestic political debate and being pressured diplomatically by South Korea, Carter suspended the withdrawal after only one brigade of the 2d Infantry Division had been removed. The U.S. relationship with the Park government deteriorated further when Carter called for an improvement in human rights in South Korea.

The ROK political situation changed abruptly in October 1979 when President Park was assassinated. During the next year, key political and military factions vied for power as students, workers, and opposition parties conducted major demonstrations that often resulted in violence. General Chun Doo Hwan slowly took power and began to arrest key political opponents, censored the press, and used loyal military units to crack down on protests. In May he deployed Special Forces units and paratroopers, ostensibly under U.S. command, to quell the Kwangju riots in southern Korea. This resulted in the deaths of hundreds of people.

A controversy arose over Chun's use of these troops who had been allegedly "released" by U.S. General John A. Wickam, commander of the Combined Forces Command. The situation was further exacerbated when President Ronald Reagan lauded Chun for his decisive response to growing chaos in the country. While Washington regarded this situation in terms of the overall regional security situation, opposition groups in the ROK saw it as U.S. complicity in support of a brutal military dictatorship. Chun successfully stabilized the situation, and in August 1980 he was "elected" ROK president. He then began a major program of political and economic reforms that quieted his critics.

The deterioration in U.S.-ROK relations during the Carter years was reversed by the close relationship that developed between Presidents Reagan and Chun. The ROK president was the first official foreign dignitary to visit Washington during the Reagan administration. President Reagan also visited Korea in 1983, and he increased the number of U.S. forces in Korea. Both were important gestures.

Two major incidents in 1983 also worked to bring the two countries together. In September the Soviets shot down Korean Airlines (KAL) Flight 007, in the process killing both Korean and American passengers. Then in October President Chun and several senior members of his government conducted a state visit to Rangoon, Burma. Two North Korean military officers had infiltrated the country and they set off a bomb that killed several members of the Chun party, including the foreign minister. As with previous incidents, no military retaliation against the DPRK was undertaken, but the two administrations worked together closely to coordinate their diplomatic responses. In a show of support, additional U.S. military forces were deployed to the region. During the next several years, the developing relationship between the Reagan administration and that of Mikhail Gorbachev in the Soviet Union, as well as Reagan's visit to the PRC, significantly lessened tensions on the Korean peninsula.

As the international situation improved, the most significant problems in South Korea were now in the domestic political arena. Chun had promised an end to military dictatorship and wanted to oversee a peaceful transition before the 1988 Seoul Olympics. In December 1987 another ROKA officer, General Roh Tae Woo, unexpectedly won the first popular election in Korea since 1971. He defeated both Kim Young Sam and Kim Dae Jung, who would both win later elections and serve as the first two elected civilian leaders of Korea since President Syngman Rhee. In 1988 the hugely successful Seoul Olympics were held. The games were attended by virtually all of the North's allies and were a major embarrassment for the DPRK. The ROK, fully supported by the United States, weathered the North's diplomatic attempts to share the games while enduring another major terrorist incident, the bombing of KAL Flight 858. The ROK, now becoming a major economic power in Asia, had conducted a peaceful transition of government and was now in a position to conduct a more independent foreign policy.

President Roh, again fully supported by the United States and taking advantage of the end of the Cold War, began to implement a policy of Nordpolitik that had its roots in the Chun era. This policy meant not only initiatives toward normalizing relations with the DPRK, but it sought improved relations with the PRC and USSR as well.

Encouraged by Washington, Roh's policies achieved dramatic results, including a reversal of Soviet support for the North and closer political and economic relations with the PRC. With the support of the major powers, in 1991 the two Koreas joined the United Nations. The Bush administration suggested that now was the time for the United States to begin the process of moving from a leading role to a supporting role on the Korean peninsula. The ROK was now being seen as more of an equal partner and a mature, independent player in the region.

As the Cold War ended in Europe and relations with China matured, the United States began to focus more on its problems in the Middle East. However, the large and well-prepared military forces of the ROK and the DPRK still confronted each other, and incidents at sea and along the DMZ continued to occur all too frequently. However, the ROK economy, military modernization program, and diplomatic initiatives toward China and Russia have put the North at a major disadvantage, and invasion seemed a more remote possibility by the early 1990s. Nevertheless, as the Clinton administration took office in early 1993, several issues cast doubt on this optimistic appraisal. Developments in missile technology, DPRK arms sales to the Middle East, and especially the possibility of a nuclear-armed North Korea increased tensions in the region.

President William J. Clinton's first foreign visit was to South Korea, where he specifically warned the North of the dire consequences of the use of nuclear weapons against the ROK. His tour of the DMZ and his visit there with U.S. troops was a symbol of the continued U.S. commitment to the defense of South Korea. The United States led the effort to negotiate with the North over the issue of nuclear weapons and technology. In July 1994, "Great Leader" Kim Il Sung died after leading the DPRK for forty-six years. His son, Kim Jong Il, took power.

In October 1994, the DPRK signed the Framework Agreement that called for an inspection regimen conducted by the International Atomic Energy Agency, a United Nations organ. North Korea was promised two light water reactors to replace its current heavy water reactors, and the United States agreed to supply oil in the interim until the new power plants came on line. Since the agreement was signed, there are indications that the DPRK may not be fully living up to the agreement. For the last several years the North's economy has been in steep decline, and there were reports of widespread famine. Millions are malnourished and hundreds of thousands of people may have died. Ominously, the North developed and launched a multistage rocket. This also increased tensions in the region. Clearly the Cold War has not ended in Korea.

U.S. policy toward the Korean peninsula remains focused on deterring the DPRK from military adventurism and defending a treaty ally. The region is the critical flash point in Asia and is specifically covered in the U.S. national security strategy as one of two areas where forces must be prepared to conduct a "Major Theater War." The United States has not relinquished its leading military role, and a U.S. officer continues to serve as commander in chief of Combined Forces Command and commander in chief of the United Nations Command. As in 1950, the United States continues to have vital and strategic interests in Korea.

—*J. G. D. Babb*

References:

Bok, Lee Suk. *The Impact of U.S. Forces in Korea.* Washington, DC: National Defense University Press, 1987.

Bunge, Frederica, M., ed. *North Korea: A Country Study* (DA Pam 550-81). Washington, DC: U.S. Government Printing Office, 1989.

Hermes, Walter G. *United States Army in the Korean War: Truce Tent and Fighting Front.* Washington, DC: Office of the Chief of Military History, 1966.

Keon, Michael. *Korean Phoenix: A Nation from the Ashes.* Englewood, NJ: Prentice-Hall International, 1977.

Kihl, Young Whan, ed. *Korea and the World: Beyond the Cold War.* Boulder, CO: Westview Press, 1994.

Oberdorfer, Don. *The Two Koreas: A Contemporary History.* Reading, MA: Addison-Wesley, 1997.

Savada, Andrea M., and William Shaw, eds. *South Korea: A Country Study* (DA Pam 550-41). Washington, DC: U.S. Government Printing Office, 1990.

See also: Eisenhower, Dwight D.; Nixon, Richard Milhous; Syngman Rhee; United States–Republic of Korea Mutual Defense Treaty.

V

Van Fleet, James Alward
(1892–1992)

U.S. Army general and commander of the Eighth Army during the Korean War. Born on 19 March 1892 in Coytesville, New Jersey, and raised in Florida, James Alward Van Fleet graduated from the U.S. Military Academy at West Point in 1915. He then served along the Mexican border. After the United States entered World War I, he led a machine-gun battalion of the U.S. Army 6th Division and saw combat in the Meuse-Argonne. In the years 1918 to 1939, Van Fleet taught military science in Reserve Officers Training Corps programs in Kansas, South Dakota, and Florida; studied and taught at the Infantry School at Fort Benning, Georgia; and eventually, as a colonel, in February 1941 became commander of the 8th Infantry Regiment. Though he remained a colonel and retained command of the 8th Infantry until 1944, his rise to general officer's rank began with the Normandy invasion, when the 8th Infantry landed at Utah Beach as a part of the U.S. 4th Division. By the time the division participated in the capture of Cherbourg, Van Fleet had earned recognition as a forceful, courageous, and competent commander. By March 1945 he was a major general and commanded III Corps.

In the postwar years Van Fleet gained valuable experience in the exigencies of Cold War generalship. After a tour of duty in the United States, he served in occupied Germany in 1947. In 1948 he was named head of the U.S. Military Advisory and Planning Group in civil war–torn Greece. Promoted to lieutenant general and appointed to the Greek National Defense Council, Van Fleet participated in one of the first confrontations between East and West in the Cold War. He helped mold the Greek army into an effective fighting force, and by 1949 that army had defeated a Communist-inspired insurgency. Van Fleet next received command of the U.S. Second Army.

In the wake of Douglas MacArthur's removal by President Truman in April 1951 and his replacement by Lieutenant General Matthew B. Ridgway, Van Fleet took over Ridgway's former position as commander of the Eighth Army. Upon his arrival in Korea Van Fleet received orders to place the Eighth Army on the defensive while inflicting the heaviest possible losses on Communist forces. Van Fleet repositioned the Eighth Army along and to the south of the 38th parallel, where a rough stalemate had by then developed between United Nations Command (UNC)

forces and the Communists. Here his troops defeated the spring offensive by the Chinese People's Volunteer Army. Van Fleet then launched a counterattack, and by June the Eighth Army had inflicted some 270,000 casualties on the Chinese and North Koreans.

Van Fleet chafed under the politically driven necessities of limited warfare in the age of the Cold War. Although fighting in Korea was certainly hot enough, larger considerations of international politics often determined action on the ground. Thus, through the fall and winter of 1951–1952, the Eighth Army fought a continuous series of defensive actions, some of them quite bloody, which Van Fleet saw as threatening morale and discipline, and which ran counter to his predilections as a leader. On the other hand, his directives for the very defensive he was ordered to implement were perceived in the press as insufficiently aggressive. He found himself thereby caught in what would become a classic Cold War bind for U.S. battlefield commanders.

Consequently, friction sometimes arose between Van Fleet and higher echelons over questions of tactics and ultimate goals. This atmosphere forced him to make extensive use of close air support along Lines Kansas and Wyoming to avoid useless losses to U.S. ground troops. It also created for him the impression that the Eighth Army was intentionally being deprived of artillery ammunition in retaliation for his being politically troublesome, a charge he made after his retirement.

Despite such differences, Van Fleet kept the Eighth Army in fighting trim during the bitter and bloody stalemate of the war's last two years. At Heartbreak Ridge and Bloody Ridge in eastern Korea in late summer 1951, in central Korea that October, and in the Iron Triangle in summer and fall 1952, Van Fleet showed himself as a pugnacious, blunt-spoken, and usually successful commander. Because of the nature of the Korean War, his troops sometimes suffered heavy casualties even in small-scale actions, but they almost always inflicted even greater losses on the enemy. Van Fleet inspired the Republic of Korea's (South Korean) political and military leadership as well.

Van Fleet relinquished his command in Korea in February 1953 and retired from the army two months later as a full general. Whatever political difficulties he may have had, he went on to serve as President Dwight D. Eisenhower's special ambassador to the Far East in 1954 and as a consultant to the secretary of the army on guerrilla warfare in 1961–1962. Van Fleet died at Polk City, Florida, on 23 September 1992.

—*D. R. Dorondo*

References:

Hermes, Walter G. *United States Army in the Korean War: Truce Tent and Fighting Front.* Washington, DC: Office of the Chief of Military History, 1966.

Mossman, Billy C. *U.S. Army in the Korean War: Ebb and Flow, November 1950–July 1951.* Washington, DC: U.S. Army Center of Military History, 1990.

New York Times, 24 September 1992.

See also: Cold War, Origins to 1950; Eighth United States Army; MacArthur, Douglas; Ridgway, Matthew Bunker.

"Van Fleet Load"

In 1950 artillery ammunition requirements for the U.S. Army in the field were expressed in terms of "days of fire" (DOF), a DOF being the number of rounds allocated per gun per day. Soon after the Korean War began, the Department of the Army approved an increase in the DOF for artillery weapons in Korea to 45 rounds per day for 155-mm howitzers and 50 rounds per day for 105-mm howitzers, 155-mm guns, and 8-inch howitzers. However, in April 1951 Lieutenant General James A. Van Fleet, commander of the Eighth U.S. Army in Korea, determined to defeat the Chinese People's Volunteer Army's (Chinese Communist) spring offensive with massive artillery firepower, stated, "We must expend steel and fire, not men." Accordingly, he increased the DOF for artillery ammunition fivefold, to 300 rounds per day for 105-mm howitzers, 250 rounds per day for 155-mm howitzers, and 200 rounds per day for 155-mm guns and 8-inch howitzers. This increased allocation of artillery ammunition came to be called the Van Fleet day of fire or the Van Fleet load. Its application significantly increased the expenditure of scarce artillery ammunition by United Nations forces in Korea. One field artillery battalion in the battle of the Soyang River in May 1951 fired 11,891 rounds of 105-mm ammunition in one twenty-four–hour period. The Chinese offensive was stopped cold by such massive artillery fire, but the United Nations logistical system was hard put to obtain, store, and distribute the large quantities of ammunition required.

—*Charles R. Shrader*

References:

Huston, James A. *Guns and Butter, Powder and Rice: U.S. Army Logistics in the Korean War.* Selinsgrove, PA: Susquehanna University Press, 1989.

———. *The Sinews of War: Army Logistics, 1775–1953.* Washington, DC: Office of the Chief of Military History, 1966.

Logistical Problems and Their Solutions. APO 301: Headquarters, Eighth U.S. Army Korea, Historical Section and Eighth Army Historical Service Detachment (Provisional), 1952.

Middleton, Harry J. *The Compact History of the Korean War.* New York: Hawthorn Books, 1965.

Mossman, Billy C. *U.S. Army in the Korean War: Ebb and Flow, November 1950–July 1951.* Washington, DC: U.S. Army Center of Military History, 1990.

See also: Artillery; Logistics in the Korean War; Van Fleet, James Alward.

Vandenberg, Hoyt S.
(1899–1954)

Born in Milwaukee, Wisconsin, on 24 January 1899, Hoyt Sanford Vandenberg was well educated and developed a clear understanding of politics from his uncle, Senator Arthur H. Vandenberg of Michigan. He graduated from the U.S. Military Academy at West Point in 1923 with an undistinguished academic record and was assigned to the Air Service.

In 1925 Vandenberg earned his wings. In the 1930s, with a reputation as a moderate between airmen advocating big bomber development and those who believed in the need for more pursuit fighters, Vandenberg attended the Command and General Staff School at Fort Leavenworth, Kansas (1936), and the Army War College (1939).

After the Japanese attack on Pearl Harbor, Vandenberg supervised the Army Air Forces' (AAF's) buildup program, and in the summer of 1942 he was assigned to General Dwight D. Eisenhower's staff to develop air plans for North African operations. He was then assigned as chief of staff for the Twelfth Air Force under Brigadier General James H. Doolittle.

In early 1943, Brigadier General Vandenberg became chief of strategic forces under Lieutenant General Carl Spaatz, commander of Northwest African Air Forces. In August he returned to AAF headquarters in Washington for four months to head the air mission to Russia under Ambassador W. Averell Harriman. From there he returned to London to serve as deputy commander of Allied Expeditionary Air Forces.

In August 1944, Eisenhower promoted Vandenberg from vice commander of the tactical Ninth Air Force to its commander, replacing Lieutenant General Lewis Brereton. Along with the Royal Air Force's Second Tactical Air Force, the Ninth Air Force covered the advance of Allied forces across France into Germany. Both Army Chief of Staff George C. Marshall and Third Army commander General George Patton agreed that the Ninth Air Force had performed a vital role in helping win the war on the western front.

In July 1945, Lieutenant General Vandenberg became assistant chief of staff for operations of USAAF. As the war ended, many younger army officers like Vandenberg had to face restoration to their permanent rank, in his case brigadier general. Instead, President Harry S. Truman successfully nominated

Vandenberg to remain a lieutenant general. In 1946 Vandenberg spent six months as chief of the intelligence division of the War Department's General Staff. He next served as director of the Central Intelligence Group (later Central Intelligence Agency, CIA). After fifteen months, he rejoined USAAF Commander General Spaatz as his deputy.

Vandenberg played an important role in helping Truman and Spaatz make the air force a separate service in September 1947. Spaatz became the first chief of staff of the air force (CSAF), with Vandenberg as his vice chief of staff. When Spaatz retired in April 1948, Vandenberg succeeded him as CSAF. His first task was to reorganize the U.S. Air Force (USAF), which was still partially tied to the army.

This was the beginning of the Cold War, and in the summer of 1948 the Soviets blockaded Berlin. It was Vandenberg who convinced Truman that the fledgling service could resupply Berlin from the air in what became known as Operation VITTLES. He also appointed his long-time colleagues Lieutenant General Curtis LeMay and Major General William Tunner to command the successful resupply of Berlin.

When the Korean War began in June 1950, it was a difficult time for the air force. Development of the B-36 had been slowed by monetary restrictions and political controversy. This meant the USAF would have to go to war with the B-29 as its primary strategic bombing platform. Worst of all, the air force still faced President Truman's strict fiscal policies. As a result, weapons and resources needed by airmen were at first simply not available. A frustrated Vandenberg called it a "shoestring air force." He refused to accept the situation, and by 1953 he had resurrected the USAF into the strongest air force in the world and the linchpin of U.S. military policy.

The first air force engagement in Korea occurred on 27 June 1950, when an F-82 escorting U.S. transport aircraft evacuating U.S. embassy personnel from Seoul shot down a North Korean YAK fighter. Despite having available only a few mostly World War II–vintage bombers and fighters, the USAF played a decisive role in saving the Pusan perimeter and in the subsequent United Nations Command (UNC) sweep north.

When the Chinese intervened in October and November 1950, the heroic UNC rear guard and a handful of mostly World War II veteran USAF fighter pilots flying new F-86 Sabres prevented total disaster. At Vandenberg's insistence, the deployment of more F-86s helped check Communist ground forces and MiG-15s and allowed Lieutenant General Matthew B. Ridgway's forces to counterattack and restore the balance of power on the ground.

When President Truman was placed in the awkward position of recalling General of the Army Douglas MacArthur, Vandenberg supported new secretary of defense George C. Marshall and chairman of the Joint Chiefs of Staff General Omar N. Bradley in deflecting congressional criticism of the president and U.S. military leadership. Vandenberg's level-headed testimony and measured counsel convinced Congress of the ultimate folly of using nuclear weapons in Korea.

As the 1952 and 1953 stalemate and negotiations unfolded, Vandenberg urged many of his fellow air force leaders to suspend close air support and focus on aerial interdiction. Many veterans and students of World War II Europe argued that interdiction efforts similar to those used in Europe would defeat Communist forces in Korea. Vandenberg believed differently. He declared, "We used to bomb and close the Brenner Pass every day, and the Germans opened it every night." Vandenberg realized that the success of interdiction depended on ground attacks and constant and consistent bombing to force Communist consumption of supplies to rise faster than they could be replenished.

Even so, he saw no alternative to at least attempting to knock out MiG bases and utilities as best he could. Thus, despite limits against attacking enemy sanctuaries in Manchuria, these targets were attacked repeatedly. Between mid-1950 and mid-1953, USAF sorties rates grew from 100 per day to 1,000 per day. But in 1953 losses to ground fire and MiG-15s rose to alarming levels that caused even veteran pilots to question the viability of USAF tactics. To solve these problems Vandenberg assigned B-29s to fly tactical night raids, increased the deployment of F-86s, and had new electronic gunsights installed on the Sabre jets. Vandenberg's trips to Korea and his personnel style convinced many reluctant pilots to continue to fly.

By the time President Dwight D. Eisenhower took office, public opinion and military policy had focused away from "brushfire" wars and toward strategic nuclear weapons aimed at the Soviet threat in Europe. It was the beginning of massive retaliation and the bomber days of the Strategic Air Command. In the face of this new posture, Vandenberg fell into a policy disagreement with new Secretary of Defense Charles E. Wilson, who sought to make drastic cuts in the air force. In the ensuing public debate, Vandenberg vigorously defended the need for a flexible and technologically advanced conventional and nuclear air force capable of strategic and tactical missions.

The 1953 summer congressional hearings on the military budget were both troubling to and hard on Vandenberg, especially as he was slowly dying of cancer and was in constant pain. An admirer of Eisenhower, he had been a conciliator and team player, so it hurt him deeply to air fundamental disagreements in public. But he believed he was right and that the country would be ill served by putting all its defense eggs in the basket of nuclear missiles. Vandenberg worried openly that a lack of conventional military preparedness would lead the nation into more Koreas, not fewer, as Wilson believed.

In the end Vandenberg lost and was forced to retire in June 1953. Even though Eisenhower was irritated by the disagreement, he never openly criticized Vandenberg or his advisers; such was his respect for his former subordinate.

After retirement, Vandenberg slowly wasted away from cancer. He died in Washington, D.C., on 2 April 1954, convinced of the correctness of his views.

—*William Head*

References:

Meilinger, Phillip S. *Hoyt S. Vandenberg: The Life of a General.* Bloomington: Indiana University Press, 1989.

Parrish, Noel F. "Hoyt S. Vandenberg: Building the New Air Force." In *Makers of the United States Air Force,* edited by John L. Frisbee. Washington, DC: Office of Air Force History, 1987: 205–228.

See also: Bradley, Omar Nelson; Eisenhower, Dwight D.; Joint Chiefs of Staff (JCS); MacArthur, Douglas; Marshall, George C.; Ridgway, Matthew Bunker; Truman, Harry S.; Wilson, Charles Edward.

Vyshinskii, Andrei Ianuarovich (1883–1954)

Soviet foreign minister from March 1949 to March 1953. Born in Odessa in 1883, Andrei Ianuarovich Vyshinskii joined the Menshevik political party in 1902. Trained as a lawyer at Kiev University, he met his future political patron, Josef Stalin, when both were in prison in Baku in 1907. But Vyshinskii did not officially become a Bolshevik until 1920. He made a name for himself as the chief state prosecutor during Stalin's bloody purges in the 1930s. The high point of Vyshinskii's legal career was his orchestration of Nikolai Bukharin's 1938 show trial.

Vyshinskii entered the foreign ministry in 1940. His rise to prominence was predicated more on opportunism than ability, but he possessed the useful knack of consistently anticipating Josef Stalin's wishes. This was essential for Vyshinskii, because Stalin maintained tight personal control over Soviet foreign policy for the last four years of his life. Vyshinskii served as one of Viacheslav Molotov's chief deputies at the Allied conferences in Yalta and Potsdam.

In 1949 Stalin removed Molotov as foreign minister and elevated Vyshinskii in his place. Unlike his former boss, the new foreign minister did not have a significant following within the Party or the general populace. The Korean War was the watershed event in Vyshinskii's four-year tenure in this post. He alternately blasted the United States and searched for nego-

tiated settlements, depending on the exigencies of the situation.

Stalin occasionally used Vyshinskii to attack while at the same time another official offered a small olive branch, or vice versa. Such a contradictory foreign policy might be hard on his subordinates, but it allowed Stalin to keep several options open at once. Under Vyshinskii's direction, the Soviet foreign ministry condemned United Nations (UN) intervention in Korea with considerable ferocity. Vyshinskii himself accused UN commanders of using disguised Japanese troops, blamed the South Koreans for starting the war, and painted the United States as an aggressor in the internal affairs of another country. After General Douglas MacArthur's daring September 1950 landing at Inch'ŏn, which put Korean People's Army (KPA, North Korean) forces into retreat, the Soviet position softened. Addressing the UN General Assembly, Vyshinskii focused his standard rhetorical attacks on specific hawks in President Harry S. Truman's administration and signaled a willingness to negotiate without the usual demand that U.S. forces withdraw first.

U.S. policymakers, believing that they had the diplomatic and military momentum, ignored these overtures. Vyshinskii, using unofficial intermediaries, again sought to open negotiations when United Nation Command (UNC) forces neared the 38th parallel in October 1950 but broke off contacts once the line had been crossed. Incensed that U.S. officials, ignoring his explicit warnings, decided to invade North Korea, on 2 November 1950 Vyshinskii unleashed a vicious tirade in the UN against Truman's advisor, John Foster Dulles. The next month, also in the UN, Vyshinskii justified the recent flood of Chinese "volunteers" into the DPRK, continued his verbal assault against U.S. aggression in Korea, and demanded that all foreign troops be withdrawn so that "the Korean question [could] be entrusted to the Korean people themselves." Other than repetitions of such rhetoric, Soviet diplomats saw their role in the conflict diminish for a few months after the Chinese intervened while events played themselves out on the battlefield.

Truce talks in Kaesŏng between the four combatants—the Republic of Korea (South Korea), the United States, the People's Republic of China, and the DPRK—began in July 1951 after the fighting had bogged down near the 38th parallel. The Soviets suggested a cease-fire in a 23 June radio address by Soviet UN delegate Jacob Malik, which got things going. On 23 August the talks were suspended over several disagreements, including the location of the demilitarized zone (DMZ) demarcation line.

Unexpectedly, Vyshinskii helped restart the talks two months later. After a little more than two years of service, U.S. Ambassador to the USSR Alan G. Kirk paid a farewell visit on 5 October to the Soviet foreign minister (Stalin was unavailable). Acting on instructions from the U.S. State Department, Kirk expressed frustration over the suspension of the truce talks and asked the Soviet government to use its influence with the Chinese and North Koreans to convince them to return to the table. Vyshinskii responded by shifting blame for the collapse of the negotiations onto commander of UNC forces Lieutenant General Matthew Ridgway. After this face-saving maneuver, the Soviet government agreed to intercede. Truce talks were restarted on 25 October 1951 in P'anmunjŏm.

Although not an official participant in the P'anmunjŏm negotiations, the Soviet Union provided considerable diplomatic support for its two allies. On several occasions during the war, Vyshinskii advocated the following formula as the basis for a truce: use of the 38th parallel as the center of the DMZ, withdrawal of all foreign troops, and the repatriation of all prisoners of war (POWs). Once all parties agreed to accept the current battle lines as the basis for the DMZ, the main sticking point became the issue of involuntary POW repatriation. Many Chinese and North Korean prisoners did not want to return home. UN Indian delegate V. K. Krishna Menon proposed a compromise on the POW question that was reluctantly accepted by the United States. Vyshinskii preempted any possibility of a favorable Chinese response by condemning the proposal and its author in a surprisingly blunt speech in the UN on 24 November 1952. This interference maintained the

deadlock in the talks for another three months until Stalin's death and Vyshinskii's subsequent demotion.

The two Communist combatants in the Korean War looked to USSR Foreign Minister Andrei Vyshinskii for diplomatic leadership. He, in turn, worked under the very close supervision of Josef Stalin, who wished to control all aspects of Soviet foreign policy. As a result, Vyshinskii's actions were occasionally unpredictable, belligerent, and contradictory. After being demoted in March 1953 to deputy foreign minister, Vyshinskii returned to his former position as the chief Soviet delegate to the UN, where he had served previously from 1946 to 1949. This appointment continued until his death in New York City on 22 November 1954.

—Edward Sharp

References:

Stueck, William W., Jr. *The Korean War: An International History.* Princeton, NJ: Princeton University Press, 1995.

Tucker, Robert C., ed. *Stalinism: Essays in Historical Interpretation.* New York: W. W. Norton, 1977.

Zubok, Vladislav, and Constantine Pleshakov. *Inside the Kremlin's Cold War: From Stalin to Khrushchev.* Cambridge, MA: Harvard University Press, 1996.

See also: Armistice Agreement; China, People's Republic of; Cold War, Origins to 1950; Dulles, John Foster; Inch'ŏn Landings: Operation CHROMITE; Kaesŏng Truce Talks; Kim Il Sung; Kirk, Alan Goodrich; MacArthur, Douglas; Malik, Jacob (Iakov) Alexandrovich; Mao Zedong; Menon, V. K. Krishna; Molotov, Viacheslav Mikhailovich; P'anmunjŏm Truce Talks; Ridgway, Matthew Bunker; Stalin, Josef; Union of Soviet Socialist Republics.

W

Wage Stabilization Board (WSB)

U.S. government agency created by executive order on 9 September 1950, to carry out the exigencies of the Defense Production Act. Reporting directly to the Economic Stabilization Agency as with its Office of Price Stabilization (OPS) counterpart, the Wage Stabilization Board (WSB) planned and implemented wage controls during the Korean War. In January 1951, the WSB froze wages simultaneously with the OPS price freeze. The freeze and subsequent wage policy adjustments that followed applied to all hourly wages, salaries, and other forms of compensation. Later in 1951 the WSB created a separate Salary Stabilization Board that handled all controls pertaining to salaried employees.

During the war the WSB underwent several structural and jurisdictional changes, the most important one occurring in April 1951, when President Harry S. Truman enlarged the board from nine to eighteen members. The makeup of the WSB was tripartite, that is, it comprised equal representation from industry, the ranks of organized labor, and the public at large. The president appointed members to the board first without congressional oversight. After the steel strike of 1952, however, Congress insisted that members of the WSB be subjected to a formal approval process. In fact, the WSB played a large role in the adjudication of the steel strike.

In December 1952, as a result of a wage dispute between the United Mine Workers and the nation's coal mine operators, the WSB voluntarily disbanded, all but ceasing the activities of the board. President Dwight D. Eisenhower formally liquidated the WSB by law in the spring of 1953.

—Paul G. Pierpaoli, Jr.

References:

Hogan, Michael J. *A Cross of Iron: Harry S. Truman and the Origins of the National Security State, 1945–1954*. Cambridge, UK: Cambridge University Press, 1998.

Pierpaoli, Paul G., Jr. *Truman and Korea: The Political Culture of the Early Cold War*. Columbia: University of Missouri Press, 1999.

Rockoff, Hugh. *Drastic Measures: History of Wage and Price Controls in the United States*. New York: Cambridge University Press, 1984.

See also: Defense Production Act; Economic Stabilization Agency (ESA); Mobilization; Office of Price Stabilization (OPS); Steel Plants, Truman's Seizure of; United States: Home Front.

Wake Island Conference
(15 October 1950)

On 7 October 1950, President Harry S. Truman decided he needed to confer with United Nations commander in Korea General Douglas MacArthur. The meeting was to take place at some point in the Pacific before the end of the month. The idea of presidential administrative assistant George M. Elsey and other executive branch officials, the meeting was prompted by military and political developments in the Korean War. As Republic of Korea Army (South Korean) forces drove into the Democratic People's Republic of Korea (North Korea), premier and foreign minister of the People's Republic of China (PRC, Communist China) Zhou Enlai warned the United States about an advance beyond the 38th parallel. After the United Nations General Assembly accepted a proposal for the unification of Korea, two U.S. aircraft strafed a Russian air installation sixty miles above the North Korean frontier near Vladivostok.

Once MacArthur repeated his capitulation demand to North Korea on 9 October without result, the U.S. Eighth Army moved above the dividing line. With partisan Republicans urging Truman to thrust northward, administration officials sought political advantage for the Democrats in the upcoming midterm elections. At first opposed to a meeting as "too political, too much showmanship" and seeing no "real need" to confer with MacArthur, Truman eventually consented. White House press secretary Charles Ross apparently influenced Truman's decision by recalling President Franklin D. Roosevelt's conference with the general in Hawaii before the 1944 presidential contest during World War II.

President Truman publicly announced two reasons for a meeting with General MacArthur. He wanted to discuss urgent Korean and Asian matters, and he desired face-to-face contact with the general. On 9 October Truman asked Secretary of Defense George C. Marshall to select a date and site for the meeting. Despite Truman's preference for a mid-October conference at Pearl Harbor, MacArthur chose Wake Island as the scene for a 15 October meeting. The president concurred, and on 10 October Ross reported the news to the media.

The Truman and MacArthur entourages contrasted in number and composition. Included in the president's twenty-four–person party were Special Presidential Assistant on Foreign Affairs W. Averell Harriman, Joint Chiefs of Staff Chairman General

President Harry S. Truman and General Douglas MacArthur at Wake Island, 15 October 1950. (National Archives)

Omar N. Bradley, Secretary of the Army Frank Pace, Assistant Secretary of State for Far Eastern Affairs Dean Rusk, Ambassador-at-Large Philip C. Jessup, and Commander in Chief, Pacific and Commander in Chief, Pacific Fleet Arthur W. Radford. A group of five accompanied the general from Japan, but only Ambassador to South Korea John J. Muccio and MacArthur actually took part in the Wake Island discussions.

In a private conversation with Truman before the main meeting, MacArthur downplayed the chance of the PRC entering the war. Yet he claimed that if such a circumstance arose, his armies could manage. MacArthur reassured Truman that the battlefield victory was won and, when asked about Europe's defense, said one combat division could be transferred out of Korea in early 1951. MacArthur likewise asserted Japan's readiness for a peace treaty and apologized for any embarrassment caused by his August message to the Veterans of Foreign Wars concerning Formosa.

During the general session of about ninety minutes,

equal attention focused on postwar Korean matters and other issues. MacArthur answered most of the inquiries addressed to his party. Some conferees and Jessup's secretary, Miss Vernice Anderson, herself in an adjacent room, took notes. Hopping quickly and often inconsistently from subject to subject without an agenda, the participants dealt with such questions as Korea's economic reconstruction, the military situation, Syngman Rhee's political security, and North Korean war crimes. Other Asian topics discussed included a Japanese peace treaty, a possible Pacific alliance, French Indo-China, and Philippine economic difficulties. MacArthur denied the need for more United Nations troops and restated his conviction that there was "very little" likelihood of Chinese or Soviet intervention.

Truman ended the parley by remarking, "This has been a most satisfactory conference." While he rested, MacArthur and Muccio chatted with several of his staff. Then the president and the general endorsed the meeting's communiqué. Written by administration officials, it cited some of the issues raised and imparted the upbeat mood of the conferees. As Truman and MacArthur rode together to the air terminal, they spoke of the upcoming 1952 presidential contest. Before the general's departure, Truman gave MacArthur a box of candy for his family and presented him with a fourth Oak Leaf Cluster for his Distinguished Service Medal. In San Francisco twenty-four hours afterward, he praised the general and called the Wake gathering an important dialogue on Asian policies. For a short time thereafter, Truman and MacArthur traded agreeable exchanges regarding the Wake Island meeting. However, Truman's satisfaction with the general soon began to erode, particularly over the Formosa question. Once the PRC entered the Korean War, the president and his staff complained that MacArthur had misled them.

—*Rodney J. Ross*

References:
Donovan, Robert J. *Tumultuous Years: The Presidency of Harry S. Truman.* New York: W. W. Norton, 1982.
James, D. Clayton. *The Years of MacArthur.* Vol. 3, *Triumph and Disaster, 1945–1964.* Boston: Houghton Mifflin, 1985.
Schaller, Michael. *Douglas MacArthur: The Far Eastern General.* New York. Oxford University Press, 1989.
Spanier, John W. *The Truman-MacArthur Controversy and the Korean War.* Cambridge, MA: Belknap Press, 1959.

See also: Bradley, Omar Nelson; Elsey, George M.; Harriman, William Averell; Jessup, Philip C.; MacArthur, Douglas; Marshall, George C.; Muccio, John J.; Pace, Frank, Jr.; Radford, Arthur W.; Rusk, David Dean; Soviet Airfield Incident; Syngman Rhee; Truman, Harry S.; Zhou Enlai.

Walker, Walton Harris
(1889–1950)

U.S. Army lieutenant general and commander of the Eighth Army during the Korean War. Born on 3 December 1889 in Belton, Texas, Walton Harris Walker graduated from the U.S. Military Academy at West Point in 1912. During World War I he served with the 13th Machine Gun Battalion of the 5th Infantry Division in France. He saw action in the Saint-Mihiel and Meuse-Argonne offensives and earned the Silver Star for gallantry in action.

In the interwar years Walker attended the Field Artillery School at Fort Sill, the Command and General Staff College, and the Army War College. He served with the 15th Infantry Regiment in Tianjin (Tientsin), China, and he taught at the Infantry School, the Coast Artillery School, and at West Point. He also served on the General Staff's War Plans Division in Washington. Just before U.S. entry into World War II, Walker commanded the 36th Infantry Regiment and the 3d Armored Brigade.

Promoted to major general in February 1942, Walker took command of the 3d Armored Division. Seven months later he assumed command of the IV

Armored Corps at Camp Young, California. There he established the Desert Training Center, responsible for training armored units for desert warfare in North Africa.

In February 1944 IV Armored Corps was redesignated XX Corps and ordered to Britain. Walker's corps was committed in Normandy in July and became part of General George S. Patton's Third Army. XX Corps became known as the "Ghost Corps" for the speed of its advance. Pushing into France from the Loire River to the Moselle, Walker's corps reduced German fortifications at Metz in November 1944.

Walker's greatest challenge in World War II came during the Ardennes offensive, when Patton swung the bulk of the Third Army north to counterattack into the southern flank of the German thrust. Walker's XX Corps was left in place to cover the front that had been held by an entire field army. In April 1945 Walker's units liberated Buchenwald concentration camp near Weimar. By May 1945 Walker's units reached Linz, Austria, the farthest advance east of any of Patton's units. In that same month, he was promoted to lieutenant general.

Walker finished World War II as commander of the 8th Service Command in Dallas, Texas. In June 1948 he took command of the Fifth Army, headquartered in Chicago. In September 1948 Walker went to Japan to assume command of the Eighth Army, the army ground force element of General Douglas MacArthur's Far East Command.

In 1948 the Eighth Army was what would today be called a "hollow force." Walker's four divisions in Japan had only two-thirds of their authorized wartime strength in men and equipment, and the soldiers were untrained and out of shape from several years of occupation duty. Despite the recent end of World War II, only 10 percent of Walker's troops had combat experience.

When the Korean War began, Walker became the primary United Nations Command (UNC) ground forces commander. On 13 July 1950 he established the Eighth Army forward headquarters at Taegu. Four days later Walker also received operational control of the units of the Republic of Korea Army (ROKA, South Korean), and eventually of the rest of UN ground forces in Korea.

Despite being almost equal in numbers to the invading Korean People's Army (KPA, North Korean), Walker's poorly trained and equipped field army was no match for them. KPA forces steadily pushed the UNC forces southward down the Korean peninsula until Walker finally managed to stabilize a defensive perimeter around the major port of Pusan. Bounded on the east and south by the sea and on the west by the Naktong River, the Pusan perimeter formed a rectangle roughly 100 by 50 miles. With his back to the sea, but with the advantage of operating on interior lines, Walker on 29 July issued his famous "Stand or Die" order, in which he bluntly declared, "there will be no Dunkirk, there will be no Bataan."

During the next six weeks, Walker conducted one of the most skillful mobile defense operations in military history. Aided by the fact that his intelligence assets had broken the KPA operational codes, Walker continually shifted his mobile reserves to parry every KPA thrust. The North Koreans often broke through the UN defensive lines, but Walker always managed to find the means to close the gaps. Holding firm along the line of the Naktong River, Walker traded space for time in the north, as the Communist attacks slowly collapsed the rectangular defense position from north to south. Throughout the entire campaign Walker himself spent a great deal of time at the front lines, personally appraising the situation and issuing necessary orders to commanders on the spot.

At the operational and strategic levels, Walker's primary objectives were to maintain the UNC foothold on the Korean peninsula and buy time for the forces in Japan to prepare for and launch the landings at Inch'ŏn, deep in the KPA rear. Walker succeeded, and X Corps landed at Inch'ŏn on 15 September. The result was a turning movement at operational depth, with some 100,000 KPA troops cut off from their lines of communication. Despite an initial rough start, Walker's forces counterattacked across the Naktong on 16 September and drove north. The Eighth Army linked up with X Corps on 26 September. Only 25,000 to 30,000 of KPA troops that had besieged the Pusan perimeter ever made it back to North Korea.

Walker protested MacArthur's decision to separate the Eighth Army and X Corps in the drive into North Korea. On 24 October Walker established his advanced command post in the Democratic People's Republic of Korea (North Korean) capital of P'yŏngyang.

On 25 October, Chinese troops first intervened in the war. Walker believed this was no minor counterattack. A U.S. regiment that went to the relief of the South Koreans was overwhelmed in fierce fighting (at Unsan) between 1 and 3 November. Walker now wisely brought the bulk of his forces back behind the Ch'ŏngch'ŏn River. MacArthur wanted an immediate resumption of the offensive, but Walker disagreed. One problem was that MacArthur had made X Corps dependent logistically on the Eighth Army, rather than being supplied from Japan as should have been the case, and this meant that both were critically short of supplies. MacArthur pushed for an attack on 15 November, but Walker resisted. Not until 20 November were supply elements able to deliver the 4,000 tons daily required for offensive operations.

Finally, Walker agreed to resume the offensive on 24 November.

On the night of 25–26 November, the Chinese intervened on massive scale, counterattacking the Eighth Army. This attack threatened the very survival of the Eighth Army and drove it back down the Korean peninsula.

In the face of overwhelming odds, Walker conducted a series of delaying actions as he pulled his army back south. His withdrawal was a mixed success. Although the 24th and 25th Infantry Divisions escaped largely intact, the rear-guard 2d Infantry Division was almost annihilated. On 15 December Walker established a new defensive line roughly along the 38th parallel.

On the morning of 23 December 1950, Walker left Seoul to visit units in the vicinity of Ŭijŏngbu. Along the way his jeep was hit by a Korean civilian truck. Walker was thrown from the open vehicle and suffered multiple head injuries. He was taken to a 24th Infantry Division clearing station, where doctors pronounced him dead. Walker was promoted posthumously to (four star) general on 2 January 1951.

Walker's performance in Korea remains a subject of debate among historians. One of his nicknames was "Bulldog," and he looked like one. His other nickname was "Johnnie Walker," because of his reputation for being able to consume large quantities of his favorite brand of Scotch. He had a flamboyant manner reminiscent of his mentor, Patton.

Although Walker's handling of the Pusan perimeter defense had been masterful, the Eighth Army suffered a number of serious setbacks after it moved north of the 38th parallel. Walker, however, was continually handicapped by serious command problems beyond his control. He started the war with understrength, underequipped, and untrained units. In addition to the U.S. units, Walker was also responsible for the disorganized and demoralized ROKA divisions. Never one of MacArthur's favorites, Walker had an uneasy relationship with his theater commander. MacArthur compounded Walker's problems by keeping X Corps independent of the Eighth Army, making it impossible for a single commander to synchronize all ground operations in Korea. Walker did not get along with X Corps commander Major General Edward Almond—but then, almost no one else could either. Walker's concern in October and November over the indicators of a large-scale Chinese intervention to the Yalu River had earned him more animosity from MacArthur's staff in Tokyo. At the time Walker died, MacArthur was considering relieving him.

Walker was not a good organizer, and he probably was not a great tactician, but he was a brave and tenacious warrior who believed in leading from the front.

Patton once called him "a fighter in every sense of the word." Army Chief of Staff General J. Lawton Collins called Walker "a fine battlefield commander." Whether his success at the Pusan perimeter was the result of effective tactics, excellent intelligence, or just sheer determination, the important thing is that he held out. Had he not done so, the Korean War could have been lost almost as soon as it started.

—*David T. Zabecki*

References:

Appleman, Roy E. *South to the Naktong, North to the Yalu.* Washington, DC: Office of the Chief of Military History, 1961.

Blair, Clay. *The Forgotten War: America in Korea, 1950–1953.* New York: Times Books, 1987.

Mossman, Billy C. *U.S. Army in the Korean War: Ebb and Flow, November 1950–July 1951.* Washington, DC: U.S. Army Center of Military History, 1990.

Robertson, William G. *Counterattack on the Naktong, 1950.* Ft. Leavenworth, KS: Combat Studies Institute, 1985.

See also: Collins, Joseph Lawton; Far East Command (FEC); MacArthur, Douglas; Pusan Perimeter and Breakout.

War Crimes Trials

U.S. State Department official and staunch anti-Communist Arthur B. Emmons III initiated the debate over whether to bring war criminals of the Korean conflict to justice. A veteran foreign service official with impressive credentials and international service, Emmons became chief of Korean affairs at the State Department in 1950. Relegated to a secondary role in policy formation, he nonetheless formulated U.S. policy regarding war crimes trials in a series of recommendations to Assistant Secretary of State Dean D. Rusk. Despite State Department efforts, opposition from the highest ranks of the military—as well as the abandonment of United Nations (UN) aims to unify Korea after the Chinese military intervention—ultimately quashed the movement to punish war criminals.

In a memorandum of 10 October 1950, Emmons drew a distinction between war crimes of aggression and war crimes involving violation of the law, the breach of customs of war, and atrocities committed against civilians. The United Nations Command (UNC) had instructions to arrest and detain alleged North Korean war criminals until the UN charged them, but even at this early phase in the war, Emmons recognized the volatility of the issue. He cautioned Rusk that it might only intensify hatred between North and South Korea already engendered by intensive Communist propaganda. Emmons warned that war crimes trials might counteract the greater goal of political reunification. At the very least, the United States should minimize or avoid altogether discussion of punishment in the UN, Emmons wrote.

The U.S. State Department and the UN found little support from military authorities to prosecute war criminals. Citing his own experiences with the post–World War II trials of Japanese war criminals, commander in chief of UNC General Douglas MacArthur repeatedly expressed his opposition in principle. He told U.S. president Harry S. Truman to avoid the issue because he believed that punishing individuals in the military for war crimes was no deterrent and was of questionable propriety, since "military commanders obey the orders of their governments and have no option about waging war." In the event that the UN did adopt a policy to bring war criminals to justice, MacArthur suggested that instead of UN-sanctioned tribunals, there should be special military commissions to try, convict, and punish those guilty of wartime atrocities.

MacArthur was well aware that civilians were often innocent victims in war. He himself supported the use of U.S. firepower with little regard for civilian casualties. This reckless expenditure of ordnance reduced U.S. casualties but took a fearsome toll on both North Korean and South Korean civilians. MacArthur was also aware of American servicemen calling in air strikes and artillery barrages on the slightest resistance. U.S. officers often destroyed entire villages to flush out single snipers. There was also the incident at Nogŏn-nl Railroad Bridge in July 1950. And racist American attitudes toward Koreans, whom they often called "gooks," caused one army chaplain to complain to Lieutenant General Matthew B. Ridgway that the refusal to investigate serious crimes made "murder, rape, and pillage easy for the criminally inclined." He cited as evidence one U.S. soldier who had slit the throats of eight civilians near P'yŏngyang in 1951.

MacArthur opposed the prosecution of war criminals because he doubted the existence of a general Democratic People's Republic of Korea (DPRK, North Korean) policy toward the treatment of prisoners or civilians. There were indications that the Korean People's Army (KPA, North Korean) opposed the execution of UNC prisoners, and that special circumstances dictated the severity with which prisoners of war (POWs) and South Korean citizens were treated. The UNC estimated that some 20,000 to 22,000 South Korean soldiers, politicians, and civilians were summarily executed by the KPA during the North Korean occupation of South Korea between June and September 1950. The KPA also executed several groups of thirty to forty captured U.S. soldiers each in the wake of the Inch'ŏn landing. Some American POWs testified that these executions took place when it became impossible for the Communists to transport their prisoners north.

The greatest massacres of civilians by Communist forces occurred as the North Koreans withdrew from South Korea in late 1950 and when the KPA and the

Chinese People's Volunteer Army (Communist Chinese) troops reoccupied North Korea during winter and spring 1950–1951. Up to one thousand South Koreans were massacred at Mokp'o and Wŏnsan after the 15 September 1950 UNC Inch'ŏn landing. Later the DPRK executed tens of thousands of its own citizens in areas formerly occupied by the UNC. Many North Korean noncombatants were massacred for alleged collaboration.

Some South Korean civilian officials and military officers were also guilty of war crimes. After the DPRK invasion of June 1950, the Rhee administration executed thousands of political prisoners as it retreated from Seoul, Inch'ŏn, and Taejŏn. The victims included two DPRK emissaries, Kim Sam-yong and Yi Chu-ha, and the "Mata Hari" of Korean communism, Kim Su-in.

Among Republic of Korea Army (ROKA, South Korean) unpunished war criminals was the ruthless "Tiger of Mount Paekdu," Kim Chong-wŏn. Kim earned his notoriety during the Yŏsu-Sunch'ŏn incident of 1950, during which his soldiers beat, maimed, and executed hundreds of poor farmers and fishermen who purportedly had cooperated with Communist guerrillas. After the UNC invasion of North Korea, as deputy provost marshal general of the ROKA occupational force in P'yŏngyang, Kim oversaw the systematic persecution and mass execution of North Korean Communists during October and November 1950.

The UN continued to discuss the issue of war crimes. In late 1950 MacArthur received explicit instructions from the UN to apprehend and hold for trial "all persons who are or may be charged with atrocities or violations of the law and customs of war." But the directive quickly became a dead letter when the People's Republic of China entered the war in late October 1950. After the Chinese intervention, the UN abandoned its goal of unifying Korea. In the armistice negotiations that followed, the matter of punishment of war criminals was conveniently forgotten.

—*Matthew D. Esposito*

References:

Cumings, Bruce. *The Origins of the Korean War.* Vol. 2, *The Roaring of the Cataract, 1947–1950.* Princeton, NJ: Princeton University Press, 1990.

U.S. Department of State, Bureau of Public Affairs. *Foreign Relations of the United States, 1950.* Vol 7, *Korea.* Washington DC: U.S. Government Printing Office, 1976.

See also: Emmons, Arthur B., III; Kim Chong-wŏn; MacArthur, Douglas; Missing in Action; Nogŏn-nl Railroad Bridge Incident; Ridgway, Matthew Bunker; Rusk, David Dean.

Washington Conference
(26 March–7 April 1951)

Fourth Meeting of Consultation of Foreign Ministers of American States, held in Washington, D.C., to discuss Latin America's contribution to United Nations (UN) and U.S. efforts in the Korean War and to prevent the spread of communism in the western hemisphere. The general declaration concluding the conference emphasized the importance of military cooperation and readiness in case of a crisis. It also called for economic cooperation in the hemisphere and elimination of economic conditions conducive to the spread of communism.

The three previous meetings of foreign ministers occurred during World War II. The Panama (1939), Havana (1940), and Rio de Janeiro (1942) conferences were to harmonize war efforts of states of the American continents. The United States promised economic help in return for substantial military and economic assistance and cooperation of the countries of Latin America during the war. Beginning with the 1947 Rio treaty, however, Washington pushed the defense issue and opposed Latin American initiatives regarding U.S. economic assistance. Washington gave priority to Cold War issues for its own security and neglected to fulfill its previous commitments. Latin American leaders believed that the United States had neglected their countries and forgotten their cooperation during World War II.

Thus, when the foreign ministers met at the initiative of U.S. secretary of state Dean Acheson in Washington, the Latin American leaders did not embrace the U.S. proposal for joint participation in the Korean conflict. The Truman administration received only rhetorical support from its southern neighbors. The Latin American leaders approved general resolutions backing the UN but declined to make specific commitments. The United States tied its call for increased production of strategic materials to a statement demanding economic development in Latin America. Colombia offered military assistance, but with only a battalion of volunteers.

—*Zsolt Varga*

References:

Davis, Harold Eugene, and C. Wilson Larman. *Latin American Foreign Policies: An Analysis.* Baltimore: John Hopkins University Press, 1975.

Matray, James I., ed. *Historical Dictionary of the Korean War.* Westport, CT: Greenwood Press, 1991.

Stebbins, R. P. *The United States in World Affairs, 1951.* New York: Harper & Row, 1952.

See also: Acheson, Dean Goodersham; Colombia; Latin America; Mexico; Peruvian Prisoner-of-War Settlement Proposal.

Webb, James E.
(1906–1992)

U.S. undersecretary of state during the Korean War. Born in Tally Ho, North Carolina, on 7 October 1906, James Edwin Webb graduated from the University of North Carolina in 1928. Two years later he joined the

Marine Corps Reserve, earning his wings as a marine aviator. In 1931 Webb worked as a clerk for Congressman Edward W. Pou of North Carolina. He studied law at George Washington University between 1933 and 1936 and was admitted to the bar in the District of Columbia. Webb then became personnel director and assistant to the president of the Sperry Gyroscope Company, which manufactured and sold airplane equipment. He served as a major of the 1st Marine Air Warning Group during World War II but was not in combat.

In 1946 Webb was named executive assistant to the undersecretary of the treasury. That same year, President Harry S. Truman appointed Webb as director of the budget, and he presented the president with the first balanced budget since 1930. Fiscally conservative, Webb supported cutting the Pentagon budget. Frank Pace, Jr., who became a general in the Korean War, worked for Webb and became budget director when Truman named Webb undersecretary of state in 1949. Secretary of State Dean G. Acheson and Webb were both experienced in economic planning and worked well together as they reorganized the department. Webb remained undersecretary of state until 1952.

Acheson directed Webb's work to secure a Korea aid bill in 1949 and 1950 to help South Korea recover economically and reestablish trade with Japan. Webb convinced Truman to send a supportive message to Congress about economic assistance for Korea and planned expert testimony to promote the plan, which lost by one vote. A revised aid bill passed because of changes to the bill and increased administrative lobbying.

After the 25 June 1950 invasion of the Republic of Korea (ROK, South Korea) by the Democratic People's Republic of Korea (North Korea), Webb worked with other State Department officials to develop a policy position. When questioned about the U.S. decision to intervene, Webb emphasized that if North Korea conquered the South it "would have been a dagger pointed at Japan" and "affected the whole economy of that region."

When Truman returned to Washington on the second day of the war, Webb accompanied Acheson and Secretary of Defense Louis A. Johnson to the airport in the presidential limousine. Knowing that Acheson and Johnson did not get along, Webb suggested that Truman consider joint recommendations from his secretaries of state and defense before deciding on issues. At the first Blair House meeting, Webb spoke to the issues of military aid for the ROK, air support to evacuate American dependents, and placing the U.S. Seventh Fleet between Taiwan and the mainland. Webb commented that he and Acheson supported the first two suggestions but thought the United States should delay in the third. Truman agreed with this

position, although he rejected Webb's recommendations that economic steps be taken to prepare the United States for war.

Webb's influence in the State Department weakened as the department focused on the Korean War. His administrative and organizational talents were not as highly valued as the expertise of other officials in foreign policy.

The relationship between Webb and Acheson became strained. Webb, who suffered migraines and endured declining health during this time, resigned in January 1952, largely because of conflicts with Paul Nitze, who enjoyed Acheson's support.

Webb then became president of the Republic Supply Company and assistant to the president of Kerr-McGee Oil Industries. He also was a director of McDonnell Aircraft and president and board chairman of the Oak Ridge Institute of Nuclear Studies. Known for his excellent organizational skills, Webb in 1961 agreed to become administrator of the National Aeronautics and Space Administration (NASA). Until 1968, Webb skillfully guided NASA during its major scientific and technological successes, culminating in the Apollo XI manned moon landing shortly after his retirement. Colleagues cited Webb's excellent management techniques. Webb died on 27 March 1992, in Washington, D.C.

—Elizabeth D. Schafer

References:

Acheson, Dean. *Present at the Creation: My Years at the State Department.* New York: W. W. Norton, 1969.

Callahan, David. *Dangerous Capabilities: Paul Nitze and the Cold War.* New York: HarperCollins, 1990.

Lambright, W. Henry. *Powering Apollo: James E. Webb of NASA.* Baltimore: Johns Hopkins University Press, 1995.

McGlothlen, R. L. "Acheson, Economics, and the American Commitment in Korea." *Pacific Historical Review* 58 (February 1989): 23–54.

Webb, James E. *Space Age Management, the Large-Scale Approach.* New York: McGraw-Hill, 1969.

See also: Acheson, Dean Goodersham; Blair House Meetings; Johnson, Louis A.; Korea Aid Bill of 1950; Nitze, Paul H.; Pace, Frank, Jr.; Rusk, David Dean; Truman, Harry S.; Truman's Domestic Agenda and the Korean War; U.S. Policy toward Korea before 1950.

West, Sir Michael M. A. R.
(1905–1978)

British army general who served as commander of the Commonwealth Division from 1952 to the end of the Korean War in 1953. Born on 27 October 1905, Michael M. A. R. West was educated at Sandhurst military academy, graduating in 1925. Commissioned an army officer, he spent the remainder of the interwar years serving in Germany, Great Britain, and India. In World War II West commanded at the regimental and brigade levels in the European theater. His performance during the war produced an appointment in 1950 as the commander of British occupation forces in Austria.

West replaced General Archibald Cassels as commander of the Commonwealth Division in September 1952 and confronted the same problems faced by Cassels. The most serious issue was the lack of manpower in the division, particularly in British units, which were always understrength. The British had too many overseas commitments, and defense spending burdened the British economy, already damaged by the world war and the spending on the welfare state at home. West attempted to solve this problem by reorganizing the division in November 1952 so that all his forces were continually in service. This replaced the old method of having one brigade withdrawn while the other two remained in action.

West also implemented a new program named the Korean Augmentation Troop Commonwealth (KATCOM). Cassels first advocated this scheme, which was based on the U.S. program used to augment its divisions with Koreans (Korean Augmentation to U.S. Army, or KATUSA). It incorporated Koreans into the Commonwealth Division to relieve personnel shortages. Koreans did not see active service with the Commonwealth Division, however, until March 1953, in the last months of the war. The program did, however, ease the manpower problem.

West had a somewhat rocky relationship with his U.S. counterparts. He objected to the U.S. prosecution of the war, which was governed by political concerns as much as military ones. The chief issue was continuing United Nations Command offensives toward the end of the conflict, which West saw as a waste of manpower. The struggle to retain Pork Chop Hill in mid-1953 illustrated West's point of view. He saw the hill as only an outpost with little military significance.

General West served after the Korean War as director of the Territorial Army. After this he served as general officer commanding (GOC) of the First Corps of the British Army of the Rhine and then as GOC of the Northern Command in Britain. West ended his career as chairman of the British Defense Staff in Washington and retired in 1965. West died on 14 May 1978.

—Eric W. Osborne

References:

Barclay, C. N. The First Commonwealth Division: The Story of British Commonwealth Land Forces in Korea, 1950–1953. Aldershot, UK: Gale & Polden, 1954.

Grey, Jeffrey. The Commonwealth Armies and the Korean War. An Alliance Study. Manchester: Manchester University Press, 1988.

Hastings, Max. The Korean War. New York: Simon & Schuster, 1987.

See also: Australia; Canada; Cassels, Sir Archibald James H.; New Zealand; United Kingdom (UK).

Weyland, Otto P.
(1902–1979)

U.S. Air Force general and commander of the Far East Air Force (FEAF) from 1951 to 1953. Born on 27 January 1902, at Riverside, California, Otto Paul Weyland graduated from Texas A&M University in 1923 with a mechanical engineering degree and was commissioned into the U.S. Army Air Corps Reserve. Weyland finished flight instruction at Kelly Field, Texas, then served with the 12th Observation Squadron at Fort Sam Houston, Texas. He next was a flight instructor at Kelly Field from 1927 to 1931, when he became commander of the 4th Observation Squadron. Weyland graduated from the Air Corps Tactical School in 1938 and from the Army Command and General Staff School in 1939. Two years later he was named assistant commander of the aviation division of the National Guard Bureau in Washington, D.C. Weyland was commander of the 16th Pursuit Group in the Panama Canal Zone when the United States joined World War II.

Weyland was deputy chief of staff for the Sixth Air Force and served on the Air Corps Staff, then went to England as commander of the 84th Fighter Wing. By February 1944 he was commander of the Nineteenth Tactical Air Command, which was part of the Ninth Air Force, providing aerial support for Patton's Third Army. Patton considered Weyland "the best damn General in the Air Corps." In 1945 Weyland was named commander of the Ninth Air Force.

After World War II, Weyland was deputy commandant of the Army Command and General Staff School at Fort Leavenworth, Kansas. When the U.S. Air Force (USAF) became a separate service, Weyland was first put in charge of devising plans and operations and then was named deputy commandant of the National War College in Washington, D.C. He became commanding general of the Tactical Air Command in July 1950.

Serving in the Far East on temporary duty when the Korean War began, Weyland was FEAF's vice commander for operations. On 10 June 1951, Weyland became commanding general of FEAF, replacing General George E. Stratemeyer, who had suffered a heart attack. Weyland served in this position until the end of the Korean War.

As FEAF commander, Weyland advised military strategists about air operations. He asked for reinforcements, and the 116th Fighter-Bomber Wing joined the FEAF. Worried that the Communists might gain air superiority, Weyland demanded more planes and pilots, but USAF leaders claimed they had no additional aircraft available.

Weyland told General Hoyt S. Vandenberg that he wanted to prove that air power provided more than a supporting role for combat troops, but a year would pass until he would receive authority to pursue this course. At the beginning of the war, FEAF had attained air superiority, losing control of some North Korean air space because of Chinese sanctuaries protecting Communist aircraft. When truce negotiations began on 10 July 1951, a new phase of the war began, with its primary goal of forcing the Communists to concede. Weyland oversaw a summer campaign of interdiction against crucial targets. Known as Operation STRANGLE, these air-power assaults on North Korean railways impeded transportation of supplies but did not force the Communist side to capitulate.

During fall 1951 Weyland wanted to use air power to stop Communist ground attacks and pressure settlement of the armistice on acceptable terms. USAF leaders in Washington were unsure that air power alone could achieve these goals. Weyland also came under criticism for favoring strategic bombing over close air support of ground troops. Weyland claimed that he had "leaned over backwards to provide more than adequate close air support." Weyland struggled with trying to carry out strategic bombing at the same time as his assets provided close air support and secured air superiority over North Korea. He chafed under the constraints of limited war, which he believed had been forced on him by military tacticians unfamiliar with air power.

When Lieutenant General Mark W. Clark replaced Lieutenant General Matthew B. Ridgway as United Nations Command (UNC) commander in May 1952, he granted Weyland the authority to initiate a sustained air-pressure campaign against strategic Communist targets. Ordering air attacks against targets in the Communist rear areas necessary to launch and supply offensives, Weyland emphasized stopping Communist forces there before they reached the battle lines. On 11 July 1952, Weyland initiated Operation PRESSURE PUMP, in which thirty targets in P'yŏngyang were struck, including the largest air attack in the war, 1,254 sorties.

Lacking adequate resources to attack all Communist airfields, Weyland determined which North Korean airfields were most threatening to UNC forces and ordered air attacks to neutralize them. In May 1953 he proposed bombing earthen irrigation dams north of P'yŏngyang to flood rice paddies. He believed some 283,000 tons of rice might be destroyed, leading to starvation and forcing the Communists to accept an armistice. Reconnaissance photographs confirmed widespread flooding from the air attacks, which Weyland called "perhaps the most spectacular of the war." The Communists retaliated with offensives against Allied troops along the truce lines. During the war Weyland personally led an unescorted bomber attack over North Korea, and he was the first U.S. Air Force general shot at by MiG jet fighters.

Returning to the United States in summer 1953, Weyland became commanding general of the Tactical Air Command at Langley Air Force Base, Virginia, in April 1954. He remained in that post until his retirement from active duty on 31 July 1959. Weyland then worked as a consultant for McDonnell Aircraft Corporation and was the director of a life insurance company. He died on 2 September 1979, in San Antonio, Texas.

—*Elizabeth D. Schafer*

References:
Futrell, Robert F. *The United States Air Force in Korea, 1950–1953*. Rev. ed. Washington, DC: Office of the Chief of Air Force History, 1983.
Washington Post, 6 September 1979.
Weyland, Otto P. "The Air Campaign in Korea." *Air University Quarterly Review* 6 (Fall 1953): 3–28.
See also: Aerial Combat; Air Power in the War; Airborne Operations; Aircraft (Principal Combat); China, People's Republic of: Air Force; Clark, Mark W.; Close Air Support; Far East Air Force (FEAF); Korea, Democratic People's Republic of, Air Force (Korean People's Air Force [KPAF]); MiG Alley; P'yŏngyang; Ridgway, Matthew Bunker; STRANGLE, Operation; Stratemeyer, George E.; Truman, Harry S.; United Nations Command Air Forces; United States Air Force (USAF); U.S. Naval Air Operations; Vandenberg, Hoyt S.

White Horse Hill, Battle of
(6–15 October 1952)

One of a series of Chinese-initiated hill battles fought largely for political reasons to improve the Communist negotiating position at the armistice talks. White Horse Hill, Hill 395, is five miles northwest of Ch'ŏrwŏn; it overlooks the Yŏkgok-ch'ŏn Valley and dominates western approaches to Ch'ŏrwŏn.

On 3 October 1952, Eighth Army intelligence officers learned from a Chinese deserter that the Chinese People's Volunteer Army (CPVA, Chinese Communist) forces intended to attack strategically situated White Horse Hill. If the defending IX Corps lost this position, it would have to withdraw to higher ground south of the Yŏkgok-ch'ŏn River in the Ch'ŏrwŏn area, denying IX Corps the use of the Ch'ŏrwŏn road net and leaving the Iron Triangle exposed to Chinese attack.

The Chinese attack began on 6 October 1952 and was the largest offensive of the year. The Chinese timed their attack to take advantage of the upcoming U.S. presidential elections to pressure the United States to quit the war and also to improve their defensive positions before the onset of winter. Two battalions of the 340th Regiment, 114th Division, Thirty-eighth Army of the CPVA targeted Major General Kim Chong-o's Republic of Korea Army (ROKA, South Korean) 9th Division. But the ROKA troops were no longer the untrained troops the Chinese had once faced. During the previous year they had greatly improved in leadership, training, and equipment. Additionally, the ROKA 9th Division was reinforced with tanks, artillery, rocket launchers, and antiaircraft weapons, and it was supported by the U.S. Fifth Air Force.

The Chinese began the attack with the diversionary tactic of opening the floodgates of the Pongnae-ho Reservoir in hopes of preventing the U.S. 2d Division from reinforcing the ROKA 9th Division. They also attacked adjacent Arrowhead Hill (Hill 281) to fix the French Battalion and U.S. 2d Division there. Chinese artillery and mortars fired some 4,500 rounds per day, and Chinese commanders regularly fed fresh troops into the battle. Casualties climbed as the Chinese sent wave after wave of troops in an effort to gain the objective.

ROKA defenders were aided by the fact that Chinese commanders had little latitude to change their tactics once ordered to attack. The ROKA also received excellent air, armor, and artillery support. The Fifth Air Force flew 669 daylight sorties and 76 night sorties, dropping more than 2,700 general-purpose bombs and 358 napalm bombs and launching more than 750 5-inch rockets. On 9 October one Fifth Air Force attack hit the Chinese 335th Regiment of the 112th Division in its assembly area. Also, IX Corps artillery fired 185,000 rounds against the attacking Chinese.

Beginning on 12 October, ROKA troops leap-frogged battalions within the leading regiment, which allowed them to inject fresh troops into the battle and to gain steadily on their objective. This helped them win the battle by 15 October.

Although White Horse Hill changed hands a total of twenty-four times, 23,000 Chinese (seven of the Thirty-eighth Army's nine regiments) were unable to dislodge the ROKA 9th Division, and the Chinese lost some 15,000 men. By contrast, ROKA 9th Division casualties were only 3,500 men. Not only had the Chinese failed to seize White Horse Hill, they had also failed to pressure the United States to end the war.

—*Carol J. Yee*

References:
Fehrenbach, T. R. *This Kind of War: A Study in Unpreparedness.* New York: Macmillan, 1962.
Hermes, Walter G. *United States Army in the Korean War: Truce Tent and Fighting Front.* Washington, DC: Office of the Chief of Military History, 1966.
Toland, John. *In Mortal Combat: Korea, 1950–1953.* New York: William Morrow, 1991.
See also: Iron Triangle.

Whitney, Courtney (1897–1969)

Military secretary and close friend and advisor to commander in chief of United Nations Command General Douglas MacArthur during the Korean War. The son of a U.S. Department of Agriculture official, Courtney Whitney was born in Takoma Park, Maryland, on 20 May 1897. Whitney enlisted as a private in the Maryland National Guard in 1917. The following year he transferred to the aviation section of the fledgling U.S. Army Signal Corps Reserve, where he was commissioned a second lieutenant in March 1918. He received a commission in the regular U.S. Army in 1920. After attending the aviation school, Whitney was named assistant adjutant and then adjutant at Payne Field in Mississippi. Three years later, he earned a law degree from National University and then went to the Philippines as adjutant for the 66th Service Squadron. From 1926 to 1927 Whitney was chief of the Publications Section of the Information Division in the Office of the Chief of the U.S. Army Air Corps.

Whitney resigned his commission in 1927 and spent the next thirteen years practicing corporate law in Manila, Philippine Islands. There he forged ties with many influential Filipinos and with General Douglas MacArthur, whom he had met in Washington in the early 1920s and who from 1936 was field marshal of the Philippine armed forces. In 1941 MacArthur became commander of U.S. Army Forces Far East.

In 1940 Whitney was commissioned a major in the Organized Reserve Corps and became assistant chief of the legal division of the U.S. Army Air Forces. Still assigned to that branch after the United States entered World War II, he also became a member of MacArthur's "Bataan Gang" and accompanied the general to Australia in March 1942. The following February Whitney became assistant judge advocate of the U.S. Army Air Forces before MacArthur had him transferred to his Southwest Pacific area general headquarters to lead the Philippine Regional Section. This organization promoted guerrilla and intelligence activities in the Philippines during the Japanese occupation in preparation for U.S. landings. After U.S. forces returned to the Philippines in the fall of 1944, Whitney became chief of the civil affairs section of MacArthur's headquarters, and into 1945 he assisted Filipino officials in restoring civil government to the liberated islands.

Whitney's capacity for hard work and his loyalty impressed MacArthur, and by the end of the war he had emerged as one of the general's closest advisors and confidants. Whitney had many critics among his staff colleagues and in the media, however; they saw him as little more than an unintelligent, arrogant, and pompous sycophant.

Early in 1946, Brigadier General Whitney joined MacArthur's occupation headquarters (Supreme Commander, Allied Powers) in Tokyo as chief of the government section. Putting together an able civilian and military staff, he purged militarists and ultranationalists from Japanese public life, advised the Japanese on the revision of their statutes and the writing of a new constitution, and implemented a host of administrative, civil service, electoral, fiscal, and police reforms. Although criticized by some as being unfair and heavy-handed in his methods and treatment of the Japanese, Whitney ably completed the job MacArthur wanted accomplished, and at the same time he became essential to the general.

After the outbreak of the Korean War in June 1950, Whitney was appointed military secretary of MacArthur's United Nations Command. He accompanied MacArthur on his trips to Korea as well as to the October 1950 Wake Island meeting with President Harry S. Truman. When Truman relieved MacArthur from command in April 1951, Whitney returned to the United States and served as the general's counsel and advisor during the Senate's inquiry into MacArthur's relief and Truman's Far Eastern policies.

At the end of May 1951, Whitney retired from the army with the permanent rank of major general to serve as MacArthur's personal secretary. Following MacArthur even into civilian life, he joined the Remington Rand Corporation as MacArthur's assistant when the general became chairman of the board. The two men remained inseparable until MacArthur's death in 1964, when Whitney was at the general's bedside. Whitney spent the remainder of his life defending his former boss, and in 1956 he published *MacArthur: His Rendezvous With History*, a book that was panned by the critics but that nonetheless earned him significant royalties. Courtney Whitney died in Washington, D.C., on 21 May 1969.

—*Clayton D. Laurie*

References:

Blair, Clay. *The Forgotten War: America in Korea, 1950–1953.* New York: Times Books, 1987.

James, D. Clayton. *The Years of MacArthur.* Vol. 3, *Triumph and Disaster, 1945–1964.* Boston: Houghton Mifflin, 1985.

Manchester, William. *American Caesar: Douglas MacArthur, 1880–1964.* Boston: Little, Brown, 1978.

New York Times, 22 March 1969.

Whitney, Courtney. *MacArthur: His Rendezvous with History.* New York: Alfred A. Knopf, 1956.

Who Was Who in America, 1969–1973. Chicago: Marquis, 1973.

See also: MacArthur, Douglas; MacArthur Hearings; Truman, Harry S.; Truman's Relief of MacArthur.

Willoughby, Charles A.
(1892–1972)

U.S. Army major general and assistant chief of staff for intelligence to General Douglas MacArthur and his various commands in the Far East after 1940. Willoughby's origins and ancestry are still a matter of dispute. Born on 8 March 1892, in Heidelberg,

Germany, Charles A. Willoughby claimed he had an American mother and a German aristocratic father.

Willoughby emigrated to the United States in 1910, was naturalized, and joined the 5th Infantry, U.S. Army, as Private Adolphe Charles Weidenbach. In 1914 he earned a B.A. at Gettysburg College. Upon receiving a U.S. Army commission in 1916, he changed his name to Charles Andre Willoughby.

Between 1916 and 1918 Willoughby served on the Mexican border with the 35th Infantry and then in France in the American Expeditionary Force with the 16th Infantry, 1st Division. Late in the war he joined the U.S. Army Air Corps and served as a pilot.

During the decade following World War I, Willoughby served in ground units on the Mexican border, then in Puerto Rico, and as a military attaché in Venezuela, Colombia, and Ecuador. He graduated from the Infantry School at Fort Benning, Georgia, in 1929 and from the Command and General Staff School at Fort Leavenworth, Kansas, in 1931. Later he spent some time studying at the University of Kansas and attended the Army War College at Carlisle, Pennsylvania.

Willoughby first met General MacArthur in the mid-1930s when Willoughby was a captain at Fort Leavenworth. Then in 1940 MacArthur summoned him to the Philippines to be assistant chief of staff for intelligence of U.S. Army Forces in the Far East. In this capacity Willoughby helped to plan the defense of the Philippines, especially Bataan and Corregidor, before the Japanese invasion in December 1941. Willoughby accompanied MacArthur to Australia in March 1942 and remained with the general throughout the war.

MacArthur commissioned Willoughby to write the official campaign history of General Headquarters, Southwest Pacific Area. He had enormous confidence in Willoughby's ability as an intelligence chief and as a scholar. Willoughby had already written two books, *U.S. Economic Participation in the World War, 1917–1918* (1931) and *The Element of Maneuver in War* (1935), and from 1931 to 1935 he had served as the editor in chief of the *General Staff Quarterly*.

Willoughby's vague personal and family background, his origins, his pompous personality, and his extraordinarily close relationship with MacArthur produced many enemies and critics over the years, who among other things alleged that his adoration and desire to please the general often jeopardized the quality of the intelligence that Willoughby provided to MacArthur. As one historian has stated, Willoughby's views influenced the entire intelligence community in the Far East Command, and a challenge to Willoughby was seen as being tantamount to a challenge to MacArthur. It was said that Willoughby only provided MacArthur with news he knew the general wanted to hear.

Remaining with MacArthur during the occupation of Japan throughout the late 1940s, Willoughby was criticized for failing to provide warning of the North Korean invasion of South Korea. It does appear, however, that Willoughby, a vehement anti-Communist, did send several reports to Washington in 1949 and 1950 indicating the possibility of a North Korean invasion in March or April 1950. However, like those in the Central Intelligence Agency and the State Department, Willoughby thought an invasion was very unlikely anytime in the foreseeable future.

When the North Koreans did invade the South in June 1950, Willoughby repeatedly overestimated the ability of the Republic of Korea Army (ROKA, South Korean) forces to stem the invasion during the early weeks of the war, and he underestimated the quality of Korean People's Army (KPA, North Korean) forces and the strength of their attack. But in spite of what some critics called egregiously bad intelligence collection and reporting, MacArthur continued to rely on Willoughby's interpretations of events through the fall of 1950.

Willoughby and others ignored the first hints, as early as August 1950, of a possible Chinese intervention. The same was true with later indicators that the Chinese were massing troops on the North Korean border in October and November 1950. Willoughby continued to insist that neither the Chinese nor the Soviets would seek to widen the war because he believed that the Chinese were utterly incapable of fighting a military power such as the United States. Even as evidence continued to come in, Willoughby persisted in explaining it away as insignificant.

After the Chinese did intervene, Willoughby, who had undergone an eleventh-hour conversion to realize the true nature and purpose of the Chinese presence on the border, wildly underestimated the numbers of troops involved, much to the chagrin of United Nations Command (UNC) field commanders, who were facing a much more numerous and determined enemy than had been predicted or initially realized. The charges that he steadfastly underestimated the presence, number, and danger of Communist forces facing UN forces in Korea dogged Willoughby for the rest of his life.

After President Truman's recall of MacArthur in April 1951, Willoughby also retired from the military. He later became editor of the *Foreign Intelligence Digest* and author of *MacArthur: 1941–1951* (1954), a book based on his personal knowledge of the general and his actions during those years. He died in Naples, Florida, on 26 October 1972.

—*Clayton D. Laurie*

References:

Blair, Clay. *The Forgotten War: America in Korea, 1950–1953.* New York: Times Books, 1987.

Goulden, Joseph C. *Korea: The Untold Story of the War.* New York: Times Books, 1982.

McGovern, James. *To the Yalu: From the Chinese Invasion to MacArthur's Dismissal.* New York: William Morrow, 1972.

New York Times, 26 October 1972.

201 File, Charles Andre Willoughby, U.S. Army Center of Military History, Washington, DC.

Washington Post, 27 October 1972.

Who Was Who in America. Vol. 5, *1969–1973.* Chicago: Marquis, 1973.

See also: MacArthur, Douglas; Military Intelligence.

Wilson, Charles Edward
(1886–1972)

President of General Electric Company and the first director of the Office of Defense Mobilization (ODM), from 1950 to 1952. Born in New York City on 18 November 1886, Charles E. Wilson suffered tragedy when his father died when he was three. This reduced the family to poverty. Raised in the infamous Hell's Kitchen neighborhood of New York City, Wilson left school at age twelve to work as an office boy at General Electric. Despite his curtailed education, Wilson—often known as "Electric" Charlie to distinguish him from his namesake Charles E. "Engine" Wilson, the president of General Motors—rose from the bottom and served successively in the departments of accounting, production, engineering, manufacturing, and marketing to become president of General Electric in 1939. In September 1942 he joined the ranks of businessmen flocking to the Roosevelt administration's war mobilization effort and joined the War Production Board, facilitating manufacture of an unprecedented 93,369 military airplanes in 1944. Differences with board chairman Donald Nelson over what Wilson considered to be unduly rapid plans for reconversion to peacetime led to his resignation in August 1944 and his return to the presidency of General Electric.

Despite, or perhaps because of, Wilson's political affiliation as a registered Republican, President Harry S. Truman regularly appointed Wilson to serve on advisory panels, including the National Security Resources Board, the National Labor-Management Panel, the University Military Training Commission, and the Taft-Hartley Advisory Board, assignments that culminated in 1946 in Wilson's chairmanship of the President's Commission on Civil Rights. In this capacity Wilson submitted a notably liberal report that demanded the legal eradication of racial violence, segregation, harassment, and discrimination in the United States.

In December 1950, after the intervention by the People's Republic of China (Communist China) in the

Korean War and the consequent disastrous impact on U.S. military fortunes, Truman appointed Wilson as director of the newly created ODM, an indication that the administration anticipated a lengthy and difficult conflict. Truman charged Wilson with the task of mobilizing American industry and the economy for the accelerated war effort in Korea. Wilson accepted the post on condition that he would have complete authority over all aspects of this task and be answerable only to the president. As ODM director, Wilson's statutory powers exceeded those of any other civilian mobilization chief. At the time, the nation's press likened Wilson's position to a co-presidency.

Wilson oversaw and facilitated a massive defense expansion, essentially that envisaged in the National Security Council's 1950 report NSC-68, which rearmed the nation for a potential global conflict even as it simultaneously waged a limited war in Korea. In 1951, military expenditures quadrupled from $15 billion to $60 billion. In this sense, Wilson presided over the birth of the permanent national security state in the United States.

One of Wilson's first priorities was to stabilize the nation's overheating economy, mainly by implementing mandatory wage and price controls through the Wage Stabilization Board and the Office of Price Stabilization. This he did in late January 1951. Wilson also began to assemble industrial advisory committees from diverse sectors of the economy that aided in developing and implementing mobilization and production priorities. Although Wilson's job was never easy, he proved to be an able administrator, negotiating the political minefields of wage and price controls, raw materials controls, and industrial expansion with much skill and success. During his tenure, the United States' military and industrial output soared, inflation and economic dislocations remained largely at bay, and raw materials shortages eased considerably.

Wilson's methods were uncompromising. A staunch supporter of wage and price controls to prevent inflation—an objective in which he largely succeeded—and facilitate mobilization, he was also a long-standing opponent of labor unions. In October 1946 he stated, "The problem of the United States can be captiously summed up in two words: Russia abroad, labor at home." In February 1951, when a national railroad strike jeopardized rearmament, Wilson went on the radio to appeal to the patriotism of American workers to end industrial action and defeat communism abroad. In March 1952, Wilson, infuriated by Truman's decision to veto price increases in steel while accepting a Wage Stabilization Board recommendation to increase steelworkers' pay and other benefits, resigned his position and moved to W. R. Grace and Co. When management refused to acqui-

esce in the president's decision, a strike ensued, and in April Truman used his emergency powers to take over the steel plants, a move that the Supreme Court declared unconstitutional in the absence of an official state of war. A second strike followed, and ultimately the steel makers obtained price increases about half of those they had originally requested.

Perhaps Wilson's greatest contribution to the Korean mobilization effort was his management technique. An early pioneer in centralized/decentralized corporate structures, Wilson sought to keep the ODM and its constituent agencies lean and compact, yet powerful. He accomplished this by combining centralized management and policymaking with decentralized policy implementation and operations. This management style kept administrative costs down and bureaucracies small. It also resembled the multidivisional management forms that Wilson had implemented at General Electric.

During the Eisenhower administration Wilson headed the People-to-People Foundation, a program intended to promote international understanding and friendship. Wilson died on 3 January 1972, in Scarsdale, New York.

—*Paul G. Pierpaoli, Jr., and Priscilla Roberts*

References:

Antone, C. P. "Charles Edward Wilson." In *Dictionary of American Biography, Supplement Nine, 1971–1975,* edited by Kenneth T. Jackson. New York: Charles Scribner's Sons, 1994.

Hogan, Michael J. *A Cross of Iron: Harry S. Truman and the Origins of the National Security State, 1945–1954.* Cambridge, UK: Cambridge University Press, 1998.

Marcus, Maeva. *Truman and the Steel Seizure Case: The Limits of Presidential Power.* New York: Columbia University Press, 1977.

McCullough, David. *Truman.* New York: Simon & Schuster, 1992.

Pierpaoli, Paul G., Jr. *Truman and Korea: The Political Culture of the Early Cold War.* Columbia: University of Missouri Press, 1999.

"Wilson, Charles E." In *Political Profiles: The Truman Years,* edited by Eleanora W. Schoenebaum. New York: Facts on File, 1978.

See also: Mobilization; NSC-68; Office of Price Stabilization (OPS); Steel Plants, Truman's Seizure of; Truman, Harry S.; Truman's Declaration of a National Emergency; Wage Stabilization Board (WSB).

WOLFHOUND, Operation
(15–17 January 1951)

January 1951 United Nations Command (UNC)–initiated attack on Communist forces. General Matthew B. Ridgway's assumption of command of the Eighth Army marked a dramatic change in how the war would be fought. To initiate this new aggressiveness, Ridgway ordered a reconnaissance in force to find and destroy Chinese People's Volunteer Army (CPVA, Communist Chinese) troops. The attack, known as Operation WOLFHOUND, was launched at 0700 on

15 January by seven infantry battalions: the entire 27th Infantry (25th Division); the 1st Battalion, 15th Infantry Regiment and the 2d Battalion, 65th Infantry Regiment (both 3d Division); the 3d Battalion, 2d Infantry Regiment, Republic of Korea Army (ROKA, South Korean) 6th Division; and the 2d Battalion, 12th Infantry Regiment, ROKA 1st Division. Tanks of the 89th Tank Battalion (25th Division) accompanied the 27th, while a smaller tank force went with 3d Division infantry. The 8th, 10th, 39th, and 90th Field Artillery Battalions supported the operation. Operation WOLFHOUND involved in all some 6,000 men.

The 1st Battalion, 27th Infantry with a tank company advanced north over a secondary road in western Korea, while the 2d and 3d Battalions of the regiment, with the remainder of the tank battalion, followed the main highway. The regimental objective was the Suwŏn-Osan area.

Neither column of the 27th Infantry met resistance except from roads and bridges that had been damaged by withdrawing UNC forces some days previously. The 1st Battalion stopped for the night at P'ajang-ni, while the principal regimental force stopped just north of Osan, ten miles to the east.

The 1st Battalion of the 15th with two tank companies moved rapidly over a road more or less parallel to, and some seven to ten miles east of, the main highway. About dusk this force entered Kimyangjang-ni, where it surprised Communist forces, killing about fifty and taking the town. Turning west in darkness toward Suwŏn, the battalion was finally stopped by heavy Communist small arms and mortar fire. The two ROKA battalions followed the 1st Battalion of the 15th, occupying Ch'ŏn-ni and Kimyangjang-ni without opposition.

The 2d Battalion of the 65th Infantry was supposed to follow a road east of but closer to the main highway than that taken by 1st Battalion of the 15th. Finding that road "impassable," the battalion doubled back and took the road previously used by 1st Battalion to the town of Songjŏn. There it turned west and stopped for the night in Osan, which the 27th had previously cleared.

On 16 January, while the 1st Battalion approached Suwŏn from the west, the remainder of the 27th came in from the south. Although the 1st Battalion met no opposition, the 2d Battalion, leading on the main road, encountered heavy machine gun fire, while other CPVA troops attempted to cut the battalion off. The 2d Battalion of the 65th Regiment took a path northeast out of Osan that morning and became bogged down in ice and snow.

Operation WOLFHOUND revealed that large Chinese forces were assembling in the Suwŏn-Kimyangjang-ni area, threatening to cut off the 27th

Infantry. Accordingly, on the afternoon of 16 January the regiment was ordered to disengage and withdraw to Osan. Total casualties among the seven battalions were three killed and seven wounded. Communist losses were about 1,800. On 17 January Operation WOLFHOUND forces set up a strong outpost line along the Chinwi-ch'ŏn River just south of Osan.

—*Uzal W. Ent*

References:

Appleman, Roy E. *Ridgway Duels for Korea*. College Station, TX: Texas A&M Press, 1990.

Blair, Clay. *The Forgotten War: America in Korea, 1950–1953*. New York: Times Books, 1987.

Mossman, Billy C. *U.S. Army in the Korean War: Ebb and Flow, November 1950–July 1951*. Washington, DC: U.S. Army Center of Military History, 1990.

See also: Ridgway, Matthew Bunker.

Women in the Military

Women served in various noncombat support roles during Korean War, beginning soon after the invasion. In July 1950, 57 U.S. Army nurses arrived at Pusan to establish a hospital, and 12 nurses were assigned to the Mobile Army Surgical Hospital (MASH) at Taejŏn to treat casualties from the nearby front lines. At the start of the war, the Women's Army Corps (WACs) and Women in the Air Force (WAFs) had Far East bases, including a WAC detachment in support of General Headquarters, Far East Command, Tokyo, Japan. None of these women were permitted to serve in Korea because of the fluctuating battle lines.

The WACs, WAFs, WAVEs (Women in the Navy) and U.S. Marine Corps Women's Reserve totaled 22,000 women on active duty in June 1950. Seven thousand of these servicewomen were in health positions, while the rest served in line assignments. Women accounted for less than 1 percent of the U.S. military.

The WACs had only recently been integrated into the regular army. Having provided valuable service during World War II, they were rewarded in 1948 when Congress passed a law assuring WACs a permanent place in the army by granting them regular army and reserve status. Former WACs and officers could join the Organized Reserve Corps, which later became known as the Army Reserve. This group of reserve WACs was among the first women to serve in the Korean War effort. By July 1950 commanders in the Far East and overseas requested WAC officers and enlisted women to fill noncombat positions—such as supply clerk, corpsman, medical technician, stenographer, typist, and finance clerk—vacated by men sent to Korea.

The United States began issuing draft calls, and reservists were recalled to active duty, with entire units being assigned to Korea, overseas locations, or impor-

Army nurse Captain Jane Thurness using a helmet for washing while on the front lines, 14 February 1951. (National Archives)

tant support positions in the United States. A WAC training center, organized and managed by women, was established at Fort Lee, Virginia. Each week approximately 250 women enlistees and women reenlisting came to Fort Lee for basic training. The women also received instruction for specific duty assignments, such as maintenance, and completed a military leadership course.

World War II WACs provided invaluable experience, acting as mentors to new enlistees. More than 1,200 WAC inactive-duty reserve officers and enlisted women voluntarily returned to active duty. Fifty WAC reservists were involuntarily recalled. In August 1950 the army suspended the discharge of WAC personnel based on marriage so that more women could serve in Korea. Both men and women had their nondisability retirements suspended by Congress, which also provided that enlisted soldiers and officers would have their obligations extended for one year.

The Defense Advisory Committee on Women in the Services (DACOWITS) was created during the Korean War and established a legacy for women in the armed services. Assistant Secretary of Defense for Manpower Anna Rosenberg recommended a committee to address women's military interests, and Secretary of Defense George C. Marshall approved it. The initial meeting to discuss DACOWITS was held on 18 September 1951, and Marshall formally established the committee the next month. He instructed the committee, consisting of 50 influential civilian women leaders in politics, the arts, business, and academia, to work together and recruit enlistees. Chaired by Mrs. Oswald Lord, who had led a previous army women's advisory committee, DACOWITS began a national campaign sponsored by the Department of Defense to recruit more women for the services. President Harry S. Truman officially started the campaign on 11 November 1951. It featured such patriotic slogans as "Share Service for Freedom" and "America's Finest Women Stand Beside Her Finest Men."

Marshall hoped to increase the women's services by 72,000 by July 1952. Of this number, 20,000 WACs were to be recruited. DACOWITS collectively, and as individual members, presented public programs about recruiting needs and reassured parents that their daughters would be safe in a supervised environment. DACOWITS members emphasized the career opportunities available to women in the military. They worked to improve public opinion of military women and enhance their prestige. For the most part, they promoted all of the women's service branches, permitting recruits to select which unit most interested them.

The WAC band at Fort Lee toured colleges and schools throughout America to welcome recruits. Actresses Helen Hayes and Irene Dunne used their fame and talents to help with the campaign. The results, however, were disappointing. By the end of 1952 the WAC had almost 500 fewer members than it had in 1951. The other women's service branches did not achieve their goals either, but they did at least increase their numbers. Several thousand women joined the navy, air force, and Marines. The Marine Corps, usually the smallest women's service branch, increased by 400 women over the 580 women Marines on active duty when the war began.

Although there was a great need for female personnel, the Pentagon failed to attract sufficient quantities and qualities of recruits to meet quotas. Many potential recruits were underage or unqualified or scored poorly on aptitude tests.

The disappointing WAC recruitment was the catalyst for much-needed fundamental changes for army women. Congress funded construction of a training center for WACs at Fort McClellan, Alabama, and the army approved new summer and winter uniforms for women and added more military occupational specialties to the WAC assignment list. Training courses for these specialties were developed and offered. Also, the recruiting command improved methods for training recruiters for WAC officers and enlisted women, in hopes that better communication techniques might boost enlistments.

Colonel Mary A. Hallaren was director of the WACs from 1947 to 1953. She had initiated and secured the rights of regular and reserve status for WACs and servicewomen, and during her tenure she promoted expansion of WAC services in the Korean War. On 3 January 1953 Colonel Irene O. Galloway succeeded Hallaren as the new WAC director.

Most servicewomen considered an overseas posting to be the most attractive assignment. During the Korean War, most requests by eligible WACs wanting to serve in the Far East command were approved. Two WAC units were sent to Japan in 1950, and a total of nine WAC units were there in 1953. Most of these WAC units were hospital units, although the WAC unit in Okinawa had both administrative and medical personnel. The number of women assigned to the Far East command increased from 629 in 1950 to 2,600 in 1951, while only 300 new WACs were added to the European command in the same time period.

During the first year of the Korean War, the WAC unit formed at Fort Lee was expected to go to Pusan or Seoul to be attached to the Eighth Army, Forward. Army commanders, however, considered combat to be too unpredictable on the peninsula to assign WACs in Korea. When battle lines became stalemated in late 1951, the Eighth Army commander asked for a WAC unit, but recruiting had declined enough that Hallaren stated the corps strength was insufficient to keep a

WAC unit in Korea. Instead, she assigned a dozen enlisted women and an officer to major headquarters in Korea during 1951. Although the number of WACs had increased from 7,259 on 30 June 1950 to 11,932 on 30 June 1951, enlistments declined when truce talks were initiated. Women who might have been inspired to enlist because of patriotism and personnel needs believed they were not needed. The other women's services also experienced decreased enlistments. In June 1951, 28,000 women served in line assignments, accounting for just over 1 percent of the military forces.

In spring 1952, 46,000 women were on active duty, with 13,000 WAFs, 10,000 WACs, 8,000 WAVEs, and 2,400 Marines. The remaining women were in health positions. One of the greatest needs for servicewomen was as nurses. Within the first month of the start of the Korean War, more than 100 nurses arrived in the Far East to assist with casualties. Between 500 and 600 Army Nurse Corps nurses served in the war zone supporting combat troops during the Korean War, and several thousand worked in hospitals in Japan and the Far East. Flight nurses treated casualties being evacuated, and army nurses cared for the wounded in evacuation hospitals and assisted with emergency surgery. Women physicians also served with the military.

By 1953 WACs served as administrative aides, stenographers, and translators to ease the shortage of male soldiers in some commands overseas. Women had more opportunities, having a chance to serve in supervisory positions. Increased numbers of women were employed in military occupational specialties that had been closed to them before the war. For example, in U.S. military hospitals in Japan that cared for wounded combat soldiers from Korea, WAC sergeants served as ward masters, a job previously held only by men. Women also gained jobs as senior noncommissioned officers, directing motor pools, mess halls, and post offices. In such capacities they supervised men and women. When the armistice was signed in July 1953, 9,925 women were WACs and had gained military experience from the war to apply to peacetime service.

The exact number of U.S. women serving on active duty in the Korean War is unknown. In the 1980 census the Veterans Administration said that 120,300 women veterans of the Korean War claimed to be living in the United States and consisted of white, black, and Hispanic women. The number of women serving during the Korean War peaked at 48,700 in October 1952; this dropped to 35,000 in June 1955.

The Korean War experience proved valuable to women serving in Vietnam and later wars. After the Korean War, DACOWITS continued to address the role of women in peacetime and wartime military services.

In addition to American servicewomen, women from other countries accompanied troops to Korea or provided an indigenous source of support. For example, Canadian Nurse Lieutenant J. I. MacDonald received the Associate of the Royal Red Cross citation, while another Canadian woman, Captain E. B. Pense, earned the Royal Red Cross commendation.

The Republic of Korea Women's Army Corps (ROKWAC) had been established in 1948 and served throughout the Korean War. Colonel Kim Hyŏn-suk was commanding officer of the ROKWAC, which she had helped organize with Korea Military Advisory Group advisors. Kim trained qualified women to serve as officers for ROKWAC units. She and these women developed military programs for girls in high schools and colleges to prepare more support personnel. On 1 September 1950, the ROKWAC headquarters and camps were established at Pusan as part of the Special Services Section of the Republic of Korea Army (ROKA). Supervised by a U.S. advisor and a WAC officer, the ROKWAC was modeled after the American WAC organization.

As the need for more servicewomen increased, the ROKWAC recruited enlistees to defend their country, but this effort was hindered by the evacuation of civilians and other limitations. Approximately 3,000 women said they wanted to enlist in the ROKWAC, which had facilities to train only 500. Potential recruits took physical and intelligence examinations to evaluate their ability. The resulting achievement ratings were used to select the women for training. These women received basic military training such as how to use weapons as well as learning support skills. Initially, women were assigned to the regular army where they were needed; but later, as more women received specific training, they were attached with special units to army groups.

The ROKWAC was divided into five departments. Women in the communications section operated message centers with teletypes and telephones. In the First ROKA Corps, ROKWACs were in charge of corps communications. Personnel duties involved recruiting, training, and assigning ROKWACs. Administrative work monitored supply and record keeping, consisting of secretarial duties. Some ROKWACs were heads of departments of administrative sections of rear companies. ROKWACs also conducted psychological warfare, broadcasting radio messages to China and North Korea and dropping leaflets from airplanes, as well as using airplane loudspeakers to transmit information to those on the ground. ROKWACs also worked with army intelligence officers. ROKWACs in the service unit provided recreational activities, such as staffing libraries.

The Korean women did not serve as nurses or in food distribution jobs. Captain Yun Hŭi-yul, aide to

Colonel Kim, commented about gender conflicts between military men and women: "Korean men do not like to obey women but if she is an officer they have to do it. They rationalize to themselves that they are obeying the title and not the woman." After the Korean War the ROKWACs served in a peacetime reserve program.

There is little information on North Korean and Chinese women in the Korean War in histories of the war written by both Communist and non-Communist authors. Allied forces did not report women among Chinese People's Volunteer Army (CPVA, Communist Chinese) or Korean People's Army (KPA, North Korean) forces.

The constitution of the Democratic People's Republic of Korea (DPRK, North Korea) promised equal rights for women. Membership in the Worker-and-Peasant Red Guard was compulsory for men between the ages of eighteen and forty-five except individuals who were disabled or serving in active military duty. Many North Korean women also joined the Red Guard, where they learned guerilla warfare, infiltration, and antiaircraft tactics and were on twenty-four–hour alert for action. DPRK leader Kim Il Sung did not differentiate by gender when he emphasized that North Koreans "must be firmly prepared, both ideologically and militarily, for perfect self-defense."

In the People's Republic of China, Communist officials attempted to achieve gender equality through legal reform and administrative changes. Women remained subordinate to men in Chinese society; however, women in urban areas did benefit more from progress in gender relations than rural women.

During the 1930s and 1940s women had supported the Red Army by serving in the women's aid corps as nurses, transporting supplies to the front, and accompanying combat troops on spying or guerrilla missions. The Chinese Communist Party had established women's propaganda teams in which women urged their husbands and male relatives to enlist in the Red Army.

When China entered the Korean War in October 1950, women soldiers were not expected to serve in the front lines of the CPVA. Instead, they performed office work and logistical and medical tasks. Most women did not hold high administrative posts in the army. Some were World War II veterans. Domestically, women were employed by war industries and represented 8.9 percent of industrial employees in 1952, a 74 percent increase from 1951. Chinese leaders wanted women to try traditionally male roles, sponsoring such events as an all-woman air show held on Woman's Day in 1952. Chinese women might also have created and distributed leaflets and propaganda during the Korean War, and a smaller number might have furtively promoted peace, risking ostracism and

punishment. After the 1953 armistice, China encouraged more traditional views of women and family instead of militarism.

Chinese and North Korean women also conducted sabotage against the United Nations (UN) forces. North Korean women posed as refugees to infiltrate UN lines and inflict casualties or gather intelligence. In November 1950, the Chung Pong police detained two female agents. During interrogation they divulged that they had been ordered by the KPA to poison wells used by UN forces. Such activities remain largely obscure.

—*Elizabeth D. Schafer*

References:

Curtin, Ann. "Army Women on Active Duty." *Army Information Digest* 8 (1953): 22–30.

Herman, Ruby E. "Women's Army Corps Trains at Fort Lee." *Army Information Digest* 6 (1951): 26–32.

Holm, Jeanne. *Women in the Military: An Unfinished Revolution.* Novato, CA: Presidio Press, 1982.

Jancar, Barbara Wolfe. *Women under Communism.* Baltimore: Johns Hopkins University Press, 1978.

King, Helen B. "The WACs of Korea." *Korean Survey* 4 (1955): 10–11.

Morden, Bettie J. *The Women's Army Corps, 1945–1978.* Washington, DC: U.S. Army Center of Military History, 1990.

Siu, Bobby. *Women of China: Imperialism and Women's Resistance, 1900–1949.* London: Zed Press, 1981.

Soderbergh, Peter A. *Women Marines in the Korean War Era.* Westport, CT: Praeger, 1994.

Stremlow, Mary V. *A History of the Women Marines, 1946–1977.* Washington, DC: History and Museums Division, Headquarters, U.S. Marine Corps, 1986.

See also: China, People's Republic of; Far East Command (FEC); Kim Il Sung; Korea, Democratic People's Republic of, 1945–1953; Korea Military Advisory Group (KMAG); Korea, Republic of Army (ROKA); Mao Zedong; Marshall, George C.; Military Medicine; Mobile Army Surgical Hospital (MASH); Truman, Harry S.; United States Air Force (USAF); United States Army; United States Marine Corps; United States Navy.

Wŏn Yong-dŏk
(1908–1968)

Republic of Korea Army (ROKA, South Korea) lieutenant general, distinguished by his unswerving loyalty to ROK President Syngman Rhee. Born in Seoul in 1908, Wŏn Yong-dŏk graduated from the Severance Medical School in 1931. He then became a surgeon with the rank of lieutenant colonel in the Japanese-led Manchukuo Army. In December 1945 Wŏn became the assistant superintendent of the Military English Language School, established by the United States to train officers for the Constabulary army in South Korea. Wŏn himself graduated from the school in 1946 as a major. After briefly serving as the first commander of the South Korean Constabulary, in September 1946 Won became superintendent of the

Korean Military Academy. In February 1947 he commanded the 5th Brigade.

A political crisis in 1952 in the ROK saw Rhee in confrontation with the National Assembly. Rhee believed that only he could manage the country effectively and sought to retain his authoritarian hold. On 25 May 1952, Rhee declared martial law and appointed then–Major General Wŏn to implement a series of emergency measures. Wŏn utilized strong-arm tactics that ensured Rhee's tight control over Pusan, the temporary ROK capital, and the area around it. Ignoring the military chain of command, he issued decrees and meted out swift punishment to dissenters.

The new regulations included restrictions on holding meetings, strict censorship, and the authority to arrest any government official. One of Wŏn's first acts was to arrest Sŏ Min-ho, a leading ROK political figure and critic of the Rhee government. The following day, forty-five members of the National Assembly were arrested, although all but twelve were soon released. Many assembly members went into hiding to avoid arrest. Wŏn helped ensure a satisfactory vote in the National Assembly to amend the constitution and call for the popular election of the ROK president and the creation of an upper house. Rhee easily won the new elections on 6 August 1952.

As a reward for his political services, Wŏn was advanced to lieutenant general, and in June 1953 Rhee made him commander of the Provost Marshal General's office, which placed all ROK military police under his control rather than that of the army, the chief of staff of which, Paek Sŏn-yŏp, was strongly pro-American. He continued to demonstrate his loyalty to President Rhee in the sudden release on 18 June 1953 of North Korean prisoners of war. Wŏn died in 1968.

—*Spencer C. Tucker*

References:
Cumings, Bruce. *The Origins of the Korean War.* 2 vols. Princeton, NJ: Princeton University Press, 1981, 1990.
Matray, James I., ed. *Historical Dictionary of the Korean War.* Westport, CT: Greenwood Press, 1991.
See also: Paek Sŏn-yŏp; Syngman Rhee; Syngman Rhee's Release of North Korean Prisoners of War.

Wŏnju, Battle of
(14–17 February 1951)

Mid-February 1951 engagement in and around the town of Wŏnju in central Korea, sixty-five miles southeast of Seoul and five miles south of Hoengsŏng. Fighting there by the 9th and 38th Regiments of the U.S. 2d Infantry Division, companies of the 17th Regiment of the 7th Division, elements of the 187th Airborne Regiment, and support units occurred while the division's other regiment, the 23d, was locked in a perimeter defense in and around the village of Chip'yŏng-ni, about twenty miles to the northwest.

In early February 1951 Communist forces continued their attack on United Nations Command (UNC) forces after the latter's withdrawal from the far north of the country and struck in force in the central part of the Korean peninsula, scattering three Republic of Korea Army (ROKA) divisions and forcing other troops in that sector to withdraw southward. Communist forces aimed their attack at the key communications centers of Chip'yŏng-ni and Wŏnju. Since his forces at these two locations were well forward of the main line of resistance, 2d Division assistant division commander Brigadier General George Stewart expected that he would also be ordered to fall back. But new Eighth Army Commander General Lieutenant Matthew B. Ridgway was determined to end the several-week-old practice of recoiling each time Communist forces attacked, and he wanted to test the willingness and ability of his forces to withstand whatever his enemy could offer. Ridgway ordered that Chip'yŏng-ni and Wŏnju be held. The ensuing fighting at Wŏnju became known among local commanders and troops as "The Wŏnju shoot" because of the extraordinary and massive amount of artillery fired at the attacking Communist forces.

The first Communist troops arriving in the area found defending UNC troops, including the Dutch Battalion, in position around Hoengsŏng. When they came under fire, the Communists yelled "Okay, Okay, we're ROKs," whereupon the Dutch lifted their fire. The infiltrating Chinese then opened fire on the Dutch command post, killing five officers, including the commanding officer. Fourteen other men were wounded and eight were later reported missing. On the night of 12 February, orders were received to abandon Hoengsŏng. A perimeter defense was then established on high ground around Wŏnju, and all available artillery was positioned so that massed fires could be placed on any approach to the city.

At daylight on 15 February, Communist forces attacked from along the Sŏm River to the west of Wŏnju and the defending artillery opened up in all its fury. The 2d Division history [p. 107] reported:

> Thunderous barrages roared across the hills as tons of shrapnel poured into the plodding troops. Thousands of shells wreaked havoc never before seen on any army as pilots reported the river running red with the blood of the massacred troops. Still they came.... Hour after hour the unbelievable slaughter mounted as dog-tired, exhausted artillerymen slammed an endless stream of shells into the exposed masses of Chinese.... The staggering losses began to tell. The once full ranks

Vehicles of the U.S. 2d Division jam up in an icy mountain pass south of Wŏnju. (National Archives)

were now thin, blasted, shocked remnants without leaders, without hope. Now only unorganized bands of useless bodies, they tried to escape north out of reach of the murderous guns.

The "Wŏnju shoot" cost Communist forces more than 5,000 men casualties. Bitter fighting waged the night of the 14th and into the following day at Wŏnju and further south involving troops that had bypassed Wŏnju. The Communists then shifted their main effort to Chip'yŏng-ni to the west and the threat to Wŏnju was eliminated.

—*Sherman W. Pratt*

References:

Blair, Clay. *The Forgotten War: America in Korea, 1950–1953.* New York: Times Books, 1987.

Munroe, Clark C. *The Second United States Infantry Division in Korea.* Tokyo: Toppan Printing, n.d. [c. 1951]

Pratt, Sherman W. *Decisive Battles of the Korean War. An Infantry Company Commander's View of the War's Most Critical Engagements.* New York: Vantage Press, 1992.

Schnabel, James F. *United States Army in the Korean War: Policy and Direction, the First Year.* Washington, DC: Office of the Chief of Military History, Department of the Army, 1972.

See also: Ridgway, Matthew Bunker.

Wŏnsan

Port city 110 air miles north of the 38th parallel on the east coast of the Korean peninsula. At present Wŏnsan is the provincial capital of North Korean Kangwŏn Province. The provincial capital of South Korean Kangwŏn-do [province] is Ch'unch'ŏn.

During the Korean War, on 11 October 1950, the 3d and Capital Divisions of the Republic of Korea Army, moving north along the east coast of the peninsula, entered Wŏnsan, securing both the city and its airfield. On 19 October, with the city already secure, the U.S. X Corps arrived offshore the city and proceeded to conduct an amphibious landing. The main body of the marines came ashore on 26 October.

From the last week of October, United Nations Command (UNC) forces in the northwestern and northeastern sectors of North Korea encountered significant opposition from Chinese troops. In mid-November, the U.S. State Department proposed a halt to UN offensive operations in Korea and a withdrawal of UN forces to the narrow neck of the peninsula just north of P'yŏngyang and Wŏnsan. By the time he received this advice to halt short of the Yalu River, UNC commander General Douglas MacArthur had already launched his final offensive. When at the end of November Chinese forces launched their large-scale counterattack, UNC forces abandoned all of North Korea above the 38th parallel, including Wŏnsan, and conducted a hurried and deep withdrawal south of the line.

—Jinwung Kim

References:

Blair, Clay. *The Forgotten War: America in Korea, 1950–1953.* New York: Times Books, 1987.

MacDonald, Callum. *Korea: The War Before Vietnam.* New York: Free Press, 1986.

Stueck, William W., Jr. *The Korean War: An International History.* Princeton, NJ: Princeton University Press, 1995.

See also: Wŏnsan Landing.

Wŏnsan Landing
(25 October 1950)

United Nations Command (UNC) amphibious operation in October 1950. After the successful Inch'ŏn landing and recapture of Seoul, General Douglas MacArthur planned an amphibious landing of X Corps on Korea's east coast as a staging site to move northwest toward the Democratic People's Republic of Korea (DPRK, North Korean) capital of P'yŏngyang. He selected the port town of Wŏnsan because of its strategic location. Some 110 miles north of the 38th parallel, Wŏnsan had a population of 75,000 people. Site of a petroleum refinery that produced hundreds of tons of gasoline daily, Wŏnsan was also Korea's primary east coast harbor, and it had an airfield, communications facilities, and roads and railways connecting both Seoul and P'yŏngyang.

Known by the code name Operation TAILBOARD, the Wŏnsan landing was controversial. On 29 September MacArthur held conferences to plan the Wŏnsan landing, to be directed by Amphibious Force Far East (Task Force 90) commander Rear Admiral James H. Doyle, and stated that he hoped to land by 29 October. Naval officers, however, realized that the landing could be delayed because of time constraints for reembarking troops at Inch'ŏn and steaming to Wŏnsan. They also criticized the lack of information, including current maps, on Wŏnsan. Proponents of the operation believed that supplying X Corps from

Wŏnsan would relieve the supply stress on Inch'ŏn and place X Corps in an excellent strategic position to advance toward P'yŏngyang in conjunction with the Eighth Army. Commanders, however, differed on how X Corps should travel to Wŏnsan.

X Corps commander Major General Edward M. Almond stressed that "from a tactical point of view, it's cheaper to go to Wŏnsan by sea." He opposed moving there by land, because of the terrain, which he said would mean that "half of our heavy equipment—bulldozers, big guns, and heavy trucks—would have been left in ditches by the side of the road." Vice Admiral C. Turner Joy, commander of U.S. Naval Forces Far East, believed X Corps "could have marched overland to Wŏnsan in a much shorter time and with much less effort than it would take to get the Corps around to Wŏnsan by sea." Other officers protested taking troops out of action when they could have been pursuing Korean People's Army (KPA, North Korean) forces.

MacArthur's decision to continue X Corps' status as an independent command also severely affected UNC logistics. To lift X Corps from Inch'ŏn, Eighth Army transportation assets had to be diverted, delaying its movement north, and the port of Inch'ŏn was closed to other shipping until X Corps departed.

On 7 October the 1st Marine Division command post at Inch'ŏn transferred to Doyle's flagship, the *Mount McKinley.* Outloading of Marines at Inch'ŏn commenced the next day. Doyle ordered the ships, carrying a total of 30,184 passengers, to begin their eastward journey of 830 sea miles on 15 October.

When the ships reached Wŏnsan's harbor five days later, they discovered the harbor was thick with several thousand Soviet magnetic and contact mines. While minesweepers cleared a channel, Doyle ordered the ships to steam north and then return south, which the Marines called "Operation Yo-Yo." The crowded ships spent five days moving up and down the Korean coast, and many of those confined on them suffered from gastroenteritis and dysentery. Finally, on 25 October Doyle permitted the ships to enter the mineswept channel to Wŏnsan. "In retrospect, it must be said that the landing was to pay dividends for the Navy," Admiral Joy admitted. "Had it not been undertaken we might never have become fully alerted to the menace of mine warfare nor profited from the lessons we learned about mine sweeping."

When X Corps troops landed on Wŏnsan's beach on 25 October, they were greeted by Republic of Korea (ROK, South Korean) soldiers who had advanced more quickly than expected. Members of the ROK Capital and 3d Divisions had secured Wŏnsan fifteen days earlier. Air maintenance crews also beat the Marines to Wŏnsan by a dozen days. More humiliating

Bob Hope with the men of X Corps at Wŏnsan, 26 October 1950. (National Archives)

to the Marines, entertainers Bob Hope and Marilyn Maxwell were flown to the objective on 24 October and put on a show that included quips at the expense of the Marines offshore.

Because P'yŏngyang had been captured by the ROK 1st Division on 19 October, X Corps troops headed north instead of west. The 1st Marine Division moved up the coast toward Hŭngnam and the Changjin Reservoir. Meanwhile, the U.S. Army's 3d Infantry Division arrived at Wŏnsan in early November to join X Corps' drive against retreating KPA forces.

After the massive Chinese military intervention, UNC troops withdrew to the coast, and on 3 December they were ordered to evacuate Wŏnsan. Some 7,009 civilian refugees, 3,834 military personnel, 1,146 vehicles, and 10,013 bulk tons of cargo were moved aboard ship; and on 7 December the UNC abandoned Wŏnsan. Two months later, on 16 February 1951, the navy began a 861-day blockade of Wŏnsan in which

destroyers, cruisers, battleships, and aircraft bombarded Communist airfields and entrenchments. Although subject to counterbattery land fire, the UNC captured seven of Wŏnsan's harbor islands, one of which, Yŏdo, was used for a 1,200-foot emergency airstrip. The UN blockade of Wŏnsan occupied some 80,000 KPA troops, diverting them and their artillery from military engagements in other parts of Korea. The Wŏnsan blockade, the longest in modern warfare, prevented the Communists from using the port. It ended on 27 July 1953, when the armistice became effective.

—Elizabeth D. Schafer

References:

Alexander, James Edwin. *Inchon to Wonsan: From the Deck of a Destroyer in the Korean War*. Annapolis, MD: Naval Institute Press, 1996.

Blair, Clay. *The Forgotten War: America in Korea, 1950–1953*. New York: Times Books, 1987.

Breuer, William B. *Shadow Warriors: The Covert War in Korea*. New York: Wiley, 1996.

Cagle, Malcolm W., and Frank A. Manson. *The Sea War in Korea.* Annapolis, MD: Naval Institute Press, 1957.

See also: Almond, Edward Mallory; Amphibious Force Far East (Task Force Ninety); Doyle, James H.; Inch'ŏn Landings: Operation CHROMITE; Joy, Charles Turner; MacArthur, Douglas; Mine Warfare; Tenth Corps.

Wrong, Humphrey Hume
(1894–1954)

Canadian ambassador to the United States during the Korean War. Born in Toronto on 10 September 1894, Hume Wrong had had a brief career as a history professor before joining the staff of the new Canadian legation in Washington, D.C., in 1928. It was in this post that he became a key figure in the often turbulent relationship between Canada and the United States during the Korean War.

Wrong's primary role during the war was to act as the messenger for Canadian views to the U.S. State Department. These were often in the form of suggestions that caused a growing difference of opinion between the two countries over military strategy and the role of the United Nations (UN) in the conflict. Wrong emphatically expressed Ottawa's contention that it was a UN collective security operation and not a vehicle for an anti-Communist offensive in Asia. This position was taken despite the Canadian government's own anti-Communist orientation and despite the fact that the United States provided the overwhelming preponderance of United Nations Command (UNC) troops in Korea.

It was Wrong who first informed the Canadian government of North Korea's invasion of the South, while offering his belief, widely shared in Ottawa and elsewhere, that the United States would not intervene militarily. He and his government were therefore surprised by President Harry S. Truman's quick and determined involvement. From then on Wrong was faced with the problem of relaying Canada's concerns over how the "police action" would evolve. Receiving orders from Canada's high-profile secretary of state for external affairs, Lester Pearson, Wrong found himself inundated with Ottawa's attempts to influence U.S. policy. The main issues focused on the leading role of the United Nations and the disinclination of Canadians to allow the war to escalate outside the confines of the Korean peninsula. Later, with the fortunes of war swinging briefly toward the UN forces, Wrong expressed the Canadians' concern over the rhetoric and tactics of UNC commander General Douglas MacArthur. He was especially concerned over the wisdom of violating Chinese airspace with "hot pursuit" by U.S. planes. Later still, he quietly informed Ottawa that even with MacArthur now gone, U.S. aircraft were still unofficially conducting such overflights well into 1952.

It was because of such views that the Canadian diplomatic corps in Washington, headed by Wrong, came to be seen by the U.S. State Department as a source of unsolicited and disagreeable obstruction. This animosity escalated, on occasion, to outright hostility by the Americans toward a country that they considered a very close friend and ally. Wrong was the lightning rod for these disagreements and, at times, even he would protest to Ottawa about the constant hectoring and questioning of policy that flowed across his desk aimed at U.S. actions and motives. Although he was in general agreement with the desirability of limiting American "excesses," he also believed that the U.S. State Department was often harassed enough by swiftly moving events. Overly questioning American ideas could be seen in Washington as questioning U.S. sincerity. Wrong believed, in the long run, that that would prove to be self-defeating. This was particularly a problem in the early stages of the war, when Canada was perceived as not contributing enough to the military effort in Korea. Later, Wrong also wisely counseled his government not to push Washington too hard on Asian matters following the firing of MacArthur because of the intense political pressure the Truman administration was encountering at home.

Beyond these more controversial issues, however, Wrong was still able to negotiate with U.S. authorities for permission to allow Canadian forces bound for Korea to train first at Fort Lewis, Washington. More importantly, Wrong also signed an agreement in October 1950 that revived the concepts of the Hyde Park Declaration between Canada and the United States during World War II. This encouraged economic cooperation between the two countries in defense production that contributed, for better or worse, in tying the two national economies closer together during the Cold War era.

After the Korean War, Wrong returned to Ottawa to begin a posting as undersecretary for external affairs, but he died in Ottawa on 24 January 1954, before he could assume that position.

—*Eric Jarvis*

References:

Granatstein, J. L., and Norman Hillmer. *For Better or for Worse, Canada and the United States to the 1990s.* Toronto: Copp Clark Pitman, 1991.

Stairs, Denis. *The Diplomacy of Constraint: Canada, the Korean War, and the United States.* Toronto: University of Toronto Press, 1974.

Stueck, William W., Jr. *The Korean War: An International History.* Princeton, NJ: Princeton University Press, 1995.

Wood, Herbert Fairlie. *Strange Battleground: The Official History of the Canadian Army in Korea.* Ottawa: Queen's Printer, 1966.

See also: Canada; Hot Pursuit; MacArthur, Douglas; Pearson, Lester B.; St. Laurent, Louis S.; Truman, Harry S.

Wu Xiuquan (Wu Hsiu-Ch'uan)
(1908–)

Diplomat, People's Republic of China (PRC) and chief representative to the United Nations special meeting on the Korean War and the Taiwan Strait situation in New York in November 1950. Born in the city of Wuchang, Hubei Province, China, on 6 March 1908, Wu Xiuquan entered Sun Yat-sen University in Moscow when he was seventeen. Later he worked as an interpreter for the Communist International at the university. Returning to China, he was an interpreter for the Communist International's adviser to China between 1930 and 1935. In that capacity, he attended the Chinese Communist Party (CCP) Zunyi Conference, a historic meeting in January 1935 that established Mao Zedong as leader of the entire CCP. In 1945, just before the end of the War of Resistance against the Japanese, he was transferred to northeast China as chief of staff, Northeast China Anti-Japanese Army.

Although he had excellent potential for advancement in the military, Wu was transferred to a diplomatic career, one of a group of senior military officers selected by Mao Zedong and Zhou Enlai to hold key positions in the new Ministry of Foreign Affairs after the founding of the PRC. In the Ministry of Foreign Affairs, Wu was responsible for assisting Premier and Foreign Minister Zhou Enlai and Vice Minister of Foreign Affairs Wang Jiaxiang in dealing with Moscow and Eastern European Communist bloc countries.

When the Korean War began, Wu was director of the Department of Soviet and Eastern European Affairs of the Ministry of Foreign Affairs. He was involved in negotiations with Moscow concerning the USSR's military assistance to China for the Korean War. Because of Wu's language skills and foreign experience, Zhou Enlai selected him to head the high-profile PRC delegation to the United Nations (UN) special meeting in November 1950. Wu was the first PRC official to appear at the UN after the 1949 revolution. His job at the UN special meeting was to deliver a tough-worded condemnation of U.S. "aggression" in the Taiwan Strait and Washington's intervention in the Korean War. He later recalled this speech as one of the most important events of his life.

In 1952, when General Li Kenong fell ill, Zhou Enlai sent Wu to assist him in the Korean War armistice negotiations with the idea that Wu would replace him. But General Li insisted on completing the talks before returning to Beijing. After returning from Korea in 1953, Wu became vice minister of foreign affairs and later PRC ambassador to Yugoslavia. After the Cultural Revolution, he returned to the military, and in 1975 he became deputy chief of staff in charge of intelligence affairs. He retired in 1988.

—*Richard Weixing Hu*

References:

Guo Huaruo et al. *Jiefangjun Junshi Dacidian* [Dictionary of PLA military history]. Changchun: Jilin People's Press, 1993.

Wu Rugao et al. *Zhongguo Junshi Renwu Dacidian* [Dictionary of Chinese military figures]. Beijing: Xinhua Chubanshe, 1989.

Zhongguo Junshi Dabaike Quanshu [Chinese military encyclopedia]. Military History, Vol. 3. Beijing: Military Science Press, 1997.

Zhongguo Renmin Jiefangjun Jiangshuai Minlu [Brief bibliographies of PLA's marshals and generals]. Vols. 1–3. Beijing: PLA Press, 1986, 1987.

See also: China, People's Republic of; Mao Zedong; Zhou Enlai.

X

Xie Fang (Hsieh Fang)
(1908–1984)

People's Liberation Army general and chief of staff, Chinese People's Volunteer Army (CPVA, Communist Chinese). Born in Dongfeng, Jilin Province, China, in 1908, Xie Fang attended the Japanese Infantry School in 1922. He first became known to the Chinese Communist Party (CCP) for his role in the "Xi'an Incident" in December 1936, when Jiang Jieshi (Chiang Kai-shek) was kidnapped by former warlord and Nationalist supporter General Zhang Xueliang, who forced Jiang to cooperate with the CCP forces in the fight against the Japanese. Xie was a protégé of General Zhang. Xie joined the CCP in 1936 and was the deputy commander of the North China Field Army during 1936–1937. In the early 1940s Xie studied at the Sun Yat-sen University in Moscow. He worked at the Central Party School in Yenan beginning in 1943. Beginning in the mid-1940s, Xie was associated with Lin Biao in northeast China. At the time of the outbreak of the Korean War, Xie was an experienced combat veteran and political commissar, serving as the chief of propaganda of the Northeast Military District. He was fluent in Russian, Japanese, and English and was a skilled educator and propagandist.

Xie was appointed chief of staff of the newly designated VIII Army Corps in the Central Military Commission "Orders to Defend the Northeast Border Security," signed by Mao Zedong on 13 July 1950. The following month, Xie drafted a report, sent to Beijing on 31 August 1950, that analyzed likely U.S. strategies and China's ability to intervene. Xie believed that the United States would launch an amphibious operation somewhere on the North Korean coast, or (with a larger force) at Seoul or P'yŏngyang. Although he thought the Korean People's Army (North Korean) would not be able to withstand a U.S. counterattack, Xie recommended that the Chinese forces not intervene until after the U.S. forces crossed the 38th parallel, since it would help Chinese forces both politically and militarily. Xie argued that strong air support and more equipment from the Soviet Union were essential to assisting the North Koreans. He recommended adding two additional corps with artillery and tank support to the Thirteenth Army force structure. Xie also recommended strengthening logistics and sending reconnaissance groups in advance to assess the terrain and the overall situation in North Korea.

Xie played a major role in preparing the intervention forces to advance into North Korea. He was officially named chief of staff of the CPVA on 23 October 1950, but he was recognized as chief of staff of the intervention forces from at least early October 1950.

During November 1950, after the First Campaign (October 1950), Peng Dehuai is said to have observed that U.S. forces were "inexperienced." Xie's opinion was more derisive, noting the "American soldiers panic easily. Their riflemen prefer to ride in trucks. They are afraid to die." Still he was concerned about logistical shortcomings that could seriously affect follow-on operations. He highlighted the shortage of sufficient transportation, which required reliance on about 500,000 coolies from northeast China. Supply lines were overextended, which would cause shortages in food and ammunition. Air support, artillery, and armor were all lacking.

Unlike Deng Hua, Xie was not a rising political figure, but he was specially selected for the Chinese negotiation team. Although he served as a junior member of the Chinese negotiation team, he played a prominent role in the day-to-day negotiations, in which he participated from July 1951 to October 1952. During negotiations Xie was sometimes profane, and he often insulted U.S. negotiators. He could shift overnight from harsh, brow-beating, name-calling attacks, designed to harass and secure further concessions, to a quiet, reasonable, and businesslike approach. U.S. Admiral C. Turner Joy described Xie as "dangerous," with "a bitterly sharp mind." Joy observed that Xie "rarely spoke from prepared material." His remarks appeared to be "extemporaneous and fluent." A confident negotiator, Xie would end a session if nothing could be accomplished.

Xie returned to Beijing from Korea in 1952; Chai Chengwen replaced him. Until the Cultural Revolution (1966–1976), Xie worked in a series of military training and education assignments as a close associate of Xiao Ke, a Long March veteran. During the Cultural Revolution, Xie was purged for his association with He Long, a leader of the Nanchang Uprising on 1 August 1927, and a Long March veteran. After the Cultural Revolution, Xie was rehabilitated and returned to work in military education as deputy director of the People's Liberation Army Logistics Academy in Wuhan. He died in 1984.

—*Susan M. Puska*

References:

Joy, C. Turner. *How Communists Negotiate*. New York: Macmillan, 1955.

Spurr, Russell. *Enter the Dragon: China's Undeclared War against the U.S. in Korea, 1950–1951*. New York: Henry Holt, 1988.

Wilhelm, Alfred D. *The Chinese at the Negotiating Table: Style and Characteristics*. Washington, DC: National Defense University Press, 1994.

Zhang, Shu Guang. *Mao's Military Romanticism: China and the Korean War, 1950–1953*. Lawrence: University of Kansas Press, 1995.

See also: China, People's Republic of: Army; Deng Hua (Teng Hua); Gao Gang (Kao Kang); Jiang Jieshi (Chiang Kai-shek); Peng Dehuai (Peng Te-huai).

Y

Yalu Bridges Controversy

Issue that strained relations between the United States and the People's Republic of China (PRC, Communist China) and also accelerated the deterioration of relations between President Harry S. Truman and United Nations (UN) commander in Korea General Douglas MacArthur. MacArthur's 15 September 1950 Inch'ŏn landing completely reversed the progress of the war. In the following months, MacArthur steadily pushed the Korean People's Army (KPA, North Korean) forces back across the 38th parallel and then pursued them into the Democratic People's Republic of Korea (DPRK, North Korea).

The Truman administration became increasingly concerned as MacArthur drove north toward the Yalu River, the border with China. Truman was well aware of the PRC warning that it would not tolerate a United Nations Command (UNC) invasion of the DPRK, but he dismissed it as propaganda. Beijing, however, worried that a U.S. presence in North Korea would endanger its heavy industry in Manchuria. The route across the Yalu River had also been the traditional one taken by invaders into China.

In late 1950 MacArthur had pushed DPRK forces far north of the 38th parallel. The North Koreans increasingly began regrouping close to the Yalu River or crossed it into China. Meanwhile MacArthur and the administration had received intelligence reports that the number of Chinese troops in Manchuria almost quadrupled between July and September 1950. By October, UNC forces reported increasing contact with Chinese ground troops on the Korean side of the Yalu.

Although he did not believe that these engagements signaled a major offensive by the Chinese, MacArthur did want to bomb the bridges over the Yalu. He argued that this would serve the dual purpose of cutting off the North Koreans and Chinese from supply and hampering the potential flow of Chinese troops into Korea.

On 6 November 1950, MacArthur prepared to send ninety B-29 bombers to destroy a bridge over the Yalu. Truman and the Joint Chiefs of Staff quickly instructed the general to postpone the attack. They feared that any damage inflicted on the Chinese side of the Yalu would provoke a full-scale Chinese attack. World war also became a possibility because of the Sino-Soviet Treaty of Friendship and Alliance, signed on 14 February 1950. MacArthur strongly protested the orders from Washington.

MacArthur did not let the issue drop and continued to insist that the bombing was necessary, especially with U.S. forces only thirty-five miles from the Yalu River border. After protracted discussions, the Truman administration reached a solution that it believed would placate MacArthur and serve the needs of U.S. foreign policy. MacArthur received permission to destroy the Korean side of the bridges.

There were sixteen bridges across both the Yalu River border with China and the Tumen River border with the Soviet Union. MacArthur first envisioned bombing them all, but he dropped some as targets to concentrate on others deemed more vital. Some of the bridges were damaged, but skirmishes with the Chinese air force increased the prospects of war with China. Also, the diplomatic cost of the bombing outweighed its effectiveness. The bombing did not seriously interrupt the flow of supplies or troops because half of the bridges bombed remained intact, while the frozen condition of the Yalu River permitted military transport across its surface.

Throughout the operation, the Truman administration proclaimed that the United States did not want a widened war with China or any other power. These statements did little good as far as Beijing was concerned, because the bombing was perceived as a military threat. On 25 November 1950, Chinese People's Volunteer Army (Chinese Communist) forces intervened in the war on a massive scale. As Chinese forces battered his command and drove UN troops back south, MacArthur criticized the Truman administration for not allowing him to completely destroy the Yalu bridges. Nonetheless, Truman's decision solidified Chinese policy in favor of intervention and led to deteriorating relations between Washington and its field commander over how to prosecute the war.

—*Eric W. Osborne*

References:

Hastings, Max. *The Korean War.* New York: Simon & Schuster, 1987.

MacDonald, Callum. *Korea: The War Before Vietnam.* New York: Free Press, 1986.

Spanier, John W. *The Truman-MacArthur Controversy and the Korean War.* Cambridge, MA: Belknap Press, 1959.

See also: Joint Chiefs of Staff (JCS); MacArthur, Douglas; Sino-Soviet Treaty of Friendship and Alliance; Truman, Harry S.; Truman's Recall of MacArthur.

Yang Yu-ch'an
(1897–1975)

Republic of Korea (ROK, South Korean) diplomat. Born in Pusan on 3 February 1897, Yang Yu-ch'an spent most of his youth in the United States. He graduated from high school and attained a B.A. degree, and then earned his M.D. at Boston University in 1923. Yang then managed a hospital in Honolulu, Hawaii. Before the end of the Second World War, he also served as secretary-general of the Korean YMCA in Hawaii and as president of the Korean Christian Foundation in Honolulu. It was in this period that Yang became acquainted with Syngman Rhee and other leaders of the Korean independence movement who were active in the exile community in the United States. It was because of his acquaintance with Rhee that Yang, a medical doctor, became a professional diplomat.

In March 1951 Rhee appointed Yang as Korean ambassador to the United States. Yang held that post until April 1960 and was thus the longest-serving ROK ambassador to the United States. He played a key role in securing U.S. defense and aid commitments to the ROK, and he also mediated between the Rhee administration and Washington. He became the deputy head of the ROK delegation to the 1954 Geneva Conference, held in accordance with the Korean Armistice Agreement. He also served as chief delegate to the ROK-Japan talks held during the 1950s. In 1960 Yang became ROK ambassador to Brazil as well as to the United States. From 1965 until his retirement in 1972, he served as ROK ambassador-at-large. Yang died in Seoul on 20 October 1975.

—Jinwung Kim

References:

Matray, James I., ed. *Historical Dictionary of the Korean War.* Westport, CT: Greenwood Press, 1991.

Tonga Ilbo. *Taehan Min'guk Yŏkdae Sambu Ch'ongram* [General collections of the Republic of Korea's successive legislative, administrative, and judiciary branch figures]. Seoul: Tonga Ilbo-sa, 1981.

See also: Syngman Rhee.

Yi Chong-ch'an
(1916–1983)

Chief of staff of the Republic of Korea Army (ROKA, South Korea) from June 1951 to July 1952. Born in Seoul on 10 March 1916, Yi Chong-ch'an graduated from the Japanese Military Academy in 1937. During World War II, Yi served as a major in an engineer corps of the Japanese army. In June 1946 Yi returned to Korea but refused an offer from the U.S. military government to lead the Korean Constabulary, predecessor to the ROKA. In June 1949, Yi accepted the post of director of the Information and Education Bureau at the Defense Ministry with the rank of colonel. On 18 June 1950, only a week before the North Korean invasion of South Korea, he was appointed to head the Capital Security Command at

Seoul. In September Yi became commander of the 3d Division on the east coast in the defense of the Pusan perimeter. In the pursuit phase of the breakout from the front along the Naktong River in the second half of September, Yi's troops led all units of both the ROKA and the U.S. Eighth Army in the drive northward. The 3d Division reached the 38th parallel on the last day of September and crossed it the next day.

On 23 June 1951 Yi was promoted to major general to take the place of Chŏng Il-kwŏn as ROKA chief of staff. He worked both to augment the ROKA and to improve its fighting ability. During the time he was chief of staff, and with support from the United States, ROKA forces expanded from about 250,000 to 460,000 men. In 1952, however, Yi found himself in conflict with President Syngman Rhee, who was then attempting to amend the constitution in his favor. On 23 May Rhee placed Pusan under martial law and ordered the arrest of some of his Assembly opponents, charging them with complicity in a Communist conspiracy. Rhee justified martial law as being necessary to counteract Communist guerrilla operations, but his actions were much criticized both from within and outside Korea. Yi tried without success to persuade Rhee to lift the martial law decree, and he refused Rhee's order to pull two combat divisions from the front line to reinforce the weak forces in Pusan. Yi thought this might endanger military operations at the front, and he also believed that the military should not be a tool for politicians. Although Yi enjoyed strong support from his staff, the ROKA in general, and such U.S. generals as Eighth Army commander Lieutenant General James A. Van Fleet and Commander in Chief of the United Nations Command Lieutenant General Mark W. Clark, Rhee dismissed him in July. During the last year of the war, Yi was in the United States to attend the Command and General Staff College, from which he graduated in July 1953. The next month he was appointed president of the ROKA College. On his retirement from the military in May 1960, after Rhee's ouster following the April student uprising, Yi joined the interim government as defense minister. In 1961 he was appointed ambassador to Italy. Held in high regard by the Korean people because of his firm advocacy of a politically neutral military, Yi Chong-ch'an died in Seoul on 10 February 1983.

—To-Woong Chung

References:

Hermes, Walter G. *United States Army in the Korean War: Truce Tent and Fighting Front.* Washington, DC: Office of the Chief of Military History, 1966.

Kang Sŏng-jae. *Ch'am Kunin Yi Chong-ch'an Changgun* [The true soldier: General Yi Chong-ch'an]. Seoul: Tonga Ilbo, 1986.

See also: Chŏng Il-kwŏn; Clark, Mark W.; Syngman Rhee; Van Fleet, James Alward.

Yi Hak-gu
(1920–?)

Senior colonel of Korean People's Army (KPA, North Korea), Thirteenth Division chief of staff, and one of the highest-ranking Communist prisoners of war (POWs). Born in Myŏngch'ŏn, North Hamgyŏng Province, North Korea, Yi Hak-gu was a primary school teacher before joining the army. Before the start of the Korean War, Yi was chief of the planning section of the Operations Planning Bureau in the KPA.

Although his wife and family remained in North Korea, Yi surrendered of his own volition with some of his men in September 1950 after the United Nations Command (UNC) landing at Inch'ŏn, when it was apparent that the Democratic People's Republic of Korea (DPRK, North Korea) had lost the war. There were even reports that Yi had shot and wounded Ch'oe Yongjin, the 13th Division commander. Yi also volunteered to make a broadcast urging KPA troops to stop

fighting. UNC authorities segregated him from other POWs and gave him special treatment in the prison camp where he was held at Pusan.

But the UNC soon determined that the KPA had ordered Yi to surrender. Sent to the POW camp on Kŏje-do, Yi vowed before North Korean officer POWs to devote all of his energies to resisting the "American capitalists," and he soon became popular among the POWs.

Yi, along with other POW Senior Colonels Hong Ch'ŏl and Pak Sang-hyŏn, acted as liaisons with the UNC camp authorities and presented POW demands and complaints. Yi came to Compound 76 on 7 May 1952 and conducted negotiations with the UNC authorities after the POWs had captured Brigadier General Francis T. Dodd.

On 10 June 1952, in Operation BREAKUP, Brigadier General Haydon L. Boatner summoned Yi as the spokesman of Compound 76 and instructed him

Brigadier General George I. Back with KPA Senior Colonel Yi Hak-gu, former chief of staff of the KPA 13th Division, now a POW at POW Camp No. 2, Pusan, January 1951. (National Archives)

to form the POWs in groups of 150 men before moving them to another compound. After prisoners failed to move out, security troops opened fire, resulting in many casualties among the POWs. The camp authorities then segregated Yi from the other POWs and placed him in solitary confinement.

Yi returned to North Korea during Operation BIG SWITCH in 1953, but the DPRK might have then purged him. A 1998 defector from North Korea said that the DPRK officials distrusted the returned POWs and put most of them to work in mines.

—Sunghun Cho

References:

Chu, Yŏng-bok. Nae ga Kyŏkkŭn Chosŏn Chŏnjaeng [The Korean War I experienced]. Seoul: Koryŏwŏn, 1990.

Kim, Sun-ho. "Koje-Do in Complication: An Analysis of the Social and Political Organization of Korean Prisoners of War in UNC POW Camps, 1950–1951." Washington, DC: Human Resources Research Office, George Washington University, 1955.

Office of the Assistant Chief of Staff G 2, Intelligence, HQ, U.S. Army Forces, Far East, Advanced. "Communist Utilization of Prisoners of War," 1953. Unpublished document.

See also: Dodd-Colson Prisoner-of-War Incident; Prisoner-of-War Administration, United Nations Command.

Yi Hyŏng-kŭn
(1920–)

Commander of the 2d Division of the Republic of Korea Army (ROKA, South Korean) at the outbreak of the Korean War. Born in Kongju, South Ch'ungch'ŏng Province, on 2 November 1920, Yi Hyŏng-kŭn graduated from the Japanese Military Academy in 1942 and rose to the rank of captain in the Japanese Army during the Second World War. Upon his return to Korea in 1945, Yi attended the Military English-Language School run by the U.S. military government in Korea. He then served as an officer in the Korean Constabulary, predecessor to the ROKA. Thanks to his high marks at the Language School, Yi received serial number 1 of all commissioned officers in the history of the ROKA. In June 1949 he became the first commanding officer of the Eighth Division, stationed at Kangnŭng, and on 10 June 1950, just before the Korean People's Army (KPA, North Korean) invasion of South Korea, he became commander of the 2d Division at Taejŏn, ninety miles below Seoul. Yi immediately complained to ROKA Chief of Staff Ch'ae Pyŏng-dŏk about the transfer. Yi remarked in his memoirs that shuffling divisional commanders about at such a critical time could not be justified.

On 25 June 1950, after the KPA invasion, Ch'ae ordered Yi to move his division northward and reinforce the 7th Division fighting in the area of Ŭijŏngbu about thirty miles north of Seoul. Ch'ae's plan was for the two divisions to counterattack the next day. This was completely impossible, and Ch'ae should have planned a delaying action, in which the ROKA could have escaped southward. Instead Ch'ae ordered Yi to bring his forces into battle piecemeal as they arrived on the battlefield. Yi objected to this and told Ch'ae he could not launch any counterattack until he had the major part of his division in place. On the spot Ch'ae then threatened Yi with a pistol to his head, removed Yi from his position, and ordered the commander of the 7th Division to assume command of the 2d Division as well as his own. U.S. advisor with the ROKA Chief of Staff Captain James H. Hausman agreed with Yi's stance but could not prevent Ch'ae's precipitous action at this critical time.

Ch'ae, who was largely responsible for the disastrous defeat of the ROKA at the beginning of the war, was subsequently removed from command, and Yi returned to field command. He had charge of the ROKA III Corps in October 1950 and I Corps in January 1952. After the war, in February 1954, he was promoted to full (four-star) general and become the first chairman of the ROK Armed Forces Joint Chiefs of Staff and, in June 1956, chief of staff of the ROKA.

—To-Woong Chung

References:

Appleman, Roy E. South to the Naktong, North to the Yalu. Washington, DC: Office of the Chief of Military History, 1961.

Hausman, James and H. Chung, Il-wha. Hausman's Witness. Seoul: Hankuk Moonwon, 1995.

Yi, Hyŏng-kŭn. Kunbŏn Ibŏn ŭi Oegil Insaeng [Memoirs: the one-road life of the service number one soldier]. Seoul: Chung'ang Ilbo-sa, 1993.

See also: Ch'ae Pyŏng-dŏk.

Yi Kwŏn-mu
(1910–)

Korean People's Army (KPA, North Korean) major general and commander of the 4th Division when the Korean War began, in October 1950 commander of II Corps. Born in Manchuria in 1910 to a Korean refugee family, Yi Kwŏn-mu was a close friend of North Korea's leader Kim Il Sung. During the Second World War he fought with the Chinese Communist Eighth Road Army against the Japanese and after the war remained with his comrades until their victory over the Guomindang was ensured. Soviet officials apparently advised Yi and other North Korean military men, who went under the name of the Korean Volunteer Army, to remain attached to Communist Chinese units even after Korea's liberation from Japanese rule in 1945, on the grounds that this would enable Korean Communists to gain valuable fighting experience that they could later utilize in their own country.

In North Korea's internal politics, Yi was regarded as a member of the China-oriented "Yenan faction," which some believed was not entirely sympathetic to Kim Il Sung. According to some accounts, during the Second World War Yi also spent some time as a lieutenant in the Red Army, and after the Chinese Communist victory he apparently went to the Soviet Union for further military training.

Yi served as the KPA's first chief of staff but was temporarily relieved of his command for reasons that remain unclear. Before the Korean War began, Yi was called back to command the 4th Division, which, along with the 3d Division, was one of the KPA's crack units. The 4th Division spearheaded North Korea's attack on South Korea and, on 28 June 1950, distinguished itself by occupying the capital, winning the name the "Seoul Division."

Yi was one of the commanders of the ultimately unsuccessful North Korean attempt to breach the Naktong River line in August 1950, but the courage and determination he and his men displayed won the respect and admiration even of their opponents. In October 1950 Yi received command of the KPA II Corps.

After the war Yi became commander of the KPA. In 1958 Kim Il Sung purged Yi and numerous other adherents of both North Korea's "Yenan" and "Soviet" political factions.

—*Priscilla Roberts*

References.

Appleman, Roy E. *South to the Naktong, North to the Yalu.* Washington, DC: Office of the Chief of Military History, 1961.

Cumings, Bruce. *The Origins of the Korean War.* 2 vols. Princeton, NJ: Princeton University Press, 1981, 1990.

Fehrenbach, T. R. *This Kind of War. A Study in Unpreparedness.* New York: Macmillan, 1962.

Kim, Joungwoon A. *Divided Korea: The Politics of Development, 1945–1972.* Cambridge, MA: Harvard University Press, 1975.

Leckie, Robert. *Conflict: The History of the Korean War, 1950–1953.* New York: Putnam, 1962.

Matray, James I., ed. *Historical Dictionary of the Korean War.* New York: Greenwood Press, 1991.

See also: Korea, Democratic People's Republic of: Army (Korean People's Army [KPA]).

Yi Pŏm-sŏk (Lee Bum Suk)
(1900–1972)

Prime minister and concurrently defense minister of the Republic of Korea (ROK, South Korea) from 1948 to 1950 before the start of the Korean War. Born on 20 October 1900 in Seoul, Yi went to China and graduated from the Yunnan Military Academy Cavalry School in 1919. The following year he led a dashing attack on Japanese forces at Ch'ŏngsan-ni in northern Manchuria, gaining a reputation as one of the most famous of Korean fighters against Japanese colonial rule. Serving for a time in Jiang Jieshi's (Chiang Kai-shek's) Nationalist Chinese forces, Yi taught at Loyang Military Academy between 1933 and 1936.

In 1940 Yi was one of leaders of the Kwangbok Army established by the Korean Provisional Government with Jiang Jieshi's support to win independence for Korea. The U.S. Office of Strategic Services (OSS) contacted Yi in the summer of 1945 and planned to use his forces in a guerrilla operation in Korea. Although Japan's sudden surrender prevented the plan from being carried out, the OSS assisted Yi by providing him air transport to Korea and then back to China in August 1945.

Although disappointed at the decision by the U.S. Army Military Government in Korea not to recognize the Korean Provisional Government as the legitimate Korean government, Yi returned to Korea in the spring of 1946. He refused to participate in the Constabulary, which he believed included too many who were formerly pro-Japanese and too many Communists. In October 1946 Yi organized the Korean National Youth Corps, which was originally intended to provide the basis for a future Korean army. This organization soon grew into a strong rightist association, which the U.S. military government later came to favor as a means of consolidating its interests in South Korea. In August 1948 Yi became both the first prime minister and first defense minister of the ROK.

Yi resigned as defense minister in February 1949 and as prime minister in April 1950, just before the start of the Korean War. After the North Korean invasion of South Korea on 25 June 1950, President Syngman Rhee requested that Yi provide military advice to the cabinet. Although neither an active-duty military officer nor a cabinet member, he participated in the initial meeting of senior military men on 26 June. This resulted in the controversial decision insisted upon by Defense Minister Sin Sŏng-mo and Army Chief of Staff General Ch'ae Pyŏng-dŏk for ROK Army troops to launch a counterattack against Korean People's Army (KPA, North Korean) forces. Disappointed at the results of that meeting, Yi took the initiative in pushing for an emergency cabinet meeting held at 0200 the next day. Faced with a rapidly deteriorating military situation, Yi urged evacuation of the government from Seoul. He also suggested that after the departure of the government, bridges over the Han River be blown up to deny the KPA an easy crossing.

President Rhee and his staff left Seoul for Taejŏn about 0400, immediately after the cabinet meeting. During the day of 27 June, ROK government officials and their families also evacuated Seoul in two special trains. Learning of this evacuation, members of the Assembly accused the government of deserting the people and decided that the Assembly would not leave Seoul and would instead remain with the people. However, most of them had crossed the Han by that same evening.

Yi vainly sought reappointment to his former positions of prime minister or defense minister or a position as a military commander in the field. But President Rhee, who sought to capitalize on Yi's experiences in waging guerrilla warfare against the Japanese in Manchuria, offered him the task of creating a guerrilla organization in the Chŏlla Provinces, then occupied by the North Koreans. Yi sought a higher post and refused the offer.

In 1951 Yi served as ambassador to Taipei during an eight-month period. Appointed home minister in May 1952, he used police powers to coerce the Assembly in the temporary capital of Pusan into accepting Rhee's demand to amend the constitution from indirect election of the president by the Assembly to direct election by the people. Rhee made Yi a scapegoat for illegal methods used against the Assembly, relieving him of his position as home minister.

Yi ran unsuccessfully for vice-president in the elections of August 1952 and again in 1956. He died in Seoul on 11 May 1972.

—To-Woong Chung

References:

Noble, Harold J. *Embassy at War.* Seattle: University of Washington Press, 1975.

War History Compilation Committee. *Han'guk Chŏnjaeng-sa* [History of the Korean War]. Vol. 2. Seoul: Ministry of National Defense, 1968.

Yi Pŏm-sŏk. *Ch'ulgi Yi Pŏm-sŏk Chajŏn* [The autobiography of Ch'ulgi Yi Pŏm-sŏk]. Seoul: Oekil-sa, 1991.

See also: Jiang Jieshi (Chiang Kai-shek); Syngman Rhee.

Yi Sang-jo
(1915–1996)

Democratic People's Republic of Korea (DPRK, North Korean) deputy chief delegate and later chief delegate to the P'anmunjŏm truce talks. Born in 1915 at Tongnae, South Korea, now a part of Pusan, in 1932 Yi Sang-jo emigrated to China with his parents. After graduating from a Chinese military officers' training school at Nanjing, he fought with the Chinese Communists against the Japanese. Later he became one of the unit commanders of the Korean Volunteer Army supported by the Chinese Communist Party. He returned to northern Korea in 1946 to become deputy chief of the organization department of the [North] Korean Workers' Party and to become an architect of the Korean People's Army (KPA).

At the time of the North Korean invasion of South Korea, Yi was vice-minister of commerce of the DPRK. Immediately he became deputy chief of staff of the KPA. In September 1950, after the Inch'ŏn landing, he secretly traveled to Beijing at the request of Kim Il Sung to appeal for Chinese military intervention in the war to prevent the destruction of the DPRK

and to ask for winter clothing for the KPA. In 1951 he was transferred to director of the Inspection Bureau of the KPA.

During the entire period of the armistice negotiations—10 July 1951 to 27 July 1953—Major General Yi served as a member of the DPRK delegation. According to Joseph C. Goulden, "chunky and often physically filthy, Lee [Yi] had one impressive characteristic: He would permit flies to crawl over his face without brushing them away. Apparently he thought this showed iron self control."

After the cease-fire Yi served as chief of the DPRK component of the Military Armistice Commission. In August 1955, after retiring from the army, he was appointed ambassador to Moscow. In April 1956 he was elected a candidate member of the central committee of the Korean Workers' Party. That same year, encouraged by the de-Stalinization campaign in the Soviet Union, the Chinese exile (Yenan) faction and the Soviet exile faction challenged the personality cult of Kim Il Sung. However, Kim purged the opposition in the so-called Ch'oe Ch'ang-ik incident of 1957, and Yi was one of its victims. Defying a recall order, he sought political asylum in Moscow. Yi never returned to the DPRK from the Soviet Union, subsequently serving as a researcher at a Soviet state-run research institute in Minsk, where he received his doctorate in political science. He resided in Minsk, living on a Soviet pension. In September 1989 Yi visited South Korea and in a press conference stated that Kim Il Sung had initiated the Korean War. He died in Minsk in 1996.

—Hakjoon Kim

References:

Goulden, Joseph C. *Korea: The Untold Story of the War.* New York: Times Books, 1982.

Korea Herald, September 13, 1989.

Korea Times, September 10, 1989.

See also: Korea, Democratic People's Republic of, 1945–1953; Korea, Democratic People's Republic of, 1953 to the Present.

Yi Sŭng-yŏp
(1905–1953)

Minister of Justice of the Democratic People's Republic of Korea (DPRK, North Korea). Born in 1905 on Yŏnghŏng Island near Inch'ŏn, Yi Sŭng-yŏp was educated at Inch'ŏn Commercial School. In 1919 he participated in the March First Movement and was expelled from the school. He joined the Korean Communist Party in September 1925 and was a reporter for the *Chosŏn Ilbo* [Chosŏn Daily], a nationalist daily newspaper. His Communist activities led to his imprisonment in 1931, 1937, and 1940, each time for nearly four years. From 1941 to 1945 he was a board member of the Inch'ŏn District Rice

Distribution Corporation, the post that would become a target for his opponents to label him pro-Japanese.

Immediately after liberation, Yi helped Pak Hŏn-yŏng in reconstructing the Korean Communist Party, and he became a member of its central committee. At the same time he became a member of the Central People's Committee at the Committee for Preparation of Korean Independence. In November 1946, when the major leftist parties merged into a single South Korean Worker's Party, he became a member of its central committee, chairman of its Kyŏnggi Province branch, and editor in chief of the party organ, *Haebang-Ilbo* [Liberation Daily]. In early 1948 Yi fled to North Korea and joined in the establishment of the DPRK, becoming its minister of justice. In June 1949 the North Korean Worker's Party absorbed the South Korean Workers' Party, thus becoming the Korean Workers' Party. Yi became its Politburo member and a secretary of its central committee. In this capacity, he was regarded as second to Pak Hŏn-yŏng in the South Korean Workers' Party, or domestic faction in North Korean politics.

On 28 June 1950, with the start of the North Korean occupation of South Korea, Yi became chairman of the Seoul People's Committee. Six months later he was engaged in the secret cease-fire negotiations of 1951 with the South Korean leftists under U.S. auspices. About this time the power struggle between Kim Il Sung's Kapsan (Manchurian) faction and Pak Hŏn-yŏng's domestic Communist faction became extremely intense. Indicative of Pak's impending demise, Yi was relieved in December 1951 as minister of justice. Five months later, he was ousted from the secretariat and demoted to chairman of the People's Inspection Committee, a post he lost ten months later. In early 1953 he, Pak, and Pak's supporters supposedly attempted a coup d'état against Kim. In April 1953 he was arrested with the other leaders of the South Korean Workers' Party faction. In August 1953 a military court sentenced him to death. Shortly thereafter he was executed as a "state enemy who colluded with the American imperialists" to overthrow the North Korean regime.

—*Hakjoon Kim*

References:
Suh, Dae-Sook. *Kim Il Sung: The North Korean Leader*. New York: Columbia University Press, 1988.
See also: Korea, Republic of: History, 1947–1953; Korea, Republic of: History, 1953 to the Present; March First Movement; Pak Hŏn-yŏng.

Yim, Louise (Yŏng-sin)
(1899–1977)

First Korean United Nations (UN) delegate, from 1945 to 1948. Louise Yim's turbulent life as political activist, educator, and feminist ultimately earned her the sobriquet "Korea's Joan of Arc." Yim's life was spent in causes, some long before they gained popular acceptance. Born into a wealthy family at Kŭmsan in central South Korea on 21 November 1899, Yŏng-sin Yim undertook a hunger strike against her parents at the age of twelve to gain permission to attend high school. Once at school, she refused an arranged marriage. She also formed an underground organization of students against the Japanese, who had annexed Korea in 1910. The student revolutionaries served as messengers and distributed anti-Japanese pamphlets. After the 1 March 1919 nationwide demonstration against Japan, Yim was imprisoned for seven months for her activities.

Ultimately, Yim found her way to the United States, where, on advice of a teacher, she changed her name to Louise. She earned an M.A. in political science from the University of Southern California even as she managed a gasoline station and vegetable market. As her country's first UN delegate from 1945 to 1948, she had helped draft the UN resolution that granted Korean independence. In June 1950 she was visiting New York as a Korean National Assembly member when North Korea invaded the South. Yim embarked on a personal campaign to force the United States to resolve the crisis.

Yim demanded that Republic of Korea (ROK) ambassador to the United States John M. Chang (Chang Myŏn) place the Korean Issue before the UN Security Council. She gave interviews to major media outlets, visited the White House, and lobbied an important friend from her UN days, Secretary-General Trygve Lie. Yim could take some satisfaction in that three days later, on 27 June, a Security Council resolution passed dispatching UN forces to restore the peace in Korea.

In May 1951 ROK president Syngman Rhee called Yim back from her efforts to enlist support for Korea in America. He directed her to organize a women's movement to supplement rear-echelon war efforts. Over the years Yim became a close political ally of and adviser to Syngman Rhee. She established the United Women's Service Association and a refugee school campus in Pusan to continue higher education for youth.

After the recapture of Seoul, Yim returned there and created two publications, the *Women's World Magazine* and the *Commerce Daily*. She then organized the Korean Women's National Defense Association, to assist veterans. Her many other accomplishments include being the first woman cabinet member in Korea (Minister of Commerce and Industry), establishing the first YWCA in Korea, and founding Chung'ang (Central) University in Seoul, where she served as president. Louise Yim died in Seoul on 17 February 1977.

—*Richard A. Garver*

References:

Oliver, Robert T. *Syngman Rhee: The Man Behind the Myth.* New York: Dodd, Mead, 1955.

Yim, Louise. *My Forty Year Fight for Korea.* Seoul: Chung-ang University, 1951.

See also: Lie, Trygve; Syngman Rhee.

Yŏngch'ŏn, Battle of
(2–12 September 1950)

Battle in early September 1950 along the Pusan perimeter between United Nations Command (UNC) and Korean People's Army (KPA, North Korean) forces. Having been forced steadily back by KPA forces in the weeks following the 25 June 1950 invasion, UNC forces were by the end of August fighting to hold the Pusan perimeter around the port city of Pusan. Lieutenant General Walton H. Walker's UN forces there faced the most perilous crisis of the war. Following initial defeats around the edge of the perimeter in late August, the KPA regrouped for a final concerted push. Its ultimate military objective was to collapse the perimeter, capturing the UNC forces or driving them into the sea and thereby reunifying the entire peninsula under the North Korean government.

Crucial to the defense of the perimeter was the east-west road running across the perimeter's northern end. This linked the eastern coastal port of P'ohang with the interior city of Taegu and ran through the town of Yŏngch'ŏn, which lay roughly midway between them. The battle in early September for control of Yŏngch'ŏn, which also had roads running from there to the south, constituted one of at least five major battles around the perimeter that occurred more or less simultaneously.

On 2 September a two-division KPA offensive drove into the Republic of Korea Army (ROKA, South Korean) lines located between twenty and thirty-five miles north of Yŏngch'ŏn. The KPA's 8th Division attacked toward Yŏngch'ŏn from the northwest, while the 15th Division came from the northeast. Yŏngch'ŏn thus became the apex of a triangle pointing southward.

In ten days' heavy fighting, the KPA 8th Division never reached closer than about twelve miles from the road junction. Instead, the ROKA 6th Division fought the KPA to a standstill near the mountainous locality known as Hwajŏng. Using artillery and close air support, the South Koreans virtually destroyed the attackers.

The second prong of the KPA advance by the 15th Division made rapid initial progress, as the attackers fought their way into, and in some cases south of, Yŏngch'ŏn. They also severed the vital roadway linking P'ohang and Taegu and established roadblocks to the southeast. While ROKA 8th Division defenders suffered initial disorder in their retreat—one regiment broke and ran—they rallied beginning about 8 September. Reinforced by Korea Military Advisory Group (KMAG) cadre and two hastily deployed regiments from other ROKA divisions, the ROKA 8th Division defeated the North Koreans in fierce fighting southeast of Yŏngch'ŏn. Important in this was the decimation of North Korean divisional artillery that had advanced near the town without supporting infantry and then found itself caught in counterbattery fire.

By 12 September the KPA 15th Division was in full retreat. In the process it abandoned significant quantities of equipment, including large numbers of small arms, several vehicles, and at least one self-propelled gun. The KPA also left behind large numbers of killed and wounded. At about the same time the breach in the South Korean lines was sealed, as other ROKA troops from farther east reestablished contact with 8th Division.

This ROKA victory, which came despite a relative weakness in organic artillery, helped preserve the integrity of the northern end of the perimeter at a vital point. Close air support provided by the U.S. Air Force, U.S. Navy, and U.S. Marine Corps also contributed to the South Korean success, even though the Americans' early efforts in the air frequently constituted operational improvisations. The Battle of Yŏngch'ŏn helped make possible the UNC breakout from the perimeter after the 15 September Inch'ŏn landing.

—*D. R. Dorondo*

References:

Appleman, Roy E. *South to the Naktong, North to the Yalu.* Washington, DC: Office of the Chief of Military History, 1961.

Ent, Uzal W. *Fighting on the Brink: Defense of the Pusan Perimeter.* Paducah, KY: Turner, 1996.

Millett, Allan R. "Korea, 1950–1953." In *Case Studies in the Development of Close Air Support,* edited by Benjamin Franklin Cooling. Washington, DC: Office of Air Force History, 1990.

Mossman, Billy C. *U.S. Army in the Korean War: Ebb and Flow, November 1950–July 1951.* Washington, DC: U.S. Army Center of Military History, 1990.

See also: Pusan Perimeter and Breakout; Walker, Walton Harris.

Yŏsu-Sunch'ŏn Rebellion
(October 1948)

Rebellion involving the 14th Regiment of the Republic of Korea Army (South Korean). The 14th came into being on 14 May 1948, based on a battalion detached from the 4th Regiment stationed in Kwangju. However, by 19 October 1948, the regiment had become embroiled in rebellion. At that time one of the main strategies of the South Korean Worker's Party (SKWP) was to infiltrate and influence military units. The 14th Regiment was one such target. This was aided by the fact that the original battalion commander, Captain An Yŏng-gil, was a leftist supporter. The regiment was split into three factions. Its overall commander, Colonel O Tong-gi, sympathized with the nationalists and belonged to the Korean Independence Party, which opposed the establishment of a separate South Korean government. The other two factions included officers and regular soldiers who were effectively controlled by the SKWP.

The SKWP in South Chŏlla placed representatives from its Military Direction Section in the 14th Regiment. They were quite successful in influencing recruitment of leftist supporters recommended by the SKWP and blocking right-wing conscripts. They even managed to eliminate many right-wing supporters who had previously been recruited. As a result, the majority of the regiment became either leftist activists or sympathizers. The seeds of rebellion had been sown.

The Cheju Island rebellion was also under way at this time, and on 19 October 1948, army headquarters ordered the 1st Battalion of the 14th Regiment to leave for Cheju to help quell the riots. Its departure was scheduled for 2100 that day; however, at 2000 Sergeant-Major Chi Ch'ang-su, a lower-ranking SKWP activist in the regiment, spontaneously ordered 40 soldiers to occupy the armory and ammunition locker. Shortly thereafter he assembled the 1st Battalion, along with soldiers from the other two battalions, and proceeded to incite them to reject their reassignment to Cheju Island, overthrow the police authorities, and establish themselves as a people's army for national unification.

Some 3,000 soldiers decided to follow Chi. They moved into the city of Yŏsu, where they were joined by another 600 leftist supporters and students. They then attacked police stations, killing many police officers, and stormed the city government buildings. By dawn on 20 October the rebels had taken control of Yŏsu, instituted a People's Committee, and were summarily executing right-wing activists.

On the morning of 20 October, between 500 and 600 rebel troops advanced on Sunch'ŏn to join forces with two other companies of the 14th Regiment already stationed there. By early afternoon Sunch'ŏn was controlled by the rebel forces. Their next maneuver was to proceed in three directions toward Hakgu-ri to the northwest, Kwangyang to the east, and Pŏlgyo to the southwest. En route they attacked police stations, killed police officers, and executed right-wing activists.

To deal with this threat, on 21 October the South Korean government established a combat command in Kwangju with seven battalions and declared a state of martial law in the region. Government forces planned to encircle the Yŏsu Peninsula to entrap the rebel troops and cut off any escape to the mountains in the

northeast. However, the operation failed because of inefficient coordination. The commander of the 15th Regiment was apathetic in his approach to the operation and ultimately surrendered to the rebel troops without resistance, and one company of soldiers even joined the rebels. In addition, unrealistic government pressure forced troops to advance in columns rather than encircling the peninsula; consequently, many rebels were able to escape into the mountains and continue their fight by means of guerilla warfare.

The overall cost in human lives from the rebellion was substantial. A journal record from 9 November 1948 fixed the number of deaths in South Chŏlla at 2,533, with a further 883 seriously wounded. However, the number of victims continued to mount from the persistent guerilla warfare and quest for bloody revenge.

Officially, the SKWP neither planned nor authorized the rebellion. Apparently, the uprising was rather a spontaneous event initiated from within the 14th Regiment itself. Sergeant-Major Chi decided on his own to begin the rebellion, disobeying instructions to desist from a superior SKWP officer, Lieutenant Kim Chi-hoe. However, once the rebellion was under way, the SKWP assumed the credit, and this event then paved the way for the spread of guerrilla warfare throughout most of South Korea during 1949.

The rebellion forced South Korean authorities to accelerate their efforts to eliminate SKWP influence in the army. By July 1949 more than 4,700 officers and soldiers had been dismissed. Thereafter, there were no further military revolts.

—*Man-ho Heo*

References:

Cumings, Bruce. *The Origins of the Korean War.* Vol. 2, *The Roaring of the Cataract, 1947–1950.* Princeton, NJ: Princeton University Press, 1990.

Headquarters, U.S. Armed Forces in Korea (USAFIK). *History of the United States Armed Forces in Korea* (HUSAFIK). Vols. 1–3. Seoul: Dolbegye, 1989.

———. *G-2 Periodic Report.* Vols. 1–7. Ch'unch'ŏn, ROK: The Institute of Asian Culture Studies, Hallym University, 1988–1989.

Kim, Chŏm-gon. *Han'guk Chŏnjaeng kwa Rodongdang Chŏnryak* [The Korean War and the strategy of the Korean Worker's Party]. Seoul: Pakyŏngsa, 1983.

See also: Cheju-do Rebellion.

Younger, Kenneth
(1908–1976)

Minister of state at the British Foreign Office from 1946 to 1951. Born on 15 December 1908, at Colton, Dunfermline, in Scotland, Kenneth Younger was educated at New College, Oxford, where he obtained third-class honors in philosophy, politics, and economics in 1930. As an Oxford undergraduate he also broke with his family's Conservative Party allegiance to join the Labour Party. In 1932 he was called to the bar, practicing law until 1939. During World War II he served in the Intelligence Corps, eventually holding the rank of major under Field Marshal Bernard Montgomery.

Younger won a parliamentary seat in 1945 and was quickly regarded as one of the most promising younger Labour members. Within a year he was appointed minister of state in the Foreign Office, deputy to Foreign Secretary Ernest Bevin, whose deteriorating health meant that much responsibility fell on Younger's shoulders. The two men were described as resembling "an old polar bear attended by a lively cub," and Bevin quickly came to rely heavily upon Younger's outstanding efficiency. Some senior Foreign Office figures, by contrast, thought him a "conceited young man" and were irritated by his readiness to accept that Britain's international position and world stature had altered and its foreign policies should be adapted to suit changing circumstances.

During the Korean War, Younger initiated the discussion of several important issues that badly needed consideration by both the Foreign Office and the cabinet. In September 1950 he was the first to speculate as to whether United Nations (UN) forces should cross the 38th parallel if and when the Inch'ŏn landing succeeded, a question that senior Foreign Office officials had not considered.

Younger was the leader of the British delegation at the UN that argued strongly in support of the resolution of 7 October 1950 authorizing the offensive beyond the parallel. Younger also raised the difficult problem of—in the event that the People's Republic of China (PRC, Communist China) and the United States should go to war over Taiwan—whether Britain should support its U.S. ally. The Foreign Office reluctantly concluded that Britain could not remain aloof from such a conflict and would be forced to assist the United States against China. Bevin, at that time ill in hospital, agreed but declined to bring the matter up in cabinet, partly because he feared that the issue might prove divisive and partly to preserve his freedom of action. To Younger's surprise, when he brought the subject up with Minister of Labour Aneurin Bevan, the latter concurred that, given Britain's global international alliance with the United States, the country had no choice but to join forces with its patron in the event of such a war.

In January 1951, however, Younger urged Prime Minister Clement Attlee to withstand American pressure for a limited war against Communist China involving the mainland's own territory, the imposition of economic sanctions, and the passage of a UN resolution condemning the PRC as an aggressor. While Attlee and Bevin believed that the need to retain American goodwill was ultimately their highest priority, they followed Younger's advice insofar as was possible, attempting to restrain U.S. condemnation of China and the imposition of sanctions, successfully avoiding the war's extension to Chinese territory, and urging the opening of negotiations with the Communist forces with the objective of reaching a compromise peace settlement.

Younger lost his Foreign Office post in the general election of 1951 but retained his seat in Parliament. Finding the opposition benches somewhat unrewarding and plagued by poor health, in 1959 he left Parliament to become director of the Royal Institute of International Affairs, where he constantly urged that Britain should adjust to the loss of superpower status by placing more emphasis on its role in the UN and regional and world cooperative organizations. In addition, Younger served on numerous government and private commissions, committees, and organizations. He died in London on 19 May 1976.

—*Priscilla Roberts*

References:

Bullock, Alan. *Ernest Bevin: Foreign Secretary, 1945–1951.* New York: W. W. Norton, 1983.

Butler, Rohan, and M. E. Pelly, eds. *Documents on British Policy Overseas. Series II,* Vol. 4, *Korea, 1950–1951.* London: Her Majesty's Stationery Office, 1995.

Grimond, J. "Younger, Sir Kenneth Gilmour." In *Dictionary of National Biography 1979–1980,* edited by Lord Blake and C. S. Nicholls. Oxford: Oxford University Press, 1986.

Lowe, Peter. *Containing the Cold War in East Asia: British Policies toward Japan, China and Korea, 1948–1953.* Manchester: Manchester University Press, 1997.

MacDonald, Callum A. *Britain and the Korean War.* Oxford: Blackwell, 1990.

See also: Attlee, Clement R.; Bevan, Aneurin; Bevin, Ernest; Morrison, Herbert S.; United Kingdom (UK).

Yu Jae-hŭung
(1921–)

Republic of Korea Army (ROKA, South Korean) general and commander of the 7th Division at the beginning of the Korean War. Born in Japan on 3 August 1921, Yu Jae-hŭung graduated from the Japanese Military Academy in 1940. His father, Yu Sŭng-yŏl, had graduated from the same school in 1914. At the time of the liberation of Korea in 1945, both Yu and his father were officers (major and colonel, respectively) in the Japanese army.

Upon his return to Korea after the end of Japanese colonial rule in 1945, Yu entered the U.S. military government's Military English-Language School in Seoul, as did many other Koreans who had served as officers in the Japanese Army. From January 1946 until August 1948, Yu served as a high-ranking officer in the Korean Constabulary and contributed much to the creation of the ROKA. After establishment of the ROK in August 1948, he was advanced to brigadier general; in May 1949 he became the commander of the 6th ROKA Division at Ch'unch'ŏn. In January 1950 he became commander of the 2d Division at Taejŏn, and the next May he commanded the 7th Division at Ŭijŏngbu. Undoubtedly such frequent change of commanding officers affected the combat readiness of the ROKA at the beginning of the Korean War.

The Ŭijŏngbu corridor, only thirty miles north of Seoul, was the site of the principal Korean People's Army (KPA, North Korean) attack on 25 June 1950. Caught by surprise by the KPA 3d and 4th Divisions, and supported by tanks of the 105th Armored Brigade, Yu's 7th Division suffered heavily. Nonetheless, in the morning of 26 June Yu counterattacked and achieved a short-term success. Heavily outnumbered, his troops could not hold off the KPA advance for long. ROKA Chief of Staff Ch'ae Pyŏng-dŏk's effort to bring up reserves and to counterattack proved inept and futile.

Promoted to command the ROKA II Corps in July 1950, Yu showed competent and aggressive leadership in the September Battle of Yŏngch'ŏn and in the United Nations offensive across the 38th parallel during October and November. At Yŏngch'ŏn, where the KPA hoped to break through the Pusan perimeter, Yu took a leading role in the destruction of the KPA 15th Division; and it was his 6th Division that first reached the Yalu River, on 26 October. Most in the ROKA regarded Yu as their most knowledgeable general.

After the Chinese People's Volunteer Army (CPVA, Chinese Communist) entered the war, Yu and the units under his command encountered serious problems. In the first phase of the Chinese military intervention, from late October to early November, the CPVA hit Yu's corps at Onchŏng and Hŭich'ŏn in the Ch'ŏngch'ŏn River Valley on the right flank of the U.S. Eighth Army. The Chinese second-phase offensive at the end of November again struck the ROKA II Corps, but this much stronger attack brought its collapse and the disastrous defeat of the U.S. Eighth Army.

In January 1951, Yu became commander and concurrently deputy chief of staff of the ROKA. Then in May 1951 during the Chinese sixth offensive, Yu's III Corps at Hyŏn-ni suffered one of the worst defeats during the war. Facing a situation in which the corps would have been cut off, Yu ordered the 9th Division to withdraw, covered by the 3d Division. But the Chinese succeeded in cutting off both divisions, the men of which simply fled in disorder into the hills, abandoning their equipment. This defeat was largely attributable to the fact that Yu and the two division commanders were not getting along with one another.

Eighth Army commander Lieutenant General James A. Van Fleet pointed out at the time that the most pressing problem in the ROKA at the time was development of leadership qualities.

After the war, Yu attended and graduated from the U.S. Army Command and General Staff College in 1954. He then served as ROKA deputy chief of staff in 1956, chairman of the Joint Chiefs of Staff in 1957, and commander of First Army in 1959. Retiring from the army in 1960, he became minister of defense in 1971.

—To-Woong Chung

References:

Appleman, Roy E. *South to the Naktong, North to the Yalu.* Washington, DC: Office of the Chief of Military History, 1961.

Mossman, Billy C. *U.S. Army in the Korean War: Ebb and Flow, November 1950–July 1951.* Washington, DC: U.S. Army Center of Military History, 1990.

Yu, Jae-hŭng. *Kyŏkdong ŭi Sewŏl* [The turbulent years: memoirs]. Seoul: Ŭlyu Munhwa-sa, 1994.

See also: Ch'ae Pyŏng-dŏk; 38th parallel, Decision to Cross; Van Fleet, James Alward; Yŏngch'ŏn, Battle of.

Yun Ch'i-yŏng
(1898–1996)

Republic of Korea (ROK, South Korean) conservative politician. Born to an important family in Seoul on 10 February 1898, Yun Ch'i-yŏng was educated in Japan (at Waseda University) and in the United States (at the University of Hawaii and at Princeton, Columbia, George Washington, and American Universities). After 1923 he worked for Syngman Rhee in the United States, but he returned to Korea in 1937. After Korea's liberation at the end of World War II, Yun, Song Chin-u, and Kim Sŏng-su formed the Korean Democratic Party, a conservative, right-wing political party.

Yun was one of ROK president Syngman Rhee's most trusted advisers. From August 1945 until the outbreak of the Korean War, Yun was chief secretary to Rhee. After the establishment of the ROK, Yun became vice speaker of the National Assembly and the first ROK minister of home affairs. During the early years of the ROK, Yun was consistent in his activities as a staunch anti-Communist conservative politician.

In August 1950 Yun was appointed minister to France. He never assumed the post, as he was a member of the ROK delegation to the United Nations. He returned to Korea in January 1951. The next year he was elected to the National Assembly, defeating former minister of home affairs and chief opponent of Rhee Cho Pyŏng-ok.

Yun was an interesting figure, noteworthy as the only prominent conservative politician in South Korea who argued that the Korean War resulted from a U.S. attempt to test the Soviet Union's Far Eastern policy by using South Korea as bait. This position, that the Korean War was provoked by the United States, was also held by Louise Yim (Yim Yŏng-sin), first ROK minister of commercial affairs and a staunch Rhee supporter.

After Park Chung Hee's May 1961 military coup d'etat, Yun helped found the Democratic Republican Party, the government party, and he served as chairman of its executive committee. He was Park's chief campaign manager in the 1963 presidential election and, after Park's victory, he became mayor of Seoul. Yun remained a loyal Park supporter and a leading member of the National Assembly. He died in Seoul on 9 February 1996.

—*Jinwung Kim*

References:

Matray, James I., ed. *Historical Dictionary of the Korean War.* Westport, CT: Greenwood Press, 1991.

Taehan Min'guk Kuksa Och'ŏn Nyŏnsa P'yŏnch'an Wiwŏn-hoe. *Taehan Min'guk Hyŏndae Immulsa Taejŏn* [The great contemporary biographical dictionary of the Republic of Korea]. Seoul: Taehan Min'guk Kuksa Och'ŏn Nyŏnsa P'yŏnch'an Wiwŏn-hoe, 1998.

See also: Syngman Rhee; Yim, Louise (Yŏng-sin).

Z

Zhang Hanfu (Chang Han-Fu) (1905–1972)

Vice–foreign minister of the People's Republic of China (PRC, Communist China) during the Korean War. Born in 1905, Zhang Hanfu studied in the United States, where he became a Communist and acquired a good command of English, which was to stand him in good stead in his years in the foreign ministry after the establishment of the PRC.

On his return to China, Zhang Hanfu immediately joined the Chinese Communist Party. From 1931 he assumed positions of leadership, first in the Guangdong and then in the Jiangsu party machineries. While working in Jiangsu, in the mid-1930s he was arrested by Guomindang authorities, who did nothing more than imprison him in Suzhou.

After his release from prison, Zhang embarked on the first of the two main facets of his career—journalism in support of the Communist position. This phase lasted until the end of 1948. During this period of some fifteen years Zhang lived and wrote prolifically in Shanghai, Wuhan, Chongqing, and Hong Kong. He published numerous articles in many of the well-known journals and newspapers of the time, the more important examples of which were *Dushu Shenghuo*, *Qunzhong*, and *Xinhua Ribao*. In fact, Zhang was instrumental in starting or sustaining the last two named publications. He wrote under aliases, according to the political necessity of those days. Even Zhang Hanfu was not his real name.

Zhang was in Hong Kong for two years from the beginning of the civil war, playing a pivotal role in Communist propaganda work in the British colony. It was after his return to China at the end of 1948 that he began to shift to the second important aspect of his career, namely foreign affairs. The beginning of the change of course can be traced to fall 1944, when he helped Dong Biwu prepare for the founding conference of the United Nations, which took place the next year. Zhang attended the conference as Dong Biwu's assistant.

During the Chinese Civil War (1946–1949), Zhang was in Hong Kong and Shanghai. After the January 1949 Communist victory in Tianjin, Zhang took charge of its foreign affairs; and he assumed the same post in Shanghai after its liberation in May 1949.

Zhang's performance in Tianjin and Shanghai, though brief, must have been impressive enough, as he was then transferred to Beijing, where he was appointed as a vice-minister in the foreign ministry of the newly established Communist regime, working under Foreign Minister Zhou Enlai.

During the Korean War, Zhang Hanfu was one of the key people dealing with the diplomatic aspects of the war. However, as expected, his work and contribution in the foreign ministry could hardly attract attention, the bulk of which was naturally drawn to the charismatic foreign minister. This situation persisted even after Chen Yi replaced Zhou Enlai as foreign minister early in 1958, in that Chen also was overshadowed by Zhou, who retained considerable influence in the ministry.

Until the mid-1960s Zhang Hanfu traveled widely to many parts of Asia, the Middle East, and Europe as deputy to either Zhou Enlai or Chen Yi and participated in a number of important conferences and events. With the onslaught of the Cultural Revolution, Zhang, as with so many others who had long supported the Communist cause, suddenly found himself the target of persecution. He died a painful and humiliating death in prison in 1972.

—*Chan Lau Kit Ching*

References:

Klein, Donald W., and Anne B. Clark, eds. *Biographic Dictionary of Chinese Communism, 1921–1965*. Cambridge, MA: Harvard University Press, 1971.

Matray, James I., ed. *Historical Dictionary of the Korean War*. Westport, CT: Greenwood Press, 1991.

Xia, Yan. "'Zhang Han-fu Wenji' daixu." In *Zhang Hanfu Wenji*. n.p.: Jiangsu Renmin Chubanshe, 1986: 1–6.

Xu Dixin, "Zui jiannanchu xian qicai—I Zhang Hanfu Tongzhi." In *Zhang Hanfu Wenji*. n.p.: Jiangsu Renmin Chubanshe, 1986: 7–11.

See also: China, People's Republic of; Zhou Enlai.

Zhang Tingfa (Tsang Ting-fa) (1918–)

General and deputy commander of the Chinese People's Volunteer Army (Communist Chinese) Eleventh Army during the Korean War. Promoted to commander of the People's Liberation Army (PLA) Air Forces in 1977, he was a member of the powerful Political Bureau of the Chinese Communist Party Central Committee from 1978 to 1985. Born in Sha Xian, Fujian Province, on 9 April 1918, Zhang joined the Red Army in 1933. After participating in the Long March, between 1935 and 1942 he was on the staff of the 129th Division in the Eighth Route Army. In 1942 he was promoted to director of operations in the Taihang Military District.

When the Korean War began, Zhang's Eleventh Army was in Sichuan Province, Southwest China. In early 1951 the Eleventh Army moved to north China and one of its divisions, the 31st, was transferred to the Twelfth Army, which entered Korea in early 1951. The remainder of the Eleventh Army, the 32d and 33d Divisions, was combined with the 182d Division of the Sixty-first Army to form the reorganized Eleventh Army and entered Korea in the mid-1951. Zhang's Eleventh Army was in Korea until October 1952, when it returned home to transfer to the new PLA Air Forces' Fifth Army in Zhejiang Province. Upon returning to China, Zhang was promoted to deputy chief of staff of the PLA Air Forces and later became chief of staff of the PLA Air Forces.

Zhang was promoted to major general in 1955. After seven years as commander of the PLA Air Forces (1977–1985), he retired in 1985.

—*Richard Weixing Hu*

References:

Guo Huaruo et al. *Jiefangjun Junshi Dacidian* [Dictionary of CPLA military history]. Changchun: Jilin People's Press, 1993.

Wu Rugao et al. *Zhongguo Junshi Renwu Dacidian* [Dictionary of Chinese military figures]. Beijing: Xinhua Chubanshe, 1989.

Zhongguo Junshi Dabaike Quanshu [The Chinese military encyclopedia]. Military History, Vol. 3. Beijing: Military Science Press, 1997.

Zhongguo Renmin Jiefangjun Jiangshui Minlu [Brief biographies of CPLA marshals and generals]. Vols. 1–3. Beijing: PLA Press, 1986, 1987.

See also: China, People's Republic of: Air Force.

Zhou Enlai
(1898–1976)

Senior Communist Party leader and prime minister of the People's Republic of China (PRC). In a career spanning nearly six turbulent decades, Zhou Enlai became known as the "indispensable man" of China's Communist regime. A superhuman administrator, master diplomat, and supremely skilled political tactician, Zhou was a key party leader during the Communists' long struggle for power. Named China's prime minister on the day the People's Republic was founded, he remained in that post for more than twenty-six years until his death. For the first eight years of that period, he served concurrently as foreign minister as well.

Born 5 March 1898 in Jiangsu Province, though his family's ancestral home was in Zhejiang on the East China Sea coast south of the Yangtze River, Zhou Enlai as a student was known as a talented actor in school plays. At nineteen he went to Japan to study but returned two years later to join the ferment of the May Fourth Movement, named for the date of massive student demonstrations in 1919 calling for modernization and democracy (the same slogans would be revived seventy years later by student protesters in Tiananmen Square).

After being imprisoned briefly for his political activities, Zhou left China in late 1920 for France, where he helped organize a branch of the brand-new Chinese Communist Party. Returning after four years abroad, Zhou embarked on his revolutionary career, participating in the Shanghai uprising, the Long March, the guerrilla war against Japan, and the civil war against Jiang Jieshi's (Chiang Kai-shek's) Nationalists. In his early years in the party, Zhou outranked Mao Zedong in the leadership. But when Mao took command during the Long March, Zhou willingly assumed a subordinate role in their partnership. For more than forty years he would be the movement's supreme survivor—the only one of Mao's inner circle never to fall victim to the incessant purges, intrigues, power struggles, and policy shifts that characterized Mao's long reign.

When the Korean War broke out in June 1950, less than a year after the PRC was founded, Zhou played a key role in carrying out Mao's decisions and in orchestrating Chinese diplomacy. In early July, Zhou presided over the initial deliberations that led to the creation of the Northeast Border Defense Army and the Chinese military buildup in the border region. Thereafter, Zhou supervised the military preparations, chairing a series of crucial meetings to decide on the structure, strategy, deployment, and logistical needs of the border force.

Meanwhile Zhou was also responsible for managing China's relations with both its allies and prospective enemy. Zhou personally instructed Indian ambassador in Beijing K. M. Panikkar to warn the United States that China would enter the war if U.S. forces crossed the thirty-eighth parallel into North Korea; it was also Zhou who led a Chinese delegation to Moscow to redeem a Soviet promise of military support, including air strikes, for Chinese troops in Korea. However, neither move achieved the desired result. U.S. leaders dismissed Zhou's warning as a bluff; in Moscow, Josef Stalin reneged on providing air cover.

As the Korean peace negotiations entered their climactic phase following Stalin's death on 5 March 1953, it was Zhou, again, who signaled that China was ready to end the conflict. Shortly after returning from Stalin's funeral, Zhou offered a compromise on the prisoner-of-war (POW) issue that had knotted the truce talks for many months. Though the wording was oblique, Zhou in effect withdrew Beijing's demand for the forced repatriation of Chinese POWs who did not wish to return to China. The concession cleared the way for the signing of the Korean armistice four months later.

The following year Zhou headed China's delegation to the 1954 Geneva negotiations on settling the French

Indo-China War. Soon after arriving, he unexpectedly encountered U.S. Secretary of State John Foster Dulles in an anteroom. Zhou offered his hand, but Dulles coldly turned his back and walked out of the room. The incident symbolized the deep-frozen U.S.-Chinese hostility that would endure for nearly two more decades. Despite Dulles' snub, Zhou became the crucial conciliator in the Geneva talks, personally persuading the Vietnamese Communist leader Ho Chi Minh to make substantial concessions in return for a settlement.

During his long tenure as prime minister, working in enigmatic partnership with the mercurial Mao, Zhou used his extraordinary organizational talent to keep China's vast administrative and economic bureaucracy functioning through the constant upheavals of Mao's policies. As the party's most skilled, supple, and polished negotiator, he continued to serve as China's chief emissary to the outside world, seldom failing to charm even the most wary foreigners. He also played a crucial role as mediator and conciliator in disputes inside the party leadership.

In 1971 Zhou received President Richard Nixon's emissary Henry Kissinger in Beijing, paving the way for the restoration of U.S.-Chinese relations and erasing, at last, the memory of Dulles' rebuff in Geneva seventeen years before.

Zhou died on 9 January 1976, leaving behind a widely accepted image of a wise, flexible, humane statesman.

—Arnold R. Isaacs

References:

Han Suyin. *Eldest Son: Zhou Enlai and the Making of Modern China, 1898–1976.* New York: Hill & Wang, 1994.

Wilson, Dick. *Zhou Enlai: A Biography.* New York: Viking Press, 1984.

See also: China, People's Republic of; Dulles, John Foster; Mao Zedong; Panikkar, Sardar K. M.

Zinchenko, Constantin
(1909–)

Assistant secretary-general at the United Nations (UN) Department of Political and Security Affairs during the Korean War. Born in Ukraine in 1909, Zinchenko graduated from the Mining Academy in Moscow in 1931. He joined the Soviet Foreign Ministry in 1940, and in 1942 was counselor at the embassy in London. He returned to Moscow at the end of the war, and in June 1948 he became first counselor and secretary-general of the Soviet Union to the UN. In April 1949 he joined the UN Secretariat.

At the UN, Zinchenko was an enigmatic presence in discussions concerning the Korean War. He often attempted to influence negotiations between Communist and non-Communist delegations, usually through unofficial gatherings and informal receptions. At first U.S. diplomats took seriously his usefulness as a possible conduit for Soviet intentions; over time, as his suggestions proved to be seemingly unconnected to any Communist authority, he became less and less credible.

In June 1950, as the UN voted on intervening in the Korean conflict, Zinchenko arranged a luncheon at a New York restaurant for Secretary-General Trygve Lie and nine of the eleven Security Council members, including Soviet ambassador Jakob Malik. The USSR was then boycotting the Security Council, and discussion revolved around Lie's attempts to convince Malik to return and U.S. diplomat Ernest Gross's maneuvering to prevent it. As it worked out, Malik did not return for the crucial vote on intervention.

On 20 August 1950, Zinchenko received a copy of the secretary-general's memorandum concerning the legal basis for UN resolutions passed earlier in the summer that had authorized intervention. Sensing the potential difficulties of Zinchenko's position, Lie created a special committee within his office to deal with Korean matters, thereby avoiding Zinchenko's post of assistant secretary-general.

In April 1951, at a UN reception at Lake Success, New York, Zinchenko assembled an informal group of diplomats, including Gross, to discuss a note recently received from the Democratic People's Republic of Korea (North Korea) suggesting withdrawal of all foreign forces from Korea. Zinchenko insisted that the North Korean request be taken seriously and, because of his involvement, many Western diplomats believed that the USSR had orchestrated a proposal that could lead to substantive negotiations. This proved illusory, however, as the Communists soon launched a spring offensive.

Early in 1952 Zinchenko again became a player, this time in the matter of repatriation of prisoners of war (POWs). His idea that a cease-fire could be initiated without dealing with this very divisive issue was proposed to an Israeli diplomat in New York, who then passed it on to the Americans and British. It was hinted that an armistice could be secured on the basis of items already settled and that it would be activated when the POW problem was finally resolved. Nothing came of this, however.

Finally, in June 1952, Zinchenko once again sought out Gross. The issue revolved around repatriation of POWs and possible Chinese compromise on the topic. Zinchenko indicated to Gross that the Soviet Union might be willing to agree to de facto voluntary repatriation as long as the UN agreed to the principle of general repatriation. Before Gross could meet with him again, however, Zinchenko had left New York on 9 July 1952 for "vacation" in the Soviet Union. He never returned to New York. In September, after failing to reappear as scheduled, Soviet authorities informed UN officials that he was ill.

On 26 May 1953, UN Secretary-General Dag Hammarskjöld accepted Zinchenko's resignation from a term that was not to have expired until 1 February 1954. Three years after he left New York, Zinchenko surfaced as a staff member on the English-language journal *Moscow News*. There were rumors that he had spent the intervening time in prison and that his Western lifestyle and ability to mix in New York society may have contributed to his downfall. It is not clear even now that he ever represented official Soviet views on the Korean War. It seems likely that he generally exceeded his instructions and simply offered his own opinions on the war, a practice that ultimately undercut his bureaucratic position.

—Eric Jarvis

References:

Bailey, Sydney D. *The Korean Armistice*. London: Macmillan, 1992.

Detzer, David. *Thunder of the Captains: The Short Summer of 1950*. New York: Cromwell, 1977.

Kaufman, Burton I. *The Korean War: Challenges in Crisis, Credibility and Command*. Philadelphia: Temple University Press, 1986.

Stueck, William W., Jr. *The Korean War: An International History*. Princeton, NJ: Princeton University Press, 1995.

Yearbook of the United Nations, 1951,1952. New York: United Nations Department of Public Information, 1952, 1953.

See also: Cease-Fire Negotiations; Gross, Ernest Arnold; Lie, Trygve; Malik, Jacob (Iakov) Alexandrovich; Repatriation, Voluntary; Soviet Security Council Boycott; Union of Soviet Socialist Republics.

Zorin, Valerian Alexandrovitch
(1902–1986)

Soviet diplomat and permanent Soviet representative to the United Nations (UN) in the last year of the Korean War, 1952–1953. Born on 13 January 1902, in Novocherkassk, Rostov, Valerian Alexandrovitch Zorin was educated at the High Communist Institute of Education. From 1922 until 1932 he held an important post in the Central Committee of Komsomol; from 1933 to 1935 he pursued postgraduate education at the High Communist Institute of Education. In 1941 he transferred to the Ministry of Foreign Affairs, where until 1942 he was assistant general secretary. He then headed its European Department. In 1945 he became the first post–World War II Soviet ambassador to the Republic of Czechoslovakia.

In 1947 Zorin became deputy minister of foreign affairs, a post he held until 1955 and again during 1956 and 1957. He was the Soviet delegate to the UN Economic Commission on Europe, and used that position to denounce U.S. aid to Greece and Turkey. In July 1947 he announced that the Soviet Union would not participate in the Marshall Plan.

As deputy foreign minister, Zorin informed U.S. representatives that the Soviet Union would not intervene in the Korean War. Concurrent with his foreign ministry post, Zorin was ambassador to the United Nations in 1952 and 1953. He replaced Jacob Malik at the UN in October 1952 and served there until April 1953, a month after Soviet Premier Josef Stalin's death, when Andrei Y. Vyshinskii took over at the UN.

From 1955 to 1960 Zorin was ambassador to the Federal Republic of Germany. He returned to the UN as Soviet permanent representative from 1960 until 1962. In 1956 he was made a candidate member of the Communist Party Central Committee, and in 1961 he became a full member. From 1965 to 1971 he was ambassador to France. He also served as the USSR's representative to disarmament talks in Geneva. He retired from government service in 1971. Zorin died in Moscow on 14 January 1986.

—Spencer C. Tucker

References:

International Who's Who, 1972–73, 36th ed. London: Europa, 1972.

Moritz, Charles, ed. *Current Biography Yearbook, 1986*. New York: H. W. Wilson, 1986.

New York Times, 19 January 1986

See also: Malik, Jacob (Iakov) Alexandrovich; Stalin, Josef; Union of Soviet Socialist Republics; Vyshinskii, Andrei Ianuarovich.

Timeline for Korean History

70000–30000 B.C.
Paleolithic culture emerges.

5000–6000 B.C.
Neolithic culture emerges.

2333 B.C.
Date for the founding of the Kingdom of Old Chosŏn ("land of the morning calm") by Tan-gun.

1200–1000 B.C.
Bronze Age emerges.

1122 B.C.
Kija Chosŏn established.

500–300 B.C.
Iron Age begins.

194 B.C.
Wiman Chosŏn takes control in North and of the three Han tribes in the south.

109–108 B.C.
Chinese invasion of Korea by Emperor Wu of the Han dynasty, signaling the fall of Wiman Chosŏn.

57 B.C.
State of Saro (later Silla) founded.

37 B.C.
Koguryŏ emerges.

18 B.C.
Paekche emerges.

313 A.D.
China loses control of Lolang in Korea.

372
Buddhism adopted; school of Confucianism started in Koguryŏ.

384
Buddhism adopted in Paekche.

427
New capital of Koguryŏ at Wanggŏm-sŏng.

503
Saro renamed Silla.

527
Buddhism adopted in Silla.

612–618
Chinese forces invade; Koguryŏ forces victorious.

644–668
Tang forces invade.

660
Paekche destroyed by forces of both Silla and China.

668
Koguryŏ destroyed by forces of both Silla and China.

674
Tang China calendar adopted.

676
Silla unifies the Korean peninsula for the first time.

682
Confucian school of learning established.

846
Rebellion of Chang Po-go.

892
Later Paekche founded by Kyŏnhwŏn.

918
Kungye's Later Koguryŏ overthrown and Kingdom of Koryŏ founded.

935
Last Silla king surrenders to Koryŏ.

993
First Khitan invasion.

1010
Second Khitan invasion.

1018
Third Khitan invasion.

1104
Jurchen invasion.

1170
Rebellion of Chŏng Chung-bu.

1231
First Mongol invasion.

1232
Second Mongol invasion.

1235–1239
Third Mongol invasion.

1259
Peace concluded with Mongols, accepting Mongol domination.

1270
Sambyŏlch'o rebellion begins.

1273
Sambyŏlch'o rebellion ends.

1274
First Mongol expedition to Japan.

1281
Second Mongol expedition to Japan.

1313
First census.

1392
Koryŏ kingdom ends.

1392–1910
Chosŏn Dynasty.

1446
Hun'gŭl (Korean written alphabet) finally completed.

1592
Japanese invade; construction of ironclad vessels.

January 1597
Japanese invade a second time.

October 1598
Japanese withdraw.

1627
First Manchu invasion.

December 1636
Second Manchu invasion.

1654
Korean troops sent on behalf of the Manchus against the Russians.

1812
Rebellion of Hong Kyŏng-nae.

1844
Treaty signed establishing trade relations between China and United States.

1845–1846
British, Americans, and French arrive.

1855
Vaccine for smallpox introduced.

August 1866
Crew of U.S. schooner *General Sherman* massacred.

10–11 June 1871
U.S. forces bombard Korean shore installations and take several forts on Kanghwa Island in response to Koreans firing on U.S. vessels.

1875
Japanese troops land at Pusan.

1880s
Japanese merchant and mining companies move into Korea.

May 1882
Treaty of Peace, Amity, Commerce, and Navigation concluded at Chemulpo (later Inch'ŏn) between Korea and the United States.

1894
China and Japan go to war over Korea; Korea backs Japan.

17 April 1895
Japan defeats China; Treaty of Shimonoseki signed.

8 October 1895
Queen Min assassinated by Japanese; King Kojong forced to work for Japanese.

1904
Japan and Russia go to war.

27 July 1905
Taft-Katsura Memorandum, by which the United States sanctions the Japanese takeover of Korea and, in return, Japan promises not to take any aggressive action against the Philippines.

5 September 1905
Russo-Japanese War ends in Treaty of Portsmouth.

October 1905
King Kojong writes to U.S. President Theodore Roosevelt, requesting the United States offer its "good offices" as stated in the 1882 treaty and intervene on behalf of Korea to prevent Japanese encroachment; Washington ignores the request.

11 November 1905
United States withdraws its legation from Seoul.

17 November 1905
Japanese General Hasekawa orders troops to march on Seoul; they take control of the palace and try to force Prime Minister Han Kyu-sŏl to sign over control to Japan; he refuses and is shot; Korea becomes protectorate of Japan.

1906
Hirobumi Ito made prince and resident general.

1907
King Kojong forced to abdicate.

30 November 1908
Root-Takahira Agreement between U.S. Secretary of State Elihu Root and Japanese Minister to the United States Kogor Takahira recognizing the "status quo" in the Pacific and each other's interests: Japan in Korea and southern Manchuria, the United States in the Philippines; both agreed to support the Open Door policy in China and to maintain its territorial integrity.

August 1910
Japan formally annexes Korea when last ruler of House of Yi signs rights away to Japan; Japanese attempt to destroy Korean culture, history, and art.

December 1918
Koreans in the United States petition President Woodrow Wilson to aid Koreans in their "aspirations for self-determination" as an obligation of the 1882 Treaty of Chemulpo.

March–April 1919
Manse Revolution, a Korean patriotic demonstration crushed by Japanese troops, who kill many Koreans; others flee abroad.

1922
Formation of the Seoul Young Men's Association.

1923
Founding of the North Star Society.

18 April 1925
Establishment of the Korean Communist Party.

1926
Death of Sunjong, last king of the Chosŏn Dynasty.

1929–1930
Uprising of 54,000 students against Japan.

19 September 1931
Mukden incident; beginning of Japanese conquest of all Manchuria.

1938
Proclamation by Japan of the Greater East Asian Co-Prosperity Sphere.

September 1940
Japan moves into north Indo-China, straining relations with United States.

July 1941
Japan moves into southern Indo-China, placing Japanese long-range bombers within striking distance of Malaya, the Dutch East Indies, and the Philippines; alarmed by this development and endeavoring to force Japan to withdraw, the United States, Great Britain, and the Netherlands impose an embargo on scrap iron and oil on Japan; with this decision Tokyo opts for war against the United States.

7 December 1941
Japan attacks Pearl Harbor.

1 December 1943
At Cairo Conference, U.S., British, and Chinese leaders declare that Korea should become free and independent "in due course," implying some temporary period of external supervision, which is condemned by Korean nationalists.

1945

February
At Yalta Conference, Soviet leader Josef Stalin confirms earlier promise to enter the Pacific War two or three months after the defeat of Germany; U.S. and British leaders consent to Soviet concessions in

Sakhalin, the Kuril Islands, and northern China; the Allies also agree to four-power Korean trusteeship but details are left ill-defined.

July

Formation of the North Korean Democratic People's Front and North Korean Labor Party, both drawn from the Communist Party.

25 July

After discussions at Potsdam, U.S. Army Chief of Staff George C. Marshall orders U.S. Army to prepare to move troops into Korea.

6 August

United States drops atomic bomb on Hiroshima.

8 August

Soviet Union enters war against Japan.

9 August

United States drops atomic bomb on Nagasaki; Soviet troops invade Manchuria.

10 August

Japan requests an armistice.

15 August

Tokyo orders Japanese forces to lay down their arms; U.S. President Harry S. Truman approves General Order 1, sending copies to Moscow and London, fixing 38th parallel as temporary dividing line between U.S. and Soviet forces in Korea; Stalin does not object.

August–September

Soviet and U.S. forces occupy Korea to accept Japanese surrender.

2 September

Formal Japanese surrender signed; Japan stripped of overseas holdings, including Korea.

8 September

Lead elements of U.S. occupation force land at port of Inch'ŏn.

December

Foreign ministers of victorious Allied powers agree to implement four-power trusteeship and establish a U.S.-Soviet Joint Commission to work out the details and begin process toward Korean independence.

1946

February

North Korean People's Committee formed, led by Kim Il Sung.

March

Land reform in North Korea; meeting of U.S.–U.S.S.R. representatives to discuss provisional Korean government.

May

U.S.–U.S.S.R. meeting over Korea breaks up with no agreement.

September

U.S. State Department agrees that Korea should be left to its fate.

1947

May

Second U.S.–U.S.S.R. meeting on Korea ends without agreement.

17 September

Washington refers the Korean situation to the General Assembly of the United Nations.

14 November

General Assembly adopts U.S.–sponsored plan, despite opposition from USSR that calls for general elections in Korea and united government.

November

North Korean People's Congress constitutes a constitutional committee.

1948

January

United Nations Temporary Commission on Korea (UNTCOK) arrives in Seoul, but Soviet authorities deny it access to North Korea.

February

UNTCOK calls for "elections in that part of Korea accessible to the Commission"; Korean People's Army (KPA) activated in North Korea; U.S. Joint Chiefs of Staff (JCS) recommends pulling U.S. forces out of South Korea even though such a move will probably result in "eventual domination of Korea by the U.S.S.R."

7 February
South Korean Labor Party (SKLP) led by Pak Hŏ-yŏng stages general strike.

April
Against backdrop of election in the South alone and possible division of Korea, North-South Political Leaders' Coalition Conference is held in P'yŏngyang but without result.

2 April
U.S. National Security Council (NSC) paper NSC-8 argues that United States should build up Republic of Korea (ROK) economy and armed forces, but that defense of South Korea should be left to the Koreans themselves; accepted by President Truman as basis for U.S. Korea policy.

3 April
In Cheju-do Rebellion, Communist guerrilla units and supporters occupy most towns on Cheju Island and disrupt May general elections there.

10 May
General election held under UN auspices, but only in South Korea.

June
National Assembly established in South Korea.

10 July
North Korean People's Congress adopts constitution.

17 July
ROK constitution promulgated; Syngman Rhee elected as first president.

15 August
ROK formally established.

25 August
North Korean People's Congress elects representatives to a Supreme People's Congress.

September
Soviet troops withdraw from North Korea.

9 September
Supreme People's Congress proclaims Democratic People's Republic of Korea (DPRK) with Kim Il Sung as premier.

October
Soviet Union recognizes DPRK.

19 October
In the Yŏsu-Sunch'ŏn Rebellion, ROK troops rebel at port of Yŏsu under SKLP instigation; ROK government sends additional troops to suppress the rebellion.

December
Soviet military delegation arrives in DPRK.

12 December
UN declares ROK as only legitimate Korean government.

31 December
Moscow announces that all Soviet troops have left North Korea.

1949

January
General Douglas MacArthur informs JCS that ROK forces could not defeat a North Korean invasion of the South, that the United States should not commit combat troops in the event of such an invasion, and that the United States should remove its armed forces from South Korea as soon as possible.

27 June
U.S. State Department recommends that the United States should deal with a North Korean invasion of the South by working through the UN.

29 June
United States completes withdrawal of its combat troops from South Korea.

1 July
U.S. Korea Military Advisory Group (KMAG) activated.

September
Communists win in China.

1 October
In Beijing, Mao Zedong proclaims the People's Republic of China (PRC); Republic of Korea Air Force (ROKAF) becomes separate service branch.

1950

January–March
U.S. Far East Command (FEC) Intelligence Section evaluates reports of an impending North Korean invasion of South Korea but concludes that it is not imminent.

12 January
U.S. Secretary of State Dean Acheson, in the course of a speech to the National Press Club in Washington, draws a defense perimeter for the United States in Asia that excludes Korea; omitted nations will have to fend for themselves until UN action can be mobilized.

19 January
U.S. House of Representatives defeats Korean aid bill for 1949–1950.

14 February
Sino-Soviet Treaty of Friendship, Alliance, and Mutual Assistance signed.

30 May
ROK elections produce a majority of National Assembly representatives hostile to the Rhee government.

7 June
Democratic Front proposes general elections in North and South Korea; three envoys sent to the ROK, which turns down offer and imprisons them.

19 June
DPRK presents plan to unify Korea.

25 June
At 0400, KPA troops, supported by tanks, heavy artillery, and aircraft, cross 38th parallel and invade the South, which can do little to slow the offensive; Washington caught by surprise.

26 June
KPA 3d and 4th Divisions move against Ŭijŏngbu; U.S. Ambassador to the ROK John J. Muccio orders all nonessential embassy personnel and all U.S. dependents evacuated to Japan.

27 June
U.S. Far East Air Force (FEAF) provides evacuation and cover of U.S. personnel from Seoul and Inch'ŏn; President Truman authorizes U.S. naval and air operations against KPA south of the 38th parallel in support of ROK forces; USAF F-82 shoots down a North Korean Yak fighter; Brigadier General John H. Church arrives in Seoul from Japan to survey the situation; call-up of U.S. reserve components initiated; UN proclaims KPA attack a breach of world peace, asks for assistance to the ROK; Seventh Fleet moves to neutralize Formosa Strait.

28 June
ROK engineers prematurely blow bridges over the Han River in Seoul, trapping many ROK soldiers and

their equipment north of the river; Seoul falls to KPA; United Kingdom sends naval support to Korea to be placed under U.S. control.

29 June
U.S. FEC Commander General Douglas MacArthur informs Washington that ROK Army (ROKA) is at half strength; Truman authorizes sea blockade of Korea; U.S. cruiser *Juneau* shells Mukho; Truman authorizes bombing of North Korea, and P'yŏngsŏng Airfield at P'yŏngyang struck.

30 June
President Truman commits U.S. ground troops to Korea; Congress authorizes call up of reserve components for up to 21 months; Truman agrees with reporter describing situation in Korea as a police action.

1 July
First U.S. ground troops arrive in Korea: members of 24th Infantry Division formed into Task Force Smith named for their commander, Lieutenant Colonel Charles B. Smith; lacking heavy weapons, they take up position on the road between Suwŏn and Osan.

2 July
Anglo-American naval flotilla engages and sinks five of six North Korean torpedo boats and gun boats in the one major naval engagement of the war.

3 July
Major General William F. Dean, commander of 24th Infantry Division, arrives in South Korea; first U.S. Navy operations begin against North Korea as carriers USS *Valley Forge* and HMS *Triumph* send fighters against airfields in the P'yŏngyang-Chinnamp'o area; KPA takes Inch'ŏn.

5 July
Task Force Smith in action against KPA just north of Osan; it holds up the KPA advance for seven hours before withdrawing, but loses a third of its force in the process.

7 July
UN asks United States to take control of UN efforts in Korea.

8 July
President Truman names General MacArthur to command United Nations Command (UNC) forces.

10 July
25th Infantry Division begins to arrive in Korea from Japan.

12 July
Lieutenant General Walton H. Walker takes command of UNC ground troops in Korea.

18 July
1st Cavalry Division begins to arrive in Korea.

19 July
24th Infantry Division begins defense of Taejŏn.

20 July
KPA takes Taejŏn; 24th and 25th Infantry Divisions launch counterattack at Okch'ŏn, helping to buy time to develop defenses along the Naktong River to the south.

29 July
Lead elements of 2d Infantry Division arrive in Korea.

1 August
Soviet UN delegate Yakov Malik ends USSR boycott and assumes presidency of the UN Security Council.

2 August
U.S. 1st Provisional Marine Brigade arrives in Korea; I Corps activated at Fort Bragg, North Carolina, and ordered to Korea.

3 August
Congress removes existing limitations on U.S. Army size.

4 August
UNC establishes Naktong River defenses, in what becomes known as the Pusan perimeter; first evacuation of casualties by Marine Corps helicopter.

7 August
1st Marine Brigade enters combat at Chinju.

15 August
Eighth Army directed to employ Korean recruits in its units, beginning what is known as Korean Augmentation to the U.S. Army (KATUSA).

18 August
First tank-to-tank battle of Korean War.

25 August
Major General William Dean, commander of the 24th Division, taken prisoner after eluding capture for a month and a half after fall of Taejŏn.

26 August
X Corps activated in Japan for Inch'ŏn landing.

29 August
British 27th Brigade arrives from Hong Kong; KPA offensive opens on west side of the Pusan perimeter.

15 September
Operation CHROMITE; X Corps lands at Inch'ŏn.

16 September
Eighth Army breaks out of Naktong perimeter and drives north.

19 September
X Corps moves to take Seoul; 2d Logistical Commander replaces Pusan Logistical Command; 3d Logistical Command activated to support X Corps; Louis Johnson resigns as U.S. secretary of defense.

21 September
George C. Marshall becomes U.S. secretary of defense.

23 September
IX Corps operational at Miryang.

27 September
UNC forces regain Seoul; President Truman authorizes operations north of 38th parallel.

29 September
MacArthur and Syngman Rhee reenter Seoul.

1 October
ROK troops cross 38th parallel.

4 October
PRC leader Mao Zedong makes final decision to intervene militarily.

7 October
UN General Assembly authorizes use of UN troops north of 38th parallel to establish a unified and democratic Korea.

8 October
Mao Zedong issues official directive turning Northeast Border Defense Army into Chinese People's Volunteers, a fig leaf enabling the PRC to go to war with the United States without formally avowing it; Mao orders that "the Chinese People's Volunteers move immediately into the territory of Korea to assist the Korean comrades in their struggle."

9 October
Eighth Army (EUSAK), led by 1st Cavalry Division, crosses 38th parallel and attacks north toward DPRK capital of P'yŏngyang.

10 October
ROK troops take Wŏnsan.

15 October
President Truman meets with General MacArthur at Wake Island.

18 October
Chinese People's Volunteer Army (CPVA) troops begin crossing Yalu River into North Korea.

19 October
ROK and Eighth Army troops take P'yŏngyang.

20 October
187th Airborne Regimental Combat Team makes parachute assault on Sukch'ŏn and Sunch'ŏn north of P'yŏngyang.

21 October
Kim Il Sung establishes new DPRK capital at Sinŭiju on Yalu River.

25 October
CPVA troops enter the war, clashing with ROK forces south of the Yalu River.

26–28 October
1st Marine Division lands at Wŏnsan.

6 November
MacArthur condemns Chinese intervention.

8 November
Seventy-nine B-29 Superfortresses bomb Yalu River bridges at Sinŭiju; first jet-on-jet air battle in history, over Sinŭiji in which F-80 Shooting Star shoots down a MiG-15.

16 November
President Truman announces that he has no intentions of fighting in China.

24 November
Eighth Army renews offensive toward Yalu River.

25 November
Chinese release fifty-seven U.S. prisoners; CPVA launches second and massive phase of its intervention in the war.

29 November
Lieutenant General Walton Walker orders general withdrawal of EUSAK from Ch'ŏngch'ŏn River south.

30 November
Marine 5th and 7th Regiments commence fighting withdrawal south from Changjin Reservoir to Hŭngnam perimeter.

3 December
UNC troops begin leaving P'yŏngyang; supply depots there burned.

5 December
P'yŏngyang taken by CPVA.

11 December
Hŭngnam evacuation begins.

14 December
UN resolution seeking cease-fire.

15 December
Eighth Army withdraws below 38th parallel.

16 December
President Truman declares a State of National Emergency in United States.

22 December
Chinese reject cease-fire.

23 December
Eighth Army commander Lieutenant General Walton Walker killed in jeep accident; Lieutenant General Matthew B. Ridgway named as successor.

24 December
X Corps completes evacuation of port of Hŭngnam.

26 December
General Ridgway arrives in Korea and takes command of Eighth Army.

31 December
CPVA begins its third offensive.

1951

1 January
3d Logistical Command made subordinate element of 2d Logistical Command.

4 January
UNC forces evacuate Seoul as ROK capital again falls to Communists.

5 January
UNC forces abandon Inch'ŏn.

7–15 January
UNC halts CPVA at 38th parallel and south of Wŏnju.

17 January
PRC refuses to accept cease-fire.

25 January
Operation THUNDERBOLT, first UNC counterattack since Chinese intervention in war, to push CPVA north of the Han River, ending all talk of UNC evacuation from Korea.

11–17 February
Fourth CPVA offensive against X Corps in central Korea.

13 February
General MacArthur issues statement critical of UN/U.S. military policy in Korea.

15 February
Communist advance contained in Battle of Chip'yŏng-ni.

21 February
UNC Operation KILLER forces CPVA north of Han River.

7 March
In Operation RIPPER, EUSAK crosses Han River.

14 March
UNC forces retake Seoul.

23 March
187th Airborne Regimental Combat Team makes air assault at Munsan-ni.

24 March
General MacArthur demands that Communist forces surrender.

5 April
Operation RUGGED begins as U.S. troops move to Line Kansas; in U.S. House of Representatives, Republican minority leader Joseph Martin receives letter from MacArthur saying there is "no substitute for victory" in Korea.

11 April
President Truman relieves General MacArthur of his command, replacing him with Lieutenant General Matthew Ridgway.

14 April
Lieutenant General James A. Van Fleet arrives in Korea to succeed General Ridgway as Eighth Army commander; UNC forces reach Line Kansas.

19 April
General MacArthur addresses joint session of Congress.

22 April
CPVA begins Fifth Offensive, initiating Battle of Imjin River, largest battle of the war; Chinese suffer heavy losses, but drive almost to Seoul before being halted at the end of May.

30 April
UNC stops Communist forces north of Seoul.

9 May
300 UNC aircraft strike Sinŭiju on Yalu River in largest air attack of the war to date.

20 May
Chinese advance halted; UNC again advances.

21 May
Eighth Army begins drive to expel Communist forces from South Korea.

30 May
UNC forces return to Line Kansas.

31 May
Far East Air Force (FEAF) launches Operation STRANGLE, air interdiction campaign.

1 June
Operation PILEDRIVER begins; Eighth Army moves to Line Wyoming in Iron Triangle; U.S. Secretary of State Acheson announces United States is prepared to accept truce line in vicinity of 38th parallel.

12 June
UNC forces secure Iron Triangle.

23 June
Soviet UN delegate Malik calls for negotiations for a cease-fire in Korea.

25 June
PRC supports idea of cease-fire.

30 June
On instructions from Washington, General Ridgway announces the UNC is willing to discuss an armistice.

1 July
Kim Il Sung and CPVA commander General Peng
Dehuai agree to armistice talks at Kaesŏng.

10 July
Armistice talks begin at Kaesŏng.

22 August
Communist side suspends talks.

17 September
Robert A. Lovett replaces George C. Marshall as secretary of defense.

25 October
Armistice talks resume at P'anmunjŏm.

12 November
General Ridgway orders end to UNC offensive operations and start of "active defense" strategy.

2 December 1951–15 March 1952
Operation RATKILLER, effort to eliminate guerrilla
activities in southwest Korea, is conducted.

1952

January–April
Disorder erupts in prisoner-of-war (POW) camps as
POW screening process begins.

1 January
UNC air and artillery attacks on Communist positions
begin.

2 January
At P'anmunjŏm negotiations, UNC proposes voluntary repatriation of all POWs.

18 February
Major clash between UN guards and Communist prisoners at Kŏje-do POW camp.

22 February
Communists accuse United States of using germ warfare in Korea.

8 April
President Truman orders seizure of strike-bound U.S.
steel mills.

7 May
Truce negotiations stall over the issue of repatriation
of Chinese and North Korean POWs; Communist
POWs capture commander of Kŏje-do POW camp

Brigadier General Francis T. Dodd and hold him
hostage.

11 May
General Dodd released.

12 May
Lieutenant General Mark Clark replaces Lieutenant
General Ridgway as U.S. commander in chief Far East
and UN commander in chief.

2 June
U.S. Supreme Court declares President Truman's
seizure of steel mills unconstitutional.

23 June
UNC air attacks of power plants along Yalu River to
hasten conclusion of armistice agreement.

25 June
Possible assassination attempt on Syngman Rhee.

29 August
Largest bombing raid of war against P'yŏngyang,
involving 1,403 aircraft, part of a July–August effort
that virtually destroys city.

8 October
Communist side rejects POW settlement proposal.

24 October
Republican presidential candidate Dwight D.
Eisenhower declares he will go to Korea if elected.

4 November
Eisenhower elected U.S. president.

2–5 December
President-elect Eisenhower visits Korea.

1953

10 February
Lieutenant General Maxwell Taylor replaces Lieutenant
General Van Fleet as Eighth Army commander.

5 March
Soviet Premier Josef Stalin dies in Moscow.

20 April–3 May
Operation LITTLE SWITCH, exchange of sick and
wounded POWs.

28 May
CPVA attacks five U.S. outposts.

10–17 June
CPVA pushes ROK II Corps back 4,000 yards, demonstrating ROK could not survive without U.S. assistance and puncturing Rhee's calls of "on to the North."

15–30 June
CPVA attacks I Corps.

18 June
Rhee orders release of North Korean POWs.

July
U.S. Navy Task Force 77 equipped with nuclear weapons.

11 July
UNC evacuates Pork Chop Hill.

27 July
Korean armistice signed at P'anmunjŏm; goes into effect at 2200 hours.

28 July
First meeting of Military Armistice Commission.

5 August–6 September
Operation BIG SWITCH, final exchange of POWs.

26 April 1954
Opening of Geneva Conference to resolve Korean reunification and deal with other Asian matters.

—Compiled by Kim Jinwung, Lee Rees,
and Spencer C. Tucker

Glossary of Terms, Acronyms and Abbreviations

A—Army airstrip (with number designation following, e.g., A-2).

AE—Army emergency airstrip (with number designation following).

AFB—Air force base.

A-frame (*chige* in Korean)—Back carrier used by porters during the war. GIs dubbed this an "A-frame," because it resembled a capital A. The outer legs of the carrier were wide-spread at the bottom and came close together at the top. A bearer often could carry his own weight on an A-frame. However, for sustained operations, or long hauls, fifty pounds per porter was the norm. Daily a bearer could carry fifty pounds for up to ten miles.

Anyang hasham niko—Fractured American version of saying hello in Korean language for *annyŏng hasimnigga.*

ASAP—As soon as possible.

Battalion—Army unit, composed of a headquarters and two or more companies or batteries, from 300 to 1,000 soldiers usually commanded by a lieutenant colonel; may be part of a regiment, brigade, or division artillery.

Battery—Army tactical and administrative artillery unit corresponding to an infantry company. Usually composed of about 100 officers and men; normally commanded by a captain.

Benjo—Outhouse or slit trench for body functions.

Boonies or boon docks—Remote woods, ridges, rice paddies, or rural areas far away from villages and settlements.

Boy san—Japanese slang for Korean male youth either civilian or military (Korean would be *sonyŏn*).

Brigade—Army unit, usually smaller than a division, to which are attached groups and/or battalions and smaller units tailored to meet anticipated requirements. During the Korean War, this was an organizational structure used by the British, Canadians, and Turks and in those cases was similar to a U.S. Army regimental combat team.

Bug out or bugging—To retreat rapidly and in panic without orders or authority when confronted with an advancing enemy and usually leaving all weapons and equipment behind; the opposite of an orderly, organized, and authorized withdrawal or relocation.

CAS—Close air support.

CCF—Chinese Communist forces. UNC term for Chinese People's Volunteer Army.

CG—Commanding general.

Chinks—Racist and derogatory term used by Americans in Korea for the Chinese.

Chuggie chuggie—Term used to hurry Koreans working with Americans.

Chop chop—Same as *chuggie chuggie* and sometimes used interchangeably.

CINCFE—Commander in chief, Far East. Commander of U.S. forces in the Far East.

CINCUNC—Commander in chief, United Nations Command. Commander of United Nations military forces in Korea.

CO—Commanding officer.

Corps—Army tactical unit larger than a division and smaller than a field army. Usually consists of two or more divisions together with auxiliary arms and services. Normally commanded by a lieutenant general.

CP—Command post.

CPVA—Chinese People's Volunteer Army. Chinese name for their People's Liberation Army (PLA) forces in the Korean War, indicating Beijing's desire to avoid a full-scale conflict with the United States.

Defense perimeter—A defense without an exposed flank, consisting of forces deployed along the perimeter of a defended area.

Division—Army basic tactical unit, larger than a regiment or brigade and smaller than a corps. A combined arms unit for waging war, generally commanded by a major general with an authorized strength (U.S. Army) of some 20,000 men.

DOF—Days of fire. Artillery term used to express the number of rounds allocated per gun per day.

DPRK—Democratic People's Republic of Korea, North Korea.

DZ—Drop zone. Area where airborne forces are to be parachuted.

ECB—Engineer (combat) battalion.

EUSAK—Eighth U.S. Army in Korea.

FAA—Fleet Air Arm. British naval aviation.

FAB—Field artillery battalion.

FAC—Forward air controller.

FEAF—Far East Air Force. Primary U.S. Air Force component serving in Korea during the Korean War.

FEC—Far East Command, today FECOM.

FO—Forward observer, artillery and mortars.

GHQ—General headquarters.

Girl san—Slang (part Japanese) for a Korean female civilian too young to bear children (Korean would be *sonyŏ*).

Gook—Racist and derogatory term for an Asian.

Group—A flexible administrative and tactical unit, composed of either two or more squadrons (U.S. Air Force) or two or more battalions (U.S. Army).

Hubba hubba—Term, directed at Koreans and sometimes Americans, meaning to speed up or move faster.

I&R—Intelligence and reconnaissance (platoons).

Ichi bahn—Japanese term meaning top rated, number one, the best; used widely by Americans when speaking with Koreans or among other Americans (Korean would be *ilbŏn*).

JATO—Jet-assisted takeoff. A pack of rockets was attached to an aircraft fuselage centerline and then ignited to add speed for liftoff. The pack was jettisoned as soon as the thrust was exhausted.

JLC—Japan Logistical Command.

JOC—Joint operations center.

K—Air force airfield (with number designation following, e.g., K-14 [Kimpŏ]).

KCOMZ—Korean communications zone. In U.S. Army doctrine, a communications zone is the specified area behind the front lines where supply and administrative facilities could be established and operated to relieve the front-line commander of responsibility for functions not directly related to combat operations.

KIA—Killed in action.

KPA—Korean People's Army, North Korean Army.

LD—Line of departure. Prominent terrain feature used to coordinate an attack.

LLC—Loudspeaker and leaflet company. U.S. Army unit involved in psychological warfare operations.

Mama san—Japanese term widely used by GIs for Korean mother or woman, usually older than a girl san (Korean is *Ŏmŏni*).

MATS—Military Air Transport Service (U.S. Air Force).

MLR—Main line of resistance.

MSR—Main supply route.

MSTS—Military Sea Transport Service.

NAVFE—Naval Forces, Far East.

Off and on—Command to troops to get up and start moving, i.e., "off your ass and on your feet."

OPLR—Outpost line of resistance.

Papa san—Japanese term widely used by GIs for Korean male old enough to be a father and especially a very old Korean man dressed in native costume with a stovepipe hat and pipe, marking him as a very senior citizen.

PLA—People's Liberation Army. People's Republic of China (Communist China's) military forces. The Chinese referred to their units in the Korean War as the Chinese People's Volunteer Army (CPVA).

Platoon—Army unit, usually four squads, of a tactical unit such as a company; usually commanded by a lieutenant.

Poggy bait—Candy, rations, or other military items thought to be sufficient to provide payment and inducement for Korean females from whom amorous or sexual favors were solicited.

PVA—People's Volunteer Army; *see* CPVA.

PWO—Psychological warfare officers. U.S. Army officers attached to Eighth Army headquarters who decided on suitable psychological warfare targets.

R&R—Rest and recuperation.

RAF—Royal Air Force; United Kingdom's air force.

RCT—Regimental combat team.

Regiment—Army administrative and tactical unit larger than a battalion and smaller than a brigade, usually consisting of three infantry battalions plus heavy mortar, intelligence and reconnaissance, heavy tank, medical, signal, and limited transportation elements; commanded by a colonel.

ROK—Republic of Korea, South Korea.

ROKA—Republic of Korea Army.

ROKAF—Republic of Korea Air Force.

ROKN—Republic of Korea Navy.

SCAP—Supreme commander, Allied Powers.

Scapjap—Shipping Control Administration Japan.

SOP—Standard operating procedure.

Sortie—One flight by one aircraft.

SOS—"Shit on a shingle." Menu item in the GI mess consisting of ground beef in cream sauce served on bread or toast usually in the breakfast meal.

SP gun—Self-propelled gun.

Squad—Smallest basic tactical infantry unit, below platoon, usually eight to twelve men; normally commanded by a sergeant.

Squadron—Basic U.S. Air Force, Navy, and Marine administrative aviation unit, consisting of several flights of approximately five aircraft each.

TACP—Tactical air-control party.

TD—Table of distribution.

TF—Task force. A group of units assembled temporarily for a particular mission.

TO&E—Tables of organization and equipment. Official authorized strength, organization, and equipment of particular units.

USAFIK—U.S. Army Forces in Korea (designation for U.S. command in Korea at the end of World War II).

WIA—Wounded in action.

Wing—U.S. Air Force unit, normally composed of one primary mission group, i.e., designated for combat, training, airlift, or service; commanded by a colonel. A typical U.S. Air Force fighter wing consists of three fighter squadrons of twenty-five aircraft each. U.S. Navy wings are similar. A U.S. Marine air wing contains the elements required for the air support of a Marine Corps division; commanded by a major general, it may include hundreds of aircraft.

XO—Executive officer.

Yard bird—Derogatory term for a common soldier usually not known for high intelligence, ambition, or performance.

ZI—Zone of the interior. During the Korean War, designation for the continental United States.

—Compiled by Sherman Pratt, Spencer C. Tucker, and Norman R. Zehr

Selected Bibliography of the Korean War

Acheson, Dean. *The Korean War*. New York: W. W. Norton, 1971.

———. *Present at the Creation: My Years at the State Department*. New York: W. W. Norton, 1969.

Aerospace Studies Institute, Air University. *Guerrilla Warfare and Airpower in Korea, 1950–1953*. Maxwell Air Force Base, AL: Air University Press, 1964.

Alexander, Bevin. *Korea: The First War We Lost*. New York: Hippocrene Books, 1986.

Allen, Richard C. *Korea's Syngman Rhee: An Unauthorized Portrait*. Rutland, VT: Charles E. Tuttle, 1960.

Appleman, Roy E. *Disaster in Korea: The Chinese Confront MacArthur*. College Station, TX: Texas A&M Press, 1989.

———. *East of Chosin: Entrapment and Breakout in Korea*. College Station, TX: Texas A&M Press, 1987.

———. *Escaping the Trap: The US Army X Corps in Northeast Korea, 1950*. College Station, TX: Texas A&M Press, 1990.

———. *Ridgway Duels for Korea*. College Station, TX: Texas A&M Press, 1990.

———. *South to the Naktong, North to the Yalu*. Washington, DC: Office of the Chief of Military History, 1961.

Baldwin, Frank, ed. *Without Parallel: The American-Korean Relationship Since 1945*. New York: Random House, 1973.

Barclay, C. N. *The First Commonwealth Division: The Story of British Commonwealth Land Forces in Korea, 1950–1953*. Aldershot, UK: Gale & Polden, 1954.

Bartlett, Norman. *With the Australians in Korea*. Canberra: Australian War Memorial, 1954.

Berebitsky, William. *A Very Long Weekend: The Army National Guard in Korea*. Shippensburg, PA: White Mane Press, 1996.

Berger, Carl. *The Korea Knot: A Military and Political History*. Philadelphia: University of Pennsylvania Press, 1957.

Berry, Henry. *Hey Mac, Where Ya Been? Living Memories of the U.S. Marines in the Korean War*. New York: St. Martin's Press, 1988.

Biderman, Albert D. *Communist Techniques of Coercive Interrogation*. Lackland Air Force Base, TX: U.S. Air Force, 1956.

———. *March to Calumny: The Story of American POWs in the Korean War*. New York: Macmillan, 1963.

Biderman, Albert D., and Herbert Zimmer, eds. *The Manipulation of Human Behavior*. New York: Wiley, 1961.

Black, Robert W. *Rangers in Korea*. New York: Ivy Books, 1989.

Blair, Clay. *Beyond Courage*. New York: David McKay, 1955.

———. *The Forgotten War: America in Korea, 1950–1953*. New York: Times Books, 1987.

Blanchard, Carroll H., Jr. *Korean War Bibliography and Maps of Korea*. Albany, NY: Korean Conflict Research Foundation, 1964.

Blunk, Chester L. *"Every Man a Tiger": The 731st USAF Night Intruders over Korea*. Manhattan, KS: Sunflower University Press, 1988.

Bowers, William T., William M. Hammond, and George L. MacGarrigle. *Black Soldier, White Army*. Washington, DC: U.S. Army Center of Military History, 1996.

Bradley, Omar N. *A Soldier's Story*. New York: Henry Holt, 1951.

Bradley, Omar N., and Clay Blair. *A General's Life: An Autobiography*. New York: Simon & Schuster, 1983.

Breen, Bob. *The Battle of Kapyong*. Syndey: Australian Army Training Command, 1992.

———. *The Battle of Maryang San*. Sydney: Australian Army Training Command, 1991.

Breuer, William B. *Shadow Warriors: The Covert War in Korea*. New York: Wiley, 1996.

Brinkley, Douglas, ed. *Dean Acheson and the Making of U.S. Foreign Policy*. New York: St. Martin's Press, 1993.

Brune, Lester H., ed. *The Korean War: Handbook of the Literature and Research*. Westport, CT: Greenwood Press, 1996.

Bussey, Charles M. *Firefight at Yechon: Courage and Racism in the Korean War*. Washington, DC: Brassey's, 1991.

Cagle, Malcolm W., and Frank A. Manson. *The Sea War in Korea*. Annapolis, MD: Naval Institute Press, 1957.

Caldwell, John C. *The Korean Story*. Chicago: Henry Regnery, 1952.

Cameron, Craig M. *American Samurai: Myth, Imagination, and the Conduct of Battle in the First Marine Division, 1941–1951*. New York: Cambridge University Press, 1994.

Camilleri, Joseph. *Chinese Foreign Policy: The Maoist Era and Its Aftermath*. Oxford: Martin Robertson, 1980.

Canada, Historical Section, General Staff, Canadian Army. *Canada's Army in Korea*. Ottawa: Queen's Printer, 1956.

Cardwell, Thomas A., III. *Command Structure for Theater Warfare: The Quest for Unity of Command*. Maxwell Air Force Base, AL: Air University Press, 1984.

Carew, Tim. *Korea: The Commonwealth at War*. London: Cassell, 1967.

Carter, Gregory A. *Some Historical Notes on Air Interdiction in Korea.* Santa Monica, CA: Rand, 1966.

Chen, Jian. *China's Road to the Korean War: The Making of the Sino-American Confrontation.* New York: Columbia University Press, 1994.

Cho, Soon-Sung. *Korea in World Politics, 1940–1950.* Berkeley: University of California Press, 1967.

Ch'oe, Chang-jip, et al. *Han'guk Chŏnjaeng Yon'gu: Han'guk Hyŏndaesa ŭi Ihae* [A study on the Korean War: understanding Korean modern history]. Seoul: T'aeam, 1990.

Ch'oe, T'ae-hwan, and Pak Hye-gyŏng. *Chŏlmŭn Hyŏngmyŏngga ŭi Ch'osang: Inmingun Changgyo Ch'oe T'ae-hwan Chungjwa ŭi Han'guk Chŏnjaeng Ch'amjŏngi* [A portrait of a young revolutionary: a war account by a North Korean Army lieutenant colonel, Ch'oe T'ae-hwan]. Seoul: Kongdongch'e, 1989.

Choi, Bong-Youn. *Korea—A History.* Rutland, VT: Charles E. Tuttle, 1971.

Chu, Yŏng-bok. *Nae ga Kyŏkkŭn Chosŏn Chŏnjaeng* [The Korean War I had experienced]. Seoul: Koryŏwŏn, 1990.

Clark, Mark W. *From the Danube to the Yalu.* New York: Harper & Row, 1954. Reprint, Blue Ridge Summit, PA: TAB Books, 1988.

Cochran, Bert. *Harry Truman and the Crisis Presidency.* New York: Funk & Wagnalls, 1973.

Collins, J. Lawton. *War in Peacetime: The History and Lessons of Korea.* Boston: Houghton Mifflin, 1969.

Condit, Doris M. *History of the Office of the Secretary of Defense.* Vol. 2, *The Test of War, 1950–1953.* Washington, DC: Office of the Secretary of Defense, 1988.

Cotton, James, and Ian Neary. *The Korean War As History.* Atlantic Highlands, NJ: Humanities Press, 1989.

Cowdrey, Albert E. *United States Army in the Korean War: The Medic's War.* Washington, DC: U.S. Army Center of Military History, 1987.

Crane, Conrad C. *American Air Power Strategy in Korea, 1950–1953.* Lawrence: University Press of Kansas, 1999.

Crews, Thomas. *Thunderbolt through Ripper: Joint Operations in Korea, 25 January–31 March 1951.* Carlisle Barracks, PA: Army War College, 1991.

Cumings, Bruce. *Child of Conflict: The Korean-American Relationship, 1943–1953.* Seattle: University of Washington Press, 1983.

———. *Korea's Place in the Sun: A Modern History.* New York: W. W. Norton, 1997.

———. *The Origins of the Korean War.* 2 vols. Princeton, NJ: Princeton University Press, 1981, 1990.

Cutforth, Rene. *Korean Reporter.* London: Allan Wingate, 1952.

Dean, William F. *General Dean's Story.* New York: Viking Press, 1954. Reprint, Westport, CT: Greenwood Press, 1973.

Deane, Phillip [Gerassimos Svoronos-Gigant]. *I Was a Captive in Korea.* New York: W. W. Norton, 1953.

Degovanni, George. *Air Force Support of Army Ground Operations: Lessons Learned during World War II, Korea, and Vietnam.* Carlisle Barracks, PA: Army War College, 1989.

Democratic People's Republic of Korea. *The U.S. Imperialists Started the Korean War.* Pyongyang: Foreign Languages Publishing House, 1977.

Detzer, David. *Thunder of the Captains: The Short Summer of 1950.* New York: Cromwell, 1977.

Dille, John. *Substitute for Victory.* New York: Doubleday, 1954.

Dobbs, Charles M. *The Unwanted Symbol: American Foreign Policy, the Cold War, and Korea, 1945–1950.* Kent, OH: Kent State University Press, 1981.

Donovan, Robert J. *Tumultuous Years: The Presidency of Harry S. Truman.* New York: W. W. Norton, 1982.

Eckert, Carter Jay, Lee Ki-Baik, Young Ick Lew, Michael Robinson, and Edward W. Wagner. *Korea: Old and New.* Seoul: Ilchokak, Publishers for the Korea Institute, Harvard University, 1990.

Ent, Uzal W. *Fighting on the Brink: Defense of the Pusan Perimeter.* Paducah, KY: Turner, 1996.

Evanhoe, Ed. *Dark Moon: Eighth Army Special Operations in the Korean War.* Annapolis, MD: Naval Institute Press, 1995.

Evans, Douglas. *Sabre Jets over Korea: A Firsthand Account.* Blue Ridge Summit, PA: Tab Books, 1984.

Farmer, James A. *Strumwasser, M.J. The Evolution of the Airborne Forward Air Controller: An Analysis of Mosquito Operations in Korea.* Santa Monica, CA: Rand, 1967.

Farrar-Hockley, Sir Anthony. *The British Part in the Korean War.* Vol. 1, *A Distant Obligation.* London: Her Majesty's Stationery Office, 1990.

———. *The British Part in the Korean War.* Vol. 2, *An Honourable Discharge.* London: Her Majesty's Stationery Office, 1994.

Fehrenbach, T. R. *The Fight for Korea.* New York: Grosset & Dunlap, 1969.

———. *This Kind of War: A Study in Unpreparedness.* New York: Macmillan, 1962.

Ferrell, Robert H. *Harry S. Truman and the Modern American Presidency.* Boston: Little, Brown, 1983.

Field, James A., Jr. *History of United States Naval Operations: Korea.* Washington, DC: U.S. Government Printing Office, 1962.

Foot, Rosemary J. *A Substitute for Victory: The Politics of Peacemaking at the Korean Armistice Talks.* Ithaca, NY: Cornell University Press, 1990.

———. *The Wrong War: American Policy and the Dimensions of the Korean Conflict, 1950–1953.* Ithaca, NY: Cornell University Press, 1985.

Forrestal, James V. *The Forrestal Diaries,* edited by Walter Millis. New York: Viking Press, 1951.

Futrell, Robert F. *The United States Air Force in Korea, 1950–1953.* Rev. ed. Washington, DC: Office of the Chief of Air Force History, 1983.

Gallaway, Jack. *The Last of the Bugle: The Long Road to Kapyong.* St. Lucia: University of Queensland Press, 1994.

Gardner, Lloyd, ed. *The Korean War.* New York: Quadrangle Books, 1972.

George, Alexander L. *The Chinese Communist Army in Action: The Korean War and Its Aftermath.* New York: Columbia University Press, 1967.

Giusti, Ernest H. *The Mobilization of the Marine Corps Reserve in the Korean Conflict.* Washington, DC: Historical Branch, G-3 Division Headquarters, U.S. Marine Corps, 1967.

Goncharov, Sergei N., John W. Lewis, and Xue Litai. *Uncertain Partners: Stalin, Mao and the Korean War.* Stanford, CA: Stanford University Press, 1993.

Goodrich, Leland Matthew. *Korea: A Study of U.S. Policy in the United Nations.* New York: Council on Foreign Relations, 1956.

Gordenker, Leon. *The United Nations and the Peaceful Unification of Korea: The Politics of Field Operations, 1947–1950.* The Hague: Martinus Nijhoff, 1959.

Gough, Terrence J. *U.S. Army Mobilization and Logistics in the Korean War.* Washington, DC: U.S. Army Center of Military History, 1987.

Goulden, Joseph C. *Korea: The Untold Story of the War.* New York: Times Books, 1982.

Grey, Jeffrey. *The Commonwealth Armies and the Korean War: An Alliance Study.* Manchester: Manchester University Press, 1988.

Gugelar, Russel A. *Combat Actions in Korea.* Rev. ed. Washington, DC: U.S. Army Center of Military History, 1987.

Gurtov, Melvin, and Byoong-Mao Hwang. *China under Threat: The Politics of Strategy and Diplomacy.* Baltimore: Johns Hopkins University Press, 1980.

Guttmann, Allen, ed. *Korea and the Theory of Limited War.* Boston: D. C. Heath, 1967.

Ha, Yŏng-sŏn, ed. *Han'guk Chŏnjaeng ŭi Saeroun Chŏpgŭn: Chŏnt'ongjuŭi wa Sujŏngjuŭi vŭl Nŏmŏsŏ.* [New approaches to the study of the Korean War: beyond traditionalism and revisionism]. Seoul: Nanam, 1990.

Hagiwara, Ryo. *The Korean War: The Conspiracies by Kim Il Sung and MacArthur.* Tokyo: Bungei Shunju Press, 1993.

Halliday, Jon, and Bruce Cumings. *Korea: The Unknown War.* New York: Pantheon, 1988.

Hallion, Richard P. *The Naval Air War in Korea.* Baltimore: Nautical and Aviation Publishing Co. of America, 1986.

Hamby, Alonzo L. *Man of the People: A Life of Harry S. Truman.* New York: Oxford University Press, 1995.

Hammel, Eric. *Chosin: Heroic Ordeal of the Korean War.* New York: Vanguard Press, 1081. Reprint, Novato, CA: Presidio Press, 1990.

Han'guk, Chŏnjaeng Saŏp-hoe, ed. *Han'guk Chŏnjaeng-sa* [History of the Korean War]. 6 vols. Seoul: Hanegrim, 1990–1992.

Harding, Harry, and Yuan Ming, eds. *Sino-American Relations, 1945–1955.* Wilmington, DE: Scholarly Resources, 1989.

Hastings, Max. *The Korean War.* New York: Simon & Schuster, 1987.

Haynes, Richard F. *The Awesome Power: Harry S. Truman As Commander in Chief.* Baton Rouge: Louisiana State University Press, 1973.

Heinl, Robert D. *Victory at High Tide: The Inchon-Seoul Campaign.* Philadelphia: J. B. Lippincott, 1968.

Heller, Francis H., ed. *The Korean War: A 25-Year Perspective.* Lawrence, KS: Regents Press of Kansas, 1977.

Henderson, Gregory. *Korea: The Politics of the Vortex.* Cambridge, MA: Harvard University Press, 1968.

Hermes, Walter G. *United States Army in the Korean War: Truce Tent and Fighting Front.* Washington, DC: Office of the Chief of Military History, 1966.

Higgins, Marguerite. *War in Korea.* Garden City, NY: Doubleday, 1951.

Higgins, Trumbell. *Korea and the Fall of MacArthur: A Précis in Limited War.* New York: Oxford University Press, 1960.

Higham, Robin, and Donald Mrozek. *Guide to the Sources of U.S. Military History: Supplement III.* Hamden, CT: Archon Books, 1993.

Hightower, Charles D. *The History of the United States Air Force Airborne Forward Air Controller in World War II, the Korean War, and the Vietnam Conflict.* Fort Leavenworth, KS: Army Command and General Staff College, 1984.

Hinshaw, Arned L. *Heartbreak Ridge: Korea, 1951.* New York: Praeger, 1989.

Hogan, Michael J. *A Cross of Iron: Harry S. Truman and the Origins of the National Security State, 1945–1954.* Cambridge, UK: Cambridge University Press, 1998.

Hoopes, Townsend, and Douglas Brinkley. *Driven Patriot: The Life and Times of James Forrestal.* New York: Alfred A. Knopf, 1992.

Hopkins, William B. *One Bugle, No Drums: The Marines at Chosin Reservoir.* Chapel Hill, NC: Algonquin Books, 1986.

Hoyt, Edwin P. *The Bloody Road to Panmunjom.* New York: Stein & Day, 1985.

———. *On to the Yalu.* New York: Stein & Day, 1984.

———. *The Pusan Perimeter.* New York: Stein & Day, 1984.

Huston, James A. *Guns and Butter, Powder and Rice: U.S. Army Logistics in the Korean War.* Selinsgrove, PA: Susquehanna University Press, 1989.

———. *Outposts and Allies: U.S. Army Logistics in the Cold War, 1945–1953.* Selinsgrove, PA: Susquehanna University Press, 1988.

Hyatt, John. *Korean War, 1950–1953: Selected References.* Maxwell Air Force Base, AL: Air University Library, 1992.

Jackson, Robert. *Air War Korea, 1950–1953.* Osceola, WA: Motorbooks International, 1998.

———. *Air War over Korea.* New York: Charles Scribner's Sons, 1973.

James, D. Clayton. *The Years of MacArthur.* Vol. 3, *Triumph and Disaster, 1945–1964.* Boston: Houghton Mifflin, 1985.

James, D. Clayton, with Anne Sharp Wells. *Refighting the Last War: Command and Crises in Korea, 1950–1953.* New York: Free Press, 1993.

Johnson, U. Alexis, with J. Olivarius McAllister. *The Right Hand of Power.* Englewood Cliffs, NJ: Prentice-Hall, 1984.

Kaufman, Burton I. *The Korean War: Challenges in Crisis, Credibility, and Command.* Philadelphia: Temple University Press, 1986.

Keefer, Edward C., ed. *Foreign Relations of the United States, 1952–1954, Korea.* Vol. 15. Washington, DC: U.S. Government Printing Office, 1984.

Kennedy, Edgar S. *Mission to Korea.* London: Derek Verschoyle, 1952.

Kim, Byong Sik. *Modern Korea.* New York: International Publishers, 1970.

Kim, Ch'ŏl-bŏm, ed. *Chinsil kwa Chŭngŏn: Sasimnyŏn mane Palk'yŏjin Han'guk Chŏnjaeng ŏi Chinsang* [Truth and testimonies: the true picture of the Korean War unmasked 40 years afterward]. Seoul: Ŭlyu, 1990.

———, ed. *Han'guk Chŏnjaeng: Kangdaeguk Chŏngch'i wa Nambukhanm Koldŭng* [The Korean War: great power politics and South-North discord]. Seoul: P'yŏngmin-sa, 1989.

———, ed. *Han'guk Chŏnjaeng kwa Miguk* [The Korean War and the United States]. Seoul: P'yŏngmin-sa, 1990.

———, ed. *Han'guk Chŏnjaeng ŭl Ponŭn Sigak* [Perspectives of the Korean War]. Seoul: Ŭlyu, 1990.

Kim, Chull-Baum, and James I. Matray. *Korea and the Cold War.* Claremont, CA: Regina Books, 1993.

Kim, Chum-gon. *The Korean War, 1950–1953.* Seoul: Kwangmyong, 1980.

Kim, Gye-Dong. *Foreign Intervention in Korea.* Aldershot, UK: Dartmouth, 1993.

Kim, Hak-jun. *Han'guk Chŏnjaeng: Kiwŏn, Kwajŏng, Hyujŏn, Yŏnghyang* [The Korean War: origins, process, truce and influence]. Seoul: Pakyŏng-sa, 1989.

Kim, Il Sung. *Kim Il Sung: Selected Works.* 2 vols. Pyongyang: Foreign Languages Publishing House, 1965.

Kim, Joungwoon A. *Divided Korea: The Politics of Development, 1945–1972.* Cambridge, MA: Harvard University Press, 1975.

Kim, Myung-Ki. *The Korean War and International Law.* Clairmont, CA: Paige Press, 1991.

Kim, Richard, and Donald K. Chung. *The Three Day Promise.* Tallahassee, FL: Father & Son Publishing, 1989.

Kim, Se-Jin. *The Politics of the Military Revolution in Korea.* Chapel Hill: University of North Carolina Press, 1971.

Kinkead, Eugene. *In Every War but One.* New York: W. W. Norton, 1959.

———. *Why They Collaborated.* New York: Longman, 1960.

Knox, Donald, and Albert Coppel. *The Korean War: An Oral History, Uncertain Victory.* San Diego: Harcourt Brace Jovanovich, 1988.

Koh, Byung Chul. *The Foreign Policy of North Korea.* New York: Praeger, 1969.

Kohn, Richard H., and Joseph P. Harahan, eds. *Air Interdiction in World War II, Korea, and Vietnam: An Interview with General Earle E. Partridge, General Jacob E. Smart, General John W. Vogt, Jr.* Washington, DC: Office of Air Force History, 1986.

———, eds. *Air Superiority in World War II and Korea: An Interview with General James Ferguson, General Robert M. Lee, General William W. Momyer, and General Elwood R. Quesada.* Washington, DC: Office of Air Force History, 1983.

Korean War Research Committee, War Memorial Service–Korea. *The Historical Reillumination of the Korean War.* Seoul: War Memorial Service, 1990.

Kwak, Tae-Han, John Chay, Cho Soon-Sung, and Shannon McCune, eds. *U.S.-Korean Relations, 1882–1982.* Seoul: Institute for Far Eastern Studies, Kyungnam University, 1982.

Langley, Michael. *Inchon Landing: MacArthur's Last Triumph.* New York: Times Books, 1979.

Lansdown, John R. P. *With the Carriers in Korea: The Sea and Air War in SE Asia, 1950–1953.* Winslow, Cheshire, UK: Crécy, 1997.

Leckie, Robert. *Conflict: The History of the Korean War, 1950–1953.* New York: Putnam, 1962.

———. *The March to Glory.* Cleveland: World, 1960.

Lee, Chae-Jin. *The Korean War: A 40-Year Perspective.* Claremont, CA: Keck Center for International and Strategic Studies, 1991.

Lee, Chong-Sik. *The Politics of Korean Nationalism.* Berkeley: University of California Press, 1963.

Lott, Arnold S. *Most Dangerous Sea: A History of Mine Warfare and an Account of U.S. Navy Mine Warfare Operations in World War II and Korea.* Annapolis, MD: U.S. Naval Institute, 1959.

Love, Robert W., Jr., ed. *The Chiefs of Naval Operations.* Annapolis, MD: Naval Institute Press, 1980.

Lyons, Gene M. *Military Policy and Economic Aid: The Korean Case, 1950–1953.* Columbus: Ohio State University Press, 1961.

MacDonald, Callum. *Korea: The War Before Vietnam.* New York: Free Press, 1986.

MacDonald, Donald Stone. *The Koreans*. Boulder, CO: Westview Press, 1988.

Mahurin, Walker M. *Honest John*. New York: Putnam, 1962.

Malcom, Ben S. *White Tigers: My Secret War in North Korea*. Washington, DC: Brassey's, 1996.

Marshall, S. L. A. *Infantry Operations and Weapons in Korea*. San Francisco: Presidio Press, 1988.

———. *Military History of the Korean War*. New York: F. Watts, 1963.

———. *Pork Chop Hill: The American Fighting Man in Action, Korea, Spring 1953*. New York: William Morrow, 1956.

———. *The River and the Gauntlet: Defeat of the Eighth Army by the Chinese Communist Forces, November 1950, in the Battle of the Chongchon River, Korea*. New York: William Morrow, 1953.

Matray, James I., ed. *Historical Dictionary of the Korean War*. Westport, CT: Greenwood Press, 1991.

———. *The Reluctant Crusade: American Foreign Policy in Korea, 1941–1950*. Honolulu: University of Hawaii Press, 1985.

McCoy, Donald R. *The Presidency of Harry S. Truman*. Lawrence: University Press of Kansas, 1984.

McCullough, David. *Truman*. New York: Simon & Schuster, 1992.

McCune, George M., and Arthur L. Grey. *Korea Today*. Cambridge, MA: Harvard University Press, 1950.

McFarland, Keith D. *The Korean War: An Annotated Bibliography*. New York: Garland, 1986.

McGibbon, Ian C. *New Zealand and the Korean War*. Vol. 1, *Politics and Diplomacy*. Wellington, New Zealand: Oxford University Press, 1992.

McGlothlen, Ronald L. *Controlling the Waves: Dean Acheson and U.S. Foreign Policy in Asia*. New York: W. W. Norton, 1993.

Meid, Pat, and James M. Yingling. *U.S. Marine Operations in Korea, 1950–1953*. Vol. 5, *Operations in West Korea*. Washington, DC: U.S. Marine Corps Historical Branch, 1972.

Meilinger, Philip S. *Hoyt S. Vandenberg: The Life of a General*. Bloomington: Indiana University Press, 1989.

Merrill, Frank. *A Study of the Aerial Interdiction of Railways during the Korean War*. Fort Leavenworth, KS: Army Command and General Staff College, 1965.

Merrill, John. *Korea: The Peninsular Origins of the War*. Newark: University of Delaware Press, 1989

Meyers, Samuel M., and Albert D. Biderman, eds. *Mass Behavior in Battle and Captivity*. Chicago: University of Chicago Press, 1968.

Michener, James. *The Bridges at Toko-Ri*. New York: Random House, 1953.

Middleton, Harry J. *The Compact History of the Korean War*. New York: Hawthorn Books, 1965.

Millar, Ward M. *Valley of the Shadow*. New York: David McKay, 1955.

Momyer, William W. *Air Power in Three Wars: WWII, Korea, Vietnam*. Washington, DC: Department of the Air Force, 1978.

Montross, Lynn. *Cavalry of the Sky: The Story of U.S. Marine Combat Helicopters*. New York: Harper & Brothers, 1954.

Montross, Lynn, and Nicholas A. Canzona. *U.S. Marine Operations in Korea, 1950–1953: The Chosin Reservoir Campaign*. Washington, DC: U.S. Marine Corps Historical Branch, 1957.

———. *U.S. Marine Operations in Korea, 1950–1953: The Inchon-Seoul Operations*. Washington, DC: U.S. Marine Corps Historical Branch, 1955.

———. *U.S. Marine Operations in Korea, 1950–1953: The Pusan Perimeter*. Washington, DC: U.S. Marine Corps Historical Branch, 1954.

Montross, Lynn, Hubard D. Kuokka, and Norman W. Hicks. *U.S. Marine Operations in Korea, 1950–1953: The East-Central Front*. Vol. 4. Washington, DC: U.S. Marine Corps Historical Branch, 1962.

Mossman, Billy C. *U.S. Army in the Korean War: Ebb and Flow, November 1950–July 1951*. Washington, DC: U.S. Army Center of Military History, 1990.

Nahm, Andrew C. *Korea, Tradition and Transformation: A History of the Korean People*. Elizabeth, NJ: Hollym International, 1988.

Nichols, Jack C., and Warren E. Thompson. *Korea: The Air War, 1950–1953*. London: Osprey, 1991.

No, Kum-Sok, with J. Roger Osterholm. *A MiG-15 to Freedom: Memoirs of the Wartime North Korean Defector Who Delivered the Secret Fighter Jet to the Americans in 1953*. Jefferson, NC: McFarland, 1996.

Noble, Harold J. *Embassy at War*. Seattle: University of Washington Press, 1975.

O'Ballance, Edgar. *Korea, 1950–1953*. London: Faber & Faber, 1969.

Odgers, George. *Across the Parallel: The Australian 77th Squadron with the United States Air Force in the Korean War, 1950–1953*. London: Heinemann, 1952.

Oliver, Robert T. *Syngman Rhee and American Involvement in Korea, 1942–1960: A Personal Narrative*. Seoul: Panmun Books, 1978.

———. *Syngman Rhee: The Man Behind the Myth*. New York: Dodd, Mead, 1955.

———. *Verdict in Korea*. State College, PA: Bald Eagle Press, 1952.

———. *Why War Came in Korea*. New York: Fordham University Press, 1950.

O'Neill, Robert J. *Australia in the Korea War, 1950–1953*. Vol. 1, *Strategy and Diplomacy*. Canberra: Australian War Memorial/Australian Government Publishing Service, 1981.

———. *Australia in the Korean War, 1950–1953.* Vol. 2, *Combat Operations.* Canberra: Australian War Memorial, 1985.

O'Quinlivan, Michael, and James S. Santelli. *An Annotated Bibliography of the United States Marine Corps in the Korean War.* Rev. ed. Washington, DC: Historical Division, Headquarters U.S. Marine Corps, 1970.

Paige, Glenn D. *The Korean Decision, June 24–30, 1950.* New York: Free Press, 1968.

Paik, Sun Yup. *From Pusan to Panmunjom.* New York: Brassey's, 1992.

Pak, Chi-Young. *Political Opposition in Korea, 1945–1960.* Seoul: Seoul National University Press, 1980.

Pemberton, William E. *Harry S. Truman: Fair Dealer and Cold Warrior.* Boston: Twayne, 1989.

Pierpaoli, Paul G., Jr. *Truman and Korea: The Political Culture of the Early Cold War.* Columbia: University of Missouri Press, 1999.

Pogue, Forrest C. *George C. Marshall, Statesman, 1945–1959.* New York: Viking Press, 1987.

Politella, Dario. *Operation Grasshopper.* Wichita, KS: Robert R. Longo, 1958.

Poole, Walter. *The History of the Joint Chiefs of Staff: The Joint Staff and National Policy.* Vol. 4, *1950–1952.* Washington, DC: History Division, Joint Chiefs of Staff, 1979.

Portway, Donald. *Korea, Land of the Morning Calm.* London: George G. Harrap, 1953.

Pratt, Sherman W. *Decisive Battles of the Korean War. An Infantry Company Commander's View of the War's Most Critical Engagements.* New York: Vantage Press, 1992.

Ransom, Frank E. *Air-Sea Rescue, 1941–1952.* U.S. Air Force Historical Study, no. 95. Washington, DC: U.S. Air Force, 1953.

Rees, David. *Korea: The Limited War.* New York: St. Martin's Press, 1964.

———, ed. *The Korean War: History and Tactics.* London: Crescent Books, 1984.

Reeve, W. D. *The Republic of Korea.* London: Oxford University Press, 1963.

Reid, Escott. *Envoy to Nehru.* Delhi: Oxford University Press, 1981.

Republic of Korea, Ministry of National Defense. *The Account of Defensive Operations along the Nak Dong River.* Seoul: South Korean Defense Ministry, 1970.

———. *All Out Counter Attack Operations.* Seoul: South Korean Defense Ministry, 1971.

———. *The Brief History of ROK Armed Forces.* Seoul: Troop Information and Education Bureau, 1986.

———. *The History of the United Nations Forces in the Korean War.* 6 vols. Seoul: War History Compilation Commission, 1967–1975.

———. *The Invasion by Chinese Forces.* Seoul: South Korean Defense Ministry, 1972.

———. *The Invasion of the North Korean Puppet Forces.* Seoul: South Korean Defense Ministry, 1967.

———. *Liberation and the Building of Armed Forces.* Seoul: South Korean Defense Ministry, 1967.

———. *The Participation of UN Forces.* Seoul: South Korean Defense Ministry, 1980.

Rhee, Syngman. *Korea Flaming High.* Seoul: Office of Public Information, Republic of Korea, 1954.

Ridgway, Matthew B. *The Korean War.* Garden City, NY: Doubleday, 1967.

———. *The Korean War: History and Tactics.* New York: Doubleday, 1967.

———. *Soldier: The Memoirs of Matthew B. Ridgway.* New York: Harper, 1956.

Robertson, William G. *Counterattack on the Naktong, 1950.* Fort Leavenworth, KS: Combat Studies Institute, 1985.

Rose, Lisle. *Roots of Tragedy: The United States and the Struggle for Asia, 1945–1953.* Westport, CT: Greenwood Press, 1976.

Russ, Martin. *The Last Parallel: A Marine's War Journal.* New York: Rinehart, 1957.

Ryan, Mark A. *Chinese Attitudes toward Nuclear Weapons: China and the United States during the Korean War.* Armonk, NY: M. E. Sharpe, 1990.

Sandler, Stanley, ed. *The Korean War: An Encyclopedia.* New York: Garland, 1995.

Sawyer, Robert K. *Military Advisors in Korea: KMAG in Peace and War.* Washington, DC: Office of the Chief of Military History, U.S. Army, 1962.

Scalapino, Robert A., and Lee Chong-Sik. *Communism in Korea.* 2 vols. Berkeley: University of California Press, 1973.

Schaller, Michael. *The American Occupation of Japan: The Origins of the Cold War in Asia.* New York: Oxford University Press, 1985.

Schnabel, James F. *United States Army in the Korean War: Policy and Direction, the First Year.* Washington, DC: Office of the Chief of Military History, Department of the Army, 1972.

Schnabel, James F., and Robert J. Watson. *The History of the Joint Chiefs of Staff: The Joint Chiefs of Staff and National Policy.* Vol. 3, *The Korean War.* Wilmington, DE: Michael Glazier, 1979.

Schonberger, Howard B. *Aftermath of War: Americans and the Remaking of Japan, 1945–1952.* Kent, OH: Kent State University Press, 1989.

Scutts, Jerry. *Air War over Korea.* London: Arms and Armour, 1982.

Sheldon, Walt J. *Hell or High Water: MacArthur's Landing at Inchon.* New York: Macmillan, 1968.

Shinn, Bill. *The Forgotten War Remembered, Korea: 1950–1953.* Elizabeth, NJ: Hollym International, 1996.

Simmons, Robert R. *The Strained Alliance: Peking, Pyongyang, Moscow, and the Politics of the Korean Civil War.* New York: Free Press, 1975.

Smith, Gaddis. *Dean Acheson.* New York: Cooper Square, 1971.

Spanier, John W. *The Truman-MacArthur Controversy and the Korean War.* Cambridge, MA: Belknap Press, 1959.

Spurr, Russell. *Enter the Dragon: China's Undeclared War against the U.S. in Korea, 1950–1951.* New York: Henry Holt, 1988.

Stairs, Denis. *The Diplomacy of Constraint: Canada, the Korean War, and the United States.* Toronto: University of Toronto Press, 1974.

Stanton, Shelby. *America's Tenth Legion: X Corps in Korea.* Novato, CA: Presidio Press, 1989.

Stewart, James T., ed. *Airpower: The Decisive Force in Korea.* Princeton, NJ: Van Nostrand, 1957.

Stokesbury, James L. *A Short History of the Korean War.* New York: William Morrow, 1988.

Stone, I. F. *The Hidden History of the Korean War.* New York: Monthly Review Press, 1952.

Strawbridge, Dennis, and Nannette Kahn. *Fighter Pilot Performance in Korea.* Chicago: University of Chicago Press, 1955.

Stueck, William W., Jr. *The Korean War: An International History.* Princeton, NJ: Princeton University Press, 1995.

———. *The Road to Confrontation: American Policy toward China and Korea, 1947–1950.* Chapel Hill: University of North Carolina Press, 1981.

Suh, Dae-Sook. *Kim Il Sung: The North Korean Leader.* New York: Columbia University Press, 1988.

———. *The Korean Communist Movement, 1918–1948.* Princeton, NJ: Princeton University Press, 1967.

Summers, Harry G., Jr. *Korean War Almanac.* New York: Facts on File, 1990.

Taylor, Maxwell D. *Swords and Plowshares.* New York: W. W. Norton, 1972.

Thompson, Annis G. *The Greatest Airlift: The Story of Combat Cargo.* Tokyo: Dai-Nippon Printing Co., 1954.

Thorgrimsson, Thor, and E. C. Russell. *Canadian Naval Operations in Korean Waters, 1950–1953.* Ottawa: Queen's Printer, 1965.

Thornton, John W. *Believed to Be Alive.* Middlebury, VT: Ericksson, 1981.

Toland, John. *In Mortal Combat: Korea, 1950–1953.* New York: William Morrow, 1991.

Tomedi, Rudy. *No Bugles, No Drums: An Oral History of the Korean War.* New York: Wiley, 1993.

Truman, Harry S. *Memoirs.* Vol. 2, *Years of Trial and Hope.* Garden City, NY: Doubleday, 1956.

Tsou, Tang. *America's Failure in China: 1941–1950.* Chicago: University of Chicago Press, 1963.

Tyrrell, John V. *Air Power in Korea.* Norfolk, VA: Armed Forces Staff College, 1985.

U.S. Air Force. *Far East Air Force (FEAF) Report on the Korean War.* Washington, DC: U.S. Government Printing Office for U.S. Air Force, 1954.

———. *Operations in Korea, 1951.* Vol. 71. U.S. Air Force Studies. Washington, DC: U.S. Air Force Office, 1952.

U.S. Department of State, Bureau of Public Affairs. *Foreign Relations of the United States, 1950.* Vol. 7, *Korea.* Washington, DC: U.S. Government Printing Office, 1976.

U.S. Senate. *Military Situation in the Far East. Hearings Before the Armed Services and Foreign Relations Committee.* 82d Cong., 1st sess. Washington, DC: U.S. Government Printing Office, 1951.

Van Ree, Eric. *Socialism in One Zone: Stalin's Policy in Korea, 1945–1947.* Oxford: Oxford University Press, 1988.

Vetter, Harold J. *Mutiny on Koje Island.* Rutland, VT: Charles E. Tuttle, 1965.

Walker, Adrian. *A Barren Place: National Servicemen in Korea, 1950–1954.* London: Leo Cooper, 1994.

Watson, George M., Jr. *The Office of the Secretary of the Air Force.* Washington, DC: Center for Air Force History, 1993.

Westover, John G. *Combat Support in Korea.* Washington, DC: Combat Forces Press, 1955.

White, William L. *Captives of Korea: An Unofficial White Paper on the Treatment of War Prisoners, Our Treatment of Theirs; Their Treatment of Ours.* New York: Charles Scribner's Sons, 1955.

Whiting, Allen S. *China Crosses the Yalu.* Stanford, CA: Stanford University Press, 1960.

Wilkinson, Allen B. *Up Front Korea.* New York: Vantage Press, 1967.

Williams, William J., ed. *A Revolutionary War: Korea and the Transformation of the Postwar World.* Chicago: Imprint, 1993.

Wilson, David. *Lion over Korea: 77 Fighter Squadron RAAF, 1950–1953.* Canberra: Banner Books, 1994.

Wood, Herbert Fairlie. *Strange Battleground: The Official History of the Canadian Army in Korea.* Ottawa: Queen's Printer, 1966.

Yim, Louise. *My Forty Year Fight for Korea.* London: Gollanez, 1952.

Yonosuke, Nagai, and Akira Iriye. *The Origins of the Cold War in Asia.* New York: Columbia University Press, 1977.

Yoo, Tae-Ho. *The Korean War and the United Nations.* Louvain, Belgium: Librairie Desbarax, 1964.

Zelman, Walter A. *Chinese Intervention in the Korean War.* Los Angeles: University of California Press, 1967.

Zhang, Shu Guang. *Mao's Military Romanticism: China and the Korean War, 1950–1953.* Lawrence: University Press of Kansas, 1995.

Zonghong, Shen, et al. *Zhongguo rennin Zhiguanjun Kangmei yuanchao zhanshi* [A history of the war to resist America and assist Korea by the Chinese People's Volunteers]. Beijing: Military Science Press, 1988.

Zubok, Vladislaw, and Constantine Pleshakov. *Inside the Kremlin's Cold War: From Stalin to Khrushchev.* Cambridge, MA: Harvard University Press, 1996.

—*Compiled by Richard A. Garver and Spencer C. Tucker*

Index